SIPRI Yearbook 1996
Armaments, Disarmament and International Security

SIPRI Yearbook 1996

Armaments, Disarmament and International Security

Stockholm International Peace Research Institute

OXFORD UNIVERSITY PRESS
1996

Oxford University Press, Walton Street, Oxford OX2 6DP

Oxford New York
Athens Auckland Bangkok Bombay
Calcutta Cape Town Dar es Salaam Delhi
Florence Hong Kong Istanbul Karachi
Kuala Lumpur Madras Madrid Melbourne
Mexico City Nairobi Paris Singapore
Taipei Tokyo Toronto
and associated companies in
Berlin Ibadan

Oxford is a trade mark of Oxford University Press

Published in the United States
by Oxford University Press Inc., New York

© *SIPRI 1996*

Yearbooks before 1987 published under title
'World Armaments and Disarmament:
SIPRI Yearbook [year of publication]'

British Library Cataloguing in Publication Data
Data available
ISSN 0953–0282
ISBN 0–19–829202–3

Library of Congress Cataloging in Publication Data
Data available
ISSN 0953–0282
ISBN 0–19–829202–3

Typeset and originated by Stockholm International Peace Research Institute
Printed and bound in Great Britain by
Biddles Ltd., Guildford and King's Lynn

Contents

Part II. Military expenditure, R&D, arms production and trade, 1995

Part III. Non-proliferation, arms control and disarmament, 1995

Nuclear Weapon-Free Zone, 15 December 1995—United Nations Security Council
Resolution 984 on Security Assurances, 11 April 1995

Preface

The Stockholm International Peace Research Institute initiated its work 30 years ago, in July 1966. Three years later, the first *SIPRI Yearbook* was published. In his preface to the volume, Robert Neild summarized the joint findings from the analyses presented therein, concluding 'that the rise in world military spending, and more particularly the constant technological acceleration in weaponry, is highly dangerous, and the attempts so far made to slow down, halt or reverse the process have been incommensurate with the danger, that the arms competition, though it is not the sole or main cause of world tensions and conflict, is an important independent factor which increases and exacerbates tensions, and that arms limitation or disarmament could help considerably to reduce those tensions' (*SIPRI Yearbook of World Armaments and Disarmament 1968/69*, p. 6). This pessimistic but hopeful tone invariably characterized the *Yearbook* findings over the next 20 years.

The end of the cold war brought about a radical change of the situation. A historical accomplishment was made in 1995 with the indefinite extension of the 1968 Non-Proliferation Treaty (NPT). The next step, the completion of a comprehensive test ban treaty (CTBT), can give the people of the world the certainty 'that they really are seeing the end of the nuclear age' (US President Clinton, Moscow, 21 April 1996). The only sustainable solution to the menaces stemming from weapons of mass destruction and other inhumane weapons such as land-mines is complete and general prohibitions.

This 27th edition of the *Yearbook* addresses these 'classic' threats connected with armaments as well as the new problems which are determining the security priorities of states in the post-cold war era. These problems include civil wars and armed conflicts, predominantly of a domestic nature, and finding ways to end them and improve the mechanisms for preventing new wars and conflicts. There are also problems of regional and subregional security as well as the difficult search for political means to normalize relations between divided nations.

The facts, data, analyses and findings presented in this *Yearbook* are predominantly the result of research conducted by the Institute; 13 of the 17 chapters were written at SIPRI. Four chapters were prepared by prominent experts outside SIPRI, whom I hereby thank for their contributions. The editorial work, as in previous years, was carried out under the leadership of Connie Wall, whose professionalism was invaluable in preparing this volume. It also owes much to the experienced and competent editors—Billie Bielckus, Jetta Gilligan Borg, Eve Johansson and Don Odom—and Rebecka Charan, editorial assistant. Special thanks go to Ian Anthony, Eric Arnett, Ragnhild Ferm, Trevor Findlay and Zdzislaw Lachowski for their attention to other parts of volume in addition to their own contributions. I would like to express my gratitude to Gerd Hagmeyer-Gaverus for programming and computer support, as well as to Billie Bielckus, who prepared all the maps, and Peter Rea for indexing the volume.

Dr Adam Daniel Rotfeld
Director
May 1996

Acronyms

Additional acronyms of UN observer, peacekeeping and electoral operations and weapon systems are given in appendix 2A and appendix 11B, respectively. Acronyms not defined in this list are defined in the chapters of this volume.

ABACC	Brazilian–Argentine Agency for Accounting and Control of Nuclear Materials	ATBM	Anti-tactical ballistic missile
		ATC	Armoured troop carrier
ABM	Anti-ballistic missile	ATTU	Atlantic-to-the-Urals (zone)
ACDA	Arms Control and Disarmament Agency	AWACS	Airborne warning and control system
ACM	Advanced cruise missile	BCC	Bilateral Consultative Commission
ACRS	Arms control and regional security	BIC	Bilateral Implementation Commission
ACV	Armoured combat vehicle	BMD	Ballistic missile defence
AIFV	Armoured infantry fighting vehicle	BMDO	Ballistic Missile Defense Organization
ALCM	Air-launched cruise missile	BSA	Bosnian Serb Army
ANC	African National Congress	BSEC	Black Sea Economic Cooperation
ANZUS	Australia–New Zealand–United States Security Treaty	BTW	Biological and toxin weapon
APC	Armoured personnel carrier	BUR	Bottom–Up Review
		BW	Biological weapon/warfare
ARF	ASEAN Regional Forum	BWC	Biological Weapons Convention
ARV	Armoured recovery vehicle	CBM	Confidence-building measure
ASAT	Anti-satellite		
ASEAN	Association of South-East Asian Nations	CBSS	Council of Baltic Sea States
ASLCM	Advanced sea-launched cruise missile	CBW	Chemical and biological weapon/warfare
ASM	Air-to-surface missile	CCW	Certain Conventional Weapons (Convention)
ASW	Anti-submarine warfare		

CD	Conference on Disarmament	CSO	Committee of Senior Officials
CEE	Central and Eastern Europe	CTB(T)	Comprehensive test ban (treaty)
CEERN	Committee on Eastern Europe and Russia in NATO	CTOL	Conventional take-off and landing
		CTR	Cooperative Threat Reduction
CEFTA	Central European Free Trade Agreement	CW	Chemical weapon/warfare
CEI	Central European Initiative	CWC	Chemical Weapons Convention
CEP	Circular error probable		
CFE	Conventional Armed Forces in Europe	DEW	Directed-energy weapon
CFSP	Common Foreign and Security Policy	DOD	Department of Defense
		DOE	Department of Energy
CGE	Central government expenditure	DOP	Declaration of Principles
C^3I	Command, control, communications and intelligence	ECO	Economic Co-operation Organization
C^4I	Command, control, communications, computer and intelligence	ECOWAS	Economic Community of West African States
		ECU	European Currency Unit
CIO	Chairman-in-Office	EFA	European Fighter Aircraft
CIS	Commonwealth of Independent States	EFTA	European Free Trade Area
CJTF	Combined Joint Task Force		
		ELINT	Electronic intelligence
COCOM	Coordinating Committee (on Multilateral Export Controls)	EMP	Electromagnetic pulse
		EMU	Economic and Monetary Union
CPC	Conflict Prevention Centre	Enmod	Environmental modification
CPI	Consumer price index	EPU	European Political Union
CSBM	Confidence- and security-building measure	ERINT	Extended Range Interceptor
CSCE	Conference on Security and Co-operation in Europe	ERW	Enhanced radiation (neutron) weapon
		ESDI	European Security and Defence Identity

EU	European Union	HACV	Heavy armoured combat vehicle
EUCLID	European Cooperative Long-term Initiative on Defence	HCNM	High Commissioner on National Minorities
Euratom	European Atomic Energy Community	HDE	Hydrodynamic experiment
EUROFOR	European Force	HEU	Highly enriched uranium
EUROMARFORCE	European Maritime Force	HLTF	High Level Task Force
FIG	Financial–industrial group	HLWG	High Level Working Group
FBR	Fast-breeder reactor	HNE	Hydronuclear experiment
FBS	Forward-based system	IAEA	International Atomic Energy Agency
FMCT	Fissile Material Cut-Off Treaty	IBRD	International Bank for Reconstruction and Development
FOC	Full operational capability		
FSC	Forum for Security Co-operation	ICBM	Intercontinental ballistic missile
FSU	Former Soviet Union	ICFY	International Conference on Former Yugoslavia
FY	Fiscal year		
FYROM	Former Yugoslav Republic of Macedonia	ICJ	International Court of Justice
G7	Group of Seven (leading industrialized nations)	ICRC	International Committee of the Red Cross
G-21	Group of 21 (formerly 21 non-aligned CD member states)	IDB	Inter-American Development Bank
GATT	General Agreement on Tariffs and Trade	IEPG	Independent European Programme Group
GBR	Ground-based radar	IFOR	Implementation Force
GDP	Gross domestic product	IFV	Infantry fighting vehicle
GLCM	Ground-launched cruise missile	IGC	Intergovernmental Conference
GNP	Gross national product	IMF	International Monetary Fund
GPALS	Global Protection Against Limited Strikes	INF	Intermediate-range nuclear forces
GPS	Global Positioning System	INFCIRC	Information circular

IOC	Initial operational capability	MOU	Memorandum of Understanding
IPM	International plutonium management	MPLA	Popular Movement for the Liberation of Angola
IPP	Individual Partnership Programme	MSC	Military Staff Committee
IPS	International plutonium storage	MTCR	Missile Technology Control Regime
IRBM	Intermediate-range ballistic missile	MTM	Multinational technical means (of verification)
JCC	Joint Consultative Commission	NAC	North Atlantic Council
JCG	Joint Consultative Group	NACC	North Atlantic Cooperation Council
JCIC	Joint Compliance and Inspection Commission	NAM	Non-aligned movement
JDA	Japan Defense Agency	NATO	North Atlantic Treaty Organization
JNA	Yugoslav National Army	NBC	Nuclear, biological and chemical (weapons)
JSG	Joint Strategy Group	NGO	Non-governmental organization
LDC	Less developed country	NMP	Net material product
LDDI	Less developed defence industry	NNA	Neutral and non-aligned (states)
LEAP	Lightweight Exoatmospheric Projectile	NNWS	Non-nuclear weapon state
LEU	Low-enriched uranium	NPG	Nuclear Planning Group
MAD	Mutual assured destruction	NPR	Nuclear Posture Review
MARV	Manœuvrable re-entry vehicle	NPT	Non-Proliferation Treaty
MBT	Main battle tank	NRRC	Nuclear Risk Reduction Centre
MD	Military District		
MIC	Military–industrial complex	NSG	Nuclear Suppliers Group
Minatom	Ministry for Atomic Energy	NTI	National trial inspection
MIRV	Multiple independently targetable re-entry vehicle	NTM	National technical means (of verification)
MLRS	Multiple launch rocket system	NWFZ	Nuclear weapon-free zone

NWS	Nuclear weapon state	PHARE	*Pologne–Hongrie: action pour la reconversion économique* (Assistance for economic restructuring in the countries of Central and Eastern Europe)
OAS	Organization of American States		
OAU	Organization of African Unity		
OBDA	Official budget defence allocation		
ODA	Official development assistance	PLA	People's Liberation Army
ODIHR	Office for Democratic Institutions and Human Rights	PLO	Palestine Liberation Organization
		PNE(T)	Peaceful Nuclear Explosions (Treaty)
OECD	Organisation for Economic Co-operation and Development	PTB(T)	Partial Test Ban (Treaty)
O&M	Operation and maintenance	PrepCom	Preparatory Commission
OMB	Office of Management and Budget	R&D	Research and development
OMG	Operational Manœuvre Group	RDT&E	Research, development, testing and evaluation
OOV	Object of verification	RMA	Restricted Military Area
OPANAL	Agency for the Prohibition of Nuclear Weapons in Latin America	RPV	Remotely piloted vehicle
OPCW	Organisation for the Prohibition of Chemical Weapons	RV	Re-entry vehicle
		SACEUR	Supreme Allied Commander, Europe
OPV	Offshore patrol vessel	SALT	Strategic Arms Limitation Talks/Treaty
OSCC	Open Skies Consultative Commission	SAM	Surface-to-air missile
		SAM	Sanctions Assistance Mission
OSCE	Organization for Security and Co-operation in Europe	SCC	Standing Consultative Commission
OSI	On-site inspection	SDI	Strategic Defense Initiative
OSIA	On-Site Inspection Agency	SDIO	Strategic Defense Initiative Organization
PA	Parliamentary Assembly	SICBM	Small ICBM
PFP	Partnership for Peace	SLBM	Submarine-launched ballistic missile

SLCM	Sea-launched cruise missile	UNCLOS	United Nations Convention on the Law of the Sea
SLV	Space launch vehicle	UNHCR	UN High Comissioner for Refugees
SMTS	Space and Missile Tracking System		
SNDV	Strategic nuclear delivery vehicle	UNITA	National Union for the Total Independence of Angola
SNF	Short-range nuclear forces	UNPA	UN Protected Area
SRAM	Short-range attack missile	UNPROFOR	United Nations Protection Force
SRBM	Short-range ballistic missile	UNSCOM	United Nations Special Commission on Iraq
SSBN	Nuclear-powered, ballistic-missile submarine	UNTAG	United Nations Transition Assistance Group
SSD	Safe and Secure Dismantlement (Talks)	UNTEA	United Nations Temporary Executive Authority
SSGN	Nuclear-powered, guided-missile submarine	USAID	US Agency for International Development
SSN	Nuclear-powered attack submarine	V/STOL	Vertical/short take-off and landing
START	Strategic Arms Reduction Talks/Treaty	VCC	Verification Co-ordinating Committee
SVC	Special Verification Commission	VEREX	Verification experiment
SWS	Strategic weapon system	WEAG	Western European Armaments Group
TASM	Tactical air-to-surface missile	WEU	Western European Union
TEL	Transporter–erector–launcher	WMD	Weapon of mass destruction
THAAD	Theatre High Altitude Area Defence	WTO	World Trade Organization
TLE	Treaty-limited equipment	WTO	Warsaw Treaty Organization (Warsaw Pact)
TMD	Theatre missile defence		
TNF	Theatre nuclear forces		
TTB(T)	Threshold Test Ban (Treaty)		

Glossary

RAGNHILD FERM and CONNIE WALL

The main terms discussed in this Yearbook are defined in the glossary. For acronyms that appear in the definitions, see page xvi. For the members of global, regional and subregional organizations, see page xxxii. For brief summaries of and parties to the arms control and disarmament agreements, see annexe A.

Agency for the Prohibition of Nuclear Weapons in Latin America (OPANAL)	A forum established by the Treaty of Tlatelolco to resolve, together with the IAEA, questions of compliance with the treaty.
Anti-ballistic missile (ABM) system	*See* Ballistic missile defence.
Anti-tactical ballistic missile (ATBM)	*See* Theatre missile defence.
Arab League	The principal objective of the League of Arab States, or Arab League, established in 1945 and with headquarters in Cairo, is to form closer union among Arab states and foster political and economic cooperation. An agreement for collective defence and economic cooperation was signed in 1950. *See* list of members.
Association of South-East Asian Nations (ASEAN)	Established in the 1967 Bangkok Declaration to promote economic, social and cultural development as well as regional peace and security. The ASEAN Regional Forum (ARF) was established in 1993 to address security issues. *See* list of ASEAN and ARF members.
Atlantic-to-the-Urals (ATTU) zone	The zone of the 1990 CFE Treaty and the 1992 CFE-1A Agreement, stretching from the Atlantic Ocean to the Ural Mountains, which comprises the entire land territory of the European NATO states, the CEE states and the CIS states (i.e., it does not include the Baltic states).
Australia Group	A group of states, formed in 1985, which meets informally each year to monitor the proliferation of chemical and biological products and to discuss chemicals which should be subject to various national regulatory measures. *See* list of members.
Balkan states	The states in south-eastern Europe bounded by the Adriatic, Aegean and Black seas: Albania, Bosnia and Herzegovina, Bulgaria, Croatia, Greece, Macedonia (Former Yugoslav Republic of), Romania, Slovenia, Turkey and Yugoslavia (Serbia and Montenegro).

Ballistic missile	A missile which follows a ballistic trajectory (part of which may be outside the earth's atmosphere) when thrust is terminated.
Ballistic missile defence (BMD)	Weapon system designed to defend against a ballistic missile attack by intercepting and destroying ballistic missiles in flight. *See also* Theatre missile defence.
Baltic Council	Established in 1990, at Tallinn, for the promotion of democracy and development of cooperation between the three Baltic states. It comprises a Council of Ministers, Secretariat and Baltic Assembly (its parliamentary organ). *See* list of members.
Baltic Sea states/region	The nine littoral states of the Baltic Sea—Denmark, Estonia, Finland, Germany, Latvia, Lithuania, Poland, Russia and Sweden—and Norway, and usually also Iceland. *See also* Council of Baltic Sea States.
Baltic states	The three former Soviet republics bordering on the Baltic Sea: Estonia, Latvia and Lithuania.
Barents Euro-Arctic Council	A two-tier organization founded in 1993, in Kirkenes, Norway, for cooperation on the intergovernmental and regional levels in projects on, e.g., environmental protection, use of resources, economics and education. *See* list of members.
Bilateral Implementation Commission (BIC)	A forum established by the START II Treaty to resolve questions of compliance with the treaty.
Biological weapon (BW)	A weapon containing living organisms, whatever their nature, or infective material derived from them, which are intended for use to cause disease or death in man, animals or plants, and which for their effect depend on their ability to multiply in the person, animal or plant attacked, as well as the means of their delivery.
Black Sea Economic Cooperation (BSEC)	Established by the Summit Declaration on Black Sea Economic Cooperation in 1992, the BSEC focuses on economic cooperation and trade in the Black Sea region. *See* list of members.
Canberra Commission	The Canberra Commission on the Elimination of Nuclear Weapons was set up in 1995 to develop a programme to achieve a world totally free of nuclear weapons. It is to present its report to the 51st session of the UN General Assembly and to the Conference on Disarmament.
Central Asia	Of the former Soviet republics, this term refers to Kazakhstan, Kyrgyzstan, Tajikistan, Turkmenistan and Uzbekistan.
Central and Eastern Europe (CEE)	Bulgaria, the Czech Republic, Hungary, Poland, Romania and Slovakia. The CEE region sometimes also includes the European former Soviet republics—Armenia, Azerbaijan, Belarus, Georgia, Moldova, the European part of Russia and Ukraine—and sometimes also the Baltic states. *See also* Eastern Europe.
Central European Initiative (CEI)	Initiated in 1989 and established as the CEI in 1992, it is a regional forum for cooperation and political contacts. *See* list of members.

Chemical weapon (CW)   Chemical substances—whether gaseous, liquid or solid—which might be employed as weapons because of their direct toxic effects on man, animals or plants, as well as the means of their delivery.

Common Foreign and Security Policy (CFSP)   An institutional framework, established by the Maastricht Treaty, for consultation and development of common positions and joint action related to European security questions. It constitutes the second of the three EU 'pillars'. *See also* European Union, Pact on Stability in Europe, Western European Union.

Commonwealth of Independent States (CIS)   Organization of 12 former Soviet republics, established in 1991 to preserve and maintain under united command a common military–strategic space. *See* list of members.

Comprehensive test ban (CTB)   A ban on all nuclear explosions in all environments, under negotiation in the Conference on Disarmament (CD).

Conference on Disarmament (CD)   A multilateral arms control negotiating body, based in Geneva, composed of states representing all the regions of the world and including the permanent members of the UN Security Council. The CD reports to the UN General Assembly. *See* list of members.

Conference on Security and Co-operation in Europe (CSCE)   *See* Organization for Security and Co-operation in Europe.

Confidence- and security-building measure (CSBM)   A measure to promote confidence and security, undertaken by a state, which is militarily significant, politically binding and verifiable. The CSBMs of the CSCE are embodied in the 1986 Stockholm Document and the Vienna Documents. *See also* Confidence-building measure.

Confidence-building measure (CBM)   A measure taken by a state to contribute to reducing the dangers of armed conflict and of misunderstanding or miscalculation of military activities which could give rise to apprehension. The Document on CBMs is included in the 1975 CSCE Helsinki Final Act.

Conventional weapon   Weapon not having mass destruction effects. *See also* Weapon of mass destruction.

Conversion   The term used to denote the shift in resources from military to civilian use, usually the conversion of industry from military to civilian production.

Cooperative Threat Reduction (CTR)   A programme established in 1993 to institutionalize bilateral cooperation between the USA and the former Soviet republics with nuclear weapons on their territories (Belarus, Kazakhstan, Russia and Ukraine), primarily for US assistance in the safe and environmentally responsible storage, transportation, dismantlement and destruction of former Soviet nuclear weapons. Often referred to as the Nunn–Lugar programme after the two senators who sponsored the programme.

Coordinating Bureau of the Non-Aligned Countries	An organization to work towards the establishment of a new international economic order and to elaborate an economic strategy for the non-aligned countries. As of 1996 all the states of the Non-Aligned Movement (NAM) are members of the Coordinating Bureau; it is the forum in which NAM coordinates its actions in the UN. *See* list of NAM members.
Council of Baltic Sea States (CBSS)	An organization comprising the states bordering on the Baltic Sea plus Iceland, the CBSS was established in 1992 to assist in the development of democratic institutions in the former Soviet republics and to promote political and economic cooperation. *See also* Baltic Sea states/region and list of members.
Council of Europe	Established in 1949, with its seat in Strasbourg, the Council is open to all European states which accept the principle of the rule of law and guarantee their citizens human rights and fundamental freedoms. Its main aims are defined in the European Convention on Human Rights (1950) and the Convention for the Protection of Human Rights and Fundamental Freedoms (1953). Among its organs is the European Court of Human Rights. *See* list of members.
Counter-proliferation	Measures or policies to prevent the proliferation or enforce the non-proliferation of weapons of mass destruction.
Cruise missile	A guided weapon-delivery vehicle which sustains flight at subsonic or supersonic speeds through aerodynamic lift, generally flying at very low altitudes to avoid radar detection, sometimes following the contours of the terrain. It can be air-, ground- or sea-launched (ALCM, GLCM and SLCM, respectively) and carry a conventional, nuclear, chemical or biological warhead.
Dual-use technology/weapon	Dual-use technology is suitable for both civilian and military applications. A dual-use weapon is capable of carrying nuclear or conventional explosives.
Eastern Europe	Albania, Armenia, Azerbaijan, Belarus, Bulgaria, the Czech Republic, Georgia, Hungary, Moldova, Poland, Romania, Slovakia and Ukraine, as well as the European part of Russia.
European Union (EU)	Organization of 15 West European states established by the Maastricht Treaty, which was agreed in December 1991 and formally signed in February 1992; it entered into force in 1993. The highest decision-making body is the European Council. Other EU institutions are the Council of Ministers, the European Commission, the European Parliament and the European Court of Justice. An EU Common Foreign and Security Policy (CFSP) was established by the Maastricht Treaty. An Intergovernmental Conference (IGC) opened in Turin, Italy, on 29 March 1996 to review the treaty. Europe Agreements are made by the CEE and Baltic states with the EU as a step towards integration and harmonization with EU regulations and goals. *See also* Common Foreign and Security Policy, Western European Union, and *see* list of members.

Fissile material	Material composed of atoms which fission when irradiated by either fast or slow (thermal) neutrons. Uranium-235 and plutonium-239 are the most common fissile materials.
Forum for Security Co-operation (FSC)	*See* Organization for Security and Co-operation in Europe.
Group of Seven (G7)	The group of seven leading industrialized nations which have met informally, at the level of heads of state or government, since the late 1970s. *See* list of members.
Group of 21 (G-21)	Originally 21, now 19, non-aligned CD member states which act together on proposals of common interest. *See* list of members, under the Conference on Disarmament.
Hydrodynamic experiment (HDE)	An explosion in which fissile material is compressed but does not reach critical mass and no significant nuclear yield is released. A subcritical experiment for measuring the non-nuclear properties of fissile material.
Hydronuclear experiment (HNE)	An explosion in which fissile material is compressed until it briefly reaches critical mass and a small nuclear yield is released.
Intercontinental ballistic missile (ICBM)	Ground-launched ballistic missile with a range greater than 5500 km.
Intermediate-range nuclear forces (INF)	Theatre nuclear forces with a range of from 1000 km up to and including 5500 km.
International Atomic Energy Agency (IAEA)	An independent, intergovernmental organization within the UN system, with headquarters in Vienna. The IAEA is endowed by its Statute, which entered into force in 1957, with the twin purposes of promoting the peaceful uses of atomic energy and ensuring that nuclear activities are not used to further any military purpose. It is involved in verification of the NPT and the nuclear weapon-free zone treaties and in the activities of the UN Special Commission on Iraq (UNSCOM). *See* list of members.
Joint Consultative Group (JCG)	Established by the CFE Treaty to promote the objectives and implementation of the treaty by reconciling ambiguities of interpretation and implementation.
Joint Compliance and Inspection Commission (JCIC)	Established by the START I Treaty to resolve questions of compliance, clarify ambiguities and discuss ways to improve implementation of the treaty. It convenes at the request of at least one of the parties.
Kiloton (kt)	Measure of the explosive yield of a nuclear device equivalent to 1000 tonnes of trinitrotoluene (TNT) high explosive. (The bomb detonated at Hiroshima in World War II had a yield of about 12–15 kilotons.)
London Guidelines for Nuclear Transfers	*See* Nuclear Suppliers Group.
Maastricht Treaty	The Treaty on European Union. *See* European Union.
Maghreb states	The North African states Algeria, Libya, Mauritania, Morocco and Tunisia.

Megaton (Mt)	Measure of the explosive yield of a nuclear device equivalent to 1 million tonnes of trinitrotoluene (TNT) high explosive.
Minsk Group	Group of states acting together in the OSCE for political settlement of the conflict in the Armenian enclave of Nagorno-Karabakh in Azerbaijan (also known as the Minsk Process or Minsk Conference). *See* list of members under the Organization for Security and Co-operation in Europe.
Missile Technology Control Regime (MTCR)	An informal military-related export control regime, established in 1987, which produced the Guidelines for Sensitive Missile-Relevant Transfers. The goal is to limit the spread of weapons of mass destruction by controlling their delivery systems. The regime consists of the Guidelines, revised in 1992, and an Equipment and Technology Annex, last revised in 1995.
Multiple independently targetable re-entry vehicles (MIRV)	Re-entry vehicles (RVs), carried by a single ballistic missile, which can be directed to separate targets along separate trajectories. A missile can carry two or more RVs.
National technical means of verification (NTM)	The technical intelligence means, under the national control of a state, which are used to monitor compliance with an arms control treaty to which the state is a party.
Non-Aligned Movement (NAM)	*See* Coordinating Bureau of the Non-Aligned Countries.
Non-strategic nuclear forces	*See* Theatre nuclear forces.
Nordic Council	A political organ for cooperation between the Nordic states, founded in 1952. The Plenary Assembly is the highest political organ. The Nordic Council of Ministers, established in 1971, is an organ for cooperation between the governments of the Nordic countries and between these governments and the Nordic Council. *See* list of members.
Nordic states	The North European states Denmark, Finland, Iceland, Norway and Sweden.
North Atlantic Council (NAC)	*See* North Atlantic Treaty Organization.
North Atlantic Cooperation Council (NACC)	Created in 1991 as a NATO institution for consultation and cooperation on political and security issues between NATO and the former WTO states and former Soviet republics. *See also* Partnership for Peace, and *see* list of members.
North Atlantic Treaty Organization (NATO)	A defensive political and military alliance established in 1949 by the North Atlantic Treaty, with headquarters in Brussels. The principal organs are the North Atlantic Council, a permanent body which meets in foreign ministerial session twice a year, the Defence Planning Committee, the Military Committee and the Nuclear Planning Group. The North Atlantic Assembly is the NATO interparliamentary organization. *See also* North Atlantic Cooperation Council, Partnership for Peace, and *see* list of members.

Nuclear Risk Reduction
Centres (NRRC)

Established by the 1987 US–Soviet NRRC Agreement, the two
centres, in Washington and Moscow, exchange information by
direct satellite link in order to minimize misunderstandings
which might carry a risk of nuclear war.

Nuclear Suppliers Group
(NSG)

Also known as the London Club, the NSG coordinates multilateral export controls on nuclear materials and in 1977 agreed
the Guidelines for Nuclear Transfers (London Guidelines),
revised in 1993. The Guidelines contain a 'trigger list', adopted
from the Zangger Committee list, of equipment or material
which, if exported to a non-nuclear weapon state that was not a
party to the NPT, would be subject to IAEA safeguards. In
1992 the NSG agreed the Guidelines for Transfers of Nuclear-
Related Dual-Use Equipment, Material and Related
Technology (Warsaw Guidelines, subsequently revised). *See
also* Zangger Committee, and *see* list of members.

Open Skies Consultative
Commission (OSCC)

A forum established by the Open Skies Treaty to resolve questions of compliance with the treaty.

Organisation for
Economic Co-operation
and Development (OECD)

Established in 1961 with the objective to promote economic
growth and social welfare by coordinating national policies.
See list of members.

Organisation for the
Prohibition of Chemical
Weapons (OPCW)

A forum established by the Chemical Weapons Convention to
resolve questions of compliance with the convention. Its seat is
in The Hague.

Organization for Security
and Co-operation in
Europe (OSCE)

From 1995 the Conference on Security and Co-operation in
Europe (CSCE) became the OSCE. The OSCE comprises the
Meetings of Heads of State or Government, the Ministerial
Council (Prague), the Senior Council (meetings in Prague), the
Secretariat (Vienna), the Conflict Prevention Centre (CPC,
Vienna), the Office for Democratic Institutions and Human
Rights (ODIHR, Warsaw), the Forum for Security Co-opera-
tion (FSC, Vienna), the Chairman-in-Office (CIO, Vienna), the
High Commissioner on National Minorities (HCNM, The
Hague), the Court [on Conciliation and Arbitration] (Geneva),
the Permanent Council (Vienna) and the Parliamentary
Assembly (PA, Copenhagen). *See also* Pact on Stability in
Europe, and *see* list of members.

Organization of African
Unity (OAU)

Established in 1963, the OAU is a union of African states with
the principal objective of promoting cooperation among the
states in the region. In 1995, together with the UN, it worked
out the Pelindaba text of the African Nuclear-Weapon-Free
Zone Treaty. *See* list of members.

Organization of American
States (OAS)

Group of states in the Americas, established in 1890, which
also has member states and permanent observers from other
continents. Its principal objective is to strengthen peace and
security in the western hemisphere. *See* list of members.

Pact on Stability in Europe	A French proposal presented to the European Union in 1993 for inclusion in the framework of the EU Common Foreign and Security Policy (CFSP). The objective is to contribute to stability by preventing tension and potential conflicts connected with borders and minorities. The Pact was adopted by over 50 states in Paris on 20–21 March 1995, and the instruments and procedures were handed over to the OSCE. The Pact consists of a declaration and a large number of agreements on and arrangements for good-neighbourliness and cooperation.
Partnership for Peace (PFP)	The NATO programme launched in January 1994 for cooperation with NACC and other CSCE states, in such areas as military planning, budgeting and training, under the authority of the North Atlantic Council. It provides for enhanced cooperation to prepare for and undertake multilateral crisis-management activities such as peacekeeping. States seeking partnership must sign a Framework Document, provide Presentation Documents to NATO, identifying the steps they will take to achieve the PFP goals, and develop with NATO Individual Partnership Programmes. *See* list of partner states under North Atlantic Treaty Organization.
Peaceful nuclear explosion (PNE)	Application of a nuclear explosion for non-military purposes such as digging canals or harbours or creating underground cavities. The USA terminated its PNE programme in the 1970s. The USSR conducted its last PNE in 1988.
Re-entry vehicle (RV)	That part of a ballistic missile which carries a nuclear warhead and penetration aids to the target, re-enters the earth's atmosphere and is destroyed in the terminal phase of the missile's trajectory. A missile can have one or several RVs; each RV contains a warhead.
Safeguards agreements	Under the NPT and the nuclear weapon-free zone treaties, non-nuclear weapon states must accept IAEA safeguards to demonstrate the fulfilment of their obligation not to manufacture nuclear weapons. *See also* International Atomic Energy Agency.
Short-range nuclear forces (SNF)	Nuclear weapons, including artillery, mines, missiles, etc., with ranges of up to 500 km. *See also* Tactical nuclear weapon, Theatre nuclear forces.
South Pacific Forum	A group of South Pacific states created in 1971 which *inter alia* proposed the South Pacific Nuclear Free Zone, embodied in the 1985 Treaty of Rarotonga. *See* list of members.
Stability Pact	*See* Pact on Stability in Europe.
Standing Consultative Commission (SCC)	The consultative body established by a 1972 US–Soviet Memorandum of Understanding. The USA and Russia refer issues regarding the implementation of the ABM Treaty to the SCC.
Strategic nuclear weapons	ICBMs and SLBMs with a range usually of over 5500 km, as well as bombs and missiles carried on aircraft of intercontinental range.
Submarine-launched ballistic missile (SLBM)	A ballistic missile launched from a submarine, usually with a range in excess of 5500 km.

Tactical nuclear weapon	A short-range nuclear weapon which is deployed with general-purpose forces along with conventional weapons.
Theatre missile defence (TMD)	Defensive systems against non-strategic nuclear missiles.
Theatre nuclear forces (TNF)	Nuclear weapons with ranges of up to and including 5500 km. In the 1987 INF Treaty, nuclear missiles are divided into intermediate-range (1000–5500 km) and shorter-range (500–1000 km), also called non-strategic nuclear forces. Nuclear weapons with ranges of up to 500 km are called short-range nuclear forces. *See also* Short-range nuclear forces.
Throw-weight	The sum of the weight of a ballistic missile's re-entry vehicle(s), dispensing mechanisms, penetration aids, and targeting and separation devices.
Toxins	Poisonous substances which are products of organisms but are inanimate and incapable of reproducing themselves as well as chemically induced variants of such substances. Some toxins may also be produced by chemical synthesis.
Treaty-limited equipment (TLE)	The five categories of equipment on which numerical limits are established in the CFE Treaty: battle tanks, armoured combat vehicles, artillery, combat aircraft and attack helicopters.
Visegrad Group	The Czech Republic, Hungary, Poland and Slovakia. The Visegrad Four signed a Central European Free Trade Agreement (CEFTA) in 1992 to create a free trade area in Central Europe by 2001.
Warhead	That part of a weapon which contains the explosive or other material intended to inflict damage.
Warsaw Guidelines	*See* Nuclear Suppliers Group.
Warsaw Treaty Organization (WTO)	The WTO, or Warsaw Pact, was established in 1955 by the Treaty of Friendship, Cooperation and Mutual Assistance. The WTO was dissolved in 1991.
Wassenaar Arrangement	The Wassenaar Arrangement on Export Controls for Conventional Arms and Dual-Use Goods and Technologies, provisionally established in Wassenaar, the Netherlands, on 18 December 1995, aims to prevent the acquisition of armaments and sensitive dual-use goods and technologies for military end uses to states whose behaviour is a cause for concern to the members. *See also* Dual-use technology/weapon.
Weapon of mass destruction	Nuclear weapon and any other weapon which may produce comparable effects, such as chemical and biological weapons.

Western European Union
(WEU)

Established in the 1954 Protocols to the 1948 Brussels Treaty of Economic, Social and Cultural Collaboration and Collective Self-Defence among Western European States. Within the EU Common Foreign and Security Policy (CFSP) and at the request of the EU, the WEU is to elaborate and implement EU decisions and actions which have defence implications. The principal WEU organs are the WEU Council (comprised of the Ministerial Council and the Permanent Council) and the WEU Assembly; the WEU Institute for Security Studies is a research institute. The Western European Armaments Group (WEAG) is the WEU armaments cooperation authority with activities on harmonization of requirements, arms cooperation programmes and policies on armaments R&D and procurement. *See* list of members.

Yield

Released nuclear explosive energy expressed as the equivalent of the energy produced by a given number of tonnes of trinitro-toluene (TNT) high explosive. *See also* Kiloton, Megaton.

Zangger Committee

The Nuclear Exporters Committee, called the Zangger Committee after its first chairman, is an intergovernmental group to coordinate multilateral export controls on nuclear materials. In 1974 it agreed the original 'trigger list' (subsequently revised) of equipment or material which, if exported to a non-nuclear weapon state that was not a party to the NPT, would be subject to IAEA safeguards. *See also* Nuclear Suppliers Group, and *see* list of members.

Membership of international organizations, as of 1 January 1996

The UN member states and organizations within the UN system are listed first, followed by all other organizations in alphabetical order. Note that not all the members of organizations are UN member states. Where confirmed information on new members became available in early 1996, this is given in notes.

United Nations (UN) and year of membership

Afghanistan, 1946
Albania, 1955
Algeria, 1962
Andorra, 1993
Angola, 1976
Antigua and Barbuda, 1981
Argentina, 1945
Armenia, 1992
Australia, 1945
Austria, 1955
Azerbaijan, 1992
Bahamas, 1973
Bahrain, 1971
Bangladesh, 1974
Barbados, 1966
Belarus, 1945
Belgium, 1945
Belize, 1981
Benin, 1960
Bhutan, 1971
Bolivia, 1945
Bosnia and Herzegovina, 1992
Botswana, 1966
Brazil, 1945
Brunei Darussalam, 1984
Bulgaria, 1955
Burkina Faso , 1960
Burundi, 1962
Cambodia, 1955
Cameroon, 1960
Canada, 1945
Cape Verde, 1975
Central African Republic, 1960
Chad, 1960
Chile, 1945
China, 1945
Colombia, 1945
Comoros, 1975
Congo, 1960
Costa Rica, 1945
Côte d'Ivoire, 1960
Croatia, 1992
Cuba, 1945
Cyprus, 1960
Czech Republic, 1993
Denmark, 1945

Djibouti, 1977
Dominica, 1978
Dominican Republic, 1945
Ecuador, 1945
Egypt, 1945
El Salvador, 1945
Equatorial Guinea, 1968
Eritrea, 1993
Estonia, 1991
Ethiopia, 1945
Fiji, 1970
Finland, 1955
France, 1945
Gabon, 1960
Gambia, 1965
Georgia, 1992
Germany, 1973
Ghana, 1957
Greece, 1945
Grenada, 1974
Guatemala, 1945
Guinea, 1958
Guinea-Bissau, 1974
Guyana, 1966
Haiti, 1945
Honduras, 1945
Hungary, 1955
Iceland, 1946
India, 1945
Indonesia, 1950
Iran, 1945
Iraq, 1945
Ireland, 1955
Israel, 1949
Italy, 1955
Jamaica, 1962
Japan, 1956
Jordan, 1955
Kazakhstan, 1992
Kenya, 1963
Korea, Democratic People's
  Republic of (North Korea),
  1991
Korea, Republic of (South
  Korea), 1991
Kuwait, 1963

Kyrgyzstan, 1992
Lao People's Democratic
  Republic, 1955
Latvia, 1991
Lebanon, 1945
Lesotho, 1966
Liberia, 1945
Libya, 1955
Liechtenstein, 1990
Lithuania, 1991
Luxembourg, 1945
Macedonia, Former Yugoslav
  Republic of (FYROM), 1993
Madagascar, 1960
Malawi, 1964
Malaysia, 1957
Maldives, 1965
Mali, 1960
Malta, 1964
Marshall Islands, 1991
Mauritania, 1961
Mauritius, 1968
Mexico, 1945
Micronesia, 1991
Moldova, 1992
Monaco, 1993
Mongolia, 1961
Morocco, 1956
Mozambique, 1975
Myanmar *(Burma)*, 1948
Namibia, 1990
Nepal, 1955
Netherlands, 1945
New Zealand, 1945
Nicaragua, 1945
Niger, 1960
Nigeria, 1960
Norway, 1945
Oman, 1971
Pakistan, 1947
Palau, 1994
Panama, 1945
Papua New Guinea, 1975
Paraguay, 1945
Peru, 1945
Philippines, 1945

Poland, 1945
Portugal, 1955
Qatar, 1971
Romania, 1955
Russia, 1945[a]
Rwanda, 1962
Saint Kitts (Christopher) and
  Nevis, 1983
Saint Lucia, 1979
Saint Vincent and the
  Grenadines, 1980
Samoa, Western, 1976
San Marino, 1992
Sao Tome and Principe, 1975
Saudi Arabia, 1945
Senegal, 1960
Seychelles, 1976
Sierra Leone, 1961

Singapore, 1965
Slovakia, 1993
Slovenia, 1992
Solomon Islands, 1978
Somalia, 1960
South Africa, 1945
Spain, 1955
Sri Lanka, 1955
Sudan, 1956
Suriname, 1975
Swaziland, 1968
Sweden, 1946
Syria, 1945
Tajikistan, 1992
Tanzania, 1961
Thailand, 1946
Togo, 1960
Trinidad and Tobago, 1962

Tunisia, 1956
Turkey, 1945
Turkmenistan, 1992
Uganda, 1962
UK, 1945
Ukraine, 1945
United Arab Emirates, 1971
Uruguay, 1945
USA, 1945
Uzbekistan, 1992
Vanuatu, 1981
Venezuela, 1945
Viet Nam, 1977
Yemen, 1947
Yugoslavia, 1945[b]
Zaire, 1960
Zambia, 1964
Zimbabwe, 1980

[a] In Dec. 1991 Russia informed the UN Secretary-General that it was continuing the membership of the USSR in the Security Council and all other UN bodies.

[b] A claim by Yugoslavia (Serbia and Montenegro) in 1992 to continue automatically the membership of the former Yugoslavia was not accepted by the UN General Assembly. It was decided that Yugoslavia should apply for membership, which it had not done by 1 Jan. 1996. It may not participate in the work of the General Assembly, its subsidiary organs or the conferences and meetings convened by it.

UN Security Council

Permanent members (the P5): China, France, Russia, UK, USA

Non-permanent members in 1995 (elected by the UN General Assembly for two-year terms. The year in brackets is the year at the end of which the term expires): Argentina (1995), Botswana (1996), Czech Republic (1995), Germany (1996), Honduras (1996), Indonesia (1996), Italy (1996), Nigeria (1995), Oman (1995), Rwanda (1995)

Note: Chile, Egypt, Guinea-Bissau, Poland and South Korea were elected non-permanent members for 1996–97.

Conference on Disarmament (CD)

Members: Algeria, Argentina, Australia, Belgium, Brazil, Bulgaria, Canada, China, Cuba, Egypt, Ethiopia, France, Germany, Hungary, India, Indonesia, Iran, Italy, Japan, Kenya, Mexico, Mongolia, Morocco, Myanmar (Burma), Netherlands, Nigeria, Pakistan, Peru, Poland, Romania, Russia, Sri Lanka, Sweden, UK, USA, Venezuela, Zaire

Observers: Armenia, Austria,* Bangladesh,* Belarus,* Brunei, Cameroon,* Chile,* Colombia,* Croatia, Czech Republic, Denmark, Ecuador, Finland,* Ghana, Greece, Holy See, Iraq,* Ireland, Israel,* Jordan, Korea (North),* Korea (South), Kuwait,* Libya, Macedonia (Former Yugoslav Republic of), Madagascar, Malaysia, Malta, New Zealand,* Norway,* Oman, Philippines, Portugal, Qatar, Senegal,* Singapore, Slovakia,* Slovenia, South Africa,* Spain,* Switzerland,* Syria,* Tanzania, Thailand, Tunisia, Turkey,* Ukraine,* Viet Nam,* Zambia, Zimbabwe*

* The 23 observer states marked with an asterisk will assume membership 'at the earliest possible date', to be decided by the CD.

Members of the Group of 21: Algeria, Brazil, Cuba, Egypt, Ethiopia, India, Indonesia, Iran, Kenya, Mexico, Mongolia, Morocco, Myanmar (Burma), Nigeria, Pakistan, Peru, Sri Lanka, Venezuela, Zaire

Members of the Eastern Group: Bulgaria, Hungary, Poland, Romania, Russia

Members of the Western Group: Argentina, Australia, Belgium, Canada, France, Germany, Italy, Japan, Netherlands, Sweden, UK, USA

International Atomic Energy Agency (IAEA)

Members: Afghanistan, Albania, Algeria, Argentina, Armenia, Australia, Austria, Bangladesh, Belarus, Belgium, Bolivia, Bosnia and Herzegovina, Brazil, Bulgaria, Cambodia, Cameroon, Canada, Chile, China, Colombia, Costa Rica, Côte d'Ivoire, Croatia, Cuba, Cyprus, Czech Republic, Denmark, Dominican Republic, Ecuador, Egypt, El Salvador, Estonia, Ethiopia, Finland, France, Gabon, Germany, Ghana, Greece, Guatemala, Haiti, Holy See, Hungary, Iceland, India, Indonesia, Iran, Iraq, Ireland, Israel, Italy, Jamaica, Japan, Jordan, Kazakhstan, Kenya, Korea (South), Kuwait, Lebanon, Liberia, Libya, Liechtenstein, Lithuania, Luxembourg, Macedonia (Former Yugoslav Republic of), Madagascar, Malaysia, Mali, Marshall Islands, Mauritius, Mexico, Monaco, Mongolia, Morocco, Myanmar (Burma), Namibia, Netherlands, New Zealand, Nicaragua, Niger, Nigeria, Norway, Pakistan, Panama, Paraguay, Peru, Philippines, Poland, Portugal, Qatar, Romania, Russia, Saudi Arabia, Senegal, Sierra Leone, Singapore, Slovakia, Slovenia, South Africa, Spain, Sri Lanka, Sudan, Sweden, Switzerland, Syria, Tanzania, Thailand, Tunisia, Turkey, Uganda, UK, Ukraine, United Arab Emirates, Uruguay, USA, Uzbekistan, Venezuela, Viet Nam, Yemen, Yugoslavia,* Zaire, Zambia, Zimbabwe

* Yugoslavia (Serbia and Montenegro) has been suspended since July 1992. It is deprived of the right to participate in the IAEA General Conference and the Board of Governers' meetings but is assessed for its contribution to the budget of the IAEA.

Note: North Korea was a member of the IAEA until Sep. 1994.

Arab League

Members: Algeria, Bahrain, Comoros, Djibouti, Egypt, Iraq, Jordan, Kuwait, Lebanon, Libya, Mauritania, Morocco, Oman, Palestine, Qatar, Saudi Arabia, Somalia, Sudan, Syria, Tunisia, United Arab Emirates, Yemen

Association of South-East Asian Nations (ASEAN)

Members: Brunei, Indonesia, Malaysia, Philippines, Singapore, Thailand, Viet Nam

ASEAN Post Ministerial Conference (ASEAN–PMC)

Members: The ASEAN states plus Australia, Canada, European Union (EU), Japan, South Korea, New Zealand, USA

ASEAN Regional Forum (ARF)

Members: The ASEAN states plus Australia, Cambodia, Canada, China, European Union (EU), Japan, South Korea, Laos, New Zealand, Papua New Guinea, Russia, USA

Australia Group

Members: Argentina, Australia, Austria, Belgium, Canada, Czech Republic, Denmark, Finland, France, Germany, Greece, Hungary, Iceland, Ireland, Italy, Japan, Luxembourg, Netherlands, New Zealand, Norway, Poland, Portugal, Romania, Slovakia, Spain, Sweden, Switzerland, UK, USA

Observer: European Commission

Baltic Council

Members: Estonia, Latvia, Lithuania

Barents Euro-Arctic Council

Core members: Finland, Norway, Russia, Sweden

Other members: Denmark, European Union (EU), Iceland

Observers: Canada, France, Germany, Japan, Netherlands, Poland, UK, USA

Members of the Regional Council: Five Nordic provinces north of the north polar circle—3 provinces of Norway (Finnmark, Troms and Nordland) and 1 each from Sweden and Finland (Norrbotten and Lappland, respectively)—plus 3 regions of Russia (Murmansk *oblast*, Archangelsk *oblast* and Karelian Republic)

Black Sea Economic Cooperation (BSEC)

Members: Albania, Armenia, Azerbaijan, Bulgaria, Georgia, Greece, Moldova, Romania, Russia, Turkey, Ukraine

Observers: Austria, Egypt, Israel, Italy, Poland, Slovakia, Tunisia

Central European Initiative (CEI)

Members: Austria, Bosnia and Herzegovina, Croatia, Czech Republic, Hungary, Italy, Macedonia (Former Yugoslav Republic of), Poland, Slovakia, Slovenia

Associate members: Albania, Belarus, Bulgaria, Romania, Ukraine

Commonwealth of Independent States (CIS)

Members: Armenia, Azerbaijan, Belarus, Georgia, Kazakhstan, Kyrgyzstan, Moldova, Russia, Tajikistan, Turkmenistan, Ukraine, Uzbekistan

Council of Baltic Sea States (CBSS)

Members: Denmark, Estonia, European Union (EU), Finland, Germany, Iceland, Latvia, Lithuania, Norway, Poland, Russia, Sweden

Council of Europe

Members: Albania, Andorra, Austria, Belgium, Bulgaria, Cyprus, Czech Republic, Denmark, Estonia, Finland, France, Germany, Greece, Hungary, Iceland, Ireland, Italy, Latvia, Liechtenstein, Lithuania, Luxembourg, Macedonia (Former Yugoslav Republic of), Malta, Moldova, Netherlands, Norway, Poland, Portugal, Romania, San Marino, Slovakia, Slovenia, Spain, Sweden, Switzerland, Turkey, UK, Ukraine

Note: Russia was admitted in Feb. 1996 and Croatia in Apr. 1996.

European Union (EU)

Members: Austria, Belgium, Denmark, Finland, France, Germany, Greece, Ireland, Italy, Luxembourg, Netherlands, Portugal, Spain, Sweden, UK

Group of Seven (G7)

Members: Canada, France, Germany, Italy, Japan, UK, USA

Missile Technology Control Regime (MTCR)

MTCR partners: Argentina, Australia, Austria, Belgium, Brazil, Canada, Denmark, Finland, France, Germany, Greece, Hungary, Iceland, Ireland, Italy, Japan, Luxembourg, Netherlands, New Zealand, Norway, Portugal, Russia, South Africa, Spain, Sweden, Switzerland, UK, USA

Non-Aligned Movement (NAM)

Members: Afghanistan, Algeria, Angola, Bahamas, Bahrain, Bangladesh, Barbados, Belize, Benin, Bhutan, Bolivia, Botswana, Brunei, Burkina Faso, Burundi, Cambodia, Cameroon, Cape Verde, Central African Republic, Chad, Chile, Colombia, Comoros, Congo, Côte d'Ivoire, Cuba, Cyprus, Djibouti, Ecuador, Egypt, Equatorial Guinea, Eritrea, Ethiopia, Gabon, Gambia, Ghana, Grenada, Guatemala, Guinea, Guinea-Bissau, Guyana, Honduras, India, Indonesia, Iran, Iraq, Jamaica, Jordan, Kenya, Korea (North), Kuwait, Laos, Lebanon, Lesotho, Liberia, Libya, Madagascar, Malawi, Malaysia, Maldives, Mali, Malta, Mauritania, Mauritius, Mongolia, Morocco, Mozambique, Myanmar (Burma), Namibia, Nepal, Nicaragua, Niger, Nigeria, Oman, Pakistan, Palestine, Panama, Papua New Guinea, Peru, Philippines, Qatar, Rwanda, Saint Lucia, Sao Tomé and Principe, Saudia Arabia, Senegal, Seychelles, Sierra Leone, Singapore, Somalia, South Africa, Sri Lanka, Sudan, Suriname, Swaziland, Syria, Tanzania, Thailand, Togo, Trinidad and Tobago, Tunisia, Turkmenistan, Uganda, United Arab Emirates, Uzbekistan, Vanuatu, Venezuela, Viet Nam, Yemen, Yugoslavia,* Zaire, Zambia, Zimbabwe

* Yugoslavia (Serbia and Montenegro) has not been permitted to participate in NAM activities since 1992.

Nordic Council

Members: Denmark (including the Faroe Islands and Greenland), Finland (including Åland), Iceland, Norway, Sweden

North Atlantic Treaty Organization (NATO)

Members: Belgium, Canada, Denmark, France,* Germany, Greece, Iceland, Italy, Luxembourg, Netherlands, Norway, Portugal, Spain,* Turkey, UK, USA

* France and Spain are not in the integrated military structures of NATO.

North Atlantic Assembly

Associate Delegations: Albania, Belarus, Bulgaria, Czech Republic, Estonia, Hungary, Latvia, Lithuania, Macedonia (Former Yugoslav Republic of), Moldova, Poland, Romania, Russia, Slovakia, Slovenia, Ukraine

NATO North Atlantic Cooperation Council (NACC)

Members: Albania, Armenia, Azerbaijan, Belarus, Belgium, Bulgaria, Canada, Czech Republic, Denmark, Estonia, France, Georgia, Germany, Greece, Hungary, Iceland, Italy, Kazakhstan, Kyrgyzstan, Latvia, Lithuania, Luxembourg, Moldova, Netherlands, Norway, Poland, Portugal, Romania, Russia, Slovakia, Spain, Tajikistan, Turkey, Turkmenistan, UK, Ukraine, USA, Uzbekistan

Observers: Austria, Finland, Malta, Slovenia and Sweden have observer status, as participants in the Partnership for Peace.

Partnership for Peace (PFP)

Partner states with approved PFP Framework Documents: Albania, Armenia, Austria, Azerbaijan, Belarus, Bulgaria, Czech Republic, Estonia, Finland, Georgia, Hungary, Kazakhstan, Kyrgyzstan, Latvia, Lithuania, Macedonia (Former Yugoslav Republic of), Malta, Moldova, Poland, Romania, Russia, Slovakia, Slovenia, Sweden, Turkmenistan, Ukraine, Uzbekistan

Partner states with approved PFP Presentation Documents: Albania, Bulgaria, Czech Republic, Estonia, Finland, Hungary, Kazakhstan, Latvia, Lithuania, Moldova, Poland, Romania, Russia, Slovakia, Slovenia, Sweden, Ukraine

Note: Austria's Presentation Document was approved in Feb. 1996.

Partner states with approved PFP Individual Partnership Programmes (IPP): Albania, Bulgaria, Czech Republic, Estonia, Finland, Hungary, Latvia, Lithuania, Moldova, Poland, Romania, Russia, Slovakia, Slovenia, Sweden, Ukraine

Nuclear Suppliers Group (NSG)

Members: Argentina, Australia, Austria, Belgium, Bulgaria, Canada, Czech Republic, Denmark, Finland, France, Germany, Greece, Hungary, Ireland, Italy, Japan, Luxembourg, Netherlands, New Zealand, Norway, Poland, Portugal, Romania, Russia, Slovakia, South Africa, Spain, Sweden, Switzerland, UK, USA

Note: South Korea was accepted for membership in Oct. 1995.

Organisation for Economic Co-operation and Development (OECD)

Members: Australia, Austria, Belgium, Canada, Denmark, Finland, France, Germany, Greece, Iceland, Ireland, Italy, Japan, Luxembourg, Mexico, Netherlands, New Zealand, Norway, Portugal, Spain, Sweden, Switzerland, Turkey, UK, USA

The European Commission participates in the work of the OECD.

Note: The Czech Republic was admitted on 1 Jan. 1996.

Organization for Security and Co-operation in Europe (OSCE)

Members: Albania, Armenia, Austria, Azerbaijan, Belarus, Belgium, Bosnia and Herzegovina, Bulgaria, Canada, Croatia, Cyprus, Czech Republic, Denmark, Estonia, Finland, France, Georgia, Germany, Greece, Holy See, Hungary, Iceland, Ireland, Italy, Kazakhstan, Kyrgyzstan, Latvia, Liechtenstein, Lithuania, Luxembourg, Macedonia (Former Yugoslav Republic of), Malta, Moldova, Monaco, Netherlands, Norway, Poland, Portugal, Romania, Russia, San Marino, Slovakia, Slovenia, Spain, Sweden, Switzerland, Tajikistan, Turkey, Turkmenistan, UK, Ukraine, USA, Uzbekistan, Yugoslavia*

* Yugoslavia (Serbia and Montenegro) has been suspended since July 1992.

Members of the Minsk Group: Belarus, Finland, France, Germany, Hungary, Italy, Russia, Sweden, Switzerland, Turkey and USA, plus Armenia and Azerbaijan

Organization of African Unity (OAU)

Members: Algeria, Angola, Benin, Botswana, Burkina Faso, Burundi, Cameroon, Cape Verde, Central African Republic, Chad, Comoros, Congo, Côte d'Ivoire, Djibouti, Egypt, Equatorial Guinea, Eritrea, Ethiopia, Gabon, Gambia, Ghana, Guinea, Guinea Bissau, Kenya, Lesotho, Liberia, Libya, Madagascar, Malawi, Mali, Mauritania, Mauritius, Mozambique, Namibia, Niger, Nigeria, Rwanda, Western Sahara (Saharawi Arab Democratic Republic), Sao Tome and Principe, Seychelles, Senegal, Sierra Leone, Somalia, South Africa, Sudan, Swaziland, Tanzania, Togo, Tunisia, Uganda, Zaire, Zambia, Zimbabwe

Organization of American States (OAS)

Members: Antigua and Barbuda, Argentina, Bahamas, Barbados, Belize, Bolivia, Brazil, Canada, Chile, Colombia, Costa Rica, Cuba,* Dominica, Dominican Republic, Ecuador, El Salvador, Grenada, Guatemala, Guyana, Haiti, Honduras, Jamaica, Mexico, Nicaragua, Panama, Paraguay, Peru, Saint Kitts (Christopher) and Nevis, Saint Lucia, Saint Vincent and the Grenadines, Suriname, Trinidad and Tobago, Uruguay, USA, Venezuela

* Cuba has been excluded from participation since 1962.

Permanent observers: Algeria, Angola, Austria, Belgium, Cyprus, Egypt, Equatorial Guinea, European Union, Finland, France, Germany, Greece, Holy See, Hungary, India, Israel, Italy, Japan, Korea (South), Lebanon, Morocco, Netherlands, Pakistan, Poland, Portugal, Romania, Russia, Saudi Arabia, Spain, Switzerland, Tunisia, Ukraine

South Pacific Forum

Members: Australia, Cook Islands, Fiji, Kiribati, Marshall Islands, Micronesia, Nauru, New Zealand, Niue, Palau, Papua New Guinea, Samoa (Western), Solomon Islands, Tonga, Tuvalu, Vanuatu

Western European Union (WEU)

Members: Belgium, France, Germany, Greece, Italy, Luxembourg, Netherlands, Portugal, Spain, UK
Associate Members: Iceland, Norway, Turkey

Observers: Austria, Denmark, Finland, Ireland, Sweden

Associate Partners: Bulgaria, Czech Republic, Estonia, Hungary, Latvia, Lithuania, Poland, Romania, Slovakia

Members of WEAG: Belgium, Denmark, France, Germany, Greece, Italy, Luxembourg, Netherlands, Norway, Portugal, Spain, Turkey, UK

Zangger Committee

Members: Australia, Austria, Belgium, Bulgaria, Canada, Czech Republic, Denmark, Finland, France, Germany, Greece, Hungary, Ireland, Italy, Japan, Luxembourg, Netherlands, Norway, Poland, Portugal, Romania, Russia, Slovakia, South Africa, Spain, Sweden, Switzerland, UK, USA

Observer: South Korea

Conventions in tables

..	Data not available or not applicable
–	Nil or a negligible figure
( )	Uncertain data
b.	billion (thousand million)
m.	million
th.	thousand
$	US dollars, unless otherwise indicated

Introduction: towards a pluralistic security system

ADAM DANIEL ROTFELD

The 20th century will soon be drawing to a close. In the view of many politicians, analysts and security experts, the political watersheds of this century were marked by the gunshots fired in Sarajevo in the summers of 1914 and 1991. The former marked the beginning of World War I, which in turn led to the end of the order founded on the concert of European powers and the formation, on its ruins, of totalitarian regimes in Russia and later in Germany. The latter marked the start of a new, post-cold war reality in which governments have started to lose control of developments.

The bipolar system based on mutual deterrence is a thing of the past, but a new world order has not yet emerged. The most prevalent menace since the end of the cold war is the occurrence of civil wars and local and regional conflicts. Security organizations have proved incapable of preventing or resolving such conflicts, and the big powers seem to have lost interest in the areas that in the past were considered their zones of influence. Another severe problem is the failure of numerous states that, as a result of their domestic weakness, are sliding into anarchy and ungovernability.

I. Accomplishments and failures

In the cold war period, arms control and disarmament were given the highest priority in the pursuit of international security and stability. Today, many consider this process to be of secondary importance, although they recognize that significant achievements have been made. The 1991 Treaty on the Reduction and Limitation of Strategic Offensive Arms (START I Treaty) resulted in deep reductions (to about 75 per cent of 1990 levels) in the nuclear arsenals of the Russian Federation and the United States and in the removal of all nuclear weapons from Belarus, Kazakhstan and Ukraine.[1] Ratification and entry into force of the 1993 Treaty on Further Reduction and Limitation of Strategic Offensive Arms (START II Treaty) will result in further reductions. An historic accomplishment of 1995 was the indefinite extension of the 1968 Non-Proliferation Treaty (NPT) as the successful outcome of the NPT Review and Extension Conference.[2] The completion of a comprehensive test ban treaty (CTBT) is also within reach.[3] Worldwide public protests against French

---

[1] For more on this subject, see De Andreis, M. and Calogero, F., *The Soviet Nuclear Weapon Legacy*, SIPRI Research Report no. 10 (Oxford University Press: Oxford, 1995).

[2] See chapter 13 in this volume.

[3] See chapter 14 in this volume.

nuclear tests in 1995 contributed to an important change in France's policy: the French Government first reduced the number of tests it was to have conducted in the South Pacific and then in 1996 announced the 'definitive end' of French nuclear testing.

Two other matters remain on the nuclear arms control agenda: the negotiations on a convention to ban the production of fissile material for nuclear weapons or other nuclear devices; and further reductions of nuclear weapons with the ultimate goal of their global elimination.

The implementation of the 1990 Treaty on Conventional Armed Forces in Europe (CFE Treaty) proceeded without major interruptions, and negotiations are under way to determine the framework for conventional arms control and the reduction of armaments into the 21st century. Some progress was also made in setting up a new arrangement on export controls for conventional arms and dual-use goods and technologies (the Wassenaar Arrangement). The significant headway made in these matters shows that arms control is by no means a secondary issue on the security agenda.

The priority task in 1995 was the search for ways to extinguish local conflicts and streamline the mechanisms for preventing new conflicts. The war in the former Yugoslavia was brought to an end in 1995 with the General Framework Agreement for Peace in Bosnia and Herzegovina (the Dayton Agreement) and the Basic Agreement on the Region of Eastern Slavonia, Baranja, and Western Sirmium (Croatia). However, the agreements created only the premises and opportunity for initiating a process leading to a durable peace; whether and to what extent this opportunity will be seized remains to be seen.[4] Developments in the Middle East, especially the difficulties encountered in the peace process between Israel and the Palestinians, illustrate the long and tortuous road from signing an agreement to establishing genuine peace.[5] On the other hand, some progress has been achieved in seeking a political solution of the conflict in Nagorno-Karabakh (Azerbaijan) and other conflicts on the territory of the former Soviet Union—in the Trans-Dniester region (Moldova), South Ossetia (Georgia) and Abkhazia (Georgia).[6]

Events confirmed that the existing security institutions are not fully adequate to meet the new challenges and threats, however. There are great expectations that the international security structures—such as the United Nations, NATO, the European Union (EU), the Western European Union (WEU) and the Organization for Security and Co-operation in Europe (OSCE)—will devote unprecedented levels of human and financial resources to conflict prevention and resolution. It is also widely demanded that international principles, norms and procedures be adapted to the new situation. UN Secretary-General Boutros Boutros-Ghali asserted that '[t]he problems presented by conflicts such as those in former Yugoslavia, Afghanistan, Liberia, Rwanda, Burundi and

---

[4] See chapter 5 in this volume.
[5] See chapter 4 in this volume.
[6] See chapter 6 in this volume.

Somalia are in many ways unprecedented'.[7] In theory, the international community remains committed to giving the UN and other international organizations both the mandate and adequate resources to meet the new tasks and expectations which they face. This is also true regarding the task of determining the legal basis for multilateral interventions aimed at restoring the peace and security of states.[8] However, in practice, states are for many reasons not eager to assume the burden of peacekeeping operations or to basically revise the tenets which curtail the possibility to intervene in other states' domestic affairs, even when grave violations of human rights and the rights of national, ethnic and religious minorities are taking place. For all the warranted criticism of the international security structures, one must remember that without such organizations as the UN, on the global scale, and NATO, the EU and the OSCE, on the European regional scale, prevention and resolution of conflicts would be even more difficult, if not impossible. The paradox is that criticism of the international institutions entrusted with maintaining peace and security is growing apace with the increase in their activities since the end of the cold war. To give just one illustration—while in 1988 the United Nations had only 9950 troops in the field, in 1995 peacekeeping operations under UN auspices employed nearly 70 000 personnel.[9] After the Dayton Agreement, about 60 000 ground troops, including the 20 000-strong US contingent under NATO command, were deployed in Bosnia and Herzegovina.[10]

Even under these circumstances, the international community is not indifferent or inactive. The peace operations in Angola, Cambodia, Haiti, El Salvador and Mozambique have brought about clear and positive effects: they have contributed to saving hundreds of thousands of lives and set in motion the process of reconstruction of states based on the rule of law and democratic institutions.

Critical assessments of international security structures stem not so much from a lack of commitment as from excessive public expectations and failure or inability to fulfil them. There are many reasons for this, the most important apparently being the absence of political will on the part of parties to a conflict to cooperate in seeking solutions. The United Nations can only be as effective as its member states allow it to be. Their option to decline an active role raises the question whether the international community can simply leave afflicted populations to their fate. As a remedy, the UN Secretary-General proposed a management plan for creating a mission-driven and result-oriented UN organization by pursuing the following objectives: better management of human

[7] Boutros-Ghali, B., *Confronting New Challenges: Annual Report on the Work of the Organization from the Forty-ninth to the Fiftieth Session of the General Assembly* (UN: New York, 1995), p. 2.
[8] See appendix 2D and chapter 7 in this volume.
[9] UN, Supplement to *An Agenda for Peace*: position paper of the Secretary-General on the occasion of the 50th anniversary of the United Nations, UN document A/50/60, S/19951, 3 Jan. 1995 (see appendix 2B in this volume). See also Findlay, T., *Challenges for the New Peacekeepers*, SIPRI Research Report no. 12 (Oxford University Press: Oxford, 1996), pp. 2–3. According to the UN Secretary-General's Annual Report, the peacekeeping troops, military observers and civilian police in peacekeeping operations engaged 67 269 persons as of 31 July 1995 (note 7). See also chapter 2 in this volume.
[10] See chapter 5 in this volume.

resources and of the organization's programme, based on better and timely information; better management of and greater access to technology within the organization; and an enhanced programme for promoting efficiency and cost-effectiveness.[11]

While it is true that better management of the world organization is essential for reform of the UN system, all the other multilateral structures established in the cold war era are also in urgent need of transformation because they are not suited to the needs of today, let alone the tasks and challenges of tomorrow. However, since the new threats consist mainly in conflicts not between states but more and more within states, it is worth considering whether consolidation of these organizations, as one of the main instruments for meeting the coming challenges, can be effective and where the limits of their competence should lie.

II. New challenges and priorities

Consideration of the tasks ahead requires that an accurate diagnosis be made and that the new threats be identified. The challenge is much more serious because in some multi-ethnic states central governments are losing control of developments.[12] Threats which today undermine stability and may tomorrow threaten world security are 'ripening' on the peripheries of great-power global politics. Conflicts which might be headed off today are often played down or ignored so long as they do not spill over into open wars.[13] To prevent such conflicts it is not enough to increase the human and financial resources at the disposal of existing organizations or streamline the mechanisms of those organizations.

There is no doubt that global and regional security organizations must be strengthened.[14] The world is witnessing the globalization and multilateralization of international relations and the growing role of transnational structures,

[11] Boutros-Ghali (note 7), p. 6.

[12] In his analyses of how scarcity, crime, overpopulation, tribalism and disease are rapidly destroying the social fabric of our planet, Robert D. Kaplan concludes that more and more places will be 'ungovernable'. Kaplan, R. D., 'The coming anarchy', *Atlantic Monthly*, Feb. 1994, p. 54. See also Waslekar, S., *South Asian Drama: Travails of Misgovernance* (Konarks: Delhi, 1996).

[13] 'West Africa is becoming *the* symbol of worldwide demographic, environmental, and societal stress, in which criminal anarchy emerges as the real "strategic" danger. Disease, overpopulation, unprovoked crime, scarcity of resources, refugee migrations, the increasing erosion of nation-states and international borders, and the empowerment of private armies, security firms, and international drug cartels are now most tellingly demonstrated through a West African prism.' Kaplan (note 12), p. 46.

[14] A number of recently published reports illustrate the search for ways to increase the effectiveness of the existing organizations by strengthening them, making them more representative and creating new structures. On the global scale, see *Global Security Programme: Final Report of the Global Security Project* (prepared under the auspices of the Gorbachev Foundation and the Rajiv Gandhi Foundation: New Delhi, Oct. 1994); *Our Global Neighbourhood*, Report of the Commission on Global Governance (Co-chairmen Ingvar Carlsson and Shridath Ramphal) (Oxford University Press: Oxford, 1995); and *The United Nations in its Second Half-Century,* Report of the Independent Working Group on the Future of the United Nations (Co-chairmen Moeen Quershi and Richard von Weizsäcker) (Ford Foundation: New York, 1995). On the European regional scale, see *Die Europäische Sicherheitsgemeinschaft: Das Sicherheitsmodell für das 21. Jahrhundert* [The European security community: a security model for the 21st century] (Peace Research and Security Policy Institute: Hamburg, 1995). See also appendix 2D in this volume.

but also the breakup of the international system based on an unswerving respect for the sovereign independence of states. That system has functioned, with successes and failures, since the Peace of Westphalia of 1648 which ended the Thirty Years' War; international security was contingent on the balance of power among the major powers, with the underlying assumption that individual states are guarantors of security, prosperity and development. 'The disorder and turbulence many people experience today comes with the realization that this guarantee can no longer be taken for granted.'[15] Criticism of international organizations results in part from the fact that expectations with regard to ensuring security and prosperity are addressed today not only to individual states but also to global and regional transnational structures.

The end of bipolarism triggered the dynamic of global structural change accompanied by the dynamic of multilateralism. Of what significance are these processes for maintaining international stability and security? Will they lead to legitimization and expansion of international interventionism, and, if so, in what circumstances and to what extent? These are not rhetorical but very practical questions.

The picture presented to the US Senate by John Deutch, Director of the Central Intelligence Agency, in his 1996 *Worldwide Threat Assessment* can be summarized as consisting of four threats: (*a*) ethnic turmoil and humanitarian crises; (*b*) the process of transformation and 'metamorphosis' of two great powers (China and Russia); (*c*) 'rogue' nations (Iran, Iraq, North Korea and Libya) that have built up significant military forces and seek to acquire weapons of mass destruction; and (*d*) proliferation of weapons of mass destruction, terrorism, drugs and crime.[16]

A new phenomenon is that security experts who represent one of the most prestigious research centres in post-Soviet Russia share this view of the risks to and priorities of security policy. They draw attention to the fact that, unlike the period when international stability relied on negative factors (mutual deterrence), the primary driving force of stability and security building in the post-cold war era is interdependence of national interests and cooperation.[17] It is worth noting that Russian analysts warn against the self-complacency inherent in the assumption that Russia will become a stable state. In fact, they argue that the force of inertia driving destabilization in Russia is difficult to stop. Restoring domestic equilibrium is dependent on constant economic growth, and this cannot be expected, according to even the most optimistic forecasts, until the beginning of the next century.[18]

---

[15] Hettne, B., 'The United Nations and conflict management: the role of the "new regionalism"', *Transnational Law and Contemporary Problems* (University of Iowa, College of Law), vol. 4, no. 2 (autumn 1994), p. 644.

[16] *Worldwide Threat Assessment Brief to the Senate Select Committee on Intelligence*, Statement by John Deutch, Director of Central Intelligence, Washington, DC, 22 Feb. 1996.

[17] *Rossiya i obespechenie mezhdunarodnoy stabilnosti* [Russia and the maintenance of international stability] (IMEMO: Moscow, 1995), p. 10.

[18] IMEMO (note 17), p. 103.

III. Rethinking the security concept

It can be assumed that assessments of threats and ways of preventing them reflect the main directions of thinking in both great powers. It is striking that both the US and Russian assessments mentioned above leave out two key questions related to international security: the information revolution and the need to redefine security. Joseph S. Nye and William A. Owens rightly noted that today '[k]nowledge, more than ever before, is power'.[19] Today power is determined to a great extent by which state is ahead in the information revolution, and this will be even more true in the future. These authors draw attention to a critical fact—that the dominant position of the United States in communications and information-processing technologies stems from huge investments and its open society. Space-based surveillance, direct broadcasting, high-speed computers and an unparalleled ability to integrate complex information systems have shaped an information edge that 'can help deter or defeat traditional military threats at relatively low costs'.[20] This has permitted the United States, the European Union, Japan and other highly industrialized countries to strengthen their security and enhance international stability through attraction rather than coercion.

The United States can use its information resources to engage China, Russia and other powerful states in security dialogue to prevent them from becoming hostile. At the same time, its information edge can help prevent states like Iran and Iraq, already hostile, from becoming powerful. Moreover, it can bolster new democracies and communicate directly with those living under undemocratic regimes. This advantage is also important in efforts to prevent and resolve regional conflicts and deal with prominent post-Cold War dangers, including international crime, terrorism, proliferation of weapons of mass destruction, and damage to the global environment.[21]

The obstacles to making use of this potential are traditional, predominantly military, perceptions of security and adherence to traditional parameters of security, such as gross national product, population, energy, land, minerals, and so on, as well as the failure to realize what the information revolution has already contributed and can offer to security.

In this context, the postulate that the nature of international security must be redefined is gaining in significance. This is directly related to the debate initiated in the European Union, and in particular to the new approach taken by the EU Intergovernmental Conference (IGC) that opened in 1996 to the institution of a Common Foreign and Security Policy (CFSP). The problems encountered in forging a common security policy are often wrongly attributed to procedural and formal matters.

---

[19] Nye, J. S., Jr and Owens, W. A., 'America's information edge', *Foreign Affairs*, vol. 75, no. 2 (Mar./Apr. 1996), p. 20.
[20] Nye and Owens (note 19), p. 20. In this case the 'relatively low costs' are probably compared to cold war military expenditures.
[21] Nye and Owens (note 19), p. 22.

Another approach is also wrong: claiming that the EU members and the USA are facing a dilemma over the organizing principle of their security policy—whether it should be national interests or shared values. In his response to Michael Mandelbaum's article entitled 'Foreign policy as social work',[22] Stanley Hoffman writes: 'the distinction between interests and values is largely fallacious, and that policy which would ignore the domestic crises that affect so many states and pseudostates today would have disastrous consequences'.[23] One way of overcoming this dilemma is offered by Karl Deutsch's concept of the pluralistic security community. Defined nearly 40 years ago, it contains the following elements: sovereignty and legal independence of states; compatibility of core values derived from common institutions; mutual responsiveness, identity and loyalty; integration to the point that states entertain 'dependable expectations of peaceful change';[24] and communication cementing political communities.[25] Such a security community would need at least some common principles of global ethics.[26]

It would be naive to expect the United States or other great powers to resign from their role in world affairs or to stop pursuing their national interests for the sake of a concept that runs counter to these interests. A new definition of security should, however, take into account not only these values and interests but also the emerging new premises, including the breakup of the Westphalian international system based on the omnipotence of sovereign states.

This new reality is implicitly reflected in the ongoing debate in Europe on a common, cooperative and comprehensive security concept. It affects the negotiations conducted in the European Union, the work initiated by the NATO transformation and the debate held in the OSCE.[27] The critical question in this search has two aspects: (*a*) the extent to which the international security system can resolve existing conflicts; and (*b*) how the emergence of threats can be prevented and their causes uprooted. The latter is gaining in prominence.

IV. SIPRI findings

By collecting precise and verifiable data and information on which to base their analyses, the authors of the chapters in this *SIPRI Yearbook* contribute to

---

[22] *Foreign Affairs*, vol. 75, no. 1 (Jan./Feb. 1996).

[23] Hoffman, S., 'In defense of Mother Teresa: morality in foreign policy', *Foreign Affairs,* vol. 75, no. 2 (Mar./Apr. 1996), p. 172.

[24] Deutsch, K. W. *et al., Political Community and the North Atlantic Area* (Princeton University Press: Princeton, N.J., 1957), p. 5.

[25] Norbert Wiener wrote: 'Communication alone enables a group to think together, and to act together'. Quoted by Karl W. Deutsch in *The Nerves of Government* (Free Press: New York, 1966), p. 17. See also Adler, E. and Barnett, M., 'Pluralistic security communities: past, present, future', *Working Paper Series on Regional Security*, no. 1 (University of Wisconsin: Madison, Wisc., June 1994), p. 1.

[26] Küng, H., *Global Responsibility: In Search of a New World Ethic* (Continuum: New York, 1993); and Lewis, F., 'Globalization brings a need for global ethics', *International Herald Tribune*, 28 Mar. 1996, p. 8.

[27] See chapter 7 in this volume.

an understanding of the essence of the ongoing processes in the world and their consequences for international security on the global and regional scale.

Conflicts. It is highly symptomatic of the new world situation that all the 30 major armed conflicts registered for 1995 are intra-state rather than inter-state.[28]

Conflict prevention, management and resolution. The Dayton Agreement on Bosnia and Herzegovina and the Basic Agreement on Croatia constituted the most spectacular peacemaking achievements of the year. Progress was also made in the Middle East peace process and in establishing or restoring democracy and law and order in Haiti. A peace accord was reached in Angola, although implementation remained incomplete. There was renewed armed conflict in Chechnya (Russia), Liberia, Sri Lanka and Sudan, despite peace efforts. UN peacekeeping contracted significantly. Conflict prevention was given new emphasis in UN debates in view of the high cost of peacekeeping and the impossibility of the UN addressing all conflicts simultaneously. Regional organizations moved to enhance their capabilities for conflict prevention, management and resolution.[29]

UN reform. The UN General Assembly set September 1996 as the deadline for recommendations on reform to be submitted by its subsidiary bodies. Reform proposals from governments and non-governmental sources covered the entire spectrum of UN activities. Particularly important ideas were those for expansion and reform of the Security Council, rationalization and better management of the UN system, democratization of the UN's decision-making processes, and financial reform.

The Middle East. The multilateral track of the peace process made progress in 1995 but is limited by the need for further bilateral achievements, particularly between Israel and Syria. Progress was achieved on the Israeli–Palestinian track with the signature of the Interim Agreement, while the Palestinian Authority and the Israeli Government intensified the fight against terrorism. The Israeli–Syrian talks were stalled for much of the year but were revived after Prime Minister Rabin's assassination. Much remains to be done, and the Israeli and US elections scheduled for 1996 may affect the process. The Israeli–Jordanian Peace Treaty was implemented smoothly in 1995.[30]

Russia and the Commonwealth of Independent States (CIS). During 1995 the war in Chechnya persisted as the most destabilizing development in Russia. The conflicts on the territories of other former Soviet republics continued in less confrontational forms than in the recent past, except for Tajikistan. In the CIS area, Russia has succeeded in considerably strengthening its position and in having the CIS area recognized by the international community as a de facto zone of Russia's vital interests. The CIS countries are expected to respond with loyalty to Russia—up to the point of accepting a Russian military presence on their territories. The institutionalization of the special rela-

[28] See chapter 1 in this volume.
[29] See chapter 2 in this volume.
[30] See chapter 4 in this volume.

tionship between Russia and Belarus may be seen as the first step towards establishing a post-Soviet empire under Russian domination.[31]

Europe. In the process of shaping European security, abstract concepts, models and deliberations are of much less importance than the response to the real needs of preventing conflict and settling crisis. A new system of security will result from the evolution, enlargement and transformation of existing structures rather than a proliferation of new institutions. Apart from the main organizations (NATO, the EU/WEU, the OSCE and the Council of Europe), subregional structures such as the Barents Euro-Atlantic Council, the Council of Baltic Sea States and the Central European Initiative will also play an increasing role.[32]

Military expenditure. Aggregate world spending continued to decline in 1995. This fall was again driven by major defence spending cuts in the Western industrialized countries and Russia. Military spending is still rising in other regions, however, notably in the Middle East and South-East Asia.[33]

Military research and development. World military research and development (R&D) expenditure in the mid-1990s probably does not exceed $60 billion, a reduction of more than 50 per cent in real terms from SIPRI's last estimate, in 1987. Spending in the countries of the former Warsaw Treaty Organization has decreased dramatically and accounts for most of the difference, but France, Italy and the USA have also reduced their spending by 25 per cent or more from the cold-war peaks. Of the major investors, only India, Japan and South Korea continue to increase their spending dramatically.[34]

Arms production. The combined armed sales of the 'top 100' arms-producing companies in the Organisation for Economic Co-operation and Development (OECD) and the developing world continued to fall in 1994, although at a slower rate than in the preceding year. The drop is expected to continue, since excess capacity is far from having been eliminated in most sectors and regions. National costs in the form of structural unemployment are high in many regions.

In no other major arms-producing country has military production dropped as sharply as in the Russian Federation: by 1995 it had fallen to one-sixth of its level in 1991. Some diversification into civilian production has taken place but the transfer of resources from the military to civilian sectors has been much less than expected. China's ambitious conversion efforts have begun to show signs of strain. With domestic procurement in considerable decline and with few export options, China's military industries must contract, but are ill-prepared to meet commercial challenges.[35]

Arms trade. According to SIPRI estimates, the global trend-indicator value of foreign deliveries of major conventional weapons in 1995 was $22 797

[31] See chapter 6 in this volume.
[32] See chapter 7 in this volume.
[33] See chapter 8 in this volume.
[34] See chapter 9 in this volume.
[35] See chapter 10 in this volume.

billion in constant (1990) US dollars.[36] The estimate for 1995 represents a slight increase over the revised estimate for 1994, suggesting that the fall in the volume of deliveries of major conventional weapons recorded since the end of the cold war has come to an end. Among the suppliers, the most notable change in 1995 was the relatively high share of deliveries by Russia: it accounted for 17 per cent of total deliveries, compared with 4 per cent in 1994. The USA remained the largest supplier in 1995, accounting for 43 per cent of deliveries. Among the recipients, the most noticeable trend has been the growing share of total deliveries to North-East Asia: deliveries to China and Taiwan have increased sharply in recent years.[37]

Arms export control. In 1995 the membership of the Nuclear Suppliers Group (NSG), the Australia Group and the Missile Technology Control Regime (MTCR) continued to expand. Modifications were made to the Zangger Committee trigger list and to the lists of equipment and technologies subject to control in the NSG, the Australia Group and the MTCR. On 18 December 1995, subject to the approval of the 28 participating member governments, a new multilateral regime was provisionally established to address the issue of export controls on conventional arms and dual-use goods and technologies (the Wassenaar Arrangement).[38]

NPT extension. While the NPT was extended indefinitely in 1995 and the nuclear weapon states parties reiterated their commitment to nuclear disarmament, there was growing concern that the treaty might be used more to prevent proliferation than to facilitate complete nuclear disarmament, which is now a more open imperative of many non-nuclear weapon states, even those that continue to rely on nuclear guarantees. Although most concerns about nuclear proliferation were in remission in 1995 as new nuclear weapon-free zones were created, the continued reliance on nuclear weapons to deter conventional war and the use of weapons of mass destruction will prevent the realization of complete nuclear disarmament unless doctrine in the nuclear weapon states and their allies and security partners is reformed.[39]

Nuclear arms control. The Conference on Disarmament made progress on the CTB in 1995 and achieved a mandate for a convention banning the production of fissile material for military purposes, but there remains a possibility that the CTB will not be completed in 1996 and progress on the fissile material cut-off is likely to be slow. The US-funded programme of bilateral cooperation to facilitate denuclearization and demilitarization in Belarus, Kazakhstan, Russia and Ukraine intensified but became embroiled in domestic controversies in both the USA and the recipient countries. The year 1996 is likely to be

---

[36] The index produced using the SIPRI valuation system is not comparable to official economic statistics such as gross domestic product, public expenditure, and/or export and import figures. The index is designed as a trend-measuring device, to permit the measurement of changes in the total flow of major conventional weapons and its geographic pattern.

[37] See chapter 11 in this volume.

[38] See chapter 12 in this volume.

[39] See chapter 13 in this volume.

a watershed, in which nuclear arms control either grinds to a halt or is reinvigorated.[40]

Chemical and biological arms control. The destruction of chemical weapons (CW) in both Russia and the USA remains a matter of concern. The overall cost of destruction in the USA has grown to $11.9 billion; for Russia the cost is estimated at approximately $6 billion. The US Johnston Atoll Chemical Agent Disposal System (JACADS) destruction facility continues to operate, but programmes at the Tooele and Anniston facilities were delayed owing to lack of state and local permits. In Russia, the Chemical Weapons Destruction Act was introduced in the Duma in December, but the Russian CW destruction programme faces major financial problems, even though Germany, the Netherlands, Sweden and the USA continue to donate funds and expertise.[41] The March 1995 terrorist attack in the Tokyo underground system demonstrated the vulnerability of societies and the need to consider measures to deter individuals and states from acquiring and using these weapons.

Conventional arms control and confidence-building measures (CSBMs) in Europe. By the end of 1995, 30 states parties to the CFE Treaty had reduced their heavy weapons by nearly 50 000 items. Along with the Russian troop withdrawals from Central Europe and the Baltic states that were completed in 1994, this established an unprecedented core of military stability and predictability in Europe. The CFE flank dispute flared up in 1995, however, with repeated threats by the Russian military to withdraw from the treaty. NATO insists on full CFE implementation, but enlargement of NATO membership to the east will call for a new approach to the conventional arms balance in Europe. The negotiations on regional arms control and CSBMs in the former Yugoslavia may be able to help enhance mutual confidence, reduce the risk of conflict and inject stability into this conflict-ridden area.[42]

Inhumane weapons: anti-personnel mines. The Review Conference of the Inhumane Weapons Convention opened in 1995 but could not agree on new provisions to strengthen Protocol II on the use of land-mines, booby-traps and other devices. The most effective way to deal with the danger posed by anti-personnel land-mines is to prohibit—not restrict or regulate—their production, stockpiling, transfer and use, and to establish international control over compliance with the prohibition. A complete ban would be more easily verifiable than partial solutions.[43]

* * *

The facts, data and analyses summarized above lead to three main conclusions.

1. In the post-cold war period, new threats and risks have emerged, while some of the 'old' ones continue to exist. The risk of an outbreak of global nuclear war has diminished, but the danger of proliferation of weapons of

[40] See chapter 13 in this volume.
[41] See chapter 15 in this volume.
[42] See chapter 16 in this volume.
[43] See chapter 17 in this volume.

mass destruction has increased. The serious threat at present is the loss of control of developments by the great powers, the multilateral security organizations and the states on whose territories conflicts have broken out. The international system, based on the principles of interaction of sovereign states, is eroding.

2. The search for a new security system should prioritize common values and ways of harmonizing national interests. Establishing a new international security order will be a long-term process of accommodating existing institutions to new needs rather than of creating new organizational structures.

3. The new security system will express the political philosophy of a pluralistic community rather than a specific model or set of abstract assumptions. The comprehensive nature of such a system should reflect three fundamental objectives of peace: security; social and economic welfare; and respect for human rights, justice and organization of society based on the rule of law.

Part I. Global and regional security and conflicts, 1995

1. Major armed conflicts

MARGARETA SOLLENBERG and PETER WALLENSTEEN

I. Global patterns of major armed conflicts, 1989–95

In 1995, 30 major armed conflicts were waged in 25 locations around the world. Both the number of major armed conflicts and the number of conflict locations were lower than in 1994 (when there were 32 conflicts in 28 locations)[1] and were significantly lower than in 1989 (when there were 36 conflicts in 32 locations), the last year of the cold war.

A 'major armed conflict' is defined here as prolonged combat between the military forces of two or more governments, or of one government and at least one organized armed group, and incurring the battle-related deaths of at least 1000 people during the entire conflict.[2] A conflict 'location' is the territory of at least one state. Since certain countries are the location of more than one conflict, the number of conflicts reported is greater than the number of conflict locations.[3]

As in 1994, all the major armed conflicts in 1995 were internal, or intra-state, rather than between states;[4] that is, the issue, or incompatibility, concerned control by internal parties over the government or territory of one state. However, foreign forces were involved in some intra-state conflicts, in the sense that their regular troops were involved in the fighting—in Tajikistan (Russian/Commonwealth of Independent States [CIS] forces were used against the opposition and also staged offensives aimed at Tajik opposition bases in Afghanistan), Liberia (the Economic Organization of West African States Monitoring Group peacekeeping forces were involved), and Bosnia and Herzegovina (troops from Croatia reinforced the Bosnian Army in battles with Bosnian Serb forces).

Only one conflict—that in Bosnia and Herzegovina—was ended during the year through a comprehensive peace treaty which included military and civilian provisions as well as ways of addressing the incompatibilities behind the conflict. The General Framework Agreement was reached in Dayton, Ohio, in

---

[1] In the *SIPRI Yearbook 1995: Armaments, Disarmament and International Security* (Oxford University Press: Oxford, 1995), chapter 1, 31 conflicts in 27 locations were recorded for 1994. Because new information has become available, the conflict in Sierra Leone has been re-evaluated and has been included as a major armed conflict in 1994. Figures for 1994 have therefore been revised as 32 conflicts in 28 locations.

[2] See appendix 1A in this volume for definitions of the criteria. See also Heldt, B. (ed.), *States in Armed Conflict 1990–91* (Department of Peace and Conflict Research, Uppsala University: Uppsala, 1992), chapter 3, for the full definitions.

[3] Some countries are also the location of minor armed conflicts. The table in appendix 1A presents only the major armed conflicts in the countries listed.

[4] However, in 1995 there were brief armed conflicts between states, e.g., that between Ecuador and Peru, which did not fulfil the criteria for major armed conflicts.

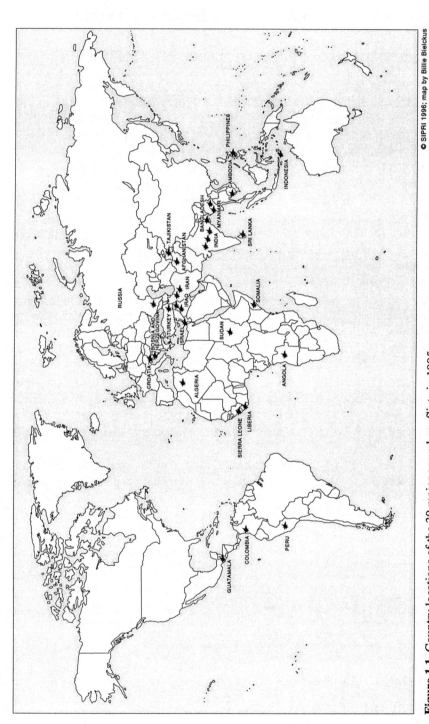

Figure 1.1. Country locations of the 30 major armed conflicts in 1995

© SIPRI 1996; map by Billie Bielckus

November and signed in Paris on 14 December 1995.[5] During the year a second conflict—that between the Croatian Government and the Croatian Serbs—ended with military victories and a peace agreement. The Croatian Government recaptured Western Slavonia and Krajina, after which an agreement was reached for the return of Eastern Slavonia to Croatian Government control.[6] In Angola and Palestine, previously agreed peace treaties were being implemented in 1995 although violence still took place.

It should be noted that the definition of 'major armed conflict' includes only those conflicts in which a government is one of the parties. In 1995, as in previous years, there were a number of cases where non-governmental actors were fighting each other, often in addition to an ongoing conflict between a government and some or all of the non-governmental parties. These included the conflicts in Afghanistan, northern Iraq, India (Kashmir), Liberia, Myanmar, Somalia and Sudan. In the Tajikistan conflict, the government side was fragmenting in the face of a united opposition made up of various interest groups.

II. Changes in the table of conflicts for 1995

New conflicts in 1995

Two new major armed conflicts were registered in 1995. The most devastating was the war in Chechnya between forces of the Russian Federation and the forces under General Dzhokhar Dudayev which demand the independence of Chechnya. The armed conflict broke out in December 1994 and intensified during the early months of 1995. A cease-fire was agreed in July 1995, but there were sporadic violations of the cease-fire and renewed fighting broke out around mid-December.[7]

The second new major armed conflict was the civil war in Sierra Leone between the government and the Revolutionary United Front (RUF). This conflict began in 1991; since then the number of battle deaths has gradually risen. The total death toll resulting directly from the conflict is now estimated to be over 3000. The future course of the Sierra Leone conflict will depend on the situation in Liberia, the location of another major armed conflict, because of the close ties between the opposition organizations in the two states.

Three of the major armed conflicts that had been active in 1993 were not recorded for 1994 but reappeared in 1995. These were the conflicts in Croatia (fighting between the Croatian Government and the Serbian Republic of Krajina in May and August 1995, which ended in a Croatian victory), Iraq (battles between the Iraqi Government and Kurdish factions in March 1995) and India (the conflict in Punjab was resumed in August by some of the

---

[5] See also chapters 2, 5, 7 and 16 in this volume. The General Framework Agreement for Peace in Bosnia and Herzegovina (Dayton Agreement, 21 Nov. 1995) is reproduced in appendix 5A in this volume.

[6] The Basic Agreement on the Region of Eastern Slavonia, Baranja and Western Sirmium, 12 Nov. 1995, is reproduced in appendix 5A in this volume.

[7] See also chapter 6 in this volume.

groups that were previously involved). In the latter two cases, fighting was at a low level and possibly temporary.

Conflicts recorded in 1994 that did not reappear in 1995

Two conflicts in 1994 were not recorded for 1995 because victory was achieved by one side and the fighting ceased: this was the case for the conflict in Yemen, where the government won decisively in July 1994, and that in Rwanda, where the Rwandan Patriotic Front (RPF) took control of most of the country by July 1994. In the latter case, there is a continuing danger that the conflict will re-ignite since the previous government fled with its troops to neighbouring Tanzania and Zaire.

In four conflicts there was no military action in 1995 because of cease-fire agreements concluded in 1994: Azerbaijan (in the conflict over Nagorno-Karabakh, a cease-fire was negotiated through the auspices of the Conference on Security and Co-operation in Europe [CSCE] in May 1994); the conflict between the Bosnian Government and the Bosnian Croat forces in Bosnia and Herzegovina (a cease-fire was agreed in February 1994 and a federation established in March between them); Georgia (in the conflict over Abkhazia, Abkhaz forces have controlled most of the territory since September 1993 and a Russian–Georgian–Abkhaz cease-fire agreement was reached in May 1994, resulting in deployment of a Russian peacekeeping force); and the United Kingdom (in Northern Ireland, following a cease-fire between the British authorities and the Irish Republican Army [IRA], agreed in September 1994). In all these conflicts, the parties retained military forces at the ready and the potential for resumption of armed conflict remained high. There were no peace agreements concluded in any of these cases.

Changes in intensity of conflicts and peace efforts

In a number of conflicts the intensity of armed conflict decreased. This was the case for the conflicts in Angola, Liberia and the Philippines and was related to major changes among the parties—involving negotiation efforts and a cease-fire in Angola, a cease-fire and the setting up of a new government involving the main warring parties in Liberia, and the declining strength of the New People's Army (NPA) in the Philippines.

Two major armed conflicts escalated markedly: in Sri Lanka, between the government and the Tamil Tigers, following a cease-fire and negotiations that appeared promising; and in Turkey, between the government and the Kurdish Worker's Party (PKK). These two conflicts were among the most violent of 1995. The conflicts in Afghanistan, Algeria, Bosnia and Herzegovina, Russia (Chechnya) and Sudan were also high-intensity conflicts, or wars—that is, more than 1000 battle-related deaths occurred in 1995—although several of them (e.g., Afghanistan and Algeria) de-escalated compared to 1994.

Peace efforts resulted in the comprehensive General Framework Agreement for Peace in Bosnia and Herzegovina as well as an agreement for Eastern Slavonia in Croatia and the end of these major armed conflicts (at least temporarily). In many other cases, negotiations focused on achieving cease-fire arrangements (e.g., in Russia and Sudan) that were maintained for limited periods.

III. Regional patterns of major armed conflicts, 1989–95

The regional distribution of locations with major armed conflicts is given in table 1.1. In the early 1990s the number of conflicts started to decline in three regions (Africa, Asia, and Central and South America) while subregions such as Southern Africa and South-East Asia began to experience fewer conflicts or less intensive conflicts. The gradual shift in incompatibilities from issues of government control (56 per cent in 1989) to those over territory (53 per cent in 1995) continued (see table 1.2).

Table 1.1. Regional distribution of locations with at least one major armed conflict, 1989–95

Region[a]	1989	1990	1991	1992	1993	1994	1995
Africa	9	10	10	7	7	7	6
Asia	11	10	8	11	9	9	9
Central and South America	5	5	4	3	3	3	3
Europe	2	1	2	4	5	4	3
Middle East	5	5	5	4	4	5	4
Total	**32**	**31**	**29**	**29**	**28**	**28**	**25**

[a] Only those regions of the world in which a conflict was recorded for the period 1989–95 are included here.

Source: Uppsala Conflict Data Project.

In 1995 Europe experienced the lowest number of conflicts and conflict locations since 1991. By the end of December 1995, following the cease-fire and peace agreements for Bosnia and Herzegovina and Croatia, there were no active major armed conflicts on this continent, except for sporadic fighting in Chechnya. However, the cease-fire agreements for conflicts involving Azerbaijan, Chechnya, Georgia and Northern Ireland were still in danger of being challenged as 1995 ended.[8]

The Middle East region, in spite of the peace agreements between Israel and the Palestinians and Jordan,[9] has shown very little variation in the number of major armed conflicts since 1989, but in 1995 many of these conflicts were at a low level of intensity. The exception was the conflict in Turkey between the

[8] The cease-fire in the UK–Northern Ireland conflict was broken by the IRA in Feb. 1996.
[9] See also chapter 4 in this volume.

Table 1.2. Regional distribution, number and types of contested incompatibilities in major armed conflicts, 1989–95[a]

Region[b]	1989 G	1989 T	1990 G	1990 T	1991 G	1991 T	1992 G	1992 T	1993 G	1993 T	1994 G	1994 T	1995 G	1995 T
Africa	7	3	8	3	8	3	6	1	6	1	6	1	5	1
Asia	6	8	5	10	3	9	5	9	4	7	4	7	4	8
Central and South America	5	–	5	–	4	–	3	–	3	–	3	–	3	–
Europe	1	1	–	1	–	2	–	4	–	6	–	5	–	3
Middle East	1	4	1	4	2	5	2	3	2	4	2	4	2	4
Total	*20*	*16*	*19*	*18*	*17*	*19*	*16*	*17*	*15*	*18*	*15*	*17*	*14*	*16*
Total	**36**		**37**		**36**		**33**		**33**		**32**		**30**	

G = Government and T = Territory, the two types of incompatibility.

[a] The total annual number of conflicts does not necessarily correspond to the number of conflict locations in table 1.1 and in table 1A, appendix 1A, since there may be more than one major armed conflict in each location.

[b] Only those regions of the world in which a conflict was recorded for the period 1989–95 are included here.

Source: Uppsala Conflict Data Project.

government and the Kurdish PKK. While the conflict in northern Iraq continued, the more intensive fighting in 1995 was recorded between Kurdish groups rather than between them and the Iraqi Government. The question of the Kurdish people, who are divided among four states, continued to generate instability in the region. In spite of internal opposition on both sides, the Israeli–Palestinian peace process continued to move forward, resulting in a further decline in armed conflict. Another set of conflict issues in the Middle East and parts of Africa concerned demands for the Islamicization of governments and states. This has resulted in a major armed conflict in Algeria. A clearly emerging major armed conflict, but still below the threshold for inclusion in the database, is that between the Egyptian Government and the Islamic opposition.[10]

Asia also continued to have a number of low-level conflicts, except for the situations in Afghanistan and Sri Lanka. Negotiations and cease-fires were attempted in several cases; often the governments had become strong enough to force the armed opposition into negotiations. This pattern was seen in Myanmar and the Philippines. In many cases the central government was still opting for military solutions, notably in India and Indonesia. The most troubling cases seemed to be those where the central government was weak (Afghanistan, Cambodia and Tajikistan).

[10] A total of 900 deaths were recorded by Oct. 1995, involving the government and the Islamic opposition (al-Gama'a al Islamiyya).

Africa shows a pattern of declining numbers of conflicts in Southern Africa, while West Africa (Sierra Leone and Liberia) and the Horn of Africa (Sudan and Somalia) remained plagued by conflicts. The lower intensity of some African conflicts may be temporary (Rwanda) and new conflicts might be brewing (Burundi and Nigeria), as governments reveal themselves as either too weak to handle opposition groups or too strong to display the necessary sensitivity to act early and constructively.

In Central and South America, there is a pattern of declining numbers of conflicts and declining intensity in the ongoing conflicts. Negotiations were attempted in two of these (Colombia and Guatemala) but not in others (Peru). The governments involved clearly opted for policies that sought to marginalize the hard-line elements of their armed opponents.

IV. Conclusions

A number of clear trends can be observed in the data on armed conflicts from 1989 to 1995. Although there were as many as 30 major armed conflicts in 1995, a very slow but steady decline in the number of both major armed conflicts and conflict locations can be observed since 1989, the end of the cold war. This trend is a result of the fact that more conflicts have been removed from the list than before, because of a military victory, cease-fire or peace agreement. However, the number of new conflicts being added each year has been fairly constant. This points to the need for not only resolving ongoing conflicts but also preventing the emergence of new ones.

Another trend is that major-power involvement has largely shifted from active support of one fighting faction against another to attempting to contain and minimize violence in localized conflicts.

Finally, there is a visible trend in the relative prominence of the key issues in major armed conflicts: more conflicts are now fought over territory than over government control.

Appendix 1A. Major armed conflicts, 1995

MARGARETA SOLLENBERG, RAMSES AMER, CARL JOHAN ÅSBERG, MARGARETA ELIASSON, MARY JANE FOX, ANN-SOFI JAKOBSSON, KJELL-ÅKE NORDQUIST, THOMAS OHLSON, ANNA SCHNELL and PETER WALLENSTEEN*

The following notes and sources apply to the locations listed in table 1A:[1]

a The stated general incompatible positions. 'Govt' and 'Territory' refer to contested incompatibilities concerning government (type of political system, a change of central government or in its composition) and territory (control of territory [interstate conflict], secession or autonomy), respectively.

b 'Year formed' is the year in which the incompatibility was stated. 'Year joined' is the year in which use of armed force began or recommenced.

c The non-governmental warring parties are listed by the name of the parties using armed force. Only those parties which were active during 1995 are listed in this column.

d The figure for 'No. of troops in 1995' is for total armed forces (rather than for army forces, as in the *SIPRI Yearbooks 1988–1990*) of the government warring party (i.e., the government of the conflict location), and for non-government parties from the conflict location. For government and non-government parties from outside the location, the figure in this column is for total armed forces within the country that is the location of the armed conflict. Deviations from this method are indicated by a note (*) and explained.

e The figures for deaths refer to total battle-related deaths during the conflict. 'Mil.' and 'civ.' refer, where figures are available, to *military* and *civilian* deaths, respectively; where there is no such indication, the figure refers to total military and civilian battle-related deaths in the period or year given. Information which covers a calendar year is necessarily more tentative for the last months of the year. Experience has also shown that the reliability of figures improves over time; they are therefore revised each year.

f The 'change from 1994' is measured as the increase or decrease in the number of battle-related deaths in 1995 compared with the number of battle-related deaths in 1994. Although based on data that cannot be considered totally reliable, the symbols represent the following changes:

+ +   increase in battle deaths of > 50%
+   increase in battle deaths of > 10 to 50%
0   stable rate of battle deaths (± 10%)
−   decrease in battle deaths of > 10 to 50%
− −   decrease in battle deaths of > 50%

[1] Note that although some countries are also the location of minor armed conflicts, the table lists only the major armed conflicts in those countries. Reference to the tables of major armed conflicts in previous *SIPRI Yearbooks* is given in the list of sources.

* R. Amer was responsible for the data for the conflict location of Cambodia; C. J. Åsberg for India; M. Eliasson and T. Ohlson for Angola, Liberia and Sierra Leone; M. J. Fox for Somalia; A.-S. Jakobsson for Israel; K.-Å. Nordquist for Colombia, Guatemala and Peru; A. Schnell for Algeria; and P. Wallensteen for Sudan. M. Sollenberg was responsible for the remaining conflict locations. Ylva Nordlander, Cecilia Backman, Ulrika Gustin and Anja Stegen provided assistance in the data collection.

n.a.   not applicable, since the major armed conflict was not recorded for 1994.

Note: In the last three columns ('Total deaths', 'Deaths in 1995' and 'Change from 1994'), '. .' indicates that no reliable figures, or no reliable disaggregated figures, were given in the sources consulted.

Sources: For additional information on these conflicts, see chapters in previous editions of the *SIPRI Yearbook:* Sollenberg, M. and Wallensteen, P., 'Major armed conflicts', *SIPRI Yearbook 1995: Armaments, Disarmament and International Security* (Oxford University Press: Oxford, 1995), chapter 1; Wallensteen, P. and Axell, K. 'Major armed conflicts', *SIPRI Yearbook 1994* (Oxford University Press: Oxford, 1994), chapter 2; Amer, R., Heldt, B., Landgren, S., Magnusson, K., Melander, E., Nordquist, K-Å., Ohlson, T. and Wallensteen, P., 'Major armed conflicts', *SIPRI Yearbook 1993: World Armaments and Disarmament* (Oxford University Press: Oxford, 1993), chapter 3; Heldt, B., Wallensteen, P. and Nordquist, K.-Å., 'Major armed conflicts in 1991', *SIPRI Yearbook 1992* (Oxford University Press: Oxford, 1992), chapter 11; Lindgren, K., Heldt, B., Nordquist, K-Å. and Wallensteen, P., 'Major armed conflicts in 1990', *SIPRI Yearbook 1991* (Oxford University Press: Oxford, 1991), chapter 10; Lindgren, K., Wilson, G. K., Wallensteen, P. and Nordquist, K.-Å., 'Major armed conflicts in 1989', *SIPRI Yearbook 1990* (Oxford University Press: Oxford, 1990), chapter 10; Lindgren, K., Wilson, G. K. and Wallensteen, P., 'Major armed conflicts in 1988', *SIPRI Yearbook 1989* (Oxford University Press: Oxford, 1989), chapter 9; Wilson, G. K. and Wallensteen, P., 'Major armed conflicts in 1987', *SIPRI Yearbook 1988* (Oxford University Press: Oxford, 1988), chapter 9; and Goose, S., 'Armed conflicts in 1986, and the Iraq–Iran War', *SIPRI Yearbook 1987* (Oxford University Press: Oxford, 1987), chapter 8.

The following journals, newspapers and news agencies were consulted: *Africa Confidential* (London); *Africa Events* (London); *Africa Reporter* (New York); *Africa Research Bulletin* (Oxford); *AIM Newsletter* (London); *Asian Defence Journal* (Kuala Lumpur); *Asian Recorder* (New Delhi); *Balkan War Report* (London); *Burma Focus* (Oslo); *Burma Issues* (Bangkok); *Conflict International* (Edgware); *Dagens Nyheter* (Stockholm); Dialog Information Services Inc. (Palo Alto); *The Economist* (London); *Facts and Reports* (Amsterdam); *Far Eastern Economic Review* (Hong Kong); *Financial Times* (Frankfurt); *Fortnight Magazine* (Belfast); *The Guardian* (London); *Horn of Africa Bulletin* (Uppsala); *Jane's Defence Weekly* (Coulsdon, Surrey); *Jane's Intelligence Review* (Coulsdon, Surrey); *The Independent* (London); *International Herald Tribune* (Paris); *Kayhan International* (Teheran); *Keesing's Contemporary Archives* (Harlow, Essex); *Latin America Weekly Report* (London); *Le Monde Diplomatique* (Paris); *Mexico and Central America Report* (London); *Middle East International* (London); *Monitor* (Washington, DC); *Moscow News* (Moscow); *Newsweek* (New York); *New Times* (Moscow); *New York Times* (New York); *OMRI (Open Media Research Institute) Daily Digest* (Prague); *Reuter Business Briefing* (London); *Prism* (Washington, DC); *RFE/RL (Radio Free Europe/Radio Liberty) Research Report* (Munich); *Pacific Report* (Canberra); *Pacific Research* (Canberra); *S.A. Barometer* (Johannesburg); *Selections from Regional Press* (Institute of Regional Studies: Islamabad); *Southern African Economist* (Harare); *Southern Africa Political & Economic Monthly* (Harare); *SouthScan* (London); *Sri Lanka Monitor* (London); *The Statesman* (Calcutta); *Sudan Update* (London); *Svenska Dagbladet* (Stockholm); *Tehran Times* (Teheran); *The Times* (London); *Transition* (Prague); *World Aerospace & Defense Intelligence* (Newtown, Conn.).

Table 1A. Table of conflict locations with at least one major armed conflict in 1995

Location	Incompatibility[a]	Year formed/ year joined[b]	Warring parties[c]	No. of troops in 1995[d]	Total deaths[e] (incl. 1995)	Deaths in 1995	Change from 1994[f]
Europe							
Bosnia and Herzegovina*			Govt of Bosnia and Herzegovina, Croatia	110 000–130 000	25 000– 55 000	800–2 000	–
	Territory	1992/1992	vs. Serbian Republic (of Bosnia and Herzegovina), Serbian irregulars	.. 75 000–85 000			

* Fighting between the Army of the Serbian Republic of Bosnia and Herzegovina and the Bosnian Croat Defence Council (or Bosnian HVO, the armed forces of the Croat Republic of Herzeg-Bosna) is not included as a conflict since neither of these parties is the government of an internationally recognized state.

Location	Incompatibility	Year formed/ year joined	Warring parties	No. of troops in 1995	Total deaths (incl. 1995)	Deaths in 1995	Change from 1994
Croatia	Territory	1990/1990	Govt of Croatia vs. Serbian Republic of Krajina, Serbian irregulars	100 000–110 000 35 000–50 000 ..	6 000– 10 000*	500–1 000	n.a.

* This figure includes the fighting during 1991 in which not just the two parties participated (see *SIPRI Yearbook 1992*, chapter 11).

Location	Incompatibility	Year formed/ year joined	Warring parties	No. of troops in 1995	Total deaths (incl. 1995)	Deaths in 1995	Change from 1994
Russia	Territory	1991/1994	Govt of Russia vs. Republic of Chechnya	1 500 000 12 000–20 000	10 000– 40 000	10 000– 40 000	n.a.
Middle East							
Iran	Govt	1970/1991	Govt of Iran vs. Mujahideen e-Khalq	513 000*	..	..	..
	Territory	1972/1979	vs. KDPI	.. 8 000			

KDPI: Kurdish Democratic Party of Iran.
* Including the Revolutionary Guard.

Iraq

Govt	1980/1991	Govt of Iraq	vs. SAIRI*	350 000–400 000	..	..
				10 000**		
Territory	1977/1980		vs. PUK	..***	..	..

SAIRI: Supreme Assembly for the Islamic Revolution in Iraq.
PUK: Patriotic Union of Kurdistan.
* Most of the Shia rebels belong to this group.
** Total strength of Shia rebels.
*** No precise figures for troops are available. PUK troop strength is possibly some 10 000 –12 000.

Israel

	1964/1964	Govt of Israel	vs. PLO groups*	170 000–180 000	1948–:	–
Territory			vs. Non-PLO groups**	..	> 12 500	250
				..		

* The Palestine Liberation Organization (PLO) is an umbrella organization; armed action is carried out by member organizations. Although Al-Fatah, the largest group within the PLO, did not use armed force in 1995, other groups (DFLP and PFLP) which reject the 1993 Declaration of Principles on Interim Self-Government Arrangements (Oslo Agreement) did. These groups opposed the PLO leadership but were still part of the PLO in 1995.
DFLP Democratic Front for the Liberation of Palestine
PFLP Popular Front for the Liberation of Palestine
** Examples of these groups are Hamas, PFLP–GC (Popular Front for the Liberation of Palestine–General Command), Islamic Jihad and Hizbollah.

Turkey

	1974/1984	Govt of Turkey	vs. PKK	500 000	>17 000	+
Territory				10 000–12 000	>4 000	

PKK: Partiya Karkeren Kurdistan, Kurdish Worker's Party, or Apocus.

Location	Incompatibility[a]	Year formed/year joined[b]	Warring parties[c]	No. of troops in 1995[d]	Total deaths[e] (incl. 1995)	Deaths in 1995	Change from 1994[f]
Asia							
Afghanistan	Govt	1978/1978	Govt of Afghanistan	..	>15 000	>1 000	– –
		1990/1990	vs. Hezb-i-Islami	..			
		1992/1992	vs. Hezb-i-Wahdat	..			
			vs. Jumbish-i Milli-ye Islami*	..			

* The National Islamic Movement (NIM), led by Dostum.

Location	Incompatibility	Year formed/year joined	Warring parties	No. of troops in 1995	Total deaths (incl. 1995)	Deaths in 1995	Change from 1994
Bangladesh	Territory	1971/1982	Govt of Bangladesh	115 500	1975–:	<25	0
			vs. JSS/SB	2 000–5 000	3 000–3 500		

JSS/SB: Parbatya Chattagram Jana Sanghati Samiti (Chittagong Hill Tracts People's Co-ordination Association/Shanti Bahini [Peace Force]).

Location	Incompatibility	Year formed/year joined	Warring parties	No. of troops in 1995	Total deaths (incl. 1995)	Deaths in 1995	Change from 1994
Cambodia	Govt	1979/1979	Govt of Cambodia	130 000*	>25 500**	..	..
			vs. PDK	5 000–10 000			

PDK: Party of Democratic Kampuchea (Khmer Rouge).
*   Including all militias.
**   For figures for battle-related deaths in this conflict prior to 1979, see *SIPRI Yearbook 1990*, p. 405, and note *p*, p. 418. Regarding battle-related deaths in 1979–89, that is, not only involving the Govt and PDK, the only figure available is from official Vietnamese sources, indicating that 25 300 Vietnamese soldiers died in Cambodia. An estimated figure for the period 1979–89, based on various sources, is >50 000, and for 1989 >1000. The figures for 1990, 1991 and 1992 were lower.

Location	Incompatibility	Year formed/year joined	Warring parties	No. of troops in 1995	Total deaths (incl. 1995)	Deaths in 1995	Change from 1994
India	Territory	../...	Govt of India	1 145 000	>37 000*	>500*	–
	Territory	../1981	vs. Kashmir insurgents**	..			
	Territory	../1992	vs. Sikh insurgents***	..			
		1982/1988	vs BdSF	..			
			vs. ULFA	..			

BdSF: Bodo Security Force.
ULFA: United Liberation Front of Assam.

* Only the Kashmir and Sikh conflicts. Of the total deaths, approximately 25 000 were killed in the Sikh conflict and at least 12 000 in the Kashmir conflict.

** Several groups are active, some of the most important being the Jammu and Kashmir Liberation Front (JKLF), the Hizb-e-Mujahideen and the Harkat-ul-Ansar.

*** Several Sikh groups exist, however, in 1995 only a few were active, i.e. the Khalistan Liberation Force (KLF).

Location	Type	Year	Warring parties	No. of troops	Total deaths	Deaths 1995	Change
Indonesia	Territory	1975/1975	Govt of Indonesia vs. Fretilin	276 000 200	15 000– 16 000 (mil.)	< 50	0
Myanmar	Territory	1948/1948	Govt of Myanmar vs. KNU	286 000 4 000	1948–50: 8 000 1981–88: 5 000–8 500	> 500	–
	Territory	.*/1993	vs. MTA	10 000–20 000	1993–94: > 1 000**		
The Philippines	Govt	1968/1968	Govt of the Philippines vs. NPA	106 500 8 000	21 000– 25 000*	< 100	–
Sri Lanka	Territory	1976/1983	Govt of Sri Lanka vs. LTTE	126 000 6 000–10 000	> 32 000	> 5 000	+ +

Fretilin: Frente Revolucionára Timorense de Libertação e Independência (Revolutionary Front for an Independent East Timor).

KNU: Karen National Union.
MTA: Mong Tai Army.

* The Mong Tai Army was formed in 1987, but it is unclear when the demand for independence was stated.

** This figure includes deaths only in the Shan conflict.

NPA: New People's Army.

* Official military sources claim that 6500 civilians were killed during 1985–91.

LTTE: Liberation Tigers of Tamil Eelam.

Location	Incompatibility[a]	Year formed/ year joined[b]	Warring parties[c]	No. of troops in 1995[d]	Total deaths[e] (incl. 1995)	Deaths in 1995	Change from 1994[f]
Tajikistan	Govt	1991/1992	Govt of Tajikistan, CIS Collective Peacekeeping Force in Tajikistan/ CIS Border Troops* vs. United Tajik Opposition**	2 000–3 000 c. 25 000	20 000–50 000	>500	n.a.

* The CIS operation includes Russian border guards and peacekeeping troops with minor reinforcements from Kazakhstan, Kyrgystan and Uzbekistan.
** The major groups constituting the United Tajik Opposition (formerly the Popular Democratic Army) are the Islamic Resistance Movement, the Democratic Party of Tajikistan and the Rastokhez People's Movement.

Africa

Location	Incompatibility[a]	Year formed/ year joined[b]	Warring parties[c]	No. of troops in 1995[d]	Total deaths[e] (incl. 1995)	Deaths in 1995	Change from 1994[f]
Algeria	Govt	1992/1992 1993/1993	Govt of Algeria vs. FIS* vs. GIA	150 000	25 000–45 000	>3 000	–

FIS: Front Islamique du Salut, *Jibhat al-Inqath* (Islamic Salvation Front).
GIA: Groupe Islamique Armé (Armed Islamic Group). It is unclear whether there are ties between GIA and FIS.
* The Islamic Salvation Army (Armée Islamique du Salut, AIS) is considered to be the armed wing of the FIS. There are also several other armed Islamic groups under the FIS military command.

Location	Incompatibility[a]	Year formed/ year joined[b]	Warring parties[c]	No. of troops in 1995[d]	Total deaths[e] (incl. 1995)	Deaths in 1995	Change from 1994[f]
Angola	Govt	1975/1975	Govt of Angola vs. UNITA	100 000 60 000	>40 000 (mil.)* >100 000 (civ.)*	500–1 500	..

UNITA: União Nacional para a Independência Total de Angola (National Union for the Total Independence of Angola).
* An estimated 1.5 million war-related deaths (military and civilian) from 1975, of which approximately 50% since the war restarted in Oct. 1992.

Location	Type	Year formed/ Year joined	Warring parties	No. of troops in 1995	Total deaths	Deaths in 1995
Liberia	Govt	1989/1989	Govt of Liberia, ECOMOG vs. NPFL*	.. / 7 000 / 10 000	1989–92: 20 000**	.. ***
Sierra Leone	Govt	1991/1991	Govt of Sierra Leone vs. RUF	5 000–6 000 / 2 000	>3 000*	>500 / n.a.
Somalia	Govt	1991/1991	Govt of Somalia* vs. USC faction (Aideed)	10 000 / 10 000	..	200–500 / ..
Sudan	Territory	1980/1983	Govt of Sudan vs. SPLA (Garang faction)	81 000 / 30 000–50 000	37 000–40 000 (mil.)*	c. 1 000 (mil.) / ..

ECOMOG: The ECOWAS (Economic Organization of West African States) Monitoring Group.
NPFL: National Patriotic Front of Liberia.
* In Aug. 1995, 7 armed factions in Liberia (including the NPFL) signed a peace agreement, and their leaders formed a transitional Council of State. Elections were scheduled for Aug. 1996.
** Note that this figure includes the fighting in 1990–91 (incurring 15 000 deaths) in which more than the two parties listed above participated.
*** No figures for battle-related deaths are available. War-related deaths (military and civilian) are estimated at 10 000–15 000 in 1995. Total war-related deaths are estimated at 150 000.

RUF: Revolutionary United Front.
* Approximately 30 000 war-related deaths since 1991.

USC: United Somali Congress.
* Taken to be the USC faction (Mahdi).

SPLA: Sudanese People's Liberation Army.
* Figure for 1991.

Location	Incompat-ibility[a]	Year formed/year joined[b]	Warring parties[c]	No. of troops in 1995[d]	Total deaths[e] (incl. 1995)	Deaths in 1995	Change from 1994[f]
Central and South America							
Colombia	Govt	1949/1978 1965/1978	Govt of Colombia vs. FARC vs. ELN	146 400 5 700 2 500	..*	<1 000	0

FARC: Fuerzas Armadas Revolucionarias Colombianas (Revolutionary Armed Forces of Colombia).
ELN: Ejército de Liberación Nacional (National Liberation Army).
* In the past three decades the civil wars of Colombia have claimed a total of some 30 000 lives.

Guatemala	Govt	1967/1968	Govt of Guatemala vs. URNG	44 200 800–1 100	<2 800 (mil.) <43 500 (civ.)	<200	0

URNG: Unidad Revolucionaria Nacional Guatemalteca (Guatemalan National Revolutionary Unity). URNG is a coalition of three main groups: Ejército Guerrillero de los Pobres (EGP), Fuerzas Armadas Rebeldes (FAR), and Organización del Pueblo en Armas (ORPA).

Peru	Govt	1980/1981 1984/1986	Govt of Peru vs. Sendero Luminoso vs. MRTA	115 000 3 000 500	>28 000	<500	0

Sendero Luminoso: Shining Path.
MRTA: Movimiento Revolucionario Tupac Amaru (Tupac Amaru Revolutionary Movement).
* Of the reported deaths for 1995, fewer than 50 were incurred between the Government of Peru and the MRTA.

2. Armed conflict prevention, management and resolution

TREVOR FINDLAY*

I. Introduction

International efforts to prevent, manage and resolve armed conflict had some striking successes in 1995 in several highly publicized cases, although the resolution of lesser known conflicts continued to elude the peacemakers. The most spectacular achievements were the Dayton Agreement on Bosnia and Herzegovina and a separate agreement on Croatia which brought armed conflict in these states to an abrupt halt in November.[1] The other notable achievement occurred in the Middle East, where further agreements between Israel and the Palestinians, although clouded by the assassination of Israeli Prime Minister Yitzhak Rabin, signalled that the peace process was still advancing.[2]

Success was also registered in Haiti, where a peace enforcement operation by a US-led multinational coalition force transferred responsibility to a UN peacekeeping operation once the situation had been stabilized. Peace accords which appeared sustainable were finally concluded for Angola and Liberia after long and bitter civil wars, although their implementation remained unsteady. The cease-fire in Northern Ireland endured but peace talks remained elusive. When the only two notable interstate conflicts in 1995 broke out, between Peru and Ecuador and between Yemen and Eritrea, cease-fires were hastily arranged. The most disheartening peacemaking failures in 1995 were in Chechnya,[3] where a cease-fire was negotiated but increasingly breached as the year progressed, and in Sudan and Sri Lanka, where cease-fires collapsed completely with disastrous upsurges in armed conflict.

While the United Nations in its 50th anniversary year played a role in almost every conflict situation, the new emphasis was unmistakably on conflict prevention or, in UN parlance, preventive diplomacy. Peacekeeping headed for a period of retraction and consolidation as five major operations of varying success, including the UN Protection Force (UNPROFOR), the largest in UN history, drew to a close in 1995. UN peacekeepers had been continually humiliated in Bosnia until rescued from their misery by NATO bombing and

---

[1] General Framework Agreement for Peace in Bosnia and Herzegovina, signed in Paris, 14 Dec. 1995. See appendix 5A in this volume for the text of the Agreement; and Basic Agreement on the Region of Eastern Slavonia, Baranja and Western Sirmium, signed in Zagreb on 12 Nov. 1995. See also chapter 5 in this volume.

[2] See chapter 4 in this volume.

[3] See chapter 6 in this volume.

* Olga Hardardóttir of the SIPRI Project on Peacekeeping and Regional Security assisted in researching this chapter.

replaced by a non-UN force. Diplomatically the UN was marginalized by the Dayton process—it was not even represented at the talks. This experience and the UN's growing financial crisis further dampened enthusiasm for major new UN peace missions. The reputation of sanctions as a tool of conflict resolution rose as those imposed on the Federal Republic of Yugoslavia (Serbia and Montenegro) appeared to be a significant factor in forcing it to the negotiating table. Peace enforcement triumphed in Bosnia and Herzegovina, but through action by NATO rather than the ill-equipped and inappropriately mandated UNPROFOR.

Regional organizations meanwhile moved frustratingly slowly to increase their own capacity for conflict prevention, management and resolution. Particular attention was devoted to Africa, where many of the world's most unstable and conflict-wracked states are extant. Individual countries, especially the USA and other great powers, again played prominent, sometimes pre-eminent, roles in preventing, managing and resolving conflict. Individuals and non-governmental actors sometimes supplemented these efforts usefully.

This chapter surveys multilateral efforts undertaken in 1995 to prevent, manage or resolve armed conflict between or within states. Section II focuses on the United Nations, the key multilateral actor in conflict prevention, management and resolution, while section III deals separately with peace-keeping, still the UN's most prominent activity in this field. Section IV surveys the UN role in peace enforcement, while section V analyses the role of regional and other multilateral organizations. Section VI provides an overview of the role of other actors, such as individual states and non-governmental organizations (NGOs).

II. The United Nations

Although the UN retained its pre-eminent position in international conflict prevention, management and resolution efforts in 1995, in its 50th anniversary year this role was under greater scrutiny than ever before. Pundits generally praised its peacekeeping record since 1945 but were sceptical of its ability to address all conflict situations or to conduct peace enforcement at all. The UN's humiliation over the fall of its 'safe areas' in Bosnia and Herzegovina, its brush with peace enforcement in that country, its worsening financial crisis and the lack of fundamental reform of its sprawling, uncoordinated system served to confirm these views. UN Secretary-General Boutros Boutros-Ghali sustained debate over the UN's role with a supplement to his 1992 *Agenda for Peace*. Conflict prevention emerged as a putative panacea for the world body's inadequacies in dealing with conflicts after they had broken out. The General Assembly's role in conflict prevention, management and resolution in 1995 was minimal, that of the Security Council crucial, and that of the Secretary-General and Secretariat expansive. Resort to the International Court of Justice (ICJ) was greater than ever before. The year saw UN peacekeeping operations contract dramatically, with several terminated, some pruned and reorganized and no completely new ones launched. Genuine reform efforts continued which in a few years will produce a much improved UN peacekeeping capability, but one for which, paradoxically, there may be neither the demand nor the requisite political and financial backing.

Supplement to *An Agenda for Peace*[4]

In January Boutros-Ghali issued a Supplement to *An Agenda for Peace*,[5] the paper in which he had systematically elaborated a United Nations approach to and instruments for the prevention, management and resolution of conflicts between and within states. The Supplement was designed to highlight unforeseen difficulties which had arisen since 1992 and the 'hard decisions' which member states now had to take.

In regard to preventive diplomacy he suggested that the greatest obstacle to success was not, as is widely supposed, a lack of information, analytical capacity or ideas, but a dearth of suitably qualified senior personnel willing to serve as his special representative or envoy. A second obstacle was a lack of finance for unforeseen, urgent, short-term missions; his suggested remedy was a contingency fund of $25 million per biennium.

In regard to peacekeeping Boutros-Ghali drew heavily on the lessons of Somalia and Bosnia and Herzegovina in noting that three types of activity had led such operations to forfeit the consent of the parties—traditionally a prerequisite for successful peacekeeping—and dangerously blurred the distinction between peacekeeping and peace enforcement. These were protecting humanitarian operations during continuing warfare, protecting civilian populations in designated safe areas and pressing parties to achieve national reconciliation at a faster pace than they were ready for. Boutros-Ghali suggested that 'peacekeeping and the use of force (other than in self-defence) should be seen as alternative techniques and not as adjacent points on a continuum, permitting each transition from one to the other'.[6] He criticized the Security Council for attempting to 'micro-manage' peacekeeping operations and the 'Friends of the Secretary-General' (influential regional states and select Security Council members assisting him in particular peace efforts) for taking initiatives without his approval. The Secretary-General also reiterated his proposal for a UN Rapid Reaction Force as a strategic reserve for use during emergencies.

---

[4] UN, Supplement to *An Agenda for Peace*: position paper of the Secretary-General on the occasion of the 50th anniversary of the United Nations, UN document A/50/60, S/1995l, 3 Jan. 1995. The bulk of the text is reproduced in appendix 2B in this volume.

[5] Boutros-Ghali, B., *An Agenda for Peace: Preventive Diplomacy, Peacemaking and Peace-keeping*, Report of the Secretary-General pursuant to the statement adopted by the Summit Meeting of the Security Council on 31 January 1992 (United Nations: New York, 1992), reproduced in *SIPRI Yearbook 1993: World Armaments and Disarmament* (Oxford University Press: Oxford, 1993), appendix 2A, pp. 66–80. For analyses see Hill, R., 'Preventive diplomacy, peace-making and peace-keeping', *SIPRI Yearbook 1993: World Armaments and Disarmament* (Oxford University Press: Oxford, 1993), pp. 45–60; and Findlay, T., 'Multilateral conflict prevention, management and resolution', *SIPRI Yearbook 1994* (Oxford University Press: Oxford, 1994), pp. 14–19 and *passim*.

[6] Supplement to *An Agenda for Peace* (note 4), p. 9.

Finally, he recognized the importance of an information strategy for peace-keeping operations, especially using UN radio broadcasts.

The Secretary-General's remarks on post-conflict peace building were rather more conceptual than practical. Perhaps in response to criticism that the UN has abandoned states to their own devices once a comprehensive peace settlement has been achieved, as in Cambodia, Boutros-Ghali suggested careful management of the 'timing and modalities' of the departure of peacekeeping missions and the transfer of their peace-building functions to others, but that each case needed consideration on its merits. A particular challenge was donors' unwillingness to finance crucial elements of peace building such as conversion of guerrilla movements into political parties, creation of new police forces or 'arms for land' programmes.

Calling sanctions 'a blunt instrument', the Secretary-General noted the problems that have arisen because of their imprecise and mutable objectives. In future, sanctions should be better targeted to avoid both harming the most vulnerable sectors of societies and giving the impression that their purpose is punishment rather than behaviour modification. The latter was a clear reference to dogged US insistence that comprehensive sanctions be maintained against Iraq in the face of pressure from others to modify or lift them. He suggested establishing a mechanism in the Secretariat to: assess the impact of sanctions before they are imposed; monitor their application; measure their effects to permit fine-tuning to maximize their political impact and minimize 'collateral damage'; ensure the delivery of humanitarian supplies to vulnerable groups; and explore ways of assisting member states suffering collateral damage and evaluate compensation claims.

To consider in detail the Secretary-General's recommendations the Security Council held special sessions in January 1995, while the General Assembly established sub-groups on various issues: preventive diplomacy and peace-making, post-conflict peace building, sanctions, coordination, and the advisory competence of the International Court of Justice. Reaction to the Supplement was mostly favourable but neither the Council nor the Assembly took up Boutros-Ghali's many suggestions in detail. The most negative comment came from US Ambassador to the UN Madeleine Albright, who criticized Boutros-Ghali's alleged attempt to assert more control over peacekeeping and to blame member states for peacekeeping failures: 'I think we have to guard against saying that every time there is a success it is due to the United Nations and every time there is a failure it is due to the member states'.[7]

Conflict prevention: a new emphasis

After gestating quietly for a number of years the idea of conflict prevention seemed suddenly an idea whose time had arrived. In 1995 there was increasing emphasis by the UN and member governments on conflict prevention as a far cheaper alternative to peacekeeping and other forms of intervention after

[7] *Wireless File* (US Information Service, US Embassy: Stockholm, 5 Jan. 1995), p. 8.

conflict has begun. The UN has long engaged in conflict prevention but could become more proficient at it given sufficient funding and better organization. Among the tools of conflict prevention identified by the Secretary-General were preventive diplomacy, preventive deployment of a military or civilian police force, preventive humanitarian intervention and preventive peace building—'an extensive menu' of political, social and economic activities to shore up weak states or rebuild devastated ones.[8]

Since effective conflict prevention is contingent on early warning of impending problems, the Secretariat moved in 1995 to strengthen further its early-warning mechanisms. It established a Framework for Co-ordination between three key Secretariat Departments—Humanitarian Affairs, Political Affairs and Peace-keeping Operations—to permit not just information sharing but also joint analysis of early-warning indicators and assessment of options for preventive action. This was intended to meet the long-standing criticism of the UN bureaucracy that while it possessed ample information throughout its system it lacked a mechanism for centrally collecting, analysing and acting on it. The UN's Humanitarian Early Warning System (HEWS) continued to develop, with 50 countries being added by April 1995 to the existing prototype based on time-series data from 5 countries.[9] However, a UN Economic and Social Council (ECOSOC) Committee warned that the UN probably would still need a single individual or unit responsible for coordinating development of its early-warning system—essentially a revived Office of Research and Collection of Information (ORCI), which had been abolished by Boutros-Ghali in 1992 as a cost-cutting measure.[10]

Despite these improvements in early warning, UN resources devoted to preventive diplomacy remained pitiful—only 40 UN officials in 1995, compared with thousands of peacekeepers. Australia reiterated its proposal for the establishment of half a dozen preventive diplomacy centres around the world, staffed by a total of 100 experts to continuously monitor their respective regions and provide instant preventive advice and assistance. The cost would be minimal, around $20 million annually (compared with the current $3 billion cost of peacekeeping), and even if only one or two conflicts were avoided the investment would be worthwhile. Australia also argued for a professional conflict-resolution service at UN headquarters. Such ideas failed to gain majority support. While many could see the wisdom of conflict prevention, it proved difficult in the prevailing financial climate to convince states to spend relatively minor amounts now to save millions in the future.

Some developing countries also expressed fear that increased preventive diplomacy would result in increased interference by the UN in their internal affairs. The most hard-line position was taken by India, which remains sensitive to any suggestion of outside involvement in Kashmir. Others opposed the

---

[8] UN, Report of the Secretary-General on the work of the Organization, UN document A/50/1, 22 Aug. 1995, p. 80.

[9] ECOSOC Committee for Programme and Co-ordination, Final Report on the in-depth evaluation of peace-keeping operations: start-up phase, UN document E/AC.51/1995/2, 17 Mar. 1995, para. 37.

[10] ECOSOC (note 9), para. 40.

concept of preventive peace building (as contrasted with post-conflict peace building after a peace settlement has been agreed), regarding it as synonymous with nation building, which they see as solely the prerogative and responsibility of the state concerned (while at the same time pressing for increased international aid for the undertaking).

Academic critics of the new enthusiasm for conflict prevention warned of several difficulties: the problem of predicting major political and military events (such as the collapse of the Soviet Union or the Iraqi invasion of Kuwait); the multiplicity of choices in dealing with a given situation; the danger that early intervention will make a situation worse; the fact that it may not necessarily be cheap or cost-free; and the difficulty of mobilizing organizations or states to meet a threat that may never eventuate.[11] Moreover, since successful conflict prevention results in a nil return—the absence of conflict—it is difficult to generate and sustain the interest of the media and therefore that of politicians. In the case of Zaire—a country that in 1995 had by many accounts 'moved well beyond candidacy for disaster'[12]—the UN Secretary-General, like other interlocutors, appeared to give up on preventive diplomacy. That Zaire did not descend into total chaos illustrated one of the pitfalls of conflict prevention—that the worst may never happen and intervention may be unnecessary.

The General Assembly, Secretary-General and Secretariat

The General Assembly's role in conflict prevention, management and resolution in 1995 continued to be mostly hortatory and it took no particularly notable initiatives in the fields of conflict prevention, management or resolution. Its main contribution was to give concentrated consideration to UN reform proposals.[13]

In contrast, the Secretary-General continued to expand his activities, especially through the use of personal representatives for preventive diplomacy and to head peacekeeping operations.[14] In 1995 he used a record 22 such emissaries. Their role has evolved more in the past 5 years than in the previous 45, especially in their increasing use in helping manage conflict within the domestic jurisdiction of member states.

During 1995 the Secretary-General again undertook several conflict prevention and peacemaking exercises, most notably in relation to Afghanistan, the Baltic states, Bougainville, Burundi, Cambodia, Cyprus, East Timor, El Salvador, Georgia/Abkhazia, Guatemala, India and Pakistan, Iraq–Kuwait, the Korean Peninsula, Liberia, the Middle East, Mozambique, Myanmar,

[11] Stedman, S. J., 'Alchemy for a new world order: overselling "preventive diplomacy"', *Foreign Affairs*, vol. 74, no. 3 (1995), pp. 14–20.

[12] Morrison, J. S., 'Zaire: looming disaster after preventive diplomacy', *SAIS Review*, vol. 15, no. 2 (summer/fall 1995), pp. 39–52.

[13] See appendix 2D in this volume for details.

[14] Hume, C. R., 'The Secretary-General's Representatives', *SAIS Review*, vol. 15, no. 2 (summer/fall 1995), pp. 75–90.

Nagorno-Karabakh, Moldova, Sierra Leone, Somalia, Tajikistan, Western Sahara and Yemen.

Less dramatically, the Secretariat continued to provide electoral assistance to states and various peacekeeping missions.[15] Since the creation of the Electoral Assistance Division in 1992 the UN has been involved in the electoral processes of 61 member states, some of them more than once. However, in July managerial responsibility for the Electoral Assistance Division was returned from the Department of Peace-keeping Operations (DPKO) to the Department of Political Affairs in view of the expected fall in the number of large-scale peacekeeping missions with electoral components.[16] In 1995 Haiti was the only such case. The number of requests from member states has also begun to decline as the initial democratic wave of the post-cold war era has passed and more states settle into democratic routine.[17] Although it is not a UN initiative, both the UN and its members will probably benefit from the establishment in Stockholm in February of the multilateral Institute for Democracy and Electoral Affairs (IDEA), which will act as a clearing-house for and promote research on electoral matters.[18]

Major activities of the Secretary-General and his representatives in 1995 are detailed below, while those conducted in connection with peacekeeping operations are considered in the peacekeeping section.

Afghanistan

The Secretary-General's efforts, through his Office of the Secretary-General in Afghanistan (OSGA), to find a negotiated solution to the multi-party civil war that has wracked Afghanistan since the Soviet withdrawal in 1989 were seriously set back in 1995 by the swift military gains of yet another armed Afghan resistance group, the Taliban. This group refused to participate in the so-called Authoritative Council, comprising representatives of all of Afghanistan's Mujahideen political forces plus UN-nominated delegates, which was to have assumed power in the country by March.[19] Intense fighting around Kabul and a reversal of Afghan President Burhanuddin Rabbani's decision to step down further prevented the transfer of power, despite the efforts of the Secretary-General's Special Mission, headed by Mahmoud Mestiri. Besides the UN, other peacemakers attempted to bring the parties to

<hr/>

[15] For further detail of UN election activities see Findlay, T., 'Conflict prevention, management and resolution', *SIPRI Yearbook 1995: Armaments, Disarmament and International Security* (Oxford University Press: Oxford, 1995), pp. 49–50. For details of electoral assistance requests received and met, see appendix 2A in this volume.
[16] UN, Enhancing the effectiveness of the principle of periodic and genuine elections: report of the Secretary-General, UN document A/50/736, 8 Nov. 1995, p. 3.
[17] UN, Press Release SC/95/63, Geneva, 12 Dec. 1995.
[18] The founding states were Australia, Barbados, Belgium, Chile, Costa Rica, Denmark, Finland, India, the Netherlands, Norway, Portugal, South Africa, Spain and Sweden. For further information see *Newsletter of International IDEA,* no. 3 (Jan. 1996).
[19] 'Afghanistan: no settlement in view', *Strategic Comments,* no. 3 (22 Mar. 1995).

agreement, including the Organization of the Islamic Conference (OIC),[20] Iran, Pakistan, Russia, Saudi Arabia, the USA and Uzbekistan.[21] By September the strategic city of Herat had fallen to the Taliban, President Rabbani's position had been weakened and Mestiri resumed his peace efforts. In a new venture the UN appointed political officers in Herat, Kabul, Kandahar and Marar-e-Sharif, considered centres of power and politics, to assist in these efforts.[22] By the end of the year Kabul itself was under virtual siege, with a humanitarian disaster looming. A sudden stalemate at the end of December prompted a new flurry of negotiations on a cease-fire and power-sharing arrangement—but a lasting peace settlement in the country will be a major challenge given its division on ethnic lines between Uzbeks, Tajiks (represented by Rabbani) and Pathans, from whom the Taliban has been formed.[23]

Burundi

During 1995 extremist elements continued to attempt to destabilize Burundi and its UN-brokered governmental power-sharing arrangement, threatening a repeat of the genocide that wracked neighbouring Rwanda in 1994. The Security Council dispatched a fact-finding mission in February, its second in six months. It recommended establishment of an international commission of enquiry into the October 1993 coup attempt and the massacres that followed, a substantial increase in the number of Organization of African Unity (OAU)[24] military observers, the strengthening of the office of the Secretary-General's Special Representative for Burundi, who had been threatened with violence, and deployment of UN human rights observers throughout the country. France also continued its efforts to broker peace through its ambassador in Bujumbura and its Co-operation Minister Bernard Debre.[25] Debre managed to broker an agreement in March between the Tutsi military and the Hutu-led FRODEBU[26] Party to disarm their militias and avoid violence, but it soon collapsed. OAU Secretary-General Salim Salim tried again in April, also to little avail.

After fighting broke out along the Tanzanian border in late November the situation in the country looked perilously close to exploding. On 29 December Boutros-Ghali formally proposed to the Security Council that it establish a UN intervention force based in Tanzania and Zaire in case the situation deteriorated dramatically.[27] The Security Council, with the ill-fated Somalia and Rwanda experiences in mind, rejected the proposal on the specious grounds that it was not clear what role such a force would play. The Burundian

---

[20] The OIC member states are : Albania, Bahrain, Benin, Burkino Faso, Cameroon, Chad, Comoros, Cyprus, Djibouti, Gabon, Gambia, Guinea, Guinea-Bissau, Kazakhstan, Kyrgyzstan, Mali, Maldives, Mauritania, Niger, Qatar, Turkmenistan, United Arab Emirates and Yemen.

[21] *The Economist*, 22 July 1995, p. 63; and *International Herald Tribune*, 31 Oct. 1995.

[22] *Financial Times*, 12 Sep. 1995, p. 8; and Saragosa, M., 'Persistent thorn in the flesh', *Financial Times*, 29 Mar. 1995, p. 12.

[23] Howard, R., 'Considering ceasing fire in Afghanistan', *Jane's Defence Weekly*, 10 Jan. 1996, p. 19.

[24] For a list of OAU member states see the Glossary at the front of this volume.

[25] Congressional Research Service, 'Burundi crisis', CRS document 95-458 F (Congressional Research Service, Library of Congress: Washington, DC, 4 Apr. 1995), p. 4.

[26] FRODEBU stands for Front pour la Démocratie au Burundi.

[27] *International Herald Tribune*, 4 Jan. 1996, p. 2.

Government itself opposed such a force, although if its country begins imploding around it such abstinence might not be sustainable.

East Timor

The fifth and sixth rounds of UN-sponsored talks between the foreign ministers of Indonesia and Portugal were held in January and July 1995 to explore a comprehensive and internationally acceptable solution to the East Timor question. A new initiative by the Secretary-General, about which Indonesia had serious reservations, saw the convening at Burg Schlaining in Austria of an All-Inclusive Intra-East Timorese Dialogue attended by 30 East Timorese of all political complexions.[28] A consensus document was adopted and a number of ideas produced which informed talks between Boutros-Ghali and the Portuguese and Indonesian foreign ministers in July. While deep differences remained, the two parties were willing to keep meeting, scheduling their next session for January 1996 in London. In East Timor itself, mysterious hooded gangs, allegedly sponsored by the Indonesian military, began a terror campaign against supporters of independence.[29]

Guatemala[30]

The UN inaugurated a new approach to conflict resolution in late 1994 when the General Assembly mandated a mission to Guatemala specifically oriented towards the protection and enhancement of human rights and the building of indigenous institutions for such purposes. This was seen as a means of achieving national reconciliation and hastening negotiation of a comprehensive peace accord to end Guatemala's 35-year civil war. The UN Mission for the Verification of Human Rights and of Compliance with the Commitments of the Comprehensive Agreement on Human Rights in Guatemala (MINUGUA), which has eight regional offices, five subregional offices and an authorized strength of 245 international staff, became fully operational in February.[31]

The Mission had early success, fostering the signing of a landmark Agreement on Identity and Rights of Indigenous Peoples at Mexico City on 31 March 1995. Negotiations later began in Mexico City between the Guatemalan Government and the opposition Unidad Revolucionaria National Guatemalteca (URNG) on socio-economic and agrarian issues, including the strengthening of civilian power, reintegration of the URNG into political life, a definitive cease-fire, constitutional reforms including an electoral regime, and a schedule for implementation, enforcement and verification. The aim was to have a comprehensive peace agreement signed in early 1996. To assist the negotiations Boutros-Ghali appointed Gilberto Schlittler as his Special Envoy

---

[28] UN, Question of East Timor: progress report of the Secretary-General, UN document A/50/436, 19 Sep. 1995, p. 2.

[29] *International Herald Tribune*, 1 Mar. 1995, p. 4.

[30] For background on Guatemala see Baranyi, S., 'Central America: a firm and lasting peace?', *SIPRI Yearbook 1995* (note 15), pp. 163–67.

[31] UN (note 8), p. 94.

for the Guatemala Peace Process. The Group of Friends of the Guatemala Peace Process (Colombia, Mexico, Norway, Spain, the USA and Venezuela) continued to be involved.

There was a two-week cease-fire during presidential elections in November 1995 which resulted in a right-wing businessman, Alvaro Arzú of the National Advancement Party (PAN), gaining more votes than Alfonso Portillo, designee of former military dictator Efraín Ríos Montt, but not by a sufficient margin to avoid a run-off vote in January 1996.[32] As 1995 ended Guatemala was in political limbo and still plagued by civil war, serious human rights abuses by Government agents and the military and widespread impunity in the commission of such offences. With its limited mandate and resources and complete dependence on the cooperation of the local parties, MINUGUA was incapable of dealing with such major challenges.

Sierra Leone

The little-noticed civil war in Sierra Leone between the venal military government which seized power in 1992 and the Revolutionary United Front of Sierra Leone (RUF) finally came to the world's attention in 1995 after the kidnapping of foreigners. The government's writ has been lost over vast areas, the country has suffered massive population displacement, with the population of the capital Freetown growing threefold, and there has been widespread devastation and a high civilian death toll.[33]

After an exploratory mission in December 1994 requested by head of state Captain Valentine Strasser, Boutros-Ghali appointed a Special Envoy for Sierra Leone, Berhanu Dinka, to cooperate with the OAU and the Commonwealth in helping the parties work towards a negotiated settlement, but he had difficulty even contacting the RUF. It was not until the government hired foreign mercenaries from Angola, Namibia and South Africa through the South African company Executive Outcomes, to help boost its limited military capability, that the RUF made moves towards contact with it.[34] Meanwhile a National Consultative Conference on Elections was held in Freetown in August 1995 and recommended elections by February 1996 despite the continuing civil war.[35] Subsequently the UN helped the government prepare an action plan for demobilization and reintegration of combatants and provided assistance to the Interim National Electoral Commission in preparing for elections.[36] An attempted military coup in October emphasized the fragility of the situation, while the dearth of resources for conducting an election and commencing reconstruction indicated the pressing need for substantial inter-

[32] *International Herald Tribune*, 14 and 15 Nov. 1995, p. 7.

[33] Dowden, R., 'Freetown follows Liberia into ruin', *The Independent*, 23 Jan. 1995, p. 9.

[34] In addition to helping secure the release of foreign hostages, International Alert, an NGO, managed, seemingly against the odds, to involve both the government and the RUF in a conflict-resolution seminar in Dakar, Senegal in Feb. 1995. *On The Alert* (International Alert) no. 5 (July 1995), p. 6.

[35] UN, Report of the Secretary-General on the situation in Sierra Leone, UN document S/1995/975, 21 Nov. 1995.

[36] UN, Press Release SC/95/53, Geneva, 27 Nov. 1995, pp. 1–2.

national assistance. In any event the RUF was unwilling to participate in an electoral process, much less cease firing and disarm.

The Security Council

In 1995 the Council maintained a busy schedule, meeting almost daily, although the hectic pace of recent years eased somewhat, with the numbers of resolutions and presidential statements both declining. While sharp disagreements did occur on several issues, only one of the permanent members resorted to a veto during the year: the USA vetoed a developing country resolution on Israeli expropriation of land in East Jerusalem.[37]

The main foci of the Council's work were the continuing conflicts in the former Yugoslavia and Africa. On Yugoslavia the Council was obliged to deal not only with recalcitrant parties, particularly the Bosnian Serbs who attacked UN safe areas and took peacekeepers hostage, but also with a restructuring, supplementation and eventual dismantling of the largest UN peacekeeping operations in the region.[38] The Council's peacemaking efforts in Africa particularly concerned Burundi and Sierra Leone. The Council dispatched an unprecedented number of fact-finding missions, all of them to Africa: Burundi (twice), Mozambique, Rwanda, Somalia and Western Sahara.[39] Cooperation with the OAU and subregional organizations was an important new feature of the Council's efforts in view of the reluctance of its members to contemplate extensive new African entanglements.

Transparency in the Council's operations, the subject of much criticism in previous years, continued to improve, with greater recourse being had to open meetings, in particular at the early stages of the Council's deliberations on a particular issue before policy was established. Briefings by the Council President for non-member states became institutionalized. However, in December 34 member states which regularly contribute troops to UN peacekeeping operations petitioned the Council to further improve consultations with them.[40] Relations between Boutros-Ghali and the Council continued to be occasionally testy, particularly because of his refusal to meet with the Council on demand. In part to alleviate this problem the Secretary-General appointed one of his Special Advisors, Chinmaya Gharekhan, as his personal representative to the Council to ensure continuous consultation.[41] Despite the fact that it was the UN's 50th anniversary, there was no forward movement on broader Security Council reform or expansion.[42]

---

[37] Draft resolution, S/1995/394, 17 May 1995. Information from Deutsche Gesellschaft für die Vereinten Nationen (DGVN) (UN Association of Germany), Bonn.
[38] See section III of this chapter for details.
[39] UN (note 8), p. 7.
[40] UN, Press Release DH/2047, Geneva, 20 Dec. 1995, p. 1.
[41] UN (note 8), p. 80.
[42] See appendix 2D in this volume for details.

International legal mechanisms

A critical component of any attempt to establish the rule of law in international relations is the international judicial system. From its inception in 1946 until 1994 the International Court of Justice had a total of just 72 contentious cases and 21 advisory cases before it and dealt with no more than one or two cases per year.[43] Recourse to the ICJ has, however, grown dramatically in recent years: in 1994–95 it had a record 14 cases before it, 4 of them new. Twelve were contentious cases involving states, while two, both submitted in 1995, were requests for advisory opinions, one submitted by the World Health Organization (WHO), the other by the General Assembly, on the legality of nuclear weapons. Two new cases between states were filed during 1995. In March Spain instituted proceedings against Canada regarding a dispute over Spanish fishing in Canadian waters, in particular the seizure on the high seas of the fishing boat the *Estai* by Canadian officials. In June New Zealand asked the Court to reopen a case it had submitted in 1973 to stop French nuclear tests in the South Pacific.[44] In record time the Court decided against New Zealand.

Apart from this decision the Court made two other judgements during 1995. In February it concluded that it had jurisdiction to adjudicate in a dispute over maritime delimitation and territory between Qatar and Bahrain.[45] In the case concerning Portugal and Australia over East Timor, in which Portugal disputed the legality of a 1989 treaty between Australia and Indonesia on exploitation of the continental shelf of the so-called Timor Gap, the ICJ ruled that, in the absence of the consent of Indonesia, it could not adjudicate.[46] Hearings in the case concerning the accidental shooting down of an Iranian airliner in 1988, brought by Iran against the USA, were postponed *sine die* at the request of the two parties.

The ICJ, despite its new-found importance, needs reform and rejuvenation. A particular difficulty is that less than one-third of UN member states have accepted compulsory jurisdiction of the ICJ. Of these less than half have accepted jurisdiction unconditionally or with only minor procedural reservations.[47]

The International Tribunal for the Former Yugoslavia, established in the Hague in 1993, continued to issue indictments, including of Bosnian Serbs, Bosnian Croats and three citizens of Serbia.[48] One Bosnian Serb, held in custody, was brought to trial. Quashing speculation that justice might be sacrificed to the exigencies of the Dayton peace process, the Chief Prosecutor of the Tribunal, Justice Richard Goldstone of South Africa, insisted that the Tribunal's activities would proceed regardless. Despite the granting of access to

---

[43] 'Lawyers and peace building', Second Annual Murdoch Student Law Society Address, by Senator Gareth Evans, QC, Minister for Foreign Affairs of Australia, Perth, 16 Aug. 1995, p. 3.
[44] *Unity* (UN Association of Australia, Canberra), July 1995, p. 3.
[45] *UN Chronicle*, vol. 32, no. 2 (June 1995), p. 75.
[46] *Insight* (Australian Department of Foreign Affairs and Trade, Canberra), 25 July 1995, p. 5.
[47] 'Lawyers and peace building' (note 43), p. 3.
[48] *International Herald Tribune*, 10 Nov. 1995, p. 6.

Table 2.1. Cases before the International Court of Justice, 1995

- Application of the Convention on the Prevention and Punishment of the Crime of Genocide (Bosnia and Herzegovina v. Yugoslavia (Serbia and Montenegro))
- Aerial Incident of 3 July 1988 (Iran v. USA)
- East Timor (Portugal v. Australia)
- Maritime Delimitation between Guinea-Bissau and Senegal
- Maritime Delimitation and Territorial Questions between Qatar and Bahrain
- Questions of Interpretation and Application of the 1971 Montreal Convention arising from the Aerial Incident at Lockerbie (Libya v. United Kingdom)
- Questions of Interpretation and Application of the 1971 Montreal Convention arising from the Aerial Incident at Lockerbie (Libya v. USA)
- Oil Platforms (Iran v. USA)
- Gabcikovo–Ngyamaros Project (Hungary/Slovakia)
- Bakassi Peninsula (Cameroon v. Nigeria)
- Legality of the Use by a State of Nuclear Weapons in Armed Conflict (WHO)*
- Legality of the Threat or Use of Nuclear Weapons (UN General Assembly)*
- Fishing Rights (Spain v. Canada)
- Nuclear Tests (New Zealand v. France)

Note: Cases listed as one party versus another are those in which one party (the first mentioned) has brought to the ICJ a case against another party; the others are cases where both parties jointly seek a Court ruling. Cases marked with an asterisk (*) are those in which an advisory opinion has been sought by one party.

Source: UN, Report of the Secretary-General on the work of the Organization, UN document A/50/1, 22 Aug. 1995, pp. 11–13.

the US-led multinational Implementation Force (IFOR), to all of Bosnia and Herzegovina, the peace process did not initially facilitate the Tribunal's work since IFOR forces were instructed not to track down alleged war criminals but only arrest them if they came upon them in the course of their other duties. IFOR was also initially reluctant to guard alleged mass grave sites. None the less the Tribunal was well advanced in amassing evidence and issuing warrants as 1995 ended.

By comparison, the International Tribunal for Rwanda, established in 1994, also with Justice Goldstone as Chief Prosecutor, struggled to cope with the aftermath of an even more systematic and brutal attempt at genocide. Hundreds of suspects were being held in custody in appalling conditions in Rwanda, while the Tribunal struggled to obtain funding and qualified personnel and overcome UN bureaucratic procedures and inter-agency rivalries.[49] Kenya was openly hostile to the Tribunal and refused to cooperate. In June the Tribunal met for the first time, in The Hague (its permanent seat will be Arusha, Tanzania), and elected Laïty Kama of Senegal as its President. It began processing its first indictments in the second half of 1995.

---

[49] McGreal, C., 'Rwanda tribunal chief struggles to win funds', *The Guardian*, 24 Oct. 1995, p. 7; and Karhilo, J., 'The establishment of the International Tribunal for Rwanda', *Nordic Journal of International Law*, vol. 64, no. 4 (1995), pp. 683–713.

One way of avoiding the convening of special international tribunals each time they are required is to establish a permanent international criminal court.[50] In April and August 1995 the Ad Hoc Committee on Establishment of an International Criminal Court, mandated by the General Assembly in December 1994 to consider the convening of an international conference to adopt a statute for such a court, held hearings in New York to discuss a draft prepared by the International Law Commission.[51] Under draft Article 20 the court would have jurisdiction over four crimes under general international law—genocide, war crimes, crimes against humanity and aggression—and exceptionally serious crimes of international concern defined by treaties. The draft statute envisaged the court as being permanent but only operating when required to consider a particular case. It would only be available to states parties to its statute and, in certain situations, to the Security Council.

While there was a wide degree of support in the Committee for establishing the court, developing states are wary of its implications for their sovereignty and national jurisdiction. One of the most controversial issues was whether or not the Security Council should be permitted to refer cases to the court. While some argued that this would enhance the Council's responsibility for international peace and security, others believed it would confer powers on the Council not envisaged by the Charter and could undermine the court's independence and impartiality.

III. UN peacekeeping operations

UN peacekeeping remained a principal tool for conflict prevention, management and resolution, but by the end of the year appeared headed for a period of consolidation in which there would be fewer, smaller, less complex and, on the whole, better managed missions. Peacekeeping remained controversial, largely because of UNPROFOR's perceived failures in the former Yugoslavia, especially after the fall of two so-called UN 'safe areas', Srebrenica and Zepa, to Bosnian Serb forces in July. Some less well-known missions also struggled to achieve their purposes, particularly those in Liberia and Western Sahara. Peacekeeping operations elsewhere, however, enjoyed quiet success, including those in Angola, Haiti and Mozambique, in helping stabilize or resolve conflict situations. Older UN missions, such as those in Cyprus, India–Pakistan and Lebanon, continued unobtrusively and successfully to fulfil their mandates of varying complexity and utility.

Boutros-Ghali and his advisers, after the set-backs suffered by the UN in Somalia and Rwanda and now in Croatia and Bosnia and Herzegovina, retreated from the more ambitious vision for peacekeeping presented in *An Agenda for Peace*. The Secretary-General's theme during much of the year was, understandably, that the UN could not deliver everything expected of it

[50] Drinan, R. F., 'Is a permanent Nuremburg on the horizon?', *Fletcher Forum of World Affairs*, vol. 18, no. 2 (summer/fall 1994), pp. 103–13.
[51] UN, Ad Hoc Committee on Establishment of International Criminal Court Ends First Segment of Initial Session, New York, 3–13 April, Press Release, GA/95/06, Geneva, 13 Apr. 1995.

unless more political support and resources were provided. By the end of the year, traumatized by the UN's inability to protect Srebrenica or Zepa, he was openly proclaiming that the UN could not engage in peace enforcement at all and even some of the more elaborate peacekeeping operations, as envisaged for Eastern Slavonia, would be beyond it.

By the end of 1995 the number of UN peacekeeping missions, compared with the end of 1994, had only dropped from 17 to 16, but this masked the termination of three large missions—the UN Operation in Somalia II (UNOSOM II), the UN Operation in Mozambique (ONUMOZ) and the UN Observer Mission in El Salvador (ONUSAL)—the splitting of UNPROFOR into three separate missions in March and the replacement of two of these by two much smaller missions following the Dayton Agreement. For the first time since 1990 no completely new mission was established.[52] By the end of 1995 total troop strength had declined to 30 000 troops from 76 countries, compared with approximately 69 000 from 77 countries at the end of 1994.[53] These numbers would continue to fall into early 1996 with the termination of the UN Confidence Restoration Operation in Croatia (UNCRO). Some 168 peacekeepers were killed in 1995.

Two of the major, largely successful missions finally terminated, ONUMOZ and ONUSAL, had both helped end civil wars, promoted national reconciliation and overseen the election of constitutional governments. In May, after the El Salvadorean parties had signed a work programme to complete implementation of outstanding points in their 1992 Chapultepec Peace Agreement, the Security Council established a new, non-peacekeeping UN Mission in El Salvador (MINUSAL) for good offices and verification purposes.[54] UNOSOM II in Somalia, one of the least successful UN missions, was terminated in March, its withdrawal assisted by a seven-nation combined task force 'United Shield'.[55] This was the first time that a UN peacekeeping force had required armed protection to withdraw, although in the end it did so safely and methodically, without casualties and with only token armed resistance.

Two peacekeeping missions that had been suspended owing to adverse political and military developments were revived. The UN Mission in Haiti (UNMIH) returned to Haiti in full strength after a US-led Multinational Force (MNF) had restored stability, while the UN Angola Verification Mission (UNAVEM II), renamed UNAVEM III, returned in force to Angola after a new peace agreement was concluded with UN assistance.

The UN Interim Force in Lebanon (UNIFIL) was cut by 10 per cent, saving $10 million per year, supposedly without affecting its operational capacity. The UN Peace-keeping Force in Cyprus (UNFICYP) continued to keep the peace despite having its strength almost halved over the past couple of years.

---

[52] UNAVEM III in Angola is not considered a new operation but a revived version of UNAVEM II.

[53] UN, Department of Peacekeeping Operations, Monthly summary of troop contributions to peacekeeping operations, 31 Dec. 1995.

[54] UN (note 8), pp. 90–91.

[55] UN (note 8), p. 105. The 7 countries involved were France, India, Italy, Malaysia, Pakistan, the UK and the USA.

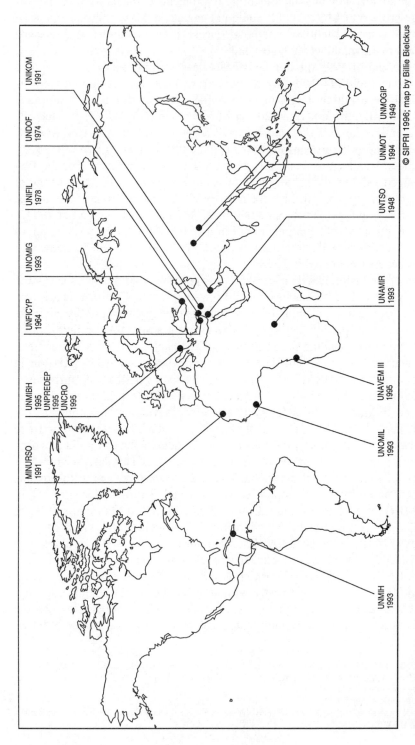

Figure 2.1. UN peacekeeping operations in the field as of 31 December 1995

Note: Dates refer to the start of operations.

© SIPRI 1996; map by Billie Bielckus

The UN Mission for the Referendum in Western Sahara (MINURSO) struggled for yet another year to fulfil its mandate to enrol electors for a referendum on the territory's future status.[56] Losing patience with the parties' uncooperativeness, Boutros-Ghali was suggesting by the end of 1995 that the UN force the issue either by pressing ahead with the referendum with a voter eligibility formula of the UN's own choosing or by abandoning the mission altogether.[57] In mid-December the Security Council authorized him to make one final effort to produce agreement, failing which he should present options for proceeding, including the 'orderly withdrawal of MINURSO'.[58]

UN Peace Forces (the former Yugoslavia)

Having spent years unsuccessfully attempting to negotiate a Yugoslavian peace settlement, the UN was unceremoniously sidelined by the USA and NATO in 1995. UNCRO, UNPROFOR and the umbrella organization UN Peace Forces (UNPF), which had been established in March to oversee all three UN peace operations in the former Yugoslavia (the third being the UN Preventive Deployment Force, UNPREDEP, in Macedonia), were disbanded in December as the implementation of the Dayton Agreement proceeded.

UNPROFOR, replaced by the US-led multinational Implementation Force on 20 December,[59] had been pilloried by the media, some international commentators and even some UN member states for its alleged failure to stop the war in Bosnia when in fact it had been neither mandated nor equipped to do so. What it had done, often against all odds, was to contain and ameliorate the consequences of the conflict. It provided humanitarian sustenance to thousands of people and, through the longest airlift in history, helped lower the death toll from 130 000 in 1992 to fewer than 4000 in 1994. It kept services running and repaired essential infrastructure where possible and prevented the Bosnian Government sectors of Bosnia and Herzegovina being swallowed completely by Croat and Serb forces. UNPROFOR went largely unmourned, with only the British representative on the Security Council paying tribute to the dedication and courage of its personnel, including more than 200 killed.[60] The UN would retain several roles in Bosnia and Herzegovina under the Dayton Agreement: the UN High Commissioner for Refugees (UNHCR) would handle humanitarian relief and refugee matters; a UN International Police Task Force (IPTF) would train and monitor the local civilian police;[61]

[56] UN, The situation concerning Western Sahara: report of the Secretary-General, UN document S/1995/779, 8 Sep. 1995. For background see Findlay (note 5), pp. 59–60; and Chopra, J., 'Breaking the stalemate in Western Sahara', International Peacekeeping, vol. 1, no. 3 (1994), pp. 303–19.
[57] International Herald Tribune, 5 Dec. 1995, p. 7.
[58] UN, Press Release SC/95/68, Geneva, 19 Dec. 1995.
[59] The Guardian, 21 Dec. 1995, p. 6.
[60] Urquhart, B. and Doyle, M., 'Peacekeeping up to now: under fire from friend and foe', International Herald Tribune, 16–17 Dec. 1995, p. 6.
[61] UN Security Council Resolution 1035, UN document S/RES/1035, 21 Dec. 1995.

and human rights work would be shared by several UN bodies. A high-ranking UN official would be appointed as UN coordinator of these activities.[62]

Having been swept aside by Croatian military victories in the second half of 1995 which returned most of Serb-held Croatia to Croatian Government control, UNCRO was already considerably downsized by the end of the year. However, it had its mandate officially extended to 15 January 1996 pending decisions on a new peace force for Eastern Slavonia, the only remaining Serb-held part of Croatia.[63] As envisaged in the Basic Agreement on Eastern Slavonia signed between Croatia and local Serbs on 12 November 1995, UNCRO's place was to be taken for a 12-month transitional period by a new UN peacekeeping force, despite opposition by Boutros-Ghali who saw this as too dangerous for UN forces already much troubled by their Balkan experiences.[64] It was envisaged that many of UNCRO's forces in Eastern Slavonia, mostly Russian and Belgian, would simply transfer to the new authority. Of the three UN operations in the former Yugoslavia only UNPREDEP in Macedonia remained intact at the end of the year.

UNAVEM III (Angola)[65]

Following the signing of the Lusaka Protocol on 20 November 1994, providing for national reconciliation between the Angolan parties, the way was cleared for the deployment of UNAVEM III, the third UN peacekeeping mission to Angola in the past seven years. It was mandated to assist the government and the opposition party, the National Union for the Total Independence of Angola (UNITA) in implementing the protocol by providing good offices and mediation; supervising, verifying and, if necessary, controlling the disengagement of forces and monitoring the cease-fire; assisting withdrawal, quartering and demobilization of UNITA forces; verifying the movement of Angolan armed forces to their barracks; and verifying and monitoring the formation of a new armed force and the free circulation of people and goods. UNAVEM III's other activities included monitoring the Angolan National Police, the quartering of the Rapid Reaction Police and coordinating and supporting humanitarian activities. A military force of 7000 was authorized, in addition to 350 monitors, 260 police observers and civilian support staff.[66] The Security Council, in order to avoid the compliance problems which caused UNAVEM II to abort its mission, decided that the deployment of infantry units would take place gradually and only if the parties complied with the

[62] In Feb. 1996 these various activities were grouped under the name UN Mission in Bosnia and Herzegovina (UNMIBH).

[63] UN Security Council Resolution 1025, UN document S/RES/1025, 30 Nov. 1995. The UN Transitional Administration for Eastern Slavonia, Baranja and Western Sirmium (UNTAES) was established on 15 Jan. 1996 by Security Council Resolution 1037 (UN document S/RES/1037, 15 Jan. 1996) and UNCRO was abolished on that date. A small separate UN peacekeeping operation, the UN Mission of Observers in Prevlaka (UNMOP) was also created in Jan. 1996 to replace UNCRO in the Prevlaka area of south-eastern Croatia.

[64] *Wireless File* (US Information Service, US Embassy: Stockholm), 14 Dec. 1995, p. 10.

[65] For background on UNAVEM II see Findlay (note 5), p. 52.

[66] UN (note 8), p. 110.

Lusaka Protocol. A Joint Commission, chaired by the Secretary-General's Special Representative for Angola, Alioune Blondin Beye, and comprising representatives of the two Angolan parties and three observer states (Portugal, Russia and the USA), was established to oversee implementation.

Despite serious violations, including unauthorized troop movements and continued mine laying, the peace process slowly advanced with the assistance of UNAVEM III.[67] Angolan President José Eduardo dos Santos, who had been elected in UN-monitored elections in September 1992, and UNITA leader Jonas Savimbi met for the first time in May in Lusaka, Zambia and in Gabon in August. These meetings and the visit of Boutros-Ghali to Angola in July helped give impetus to the peace process. Learning the lessons of previous peacekeeping missions elsewhere, the UN attempted to ensure that mine mapping and clearance proceeded well in advance of moves to quarter and demobilize the parties' troops. It also secured agreement to establish a UN radio station to familiarize the Angolan population with UNAVEM's presence and plans, support the peace process and counter anti-peace propaganda.

In August UNAVEM III's mandate was extended to February 1996 despite concerns in the Security Council about the protracted peace process.[68] In September 1995 a European Union (EU)-sponsored conference pledged $1 billion to help Angola recover.[69] Yet by October the phased billeting of government and UNITA troops to 15 UN-built quartering areas, prior to their merger into a unified Angolan Army, had still not begun. Both sides blamed the UN but continued to bolster their forces with arms acquisitions and recruitment. In December UNITA announced that it would halt the quartering of its forces, which it had only just begun, in response to government attacks against it in the oil-rich north-west of the country. During a visit to Washington the USA warned dos Santos to rein in his forces or lose Western support.[70]

After 20 years of civil war the animosity between Angola's rival political forces remains entrenched. Angola's future depends on true political reconciliation, successful demobilization and reintegration of former combatant forces, humanitarian relief and resettlement and extensive de-mining. The international community has so often in the past given Angola one last chance at peace—only to be frustrated by the machinations of one or other party—that it was not clear whether it would be willing to give it another in 1996.

UNMIH (Haiti)

In contrast to Somalia and drawing on the lessons learned there, the UN operation in Haiti increasingly looked like a relatively successful venture in failed-state restoration as 1995 unfolded. As scheduled, UNMIH resumed its mission on 31 March, assuming responsibility from the US-led Multinational Force

[67] UN, Report of the Secretary-General on the United Nations Angola Verification Mission (UNAVEM III), UN document S/1995/842, 4 Oct. 1995.
[68] UN Security Council Resolution 1008, UN document S/RES/1008, 7 Aug. 1995.
[69] Africa Research Bulletin, 9 Nov. 1995, p. 1.
[70] The Economist, 16 Dec. 1995, pp. 55–56.

which had peacefully invaded the country in October 1994 at the behest of the Security Council. The MNF had successfully overseen the restoration of the Aristide Government and the dissolution of the military and its paramilitary gangs, curtailed politically motivated violence and ended major violations of human rights.

In taking over from the MNF, UNMIH was strengthened well beyond its original size to 6000, incorporating many of the MNF forces, including 2500 US troops. UNMIH became the first UN peacekeeping mission to be headed by a serving US officer, Major General Joseph Kinzer.[71] While subordinate to the UN Secretary-General, he consulted regularly with US authorities at home and in Port-au-Prince, which reportedly led to some friction between the USA and the UN. Overall, however, the Haiti mission, conducted in a more benign environment than those in Somalia or Bosnia, was proving to be a model of cooperation between the world organization and the only remaining super-power.

One problem which UNMIH inherited from the MNF was that the unexpected total collapse of the old Haitian military in late 1994 had created a security void which, while leaving the Aristide Government and the peace-keeping forces unchallenged militarily, led to a rapid increase in crime. It also changed UNMIH's anticipated role from one of cooperating closely with the Haitian authorities in maintaining a secure environment to one of essentially providing such an environment itself. The MNF had established an Interim Public Security Force, comprised of vetted and retrained former police, but necessarily including some individuals known to have been involved in human rights violations under the previous regime. UNMIH was charged with over-seeing the creation of an entirely new National Police Force (no new Haitian military force was to be established to replace the old disbanded one) and a credible judicial system, in addition to laying the groundwork for economic reconstruction and the growth of a civil society.

The joint UN–Organization of American States (OAS)[72] International Civilian Mission in Haiti (MICIVIH) also returned to the country in full strength in 1995 to help safeguard and promote human rights.[73] In June legislative and local elections were held under generally secure conditions but were marked by organizational flaws. A partial rerun was held in August. In December Aristide's anointed successor, René Préval, was elected President in the most peaceful election in Haitian history. Both UNMIH and MICIVIH helped an OAS observer mission monitor these electoral processes. Despite continuing low-level violence and the slow pace of economic reform, Haiti at least was set to experience in January 1996 the first peaceful, democratic transfer of political power in its turbulent history.

Yet while the machinery and trappings of democracy and of law and order had been established or restored, economically and socially Haiti's plight was

[71] 'Building a new Haiti', *Strategic Comments*, no. 5 (8 June 1995).
[72] For a list of OAS member states see the Glossary at the front of this volume.
[73] UN (note 8), p. 113.

as desperate as ever.[74] Some senior US officials argued that UNMIH should stay beyond the hand-over to a new head of state in February 1996 to help safeguard the transition, continue restoring the police and judicial systems and foster economic reform. However, the UN, concerned about becoming entrenched in Haiti and eager to demonstrate a success before future problems emerged, was keen to end its mission.[75] Clearly, whether UNMIH stays or goes, Haiti will need the support of the international community for years to come if it is to overcome its deeply entrenched societal divisions and economic deprivation.[76]

UNAMIR (Rwanda)[77]

During the year relations between the UN Assistance Mission for Rwanda (UNAMIR) and the Rwandan Government deteriorated as frustration at the slow pace of refugee repatriation, national reconciliation and reconstruction boiled over. The Government accused the peacekeeping force of undermining its authority, expressed resentment at the flow of international aid to Hutu refugee camps in Zaire and Tanzania while aid for its own reconstruction efforts was slow to materialize, and criticized the swiftness and vehemence of international outrage at its forced expulsion of refugees from the Kibeho refugee camp in April compared with the tardy response to the genocide of 1994.[78] (An Independent International Commission of Enquiry quickly investigated the Kibeho incident and concluded that while not premeditated it could have been prevented.[79])

Although the situation in the country stabilized in 1995, Rwanda faced enormous problems, chief of which were the delay in bringing to justice individuals involved in the 1994 genocide, the hiatus in the safe return of refugees and internally displaced persons, and the slow arrival of international reconstruction and development assistance. In January 1995, in an unprecedented step, the UNHCR contracted with the Zairean Government to employ 1500 Zairean troops and police to improve security and prevent an armed resistance movement re-forming in Rwandan refugee camps in Zaire.[80] In a joint initiative with the OAU, a Regional Conference on Assistance to Refugees, Returnees and Displaced Persons in the Great Lakes Region was held at Bujumbura in February, resulting in several proposals for easing the humanitarian crisis in the region. Rwanda, however, opposed proposals by Boutros-Ghali to convene a similar conference on security and stability in the region[81] and to station

[74] McGeary, J., 'Did the American mission matter?', *Time*, 19 Feb. 1996, pp. 26–29.

[75] *Jane's Defence Weekly*, 12 Aug. 1995, p. 12.

[76] Mintz, S. W., 'Can Haiti change?', *Foreign Affairs*, vol. 74, no. 1 (Jan.–Feb. 1995), pp. 73–86.

[77] For background see Karhilo, J., 'Case study on peacekeeping: Rwanda', *SIPRI Yearbook 1995* (note 15), pp. 100–16.

[78] *The Economist*, 17 July 1995; McGreal, C., 'Rwanda leaders turn on UN', *Guardian Weekly*, 7 May 1995, p. 3; and Crossette, B., 'Rwanda calls for development aid', *International Herald Tribune*, 9 June 1995, p. 7.

[79] UN (note 8), p. 116.

[80] UN (note 8), p. 115.

[81] UN, Press Release DH/2021, Geneva, 13 Nov. 1995, p. 4.

military observers in several states to monitor the flow of arms to Rwanda in violation of the April 1994 UN arms embargo. Instead, in September 1995 the Security Council established an international commission to investigate allegations of illegal arms deliveries to former Rwandan Government forces.[82]

In July the Government requested that UNAMIR be phased out. After convincing it to permit some sort of UN presence, the Security Council adjusted UNAMIR's mandate from peacekeeping to 'confidence building' and reduced its force level from approximately 5700 to 1800 within four months, with a complete withdrawal by December 1995. Relations subsequently improved as UNAMIR concentrated on helping promote national reconciliation, the return of refugees and establishment of a national police force. (UNAMIR was already responsible for protecting humanitarian organizations, human rights observers and members of the International Tribunal for Rwanda.)

In November a two-day summit meeting in Cairo organized by former US President Jimmy Carter, attended by the presidents of Burundi, Rwanda, Uganda and Zaire and an envoy from Tanzania, agreed to encourage Rwandan refugees to return home but also agreed that there would be no forcible repatriation. Zaire had threatened to expel all refugees by 31 December.[83] Meanwhile the United Nations Children's Fund (UNICEF) and the Rwandan Ministry of Justice reached agreement to move an estimated 400 children accused of genocide from adult prisons to a separate location and to begin the rehabilitation of child soldiers. According to Boutros-Ghali, the creative use of various UN capabilities in dealing with the Rwanda situation demonstrated 'a new integrated approach, enlisting and combining all the resources of the United Nations family', one which should be emulated in future UN operations.[84]

None of the UN's initiatives could, however, stop increasing cross-border raids into Rwanda by Zaire-based Hutu militias belonging to the defeated former Rwandan army or a Rwandan Government assault on an island near the border with Tanzania in which more than 300 Hutu rebels were killed. The prospects were for a reigniting of the 1994 conflict in which millions were estimated to have been killed.

Although the Rwandan Government had originally demanded the complete withdrawal of what was left of UNAMIR by the end of the year, it agreed in December, in a last-minute turnaround, to a further three-month extension to March 1996.[85] This was in return for a reduction in the force to 1200 troops and 200 other military personnel, withdrawal of the civilian police component altogether and consideration of its request for the UN to turn over 'non-lethal' equipment when it departs.[86] In these circumstances the UN force commander, Canadian Major General Guy Tousignant, believed that the mission had outlived its usefulness: 'We're wasting our time here. It's worse than a token

[82] *Jane's Defence Weekly,* 25 Sep. 1995, p. 17.
[83] *Financial Times,* 30 Nov. 1995, p. 4.
[84] UN (note 8), p. 116.
[85] UN Security Council Resolution 1029, UN document S/RES/1029, 12 Dec. 1995.
[86] *Jane's Defence Weekly,* 5 Jan. 1996, p. 14.

gesture'.[87] In the Security Council, Canada lambasted Rwanda for dictating the force structure and mandate of UNAMIR, which would henceforth be confined to Kigali in 'garrison mode'. It accused the Council of 'compromising the integrity of a peace-keeping mandate and the credibility of the Organization to fulfil the short-term, politically expedient requirement of retaining the Mission at all costs'.[88] The Council, Canada warned, was demonstrating that it had not absorbed a key lesson of the recent past, namely that if member states were not prepared to provide adequate resources then the UN should not be involved.

Faced with open hostility on the part of the Rwandan Government and reluctance on the part of the five permanent Security Council members to commit substantial additional resources, the UN's options for making a substantial contribution to resolving Rwanda's problems had considerably narrowed by the end of 1995. Conflict prevention in this case, while obviously urgently needed, was forced to take a back seat to political realities both within and outside the country.

Continuing peacekeeping reforms

The DPKO, established in 1992 to take prime responsibility in the UN Secretariat for peacekeeping, continued to grow during the year despite the overall decline in peacekeeping activity. In 1995 it had one Under Secretary-General (Kofi Annan, replaced later in the year by Ismail Kittani), two Assistant Secretaries-General, some 117 professional staff and about 116 military officers, most of the latter seconded from member states at no cost to the UN. This compared with the estimated 42 professional and 49 general service officers who had direct responsibility for peacekeeping in 1991. Reorganization of the Department and the creation of functional units within it—including the Situation Centre, the Policy and Analysis Unit, the Mission Planning Service, the Training Unit, the Civilian Police Unit, the De-mining Unit and the Electoral Assistance Division—resulted by 1995 in much more coherent management of peacekeeping operations. The DPKO was, however, like other parts of the Secretariat, threatened by the UN's severe financial crisis by the end of the year. The new Under Secretary-General for Administration and Management, Joseph Connor, announced that all short-term contracts, on which the Department heavily depends, would be allowed to expire and the total staff of approximately 300 halved.[89] While these drastic measures were postponed until 1996 they do not augur well for a Department whose chief activity is in decline.

Other departments of the Secretariat retained responsibilities for activities associated with peacekeeping, thereby requiring coordination with the DPKO. The Secretary-General's Task Force on UN Operations, established in 1994,

[87] *Daily Telegraph*, 8 Dec. 1995, p. 1, URL <http://www.telegraph.co.uk>.
[88] UN, Press Release SC/95/63, Geneva, 12 Dec. 1995, p. 8.
[89] Clark, B. and Littlejohns, M., 'UN's peacekeepers live to fight another day', *Financial Times*, 25 Jan. 1996, p. 4.

was intended to improve interdepartmental coordination at the highest levels, while mission-specific interdepartmental working groups were intended to improve coordination at lower levels. These reforms were only partly success-ful and coordination problems persisted in 1995.[90] Moreover, some of the functional units, although lauded by the Secretary-General, had not performed as expected or been provided with the requisite resources. The Policy and Analysis Unit, for instance, which was expected to produce a UN peace-keeping doctrine, was staffed in 1995 with just one professional officer. The Police Unit consisted of only two professional officers and appeared to have a marginal effect on operations despite the fact that there have been major fail-ings in the civilian police component of UN missions, often resulting in unsatisfactory individuals being repatriated. While the so-called Focal Point Unit was meant to provide a point of contact for permanent UN missions to obtain answers to operational questions, it was staffed by only one profes-sional officer and tended to be bypassed by permanent missions going directly to the relevant desk officer.

One valuable institutional innovation undertaken in 1995 was the establish-ment of a Lessons-Learned Unit, to conduct systematic analyses of past peace-keeping operations to learn both positive and negative lessons from them. The first study, on Somalia, was published in December.[91]

The organizational arrangements for de-mining continued to evolve. As demining needs to continue after a peacekeeping operation has ended, a de-mining unit was established in the Department of Humanitarian Affairs, in addition to the one in DPKO, to assume responsibility for post-peacekeeping de-mining as a humanitarian and development activity. However both units remained understaffed.

The Situation Centre's operations continued to improve, especially as a result of its relocation to UN headquarters and an increase in the number of loaned officers. However, its weekly mission summaries to member states were cancelled shortly after they were begun, after some permanent missions attempted to censor them to eliminate what they perceived as embarrassing information or to use them to try to influence operational decisions.

The Mission Planning Service, expanded significantly with seconded mili-tary officers, was responsible for detailed planning for UNAVEM III and UNAMIR and the withdrawal of UNOSOM II and UNPROFOR. While the Service is gaining experience and its organizational structure is evolving, the planning process is still relatively unsystematized and interdepartmental coordination patchy. The Field Missions Procurement Section remained under considerable strain: an internal study of March 1994 showed that while profes-sional staff levels had remained constant, the total procurement dollar volume

---

[90] The following details concerning the performance of the Secretariat were obtained from Secretariat officials and permanent missions to the UN in New York.

[91] Comprehensive Report on Lessons Learned from United Nations Operation in Somalia April 1992–March 1995, Friedrich-Ebert-Stiftung (Germany), Life and Peace Institute (Sweden), Norwegian Institute of International Affairs in cooperation with the Lessons-Learned Unit of the Department of Peace Keeping Operations, Dec. 1995.

had increased by 872 per cent since 1990.[92] By 1995 there was still no UN doctrine on planning or logistics for peacekeeping.[93]

The liquidation of peacekeeping missions has long been a concern of member states, worried that the Secretariat allows too much waste, fraud and inefficiency to occur. In April the UNOSOM II Force Commander strongly criticized the Secretariat for making wasteful decisions on the recovery and disposal of equipment from his mission. In 1995, however, the UN established at Brindisi in Italy its first logistics base for storage and recycling of mission equipment, enabling the UN to launch missions more quickly and to equip troops from poorer states which are willing to volunteer personnel but cannot afford equipment.[94] Progress was made in organizing and developing 'peacekeeping start-up kits' to aid rapid deployment of UN missions. Some were used to equip UNAVEM III.

The Convention on the Safety of United Nations and Associated Personnel,[95] opened for signature in December 1994 after being negotiated in record time, was signed by 29 states by September 1995 and ratified by three—Denmark, Japan and Norway.[96]

Australia, Canada, the UK and the USA were all working on ways of improving the communications and information systems for UN peacekeeping operations, especially interoperability.[97] A decision had been taken in 1994 to upgrade the UN telecommunications system to provide improved logistical support to such operations: the new system will consist of a satellite backbone network, with strengthened European hubs servicing both the Atlantic Ocean and Indian Ocean regions, upgraded headquarters facilities and portable earth stations.[98]

The UN Stand-by Arrangements System for future contributions to peacekeeping operations continued to attract pledges. By 31 October 1995, 47 member states (up from 34 at the end of 1994) had confirmed their participation, 30 of them pledging a total of 55 000 personnel. Thirteen were finalizing their offers.[99] However only two, Denmark and Jordan, had signed the required Memoranda of Understanding (MOU) with the UN.[100] The experience of the past few years indicates that 70 000 is probably the maximum number of troops that member states are prepared to provide, globally, for UN peacekeeping at any one time. Moreover, the commitments made still did not

[92] ECOSOC (note 9), para. 87.

[93] ECOSOC (note 9), paras 49 and 73.

[94] Pagani, F., 'The first UN logistic base for peacekeeping in Italy', *International Peacekeeping*, vol. 2, no. 2/3 (Feb.–May. 1995), pp. 44 and 57.

[95] For background see Findlay (note 5), p. 67.

[96] Kirsch, P., 'The Convention on the Safety of United Nations and Associated Personnel', *International Peacekeeping*, vol. 2, no. 5 (Aug./Sep. 1995), p. 103.

[97] *Defense News*, vol. 10, no. 4 (1995); and *Asia–Pacific Defence Reporter*, Apr./May 1994, p. 37.

[98] ECOSOC (note 9), para. 79.

[99] UN, Report of the Secretary-General on Standby Arrangements for Peace-keeping, UN document S/1995/943, 10 Nov. 1995, p. 3.

[100] The first Memorandum of Understanding between the UN and a member state relating to stand-by forces was signed with Jordan on 5 Jan. 1995. See UN Press Release DH/1804, 6 Jan. 1995, p. 2. Memorandum of Understanding on Stand-by Arrangements for Peace-keeping Operations signed between United Nations and Denmark, UN Press Release PKO/40, 10 May 1995.

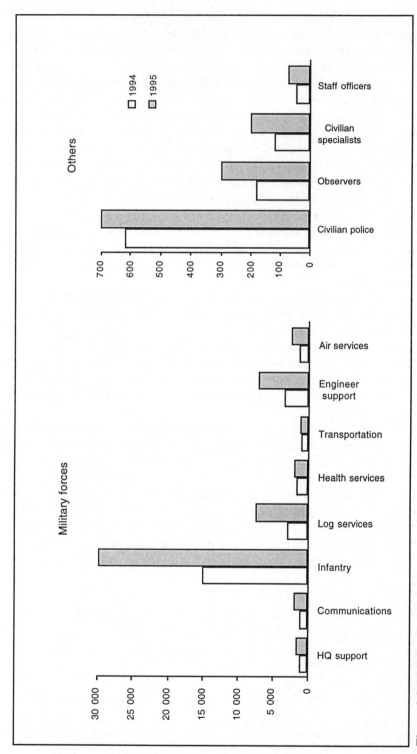

Figure 2.2. UN stand-by arrangements in 1994 and 1995

Source: Report of the Secretary-General on Standby Arrangements for Peace-keeping, UN document S/1995/943, 10 Nov. 1995, pp. 6–7.

cover the whole spectrum of resources required to mount and execute future peacekeeping operations, particularly in critical areas such as communications, multi-role logistics, health services, supply, engineering and transportation. Only 12 countries had volunteered civilian police.[101]

It was still not clear that the Stand-by Arrangements System would ever permit the UN to react quickly to an impending catastrophe, such as occurred in Rwanda in 1994. The Secretary-General noted that while there was 'certainly no lack of willingness to make troops and equipment available for peacekeeping operations, the United Nations is currently far from having a rapid reaction capability'.[102] In his *Supplement to An Agenda for Peace* he again urged that serious consideration be given to the idea. The Canadian, Danish and Netherlands governments responded to this call with major studies. All the Nordic states, meanwhile, continued debate and study on establishing their own rapid reaction forces, except Denmark, which had already established one.[103]

Denmark also initiated a Working Group on a Multinational Stand-by Forces High Readiness Brigade, with members from 11 countries and two observers, which presented its report in August.[104] It proposed that a number of UN member states could, by forming an 'affiliation' between their contributions to the UN Stand-by Arrangements System, make a pre-established 'high-readiness brigade' available to the UN for use in emergencies. The brigade would only be deployed on missions where urgent action was required and its deployment would be limited to six months.

The Netherlands proposed on the other hand that a standing infantry 'fire' brigade of 2000–5000 international volunteers, mandated by and under the control of the Security Council, be established.[105] It would be deployable within days for strictly limited periods and be accompanied by simultaneous preparations for deployment of a normal peacekeeping force—it would be first in and first out. Although it would be a 'light' brigade it would be capable of 'robust' action, while maintaining sufficient flexibility to carry out a wide variety of tasks. Equipped with armoured vehicles, it could protect itself, withstand intimidation and counter external violence. To avoid attracting 'soldiers of fortune', recruitment would be done through governments, although the UN would employ the personnel individually. Finance would be on an assessed basis with a weighting for the permanent members of the Security Council but be outside the regular UN budget.

A Canadian Government report emphasized improving UN capability at the centre first, particularly in the area of operational planning, thereby encourag-

---

[101] ECOSOC (note 9), para. 30.

[102] UN (note 99), p. 5.

[103] See appendix 2C in this volume.

[104] Report by the Working Group on a Multinational UN Stand-by Forces High Readiness Brigade, Chief of Defence Denmark, Copenhagen, Document no. AUG-9S PLU-824b (UKL), 15 Aug. 1995. Participants were Argentina, Austria, Belgium, Canada, Czech Republic, Denmark, the Netherlands, New Zealand, Norway, Poland and Sweden. Finland and Iceland were observers.

[105] UN, Letter dated 7 April 1995 from the Permanent Representative of the Netherlands to the United Nations addressed to the Secretary-General, UN document A/49/886, S/1995/276, 10 Apr. 1995.

ing states to put greater trust in and be more willing to contribute to the UN Stand-by Arrangements System.[106] It proposed a Troop Contributors Committee for each mission to formalize consultation, a Troop Contributors Forum to consider general operational issues, a unified UN peacekeeping budget, an 'early-warning alert' system, the application of advanced technology to peacekeeping, consideration of a standing UN police force and a small UN Standing Emergency Group. The main Canadian innovation was however to propose a 'Vanguard Concept', involving the establishment of 'a permanent UN operational-level headquarters which would be a standing, fully deployable, integrated, multinational group of 30–50 personnel, augmented in times of crisis, to conduct contingency planning and rapid deployment'.[107] This would be deployed to the field as required along with the tactical elements provided by member states through the Stand-by Arrangements System. The Special Committee on Peace-Keeping Operations agreed that serious consideration should be given to a UN rapid reaction capability but stressed that priority should be given to reinforcing the Stand-by Arrangements System.[108] It also endorsed something along the lines of the Canadian 'vanguard concept', urged consideration of establishing more than one UN logistics base and that special attention be paid to rapid and effective responses to emergency situations in Africa.[109] Although an influential Friends Group—Australia, Canada, Denmark, Jamaica, the Netherlands, New Zealand, Nigeria, Senegal and Ukraine—cooperated during the year to advance the Canadian ideas,[110] the state of UN finances and the reluctance of many UN members, especially the USA, to commit themselves to further financial outlays dampened enthusiasm for such major initiatives. However, Boutros-Ghali did announce the creation of a stand-by headquarters component in the Mission Planning Service of DPKO.[111] This would undoubtedly be modest to begin with but would nevertheless be a start. However, the lack of progress towards establishing a UN Rapid Reaction Force emphasized the point that the UN was unlikely to be able to conduct peace enforcement operations in the foreseeable future and would be required to rely instead on ad hoc coalitions of willing states, so-called 'sheriff's posses'.

Several UN bodies commended other reforms during the year. The Security Council proposed establishment of a comprehensive database to cover civilian and military resources for peacekeeping operations.[112] The Special Committee on Peace-Keeping Operations recommended elaboration of agreed definitions of the different kinds of command relationships applicable to peacekeeping

[106] Government of Canada, *Towards a Rapid Reaction Capability for the United Nations* (Government of Canada: Ottawa, Sep. 1995).

[107] Government of Canada (note 106), p. 70.

[108] Special Committee on Peace-keeping Operations Final Meeting (AM) and Round-Up of Session, UN document GA/PK/136, 12 May 1995, pp. 1–4.

[109] Livermore, D., 'Peacekeeping: rapid response and Canada's "Vanguard Concept"', *Pacific Research*, Aug. 1995, pp. 40–41.

[110] Hitchens, T., 'Nine nations urge allies to back crisis response plan', *Defense News,* vol. 10, no. 40 (9–15 Oct. 1995), p. 18.

[111] UN, Press Release SC/95/67, Geneva, 19 Dec. 1995.

[112] *UN Chronicle*, vol. 32, no. 2 (June 1995), p. 35.

operations, the integration into planning of improved arrangements for the safety and security of UN personnel, the strengthening of the Civilian Police Unit in DPKO, strengthening of the UN's public information capacity and the possible attachment of training assistance teams to mission headquarters. A report on the start-up phase of peacekeeping operations prepared by the ECOSOC Committee on Programme and Co-ordination also made major recommendations for peacekeeping improvements, including designating 'responsibility centres' in the UN Secretariat for the human rights and civilian police components of peacekeeping operations (incredibly, no such centres already existed, nor any doctrine or standard operating procedures for such matters).[113] The report recommended that the Centre for Human Rights be so designated for human rights and the Civilian Police Unit in DPKO for police matters.

The plethora of reform proposals, some of which had financial implications beyond the UN's current strapped resources, largely remained to be considered by a Secretariat already engaged in less spectacular but still vital reforms.[114] These included in 1995 the long-awaited delegation of significant procurement authority for peacekeeping missions away from UN headquarters to the field and the establishment of global supply contracts for all UN missions. The Department of Public Information formed an interdepartmental working group to develop proposals for public information strategies for UN peacekeeping and other political missions, a pressing need in the light of successes in Cambodia and Mozambique and failures in the former Yugoslavia and Somalia. The UN Institute for Training and Research (UNITAR) conducted a training programme in international affairs management for UN employees, including peacemaking and preventive diplomacy. To assist member states in peacekeeping training, the DPKO's Training Unit compiled a roster of 30 UN officers available for such purposes.[115] The Office of Legal Affairs, following a UN enquiry into a 1993 massacre of civilians in Liberia, prepared guidelines for UN investigators into allegations of massacres.[116] Regional peacekeeping workshops were initiated, beginning with Europe and Latin America in 1995, with those in Asia and Africa planned for 1996.[117] A pilot training programme in Haiti for the headquarters staff of UNMIH assisted in the early integration of political, military, humanitarian and administrative personnel into a cohesive team.[118] A similar model was used for UNAVEM III with reportedly encouraging results.

---

[113] ECOSOC (note 9), paras 27–30.
[114] UN (note 8), pp. 15, 16 and 18.
[115] ECOSOC (note 9), para. 96.
[116] UN (note 8), p. 15.
[117] UN, Press Release GA/95/28, Geneva, 13 Nov. 1995, p. 1.
[118] UN (note 116), p. 8.

Peacekeeping finance

The cost of peacekeeping fell to $3 billion for 1995 from almost $3.8 billion for 1994 (but still remained dramatically up from the $626 million of a decade ago).[119] The UN was only able to continue its peacekeeping operations in 1995 by halting all reimbursements to troop-contributing countries in June. By the end of the year delayed reimbursements were expected to reach $1 billion (although some payments were made when unexpected dues were received).[120] Ironically, the UN's normal operations were only able to keep functioning by borrowing from various peacekeeping accounts. The General Assembly adopted procedures to strengthen the administrative and budgetary aspects of peacekeeping, including the establishment of a common financial year, beginning 1 July, for all peacekeeping operations, a reform long mooted. The Secretary-General was also requested to submit biannually, for the Assembly's information, a table summarizing the proposed budgetary requirements of each operation.[121] However, the future financing of peacekeeping depended on overhaul of the UN's entire financing system, which remained in crisis throughout the year.[122]

National and cooperative efforts

Individual countries continued to gear up to participate more actively in peace-keeping. President Nelson Mandela indicated that after a long period of hesitation South Africa would be willing to participate.[123] Bilateral cooperation also increased. Japan and South Korea reportedly agreed to study the possibility of joint peacekeeping training and mutual use of transport aircraft.[124] In October Ukraine and Poland agreed to form a joint peacekeeping battalion, while Poland and the USA conducted their first bilateral peacekeeping exercises in July.[125] Moldova established a peacekeeping training centre in Tiraspol[126] and Malaysia established one north of Kuala Lumpur for its own troops and possibly for neighbouring states in future. In July the Lester B. Pearson Canadian International Peacekeeping Training Centre in Nova Scotia inaugurated the International Association of Peace-keeping Training Centres to promote understanding and cooperation in peacekeeping training.[127]

Russian peacekeeping efforts, for the UN, the Commonwealth of Independent States (CIS) and unilateral ventures in its 'near abroad', at last acquired a legal basis, at least in Russian if not international law. On 23 June the State Duma adopted a Federal Law 'concerning the procedure for providing by the

[119] UN (note 8), pp. 5 and 21; and UN, Press Release DH/2049, 22 Dec. 1995, p. 2.
[120] UN, Press Release DH/2009, 26 Oct. 1995, p. 1.
[121] UN (note 8), pp. 5 and 22.
[122] See appendix 2D in this volume for details.
[123] *International Peacekeeping News*, vol. 1, no. 12 (Oct. 1995), p. 2.
[124] *International Peacekeeping News*, vol. 1, no. 12 (Oct. 1995), p. 12.
[125] *International Peacekeeping News*, no. 10 (summer 1995), p. 21.
[126] *Izvestia*, 2 Dec. 1995, p. 2.
[127] *Peacekeeping Profile* (Lester B. Pearson Canadian International Peacekeeping Training Centre, Nova Scotia), vol. 1, no. 3 (Oct. 1995).

Russian Federation of military and civil personnel for the participation in activities for the maintenance or restoration of international peace and security'.[128]

IV. UN peace-enforcement measures

The two principal means which the UN Charter envisages the United Nations using to 'enforce' peace are sanctions and the threat or use of military force. Both were used in 1995, sometimes in combination against a particular party.[129]

Sanctions

Seven UN sanctions regimes were in effect in 1995, against Angola, Iraq, the former Yugoslavia, Libya, Rwanda and Somalia. In August the Security Council unanimously lifted the arms embargo on the Rwandan Government for one year, but kept it in place for non-government forces in Rwanda.[130]

One day after the initialling of the Dayton Agreement on Bosnia and Herzegovina on 21 November the UN Security Council voted to set in motion a phased lifting of the arms embargo on Bosnia and Herzegovina, Serbia and Croatia to begin on the day the three parties signed the agreement.[131] During the first 90 days the embargo, which was imposed in 1991 and banned the delivery of weapons and other military equipment, would remain in place. During the second 90 days imports of all such material except tanks, mines, military aircraft, helicopters and other heavy offensive weapons would be permitted. After 180 days the arms embargo would be automatically terminated unless the Council decided otherwise. The arms embargoes against the other former Yugoslav republics, Slovenia and Macedonia were lifted immediately. A second resolution, approved on 22 November, suspended immediately all economic sanctions imposed on the Federal Republic of Yugoslavia (Serbia and Montenegro) but kept in place the sanctions on the Bosnian Serbs until their forces were withdrawn behind the zone of separation set out in the Dayton Agreement.[132] The sanctions, which could be reimposed on either the Federal Republic or the Bosnian Serbs if at any time they failed to comply with the Dayton Agreement, would formally end 10 days after the Bosnian elections to be held in 1996. Sanctions as a conflict resolution tool have experienced mixed results in the former Yugoslavia. While those against the Federal Republic of Yugoslavia were far from watertight, they so disrupted the

[128] Siekmann, R., 'Russian law on participation in peace operations', *International Peacekeeping*, Aug./Sep. 1995, p. 110.

[129] 'Enforce' is used here in the sense of coercing a party to do something it would otherwise not wish to do or to refrain from doing something it does wish to do. The difference between an enforcement activity and a non-enforcement activity turns on the question of consent. If the consent of the party is not forthcoming then the action taken is necessarily an enforcement activity.

[130] UN Security Council Resolution 1011, UN document S/RES/1011, 16 Aug. 1995.

[131] UN Security Council Resolution 1021, UN document S/RES/1021, 22 Nov. 1995.

[132] UN Security Council Resolution 1022, UN document S/RES/1022, 22 Nov. 1995.

Serbian economy as to be a major factor in bringing the country to the negotiating table. On the other hand, sanctions against the Bosnian Serbs were consistently violated and appear to have little effect in bringing them to heel.

Although the EU imposed a sport boycott on Nigeria and withdrew EU military attachés from Lagos in protest at the hanging of writer Ken Saro-Wiwa and eight other human rights activists in November, the UN Security declined to impose sanctions despite calls for it to do so.[133] Pressure to lift sanctions against Iraq was deflated after revelations in August by defecting Iraqi generals that Iraq had kept chemical and biological weapon activities secret from UN inspectors.[134]

Use of military force

In 1995 several organizations were authorized by the Security Council to use force under Chapter VII of the UN Charter. One was the Multinational Force in Haiti, which had been so authorized in the expectation that it would meet resistance in deploying to the country in October 1994. In the event only a show of force was necessary and it withdrew in March 1995 without having used its enforcement powers.

The other organizations were all authorized to use force in the former Yugoslavia. First, UNPROFOR had been authorized in 1994 to do so in Bosnia and Herzegovina, while NATO was authorized to use force both in Bosnia and Herzegovina and later against targets in Croatia which might have supported attacks against safe areas in Bosnia and Herzegovina. (UNCRO was established under Chapter VII but its mandate was less explicit regarding its right to use force other than to defend itself.) While putatively authorized only to use force for defending UN forces and the carrying out of the UN mission, in effect both NATO and UNPROFOR were involved in peace enforcement by being mandated to deter and respond to attacks on the safe areas established around several towns in Bosnia and Herzegovina and to violations of the heavy weapon exclusion zones later added to them. Disagreement between NATO, UNPROFOR and UN headquarters simmered during the year over the so-called 'dual-key' system for authorizing NATO air strikes.[135] To avoid jeopardizing its impartiality UNPROFOR was extremely reluctant to call in air strikes for any purpose, especially after it became apparent that its troops were vulnerable to being taken hostage. Air power was used on only two occasions in 1995 before the massive attacks of August and September.

In late May 1995, at the request of UNPROFOR, NATO responded to continuing Bosnian Serb attacks on Sarajevo by bombing ammunition dumps near the Bosnian Serb capital of Pale twice over two days. The proximate cause was a refusal by the Bosnian Serbs to return four heavy weapons to a UN col-

[133] *International Herald Tribune*, 5 Dec. 1995, p. 5.
[134] See chapter 15 in this volume for details.
[135] Zucconi, M., 'The former Yugoslavia: lessons of war and diplomacy', *SIPRI Yearbook 1995* (note 15), pp. 224–28.

lection zone.[136] This was the first use of NATO air power since November 1994 and the first time that retaliation had been carried out on a target not directly connected with an attack. The Bosnian Serbs acted as predicted by surrounding or taking hostage around 400 peacekeepers and observers, chaining some in humiliating situations to gates and poles and placing them, as human shields, near presumed targets of further NATO air attacks. NATO air power and UN peace enforcement seemed to have been effectively stymied.

During the Bosnian Serb attack on the safe area of Srebrenica in July the commander of the Dutch UNPROFOR troops stationed there made repeated pleas for air support but was turned down either by UNPROFOR in Sarajevo or by UN Peace Forces commander Lieutenant-General Bernard Janvier until it was too late. On 11 July Janvier and the UN Secretary-General's Special Representative for the former Yugoslavia, Yasushi Akashi, finally approved an attack but limited it to tanks in the safe area and artillery seen firing.[137] NATO jets attacked two tanks and withdrew. Srebrenica and Zepa later both fell to the Bosnian Serbs, precipitating a crisis for the UN operation and strong pressure from NATO to move towards overt and robust peace enforcement.

After the London Conference of 21 July NATO announced that an attack on the remaining eastern enclave of Gorazde would be 'met by a substantial and decisive response'.[138] This was later extended to the other remaining safe areas. Changes to the dual-key system came on 26 July when authority was delegated from Boutros-Ghali and Akashi to Janvier.[139] A precondition for approval of air strikes would be the reduction of the vulnerability of UN personnel to an 'acceptable minimum'.

The final straw for NATO's patience with the Bosnian Serbs came on 28 August when a mortar round lobbed into a Sarajevo street killed 43 people. With operational procedures in place for air strikes, a new British–French Rapid Reaction Force fully deployed and peacekeepers withdrawn to safety, NATO waited only until the last British troops were out of Gorazde before launching the largest military operation in its history. After a brief bombing pause to allow peace talks a chance and for the Bosnian Serbs to assess their options, the raids continued for another two weeks before they capitulated. The bombing also induced the Bosnian Serbs to resume serious peace negotiations, even though they had already agreed to do so as part of a combined delegation with Serbia.

The force that replaced UNPROFOR after the NATO bombings, IFOR, was also authorized by the Security Council to use force under Chapter VII but acquired stronger rules of engagement and much greater capability to use deadly force than any UN force had ever been given.[140] Ironically, however, IFOR's role was more akin to traditional peacekeeping than UNPROFOR's

[136] *Wireless File* (US Information Service, US Embassy: Stockholm, 25 May 1995), p. 3.

[137] Block, R., "'I have to get rid of these enclaves"—UN chief', *The Independent*, 30 Oct. 1995, p. 3.

[138] *Wireless File* (US Information Service, US Embassy: Stockholm, 21 July 1995), p. 2.

[139] UN Press Statement, reproduced in *Wireless File* (US Information Service, US Embassy: Stockholm, 26 July 1995), p. 8.

[140] UN Security Council Resolution 1031, UN document S/RES/1031, 15 Dec. 1995.

since it was to help implement a peace agreement, including separation of forces, patrolling established zones between them and responding to cease-fire and other violations.

Several lessons have been painfully learned from the UN's involvement with the use of force in Bosnia. One is that the 'sub-contracting' out of peace enforcement is problematic because, in seeking to marry the differing perceptions, goals and methods of very different organizations, it complicates and weakens the chain of command. Second, an attempt to disguise peace enforcement as the use of force in self-defence (in order to avoid the escalatory implications of the former and retain support of troop contributors) will not fool the parties on the ground and will not deter them from reacting to the perceived abandonment of UN impartiality. A third lesson is a reinforcement of one supposedly learned in the Congo in the 1960s and in Somalia in 1993: that peacekeeping and peace enforcement in the same geographical space are incompatible unless peacekeepers are withdrawn to safety and peacekeeping at least temporarily abandoned, and that one type of operation should not be allowed to drift into the other. Finally, peacekeepers should not be mandated to use robust force, even in self-defence, unless they have the proper political support, military capability and other resources. The overall lesson of the UNPROFOR experience can be sloganized as: 'no peacekeeping without a peace to keep'.

Experience in the former Yugoslavia will profoundly affect UN views on its future involvement in peace enforcement. This was already apparent in late 1995 in the reluctance of Boutros-Ghali, in the wake of the Dayton accords, to see a UN force deployed to oversee the transfer of Eastern Slavonia from Serb to Croat control, particularly without the protection of a Chapter VII mandate. None the less the exigencies of particular crises may force the UN to become involved in less than optimal circumstances. While opposing a UN force for Eastern Slavonia, Boutros-Ghali was at the same time advocating an intervention force for Burundi despite the uncertainties involved in such a mission.

V. Regional and other multilateral organizations

Africa

Progress was made during 1995 towards enhanced African capacities for conflict prevention and peacekeeping.[141] Two years after the decision to establish it, the OAU's Conflict Resolution Mechanism received substantial assistance from Britain, Canada, France, Japan, the USA and the UN. US funding, provided through the 1994 Congressional African Conflict Resolution Act, assisted the establishment of a Conflict Management Centre at OAU headquarters in Addis Ababa, where a core of civilian and military officers will, on a 24-hour basis, monitor African crisis situations. In June 1995 the

[141] Much of the following is drawn from van der Donkt, C., 'The OAU's conflict management mechanism two years on', *Pacific Research*, vol. 8, no. 3 (Aug. 1995), pp. 42–45, and discussions with the author.

OAU summit meeting endorsed the establishment of an Early Warning Network at the Centre.[142] The USA also funded a 'capability package' (radios, jeeps and other equipment) for a 100-person OAU observer force to be assembled by January 1996. Britain organized a series of successful workshops on early warning, preventive diplomacy and peacekeeping in Egypt, Ghana, Zimbabwe and Botswana.

On the ground the OAU remained relatively ineffectual. Despite appointing a special representative to Burundi and increasing the strength of the OAU Mission in Burundi (OMIB) from 47 to 65 military observers, it appeared to have little effect on the extremely fragile situation in that country. It also appeared unable to affect the Red Sea border dispute between Egypt and Sudan, which heated up in June after the attempted assassination in Khartoum of Egyptian President Hosni Mubarak.[143] Peace processes in Angola, Liberia, Rwanda and Sudan proceeded without notable OAU input.

France's 1994 proposal for an African intervention force, organized at the subregional level but under OAU political direction, continued to appear too ambitious. However, several African countries, including Egypt, Ghana, Nigeria, South Africa, Zambia and Zimbabwe, did offer peacekeeping training at their staff colleges in 1995.[144] An OAU peacekeeping training centre was opened in Cairo in June. Following a meeting of international military experts in Harare in January to discuss establishing UN logistics bases in Africa, Zimbabwe announced that it may host such a base.[145] The US Department of Defence's International Military Education Training (IMET) Program, meanwhile, helped train various African militaries in peace operations.

In a report on improving preparedness for conflict prevention and peacekeeping in Africa, the UN Secretary-General made clear that the key 'lies first and foremost with the countries of the continent'.[146] Ironically, at the same time Boutros-Ghali contended that any cooperative arrangement between the UN and the OAU in such matters needed to 'respect the primacy of the United Nations'. He proposed specifically that the UN post a liaison officer to OAU headquarters to ensure effective coordination; send a technical team on a short-term mission to assist the OAU Mechanism in organizing its situation room; establish a staff exchange programme; and implement routine sharing of peacekeeping training information from UN member states. A further innovative proposal was that the UN promote 'partnerships' between nations with complementary strengths in peacekeeping, presumably developed and developing, whereby one country could make its troops available, while another could provide the necessary specialized and heavy equipment for such troops.

---

[142] Cilliers, J., 'The evolving security architecture in southern Africa', unpublished manuscript, Cape Town, Oct. 1995, p. 9.

[143] Ibrahim, Y. M., 'Egypt orders Sudan troops out of area near border', *International Herald Tribune*, 30 June 1995, p. 1.

[144] Cilliers (note 142), p. 11.

[145] *International Peacekeeping News*, vol. 1, no. 5 (May 1995), p. 2.

[146] UN, Report of the Secretary-General on the work of the organization: improving preparedness for conflict prevention and peace-keeping in Africa, UN document A/50/711, S/1995/911, 1 Nov. 1995.

Resentment appeared to be growing in the OAU, however, about the uncoordinated and unsolicited character of the external assistance being volunteered. Moreover, the views of OAU Secretary-General Salim Salim were reportedly getting ahead of many members of his organization on conflict prevention and management.[147] Many African countries tended to place more trust in subregional bodies with more modest political profiles. One of these, the Botswana-based Southern African Development Community (SADC)[148] recommended at its foreign ministers meeting in Harare in March the designation of the Association of Southern African States (ASAS), established in 1994, as the primary mechanism for conflict prevention, management and resolution in Southern Africa.[149] It would be informal, flexible, with minimum bureaucracy and have unimpeded access to members' heads of state. The August 1995 SADC summit in Johannesburg deferred a final decision on ASAS for another year, partly because of South African–Zimbabwean rivalry over chairmanship of the body.[150] The Norwegian Government meanwhile began funding a five-year 'Training for Peace' programme to improve Southern Africa's conflict resolution and peacekeeping capabilities.[151]

The only true example of a regional peacekeeping force anywhere in the world, ECOMOG in Liberia, came close to being disbanded as the warring parties continued to find a peace accord elusive.[152] The UN also began to show its frustration, threatening to withdraw its accompanying operation, the UN Observer Mission in Liberia (UNOMIL). In August the organization which sponsors ECOMOG, the Economic Organization of West African States (ECOWAS) Monitoring Group meeting in Abuja, Nigeria, managed to bring all the parties to agreement for the first time, in an accord designed to supplement previous failed ones.[153] By October this latest accord had resulted in genuine progress, including installation of an all-party Council of State and a Liberian National Transitional Government, the beginning of the disengagement of forces and agreement on a new timetable for implementation of all other aspects of the accord.[154] The Security Council, in response, decided that UNOMIL's mandate should be enhanced to assist the parties and ECOMOG in such implementation, especially in disarmament and demobilization, human

[147] See, e.g., Salim, S. A., 'Africa in crisis: response of OAU and future challenges', *Ethioscope* (Government of Ethiopia: Addis Ababa, June 1995), pp. 5–15.

[148] Its membership comprises Angola, Botswana, Lesotho, Malawi, Mauritius, Mozambique, Namibia, South Africa, Swaziland, Tanzania and Zimbabwe.

[149] Cilliers, J., Shaw, M. and Mills, G., 'Towards a South African policy on preventive diplomacy and peace support operations', ed. M. Shaw and J. Cilliers, *South Africa and Peacekeeping in Africa, Vol. 1* (Institute for Defence Policy: Cape Town, 1995), p. 5; and *International Peacekeeping News*, vol. 1, no. 12 (Oct. 1995), p. 2. ASAS is an attempt to remould the Frontline States into a security and political wing of SADC.

[150] Cilliers (note 142), p. 21.

[151] 'Editorial comment', *African Security Review*, vol. 4, no. 6 (1995), pp. 1–2.

[152] For background see Ofuatey-Kodjoe, W., 'Regional organizations and the resolution of internal conflict: the ECOWAS intervention in Liberia', *International Peacekeeping*, vol. 1, no. 3 (autumn 1994), pp. 261–302.

[153] In Cotonou, Benin (July 1993); Akosombo, Ghana (Sep. 1994); and Accra, Ghana (Dec. 1994). *International Herald Tribune*, 21 Aug. 1995, p. 7.

[154] UN, Thirteenth progress report of the Secretary-General on the United Nations Observer Mission in Liberia, UN document S/1995/881, 23 Oct. 1995, p. 1.

rights monitoring and the holding of elections.[155] The UN convened a successful pledging conference in New York in October to seek international funding for implementing the accord, including financial support for ECOMOG.[156] Boutros-Ghali noted that the cost of peacekeeping in the former Yugoslavia for five days equalled the entire budget of UNOMIL for a year.[157] Peace in Liberia was however threatened towards the end of the year by resumed fighting between two of the factions and by the late arrival of UN financial support for disarmament and demobilization.[158]

Europe

The Organization for Co-operation and Security in Europe (OSCE)[159] continued to maintain its various missions designed to prevent, manage or resolve conflict, while adding two new ones, the OSCE Assistance Group to mediate the Chechnyan conflict in the Russian Federation,[160] and the OSCE Mission to Bosnia and Herzegovina in accordance with the Dayton Agreement. However, the organization, despite being fully prepared for its first peacekeeping mission, to Nagorno-Karabakh, was still unable to deploy it because of continuing disagreement between the warring parties.[161] The cease-fire there continued to hold, despite occasional skirmishes and artillery duels, while the OSCE's Minsk Group[162] conducted yet another round of peace talks in Finland in October.

The year was an unprecedentedly active one for NATO as it undertook the largest military operation in its history and followed this with its first peacekeeping operation in the form of IFOR in Bosnia and Herzegovina. Less spectacularly, as part of its Partnership for Peace (PFP) programme, NATO vastly expanded its schedule of joint training exercises with east European states, emphasizing peacekeeping, humanitarian operations and search and rescue. In 1995 it conducted 11, compared with 3 in the first year of the partnership, including a major 12-country peacekeeping exercise at Fort Polk, Louisiana in August, the first ever held in North America.[163] The Political–Military Steering Committee/Ad Hoc Group on Cooperation in Peacekeeping continued to serve as the main NACC/PFP forum for consultations on political and conceptual, including legal, aspects of peacekeeping and for exchanges of field experience

---

[155] UN Security Council Resolution 1020, UN document S/RES/1020, 10 Nov. 1995.

[156] *International Herald Tribune*, 2 Nov. 1995, p. 6.

[157] UN, Press Release DH/2010, Geneva, 27 Oct. 1995, p. 2.

[158] The USA was forced to bolster UN efforts with 5 military logisticians. *The Guardian*, 7 Oct. 1995, p. 2.

[159] For details on OSCE activities see chapter 7 in this volume.

[160] Bloed, A., 'OSCE chronicle: active mediation in Chechnya crisis', *Helsinki Monitor 1995*, vol. 6, no. 3 (1995), pp. 81–85.

[161] For background see Nowak, J. M., 'The Organization for Security and Co-operation in Europe', ed. T. Findlay, *Challenges for the New Peacekeepers*, SIPRI Research Report no. 12 (Oxford University Press: Oxford, 1996), pp. 121–41.

[162] See the Glossary at the front of this volume for a list of members of the Minsk Group.

[163] *NATO Review*, vol. 43, no. 4 (July 1995), pp. 13–14. For further details see chapter 7 in this volume.

and planning for future cooperation.[164] Practical interoperability experience was gained through the participation of Estonian and Lithuanian platoons in the Danish battalion in UNCRO and later IFOR. NATO's new five-nation Eurocorps, launched in December, comprising forces from Belgium, France, Germany, Spain and Luxembourg, will be available for peacekeeping and humanitarian operations under UN auspices.[165]

Despite the involvement of EU representative Carl Bildt in negotiating the Dayton Agreement, a stark lesson for Europe was that, its institutional largesse and wealth of resources notwithstanding, it still lacked an effective mechanism for resolving major European conflicts and remained reliant on US leadership. While NATO took the predominant military role in IFOR, other European institutions were given the scraps of the accompanying civilian operation: the OSCE would be responsible for organizing and monitoring elections in Bosnia and Herzegovina and for guiding negotiations on confidence- and security-building measures and conventional arms control.[166] The EU would be responsible for reconstruction and rehabilitation. It would also continue to play a role in attempting reconciliation in the divided city of Mostar. Meanwhile, the joint UN–EU International Conference on the Former Yugoslavia (ICFY) was promptly wound up.

The CIS continued its two peacekeeping operations, in Abkhazia in Georgia[167] and in Tajikistan,[168] but they remained predominantly Russian affairs. Peace settlements were no closer, despite the efforts of Russia, the UN and others.[169] Meanwhile the Russian Government proposed the creation of two organs, the Council and the Secretariat of Collective State Security, which would coordinate peacekeeping operations by CIS forces.[170] Moscow also proposed a plan for sharing the financial burden of such operations. The presidents of Kazakhstan, Kyrgyzstan and Uzbekistan appealed to the UN Secretary-General to consider the possibility of a regional peacekeeping force under the aegis of the UN to be based in southern Kazakhstan.[171]

Other regions

Like the UN, the Arab League celebrated its 50th anniversary in 1995 but with little to show for its existence.[172] It continued to be unable to prevent or resolve intra-Arab conflicts.[173] Egypt and Saudi Arabia called for reform of the

[164] Meeting of the North Atlantic Cooperation Council in Noordwijk Aan Zee, Netherlands, 31 May 1995, NATO Press Release M-NACC-1 (95) 50, 31 May 1995.

[165] *Jane's Military Exercise & Training Monitor,* Oct.–Dec. 1995, p. 8.

[166] See chapter 16 in this volume for details of the CSBM and arms control arrangements.

[167] Marks, E., 'Dynamics of peacekeeping in Georgia', *Strategic Forum* (Institute for National Strategic Studies, National Defense University, Washington, DC), no. 45 (Sep. 1995).

[168] US Institute of Peace Special Report, *The War in Tajikistan Three Years On,* Washington DC, Nov. 1995.

[169] For further details see chapter 6 in this volume.

[170] *International Peacekeeping News,* vol. 1, no. 12 (Oct. 1995), p. 22.

[171] *Daily Report–Central Eurasia (FBIS-SOV),* FBIS-SOV-95-248, 27 Dec. 1995, p. 33.

[172] See the Glossary at the front of this volume for a list of members of the Arab League.

[173] Just as it had failed to prevent the 1970–71 war between Jordan and the Palestinians, the civil wars in Lebanon and Yemen and the invasion of Kuwait by Iraq.

League. One idea being touted was a court to adjudicate intra-Arab disputes.[174] The Organization of the Islamic Conference did help mediate the Muslim conflict in the southern Philippines, but in relation to Bosnia, being biased in favour of one side in the conflict, failed dismally in its efforts to affect the course of negotiations on a peace settlement.[175]

In Latin America, as a result of its history of military coups, the emphasis in conflict prevention, management and resolution continued to be on the sustenance of democracy. The Organization of American States maintained its so-called 'defence of democracy' mechanism, established by Resolution 1080 at its June 1993 summit meeting.[176] However the mechanism was not required in relation to domestic events in 1995 and was irrelevant to the Ecuador–Peru border clash.[177] Steps were taken in 1995 by the OAS Secretary-General to strengthen the OAS Unit for the Promotion of Democracy and reallocate resources to the little-known Inter-American Commission on Human Rights and the Inter-American Court.[178] Advances were also made in intra-Latin American cooperation in peacekeeping when Argentina, Brazil, Paraguay, Uruguay and the USA participated in the hemisphere's first peacekeeping exercise, FUERZAS UNIDAS–PKO '95. Sponsored by Argentina and held near Buenos Aires, the exercise involved key personnel from the Argentina Peacekeeping Training Centre, the only one in the region, and a unique combined logistics battalion.[179]

In Asia the Association of South-East Asian Nations (ASEAN) Regional Forum (ARF) established an inter-sessional working group on peacekeeping chaired jointly by Malaysia and Canada.[180] A so-called 'second-track' or non-official meeting on peacekeeping was held in Brunei in March co-chaired by a Canadian Foreign Ministry official and the head of the Malaysian Institute for Strategic and International Studies (ISIS).[181] However, Asia lagged behind regional organizations in Europe, Africa and Latin America in undertaking planning for or practical steps towards regional peacekeeping endeavours.

As to missions in the field operated neither by the UN nor by a regional organization, the most substantial, apart from the MNF in Haiti, was the Multinational Force and Observers (MFO) which remained in the eastern Sinai despite the apparent solidity of the peace between Israel and Egypt. The now tripartite Neutral Nations Supervisory Commission (NNSC) for Korea limped

---

[174] Glubb, F., 'What future for the Arab League?', *Middle East International*, 17 Mar. 1995, pp. 20–21.

[175] 'Background notes on the situation in Bosnia-Herzegovina and OIC's efforts to resolve the problem', *Iranian Journal of International Affairs*, vol. 7, no. 2 (summer 1995), pp. 478–99.

[176] This has been used with mixed results in relation to coups in Guatemala, Haiti, Peru and Venezuela, for strengthening the legislature in Paraguay and in 1994 in brokering the Pact for Democracy to resolve disputed elections in the Dominican Republic.

[177] For background see Bloomfield, R. J., 'Making the Western Hemisphere safe for democracy? The OAS defense-of-democracy regime', *Washington Quarterly*, vol. 17, no. 2 (1994), pp. 157–69.

[178] Christopher, W., 'The OAS: playing an essential role in the western hemisphere', *DISARM Journal*, vol. 18, no. 1 (fall 1995), pp. 31–32.

[179] *International Peacekeeping News*, vol. 1, no. 12 (Oct. 1995), p. 13.

[180] *Jane's Defence Weekly*, 12 Aug. 1995, p. 20. See the Glossary at the front of this volume for a list of ASEAN and ARF member states.

[181] *Insight* (Australian Department of Foreign Affairs and Trade, Canberra), 11 July 1995, p. 16.

on despite the fact that North Korea only allowed the representatives of Sweden and Switzerland, but not Poland, to have access to its territory.[182] The Military Observer Mission Ecuador/Peru (MOMEP), comprising observers from the four guarantor parties to the 1942 Rio Protocol—Argentina, Brazil, Chile and the USA—monitored the cease-fire, withdrawal and demilitarization agreement reached between Peru and Ecuador in February.[183] By October it was due to begin handing over its duties to observers from Ecuador and Peru.[184] Another ad hoc monitoring mission, made up of representatives from Canada, Norway and the Netherlands, was withdrawn from Sri Lanka after the January cease-fire collapsed.[185]

VI. Other players

A multitude of other players, seemingly more than ever before, were active in 1995 in conflict prevention, management and resolution. Sometimes they were more effective than international organizations. Often they worked in tandem or in cooperation with international organizations, particularly the UN, but also, on occasions, at cross purposes with them and each other.

Individual countries were the most prominent, the USA being involved in some way in almost every conflict situation. It used its diplomatic tools, political influence and military power to greatest effect in achieving the Dayton Agreement, with assistance (when it requested it) from the EU and the Russian Federation. It was almost a textbook example of the art of mediation, the parties being isolated in a negotiating hothouse on an unattractive US airbase in Dayton, Ohio, where chief US negotiator Richard Holbrooke and Secretary of State Warren Christopher alternatively charmed, pressured, badgered and bullied them into agreement.

The USA was again a key player in the Middle East in nudging the peace process between Israel and the Palestinians forward, tending that between Jordan and Israel and being actively involved in talks with Syria directed at an eventual Israeli–Syrian peace agreement. It continued to play a key role in conflict prevention on the Korean Peninsula by offering inducements to North Korea to forgo its nuclear option.[186]

The USA also facilitated the Northern Ireland peace process—initiated in 1994 by the British and Irish governments—through a visit by President Clinton and by offering the services of his adviser on Northern Ireland, prominent former Senator George Mitchell, to chair an international commission to pronounce on the issue of whether the Irish Republican Army (IRA) and Loyalist militia should disarm before, during or after formal peace talks. The commission, whose other members were former Prime Minister of Finland

---

[182] Information from the Swedish Foreign Ministry, Stockholm.
[183] *Wireless File* (US Information Service, US Embassy: Stockholm, 17 Feb. 1995), p. 3.
[184] *International Security Digest*, vol. 3, no. 1 (Oct. 1995), p. 2.
[185] *International Herald Tribune*, 9 Jan. 1995, p. 5.
[186] See chapter 3 in this volume.

Harri Holkeri and General John de Chastelain of Canada, was due to report in early 1996.

The Russian Federation, meanwhile, continued, with little change, its peace-keeping/peacemaking[187] efforts in two former Soviet republics: in Georgia's South Ossetia region and in eastern Moldova. It also continued to attempt to broker settlements in other armed conflicts around the Russian periphery. France engaged in conflict resolution of sorts by unilaterally putting down a military coup in the Comoros in September by force. It also mediated in Burundi and offered to do so in Sri Lanka and between Yemen and Eritrea.

Indonesia hosted a third round of talks in Jakarta, observed by the Organization of the Islamic Conference, between the Philippines Government and the Moro National Liberation Front on the conflict in Mindanao.[188] In October it also hosted the sixth informal workshop on the Spratly Islands dispute in the South China Sea.[189] The meeting acquired added urgency after Chinese forces in February occupied Mischief Reef, claimed by the Philippines, despite the fact that the previous year's workshop had discussed a voluntary halt to development of military installations on the Spratlys. Australia hosted talks in Cairns in September and December between Papua New Guinea and the Bougainville Revolutionary Army (BRA), with representatives of the Commonwealth and the UN in attendance.[190] In an unusual twist, the parties agreed to a four-month peace dialogue without a cease-fire.

Again in 1995 the parties to conflict themselves sometimes initiated a peace process, with or without external assistance. After the Algerian elections in November, the outlawed Islamic Salvation Front, which had waged a bloody war against the military government, recognized the newly elected authorities and sought peace talks.[191] Iran and the United Arab Emirates announced, apparently spontaneously, that they would meet in Qatar to resume their 1992 negotiations over three disputed islands in the Persian Gulf.[192] Saudi Arabia and Yemen, with US support, signed a memorandum in February committing them to further negotiations over their long-disputed border region.[193] After fighting broke out in Iraq between the Kurdistan Democratic Party (KDP) and the Patriotic Union of Kurdistan, leaving an estimated 500 dead, both the opposition Iraqi National Congress (INC) and the USA attempted to mediate.[194] Talks were held in Dublin, overseen by the USA and observed by Turkey and the UK. When this failed, Iran stepped in with apparently greater

---

[187] Russian political parlance does not differentiate between peacekeeping, peace making and peace enforcement. The term used in Russia—*mirotvorchestvo*—means, if directly translated, 'peace creation'; this could cover a very broad range of activities, from political mediation to combat operations aimed at 'imposing peace'.

[188] Tiglao, R., 'Under the gun: spectre of a Muslim rebellion again looms large', *Far Eastern Economic Review*, 24 Aug. 1995, pp. 23–24; and *International Herald Tribune*, 27 Nov. 1995, pp. 1, 8.

[189] *The Australian*, 11 Oct. 1995.

[190] *The Australian*, 20 Dec. 1995, p. 3; and *Insight*, 12 Feb. 1996, p. 7.

[191] *International Herald Tribune*, 21 Nov. 1995, p. 6.

[192] *International Herald Tribune*, 21 Nov. 1995, p. 2.

[193] 'Resolving the Saudi–Yemen border dispute', *Strategic Comments*, no. 3 (22 Mar. 1995).

[194] 'Conflict in Iraqi Kurdistan', *Strategic Comments*, no. 2 (22 Feb. 1995).

success.[195] Negotiations between the Mexican Government and its Zapatista rebels were initiated after a Government military offensive in February captured almost all rebel territory. The Bangladeshi Government and the Shanti Bahini insurgents extended for the 18th time their 1992 cease-fire in relation to the tribal-based conflict in the Chittagong Hill Tracts which began in 1976.[196] Negotiations between the Myanmar Government and the insurgent Mong Tai Army in December helped end decades-long fighting in the so-called Golden Triangle region and led to government forces occupying the self-declared Shan State.[197] In December after Eritrea and Yemen battled briefly over the Red Sea islands of Hanish a cease-fire was quickly reached, overseen by a committee that included a Yemeni, an Eritrean and two US military attachés.[198] Ethiopia later brokered negotiations and France made its good offices available.[199] In Colombia talks began between the government and one guerrilla group, the Jaime Bateman Command, but feelers from other groups for peace talks came to nothing.[200]

A cease-fire was arranged by the two parties to the conflict in Chechnya, but a more permanent settlement between Russia and the Chechnyan rebels, being negotiated with the help of the OSCE, was not achieved. After Peru and Ecuador skirmished briefly over their contested border area in January, agreement was quickly reached on a cease-fire and demilitarized zone during negotiations conducted by the 1942 Rio Protocol parties which had guaranteed the previous Peru–Ecuador territorial settlement. The results were embodied in the Itamaraty Peace Declaration signed in Brasilia in February, but negotiations on a new territorial settlement were still not concluded by the end of the year.

One of the greatest setbacks to peace efforts initiated by the parties themselves occurred in Sri Lanka, where the rebel Tamil Tigers violently ended peace negotiations and an internationally monitored cease-fire and spurned a substantive devolution plan offered by the Government of Chandrika Kumaratunga. The army launched a major offensive to capture the rebel's main redoubt, the Jaffna Peninsula, resulting in a substantial flare-up in the war.

Individuals and non-governmental organizations (NGOs) had an impact on some negotiation processes in 1995. Former US President Carter, after successes in Haiti and Bosnia in 1994, continued his activism, convening a regional summit to try to prevent further humanitarian tragedies in Rwanda and Burundi.[201] In March 1995 he negotiated a two-month cease-fire in Sudan between the Khartoum Government and two rebel groups, the Sudanese People's Liberation Movement/Army (SPLM/A) and the South Sudan Inde-

---

[195] *Jane's Defence Weekly,* 4 Nov. 1995, p. 25 and 24 Jan. 1996, p. 16.

[196] *Jane's Defence Weekly,* 25 Nov. 1995, p. 15.

[197] *Jane's Defence Weekly,* 10 Jan. 1996, p. 14. Since 1989 the government has struck deals with over a dozen ethnic rebel factions which has allowed them a high degree of autonomy in their own areas in return for an end to armed conflict.

[198] *International Herald Tribune,* 19 Dec. 1995, p. 7.

[199] *Financial Times,* 4 Jan 1996, p. 4 and 10 Jan. 1996, p. 4.

[200] *Latin American Weekly Report,* no. 8 (2 Mar. 1995), p. 89 and no. 41 (26 Oct. 1995), p. 482.

[201] *International Herald Tribune,* 24 Oct. 1995.

pendence Movement/Army (SSIM/A), the first in the 12-year war.[202] Kenyan President Daniel Arap Moi, chairman of the Inter-Governmental Authority on Drought and Development (IGADD), which had initiated peace efforts in Sudan, thereafter negotiated a two-month extension. Carter visited Sudan in July to seek a further extension and to pursue the peace process. Officials from the USA, Canada and four European nations formed a 'Friends of IGADD' group to support the process, which also involved a non-governmental organization, the Processes of International Negotiations (PIN).[203] However, their efforts proved unable to prevent a resumption of fighting in October after the SPLA launched a major offensive.[204]

Other non-governmental organizations were also active in 1995, including International Alert in relation to Burundi, Cameroon, Sierra Leone and Togo.[205] It is a feature of the mid-1990s that non-governmental groups—well resourced, politically neutral and equipped with the latest information technology that allows them to be as aware of the details of conflict situations as some governments—can be useful interlocutors in conflict prevention, management and resolution efforts.

VII. Conclusions

The greatest peacemaking achievement in 1995, the peace agreements on Bosnia and Herzegovina and Croatia, brought an abrupt end to several years of vicious armed conflict in the former Yugoslavia, but only after the massive use of military power by NATO. While they were an artful mixture of conflict prevention, management and resolution, the Dayton accords did not guarantee a long-term peace but possibly only a respite from armed conflict. Significant progress was also made in the Middle East towards resolution of the Palestinian–Israeli conflict, although much remained to be done. Other successful conflict resolution processes during the year included that in Haiti, which combined the strengths of a joint US-led multilateral force, a traditional UN peacekeeping mission and an OAS human rights component. Conflict resolution processes advanced in Angola and Liberia but with unsteady prospects.

Other conflicts had to be content with management efforts and arrangements, usually in the form of cease-fires, often patchily adhered to and sometimes accompanied by peace talks. Bougainville, Chechnya, Nagorno-Karabakh, the southern Philippines, the Chittagong Hill Tracts conflict, Northern Ireland and the two conflicts in Georgia fell into this category. Cease-fires were hastily arranged to end the two significant inter-state conflicts in 1995, between Peru–Ecuador and Eritrea–Yemen. Longer-term conflict management efforts continued in the form of UN peacekeeping operations in Cyprus,

---

[202] *Wireless File* (US Information Service, US Embassy: Stockholm), 18 July 1995, pp. 9–10.
[203] Zartman, I. W., 'Applying negotiation concepts in the Horn of Africa', *PIN Newsletter*, July 1995, p. 3.
[204] *Financial Times*, 7 Dec. 1995, p. 6.
[205] *On the Alert*, no. 5 (July 1995).

Lebanon and Kashmir, or Russian-led operations under a CIS mandate, as in Tajikistan. Cease-fires collapsed disastrously in Sri Lanka and Sudan.

Conflict-prevention efforts, while intrinsically difficult to survey and with the usual mixed record, were most noticeable in regard to Burundi, Iraq, Macedonia, North Korea and Rwanda.

The conflicts least amenable to prevention, management or resolution in 1995 included those in Afghanistan, Algeria, East Timor and Sierra Leone. Continuing armed conflict in Cambodia, Chad, Kenya, Peru, Somalia and Turkey seemed to be the focus of no conflict-resolution or -management efforts by anyone.

The United Nations was seemingly omnipresent in conflict-prevention, -management and -resolution efforts but often lacked the capability, resources, mandate or, most tellingly, political weight to affect outcomes significantly. Even peacekeeping, the UN's forte, was destined for downsizing, having sustained unacceptable humiliations during the year in the former Yugoslavia. While quiet successes had been achieved elsewhere, peacekeeping was straining the UN budget to breaking-point. Paradoxically this came as the UN was becoming more efficient and effective at planning and managing peacekeeping operations. Regional organizations again failed to live up to their promise, although many are becoming marginally better prepared. The most effective actors in most peacemaking efforts were, as might be expected, those with the greatest political and military power, the USA and Russia in particular, ad hoc consortia of interested regional states assisted by developed state partners and the conflicting parties themselves.

Appendix 2A. Multilateral observer, peacekeeping and electoral operations, 1995

OLGA HARDARDÓTTIR

I. Multilateral observer and peacekeeping missions

Table 2A.1 lists multilateral observer and peacekeeping operations initiated, continuing or terminated in 1995, by international organization and by starting date. Five groups of operations are presented. The 24 operations run by the United Nations are divided into two sections: UN peacekeeping operations (21) are those so designated by the UN itself (see figure 2.1 in this volume), although they may include some missions more properly described as observer missions; the other UN operations comprise substantial UN peace missions not officially described by the UN as peacekeeping operations. Of the remaining operations 10 are operated by the Organization for Security and Co-operation in Europe (OSCE), 4 by the Commonwealth of Independent States (CIS)/Russia and 9 by other organizations. Purely civilian missions are not included, although in some of the missions listed military observers may act in a civilian capacity.

Legal instruments underlying the establishment of an operation are given in the first column, which lists the resolution adopted by the UN Security Council or the date of the decision taken by the respective body or organization.

Countries ending their participation in the course of 1995 are listed in italics, and those participating for the first time in 1995 are listed in bold text. Numbers of civilian observers and international and local civilian staff are not included.

Mission fatalities are recorded from the beginning of the conflict until the last reported date for 1995 ('to date'), and as a total for the year ('in 1995'). Information on the approximate or estimated annual cost of the missions ('yearly') and the approximate cost of outstanding contributions ('unpaid') to the operation fund at the close of the 1995 budget period (the date of which varies from operation to operation) is given in current US $m. In the case of UN missions, unless otherwise noted, UN data on contributing countries and on numbers of troops, military observers and civilian police as well as on fatalities and costs are as of 31 December 1995. UN data on total mission fatalities ('to date') are for all UN missions since 1948.

While serving a peacekeeping role, and numbering some military observers, the OSCE missions are not military operations. Figures on the number of personnel involved are totals for each mission, and include both military and civilian staff in 1994. The mission to Kosovo, Sanjak and Vojvodina, expelled on 28 June 1993, could not be reinstalled because of a lack of agreement on its extension. The OSCE also maintained Sanctions Assistance Missions (SAMs) in Albania, Bulgaria, Croatia, Hungary, the Former Yugoslav Republic of Macedonia, Romania and Ukraine. Their function is to assist the host countries in the implementation of the sanctions and embargoes imposed on the republics of the former Yugoslavia in accordance with relevant UN Security Council resolutions, in particular resolutions 713, 757, 787, 820, 943, 970, 988 and 1003. In 1995 they were staffed by 45 customs officers from various OSCE participating states.

II. Selected UN-assisted electoral observer missions

Table 2A.2 lists major electoral observer missions coordinated or assisted by the UN for elections held in 1995, by country and by elections observed. Data on number of electoral observers pertain to the polling period. Only missions containing an international observer group are included. The UN may provide assistance only on the basis of a formal request or pursuant to a Security Council resolution.

III. A note on acronyms

Acronyms for the names of the individual missions are explained in the tables. Other acronyms used throughout the tables are as follows: CIS = Commonwealth of Independent States; CSO = OSCE Council of Senior Officials; ECOWAS = Economic Community of West African States; EU = European Union; GAR = General Assembly Resolution; MOU = Memorandum of Understanding; OAS = Organization of American States; OAU = Organization of African Unity; SCR = Security Council Resolution; SG = Secretary-General.

Table 2A.1. Multilateral observer and peacekeeping missions

Acronym/ (Legal instrument)	Name/type of mission (O: observer) (PK: peacekeeping)	Location	Start date	Countries contributing troops, military observers (mil. obs) and/or civilian police (civ. pol.) in 1995	Troops/ Mil. obs/ Civ. pol.	Deaths: To date In 1995	Cost: Yearly Unpaid
United Nations (UN) peacekeeping operations[1] (UN Charter, Chapters VI and VII)		(21 operations)			27 939[2] 2 004 1 088	1 450[3] 168	3 000[4] 1 700[5]
UNTSO (SCR 50)	UN Truce Supervision Organization (O)	Egypt/Israel/ Lebanon/Syria	June 1948	Argentina, Australia, Austria, Belgium, Canada, Chile, China, Denmark, Finland, France, Ireland, Italy, Netherlands, New Zealand, Norway, Russia, Sweden, Switzerland, USA	– 194 –	38 10	27 –
UNMOGIP (SCR 91)	UN Military Observer Group in India and Pakistan (O)	India/Pakistan (Kashmir)	Jan. 1949	Belgium, Chile, Denmark, Finland, Italy, South Korea, Sweden, Uruguay	– 44 –	9 3	7 –
UNFICYP (SCR 186)	UN Peace-keeping Force in Cyprus (PK)	Cyprus	Mar. 1964	Argentina, Australia, Austria, Canada, Finland, Ireland, UK	1 140 – 35	167 4	44[6] 8
UNDOF (SCR 350)	UN Disengagement Observer Force (O)	Syria (Golan Heights)	June 1974	Austria, Canada, Poland	1 036 –[7] –	36 2	32[8] 37[9]
UNIFIL (SCR 425, 426)	UN Interim Force in Lebanon (PK)	Lebanon (Southern)	Mar. 1978	Fiji, Finland, France, Ghana, Ireland, Italy, Nepal, Norway, Poland	4 739[10] –[11] –	209 9	135 204
UNIKOM (SCR 689)	UN Iraq–Kuwait Observation Mission (O)	Iraq/Kuwait (Khawr 'Abd Allah water- way and UN DMZ)[12]	Apr. 1991	Argentina, Austria, Bangladesh, Canada, China, Denmark, Fiji, Finland, France, **Germany**, Ghana, Greece, Hungary, India, Indonesia, Ireland, Italy, Kenya, Malaysia, Nigeria, Pakistan, Poland, Romania, Russia, Senegal, Singapore, Sweden, Thailand, Turkey, UK, USA, Uruguay, Venezuela	899[13] 245 –	5 2	62 31
UNAVEM II (SCR 696)	UN Angola Verification Mission II (O)	Angola	June 1991[14]	Argentina, Brazil, Congo, Guinea-Bissau, Hungary, India, Jordan, Malaysia, Morocco, Netherlands, New Zealand, Nigeria, Norway, Slovakia, Sweden, Zimbabwe	11[15] 161 107	5 1	·· –[16]

Acronym/ (Legal instrument)	Name/type of mission (O: observer) (PK: peacekeeping)	Location	Start date	Countries contributing troops, military observers (mil. obs) and/or civilian police (civ. pol.) in 1995	Troops/ Mil. obs/ Civ. pol.	Deaths: To date In 1995	Cost: Yearly Unpaid
ONUSAL (SCR 693, 729)	UN Observer Mission in El Salvador (O)	El Salvador	July 1991[17]	Brazil, Chile, Colombia, Guyana, Italy, Mexico, Spain, Venezuela	– 3[18] 31	5 2	4[19] 20[20]
MINURSO (SCR 690)	UN Mission for the Referendum in Western Sahara (O)	Western Sahara	Sep. 1991	Argentina, Austria, Bangladesh, Belgium, China, Egypt, El Salvador, France, Germany, Ghana, Greece, Guinea, Honduras, Hungary, Ireland, Italy, Kenya, Malaysia, Nigeria, Norway, Pakistan, Poland, Russia, South Korea, Togo, Tunisia, USA, Uruguay, Venezuela	48[21] 232 90	7 3	59 48
UNPROFOR (SCR 743, 776, 795, 982)[22]	UN Protection Force (PK)	Bosnia and Herzegovina	Mar. 1992[23]	Argentina, Bangladesh, Belgium, Brazil, Canada, Colombia, Czech Rep., Denmark, Egypt, Estonia, Finland, France, Ghana, Indonesia, Ireland, Jordan, Kenya, Lithuania, Malaysia, Nepal, Netherlands, New Zealand, Nigeria, Norway, Pakistan, Poland, Portugal, Russia, Senegal, Slovakia, Spain, Sweden, Switzerland, Tunisia, Turkey, Ukraine, UK, USA	2 433[24] 156 86	207[25] 69	1 664[26] 803[27]
ONUMOZ (SCR 797, 898)	UN Operation in Mozambique (PK)	Mozambique	Dec. 1992[28]	Argentina, Australia, Austria, Bangladesh, Botswana, Brazil, Canada, Cape Verde, China, Czech Rep., Egypt, Ghana, Guinea Bissau, Guyana, Hungary, India, Indonesia, Italy, Japan, Jordan, Malaysia, Nepal, Netherlands, New Zealand, Nigeria, Pakistan, Portugal, Russia, Spain, Sri Lanka, Sweden, Togo, USA, Uruguay, Zambia	3 941[29] 204 918	24 5	.. 41
UNOSOM II (SCR 814)	UN Operation in Somalia II (PK)	Somalia	May 1993[30]	Australia, Bangladesh, Egypt, Ghana, India, Indonesia, Italy, Malaysia, Netherlands, Nigeria, Pakistan, Philippines, South Korea, Zambia, Zimbabwe	7 946[31] – 27	147 13	.[32] 315[33]
UNOMIG (SCR 849, 858)	UN Observer Mission in Georgia (O)	Georgia (Abkhazia)	Aug. 1993	Albania, Austria, Bangladesh, Cuba, Czech Rep., Denmark, Egypt, France, Germany, Greece, Hungary, Indonesia, Jordan, Pakistan, Poland, Russia, South Korea, Sweden, Switzerland, Turkey, UK, USA, Uruguay	132[34] –	1 1	16 1
UNOMIL (SCR 866)	UN Observer Mission in Liberia (O)	Liberia	Sep. 1993	Bangladesh, China, Czech Rep., Egypt, Guinea-Bissau, India, Jordan, Kenya, Malaysia, Pakistan, Uruguay	8[35] 68[36] –	– –	18 8

Acronym (SCR)	Mission (type)	Location	Date	Contributing countries			
UNMIH (SCR 867)	UN Mission in Haiti (PK)	Haiti	Sep. 1993[37]	Algeria, *Antigua & Barbuda*, Argentina, Austria, Bahamas, Bangladesh, Barbados, Belize, Benin, Canada, Djibouti, France, Guatemala, *Guinea-Bissau*, Guyana, Honduras, India, Ireland, Jamaica, *Jordan*, Mali, Nepal, Netherlands, *New Zealand*, Pakistan, *Philippines*, Russia, *St Kitts & Nevis*, *St. Lucia, Suriname*, Togo, Trinidad & Tobago, *Tunisia*, USA	5 609[38] – 414	2 2	243 69
UNAMIR (SCR 872)	UN Assistance Mission for Rwanda (PK)	Rwanda	Oct. 1993[39]	*Argentina, Australia*, Austria, Bangladesh, Canada, Chad, Congo, Djibouti, *Ethiopia, Fiji, Germany*, Ghana, Guinea, Guinea-Bissau, India, Jordan, Malawi, Mali, *Niger*, Nigeria, Pakistan, *Poland*, Russia, Senegal, *Spain, Switzerland, Tunisia, UK*, Uruguay, Zambia, Zimbabwe	1 777[40] 228 17	26 10	199 59[41]
UNMOT (SCR 968)	UN Mission of Observers in Tajikistan (O)	Tajikistan	Dec. 1994	Austria, Bangladesh, Bulgaria, Denmark, *Hungary*, Jordan, Poland, Switzerland, Ukraine, Uruguay	– 40 –	1 1	7 1
UNAVEM III (SCR 976)	UN Angola Verification Mission III (O)	Angola	Feb. 1995	Algeria, *Argentina*, Bangladesh, Brazil, Bulgaria, Congo, Egypt, Fiji, France, Guinea-Bissau, Hungary, India, Italy, Jordan, Kenya, Malaysia, Mali, *Morocco*, Netherlands, New Zealand, Nigeria, Norway, Pakistan, Poland, Portugal, Romania, Russia, Senegal, Slovakia, South Korea, Sweden, Tanzania, UK, Uruguay, Zambia, Zimbabwe	5 836[42] 349 252	6 6	254 27[43]
UNCRO (SCR 981)[22]	UN Confidence Restoration Operation in Croatia (PK)	Croatia	Mar. 1995[44]	Argentina, Bangladesh, Belgium, Brazil, Canada, Czech Rep., Denmark, Egypt, *Estonia*, Finland, France, Germany, Ghana, Indonesia, Ireland, Jordan, Kenya, *Lithuania*, Malaysia, Nepal, Netherlands, New Zealand, Nigeria, Norway, Pakistan, Poland, Portugal, Russia, Senegal, Slovakia, Spain, Sweden, Switzerland, *Tunisia*, Turkey, Ukraine, UK, *USA*	3 294[45] 290 168	16 16	–[26] –[27]
UNPREDEP (SCR 983)[22]	UN Preventive Deployment Force (PK)	Macedonia	Mar. 1995	Argentina, Bangladesh, Belgium, Brazil, Canada, *Czech Rep.*, Denmark, Egypt, Finland, France, Ghana, Indonesia, Ireland, Jordan, Kenya, *Malaysia, Nepal*, Netherlands, *New Zealand*, Nigeria, Norway, Pakistan, Poland, Portugal, Russia, *Senegal*, Spain, Sweden, Switzerland, Ukraine, UK, USA	1 120 26 26	– –	–[26] –[27]

Acronym/ (Legal instrument)	Name/type of mission (O: observer) (PK: peacekeeping)	Location	Start date	Countries contributing troops, military observers (mil. obs) and/or civilian police (civ. pol.) in 1995	Troops/ Mil. obs/ Civ. pol.	Deaths: To date / In 1995	Cost: Yearly / Unpaid
UNMIBH (SCR 1035)[46]	UN Mission in Bosnia and Herzegovina (O)	Bosnia and Herzegovina	Dec. 1995	Bangladesh, Denmark, Finland, France, Germany, Greece, Indonesia, Ireland, Jordan, Kenya, Norway, Poland, Portugal, Russia, Senegal, Spain, Sweden, Switzerland, Tunisia, Ukraine	– / – / 374[47]	– / –	–[48] / –

Other United Nations (UN) operations (3 operations)[49]

Acronym/ (Legal instrument)	Name/type of mission (O: observer) (PK: peacekeeping)	Location	Start date	Countries contributing troops, military observers (mil. obs) and/or civilian police (civ. pol.) in 1995	Troops/ Mil. obs/ Civ. pol.	Deaths: To date / In 1995	Cost: Yearly / Unpaid
MINUGUA[50] (GAR 48/267)	UN Mission for the Verification of Human Rights and of Compliance with the Commitments of the Comprehensive Agreement on Human Rights in Guatemala	Guatemala	Oct. 1994	Argentina, Brazil, Canada, Colombia, Italy, Spain, Sweden, Uruguay, Venezuela[51]	– / 17 / 49[52]	– / –	22[53] / –
OSGA (SG Jan. 1995)[54]	Office of the Secretary-General in Afghanistan	Afghanistan/ Pakistan[55]	Jan. 1995	France, Germany, Ghana, Ireland	– / 2[56] / –	.. / ..	.. / ..
MINUSAL (SG Feb. 1995)[57]	Mission of the UN in El Salvador	El Salvador	May 1995	Brazil, Chile, Italy, Spain[58]	– / – / 7	.. / ..	..[59] / ..

Organization for Security and Co-operation in Europe (OSCE) (10 operations)[60]

Acronym/ (Legal instrument)	Name/type of mission (O: observer) (PK: peacekeeping)	Location	Start date	Countries contributing troops, military observers (mil. obs) and/or civilian police (civ. pol.) in 1995	Troops/ Mil. obs/ Civ. pol.	Deaths: To date / In 1995	Cost: Yearly / Unpaid
(CSO 18 Sep. 1992)[61]	OSCE Spillover Mission to Skopje (O)	Former Yugoslav Rep. of Macedonia	Sep. 1992	..	– / 8[62] / –	– / –	0.6[63] / ..
(CSO 6 Nov. 1992)[64]	OSCE Mission to Georgia (O)	Georgia (S. Ossetia; Abkhazia)	Dec. 1992	..	– / 17 / –	1 / 1	2[63] / ..

Operation	Location	Start date	Mandate/authorization	Countries involved					
OSCE Mission to Estonia (O)	Estonia	Feb. 1993	(CSO 13 Dec. 1992[65])	..	—	6	—	0.4[63]	..
OSCE Mission to Moldova (O)	Moldova	Apr. 1993	(CSO 4 Feb. 1993[66])	..	—	8	—	0.6[63]	..
OSCE Mission to Latvia (O)	Latvia	Nov. 1993	(CSO 23 Sep. 1993[67])	..	—	7	—	0.7[63]	..
OSCE Mission to Tajikistan (O)	Tajikistan	Feb. 1994	(CSO 1 Dec. 1993[68])	..	—	8	—	0.4[63]	..
OSCE Mission in Sarajevo (O)	Bosnia and Herzegovina	Oct. 1994	(2 June 1994[69])	..	—	6	—	0.7[63]	..
OSCE Mission to Ukraine (O)	Ukraine	Nov. 1994	(CSO 15 June 1994[70])	..	—	6	—	1[63]	..
OSCE Assistance Group to Chechnya (O)	Chechnya	Apr. 1995	(11 Apr. 1995[71])	..	—	6	—	2[72]	..
OSCE Mission to Bosnia and Herzegovina (O)	Bosnia and Herzegovina	Dec. 1995[74]	(8 Dec. 1995[73])	..	—	—[75]	—	..	..

CIS/Russia (4 operations)[76]

Operation	Location	Start date	Countries involved	Authorization			
'South Ossetia Joint Force' (PK)	Georgia (S. Ossetia)	July 1992	Georgia, Russia, North and South Ossetia	(Bilateral agreement[77])	1 400[78]	—	.. ..
'Moldova Joint Force' (PK)	Moldova (Trans-Dniester)	July 1992	Moldova, Russia, 'Trans-Dniester Republic'	(Bilateral agreement[79])	c. 3 000[80]	—	.. ..

Acronym/ (Legal instrument)	Name/type of mission (O: observer) (PK: peacekeeping)	Location	Start date	Countries contributing troops, military observers (mil. obs) and/or civilian police (civ. pol.) in 1995	Troops/ Mil. obs/ Civ. pol.	Deaths; To date In 1995	Cost: Yearly Unpaid
– (CIS 24 Sep. 1993[81])	CIS 'Tajikistan Buffer Force' (PK)	Tajikistan (Afghan border[82])	Aug. 1993[83]	Kazakhstan, Kyrgyzstan, Russia, Uzbekistan[84]	..[85] / – / –	75[86] / ..	..[87] / ..[88]
– (CIS 15 Apr. 1994)[89]	CIS 'Peacekeeping Forces in Georgia' (PK)	Georgian–Abkhazian border	June 1994	Russia	3000[90] / – / ..	.. / ..	.. / ..

Other (9 operations)

Acronym/ (Legal instrument)	Name/type of mission (O: observer) (PK: peacekeeping)	Location	Start date	Countries contributing troops, military observers (mil. obs) and/or civilian police (civ. pol.) in 1995	Troops/ Mil. obs/ Civ. pol.	Deaths; To date In 1995	Cost: Yearly Unpaid
NNSC (Armistice Agreement[91])	Neutral Nations Supervisory Commission (O)	North Korea/ South Korea	July 1953	Sweden, Switzerland[92]	– / 10 / –	– / –	0.7[93] / ..
MFO (Protocol to treaty[94])	Multinational Force and Observers in the Sinai (O)	Egypt (Sinai)	Apr. 1982	Australia, Canada, Colombia, Fiji, France, **Hungary**, Italy, *Netherlands*, New Zealand, Norway, Uruguay, USA	1 954[95] / – / –	.. / ..	51[96] / ..
ECOMOG (ESMC 7 Aug. 1990[97])	ECOWAS[98] Monitoring Group (PK)	Liberia	Aug. 1990	Gambia, Ghana, Guinea, Mali, Nigeria, Sierra Leone, *Tanzania*, Uganda[99]	7 269[100] / – / –	.. / ..	91[101] / ..
ECMM (Brioni Agreement[102])	European Community Monitoring Mission[103] (O)	Former Yugoslavia	July 1991	**Austria**, Belgium, Czech Rep., Denmark, **Finland**, France, Germany, Greece, Ireland, Italy, Netherlands, **Norway**, Poland, Portugal, Slovakia, Spain, Sweden, UK	– / 211 / –	6 / –	10[104] / ..
OMIB[105] (OAU 1993)	OAU Mission in Burundi (O)	Burundi	Dec. 1993	Burkina Faso, Guinea, Mali, Niger, Tunisia	65[106] / –	1 / 1	5[107] / ..
MNF (SCR 940)[108]	Operation Uphold Democracy (PK)	Haiti	Sep. 1994[109]	*Antigua & Barbuda, Argentina, Australia, Bahamas, Bangladesh, Barbados, Belgium, Belize, Benin, Bolivia, Costa Rica, Denmark, Dominica, Grenada, Guatemala, Guyana, Israel, Jamaica, Jordan, Netherlands, Philippines, Poland, St Kitts & Nevis, St Lucia, St Vincent & Grenadines, Trinidad & Tobago, UK, USA*[110]	7 143[111] / – / *654*	.. / ..	605[112] / ..

Acronym/(Legal instrument)	Name of observer coordinating unit	Location	Start date	Participating states			Observers
— (Agreement Sep. 1994; SCR 943)	Mission of the International Conference on the Former Yugoslavia[113] (O)	Serbia/Bosnia and Herzegovina border area	Sep. 1994	Belgium, Canada, Czech Rep., Denmark, Finland, France, Germany, Greece, Ireland, Italy, Netherlands, Norway, Portugal, Russia, Spain, Sweden, UK, USA	– 218 –	– –	6.5[114] ..
MOMEP (Declaration of Itamaraty)[115] Peru	Mission of Military Observers Ecuador/Peru (O)	Ecuador/Peru	Mar. 1995	Argentina, Brazil, Chile, USA	– 30 –	– –	.. ..
IFOR (SCR 1031)[116]	Implementation Force (PK)	Bosnia and Herzegovina	Dec. 1995[117]	Austria, Belgium, Canada, Czech Rep., Denmark, Egypt, Estonia, Finland, France, Germany, Greece, Hungary, Italy, Jordan, Latvia, Lithuania, Luxembourg, Malaysia, Morocco, Netherlands, Norway, Poland, Portugal, Romania, Russia, Slovakia, Spain, Sweden, Turkey, Ukraine, UK, USA[118]	60 000[119] – –	– –	.[120] ..

Table 2A.2. Selected substantial UN-assisted electoral observer missions[121]

Acronym/ (Legal instrument)	Name of observer coordinating unit	Location	Start date	Elections conducted in 1994 with UN assistance	Date of elections	Electoral observers
UNMIH (SCR 940 Request Sep. 1994)[122]	UN Mission in Haiti[123]	Haiti	Nov. 1994	Legislative, municipal and local elections Complimentary legislative and municipal elections Second round of legislative elections and additional re-runs Presidential elections[124]	25 June 13 Aug. 17 Sep.[125] 17 Dec.	293[126]
— (Request Jan. 1995)	OSCE/UN Joint Operation for the Election Monitoring in Armenia	Armenia	June 1995	Parliamentary elections Parliamentary elections, second round	5 July 19 July	90
— (Request June 1995)		Tanzania	Aug. 1995	Presidential elections in Zanzibar Presidential and parliamentary elections in Tanzania[127]	22 Oct. 29 Oct.	405
— (Request June 1995)	OSCE/UN Joint Electoral Observation Mission in Azerbaijan	Azerbaijan	Sep. 1995	Parliamentary elections Parliamentary elections, second round	12 Nov. 26 Nov.	122

Notes for tables 2A.1 and 2A.2.

[1] Sources for this section, unless otherwise noted: United Nations, Department of Peacekeeping Operations, Monthly summary of troop contributions to peace-keeping operations; United Nations, *United Nations Peace-keeping Operations*, Background Note, DPI/1634/Rev. 2, 1 Mar. 1996; United Nations, Status of contributions as at 31 December 1995, UN document ST/ADM/SER.B/484, 12 Jan. 1996; and information from UN Department of Public Information, Peace and Security Section, New York.

[2] As of 31 Dec. 1995. Operational strength varies from month to month because of rotation.

[3] Casualty figures are valid 31 Dec. 1995 and include military, civilian police and civilian international and local staff.

[4] 19 of the 21 UN peacekeeping operations conducted or ongoing in 1995 are financed from their own separate accounts on the basis of legally binding assessments on all member states in accordance with Article 17 of the UN Charter. UNTSO and UNMOGIP are funded from the UN regular budget. UNFICYP is partly funded by voluntary contributions from Cyprus and Greece. Unless otherwise indicated, figures are average annual costs as of 31 Dec. 1995.

[5] Outstanding contributions to UN peacekeeping operations as of 31 Dec. 1995.

[6] With effect from 16 June 1993, the financing of UNFICYP is inclusive of voluntary contributions of $6.5 m. annually from the Government of Greece and of one-third of the cost from the Government of Cyprus. Thus only c. $23 m. is assessed on the UN member states annually. United Nations, Report of the Secretary-General on United Nations Operation in Cyprus, UN document S/1995/1020, 10 Dec. 1995, p. 11.

[7] UNDOF comprised 4 military observers seconded by UNTSO and was in addition assisted by 84 military observers of the Observer Group Golan (OGG) of UNTSO. United Nations, Report of the Secretary-General on the United Nations Disengagement Observer Force, UN document S/1995/952, 17 Nov. 1995, p. 2.

[8] Initially financed from a special account established for UNEF II (Second UN Emergency Force, Oct. 1973–July 1979). At the termination of UNEF II, the account remained open for UNDOF.

[9] Total approximate value of outstanding contributions to UNEF II and UNDOF.

[10] SCR 1006 (28 July 1995) reduced the overall strength of the Force by 10%.

[11] 57 UNTSO military observers assisted. UN, Report of the Secretary-General on the United Nations Interim Force in Lebanon, UN document S/1996/45, 22 Jan. 1996, p. 4.

[12] SCR 687 (3 Apr. 1991) established a demilitarized zone (DMZ) stretching about 200 km along the Iraq-Kuwait border, extending 10 km into Iraq and 5 km into Kuwait.

[13] Authorized strength: 910 troops and 300 military observers. United Nations, Financing of the activities arising from Security Council Resolution 687 (1991): United Nations Iraq–Kuwait Observation Mission, Report of the Secretary-General, UN document A/49/863, 20 Mar. 1995, p. 5.

[14] Replaced by UNAVEM III when its mandate expired on 8 Feb.

[15] As of 31 Jan. 1995.

[16] Total approximate value of outstanding contributions to UNAVEM I (Jan. 1989–June 1991), UNAVEM II and UNAVEM III (from Feb. 1995).

[17] Mandate expired 30 Apr. 1995 pursuant to SCR 961 (23 Nov. 1994).

[18] As of 31 Mar. 1995.

[19] UN Department of Public Information, Peace and Security Section, New York.

[20] Total approximate value of outstanding contributions to ONUCA (UN Observer Group in Central America, Nov. 1989–Jan. 1992) and ONUSAL.

[21] Authorized strength: 1695 troops and military observers and 160 civilian police. United Nations, The Situation concerning Western Sahara. Report of the Secretary-General, UN document S/1995/240, 30 Mar. 1995, p. 8.

[22] Force previously divided into 3 separate operational commands: UNPROFOR I (Croatia); UNPROFOR II (Bosnia and Herzegovina); and UNPROFOR III (Former Yugoslav Republic of Macedonia, FYROM). SCRs 981, 982 and 983 (31 Mar. 1995) authorized the replacement of UNPROFOR by 3 separate but interlinked operations: UNCRO (UN Confidence Restoration Operation in Croatia); UNPROFOR (Bosnia and Herzegovina); and UNPREDEP (UN Preventive Deployment Force, operating in FYROM). Overall command and control of the 3 missions was exercised by United Nations Peace Forces Headquarters (UNPF-HQ) in Zagreb. United Nations, Report of the Secretary-General pursuant to Security Council Resolution 947 (1994), UN document S/1995/222, 22 Mar. 1995, p. 24.

23 Mandate terminated 20 Dec. 1995 when authority was transferred from UNPROFOR to the non-UN Implementation Force (IFOR) in accordance with SCR 1031 (15 Dec. 1995) (see note 116).

24 As of 20 Mar. 1995 UNPROFOR consisted of a total of 37 915 troops, 684 military observers and 803 civilian police, distributed as follows: UNPROFOR I—14 825 troops, 283 military observers and 731 civilian police; UNPROFOR II—21 994 troops, 352 military observers and 45 civilian police; and UNPROFOR III—1096 troops, 24 military observers and 24 civilian police. SCR 998 (16 June 1995) authorized an increase of up to 12 500 additional troops for UNPF/UNPROFOR to permit establishment of largely French–British Rapid Reaction Force (RRF). Of the approximately 21 000 UNPROFOR and RRF troops that remained on 20 Dec., about 18 500 were designated to stay on as part of IFOR (see note 117). The majority of the remaining units were to be repatriated by mid-Feb. 1996. United Nations, Further report of the Secretary-General pursuant to Security Council resolutions 1025 (1995) and 1026 (1995), UN document S/1996/83, p. 2.

25 During the first 3 months of 1995 UNPROFOR suffered 29 deaths, bringing the total to 167 deaths as of 31 Mar. Thereafter UNPROFOR suffered further 40 fatalities to the end of the deployment under that designation. UNPF had 9 deaths in 1995.

26 Overall annual expenditure in 1995 for UNPROFOR/UNCRO/UNPREDEP was $1664 m., valid as of 30 Jan. 1996 and subject to change. Information from UN Department of Public Information, Peace and Security Section, New York.

27 Total approximate value of outstanding contributions to UNPROFOR, UNCRO, UNPREDEP and UNPF-HQ.

28 Mandate terminated 31 Jan. 1995.

29 As of 31 Dec. 1994.

30 SCR 954 (4 Nov. 1994) authorized withdrawal of UNOSOM II by 31 Mar. 1995. On 2 Mar. withdrawal of the mission completed with support of combined task force 'United Shield' (France, India, Italy, Malaysia, Pakistan, UK, USA). UN Press Release, SG/SM/95/51, 2 Mar. 1995.

31 As of 31 Jan. 1995.

32 Total amount assessed for period 1 May 1993 to 30 June 1995 is $1537 m. UN Department of Public Information, Peace and Security Section, New York.

33 Total approximate value of outstanding contributions to UNOSOM I (Apr. 1993–Apr. 1994) and UNOSOM II.

34 Authorized strength: 136 military observers. SCR 937 (21 July 1994).

35 Original authorized strength: 65 troops (20 military medical staff and 45 military engineers) and 303 military observers. UN, Report of the Secretary-General on Liberia, UN document S/26422/Add. 1, 17 Sep. 1993, p. 1.

36 SCR 950 (21 Oct. 1994) authorized temporary reduction of observer force to 90 because of deteriorating security. SCR 1020 (10 Nov. 1995) decided that the number of military observers should not exceed 160.

37 Initial deployment halted following an incident on 11 Oct. 1993 in which armed civilians prevented landing of a ship carrying an UNMIH advance unit of 220 military personnel. Deployment of a 60-person UNMIH advance team commenced 23 Sep. 1994. On 30 Jan. 1995, the Security Council determined in SCR 975 that 'a secure and stable environment' existed in Haiti and authorized the build-up of UNMIH to its permitted strength to take over from the non-UN Multinational Force (note 108) by 31 Mar. 1995. On that date, the tasks of the advance team expired pursuant to SCR 940 (31 July 1994).

38 Authorized strength pursuant to SCR 975 (30 Jan. 1995): 6000 military personnel and 900 civilian police.

39 SCR 1029 (12 Dec. 1995) extended mandate of UNAMIR for a final period to 8 Mar. 1996.

40 SCR 997 (9 June 1995) authorized reduction of force level from 5500 to 2330 troops by Sep. and 1800 by Oct., and decided to maintain current level of 320 military observers and 120 civilian police personnel. SCR 1029 (12 Dec. 1995) further requested the Secretary-General to reduce force level to 1200 troops, numbers of military observers, headquarters and other military support staff to 200 and to withdraw the Civilian Police component.

41 Total approximate value of outstanding contributions to UNOMUR (June 1993–Jan. 1994) and UNAMIR.

42 Authorized strength pursuant to SCR 976 (8 Feb. 1995): 7000 military personnel, 350 military observers and 260 police observers.

43 Total approximate value of outstanding contributions to UNAVEM I (Jan. 1989–June 1991), UNAVEM II (June 1991–Feb. 1995) and UNAVEM III.

44 On 1 Dec. 1995, command and control of UNCRO military operations in Sector East transferred from UNCRO to UNPF-HQ. UN, Further report of the Secretary-General pursuant to Security Council resolutions 1025 (1995) and 1026 (1995), UN document S/1996/83, 6 Feb. 1996. Pursuant to SCR 1025 (30 Nov. 1995), the mandate of UNCRO ended on 15 Jan. 1996.

45 UNCRO's strength gradually reduced during autumn 1995 and withdrawal of military units was completed on 15 Dec. except for Sector East and small rear parties of Sectors North, South and West. When UNCRO's mandate expired all civilian police officers redeployed to Bosnia and Herzegovina or to new operation in Eastern Slavonia, Baranja and Western Sirmium (UNTAES), established by SCR 1037 (15 Jan. 1996). UN document S/1996/83 (note 44).

46 SCR 1035 (21 Dec. 1995) authorized establishment of International Police Task Force (IPTF), in accordance with annex 11 to the General Framework Agreement for Peace in Bosnia and Herzegovina (the Dayton Agreement), plus a civilian mission as proposed in the Secretary-General's report of 13 Dec. 1995, S/1995/1031. The mission was later given the name UNMIBH. UN document S/1996/83 (note 44), p. 5.

47 As of 29 Feb. 1996. Authorized strength of IPTF, the principal component of UNMIBH: 1721 police monitors. Full deployment of IPTF was delayed because many member states were unable to make police officers immediately available. As of 21 Mar. 1996, 650 officers had been deployed, 542 were scheduled for deployment before 10 Apr. and 529 before the end of Apr. UN, Report of the Secretary-General pursuant to Security Council Resolution 1035 (1995), UN document S/1996/210, 21 Mar. 1996.

48 Projected cost for 6 months $25.2 m. United Nations, *United Nations Peace-keeping Operations*, Background note, DPI/1634/Rev. 2, 1 Mar. 1996.

49 Comprises substantial UN peace missions not officially described by the UN as peacekeeping.

50 All information concerning this mission from the Guatemala Unit, Department of Political Affairs, United Nations, New York.

51 Countries providing military observers and civilian police. In addition 31 countries are contributing with civilian personnel.

52 The mission has an authorized personnel of 442, of whom 140 are local staff.

53 From 1 Oct. 1994 to 31 Dec. 1995.

54 Established by Secretary-General following discontinuation of the function of the Personal Representative of the Secretary-General for Afghanistan and Pakistan in Dec. 1994. United Nations, Strengthening of the coordination of humanitarian and disaster relief assistance of the United Nations, including special economic assistance: emergency international assistance for peace, normalcy and reconstruction of war-stricken Afghanistan. Report of the Secretary General, UN document A/50/737, 8 Nov. 1995, p. 2.

55 Headquarters in Jalalabad in Afghanistan but the mission also maintains an office in Pakistan.

56 In addition to 3 political officers and the director. Information from OSGAP office in Pakistan.

57 Established by the Secretary-General in response to a request from the Government of El Salvador and from FMLN. United Nations, Assistance for the reconstruction and development of El Salvador. Report of the Secretary-General, UN document A/50/455, 23 Oct. 1995, p. 4.

58 Countries providing civilian police at end of Sep. 1995. In addition Canada, Colombia, Mexico, Peru, Switzerland, Uruguay and Venezuela contributed with civilian observers. Information from UN Office for Verification in El Salvador.

59 Mission funded partly by the regular UN budget and partly by voluntary contributions. In May 1995 the Secretary-General established Trust Fund for MINUSAL in order to support the mission's activities, UN, The Situation in Central America: Procedures for the establishment of a firm and lasting peace, freedom, democracy and development. Report of the Secretary-General, UN document A/50/517, 6 Oct. 1995, pp. 1–2.

60 28 countries sent seconded personnel to OSCE missions in 1995; Armenia, Austria, Belarus, Bulgaria, Canada, Czech Republic, Denmark, Finland, France, Georgia, Germany, Hungary, Ireland, Italy, Japan (OSCE observer), Lithuania, Moldova, Netherlands, Norway, Poland, Russia, Slovakia, Spain, Sweden, Switzerland, Ukraine, UK, USA. Country representation is constantly changing and therefore OSCE does not provide current information on which countries contributed personnel to which operations. Sources for this section: OSCE, *Survey of OSCE Long-Term Missions and other OSCE Field Activities* (CPC: Vienna, 14 Sep. 1995); OSCE, *Survey of OSCE Long-Term Missions and other OSCE Field Activities* (CPC: Vienna, 20 Jan. 1995); OSCE, *Survey of OSCE Long-Term Missions and Sanctions Assistance Missions* (Conflict Prevention Centre: Vienna, 15 Feb. 1996); and specific information from the Conflict Prevention Centre in Vienna.

61 Decision to establish the mission taken at 16th CSO meeting, 18 Sep. 1992, Journal no. 3, Annex 1. Authorized by Government of FYROM through Articles of

Understanding (corresponding to an MOU) agreed by exchange of letters, 7 Nov. 1992.

62 Supplemented by 2 monitors from the European Community Monitoring Mission (ECMM) (note 102) under operational command of OSCE Head of Mission.

63 Budget adopted for 1995.

64 Decision to establish the mission taken at 17th CSO meeting, 6 Nov. 1992, Journal no. 2, Annex 2. Authorized by Government of Georgia through MOU, 23 Jan. 1993 and by 'Leadership of the Republic of South Ossetia' by exchange of letters on 1 Mar. 1993. Mandate expanded in Mar. 1994 to include i.a. monitoring of Joint Peacekeeping Forces in South Ossetia.

65 Decision to establish the mission taken at 18th CSO meeting, 13 Dec. 1992, Journal no. 3, Annex 2. Authorized by Estonian Government through MOU, 15 Feb. 1993.

66 Decision to establish mission taken at 19th CSO meeting, 4 Feb. 1993, Journal no. 3, Annex 3. Authorized by Government of Moldova through MOU, 7 May. An 'Understanding of the Activity of the CSCE Mission in the Pridnestrovian [Trans-Dniester] Region of the Republic of Moldova' came into force on 25 Aug. 1993 through exchange of letters between Head of Mission and 'President of the Pridnestrovian Moldovan Republic'.

67 Decision to establish the mission taken at 23rd CSO meeting, 23 Sep. 1993, Journal no. 3, Annex 3. Authorized by Government of Latvia through MOU, 13 Dec. 1993.

68 Decision to establish the mission taken at 4th meeting of the Council, Rome (CSCE/4-C/Dec. 1), Decision I.4, 1 Dec. 1993. No MOU signed.

69 Decision to establish the mission taken by Permanent Committee, 2 June 1994, Journal no. 23, Annex. According to Article 18 of 'Decision on OSCE Action for Peace, Democracy and Stability in Bosnia and Herzegovina' (MC(5).DEC/1) by the Budapest Ministerial Council on 8 Dec. 1995, '... the present OSCE Mission in Sarajevo ... will be expanded and reorganized into a distinct section of the new Mission [to Bosnia and Herzegovina]'. See note 73.

70 Decision to establish the mission taken at 27th CSO meeting, 15 June 1994, Journal no. 3, decision (c). Authorized by Government of Ukraine through MOU, 24 Jan. 1995.

71 Decision to establish the mission taken at 16th meeting of Permanent Council, 11 Apr. 1995, decision (a). No MOU signed.

72 Budget valid from 15 Apr. to 15 Oct. 1995.

73 Decision to establish the mission taken at 5th meeting, Ministerial Council, Budapest, 8 Dec. 1995 (MC(5).DEC/1) in accordance with Annex 6 of the Dayton Agreement. OSCE cooperates closely with ECMM (note 102).

74 Head of Mission started work in Sarajevo 29 Dec. 1995, relying, initially, on infrastructure of existing mission in Sarajevo (see note 69).

75 Planned strength of the mission is c. 250 internationally seconded members.

76 Figures used in this section could not be verified by official sources by time of publication. Russian-dominated peacekeeping efforts in South Ossetia and Moldova cannot be described as CIS peacekeeping operations as the agreements establishing them were bilateral, they are being undertaken by CIS and non-CIS forces, or came into being before general CIS peacekeeping agreements entered into force. See Crow, S., 'Russia promotes CIS as an international organization', RFE/RL Research Report, vol. 3, no. 11 (18 Mar. 1994), p. 35, note 11.

77 Agreement on the Principles Governing the Peaceful Settlement of the Conflict in South Ossetia, signed 24 June 1992 by Georgia and Russia. Under the Agreement, a 4-party Joint Monitoring Commission established with representatives of Russia, Georgia and North and South Ossetia. Force Commander is Russian.

78 700 Russian troops and 700 joint N/S Ossetian units. O'Prey, K., Henry L. Stimson Center, Keeping the Peace in the Borderlands of Russia, Occasional paper no. 23 (Henry L. Stimson Center: Washington, DC, July 1995), p. 16.

79 Agreement on the Principles Governing the Peaceful Settlement of the Armed Conflict in the Trans-Dniester Region, signed 21 July 1992 by presidents of Moldova and Russia. 'Moldovan Peace Agreement signed', RFE/RL Research Report vol. 1, no. 31 (31 July 1992), p. 73.

80 Originally reported to comprise: between 4 and 6 Russian battalions reportedly reduced to 640 troops in 1993–94; 3 Moldovan battalions (1200 troops); 3 Dniester battalions (1200 troops); and 10 military observers from each of the parties involved in the conflict. Gribincea, M., 'Rejecting a new role for the former 14th Russian Army', Transition, vol. 2, no. 6 (22 Mar. 1996), pp. 38–39.

81 CIS Agreement on the Collective Peace-keeping Forces and Joint Measures on their Logistical and Technical Maintenance, Moscow, 24 Sep. 1993. Tajikistan operation is

first application of Agreement on Groups of Military Observers and Collective Peacekeeping Forces in the CIS, signed at Kiev 20 Mar. 1992.

82 Mandate limited to guarding Afghan border. Russian and other CIS forces stationed or operating elsewhere in Tajikistan are not part of this operation.

83 An earlier CIS operation in Tajikistan began Dec. 1992 as decided by meeting of CIS defence ministers, 30 Nov. 1992. O'Prey (note 78), p. 37.

84 Conflicting reports as to whether the force included units from Kazakhstan in 1995. O'Prey (note 78), p. 16; *Krasnaya Zvezda*, 23 Sep. 1995, p. 2; and *Nezavisimaya Gazeta*, 23 May 1995, p. 2, (see note 121 in chapter 6 in this volume); 'Mandate of CIS peacekeepers in Tajikistan extended', Open Media Research Institute (hereafter OMRI), *OMRI Daily Digest*, vol. 2, no. 15 (22 Jan. 1996), URL <http://www.omri.cz/Publications/Digests/9601/Digest.960122.html>; Moscow INTERFAX in English, in Foreign Broadcast Information Service, Daily Report–Central Eurasia (*FBIS-SOV*), FBIS-SOV-95-199, 16 Oct. 1995, p. 83.

85 Force reportedly includes part of Russian 201st Motor Rifle Division at reduced strength, an Uzbek battalion, a Kyrgyz battalion, company or platoon and, according to some sources, a Kazakh battalion and/or two Kazakh officers. Estimates of number of troops range from less than 10 000 to 25 000. O'Prey (note 78), pp. 16 and 38; FBIS-SOV-95-199, 16 Oct. 1995, p. 83; and Masyuk, Y., Moscow NTV, video report 23 Oct. 1995, in FBIS-SOV-95-207, 26 Oct. 1995, p. 14.

86 As of 28 Sep. 1995. Masyuk (note 85). By the end of Nov., more than 30 soldiers and officers had been killed in 1995. Gridneva, G., Moscow ITAR-TASS in English 30 Nov. 1995, FBIS–SOV-95-231, 1 Dec. 1995, p. 55. Fatal casualties in the 201st MRD reportedly numbered 39 in 1993, 35 in 1994 and 23 in 1995. *Krasnaya Zvezda*, 19 Jan. 1996, p. 2 (see note 125 in chapter 6 in this volume).

87 National contingents fully financed by the state sending them. Only command of the collective force and combat support units are financed from joint budget, shared as follows: Kyrgyzstan 10%; Tajikistan 10%; Kazakhstan 15%; Uzbekistan 15%; and Russia 50%. O'Prey (note 78), p. 38.

88 Only Russia had fully paid its dues by Oct. 1995. Masyuk (note 85).

89 CIS Council of Heads of States on 15 Apr. expressed readiness to send a 'peacemaking' force of military contingents from interested parties to the CIS Treaty on Collective Security. Georgian–Abkhazian Agreement on a Cease-fire and Separation of Forces, 14 May 1994, stipulated that Georgian and Abkhazian units move 12 km away from the Inguri river and a CIS peacekeeping contingent take up positions inside the 24-km buffer zone. In an unusual procedure not provided for in any CIS document, the Chairman of the Council, President Yeltsin, decided to deploy the force in June following CIS Executive Secretary mission to other CIS states to obtain support. Mandate approved by Heads of States members of the CIS Council of Collective Security, 21 Oct. 1994.

90 *OMRI Daily Digest*, vol. 2, no. 10 (15 Jan. 1996); and 'Abkhazia attack condemned', *Financial Times*, 6–7 Jan. 1996, p. 2.

91 Agreement concerning a military armistice in Korea, signed at Panmunjom on 27 July 1953 by Commander-in-Chief, UN Command; Supreme Commander of the Korean People's Army; and Commander of the Chinese People's Volunteers. Entered into force 27 July 1953. US Department of State, *Treaties in Force: A List of Treaties and Other International Agreements of the United States in Force on January 1, 1994*, Department of State Publication 9433 (Department of State, Office of the Legal Adviser: Washington, DC, June 1994), p. 359.

92 By end of 1995, Korean People's Army/Chinese People's Volunteers had not nominated replacement for the former Czechoslovak member of the Commission, whose nomination they had withdrawn in Jan. 1993 following the division of Czechoslovakia into two separate states. North Korea announced withdrawal of its consent to Polish participation in Nov. 1994. In diplomatic notes of 23 Jan. and 8 Feb. 1995 it demanded withdrawal of the Polish delegation by 28 Feb. 1995. Polish personnel left North Korea but Poland remains a Commission member. Information from Swedish Foreign Office; and United Nations, Letter dated 9 May 1995 from the Deputy Permanent Representative of the United States of America to the United Nations addressed to the President of the Security Council, UN document S/1995/378, 11 May 1995, p. 7.

93 Cost of the Swedish delegation.

94 1981 Protocol to Peace Treaty between Egypt and Israel of 26 Mar. 1979. Established following withdrawal of Israeli forces from Sinai. Deployment began 20 Mar. and mission commenced 25 Apr. 1982. Multinational Force and Observers, *Annual Report of the Director General* (MFO: Rome, Jan. 1996).

95 Strength as of Nov. 1995.

96 Operating budget for FY 1995. Force funded by Egypt, Israel, and USA and voluntary contributions from Germany (since 1992), Japan (since 1989) and Switzerland (since 1994).

97 Decision to establish force taken by the ECOWAS Standing Mediation Committee (ESMC) at its first session on 7 Aug. 1990. ESMC composed of Gambia, Ghana, Guinea, Nigeria, Sierra Leone and Mali.

98 ECOWAS membership: Benin, Burkina Faso, Cape Verde, Côte d'Ivoire, Gambia, Ghana, Guinea, Guinea-Bissau, Liberia, Mali, Mauritania, Niger, Nigeria, Senegal, Sierra Leone and Togo.

99 Pursuant to the Cotonou Peace Agreement of 25 July 1993 (UN document S/26272) signed by 3 Liberian parties, ECOMOG expanded to include troops from outside West Africa.

100 All ranks as of Oct. 1995. United Nations. Thirteenth progress report of the Secretary-General on the United Nations Observer Mission in Liberia, UN document S/1995/881, 23 Oct. 1995, p. 8. Estimated troop strength required to implement Accra Agreement of 21 Dec. 1994 (UN document S/1995/7, 5 Jan. 1995, annexes I and II): 12 000.

101 Mainly financed by ECOWAS countries with additional voluntary contributions from UN member states through Trust Fund for the Implementation of the Cotonou Agreement. United Nations, Ninth progress report of the Secretary-General on the United Nations Observer Mission in Liberia, UN document S/1995/158, 24 Feb. 1995, p. 6.

102 Mission established by Brioni Agreement, signed at Brioni (Croatia), 7 July 1991 by representatives of European Community (EC) and governments of Croatia, the Federal Republic of Yugoslavia (Serbia and Montenegro) and Slovenia. Mandate confirmed by EC foreign ministers meeting, The Hague, 10 July 1991. Mission authorized by governments of Croatia, Yugoslavia and Slovenia through MOU, 13 July 1991. Information from Swedish delegation to ECMM, Zagreb.

103 EC established mission maintained with OSCE cooperation, including monitors from 3 non-EU OSCE participating states: Czech Republic, Poland and Slovakia.

104 Not including national expenditures.

105 In French MIOB: Mission de l'OUA au Burundi. Both names are official. Information from Permanent Delegation of the OAU in Geneva and OMIB Office in Bujumbura.

106 In addition there are 6 civilian officers.

107 Funded by regular budget of the OAU and voluntary contributions.

108 SCR 940 (31 July 1994) authorized member states to form a 'multinational force under unified command and control'. The Force operated under US command.

109 MNF terminated its mission on 31 Mar. 1995 and UNMIH assumed full range of its functions pursuant to SCR 975 (30 Jan. 1995) (see note 38).

110 Participating states as of 19 Jan. 1995. UN documents S/1995/55, 19 Jan. 1995 and S/1995/55/Add. 1, 20 Jan. 1995.

111 As of Mar. 1995. Thirteenth, and final, report of the Multinational Force in Haiti, reproduced as annex to United Nations, Letter dated 20 March 1995 from the Permanent Representative of the United States of America to the United Nations addressed to the President of the Security Council, UN document S/1995/211, 20 Mar. 1995, p. 3.

112 Incremental costs incurred by USA for period 1 Oct. 1993 to 28 Feb. 1995 for support of foreign monitors, police and military and for US troops in MNF coalition. The White House, Office of the Press Secretary, Report to Congress on the Situation in Haiti, 1 Apr. 1995.

113 Established pursuant to exchange of letters 17 Sep. 1994 between Co-Chairmen of the Steering Committee of the International Conference on the Former Yugoslavia (ICFY) and Foreign Minister of Yugoslavia to monitor border closure between Yugoslavia and Bosnia and Herzegovina to all traffic except deliveries of humanitarian assistance. ICFY closed down on 31 Jan. 1996. Mission continues its work reporting to High Representative for Bosnia. Information from the ICFY in Geneva; Office of the High Representative in Brussels; and Operations of the Mission of the International Conference on the Former Yugoslavia to the Federal Republic of Yugoslavia (Serbia and Montenegro), reproduced as annex to United Nations, Letter dated 10 November 1995 from the Secretary-General addressed to the President of the Security Council, UN document S/1995/944, 10 Nov. 1995.

114 Estimated total cost of the operation in 1995 in ICFY Mission budget as financed through assessed and voluntary contributions from participating states.

115 First article of Declaration, dated 17 Feb. 1995, states the willingness of the guarantor countries of the Protocol of Rio de Janeiro of 1942—Argentina, Brazil, Chile and USA—to send observer mission to the region in conflict, as well as the acceptance of this offer by the conflicting parties. Information from Brazilian Embassy in Stockholm.

116 SCR 1031 (15 Dec. 1995) authorized member states to establish a multinational military Implementation Force, under unified control and command and composed of

ground, air and maritime units from NATO and non-NATO nations, to ensure compliance with the Dayton Agreement (UN document A/50/790–S/1995/999).

117 An advance enabling force of 2600 troops began deploying to Bosnia and Croatia on 2 Dec. 1995. Deployment of the main body of troops was activated 16 Dec. and on 20 Dec., after transfer of authority from UNPF to IFOR (see note 23), all NATO and non-NATO forces participating in the operation came under command and/or control of IFOR commander, resulting in a force of over 17 000 troops. NATO, *NATO's role in the implementation of the Bosnian Peace Agreement*, NATO Basic Fact Sheet No. 11, Feb. 1996, p. 3; and IFOR Fact Sheet, 4 Mar. 1996, URL <gopher://marvin.stc.nato.int:70/yugo/iffs0403.96>.

118 As of Feb. 1996. Every NATO nation with armed forces has committed troops to IFOR. Non-NATO participating states are Austria, Czech Rep., Estonia, Finland, Hungary, Latvia, Lithuania, Poland, Romania, Russia, Slovakia, Sweden and Ukraine—all Partnership for Peace participants—plus, Egypt, Jordan, Malaysia and Morocco. NATO (note 117), pp. 2–3.

119 As of 18 Feb. 1996. 50 000 provided by NATO states and approximately 10 000 from non-NATO contributors. IFOR (note 117).

120 Mix of common and national funding. NATO common-funded costs will be borne by the Military Budget and the NATO Security Investment Programme. Non-NATO countries will pay their own national contributions to IFOR, but NATO will not seek reimbursement from them for NATO common-funded costs. NATO (note 117), p. 4.

121 During 1995 UN received 22 requests for electoral assistance from Algeria, Armenia, Azerbaijan, Bangladesh, Benin, Cape Verde, Chad, Comoros, Congo, Côte d'Ivoire, El Salvador, Ethiopia, Fiji, Gabon, Gambia, Guinea, Nicaragua, Moldova, Sao Tome and Principe, Uganda, Zimbabwe and Tanzania. Of these 4 could not be met, Cape Verde, Congo, Moldova and Palestine (not a UN member). In addition to these new requests, assistance, based on requests received before 1995, was provided in 11 cases: to Brazil, Equatorial Guinea, Haiti, Honduras, Kyrgyzstan, Liberia, Mexico, Mozambique, Niger, Panama and Sierra Leone. Sources for this section (unless otherwise noted): United Nations, Human rights questions: human rights questions, including alternative approaches for improving the effective enjoyment of human rights and fundamental freedoms, enhancing the effectiveness of the principle of periodic and genuine elections, Report of the Secretary-General. UN document A/50/736, 8 Nov. 1995.

122 SCR 940 (31 July 1994) requested that UNMIH assist the legitimate constitutional authorities of Haiti in establishing an environment conducive to the organization of free and fair legislative elections.

123 Based on an agreement between the UN and OAS, UN was responsible for technical and advisory services to Provisional Electoral Council. OAS took responsibility for organizing international observation of elections. The International Civilian Mission in Haiti (MICIVIH), a joint operation of the UN and OAS, monitored human rights aspects of the electoral campaign.

124 Second round not required as the winning candidate obtained more than 50% of the vote.

125 On 8 Oct. additional run-offs held in 4 constituencies and elections re-run in 7 communal sections. United Nations, Report of the Secretary-General on the United Nations Mission in Haiti, UN document S/1995/922, 6 Nov. 1995, p. 6.

126 *Wireless File* (United States Information Service, US Embassy: Stockholm, 14 July 1995), p. 19.

127 Because of significant administrative and other problems, elections in Dar-es-Salaam were re-run on 19 Nov. 1995.

Appendix 2B. Supplement to *An Agenda for Peace*

SUPPLEMENT TO AN AGENDA FOR PEACE: POSITION PAPER OF THE SECRETARY-GENERAL ON THE OCCASION OF THE FIFTIETH ANNIVERSARY OF THE UNITED NATIONS

Excerpts

I. Introduction

1. On 31 January 1992, the Security Council met for the first time at the level of heads of State or Government. The cold war had ended. It was a time of hope and change and of rising expectations for—and of—the United Nations. The members of the Council asked me to prepare an 'analysis and recommendations on ways of strengthening and making more efficient within the framework and provisions of the Charter the capacity of the United Nations for preventive diplomacy, for peacemaking and for peace-keeping' (see S/23500). Five months later, in June 1992, I submitted my report entitled 'An Agenda for Peace' (A/47/277-S/24111). It dealt with the three problems the Council had requested me to consider, to which I added the related concept of post-conflict peace-building. It also touched on peace enforcement.

2. In submitting my recommendations on how to improve the Organization's capacity to maintain peace and security, I said that the search for improved mechanisms and techniques would be of little significance unless the new spirit of commonality that had emerged, of which the Summit was such a clear manifestation, was 'propelled by the will to take the hard decisions demanded by this time of opportunity' (ibid., para. 6).

3. Subsequent discussion of 'An Agenda for Peace' in the General Assembly, in the Security Council and in Member States' parliaments established that there was general support for the recommendations I had put forward. That discussion, and the new process initiated in 1994 for the elaboration of 'An Agenda for Development' (see A/48/935), have also served to advance international consensus on the crucial importance of economic and social development as the most secure basis for lasting peace.

4. Since the Security Council Summit the pace has accelerated. There have been dramatic changes in both the volume and the nature of the United Nations activities in the field of peace and security. New and more comprehensive concepts to guide those activities, and their links with development work, are emerging. Old concepts are being modified. There have been successes and there have been failures. The Organization has attracted intense media interest, often laudatory, more often critical, and all too often focused on only one or two of the many peace-keeping operations in which it is engaged, overshadowing other major operations and its vast effort in the economic, social and other fields.

5. All this confirms that we are still in a time of transition. The end of the cold war was a major movement of tectonic plates and the after-shocks continue to be felt. But even if the ground beneath our feet has not yet settled, we still live in a new age that holds great promise for both peace and development.

6. Our ability to fulfil that promise depends on how well we can learn the lessons of the Organization's successes and failures in these first years of the post-cold-war age. Most of the ideas in 'An Agenda for Peace' have proved themselves. A few have not been taken up. The purpose of the present position paper, however, is not to revise 'An Agenda for Peace' nor to call into question structures and procedures that have been tested by time. Even less is it intended to be a comprehensive treatise on the matters it discusses. Its purpose is, rather, to highlight selectively certain areas where unforeseen, or only partly foreseen, difficulties have arisen and where there is a need for the Member States to take the 'hard decisions' I referred to two and a half years ago.

7. The Organization's half-century year will provide the international community an opportunity to address these issues, and the related, major challenge of elaborating 'An Agenda for Development', and to indicate in a comprehensive way the direction the Member States want the Organization to take. The present position paper is offered as a contribution to the many debates I hope will take place during 1995 and perhaps beyond, inside and outside the intergovernmental bodies, about the current performance and future role of our Organization.

II. Quantitative and qualitative changes

8. It is indisputable that since the end of the cold war there has been a dramatic increase in the United Nations activities related to the maintenance of peace and security. The figures speak for themselves. The following table gives them for three dates: 31 January 1988 (when the cold war was already coming to an end); 31 January 1992 (the date of the first Security Council Summit); and today, on the eve of the fiftieth anniversary of the United Nations.

9. This increased volume of activity would have strained the Organization even if the nature of the activity had remained unchanged. It has not remained unchanged, however: there have been qualitative changes even more significant than the quantitative ones.

10. One is the fact that so many of today's conflicts are within States rather than between States. The end of the cold war removed constraints that had inhibited conflict in the former Soviet Union and elsewhere. As a result there has been a rash of wars within newly independent States, often of a religious or ethnic character and often involving unusual violence and cruelty. The end of the cold war seems also to have contributed to an outbreak of such wars in Africa. In addition, some of the proxy wars fuelled by the cold war within States remain unresolved. Inter-state wars, by contrast, have become infrequent.

11. Of the five peace-keeping operations that existed in early 1988, four related to inter-state wars and only one (20 per cent of the total) to an intra-state conflict. Of the 21 operations established since then, only 8 have related to inter-state wars, whereas 13 (62 per cent) have related to intra-state conflicts, though some of them, especially those in the former Yugoslavia, have some inter-state dimensions also. Of the 11 operations established since January 1992 all but 2 (82 per cent) relate to intra-state conflicts.

12. The new breed of intra-state conflicts have certain characteristics that present United Nations peace-keepers with challenges not encountered since the Congo operation of the early 1960s. They are usually fought not only by regular armies but also by militias and armed civilians with little discipline and with ill-defined chains of command. They are often guerrilla wars without clear front lines. Civilians are the main victims and often the main targets. Humanitarian emergencies are commonplace and the combatant authorities, in so far as they can be called authorities, lack the capacity to cope with them. The number of refugees registered with the Office of the United Nations High Commissioner for Refugees (UNHCR) has increased from 13 million at the end of 1987 to 26 million at the end of 1994. The number of internally displaced persons has increased even more dramatically.

13. Another feature of such conflicts is the collapse of state institutions, especially the police and judiciary, with resulting paralysis of governance, a breakdown of law and order, and general banditry and chaos. Not only are the functions of government suspended, its assets are destroyed or looted and experienced officials are killed or flee the country. This is rarely the case in inter-state wars. It means that international intervention must extend beyond military and humanitarian tasks and must include the promotion of national reconciliation and the re-establishment of effective government.

14. The latter are tasks that demand time and sensitivity. The United Nations is, for good reasons, reluctant to assume responsibility for maintaining law and order, nor can it impose a new political structure or new state institutions. It can only help the hostile factions to help themselves and begin to live together again. All too often it turns out that they do not yet want to be helped or to resolve their problems quickly.

15. Peace-keeping in such contexts is far more complex and more expensive than when its tasks were mainly to monitor cease-fires and control buffer zones with the consent of the States involved in the conflict. Peace-keeping today can involve constant danger.

16. I cannot praise too highly or adequately express my gratitude and admiration for the courage and sacrifice of United Nations personnel, military and civil, in this new era of challenge to peace and security. The conditions under which they serve are often extremely harsh. Many have given their lives. Many must persevere despite the loss of family members and friends.

17. It must also be recognized that the vast increase in field deployment has to be supported by an overburdened Headquarters staff that resource constraints have held at levels appropriate to an earlier, far less demanding, time.

18. A second qualitative change is the use of United Nations forces to protect humanitarian operations. Humanitarian agencies endeavour to provide succour to civilian victims

of war wherever they may be. Too often the warring parties make it difficult or impossible for them to do so. This is sometimes because of the exigencies of war but more often because the relief of a particular population is contrary to the war aims of one or other of the parties. There is also a growing tendency for the combatants to divert relief supplies for their own purposes. Because the wars are intra-state conflicts, the humanitarian agencies often have to undertake their tasks in the chaotic and lawless conditions described above. In some, but not all, such cases the resulting horrors explode on to the world's television screens and create political pressure for the United Nations to deploy troops to facilitate and protect the humanitarian operations. While such images can help build support for humanitarian action, such scenes also may create an emotional environment in which effective decision-making can be far more difficult.

19. This has led, in Bosnia and Herzegovina and in Somalia, to a new kind of United Nations operation. Even though the use of force is authorized under Chapter VII of the Charter, the United Nations remains neutral and impartial between the warring parties, without a mandate to stop the aggressor (if one can be identified) or impose a cessation of hostilities. Nor is this peace-keeping as practised hitherto, because the hostilities continue and there is often no agreement between the warring parties on which a peace-keeping mandate can be based. The 'safe areas' concept in Bosnia and Herzegovina is a similar case. It too gives the United Nations a humanitarian mandate under which the use of force is authorized, but for limited and local purposes and not to bring the war to an end.

20. A third change has been in the nature of United Nations operations in the field. During the cold war United Nations peace-keeping operations were largely military in character and were usually deployed after a cease-fire but before a settlement of the conflict in question had been negotiated. Indeed one of their main purposes was to create conditions in which negotiations for a settlement could take place. In the late 1980s a new kind of peace-keeping operation evolved. It was established after negotiations had succeeded, with the mandate of helping the parties implement the comprehensive settlement they had negotiated. Such operations have been deployed in Namibia, Angola, El Salvador, Cambodia and Mozambique. In most cases they have been conspicuously successful.

21. The negotiated settlements involved not only military arrangements but also a wide range of civilian matters. As a result, the United Nations found itself asked to undertake an unprecedented variety of functions: the supervision of cease-fires, the regroupment and demobilization of forces, their reintegration into civilian life and the destruction of their weapons; the design and implementation of de-mining programmes; the return of refugees and displaced persons; the provision of humanitarian assistance; the supervision of existing administrative structures; the establishment of new police forces; the verification of respect for human rights; the design and supervision of constitutional, judicial and electoral reforms; the observation, supervision and even organization and conduct of elections; and the coordination of support for economic rehabilitation and reconstruction.

22. Fourthly, these multifunctional peace-keeping operations have highlighted the role the United Nations can play after a negotiated settlement has been implemented. It is now recognized that implementation of the settlement in the time prescribed may not be enough to guarantee that the conflict will not revive. Coordinated programmes are required, over a number of years and in various fields, to ensure that the original causes of war are eradicated. This involves the building up of national institutions, the promotion of human rights, the creation of civilian police forces and other actions in the political field. As I pointed out in 'An Agenda for Development' (A/48/935), only sustained efforts to resolve underlying socio-economic, cultural and humanitarian problems can place an achieved peace on a durable foundation.

III. Instruments for peace and security

23. The United Nations has developed a range of instruments for controlling and resolving conflicts between and within States. The most important of them are preventive diplomacy and peacemaking; peace-keeping; peace-building; disarmament; sanctions; and peace enforcement. The first three can be employed only with the consent of the parties to the conflict. Sanctions and enforcement, on the other hand, are coercive measures and thus, by definition, do not require the consent of the party concerned. Disarmament can take place on an agreed basis or in the context of coercive action under Chapter VII.

24. The United Nations does not have or claim a monopoly of any of these instru-

ments. All can be, and most of them have been, employed by regional organizations, by ad hoc groups of States or by individual States, but the United Nations has unparalleled experience of them and it is to the United Nations that the international community has turned increasingly since the end of the cold war. The United Nations system is also better equipped than regional organizations or individual Member States to develop and apply the comprehensive, long-term approach needed to ensure the lasting resolution of conflicts.

25. Perceived shortcomings in the United Nations performance of the tasks entrusted to it have recently, however, seemed to incline Member States to look for other means, especially, but not exclusively, where the rapid deployment of large forces is required. It is thus necessary to find ways of enabling the United Nations to perform better the roles envisaged for it in the Charter.

A. Preventive diplomacy and peacemaking

26. It is evidently better to prevent conflicts through early warning, quiet diplomacy and, in some cases, preventive deployment than to have to undertake major politico-military efforts to resolve them after they have broken out. The Security Council's declaration of 31 January 1992 (S/23500) mandated me to give priority to preventive and peacemaking activities. I accordingly created a Department of Political Affairs to handle a range of political functions that had previously been performed in various parts of the Secretariat. That Department has since passed through successive phases of restructuring and is now organized to follow political developments worldwide, so that it can provide early warning of impending conflicts and analyse possibilities for preventive action by the United Nations, as well as for action to help resolve existing conflicts.

27. Experience has shown that the greatest obstacle to success in these endeavours is not, as is widely supposed, lack of information, analytical capacity or ideas for United Nations initiatives. Success is often blocked at the outset by the reluctance of one or other of the parties to accept United Nations help. This is as true of inter-state conflicts as it is of internal ones, even though United Nations action on the former is fully within the Charter, whereas in the latter case it must be reconciled with Article 2, paragraph 7.

28. Collectively Member States encourage the Secretary-General to play an active role in this field; individually they are often reluctant that he should do so when they are a party to the conflict. It is difficult to know how to overcome this reluctance. Clearly the United Nations cannot impose its preventive and peacemaking services on Member States who do not want them. Legally and politically their request for, or at least acquiescence in, United Nations action is a sine qua non. The solution can only be long-term. It may lie in creating a climate of opinion, or ethos, within the international community in which the norm would be for Member States to accept an offer of United Nations good offices.

29. There are also two practical problems that have emerged in this field. Given Member States' frequently expressed support for preventive diplomacy and peacemaking, I take this opportunity to recommend that early action be taken to resolve them.

30. The first is the difficulty of finding senior persons who have the diplomatic skills and who are willing to serve for a while as special representative or special envoy of the Secretary-General. As a result of the streamlining of the senior levels of the Secretariat, the extra capacity that was there in earlier years no longer exists.

31. The second problem relates to the establishment and financing of small field missions for preventive diplomacy and peacemaking. Accepted and well-tried procedures exist for such action in the case of peacekeeping operations. The same is required in the preventive and peacemaking field. Although special envoys can achieve much on a visiting basis, their capacity is greatly enhanced if continuity can be assured by the presence on the ground of a small support mission on a full-time basis. There is no clear view amongst Member States about whether legislative authority for such matters rests with the Security Council or the General Assembly, nor are existing budgetary procedures well-geared to meet this need.

32. Two solutions are possible. The first is to include in the regular budget a contingency provision, which might be in the range of $25 million per biennium, for such activities. The second would be to enlarge the existing provision for unforeseen and extraordinary activities and to make it available for all preventive and peacemaking activities, not just those related to international peace and security strictly defined.

B. Peace-keeping

33. The United Nations can be proud of the

speed with which peace-keeping has evolved in response to the new political environment resulting from the end of the cold war, but the last few years have confirmed that respect for certain basic principles of peace-keeping are essential to its success. Three particularly important principles are the consent of the parties, impartiality and the non-use of force except in self-defence. Analysis of recent successes and failures shows that in all the successes those principles were respected and in most of the less successful operations one or other of them was not.

34. There are three aspects of recent mandates that, in particular, have led peace-keeping operations to forfeit the consent of the parties, to behave in a way that was perceived to be partial and/or to use force other than in self-defence. These have been the tasks of protecting humanitarian operations during continuing warfare, protecting civilian populations in designated safe areas and pressing the parties to achieve national reconciliation at a pace faster than they were ready to accept. The cases of Somalia and Bosnia and Herzegovina are instructive in this respect.

35. In both cases, existing peace-keeping operations were given additional mandates that required the use of force and therefore could not be combined with existing mandates requiring the consent of the parties, impartiality and the non-use of force. It was also not possible for them to be executed without much stronger military capabilities than had been made available, as is the case in the former Yugoslavia. In reality, nothing is more dangerous for a peace-keeping operation than to ask it to use force when its existing composition, armament, logistic support and deployment deny it the capacity to do so. The logic of peace-keeping flows from political and military premises that are quite distinct from those of enforcement; and the dynamics of the latter are incompatible with the political process that peace-keeping is intended to facilitate. To blur the distinction between the two can undermine the viability of the peace-keeping operation and endanger its personnel.

36. International problems cannot be solved quickly or within a limited time. Conflicts the United Nations is asked to resolve usually have deep roots and have defied the peacemaking efforts of others. Their resolution requires patient diplomacy and the establishment of a political process that permits, over a period of time, the building of confidence and negotiated solutions to long-standing differences. Such processes often encounter frustrations and set-backs and almost invariably take longer than hoped. It is necessary to resist the temptation to use military power to speed them up. Peace-keeping and the use of force (other than in self-defence) should be seen as alternative techniques and not as adjacent points on a continuum, permitting easy transition from one to the other.

37. In peace-keeping, too, a number of practical difficulties have arisen during the last three years, especially relating to command and control, to the availability of troops and equipment, and to the information capacity of peace-keeping operations.

38. As regards command and control, it is useful to distinguish three levels of authority:

(a) Overall political direction, which belongs to the Security Council;

(b) Executive direction and command, for which the Secretary-General is responsible;

(c) Command in the field, which is entrusted by the Secretary-General to the chief of mission (special representative or force commander/chief military observer).

The distinctions between these three levels must be kept constantly in mind in order to avoid any confusion of functions and responsibilities. It is as inappropriate for a chief of mission to take upon himself the formulation of his/her mission's overall political objectives as it is for the Security Council or the Secretary-General in New York to decide on matters that require a detailed understanding of operational conditions in the field.

39. There has been an increasing tendency in recent years for the Security Council to micro-manage peace-keeping operations. Given the importance of the issues at stake and the volume of resources provided for peace-keeping operations, it is right and proper that the Council should wish to be closely consulted and informed. Procedures for ensuring this have been greatly improved. To assist the Security Council in being informed about the latest developments I have appointed one of my Special Advisers as my personal representative to the Council. As regards information, however, it has to be recognized that, in the inevitable fog and confusion of the near-war conditions in which peace-keepers often find themselves, as for example in Angola, Cambodia, Somalia and the former Yugoslavia, time is required to verify the accuracy of initial reports. Understandably, chiefs of mission have to be more restrained than the media in broadcasting facts that have not been fully substantiated.

40. Troop-contributing Governments, who are responsible to their parliaments and electorates for the safety of their troops, are also understandably anxious to be kept fully informed, especially when the operation concerned is in difficulty. I have endeavoured to meet their concerns by providing them with regular briefings and by engaging them in dialogue about the conduct of the operation in question. Members of the Security Council have been included in such meetings and the Council has recently decided to formalize them. It is important that this should not lead to any blurring of the distinct levels of authority referred to above.

41. Another important principle is unity of command. The experience in Somalia has underlined again the necessity for a peace-keeping operation to function as an integrated whole. That necessity is all the more imperative when the mission is operating in dangerous conditions. There must be no opening for the parties to undermine its cohesion by singling out some contingents for favourable and others for unfavourable treatment. Nor must there be any attempt by troop-contributing Governments to provide guidance, let alone give orders, to their contingents on operational matters. To do so creates division within the force, adds to the difficulties already inherent in a multinational operation and increases the risk of casualties. It can also create the impression amongst the parties that the operation is serving the policy objectives of the contributing Governments rather than the collective will of the United Nations as formulated by the Security Council. Such impressions inevitably undermine an operation's legitimacy and effectiveness.

42. That said, commanders in the field are, as a matter of course, instructed to consult the commanders of national contingents and make sure that they understand the Security Council's overall approach, as well as the role assigned to their contingents. However, such consultations cannot be allowed to develop into negotiations between the commander in the field and the troop-contributing Governments, whose negotiating partner must always be the Secretariat in New York.

43. As regards the availability of troops and equipment, problems have become steadily more serious. Availability has palpably declined as measured against the Organization's requirements. A considerable effort has been made to expand and refine stand-by arrangements, but these provide no guarantee that troops will be provided for a specific operation. For example, when in May 1994 the Security Council decided to expand the United Nations Assistance Mission for Rwanda (UNAMIR), not one of the 19 Governments that at that time had undertaken to have troops on stand-by agreed to contribute.

44. In these circumstances, I have come to the conclusion that the United Nations does need to give serious thought to the idea of a rapid reaction force. Such a force would be the Security Council's strategic reserve for deployment when there was an emergency need for peace-keeping troops. It might comprise battalion-sized units from a number of countries. These units would be trained to the same standards, use the same operating procedures, be equipped with integrated communications equipment and take part in joint exercises at regular intervals. They would be stationed in their home countries but maintained at a high state of readiness. The value of this arrangement would of course depend on how far the Security Council could be sure that the force would actually be available in an emergency. This will be a complicated and expensive arrangement, but I believe that the time has come to undertake it.

45. Equipment and adequate training is another area of growing concern. The principle is that contributing Governments are to ensure that their troops arrive with all the equipment needed to be fully operational. Increasingly, however, Member States offer troops without the necessary equipment and training. In the absence of alternatives, the United Nations, under pressure, has to procure equipment on the market or through voluntary contributions from other Member States. Further time is required for the troops concerned to learn to operate the equipment, which they are often encountering for the first time. A number of measures can be envisaged to address this problem, for example, the establishment by the United Nations of a reserve stock of standard peace-keeping equipment, as has been frequently proposed, and partnerships between Governments that need equipment and those ready to provide it.

46. An additional lesson from recent experience is that peace-keeping operations, especially those operating in difficult circumstances, need an effective information capacity. This is to enable them to explain their mandate to the population and, by providing a credible and impartial source of information, to counter misinformation disseminated about them, even by the parties themselves. Radio is the most effective medium for this

purpose. In all operations where an information capacity, including radio, has been provided, even if late in the day, it has been recognized to have made an invaluable contribution to the operation's success. I have instructed that in the planning of future operations the possible need for an information capacity should be examined at an early stage and the necessary resources included in the proposed budget.

C. Post-conflict peace-building

47. The validity of the concept of post-conflict peace-building has received wide recognition. The measures it can use—and they are many—can also support preventive diplomacy. Demilitarization, the control of small arms, institutional reform, improved police and judicial systems, the monitoring of human rights, electoral reform and social and economic development can be as valuable in preventing conflict as in healing the wounds after conflict has occurred.

48. The implementation of post-conflict peace-building can, however, be complicated. It requires integrated action and delicate dealings between the United Nations and the parties to the conflict in respect of which peace-building activities are to be undertaken.

49. Two kinds of situation deserve examination. The first is when a comprehensive settlement has been negotiated, with long-term political, economic and social provisions to address the root causes of the conflict, and verification of its implementation is entrusted to a multifunctional peace-keeping operation. The second is when peace-building, whether preventive or post-conflict, is undertaken in relation to a potential or past conflict without any peace-keeping operation being deployed. In both situations the essential goal is the creation of structures for the institutionalization of peace.

50. The first situation is the easier to manage. The United Nations already has an entrée. The parties have accepted its peace-making and peace-keeping role. The peace-keeping operation will already be mandated to launch various peace-building activities, especially the all-important reintegration of former combatants into productive civilian activities.

51. Even so, political elements who dislike the peace agreement concluded by their Government (and the United Nations verification provided for therein) may resent the United Nations presence and be waiting impatiently for it to leave. Their concerns may find an echo among Member States who fear that the United Nations is in danger of slipping into a role prejudicial to the sovereignty of the country in question and among others who may be uneasy about the resource implications of a long-term peace-building commitment.

52. The timing and modalities of the departure of the peace-keeping operation and the transfer of its peace-building functions to others must therefore be carefully managed in the fullest possible consultation with the Government concerned. The latter's wishes must be paramount; but the United Nations, having invested much effort in helping to end the conflict, can legitimately express views and offer advice about actions the Government could take to reduce the danger of losing what has been achieved. The timing and modalities also need to take into account any residual verification for which the United Nations remains responsible.

53. Most of the activities that together constitute peace-building fall within the mandates of the various programmes, funds, offices and agencies of the United Nations system with responsibilities in the economic, social, humanitarian and human rights fields. In a country ruined by war, resumption of such activities may initially have to be entrusted to, or at least coordinated by, a multifunctional peace-keeping operation, but as that operation succeeds in restoring normal conditions, the programmes, funds, offices and agencies can re-establish themselves and gradually take over responsibility from the peace-keepers, with the resident coordinator in due course assuming the coordination functions temporarily entrusted to the special representative of the Secretary-General.

54. It may also be necessary in such cases to arrange the transfer of decision-making responsibility from the Security Council, which will have authorized the mandate and deployment of the peace-keeping operation, to the General Assembly or other inter-governmental bodies with responsibility for the civilian peace-building activities that will continue. The timing of this transfer will be of special interest to certain Member States because of its financial implications. Each case has to be decided on its merits, the guiding principle being that institutional or budgetary considerations should not be allowed to imperil the continuity of the United Nations efforts in the field.

55. The more difficult situation is when post-conflict (or preventive) peace-building

activities are seen to be necessary in a country where the United Nations does not already have a peacemaking or peace-keeping mandate. Who then will identify the need for such measures and propose them to the Government? If the measures are exclusively in the economic, social and humanitarian fields, they are likely to fall within the purview of the resident coordinator. He or she could recommend them to the Government. Even if the resident coordinator has the capacity to monitor and analyse all the indicators of an impending political and security crisis, however, which is rarely the case, can he or she act without inviting the charge of exceeding his or her mandate by assuming political functions, especially if the proposed measures relate to areas such as security, the police or human rights?

56. In those circumstances, the early warning responsibility has to lie with United Nations Headquarters, using all the information available to it, including reports of the United Nations Development Programme (UNDP) resident coordinator and other United Nations personnel in the country concerned. When analysis of that information gives warning of impending crisis, the Secretary-General, acting on the basis of his general mandate for preventive diplomacy, peacemaking and peace-building, can take the initiative of sending a mission, with the Government's agreement, to discuss with it measures it could usefully take.

D. Disarmament

. . .

E. Sanctions

66. Under Article 41 of the Charter, the Security Council may call upon Member States to apply measures not involving the use of armed force in order to maintain or restore international peace and security. Such measures are commonly referred to as sanctions. This legal basis is recalled in order to underline that the purpose of sanctions is to modify the behaviour of a party that is threatening international peace and security and not to punish or otherwise exact retribution.

67. The Security Council's greatly increased use of this instrument has brought to light a number of difficulties, relating especially to the objectives of sanctions, the monitoring of their application and impact, and their unintended effects.

68. The objectives for which specific sanctions regimes were imposed have not always been clearly defined. Indeed they sometimes seem to change over time. This combination of imprecision and mutability makes it difficult for the Security Council to agree on when the objectives can be considered to have been achieved and sanctions can be lifted. While recognizing that the Council is a political body rather than a judicial organ, it is of great importance that when it decides to impose sanctions it should at the same time define objective criteria for determining that their purpose has been achieved. If general support for the use of sanctions as an effective instrument is to be maintained, care should be taken to avoid giving the impression that the purpose of imposing sanctions is punishment rather than the modification of political behaviour or that criteria are being changed in order to serve purposes other than those which motivated the original decision to impose sanctions.

69. Experience has been gained by the United Nations of how to monitor the application of sanctions and of the part regional organizations can in some cases play in this respect. However, the task is complicated by the reluctance of Governments, for reasons of sovereignty or economic self-interest, to accept the deployment of international monitors or the international investigation of alleged violations by themselves or their nationals. Measuring the impact of sanctions is even more difficult because of the inherent complexity of such measurement and because of restrictions on access to the target country.

70. Sanctions, as is generally recognized, are a blunt instrument. They raise the ethical question of whether suffering inflicted on vulnerable groups in the target country is a legitimate means of exerting pressure on political leaders whose behaviour is unlikely to be affected by the plight of their subjects. Sanctions also always have unintended or unwanted effects. They can complicate the work of humanitarian agencies by denying them certain categories of supplies and by obliging them to go through arduous procedures to obtain the necessary exemptions. They can conflict with the development objectives of the Organization and do long-term damage to the productive capacity of the target country. They can have a severe effect on other countries that are neighbours or major economic partners of the target country. They can also defeat their own purpose by provoking a patriotic response against the international community, symbolized by the United Nations, and by rallying the population

behind the leaders whose behaviour the sanctions are intended to modify.

71. To state these ethical and practical considerations is not to call in question the need for sanctions in certain cases, but it illustrates the need to consider ways of alleviating the effects described. Two possibilities are proposed for Member States' consideration.

72. The first is to ensure that, whenever sanctions are imposed, provision is made to facilitate the work of humanitarian agencies, work that will be all the more needed as a result of the impact of sanctions on vulnerable groups. It is necessary, for instance, to avoid banning imports that are required by local health industries and to devise a fast track for the processing of applications for exemptions for humanitarian activities.

73. Secondly, there is an urgent need for action to respond to the expectations raised by Article 50 of the Charter. Sanctions are a measure taken collectively by the United Nations to maintain or restore international peace and security. The costs involved in their application, like other such costs (e.g. for peacemaking and peace-keeping activities), should be borne equitably by all Member States and not exclusively by the few who have the misfortune to be neighbours or major economic partners of the target country.

74. In 'An Agenda for Peace' I proposed that States suffering collateral damage from the sanctions regimes should be entitled not only to consult the Security Council but also to have a realistic possibility of having their difficulties addressed. For that purpose I recommended that the Security Council devise a set of measures involving the international financial institutions and other components of the United Nations system that could be put in place to address the problem. In response, the Council asked me to seek the views of the heads of the international financial institutions. In their replies, the latter acknowledged the collateral effects of sanctions and expressed the desire to help countries in such situations, but they proposed that this should be done under existing mandates for the support of countries facing negative external shocks and consequent balance-of-payment difficulties. They did not agree that special provisions should be made.

75. In order to address all the above problems, I should like to go beyond the recommendation I made in 1992 and suggest the establishment of a mechanism to carry out the following five functions:

(a) To assess, at the request of the Security Council, and before sanctions are imposed, their potential impact on the target country and on third countries;

(b) To monitor application of the sanctions;

(c) To measure their effects in order to enable the Security Council to fine tune them with a view to maximizing their political impact and minimizing collateral damage;

(d) To ensure the delivery of humanitarian assistance to vulnerable groups;

(e) To explore ways of assisting Member States that are suffering collateral damage and to evaluate claims submitted by such States under Article 50.

76. Since the purpose of this mechanism would be to assist the Security Council, it would have to be located in the United Nations Secretariat. However, it should be empowered to utilize the expertise available throughout the United Nations system, in particular that of the Bretton Woods institutions. Member States will have to give the proposal their political support both at the United Nations and in the intergovernmental bodies of the agencies concerned if it is to be implemented effectively.

F. Enforcement action

77. One of the achievements of the Charter of the United Nations was to empower the Organization to take enforcement action against those responsible for threats to the peace, breaches of the peace or acts of aggression. However, neither the Security Council nor the Secretary-General at present has the capacity to deploy, direct, command and control operations for this purpose, except perhaps on a very limited scale. I believe that it is desirable in the long term that the United Nations develop such a capacity, but it would be folly to attempt to do so at the present time when the Organization is resource-starved and hard pressed to handle the less demanding peacemaking and peace-keeping responsibilities entrusted to it.

78. In 1950, the Security Council authorized a group of willing Member States to undertake enforcement action in the Korean peninsula. It did so again in 1990 in response to aggression against Kuwait. More recently, the Council has authorized groups of Member States to undertake enforcement action, if necessary, to create conditions for humanitarian relief operations in Somalia and Rwanda and to facilitate the restoration of democracy in Haiti.

79. In Bosnia and Herzegovina, the Security Council has authorized Member States, acting nationally or through regional arrangements, to use force to ensure compliance with its ban on military flights in that country's air space, to support the United Nations forces in the former Yugoslavia in the performance of their mandate, including defence of personnel who may be under attack, and to deter attacks against the safe areas. The Member States concerned decided to entrust those tasks to the North Atlantic Treaty Organization (NATO). Much effort has been required between the Secretariat and NATO to work out procedures for the coordination of this unprecedented collaboration. This is not surprising given the two organizations' very different mandates and approaches to the maintenance of peace and security. Of greater concern, as already mentioned, are the consequences of using force, other than for self-defence, in a peace-keeping context.

80. The experience of the last few years has demonstrated both the value that can be gained and the difficulties that can arise when the Security Council entrusts enforcement tasks to groups of Member States. On the positive side, this arrangement provides the Organization with an enforcement capacity it would not otherwise have and is greatly preferable to the unilateral use of force by Member States without reference to the United Nations. On the other hand, the arrangement can have a negative impact on the Organization's stature and credibility. There is also the danger that the States concerned may claim international legitimacy and approval for forceful actions that were not in fact envisaged by the Security Council when it gave its authorization to them. Member States so authorized have in recent operations reported more fully and more regularly to the Security Council about their activities.

IV. Coordination

. . .

V. Financial resources

97. None of the instruments discussed in the present paper can be used unless Governments provide the necessary financial resources. There is no other source of funds. The failure of Member States to pay their assessed contributions for activities they themselves have voted into being makes it impossible to carry out those activities to the

standard expected. It also calls in question the credibility of those who have willed the ends but not the means—and who then criticize the United Nations for its failures. On 12 October 1994, I put to the Member States a package of proposals, ideas and questions on finance and budgetary procedures that I believe can contribute to a solution (see A/49/PV.28).

. . .

VI. Conclusion

102. The present position paper, submitted to the Member States at the opening of the United Nations fiftieth anniversary year, is intended to serve as a contribution to the continuing campaign to strengthen a common capacity to deal with threats to peace and security.

103. The times call for thinking afresh, for striving together and for creating new ways to overcome crises. This is because the different world that emerged when the cold war ceased is still a world not fully understood. The changed face of conflict today requires us to be perceptive, adaptive, creative and courageous, and to address simultaneously the immediate as well as the root causes of conflict, which all too often lie in the absence of economic opportunities and social inequities. Perhaps above all it requires a deeper commitment to cooperation and true multilateralism than humanity has ever achieved before.

104. This is why the pages of the present paper reiterate the need for hard decisions. As understanding grows of the challenges to peace and security, hard decisions, if postponed, will appear in retrospect as having been relatively easy when measured against the magnitude of tomorrow's troubles.

105. There is no reason for frustration or pessimism. More progress has been made in the past few years towards using the United Nations as it was designed to be used than many could ever have predicted. The call to decision should be a call to confidence and courage.

Notes
[1] Official Records of the General Assembly, Forty-seventh Session, Supplement No. 27 (A/47/27), appendix I.
[2] See The United Nations Disarmament Yearbook, vol. 5: 1980 (United Nations publication, Sales No. G.81.IX.4), appendix VII.

Source: UN document A/50/60 (S/1995/1), 3 Jan. 1995.

Appendix 2C. Redesigning Nordic military contributions to multilateral peace operations

JAANA KARHILO

I. Introduction

The Nordic countries have been actively involved in peacekeeping since the early observer missions.[1] Their commitment was initially partly due to the close connections between Nordic politicians and the UN Secretariat and partly to the wish of small nations to support multilateralism and collective security. With no great-power ambitions or colonial legacies the Nordic countries were well suited to peacekeeping. It also permitted cooperation between the Nordic defence establishments, otherwise unthinkable between NATO and non-NATO states during the East–West confrontation.[2]

Responding to a call by UN Secretary-General Dag Hammarskjöld, the Nordic countries discussed possible concepts for troop contributions in the early 1960s. By 1964 it was decided that each country would establish and train a stand-by force for peacekeeping which, upon the request of the Secretary-General and subject to national decision, could be put at the disposal of the UN. In 1968 the four countries each forwarded data on their stand-by forces to the UN Special Committee on Peacekeeping Operations. These units were not available for enforcement operations nor did they constitute standing forces. According to the system established in each country, regular officers as well as reserves signed contracts indicating their willingness to be available for UN service or training on short notice, usually within a few days. The number of personnel each country trained and prepared for UN service remained relatively constant until the increase in demand in the early 1990s: Norway has raised the maximum number of personnel from 1330 to 2022, Denmark from 950 to 1500, while Finland's limit remains at 2000 and Sweden's at 3000.[3]

During the past 30 years the Nordic countries have developed extensive institutional and operational cooperation in peacekeeping. Nordic defence ministers exchange views on ongoing missions in biannual meetings, and joint proposals have been presented to the UN Special Committee on Peacekeeping, of which Denmark is

---

[1] The Nordic countries in this context include Denmark and Norway (NATO members) and Finland and Sweden (non-aligned). Iceland, which has no armed forces, is not included in the discussion. This appendix is an abbreviated version of Karhilo, J., 'Nordic responses to the new requirements of conflict management', SIPRI Project on Peacekeeping and Regional Security, Working Paper (SIPRI: Stockholm, 1996).

[2] Eknes, Å., 'Prepared for peace-keeping: the Nordic countries and participation in UN military operations', Stiftung Wissenschaft und Politik, *Blauhelme in einer turbulenten Welt: Beiträge internationaler Experten zur Fortentwicklung des Völkerrechts und der Vereinten Nationen* [Blue helmets in a turbulent world: the contributions of international experts to the development of international law and the United Nations], (Nomos: Baden Baden, 1993), pp. 510–11; and Eknes, Å., 'Norden og FNs fredsbevarende operasjoner' [The Nordic countries and UN peacekeeping operations], ed. Å. Eknes, *Norden i FN: Status och framtidsutsikter* [The Nordic countries in the UN: status and future prospects], (Nordic Council: Copenhagen, 1994), p. 62.

[3] The ratio of Nordic citizens among peacekeepers had declined from up to 1 : 4 during parts of the cold war period to 1 : 10 in 1993. From the beginning of UN peacekeeping until the end of 1995, Denmark has contributed over 45 000 military personnel, Finland over 32 000, Norway over 49 000 and Sweden over 68 000 to UN operations.

a member. Practical coordination is handled by the Nordic Committee for Military UN Matters (NORDSAMFN), while the Nordic Economic Working Committee deals with financial issues related to peacekeeping. Each country provides training for the Nordic observers and troops participating in UN missions according to an agreed division of labour.[4] Recently they have cooperated with the British in training a joint Baltic battalion for United Nations duty. Joint Nordic contingents have served in the United Nations Emergency Force (UNEF I),[5] in the first UN preventive deployment in Macedonia[6] and most recently in the UN Protection Force (UNPROFOR) in Bosnia and Herzegovina.[7] In late 1995 a joint Nordic–Polish brigade was established to serve with the US Division in the Implementation Force (IFOR).[8]

In the past few years each of the four countries has conducted policy reviews in response both to the greater demands imposed on troop contributors by UN operations with complex civil–military mandates and increased emphasis on cooperative conflict management efforts by the European security organizations. In 1991 NATO adopted both a new strategic concept, emphasizing force mobility and flexibility as well as greater reinforcement capability, and a new force structure divided into Main Defence Forces, Rapid Reaction Forces (RRF) and Augmentation Forces. Sub-units of the RRF will form a smaller Immediate Reaction Force (IRF). A major task of the renewed Alliance besides collective defence, is conflict management outside NATO's central region in keeping with a broader definition of security. All the Nordic states have joined NATO's Partnership for Peace (PFP) programme in which peacekeeping is an important component. Their resources may also be tasked in the future by the development of the Combined Joint Task Force (CJTF) concept and Western European Union (WEU) conflict management as well as the prospect of Organization for Security and Co-operation in Europe (OSCE) peacekeeping activities.

As each country has re-evaluated the basis and most appropriate means of its international engagement, the arrangements whereby Nordic countries contribute forces to international operations have begun to diverge somewhat. It has become apparent in this process that the international, regional and national levels of security are intertwined in more complex ways than before: international operations are perceived as constituting an increasingly important function of the defence forces and contributing to the security of the country itself, at least indirectly. Discussion on the doctrinal, political and military implications of multilateral operations, particularly those calling

[4] Finland is responsible for the training of military observers, Sweden for staff officers, Denmark for military police, and Norway for movement control personnel and logistics officers.

[5] A joint Danish–Norwegian battalion (DANOR) served in UNEF I from shortly after the deployment of the national contingents in 1956 to the withdrawal of the mission in 1967. Garde, H., 'Dansk forsvars internationale engagement' [The international commitment of Danish defence], *Dansk Udenrigspolitisk Årbog 1993* [Danish Foreign Policy Yearbook 1993], (Danish Institute of International Studies: Copenhagen, 1994), p. 53.

[6] An infantry battalion (NORDBATT 1) was provided jointly by Finland, Norway and Sweden and staff personnel by Denmark. Archer, C., 'Conflict prevention in Europe: the case of the Nordic states and Macedonia', *Cooperation & Conflict*, vol. 29, no. 4 (1994), pp. 367–86.

[7] NORDBATT 2, consisting of a Swedish infantry battalion, a Norwegian logistics battalion and a Danish battle tank squadron, and supported by a Finnish delivery of wheeled armoured personnel carriers, has been considered a tactical success in a strategically failed mission. Dalsjö, R., 'Sweden and Balkan Blue Helmet operations', ed. L. Ericson, *Solidarity and Defence: Sweden's Armed Forces in International Peace-keeping Operations during the 19th and 20th Centuries* (Swedish Military History Commission: Stockholm, 1995), pp. 95–118.

[8] The joint Nordic–Polish brigade contains infantry battalions from Denmark, Sweden and Poland, a Norwegian logistics battalion and a Finnish construction company. The Nordic contributions comprise 1040 personnel from Norway, 800 from Denmark, 750 from Sweden and 450 from Finland.

for the use of force beyond self-defence, has also led to different conclusions in each Nordic country regarding the desirability of its involvement.

II. Denmark

In Danish security policy the end of the cold war has led to an increased emphasis on preventive diplomacy, peacekeeping and peace making in lieu of the earlier concern with military aggression.[9] There is wide agreement that there is no military threat to Denmark—an assessment which is more unequivocal and which has led to a restructuring of the army earlier than in the other Nordic countries. The official purpose of Denmark's defence is now de facto two-tiered: conflict prevention, peacekeeping, peace making and humanitarian missions in the context of the UN or the OSCE and conflict prevention, crisis management and defence in the NATO context.[10] In keeping with this concept, the army's wartime organization will have changed dramatically by the end of the decade. While in 1990, 61 per cent of the army had tasks related to the defence of Denmark and its surroundings, in 1999 the figure will be only 43 per cent with 57 per cent allocated to international tasks and NATO.[11]

In November 1993 the Danish Parliament authorized the formation of the Danish International or Reaction Brigade (DRB), to be available by the end of 1995 for peacekeeping, peace making or humanitarian operations under the auspices of the UN or the OSCE.[12] It will also be assigned to NATO's Allied Command Europe Rapid Reaction Corps (ARRC) and used for national defence tasks.[13] The DRB was set up with broad parliamentary and public support, political discussion focusing mainly on financing and how international obligations would affect the traditional functions of the Defence Forces.

The DRB comprises: a headquarters and HQ company; an armoured battalion with three tank squadrons and a mechanized infantry company; two mechanized infantry battalions; a reconnaissance squadron; an artillery battalion; an air defence missile battery; a reinforced engineer company; a service support battalion; a logistics support battalion including a field hospital; and a military police detachment. If required the Brigade could be reinforced with anti-tank helicopters, long-range reconnaissance patrols and additional artillery.

[9] The terminology on multilateral conflict management is that used in the defence documents of the respective country. For a critical discussion of the concepts used in Boutros-Ghali, *An Agenda for Peace: Preventive Diplomacy, Peacemaking and Peace-keeping*, Report of the Secretary-General pursuant to the statement adopted by the Summit Meeting of the Security Council on 31 January 1992 (United Nations: New York, 1992), see Findlay, T., 'Multilateral conflict prevention, management and resolution', *SIPRI Yearbook 1994* (Oxford University Press: Oxford, 1994), pp. 13–52.

[10] Lov nr 909 af 8 Dec. 1993 om forsvarets formål, opgaver og organisation m.v. [Act no. 909 of 8 Dec. 1993 on the aims, tasks and organization, etc., of the Armed Forces], para. 1, entered into force 1 Jan. 1994.

[11] 'Et forsvar for fremtiden—på vej mod år 2000' [A defence for the future—towards 2000], Chief of Defence, Denmark, 1996, p. 20.

[12] Folketingsbeslutning nr B1 af 25 Nov. 1993 om etablering af en dansk international brigade [Parliamentary resolution B1 on the establishment of a Danish International Brigade], adopted 25 Nov. 1993.

[13] Denmark's contribution to ARRC consists additionally of patrols of the Jaeger Corps, an electronic reconnaissance company, a submarine, a FLEX-300 in a mine-hunting role and a HAWK squadron. Denmark's contribution to NATO's IRF consists of a light reconnaissance unit, a corvette and a FLEX-300 mine-hunter. An F-16 squadron can be deployed either with the RRF or IRF. Speech by Leif Simonsen at the Defence Command on the Defence Agreement for 1995–1999, Vedbaek, 18 Jan. 1996, p. 8.

The multi-purpose role of the Brigade is reflected in the special organization, equipment and training of its units. The DRB is equipped with material necessary for UN operations, such as mine-clearance and night-vision equipment, and has its own air-defence battery and service-support battalion, allowing the units to operate independently in areas where infrastructure is limited or destroyed. The logistics and engineer components are stronger than usual because of the special demands for increased protection, flexibility and mobility. The Brigade trains to maintain a capability to carry out a broad spectrum of missions, from peacekeeping and humanitarian to peace enforcement and 'pure war fighting'.

Expected to reach its full strength by the end of 1996, the Brigade will comprise 4550 personnel with 360 officers, 740 NCOs and 3450 privates. Only 20 per cent will be regular personnel; the majority will be reservists on three-year contracts. The Army hopes to identify conscripts for the DRB as early as possible to group them into sub-units for mandatory basic training, which lasts 8–12 months. Volunteers accepted for the DRB receive a further five weeks of training for international duties and two weeks of mission-oriented training before their first six-month tour of UN duty. Over the next two years the reservists participate in annual refresher training and are available for immediate mobilization. The three-year period may end with another six months in a UN operation, whereupon personnel are assigned to the mobilization force to complete standard reserve service.

In 1994–95, during the initial phase of establishing the Brigade, the aim was to recruit 2000 conscripts annually.[14] Once the DRB has reached its full strength, recruitment will level off at 1200 annually. The DRB will be able to maintain approximately 1500 personnel on UN duty at any one time, although more could be deployed for a limited period. In exceptional circumstances, the Brigade could be used in its entirety for at most a one-year mission. Deployment will concentrate on Europe, the Middle East and North Africa for logistical and practical, not political reasons. Smaller units and individuals will be available for operations in other parts of the world.

Since its inauguration on 1 July 1994, units trained for the DRB have served in UN operations alongside other reservists, such as two of the four rifle companies deployed to Croatia in August 1995. Although specialists from outside the Brigade will still be used for UN operations when necessary, the DRB will constitute the basis of Denmark's future UN commitments. The most substantial contribution has been to various missions in the former Yugoslavia, where Denmark maintained an average of 1300 personnel in 1995 (the DRB contingent in UNPROFOR was the most power-fully armed contingent).[15] Given the DRB's constant deployment, unit by unit, to UN contingencies, questions have been raised about its operational standards for NATO since it cannot be mustered as a formation and trained in its conventional role.[16]

Denmark has also been able to draw on the Brigade to pledge contributions to the UN Stand-by Arrangements System and the proposed Multinational UN Stand-by Forces High Readiness Brigade (SHIRBRIG). In May 1995 Denmark became the second country after Jordan to sign a Memorandum of Understanding (MOU) with

[14] This target was met to only 80%, while a growing number of recruits have not enlisted for a second period of UN service as originally planned for the end of the contract. Information from the Chief of Defence, Denmark, 27 Mar. 1996.

[15] Danish contingents also included troops from Lithuania in 1994 and Estonia in 1995. Kemp, I., 'Denmark: rebuilding its army for peace', *Jane's Defence Weekly,* 19 Aug. 1995, p. 23.

[16] Mackinlay, J. and Olsen, J., 'Squaring the circle', *International Defense Review,* vol. 28 (Oct. 1995), p. 78.

the UN confirming its participation in the Stand-by Arrangements System with a preliminary commitment of DRB staff officers and a headquarters company, ready to deploy in 5–7 days.[17] In August 1995 an international Working Group led by Denmark submitted a plan for the establishment by 1998 of a High Readiness Brigade to be generated by nations pooling their contributions to the Stand-by Arrangements System.[18] The Brigade Pool, to which Denmark will contribute a headquarters element, is to contain duplicates of the component units to ensure deployment even in case of non-participation by some contributor. To secure a high degree of legitimacy, the project is to be open to all interested countries after June 1996, when the original group of countries are to sign a letter of intent to participate and an MOU on contributions to a permanent planning element, which Denmark hopes to host.[19]

Danish policy planners have envisaged increasingly operative roles for NATO and even the North Atlantic Cooperation Council (NACC) in international peace operations, while awaiting the 1996 European Union (EU) Intergovernmental Conference for clarification on the future WEU role in crisis management.[20] Although a member of the EU since 1973, Denmark has traditionally been wary of intensified European security and defence cooperation. After the Danes had rejected the Maastricht Treaty in a referendum in June 1992, the Danish Government negotiated several exemptions including not participating in EU decisions and actions that have defence implications. A 1995 expert committee recommended a re-evaluation of Denmark's observer status in the WEU in the light of the organization's aspiration for a stronger role in future peace operations.[21]

III. Norway

Participation in UN peacekeeping operations has long been an important part of Norwegian security policy and since the 1980s has been designated one of the main tasks of the defence forces.[22] As in the case of the other Nordic countries, peacekeeping has provided Norway 'a committed and partisan role with regard to the vision of an international order based on the rule of law and the collective will of the states which make up the community of nations'.[23] In the past four years, however, Norway's military participation in international operations has become more intimately connected to its own defence interests than during the cold war.

---

[17] OSCE Forum for Security Co-operation, *Denmark: Annual Exchange of Information on Defence Planning* (Feb. 1996), p. 4. Other DRB units have the same standard of readiness for UN missions as they do for NATO operations, namely 10–15 days.

[18] 'Report by the Working Group on a Multinational UN Stand-by Forces High Readiness Brigade', Chief of Defence, Denmark, 15 Aug. 1995. For details of the proposal, see chapter 2 in this volume.

[19] Information from the Chief of Defence, Denmark, 27 Mar. 1996.

[20] Odlander, J., 'Dansk säkerhetspolitik: Att vara eller inte vara med?' [Danish security policy: To join in or not?], *Internationella Studier*, no. 3 (1995), p. 21.

[21] The report points out that Denmark's WEU observer status can restrict its influence on the so-called 'Petersberg operations' for peacekeeping and humanitarian assistance and should be re-evaluated in the light of its otherwise substantial contribution to peacekeeping. *Dansk og europæisk sikkerhed* [Danish and European security], (Danish Commission on Security and Disarmament: Copenhagen, 1995).

[22] Eknes, Å., *FNs fredsbevarende operasjoner: Sikkerhet, Nødhjelp, Utvikling* [UN peacekeeping operations: security, emergency relief, development], Utenrikspolitiske skrifter no. 84 (Norwegian Institute of International Affairs: Oslo, 1995), p. 102.

[23] J. J. Holst, cited in Myhrengen, H., 'Norges militære FN-engasjement i en ny tid' [Norway's military commitment to the UN in a new era], *Internasjonal Politikk*, vol. 53, no. 1 (1995), p. 85.

Following the reorganization of NATO's force structure, and increasingly since the Norwegians rejected EU membership in a national referendum in late 1994, Norway has become more concerned about its potential isolation on NATO's northernmost flank. Traditionally a designated recipient of Allied reinforcements in time of war, Norway now needs to engage more forcefully in mutual security arrangements to be assured of defence assistance. A government White Paper of 1994 noted that:

To participate actively in maintaining international peace and security means as its extreme consequence that we can feel more secure if in the future a situation should arise whereby Norway should need military assistance from other countries. Norway's active and extensive participation in international peacekeeping operations are noticed amongst our allies in NATO. Utilisation of Norwegian forces abroad thus contributes to strengthening the defence of Norway.[24]

As an associate member of the WEU, Norway in 1995 also registered forces as part of the WEU pool (Forces Answerable to WEU).

Norway's stand-by force for UN duty, established in 1964, was reorganized in 1993.[25] Parliament, in agreement on Norwegian participation in the new generation of peace operations and responding to the UN's need for more troops, decided to expand the force from 1330 to 2000. The structure of the force was altered to comprise: an infantry battalion, an engineer company, a military police unit, a transport control unit, a logistics support company, a maintenance company and a medical company. In addition, it included naval vessels, an air transport unit (helicopters and two C-130 Hercules aircraft), headquarters personnel and military observers. The reorganized force comprised 1600 personnel from the army, 250 from the navy and 92 from the air force, totalling 2022.[26] Norway has listed components of this force in the Stand-by Arrangements System. Although units from outside the stand-by force have also occasionally been provided for UN service, a numerical upper limit has been reached within existing resources, according to the Defence Ministry. In 1995 Norway continued to concentrate on fewer operations, primarily the UN Interim Force in Lebanon (UNIFIL) and UNPROFOR.[27]

In response to the reorganization of NATO's force structure, the Storting decided in June 1993 to contribute to the Immediate Reaction Force and outlined the principles governing the operation of its forces. Norway's contribution would consist of an infantry battalion, an F-16 squadron, a frigate and a mine-countermeasure vessel. The so-called Telemark Battalion, to be established in the beginning of 1995 and to be operational in August, would comprise 900 officers and privates, all volunteers. Minimum service time for conscripts was set at 12 months. The battalion would have a readiness to deploy to a crisis area with seven days' notice and to send an advance

---

[24] Norwegian Ministry of Defence, 'The Defence Budget 1995: Unofficial translation of the main themes in the defence budget proposals to the Storting, submitted 4 Oct. 1994', Fact Sheet no. 9 (Oct. 1994), p. 27.

[25] The government has also supported the establishment of a civilian stand-by capability, the Norwegian Emergency Preparedness Systems (NOREPS), as a joint venture of many non-governmental organizations (NGOs) coordinated by the Norwegian Refugee Council. A field hospital deployed in 1995 as an integral part of UNAMIR in Rwanda is the first time such a civilian structure has been integrated in a UN peacekeeping operation.

[26] Norwegian Parliament, Beredskap for fred: Om Norges framtidige militære FN-engasjement og FNs rolle som konfliktløser [Report on readiness for peace: on Norway's future military commitment to the UN and the UN's role in resolving conflicts], St.meld.nr. 14 (1992/93), 18 Dec. 1992, p. 65.

[27] Norway also had military observers in the UN Truce Supervision Organization (UNTSO), the UN Angola Verification Mission (UNAVEM) and UNPROFOR.

party within three days. It is an activated unit which must be operative at all times in terms of both personnel and equipment.[28] The level of training is to be such that the unit can be sent on missions, including combat operations, at any time.[29] Although the IRF battalion can also be used in operations mandated by the UN or OSCE, it was set up specifically for NATO's Immediate Reaction Force in order to maintain Norway's credibility in the Alliance.[30] Its establishment constitutes a break with both traditional Norwegian defence policy and traditional defence structure.[31] That Norway was now ready to send forces abroad potentially for combat was politically novel, challenging for the Defence Forces and not entirely uncontroversial. The battalion has been criticized as the first step towards a standing army, eroding a defence tradition based on universal conscription.

In June 1994 the government adopted further guidelines for the participation of Norwegian forces in international operations, which established a certain division of labour between the UN stand-by force and the IRF battalion.[32] According to these guidelines, four factors were to be considered: Norway's experience of past operations; the structure and development of the Defence Forces; the risks inherent in the proposed operation; and whether Norwegian participation would be cost-effective and contribute substantially to the UN's capability. Applying these criteria to four types of operation, the report outlined various modes of participation in the future. The UN stand-by force was specifically adapted to traditional peacekeeping operations where Norway had already built up a special competence. Traditional operations did not require large units and they should remain a priority. Participation in preventive deployment was likely to pose the same requirements regarding training and equipment of forces but would call for troops, already structured as a unit, on short notice. Their tasks in such a UN mission would resemble those of NATO's IRF, so the Telemark Battalion could be sent in at an early stage to be replaced later by the UN stand-by force. The wider rules of engagement utilized in humanitarian operations make them more demanding of forces and equipment. Norway should also be able to take part in these operations, as it has already done in Somalia and the former Yugoslavia, but preferably with support units or in maritime missions.

As a small country, Norway has limited possibilities to contribute troops beyond the battalion level to enforcement operations, which require larger units to ensure an effective chain of command and control. Norwegian participation in combat would

[28] In practice the IRF will contain up to 2 rifle companies and up to 7 special units from the reserves which can be called up and outfitted for deployment with the main force within 7 days. It is thus a combined standing and mobilization battalion. Druglimo, A., 'En bataljonssjefs tanker om IRF-bataljonen' [A battalion commander's thoughts on the IRF battalion], *Norsk Militær Tidskrift*, vol. 164, no. 1 (1994), p. 11.

[29] Norwegian Parliament, Om visse organisasjonsendringer mv i Forsvaret [Bill on certain organizational changes, etc., in the Defence Forces], St.Prp.nr. 83 (1992/93), 14 May 1993, pp. 5–6.

[30] Information from the Norwegian Ministry of Defence, 19 Dec. 1995. The Danish model has been advocated by researchers who argue that NATO and UN commitments are interlinked and that international functions should be integrated more closely into the structure of the Defence Forces. Eknes, Å. and Knudsen, T. H., 'Flernasjonale operasjoner og norsk deltakelse' [Multinational operations and Norwegian participation], *Norsk Militær Tidskrift*, vol. 164, no. 6–7 (1994).

[31] Hammerstad, J. and Jahr, K., 'Telemark bataljon: NATOs nye styrkestruktur og Norges deltakelse i IRF' [The Telemark battalion: NATO's new force structure and Norwegian participation in IRF], IFS Info 2/1995 (Norwegian Institute for Defence Studies: Oslo, 1995).

[32] Norwegian Parliament, Bruk av norske styrker i utlandet [Report on the use of Norwegian forces abroad], St.meld.nr. 46 (1993/94), 16 June 1994.

therefore be limited to the IRF battalion operating within a NATO framework.[33] However, Norway would prefer to send support units such as engineer companies, and maintenance, supply and medical staff if required.

The most controversial question in recent parliamentary debate has been over how Norwegian military personnel can be ordered to take part in operations outside the NATO framework. While officers and conscripts can be ordered to serve within the NATO area, participation outside it has been voluntary. For conscripts this will continue in the future according to a bill proposed in 1995, but if the IRF battalion were needed on short notice for UN service officers may be ordered to participate unless vacancies for key positions can be filled voluntarily.[34] The bill was denounced by representatives of the officers and caused a drop in recruitment to the new battalion. Uncertainty over the possible future missions of the IRF has also made it less popular than the UN stand-by force. The Defence Forces have consequently delayed the deadline for the Telemark Battalion to become operational.[35]

IV. Finland

In the 1980s Finland could still boast of having contributed to every UN peacekeeping operation since that in the Congo with troops, observers or financial resources. With firm political and public support, Finnish participation in UN peacekeeping was viewed primarily as a foreign policy tool aimed at bolstering multilateral management of conflict in the cold war bipolar confrontation.

Ten years later the radical changes in Europe have had a greater impact on Finland than the other Nordic countries. A new foreign policy was launched in the autumn of 1990, with a unilateral reinterpretation of two post-war treaties which had been the cornerstones of Finland's foreign policy, the 1947 Paris Peace Treaty and the 1948 Treaty of Friendship, Cooperation and Mutual Assistance with the USSR. Thereafter Finnish policy has increasingly emphasized participation and cooperative security. Finland became an observer in NACC and applied for EU membership in 1992, entered a dialogue with the WEU in 1993 and joined the PFP in early 1994. In 1995 Finland became a member of the EU and an observer in the WEU. While the political leadership has repeatedly emphasized that membership in a military alliance is not a goal of Finnish foreign policy, recent analyses suggest that the option is being kept open.

These new links have led to an increased emphasis on Finland's European policy alongside its traditional UN policy as a determining factor in the development of its force capabilities for international duty. Two recent policy reviews have outlined Finland's future participation in peace operations. In 1993 a committee established by the Ministry of Defence was tasked with considering the changes necessary in the existing 1984 peacekeeping law which regulated Finnish participation, to take account of the 'second-generation' missions launched by the UN after 1990. In 1995 a major review of Finnish security policy proposed the establishment of a rapid reaction force alongside Finland's UN stand-by force. Established in the 1960s, this

[33] While there are no set criteria for participation with fighting units, factors such as the safety of the personnel, the quality of the command and control structure, and the ability of the proposed force to carry out its mission should be taken into account.
[34] Norwegian Parliament, Om lov om tjenestegjøring i internasjonale fredsoperasjoner [Bill on the law on service in international peace operations], Ot.prp.nr. 56 (1994/95), 19 May 1995, pp. 12–15.
[35] Information from the Norwegian Defence Command, 18 Dec. 1995.

force draws on a pool of candidates interested in UN service who have completed their national military service in all service branches and possess useful civilian skills; it is not part of the defence structure.[36]

In the first half of the 1990s Finnish participation in peace operations was, in principle, still confined to the deployment of troops and observers in traditional missions. While the 1984 peacekeeping law contained no definition of peacekeeping activities,[37] the background documentation specified that both Finnish participation and the multilateral operation as a whole required the consent of all parties to the crisis, the cooperation of all parties and the full support of the UN Security Council.[38] Operations involving the use of military force under Chapter VII of the UN Charter were excluded from the purview of the law.[39] Its interpretation, however, has not been completely consistent. Even though Finnish participation in UNPROFOR in Bosnia and Herzegovina was excluded as falling outside the traditional peacekeeping allowed by the law, Finland took part in the UN Iraq–Kuwait Observation Mission which was established under Chapter VII without the consent of Iraq.[40]

The 1993 Committee proposed giving policy makers greater latitude to decide on Finnish participation. 'Wider peacekeeping' was not to be defined in the text of the new law; instead, enforcement action under articles 42 or 51 of the UN Charter was to be excluded. Regarding the military requirements of enforcement action, the Committee noted that the current Finnish UN stand-by force was incapable of providing ground troops for combat. Moreover, the Finnish Defence Forces and reserves, structured, equipped and trained as part of the national territorial defence system, have neither the organization nor the equipment to allow the interoperability required in an international force. Only a brigade could operate independently and thus serve as part of a large multinational operation, but its establishment was not considered possible within Finland's personnel, material or economic resources. Instead, the Committee proposed improving the existing stand-by system to prepare for Finnish participation in 'wider peacekeeping' operations.[41] Improvements in organization, recruitment, training, terms of contract and especially equipment were considered necessary. If reaction capacity was to be upgraded, a core group (10–20 per cent) of personnel on active duty should be given responsibility for training, planning and equipment.

---

[36] In 1995 the Finnish Stand-by Force comprised an infantry battalion of 954 and a construction battalion of 415 personnel. Finnish Ministry of Defence, *The Finnish Peacekeepers,* Helsinki, 1995, p. 20.

[37] Laki Suomen osallistumisesta Yhdistyneiden Kansakuntien ja Euroopan turvallisuus- ja yhteistyökonferenssin rauhanturvaamistoimintaan [Law on the participation of Finland in the peacekeeping activities of the UN and the CSCE], 514/84, entered into force 1 Jan. 1985, amended to include the CSCE in 520/93.

[38] Rauhanturvaamislainsäädännön kehittämistoimikunnan osamietintö I [Partial report of the Commission for the Development of Peacekeeping Legislation I], KM 1982:62, 30 Nov. 1982, p. 53.

[39] Finnish Parliament, Hallituksen esitys Eduskunnalle laiksi Suomen osallistumisesta Yhdistyneiden Kansakuntien rauhanturvaamistoimintaan [Government bill to the Parliament for a law on Finnish participation in United Nations peacekeeping activities], HE 193/1983, pp. 7–8.

[40] It has been argued that Finnish participation was possible because the tasks of the peacekeepers were the same as in traditional missions. Hallituksen esitys Eduskunnalle laiksi Suomen osallistumisesta Yhdistyneiden Kansakuntien ja Euroopan turvallisuus- ja yhteistyökonferenssin rauhanturvaamistoimintaan annetun lain muuttamisesta [Government bill to the Parliament for an amendment to the law on the participation of Finland in the peacekeeping activities of the UN and the CSCE], HE 185/1995, p. 5.

[41] According to the Committee's definition, a 'wider' peacekeeping operation is one in which a limited amount of armed force is permitted in defence of the mission and/or which does not enjoy the guaranteed cooperation of all parties to the conflict. The term has been used in subsequent discussions of Finland's participation in multilateral missions.

Immediate availability would require a standing force, which was judged too expensive for Finland.[42]

The debate on 'peace enforcement' which accompanied the discussion on possible participation in Bosnia and Herzegovina in 1993–94 was coloured by a traditional Finnish aversion to potential embroilment in foreign conflicts and the bill never came before parliament. Military leaders were quick to point out that Finland had neither the tradition, the capabilities nor the required professional army to participate in robust missions beyond its borders.[43] When the other Nordic countries redeployed their forces in a joint battalion in Bosnia and Herzegovina, Finland increased its UNPROFOR contingent in the less dangerous preventive deployment mission in Macedonia. After Finland joined the PFP, however, political and military leaders mooted a more active role for Finland despite the previous public controversy.[44] In a speech in August 1994, new Commander-in-Chief General Gustav Hägglund foresaw the possibility of situations in which 'Finland would, for reasons of its own security, consider it necessary to participate in crisis management functions outside our own borders'.[45] In the latter half of 1994 discussion focused on the need to establish a new force, better trained and equipped and more capable of operating as part of a multinational force than the existing Finnish UN stand-by force.

The blueprint for a proposed new Rapid Deployment Force within the Defence Forces was presented in a cabinet report on Finnish security policy on 6 June 1995.[46] The force would enhance Finland's readiness for military crisis management 'as part of the country's own defence readiness and capability'. It could be used as part of a multinational force in addition to performing normal military and peacekeeping duties. It would consist of at least one battalion which could become operational in 2–3 years.[47] Training of the recruited group would begin during their 8- to 11-month military service and continue thereafter during their two-year service contract with the Defence Forces.[48] For overseas duty the battalion would be assembled from trained personnel in the reserve who would be placed in the same infantry (Jaeger) brigade, which in turn—unlike the current Finnish UN stand-by force—would be part of the Finnish defence system. The composition of the brigade would allow for the deployment of engineering, signal or transport units in addition to or instead of the battalion. The new force would require training and equipment to handle demanding tasks involving the possible use of force beyond self-defence.[49] The maximum

---

[42] Finnish Ministry of Defence, Suomen osallistuminen rauhanturvaamistoimintaan [Report on Finland's participation in peacekeeping activities], Helsinki, 15 Sep. 1993, pp. 16–19.

[43] Penttilä, R., Finland's Security in a Changing Europe: A Historical Perspective, Finnish Defence Studies no. 7 (National Defence College: Helsinki, 1994), p. 65.

[44] In its PFP Presentation Document, Finland expressed an interest in cooperation regarding peacekeeping training, search and rescue and humanitarian operations, training and information exchange and environmental protection. The Individual Partnership Programme was finalized in Nov. 1994.

[45] General Gustav Hägglund in Joensuu on 19 Aug. 1994, cited in Penttilä (note 43), p. 66.

[46] Finnish Ministry for Foreign Affairs, Security in a Changing World: Guidelines for Finland's Security Policy, Report by the Council of State to the Parliament, Helsinki, 6 June 1995.

[47] The military have subsequently fine-tuned the proposal, calling for the training of an entire brigade over time. Helsingin Sanomat, 29 Sep. 1995; and Iltalehti, 23 Feb. 1996.

[48] Conscripts could only be sent outside Finland for exercises. When 50 conscripts attended the PFP exercise 'Cooperative Jaguar' in Oct. 1995, the Commander of the Navy, Vice-Admiral Sakari Visa, confirmed that such participation must be voluntary. Ruotuväki, vol. 33, no. 20 (729), 8 Nov. 1995, p. 4.

[49] According to the estimates updated since the 1993 Committee report, the force would require improved personal equipment, diversified transport capacity and communications systems, new support system containers and new night vision devices. Finnish Parliament, Puolustusvaliokunnan lausunto [Statement of the Defence Committee], PuVL 2/1995 vp - VNS 1/1995 vp, 26 Sep. 1995, p. 12.

number of troops serving abroad at any one time would remain at the current level of 2000.[50]

The report was initially criticized by opposition parties and members of the governing coalition alike. Discussion focused on the rapid reaction force proposal, which elicited a negative response from the Defence Committee in an October report opposing Finland's participation in operations that require functions beyond traditional peacekeeping. Since the limits of humanitarian action were hard to define and a 'wider' peacekeeping operation might later turn into enforcement, the committee thought Finland should limit its participation to operations that do not require the use of force beyond self-defence. For that the present stand-by system was sufficient, although it could be made more effective.[51] Opponents of the force also objected to the costs of its establishment and feared the introduction, albeit in embryonic form, of a standing army in Finland and a hidden agenda to move Finland towards NATO membership.

The Parliamentary Foreign Affairs Committee, by contrast, was favourably inclined towards Finnish participation in 'wider peacekeeping' but took no firm stand on the establishment of a new rapid reaction force. It did, however, indirectly endorse the idea by suggesting that military crisis-management tools should be part of Finland's own defence capability and readiness. Training should be such that tasks could be undertaken more quickly than before and the capacity for flexible cooperation between different Nordic units could be maintained.[52] Greater use of Finnish civilian personnel in humanitarian and rescue operations, the establishment of a trained civilian reaction force and the pre-stocking of *matériel* were also advocated.

No decision was taken in 1995 on the proposed Rapid Deployment Force, but plans for its establishment were ready early in the new year. Outlining the needs of the Defence Forces in the near future, General Hägglund in November 1995 singled out the importance of maintaining the basis of defence, improving quality and creating the capacity required in international cooperation, such as interoperability. The latter implies a coordination of the 'software' in operations, developing a common language rather than adopting the same weapon systems. However, he still emphasized that at least for now the intention is to cooperate, not change the operating procedures of the Finnish Defence Forces to make them interoperable with NATO.[53] He also reiterated his view that Finnish membership of NATO is not an issue, a stand repeated by the President in December.[54]

The debate on the proposed rapid reaction forces subsided in November to give way to a consideration of Finnish participation in IFOR. Impossible without a change in the peacekeeping law, the necessary legislation was pushed through in December. It allows for participation in peacekeeping and humanitarian operations authorized by the UN or the OSCE, even under Chapter VII, if they involve only limited use of force to protect the mission. Participation in 'activity which can be considered peace enforcement' is excluded, and Parliament must be consulted on proposed Finnish participation in a mission mandated to use force beyond that necessary in traditional

[50] Note 46, pp. 37–38. The report also notes that Finland has good potential for increasing participation by civilian personnel, especially in humanitarian operations.

[51] Puolustusvaliokunnan lausunto (note 49).

[52] Finnish Parliament, Ulkoasiainvaliokunnan mietintö [Report of the Parliamentary Foreign Affairs Committee], UaVM 12/1995 vp - VNS 1/1995 vp, 19 Oct. 1995, pp. 32–34.

[53] *Ruotuväki* (note 48), p. 4.

[54] *Helsingin Sanomat*, 24 Dec. 1995.

peacekeeping.[55] The law was implemented for the first time a few days later when parliament approved Finnish participation in IFOR, classified as a 'wider peace-keeping' operation.[56]

V. Sweden

In 1964, after an appeal from Dag Hammarskjöld, Sweden decided to maintain a stand-by force of two battalions in permanent readiness for peacekeeping operations, augmented in 1974 to include special units comprising at most one battalion in strength.[57] Of the 530 000 troops that had taken part in UN operations by the end of 1991, nearly 12 per cent were Swedes.[58]

While in Finland the old restrictive legislation has provided a framework and jus-tification for a cautious policy, in Sweden, despite what could have been construed as equally restrictive legislation, the political grounds for participation in peace opera-tions have been weighed in each individual case. Although the most recent amend-ment to the law, in 1992, allowing for participation by a Swedish armed force in UN or OSCE peacekeeping, does not define 'peacekeeping' in either the text of the law or the background documentation, this activity is to be understood as in the 1974 law, that is, as being of the 'first-generation' variety.[59] Less hampered by self-imposed restraints and desiring a more visible presence, Sweden has taken part in a more ambitious range of multinational operations than Finland, including troop contribu-tions to the UN Operation in the Congo (ONUC), field hospitals in Operation Desert Storm and the United Task Force (UNITAF) in Somalia and most recently a battalion in UNPROFOR in Bosnia. Authorized by a special decision of parliament, the latter is the heaviest, best-equipped and most highly trained unit Sweden has sent into UN service and the first to take a major part in combat or combat-like operations since the Congo in which substantial force beyond the requirements of self-defence was used by the Swedish contingent. The decision, following the reinforcement of the bat-talion with Danish tanks and forward air controllers, was a departure from previous

[55] Laki Suomen osallistumisesta Yhdistyneiden Kansakuntien ja Euroopan turvallisuus- ja yhteistyöjärjestön päätökseen perustuvaan rauhanturvaamistoimintaan [Law on the participation of Fin-land in peacekeeping activities based on a decision of the UN and the OSCE], 1465/95, entered into force 19 Dec. 1995.

[56] The government also emphasized that the parties had consented to the use of force by IFOR. Finnish Parliament, Suomen osallistuminen Bosnia-Hertsegovinan rauhansopimuksen sotilaalliseen toimeenpanoon [Finland's participation in the military implementation of the Peace Agreement on Bosnia and Herzegovina], Report of the Council of State to Parliament, VNS 3/1995 vp, 18 Dec. 1995, p. 2. The Foreign Affairs Committee noted that the tasks of the Finnish contingent fell within the confines of traditional peacekeeping. Finnish Parliament, Ulkoasiainvaliokunnan mietintö [Report of the Foreign Affairs Committee], UaVM 22/1995 vp - VNS 3/1995 vp, 19 Dec. 1995, pp. 4–6.

[57] Lag om beredskapsstyrka för FN-tjänst [Law on a stand-by force for UN duty], SFS 1974:614, para. 3, entered into force 1 Jan. 1975. The underlying proposal specified that this amounted to at most 3000 troops. Swedish Parliament, Kungl. Maj:ts proposition angående vissa organisationsfrågor m.m. rörande försvaret [His Majesty's bill on certain organizational questions etc. affecting defence], Prop. 1974:50, 22 Mar. 1974, p. 34. In 1992, an upper limit of 3000 serving abroad was included in the text of the law. Lag om väpnad styrka för tjänstgöring utomlands [Law on armed forces for service abroad], SFS 1992:1153, entered into force 1 Jan. 1993 and amended in SFS 1995:597.

[58] Persson, S., 'Peace enforcement: Sweden's role in changing pattern of UN activities 1991–1992', ed. Ericson (note 7), p. 93.

[59] SFS 1992:1153 (note 57); and Swedish Parliament, Regeringens proposition om väpnad styrka för tjänstgöring utomlands [Government bill on armed forces for service abroad], Prop. 1992/93:77, 15 Oct. 1992.

practice and was neither easily made nor uncontroversial.[60] An important factor underlying Swedish participation appears to have been its pending application for EU membership. Sweden was keen to demonstrate its active contribution to building a common European security order to alleviate fears that the admission of neutral states would cripple the EU's ability to act forcefully in foreign and security policy.

In parallel with the new requirements imposed by Sweden's participation in UN operations in Macedonia and Bosnia and Herzegovina and in NATO's PFP since August 1994, the Swedish UN stand-by system has been developed in the 1990s and supported since 1993 by the Swedish Armed Forces' International Centre (SWEDINT), in charge of training and national logistics support to Swedish elements abroad.[61] Responsibility for setting up and training Swedish contingents is delegated regionally to a division commander. For larger longer-term operations, such as that in Bosnia and Herzegovina, the responsibility for setting up each battalion rotates among the brigades while the training of companies for a battalion can be divided between regiments from different brigades simultaneously with support and coordination by SWEDINT. Spreading the responsibility for force generation is regarded as beneficial to the armed forces since a larger portion of their personnel will feel involved and gain experience from international operations.[62]

Personnel for international operations are recruited on a voluntary basis from reserves in all three services. As a complement to the present system of recruitment in regiments and by general announcements, the armed forces in 1994 started an experimental project of asking enlisting conscripts whether they would be willing, on a voluntary basis, to be available for international duty upon completion of their 7- to 15- month national service. The non-legally binding declaration of intent is meant to stay in force for three years. The intention is to generate a company for international duty in each battalion trained during national service and to enable such units to train together as much as possible during their basic military service. In a report to the government, the Commander-in-Chief has suggested that Sweden also consider changing its legislation to allow officers to be ordered to participate in overseas operations, but this initiative has been deferred to the Parliamentary Defence Commission preparing the next long-term defence decision to be finalized in late 1996.

A fundamental reorganization of Sweden's participation in international military operations has been included in the extensive defence review. Sweden's intention to set up a brigade for international operations was announced by the first cabinet of the new Social Democratic Government in its initial policy statement in 1994 and has since been repeated in international forums.[63] In the wake of Sweden's participation in UNPROFOR, the Defence Ministry was preparing for future involvement in a broad spectrum of international missions. In early 1994, policy makers evaluated the requirements of qualitatively different missions for the defence establishment, pointing out that it would be necessary to consider these factors from the outset and shape

[60] Dalsjö (note 7), p. 96.

[61] *Nordic UN Stand-by Forces,* 4th edn (NORDSAMFN: Helsinki, 1993), pp. 159–60.

[62] Swedish Ministry for Foreign Affairs, Sveriges deltagande i internationella fredsfrämjande insatser [Swedish participation in international peace-promotion activities], Ds 1995:24, p. 12.

[63] 'Regeringsförklaring' [Government statement], *R&D*, no. 31 (1994), p. 7. In her address to the UN General Assembly, Foreign Minister Lena Hjelm-Wallén indicated Sweden's willingness to set up a Swedish international rapid-reaction force for peacekeeping tasks at short notice. Swedish Ministry for Foreign Affairs, 'The Foreign Minister at the United Nations', Press Release, 28 Sep. 1995.

the organization, units and training of the Swedish armed forces accordingly.[64] Late in the year the Foreign Ministry appointed a rapporteur to evaluate the requirements of international operations and lay the groundwork for a Swedish policy on participation.[65]

The published blueprint for a new Swedish international force, prepared by the defence review and endorsed by the cabinet and the Parliamentary Defence Committee, is still rather vague.[66] According to the government proposal, the armed forces should establish an international force for use in peace operations under a UN or OSCE mandate. The size of a brigade,[67] it should contain infantry units as well as special units for headquarters, medical care and transport, and support of civilian missions. Its composition should reflect international demand, with personnel and resources from all the service branches. SWEDINT is to be part of the force, which should also include a pool of readily available military observers, monitors and staff officers. It would comprise a commander with staff, personnel and units in readiness, in training and in ongoing operations. Normally 800–1400 personnel from the force could serve abroad at a time, with flexibility to exceed this limit for short periods given sufficient lead time.

One or two companies of the force should be kept in especially high readiness on special contracts for use in, for example, multinational rapid reaction forces with a deployment time of 15–30 days from the Swedish Cabinet decision. A reconnaissance team should be operable within a week. To give this type of contribution maximum effect, the government proposed coordination with other countries, especially on the basis of traditional Nordic cooperation. Perhaps surprisingly, Sweden, unlike the other Nordic countries, has not pledged forces to the UN Stand-by Arrangements System. It has argued that its substantial contributions to ongoing operations, especially UNPROFOR, do not allow for the earmarking of additional units for the UN roster and that the current organization cannot accommodate the required two-week readiness time. However, one of the justifications given for a Swedish international force is that Sweden should be able to participate more quickly and be able to back up its demands for an improved UN rapid reaction capability with its own contribution.[68]

In keeping with heightened ambitions for future Swedish participation, the proposed international force would be suitable for traditional as well as wider peace-keeping operations. A limited contribution to peace-enforcement operations with small units might also be possible to show solidarity, but the proposed policy is for restraint and a humanitarian orientation.[69] Sweden would strive to meet international demand for special units, in spite of previous difficulties in recruiting certain special-

[64] 'Sveriges försvar får ökat internationellt ansvar' [Sweden's defence gets more international responsibility], *Folk och Försvar*, vol. 54, no. 1 (1994), p. 7.

[65] Swedish Ministry for Foreign Affairs, PM, 1 Dec. 1994. The report Ds 1995:24 (note 62) was submitted in Mar. 1995.

[66] Swedish Ministry of Defence, Totalförsvarets utveckling och förnyelse: rapport från försvars-beredningen hösten 1995 [The development and renewal of the total defence: report by the Swedish Parliamentary Defence Commission, Autumn 1995], Ds 1995:51, pp. 128–31; Swedish Parliament, Regeringens proposition, *Totalförsvar i förnyelse* [Government bill: renewal of the total defence], Prop. 1995/96:12, 21 Sep. 1995, pp. 106–108; and Swedish Parliament, Försvarsutskottets betänkande, Total-försvarets förnyelse 1995/96 [Report of the Defence Committee: the renewal of the total defence, 1995/96], FöU 1 (1995), 23 Nov. 1995, pp. 68–71.

[67] The government proposal does not contain figures on the overall size of the force, but early in the year it was estimated at c. 5000. *Svenska Dagbladet*, 30 Jan. 1995.

[68] FöU 1 (note 66), p. 68; and Ds 1995:24 (note 62), pp. 99–101.

[69] Ds 1995:24 (note 62), pp. 90–91.

ists, for instance, for the military hospitals sent to the Gulf and Somalia. Consequently the structure of economic incentives should be re-evaluated. Personnel should continue to be recruited on a voluntary basis except possibly in the case of career officers if it turns out to be difficult for Sweden to fulfil its international obligations. Training should be improved with a view to developing cooperation between civilian and military units in multifunctional operations. Greater weight should be given to developing forms of civilian assistance and a special force should be set up for this purpose.[70]

The timetable for their establishment and the substance of the proposed international forces is an integral part of Sweden's next long-term defence decision and dependent on the overall aims and structure of the armed forces, which are to be downsized from the current 16 to 13 brigades. The Defence Commission has determined that an armed attack against Sweden is now highly unlikely and has defined four functions for the enlarged Swedish total defence concept: assertion of territorial integrity; crisis management; international operations; and maintaining the ability to meet any military threat which may nevertheless arise. Participation in international peacekeeping is now identified as one of the principal tasks.[71] Exactly how these contributions are organized will depend on the totality of tasks entrusted to the armed forces, derived from the desired level of ambition in maintaining a credible, independent territorial defence. This will in turn depend on future decisions about Sweden's long-standing policy of non-alignment which has been re-evaluated especially since Sweden's application for EU membership.

Supported by the majority of public opinion, the interim report of the defence review has concluded that membership of NATO or the WEU would benefit neither Swedish security interests nor stability in the Nordic subregion. The Moderate and Liberal Party representatives left the Defence Commission in April 1995 in protest at its refusal to even investigate the implications of security alternatives involving an alliance. This deep-seated apprehension was voiced by the Green and Left parties in their joint registration of dissent from Sweden's decision to participate in IFOR, which they feared would bring the country closer to NATO. Contrary to majority opinion in Parliament, they demanded that the government clearly announce this to be a one-off event and revert to UN-led operations in the future.[72] The formal decision making on IFOR was surrounded by debate about the capabilities and possible restrictions on the operations of the Swedish contingent. With opinion divided over the implications of EU membership for national security, the Swedish debate has nevertheless taken on new dimensions following Sweden's commitment to the EU Common Foreign and Security Policy and subsequent statements by former Prime Minister Carl Bildt (Moderate) that Sweden could not remain neutral in its reactions in the event of an armed conflict in the Baltic region or within the EU. Even

[70] Swedish Ministry of Defence, Svenska insatser för internationell katastrof- och flyktinghjälp: Kartläggning, analys och förslag. Betänkande av Utredningen om civila insatser för katastrof- och flyktinghjälp [Swedish contributions to international disaster and refugee relief: Survey, analysis and proposals: report of the investigation of civilian contributions to disaster and refugee relief], SOU 1995:72, 29 June 1995.
[71] Swedish Ministry of Defence, Sverige i Europa och Världen: Säkerhetspolitisk rapport från försvarsberedningen våren 1995 [Sweden in Europe and in the world: Report on security policy by the Swedish Parliamentary Defence Commission, spring 1995], Ds 1995: 28.
[72] Nilsson, M., '870 svenskar till Nato' [870 Swedes to NATO], R&D, no. 40 (1995), p. 16. The government described IFOR's tasks as being mainly traditional peacekeeping. Swedish Parliament, Regeringens proposition, Svenskt deltagande i fredsstyrka i f.d. Jugoslavien [Government bill, Swedish participation in the peace force in the former Yugoslavia], Prop. 1995/96:113, 30 Nov. 1995.

Prime Minister Ingvar Carlsson (Social Democrat) opened the door to a re-evaluation of Swedish non-alignment in 6–7 years.[73]

VI. Conclusions

After having remained very similar for 30 years, the organization of military forces for international operations now differs considerably from one Nordic country to the other. The 1964 stand-by forces model has been abolished in Denmark and Sweden, retained alongside an IRF commitment in Norway and is being reconsidered in Finland. Following decisions in 1993 on the RRF contributions of the two NATO members, the Danish DRB and Norwegian IRF battalion will be operational in 1996. Finnish and Swedish plans to set up international brigades contain elements from the Danish model, but remain to be finalized in 1996. All the Nordic reorganization schemes seek to increase the versatility, flexibility and capability of the newly established forces, which are assigned a role in the national defence structure.

Although participation in international operations is becoming an increasingly important task for the armed forces of all the Nordic countries, variations in security perceptions and alignments result in different equations between national security and international commitment. Whereas Norway, Sweden and Finland share a residual security concern over political volatility in Russia, Denmark has been able to reorient its Defence Forces towards international missions relatively more forcefully. The gamut of possible peace operations is most extensive for Denmark and most restrictive for Finland, the decisive factor being the extent to which use of force by national contingents is considered permissible. Sweden, actively pursuing the formulation of a new policy on peace operations, and Finland, having moved towards broadening its traditionally cautious approach, continue to reflect on the policy implications of continued non-alignment within the EU. Although they still hold consultations and exchange early information, the Nordic caucus at the UN no longer issued joint statements in 1995, having been superseded by the EU allegiance of the three Nordic members. Norway's fear of isolation has paradoxically rejuvenated the meetings of Nordic defence ministers, which were previously used to compare experiences from UN missions but now include a varied agenda of security policy issues.

In spite of differences in national peacekeeping organization and policy, the tradition of cooperation fostered by the Nordic countries is still one of their great strengths. They have been able to assemble and deploy joint battalions quickly, as in the case of Macedonia, and to coordinate the joint operation of their units in UNPROFOR. They have pooled their resources in training peacekeepers and sought other like-minded countries for larger international projects like the SHIRBRIG. Their joint participation in IFOR will provide the next indicator for the desired future development of their international forces.

---

[73] Eneberg, K., 'Dörr mot Nato öppnad' [Door to NATO opened], *Dagens Nyheter,* 31 Jan. 1996.

Appendix 2D. Reform of the United Nations

TREVOR FINDLAY

I. Introduction

In 1995 the 50th anniversary of the founding of the United Nations was marked by pomp, ceremony and celebration, including, in October, the largest gathering of heads of state in history at UN headquarters in New York. Innumerable conferences and symposia, educational programmes, television series and press articles pushed the often neglected body to the forefront of world attention. UN triumphs, from eradicating smallpox to facilitating decolonization, were deservedly eulogized and its failures rudely trumpeted and dissected. Some of these failures were rightly excused on the grounds that member states had consistently failed to provide the UN with the requisite power and resources to carry out its ambitious mandates. Indeed the celebrations were haunted by the UN's growing financial crisis, its worst since the Congo crisis of the early 1960s, and overwhelming evidence that UN peacekeeping forces in the former Yugoslavia had been poorly mandated and provided for. Even more worrying was the realization that even with substantial additional resources the United Nations in its present state could not meet the needs of the next five years, much less those of the 21st century. Fundamental reform was urgently required. As US Ambassador to the UN Madeleine Albright so melodramatically put it, 'the UN must reform or die'.[1]

Throughout 1995 (and in the preceding two or three years) UN reform proposals proliferated. Some were Utopian and stood no chance of general acceptance. Others were opposed early, usually by one or more of the great powers. Still others were noted for further study. None reached fruition immediately. The 7-page Declaration on the Occasion of the Fiftieth Anniversary of the United Nations adopted unanimously by the General Assembly on 24 October contained only the vaguest of admonitions and no specific reform proposals.[2] The anniversary year was clearly not the time for reaching agreement on major UN reform, much less implementing it. Indeed the deadline for agreement on specific reform proposals was officially declared to be the opening of the 51st session of the General Assembly in September 1996. While 1995 was to be a year of celebration and contemplation of reform, 1996 would, it was hoped, be the year of decision.

II. The vision of a reformed UN

Fifty years after its establishment the UN is patently in need of a major overhaul. It is generally regarded as inefficient, over-bureaucratized, unresponsive to real human needs, undemocratic and aloof. For the 21st century the international community demands a more efficient and professional UN, one with a holistic approach to human security that integrates human rights, economic and social advancement, the

---

[1] Walsh, J., 'The UN at 50', *Time*, 23 Oct. 1995, p. 26.
[2] Declaration on the Occasion of the Fiftieth Anniversary of the United Nations, 24 Oct. 1995, para. 14, reproduced in *Wireless File* (United States Information Service, US Embassy: Stockholm, 25 Oct. 1995), pp. 10–13.

promotion of democracy and effective conflict prevention, management and resolution.[3] The organ charged with safeguarding international peace and security, the Security Council, should be more representative of the UN membership, never again stultified by the veto power, more transparent in its deliberations, and have access to the best advice and information available. A new and improved UN should have information-gathering and -processing capabilities that provide early warning of impending humanitarian or politico-military events, which in turn trigger the appropriate response. Such responses could range from the early dispatch of conflict-resolution experts, perhaps from regional UN centres, through the prompt and efficient delivery of humanitarian assistance, to the deployment within days of a UN rapid reaction force. Larger, less urgent missions would be conducted by peacekeeping forces headed by a pre-formed, operational command, combining troops well versed in peacekeeping techniques, provided with essential equipment from UN logistics bases and guided by crisp mandates, clear rules of engagement, and streamlined command and control arrangements. A reformed UN would have a doctrine for the use of force that avoids 'mission drift' from peacekeeping into peace enforcement. As for peace enforcement itself, while no UN army is yet seriously contemplated, 'coalitions of the willing and able' would be standard but would be guided more closely by the Security Council to avoid their misuse for national ends that differed from those of the UN. Economic sanctions would be more carefully targeted and unintended consequences foreseen and ameliorated.

In the area of human rights a remodelled UN would accord them a more prominent place on its agenda, it would monitor them more thoroughly and have mechanisms to counterbalance the *droit de regard* that many states wish to retain over such matters. In the economic and social fields the new UN would have rationalized and consolidated its myriad agencies, abolishing some, amalgamating others. The Economic and Social Council (ECOSOC) would either have been replaced or strengthened. The UN as a whole would have a much clearer role in helping marry national development efforts with sustainable development goals, global environmental concerns, the booming international private business sector, expanding world trade and maverick financial markets. The World Bank and the International Monetary Fund (IMF) would have been brought closer to the UN and imbued with a heightened social and environmental conscience. In the social sphere the UN would have trimmed its agenda to suit its capabilities, having sorted through the vast number of issues tackled at its series of summit meetings held in the 1990s on the environment, sustainable development, social development and women's issues.[4]

To carry out these daunting tasks the UN should operate from a stable and secure financial base, provided not only through a reformed and just assessment system but by non-state-based levies. The UN's accounting, procurement and financial delegation procedures would have been transformed, especially for large field missions. UN staff would be recruited competitively, trained continuously and held to the most rigorous standards of accountability and responsibility. 'Best practice' management techniques would prevail, including those relating to gender equity. Professional

---

[3] The following discussion of a UN vision is inspired by *The United Nations in its Second Half-Century*, Report of the Independent Working Group on the Future of the United Nations (Ford Foundation: New York, 1995), pp. 7–10.

[4] The 1995 World Summit for Social Development in Copenhagen, the 1995 UN Women's Conference in Beijing, the 1992 UN Conference on Environment and Development in Rio de Janeiro and the 1993 World Conference on Human Rights in Vienna.

searches would be conducted for all high-level appointments from the Secretary-General down.

Multitudinous reform proposals directed at all these areas were contained in the 185 statements by heads of state or other national representatives to the 50th anniversary session. As might be expected, however, the most imaginative and far-reaching reform proposals have tended to come from outside the UN system.[5] Favourite areas for reform included the Security Council, the need for 'democratization' of the UN, the institutional framework of the UN 'system' and finance.[6]

III. Security Council reform

Probably the most popular target of UN reform is the Security Council. Including as it does five permanent members (China, France, Russia, the UK and the USA), each with a veto and considerable control over Council deliberations and decisions, it naturally attracts criticism from those who wish to 'democratize' the UN and lessen the influence of the great powers.[7] It is regarded by many states as secretive, arbitrary and beholden in particular to the 'permanent three', the USA, the UK and France.

Proposals for reform have centred on increasing the size of the Council and amending or abolishing the veto. Although the Council was increased from 11 to 15 in 1963 it is now universally recognized that a Council of this size cannot adequately reflect a UN membership that has grown from the original 49 signatories of the 1945 Treaty of San Francisco to 185 at the end of 1995. A consensus seems to be forming around adding an additional five members, raising membership to 20, although some states prefer up to 25. The candidates almost universally favoured for permanent membership are Germany and Japan, but adding these alone would increase the predominance of the developed world among the permanent members. The leading contenders for boosting developing country representation are Brazil, India, Indonesia and Nigeria. Alternatives are Argentina, Pakistan, Egypt and, most recently, South Africa.

There remain vastly differing views on the number of new permanent and non-permanent members that should be added and whether the permanent members should be granted the veto power. Tanzania, submitting the ambit claim of the African group, has proposed that Africa receive two permanent seats and more non-

---

[5] Among them were proposals from a number of high-level commissions comprised of eminent personalities, such as the Yale–Ford Independent Working Group on the Future of the United Nations and the Carlsson–Ramphal Commission on Global Governance. *The United Nations in its Second Half-Century* (note 3); and *Our Global Neighbourhood*, Report of the Commission on Global Governance (Oxford University Press: Oxford, 1995). Further grist to the reform mill was provided by Australian Foreign Minister Gareth Evans in Evans, G., *Cooperating for Peace: The Global Agenda for the 1990s and Beyond* (Allen & Unwin: Sydney, 1993); in Childers, E. and Urquhart, B., *Towards A More Effective United Nations* (Dag Hammarskjöld Foundation: Uppsala, 1991); and in Childers, E. with Urquhart, B., *Renewing the United Nations System* (Dag Hammarskjöld Foundation: Uppsala, 1994). Also important were the *The UN and the Health of Nations,* Final Report of the United States Commission on Improving the Effectiveness of the United Nations, Washington, DC, Sep. 1993, and the only major report from the developing world, *Reform of the United Nations Organization*, Rajiv Gandhi Memorial Initiative for the Advancement of Human Civilization, New Delhi, Apr. 1994.

[6] Reform proposals relating to conflict prevention, management and resolution, including peacekeeping and a UN Rapid Reaction Force, are considered in chapter 2 in this volume.

[7] See Ciechanski, J., 'Restructuring of the UN Security Council', *International Peacekeeping*, vol. 1, no. 4 (winter 1994), pp. 413–39.

permanent seats.[8] The Association of South-East Asian States (ASEAN) has suggested that it also be permanently represented on the Council by one of its members. Proposals for a single European Union seat, advanced by Italy, are unlikely to be realized, especially if they involve France and the UK surrendering their individual seats. A meeting of the Foreign Ministers of the permanent five members of the Council agreed in September 1995 that the Council should be expanded and continue to be reformed but without specifying how.[9] The USA favours adding Germany and Japan as permanent members, in addition to three new non-permanent seats.[10] Russia and the UK support limited enlargement up to 20 members and preservation of the status of permanent members.[11] Ultimately the number of seats and regional mix will depend on inter-regional bargaining and political trade-offs.

The veto question is more vexed, especially since UN members are sharply divided between wanting it abolished, curtailed, accorded to new permanent members or restricted to the existing ones. Many members view the extension of the veto to even more states as compounding an already untenable power disparity. Moreover, any extension or modification of the veto—or indeed any Council reform—requires the support of the current veto holders. Malaysia favours abolishing it altogether, a view not shared by all the developing countries, especially not those that aspire to permanent membership.[12] While the permanent five are unlikely to surrender their veto power they may be willing to formally or informally agree to restrict their use of it to non-procedural matters of vital national interest—a situation that has in effect pertained since the end of the cold war.

Some aspects of Security Council reform are already being attended to. The Council now publishes an agenda, provides regular briefings for non-members on its deliberations, and holds consultations with non-members on such issues as the establishment and operation of peacekeeping missions. However, calls for Council meetings to operate completely openly are unlikely to be heeded, since secrecy is often vital to effective Council diplomacy and action. Were Council meetings forced into the open it is apparent that additional secret meetings would simply be conducted outside the Council chamber. Similarly, even the addition of a more representative group of permanent members and expansion of the numbers of non-permanent members will hardly render the Council democratic: it was deliberately designed to reflect the base realities of political, economic and military power so that its enforcement powers would be taken seriously. One way of establishing a check or balance on the Council's current unlimited powers would be a 'Chapter VII Consultation Committee' of 21 members of the General Assembly, which would consider Council proposals for peace enforcement operations.[13] An alternative would be some sort of constitutional review, as proposed by Colombia, presumably by the International Court of Justice.[14] Even without a formal veto power and permanent membership the great

---

[8] UN, Question of equitable representation on and increase in the membership of the Security Council: Report of the Secretary-General, UN document A/48/264/Add.5, 30 Nov. 1993.

[9] Statement of the Foreign Minister of the Five Permanent Members of the Security Council following meeting with the Secretary-General on 27 September, UN Press Release, UN Information Centre for the Nordic Countries, 28 Sep. 1995, Copenhagen, p. 5.

[10] Address of US Ambassador Madeleine Albright to UN General Assembly, 27 Oct. 1994, reproduced in *Wireless File* (US Information Service, US Embassy: Stockholm, 28 Oct. 1994), p. 15.

[11] UN, Press Release DH/1752, Geneva, 17 Oct. 1994, p. 6.

[12] *Unity*, UN Association of Australia, no. 56 (Nov. 1994), p. 8.

[13] Proposed by Michael Reisman. See Alvarez, J. E., 'The once and future Security Council', *Washington Quarterly*, spring 1995, p. 14.

[14] Alvarez (note 13), p. 17.

powers will always exercise disproportionate influence on Council decision making. Conversely, they will also be expected to bear a heavier burden in implementing Council decisions, such as in supporting peacekeeping and peace-enforcement operations.

IV. Democratization of the UN system

The UN Charter begins grandly with 'We the peoples of the United Nations' and promises them peace and security, food, shelter, social and economic advancement, and human rights. Unfortunately 'we the peoples' are never heard of again in the Charter and seldom in much of what the UN has done in their name. The UN was designed to be an organization of nation-states and naturally state interests were seen to be paramount: the interests of humanity were to be secured not by direct UN interaction with peoples, especially in such sensitive areas as human rights and human security, but by 'harmonizing the actions of nations'.[15]

The interests of states and peoples are not synonymous or always in harmony, however. Most UN member states are not democracies and even democracies represent the will of their peoples imperfectly. Many states, far from being the protectors of human rights or guardians of the welfare of their peoples, are their chief oppressors, as countless reports of Amnesty International attest. At the UN, many member states vote for resolutions and sign conventions without the slightest intention of complying with them. In the human rights area UN bodies have been dominated by state interests, preventing individual states being called to account for their actions.[16] In the field, where the UN has done some of its best work, programmes often appear geared more to the needs of donor and host governments than people in need, again because the state acts as a filter between the UN and direct interaction with peoples. The chief legal constraint on more independent UN action has been Article 2.7 of the Charter, which prohibits the UN from intervening 'in matters which are essentially within the jurisdiction of any state'.

Some changes are occurring: the impact of non-governmental organizations (NGOs) on UN proceedings was starkly apparent at the UN Women's Conference in Beijing in 1995, a trend first witnessed at the Rio de Janeiro UN Conference on Environment and Development in 1992. The UN has now conceded that NGOs are important to its work and is increasingly prepared to cooperate with them in areas ranging from early warning of humanitarian disasters to mine-clearance. The UN now has a Human Rights Commissioner, appointed after decades of debate, whose job is to concern himself with violations of human rights brought to his attention by individuals and groups rather than governments. Over the years the Human Rights Commission in Geneva has become bolder in investigating and castigating member states for their human rights records.

One reform proposal originally proposed at the UN's inception, is a People's Assembly that would meet in New York at the same time as the UN General

---

[15] Charter of the United Nations, Article 1.4.

[16] Even in its 50th anniversary year the UN Secretariat attempted to censor a work it had commissioned to celebrate the event by expunging a quotation from the Dalai Lama on the grounds that it was 'not acceptable'—presumably to China. Press Release, Transnational Foundation for Peace and Future Research, Lund, Sweden, 26 June 1995. The publication in question was Power, J. (ed.), *A Vision of Hope: The Fiftieth Anniversary of the United Nations* (Regency Corporation: London, 1995).

Assembly.[17] It would have representatives elected directly by the people or by democratic parliaments where that was possible and selected by other means where it was not. Given that most representatives would still not be representative of 'we the peoples', the idea is problematic, but worth further debate. The Carlsson–Ramphal Commission on Global Governance, which set great store on the 'security of peoples', in 1995 suggested a Forum of Civil Society, consisting of accredited representatives of NGOs, who would meet in the General Assembly hall before the annual session of the Assembly.[18] This would not be democratic but would certainly represent a different perspective from that of governments. An alternative is a UN Lower Chamber, still comprised of national representatives, but where voting power would be weighted by a variety of indicators, including share of world gross national product (GNP), trade or even adherence to democratic or human rights values, rather than according to a one-country one-vote system. This would be extremely complex to administer, with endless possibilities for dispute, and would in any case be unlikely to result in a greater level of democratic governance at the UN or provide a voice for 'we the peoples'.

The problem with all these schemes for more or less democratic second chambers is that there would be no mechanism for reconciling the different resolutions passed by them and by the existing state-based General Assembly and Security Council. Unlike democratic parliamentary systems there is no executive branch in the UN system to interpret the 'will of the people' as expressed through the legislature and to act accordingly. The UN Secretary-General is decidedly not a chief executive in the sense of a prime minister or president but rather a cipher required to act on instructions from the General Assembly and the Security Council. While attempts to inject a 'democratic voice' into the UN are admirable and may lead to member states taking greater notice of such opinion, any democratic assembly will remain simply advisory—like the General Assembly itself on most issues—until there is a drastic reconstitution of the UN system. Such radical reform, in which states would essentially create the beginnings of a supranational world body, are way beyond the realms of possibility in the closing years of this century.

However, less ambitious measures than a peoples' assembly might have the effect of injecting new perspectives into the state-bound UN system. The Commission on Global Governance suggested, for instance, a right of petition for non-state actors to bring situations massively endangering the security of people to the attention of the Security Council. While these would still be 'filtered' by a process dominated by states, they would at least in some cases reach the agenda of the most powerful organ in the UN system. The Yale–Ford study on the other hand proposed bringing the views of NGOs and other non-state actors into the UN system through better consultation mechanisms built into reformed economic and social councils that would replace ECOSOC.[19] This would be more acceptable to UN member states and may in the long run be more effective by being insidious rather than confrontational and rhetorical, as a people's assembly would undoubtedly be.

In the long run, however, one of the most effective ways to bring the UN to the people may be institutional reform of the UN 'system' itself.

---

[17] Childers with Urquhart (note 5), pp. 212–13.
[18] *Our Global Neighbourhood* (note 5), p. 345.
[19] *The United Nations in its Second Half-Century* (note 3), pp. 52–53.

V. Restructuring the UN system

To call the UN a system—in the sense of a coordinated and integrated constellation of organizations and agencies—is a misnomer. The UN comprises over 100 separate entities, most of them not under the direct control of UN headquarters in New York. While there is an Administrative Committee on Co-ordination which is meant to coordinate the programmes and activities of the entire UN system, it meets only three times annually and has mainly a reporting function. The 'system' is in effect out of control: neither the Secretary-General, the UN Secretariat in New York, the General Assembly, the most powerful of states, nor any group of states, like the Western Group, has even a good overview of the varied activities of the system, much less sustained influence or control. The most assiduous delegations, mostly from the Western states, are unable even to read the huge array of UN documents, plans and budgets, much less critically analyse and react to them all.

The specialized agencies, such as the ILO, FAO, UNESCO and WHO, all have separate charters, organizational structures and financing arrangements, and their governing boards and directors are elected by the member states of each respective organization. Some of them predate the UN. They operate like entirely separate corporations, their heads are almost impossible to remove and even 'coordination', which in the UN system is usually minimal, is resented and resisted. Even the non-specialized agencies which are theoretically part of the main UN system, such as UNCTAD, UNICEF and UNHCR, are difficult to control from New York. UN agencies are run like fiefdoms—the 'last of the world's absolute monarchies'.[20]

The result is overlapping functions, competing mandates, inefficiency, waste and poor performance. Without systemic and systematic oversight staff recruitment has been politically tainted—with the connivance of member states. Until recently staff training has been negligible, promotion chaotic and the gender balance skewed determinedly away from women.

The economic and social agencies in particular are a problem. They have strayed from their original mandates as intellectual clearing-houses and become competing providers of technical assistance in the field, normally in the form of highly paid Western experts. Financial resources have been spread too thinly across too many small-scale, inconsequential projects. Up to now this has suited both aid receivers and aid providers; but it has had so little impact on the ground that it is being widely questioned: some reformers have called for the outright abolition of technical assistance. Overlapping functions are rife. Some 23 UN entities have development assistance funds to spend at country level.[21] When one UN body has failed to perform, another has been created. There are, for example, four UN agencies concerned with food production and seven with industrial development in the developing countries.

There are exceptions to the pattern. Good performers among the agencies include the UNHCR and the IAEA. The World Bank and the IMF (the Bretton Woods institutions), although members of the UN family, are run along quite different lines, with weighted voting according to economic contribution, proper management and recruitment systems and procedures for in-house review and reform. The World Bank has largely taken over the financing of development in the developing countries.

---

[20] Righter, R., *Utopia Lost: The United Nations and World Order* (Twentieth Century Book Fund: New York, 1995), p. 55.
[21] Childers with Urquhart (note 5), p. 89.

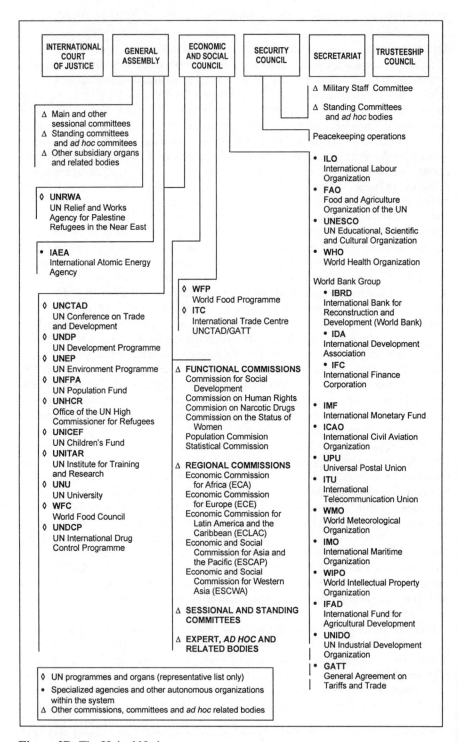

Figure 2D. The United Nations system

While both Bretton Woods institutions have been criticized for their lack of attention to social and environmental values they have, unlike other UN agencies, had the flexibility and ability to respond appropriately to such criticisms.

A radical 'root and branch' reform of this system would bring all UN agencies under central UN control, with oversight and coordination by the Secretary-General, and common management, financial and staffing procedures. The Secretary-General would in this situation need to devolve much of his day-to-day workload to several new Deputy Secretaries-General, as proposed by Australia.[22] A single 7-year term for the Secretary-General rather than renewable 5-year terms should also be considered to help avoid politicization of the position that invariably comes with re-election campaigns (however informal and discreet they might be in the UN's case).[23]

Radical reform would also involve 'picking winners and losers' among the agencies, abolishing some, amalgamating others, and changing the mandates of still others. Brian Urquhart and Erskine Childers even recommend relocating all UN agencies to New York to facilitate coordination and cooperation.[24]

ECOSOC is a particular target for reform. It has never functioned as originally intended, as an economic security council capable of coordinating all UN activities in the economic and social area and initiating high-level studies that would contribute to global economic policy. Some proposals for ECOSOC envisage its outright abolition and replacement by a genuine Economic Security Council.[25] The Yale–Ford study envisages two 23-member bodies modelled on the Security Council—an Economic Council and a Social Council—which would periodically meet together at the highest levels in what is grandiloquently called a Global Alliance for Sustainable Development. This would have the advantage of allowing economic and social issues to be considered separately when that is preferable and together as required. It would also enable each body to target much better its appropriate 'clientele' among NGOs and individuals such as academics and professional advisers. Hanna Suchocka, former Polish Prime Minister, who was on the Yale–Ford panel, finds the splitting of economic and social matters between two councils, at the very time when the interrelationship between them has become more apparent than ever, to be infelicitous.[26] Others, including ECOSOC itself, see the organization as reformable. Indeed the 50th anniversary heads of state declaration appeared to pre-empt moves to abolish ECOSOC by calling for its 'strengthening', a plaint that has been heard before to no effect.[27]

In the development assistance field rationalization is urgently required. One proposal is to give UNDP coordinating responsibility for all development work done by the UN, its offices in developing countries being mandated to represent all the UN agencies. Others would have UNDP become the funding authority for all UN development activity in the field: the work itself would still be carried out by separate agencies.[28] The various UN bodies dealing with food issues—the World Food Council, the lacklustre FAO and the World Food Programme—should be merged

[22] Neuhaus, M. E. K., 'The United Nations' security role at fifty—the need for realism', *Australian Journal of International Affairs*, vol. 49, no. 2 (Nov. 1995), p. 279.

[23] Sheridan, M., 'UN seeks deal for new Boutros term', *The Independent*, 24 Jan. 1996, p. 10.

[24] Childers with Urquhart (note 5), pp. 189–90.

[25] *Our Global Neighbourhood* (note 5), p. 346.

[26] Suchocka, H., 'The United Nations in its second half-century: the report of the Independent Working Group on the Future of the United Nations', *Polish Quarterly of International Affairs*, vol. 4, no. 1, (1995), p. 68.

[27] Declaration on the Occasion of the Fiftieth Anniversary of the United Nations (note 2), para. 14.

[28] Power (note 16), p. 238.

into one. UNIDO, a particularly poor performer, should be abolished. The USA served notice in late 1995 that it was leaving the organization, although as previously witnessed in the case of UNESCO this does not automatically bring about the demise of a UN agency.[29] A number of countries, including the USA and the UK, have also called for the abolition of UNCTAD, which has never lived up to its promise. Its trade functions could now be given to the World Trade Organization (WTO), which replaced the temporary GATT Agreement in January 1995, and its development functions to UNDP. This would be contested by the developing states which urged the establishment of UNCTAD as a lead agency for promoting their ill-fated New International Economic Order (NIEO) and have regarded it as 'their' agency ever since. Trade-offs will need to be made to ensure their assent.

As for humanitarian emergencies, real coordinating authority for providing relief and marshalling the appropriate resources should be given to the Under-Secretary General for Humanitarian Affairs as was intended when the post was created in 1992. The original appointee, Jan Eliasson of Sweden, resigned in frustration at the lack of authority and resources his office had been given.[30]

Other UN organizations have also outlived their usefulness. With the achievement of independence in 1994 of Palau, the last UN trusteeship, the Trusteeship Council has lost its *raison d'être* and should be abolished. Alternatively it could be given responsibility for nurturing so-called 'failed' states like Somalia back to health, but this would require amendment of the Charter, which currently forbids the UN to adopt sovereign UN member-states in this fashion.[31] It might also smack too much of paternalism to be swallowed by the developing states. Another role for the Trusteeship Council might be to keep a watch on the last of the dependent territories, scattered remnants of empire like New Caledonia, that have yet to achieve independence. Other small UN bodies deserve the axe. A particularly useless one is the Ad Hoc Committee on the Indian Ocean, which feebly attempts to address a lost and forgotten cause—demilitarization of the Indian Ocean—with outdated concepts and an unrepresentative membership.

Substantial institutional reform will require leadership from Boutros Boutros-Ghali (who has demonstrated fluctuating reformist zeal up to now) and his agency heads (some of whom stand to lose their jobs or their influence), the Permanent Five members of the Security Council and the biggest financial contributors—the EU states, the Nordic countries, Canada, Japan and the USA. It has never been achievable before and will be extraordinarily difficult now. Both piecemeal and grand reforms have been proposed in the past, for instance by the Nordic countries and by special internally inspired reports on the UN system,[32] but they have never had concerted political support, either from the reform-inclined Western group or others. Developing country majorities have stifled reform proposals because of fear that the UN, which they see as helping them redress global political and economic power imbalances stacked against them, might be subverted. Drastic reform is, however, made more likely with the end of the cold war and the collapse of its attendant power blocs, a dramatic increase in the number of democratic states, especially in Latin America and southern Africa, the financial strictures currently affecting many countries both rich and poor,

[29] *Wireless File* (US Information Service, US Embassy: Stockholm), 5 Dec. 1995, p. 17.
[30] Righter (note 20), p. 293.
[31] Article 78, Charter of the United Nations.
[32] See, for instance, Sir Robert Jackson's *A Study of the Capacity of the UN Development System* UNDP/5 (United Nations: Geneva, 1969), which recommended a major overhaul of the UN system.

the increasing impatience of Western states with UN deficiencies, the emergence of East European states with reform-minded governments and, finally, a realization by the developing states that they have not been getting value for money. All these factors could make a difference this time.

Rosemary Righter warns that attempts to *negotiate* reform always end in failure since the opportunities for railroading, postponement of hard decisions and lowest common denominator politics increase exponentially.[33] The alternative (other than cosmetic reform) is for the UN's biggest financial contributors to wield the power of the purse systematically and ruthlessly. Useless agencies would be left to wither away while useful ones were strengthened. Most of the funding of the UN specialized agencies is voluntary so this is possible in their case. However, this would be confrontational and require solidarity and perseverance that the West probably does not have. It also has the major drawback, as the USA has discovered, that withholding funds may put a member state in a worse, not better, position to press for UN reform. In any event the negotiation of reform and the use of financial incentives or disincentives by the wealthiest states are not mutually exclusive. If the Western states bent on reform can convince enough of the now vastly expanded and very differently oriented UN membership that greater benefits will be forthcoming from a reformed UN, they may just carry the day. In any event, fundamental reform of the UN system is impossible without fundamental financial reform.

VI. Financial reform

Considering the breadth of its mandate and responsibilities the UN is a bargain: its central budget is less than that of the New York police and fire departments; its central offices employ fewer people than the city of Stockholm; and worldwide it has fewer employees than McDonalds. UN peacekeeping expenditure is less than 1 per cent of the estimated $868 billion in military spending by all the world's states combined.[34] Yet the UN is starved of cash and on the verge of insolvency. With no major income-generating capacity of its own, it is almost entirely dependent for revenue on the contributions of its member states, both compulsory assessed contributions and voluntary contributions.

The anniversary year was clouded by a worsening financial situation as the peacekeeping bill continued to rise, more member states fell behind in their payments and the UN's biggest debtor, the USA, slid further into arrears. As of 15 January 1996 unpaid assessments by member states totalled $3.3 billion, more than the annual running costs, including $1.6 billion for the regular budget and $1.7 billion for peacekeeping.[35] Also rising was the number of states (17, nearly 10 per cent of total UN membership, as of August 1995) whose arrears exceeded their assessed contributions for the past two years and which, under Article 19 of the UN Charter, were liable to lose their vote in the General Assembly. By 31 December only 94 member states had paid their regular budget contributions in full and 22 had made no payment at all.[36]

---

[33] Righter (note 20), p. 264.
[34] 'The future of the United Nations: an Australian perspective', address by Senator Gareth Evans, Minister of Foreign Affairs of Australia, to the Women's International Forum, New York, 21 Oct. 1995, p. 9.
[35] Goshko, J. M., 'To help ward off bankruptcy, UN may lay off more than 1,000 staff', *Washington Post*, 3 Feb. 1996.
[36] *Wireless File* (US Information Service, US Embassy: Stockholm, 31 Jan. 1996).

The USA, the largest contributor as well as the largest debtor, owed $1.4 billion. It fell further into arrears not only because the US Congress continued withholding due payments purportedly to force radical reform on the UN, but because the Administration, to appease congressional critics, unilaterally reduced the US share of the UN's peacekeeping expenses from 31 to 25 per cent as of 1 October.[37] The Clinton Administration, which opposes congressional attempts to decimate US contributions to the UN budget generally, estimated that by the end of US fiscal year 1996 the USA would owe $1.5–2 billion—43 per cent of the total UN debt.[38] This situation incurred scathing criticism from delegates to the General Assembly's 50th anniversary session, even from the USA's closest allies, especially since assessed contributions are a legally binding obligation. British Foreign Secretary Douglas Hurd scathingly called for no 'representation without taxation'.[39] The foreign ministers of the Nordic states—Denmark, Finland, Iceland, Norway and Sweden—declared that the unilateral withholding of assessed contributions was 'a clear violation of the obligations of member states'.[40] *The New York Times* labelled the USA the 'champion UN deadbeat'.[41] The USA of course could not be deprived of its vote without a major crisis and the UN is powerless to compel the USA to pay.

The USA is not the only defaulter, but others have rather more serious reasons: they include Iraq (in dispute with the UN), Russia (in the midst of economic reconstruction), South Africa (with a backlog inherited from the apartheid years),[42] Ukraine (desperately poor) and Yugoslavia (under UN sanctions and suspended from participation in UN bodies). Most of the 25 states with a 2-year backlog are poor developing states such as Burkina Faso, the Dominican Republic and Somalia.

The General Assembly's Group of Experts on the Principle of Capacity to Pay continued to wrangle over methodology. The scale of assessments has caused controversy for years. One problem is that countries that have become richer have not had their assessments increased accordingly. These include the Bahamas, South Korea, Qatar, Saudi Arabia, Singapore and the United Arab Emirates. Discounts for low-income countries adopted in 1974 had by 1994 almost wiped out China's assessment for the regular UN budget altogether, having reduced it from 5.5 per cent to 0.77 per cent.[43] At the lowest end of the scale the fixed minimum rate of assessment, designed to make all member states pay a minimum amount, had resulted in 27 small states paying more than their share of global income would indicate that they should pay. In 1995 the Marshall Islands, supported by six other South Pacific nations, attempted to garner support to abolish this, pointing out that the Marshallese pay $2.5 per person

[37] This unilateral move would produce a 'structural' deficit for the UN of approximately $300 million by the end of 1996. *Wireless File* (US Information Service, US Embassy: Stockholm), 23 Oct. 1995, p. 25.

[38] White House Press Release, 'US funding of the UN and other international organizations', 22 Oct. 1995, in *Wireless File* (US Information Service, US Embassy: Stockholm, 23 Oct. 1995, p. 25.

[39] *International Herald Tribune*, 1 Nov. 1995, p. 5.

[40] *International Peacekeeping News*, vol. 1, no. 12 (Oct. 1995), p. 23.

[41] Rosenthal, A. M., 'The champion UN deadbeat ought to be ashamed of itself', *New York Times*, republished in *International Herald Tribune*, 4 Oct. 1995, p. 8. Indignation was exacerbated by the fact that the 25% ceiling on the USA's contributions to the regular UN budget had for decades given it an effective discount compared with its share of global income, a shortfall made up by the Western European states and Canada. Laurenti, J., *National Taxpayers, International Organizations: Sharing the Burden of Financing the United Nations* (UN Association of the USA: New York, 1995), p. 31.

[42] At the end of 1995 the UN General Assembly voted to relieve South Africa of the dues incurred by it during the apartheid era.

[43] Laurenti (note 41), pp. 22 and 28.

per year to the UN, while the USA pays only 85 cents.[44] Opponents of abolition responded that such states make practically no voluntary financial contributions to UN activities while receiving substantial sums, such as development aid, from the multilateral system. Some argue, as Swedish Prime Minister Olof Palme once did, that as well as a lower limit there should also be an upper limit for any one contributor, such as the USA, in order to avoid 'blackmail'.[45]

The General Assembly's High-level Open-ended Working Group on the Financial Situation of the Organization failed to produce any agreed recommendations in 1995. Efficiency and cost-cutting measures currently being implemented will save some money. The new Under-Secretary for Administration and Management, Joseph Connor, former head of the US management firm Price Waterhouse, in 1995 became the first businessman ever to hold a senior administrative position at UN headquarters. Appointed in response to strong US pressure for UN managerial reforms, he immediately established an efficiency board charged with identifying during the next biennium further significant savings. In December the General Assembly took the radical step of adopting, for the first time in its history, a zero growth budget. The Secretary-General was also asked to identify additional savings of up to $100 million.[46] However much of Connor's time in 1995 was spent keeping the UN from insolvency through creative accounting, such as using funds earmarked for peacekeeping to pay for normal UN operating expenses. The new UN inspector, Under-Secretary General for Internal Oversight Services Karl Paschke, meanwhile revealed in his first report that his office had uncovered in less than a year $16 million lost to fraud, waste and abuse in the central UN system. He had not, however, found the UN to be a more corrupt organization than any comparable, sizeable public administration.[47]

Connor estimates that his creative accounting can, however, only carry the UN through 1996 before bankruptcy becomes a reality.[48] Cost-cutting and efficiency gains can, moreover, only go so far before beginning to bite into essential functions. Many UN activities are already pared to the bone. Staff cuts cannot be made because there are no funds for paying them off. Even drastic amalgamations of agencies, large-scale sackings and a major paring back of UN activity, while ultimately saving millions, would be slow and require large payments to effect. Finally, many of the reforms so far initiated affect only the central UN Secretariat and related agencies, not the specialized agencies. These agencies range from the reform-minded (some are way ahead of the UN Secretariat) to the stubbornly resistant.

Several long-term solutions to the UN's perennial financial difficulties have been suggested. One would be to borrow from commercial sources or the World Bank. UN bonds might be sold (this was done in the 1960s to raise funds for the Congo operation) or Special Drawing Rights accorded the UN through the World Bank. But as the UN as yet has no revenue-generating ability of its own, apart from sales of stamps and publications, this is a large financial risk. Connor has suggested 'selling' UN debt for a discounted cash amount to private intermediaries who would then take on the task of collecting from debtors. Other possibilities include 'global taxes' on military budgets (unlikely because of the lack of transparency of such budgets), international

---

[44] *International Report*, 9 June 1995, pp. 6 and 32.

[45] Childers with Urquhart (note 5), p. 153.

[46] *Wireless File* (US Information Service, US Embassy: Stockholm, 31 Jan. 1996.)

[47] Aita, J., 'Inspector identifies $16 million in misspent UN funds', *Wireless File* (US Information Service, US Embassy: Stockholm, 26 Oct. 1995), p. 16.

[48] Wren, C., 'The UN's financial juggler', *New York Times*, 8 Dec. 1995, p. D1.6.

financial transactions, petroleum and hydrocarbons, and air tickets.[49] These would be justified on the grounds that such activities depend fundamentally on the existence of peace and security. All of them face difficulties in achieving consensus, much less implementation. In the long run, however, the UN must be given some independent source of income if it is to avoid perpetual financial crises. Boutros-Ghali has called for a special session of the General Assembly in 1996 to consider the financial future of the UN.[50]

VII. The machinery of UN reform

Paradoxically, one of the stumbling blocks to UN reform is that the organization is using its existing flawed machinery, with its ponderous procedures and need to consider the views of all member states, to pursue reform. While this was inevitable, given the state-centric nature of the organization, it stands in stark contrast to the business world, where outside consultants are engaged whenever radical reorganizational changes are contemplated.

The chief means by which reform is being pursued is through ad hoc subsidiary bodies of the General Assembly. These bodies, some of them formed as long ago as 1992, spent 1995 gathering and dissecting a myriad of reform proposals but without reaching any conclusions.

In 1992 the Informal Open-ended Group on An Agenda for Peace was created to examine Boutros-Ghali's *An Agenda for Peace*, which contained proposals for extensive reform in the area of peace and security, some of them clearly ahead of their time.[51] In January 1995 he released a *Supplement to An Agenda for Peace* containing further proposals, many inspired by stark lessons drawn from the UN's previous three tumultuous years of preventive diplomacy, peacekeeping, peace making and peace enforcement.[52] These were still being considered as 1995 ended. In 1996 the Group will concentrate on the issues of preventive diplomacy and UN sanctions.

In 1993 the Assembly established the Open-ended Working Group on Membership of the Security Council. Although there were intense consultations in the group throughout 1995 and all permutations of Council reform were tabled and considered, no decisions were made.

In 1994 the Ad Hoc Open-ended Working Group of the General Assembly on An Agenda for Development was established, not to consider Boutros-Ghali's recommendations, of which there were surprisingly few, but to draw practical proposals

[49] 'The UN at fifty: looking back and looking forward', Statement to the Fiftieth General Assembly of the United Nations by Senator Gareth Evans, Foreign Minister of Australia, New York, 2 Oct. 1995, p. 10.

[50] UN, Interview with the Secretary-General of the United Nations, New York, UN document SG/SM/95/331, 18 Dec. 1995, p. 11.

[51] Boutros Boutros-Ghali, An Agenda for Peace: Preventive Diplomacy, Peacemaking and Peace-keeping, Report of the Secretary-General pursuant to the statement adopted by the Summit Meeting of the Security Council on 31 January 1992 (United Nations: New York, 1992), reproduced in *SIPRI Yearbook 1993: World Armaments and Disarmament* (Oxford University Press: Oxford, 1993), appendix 2A, pp. 66–80. For analyses see Hill, R., 'Preventive diplomacy, peace-making and peace-keeping', in the same volume, pp. 45–60; and Findlay, T., 'Multilateral conflict prevention, management and resolution', *SIPRI Yearbook 1994* (Oxford University Press: Oxford, 1994), pp. 14–19 and *passim*.

[52] UN, Supplement to an Agenda for Peace: position paper of the Secretary-General on the occasion of the 50th anniversary of the United Nations, UN document A/50/60, S/19951, 3 Jan. 1995. See chapter 2 in this volume for details. Excerpts from the text are reproduced in appendix 2B in this volume.

from the philosophical approach to development he outlined.[53] Also in 1994 a High-Level Open-ended Working Group on the Financial Situation of the Organization was convened to consider remedies for the UN's dire financial situation, especially assessments and arrears.

Finally, in September 1995, in the last days of the year's General Assembly session, a High Level Open-ended Working Group on the Strengthening of the United Nations System was inaugurated to review proposals to revitalize, strengthen and reform the UN system. It was mandated to report to the Assembly by 14 September 1996.[54]

This tangle of committees with overlapping membership and subject-matter clearly needed its own process of reform and rationalization. The President of the General Assembly in 1995, Diogo Freitas do Amaral of Portugal, chairman of all five working groups except that on the *Agenda for Peace* (chaired by Egypt), devised a coordinated plan of action to achieve this.[55] The working groups on the agendas for peace and development were to be considered as dealing with purposes and objectives, while the remaining three groups were considered to be dealing with 'ways and means'. Their work programmes would be structured accordingly to avoid overlap, and the groups 'interlinked' to facilitate coordination and complementarity and sustain progress in all of them. A common meeting timetable was agreed (they would all begin their substantive work on 15 January 1996), a trust fund was established to fund reform proposals and a schedule of topics to be dealt with was determined. Towards the end of 1996 the work of all the committees will be pooled to produce a global package for UN reform.

Meanwhile, the Special Committee on the Charter of the United Nations and on the Strengthening of the Role of the Organization, established as long ago as 1974, recommended just one reform measure in 1995: the deletion of those parts of Articles 53, 77 and 107 of the Charter which brand Germany, Italy and Japan and their World War II allies as 'enemy states' of the UN membership. By the end of the year the General Assembly had put in motion the procedure for securing this Charter amendment.[56] While these provisions were startlingly anachronistic in the 50th anniversary year, their justifiable deletion could hardly be labelled major UN reform.[57]

A harbinger of a much more significant reform came with the Assembly's decision in December to establish a Preparatory Committee to draft a widely acceptable convention for an International Criminal Court.[58] The establishment of such a court would obviate the need for convening ad hoc tribunals as in the cases of the former Yugoslavia and Rwanda to try suspects accused of committing gross human rights abuses, including genocide.[59]

The recommendations of all these committees will eventually be considered by the plenary of the General Assembly at its 1996 session. Reforms necessitating Charter amendment require a two-thirds majority of the Assembly and subsequent ratification

[53] UN, An Agenda for Development, Report of the Secretary-General, UN document A/48/935, 6 May 1994.
[54] *International Report*, 15 Sep. 1995, p. 1.
[55] Transcript of press conference by General Assembly President Prof. Diogo Freitas do Amaral, UN, Press Release GA/95/43, 21 Dec. 1995, pp. 3–4.
[56] UN, Press Release DH/2040, 11 Dec. 1995, p. 2.
[57] *UN Chronicle*, June 1995, p. 74.
[58] UN, Press Release DH/2040, 11 Dec. 1995, p. 2.
[59] For further details see chapter 2 in this volume.

by two-thirds of the UN membership, including the five permanent members of the Security Council. Other reforms may be implemented by decision of a majority of the Assembly. The specialized and other agencies will have their own problematic decision-making processes to go through in response to reform proposals that affect them.

VIII. Conclusions

In its first 50 years the UN saved millions of lives, clothed, fed and sheltered millions more, oversaw decolonization, kept the peace in war-torn situations, and helped resolve and prevent conflict in others. For its member states it has provided a talking shop, a scapegoat and a punching bag. It must be borne in mind that, as in the past, the future UN will only be as effective as its member states allow it to be. Formidable obstacles stand in the way of radical reform, including a lack of political will and financial constraints. None the less these constraints, whether of power, finance or bureaucratization, are all within the ability of member states to change. There is no dearth of creative ideas on the table. It remains to be seen in 1996 whether member states will have the political will to begin the reform process so urgently required.

3. The divided nations of China and Korea: discord and dialogue

BATES GILL*

I. Introduction

Five years into the post-cold war era and at the dawn of the 'Pacific Century', the bitter legacies of the cold war carry on in the discordant relations between mainland China and Taiwan and between North and South Korea.[1] These tense areas of potential conflict stand out as the greatest threats to regional stability in East Asia for the foreseeable future.

Developments in the first half of the 1990s have had a particularly profound influence on the divisive relations on the Korean peninsula and across the Taiwan Strait. On the one hand, there were the most hopeful developments to date regarding the resolution of these two disputes: new channels of dialogue and contact were established in the political, economic, humanitarian and cultural spheres. On the other hand, tensions continue to threaten a peaceful settlement of differences.

This chapter documents and analyses the ongoing processes of bilateral dialogue which have been initiated in China and Korea. The concluding section of the chapter comparatively analyses these dialogue processes, identifies the key successes and problems which they face, and suggests how these processes affect the prospects for regional stability.[2] The prospects for 'reunification' of Taiwan and mainland China and of North and South Korea remain an open question and are not directly addressed here. Furthermore, while recognizing the critical importance of third parties in influencing the outcome of settlements across the Taiwan Strait and in Korea, this chapter focuses largely on the bilateral aspects of these divisions.

---

[1] In this chapter, 'China' refers to the geographic entity encompassing the mainland of China and Taiwan. Similarly, 'Korea' refers to the geographic entity encompassing North and South Korea. As necessary, the chapter refers to 'mainland China' (People's Republic of China), 'North Korea' (Democratic People's Republic of Korea), 'South Korea' (Republic of Korea) and 'Taiwan'. The government on Taiwan uses the term 'Republic of China', but the 'Republic of China' is not recognized by the United Nations; as of 31 Dec. 1995, 31 countries recognize and conduct formal diplomatic relations with the Republic of China.

[2] Background information and references on historic and contemporary divisions and tensions in North-East Asia are found in Gill, B., 'North-East Asia and multilateral security institutions', *SIPRI Yearbook 1994* (Oxford University Press: Oxford, 1994), pp. 149–68.

* The author gratefully acknowledges the helpful research assistance of Kristina Han and Wu Yun in the preparation of this chapter.

II. Channels of dialogue on the Korean peninsula

Formally separated since the Korean Armistice Agreement of 1953, North and South Korea have remained militarily poised against one another and make the areas on either side of the demilitarized zone (DMZ) which divides the peninsula one of the most heavily militarized in the world. Trust is nearly absent in the relationship, and both sides take actions which undermine mutual confidence.

In spite of these constant and threatening animosities, the two sides achieved some slow progress in reconciliation in the first half of the 1990s and in 1994–95. Inter-Korean dialogue is a complex of bilateral relations and developments of which three aspects can be identified and examined: official, economic, and humanitarian and cultural contacts.

Official contacts

On 4 July 1972, North and South Korea published a seven-point communiqué agreeing to end hostility and to work together for peaceful reunification. However, owing to frequent disagreements this official channel of dialogue has often been suspended for long periods (e.g., from June 1973 to February 1979 and from December 1985 to August 1988). As a result of discussions initiated in August 1988, the two sides reached agreement to hold the first meeting between their prime ministers in September 1990.[3] These ministerial meetings—known as 'high-level talks'—proved to be the critical conduit for several breakthroughs in the North–South dialogue in 1991–92.

Inter-Korean accords

A significant breakthrough was reached in October 1991 at the fourth high-level talks when North and South Korea agreed to work on the first formal inter-Korean accords since 1972. As a result at the fifth round of high-level talks in Seoul, in December 1991, the two sides signed the Agreement on Reconciliation, Nonaggression, and Exchanges and Cooperation (the 'Basic Agreement'). The document was ratified by both sides and formally entered into effect in February 1992 at the sixth round of high-level talks, held in Pyongyang (see table 3.1). At that meeting the two sides also signed the North–South Joint Declaration on the Denuclearization of the Korean Peninsula. It declares that North and South Korea 'shall not test, manufacture, produce, receive, possess, store, deploy or use nuclear weapons'.[4] This agreement goes significantly beyond the commitments both governments made in the

---

[3] The text of the Agreement on Opening of the South–North High-Level Talks is found in *Intra-Korean Agreements* (National Unification Board: Seoul, Oct. 1992), pp. 55–60.
[4] Texts of the Basic Agreement and the Joint Declaration on the Denuclearization of the Korean Peninsula are found in *Intra-Korean Agreements* (note 3), pp. 3–9, 49–50.

Table 3.1. Summary of key articles in the Agreement on Reconciliation, Non-Aggression and Exchanges and Cooperation, 13 December 1991

Section/article	Article description
Section 1. Reconciliation	
Article 1	Mutual respect for political systems of one another
Article 2	Mutual non-interference in internal affairs of one another
Article 3	Agreement not to 'slander or vilify' one another
Article 4	Agreement not to 'sabotage or overthrow' one another
Article 5	Agreement to 'transform the present state of armistice regime into a solid state of peace' and to abide by the armistice until a state of peace is realized
Section 2. Non-aggression	
Article 9	Agreement not to use armed force nor armed aggression against one another
Article 12	Agreement to establish a Joint Military Committee to discuss and carry out military confidence-building and arms reduction measures
Section 3. Exchanges and Cooperation	
Article 15	Agreement to conduct economic exchanges and cooperation, including resource development, investment and trade
Article 16	Agreement to conduct exchanges and cooperation in a broad range of fields, including science, technology, education, culture, sports, and print and broadcast media
Articles 17–18	Agreement to permit free inter-Korean travel, correspondence, reunions and visits
Articles 19–20	Agreement to open transport links between each other, and to facilitate North–South post and telecommunication services

Source: *Intra-Korean Agreements* (National Unification Board: Seoul, Oct. 1992), pp. 3–7.

1968 Non-Proliferation Treaty (NPT)—which prohibits them from acquiring nuclear weapons—in that it bans the stationing of nuclear weapons in North and South Korea, forbids the production of fissile material in North and South Korea, and includes a potentially highly intrusive verification procedure. However, to date neither side has taken steps towards formally implementing this agreement.

With these accords in place a number of important steps were taken to improve dialogue and confidence. A Joint Nuclear Control Commission was established and held its first meeting in March 1992 to facilitate the implementation of the denuclearization declaration. The military, political and cooperative exchange subcommittees began holding regular meetings in March 1992. In May 1992, at the seventh round of high-level talks, the two sides formally established several working commissions: the Joint Military Commission, the Joint Commission for Economic Exchanges and Cooperation, and the Joint Commission for Social and Cultural Exchanges and Cooperation. In addition, at the May 1992 meeting government liaison offices were opened at the Panmunjom truce village in the DMZ, marking the first time that the two sides established official organizations to facilitate North–South contact.[5] In September 1992, at the eighth round of high-level talks, the two sides signed three auxiliary protocols intended to more specifically supplement the chapters of the Basic Agreement.

By the end of 1992, however, these channels for inter-Korean dialogue became increasingly strained and embroiled in broader issues. The North Korean threat to withdraw from the NPT in March 1993 brought an abrupt halt to North–South Korean dialogue. Subsequent efforts in 1994 to regenerate discussions included plans to hold the first-ever Korean presidential summit meeting. The planned July 1994 meeting between North Korean President Kim Il Sung and South Korean President Kim Young Sam promised an historic opportunity for reconciliation on the Korean peninsula. However, the summit meeting was cancelled and political talks between North and South Korea were suspended with the death of Kim Il Sung on 8 July 1994.

The Agreed Framework and KEDO

On 21 October 1994 the United States and North Korea signed an 'Agreed Framework' derived from an effort, in the words of the document, 'to negotiate an overall resolution of the nuclear issue on the Korean Peninsula'.[6] Articles 2 and 3 in Section 3 of the Agreed Framework state that North Korea 'will consistently take steps to implement the North–South Joint Declaration on the Denuclearization of the Korean Peninsula' and 'will engage in North–South dialogue, as this Agreed Framework will help create an atmosphere that promotes such dialogue.'

The Agreed Framework also stipulates that the USA will lead a project to build two light-water reactors (LWRs) for North Korea. While the accord explicitly states that the 'U.S., representing the international consortium, will serve as the principal point of contact' with North Korea on the LWR project, it is clearly the intention of the USA and South Korea that the LWR project serve as a conduit for North–South Korean exchange and dialogue. Indeed, from the outset of US–North Korean discussions to resolve the issue of North Korea's adherence to its NPT commitments, Washington insisted that progress on nuclear issues and normalization must be linked to good-faith efforts by Pyongyang to engage in dialogue with the South. South Korea supports this

---

[5] For a discussion of the establishment of the commissions and liaison office, see Yim Young-kyu (ed.), *Korea Annual 1992* (Yonhap News Agency: Seoul, 1992), pp. 90–95, 399–402. The texts of the agreements to establish the Joint Nuclear Control Commission, the Joint Military Commission, and the Joint Commissions for Exchanges and Cooperation, and the liaison offices are found in *Intra-Korean Agreements* (note 3), pp. 39–48, 51–54.

[6] Agreed Framework of 21 October 1994 between the United States of America and the Democratic People's Republic of Korea, IAEA document INFCIRC/457, 2 Nov. 1994. For analyses of the agreement, see chapter 13 in this volume; Davis, Z. and Donnelly, W., *The U.S.–North Korea 'Agreed Framework' to End North Korea's Nuclear Weapons Program* (Congressional Research Service: Washington, DC, 3 Aug. 1995); and Wilborn, T. L., *Strategic Implications of the U.S.–DPRK Framework Agreement* (Strategic Studies Institute US Army War College: Carlisle Barracks, Pa., 3 Apr. 1995). For in-depth studies detailing the development of the North Korean nuclear programme and the events related to the Agreed Framework, see Mazarr, M. J., *North Korea and the Bomb: A Case Study in Nonproliferation* (Macmillan: London, 1995); and Reiss, M., *Bridled Ambitions: Why Countries Constrain Their Nuclear Ambitions* (Woodrow Wilson Center: Washington, DC, 1995).

stance, but the North—fearful of absorption by the South and seeking greater international recognition, especially from Washington—hopes to radically improve ties with the USA while de-linking them from the issue of North–South Korean dialogue.[7] With the South expected to make the largest financial contribution to the Agreed Framework (approximately 70 per cent of the expected $4.5-billion cost for the two LWRs) and with clear political, economic and security interests at stake, Seoul seeks a central role in its implementation.

However, the issue of North–South dialogue is not explicitly linked to any steps undertaken or achieved within the Agreed Framework. Moreover, it is not explicitly stated in the Agreed Framework who will provide the LWRs, although the Clinton Administration understood that the LWRs would be acquired from South Korea. However, even before the Agreed Framework was signed North Korea refused for political reasons to accept a package which included South Korean LWRs. An 'international consortium' was created to act as the provider of the LWRs precisely to avoid this potential obstacle to progress. That international consortium—the Korean Peninsula Energy Development Organization (KEDO)—was formally established in March 1995. Article II (a) of the agreement establishing KEDO stipulates that the LWR project in North Korea is to consist of two reactors of the South Korean standard nuclear plant and that the Ulchin 3 and Ulchin 4 South Korean reactors are to be the reference models.[8]

After lengthy negotiations between the USA and North Korea in the spring of 1995, the two issued a joint press release on 13 June 1995 stating that the reactor model would be 'selected by KEDO', that it would be 'the advanced version of U.S.-origin design and technology' and that 'KEDO will select a prime contractor to carry out the project'.[9] On the same day, the KEDO Executive Board issued a resolution which noted the joint US–North Korean press statement and stated that 'KEDO will select a qualified firm from the Republic of Korea [South Korea] as prime contractor' for the LWRs project, and that KEDO should 'begin discussions with Korea Electric Power Corporation (KEPCO) in connection with the prime contract'. In addition, the resolution stated that KEDO would begin negotiations with North Korea to arrange necessary site surveys and continued implementation of the LWR project, and that KEDO delegations and teams would include 'nationals of each

---

[7] South Korean President Kim Young Sam noted in early Jan. 1994 that 'international inspections of suspected North Korean nuclear sites should be carried out simultaneously with inter-Korean dialogue'. 'Chronicle of selected events on security concerning Korea (October 1993 through March 1994)', *Korean Journal of Defense Analysis*, vol. 6, no. 1 (summer 1994), p. 288. However, in Apr. 1994 under pressure from Washington, which wished to resume high-level talks, the South dropped its insistence for a North–South exchange of presidential envoys as a precondition for those talks. 'Chronicle of selected events on security concerning Korea (April 1994 through September 1994)', *Korean Journal of Defense Analysis*, vol. 6, no. 2 (winter 1994), p. 367. See also Mazarr (note 6), p. 156.

[8] Ulchin 3 and Ulchin 4 are 2 nuclear power plants under construction in North Kyongsang Province, South Korea, set to begin operation in 1998 and 1999, respectively. 'Ulchin power plants set "Korean-standard"', *Korea Newsreview* (Seoul), 24 June 1995, p. 6. This plant model was originally developed and designed in the USA.

[9] 'Joint U.S.–North Korean press statement', 13 June 1995, reprinted in *Arms Control Today*, vol. 25, no. 6 (July/Aug. 1995), p. 26.

member country of the Executive Board'.[10] These twin statements created a situation in which North Korea accepted an LWR of US design but one which would be supplied by a South Korean contractor. Furthermore, it is intended that South Korea will be fully represented in all future dealings between KEDO and North Korea.

The LWR project serves as the centrepiece of KEDO's work in North Korea and will function as a principal point of contact between North and South Korea. KEDO is also tasked with financing and implementing heavy-oil shipments to North Korea totalling 500 000 tonnes (t) annually pending completion of the first LWR. In addition, KEDO is charged with the safe storage and eventual removal from North Korea of 8000 spent fuel rods located in a cooling pond at the Yongbyon nuclear facility. These responsibilities offer additional opportunities within the Agreed Framework to develop North–South ties and provide a long-term venue for official discussions with North Korea on the nuclear issue.

It is also possible that economic relations between the two Korean states might be enhanced with the provision by South Korean firms of certain 'accessory' services and facilities which North Korea has said it will require to fully implement the Agreed Framework. Such items might include road construction and other infrastructure improvements.

Economic and trade relations

North and South Korea share complementary advantages in trade and other economic relations, but the realities of politics have thus far hindered the full development of this aspect of their bilateral ties. Yet the nature of North–South economic relations cannot be seen as distinct from politics. Efforts by the South to create broader economic linkages are part of Seoul's long-term unification strategy to the extent that they contribute to the social, political and economic transformation of North Korea. For the North, economic relations with the South carry with them both the prospect of economic benefits and potentially enormous political disadvantages.

In recent years, particularly since 1991, inter-Korean trade has grown considerably, but numerous problems attend the relationship. Trade with the North remains a small portion of the South's overall trade. Since 1989, when trade relations between the two sides officially opened, the volume of two-way trade between North and South Korea has expanded more than thirteen-fold.[11] In the period 1989–94, North Korean exports to the South accounted for 93 per cent of the total bilateral trade. The value of total inter-Korean trade

---

[10] Korean Peninsula Energy Development Organization Executive Board Resolution 1995-12, 13 June 1995, reprinted in *Arms Control Today*, vol. 25, no. 6 (July/Aug. 1995), p. 26.

[11] Offers to open trade between North and South Korea were first officially made in statements by South Korean President Roh Tae Woo and Economic Planning Minister Rha Woong Bae in mid- to late 1988. See Lee Chung-moo, 'Nurturing friendly ties', *Korea Economic Report*, Nov. 1988, pp. 10–15.

Table 3.2. Inter-Korean trade, 1988–95*ᵃ*

Figures are in US $m. Figures in italics show per cent annual change over the previous year.

Year	North to South	Change	South to North	Change	Total trade	Change
1988	1.0	–	–	–	1.0	–
1989	22.2	*2044.1*	0.1	–	22.3	*2050.8*
1990	20.3	*– 8.5*	4.7	*6756.5*	25.1	*12.5*
1991	165.9	*715.1*	26.2	*453.3*	192.2	*666.1*
1992	200.7	*20.9*	12.8	*– 51.0*	213.5	*11.1*
1993	188.5	*– 6.1*	10.3	*– 19.9*	198.8	*– 6.9*
1994	203.5	*7.9*	25.4	*– 146.6*	228.9	*15.2*
1995	228.1	*12.1*	71.2	*180.3*	299.3	*30.7*
Total	**1 030.5**		**150.7**		**1 181.1**	

ᵃ Totals may not add up due to rounding.

Source: Adapted from *Nambookkyoryuhyopryok Donghyang* [North–South exchange and cooperation trends monthly], no. 54 (National Unification Board: Seoul, Dec. 1995), p. 19.

since 1989 was over $1 billion in 1995 (see table 3.2). This level of trade has made South Korea the North's third largest trading partner, after Japan and China.[12]

Perhaps more significantly for inter-Korean relations, in 1995 there was renewed interest in South Korean private investments in North Korea. This resulted from the decision by Seoul in November 1994 to end the two-year ban on direct business investment by the South in the North and to invigorate economic relations between the two states.[13] The first approval for direct investment under the new regulations came in May 1995, when the South Korean Government approved the plan by the Daewoo Corporation to invest $5.12 million to establish a joint venture with the North Korean Samchonri Group to build a textile factory in Nampo. Daewoo later won approval in June to send 13 engineers and technicians to North Korea to begin preparing for construction of the site. In June 1995 the Kukje Corporation gained approval to invest $3.5 million, and the Hanil Synthetic Fiber Industry Company was given approval to invest $5.8 million in North Korean projects.[14]

The unprecedented Daewoo venture marked the first time that an investment arrangement was completed between North and South Korea. In addition, the engineers and technicians from Daewoo were granted the first long-term residence permits given to South Koreans since 1953. Such arrangements will allow the extremely rare opportunity for non-North Koreans to work closely

[12] Jinwook Choi, 'Inter-Korean economic cooperation: a vital element of Seoul's unification policy', *Korean Journal of National Unification*, no. 4 (1995), p. 145.
[13] Burton, J., 'South Korea eases curbs on economic ties with North', *Financial Times*, 8 Nov. 1994, p. 18.
[14] 'DPRK OKs Southern firms', *China Daily*, 27 June 1995, p. A6, cited in *NAPSNet Daily Report*, Nautilus Institute, 27 July 1995, part 2, p. 2. One source notes that in 1992 'South Korea's Kolon Corp. began original equipment manufacturing . . . of knapsacks at a joint venture plant on the outskirts of Pyongyang in January this year [1992]'. See Kim Chong-tae, 'Perfect partners?', *Korea Economic Report* (Aug. 1992), p. 17.

with North Korean citizens—such contact is normally forbidden or carefully monitored by the North Korean Government.[15]

Since November 1994 South Korean investors have stepped up exploratory visits to the North in search of investment opportunities.[16] According to a poll by the South Korean Ministry of Trade, Industry and Energy, 62.6 per cent of small and medium companies queried in the South wish to invest in North Korea.[17] Some major corporations in South Korea have ambitious—as yet unrealized—plans for the North, such as the agreement reached in January 1992 between the Daewoo Corporation and North Korea to construct a large industrial zone in Nampo for South Korean manufacturing firms.[18]

North Korea has taken steps to facilitate and expand North–South economic relations. In September 1984 North Korea enacted its first Joint Venture Law, and in 1991 North Korea announced the opening of the Ranjin–Sonbong free economic and trade zone and has since encouraged potential South Korean and other investors to locate there.[19] In order to induce greater foreign investment in North Korea the Pyongyang Government promulgated a series of laws in 1992 and 1993, including regulations on joint ventures, taxation, foreign exchange control and free-trade zones.[20] However, by the end of 1995 this area had yet to attract much foreign investment, owing to the closed and uncertain nature of the North Korean system and competition from other attractive investment opportunities in East Asia. In 1984–93 the North attracted only $150 million for 140 foreign investment projects. Fully 90 per cent of the investments in these projects were made by members of the General Association of Korean Residents in Japan.[21]

The governments of North and South Korea, along with those of mainland China, Mongolia and Russia, formally signed an inter-governmental agreement for the joint development of the Tumen River Area Development Project (TRADP) on 6 December 1995. This multilateral development project—in

[15] On the Daewoo deal and its potential for North–South ties, see Shim Jae Hoon, 'Bridging the divide', *Far Eastern Economic Review*, 14 Sep. 1995, p. 63.

[16] 'Bizmen to visit NK's Sonbong', *Korea Times*, 20 Sep. 1995, p. 8, cited in *NAPSNet Daily Report*, Nautilus Institute, 20 Sep 1995, p. 3; 'Samsung to set up in N. Korea', *Financial Times*, 17 Jan. 1995, p. 4; 'Chung Ju-yung [honorary chairman of Hyundai Business Group] to resume business activities', *Korea Herald*, 20 Aug. 1995, p. 8, cited in *NAPSNet Daily Report*, Nautilus Institute, 21 Aug. 1995, p. 5; and Shim Jae Hoon, 'Dangerous deadlock', *Far Eastern Economic Review*, 22 June 1995, p. 50.

[17] The poll noted, however, that 89.1% of those preferred to wait until after 1997—watching North–South relations—before investing. 'Small firms eager to invest in NK in electronics, machinery after '97', *Korea Times*, 25 July 1995, cited in *NAPSNet Daily Report*, Nautilus Institute, 25 July 1995, part 1, p. 3.

[18] Kim Chong-tae (note 14), p. 16. South Korea's largest cement producer, the Ssangyong Group, wishes to set up a joint venture in North Korea, and the Samsung Group has expressed an interest in developing port construction and telecommunications projects in the North. See Shim Jae Hoon (note 15).

[19] 'Western companies eager to enter N. Korea', *Korea Times*, 22 Aug. 1995, p. 8, cited in *NAPSNet Daily Report*, Nautilus Institute, 22 Aug. 1995, p. 3.

[20] 'North Korean laws on foreign investment', 'The law on free economic and trade zone', 'Law on the leasing of land' and 'Enactment of laws and enforcement decrees for foreign investment', ed. Chong Bong-uk, *North Korea: The Land That Never Changes* (Naewoe Press: Seoul, 1995), pp. 230–45, 257.

[21] Young Namkoong, 'An analysis on management and results of North Korean policy to induce foreign capital', *RINU* [Research Institute for National Unification, Seoul] *Newsletter*, vol. 4, no. 2 (June 1995), p. 8. The General Association of Korean Residents in Japan is an organization with pro-North sympathies and close ties to the national government in Pyongyang.

which North and South Korea will act as partners—may contribute to better economic and political relations in North-East Asia and open the North Korean economy and society to greater outside influence. In addition to its five member countries, Japan and international organizations participate in TRADP as observers.[22] For both North and South Korea the short-term political implications of these economic ties are more important than potential long-term economic gains.

Humanitarian ties

In 1995 two devastating developments for the North brought great pressure on Pyongyang to tolerate more humanitarian ties with South Korea and with the international community. The first was the significant shortfall of grain production in the North—estimated to be 2.6 million t short of the 1995 requirement of 6.72 million t—owing to poor weather conditions.[23] The second was the extensive losses of life and property sustained during widespread flooding in North Korea in August 1995.

The rice talks

In June 1995, the chairman of North Korea's International Trade Promotion Committee stated in discussions with Japanese officials that North Korea would accept rice aid from South Korea if it were provided without political preconditions.[24] The South responded favourably and officials from both sides held the first round of 'rice talks' in Beijing beginning on 17 June 1995.

Agreement was reached on 21 June that South Korea would ship 150 000 t of rice to the North free of charge. In order to alleviate political sensitivities the agreement did not mention the names of the negotiators; the rice was to be shipped without indication as to its place of origin and the shipment was to be handled by the quasi-governmental Korea Trade-Investment Promotion Agency (KOTRA), rather than the South Korean Government.[25] The initial shipments were marred when North Korea required a South Korean ship delivering rice—the first to arrive under the agreement—to fly the North

[22] The Tumen River development project is located in the far north-east of the Korean peninsula where the Tumen River empties into the Sea of Japan and where the borders of China, North Korea and Russia converge. The project has evolved with the support of the United Nations Development Programme from an initiative first suggested by China in July 1990. Sejong Institute, *Tumen River Area Development Project: The Political Economy of Cooperation in Northeast Asia* (Sejong Institute: Seoul, 1995). For a critical perspective on the prospects for TRADP, see Noland, M., 'The North Korean economy', *Joint U.S.–Korean Academic Studies*, vol. 6 (1995).

[23] 'South to give North 150 000 tons of rice', *Korea Newsreview*, 24 June 1995, p. 4. North Korean government statistics report that the country's annual requirement for rice is 7.639 million tonnes, and that estimate for the 1995–96 crop (before the July/Aug. 1995 floods) was 5.665 million tonnes, a 1.974 million-tonne shortfall. The two estimates show a 25–38% shortfall of annual requirements. United Nations Department of Humanitarian Affairs, *Democratic People's Republic of Korea: Assessment of Damage and Immediate Relief Requirements Following Floods*, 12 Sep. 1995, as transcribed in *NAPSNet Daily Report*, Nautilus Institute, 18 Sep. 1995, parts 1 and 2.

[24] 'Seoul ready to provide P'yang with food grains', *Korea Newsreview*, 3 June 1995.

[25] 'South to give North 150 000 tons of rice' (note 23), p. 4.

Korean flag. After diplomatic *démarches*, rice shipments resumed in mid-July 1995.[26]

In the second round of talks, in mid-July, the North expressed interest in the possibility of South Korean investments in the Rajin–Sonbong special economic zone, and the two sides discussed improvements in shipping communications as well as further rice aid.[27] However, North Korea resisted South Korean efforts to link other issues to the rice talks, such as the detention of a South Korean fishing crew and trawler, the *Woosung No. 8*, held in North Korea since late May 1995. The third round of rice talks was intended to continue discussions on economic cooperation and rice aid, but it was cancelled by Pyongyang on 10 August as a result of another incident involving a South Korean ship delivering rice to the North. The ship and its crew were detained by North Korean authorities on the grounds that a crew member who photographed the port where the deliveries were made had engaged in spying activities. After negotiations the ship and its crew were released on 13 August.

The third round of talks was held in late September 1995, but no progress was made since the North wished to keep the discussions focused on the issue of rice shipments while the South tried to expand the agenda to consider other items. The two sides did not agree to hold a fourth round of talks, and the last delivery of the originally pledged 150 000 t of rice was made on 7 October 1995.[28] Even after the release of the crew of the *Woosung No. 8*, South Korea refused to discuss further rice aid until North Korea agreed to broader North–South dialogue at an official level.[29]

Owing to the fact that the 1995 rice talks represented the first official dialogue between North and South at any level since the death of Kim Il Sung in July 1994, they were appreciated more for their political than their humanitarian potential, particularly in South Korea.[30] South Korean negotiators sought to broach a number of issues in addition to rice aid, and the offer of further humanitarian assistance was explicitly linked to progress on the political front. In the words of South Korean Vice-Minister for Unification Song Young-dae,

---

[26] 'Rice aid to North Korea will go on as scheduled', *Korea Herald*, 11 July 1995, p. 2, cited in *NAPSNet Daily Report*, Nautilus Institute, 13 July 1995, p. 3.

[27] 'Issues other than rice aid to be tackled', *Korea Times*, 15 July 1995, p. 2; '"Rice talks" said to focus on a variety of issues', *Korea Herald*, 16 July 1995, p. 1; and 'South, North, discuss rice, other inter-Korean issues', *Korea Times*, 17 July 1995, p. 1 as cited in *NAPSNet Daily Report*, Nautilus Institute, 19 July 1995, p. 4.

[28] See note 27.

[29] Five crew members returned to South Korea on 26 Dec. 1995. The ashes of the remaining 3 crewmen—2 were killed during the ship's capture and one later died of illness—were also returned on that day. The ship was not returned. '5 in crew set free by North Koreans', *International Herald Tribune*, 23–25 Dec. 1995, p. 5; and 'Captives release fails to restart Seoul rice aid', *International Herald Tribune*, 28 Dec. 1995, p. 4.

[30] An analysis of the possible political and economic significance of the rice talks is offered in Choi Jin-wook, 'The meaning of South Korea's rice supply to the North', *RINU Newsletter*, vol. 4, no. 2 (June 1995), p. 9. See also Choi Nam-hyun, 'Food aid accord may serve as icebreaker in S–N talks', *Korea Newsreview*, 24 June 1995, p. 5; and 'Seoul seeks S–N economic panel at rice talks', *Korea Herald*, 14 July 1995, p. 1, cited in *NAPSNet Daily Report*, Nautilus Institute, 14 July 1995, part 1, p. 2.

'for additional rice assistance, there must be a change in North Korea's attitude toward us'.[31]

Flood relief

According to United Nations reports, widespread flooding in North Korea in July and August 1995 killed nearly 100 persons, left some 500 000 persons homeless and swept away an estimated 1.9 million t of food grains and 1.195 million hectares of crop land. The flooding also caused extensive damage to hospitals, clinics and schools, engendered the spread of disease, and destroyed portions of the national transport and communication infrastructure. In September Pyongyang estimated the cost of the flood damage at $15 billion.[32]

Reports of the disaster first came out of North Korea in mid-August,[33] and at the request of the North Korean Government a UN team led by the Department of Human Affairs arrived in North Korea to assess the damage on 29 August. The UN team was allowed access to three principal areas of North Korea in making its assessment from 29 August until 9 September.[34] It issued an appeal to the international community for $16 million worth of assistance.[35]

The official response of the South Korean Government to these appeals was muted at first. On 7 September 1995, the South Korean Vice-Prime Minister and Minister of Unification declined to offer aid to North Korea, citing the unresolved problem of the *Woosung No. 8*, persistently negative propaganda from the North and the turning of South Korean public opinion against the North. On 15 September Seoul announced that it would provide medicine, clothes and blankets worth $50 000 to the North through the South Korean Red Cross. This was a significant cut-back from the $2 million in aid which the Ministry of Unification initially sought from the South Korean Government. The position of the government did not preclude the assistance of private organizations, although the South Korean Minister for Unification said that 'it is inappropriate for large conglomerates to offer aid' with an eye to generating business contracts.[36] The South Korean Government preferred that

[31] Quoted in 'Captives release fails to restart Seoul rice aid', *International Herald Tribune*, 28 Dec. 1995, p. 4.

[32] An initial assessment of the flood damage is offered in United Nations Department of Humanitarian Affairs (note 23). With an estimated GNP of approximately $20 billion, the figure of $15 billion is considered extremely high.

[33] Reuter, 'Flood damage feared in food-shortage [*sic*] North Korea', 18 Aug. 1995, cited in *NAPSNet Daily Report*, Nautilus Institute, 20 Aug. 1995, p. 1.

[34] The areas were in North Hwanghae, North Pyongan and Chagang provinces, including areas on the Amnok river basin along the Chinese border near Sinuiju city, along the Chongchon river near Pakchon and Anju cities, and to the south of Pyongyang near Pongean Rinsan and Chonggye-ri cities. United Nations Department of Humanitarian Affairs (note 23).

[35] Office of the United Nations Resident Coordinator and United Nations Development Programme Resident Representative, 'Flood relief target within sight', *Press Release*, no. 3, 15 Sep. 1995 as transcribed in *NAPSNet Daily Report*, Nautilus Institute, 15 Sep. 1995, part 1, p. 1. A South Korean publication notes that North Korea requested some $491 million worth of aid from the United Nations. 'North Korean diplomats make all-out efforts to obtain foreign aid', *Vantage Point*, Oct. 1995, p. 17.

[36] Remarks attributed to Rha Woong-bae in 'KNRC to convey southern relief to NK', *Korea Times*, 15 Sep. 1995, p. 1, cited in *NAPSNet Daily Report*, Nautilus Institute, 19 Sep. 1995, part 1, p. 5.

the North make official government-to-government contact to discuss the issue, but such requests were not made in 1995.

At the end of 1995 it was too early to discern precisely what effect the flooding and subsequent international response would have on the further opening of North Korea. The fact that North Korea made the mid-August appeal and opened its doors to short-notice visits by international delegations and emergency teams marks a significant step towards broader possibilities for dialogue between North Korea and the international community. However, it appeared that the North would remain extremely cautious in opening up to the international community.

III. Channels of dialogue across the Taiwan Strait

Since the mid- to late 1980s, reformist policies in mainland China and on Taiwan have resulted in a dramatic lessening of restrictions on contacts across Taiwan Strait. In March 1991 the Straits Exchange Foundation (SEF) was formally established on Taiwan as a nominally unofficial body to handle cross-Strait ties with the mainland. In December 1991 Beijing established the Association for Relations Across the Taiwan Straits (ARATS) with the aim of establishing a semi-official conduit for dialogue with Taiwan. As a result of these policies, the two sides have increased semi-official, economic and cultural ties with one another.

In 1995 the dialogue between mainland China and Taiwan experienced both encouraging progress and problematic set-backs. In early 1995 leaders in mainland China and those on Taiwan issued conciliatory statements that set out broad parameters for peaceful unification. In addition, economic relations between the two sides continued to experience considerable growth. However, this goodwill diminished in the wake of a June 1995 private visit by Taiwan's President Lee Teng-hui to the United States. Following that visit, high-level and working-level talks between ARATS and SEF were suspended, and political and military tensions rose to volatile levels.[37]

Semi-official dialogue

The ARATS–SEF talks

From both a symbolic and practical point of view, the most important recent development for cross-Taiwan Strait relations was the establishment in 1991

[37] This controversy is rooted in the fundamental differences of the 2 sides over the issue of Taiwan's political status. The mainland holds that Taiwan is an integral and subordinate part of the People's Republic of China. The government on Taiwan holds that Taiwan is a part of China, but that it currently possesses a separate identity as a 'political entity' equal to that of the mainland. All governments having official relations with mainland China accept Beijing's 'one-China' principle, and the mainland condemns efforts which may lead to a broader interpretation of Taiwan's political status. Official policies for cross-Strait relations for Taiwan and China are set out, respectively, in Mainland Affairs Council, *Relations Across the Taiwan Straits* (Mainland Affairs Council: Taipei, July 1994) and Taiwan Affairs Office and Information Office, *The Taiwan Question and Reunification of China* (State Council: Beijing, Aug. 1993).

of ostensibly private agencies—SEF and ARATS—to carry out semi-official dialogue across the Taiwan Strait. SEF is funded in part (approximately two-thirds) by the government on Taiwan and in part (approximately one-third) by private support, and is overseen by a government agency, the Mainland Affairs Council (MAC). Koo Chen-fu, head of the National Association of Industry and Commerce and a member of the Central Standing Committee of the KMT, is its chairman. The chairman of ARATS, Wang Daohan, was formerly mayor of Shanghai. These two leaders first met in Singapore for the ground-breaking Koo-Wang talks in April 1993, and by the end of 1995 a total of 11 rounds of ARATS–SEF meetings had been held—7 rounds at the working level and 4 rounds at the vice-chairman level (see table 3.3).

Four agreements were signed as a result of the first Koo-Wang talks.[38] In practical terms, these agreements set the framework for future discussions between the two sides, created a channel through which matters of urgency could be handled more effectively, and set out basic rules concerning the authentication of documents and the handling of registered mail deliveries. In a Joint Statement the two sides also agreed to 'definitely hold' discussions before the end of 1993 on five topics: repatriation of illegal immigrants, joint efforts to suppress criminal activities in the Taiwan Strait, handling of fishery disputes, protection of intellectual property, and mutual assistance to judicial organs. In addition, in the Joint Statement the two sides agreed to work together on enhancing economic cooperation and to promote mutual exchanges of young people, members of the press, and science and technology personnel. The meeting also kept discussions narrowly focused on practical and functional matters, avoiding political rhetoric or exchanges. Most importantly, the meeting had the symbolic value of demonstrating the good faith of both sides to enhance mutual confidence through dialogue.[39]

At the first round of talks held after the Koo-Wang meeting, however, the two sides were unable to reach agreement on the agenda of future talks. In addition to the five 'definite' discussion points set out in the Joint Statement, ARATS also raised such issues as opening the Taiwan labour market to mainland workers, loosening Taiwan restrictions on investments in the mainland and convening a joint economic conference, all of which SEF refused to discuss as being outside the original Koo-Wang agenda agreed in April 1993. In this sense the mainland efforts to expand and deepen the negotiating agenda beyond 'technical issues' were similar to those by South Korea to broaden discussions with the North. The issuance at this time of the mainland China White Paper on Taiwan—which was viewed by many on Taiwan as a tough-worded and inflexible document—probably also contributed to the lack of progress at the talks. Following the Koo-Wang meetings a second round of

---

[38] For a full discussion of the first Koo-Wang meeting, see Koo Chen-fu, *A Résumé of the Koo-Wang Talks* (Straits Exchange Foundation: Taipei, Dec. 1993), pp. 17–18.

[39] A detailed review and analysis of the Koo-Wang process up to Sep. 1993 is offered in Hungdah Chiu, 'The Koo-Wang talks and intra-Chinese relations', *American Journal of Chinese Studies,* vol. 2, no. 2 (Oct. 1994), pp. 219–62.

Table 3.3. ARATS–SEF meetings, 1993–95[a]

Date	Description
25–27 Mar. 1993	Working-level preparatory meeting held in Beijing for first Koo-Wang talks
11 Apr. 1993	Vice-chairman preparatory meeting held in Beijing for first Koo-Wang talks
25–26 Apr. 1993	Vice-chairman preparatory meeting held in Singapore for first Koo-Wang talks
27–29 Apr. 1993	First Koo-Wang talks held in Singapore between chairman of ARATS Wang Daohan and the chairman of SEF Koo Chen-fu
30 Aug.–3 Sep. 1993	First working-level meeting held in Beijing between deputy secretary general of ARATS Sun Yafu and deputy secretary general of SEF Shi Hwei-you
2–7 Nov. 1993	Second working-level meeting held in Xiamen between deputy secretary general of ARATS Sun Yafu and deputy secretary general of SEF Shi Hwei-you
18–22 Dec. 1993	Third working-level meeting held in Beijing between deputy secretary general of ARATS Sun Yafu and deputy secretary general of SEF Shi Hwei-you
31 Jan.–5 Feb. 1994	First vice-chairman meeting held in Taipei between vice-chairman of ARATS Tang Shubei and vice-chairman of SEF Chiao Jen-ho
25–31 Mar. 1994	Fourth working-level meeting held in Beijing between deputy secretary general of ARATS Sun Yafu and deputy secretary general of SEF Shi Hwei-you
31 July–3 Aug. 1994	Fifth working-level meeting held in Taibei between deputy secretary general of ARATS Sun Yafu and deputy secretary general of SEF Shi Hwei-you; first meeting since suspension of talks following Qiandao Lake incident, 31 March 1994
4–7 Aug. 1994	Second vice-chairman meeting held in Taipei between vice-chairman of ARATS Tang Shubei and vice-chairman of SEF Chiao Jen-ho
22–27 Nov. 1994	Sixth working-level meeting held in Nanjing between deputy secretary general of ARATS Sun Yafu and the deputy secretary general of SEF Shi Hwei-you
21–27 Jan. 1995	Seventh working-level meeting held in Beijing between deputy secretary general of ARATS Sun Yafu and deputy secretary general of SEF Shi Hwei-you
21–27 Jan. 1995	Third vice-chairman meeting held in Beijing between vice-chairman of ARATS Tang Shubei and vice-chairman of SEF Chiao Jen-ho
27–29 May 1995	Fourth vice-chairman meeting held in held in Taipei between vice chairman of ARATS Tang Shubei and vice-chairman of SEF Chiao Jen-ho
16 June 1995	Beijing suspends ARATS–SEF meetings in response to visit to the USA by Lee Teng-hui

[a] Technical and vice-chairman meetings taking place in accordance with agreement reached at the first Koo-Wang talks of 27–29 April 1993 are ordered numerically following that date.

Sources: Various issues of *Beijing Review*, *Far Eastern Economic Review*, *Financial Times*, *Free China Journal* and *International Herald Tribune*.

talks took place in November 1993, but the two sides were again unable to reach significant agreement.[40]

In 1994 a total of 5 ARATS–SEF meetings were held: 3 technical meetings, and 2 meetings at the vice-chairman level. Very little of promise emerged from the meetings. At the technical-level meetings on 31 July–2 August 1994, the two sides reached a minor agreement: that if air hijackers are returned to mainland China they will receive credit for time served in imprisonment in Taiwan. At the vice-chairman level meeting in early August 1994, the two sides reached 'consensus' on the importance of several issues:[41] enhancing contacts and keeping each other informed in times of tension; finalizing a draft for signing 'as soon as possible' on the issues of illegal entrants, repatriation of mainland hijackers and fishery disputes; verifying documents; improving cross-Strait mail and telephone communications; handling matters related to inheritances; and expanding economic, cultural and technological exchanges. Subsequent technical meetings in November and vice-chairmen meetings in January 1995 to work out the precise details of the draft agreements failed to reach an accord.

As a result of these failures, interest was generated on both sides to upgrade the level of the talks once again to the vice-chairman level and to hold another Koo-Wang meeting in 1995. In 1995 speculation grew that the second Koo-Wang talks would focus on 'two tiers': mutual concerns (e.g., illegal entrants, trade and economic exchanges) and 'mainland–Taiwan policies'.[42] However, following Lee's visit to the USA, on 16 June 1995 all technical and high-level talks between ARATS and SEF were suspended by Beijing in protest.

Tension mounted in the summer of 1995 as China staged military exercises and missile tests in July and August in waters approximately 145 km north of Taiwan and expressed through discrete channels its intention to conduct several more exercises running up to the 23 March 1996 first democratic presidential elections on Taiwan. Taiwan countered with war games of its own in July, and comments in the summer of 1995 by Taiwan's leadership suggested the possibility of Taiwan studying the development of nuclear weapons.[43]

Under these conditions, statements issued by officials from both sides were understandably cautious about the prospects for restarting the cross-Strait dialogue. ARATS vice-chairman Tang Shubei expressed his dissatisfaction with the talks on 19 September, saying that there was no point in holding ARATS

[40] 'China and Taiwan fail to make headway', *International Herald Tribune*, 8 Nov. 1993, p. 7.

[41] Joint Press Release by the Straits Exchange Foundation and the Association for Relations Across the Taiwan Straits, 8 Aug. 1994, provided to SIPRI by the Straits Exchange Foundation.

[42] Su Chi, 'Second Koo-Wang talks appear set for summer', *Free China Journal*, 12 May 1995, p. 1; and 'Across Straits summit scheduled', *Beijing Review*, 19–25 June 1995, p. 4.

[43] Richburg, K. B., 'In new show of force, China fires missiles near Taiwan', *International Herald Tribune*, 16 Aug. 1995, p. 4; 'Taipei opens rival war games', *International Herald Tribune*, 26 July 1995, p. 4; Tyson, L., 'Taiwan may revive nuclear weapons defence programme', *Financial Times*, 30 July 1995, p. 24; Murphy, K., 'Taiwan dusts off nuclear threat in its dispute with Beijing', *International Herald Tribune*, 29–30 July 1995, p. 1; and Faison, S., 'Taiwan reports nearby firing of 4 test missiles by China', *New York Times*, 24 July 1995, p. A2.

Table 3.4. Key points of unification speeches by Jiang Zemin and Lee Teng-hui, 1995

Jiang Zemin's eight points	Lee Teng-hui's six points
1. Adherence to 'one China' principle	1. Pursuit of reunification based on the reality that two sides are governed by two different governments
2. Allow non-governmental economic and cultural ties with Taiwan	
3. Hold negotiations with Taiwan on peaceful reunification of China	2. Strengthen bilateral ties based upon Chinese culture
4. Chinese should not fight fellow Chinese	3. Improve the bilateral economic and trade ties
5. Expand economic exchange and cooperation between Taiwan and the mainland	4. Allow both sides to join international organizations on an equal basis, and ensure that leaders from both sides meet in a natural setting
6. The two sides should jointly carry forward and enhance the tradition of Chinese culture, an important basis for reunification	
7. Extend respect to and strengthen ties with Taiwan-based compatriots	5. Adhere to principle of peaceful settlement of disputes
8. Leaders from Taiwan are welcome to visit China in appropriate capacities, China prepared to accept invitations to visit Taiwan	6. Jointly ensure prosperity and democracy for Hong Kong and Macao

Sources: Jiang Zemin, 'Continue to promote the reunification of the motherland', in British Broadcasting Corporation, *Summary of World Broadcasts: Far East*, FE/2215, 31 Jan. 1995 pp. G/1–G/4; and Lee Teng-hui, 'Address to National Unification Council', 8 Apr. 1995, transcript in English made available to SIPRI by the Straits Exchange Foundation.

and SEF consultations as long as the 'one-China' position was not upheld by the Taiwan side. Tang reiterated this point on 20 December, noting that the talks could not resume until Taiwan accepted the mainland's version of the one-China policy, that is, 'one China, two systems', as opposed to the Taiwan approach of 'one China, two equal political entities'.

By the end of 1995 there was little enthusiasm for the talks. In their new year's messages for 1996, Jiang Zemin, President of the People's Republic of China and General Secretary of the Chinese Communist Party, and Lee Teng-hui expressed their desire to restart semi-official dialogue. While these statements indicated some willingness on both sides to renew the dialogue, such talks were likely to be postponed until after the presidential elections on Taiwan.

The Jiang and Lee proposals

In 1995 the political leaders of China and Taiwan issued important declarations regarding unification. On 30 January 1995, Jiang Zemin gave an eight-point message on reunification, and on 8 April 1995 Lee Teng-hui offered a six-point response (see table 3.4). These exchanges had several points of agreement—regarding economic exchanges and advancing Chinese culture—

but there continued to be disagreement on the critical question of Taiwan's status.

On a number of occasions since late 1994 the two leaders have expressed a willingness to meet, raising the possibility of a cross-Strait summit meeting. In October 1994 in an interview with the *Asian Wall Street Journal,* Lee said that it might be possible to meet with Jiang at an international venue. Jiang was quoted twice in late 1994 as saying that he wished to meet with Lee. During the late January 1995 ARATS–SEF meeting in Shanghai, ARATS chairman Wang Daohan told visiting SEF vice-chairman Chiao Jen-ho that Jiang was willing to meet Lee 'at any time and under any conditions agreed to by both sides'.[44] In Jiang's eight-point speech, he also declared that the 'leader of the Taiwan authorities' was welcome to visit the mainland in an 'appropriate status' and that he would welcome an invitation to Taiwan.

Mainland China wishes to establish talks which are clearly aimed at reunification and has pushed strongly for high-level talks—either between the ARATS and SEF chairmen or between Jiang and Lee—as it hopes that such meetings will get beyond 'technical issues' to discussion of unification. Taiwan, on the other hand, seeks to keep discussions focused on technical and non-political issues so as to build confidence and not rush reunification talks. The mainland's official policy remains centred on the achievement of reunification and the prevention of independence or the permanent separation of Taiwan. Reunification is a goal of official Taiwan policy, but the differences between the two political and economic systems must be acknowledged and addressed before reunification can proceed. Prior to agreement on these issues the question of Taiwan's diplomatic and political status *vis-à-vis* the mainland must be resolved. It is on this fundamental difference that cross-Strait political dialogue has foundered.

Economic relations

One of the most prominent features of recent cross-Strait relations is the enormous growth in economic activity between Taiwan and mainland China. Indeed, in spite of heated political rhetoric and military-related manoeuvres in the Taiwan Strait the two sides have enjoyed considerable growth in their economic relationship (see table 3.5).

The relationship is largely a one-way street, with Taiwan exports and investments in mainland China far outweighing such economic activity in the other direction. Trade grew some 30 per cent or more per year in the first half of the 1990s. In the first five months of 1995 trade grew nearly 40 per cent over the same period in 1994, for a total of $8.7 billion during this period. By mid-1995 trade had reached $10.43 billion, and estimates placed the 1995 total at between 17 and 21 billion.[45] According to figures released in 1995 China had

---

[44] 'No accord as cross-Straits talk ends', *Free China Journal*, 10 Feb. 1995, p. 2.
[45] 'Aufstieg Chinas zur zehntgrössten Handelsmacht' [The rise of China to the tenth largest trade power], *Neue Zürcher Zeitung*, 16 Jan. 1996, p. 11; Zhang Tien and Zheng Liedong, 'Taiwan–Mainland

Table 3.5. Cross-Taiwan Strait trade, 1986–95[a]

Figures are in US $m. Figures in italics show per cent annual change over the previous year.

Year	Taiwan to mainland	Change	Mainland to Taiwan	Change	Total trade	Change
1986	811.3	–	144.2	–	955.6	–
1987	1 226.5	*51.2*	288.9	*100.3*	1 515.5	*58.6*
1988	2 242.2	*82.8*	478.7	*65.7*	2 720.9	*79.5*
1989	2 869.5	*28.0*	586.9	*22.6*	3 456.4	*27.0*
1990	3 278.3	*14.2*	765.4	*30.4*	4 043.6	*17.0*
1991	4 667.2	*42.4*	1 126.0	*47.1*	5 793.1	*43.3*
1992	6 287.9	*34.7*	1 119.0	*– 6.2*	7 406.9	*27.9*
1993	7 585.4	*20.6*	1 103.6	*– 1.4*	8 689.0	*17.3*
1994	8 517.2	*12.3*	1 292.3	*17.1*	9 809.5	*12.9*
1995[b]	9 794.8	*15.0*	1 486.1	*15.0*	11 280.9	*15.0*
Total	**47 280.3**		**8 391.1**		**55 671.3**	

[a] Totals may not add up due to rounding.
[b] Figures for 1995 are estimated.

Source: Adapted from *Liangan Jingji Tongji Yuebao* [Cross-Strait economic statistics monthly], no. 37, Sep. 1995, p. 19.

become Taiwan's second-largest export market. It is likely that there is a great deal more trade being conducted than is officially reported.[46]

Taiwan is estimated to be the second-largest investor in the mainland after Hong Kong and in late 1994 was estimated to have invested nearly $20 billion in some 26 000 projects.[47] In the first 10 months of 1995 Taiwan-based entrepreneurs invested $5.58 billion in new mainland projects.[48] When Hong Kong is turned over to China in mid-1997 Taiwan is likely to become the largest source of investment outside the mainland.[49]

By the end of 1995 a number of factors contributed to a slight slowdown in the growth of investment and trade between the two sides. Perhaps most important were the intensified political and military tensions following Lee's visit to the USA in June 1995. Second, Beijing took steps in April 1995 to tighten regulations on foreign investment and began to impose an incremental tax on imports.[50] The development of two-way trade and investment is also

trade jumps despite cooling relations', *China News Digest Global News*, 2 Aug. 1995, p. 2; Her, K., 'Trade with mainland rising sharply', *Free China Journal*, 4 Aug. 1995, p. 3; and Shen, D., 'Taiwan–mainland trade ties increase in first half of year', *Free China Journal*, 8 Sep. 1995, p. 8.

[46] Tyler, P. E., 'In the mists of Taiwan, a war is ending', *International Herald Tribune*, 5 Oct. 1995, p. 1.

[47] Ren Xin, 'Mainland, Taiwan economic ties enhanced', *Beijing Review*, 13–19 Mar. 1995, p. 16.

[48] Shen, D., 'Record trade with the mainland in 1995', *Free China Journal*, 6 Jan. 1996, p. 3.

[49] The island of Hong Kong was ceded to the United Kingdom 'in perpetuity' according to the 1842 Treaty of Nanjing between the UK and China. The 'New Territories' on the mainland of China opposite Hong Kong island and islands adjoining the New Territories, were 'leased' to the UK for 99 years beginning in 1898. By agreement between China and the UK in Aug. 1984 the UK agreed to restore sovereignty of Hong Kong to China on 1 July 1997, the expiry date of the New Territories' lease.

[50] Shen, D., 'Mainland's war games impede cross-Straits business activities', *Free China Journal*, 15 Dec. 1995, p. 3.

hampered by policies on both sides which continue to hinder postal, transport and trade links. Official Taiwan policy prohibits direct transport and trade ties. In addition, owing to concerns about over-dependence on the mainland, the government on Taiwan has encouraged a 'go south' strategy for investors to develop links with South-East Asia. As a result, while trade continues to grow, the pace of growth slowed from 30–40 per cent at the beginning of 1995 (compared to the same period in 1994) to approximately 15 per cent by the end of 1995.

As in the case of North and South Korea, it appears that economic exchanges and development present a promising avenue to assist in peaceful settlement of differences between mainland China and Taiwan. Both Jiang and Lee emphasized the importance of economic exchanges in their 1995 speeches on reunification. Taiwan's entrepreneurs could make significant economic gains from investing on the mainland, while simultaneously laying the groundwork for the building of mutual confidence and trust between the two sides. In the long term the economic development of the mainland is in the interest of Taiwan to the degree it can raise the standard of living on the mainland, introduce and spread free-market principles, and assist in establishing an atmosphere more conducive to the peaceful resolution of differences. China will also gain from investment and trade with Taiwan and aims to link Taiwan more closely to the mainland through economic means.

Cultural and people-to-people exchanges

In recent years there has been remarkable growth in cross-Strait channels of dialogue in the areas of cultural and people-to-people ties.[51] Prior to the mid-1980s tight restrictions both in the mainland and on Taiwan made these kinds of relations extremely difficult and rare. It was not until November 1987 that Taiwan first allowed a partial lifting of the ban on cross-Strait travel. Even under the November 1987 travel law, government employees and people in other professions concerned with 'security', as broadly defined, were not allowed to travel to the mainland, and prospective travellers needed first to apply to the Taiwan Red Cross. Nevertheless, a total of 6000 persons from Taiwan travelled to the mainland in the first half of November 1987. One year later Taiwan loosened the restrictions to allow mainlanders to enter Taiwan to visit sick family members or to attend funerals of relatives. Almost one million visitors from Taiwan travelled to mainland China in 1990; in 1987–92 the figure was more than 4.2 million, with approximately 40 000 mainland visitors going to Taiwan in the six-year period. By the end of 1995 an estimated 7 million visitors had travelled from Taiwan to the mainland.[52] According to

---

[51] For this section, see the chronologies offered in 'Cross-Straits chronology, 1987–1995', *Free China Review*, Aug. 1995 pp. 24–25; and Chi Huang and Wu, S. S. G., 'Inherited rivalry: a chronology', eds Tun-jen Chung *et al.*, *Inherited Rivalry: Conflict Across the Taiwan Straits* (Lynne Reinner: Boulder, Colo., 1995), pp. 229–60. See also Hungdah Chiu (note 39); and Chen Qiuping, 'From confrontation to communication', *Beijing Review*, 6–13 June 1993, pp. 16–17.

[52] Information provided to SIPRI by the Taipei Mission in Sweden, Feb. 1996.

mainland Chinese statistics, in 1995 alone 1.53 million trips were made by Taiwan tourists to the mainland, an increase of 10.3 per cent over 1994.[53]

Cultural exchanges also began to accelerate in this period. The mainland allowed the first Taiwan-based journalists on reporting assignments to enter China in September 1987 (in defiance of a ban on such visits by Taiwan). In April 1989 Taiwan began to allow its reporters to travel to the mainland and to gather information there, and in August 1990 the first mainland reporters were allowed into Taiwan (although the mainland reporters were required to renounce their membership in the Chinese Communist Party before entering Taiwan). In November 1988 Taiwan began to allow entry to mainland artistic performers and, beginning in December 1988, mainland theatre plays written after 1949 were permitted to be staged in Taiwan. In July 1992 the first visit by leading Taiwan-based scientists to the mainland took place, and the first contact between legal officials on the two sides occurred at a conference in August 1993. The pace and scope of cultural, professional, youth and sports exchanges were stepped up as a further result of the Koo-Wang process inaugurated in April 1993, which specifically reached consensus on the promotion of such activities as conducive to building mutual confidence and understanding. In January 1994 the official Taiwan Mainland Affairs Council established a $2 million fund to support cross-Strait cultural and academic exchange activities.

The two sides reached a humanitarian breakthrough in September 1990 when their respective Red Cross societies signed the Quemoy Agreement on the Strait island of Quemoy to govern the repatriation of illegal immigrants. This agreement was the first such accord between the two sides. By 1993, under the Quemoy Agreement, some 24 000 illegal immigrants were returned to the mainland from Taiwan through the Red Cross societies.[54] The establishment of ARATS and SEF also provided a channel through which humanitarian aid and delegations could pass.

As with trade relations, the rapid expansion of cross-Strait cultural and people-to-people ties is characterized largely by a flow from Taiwan to the mainland. Typically citing security and population concerns, Taiwan has tried to keep the number of legal entrants to Taiwan at a manageable level, while gradually allowing increasing numbers of academic, youth and cultural exchanges. However, difficult and unpleasant experiences for some visitors from Taiwan on the mainland, from entrepreneurs to tourists, and the continued military threat from the mainland, underscore the fact that the two sides represent distinctly different social and political systems.[55]

[53] 'Taiwanese tourism to mainland up 10%', *China News Digest Global News*, no. GL96-020, 14 Feb. 1996, p. 1.

[54] Sheng, V., 'Cross-Straits talks reach accord on fishing, illegal entrants', *Free China Journal*, 5 Nov. 1993 p. 1.

[55] In one recent poll taken in Taiwan, 57.3% of respondents said relations with the mainland had worsened in 1995. In another poll, only 36% said they favoured reunification with the mainland. 'For the record', *International Herald Tribune*, 2 Jan. 1996, p. 2; and 'Taiwanese turn sour on rejoining the mainland', *International Herald Tribune*, 21 June 1995, p. 4.

It is far too early to know what impact such relations might have on the prospects for a peaceful settlement of the cross-Strait confrontation. Leaders on both sides of Taiwan Strait appeal to 'Chinese culture' and claim that they wish to avoid a conflict in which Chinese fight Chinese. Unlike the situation between North and South Korea, exchanges of persons from all walks of life across the Taiwan Strait have been extensive, even in the face of the tense political relations between the two sides.

IV. Prospects for dialogue and regional security

Despite encouraging developments for the peaceful resolution of differences the root causes of difference and tension remain strong in inter-Korean and cross-Strait relations. At best, a note of cautious optimism can be voiced that the fledgling attempts at dialogue may progress, but in order to do so they must overcome decades of animosity and deep-seated disagreements. In the foreseeable future little progress is likely to be made in alleviating military tensions and political differences. Economic ties and humanitarian and cultural exchanges appear to offer the best channels for continuing positive interaction. As a result, despite some encouraging developments, the confrontations across the Taiwan Strait and on the Korean peninsula will continue to pose the greatest threats to regional security in East Asia.

Military tensions

The highly charged military situations across the Taiwan Strait and on the Korean peninsula are rooted in civil wars which have not reached conclusions, peaceful or otherwise. On 30 April 1991, Taiwan formally terminated the 'Period of National Mobilization for Suppression of the Communist Rebellion' and recognized that a 'political entity' governed the mainland. These steps effectively ended Taiwan's state of war with the mainland. However, while Jiang Zemin's eight-point speech in January 1995 declared that 'Chinese should not fight fellow Chinese' the mainland has not renounced the use of force against Taiwan under certain conditions: if Taiwan obtains nuclear weapons; if Taiwan is overtaken by 'foreign forces'; or if Taiwan moves towards independence or permanent separation from the mainland. In the second half of 1995 mainland Chinese military activities directed at Taiwan— such as military exercises and missile tests near the island—raised cross-Strait military tension to its highest level since the 1950s and undermined the short-term prospects for positive dialogue between the two sides. While it is highly unlikely that mainland China would launch an invasion or direct attack on Taiwan, continued lower-level military intimidation can be expected.

The military situation on the Korean peninsula has a long history of more immediate and tense confrontation. The inter-Korean military stand-off is punctuated by flashpoints such as incidents in 1995 in which suspected North Korean infiltrators were killed in the DMZ and in which a US military helicopter was brought down by North Korean fire, killing one crew member. Directly poised against one another, the two sides of the inter-Korean conflict are heavily armed and in a constant state of alert. The close proximity of the antagonists, which share a border of some 250 km with Seoul only 40 km from North Korean territory, further contributes to the tense military situation.

The US presence looms large as a critical factor affecting both the military relations across the Strait and those on the Korean peninsula. The US–South Korean security relationship is viewed by North Korea as a provocation and is often cited by Pyongyang as a reason to stall or break off opportunities for dialogue with the South. In the past North Korea has demanded the withdrawal of US troops, although in 1995 there were indications that it was willing to accept the presence of US troops and wished to negotiate a separate peace with the USA outside the 1953 Korean Armistice Agreement.[56] The presence of some 37 000 US troops in South Korea and the guarantee of the security pact between the USA and South Korea ensures the direct involvement of the US military should conflict erupt on the Korean peninsula.

The 1979 Taiwan Relations Act, the US legislation governing unofficial relations between Washington and Taipei, leaves open the possibility of US military involvement in the event of escalating tension and conflict between mainland China and Taiwan. The act states that the USA would view 'any effort to determine the future of Taiwan by other than peaceful means . . . a threat to the peace and security of the Western Pacific area and of grave concern to the United States'. It further states that the USA 'will make available to Taiwan such defense articles and defense services in such quantity as may be necessary to enable Taiwan to maintain a sufficient self-defense capability'.[57] The language is purposely vague but is intended to ensure continued stability in the Strait. The mainland must calculate its actions with the possibility of US military intervention in mind, and Taiwan must make its calculations without a guarantee of a full US military intervention.

The North Korean nuclear issue tends to exacerbate the situation on the Korean peninsula in a way that is absent in cross-Strait relations. Indeed, in the early 1990s this issue repeatedly led to delays and lack of progress in the political, economic and humanitarian spheres of North–South dialogue. Even when under the Agreed Framework full verification measures can be taken to ensure the end of the suspected North Korean nuclear weapon programme, it may be impossible to guarantee that no clandestine activities occurred.

The very real threat of military hostilities on the Korean peninsula and across the Taiwan Strait cannot be downplayed. The military confrontation will continue to characterize these two stand-offs for years to come.

---

[56] Sullivan, K. and Jordan, M., 'North Korea said to drop objection to U.S. troops', *International Herald Tribune*, 29 Sep. 1995, p. 1; and 'DPRK–US military talks demanded', *Pyongyang Times*, 22 July 1995, p. 8. The Armistice Agreement which brought a de facto end to the Korean War in 1953 was signed between North Korea and representatives of the United Nations command. Neither South Korea nor the United States were formal parties to this agreement.

[57] *Taiwan Relations Act*, Public Law 96-8, sec. 2 and sec. 3, 10 Apr. 1979.

Political factors

While military tensions undermine confidence and threaten hostilities, fundamental political differences present the most immediate problems to near-term progress in reconciliation. Moreover, domestic political difficulties in mainland China, Taiwan, North Korea and South Korea exacerbate the problems associated with settlements across the Taiwan Strait and on the Korean peninsula.

In both cases the disputing parties have entirely different economic, social and political systems: North Korea has a communist leadership and a tightly controlled planned economy while South Korea is a fledgling democracy with a strong free market orientation; China has a communist political system, and is undergoing market-oriented reforms, while Taiwan is a free market economy which has made the transition to multi-party democracy.

Currently, neither side in these stand-offs is prepared to accept the other's form of political, social and economic organization. On the Korean peninsula, the North fears possible absorption by its economically more vibrant and more heavily populated southern counterpart—hence the calls by Pyongyang to establish a confederated Korean state which would preserve its political system and its thus-far persistent reluctance to open its doors to influences from the South. For its part the South rejects the North's political system but at the same time does not wish to be prematurely overwhelmed by North Korean refugees should the situation in North Korea deteriorate.

Taiwan faces a somewhat similar problem: the enormous cultural, geographic and demographic weight of the mainland appears easily capable of absorbing the smaller island society. In economic terms, such a process may already be under way, as Taiwan has become increasingly tied to the mainland through trade and investments. Stressing that it is distinctly different from the mainland in political, economic and social terms, Taiwan seeks to define itself as an equal political entity, distinguished from the mainland. The mainland has few concerns in the sense of quantitative absorption, but the Beijing leadership may fear the democratic and economic success of Taiwan to the extent that it undermines the legitimacy of the mainland's forms of political, economic and social organization. This reluctance, shared by all parties, to be prematurely overtaken by strong but undesirable influences ensures that the negotiated resolution of differences across the Taiwan Strait and on the Korean peninsula will move slowly.

In addition, the current domestic political situation in each of the four parties undermines political processes which might lead to negotiated settlements. In mainland China, although the early stages of succession to political patriarch Deng Xiaoping were complete by the end of 1995, the long-term stability of the 'collective leadership with Jiang Zemin at the core' nevertheless remains in some question. In any event, no leader in mainland China can afford to appear weak *vis-à-vis* Taiwan, making gestures of political conciliation difficult. Similarly, in Taiwan, while Lee Teng-hui handily won the March 1996 presidential election, he nevertheless must constantly account for powerful forces at home—some of which advocate independence, others of which demand an accelerated reunification process—as he charts the course for Taiwan's mainland policy.

The domestic situations in North and South Korea create similar difficulties for political settlement on the peninsula. As in the cross-Strait relationship the leaders in Pyongyang and Seoul must not appear to be 'selling out' to the other side, which stiffens resolve aga

inst compromise. The spring 1996 national assembly elections in South Korea also narrowed the chances for the presentation of new and accommodating initiatives towards the North. Moreover, political scandal at the highest reaches of the South Korean power structure in 1995 weakened the ability of the political leadership to make assertive moves on the highly sensitive relationship with North Korea. By the end of 1995, a year and a half after the death of North Korean leader Kim Il Sung, uncertainty surrounded the succession prospects for his son, Kim Jong Il: he retained his title as supreme commander of the armed forces but the positions of president and party leader remained open. These uncertainties of succession in North Korea, coupled with the country's apparent economic deterioration, further weaken near-term prospects for political settlements.[58]

Even in the so-called 'second track' processes in East Asia, unresolved political problems undermine potential opportunities for unofficial dialogue. Established in part as a means to discuss controversial issues in an unofficial setting, such second-track organizations as the Council for Security Cooperation in the Asia Pacific (CSCAP)[59] grapple with the one-China principle and have yet to seat mainland China, the representatives of which have effectively barred participation by Taiwan. Second-track processes set up to include North Korean representatives have encountered difficulties in securing North Korean participation—although the North has formally joined the CSCAP—probably owing to the North's reluctance to have its representatives exposed to outside political influences and ideas.

However, while the political situations affecting the situation in cross-Strait and Korean peninsula relations are similar in many respects, there are a number of subtle but important differences. First, the two sets of relations differ as to how the parties view one another as political entities. The Korean dialogue process has been characterized by a relatively high-level, high-profile and official set of discussions, while the cross-Strait talks have been low-key and

---

[58] In addition to the destruction brought by floods and bad harvests in 1995, North Korea's economy, as measured by GNP growth, had declined by an estimated annual average of 4.5% from 1990 through 1994. See *Daebukkyoyok-tuja sulmyonghoe* [Briefing on trade and investment with North Korea] (Korea Trade-Investment Promotion Agency: Seoul, Dec. 1995), p. 3. Total trade also declined slightly for the North in 1995 as exports ($590 million) dropped by 30% and imports ($1.47 billion) grew by 16%. 'Worsening trade', *Korea Times*, 28 Feb. 1996, p. 2, cited in *NAPSNet Daily Report*, Nautilus Institute, 28 Feb. 1996, p. 3.

[59] CSCAP was founded by a group of 10 non-governmental research institutes from the region (Australia, Canada, Indonesia, Japan, South Korea, Malaysia, the Philippines, Singapore, Thailand and the USA), meeting under the auspices of the Pacific Forum/Center for Strategic and International Studies (CSIS). It was officially launched on 9 June 1993 in Kuala Lumpur. Since then North Korea, New Zealand and Russia have also joined the group. The European Union and India have joined as associate members.

unofficial. This is because the two Korean states recognize one another as political entities, while China does not recognize Taiwan as a distinct political entity. By acknowledging one another politically, the two Korean states appear to be in a better position than China and Taiwan to achieve some progress in reconciliation at the political level.

Second, while on the Korean peninsula there appears to be consensus about the desirability of unifying the two Korean states at some stage, the scope of consensus is not so great across the Taiwan Strait. In particular, a growing body of opinion on Taiwan, led by the Democratic Progressive Party (DPP), openly advocates independence from the mainland. This opinion is quite distinct from the ruling party's approach, which continues to seek eventual reunification, but under terms negotiated between mainland China and Taiwan as 'two equal political entities'. Since Taiwan opened up to democratic processes in the late 1980s the DPP has made significant political gains in local and island-wide elections. The presence of an important domestic political force which is officially opposed to reunification presents complications for dialogue across the Strait, the implications of which are likely to increase rather than decrease tensions.

Under these political conditions, significant and mutually agreed progress towards political settlement remains out of reach for the time being. The parties recognize this, which explains their attempts to pursue other means in addition to bilateral political discussions to achieve their goals. North Korea and Taiwan both appeal to the international community for greater recognition and understanding as a means to strengthen their political hand against their respective counterparts: Taiwan pursues an ambitious campaign to raise its international profile, including its effort to gain an independent seat in the United Nations; North Korea seeks to normalize relations with the USA and Japan, and to dismantle the current Korean armistice agreement in order to reach a 'new peace mechanism' directly with the United States.[60] South Korea and mainland China seek to expand the agenda in their respective negotiations with Taiwan and North Korea as a means to ease the reunification process forward on their terms. South Korea and mainland China also seem to favour playing the economic card more strongly than their counterparts as an approach to engendering closer ties. In mainland China the phrase for such indirect tactics—'use the people to influence the government' (*yimin biguan*)—implies that perhaps the best way to achieve political results is not through direct bilateral talks, but through other less direct means.

The political channels described here, while cautious and deliberate, thus serve the important function of buying time: allowing for evolutionary change to take place so the parties can find mutually satisfactory resolutions to their differences. This pathway to settlement may be the most difficult and frustrating, but it is also likely to be the least calamitous. For this reason it appears to be a path that all of the parties—with different degrees of interest—are willing to follow for the time being.

---

[60] 'DPRK–US military talks demanded', *Pyongyang Times*, 22 July 1995, p. 8.

Conducive elements

For the near-term future, economic and trade relations appear to hold the greatest promise for improving relations between North and South Korea and between mainland China and Taiwan. Not only do such relations hold out immediate economic benefits, but they can also serve the parties' political aims. For the mainland, building closer economic relations with Taiwan knits the two sides together in a way that Beijing sees as favourable to its goal of reunification. For Taiwan, the development of China's standard of living and socio-economic situation can contribute to establishing a more open and prosperous mainland, a goal which is in Taiwan's long-term interest regardless of the outcome on reunification. South Korea sees political benefits in opening up the North to economic relations and trade. Such relations might ease the process should the two sides reunify, and they also tie the North closer to the South, which will ease progress towards dialogue and reunification. For the North, a properly managed economic opening will attract hard currency exchange and investment, strengthen the regime's influence and legitimacy, and possibly prevent an undesirable reunification scenario on the South's terms. In any event, each side will find benefits in pursuing economic relations and will seek to use them as a means to gain concessions in their ongoing adversarial relations.

However, the promises of economic ties have their drawbacks. For South Korea, economic ties need to be managed in a way that does not bring rapid disintegration of the North on the one hand, and avoids contributing to the political and military resources of Pyongyang on the other. For the North, over-exposure to the economic dynamism and growth of the South would threaten the legitimacy and survival of the leadership in Pyongyang, which explains the North's go-slow approach to economic ties. For Taiwan, entrepreneurs remain concerned that the mainland exercise proper protection over trade and investments. In addition, fearing the development of over-dependency, the government on Taiwan has thus far resisted most attempts at opening direct trade links between the island and the mainland. Of the four parties, it would appear that only the mainland would benefit from a rapid opening of economic ties with its adversary.

Cultural and humanitarian exchanges remain undeveloped on the Korean peninsula as opposed to those across the Taiwan Strait. On the Korean peninsula, the ideological, political and military stand-off renders such exchanges highly difficult and politicized affairs. The reported deteriorating conditions in North Korea suggest that humanitarian aid will continue to be a likely channel for dialogue and exchange between the North and South, as well as between the North and the international community, although it will be marked by disruptive periods of ambivalence and animosity on all sides.

For China–Taiwan relations, cultural exchanges have flourished in recent years and offer a considerable level of people-to-people contact. The process of dialogue and consensus building within the Koo-Wang framework has facilitated these developments, as have the general social, political and economic reforms experienced on both sides of the Taiwan Strait since the early 1980s. Such ties across the Taiwan Strait have continued in the face of often acrimonious relations at political and military levels and will probably serve in the future to facilitate progress towards a peaceful settlement of differences, albeit in a way that is less tangible and more difficult to assess with certainty.

While the bitter divisions across the Taiwan Strait and on the Korean peninsula need to be addressed by the parties directly involved, the security interests of other powers in the region and those of the international community as a whole are best served by a peaceful outcome to these disputes. A major military confrontation in either or both of these disputes would have disastrous consequences, which would require years if not decades to overcome. This is particularly true for the parties involved, but also for the strategic and economic security of all of East Asia.

In this sense the degree to which dialogue across the Taiwan Strait and on the Korean peninsula contributes to a peaceful solution of differences—or lack thereof—deserves close scrutiny by concerned observers both inside and outside East Asia. In 1996 and beyond, the degree of political and military tensions in these disputes will remain dangerously high, and renewed efforts are needed to develop the several promising dialogue channels.

4. The Middle East peace process

PETER JONES

I. Introduction

In 1995 there was both success and tragedy in the Middle East peace process. Israeli Prime Minister Yitzhak Rabin was murdered by a Jewish extremist on 4 November. The Labour Party continued negotiations under his successor, Shimon Peres. A critical agreement, the Israeli–Palestinian Interim Agreement on the West Bank and the Gaza Strip (also known as the Oslo II Agreement), was signed between Israel and the Palestinian Authority (PA) on 28 September 1995,[1] almost two years behind the schedule set in the Declaration of Principles on Interim Self-Government Arrangements (DOP) of 13 September 1993 (also known as the Oslo Agreement).[2]

The negotiations between Israel and Syria made little progress for most of 1995, but talks resumed in the wake of the Rabin assassination. As 1995 ended it was apparent that quick action would be required if an agreement was to be achieved before the Israeli and US elections in 1996. The implementation of the Israeli–Jordanian Treaty of Peace[3] of 26 October 1994 proceeded smoothly in 1995.

Progress was made on the multilateral track of the process. However, some participants in the process continued to refuse to take part in initiatives designed to normalize relations with Israel before the Israeli–Syrian talks have concluded and such issues as the future status of Jerusalem are decided.

This chapter describes and analyses events in the Middle East peace process in 1995. Following discussion of the key bilateral negotiations in 1995, the multilateral process is reviewed. The conclusion offers a brief outline of issues likely to be of importance in 1996 and of broader security issues in the region.

II. The Israeli–Palestinian talks

The Israeli–Palestinian talks derive their agenda from the DOP, which includes provisions for immediate Palestinian self-rule in the Gaza Strip and Jericho, the transfer of specific government functions on the West Bank to the Palestinians and the establishment of a Palestinian Council (which will serve as the interim self-government authority) through elections in Gaza and the West Bank. The intention is to initiate a five-year interim period of limited

---

[1] Excerpts from the text of the agreement are reproduced in appendix 4A in this volume.

[2] The text of the DOP is reproduced in *SIPRI Yearbook 1994* (Oxford University Press: Oxford, 1994), pp. 117–22.

[3] The treaty is reproduced in *SIPRI Yearbook 1995: Armaments, Disarmament and International Security* (Oxford University Press: Oxford, 1995), pp. 197–203.

Palestinian self-rule. During this time, Israel will retain responsibility for foreign affairs, defence, the security of Israeli settlements, and the patrolling of international borders and cease-fire lines.

It was also agreed in the DOP that talks would commence no later than May 1996 to address the outstanding issues between Israel and the PA. These Final Status talks will include such issues as the status of the Palestinian Government, Jerusalem, Israeli settlements, borders, security arrangements and the rights of return of Palestinian refugees. Although formal talks will not begin until May 1996, informal talks, led by academics, were under way in 1995.

The DOP established deadlines, none of which was met and which may have been unrealistic. Israeli troops were to withdraw from Gaza and from Jericho by 13 April 1994 but did not do so until 18 May. Withdrawal was to be followed by elections to the Palestinian Council in Gaza and the West Bank by 13 July 1994, and the further redeployment, also by 13 July, of Israeli troops from West Bank population centres was to be agreed.[4] Neither of these events took place in 1994, and for much of 1995 it could not be said with certainty when or if they would occur.

A combination of interrelated factors accounted for this delay. Since the signing of the DOP those Israelis and Palestinians opposed to it have used confrontation and terror to undermine the agreement. With each attack, concerns for personal security have increased and support for the process has dropped in Israel. Rabin argued that he could not adhere to the original timetable in the face of diminishing support.[5]

In response to terrorism, Israel temporarily suspended talks after each attack and sealed off the occupied territories as a security measure thereby preventing Palestinian residents from entering Israel proper. Such 'closures' punished the Palestinians as a group since the income of a significant number of residents in the West Bank and Gaza comes from work in Israel. This further exacerbated the second reason why progress could not be made according to the original timetable: the difficulties faced by the Palestinian Authority in establishing itself in Jericho and Gaza.

The effect of the closures was compounded by the fact that international aid was not delivered to the PA as promised.[6] This affected the PA's attempt to establish itself and to meet the needs of the people and also made the argu-

---

[4] This schedule is derived from Article XVII, paragraph 1; Annex II, paragraphs 1 and 2; Article III; and Article XIII of the DOP. See also Kemp, G. and Pressman, J., 'The Middle East: continuation of the peace process', *SIPRI Yearbook 1995* (note 3), p. 174; and chapter 1 in this volume.

[5] For more on the fragile support in Israel for the process, see Ben Meir, Y., *Israeli Public Opinion, Final Status Issues: Israel Palestinians*, Study no. 6 (Jaffe Centre for Strategic Studies: Tel Aviv, 1995). See also Peace Watch, 'Israelis and Palestinians killed in terrorist acts since the Israel–PLO Accord', *The Arab–Israeli Peace Process and US Policy: Documents and Analysis, January 1993–March, 1994* (Washington Institute for Near East Policy: Washington, DC, 1994), pp. 253–55.

[6] After the signing of the DOP $2.5 billion was promised to the PA over 5 years, but only a fraction was disbursed initially. In 1994, $700–800 million was promised (depending on how various pledges are counted); $228 million was delivered. In Nov. 1994 an emergency fund, in honour of the late Norwegian Foreign Minister Johan Jørgen Holst, was created to make up shortfalls in the PA's operating expenses and was to be supported by $60 million. By Mar. 1995, $36 million in pledges had not been honoured. Greenberg, J., 'Failure by pledged donors drains Gaza–Jericho fund', *New York Times,* 13 Mar. 1995, p. A6; and Black, I., 'Prop up the peace tent', *The Guardian,* 24 Jan. 1995, p. 2.

ments of those opposed to the process more appealing than might otherwise have been the case. There are two reasons for the initially poor delivery of aid, in addition to parsimony on the part of some donors: the early operating procedures of the PA did not inspire confidence, and the priorities of the PA and donors were at variance.

First, aid officials and former Palestine Liberation Organization (PLO) associates argued that PLO Chairman Yasser Arafat's desire to approve all decisions resulted in a sclerotic system incapable of providing a dynamic, open economy. Second, donors wanted their foreign aid to be used to provide schools, roads, hospitals and sewers. While this infrastructure is lacking, Arafat's most pressing need as he moved to gain control over the area of Palestinian self-government was not infrastructure but funds to pay supporters and to persuade others to join him. However, owing to the PA's autocratic tendencies, donors were reluctant to provide the desired funds.[7]

Completing the circle, the PA's difficulties provided an opening for Palestinians opposed to the peace process. The most effective group was Hamas, an Islamic movement active in the West Bank and Gaza Strip, which has carried out much of the terrorism since the signing of the DOP.

Despite these problems, the two sides had implemented much of the DOP in 1994.[8] Agreements had been reached on translating the general formulations of the DOP into firm text on: the boundaries of Jericho, procedures for border crossings, procedures for cooperation between the PA police and Israeli security, and economic agreements between the two parties on taxation and customs. On 4 May 1994, Israel and the PLO signed the Agreement on the Gaza Strip and the Jericho Area in Cairo.[9] The remainder of 1994 was spent implementing this document and combating terrorism.

The 1995 agenda

The central item on the 1995 agenda was to achieve an agreement that would complete the implementation of the DOP in time for the beginning of the Final Status talks. The main issues were: the transfer of more territory and powers to the PA, and the related issue of the status of Israeli settlements in areas to be ceded to the PA; elections to the Palestinian Council, which itself had to be designed; the release of Palestinian prisoners in Israeli jails; and access to water. Although not officially on the agenda, the related questions of Israeli settlements around Jerusalem and Palestinian political activity in Jerusalem were also much disputed in 1995.

Beyond the official agenda, the primary Israeli concern in early 1995 was the control of acts of terror by Palestinians opposed to the peace process. The question repeatedly arose in Israel as to how the PA could be entrusted with

---

[7] Lederman, J., 'Economics of the Arab–Israeli peace process', *Orbis,* vol. 39, no. 4 (fall 1995), especially pp. 550–56. In the wake of the Interim Agreement of Sep. 1995 it appears that international aid is now flowing more freely to the PA.

[8] The following summary is drawn from Kemp and Pressman (note 4), pp. 174–80.

[9] The text of the agreement is reproduced in *SIPRI Yearbook 1995* (note 3), pp. 203–10.

more land and power if it could not control that which it had received under the DOP. Israel stated that it would not go forward until the PA stopped attacks which used land controlled by the PA as a base.[10] The Israeli Government expressed sympathy with the hardship caused by its policy of closures after attacks, but many in Israel were suspicious that Arafat was not sufficiently committed to the process to confront the Palestinian opposition. As attacks mounted in the first months of 1995, even Israeli President Ezer Weizman, traditionally a supporter of peace, began to wonder about Arafat's commitment to the peace process.[11]

Growing unease in Israel over personal security led the government to redefine its aims in the first months of 1995 towards the vague concept of 'separation'.[12] Few analysts could authoritatively state what separation meant or believed that it would work, arguing that the Israeli and Palestinian economies were too intertwined. However, discussion of separation seemed to reassure the Israeli public in the aftermath of violent attacks.[13]

Right-wing opposition to the peace process grew throughout 1995 in Israel. As the government appeared prepared to make territorial concessions on the West Bank, right-wing settlers became increasingly strident. During the summer they launched an effort to create divisions within Israel by forcing the army to confront them physically over illegal attempts to expand settlements. The settlers believed that the sight of Israelis being dragged off land in Judaea and Samaria, the heart of biblical Israel, would heighten opposition to the peace process.[14] Their campaign was strengthened when a few right-wing rabbis issued a religious edict that it was morally right and permissible under Jewish law for soldiers to disobey orders to remove settlers or Israeli Army bases from Judaea and Samaria.[15] By August it seemed that these tactics had failed. Although Israeli citizens expressed concern, the government felt that a majority of them supported the peace process.

However, the protests crystalized, increasing right-wing opposition to the peace process around an emotive issue, and a concerted campaign was begun to heckle and threaten supporters of the peace process. In August and Septem-

---

[10] Haberman, C., 'Rabin plans to limit building by settlers on the West Bank', *New York Times*, 21 Jan. 1995, p. A2; and Reuter, 'Once more, Israel links talks with PLO action', 14 Feb. 1995.

[11] Honig, S., 'Weizman: halt talks with PLO', *Jerusalem Post* (international edn), week ending 4 Feb. 1995, p. 2. The cause of Weizman's remarks was a suicide attack on people waiting at a bus-stop at Beit Lid on 22 Jan. For more on the Beit Lid incident and its impact on Israeli public opinion, see Haberman, C., 'Israelis mourn, but Rabin says talks continue', *New York Times*, 24 Jan. 1995, pp. A1, A6.

[12] 'Rabin's peace goal: "total separation": talks go on despite uproar after bombing', *International Herald Tribune*, 24 Jan. 1995, pp. 1, 6; Haberman, C., 'A wall around Israel?', *New York Times*, 25 Jan. 1995, pp. A1, A9; and Brown, D., 'Rabin moves closer to final separation', *The Guardian*, 25 Jan. 1995, p. 4.

[13] Friedman, T. L., 'Israel's economic bomb', *New York Times*, 8 Feb. 1995, p. A19; Gellman, B., 'For Israelis, appeal of "separation" is its vagueness', *International Herald Tribune*, 7 Apr. 1995, pp. 1, 6; and Ozanne, J., 'A fence that may make better neighbours', *Financial Times*, 2 Feb. 1995, p. 7.

[14] Keinon, H., 'The battle is joined', *Jerusalem Post* (international edn), week ending 12 Aug. 1995, p. 3.

[15] Keinon, H., 'Rabbis: Halacha forbids moving army bases from Judea, Samaria', *Jerusalem Post* (international edn), week ending 22 July 1995, p. 1. By Aug. the army had court-martialled its first soldier for refusing to remove settlers. He was sentenced to 28 days in jail. Gellman, B., 'Torn between the Torah and the army', *International Herald Tribune*, 26–27 Aug. 1995, pp. 1, 5.

ber 1995 concern was expressed that the mood of intolerance might lead to violence against a political figure.[16]

For its part, the PA argued that the talks were being impeded by the slow implementation of the DOP and by Israel's policy of settlement expansion, especially around Jerusalem.[17] PA officials expressed frustration that by the time the Final Status talks began there would be little land of value left for negotiation.

Acts of terrorism continued to occur, but Arafat began to deal more firmly with those who attacked Israel from PA territory. After bombings on 11 April, the PA rounded up 100 members of Hamas and Islamic Jihad. More significantly, courts were established and began to sentence law-breakers.[18] While some criticized the courts for practising 'rough justice', their establishment was taken as a sign that Arafat was becoming less tolerant of those who used PA areas for attacks on Israel.

April was apparently the turning-point in Arafat's determination to rein in the Palestinian militants in order to protect the gains already made in the peace process and to protect its future. As 1995 progressed, the PA took increasing action against those trying to disrupt the peace process. Although terror continued, such as the 24 July, 21 August and 28 August bus bombings, Israeli leaders quickly praised the efforts of the PA in combating it. They also moved to limit the damage such actions caused to the peace process.[19] Throughout 1995 signs emerged of cooperation in the fight against terrorism.[20]

At the same time, Arafat recognized the need to reconcile with Hamas. In particular, he appears to have believed that Hamas still had significant support in some areas and to have been reluctant to press it too hard lest it rebel openly and threaten the PA's grip on power. Accordingly, Arafat did not take the steps to destroy the Hamas infrastructure which were requested by some in Israel. Instead, the PA met with Hamas and intensified efforts to persuade it to

[16] 'Rabin, ministers warned of likely attempts on their lives by the ultra-right', *Mideast Mirror*, 30 Aug. 1995, p. 2; and Claude, P., 'Terrorism by Jewish settlers alarms Israel', *Guardian Weekly*, 24 Sep. 1995, p. 16.

[17] Ozanne, J., 'Jewish settlers undermine peace process', *Financial Times*, 19 Jan. 1995, p. 6; and 'Israel acts to confiscate land in East Jerusalem for housing', *International Herald Tribune*, 28 Apr. 1995. Senator Robert Dole added to the tension by introducing legislation requiring the movement of the US Embassy to Jerusalem by 1999. It is believed that his action was motivated by domestic political ambitions. Haberman, C., 'Muslims say they own site proposed for US Embassy in Jerusalem', *New York Times*, 11 May 1995, p. A8.

[18] The day after the bombings a PA court sentenced an Islamic militant to a 15-year prison term on charges of training Palestinian youths to carry out suicide attacks. Ibrahim, Y. M., 'Palestinians seize 100 militants who oppose talks with Israel', *New York Times*, 11 Apr. 1995, pp. A1, A10. Four more Islamic militants were sentenced by 17 Apr. Reuter, 'Palestinian groups meet over attacks', *International Herald Tribune*, 18 Apr. 1995.

[19] After the July bombing, polls in Israel showed that 64% of Israelis believed that terrorism would increase after withdrawal. At the same time, slightly over 50% of all Israelis wanted the peace process to continue. Lancaster, J., 'Suicide bomber kills 5 Israelis on a bus', *International Herald Tribune*, 25 July 1995, pp. 1, 6. See also Schmemann, S., 'Israel passes point of no return', *New York Times*, 26 July 1995, p. A6; and Silver, E., 'Bus bombing will not halt peace process', *The Independent*, 25 July 1995, p. 10.

[20] Silver, E., 'Israelis net suicide bomb suspects', *The Independent*, 24 Aug. 1995, p. 14; Immanuel, J., 'Palestinian police foil suicide bomb plot', *Jerusalem Post* (international edn), week ending 26 Aug. 1995, pp. 1, 2; and Reuter, 'Israeli army kills 2 Hamas militants in Hebron clash', *International Herald Tribune*, 26–27 Aug. 1995, p. 5.

accept the new situation and to confine itself to political protests.[21] By September the Hamas leadership appeared to have concluded that defiance of the increasingly effective PA police was unproductive. However, reports surfaced of a campaign to organize politically and to recruit for the coming political battles within the self-rule areas, while maintaining the ability to resume violence should Arafat's policies fail.[22]

Meanwhile, polls showed that Palestinians on the Gaza Strip were starting to see benefits from the peace process and that they credited Arafat with them. Foreign aid programmes seemed to be delivering tangible benefits, and small businesses such as restaurants began to open. Most importantly, there appeared to be relief in Gaza that the Islamic fundamentalist excesses of the intifada period were over and that those living there could again enjoy a more secular lifestyle.[23]

The issues explored

Territorial questions

The questions of more territory and powers for the PA and of Israeli settlements are related, and it appeared in early 1995 that the two sides had tentatively agreed that the areas to be handed to the PA would resemble a patchwork of various levels of autonomy in different areas of the West Bank.[24] The rest of 1995 was spent working out how much land would be transferred to the PA and what its authority would be in various areas.

In March the two sides agreed to a 1 July deadline for the conclusion of an agreement on the transfer of areas and powers to the PA. Implementation was to begin thereafter and to include such difficult issues as the withdrawal of the Israeli Army from areas ceded to the PA. Given that these areas were close to Jewish settlements, the fate of which Rabin vowed to leave untouched until the Final Status talks concluded, withdrawal would be difficult.

Israel agreed in July to withdraw from either six or seven towns on the West Bank, ceding them to the PA, before the PA elections and leaving security and internal administration to the Palestinian Authority. Israel would remain in charge of security in rural areas, although more land would be handed over in a phased manner. Israel would continue to provide security for Israeli settlements on the West Bank.

[21] Reuter, 'Palestinian groups meet over attacks', 18 Apr. 1995. Talks continue. Brown, D., 'PLO opens talks with Hamas', *Guardian Weekly*, 12 Nov. 1995, p. 3.

[22] Ozanne, J. and Dennis, M., 'Advances in peace undermine Palestinian opposition', *Financial Times*, 1 Dec. 1995, p. 6.

[23] Gellman, B., 'In Gaza, revolution is out and government is in', *International Herald Tribune*, 3 July 1995, p. 2.

[24] See the comments of an unnamed Israeli official in Makovsky, D., 'Self-rule areas to be a patchwork', *Jerusalem Post* (international edn), week ending 28 Jan. 1995, p. 1.

The Palestinian Council

Progress was also achieved in establishing rules for the long-delayed elections to the Palestinian Council, its powers and an election date. In March 1995 it was agreed that candidates for the Council would seek office as individuals rather than in groups. This allowed members of Hamas and Islamic Jihad to run for office, circumventing Israeli laws forbidding political activities by groups pledged to the destruction of Israel.[25]

The two sides also agreed that the Council would have legislative and executive powers. Israel had argued that the Palestinian Council should be an executive body on the grounds that law-making authority can only be held by the representatives of a state, not by the government of a limited autonomy area. The agreement that the Council should have legislative and executive powers was a breakthrough for the PA in its campaign for eventual status as an independent nation.

There was still dispute as to whether the Palestinian residents of East Jerusalem would be permitted to vote and where (in East Jerusalem or not). The establishment of Palestinian voting booths in the city would strengthen the PA's claim that at least part of the city should be regarded as the future capital of a Palestinian state.

By July 1995 it was agreed that Palestinians living in Jerusalem could run for office, provided they had or could use an address in the West Bank or Gaza. Israel also offered to allow Jerusalem Palestinians to vote in polling stations on the municipal border. Although not yet acceptable to the Palestinians, these offers constituted a breakthrough for residents of the Palestinian-claimed areas of Jerusalem in their quest to participate in the Palestinian elections. Questions remained on the size and functions of the Council. Israel had initially argued that the Council should have 24 members but then offered to increase the number to 50. The PA held to 100 members. Finally, Israel argued that the Council should be administrative, while the PA wanted to give it the powers of a parliament in the making.[26]

Palestinian prisoners

The PA maintained that the estimated 5000 Palestinian prisoners in Israeli jails were freedom fighters who should be released. Israel was prepared to release some prisoners but said that those convicted of violent crimes should be treated as criminals and held in jail. In July it was revealed that Israel would release up to 1000 of these prisoners as part of the emerging agreement. President Weizman began examining the question of granting pardons to women prisoners.[27]

---

[25] Associated Press, 'Palestinian election likely by September as talks progress', *International Herald Tribune*, 17 Mar. 1995.

[26] Silver, E., 'Israel may set free 1000 PLO prisoners', *The Independent*, 21 July 1995, p. 11.

[27] Silver (note 26).

Water rights

The PA sought rights over water originating from the West Bank. Israel did not agree to this, as underground aquifers there supply 25 per cent of its water. However, Israel recognized the current inequities (the average Israeli uses approximately 100 cubic metres (m³) of water per year while the average Palestinian uses 31 m³) and proposed joint efforts to increase the supply. Israel also hinted that it would allow the PA the first right to drill in areas not yet fully tapped.[28]

The Taba Joint Statement

After months of difficult negotiation, Arafat and Peres announced a partial deal, the Taba Israeli–Palestinian Joint Statement, on 11 August 1995, at the Egyptian resort at Taba.[29] Specifically, they achieved framework agreements on the transfer of many civilian functions of West Bank administration to the PA, the definition of many areas in which the PA would exercise self-rule, the election and composition of the Palestinian Council, the release of Palestinian prisoners, and the control of water rights. It proved difficult to translate the agreements into legal text, however.[30] Sticking-points remained on the questions of security—who would administer it and under what conditions, and who would provide security for the Israeli settlers in the West Bank areas to be handed over—and the status of Hebron.

Hebron was a particularly difficult issue as it holds religious significance for both sides as the burial place of their common biblical patriarch, Abraham. Only 450 ultra-religious Jewish settlers live in Hebron together with over 100 000 Palestinians. However, Israel insisted that its army remain in Hebron to protect the settlers, unlike the other six towns which have no settlements within them and from which it would redeploy. Concerned about establishing a precedent if Israel partially withdrew from one place, the PA refused, stating that the settlers in Hebron need not move but that it would provide security.[31]

The response to the Taba Joint Statement was mixed. Some Israelis believed that the framework for army withdrawal from the West Bank would create problems in defending remaining settlements.[32] Palestinians said that Hebron was a breaking-point. Although the Taba Statement was not the overdue successor to the DOP, it laid out the direction of the talks and attracted opposition

[28] For more on the issue of water in the discussions, see Lancaster, J., 'Water, a West Bank symbol', *International Herald Tribune*, 24 July 1995, p. 2.

[29] The Joint Statement is reproduced in appendix 4A in this volume.

[30] Associated Press, 'Peres and Arafat seem to be making headway on accord', *International Herald Tribune*, 10 Aug. 1995, p. 7.

[31] A PA delegate to Taba was quoted as saying, 'Without solving the outstanding problems of Hebron, there won't be an agreement. . . . One hundred thousand Palestinians cannot be held hostage to 450 Jews. They are welcome to stay there, but under our rule'. Silver, E., 'Hebron "biggest obstacle to deal"', *The Independent*, 11 Aug. 1995, p. 10. The number 450 is subject to some dispute. The Jewish settlement Kiryat Arba, on the outskirts of the city, contains several thousand religious settlers and is noted for its militancy.

[32] Makovsky, D. and Lahoud, L., '"Partial agreement" initialed on autonomy', *Jerusalem Post* (international edn), week ending 19 Aug. 1995, pp. 1, 2.

from the Israeli right, who saw it as proof that the government would 'give up' Judaea and Samaria.

Any doubts vanished when the cabinet debated the Taba Joint Statement. Rabin stated that the next phase of the process would constitute a 'mighty blow to the delusion of Greater Israel . . . This Government does not believe in Greater Israel, nor does it want to rule another people'. He went on to state in the clearest terms used thus far what Israel wanted: 'We want Jerusalem, we want the Jordan River to be our security border, and we want other areas here and there'.[33]

On 27 August Israel and the PA agreed to transfer eight civilian powers to the PA to signal that the Taba Statement was being translated into action. The PA gained control over agriculture, insurance, labour, local government, postal services, oil and petrol, statistics, and trade and industry. The committees remained at work on the 32 other areas to be handed over.[34]

However, Israel took steps to halt PA activity in East Jerusalem. Fearing that this might create an impression that the PA had rights in the city prior to the Final Status talks, Israel threatened to close the self-designated Palestinian statistics 'ministry', health 'ministry' and broadcasting authority. Israel warned the PA to cease political activities at its headquarters in East Jerusalem, Orient House, or that it, too, would be closed. The PA meanwhile complained that Israel's celebration of the 3000th anniversary of Jerusalem was too heavily oriented to the Jewish aspect of the city's history and that it was intended to cement the status of Jerusalem as the capital of Israel only.[35]

The Interim Agreement

On 24 September the two sides reached agreement on the successor to the DOP, which translated the Taba Joint Statement into a formal agreement. Peres and Arafat initialed the 400-page Israeli–Palestinian Agreement on the West Bank and the Gaza Strip and announced that the signing ceremony would take place in Washington on 28 September. Known as the Interim Agreement,[36] it is complex and lengthy. It creates three zones on the West Bank (see figure 4.1):

1. Area A consists of those zones for which the Palestinians will have full responsibility for internal security and public order as well as for civil affairs (the cities of Bethlehem, Jenin, Nablus, Qalqilya, Ramallah and Tulkarem, in

---

[33] All quotations taken from Makovsky, D. and Yudelman, M., 'PM: Oslo II is "blow to greater Israel"', *Jerusalem Post* (international edn), week ending 26 Aug. 1995, pp. 1, 2. The cabinet approved the Taba Statement by a vote of 15 to 1, with 2 abstentions.

[34] 'Protocol on further transfer of powers and responsibilities', 27 Aug. 1995. Version current on 6 Sep. 1995, URL <gopher://israel-info.gov.il:70/0R91163-118275-/new/pprocess1>. These powers were in addition to others which had been transferred in earlier agreements on PA empowerment.

[35] Cockburn, P., 'Jerusalem's 3000th starts a capital row', *The Independent*, 5 Sep. 1995, p. 11.

[36] Excerpts from the text of the Interim Agreement are reproduced in appendix 4A in this volume.

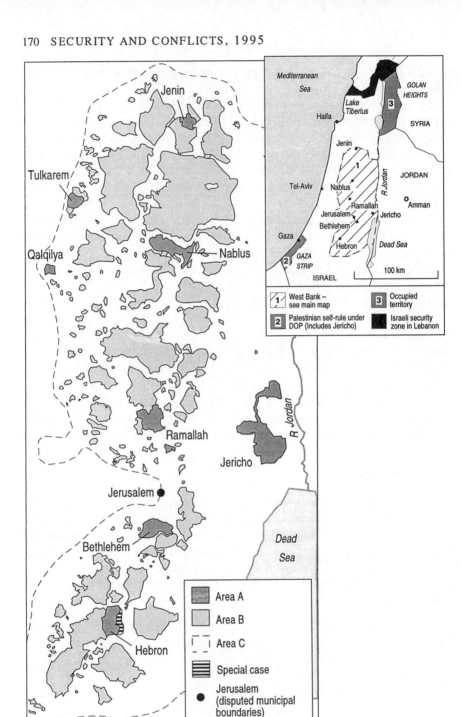

© SIPRI 1996; map by Billie Bielckus

Figure 4.1. The West Bank under the Israeli–Palestinian Interim Agreement
Source: Israeli–Palestinian Interim Agreement on the West Bank and the Gaza Strip, map no. 1, First Phase of Redeployment, map delineating areas A and B.

addition to Jericho), and parts of the city of Hebron outside specific areas where the Israeli Army will be responsible for security.[37]

2. Area B consists of Palestinian towns and villages on the West Bank in which the PA will have civil authority and be charged with maintaining order within specified hamlets in area B.[38] Twenty-five PA police stations will be established, although the movement of the PA police between the towns and villages will be 'coordinated and confirmed' with Israel. Notwithstanding the powers of the Palestinian police, Israel will maintain overriding security authority.[39]

3. Area C consists of unpopulated areas of the West Bank, areas of strategic importance to Israel and Jewish settlements. Israel will retain full authority for order and security, although the Palestinians will gradually assume all civil responsibilities not related to territory (health, education, the economy and so on) except in the areas to be discussed in the Final Status talks.[40] The fact that the PA is to gradually assume civilian powers in much of this area has political implications for its status within those talks.

The Interim Agreement established a timetable for the redeployment of the Israeli Army. The first stage requires the army to begin redeployment within 10 days of the signing of the agreement and to have left the six cities by 31 December 1995. The areas of Hebron will be vacated by late March 1996 after Israel has constructed bypass roads so that the Israeli settlers need not enter Arab areas. Civilian authority in the 450 villages in area B will be handed over in intervals.[41] Further redeployments will take place in area C at six-month intervals; additional territorial jurisdictions in area C will be transferred so that the only areas under the direct jurisdiction of the Israeli Army will be those whose jurisdiction is to be determined in the Final Status talks. In order to facilitate movement between Jewish settlements and other strategic sites retained by Israel, roads will be built for the exclusive use of Israelis.[42]

The Interim Agreement established the size of the Palestinian Council at 82 members, but the number was subsequently raised to 88 members. The Council was given legislative and executive powers and will sit until May 1999, when new elections will be held. In addition to the Council election (of individual candidates by district), a separate election was to be held simultaneously for the post of Head (Ra'ees) of the Executive Authority of the Council, a decision-making body of selected Council members and top officials. Palestinians in Jerusalem were permitted to vote by means of special envelopes

[37] Interim Agreement, Annex 1, Article VII. The Arab mayor of Hebron later accused Arafat of caving in to the Israelis on a fundamental issue. Cockburn, P., 'Hebron fears the worst as settlers hang on', *The Independent*, 26 Sep. 1995, p. 8.

[38] Interim Agreement, Annex 1, Appendix 6 lists the hamlets included in area B.

[39] Interim Agreement, Article XIII (Annex 1, Appendix 3 lists the locations of the stations).

[40] Interim Agreement, Annex III (particularly Article IV).

[41] Interim Agreement, Article XIII. The timetable in the Taba Joint Statement called for Israeli withdrawal from the 6 towns by Feb. The schedule was brought forward in last-minute negotiations. 'Israel sets schedule for West Bank pullout', *International Herald Tribune*, 6 Oct. 1995, p. 1.

[42] According to one source, the total cost of the move, including the access roads, will be at least $1 billion. Dennis, M., 'Israelis bypass Palestinian areas', *Financial Times*, 21 Dec. 1995.

which were deposited in 'receptacles' in five post offices in Jerusalem and then sent to the Elections Committee.[43] Palestinians from Jerusalem wishing to stand for the Council were allowed to do so if they had a valid alternate address in the West Bank or Gaza.

On the issue of water rights, Israel had earlier held that it would not provide any of its current water supply to the PA but would assist it to tap new sources. In the Interim Agreement, Israel modified its position and committed itself to increase the water allocated to the PA by 28.6 million m^3 per year. Further increases will come from the development of new sources. The two sides also agreed to establish a joint committee to enforce policies pertaining to uncontrolled drilling and water quality.[44]

The Interim Agreement called for Joint Security Committees to coordinate the joint actions of the PA police and the Israeli Defence Forces (IDF) and to promote information sharing. Joint patrols will be established to facilitate free movement by Israeli citizens in the West Bank, particularly on designated roads in area A. It is stipulated that only Israelis on a joint patrol can ask an Israeli citizen for personal or vehicle documents; the PA police cannot under any circumstances arrest or place in custody an Israeli.[45] On prisoner release, Israel agreed to release Palestinian prisoners in three stages: upon signature of the agreement, on the eve of Council elections and at a third stage to be agreed.[46]

The PA agreed to revoke the sections of the Charter of the PLO calling for the destruction of Israel within two months of the Council's inauguration, although the entire Palestinian National Council will have to meet to make this change.[47] The issue of the Charter is an important one. Israel views it as a basic litmus test of the PA's seriousness and has said that it will not move forward with the peace process unless the change is made. Some feeling exists in Israel that the Charter should have been altered immediately after the signing of the DOP in 1993.

Other sections of the Interim Agreement deal with legal issues,[48] joint and single custody of religious sites (whoever controls a site must ensure equal access for all religions),[49] cooperation and economic relations,[50] and 'education for peace' (the two sides agree to enhance understanding and tolerance by using their educational systems to promote peace).[51]

[43] Interim Agreement, Annex II, Article VI, 'Election arrangements concerning Jerusalem'. This provision was later attacked by the Israeli right as a sign that Palestinians would be allowed to vote in Jerusalem, despite the government's earlier claim that they would not. See the exchange on this subject between Rabin and Binyamin Netanyahu in Collins, L., 'Rabin offers vision for final settlement', *Jerusalem Post* (international edn), week ending 14 Oct. 1995, pp. 1, 2. See also the comments by the right-wing Mayor of Jerusalem, reprinted in *Mideast Mirror*, 23 Oct. 1995, pp. 7–8.

[44] Interim Agreement, Annex III, Article 40.
[45] Interim Agreement, Annex I, Article III.
[46] Interim Agreement, Annex VII.
[47] Interim Agreement, Article XXXI, para. 9.
[48] Interim Agreement, Articles XVII–XXI and Annex IV.
[49] Interim Agreement, Annex III, Appendix I, Article 32.
[50] Interim Agreement, Annex V.
[51] Interim Agreement, Annex VI, Article 8.

Fundamentalists on both sides objected to the agreement and accused its authors of treason.[52] Hamas said that the agreement meant that Palestinians would never have a state. Others criticized it for ignoring the '1948 refugees' (those who fled or were expelled from Palestine during the war that attended the creation of Israel), stating that the PA's acceptance of the West Bank and Gaza as the limits of a future Palestine amounted to acquiescence that they could never return to their homes.[53]

In Israel some opponents saw the deal as flawed in security terms, while others could not accept any deal involving compromises on the West Bank. Opposition leader Benjamin Netanyahu was particularly adamant in his view that the deal was deeply flawed. Despite criticism, polls showed that a slim majority of Israelis supported the Interim Agreement.[54] This was translated into the result of the Knesset vote on the agreement on 6 October 1995, which the government won by a margin of 61 to 59. The intensity of the protests increased, and the extreme right-wing presented Rabin's likeness in Nazi uniform and disrupted Rabin at public rallies with vicious verbal attacks. Concern was expressed that the intensity of the hatred could lead to an act of violence against the political leadership.[55]

One of the reasons the debate was difficult was because many did not understand where the peace process was headed. In remarks to the Knesset on 5 October, Rabin made a clear statement of his vision of peace and outlined specific positions which Israel would take in the forthcoming Final Status talks. He stated that a united Jerusalem under Israeli sovereignty would continue to be Israel's capital and that its boundaries would extend beyond the recently expanded municipal boundaries of the city. In addition he said that 'The security border of the state of Israel will be located in the Jordan Valley in the broadest meaning of that term'. He promised that 'The borders of the State of Israel, during the permanent solution, will be *beyond* the lines which existed before the Six-Day War. We will not return to the June 4, 1967 lines'. Speaking of the PA's future, Rabin said, 'We see the final arrangements as including most of the Land of Israel, as it was under the British Mandate, and alongside it a Palestinian entity, which is less than a state, and which will independently run the lives of most of the Palestinians living in the Gaza Strip and the West Bank'. Finally, Rabin justified the course he had chosen; 'We had to choose between the Greater Land of Israel, which means a bi-national state and whose population would comprise, as of today, 4.5 million Jews and more than 3 million Palestinians, which are a separate entity—religious, polit-

---

[52] Brown, D., 'Israel agrees to quit West Bank', *Guardian Weekly*, 1 Oct. 1995, p. 1.

[53] Ozanne, J., 'Islamic group slams PLO–Israel accord', *Financial Times*, 26 Sep. 1995, p. 7; and Fisk, R., 'Despair greets deal in the Palestinian refugee camps', *The Independent*, 26 Sep. 1995, p. 8.

[54] Ozanne, J., 'Israelis back deal by slim majority', *Financial Times*, 29 Sep. 1995.

[55] See the summaries of Israeli press stories in 'Fear of peace opponents turning verbal abuse to physical violence is real', *Mideast Mirror*, 12 Oct. 1995, pp. 2–5; and 'Columnists warn of civil violence erupting out of angry political debate', *Mideast Mirror*, 13 Oct. 1995, pp. 8, 9.

ical and national—and a state smaller in area, but which would be a Jewish state. We choose to be a Jewish state'.[56]

Although Rabin's remarks seemed clear, there was disagreement over whether the PA would become a state. Arafat took the view that this was the only logical outcome of the peace process, and even some of Rabin's cabinet appeared to hold divergent views.[57]

Implementation of the Interim Agreement was accompanied by problems. The first arose over prisoner release. President Weizman refused to release all of the prisoners agreed, particularly those convicted of killing Israelis, who required presidential pardons. When Weizman would not pardon two women convicted of murder, another 20 women, who had been pardoned, refused to leave prison in sympathy.[58] Since the agreement committed Israel to release 'all female detainees and prisoners in the first stage' of releases,[59] this became the first crisis in its implementation. The situation worsened when General Ilan Biran, the military governor of the West Bank, denied pardons to three other women. However, 950 prisoners were released by Israel by mid-October, constituting the bulk of the first stage of the release process. Moreover, the female prisoners were eventually released by Weizman.

Questions also arose over the schedule for redeployment of the Israeli Army from area A. On 5 October Arafat wrote Rabin a letter accusing Israel of delaying its commitment to begin redeployment within 10 days of signing the Interim Agreement by handing over only modest authority in small villages.[60] Peres and Arafat met on 15 October to resolve the dispute, and a timetable for withdrawal was agreed.[61]

The assassination of Prime Minister Rabin and preparations for the Palestinian elections

In early November 1995 concern over the intensity of the domestic opposition to the peace process caused many Israelis to unite in support of the government. Supporters of the peace process organized a rally on 4 November in Tel Aviv. As Rabin left the rally he was murdered by Yigal Amir, a right-wing religious extremist who regarded Rabin's peace policy as traitorous.[62] A few

[56] Rabin quotations from Collins, L., 'Rabin offers vision for final settlement', *Jerusalem Post* (international edn), week ending 14 Oct. 1995, pp. 1, 2; and excerpts from the text of the speech in *Mideast Mirror*, 6 Oct. 1995, pp. 3–5, emphasis in original.

[57] Environment Minister Yossi Sarid commented that eventual Palestinian statehood was inevitable shortly before the ceremony in Washington. 'A Palestinian state on the way?', *Jerusalem Post* (international edn), week ending 7 Oct. 1995, p. 3.

[58] 'Talks on redeployment schedule continue, but snag hits release of women prisoners', *Mideast Mirror*, 9 Oct. 1995, pp. 2–3.

[59] Interim Agreement, Annex VII, 'Release of Palestinian prisoners and detainees', para. 2a.

[60] The letter and its contents are referred to in 'Rabin confers with senior aides over Arafat's protestation', *Mideast Mirror*, 12 Oct. 1995, pp. 5–7; and Reuter, 'Israel's Peres, PLO's Arafat to meet', 11 Oct. 1995.

[61] The schedule is reprinted in 'Accelerated timetable', *Mideast Mirror*, 16 Oct. 1995, p. 4. The schedule was kept despite the assassination of Rabin.

[62] Gellman, B. and Blumenfeld, L., 'The religious obsessions that drove Rabin's killer', *International Herald Tribune*, 13 Nov. 1995, pp. 1, 6.

hours later Peres assumed office. The impact of Rabin's assassination upon Israel was profound: most Israelis were incredulous that a Jew could murder another Jew for political reasons. For many, the illusion that Israel was a country where heated internal debate could never lead to civil war was shattered.[63]

Politically, the assassination appeared, at least in the short term, to have discredited the Israeli right wing.[64] Peres experienced a dramatic boost in the opinion polls, although it was short-lived. Over the longer term, concerns over personal security may lead many Israelis to return to the Likud banner once the shock of Rabin's murder fades.

When he became prime minister, Peres stated his determination to continue the peace process and committed himself to the redeployment schedule. By early December Israeli officials conceded that redeployment meant that the peace process had passed 'the point of no return'.[65] Any attempt by Israel to forcibly return to the previous state of affairs would not be politically feasible or militarily easy. The large number of international representatives who attended Rabin's funeral, including several Arab leaders and representatives of Arab states with which Israel does not yet have diplomatic ties, signalled the extent to which the political situation in the region has changed and that it is unlikely to return to the pre-1993 status quo.

By the end of 1995 the redeployments had been accomplished (with the exception of Hebron, as agreed) and preparations were under way for the Palestinian elections. Concerns were expressed by observers that the elections would not be entirely fair, but a heavy turnout was anticipated.[66] (The elections took place on 20 January 1996 and resulted in a large majority for Arafat, who was also elected Head (Ra'ees) of the Executive Authority of the Council. The turnout was heavy despite calls for a boycott by opponents of the process. International observers declared the elections substantially free and fair.)

III. The Israeli–Syrian talks

In 1995 the talks between Syria and Israel were dominated by the nature and timetable of the Israeli withdrawal from the Golan Heights and the character of the peace and security guarantees which Syria would offer Israel. At times the talks made progress. The Israeli and Syrian chiefs of staff met in Washington in June and reportedly developed a set of understandings on security. Unfortunately, subsequent disagreement over exactly what had been discussed prevented further high-level meetings until December 1995. For much of 1995 the talks consisted of hopeful signs, missed opportunities and revised dead-

---

[63] Dennis, M., 'Death opens "deep wound in nation's spirit"', *Financial Times*, 6 Nov. 1995, p. 1.

[64] Ozanne, J., 'Likud leader struggles to avoid taking blame', *Financial Times*, 8 Nov. 1995, p. 7. Netanyahu's struggle became more difficult when Rabin's widow publicly blamed him for having contributed to the atmosphere of violence which led to her husband's death.

[65] Cockburn, P., 'Israeli pull-out passes the point of no return', *The Independent*, 1 Dec. 1995, p. 16.

[66] Brown, D., 'Arafat "tinkers with polls"', *The Guardian*, 2 Jan. 1996, p. 7.

lines. The process followed the 1994 pattern:[67] sporadic meetings between officials in Washington, extensive US mediation and an apparent unwillingness on the part of Syrian President Hafez al-Assad to engage in the type of secret face-to-face talks which had taken place in the other bilateral negotiations.

For Israel the goal of the negotiation with Syria (and by extension with Lebanon) is relatively straightforward: a peace treaty, including provisions for full exchanges between the two societies on all levels, leading to an end to the war between Israel and Syria. Such a treaty would have to include security arrangements to compensate for the loss of the Golan Heights and to ensure the protection of Israel's water supplies. Peace with Syria would also be the signal for the other Arab participants in the peace process (primarily Saudi Arabia and a few Gulf states) to enter into normal relations with Israel.

In addition to the basic requirement of getting the Golan Heights back, Syria's strategic goals are more complex. First, with the end of the cold war, and with it Syria's ability to count on Soviet political assistance and military cooperation on favourable conditions, Syria needs to reorient its foreign policy to the West and particularly to the USA. This requires peace with Israel and other acts designed to convince the US State Department to no longer list Syria as a sponsor of terrorism. Second, President Assad must be able to show his people and the rest of the Arab world that he has achieved peace on his terms in order to solidify his position in the post-peace Middle East and to justify waiting so much longer than Egypt to make peace with Israel. Third, Israel's desire for 'normalized' relations as part of a peace treaty, including personal and economic links between the two countries, may pose a problem for the Syrian Government, which has demonstrated a desire to retain close control over such links with the outside world. Fourth, any peace deal will have to take into account Syria's special situation in Lebanon, while also providing for the security of Israel's northern border.

In early 1995 there was little activity in the talks between the Israeli and Syrian ambassadors in Washington. Meanwhile, it became known that Israel had proposed a four-year timetable for withdrawal from the Golan Heights.[68] In March 1995 US Secretary of State Warren Christopher visited the region to try to breathe new life into the peace process. However, Israel warned that time was running out in view of the impending Israeli elections.[69]

During the Christopher visit it was agreed that the ambassadorial talks in Washington would be resumed, that the chiefs of staff would meet and that a committee of Israel, Syria and the USA would oversee the talks, although it was not reported what the committee would do.[70] In addition, Israel intimated

[67] Kemp and Pressman (note 4), pp. 186–91.

[68] Izenberg, D., Makovsky, D. and Collins, L., "'Israel wants four years for Golan Heights withdrawal'", *Jerusalem Post* (international edn), week ending 14 Jan. 1995, p. 3.

[69] Reuter, 'Israel to Syria: make peace deal now or lose the chance for several years', *International Herald Tribune*, 7 Mar. 1995.

[70] Associated Press, 'Israel and Syria to reopen talks', *International Herald Tribune*, 15 Mar. 1995, p. 6; and Hudson, D., 'Syria and Israel agree to resume peace negotiations', *The Guardian*, 15 Mar. 1995, p. 5.

that it was prepared to give up the Golan Heights in return for peace, while President Assad indicated a willingness to confer some form of recognition on Israel before the completion of withdrawal.[71] The ambassadorial talks resumed on 25 March, and progress was made on security arrangements, troop reductions and foreign monitors.

The talks then stalled over the lines to which Israel would withdraw and how deeply into each country the demilitarization would extend. The first issue was Syria's insistence that the boundaries be those of 4 June 1967, rather than the 1923 boundary agreed by Britain and France when they were the Mandatory Powers for the region, which Israel recognizes as the international border. Syria does not accept the 1923 boundary, which also formed much of the agreed border between the two countries in the 1948 Armistice Agreement, and had extended its control over the Golan Heights between 1948 and 1967. A return to the 1967 boundaries would give slightly more land to Syria, including a small piece of territory that would provide Syria access to Lake Tiberius, a critical source of water.

In May the stalled talks moved forward when the Syrians reportedly showed flexibility on a key security issue: the relative distances Israeli and Syrian troops would be withdrawn from the Golan. Syria is reported to have accepted Israel's view that the distances be asymmetrical in view of Syria's strategic depth.[72] Israel had long argued that security arrangements should be mutual and reciprocal, but not equal or symmetrical.

On 24 May the USA announced that Israel and Syria had agreed to what was called a framework understanding on security arrangements.[73] The framework is said to have enshrined earlier progress on asymmetrical security arrangements and contained agreements on issues such as early warning, demilitarized areas and weapon deployment limits. The USA announced that talks would intensify and that the chiefs of staff would meet to discuss detailed provisions but warned that much remained to be done, including the reaching of agreement on non-military issues.

On 25 May Peres made a far-reaching statement on Israel's possible withdrawal from the Golan Heights. Perhaps to prepare the Israeli public for the eventual agreement, Peres stated that Syria would demand no less for peace than Egypt had.[74] Further progress came a few days later when Prime Minister Rabin stated that one Golan settlement would have to be relinquished in the first stage of Israeli withdrawal from the Golan, with others following.[75] A few

---

[71] Haberman, C., 'Israel says Syria is promising ties for Golan return', *New York Times*, 1 Apr. 1995, pp. A1, A5.

[72] Greenhouse, S., 'Israel–Syria talks move ahead, U.S. says', *New York Times*, 16 May 1995, p. A6.

[73] Reuter, 'Security plan agreed upon by Israelis and Syrians', *International Herald Tribune*, 25 May 1995, p. 1; and Greenhouse, S., 'Damascus making a big concession in talks on Golan', *New York Times*, 25 May 1995, pp. A1, A8.

[74] Haberman, C., 'Peres inches toward ceding Golan for peace with Syria', *New York Times*, 26 May 1995, p. A2.

[75] 'PM: "One Golan settlement must go"', *Jerusalem Post* (international edn), week ending 3 June 1995, pp. 1, 2. Rabin was confident that a majority of Israelis would approve withdrawal from the Golan once they saw the agreement, although a majority were sceptical at this point. Reuter, 'Rabin confident on Golan plan', *International Herald Tribune*, 3–4 June 1995, p. 5.

days later President Assad made a similarly encouraging statement on Syrian radio, one of the few occasions on which he has commented on the talks at length.[76]

The chiefs of staff met in Washington on 27 June and appeared to make progress on the question of asymmetrical withdrawals. However, Syria would not agree to demilitarize some of the sectors requested by Israel, arguing that to do so would leave the approaches to Damascus undefended. Syria also continued to oppose Israel's desire to retain access to its early-warning stations on the Golan, saying that this function should be carried out aerially, possibly with US assistance.[77]

In July Assad referred to the possibility of a third party operating the stations on behalf of Israel, but he subsequently repudiated the idea.[78] This question had been discussed before, with the USA suggested as the logical choice. There had also been a proposal that Israelis might serve in the stations under US command. This was rejected by Syria. Israel was also opposed to the idea unless it could have its own officers in the stations as it feared disputes with the USA over data and that in a crisis the USA might not reveal all information in an attempt to prevent a situation from escalating.

Some in Israel began to consider a formal security arrangement with the USA to counterbalance the security concessions that Israel would have to make to Syria for peace. Discussion of these ideas continued into 1996.

Unfortunately, the talks slowed in July and did not regain momentum until after Rabin's assassination. President Assad, claiming that there was misunderstanding over what had been agreed by the chiefs of staff, refused to allow follow-on meetings between military officers and proposed that the process revert to meetings between diplomats. Rabin refused, stating that the process had evolved and should not move backwards. Israel's insistence that it retain access to the Golan early-warning stations seemed the primary cause of the slow-down. President Assad maintained his position that aerial surveillance was adequate,[79] but Israel did not agree.

As the Israeli–Palestinian talks neared their climax, both Assad and Rabin seemed to abandon the goal of peace in 1995 or perhaps until after the 1996 elections. Both leaders demonstrated indifference to the need for haste.[80] Whether their statements were tactical or genuine is difficult to assess, but there was little indication of talks between July and November.

---

[76] Sheridan, M., 'Syria edges closer to treaty with Israel', *The Independent*, 13 June 1995, p. 14. Israel's response to Assad's comments was swift. On 5 June Peres stated that 'the Golan Heights were never historically part of Israel'.

[77] Gold, D., 'Forewarned is forearmed', *Jerusalem Post* (international edn), week ending 29 July 1995, p. 7.

[78] 'Peres thanks Syria for "positive" signs on peace', *International Herald Tribune*, 12 July 1995, p. 2.

[79] See, for example, his comments to the Egyptian daily *al-Ahram*, in *Mideast Mirror*, 11 Oct. 1995, p. 14.

[80] See, for example, 'Assad can afford to wait, even for Likud', *Mideast Mirror*, 13 Oct. 1995, pp. 10–15. See also 'US thinks neither Rabin nor Assad is interested in peace deal', *Mideast Mirror*, 20 Oct. 1995, pp. 2–6.

The situation worsened when nine Israelis were killed in attacks by the Iranian-supported Hizbollah group in Israel's self-declared 'security zone' in southern Lebanon in mid-October. The Israeli Government charged that the attacks were ordered by Syria to remind Israel that Syria held the key to peace in southern Lebanon.[81] Syria denied the accusation, saying that the attacks demonstrated the desire of the Lebanese people to resist the Israeli occupation.[82]

The assassination of Rabin and the succession of Peres as prime minister was accompanied by apparent progress. Shortly after the assassination, the Syrian press urged Israel to adopt a fresh approach.[83] The new mood was exemplified by the 20 November statement by the Syrian Foreign Minister that Syria would 'play its role' to convince the Lebanese 'resistance' that 'its aims have been realized' if peace were achieved between Israel and Syria.[84] This was the clearest statement yet that Syria could and would bring the violence in southern Lebanon to an end in the wake of a peace treaty. Such a step could have adverse implications for Syria's relationship with Hizbollah's main supporter, Iran, which Damascus has striven to cultivate.

At the same time, Peres signalled his intention to diverge from Rabin's tactic of concentrating only on security. In his speech to the Knesset on 22 November upon forming his new government, Peres hinted that the time had come to consider all aspects of the Israeli–Syrian talks simultaneously, rather than just focusing on security.[85] Following discussions between Prime Minister Peres and President Bill Clinton in Washington, Secretary of State Christopher was sent to the region to restart the talks.

After meeting with Assad and Peres, Christopher reported that direct talks would resume between the two sides without preconditions in late December in the USA. In a change from previous rounds, it was agreed that the USA would play a more active role, presenting ideas for compromise. Amid uncharacteristically positive statements from Christopher and his aides, it was announced that the talks would recommence in the USA on 27 December.[86]

It subsequently emerged that Israel had hinted that it might reduce the time period required for withdrawal from the Golan Heights and rely on aerial surveillance and other means to replace its early-warning stations there, if

---

[81] 'PM slams Syrian support for terror', *Jerusalem Post* (international edn), week ending 28 Oct. 1995, pp. 1, 2.

[82] 'The Lebanese option', *Mideast Mirror*, 16 Oct. 1995, pp. 10–11.

[83] 'Syria urges Peres to adopt a fresh approach to peace', *Mideast Mirror*, 7 Nov. 1995, pp. 14–15; 'A Syrian olive branch to Peres', *Mideast Mirror*, 8 Nov. 1995, pp. 12–13; and 'Moves to accelerate Syria track, with Peres way ahead in opinion ratings', *Mideast Mirror*, 17 Nov. 1995, pp. 1–2.

[84] 'Syria will curb Hizbollah after peace—Sharaa', *Mideast Mirror*, 20 Nov. 1995, p. 12. The Foreign Minister also made a statement appealing for 'calm' in Southern Lebanon during the talks on 20 Dec. 'Sharaa applauds Peres's "flexibility" opposes "escalation" in South Lebanon', *Mideast Mirror*, 20 Dec. 1995, pp. 8–9.

[85] See the text of his remarks in 'Peres appeals to Assad before winning 62–8 Knesset confidence vote', *Mideast Mirror*, 22 Nov. 1995. On 7 December word surfaced that Israel was preparing a new strategy, based on the Prime Minister's comments. Ozanne, J. ,'Israel to present new initiative to break deadlock in talks with Syria', *Financial Times*, 7 Dec. 1995, p. 5.

[86] Lippman, T. W., 'Syria drops conditions for peace negotiations', *International Herald Tribune*, 16–17 Dec. 1995; and Brown, D., 'Peres ready to give up Golan Heights', *The Guardian*, 18 Dec. 1995, p. 6.

Syria would agree to a sufficiently deep demilitarization of the area. Mention was made of the possibility of other nationals occupying the early-warning stations and transmitting data to Israel in 'real time' via fibre optic cables.[87]

The year thus ended with Israel and Syria back at the negotiating table. Despite the more positive atmosphere officials pointed out that months of bargaining lay ahead and that the Israeli elections were drawing closer. As 1995 ended Peres faced the decision of whether to hold elections in the spring in order to secure his own mandate while memories of Rabin's murder were fresh or to wait until October when elections were scheduled. His decision was rumoured to be contingent on whether he believed that the prospects for progress on the Syrian track justified delaying the elections. Peres ultimately decided to move the elections forward to 29 May 1996.

IV. The Israeli–Jordanian talks

Talks between Jordan and Israel aimed at implementing the Treaty of Peace of 26 October 1994[88] made steady progress in 1995. The treaty calls for 15 functional agreements to be negotiated between the two states in such areas as economic cooperation, tourism and agriculture. By December 1995 most of these had been achieved and the others were at an advanced stage. Also, joint economic projects, such as the sharing of tourism infrastructure in the Aqaba–Eilat region, were under way.

However, signs emerged towards the end of 1995 that King Hussein was concerned over what he perceived to be lack of support for the treaty among academics, writers and others in Jordan. Shortly after Rabin's death, the king remonstrated against those whom he claimed were undermining stability in Jordan through opposition to peace and called on 'the silent majority' of supporters of his policies to become more active.[89] Jordan also continued to express a desire to develop economic ties to demonstrate that a 'peace dividend' was being realized.

The year began with Israeli withdrawal from small areas of Jordanian land near the Dead Sea. Much of this land is arid, but two small areas were handed back which Israeli farmers will continue to farm under a 'leaseback' arrangement with Jordan.[90] By the end of 1995, Peres was speculating that Israel might in future locate some of its infrastructure in Jordan. He argued that Israeli land could thus be set aside for housing and agriculture. Peres advocated that airports, oil terminals, railway lines and highways be located in Jordan, which is five times larger than Israel. When asked about the danger of

---

[87] See the comments of Israeli Deputy Defence Minister Ori Orr in an interview with the Associated Press, reprinted in *Mideast Mirror*, 20 Dec. 1995, pp. 4–5.

[88] See note 3.

[89] See the text of the king's remarks and associated press coverage translated in 'King Hussein warns local opponents of peace process', *Mideast Mirror*, 10 Nov. 1995, pp. 10–14.

[90] The leaseback arrangement is detailed in Annex 1(c) of the treaty between Israel and Jordan. See also Greenberg, J., 'Israel's crops in Jordan's fields? It must be peace', *New York Times*, 28 Mar. 1995, p. A4.

Israel losing access to these facilities in a war, Peres scoffed, 'Where will the lion come [from]—from Jordan? Egypt? We have peace with them!'[91]

The improving relations between the two countries were strained over certain issues in 1995. Israel's expansion of settlements around Jerusalem and the proposed move of the US embassy to Jerusalem were criticized by Jordan.[92] However, the relationship had matured sufficiently for criticism over specific issues not to be a threat to ties generally.

Perhaps the greatest long-term impediment will be if the economic situation in Jordan does not improve following peace. Accordingly, the promises of the international community to provide economic relief to Jordan in return for peace assume strategic importance. In this context, the difficulty which the Clinton Administration had in persuading Congress to honour pledges to provide debt relief to Jordan was critical. King Hussein lobbied Congress personally on the issue,[93] and Prime Minister Rabin publicly reminded the USA how much it stood to lose if a relatively small investment in debt relief was not made. On 21 July, the US Congress passed a bill which financed the write-off of Jordan's $480 million debt to the USA. At the end of 1995 Israel supported Jordan's request to the USA for F-16 fighter aircraft for the Jordanian Air Force. Overall, the ability to translate the political accomplishments of the peace process into tangible gains for Jordan will be the true test of the peace between Israel and Jordan.[94]

V. The multilateral track in 1995

The multilateral track of the Middle East peace process has not received significant attention outside a small group of specialists.[95] In 1994 the US Deputy Assistant Secretary of State who oversaw the multilateral negotiations referred to them as 'the stealth peace process'.[96]

The procedures for the multilateral track were agreed in Moscow in January 1992.[97] It was decided that there would be five working groups which would report to a Steering Group, that all decisions would be made by consensus, that states outside the Middle East (and international organizations such as the

[91] Quoted in Shapiro, H., 'Israel, Amman agree on transport, tourism', *Jerusalem Post* (international edn), week ending 28 Oct. 1995, p. 24.

[92] Haberman (note 17).

[93] Sciolino, E., 'As a lobbyist, King Hussein finds it cool on Capitol Hill', *New York Times*, 29 Mar. 1995, pp. A8.

[94] Gardner, D., 'Jordan: a new stake in stability', *Financial Times*, 25 Oct. 1995, p. 27.

[95] For exceptions, see Peters, J., *Pathways to Peace: The Multilateral Arab–Israeli Peace Talks* (Royal Institute for International Affairs: London, 1996); and Kemp and Pressman (note 4), pp. 191–94.

[96] Quoted in Greenberger, R., 'Israel, Arab nations ease tensions, make modest gains in low-key talks', *Wall Street Journal*, 19 Sep. 1994, p. A11.

[97] See the comments of Secretary of State James Baker at the organizational meeting for the multilateral process in Moscow in Jan. 1992. 'Organizational meeting for multilateral negotiations on the Middle East', *US Department of State Dispatch (Supplement)*, Jan. 1992, pp. 27–28. For an in-depth examination of the multilateral process in the Middle East, see Peters (note 95). See especially pp. 5–8 for a discussion of the basic aims of the process.

United Nations) would be involved in the multilateral process and that initial projects would be practically oriented.[98]

The relationship between the bilateral and the multilateral tracks is crucial. The bilateral negotiations retain primary importance. In practical terms, many issues dealt with in the multilateral negotiations are also part of the bilateral negotiations, and there is reluctance to push too far on these issues in the multilateral forum until appropriate understandings are reached bilaterally. More broadly, some Arab delegations believe that the multilateral negotiations should not promote the normalization of relations between Israel and the region until all bilateral issues have been addressed. The strongest proponent of this view is Syria's President Assad, who has refused to join the multilateral track until the bilateral negotiations between Israel and Syria are concluded.[99] He has urged other Arab leaders to do the same. Not all have followed suit—Jordan, Morocco, Oman, Qatar and Tunisia have taken tentative steps to develop relations with Israel in advance of the resolution of all bilateral issues.

The multilateral negotiations promote a pan-regional approach to the issues of concern. President Assad has stated that the emergence of a sense of 'Middle-Easternism', particularly in economic terms, represents an attempt 'to eliminate the concept of Arabism. . . . The Middle East is posited as a substitute for Arabism', warning that the concept is a tool of outsiders to diminish the Arab nation.[100] Others take the view that a pan-regional approach is necessary to address the underlying problems of the region beyond the Arab–Israeli dispute and to release its economic potential. The two economic summit meetings held in the region can be viewed in this light.

The Steering Group is developing a Vision Paper, which is intended to promote a common vision of a Middle East at peace. It outlines the desired norms for relations between the states of the region and establishes goals towards these ends. Discussion of the Vision Paper continued throughout 1995 without result. The Steering Group also heard proposals in 1995 for the creation of new multilateral working groups on human rights and Jerusalem. Neither proposal received the necessary consensus required for action.[101]

The Arms Control and Regional Security Working Group

The Arms Control and Regional Security (ACRS) Working Group was the only group which did not hold a plenary meeting in 1995. Its last such meeting was held in December 1994, and the group had previously met every six months since 1992. Although a plenary meeting was scheduled for the spring of 1995, a dispute between Israel and Egypt over Israeli policy towards the

---

[98] Peters (note 95).

[99] For a statement from Madrid on Syria's position, see Foreign Broadcast Information Service, *Daily Report–Near East and South Asia (FBIS-NES)*, 10 May 1993, p. 5.

[100] See President Assad's comments to *al-Aharam* in *Mideast Mirror*, 11 Oct. 1995, p. 15.

[101] Peters (note 95), pp. 14–15.

1968 Non-Proliferation Treaty (NPT) prevented the meeting.[102] As the NPT was up for renewal in May 1995, it was believed that a divisive ACRS Plenary would serve no purpose.

The Egyptian–Israeli dispute, which manifests itself in debate over the wording of a reference to the NPT in the draft ACRS Statement on Arms Control and Regional Security, is central to discussion of the role and function of ACRS. Egypt argued that ACRS should regard the possible existence in the region of weapons of mass destruction as a priority issue for immediate discussion and action. Cairo is concerned by the security and political ramifications of Israel's status as an alleged possessor of nuclear weapons, believes that this creates a dangerous and unequal situation in the region and wants to use ACRS to address that situation.[103]

Israel held that its policy of nuclear ambiguity was a symptom of a larger problem—lack of security. Accordingly, it was important to foster a new security environment through the development of mutual confidence. As confidence grew, according to Israel, the nuclear problem would wither away. The task of ACRS, in the Israeli view, was to begin developing confidence in the region through the adoption of progressively more ambitious confidence-building measures (CBMs) leading to arms control agreements.[104] Towards the end of 1995, Israel implied that it would sign the NPT after peace had been achieved in the region, including peace with Iran, Iraq and Libya, states not currently represented in the peace process.[105] However, this ambiguous statement does not seem to have been enough to restart the ACRS process.

Although the plenary did not meet, ACRS continued its work in functional areas. In 1993 ACRS had created two subgroups dealing, respectively, with 'operational' questions (CBMs) and 'conceptual' matters, such as verification. Both subgroups report to the plenary. On the basis of the Tunis plenary meeting of December 1994, ACRS established an interim Regional Communications Network, modelled on that of the Organization for Security and Co-operation in Europe (OSCE), in March 1995. The initial network hub is collocated with the OSCE hub in The Hague. It is expected that a regional hub will be created in Cairo. End-user stations have been installed or ordered by Egypt, Israel, Jordan, the Palestinians and Qatar.[106] It is hoped that other stations will become operational shortly. The development of the network is facilitated by the Netherlands, and it was demonstrated at an ACRS meeting on operational matters in Antalya, Turkey, in March 1995. Also in 1995, a five-day training

---

[102] See also chapter 13 in this volume.

[103] For a statement of the Egyptian position, see Karem, M., 'The proliferation of weapons of mass destruction and of ballistic missiles', ed. C. Oudraat, *United Nations Institute for Disarmament Research: Conference of Research Institutes in the Middle East* (UNIDIR: Geneva, 1994), pp. 39–50.

[104] For the Israeli view, see Levite, A., 'Confidence and security-building measures in the Middle East', ed. C. Oudraat (note 103), pp. 97–103. Furthermore, Israel does not wish to discuss the nuclear issue without Iranian participation in the ACRS, as Iran's alleged nuclear ambitions are a source of considerable concern in Israel.

[105] Collins, L., 'Peres ready to "give up atom" after peace', *Jerusalem Post* (international edn), week ending 30 Dec. 1995, p. 1.

[106] Lok, J. J., 'Security in numbers on the OSCE network', *Jane's Defence Weekly*, 24 Jan. 1996, p. 27.

course was held in Cairo for Middle East operators.[107] Associated with the network is a Russian project to develop an ACRS data bank on arms control and security matters which will be accessible through the network.

The texts of two maritime CBMs were completed at the March 1995 Antalya meeting, and discussion began on implementation. The texts are a multilateral regional Prevention of Incidents at Sea Agreement and a regional framework for maritime search and rescue cooperation. The discussion of maritime CBMs was facilitated by Canada. Other discussions in 1995 included a planning meeting in Tunis in January for a proposed maritime 'activity' involving regional assets,[108] and a planning meeting in Canada for the second in a series of meetings involving senior naval officers from the region. However, the meeting of senior naval officers did not take place in 1995.

The exchange of 'non-sensitive' military information and prior notification of military exercises continued to be discussed in 1995. Turkey has been facilitating this issue, and agreed texts were adopted at the Tunis plenary meeting.[109] They were further refined in 1995 with respect to the information to be exchanged.

A meeting was held on conceptual issues in Helsinki in late May. It heard presentations on the possible definition of the Middle East for arms control purposes and continued a long-standing discussion of the ACRS Statement on Arms Control and Regional Security. Issues such as the definition of long-term goals for regional arms control and security continued to present difficulty, and the ACRS Statement was not finalized. It was agreed, however, that a seminar on military doctrines would be held in the future.

Finally, a meeting was held in Amman in September to discuss the establishment of a Regional Security Centre (RSC). The RSC proposal, made by Jordan, had been approved by the Tunis plenary meeting. The plenary meeting had also approved the establishment of such a centre in Jordan, with other facilities in Qatar and Tunisia. The suggested purposes of the RSC are: to facilitate seminars and meetings on topics relevant to the ACRS process, to facilitate and provide training for regional parties in arms control matters, and to function as a part of the ACRS Communications System and data bank.[110] The meeting made considerable progress in drafting a mandate for the RSC but did not achieve consensus because of the nuclear issue.

It appeared that it might be possible to resume work in ACRS in 1996 when Peres and Egyptian President Hosni Mubarak seemed to agree not to address the dispute over nuclear weapons for a year. Indications are, however, that this understanding did not create the circumstances required for a resumption of

[107] Institute for Defense and Disarmament Studies, *Arms Control Reporter* (IDDS: Brookline, Mass.), sheet 453.B.186, Dec. 1994.

[108] Although the planning meeting took place, the actual activity had to be postponed after adverse press coverage caused some regional states to request that a more propitious moment be found. At the time of writing the maritime activity has not been rescheduled. For more on the activity, see Downing, J., 'Flying the flag for peace', *Jane's Defence Weekly*, 11 Mar. 1995, p. 30.

[109] It text is reprinted in *Arms Control Reporter,* sheets 453.D.17–D.20, Dec. 1994.

[110] See note 107.

ACRS. The ACRS group may have to rely on unofficial meetings for much of 1996.

The Regional Economic Development Working Group

The Regional Economic Development Working Group (REDWG) addresses issues relating to the region's economic infrastructure. It is implementing the Copenhagen Action Plan of 1993, which created a framework of projects to promote economic integration. A Monitoring Committee, established in Rabat in June 1994 oversees this activity. The Monitoring Committee has in turn established various Sectoral Committees to deal with different types of economic projects.[111]

Representative of the REDWG meetings in 1995 were seminars organized by France on the port and maritime sector, civil aviation and railways in the region. These explored ways in which national transport infrastructures in the region could cooperate. In 1995 seminars were also held on the role of the private sector in the construction of public infrastructure, and studies were completed on regional approaches to trade and tourism.[112]

Closely associated with the REDWG, although not formally part of it, is the series of summit meetings on economic cooperation sponsored by the New York-based Council on Foreign Relations and the Geneva-based World Economic Forum. The first regional economic summit meeting was held in Casablanca in October 1994 and resulted in a number of proposals for the stimulation of regional trade and development.[113] The second summit meeting was held in Amman in October–November 1995 and approved a number of ambitious projects such as: the creation of a regional Bank for Economic Development in the Middle East and North Africa, based in Cairo, to promote infrastructure projects and develop regional economic cooperation; the creation of a Regional Business Council to promote regional trade; the creation of an Economic Summit Executive Secretariat in Rabat to foster private sector cooperation; and the establishment of a Regional Tourism Board.[114] The 1995 summit meeting emphasized the development of contacts among business leaders.

A number of Arab commentators are suspicious of the process of closer economic cooperation in the region. For example, several wealthy Gulf states have refused to provide capital for the proposed bank. Given the size of Israel's economy (equal to the Egyptian, Jordanian, Lebanese and Syrian economies combined) some believe that the economic summit meetings will provide Israel a mechanism for economic domination of the region. Worries exist that Western interests will use the Regional Development Bank to further

---

[111] Peters (note 95), pp. 46–60.
[112] A full listing of REDWG activities in support of the Copenhagen Action Plan is found in Peters (note 95), pp. 99–101.
[113] The Casablanca Declaration of 1 Nov. 1994 is reproduced in Peters (note 95), appendix 6. See also Nicholson, M. and Ozanne, J., 'Beating Mideast swords into ploughshares', *Financial Times*, 29–30 Oct. 1994.
[114] The Amman Declaration of 31 Oct. 1995 is reproduced in Peters (note 95), appendix 7.

cement what Arab nationalists believe to be an unhealthy hold on the region's economies. In addition, there are continuing concerns over the problem of normalization with Israel prior to peace.[115] Plans were announced in Amman to hold a third summit meeting in Cairo in 1996.

The EU held its own meeting with several Middle Eastern states from the Mediterranean region in November in Barcelona. The meeting was intended to launch a Euro-Mediterranean process of discussion and trade to combat instability and poverty in the region. Although there were disputes over terminology relating to non-proliferation and self-determination, the meeting produced an agreed statement calling for regular dialogue and the creation of a free-trade zone by 2010.[116]

The Environment Working Group

The Environment Working Group promotes cooperation in an area which should be non-controversial, but there have been difficulties. The Palestinians attempted to establish an environmental protection agency at early meetings of the group. Israel objected, but the issue was resolved with the signing of the DOP in September 1993, which established such an agency. A second problem was Egypt's insistence that the issue of radioactive waste in the region be dealt with. Israel resisted, fearing that this was an Egyptian ploy to introduce the nuclear dispute into another working group. The issue was finally discussed in 1995 when a seminar was held in Washington shortly before the NPT Review and Extension Conference.

Aside from these controversies the group has made progress on its agenda. An achievement of note was the adoption of the Bahrain Environmental Code of Conduct for the Middle East at the Bahrain plenary meeting on 25 October 1994.[117]

Projects and discussions were under way through 1995. The World Bank is overseeing a project on desertification intended to establish new grazing lands and to study methods for the purification of brackish water. Regional centres were established in 1995 to study this topic. Another project is the Upper Gulf of Aqaba Oil Spill Contingency Plan, intended to mesh the contingency plans of Egypt, Israel and Jordan. It is funded by the EU and Japan.[118]

---

[115] For more on the views of those who opposed the summit meeting, see the comments in the Saudi daily *Asharq al-Awsat* translated as 'Beware Israel's economic agenda', *Mideast Mirror*, 17 Oct. 1995, pp. 12–13; and those in various Arab papers translated and summarized under 'Arabs warned of Israel's economic designs ahead of Amman summit', *Mideast Mirror*, 20 Oct. 1995, pp. 9–13. Lebanon, Saudi Arabia and Syria did not attend.

[116] Nash, E., 'Mediterranean trade deal clinched', *The Independent*, 29 Nov. 1995, p. 9; and Reuter, '"Euro-Med" talks pledge era of peace', *Financial Times*, 29 Nov. 1995, p. 6.

[117] It is reproduced in Peters (note 95), appendix 3.

[118] These projects are referred to in Libiszewski, S., *Water Disputes in the Jordan Basin Region and their Role in the Resolution of the Arab–Israeli Conflict* (Centre for Security Studies and Conflict Research: Zurich, 1995), pp. 83–84.

The Water Resources Working Group

The Water Resources Working Group deals with an issue which is directly relevant to the bilateral negotiations. The group has agreed to leave discussion of the division of existing water resources to the various bilateral tracks and has concentrated instead on ways of enhancing water supplies and using water more efficiently. The group has established projects to promote water conservation, train personnel in water management, encourage research into desalination, enhance water quality and create data banks on water management issues. Concrete examples include a German study of water demand in the next century and ways in which it can be met, a Canadian project to install rainwater catchment systems in Gaza and an Omani proposal to establish a Desalination Research Centre in Oman. These projects continued throughout 1995.[119]

The Refugee Working Group

The Refugee Working Group, chaired by Canada, is the other group dealing with an issue most relevant to the bilateral negotiations. The issue of which Palestinian refugees will be allowed to return to their former homes is critical to the Final Status talks.[120] The working group does not discuss this issue but rather seeks to find ways of improving the conditions of refugees. Notwithstanding this aim, the group has run into controversy. For example, the Palestinians insisted that the subject of 'family reunification' be on the agenda. Israel views this with suspicion as possibly opening the door to an unspecified Palestinian 'right of return' to Israel proper for the purposes of reuniting families.[121]

Despite the controversy, a number of projects are under way. For example, a Norwegian project seeks to establish a database on the current situation of refugees and efforts to assist them, although this is not to be a database listing refugees. French-sponsored seminars on family reunification are intended to examine the current policies of regional states in this area.

The group has generated projects to improve the quality of life for refugees. These include a German project for vocational training for refugees, a Japanese project for the construction of schools for refugees, a Swedish project to support refugee children in the West Bank and Gaza, and a Canadian project to move refugees from a camp in Egypt back to Gaza.

[119] Libiszewski (note 118), pp. 82–85; see also Peters (note 95), pp. 16–22.
[120] Tentative discussions involving Egypt, Israel, Jordan and the Palestinians began in Mar. but were inconclusive. Haberman, C., 'Now, the tough issue: Palestinian refugees', *New York Times*, 9 Mar. 1995, p. A3.
[121] Peters (note 95), p. 30.

Summary of the multilateral negotiations

In reviewing the multilateral process and its achievements in 1995, there are several notable factors. The multilateral negotiations have succeeded in involving in the peace process a number of Arab countries beyond those which border Israel and also a large number of countries outside the region. However, the multilateral negotiations remain firmly subservient to the bilateral negotiations. Without continued progress on the bilateral track, the multilateral negotiations would not continue. At the same time, they are also beginning to take on a life of their own. This is particularly true where the questions they address are not directly germane to the Arab–Israeli dispute but rather are endemic to the region as a whole.

The Environment and Regional Economic Development working groups focus on such areas, and many states of the region are willing to proceed, provided the bilateral negotiations do not completely collapse and that the work done by the groups does not impinge upon them. It is in the direct interest of many regional states that these groups not be held hostage to the bilateral process. The Water Resources and Refugee working groups, on the other hand, remain firmly linked to the bilateral track. It is unlikely that the groups which address these issues will go beyond the technical work they have done to date until the bilateral track signals a 'go-ahead'. However, this does not mean that some of the projects they have established have not developed a life of their own.

ACRS is a hybrid. Many states conceive this working group as primarily a vehicle for addressing security concerns *vis-à-vis* Israel. While this is a valid objective, it seems clear that discussions of broader regional security issues must move beyond the immediate Arab–Israeli dynamic to address the security concerns of the region as a whole. This will be difficult as long as ACRS focuses on the Arab–Israeli issues and states critical to general regional security, such as Iran and Syria, remain outside the group.

VI. Wider regional issues and conclusions

The Middle East peace process continued its difficult course in 1995. The bilateral talks made progress, although not as much as had been hoped, especially in the Syrian talks. The progress made in the Palestinian negotiations was fundamental, but what occurred in 1995 was intended to have happened many months earlier. Nevertheless, the two sides seem to be on course, and the election of the Palestinian Council should provide President Arafat and his peace policy with even greater legitimacy. That progress was slower than expected may not prove to be detrimental in the long term.

However, the price of progress, particularly in Israel, was high. The murder of Prime Minister Rabin will likely count as one of the great tragedies in the history of Israel. Although Peres has all the qualifications to succeed him and may well prove willing to move ahead more quickly than was Rabin, Rabin's standing as a champion of security seemed to cause an Israeli public already sceptical on security issues to look even more closely at the process. Much will depend on the outcome of the Israeli elections scheduled for 29 May 1996.

More broadly, the assassination of Rabin indicates that the political landscape of the Middle East remains subject to violent disruption at the hands of extremists. Events in Algeria, Bahrain, Egypt and Saudi Arabia,[122] and the continuing efforts in the region by groups which justify their acts on religious grounds, are a reminder that a radical change in any nation's leadership and policies as a result of violence remains a possibility.

Clearly, those who oppose the objectives of the peace process are still active and working to undermine it and to reverse the course of the past few years. Indeed, as the process moves closer to finding solutions, the activities of terrorists on all sides can be expected to increase.

Moving beyond the Arab–Israeli peace process, and looking at the region as a whole, it seems unlikely that true regional security will be achieved in the absence of Iran and Iraq. Both states, although weakened by war and economic embargoes, retain the power to fundamentally upset the most careful calculations of regional stability, and they have demonstrated that they are prepared to use that power.

These points being made, the peace process has proved itself to be more resilient than many had thought. It is worth remembering how much has been accomplished since the 1991 Madrid Conference, much of it unthinkable at that time. In 1996 the Israeli, Palestinian and US elections will have an impact on the peace process. The Iranian parliamentary election will also provide some clues as to future political developments in that country. Other events and trends likely to be of significance include: the beginning of the Final Status talks, developments on the Syrian track and the general economic development of the region. It is in this last area that the multilateral negotiations can make their greatest contribution to stability in the region by convincing people in the Middle East that an end to the cycle of bloodshed will improve their daily lives in measurable ways.

---

[122] Each of these countries has to some degree suffered internal upheaval owing to violent protests against the established government by dissident groups claiming to be acting for religious motives.

Appendix 4A. Documents on the Middle East peace process

THE TABA ISRAELI–PALESTINIAN JOINT STATEMENT[1]

Taba, Egypt, 11 August 1995

The Palestinian delegation, headed by President Yasser Arafat, and the Israeli delegation, headed by Foreign Minister Shimon Peres, met in Taba, Egypt, between 7–11 August, 1995 and agreed on some of the principles, to be elaborated in the Interim Agreement, as follows:

1. Area B

In Area B there will be a complete redeployment of Israeli military forces. The Palestinian Police shall assume responsibility for public order for Palestinians and shall establish [I: 25] [P: 30] police stations and posts in towns, villages and other places, as agreed. In Area B, Israel shall have the overriding responsibility for security for the purpose of protecting Israelis and confronting the threat of terrorism. While the [I: activities] [P: movement] of uniformed Palestinian policemen in Area B outside places where there is a Palestinian Police station will be carried out after coordination and confirmation, three months after the completion of redeployment from Area B, the DCOs (District Coordination and Cooperation Offices) may decide that movement of Palestinian policemen from the police stations in Area B to Palestinian towns and villages in Area B on roads that are used only by Palestinian traffic will take place after notifying the DCO.

These procedures will be reviewed within six months.

2. Further redeployments

The further redeployments of Israeli military forces to specified military locations will be gradually implemented in accordance with the DOP (Declaration of Principles) in three intervals, every six months, after the inauguration of the Council, to be completed by [P: February] [I: July] 1997. In Area C, while Israel will transfer civil powers and responsibilities not relating to territory in the first phase of redeployment, powers and responsibilities relating to territory will be transferred gradually to Palestinian jurisdiction that will cover West Bank and Gaza Strip territory, except for the issues that will be negotiated in the permanent status negotiations, during the further redeployment phases, to be completed by [P: February] [I: July] 1997.

3. Hebron

With regard to Hebron, both sides exchanged ideas and decided to continue negotiations on this issue.

4. Prisoners

In addition to the two stages of prisoner release agreed to in the context of the Ministerial Committee (one upon the signing of the interim agreement and the other before the Palestinian elections), there will be a third stage. The Ministerial Committee will work out the details of this third stage.

5. Revenues

The Israeli side will transfer tax revenues to the Palestinian side upon the signing of the interim agreement.

6. Joint committee

A joint Israeli–Palestinian–American committee will be formed to deal with (1) economic issues; (2) water production; and (3) political coordination.

7. The Palestinian Covenant

Two months after the inauguration of the Palestinian Council, the Palestinian Covenant will be amended in accordance with the letter of Chairman Arafat to Prime Minister Rabin, dated September 9, 1993.

Source: *Jerusalem Post* (international edn), week ending 19 Aug. 1995, p. 6.

---

[1] On points still disputed, [I] and [P] refer to Israeli and Palestinian proposals, respectively.

THE ISRAELI–PALESTINIAN INTERIM AGREEMENT ON THE WEST BANK AND THE GAZA STRIP

Washington, DC, 28 September 1995

Excerpts

The Government of the State of Israel and the Palestine Liberation Organization (hereinafter 'the PLO'), the representative of the Palestinian people;

Preamble

Within the framework of the Middle East peace process initiated at Madrid in October 1991;

Reaffirming their determination to put an end to decades of confrontation and to live in peaceful coexistence, mutual dignity and security, while recognizing their mutual legitimate and political rights;

Reaffirming their desire to achieve a just, lasting and comprehensive peace settlement and historic reconciliation through the agreed political process;

Recognizing that the peace process and the new era that it has created, as well as the new relationship established between the two Parties as described above, are irreversible, and the determination of the two Parties to maintain, sustain and continue the peace process;

Recognizing that the aim of the Israeli–Palestinian negotiations within the current Middle East peace process is, among other things, to establish a Palestinian Interim Self-Government Authority, i.e. the elected Council (hereinafter 'the Council' or 'the Palestinian Council'), and the elected Ra'ees of the Executive Authority, for the Palestinian people in the West Bank and the Gaza Strip, for a transitional period not exceeding five years from the date of signing the Agreement on the Gaza Strip and the Jericho Area (hereinafter 'the Gaza–Jericho Agreement') on May 4, 1994, leading to a permanent settlement based on Security Council Resolutions 242 and 338;

Reaffirming their understanding that the interim self-government arrangements contained in this Agreement are an integral part of the whole peace process, that the negotiations on the permanent status, that will start as soon as possible but not later than May 4, 1996, will lead to the implementation of Security Council Resolutions 242 and 338, and that the Interim Agreement shall settle all the issues of the interim period and that no such issues will be deferred to the agenda of the permanent status negotiations;

Reaffirming their adherence to the mutual recognition and commitments expressed in the letters dated September 9, 1993, signed by and exchanged between the Prime Minister of Israel and the Chairman of the PLO;

Desirous of putting into effect the Declaration of Principles on Interim Self-Government Arrangements signed at Washington, DC on September 13, 1993, and the Agreed Minutes thereto (hereinafter 'the DOP') and in particular Article III and Annex I concerning the holding of direct, free and general political elections for the Council and the Ra'ees of the Executive Authority in order that the Palestinian people in the West Bank, Jerusalem and the Gaza Strip may democratically elect accountable representatives;

Recognizing that these elections will constitute a significant interim preparatory step toward the realization of the legitimate rights of the Palestinian people and their just requirements and will provide a democratic basis for the establishment of Palestinian institutions;

Reaffirming their mutual commitment to act, in accordance with this Agreement, immediately, efficiently and effectively against acts or threats of terrorism, violence or incitement, whether committed by Palestinians or Israelis;

Following the Gaza–Jericho Agreement, the Agreement on Preparatory Transfer of Powers and Responsibilities signed at Erez on August 29, 1994 (hereinafter 'the Preparatory Transfer Agreement'); and the Protocol on Further Transfer of Powers and Responsibilities signed at Cairo on August 27, 1995 (hereinafter 'the Further Transfer Protocol'); which three agreements will be superseded by this Agreement;

Hereby agree as follows:

CHAPTER 1. THE COUNCIL

Article I

Transfer of Authority

1. Israel shall transfer powers and responsibilities as specified in this Agreement from the Israeli military government and its Civil Administration to the Council in accordance with this Agreement. Israel shall continue to exercise powers and responsibilities not so transferred.

2. Pending the inauguration of the Council, the powers and responsibilities transferred to the Council shall be exercised by the Palestinian Authority established in accordance with the Gaza–Jericho Agreement, which shall also have all the rights, liabilities and obligations to be assumed by the Council in this regard. Accordingly, the term 'Council' throughout this Agreement shall, pending the inauguration of the Council, be construed as meaning the Palestinian Authority.

3. The transfer of powers and responsibilities to the police force established by the Palestinian Council in accordance with Article XIV below (hereinafter 'the Palestinian Police') shall be accomplished in a phased manner, as detailed in this Agreement and in the Protocol concerning Redeployment and Security Arrangements attached as Annex I to this Agreement (hereinafter 'Annex I').

4. As regards the transfer and assumption of authority in civil spheres, powers and responsibilities shall be transferred and assumed as set out in the Protocol Concerning Civil Affairs attached as Annex III to this Agreement (hereinafter 'Annex III').

5. After the inauguration of the Council, the Civil Administration in the West Bank will be dissolved, and the Israeli military government shall be withdrawn. The withdrawal of the military government shall not prevent it from exercising the powers and responsibilities not transferred to the Council.

6. A Joint Civil Affairs Coordination and Cooperation Committee (hereinafter 'the CAC'), Joint Regional Civil Affairs Subcommittees, one for the Gaza Strip and the other for the West Bank, and District Civil Liaison Offices in the West Bank shall be established in order to provide for coordination and cooperation in civil affairs between the Council and Israel, as detailed in Annex III.

7. The offices of the Council, and the offices of its Ra'ees and its Executive Authority and other committees, shall be located in areas under Palestinian territorial jurisdiction in the West Bank and the Gaza Strip.

Article II

Elections

1. In order that the Palestinian people of the West Bank and the Gaza Strip may govern themselves according to democratic principles, direct, free and general political elections will be held for the Council and the Ra'ees of the Executive Authority of the

Council in accordance with the provisions set out in the Protocol concerning Elections attached as Annex II to this Agreement (hereinafter 'Annex II').

2. These elections will constitute a significant interim preparatory step towards the realization of the legitimate rights of the Palestinian people and their just requirements and will provide a democratic basis for the establishment of Palestinian institutions.

3. Palestinians of Jerusalem who live there may participate in the election process in accordance with the provisions contained in this Article and in Article VI of Annex II (Election Arrangements concerning Jerusalem).

4. The elections shall be called by the Chairman of the Palestinian Authority immediately following the signing of this Agreement to take place at the earliest practicable date following the redeployment of Israeli forces in accordance with Annex I, and consistent with the requirements of the election timetable as provided in Annex II, the Election Law and the Election Regulations, as defined in Article I of Annex II.

Article III

Structure of the Palestinian Council

1. The Palestinian Council and the Ra'ees of the Executive Authority of the Council constitute the Palestinian Interim Self-Government Authority, which will be elected by the Palestinian people of the West Bank, Jerusalem and the Gaza Strip for the transitional period agreed in Article I of the DOP.

2. The Council shall possess both legislative power and executive power, in accordance with Articles VII and IX of the DOP. The Council shall carry out and be responsible for all the legislative and executive powers and responsibilities transferred to it under this Agreement. The exercise of legislative powers shall be in accordance with Article XVIII of this Agreement (Legislative Powers of the Council).

3. The Council and the Ra'ees of the Executive Authority of the Council shall be directly and simultaneously elected by the Palestinian people of the West Bank, Jerusalem and the Gaza Strip, in accordance with the provisions of this Agreement and the Election Law and Regulations, which shall not be contrary to the provisions of this Agreement.

4. The Council and the Ra'ees of the Executive Authority of the Council shall be elected for a transitional period not exceeding five years from the signing of the Gaza–Jericho Agreement on May 4, 1994.

5. Immediately upon its inauguration, the Council will elect from among its members a Speaker. The Speaker will preside over the meetings of the Council, administer the Council and its committees, decide on the agenda of each meeting, and lay before the Council proposals for voting and declare their results.

6. The jurisdiction of the Council shall be as determined in Article XVII of this Agreement (Jurisdiction).

7. The organization, structure and functioning of the Council shall be in accordance with this Agreement and the Basic Law for the Palestinian Interim Self-Government Authority, which Law shall be adopted by the Council. The Basic Law and any regulations made under it shall not be contrary to the provisions of this Agreement.

8. The Council shall be responsible under its executive powers for the offices, services and departments transferred to it and may establish, within its jurisdiction, ministries and subordinate bodies, as necessary for the fulfilment of its responsibilities.

9. The Speaker will present for the Council's approval proposed internal procedures that will regulate, among other things, the decision-making processes of the Council.

Article IV

Size of the Council

The Palestinian Council shall be composed of 82 representatives and the Ra'ees of the Executive Authority, who will be directly and simultaneously elected by the Palestinian people of the West Bank, Jerusalem and the Gaza Strip.

Article V

The Executive Authority of the Council

1. The Council will have a committee that will exercise the executive authority of the Council, formed in accordance with paragraph 4 below (hereinafter 'the Executive Authority').

2. The Executive Authority shall be bestowed with the executive authority of the Council and will exercise it on behalf of the Council. It shall determine its own internal procedures and decision making processes.

3. The Council will publish the names of the members of the Executive Authority

immediately upon their initial appointment and subsequent to any changes.

4. a. The Ra'ees of the Executive Authority shall be an *ex officio* member of the Executive Authority.

b. All of the other members of the Executive Authority, except as provided in subparagraph c. below, shall be members of the Council, chosen and proposed to the Council by the Ra'ees of the Executive Authority and approved by the Council.

c. The Ra'ees of the Executive Authority shall have the right to appoint some persons, in number not exceeding twenty percent of the total membership of the Executive Authority, who are not members of the Council, to exercise executive authority and participate in government tasks. Such appointed members may not vote in meetings of the Council.

d. Non-elected members of the Executive Authority must have a valid address in an area under the jurisdiction of the Council.

Article VI

Other Committees of the Council

1. The Council may form small committees to simplify the proceedings of the Council and to assist in controlling the activity of its Executive Authority.

2. Each committee shall establish its own decision-making processes within the general framework of the organization and structure of the Council.

Article VII

Open Government

1. All meetings of the Council and of its committees, other than the Executive Authority, shall be open to the public, except upon a resolution of the Council or the relevant committee on the grounds of security, or commercial or personal confidentiality.

2. Participation in the deliberations of the Council, its committees and the Executive Authority shall be limited to their respective members only. Experts may be invited to such meetings to address specific issues on an *ad hoc* basis.

Article VIII

Judicial Review

Any person or organization affected by any act or decision of the Ra'ees of the Executive Authority of the Council or of any member of the Executive Authority, who believes that such act or decision exceeds the authority of the Ra'ees or of such member, or is otherwise incorrect in law or procedure, may apply to the relevant Palestinian Court of Justice for a review of such activity or decision.

Article IX

Powers and Responsibilities of the Council

1. Subject to the provisions of this Agreement, the Council will, within its jurisdiction, have legislative powers as set out in Article XVIII of this Agreement, as well as executive powers.

2. The executive power of the Palestinian Council shall extend to all matters within its jurisdiction under this Agreement or any future agreement that may be reached between the two Parties during the interim period. It shall include the power to formulate and conduct Palestinian policies and to supervise their implementation, to issue any rule or regulation under powers given in approved legislation and administrative decisions necessary for the realization of Palestinian self-government, the power to employ staff, sue and be sued and conclude contracts, and the power to keep and administer registers and records of the population, and issue certificates, licenses and documents.

3. The Palestinian Council's executive decisions and acts shall be consistent with the provisions of this Agreement.

4. The Palestinian Council may adopt all necessary measures in order to enforce the law and any of its decisions, and bring proceedings before the Palestinian courts and tribunals.

5. a. In accordance with the DOP, the Council will not have powers and responsibilities in the sphere of foreign relations, which sphere includes the establishment abroad of embassies, consulates or other types of foreign missions and posts or permitting their establishment in the West Bank or the Gaza Strip, the appointment of or admission of diplomatic and consular staff, and the exercise of diplomatic functions.

b. Notwithstanding the provisions of this paragraph, the PLO may conduct negotiations and sign agreements with states or international organizations for the benefit of the Council in the following cases only:

(1) economic agreements, as specifically provided in Annex V of this Agreement;

(2) agreements with donor countries for the purpose of implementing arrangements for the provision of assistance to the Council;

(3) agreements for the purpose of imple-

menting the regional development plans detailed in Annex IV of the DOP or in agreements entered into in the framework of the multilateral negotiations; and

(4) cultural, scientific and educational agreements.

c. Dealings between the Council and representatives of foreign states and international organizations, as well as the establishment in the West Bank and the Gaza Strip of representative offices other than those described in subparagraph 5. a above, for the purpose of implementing the agreements referred to in subparagraph 5. b above, shall not be considered foreign relations.

6. Subject to the provisions of this Agreement, the Council shall, within its jurisdiction, have an independent judicial system composed of independent Palestinian courts and tribunals.

CHAPTER 2. REDEPLOYMENT AND SECURITY ARRANGEMENTS

Article X

Redeployment of Israeli Military Forces

1. The first phase of the Israeli military forces redeployment will cover populated areas in the West Bank—cities, towns, villages, refugee camps and hamlets —as set out in Annex I, and will be completed prior to the eve of the Palestinian elections, i.e., 22 days before the day of the elections.

2. Further redeployments of Israeli military forces to specified military locations will commence after the inauguration of the Council and will be gradually implemented commensurate with the assumption of responsibility for public order and internal security by the Palestinian Police, to be completed within 18 months from the date of the inauguration of the Council as detailed in Articles XI (Land) and XIII (Security), below and in Annex I.

3. The Palestinian Police shall be deployed and shall assume responsibility for public order and internal security for Palestinians in a phased manner in accordance with Article XIII (Security) below and Annex I.

4. Israel shall continue to carry the responsibility for external security, as well as the responsibility for overall security of Israelis for the purpose of safeguarding their internal security and public order.

5. For the purpose of this Agreement, 'Israeli military forces' includes Israel Police and other Israeli security forces.

Article XI

Land

1. The two sides view the West Bank and the Gaza Strip as a single territorial unit, the integrity and status of which will be preserved during the interim period.

2. The two sides agree that West Bank and Gaza Strip territory, except for issues that will be negotiated in the permanent status negotiations, will come under the jurisdiction of the Palestinian Council in a phased manner, to be completed within 18 months from the date of the inauguration of the Council, as specified below:

a. Land in populated areas (Areas A and B), including government and Al Waqf land, will come under the jurisdiction of the Council during the first phase of redeployment.

b. All civil powers and responsibilities, including planning and zoning, in Areas A and B, set out in Annex III, will be transferred to and assumed by the Council during the first phase of redeployment.

c. In Area C, during the first phase of redeployment Israel will transfer to the Council civil powers and responsibilities not relating to territory, as set out in Annex III.

d. The further redeployments of Israeli military forces to specified military locations will be gradually implemented in accordance with the DOP in three phases, each to take place after an interval of six months, after the inauguration of the Council, to be completed within 18 months from the date of the inauguration of the Council.

e. During the further redeployment phases to be completed within 18 months from the date of the inauguration of the Council, powers and responsibilities relating to territory will be transferred gradually to Palestinian jurisdiction that will cover West Bank and Gaza Strip territory, except for the issues that will be negotiated in the permanent status negotiations

f. The specified military locations referred to in Article X, paragraph 2 above will be determined in the further redeployment phases, within the specified time-frame ending not later than 18 months from the date of the inauguration of the Council, and will be negotiated in the permanent status negotiations.

3. For the purpose of this Agreement and until the completion of the first phase of the further redeployments:

a. 'Area A' means the populated areas

delineated by a red line and shaded in brown on attached map No. 1;

b. 'Area B' means the populated areas delineated by a red line and shaded in yellow on attached map No. 1, and the built-up area of the hamlets listed in Appendix 6 to Annex I; and

c. 'Area C' means areas of the West Bank outside Areas A and B, which, except for the issues that will be negotiated in the permanent status negotiations, will be gradually transferred to Palestinian jurisdiction in accordance with this Agreement.

Article XII

Arrangements for Security and Public Order

1. In order to guarantee public order and internal security for the Palestinians of the West Bank and the Gaza Strip, the Council shall establish a strong police force as set out in Article XIV below. Israel shall continue to carry the responsibility for defense against external threats, including the responsibility for protecting the Egyptian and Jordanian borders, and for defense against external threats from the sea and from the air, as well as the responsibility for overall security of Israelis and Settlements, for the purpose of safeguarding their internal security and public order, and will have all the powers to take the steps necessary to meet this responsibility.

2. Agreed security arrangements and coordination mechanisms are specified in Annex I.

3. A Joint Coordination and Cooperation Committee for Mutual Security Purposes (hereinafter 'the JSC'), as well as Joint Regional Security Committees (hereinafter 'RSCs') and Joint District Coordination Offices (hereinafter 'DCOs'), are hereby established as provided for in Annex I.

4. The security arrangements provided for in this Agreement and in Annex I may be reviewed at the request of either Party and may be amended by mutual agreement of the Parties. Specific review arrangements are included in Annex I.

5. For the purpose of this Agreement, 'the Settlements' means, in the West Bank—the settlements in Area C; and in the Gaza Strip—the Gush Katif and Erez settlement areas, as well as the other settlements in the Gaza Strip, as shown on attached map No. 2.

Article XIII

Security

1. The Council will, upon completion of the redeployment of Israeli military forces in each district, as set out in Appendix 1 to Annex I, assume the powers and responsibilities for internal security and public order in Area A in that district.

2. a. There will be a complete redeployment of Israeli military forces from Area B. Israel will transfer to the Council and the Council will assume responsibility for public order for Palestinians. Israel shall have the overriding responsibility for security for the purpose of protecting Israelis and confronting the threat of terrorism.

b. In Area B the Palestinian Police shall assume the responsibility for public order for Palestinians and shall be deployed in order to accommodate the Palestinian needs and requirements in the following manner:

(1) The Palestinian Police shall establish 25 police stations and posts in towns, villages, and other places listed in Appendix 2 to Annex I and as delineated on map No. 3. The West Bank RSC may agree on the establishment of additional police stations and posts, if required.

(2) The Palestinian Police shall be responsible for handling public order incidents in which only Palestinians are involved.

(3) The Palestinian Police shall operate freely in populated places where police stations and posts are located, as set out in paragraph b(1) above.

(4) While the movement of uniformed Palestinian policemen in Area B outside places where there is a Palestinian police station or post will be carried out after coordination and confirmation through the relevant DCO, three months after the completion of redeployment from Area B, the DCOs may decide that movement of Palestinian policemen from the police stations in Area B to Palestinian towns and villages in Area B on roads that are used only by Palestinian traffic will take place after notifying the DCO.

(5) The coordination of such planned movement prior to confirmation through the relevant DCO shall include a scheduled plan, including the number of policemen, as well as the type and number of weapons and vehicles intended to take part. It shall also include details of arrangements for ensuring continued coordination through appropriate communication links, the exact schedule of movement to the area of the planned operation, including the destination and routes thereto, its proposed duration and the schedule for returning to the police station or post.

The Israeli side of the DCO will provide the Palestinian side with its response, following a request for movement of policemen in accordance with this paragraph, in normal or routine cases within one day and in emergency cases no later than 2 hours.

(6) The Palestinian Police and the Israeli military forces will conduct joint security activities on the main roads as set out in Annex I.

(7) The Palestinian Police will notify the West Bank RSC of the names of the policemen, number plates of police vehicles and serial numbers of weapons, with respect to each police station and post in Area B.

(8) Further redeployment is from Area C and transfer of internal security responsibility to the Palestinian Police in Areas B and C will be carried out in three phases, each to take place after an interval of six months, to be completed 18 months after the inauguration of the Council, except for the issues of permanent status negotiations and of Israel's overall responsibility for Israelis and borders.

(9) The procedures detailed in this paragraph will be reviewed within six months of the completion of the first phase of redeployment.

Article XIV

The Palestinian Police

1. The Council shall establish a strong police force. The duties, functions, structure, deployment and composition of the Palestinian Police, together with provisions regarding its equipment and operation, as well as rules of conduct, are set out in Annex I.

2. The Palestinian police force established under the Gaza–Jericho Agreement will be fully integrated into the Palestinian Police and will be subject to the provisions of this Agreement.

3. Except for the Palestinian Police and the Israeli military forces, no other armed forces shall be established or operate in the West Bank and the Gaza Strip.

4. Except for the arms, ammunition and equipment of the Palestinian Police described in Annex I, and those of the Israeli military forces, no organization, group or individual in the West Bank and the Gaza Strip shall manufacture, sell, acquire, possess, import or otherwise introduce into the West Bank or the Gaza Strip any firearms, ammunition, weapons, explosives, gunpowder or any related equipment, unless otherwise provided for in Annex I.

Article XV

Prevention of Hostile Acts

1. Both sides shall take all measures neces-

sary in order to prevent acts of terrorism, crime and hostilities directed against each other, against individuals falling under the other's authority and against their property, and shall take legal measures against offenders.

2. Specific provisions for the implementation of this Article are set out in Annex I.

Article XVI

Confidence Building Measures

With a view to fostering a positive and supportive public atmosphere to accompany the implementation of this Agreement, to establish a solid basis of mutual trust and good faith, and in order to facilitate the anticipated cooperation and new relations between the two peoples, both Parties agree to carry out confidence building measures as detailed herewith:

1. Israel will release or turn over to the Palestinian side, Palestinian detainees and prisoners, residents of the West Bank and the Gaza Strip. The first stage of release of these prisoners and detainees will take place on the signing of this Agreement and the second stage will take place prior to the date of the elections. There will be a third stage of release of detainees and prisoners. Detainees and prisoners will be released from among categories detailed in Annex VII (Release of Palestinian Prisoners and Detainees). Those released will be free to return to their homes in the West Bank and the Gaza Strip.

2. Palestinians who have maintained contact with the Israeli authorities will not be subjected to acts of harassment, violence, retribution or prosecution. Appropriate ongoing measures will be taken, in coordination with Israel, in order to ensure their protection.

3. Palestinians from abroad whose entry into the West Bank and the Gaza Strip is approved pursuant to this Agreement, and to whom the provisions of this Article are applicable, will not be prosecuted for offenses committed prior to September 13, 1993.

CHAPTER 3. LEGAL AFFAIRS

Article XVII

Jurisdiction

1. In accordance with the DOP, the jurisdiction of the Council will cover West Bank and Gaza Strip territory as a single territorial unit, except for:

a. issues that will be negotiated in the permanent status negotiations: Jerusalem, settlements, specified military locations, Palestinian refugees, borders, foreign relations and Israelis; and

b. powers and responsibilities not transferred to the Council.

2. Accordingly, the authority of the Council encompasses all matters that fall within its territorial, functional and personal jurisdiction, as follows:

a. The territorial jurisdiction of the Council shall encompass Gaza Strip territory, except for the Settlements and the Military Installation Area shown on map No. 2, and West Bank territory, except for Area C which, except for the issues that will be negotiated in the permanent status negotiations, will be gradually transferred to Palestinian jurisdiction in three phases, each to take place after an interval of six months, to be completed 18 months after the inauguration of the Council. At this time, the jurisdiction of the Council will cover West Bank and Gaza Strip territory, except for the issues that will be negotiated in the permanent status negotiations.

Territorial jurisdiction includes land, subsoil and territorial waters, in accordance with the provisions of this Agreement.

b. The functional jurisdiction of the Council extends to all powers and responsibilities transferred to the Council, as specified in this Agreement or in any future agreements that may be reached between the Parties during the interim period.

c. The territorial and functional jurisdiction of the Council will apply to all persons, except for Israelis, unless otherwise provided in this Agreement.

d. Notwithstanding subparagraph a. above, the Council shall have functional jurisdiction in Area C, as detailed in Article IV of Annex III.

3. The Council has, within its authority, legislative, executive and judicial powers and responsibilities, as provided for in this Agreement.

4. a. Israel, through its military government, has the authority over areas that are not under the territorial jurisdiction of the Council, powers and responsibilities not transferred to the Council and Israelis.

b. To this end, the Israeli military government shall retain the necessary legislative, judicial and executive powers and responsibilities, in accordance with international law. This provision shall not derogate from Israel's applicable legislation over Israelis *in personam*.

5. The exercise of authority with regard to the electromagnetic sphere and air space shall be in accordance with the provisions of this Agreement.

6. Without derogating from the provisions of this Article, legal arrangements detailed in the Protocol Concerning Legal Matters attached as Annex IV to this Agreement (hereinafter 'Annex IV') shall be observed. Israel and the Council may negotiate further legal arrangements.

7. Israel and the Council shall cooperate on matters of legal assistance in criminal and civil matters through a legal committee (hereinafter 'the Legal Committee'), hereby established.

8. The Council's jurisdiction will extend gradually to cover West Bank and Gaza Strip territory, except for the issues to be negotiated in the permanent status negotiations, through a series of redeployments of the Israeli military forces. The first phase of the redeployment of Israeli military forces will cover populated areas in the West Bank— cities, towns, refugee camps and hamlets, as set out in Annex I—and will be completed prior to the eve of the Palestinian elections, i.e. 22 days before the day of the elections. Further redeployments of Israeli military forces to specified military locations will commence immediately upon the inauguration of the Council and will be effected in three phases, each to take place after an interval of six months, to be concluded no later than eighteen months from the date of the inauguration of the Council.

Article XVIII

Legislative Powers of the Council

1. For the purposes of this Article, legislation shall mean any primary and secondary legislation, including basic laws, laws, regulations and other legislative acts.

2. The Council has the power, within its jurisdiction as defined in Article XVII of this Agreement, to adopt legislation.

3. While the primary legislative power shall lie in the hands of the Council as a whole, the Ra'ees of the Executive Authority of the Council shall have the following legislative powers:

a. the power to initiate legislation or to present proposed legislation to the Council;

b. the power to promulgate legislation adopted by the Council; and

c. the power to issue secondary legislation, including regulations, relating to any matters specified and within the scope laid down in any primary legislation adopted by the Council.

4. a. Legislation, including legislation which amends or abrogates existing laws or military orders, which exceeds the jurisdiction of the Council or which is otherwise inconsistent with the provisions of the DOP, this Agreement, or of any other agreement that may be reached between the two sides during the interim period, shall have no effect and shall be void *ab initio*.

b. The Ra'ees of the Executive Authority of the Council shall not promulgate legislation adopted by the Council if such legislation falls under the provisions of this paragraph.

5. All legislation shall be communicated to the Israeli side of the Legal Committee.

6. Without derogating from the provisions of paragraph 4 above, the Israeli side of the Legal Committee may refer for the attention of the Committee any legislation regarding which Israel considers the provisions of paragraph 4 apply, in order to discuss issues arising from such legislation. The Legal Committee will consider the legislation referred to it at the earliest opportunity.

Article XIX

Human Rights and the Rule of Law
Israel and the Council shall exercise their powers and responsibilities pursuant to this Agreement with due regard to internationally-accepted norms and principles of human rights and the rule of law.

Article XX

Rights, Liabilities and Obligations
1. a. The transfer of powers and responsibilities from the Israeli military government and its civil administration to the Council, as detailed in Annex III, includes all related rights, liabilities and obligations arising with regard to acts or omissions which occurred prior to such transfer. Israel will cease to bear any financial responsibility regarding such acts or omissions and the Council will bear all financial responsibility for these and for its own functioning.

b. Any financial claim made in this regard against Israel will be referred to the Council.

c. Israel shall provide the Council with the information it has regarding pending and anticipated claims brought before any court or tribunal against Israel in this regard.

d. Where legal proceedings are brought in respect of such a claim, Israel will notify the Council and enable it to participate in defending the claim and raise any arguments on its behalf.

e. In the event that an award is made against Israel by any court or tribunal in respect of such a claim, the Council shall immediately reimburse Israel the full amount of the award.

f. Without prejudice to the above, where a court or tribunal hearing such a claim finds that liability rests solely with an employee or agent who acted beyond the scope of the powers assigned to him or her, unlawfully or with willful malfeasance, the Council shall not bear financial responsibility.

2. a. Notwithstanding the provisions of paragraphs 1.d through 1.f above, each side may take the necessary measures, including promulgation of legislation, in order to ensure that such claims by Palestinians, including pending claims in which the hearing of evidence has not yet begun, are brought only before Palestinian courts or tribunals in the West Bank and the Gaza Strip, and are not brought before or heard by Israeli courts or tribunals.

b. Where a new claim has been brought before a Palestinian court or tribunal subsequent to the dismissal of the claim pursuant to subparagraph a. above, the Council shall defend it and, in accordance with subparagraph 1.a above, in the event that an award is made for the plaintiff, shall pay the amount of the award.

c. The Legal Committee shall agree on arrangements for the transfer of all materials and information needed to enable the Palestinian courts or tribunals to hear such claims as referred to in subparagraph b. above, and, when necessary, for the provision of legal assistance by Israel to the Council in defending such claims.

3. The transfer of authority in itself shall not affect rights, liabilities and obligations of any person or legal entity, in existence at the date of signing of this Agreement.

4. The Council, upon its inauguration, will assume all the rights, liabilities and obligations of the Palestinian Authority.

5. For the purpose of this Agreement, 'Israelis' also includes Israeli statutory agencies and corporations registered in Israel.

Article XXI

Settlement of Differences and Disputes
Any difference relating to the application of this Agreement shall be referred to the appropriate coordination and cooperation mechanism established under this Agreement. The provisions of Article XV of the DOP shall

apply to any such difference which is not settled through the appropriate coordination and cooperation mechanism, namely:

1. Disputes arising out of the application or interpretation of this Agreement or any related agreements pertaining to the interim period shall be settled through the Liaison Committee.

2. Disputes which cannot be settled by negotiations may be settled by a mechanism of conciliation to be agreed between the Parties.

3. The Parties may agree to submit to arbitration disputes relating to the interim period, which cannot be settled through conciliation. To this end, upon the agreement of both Parties, the Parties will establish an Arbitration Committee.

CHAPTER 4. COOPERATION

Article XXII

Relations between Israel and the Council

1. Israel and the Council shall seek to foster mutual understanding and tolerance and shall accordingly abstain from incitement, including hostile propaganda, against each other and, without derogating from the principle of freedom of expression, shall take legal measures to prevent such incitement by any organizations, groups or individuals within their jurisdiction.

2. Israel and the Council will ensure that their respective educational systems contribute to the peace between the Israeli and Palestinian peoples and to peace in the entire region, and will refrain from the introduction of any motifs that could adversely affect the process of reconciliation.

3. Without derogating from the other provisions of this Agreement, Israel and the Council shall cooperate in combating criminal activity which may affect both sides, including offenses related to trafficking in illegal drugs and psychotropic substances, smuggling, and offenses against property, including offenses related to vehicles.

Article XXIII

Cooperation with Regard to Transfer of Powers and Responsibilities

In order to ensure a smooth, peaceful and orderly transfer of powers and responsibilities, the two sides will cooperate with regard to the transfer of security powers and responsibilities in accordance with the provisions of Annex I, and the transfer of civil powers and responsibilities in accordance with the provisions of Annex III.

Article XXIV

Economic Relations

The economic relations between the two sides are set out in the Protocol on Economic Relations, signed in Paris on April 29, 1994, and the Appendices thereto, and the Supplement to the Protocol on Economic Relations, all attached as Annex V, and will be governed by the relevant provisions of this Agreement and its Annexes.

Article XXV

Cooperation Programs

1. The Parties agree to establish a mechanism to develop programs of cooperation between them. Details of such cooperation are set out in Annex VI.

2. A Standing Cooperation Committee to deal with issues arising in the context of this cooperation is hereby established as provided for in Annex VI.

Article XXVI

The Joint Israeli–Palestinian Liaison Committee

1. The Liaison Committee established pursuant to Article X of the DOP shall ensure the smooth implementation of this Agreement. It shall deal with issues requiring coordination, other issues of common interest and disputes.

2. The Liaison Committee shall be composed of an equal number of members from each Party. It may add other technicians and experts as necessary.

3. The Liaison Committee shall adopt its rules of procedures, including the frequency and place or places of its meetings.

4. The Liaison Committee shall reach its decisions by agreement.

5. The Liaison Committee shall establish a subcommittee that will monitor and steer the implementation of this Agreement (hereinafter 'the Monitoring and Steering Committee'). It will function as follows:

a. The Monitoring and Steering Committee will, on an ongoing basis, monitor the implementation of this Agreement, with a view to enhancing the cooperation and fostering the peaceful relations between the two sides.

b. The Monitoring and Steering Committee will steer the activities of the various joint committees established in this Agreement (the JSC, the CAC, the Legal Committee, the Joint Economic Committee and the Standing

Cooperation Committee) concerning the ongoing implementation of the Agreement, and will report to the Liaison Committee.

c. The Monitoring and Steering Committee will be composed of the heads of the various committees mentioned above.

d. The two heads of the Monitoring and Steering Committee will establish its rules of procedures, including the frequency and places of its meetings.

Article XXVII

Liaison and Cooperation with Jordan and Egypt

1. Pursuant to Article XII of the DOP, the two Parties have invited the Governments of Jordan and Egypt to participate in establishing further liaison and cooperation arrangements between the Government of Israel and the Palestinian representatives on the one hand, and the Governments of Jordan and Egypt on the other hand, to promote cooperation between them. As part of these arrangements a Continuing Committee has been constituted and has commenced its deliberations.

2. The Continuing Committee shall decide by agreement on the modalities of admission of persons displaced from the West Bank and the Gaza Strip in 1967, together with necessary measures to prevent disruption and disorder.

3. The Continuing Committee shall also deal with other matters of common concern.

Article XXVIII

Missing Persons

1. Israel and the Council shall cooperate by providing each other with all necessary assistance in the conduct of searches for missing persons and bodies of persons which have not been recovered, as well as by providing information about missing persons.

2. The PLO undertakes to cooperate with Israel and to assist it in its efforts to locate and to return to Israel Israeli soldiers who are missing in action and the bodies of soldiers which have not been recovered.

CHAPTER 5. MISCELLANEOUS PROVISIONS

Article XXIX

Safe Passage between the West Bank and the Gaza Strip

Arrangements for safe passage of persons and transportation between the West Bank and the Gaza Strip are set out in Annex I.

Article XXX

Passages

Arrangements for coordination between Israel and the Council regarding passage to and from Egypt and Jordan, as well as any other agreed international crossings, are set out in Annex I.

Article XXXI

Final Clauses

1. This Agreement shall enter into force on the date of its signing.

2. The Gaza–Jericho Agreement, except for the article XX (Confidence-Building Measures), the Preparatory Transfer Agreement and the Further Trade Protocol will be superseded by this agreement.

3. The Council, upon its inauguration, shall replace the Palestinian Authority and shall assume all the undertakings and obligations of the Palestinian Authority under the Gaza–Jericho Agreement, the Preparatory Transfer Agreement, and the Further Transfer Protocol.

4. The two sides shall pass all necessary legislation to implement this Agreement.

5. Permanent status negotiations will commence as soon as possible, but not later than May 4, 1996, between the Parties. It is understood that these negotiations shall cover remaining issues, including: Jerusalem, refugees, settlements, security arrangements, borders, relations and cooperation with other neighbors, and other issues of common interest.

6. Nothing in this Agreement shall prejudice or preempt the outcome of the negotiations on the permanent status to be conducted pursuant to the DOP. Neither Party shall be deemed, by virtue of having entered into this Agreement, to have renounced or waived any of its existing rights, claims or positions.

7. Neither side shall initiate or take any step that will change the status of the West Bank and the Gaza Strip pending the outcome of the permanent status negotiations.

8. The two Parties view the West Bank and the Gaza Strip as a single territorial unit, the integrity and status of which will be preserved during the interim period.

9. The PLO undertakes that, within two months of the date of the inauguration of the Council, the Palestinian National Council will convene and formally approve the necessary changes in regard to the Palestinian Covenant, as undertaken in the letters signed by the Chairman of the PLO and addressed to

the Prime Minister of Israel, dated September 9, 1993 and May 4, 1994.

10. Pursuant to Annex I, Article VII of this Agreement, Israel confirms that the permanent checkpoints on the roads leading to and from the Jericho Area (except those related to the access road leading from Mousa Alami to the Allenby Bridge) will be removed upon the completion of the first phase of redeployment.

11. Prisoners who, pursuant to the Gaza–Jericho Agreement, were turned over to the Palestinian Authority on the condition that they remain in the Jericho Area for the remainder of their sentence, will be free to return to their homes in the West Bank and the Gaza Strip upon the completion of the first phase of redeployment.

12. As regards relations between Israel and the PLO, and without derogating from the commitments contained in the letters signed by and exchanged between the Prime Minister of Israel and the Chairman of the PLO, dated September 9, 1993 and May 4, 1994, the two sides will apply between them the provisions contained in Article XXII, paragraph 1, with the necessary changes.

13. a. The Preamble to this Agreement, and all Annexes, Appendices and maps attached hereto, shall constitute an integral part hereof.

b. The Parties agree that the maps attached to the Gaza–Jericho Agreement as:

a. map No. 1 (The Gaza Strip), an exact copy of which is attached to this Agreement as map No. 2 (in this Agreement 'map No. 2');

b. map No. 4 (Deployment of Palestinian Police in the Gaza Strip), an exact copy of which is attached to this Agreement as map No. 5 (in this Agreement 'map No. 5'); and

c. map No. 6 (Maritime Activity Zones), an exact copy of which is attached to this Agreement as map No. 8 (in this Agreement 'map No. 8');

are an integral part hereof and will remain in effect for the duration of this Agreement.

14. While the Jeftlik area will come under the functional and personal jurisdiction of the Council in the first phase of redeployment, the area's transfer to the territorial jurisdiction of the Council will be considered by the Israeli side in the first phase of the further redeployment phases.

Done at Washington DC, this 28th day of September, 1995.

For the Government of the State of Israel
For the PLO

Witnessed by:

The United States of America
The Russian Federation
The Arab Republic of Egypt
The European Union
The Kingdom of Norway
The European Union

_____

Source: Israeli–Palestinian Agreement on the West Bank and the Gaza Strip, 28 Sep. 1995, Israeli Ministry of Foreign Affairs, Jerusalem.

5. The former Yugoslavia: the war and the peace process

ANTHONY BORDEN and RICHARD CAPLAN*

I. Introduction

The year 1995 culminated with the formal signing in Paris on 14 December of an agreement to end the war in Bosnia and Herzegovina. After an extraordinary 12 months of military and diplomatic developments, including the largest military operation in NATO's history and a three-week negotiating marathon in Dayton, Ohio, with the presidents of Bosnia and Herzegovina, Croatia and Serbia, peace throughout the region was declared. According to some estimates, 250 000 had died and there were 2.7 million refugees and displaced persons in Bosnia and Herzegovina—one-third of the pre-war population.

If there was, for the first time, something in the Balkans to celebrate, it came only after the gravest humanitarian tragedies of the war, including shellings, mass executions and enormous population displacements. Moreover, despite the proliferation of peace conferences, diplomatic missions and UN resolutions, it was military developments which ultimately brought the war towards a conclusion, raising questions about what the 'peace process' had actually achieved and whether it had all along been properly conceived.

These questions were underlined by the stipulations of the Dayton Agreement on Bosnia and Herzegovina,[1] which entrenched, rather than resolved, the fundamental causes of the conflict, most importantly the territorial division of the country. Other serious concerns also remained. While a breakthrough was reached in the dispute between Greece and the Former Yugoslav Republic of Macedonia, the political stability of the latter, highlighted by the assassination attempt on the president and by continued unrest among the Albanians, remained fragile. The treatment of the Serb minority in Croatia raised fresh concern over that country's democratic credentials, and Serbia's purportedly constructive role in Bosnia and Herzegovina was belied by its continued support for the Bosnian Serbs and by the failure to take any steps towards settling the problem in Kosovo, where, it is often argued, the wars of Yugoslav secession actually began.

This chapter reviews the primary events in Croatia, Bosnia and Herzegovina and Macedonia, and then offers an assessment of future prospects for the

---

[1] The text of the Framework Agreement and annexes 1A, 1B and 4 are reproduced in appendix 5A in this volume.

* The authors would like to thank Jennifer Pearce for assistance with this chapter.

SIPRI Yearbook 1996: Armaments, Disarmament and International Security

region, including a consideration of the provisions and likely implementation of the Dayton Agreement.

II. Croatia

The year witnessed a dramatic turn of events in the Croatian conflict, with consequences for the wider region. Abandoning efforts to achieve a peaceful reintegration of Serb-controlled territories, the Croatian Government launched two military offensives—one in May and another in August—that decisively ended the three-year stalemate in its favour. By late summer the radically altered circumstances were producing knock-on effects for the Bosnian conflict which culminated in the Dayton accord.

The year began on a relatively hopeful note from the standpoint of a negotiated solution to Croatia's 'Serbian question'.[2] Although shaky, the 29 March 1994 cease-fire agreement between the Croatian Government and the Croatian Serbs[3] was still holding, and an economic agreement signed on 2 December 1994[4] had begun to be implemented. The latter envisaged the restoration of major services between Croatia and the 'Republic of Serb Krajina', the Serb-held enclaves of Croatia. Thus on 21 December 1994 a 27-km stretch of the Zagreb–Belgrade motorway running through Serb-held territory was reopened; on 9 January 1995 the Croatian Government returned electricity poles it had removed from the Obrovac power plant in Krajina; and on 27 January the northern track of the Adriatic oil pipeline, also cutting across Serb-held territory, was put back into service.[5]

Croatia's impatience became apparent, however, when on 12 January President Franjo Tudjman wrote to UN Secretary-General Boutros Boutros-Ghali indicating that Croatia would not renew the mandate of the UN Protection Force (UNPROFOR) in Croatia, due to expire at the end of March.[6] 'Croatia finds the present situation in the occupied territories wholly unacceptable', Tudjman wrote. 'Moreover, given the present inefficient UNPROFOR mission, Croatia finds the continued presence of UNPROFOR troops in the occupied territories to be significantly counterproductive to the peace process.'[7] Despite Tudjman's stated commitment to a 'constructive peace policy', there was concern about renewed fighting. Indeed, in a 23 January interview

[2] Following Croatia's declaration of independence on 25 June 1991, Croatian Serb forces, with the support of the Yugoslav National Army (JNA), seized nearly one-third of Croatia in a region known as Krajina. For background to the Croatian conflict, see Cohen, L. J., *Broken Bonds: Yugoslavia's Disintegration and Balkan Politics in Transition*, 2nd ed. (Westview Press: Boulder, Colo., 1995), chapter 8; and Woodward, S. L., *Balkan Tragedy: Chaos and Dissolution after the Cold War* (Brookings Institution: Washington, DC, 1995), chapters 5 and 6.

[3] United Nations, Report of the Secretary-General, UN document S/1994/367, 29 Mar. 1994.

[4] United Nations, Report of the Secretary-General, UN document S/1994/1375, 2 Dec. 1994.

[5] United Nations, Report of the Secretary-General, UN document S/1995/626, 26 July 1995.

[6] UN Security Council Resolution 743, 21 Feb. 1992 (UN document S/RES/743) authorized the deployment. For background to UNPROFOR's mandate in Croatia, see Claesson, P. and Findlay, T., 'Case studies on peacekeeping: UNOSOM II, UNTAC and UNPROFOR', *SIPRI Yearbook 1994* (Oxford University Press: Oxford, 1994), pp. 70–74.

[7] United Nations, Letter from the Permanent Representative of Croatia to the Secretary-General, UN document A/50/64 and S/1995/28, 12 Jan. 1995.

with *Der Spiegel*, Tudjman declared that Croatia would retake Serb-held territory, if necessary by force.[8]

In an effort to forestall violence, the Zagreb-4 group, representing the UN, Russia, the USA and the European Union (EU), presented a plan for Krajina on 30 January that would have given a large measure of autonomy to the Serbs while maintaining the formal unity of Croatia. Under the plan the Knin and Glina districts of Krajina were to be granted extensive control over taxation, police, education, tourism and public services, while Western Slavonia was to revert to Croatian Government control and Eastern Slavonia would be placed under temporary international administration.[9] Representatives of Serb Krajina, however, announced on 30 January that they would not discuss the plan unless Croatia agreed to renew UNPROFOR's mandate;[10] they seemed unwilling to cede much authority anyway.[11] The Croatian Government also objected that the plan granted the Serbs too much autonomy; on 3 February an aide to Tudjman, Smiljko Soko, deemed it 'unacceptable'.[12]

The situation continued to deteriorate: in reaction to Croatia's stance towards UNPROFOR, the Krajina 'parliament' voted on 8 February to suspend political negotiations with the Croatian Government as well as talks on further implementation of the economic agreement. Two weeks later, top Croatian Serb and Bosnian Serb military leaders met in Banja Luka to establish a joint military council to provide for mutual defence and assistance[13] (Croatian Serb assistance to the Bosnian Serbs had already been observed by the UN, most recently in the Bosnian Serb campaign against the Bihac pocket in Bosnia and Herzegovina in December 1994).[14] Croatia and the Croatian–Muslim Federation of Bosnia and Herzegovina, in turn, announced a new military alliance on 7 March 1995.[15]

There had been hints from the beginning of the year that Croatia might accept a modified international presence in Croatia.[16] In view of the deteriorating situation, the major powers thus concentrated on persuading Tudjman to

[8] 'Die Uno stört uns' [The UN disturbs us], *Der Spiegel*, 23 Jan. 1995, p. 131.
[9] Draft Agreement on the Krajina, Slavonia, Southern Baranja and Western Sirmium, 18 Jan. 1995. Text provided by the US Information Service, Zagreb.
[10] *Keesing's Record of World Events*, vol. 41, no. 1 (Jan. 1995), p. 40371.
[11] 'The RSK will never be part of Croatia', Rajko Lezajic, speaker of the parliament of the 'Republic of Serb Krajina', stated on 27 Feb. 1995. *Keesing's Record of World Events*, vol. 41, no. 2 (Feb. 1995), p. 40419.
[12] *Keesing's Record of World Events* (note 11).
[13] 'Bosnian and Krajina Serbs form joint war council', Open Media Research Institute (hereafter OMRI), *OMRI Daily Digest*, 21 Feb. 1995, URL <http://www.omri.cz/Index.html> (hereafter, references to the *OMRI Daily Digest* refer to the Internet edition at this URL address).
[14] United Nations, Report of the Secretary-General, UN document S/1994/1454, 29 Dec. 1994.
[15] 'Croats form anti-Serbia military pact with Bosnia', *International Herald Tribune*, 7 Mar. 1995, p. 1. On the 1994 agreements between the Bosnian Government and the Bosnian Croats, and between the governments of Bosnia and Herzegovina and Croatia, see Zucconi, M., 'The former Yugoslavia: lessons of war and diplomacy', *SIPRI Yearbook 1995: Armaments, Disarmament and International Security* (Oxford University Press: Oxford, 1995), pp. 218–19.
[16] On 26 Feb., for instance, Foreign Minister Mate Granic indicated that Croatia would consider the involvement of a multinational task force of observers after 31 Mar.

© SIPRI 1996; map by Billie Bielckus

Figure 5.1. Croatia and the UN Protected Areas

temper his hard line. Following discussions with US Vice-President Al Gore at the United Nations World Summit on Social Development in Copenhagen on 12 March, Tudjman announced that he would be willing to accept a scaled-down UN force (from 12 000 to 5000) whose tasks would be fourfold: to control Croatia's borders with Serbia and Bosnia and Herzegovina, to control the passage of aid through Croatia to Bosnia, to expedite implementation of the agreements between Croatia and the Croatian Serbs and to assist the repatriation of Croatian refugees to Krajina. Tudjman clearly was seeking to put an end to the de facto partition of Croatia which in his view UNPROFOR was only serving to reinforce.[17] This would explain his insistence that any extended UN presence reorient itself away from the UN Protected Areas (UNPAs) inside Croatia[18] and towards the state's internationally recognized borders—to place themselves, in other words, between the Croatian Serbs and their allies in Serbia and Bosnia and Herzegovina.

---

[17] This view was echoed by Boutros-Ghali: 'The Serb side has taken advantage of the presence of UNPROFOR in its efforts to freeze the status quo, under UNPROFOR "protection", while establishing a self-proclaimed "State" of the "Republic of Serb Krajina" in UNPROFOR's area of responsibility'. United Nations, Report of the Secretary-General to the Security Council, UN document S/1994/300, 16 Mar. 1994.

[18] The UNPAs were areas where Serbs constituted a majority or a substantial minority of the population and where intercommunal tensions had erupted in the past. UN forces were deployed to these areas in Apr. 1992 to help prevent the recurrence of hostilities. United Nations, Report of the Secretary-General, UN document S/23280, 11 Dec. 1991, Annex III.

On 31 March the Security Council voted to reorganize its peacekeeping operations in the former Yugoslavia, establishing a separate UN Confidence Restoration Operation in Croatia (UNCRO) essentially along the lines Tudjman had requested.[19] The Krajina Serb leadership protested, maintaining that as a party to the original agreement to deploy UNPROFOR any change in the mandate required its approval. Their protests fell on deaf ears.

On 1 May, however, even before the newly organized UNCRO could be deployed, the Croatian Army launched a military offensive (Operation Flash) against UNPA Sector West in Western Slavonia.[20] The official explanation for the operation was that it was aimed at ending Serb attacks on vehicles travelling along the Zagreb–Belgrade highway, which on 28 April had resulted in the deaths of five Croat civilians. By 3 May, however, Croatia was in control of the entire sector.[21] The Serbs retaliated by shelling Zagreb with cluster anti-personnel bombs, killing six and wounding 175 people. Karlovac, Sisak and Novska were also hit. The UN Security Council condemned the Croatian offensive[22] and although Peter Galbraith, the US Ambassador to Zagreb, stated that Croatia received 'not a green light but a red light' from the USA regarding the move,[23] there was speculation that the USA had indicated that it would turn a blind eye and that it had quietly been providing Croatia with military aid.[24] There were also allegations of massive human rights abuses of the local Serb population by Croatian authorities.[25] These charges were challenged by the government as well as by some independent observers,[26] and the issue still has not been fully clarified.[27] What is clear is that all but 2000–2500 Serbs out of an estimated pre-offensive population of 12 000–15 000 had fled the sector by 12 May, whether out of fear or in response to actual harassment.[28]

The significance of Operation Flash was not only military. In the absence of any intervention by the Federal Republic of Yugoslavia (Serbia and Montenegro), the offensive had the effect of radicalizing the Croatian Serb leader-

[19] UN Security Council Resolution 981, 31 Mar. 1995 (UN document S/RES/981). The Security Council did not actually authorize the deployment of UNCRO (8750 troops) until 28 Apr. 1995 (UN document S/RES/990).

[20] Borger, J., 'Balkan war erupts on new front', *The Guardian*, 2 May 1995.

[21] UN High Commissioner for Refugees, *Information Notes on Former Yugoslavia*, no. 5/95 (May 1995), p. ii.

[22] Presidential Statement of 4 May 1995, UN document S/PRST/1995/26.

[23] 'What role for the US in Western Slavonia?', *OMRI Daily Digest*, 15 May 1995.

[24] Both Britain and France voiced concerns to this effect. Clark, B., 'West's antidote for Balkans war fever', *Financial Times*, 14 Dec. 1995, p. 3; and Cohen, R., 'US cooling ties to Croatia after winking at its buildup', *New York Times*, 28 Oct. 1995, p. 1.

[25] UN officials claimed that 'massive' human rights abuses were taking place in Western Slavonia during the first few days of the offensive. 'The Croatian army offensive in Western Slavonia and its aftermath', *Human Rights Watch*, July 1995, p. 2.

[26] EU monitor Gunter Baron, for instance, described the Croatian operation as 'excellent, professional, competent and correct'. *Keesing's Record of World Events*, vol. 41, no. 5 (May 1995), p. 40565. Human Rights Watch, while it found evidence of some human rights violations, concluded that they were not widespread. 'The Croatian army offensive in Western Slavonia and its aftermath' (note 25), pp. 2, 15–16.

[27] For the questions surrounding attacks on civilians, see Hedl, D., 'Slavonia aftermath', *WarReport*, no. 34 (June 1995), p. 13.

[28] UN High Commissioner for Refugees, *Information Notes on Former Yugoslavia*, no. 6/95 (June 1995), p. ii.

ship, who on 21 May ignored the moderates in their ranks and voted for unification of the Serb territories in Croatia and Bosnia. Yugoslav Foreign Minister Vladislav Jovanovic criticized the move, arguing that it would only spell catastrophe since it would invite the international community to extend sanctions on the Bosnian Serbs to the Croatian Serbs.[29] For its part the Croatian Government indicated that it would not tolerate the establishment of a 'United Serb Republic'. In a letter of 1 June to Boutros-Ghali, Croatian Foreign Minister Mate Granic warned that if unification were attempted Croatia 'would be forced to undertake all appropriate means to defend its sovereignty and territorial integrity'.[30]

Emboldened by the success of his offensive, Tudjman on 9 June threatened further military action unless rebel Serbs in the remaining UNPAs agreed to accept Croatian sovereignty.[31] The Krajina leadership, however, insisted on the withdrawal of Croatian forces from Western Slavonia before they would be willing to restart negotiations. Both sides began to place renewed emphasis on military options: monitors noted increased troop movements of the Croatian Army while the Krajina Serb leaders announced a general mobilization, including, with Serbian assistance and in violation of international law, the forced conscription of Krajina refugees living in Serbia.[32] (The UN High Commissioner for Refugees (UNHCR) estimated that a total of 2500 draft-age ethnic Serb refugees were rounded up in June.)[33] Croatia also protested at what it claimed to be a 'significantly higher degree of involvement of the Belgrade regime on behalf of their proxies . . . in the occupied regions', referring specifically to the transfer of military equipment and the presence of some 6000 Yugoslav National Army soldiers.[34]

Rising tensions between Croatia and the Krajina Serbs came to a head in early August. On 4 August, tens of thousands of Croatian Army troops poured into UNPA Sectors North and South, thus launching Operation Storm. Meeting little or no resistance, the army captured Knin, Petrinja, Plaski and several key roads in just two days; by 9 August it was in full control of the two sectors and Croatia announced that it was ending its operations. There were once again reports of human rights violations committed by the army against the Serb population—systematic and widespread burning and looting of houses and fields and wholesale attacks on civilians—which this time could not be denied,[35] but these violations could not alone account for the fact that an estimated 180 000 refugees fled the region, mostly to northern Bosnia, in the first

[29] 'Serbian foreign minister on unification, Bosnian crisis', *Keesing's Record of World Events*, vol. 41, no. 5 (May 1995), p. 40565; and *OMRI Daily Digest*, 30 May 1995.
[30] Letter provided to the authors by Croatia's Ministry of Foreign Affairs.
[31] *Keesing's Record of World Events*, vol. 41, no. 6 (June 1995), p. 40608.
[32] Reuter, 15 June 1995. The forcible repatriation of refugees is in violation of the 1951 Convention Relating to the Status of Refugees.
[33] UN High Commissioner for Refugees, *Information Notes on Former Yugoslavia*, no. 7/95 (July 1995), p. iii.
[34] Letter of Mate Granic to UN Secretary-General Boutros-Ghali, 29 June 1995, provided by the Croatian Ministry of Foreign Affairs.
[35] Amnesty International, 'Urgent action', EUR/64/02/95 (10 Aug. 1995); and 'Urgent action', EUR/64/05/95 (15 Sep. 1995).

week. It was the largest exodus since the war began. As Zarko Puhovski, a professor at the University of Zagreb, observed, 'Knin propaganda over the years—that Serbs could never safely live within Croatia—ultimately contributed to their flight'.[36]

Whether Croatia was in fact guilty of 'ethnic cleansing', as Britain later charged,[37] the effect was certainly to move it closer to being an ethnically pure state: out of a pre-war Serb population of 600 000, an estimated 100 000–150 000 now remained. Although Serbs were officially allowed to return, the obstacles were formidable: by mid-September no formal return procedure had been established and by executive order Serbs were given only 30 days (later extended to 90) to reclaim their property, which would otherwise be given to Croat refugees and displaced persons.[38]

In what by now had become a familiar pattern, Tudjman told cheering crowds during a post-victory train ride through Krajina on 26 August that Croatia would next 'liberate' the oil-rich region of Eastern Slavonia if its Serb population did not give up its insurrection.[39] On 3 October, however, the Croatian Government met the local Serb authorities in Erdut and, in contrast with trends of the past year, reached agreement on the 'guiding basic principles' for negotiations which led to the signing, on 12 November, of the Basic Agreement on the Region of Eastern Slavonia, Baranja, and Western Sirmium.[40] The agreement provides for the establishment of a UN transitional authority to administer the region for a period of 12 months, renewable at the request of either party for a period not to exceed 12 additional months. An international force has responsibility for maintaining peace and security and for overseeing the demilitarization of the region (which, significantly, extends to existing police forces—an obvious effort to improve upon a weakness of the original Vance Plan for the UNPAs). All refugees and displaced persons have the right to return to their places of residence or to be compensated for property that cannot be restored. Elections are to be held no later than 30 days before the end of the transitional period.

It is only possible to speculate as to why the Serbs agreed to negotiate away control of this strategic region. Twice before, however, Tudjman had demonstrated that in the absence of a negotiated settlement he would not hesitate to use force to recapture occupied territory, and each time Belgrade had refused to come to the rescue of the Croatian Serbs. There was no reason to expect that the situation would be any different with Eastern Slavonia. Moreover, Serbian President Slobodan Milosevic by this time was seeking to ingratiate himself with the Western powers. There is also evidence to suggest that

[36] Puhovski, Z., 'Cleansing "Krajina"', *WarReport*, no. 35 (May 1995), p. i.

[37] The British Defence Secretary, Michael Portillo, said: 'Where people are driven from their homes and where they have lived in those places for generations, that amounts to ethnic cleansing'. Reuter, 8 Aug. 1995. The EU later issued a report condemning Croatia's 'terror against civilians'. 'As do US and others', *OMRI Daily Digest*, 2 Oct. 1995.

[38] UN High Commissioner for Refugees, *Information Notes on Former Yugoslavia*, no. 9/95 (Sep. 1995), p. iii.

[39] Reuter, 27 Aug. 1995.

[40] UN High Commissioner for Refugees, *Information Notes on Former Yugoslavia*, no. 11/95 (Nov. 1995), p. iii.

Tudjman had an effective understanding with Milosevic to exchange Serb control of Posavina in Bosnia and Herzegovina for Croatian control of Eastern Slavonia—an exchange which was to be achieved at Dayton soon afterwards.[41]

The question remains, what next? The Croatian Government expects that the agreement will lead to reintegration of the region; the Serbs believe that they will enjoy a certain degree of autonomy or even continue effectively to live in Serbia. To US President Bill Clinton, the Croatian offensive had created 'a moment of real promise' for peace in the region.[42] Certainly, Tudjman's easy victories shattered the myth of Serbian invincibility. Given Serbia's reticence, unity among the Serbs seemed little more than a slogan. These judgements underlay the policy of 'diplomacy backed by force' which the USA now began to pursue in the Bosnian conflict.

III. Bosnia and Herzegovina

After three and a half years and a dramatic *dénouement*, the war in Bosnia and Herzegovina came to a close; the first of 60 000 NATO troops marched into Bosnia and Herzegovina to implement a complex and problematic peace accord. The country was divided and devastated and the largest mission in the UN's history had been humiliated. Nevertheless, peace offered a crucial respite for the country and some hopes that new political visions could arise in a reconstructed state.

Winter offensives

At the close of 1994 the prospects for Bosnia and Herzegovina appeared as grim as ever.[43] The peace process had been drifting since the summer, when the rebel Bosnian Serbs rejected the 'take-it-or-leave-it' plan for the 51 : 49 division of the territory brokered by the Contact Group.[44] International diplomacy had focused on encouraging the split between the Belgrade and the rebel Serbs, playing to Serbian President Slobodan Milosevic's self-appointed new role as Balkan peacemaker. The Bosnian Serb leader, Radovan Karadzic, remained intransigent, however, and Milosevic continued to bargain hard for the lifting of sanctions[45] and to support Serb forces outside the Federal Republic of Yugoslavia (Serbia and Montenegro). The focus shifted from one

---

[41] Borden, A. and Hedl, D., 'How the Bosnians were broken', *WarReport*, no. 39 (Feb./Mar. 1996), p. 28.

[42] Reuter, 10 Aug. 1995.

[43] For a summary of events to the end of 1994, see Zucconi (note 15), pp. 213–29.

[44] Woodward (note 2), pp. 314–16. The Contact Group consisted of Russia and the USA plus France, Germany and the UK, the latter 3 representing the EU. Its plan, agreed to by the Bosnian Government, Croatian representatives and Serbian President Slobodan Milosevic, was rejected by the parliament of the Bosnian Serbs. Its main feature was a map to divide Bosnia 51 : 49, with the larger portion for the Croat–Bosnian Federation and the remainder for the rebel Bosnian Serbs.

[45] Economic sanctions were originally imposed against the Federal Republic of Yugoslavia (Serbia and Montenegro) by UN Security Council Resolution 757 of 30 May 1992 with the intention of preventing further intervention by Serbia in the Bosnian conflict.

crisis to the next, such as the heavy autumn fighting around the Bihac pocket in north-west Bosnia and Herzegovina, which illustrated once again the UN's inability to protect a declared safe area.[46]

Beneath the surface fundamental changes in the conflict were taking place. Despite the territorial conquests of the rebel Bosnian Serbs, the weakness of their position was becoming increasingly apparent, from over-extended front lines and a lack of spare parts to political isolation and internal divisions. At the same time, the Bosnian Army was growing stronger, gradually obtaining more arms and better trained troops, and developing more effective military and diplomatic strategies.[47] These facts and the fragile but gradually developing Bosnian military alliance with Croatian forces led some commentators to conclude that a Bosnian Serb defeat was inevitable.

The new year did offer one hopeful note. On 1 January, a four-month cease-fire, negotiated with customary flair and controversy by former US President Jimmy Carter, brought a lull in the fighting. The Cessation of Hostilities Agreement, signed by the rebel Bosnian Serbs and the Bosnian Government on 1 January, and shortly after by Bosnian Croat officials, included a number of potentially important provisions on demilitarization and the interposition of UNPROFOR troops between hostile forces, the opening of routes for humanitarian aid and civilian traffic, and the exchange of prisoners of war.[48]

Like countless cease-fires past, this agreement was to disintegrate. Severe conflict around the Bihac pocket continued, especially around the town of Velika Kladusa, pitting the joint forces of rebel Bosnian Muslim leader Fikret Abdic and rebel Serbs from Krajina against the Bosnian Army Fifth Corps. Aid deliveries by the UNHCR were restricted, raising serious health concerns for the 155 000 people there. Other provisions of the accord were neglected or only partially implemented.[49]

Critically, despite visits by representatives of the Contact Group to Sarajevo and the Bosnian Serb stronghold of Pale in late January, Karadzic refused to rejoin negotiations on the basis of the summer's division plan. Practical as well as ideological considerations drove him, convinced that after so much bloodshed and hardship his political life would be over if he signed away any of the 70 per cent of Bosnian territory in his control.[50] The cease-fire agreement increasingly appeared more like a convenient respite for the combatants than a genuine effort to make peace, with even the Bosnian Government declaring that it only reinforced an 'unacceptable status quo'.[51]

---

[46] The 6 safe areas, established by UN Security Council Resolutions 819, 16 Apr. 1993 (UN document S/RES/819) and 824, 6 May 1993 (UN document S/RES/824), were Srebrenica, Sarajevo, Tuzla, Bihac, Gorazde and Zepa. See Zucconi (note 15), pp. 221–22, 225.

[47] Vasic, M., 'War of attrition', *WarReport*, no. 29 (Oct./Nov. 1994), p. 6.

[48] Agreement on Complete Cessation of Hostilities, 31 Dec. 1994, provided to the authors by the Carter Center, Atlanta, Georgia. Traynor, I., 'Bosnian ceasefire kindles fresh hopes for peace', *The Guardian*, 2 Jan. 1995, p. 7; and Daly, E., 'Croats agree to Bosnian truce', *The Independent*, 3 Jan. 1995.

[49] UN High Commissioner for Refugees, *Information Notes on Former Yugoslavia*, no. 1/95 (Jan. 1995), p. 2.

[50] Vasic, M., 'New war', *WarReport*, no. 34 (June 1995), p. 6.

[51] 'Bosnian government refuses to extend cease-fire', *OMRI Daily Digest*, 21 Apr. 1995, citing international news agencies.

By early February, frustration over Bosnian Serb intransigence led the US Administration to a policy reversal. In an initiative that some observers argued contravened UN Resolution 942 of September 1994, which called on members not to maintain contacts with the Bosnian Serbs,[52] during December 1994 and January 1995 the US State Department had sought to establish dialogue with the Bosnian Serb leadership. By the first week of February the USA was publicly venting its exasperation with Karadzic and confirmed that it was breaking off its attempt to build a constructive rapport with the Bosnian Serbs.

In the same week the USA shifted its policy towards the Federal Republic of Yugoslavia (Serbia and Montenegro), agreeing with its European allies a controversial proposal to offer it a full lifting of sanctions for two months if it agreed to recognize the successor states in their communist-era borders, stiffen its enforcement of the arms embargo on the Bosnian Serbs,[53] and pressure the Pale leadership to rejoin the peace talks on the basis of the Contact Group's summer 1994 plan.[54] The aim of recognition was to compel Milosevic to renounce his designs of a Greater Serbia, but the practical benefits were unclear. Certifying compliance with the embargo on the Bosnian Serbs, the UN had just voted to ease sanctions.[55] A number of states warned that, once lifted, sanctions would not be re-imposed even if the Federal Republic of Yugoslavia (Serbia and Montenegro) later flagrantly violated the embargo. Concerns over compliance with sanctions were shown to be well-grounded when UN monitors reported more than 60 flights of helicopters from Serbia to Bosnian Serb army (BSA) positions around the safe area of Srebrenica. In any event, President Milosevic adamantly ruled out recognizing the Republic of Bosnia and Herzegovina.[56]

Other factors, however, appeared to justify the approach of working through Belgrade. On the ground, the Bosnian Army was holding out in Bihac town and inflicting various tactical defeats on the Serb forces. The failure of Serb forces to score a decisive victory over the Fifth Corps caused the long-running feud between Karadzic and General Ratko Mladic, commander of the BSA, to break out into the open. The Belgrade media reported accusations by the BSA that the civilian leadership had forced it to attempt impossible tasks and had not provided sufficient men and *matériel*. Through the year these recriminations were to increase as the military fortunes of the Bosnian Serbs declined. The Western media speculated that Milosevic, tired of if not directly threatened by his uncontrollable proxy Karadzic, sided with Mladic and directly fuelled the internal divisions. This view encouraged the belief internationally

[52] UN Security Council Resolution 942, 23 Sep. 1994 (UN document S/RES/942).

[53] A complete embargo was introduced on the import of all weapons and military equipment into all the republics of Yugoslavia on 25 Sep. 1991 by UN Security Council Resolution 713. The embargo was all along seen by many, especially in the USA, as unfairly disadvantaging the Bosnian Government and its forces. Senator Robert Dole in the US Congress tried to secure the unilateral lifting of the embargo on the Bosnian Government in July 1994, and in Aug. 1994 President Clinton announced that if the Serbs did not accept the Contact Group plan by 15 Oct. he would request the UN to lift it.

[54] Graham, G. and Silber, L., 'US relents on Serb sanctions', *Financial Times*, 15 Feb. 1995, p. 2.

[55] 'Security Council resolves to continue with easing of Serbian sanctions', *OMRI Daily Digest*, 13 Jan. 1995.

[56] Cohen, R., 'Serbia rejects sanctions offer', *International Herald Tribune*, 21 Feb. 1995, p. 5.

that supporting Milosevic could bring about a decisive shift in the Bosnian Serb position.

Meanwhile tensions between Croat and Bosnian authorities in Mostar increased, raising questions about the viability of the Bosnian–Croat Federation.[57] Since March 1994, the federation had been a key element in US policy towards the Balkans. While constantly wavering on its position towards the Bosnian Serbs and the Federal Republic of Yugoslavia, the USA had initiated a clear policy of supporting Croatia. In contrast to the European approach of officially neutral mediation, championed by the UK and France, the USA moved towards a policy of regional power politics. In effect this meant a change from bowing to the military strength of rebel Serbs in Croatia and Bosnia and Herzegovina towards fortifying Croatia as a balancing factor.

Croatia, however, was hardly the most disinterested ally for Bosnia and Herzegovina. President Tudjman frequently hinted at designs on Bosnian territory and openly expressed his disrespect for Muslims.[58] The hard-line nationalist 'Herzegovina' lobby remained a strong political force in Zagreb, and the self-declared mini-state of Herceg-Bosna, in Herzegovina, featured on all Croatian state accoutrements, including the Croatian dinar. The Croatian–Bosnian border was almost non-existent, and local Croatian authorities had consistently obstructed EU-sponsored efforts to reintegrate the divided city of Mostar.

By March the cease-fire in Bosnia and Herzegovina had essentially collapsed. Numbers of civilian casualties rose throughout the country, increasing numbers of people had to flee their homes, and the humanitarian operation again faced serious obstacles at checkpoints held by the BSA, and in some instances by Bosnian government forces.[59] Bihac was completely sealed off, and humanitarian aid deliveries all but ceased.[60] Then on 19 March the Bosnian Army launched substantial, ultimately successful, offensives on Serb-held mountains around Tuzla in the north-east and around Travnik in central Bosnia. Capturing high ground increased the security of these critical government-held towns and deprived the Bosnian Serbs of important communications transmitters.[61] The escalation of fighting in Bosnia, coinciding with Tudjman's high-stakes bargaining with the UN over the renewal of its mandate in Croatia, raised serious concerns about the possibility of a broader Serbian–Croatian conflict.[62]

[57] Zucconi (note 15), p. 218.

[58] Evans, M., 'Tudjman mapped out future on city menu', *The Times*, 7 Aug. 1995, gives an account of the map of the Serb–Croat division of Bosnia allegedly drawn by Tudjman on a dinner napkin. See also 'Franjo Tudjman: Nous ne ferons aucun compromis' [We will not compromise], interview with Patrick de St-Exupéry, *Le Figaro*, 25 Sep. 1995, p. 2, on Tudjman's view of the need to integrate the Muslims into European civilization.

[59] UN High Commissioner for Refugees, *Information Notes on Former Yugoslavia*, no. 4/95 (Apr. 1995).

[60] *Keesing's Record of World Events*, vol. 41, no. 3 (Mar. 1995), p. 40466.

[61] Pecanin, S., 'Climb any mountain', *WarReport*, no. 33 (May 1995), p. 12.

[62] Magas, B., 'Partnerships for Peace?', *WarReport*, no. 32 (Mar. 1995), p. 27. The new revised mandate for UN troops in Croatia was ratified in UN Security Council Resolution 981, 31 Mar. 1995 (UN document S/RES/981). At the same time, Security Council resolutions 982 and 983, both also of 31 Mar.

The hostage crisis

The expiry of the cease-fire on 1 May brought increased violence. On 7 May, Bosnian Serb shells hit the Butmir suburb of Sarajevo, killing 11 people and seriously wounding at least 14. The next day, the UN Commander in Bosnia and Herzegovina, Lieutenant-General Sir Rupert Smith, requested air strikes against BSA positions. Fearing retaliation against UN peacekeepers, UN Special Representative Yasushi Akashi overruled the decision. France and the USA strongly criticized the failure to respond and Boutros-Ghali initiated a 'fundamental review' of UN peacekeeping operations in Bosnia and Herzegovina.[63] Clearly the safe area policy was not working. The question was whether the international community lacked the will or coherence to implement it or whether the policy itself was fundamentally flawed.

On 31 May Boutros-Ghali released his review, outlining four options for peacekeeping—maintain current operations, use air strikes, pull out or scale down. Arguing that aggressive military actions are incompatible with peacekeeping activities, the Secretary-General preferred the latter option which, he suggested, would include negotiating and monitoring local agreements, maintaining a presence in the safe areas, operating the Sarajevo airport and supporting humanitarian deliveries. The UN would use force only in self-defence.[64] NATO countered that the peacekeeping deployment should be strengthened. The US Administration expressed its willingness in the event of a withdrawal to provide up to half of the 50 000 troops believed necessary to oversee a pull-out.[65]

The major powers had their own views about options, although some of their positions underwent change in the course of the year as events at home and in Bosnia were seen to create new opportunities and imperatives. Broadly speaking, there were two strategic options. The first was to try to maintain a holding pattern through peacekeeping in the hope that exhaustion would eventually induce the warring parties to settle peacefully (even if largely on Serb terms). This was essentially the view of the British and the French, who, with the largest numbers of peacekeepers on the ground, did not want to provoke the Serbs and thus expose their soldiers to undue danger. (With the election of Jacques Chirac as President, France moved closer towards a peace-enforcement stance.) The Russians also shared this view; indeed, they would have preferred to go further and lift sanctions on Yugoslavia. This may have had less to do with any pan-Slavism than with a desire for greater influence in the region.

1995 (UN documents S/RES/982 and S/RES/983), created distinct operations for Bosnia and Macedonia, respectively, and extended the mandate in Bosnia until 30 Nov. 1995.

[63] *Keesing's Record of World Events*, vol. 41, no. 5 (May 1995), p. 40563; and Borger, J., 'UN admits it cannot protect Sarajevo', *The Guardian*, 10 May 1995, p. 13.

[64] UN High Commissioner for Refugees, *Information Notes on Former Yugoslavia*, no. 6/95 (June 1995), p. i; and United Nations, Report of the Secretary-General, UN document S/1995/444, 30 May 1995.

[65] 'Peacekeeping in Bosnia-Herzegovina', *OMRI Daily Digest*, 25 May 1995.

The second option, favoured by the USA,[66] was greater use of Allied force—notably selective NATO air strikes—to restrain the Bosnian Serbs and to pressure them to accept a negotiated settlement on the basis of the Contact Group's plan. The use of force was the biggest bone of contention between the USA and its allies. As one Canadian observer put it acerbically, 'You Americans . . . want to bomb Bosnia to the last Canadian, British and French peacekeeper'.[67] Meanwhile, against the wishes of both the administration and its allies, leading members of the US Congress were moving to lift the embargo on arms to the Bosnian Government. These differences caused one of the most serious rifts NATO has ever experienced.

Despite the lack of consensus among the great powers, on 24 May General Smith issued an ultimatum to all sides to cease firing heavy weapons or face air strikes. It demanded that the Bosnian Serbs return guns they had removed from UN collection points and surrender other heavy weapons. 'If the UN orders air strikes, we are going to treat it as the enemy', Karadzic told Reuter, threatening to take UN troops hostage and to capture the enclaves of Srebrenica, Zepa and Gorazde in eastern Bosnia.

On 25–26 May, following some of the fiercest shelling of Sarajevo in more than a year, General Smith called in air strikes. Six NATO jets bombed a BSA ammunitions dump near Pale. Bosnian Serb forces responded quickly by launching attacks on Sarajevo, Srebrenica, Tuzla, Gorazde and Bihac and clashing with French troops in Sarajevo. In Tuzla a shell fired into the centre of town killed 71 people, mostly teenagers socializing in street cafes; 165 were wounded. Bosnian Serbs also began taking hundreds of UN soldiers hostage, including British, French, Canadian, Russian and other troops. Several were chained to bridges, ammunition dumps and other potential NATO targets. The number of hostages exceeded 370.

The hostage-taking created a major crisis for the UN. The USA, although widely seen as putting pressure on the UN to allow NATO to conduct the air strikes, declined to offer ground troops, later raised the possibility of a US deployment to help 'reconfigure' UNPROFOR, and later still appeared to rule it out.[68] Russia derided the strikes as 'misconceived and one-sided'. France criticized them as 'ill-prepared', saying they exposed peacekeepers to 'thoughtless risks', and mooted the possibility of withdrawal if the deployment was not significantly strengthened. Britain, which had hitherto argued consistently against a more forceful engagement and had not taken part in the strikes, responded by announcing the dispatch of 6700 fresh troops, in addi-

---

[66] The US Administration, more than other governments, was internally divided over policy options. Thus, while some members of the Administration may have favoured the use of air strikes, the Pentagon was wary of more robust engagement.

[67] Dean, J., *Ending Europe's Wars: The Continuing Search for Peace and Security* (Twentieth Century Fund: New York, 1994), p. 145, fn. 20.

[68] 'Most governments waffle in the face of Serb defiance', *OMRI Daily Digest*, 29 May 1995; 'Clinton offers US ground troops for Bosnia', *OMRI Daily Digest*, 1 June 1995; and 'Rapid Reaction Force faces hurdles', *OMRI Daily Digest*, 6 June 1995.

tion to its contingent of 3800 on the ground.[69] For the UN itself, its mission appeared to be in serious jeopardy.

The BSA supreme command declared 'all Security Council resolutions, all NATO ultimatums, and all accords with the UN . . . null and void'.[70] The Bosnian Serbs made release of the hostages contingent upon NATO guarantees not to launch any more strikes. President Milosevic became the focus of efforts by both the international community and the Bosnian Serbs to defuse the crisis, and following a meeting between the Bosnian Serb leadership and the Serbian authorities 120 hostages were released. Following further intervention by Belgrade, the remainder of the hostages were released in groups over the first three weeks of June.

One prominent casualty of the crisis may have been EU mediator for the former Yugoslavia, Lord David Owen. Although he had expressed his intentions for some time, Owen chose the height of the hostage crisis, 31 May, to resign. He had held the position since the formation of the International Conference on the Former Yugoslavia at the London Conference of August 1992, and had co-authored, with UN mediator Cyrus Vance, the Vance–Owen Plan of January 1993. He was replaced, on 12 June, by former Swedish Prime Minister Carl Bildt.

On 3 June, amid intensified fighting throughout Bosnia and Herzegovina, NATO and Western European Union ministers meeting in Paris agreed to create a new unit, the Rapid Reaction Force, for the fresh troops being sent to Bosnia and Herzegovina. This well-equipped force, to include 14 000 troops mainly from Britain and France, represented a compromise between NATO and UN imperatives: it would wear national uniforms but operate within UN military structures. Its tasks were to include retaliating in the event of an attack on UN forces, assisting isolated units to regroup, supporting besieged enclaves in eastern Bosnia, resupplying besieged peacekeepers and policing UN-declared weapon-free zones.[71]

On 15 June, a massive deployment of some 10 000–15 000 Bosnian Army troops launched a major offensive against Serb-held positions around Sarajevo to break the siege. While the UN and other officials warned the Bosnians against seeking a 'military solution', the pressure on the capital had become severe: civilian deaths were rising, water and electricity had been deliberately cut off, and UNHCR aid flights, halted in April, remained suspended.[72] Serb forces responded by heavily shelling Sarajevo and by declaring a special mobilization, which included an unprecedented campaign in Serbia of press-ganging draft-age Serbs with links to Bosnia and Herzegovina.[73] After several weeks of combat, despite confident predictions by the government and, for the

---

[69] Only 1200 were actually sent.

[70] 'Bosnian Serbs remain defiant', *OMRI Daily Digest,* 30 May 1995.

[71] The deployment was authorized by UN Security Council Resolution 998, 16 June 1995 (UN document S/RES/998).

[72] UN High Commissioner for Refugees, *Information Notes on Former Yugoslavia,* no. 7/95 (July 1995).

[73] Schwarm, P., 'Shot by both sides', *WarReport,* no. 34 (June 1995), p. 9.

first time, Croatian artillery support, the Bosnian Army offensive petered out.[74]

The fall of Srebrenica

The summer had already seen intensive international diplomacy and renewed assertions of Western resolve. Any expectations of a more unified and forceful international policy towards Bosnia and Herzegovina were shattered, however, in the second week of July with the Bosnian Serbs' capture of Srebrenica, their subsequent massacre of thousands of Bosnian Muslims of fighting age and other atrocities. The fall of the enclave, a declared safe area, was the first explicit defeat of the international forces in Bosnia and Herzegovina, and was widely proclaimed as one of the gravest humiliations not just of the UN but of the Western alliance itself.

Srebrenica was home to roughly 42 000 Bosnians, mainly Muslims displaced from elsewhere, and was defended by around 4000 poorly armed Bosnian soldiers. Seventy Dutch UN peacekeepers were deployed in the besieged town, with an additional 400 based at Potocari, five kilometres to the north. The BSA assault began on 6 July, with heavy shelling and artillery fire. Several times, over the following days, the Dutch troops called for close air support to rebuff the attacking forces. The UN Commander for Bosnia and Herzegovina and Croatia, Lieutenant-General Bernard Janvier, refused the request several times—a refusal that is still controversial.[75] By 8 July, the Serb forces easily overran UN positions, taking 32 Dutch soldiers hostage, and by the next day BSA tanks were less than two kilometres from the centre of the town. On 11 July two air strikes by NATO jets slowed an advancing BSA tank column, but a third strike was halted after the Bosnian Serbs threatened to kill some of the Dutch hostages.[76]

Shortly after, Srebrenica fell to the Bosnian Serbs. The Dutch troops fled to their base at Potocari, followed by thousands of refugees. General Mladic personally supervised the loading of Muslim women and children onto buses to expel them towards government-held territory. Men of fighting age were detained and transported to detention camps. In the aftermath thousands of refugees and the fleeing Bosnian soldiers endured mines, ambushes and live front lines in a six-day trek to Sapna, north of Tuzla. In graphic interviews given later to human rights organizations and the media, refugees described rapes and executions. Many of those fleeing lost their minds with fear.[77] Others fared worse. As the days passed thousands of people remained missing. Subsequent documentation by media and human-rights monitors revealed

[74] Block, R., 'Dead Muslim warriors erode Serb morale', *Independent on Sunday,* 25 June 1995, p. 17.
[75] Block, R., 'Betrayal of Srebrenica', *The Independent,* 30 Oct. 1995, p. 3.
[76] Bellamy, C., 'Serbs humiliate UN in "safe area"', *The Independent,* 12 July 1995.
[77] 'Bosnia–Herzegovina: the fall of Srebrenica and the failure of UN peacekeeping', *Human Rights Watch,* vol. 7, no. 13 (Oct. 1995); Borger, J., 'Lonely death in a crowded cornfield', *The Guardian,* 15 July 1995; and Dobbs, M., and Spolar, C., '12 000 Muslims and a trek through Serb killing fields', *International Herald Tribune,* 27 Oct. 1995, p. 1.

evidence of mass executions. The USA, releasing satellite reconnaissance photographs it claimed showed recent mass graves, set the numbers of persons killed at 2700; other organizations estimated 4000–8000.[78] This was the worst single atrocity of the war; many commentators deemed it the largest single mass killing in post-World War II Europe. On 27 July, the International Criminal Tribunal for the Former Yugoslavia in The Hague announced indictments against Karadzic and Mladic on charges of genocide; on 17 November the indictments were amended to include responsibility for the deaths of up to 8000 people at Srebrenica.

The international response was vociferous but divided. The sharpest words came from the newly elected French President, Jacques Chirac. Speaking on Bastille Day, he compared the Bosnian Serb crimes to those of the Nazis and linked Western inaction to the appeasement of Hitler. Hardly endearing himself to the more reserved British or the hesitant Americans, he declared that France was willing to retake the enclave by force.[79] In the coming weeks, Dutch officers and politicians were to face hard questioning over the loss of the enclave. (A Dutch Government report absolved them of responsibility, blaming the undermanning of UNPROFOR and its lack of authority to use force.) Subsequent media reports suggested that General Janvier, at a 'closed-doors' briefing in New York for members of the UN Security Council six weeks before, had intimated that the position of the enclaves was hopeless and that they would have to be abandoned to the BSA.[80]

The great powers responded with a conference in London on 21 July of the foreign and defence ministers of the Contact Group and other UNPROFOR contributors at which they called for a 'substantial and decisive response' against any attacks on Gorazde. 'Pinprick' strikes would no longer be used, but none of the other remaining safe areas was cited.

Zepa finally fell on 25 July, when Bosnian government troops fled to the hills. This time the 15 000 civilians trapped there were 'humanely' expelled, with a UN soldier riding on each outward-bound bus. Again, however, the BSA separated out draft-age men. Two days later, protesting at 'the world's hypocrisy' both in the fall of Srebrenica and in the indecisive response immediately following, former Polish Prime Minister Tadeusz Mazowiecki resigned his post as UN special rapporteur for human rights in the former Yugoslavia. 'The very stability of international order and the principle of civilization is at stake over the question of Bosnia', he warned in his resignation letter.[81]

Meanwhile the Bosnian Serbs avoided the expected confrontation at Gorazde, the remaining eastern enclave, and launched a renewed attack around Bihac in alliance with the joint forces of Abdic and rebel Croatian

---

[78] The higher figure has been cited by the International Committee of the Red Cross in 'Perspective on the humanitarian situation in the Former Yugoslavia', Annexe 3: Srebenica (8 Dec. 1995), p. 3. The lower figure is cited by Amnesty International in 'Bosnia–Herzegovina: The missing of Srebrenica', EUR/63/22/95 (Sep. 1995).

[79] Walker, M., Traynor, I. and Borger, J., 'Serbs turn on second safe haven', *The Guardian*, 15 July 1995, p. 1.

[80] Block, R., 'UN left 8000 to die in Bosnia', *The Independent*, 30 Oct. 1995, p. 1.

[81] Williams, I., 'Mazowiecki bucks the trend', *WarReport*, no. 35 (July/Aug. 1995), p. 16.

Serbs. In response, the Croatian Government dispatched thousands of troops in alliance with Bosnian Croat forces. By the end of the month the joint Croatian–Bosnian Croat forces had seized Grahovo and Glamoc, two Bosnian towns, cutting Serb supply lines into Krajina and setting the stage for the Croatian Army's Krajina offensive.[82]

Clearly, the London Conference results needed further modification. One step was to revise the 'dual-key' policy, which required air strikes to be approved by both NATO and UN civilian officials. Boutros-Ghali agreed on 25 July to turn over his and Akashi's veto power to General Janvier. No new UN resolution was passed. Another change was NATO's decision to extend the threat of air strikes to the three remaining safe areas, Sarajevo, Tuzla and Bihac.[83]

Increasingly the UN now took a back seat to the military alliance, which was itself largely driven by the USA. However, the USA's room to man-oeuvre was suddenly restricted on 26 July, when the US Senate approved a bill requiring the USA unilaterally to lift the arms embargo against Bosnia and Herzegovina imposed by the Security Council, either upon the withdrawal of the UN or 12 weeks after a request by the Bosnian Government.[84] A few days later, the House of Representatives followed suit. A personal success for the bill's champion, Senator Robert Dole, the bill was hailed by the Bosnian Government and widely criticized in Europe. President Clinton vetoed it 10 days later. The scale of its majority implied that Republican congressional leaders had the required votes to override the veto, but because of the summer recess it could not be brought back for a vote until September. This gave the administration a precious short period in which to formulate a new solution for Bosnia and Herzegovina.

Diplomacy backed by force

By August, despite the rapid military and diplomatic developments, it remained unclear what had actually changed within Bosnia and Herzegovina. Fighting continued, Karadzic continued to make provocative statements and the BSA still held the preponderance of territory. Despite several shifts in the military deployments and command structure in Bosnia and Herzegovina, the international forces had yet to demonstrate whether a new policy was actually in place.

Yet the period of forceful diplomacy, dominated by the USA, was about to begin. Although there was widespread public sympathy for the sufferings of the people of Srebrenica, it was probably not this that inspired the change. One explanation is that the president needed to 'solve' Bosnia before the arms embargo bill, which spelled the end of the UN mission as well as severe political embarrassment, returned to Congress. US officials say that Clinton

---

[82] Gorinsek, K., 'The terms of the battlefield', *WarReport*, no. 35 (July/Aug. 1995), p. 8.

[83] *Keesing's Record of World Events*, vol. 41, no. 8 (Aug. 1995), p. 40690. Until its meeting of 24–26 July the NATO guarantee had only extended air strikes to protect Gorazde.

[84] See note 53.

stiffened his resolve because of the summer's humiliations of the international community, particularly the hostage crisis and the death of three US officials who were killed when their transport vehicle left the road on Mount Igman near Sarajevo.[85] Events on the ground also provided an opportunity for US diplomacy to be employed.

Radically altering the military balance in Bosnia and Herzegovina, on 4–9 August the Croatian Army scored a stunning defeat over the rebel Serbs in Croatia, recapturing all of the Krajina region, including the Serb stronghold of Knin. In a matter of days, the Bosnian Serbs' extensive western territory around Banja Luka shrank to an enclave itself, connected to Serbia only through the narrow corridor at Brcko. At the same time, a joint Croatian–Bosnian offensive broke the siege of Bihac.

The abrupt turn of military fortunes in the Bosnian enclaves and Krajina caused enormous human displacement. In a matter of weeks, however, the reversals in Krajina and Srebrenica/Zepa had also clarified the map of the region into more compact, ethnically homogenous territories. The withdrawal of UN forces from harm's way (British troops pulled out of Gorazde on 28 August) removed the risk of hostage-taking. Recognizing this opportunity, in mid-August US Assistant Secretary of State Richard Holbrooke launched a new peace plan. Based on the earlier Contact Group plan, it maintained a 51 : 49 per cent territorial division, but more closely reflecting the current situation. While the Bosnian Serbs would retain the captured enclaves, the government would be compensated with an area around Sarajevo. The proposal allowed for the use of force against the Bosnian Serbs if they failed to comply, but it also lifted restrictions on a 'confederation' link between the Bosnian Serbs and Serbia.[86] These mixed measures helped the plan win support internationally and from the Bosnian Serbs, although the Bosnian Government remained sceptical.

Then on the morning of 28 August a single shell fell in central Sarajevo, killing 37 people and wounding more than 85 just yards from the market-place where the infamous shell of February 1994 hit, killing 68 people. The next day the UN announced that it had proved 'beyond any reasonable doubt' that the shell had been fired from Bosnian Serb territory, and on 30 August NATO launched Operation Deliberate Force, the largest military operation in its history.[87] In the first 12 hours, aircraft from France, the Netherlands, Spain, the UK and the USA flew 300 sorties. Targeting radar, communications, missile and artillery sites throughout Bosnian Serb-held territory, the aim was to disrupt the BSA's integrated air defence system. The Rapid Reaction Force around Sarajevo also fired hundreds of artillery rounds on BSA mortar sites and ammunition dumps. One French Mirage jet was downed.

[85] Gutman, R, 'Signed, sealed, undelivered', *WarReport*, no. 38 (Nov./Dec. 1995); and Cohen, R., 'Taming the bullies of Bosnia', *New York Times Magazine*, 17 Dec. 1995, pp. 58–95.

[86] Whitney, C., 'US delivers latest plan for peace to Balkan chiefs', *International Herald Tribune*, 15 Aug. 1995, pp. 1, 7; and 'Enter the Americans: America's peace plan for Bosnia is gaining support', *The Economist*, 19 Aug. 1995, pp. 31–32.

[87] Vulliamy, E., Black, I. and Palmer, J., 'The defining moment', *The Guardian*, 31 Aug. 1995, p. 1.

The attack brought immediate results. The next day the Belgrade media announced an agreement to participate in future peace negotiations as part of a Serb team headed by Milosevic.[88] Some media reports suggested that the agreement bound Milosevic to support a platform drawn up by the Bosnian Serbs.[89] The dispute between Karadzic and Mladic broke into the open, with the former declaring (unsuccessfully) the removal of the general from his post.[90] During a pause in the strikes, on 1 September, General Mladic agreed to stop shelling Sarajevo and open land routes to the capital. He declined, however, to accept NATO's principal demand, to withdraw heavy weaponry from around the city, and the attacks resumed.

On 8 September, in the first face-to-face meeting of the combatants for 18 months, the foreign ministers of Bosnia and Herzegovina, Croatia and Yugoslavia (Serbia and Montenegro), the latter also representing the Bosnian Serbs, convened in Geneva with representatives of the Contact Group. The meeting, the result of intensive shuttle diplomacy by Holbrooke, produced an agreement on basic principles for a peace settlement. The document nevertheless sustained the critical contradiction of the war, with items confirming the 'legal' existence of Bosnia and Herzegovina with its present borders, while recognizing the existence of a Republika Srpska within a federal structure. It enshrined the 51 : 49 parameter for territorial division. Raising Bosnian government suspicions of Serbian secession, it also acknowledged the right of the two entities to 'establish parallel special relationships with neighbouring countries'. It guaranteed refugees the right to return to their homes 'or receive just compensation'. Acknowledging significant differences between the sides, Holbrooke deemed it 'an important milestone in the search for peace'.[91]

By 14 September, when the bombing operation was again suspended, NATO jets had carried out some 3400 missions, including 850 bombing sorties. Bosnian Serbs claimed more than 200 civilian casualties, including the shelling of a hospital near Sarajevo. Western military sources claimed that civilian casualties had been minimal.[92] At negotiations in Belgrade, with Milosevic, Holbrooke, Karadzic and Mladic, the Bosnian Serbs agreed to withdraw weapons from the Sarajevo exclusion zone, placing some under international supervision.[93] On 15 September, the first humanitarian aid flight since April arrived in Sarajevo and land convoys entered the city unhindered.[94] Five days later a joint NATO–UN statement reported that the weapons had been withdrawn and that air strikes would not be resumed.

[88] A provisional agreement had been reached some days before, but the timing of the announcement suggested that the bombing had a clear impact.

[89] Silber, L., 'Serb leaders bury the hatchet', Financial Times, 1 Sep. 1995, p. 3; and Prentice, E. A., 'US envoy encouraged by Milosevic takeover', The Times, 1 Sep. 1995.

[90] Vasic, M., 'The taste of defeat', WarReport, no. 37 (Oct. 1995), p. 8.

[91] Silber, L. and Robinson, A., 'US envoy hails accord on Bosnia', Financial Times, 9 Sep. 1995, p. 2.

[92] Clark, B., 'Bombing raids damage diplomatic bridges', Financial Times, 14 Sep. 1995.

[93] Martin, H., Wood, P. and Clark, B., 'Serbs move to withdraw big guns: NATO welcomes gesture after UN relief flights resume into Sarajevo', Financial Times, 16 Sep. 1995, p. 22.

[94] UN High Commissioner for Refugees, Information Notes on Former Yugoslavia, no. 10/95 (Oct. 1995).

On 26 September the group of three foreign ministers, this time meeting in New York, agreed an additional list of principles, establishing the outlines for building a democratic government, human rights guarantees and the return of refugees.[95]

The constructive talks did not end the fighting within Bosnia and Herzegovina. In a joint offensive launched on 11 September, Bosnian Government and Bosnian Croat forces recaptured some 3300 km^2 of territory in central and western Bosnia, leaving both sides holding roughly half the country, as stipulated in the peace plans. More than 100 000 refugees fled the oncoming armies into Banja Luka, which itself came under threat until the USA ordered a halt.[96] Towards the end of the month the Bosnian Government resisted pressure to agree a cease-fire, setting a range of preconditions, such as the full opening of Sarajevo. However, the contours of a viable map were finally in place. On 5 October, President Clinton announced a 60-day cease-fire, to allow for the completion of 'proximity peace talks'. The agreement was to take effect upon the restoration of utilities to Sarajevo, and on 12 October, after 42 months of war and 48 hours behind schedule, the guns in Bosnia and Herzegovina fell silent.

A problematic peace

In the weeks preceding Dayton, all actors engaged in pre-talks posturing. Representatives from Bosnia and Herzegovina, Croatia and the Bosnian Serbs expressed serious concern about the negotiations. UN Special Representative Akashi chose this moment to resign, while US negotiator Holbrooke tried to play down expectations. Nevertheless, talks convened on 1 November, at Wright-Patterson Air Base in Dayton. In sterile quarters amid a media blackout, the presidents of Bosnia and Herzegovina, Croatia and Serbia, plus other representatives from the region and officials from the USA, EU and Russia, endured a mediation marathon lasting three weeks, and several times nearing collapse. The result was in question until the final moment.

On 21 November President Clinton announced an 'historic and heroic' peace agreement.[97] Consisting of dozens of articles, 11 annexes and 102 maps, the document enshrined the 51 : 49 partition between the Bosnian–Croat Federation and Republika Srpska, while proclaiming an undivided capital and central government in a unified and democratic state.[98] Underscoring the fragility of the new structure, the bulk of the document covered military agreements on the separation of forces and on the replacement of the UN by a 60 000-strong NATO implementation force, to stay for a year. In a separate

[95] 'Principles for a Comprehensive Peace Settlement in Bosnia-Herzegovina',*WarReport*, Oct. 1995, p. 10.

[96] Schwarm, P., 'Hold your nose and sign', *WarReport*, no. 37 (Oct. 1995), p. 9.

[97] Rhodes, T., 'Bosnia peace deal agreed after US talks', *The Times*, 22 Nov. 1995, p. 1; and Dobbs, M., 'Balkan leaders approve Bosnian pact', *Washington Post*, 22 Nov. 1995, p. 1.

[98] Evans, M., 'Border blockade by Milosevic seen as turning point', *The Times*, 22 Nov. 1995.

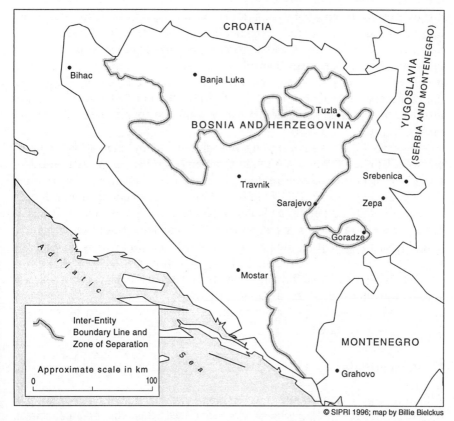

© SIPRI 1996; map by Billie Bielckus

Figure 5.2. The Dayton Peace Agreement zone of separation
Source: Courtesy Allied Command Europe Rapid Reaction Corps Headquarters

agreement signed earlier, Croatian and Bosnian representatives committed themselves to fully integrating the territory and institutions of the federation, while Bosnia and Herzegovina and the Federal Republic of Yugoslavia (Serbia and Montenegro) exchanged official recognition. Sanctions were to be lifted.[99]

'The war is now definitely over', an uncomfortable Milosevic announced on Serbian television. Bosnian President Alija Izetbegovic declared the agreement a 'useful but bitter medicine'. While the Bosnian Serbs had won their territory and international recognition, Holbrooke argued that the 'big losers' were Karadzic and Mladic. Excluded from the talks, they were apparently now

[99] Three Security Council resolutions were passed on 22 Nov. 1995: (*a*) 1021, which lifted the arms embargo on the former Yugoslav states (UN document S/RES/1021); (*b*) 1022, which lifted economic sanctions against the Federal Republic of Yugoslavia (Serbia and Montenegro) (UN document S/RES/1022); and (*c*) 1023, which approved the agreement for a Transitional Administration in Eastern Slavonia (UN document S/RES/1023). Security Council Resolution 1021 (see note 99) maintained the embargo on arms to the region for 90 days, then restricted only the transfer of heavy weapons for 90 days, and then allowed for the termination of all provisions of the arms embargo. Sanctions against Republika Srpska were lifted in Feb. 1996 in a statement by the President of the UN Security Council, citing Resolution 1022. On the effectiveness of sanctions, see also chapter 2, section IV.

disqualified from power by stipulations in the Dayton accords preventing those indicted for war crimes from holding public office. While Serbs in the Sarajevo suburbs held by Karadzic complained bitterly of provisions to return these areas to government control in exchange for Srebrenica and Zepa, people throughout government-held territory uncorked champagne. As even the embittered Karadzic ultimately stated, if the conflict issues were not resolved for the time being, at least they would be fought over by peaceful means.

The weeks following the signing were dominated by international conferences: in Brussels (29 November), to agree on NATO's deployment; in Budapest (7–8 December) to confirm the role of the Organization for Security and Co-operation in Europe (OSCE) in human-rights and elections monitoring; in London (8–9 December) to consider implementation plans; and in Brussels (20 December) to raise financial support. EU mediator Bildt was appointed coordinator of civil programmes, to be based in Sarajevo. Estimating the reconstruction bill at $5.1 billion, the pledging conference raised $500 million for immediate needs. The formal ceremony in Paris to ratify the end of the war was an anticlimax, burdened by long declarations that could not do justice to the human traumas of the dead and the refugees, and clouded by so many questions about the future.

IV. Macedonia

Although largely overshadowed by developments to the north, the situation in the Former Yugoslav Republic of Macedonia was cause for some concern in 1995. It continued to be spared the violence which has shaken the rest of the region (it is the only former Yugoslav republic to have avoided armed conflict) but it has not been an oasis of calm either. Relations between Slavs and ethnic Albanians, already tense, came under further strain in the course of the year. Meanwhile the Federal Republic of Yugoslavia (Serbia and Montenegro) remained unwilling to normalize relations with Macedonia. A sharp improvement in Greek–Macedonian relations in September, however, alleviated one major source of conflict for the strategically situated republic.

Since the deployment of UN peacekeepers along Macedonia's borders with Serbia and Albania in 1993,[100] the greatest threat to peace and stability has not been external aggression so much as internal unrest between Slav Macedonians and ethnic Albanians. The latter, who make up roughly 23 per cent of the population,[101] have been seeking improvements in their status—socially, economically and constitutionally—ever since the republic achieved independence in January 1991. Some of the worst violence the young republic has

---

[100] UN Security Council Resolution 795, 11 Dec. 1992 (UN document S/RES/795) authorized the deployment as part of UNPROFOR. Resolution 983, 31 Mar. 1995 (UN document S/RES/983) established UNPREDEP to succeed UNPROFOR in Macedonia.

[101] Although the Albanians claim to make up 30–40% of the population, a census conducted in 1994, which was judged to be free and fair by international observers, confirmed the lower estimate. See United Nations, Report of the Secretary-General, UN document S/1994/1454, 29 Dec. 1994.

experienced to date grew out of the Albanians' efforts early in the year to establish a privately funded Albanian-language university outside Tetovo in the heartland of Albanian Macedonia. University education until now has been available only in the Macedonian language, with state officials concerned that dual-language education would contribute to greater ethnic fragmentation. Acting in defiance of government warnings, Vice-Chancellor Fadil Sulejmani announced the opening of the university on 15 February, prompting a police crack-down two days later that left one Albanian dead and up to 60 wounded.[102] Sulejmani, along with four other leading members of the Albanian community, was later sentenced to prison for inciting riot.[103]

Only one week earlier, on 9 February, all 18 ethnic Albanian deputies had walked out of the parliament to protest against a draft law forbidding use of the Albanian language on Macedonian identity cards and passports.[104] In response to the police crack-down the deputies chose to boycott the next session of the parliament on 1 March—a boycott which some deputies maintained until 14 July, when by-elections would have had to be called in their constituencies as a result of their prolonged absence.[105]

While the presence of UN peacekeepers in the UN Preventive Deployment Force (UNPREDEP), among them some 500 US soldiers, has diminished any serious threat from the north, Serbia has engaged in a series of provocations that have disturbed the relative calm. Numerous border incursions—as many as 10 a month—had been observed by the UN throughout 1994.[106] In 1995 veiled pressure from Belgrade, in the form of persistent talk about the possibility of a Balkan federation with Yugoslavia, Macedonia and Greece, was resisted publicly by Macedonian President Kiro Gligorov.[107] 'The independence of the successor states has to be guaranteed', Gligorov was quoted as saying. As of 1 January 1996, the Federal Republic of Yugoslavia (Serbia and Montenegro) had still not extended recognition to Macedonia.

The fragility of peace in the republic was further underscored by the attempted assassination of Gligorov on 3 October.[108] The 78-year-old president, who was still recovering at the end of the year, is credited with having practised a politics of inclusion (there are four Albanian ministers in the government) and with performing a delicate balancing act among competing regional powers—Albania, Bulgaria, Greece, Serbia and Turkey, all with interests in Macedonia. By mid-December no one had claimed responsibility for the attack but there was speculation that either Albanian or Macedonian

[102] Perry, D. M., 'On the road to stability—or destruction?', *Transition*, vol. 1, no. 15 (25 Aug. 1995), p. 42.

[103] 'Sulejmani sentenced in Macedonia', *OMRI Daily Digest*, 4 May 1995.

[104] *Keesing's Record of World Events*, vol. 41, no. 2 (Feb. 1995), p. 40419.

[105] *Keesing's Record of World Events*, vol. 41, no. 7/8 (July 1995), p. 40659.

[106] Geroski, B., 'With a peace to keep', *WarReport*, no. 37 (Oct. 1995).

[107] In an interview with Macedonian Radio on 8 Apr. and in an address to the Parliamentary Assembly of the Western European Union on 20 June. 'Macedonia rules out federation with neighbours', *OMRI Daily Digest*, 11 Apr. 1995; and 'Macedonia President against new federation', *OMRI Daily Digest*, 21 June 1995.

[108] 'A Macedonian bomb', *The Economist*, 7 Oct. 1995.

nationalists might have carried it out, the latter perhaps in reaction to the concessions Gligorov had made recently to Greece.[109]

The concessions were part of an Interim Accord brokered with the help especially of US envoy Matthew Nimitz and signed in New York on 13 September by foreign ministers Stevo Crvenovski of Macedonia and Karolos Papoulias of Greece.[110] The treaty represented a breakthrough in Greek–Macedonian relations: it unblocked Macedonia's accession to a number of international organizations and, most important, it brought an end to the crippling economic embargo which Athens had imposed in February 1994, estimated to be costing Macedonia $40 million in lost trade and revenue each month. (The EU's own efforts to end the embargo, by seeking to bring Greece before the European Court of Justice, failed on 6 April when Advocate General Francis Jacob recommended that the case be dropped because it fell outside the jurisdiction of the Court. On 24 October the Commission of the European Communities withdrew its legal action.[111]) For its part Macedonia agreed to abandon the use on its national flag of the 16-pointed Star of Vergina, which Greece claims as part of its unique historic patrimony, and to give authoritative meaning to language in its constitution that has been interpreted by Greece to have possible irredentist implications. Negotiations are to continue over the disputed name 'Macedonia' (the first talks were held in New York on 16 December). Within a week of the attempted assassination of Gligorov, the Macedonian Parliament ratified the accord and by the end of the year Macedonia had been admitted as a member of the OSCE, the Council of Europe and the Partnership for Peace programme.[112]

V. The Dayton Agreement on Bosnia and Herzegovina

The General Framework Agreement of 21 November 1995[113] changed the name of the Republic of Bosnia and Herzegovina—it is henceforth 'Bosnia and Herzegovina'—and replaced its constitution. It remains a sovereign state in its internationally recognized borders. An effective international army of occupation has been established and a precise separation line determined between formally recognized enemy 'entities', the Federation of Bosnia and Herzegovina and Republika Srpska. Only the implementation of the accords over the coming months and years will determine whether the document signals the ultimate partition of the country or its eventual reunification.

---

[109] Allain, M.-F. and Ditchev, I., 'Fragile Macédoine' [Fragile Macedonia], *Le Monde Diplomatique*, Nov. 1995, p. 11 ((n French). It has also been suggested that Gligorov was targeted by the forces of organized crime in response to his recent anti-corruption campaign. Geroski, B., 'Gligorov is back', *WarReport*, no. 38 (Nov./Dec. 1995), p. 12.

[110] Interim Accord, Skopje, 15 Sep. 1995 , Macedonia Information Center, Skopje, 15 Sep. 1995.

[111] Krause, S., 'Redefining neighborly relations', *Transition,* vol. 1, no. 21 (17 Nov. 1995).

[112] 'Macedonia admitted into OSCE', *OMRI Daily Digest*, 13 Oct. 1995; 'Macedonia, Ukraine become members of Council of Europe', *OMRI Daily Digest*, 10 Nov. 1995; and 'Macedonia becomes member of Partnership for Peace', *OMRI Daily Digest*, 15 Nov. 1995.

[113] See note 1.

As with all the peace plans negotiated during the war, the most important element of the Dayton document—and the most heatedly argued—was the map. Indeed, on the question of territory, the talks were arguably not more successful than the Contact Group negotiations of the year before, on which the presidents of Bosnia and Herzegovina, Croatia and Serbia had also agreed. The critical difference was that at Dayton Radovan Karadzic, the man who had scuppered all previous deals, had been excluded. This was partly because he was indicted for war crimes, but also because, as a true warlord, he would not and perhaps could not agree to any territorial concessions. The absence of war is political suicide for extremist nationalists: they have nothing to offer as a political programme. Even so, despite his absence and the Bosnian Serbs' weakened military position, the territorial question remained so sensitive that Milosevic only showed the final map to the Bosnian Serb representatives at the talks just minutes before the signing.[114]

Based on the arbitrary 51 : 49 convention of earlier talks, the map primarily ratified the territorial exchanges achieved during the preceding months. Srebrenica and Zepa remain in Republika Srpska, while the capital, Sarajevo, is reunited. In a provision bitterly received and potentially resisted in Pale, the Bosnian Serbs must return suburbs under their control around Sarajevo to the government. The remaining eastern enclave of Gorazde, with roughly 60 000 people, remained in the Federation, with a widened connecting corridor, while various towns in northern Bosnia were returned to the Bosnian Serbs. Resolution of the question of the contentious 'Brcko corridor', the wafer-thin link between the western and eastern parts of Republika Srpska, was deferred for binding international arbitration, to be completed within one year.

Of the text itself, the central component was Annex 1, detailing the deployment of the Implementation Force (IFOR), predominantly made up by NATO and projected to stay for one year. Designed in the expectation that Karadzic and the Bosnian Serbs would not submit to the accord,[115] the annex established that peacekeeping and the UN mission in Bosnia and Herzegovina were finished.[116] With a peace finally to keep, IFOR was tasked with carrying out many standard peacekeeping functions such as interposition of forces, monitoring of withdrawal and disarmament, which UNPROFOR was never able to do. Its Commander was, morever, authorized to use force to protect his own troops or to carry out any of his responsibilities in implementing the accord. In particular, force could be used against any party failing to maintain the cessation of hostilities or to remove weapons from specified zones and vacate areas to be transferred to the other entity on schedule. The deadlines were tight: within 30 days of signing, all forces of non-local origin must be withdrawn, all troops and weapons pulled back from separation zones, and all armed civilian groups disbanded. Arms limitation talks must be under way, and all prisoners of war must be released. IFOR was granted the authority to arrest indicted war criminals, but was not charged with actively pursuing

---

[114] Borden and Hedl (note 41).
[115] Gutman (note 85), p. 4.
[116] Authority was transferred to IFOR on 19 Dec. 1995.

them. Most other military aspects of implementation were to be completed within three months.

Without requiring public ratification, the Framework Agreement imposed a new constitution, contained in Annex 4, with a unified but weak structure. The central government in Sarajevo was tasked with responsibility for foreign and trade policy, customs, immigration, monetary policy (including a central bank), operation of common and international communications, and air traffic control. Republika Srpska and the Federation (namely, the Croats within it) were allowed to maintain 'special parallel relationships with neighbouring states consistent with the sovereignty and territorial integrity of Bosnia and Herzegovina'. Uniquely, and potentially problematic for a unified state, the entities maintained their own separate armies.

Declaring ideals of democracy and non-discrimination, the constitution outlined a complicated structure of political institutions, including a three-person executive presidency, a 15-person upper legislative chamber selected from the entities, respective assemblies, and a 42-person lower house directly elected from each entity. The agreement stipulated that no one charged by the International Tribunal for the Former Yugoslavia may stand as a candidate or hold any appointive, elective or other public office. A range of mechanisms reminiscent of the communist era, including vetoes and quotas, sought to guarantee balance and fairness among the communities. Quorums were determined by the ethnicity, as well as number, of participants, all parliamentary majority votes must include one-third of the votes from each entity, and presidential decisions, when declared 'vital interests by one entity', could be vetoed by a two-thirds majority vote of that entity's assembly. The constitution enshrined the communal composition of the presidency—one Muslim, one Croat and one Serb—and determined which entity they represent. As under communism, such balancing mechanisms entrench ethnically oriented political parties at the expense of civil options and ethnically mixed individuals. They leave no place for leaders who are ethnically mixed or reject national determinations outright.

Refugees gained the right to go home or to receive fair compensation and to vote in their original places of residence. There was to be freedom of movement throughout the country. Several central bodies were created to ensure the 'highest levels of human rights', including a Constitutional Court, a Human Rights Commission and a Commission for Displaced Persons and Refugees. An international High Representative was appointed to coordinate and monitor the civil aspects of implementation, assist rehabilitation, facilitate dialogue among the parties, and report on progress to the UN and other international bodies and governments. The High Representative is also tasked with coordinating a new UN civilian International Police Task Force to assist in law enforcement and public order.

These stipulations aimed to ease the way towards reconciliation and reintegration. The first real indication of progress towards this goal will be elections. The OSCE was appointed to help organize and monitor 'free and fair elections' to central and entity assemblies, the presidency and municipal authorities. The Framework Agreement anticipated that by election time the return of refugees should already be under way, thus allowing many to vote in person. The willingness of refugees to return—and the ability of IFOR and other bodies to create the environment to make this possible—will therefore determine the demographics and thus the fundamental direction of the new state. The vote was scheduled for between six and nine months ahead—that is, by 14 September at the latest—so long as the OSCE considers that the proper conditions exist.

VI. Conclusions: prospects for future peace

At no other time in the past five years has the outlook for peace in Bosnia and Herzegovina seemed brighter. At the very least, the deployment of 60 000 NATO ground troops—including a sizeable US contingent—means that the country can look forward to a suspension of warring for the next 12 months, at which point IFOR is scheduled to withdraw. However, whether the cease-fire provides the basis for a more lasting peace, whether the provisions of the Dayton accord can initiate a process of reconciliation and reintegration, and whether the absence of war will strengthen the forces of tolerance and democracy not only in Bosnia and Herzegovina but also in neighbouring Croatia, Serbia (especially vis-à-vis Kosovo) and Macedonia are all questions that have critical bearing on the quality and durability of peace in the region.

In any war-ravaged nation the obstacles to post-conflict peace-building are considerable, and in Bosnia and Herzegovina the 'facts on the ground' and structural impediments suggest the magnitude of the challenge that lies ahead. To begin with, neither side has won a decisive victory and neither is satisfied with the status quo. Historically such conditions have been a prescription for renewed warring. There have been grumbling, threats and even scattered violence since Dayton, particularly but not only from the Bosnian Serb side.[117] None the less, the presence of heavily armed NATO troops and general war-weariness among the population militate against a new wave of fighting. The cantonment of heavy weapons, as mandated by the Dayton accord, should reinforce this.

Paradoxically, the Dayton accord is itself an obstacle to peace. By enshrining partition, allowing for the establishment of two states within a state and the maintenance of two separate armies, Dayton makes the task of reintegration that much more difficult to achieve. The requirements for consensus that govern the main political organs, for instance, allow for intransigent parties to thwart the effective functioning of the national parliament. It is worth recalling that a similar crisis contributed to the collapse of the Yugoslav Federation and the build-up to war.

Effective partition will also make it difficult to resettle the 2.7 million refugees and internally displaced persons.[118] Despite the formal right of return

---

[117] Bosnian Serbs held 16 Muslims hostage in early Jan. 1996 and there have been numerous attacks on IFOR. 'So far, so good', *The Economist*, 6 Jan. 1996, pp. 34, 36; and 'IFOR under constant attack in Bosnia', *OMRI Daily Digest*, 8 Jan. 1996.
[118] 'A peace still to win', *The Economist*, 16 Dec. 1995, p. 50.

these people enjoy, in practice many of them will be deterred by the prospect of having to cross lines of separation into 'hostile' territory in order to go home. Nor can they be expected to wish to return to areas that have been ethnically cleansed and where personal security is 'guaranteed' by local police forces who may have carried out the cleansing in the first place. Of critical importance, therefore, to an enduring peace is successful implementation of the civilian aspects of the Dayton plan, including the training and supervision of local police. Even then a force of 1700 UN policemen will find it impossible to monitor the activities of local policemen in every back alley of the country.

Two additional factors, time and aid, may work to erode the barrier of partition. If the guns stay silent long enough, the broken links between people from different communities may be re-established. Moreover, the flow of commerce and information, if given a chance to expand, will also help to bridge the divide. (One missed opportunity at Dayton in this regard was the establishment of a nationwide Bosnian broadcasting system.)[119] Aid, if it is administered properly—that is, if it is channelled into the hands of responsible and civic-oriented non-governmental organizations and public agencies and not into the pockets of warlords—can also help to achieve integration, much as Marshall Aid money did for Europe after World War II. Large amounts of aid are involved, however—an estimated $5–6 billion will be needed in the next three to four years[120]—and the opportunities for corruption and nepotism will be rife.

Another key to an enduring peace in the region will be the effectiveness of the International Tribunal in The Hague. Any significant return of refugees would seem unlikely unless local leaders implicated in crimes are removed. More broadly, unless individuals responsible for war crimes are brought to justice, the tendency will be for victims of those crimes to blame entire nations, and thus perpetuate the cycle of violence; but it seems likely that the two individuals most directly responsible for the war in Bosnia and Herzegovina—the presidents of Serbia and Croatia—will escape prosecution.

The Federation of Bosnia and Herzegovina, Republika Srpska, Croatia and Serbia have all pledged to 'cooperate fully' with the International Tribunal in the investigation and prosecution of war criminals, but such cooperation will be difficult to enforce. The international community's own commitment to the Tribunal appears strong, but the dependence on Milosevic and Tudjman—potential Hague defendants themselves—suggests the likely limits to that commitment. Nevertheless, by barring indicted persons from public office, the Tribunal achieves some measure of success even without trials. It is sometimes enough, as a number of Latin American and former Soviet bloc coun-

[119] Malcolm, N., 'Bosnia deconstructed', *Prospect,* Jan. 1996, p. 8. For an analysis of the role the media played in fomenting conflict in the former Yugoslavia, see Article 19, *Forging War: The Media in Serbia, Croatia and Bosnia-Hercegovina* (Article 19: London, 1994).

[120] Done, K., 'Sarajevo needs over $3bn', *Financial Times,* 24 Jan. 1996, p. 2.

tries have discovered, simply to make the truth known in order to effect a considerable degree of national healing.[121]

If time is critical to securing a lasting peace, the time-frame envisioned for implementation of the Dayton Agreement may prove to be too compressed. New political thinking, in contrast to the extreme nationalism that has predominated in some places, requires time to develop. The danger with holding elections between just six and nine months after the signing of the Dayton accord is that in a climate of fear and uncertainty the tendency will be for populations to vote along ethnic lines and thus reinforce ethnic divisions. The proposed withdrawal of NATO troops just 12 months after deployment, while it may reassure a US electorate concerned about entanglement abroad, also creates an opening for any parties bent on the resumption of fighting. In this regard the relaxation of the UN arms embargo[122] may have the effect of levelling the playing-field and thus inhibiting conflict, or it may embolden the strengthened Bosnian Muslim forces to restart the war.

The peace agreement is only a partial solution to the region's problems. The right of return, thus, does not extend to the tens of thousands of Croatian Serbs who fled the Krajina region in the face of last year's offensives. Nor does it speak to the plight of Kosovo's Albanian population, who continue to suffer violations of human rights on a systematic basis. It therefore leaves unresolved at least two critical issues that have the potential for future destabilization. Finally, because it entrenches the ethnic divisions that gave rise to the conflict in the first place, a shadow is cast over the prospects for long-term stability and reconciliation.

[121] Gow, J., 'Building on the peace', *WarReport*, no. 38 (Nov./Dec. 1995), p. 27.
[122] See note 99.

Appendix 5A. The Dayton peace agreement

GENERAL FRAMEWORK AGREEMENT FOR PEACE IN BOSNIA AND HERZEGOVINA

Initialed in Dayton, Ohio, 21 November 1995 and signed in Paris, 14 December 1995

Table of contents

The Republic of Bosnia and Herzegovina, the Republic of Croatia and the Federal Republic of Yugoslavia (the 'Parties'),

Recognizing the need for a comprehensive settlement to bring an end to the tragic conflict in the region,

Desiring to contribute toward that end and to promote an enduring peace and stability,

Affirming their commitment to the Agreed Basic Principles issued on September 8, 1995, the Further Agreed Basic Principles issued on September 26, 1995, and the cease-fire agreements of September 14 and October 5, 1995,

Noting the agreement of August 29, 1995, which authorized the delegation of the Federal Republic of Yugoslavia to sign, on behalf of the Republika Srpska, the parts of the peace plan concerning it, with the obligation to implement the agreement that is reached strictly and consequently,

Have agreed as follows:

Article I

The Parties shall conduct their relations in accordance with the principles set forth in the United Nations Charter, as well as the Helsinki Final Act and other documents of the Organization for Security and Cooperation in Europe. In particular, the Parties shall fully respect the sovereign equality of one another, shall settle disputes by peaceful means, and shall refrain from any action, by threat or use of force or otherwise, against the territorial integrity or political independence of Bosnia and Herzegovina or any other State.

Article II

The Parties welcome and endorse the arrangements that have been made concerning the military aspects of the peace settlement and aspects of regional stabilization, as set forth in the Agreements at Annex 1-A and Annex 1-B. The Parties shall fully respect and promote fulfillment of the commitments made in Annex 1-A, and shall comply fully with their commitments as set forth in Annex 1-B.

Article III

The Parties welcome and endorse the arrangements that have been made concerning the boundary demarcation between the two Entities, the Federation of Bosnia and Herzegovina and Republika Srpska, as set forth in the Agreement at Annex 2. The Parties shall fully respect and promote fulfillment of the commitments made therein.

Article IV

The Parties welcome and endorse the elections program for Bosnia and Herzegovina as set forth in Annex 3. The Parties shall fully respect and promote fulfillment of that program.

Article V

The Parties welcome and endorse the arrangements that have been made concerning the Constitution of Bosnia and Herzegovina, as set forth in Annex 4. The Parties shall fully respect and promote fulfillment of the commitments made therein.

Article VI

The Parties welcome and endorse the arrangements that have been made concerning the establishment of an arbitration tribunal, a Commission on Human Rights, a Commission on Refugees and Displaced Persons, a Commission to Preserve National Monuments, and Bosnia and Herzegovina Public Corporations, as set forth in the Agreements at Annexes 5–9. The Parties shall fully respect and promote fulfillment of the commitments made therein.

Article VII

Recognizing that the observance of human rights and the protection of refugees and displaced persons are of vital importance in achieving a lasting peace, the Parties agree to and shall comply fully with the provisions concerning human rights set forth in Chapter One of the Agreement at Annex 6, as well as the provisions concerning refugees and displaced persons set forth in Chapter One of the Agreement at Annex 7.

Article VIII

The Parties welcome and endorse the arrangements that have been made concerning the implementation of this peace settlement, including in particular those pertaining to the civilian (non-military) implementation, as set forth in the Agreement at Annex 10, and the international police task force, as set forth in the Agreement at Annex 11. The Parties shall fully respect and promote fulfillment of the commitments made therein.

Article IX

The Parties shall cooperate fully with all entities involved in implementation of this peace settlement, as described in the Annexes to this Agreement, or which are otherwise authorized by the United Nations Security Council, pursuant to the obligation of all Parties to cooperate in the investigation and prosecution of war crimes and other violations of international humanitarian law.

Article X

The Federal Republic of Yugoslavia and the Republic of Bosnia and Herzegovina recognize each other as sovereign independent States within their international borders. Further aspects of their mutual recognition will be subject to subsequent discussions.

Article XI

This Agreement shall enter into force upon signature.

DONE at Paris, this 14th day of december, 1995, in the Bosnian, Croatian, English and Serbian languages, each text being equally authentic.

(...)

Annexe 1-A. Agreement on the Military Aspects of the Peace Settlement

The Republic of Bosnia and Herzegovina, the Federation of Bosnia and Herzegovina, and the Republika Srpska (hereinafter the 'Parties') have agreed as follows:

Article I. General obligations

1. The Parties undertake to recreate as quickly as possible normal conditions of life in Bosnia and Herzegovina. They understand that this requires a major contribution on their part in which they will make strenuous efforts to cooperate with each other and with the international organizations and agencies which are assisting them on the ground. They welcome the willingness of the international community to send to the region, for a period of approximately one year, a force to assist in implementation of the territorial and other militarily related provisions of the agreement as described herein.

(a) The United Nations Security Council is invited to adopt a resolution by which it will authorize Member States or regional organizations and arrangements to establish a multinational military Implementation Force (hereinafter 'IFOR'). The Parties understand and agree that this Implementation Force may be composed of ground, air and maritime units from NATO and non-NATO nations, deployed to Bosnia and Herzegovina to help ensure compliance with the provisions of this Agreement (hereinafter 'Annex'). The Parties understand and agree that the IFOR will begin the implementation of the military aspects of this Annex upon the transfer of authority from the UNPROFOR Commander to the IFOR Commander (hereinafter 'Transfer of Authority') and that until the Transfer of Authority, UNPROFOR will continue to exercise its mandate.

(b) It is understood and agreed that NATO may establish such a force, which will operate under the authority and subject to the direction and political control of the North Atlantic Council ('NAC') through the NATO chain of command. They undertake to facilitate its operations. The Parties, therefore, hereby agree and freely undertake to fully comply with all obligations set forth in this Annex.

(c) It is understood and agreed that other States may assist in implementing the military aspects of this Annex. The Parties understand and agree that the modalities of those States' participation will be the subject of agreement between such participating States and NATO.

2. The purposes of these obligations are as follows:

(a) to establish a durable cessation of hostilities. Neither Entity shall threaten or use force against the other Entity, and under no circumstances shall any armed forces of either Entity enter into or stay within the territory of the other Entity without the consent of the government of the latter and of the Presidency of Bosnia and Herzegovina. All armed forces in Bosnia and Herzegovina shall operate consistently with the sovereignty and territorial integrity of Bosnia and Herzegovina;

(b) to provide for the support and authorization of the IFOR and in particular to authorize the IFOR to take such actions as required, including the use of necessary force, to ensure compliance with this Annex, and to ensure its own protection; and

(c) to establish lasting security and arms control measures as outlined in Annex 1-B to the General Framework Agreement, which aim to promote a permanent reconciliation between all Parties and to facilitate the achievement of all political arrangements agreed to in the General Framework Agreement.

3. The Parties understand and agree that within Bosnia and Herzegovina the obligations undertaken in this Annex shall be applied equally within both Entities. Both Entities shall be held equally responsible for compliance herewith, and both shall be equally subject to such enforcement action by the IFOR as may be necessary to ensure implementation of this Annex and the protection of the IFOR.

Article II. Cessation of hostilities

1. The Parties shall comply with the cessation of hostilities begun with the agreement of October 5, 1995 and shall continue to refrain from all offensive operations of any type against each other. An offensive operation in this case is an action that includes projecting forces or fire forward of a Party's own lines. Each Party shall ensure that all personnel and organizations with military capability under its control or within territory under its control, including armed civilian groups, national guards, army reserves, military police, and the Ministry of Internal Affairs Special Police (MUP) (hereinafter 'Forces') comply with this Annex. The term 'Forces' does not include UNPROFOR, the International Police Task Force referred to in the General Framework Agreement, the IFOR or other elements referred to in Article I, paragraph 1 (c).

2. In carrying out the obligations set forth in paragraph 1, the Parties undertake, in particular, to cease the firing of all weapons and explosive devices except as authorized by this Annex. The Parties shall not place any additional minefields, barriers, or protective obstacles. They shall not engage in patrolling, ground or air reconnaissance forward of their own force positions, or into the Zones of Separation as provided for in Article IV below, without IFOR approval.

3. The Parties shall provide a safe and secure environment for all persons in their respective jurisdictions, by maintaining civilian law enforcement agencies operating in accordance with internationally recognized standards and with respect for internationally recognized human rights and fundamental freedoms, and by taking such other measures as appropriate. The Parties also commit themselves to disarm and disband all armed civilian groups, except for authorized police forces, within 30 days after the Transfer of Authority.

4. The Parties shall cooperate fully with any international personnel including investigators, advisors, monitors, observers, or other personnel in Bosnia and Herzegovina pursuant to the General Framework Agreement, including facilitating unimpeded access and movement and by providing such status as is necessary for the effective conduct of their tasks.

5. The Parties shall strictly avoid committing any reprisals, counterattacks, or any unilateral actions in response to violations of this Annex by another Party. The Parties

shall respond to alleged violations of the provisions of this Annex through the procedures provided in Article VIII.

Article III. Withdrawal of foreign forces

1. All Forces in Bosnia and Herzegovina as of the date this Annex enters into force which are not of local origin, whether or not they are legally and militarily subordinated to the Republic of Bosnia and Herzegovina, the Federation of Bosnia and Herzegovina, or Republika Srpska, shall be withdrawn together with their equipment from the territory of Bosnia and Herzegovina within thirty (30) days. Furthermore, all Forces that remain on the territory of Bosnia and Herzegovina must act consistently with the territorial integrity, sovereignty, and political independence of Bosnia and Herzegovina. In accordance with Article II, paragraph 1, this paragraph does not apply to UNPROFOR, the International Police Task Force referred to in the General Framework Agreement, the IFOR or other elements referred to in Article I, paragraph 1 (*c*).

2. In particular, all foreign Forces, including individual advisors, freedom fighters, trainers, volunteers, and personnel from neighboring and other States, shall be withdrawn from the territory of Bosnia and Herzegovina in accordance with Article III, paragraph 1.

Article IV. Redeployment of forces

1. The Republic of Bosnia and Herzegovina and the Entities shall redeploy their Forces in three phases:

2. PHASE I

(*a*) The Parties immediately after this Annex enters into force shall begin promptly and proceed steadily to withdraw all Forces behind a Zone of Separation which shall be established on either side of the Agreed Cease-Fire Line that represents a clear and distinct demarcation between any and all opposing Forces. This withdrawal shall be completed within thirty (30) days after the Transfer of Authority. The precise Agreed Cease-Fire Line and Agreed Cease-Fire Zone of Separation are indicated on the maps at Appendix A of this Annex.

(*b*) The Agreed Cease-Fire Zone of Separation shall extend for a distance of approximately two (2) kilometers on either side of the Agreed Cease-Fire Line. No weapons other than those of the IFOR are permitted in this Agreed Cease-Fire Zone of Separation except as provided herein. No individual

may retain or possess any military weapons or explosives within this four kilometer Zone without specific approval of the IFOR. Violators of this provision shall be subject to military action by the IFOR, including the use of necessary force to ensure compliance.

(*c*) In addition to the other provisions of this Annex, the following specific provisions shall also apply to Sarajevo and Gorazde:

Sarajevo

(1) Within seven (7) days after the Transfer of Authority, the Parties shall transfer and vacate selected positions along the Agreed Cease-Fire Line according to instructions to be issued by the IFOR Commander.

(2) The Parties shall complete withdrawal from the Agreed Cease-Fire Zone of Separation in Sarajevo within thirty (30) days after the Transfer of Authority, in accordance with Article IV, paragraph 2. The width of this Zone of Separation will be approximately one (1) kilometer on either side of the Agreed Cease-Fire Line. However, this Zone of Separation may be adjusted by the IFOR Commander either to narrow the Zone of Separation to take account of the urban area of Sarajevo or to widen the Zone of Separation up to two (2) kilometers on either side of the Agreed Cease-Fire Line to take account of more open terrain.

(3) Within the Agreed Cease-Fire Zone of Separation, no individual may retain or possess any weapons or explosives, other than a member of the IFOR or the local police exercising official duties as authorized by the IFOR in accordance with Article IV, paragraph 2 (*b*).

(4) The Parties understand and agree that violators of subparagraphs (1), (2) and (3) above shall be subject to military action by the IFOR, including the use of necessary force to ensure compliance.

Gorazde

(1) The Parties understand and agree that a two lane all-weather road will be constructed in the Gorazde Corridor. Until such road construction is complete, the two interim routes will be used by both Entities.

(. . .)

There shall be complete freedom of movement along these routes for civilian traffic. The Parties shall only utilize these interim routes for military forces and equipment as authorized by and under the control and direction of the IFOR. In this regard, and in order to reduce the risk to civilian traffic, the IFOR shall have the right to manage movement of military and civilian traffic from both Entities along these routes.

(2) The Parties understand and agree that violators of subparagraph (1) shall be subject to military action by the IFOR, including the use of necessary force to ensure compliance.

(3) The Parties pledge as a confidence building measure that they shall not locate any Forces or heavy weapons as defined in paragraph 5 of this Article within two (2) kilometers of the designated interim routes. Where those routes run in or through the designated Zones of Separation, the provisions relating to Zones of Separation in this Annex shall also apply.

(d) The Parties immediately after this Annex enters into force shall begin promptly and proceed steadily to complete the following activities within thirty (30) days after the Transfer of Authority or as determined by the IFOR Commander: (1) remove, dismantle or destroy all mines, unexploded ordnance, explosive devices, demolitions, and barbed or razor wire from the Agreed Cease-Fire Zone of Separation or other areas from which their Forces are withdrawn; (2) mark all known mine emplacements, unexploded ordnance, explosive devices and demolitions within Bosnia and Herzegovina; and (3) remove, dismantle or destroy all mines, unexploded ordnance, explosive devices and demolitions as required by the IFOR Commander.

(e) The IFOR is authorized to direct that any military personnel, active or reserve, who reside within the Agreed Cease-Fire Zone of Separation register with the appropriate IFOR Command Post referred to in Article VI which is closest to their residence.

3. PHASE II (AS REQUIRED IN SPECIFIC LOCATIONS)

This phase applies to those locations where the Inter-Entity Boundary Line does not follow the Agreed Cease-Fire Line.

(a) In those locations in which, pursuant to the General Framework Agreement, areas occupied by one Entity are to be transferred to another Entity, all Forces of the withdrawing Entity shall have forty-five (45) days after the Transfer of Authority to completely vacate and clear this area. This shall include the removal of all Forces as well as the removal, dismantling or destruction of equipment, mines, obstacles, unexploded ordnance, explosive devices, demolitions, and

weapons. In those areas being transferred to a different Entity, in order to provide an orderly period of transition, the Entity to which an area is transferred shall not put Forces in this area as required for ninety (90) days after the Transfer of Authority or as determined by the IFOR Commander. The Parties understand and agree that the IFOR shall have the right to provide the military security for these transferred areas from thirty (30) days after the Transfer of Authority until ninety-one (91) days after the Transfer of Authority, or as soon as possible as determined by the IFOR Commander, when these areas may be occupied by the Forces of the Entity to which they are transferred. Upon occupation by the Entity to which the area is transferred, a new Zone of Separation along the Inter-Entity Boundary Line as indicated on the map at Appendix A shall be established by the IFOR, and the Parties shall observe the same limitations on the presence of Forces and weapons in this Zone as apply to the Agreed Cease-Fire Zone of Separation.

(b) The IFOR is authorized to direct that any military personnel, active or reserve, who reside within the Inter-Entity Zone of Separation register with the appropriate IFOR Command Post referred to in Article VI which is closest to their residence.

4. GENERAL

The following provisions apply to Phases I and II:

(a) In order to provide visible indication, the IFOR shall supervise the selective marking of the Agreed Cease-Fire Line and its Zone of Separation, and the Inter-Entity Boundary Line and its Zone of Separation. Final authority for placement of such markers shall rest with the IFOR. All Parties understand and agree that the Agreed Cease-Fire Line and its Zone of Separation and the Inter-Entity Boundary Line and its Zone of Separation are defined by the maps and documents agreed to as part of the General Framework Agreement and not the physical location of markers.

(b) All Parties understand and agree that they shall be subject to military action by the IFOR, including the use of necessary force to ensure compliance, for:

(1) failure to remove all their Forces and unauthorized weapons from the four (4) kilometer Agreed Cease-Fire Zone of Separation within thirty (30) days after the Transfer of Authority, as provided in Article IV, paragraph 2 (a) and (b) above;

(2) failure to vacate and clear areas being transferred to another Entity within forty-five (45) days after the Transfer of Authority, as provided in Article IV, paragraph 3 (*a*) above;

(3) deploying Forces within areas transferred from another Entity earlier than ninety (90) days after the Transfer of Authority or as determined by the IFOR Commander, as provided in Article IV, paragraph 3 (*a*) above;

(4) failure to keep all Forces and unauthorized weapons outside the Inter-Entity Zone of Separation after this Zone is declared in effect by the IFOR, as provided in Article IV, paragraph 3 (*a*) above; or

(5) violation of the cessation of hostilities as agreed to by the Parties in Article II.

5. PHASE III
The Parties pledge as confidence building measures that they shall:

(*a*) within 120 days after the Transfer of Authority withdraw all heavy weapons and Forces to cantonment/ barracks areas or other locations as designated by the IFOR Commander. 'Heavy weapons' refers to all tanks and armored vehicles, all artillery 75 mm and above, all mortars 81 mm and above, and all anti-aircraft weapons 20 mm and above. This movement of these Forces to cantonment/barracks areas is intended to enhance mutual confidence by the Parties in the success of this Annex and help the overall cause of peace in Bosnia and Herzegovina.

(*b*) within 120 days after the Transfer of Authority demobilize Forces which cannot be accommodated in cantonment/barracks areas as provided in subparagraph (*a*) above. Demobilization shall consist of removing from the possession of these personnel all weapons, including individual weapons, explosive devices, communications equipment, vehicles, and all other military equipment. All personnel belonging to these Forces shall be released from service and shall not engage in any further training or other military activities.

6. Notwithstanding any other provision of this Annex, the Parties understand and agree that the IFOR has the right and is authorized to compel the removal, withdrawal, or relocation of specific Forces and weapons from, and to order the cessation of any activities in, any location in Bosnia and Herzegovina whenever the IFOR determines such Forces, weapons or activities to constitute a threat or potential threat to either the IFOR or its

mission, or to another Party. Forces failing to redeploy, withdraw, relocate, or to cease threatening or potentially threatening activities following such a demand by the IFOR shall be subject to military action by the IFOR, including the use of necessary force to ensure compliance, consistent with the terms set forth in Article I, paragraph 3.

Article V. Notifications

1. Immediately upon establishment of the Joint Military Commission provided for in Article VIII, each Party shall furnish to the Joint Military Commission information regarding the positions and descriptions of all known unexploded ordnance, explosive devices, demolitions, minefields, booby traps, wire entanglements, and all other physical or military hazards to the safe movement of any personnel within Bosnia and Herzegovina, as well as the location of lanes through the Agreed Cease-Fire Zone of Separation which are free of all such hazards. The Parties shall keep the Joint Military Commission updated on changes in this information.

2. Within thirty (30) days after the Transfer of Authority, each Party shall furnish to the Joint Military Commission the following specific information regarding the status of its Forces within Bosnia and Herzegovina and shall keep the Joint Military Commission updated on changes in this information:

(*a*) location, type, strengths of personnel and weaponry of all Forces within ten (10) kilometers of the Agreed Cease-Fire Line and Inter-Entity Boundary Line;

(*b*) maps depicting the forward line of troops and front lines;

(*c*) positions and descriptions of fortifications, minefields, unexploded ordnance, explosive devices, demolitions, barriers, and other man-made obstacles, ammunition dumps, command headquarters, and communications networks within ten (10) kilometers of the Agreed Cease-Fire Line or Inter-Entity Boundary Line;

(*d*) positions and descriptions of all surface to air missiles/launchers, including mobile systems, anti-aircraft artillery, supporting radars and associated command and control systems;

(*e*) positions and descriptions of all mines, unexploded ordnance, explosive devices, demolitions, obstacles, weapons systems, vehicles, or any other military equipment which cannot be removed, dismantled or destroyed under the provisions of Article IV, paragraphs 2 (*d*) and 3 (*a*); and

(*f*) any further information of a military nature as requested by the IFOR.

3. Within 120 days after the Transfer of Authority, the Parties shall furnish to the Joint Military Commission the following specific information regarding the status of their Forces in Bosnia and Herzegovina and shall keep the Joint Military Commission updated on changes in this information:

(*a*) location, type, strengths of personnel and weaponry of all Forces;

(*b*) maps depicting the information in sub-paragraph (*a*) above;

(*c*) positions and descriptions of fortifications, minefields, unexploded ordnance, explosive devices, demolitions, barriers, and other man-made obstacles, ammunition dumps, command headquarters, and communications networks; and

(*d*) any further information of a military nature as requested by the IFOR.

Article VI. Deployment of the Implementation Force

1. Recognizing the need to provide for the effective implementation of the provisions of this Annex, and to ensure compliance, the United Nations Security Council is invited to authorize Member States or regional organizations and arrangements to establish the IFOR acting under Chapter VII of the United Nations Charter. The Parties understand and agree that this Implementation Force may be composed of ground, air and maritime units from NATO and non-NATO nations, deployed to Bosnia and Herzegovina to help ensure compliance with the provisions of this Annex. The Parties understand and agree that the IFOR shall have the right to deploy on either side of the Inter-Entity Boundary Line and throughout Bosnia and Herzegovina.

2. The Parties understand and agree that the IFOR shall have the right:

(*a*) to monitor and help ensure compliance by all Parties with this Annex (including, in particular, withdrawal and redeployment of Forces within agreed periods, and the establishment of Zones of Separation);

(*b*) to authorize and supervise the selective marking of the Agreed Cease-Fire Line and its Zone of Separation and the Inter-Entity Boundary Line and its Zone of Separation as established by the General Framework Agreement;

(*c*) to establish liaison arrangements with local civilian and military authorities and other international organizations as necessary for the accomplishment of its mission; and

(*d*) to assist in the withdrawal of UN Peace Forces not transferred to the IFOR, including, if necessary, the emergency withdrawal of UNCRO Forces.

3. The Parties understand and agree that the IFOR shall have the right to fulfill its supporting tasks, within the limits of its assigned principal tasks and available resources, and on request, which include the following:

(*a*) to help create secure conditions for the conduct by others of other tasks associated with the peace settlement, including free and fair elections;

(*b*) to assist the movement of organizations in the accomplishment of humanitarian missions;

(*c*) to assist the UNHCR and other international organizations in their humanitarian missions;

(*d*) to observe and prevent interference with the movement of civilian populations, refugees, and displaced persons, and to respond appropriately to deliberate violence to life and person; and

(*e*) to monitor the clearing of minefields and obstacles.

4. The Parties understand and agree that further directives from the NAC may establish additional duties and responsibilities for the IFOR in implementing this Annex.

5. The Parties understand and agree that the IFOR Commander shall have the authority, without interference or permission of any Party, to do all that the Commander judges necessary and proper, including the use of military force, to protect the IFOR and to carry out the responsibilities listed above in paragraphs 2, 3 and 4, and they shall comply in all respects with the IFOR requirements.

6. The Parties understand and agree that in carrying out its responsibilities, the IFOR shall have the unimpeded right to observe, monitor, and inspect any Forces, facility or activity in Bosnia and Herzegovina that the IFOR believes may have military capability. The refusal, interference, or denial by any Party of this right to observe, monitor, and inspect by the IFOR shall constitute a breach of this Annex and the violating Party shall be subject to military action by the IFOR, including the use of necessary force to ensure compliance with this Annex.

7. The Army of the Republic of Bosnia and Herzegovina, the Croat Defense Council Forces, and the Army of Republika Srpska shall establish Command Posts at IFOR brigade, battalion, or other levels which shall be co-located with specific IFOR command locations, as determined by the IFOR Commander. These Command Posts shall exercise command and control over all Forces of their respective sides which are located within ten (10) kilometers of the Agreed Cease-Fire Line or Inter-Entity Boundary Line, as specified by the IFOR. The Command Posts shall provide, at the request of the IFOR, timely status reports on organizations and troop levels in their areas.

8. In addition to co-located Command Posts, the Army of the Republic of Bosnia and Herzegovina, the Croat Defense Council Forces, and the Army of Republika Srpska shall maintain liaison teams to be co-located with the IFOR Command, as determined by the IFOR Commander, for the purpose of fostering communication, and preserving the overall cessation of hostilities.

9. Air and surface movements in Bosnia and Herzegovina shall be governed by the following provisions:

(a) The IFOR shall have complete and unimpeded freedom of movement by ground, air, and water throughout Bosnia and Herzegovina. It shall have the right to bivouac, maneuver, billet, and utilize any areas or facilities to carry out its responsibilities as required for its support, training, and operations, with such advance notice as may be practicable. The IFOR and its personnel shall not be liable for any damages to civilian or government property caused by combat or combat related activities. Roadblocks, checkpoints or other impediments to IFOR freedom of movement shall constitute a breach of this Annex and the violating Party shall be subject to military action by the IFOR, including the use of necessary force to ensure compliance with this Annex.

(b) The IFOR Commander shall have sole authority to establish rules and procedures governing command and control of airspace over Bosnia and Herzegovina to enable civilian air traffic and non-combat air activities by the military or civilian authorities in Bosnia and Herzegovina, or if necessary to terminate civilian air traffic and non-combat air activities.

(1) The Parties understand and agree there shall be no military air traffic, or non-military aircraft performing military mis-

sions, including reconnaissance or logistics, without the express permission of the IFOR Commander. The only military aircraft that may be authorized to fly in Bosnia and Herzegovina are those being flown in support of the IFOR, except with the express permission of the IFOR. Any flight activities by military fixed-wing or helicopter aircraft within Bosnia and Herzegovina without the express permission of the IFOR Commander are subject to military action by the IFOR, including the use of necessary force . . .

(. . .)

10. The IFOR shall have the right to utilize such means and services as required to ensure its full ability to communicate and shall have the right to the unrestricted use of all of the electromagnetic spectrum for this purpose. In implementing this right, the IFOR shall make every reasonable effort to coordinate with and take into account the needs and requirements of the appropriate authorities.

11. All Parties shall accord the IFOR and its personnel the assistance, privileges, and immunities set forth at Appendix B of this Annex [not reproduced here], including the unimpeded transit through, to, over and on the territory of all Parties.

12. All Parties shall accord any military elements as referred to in Article I, paragraph 1 (c) and their personnel the assistance, privileges and immunities referred to in Article VI, paragraph 11.

Article VII. Withdrawal of UNPROFOR

It is noted that as a consequence of the forthcoming introduction of the IFOR into the Republic of Bosnia and Herzegovina, the conditions for the withdrawal of the UNPROFOR established by United Nations Security Council Resolution 743 have been met. It is requested that the United Nations, in consultation with NATO, take all necessary steps to withdraw the UNPROFOR from Bosnia and Herzegovina, except those parts incorporated into the IFOR.

Article VIII. Establishment of a Joint Military Commission

1. A Joint Military Commission (the 'Commission') shall be established with the deployment of the IFOR to Bosnia and Herzegovina.

2. The Commission shall:

(a) Serve as the central body for all Parties to this Annex to bring any military complaints, questions, or problems that require resolution by the IFOR Commander, such as allegations of cease-fire violations or other noncompliance with this Annex.

(b) Receive reports and agree on specific actions to ensure compliance with the provisions of this Annex by the Parties.

(c) Assist the IFOR Commander in determining and implementing a series of local transparency measures between the Parties.

3. The Commission shall be chaired by the IFOR Commander or his or her representative and consist of the following members:

(a) the senior military commander of the forces of each Party within Bosnia and Herzegovina;

(b) other persons as the Chairman may determine;

(c) each Party to this Annex may also select two civilians who shall advise the Commission in carrying out its duties;

(d) the High Representative referred to in the General Framework Agreement or his or her nominated representative shall attend Commission meetings, and offer advice particularly on matters of a political–military nature.

4. The Commission shall not include any persons who are now or who come under indictment by the International Tribunal for the Former Yugoslavia.

5. The Commission shall function as a consultative body for the IFOR Commander. To the extent possible, problems shall be solved promptly by mutual agreement. However, all final decisions concerning its military matters shall be made by the IFOR Commander.

6. The Commission shall meet at the call of the IFOR Commander. The High Representative may when necessary request a meeting of the Commission. The Parties may also request a meeting of the Commission.

7. The IFOR Commander shall have the right to decide on military matters, in a timely fashion, when there are overriding considerations relating to the safety of the IFOR or the Parties' compliance with the provisions of this Annex.

8. The Commission shall establish subordinate military commissions for the purpose of providing assistance in carrying out the functions described above. Such commissions shall be at the brigade and battalion level or at other echelons as the local IFOR Commander shall direct and be composed of commanders from each of the Parties and the

IFOR. The representative of the High Representative shall attend and offer advice particularly on matters of a political–military nature. The local IFOR Commander shall invite local civilian authorities when appropriate.

9. Appropriate liaison arrangements will be established between the IFOR Commander and the High Representative to facilitate the discharge of their respective responsibilities.

Article IX. Prisoner exchanges

1. The Parties shall release and transfer without delay all combatants and civilians held in relation to the conflict (hereinafter 'prisoners'), in conformity with international humanitarian law and the provisions of this Article.

(a) The Parties shall be bound by and implement such plan for release and transfer of all prisoners as may be developed by the ICRC, after consultation with the Parties.

(b) The Parties shall cooperate fully with the ICRC and facilitate its work in implementing and monitoring the plan for release and transfer of prisoners.

(c) No later than thirty (30) days after the Transfer of Authority, the Parties shall release and transfer all prisoners held by them.

(d) In order to expedite this process, no later than twenty-one (21) days after this Annex enters into force, the Parties shall draw up comprehensive lists of prisoners and shall provide such lists to the ICRC, to the other Parties, and to the Joint Military Commission and the High Representative. These lists shall identify prisoners by nationality, name, rank (if any) and any internment or military serial number, to the extent applicable.

(e) The Parties shall ensure that the ICRC enjoys full and unimpeded access to all places where prisoners are kept and to all prisoners. The Parties shall permit the ICRC to privately interview each prisoner at least forty-eight (48) hours prior to his or her release for the purpose of implementing and monitoring the plan, including determination of the onward destination of each prisoner.

(f) The Parties shall take no reprisals against any prisoner or his/her family in the event that a prisoner refuses to be transferred.

(g) Notwithstanding the above provisions, each Party shall comply with any order or request of the International Tribunal for the

Former Yugoslavia for the arrest, detention, surrender of or access to persons who would otherwise be released and transferred under this Article, but who are accused of violations within the jurisdiction of the Tribunal. Each Party must detain persons reasonably suspected of such violations for a period of time sufficient to permit appropriate consultation with Tribunal authorities.

2. In those cases where places of burial, whether individual or mass, are known as a matter of record, and graves are actually found to exist, each Party shall permit graves registration personnel of the other Parties to enter, within a mutually agreed period of time, for the limited purpose of proceeding to such graves, to recover and evacuate the bodies of deceased military and civilian personnel of that side, including deceased prisoners.

Article X. Cooperation

The Parties shall cooperate fully with all entities involved in implementation of this peace settlement, as described in the General Framework Agreement, or which are otherwise authorized by the United Nations Security Council, including the International Tribunal for the Former Yugoslavia.

Article XI. Notification to military commands

Each Party shall ensure that the terms of this Annex, and written orders requiring compliance, are immediately communicated to all of its Forces.

Article XII. Final authority to interpret

In accordance with Article I, the IFOR Commander is the final authority in theatre regarding interpretation of this agreement on the military aspects of the peace settlement, of which the Appendices constitute an integral part.

Article XIII. Entry into force

This Annex shall enter into force upon signature.

Appendix A to Annex 1A

Appendix A to Annex 1-A consists of (a) a 1 : 600 000 scale UNPROFOR road map consisting of one map sheet, attached hereto; and (b) a 1 : 50 000 scale Topographic Line Map, attached hereto.

Such maps are an integral part of this Appendix, and the Parties agree to accept such maps as controlling and definitive for all purposes.

(...)

Annex 1-B. Agreement on Regional Stabilization

The Republic of Bosnia and Herzegovina, the Republic of Croatia, the Federal Republic of Yugoslavia, the Federation of Bosnia and Herzegovina, and the Republika Srpska (hereinafter the 'Parties') have agreed as follows:

Article I. General obligations

The Parties agree that establishment of progressive measures for regional stability and arms control is essential to creating a stable peace in the region. To this end, they agree on the importance of devising new forms of cooperation in the field of security aimed at building transparency and confidence and achieving balanced and stable defense force levels at the lowest numbers consistent with the Parties' respective security and the need to avoid an arms race in the region. They have approved the following elements for a regional structure for stability.

Article II. Confidence- and security-building measures in Bosnia and Herzegovina

Within seven days after this Agreement (hereinafter 'Annex') enters into force, the Republic of Bosnia and Herzegovina, the Federation of Bosnia and Herzegovina, and the Republika Srpska shall at an appropriately high political level commence negotiations under the auspices of the Organization for Security and Cooperation in Europe (hereinafter 'OSCE') to agree upon a series of measures to enhance mutual confidence and reduce the risk of conflict, drawing fully upon the 1994 Vienna Document of the Negotiations on Confidence- and Security-Building Measures of the OSCE. The objective of these negotiations is to agree upon an initial set of measures within forty-five (45) days after this Annex enters into force including, but not necessarily limited to, the following:

(a) restrictions on military deployments and exercises in certain geographical areas;

(b) restraints on the reintroduction of foreign Forces in light of Article III of Annex 1-A to the General Framework Agreement;

(c) restrictions on locations of heavy weapons;

(*d*) withdrawal of Forces and heavy weapons to cantonment/barracks areas or other designated locations as provided in Article IV of Annex 1-A;

(*e*) notification of disbandment of special operations and armed civilian groups;

(*f*) notification of certain planned military activities, including international military assistance and training programs;

(*g*) identification of and monitoring of weapons manufacturing capabilities;

(*h*) immediate exchange of data on the holdings of the five Treaty on Conventional Armed Forces in Europe (hereinafter 'CFE') weapons categories as defined in the CFE Treaty, with the additional understanding that artillery pieces will be defined as those of 75mm calibre and above; and

(*i*) immediate establishment of military liaison missions between the Chiefs of the Armed Forces of the Federation of Bosnia and Herzegovina and the Republika Srpska.

Article III. Regional confidence- and security-building measures

To supplement the measures in Article II above on a wider basis, the Parties agree to initiate steps toward a regional agreement on confidence- and security-building measures. The Parties agree:

(*a*) not to import any arms for ninety (90) days after this Annex enters into force;

(*b*) not to import for 180 days after this Annex enters into force or until the arms control agreement referred to in Article IV below takes effect, whichever is the earlier, heavy weapons or heavy weapons ammunition, mines, military aircraft, and helicopters. Heavy weapons refers to all tanks and armored vehicles, all artillery 75 mm and above, all mortars 81 mm and above, and all anti-aircraft weapons 20 mm and above.

Article IV. Measures for sub-regional arms control

1. Recognizing the importance of achieving balanced and stable defense force levels at the lowest numbers consistent with their respective security, and understanding that the establishment of a stable military balance based on the lowest level of armaments will be an essential element in preventing the recurrence of conflict, the Parties within thirty (30) days after this Annex enters into force shall commence negotiations under the auspices of the OSCE to reach early agreement on levels of armaments consistent with this goal.

Within thirty (30) days after this Annex enters into force, the Parties shall also commence negotiations on an agreement establishing voluntary limits on military manpower.

2. The Parties agree that the armaments agreement should be based at a minimum on the following criteria: population size, current military armament holdings, defense needs, and force levels in the region.

(*a*) The agreement shall establish numerical limits on holdings of tanks, artillery, armored combat vehicles, combat aircraft, and attack helicopters, as defined in the relevant sections of the CFE Treaty, with the additional understanding that artillery pieces will be defined as those of 75 mm calibre and above.

(*b*) In order to establish a baseline, the Parties agree to report within thirty (30) days after this Annex enters into force their holdings as defined in sub-paragraph (*a*) above, according to the format prescribed in the 1992 Vienna Document of the OSCE.

(*c*) This notification format shall be supplemented to take into account the special considerations of the region.

3. The Parties agree to complete within 180 days after this Annex enters into force the negotiations above on agreed numerical limits on the categories referred to in paragraph 2(*a*) of this Article. If the Parties fail to agree to such limits within 180 days after this Annex enters into force, the following limits shall apply, according to a ratio of 5:2:2 based on the approximate ratio of populations of the Parties:

(*a*) the baseline shall be the determined holdings of the Federal Republic of Yugoslavia (hereinafter the 'baseline');

(*b*) the limits for the Federal Republic of Yugoslavia shall be seventy-five (75) percent of the baseline;

(*c*) the limits for the Republic of Croatia shall be thirty (30) percent of the baseline;

(*d*) the limits for Bosnia and Herzegovina shall be thirty (30) percent of the baseline; and

(*e*) the allocations for Bosnia and Herzegovina will be divided between the Entities on the basis of a ratio of two (2) for the Federation of Bosnia and Herzegovina and one (1) for the Republika Srpska.

4. The OSCE will assist the Parties in their negotiations under Articles II and IV of this Annex and in the implementation and verification (including verification of holdings declarations) of resulting agreements.

Article V. Regional arms control agreement

The OSCE will assist the Parties by designating a special representative to help organize and conduct negotiations under the auspices of the OSCE Forum on Security Cooperation ('FSC') with the goal of establishing a regional balance in and around the former Yugoslavia. The Parties undertake to cooperate fully with the OSCE to that end and to facilitate regular inspections by other parties. Further, the Parties agree to establish a commission together with representatives of the OSCE for the purpose of facilitating the resolution of any disputes that might arise.

Article VI. Entry into force

This Annex shall enter into force upon signature.

(...)

Annex 4. Constitution of Bosnia and Herzegovina

Preamble

Based on respect for human dignity, liberty, and equality,

Dedicated to peace, justice, tolerance, and reconciliation,

Convinced that democratic governmental institutions and fair procedures best produce peaceful relations within a pluralist society,

Desiring to promote the general welfare and economic growth through the protection of private property and the promotion of a market economy,

Guided by the Purposes and Principles of the Charter of the United Nations,

Committed to the sovereignty, territorial integrity, and political independence of Bosnia and Herzegovina in accordance with international law,

Determined to ensure full respect for international humanitarian law,

Inspired by the Universal Declaration of Human Rights, the International Covenants on Civil and Political Rights and on Economic, Social and Cultural Rights, and the Declaration on the Rights of Persons Belonging to National or Ethnic, Religious and Linguistic Minorities, as well as other human rights instruments,

Recalling the Basic Principles agreed in Geneva on September 8, 1995, and in New York on September 26, 1995,

Bosniacs, Croats, and Serbs, as constituent peoples (along with Others), and citizens of Bosnia and Herzegovina hereby determine that the Constitution of Bosnia and Herzegovina is as follows:

Article I. Bosnia and Herzegovina

1. Continuation

The Republic of Bosnia and Herzegovina, the official name of which shall henceforth be 'Bosnia and Herzegovina,' shall continue its legal existence under international law as a state, with its internal structure modified as provided herein and with its present internationally recognized borders. It shall remain a Member State of the United Nations and may as Bosnia and Herzegovina maintain or apply for membership in organizations within the United Nations system and other international organizations.

2. Democratic principles

Bosnia and Herzegovina shall be a democratic state, which shall operate under the rule of law and with free and democratic elections.

3. Composition

Bosnia and Herzegovina shall consist of the two Entities, the Federation of Bosnia and Herzegovina and the Republika Srpska (hereinafter 'the Entities').

4. Movement of goods, services, capital, and persons

There shall be freedom of movement throughout Bosnia and Herzegovina. Bosnia and Herzegovina and the Entities shall not impede full freedom of movement of persons, goods, services, and capital throughout Bosnia and Herzegovina. Neither Entity shall establish controls at the boundary between the Entities.

5. Capital

The capital of Bosnia and Herzegovina shall be Sarajevo.

6. Symbols

Bosnia and Herzegovina shall have such symbols as are decided by its Parliamentary Assembly and approved by the Presidency.

7. Citizenship

There shall be a citizenship of Bosnia and Herzegovina, to be regulated by the Parliamentary Assembly, and a citizenship of each Entity, to be regulated by each Entity, provided that:

(a) All citizens of either Entity are thereby citizens of Bosnia and Herzegovina.

(b) No person shall be deprived of Bosnia and Herzegovina or Entity citizenship arbitrarily or so as to leave him or her stateless.

No person shall be deprived of Bosnia and Herzegovina or Entity citizenship on any ground such as sex, race, color, language, religion, political or other opinion, national or social origin, association with a national minority, property, birth or other status.

(c) All persons who were citizens of the Republic of Bosnia and Herzegovina immediately prior to the entry into force of this Constitution are citizens of Bosnia and Herzegovina. The citizenship of persons who were naturalized after April 6, 1992 and before the entry into force of this Constitution will be regulated by the Parliamentary Assembly.

(d) Citizens of Bosnia and Herzegovina may hold the citizenship of another state, provided that there is a bilateral agreement, approved by the Parliamentary Assembly in accordance with Article IV (4) (d), between Bosnia and Herzegovina and that state governing this matter.

Persons with dual citizenship may vote in Bosnia and Herzegovina and the Entities only if Bosnia and Herzegovina is their country of residence.

(e) A citizen of Bosnia and Herzegovina abroad shall enjoy the protection of Bosnia and Herzegovina. Each Entity may issue passports of Bosnia and Herzegovina to its citizens as regulated by the Parliamentary Assembly. Bosnia and Herzegovina may issue passports to citizens not issued a passport by an Entity. There shall be a central register of all passports issued by the Entities and by Bosnia and Herzegovina.

Article II. Human rights and fundamental freedoms

1. Human rights
Bosnia and Herzegovina and both Entities shall ensure the highest level of internationally recognized human rights and fundamental freedoms. To that end, there shall be a Human Rights Commission for Bosnia and Herzegovina as provided for in Annex 6 to the General Framework Agreement.

2. International standards
The rights and freedoms set forth in the European Convention for the Protection of Human Rights and Fundamental Freedoms and its Protocols shall apply directly in Bosnia and Herzegovina. These shall have priority over all other law.

3. Enumeration of rights
All persons within the territory of Bosnia and Herzegovina shall enjoy the human rights and fundamental freedoms referred to in paragraph 2 above; these include:

(a) The right to life.

(b) The right not to be subjected to torture or to inhuman or degrading treatment or punishment.

(c) The right not to be held in slavery or servitude or to perform forced or compulsory labor.

(d) The rights to liberty and security of person.

(e) The right to a fair hearing in civil and criminal matters, and other rights relating to criminal proceedings.

(f) The right to private and family life, home, and correspondence.

(g) Freedom of thought, conscience, and religion.

(h) Freedom of expression.

(i) Freedom of peaceful assembly and freedom of association with others.

(j) The right to marry and to found a family.

(k) The right to property.

(l) The right to education.

(m) The right to liberty of movement and residence.

4. Non-discrimination
The enjoyment of the rights and freedoms provided for in this Article or in the international agreements listed in Annex I to this Constitution shall be secured to all persons in Bosnia and Herzegovina without discrimination on any ground such as sex, race, color, language, religion, political or other opinion, national or social origin, association with a national minority, property, birth or other status.

5. Refugees and displaced persons
All refugees and displaced persons have the right freely to return to their homes of origin. They have the right, in accordance with Annex 7 to the General Framework Agreement, to have restored to them property of which they were deprived in the course of hostilities since 1991 and to be compensated for any such property that cannot be restored to them. Any commitments or statements relating to such property made under duress are null and void.

6. Implementation
Bosnia and Herzegovina, and all courts, agencies, governmental organs, and instrumentalities operated by or within the Entities, shall apply and conform to the human rights and fundamental freedoms referred to in paragraph 2 above.

7. International agreements
Bosnia and Herzegovina shall remain or become party to the international agreements listed in Annex I to this Constitution.

8. Cooperation
All competent authorities in Bosnia and Herzegovina shall cooperate with and provide unrestricted access to: any international human rights monitoring mechanisms established for Bosnia and Herzegovina; the supervisory bodies established by any of the international agreements listed in Annex I to this Constitution; the International Tribunal for the Former Yugoslavia (and in particular shall comply with orders issued pursuant to Article 29 of the Statute of the Tribunal); and any other organization authorized by the United Nations Security Council with a mandate concerning human rights or humanitarian law.

Article III. Responsibilities of and relations between the institutions of Bosnia and Herzegovina and the Entities

1. Responsibilities of the institutions of Bosnia and Herzegovina
The following matters are the responsibility of the institutions of Bosnia and Herzegovina:

(*a*) Foreign policy.

(*b*) Foreign trade policy.

(*c*) Customs policy.

(*d*) Monetary policy as provided in Article VII.

(*e*) Finances of the institutions and for the international obligations of Bosnia and Herzegovina.

(*f*) Immigration, refugee, and asylum policy and regulation.

(*g*) International and inter-Entity criminal law enforcement, including relations with Interpol.

(*h*) Establishment and operation of common and international communications facilities.

(*i*) Regulation of inter-Entity transportation.

(*j*) Air traffic control.

2. Responsibilities of the entities
(*a*) The Entities shall have the right to establish special parallel relationships with neighboring states consistent with the sovereignty and territorial integrity of Bosnia and Herzegovina.

(*b*) Each Entity shall provide all necessary assistance to the government of Bosnia and Herzegovina in order to enable it to honor the international obligations of Bosnia and Herzegovina, provided that financial obligations incurred by one Entity without the consent of the other prior to the election of the Parliamentary Assembly and Presidency of Bosnia and Herzegovina shall be the responsibility of that Entity, except insofar as the obligation is necessary for continuing the membership of Bosnia and Herzegovina in an international organization.

(*c*) The Entities shall provide a safe and secure environment for all persons in their respective jurisdictions, by maintaining civilian law enforcement agencies operating in accordance with internationally recognized standards and with respect for the internationally recognized human rights and fundamental freedoms referred to in Article II above, and by taking such other measures as appropriate.

(*d*) Each Entity may also enter into agreements with states and international organizations with the consent of the Parliamentary Assembly. The Parliamentary Assembly may provide by law that certain types of agreements do not require such consent.

3. Law and responsibilities of the entities and the institutions
(*a*) All governmental functions and powers not expressly assigned in this Constitution to the institutions of Bosnia and Herzegovina shall be those of the Entities.

(*b*) The Entities and any subdivisions thereof shall comply fully with this Constitution, which supersedes inconsistent provisions of the law of Bosnia and Herzegovina and of the constitutions and law of the Entities, and with the decisions of the institutions of Bosnia and Herzegovina. The general principles of international law shall be an integral part of the law of Bosnia and Herzegovina and the Entities.

4. Coordination
The Presidency may decide to facilitate inter-Entity coordination on matters not within the responsibilities of Bosnia and Herzegovina as provided in this Constitution, unless an Entity objects in any particular case.

5. Additional responsibilities
(*a*) Bosnia and Herzegovina shall assume responsibility for such other matters as are agreed by the Entities; are provided for in Annexes 5 through 8 to the General Framework Agreement; or are necessary to preserve the sovereignty, territorial integrity, political independence, and international personality of Bosnia and Herzegovina, in accordance with the division of responsibili-

ties between the institutions of Bosnia and Herzegovina. Additional institutions may be established as necessary to carry out such responsibilities.

(b) Within six months of the entry into force of this Constitution, the Entities shall begin negotiations with a view to including in the responsibilities of the institutions of Bosnia and Herzegovina other matters, including utilization of energy resources and cooperative economic projects.

Article IV. Parliamentary Assembly

The Parliamentary Assembly shall have two chambers: the House of Peoples and the House of Representatives.

1. House of Peoples

The House of Peoples shall comprise 15 Delegates, two-thirds from the Federation (including five Croats and five Bosniacs) and one-third from the Republika Srpska (five Serbs).

(a) The designated Croat and Bosniac Delegates from the Federation shall be selected, respectively, by the Croat and Bosniac Delegates to the House of Peoples of the Federation. Delegates from the Republika Srpska shall be selected by the National Assembly of the Republika Srpska.

(b) Nine members of the House of Peoples shall comprise a quorum, provided that at least three Bosniac, three Croat, and three Serb Delegates are present.

2. House of Representatives

The House of Representatives shall comprise 42 Members, two-thirds elected from the territory of the Federation, one-third from the territory of the Republika Srpska.

(a) Members of the House of Representatives shall be directly elected from their Entity in accordance with an election law to be adopted by the Parliamentary Assembly. The first election, however, shall take place in accordance with Annex 3 to the General Framework Agreement.

(b) A majority of all members elected to the House of Representatives shall comprise a quorum.

3. Procedures

(a) Each chamber shall be convened in Sarajevo not more than 30 days after its selection or election.

(b) Each chamber shall by majority vote adopt its internal rules and select from its members one Serb, one Bosniac, and one Croat to serve as its Chair and Deputy Chairs, with the position of Chair rotating among the three persons selected.

(c) All legislation shall require the approval of both chambers.

(d) All decisions in both chambers shall be by majority of those present and voting. The Delegates and Members shall make their best efforts to see that the majority includes at least one-third of the votes of Delegates or Members from the territory of each Entity. If a majority vote does not include one-third of the votes of Delegates or Members from the territory of each Entity, the Chair and Deputy Chairs shall meet as a commission and attempt to obtain approval within three days of the vote. If those efforts fail, decisions shall be taken by a majority of those present and voting, provided that the dissenting votes do not include two-thirds or more of the Delegates or Members elected from either Entity.

(e) A proposed decision of the Parliamentary Assembly may be declared to be destructive of a vital interest of the Bosniac, Croat, or Serb people by a majority of, as appropriate, the Bosniac, Croat, or Serb Delegates selected in accordance with paragraph 1 (a) above. Such a proposed decision shall require for approval in the House of Peoples a majority of the Bosniac, of the Croat, and of the Serb Delegates present and voting.

(f) When a majority of the Bosniac, of the Croat, or of the Serb Delegates objects to the invocation of paragraph (e), the Chair of the House of Peoples shall immediately convene a Joint Commission comprising three Delegates, one each selected by the Bosniac, by the Croat, and by the Serb Delegates, to resolve the issue. If the Commission fails to do so within five days, the matter will be referred to the Constitutional Court, which shall in an expedited process review it for procedural regularity.

(g) The House of Peoples may be dissolved by the Presidency or by the House itself, provided that the House's decision to dissolve is approved by a majority that includes the majority of Delegates from at least two of the Bosniac, Croat, or Serb peoples. The House of Peoples elected in the first elections after the entry into force of this Constitution may not, however, be dissolved.

(h) Decisions of the Parliamentary Assembly shall not take effect before publication.

(i) Both chambers shall publish a complete record of their deliberations and shall, save in exceptional circumstances in accordance with their rules, deliberate publicly.

(*j*) Delegates and Members shall not be held criminally or civilly liable for any acts carried out within the scope of their duties in the Parliamentary Assembly.

4. Powers

The Parliamentary Assembly shall have responsibility for:

(*a*) Enacting legislation as necessary to implement decisions of the Presidency or to carry out the responsibilities of the Assembly under this Constitution.

(*b*) Deciding upon the sources and amounts of revenues for the operations of the institutions of Bosnia and Herzegovina and international obligations of Bosnia and Herzegovina.

(*c*) Approving a budget for the institutions of Bosnia and Herzegovina.

(*d*) Deciding whether to consent to the ratification of treaties.

(*e*) Such other matters as are necessary to carry out its duties or as are assigned to it by mutual agreement of the Entities.

Article V. Presidency

The Presidency of Bosnia and Herzegovina shall consist of three Members: one Bosniac and one Croat, each directly elected from the territory of the Federation, and one Serb directly elected from the territory of the Republika Srpska.

1. Election and term

(*a*) Members of the Presidency shall be directly elected in each Entity (with each voter voting to fill one seat on the Presidency) in accordance with an election law adopted by the Parliamentary Assembly. The first election, however, shall take place in accordance with Annex 3 to the General Framework Agreement. Any vacancy in the Presidency shall be filled from the relevant Entity in accordance with a law to be adopted by the Parliamentary Assembly.

(*b*) The term of the Members of the Presidency elected in the first election shall be two years; the term of Members subsequently elected shall be four years. Members shall be eligible to succeed themselves once and shall thereafter be ineligible for four years.

2. Procedures

(*a*) The Presidency shall determine its own rules of procedure, which shall provide for adequate notice of all meetings of the Presidency.

(*b*) The Members of the Presidency shall appoint from their Members a Chair. For the first term of the Presidency, the Chair shall be the Member who received the highest number of votes. Thereafter, the method of selecting the Chair, by rotation or otherwise, shall be determined by the Parliamentary Assembly, subject to Article IV (3).

(*c*) The Presidency shall endeavor to adopt all Presidency Decisions (i.e., those concerning matters arising under Article III (l) (*a*)–(*e*)) by consensus. Such decisions may, subject to paragraph (*d*) below, nevertheless be adopted by two Members when all efforts to reach consensus have failed.

(*d*) A dissenting Member of the Presidency may declare a Presidency Decision to be destructive of a vital interest of the Entity from the territory from which he was elected, provided that he does so within three days of its adoption. Such a Decision shall be referred immediately to the National Assembly of the Republika Srpska, if the declaration was made by the Member from that territory; to the Bosniac Delegates of the House of Peoples of the Federation, if the declaration was made by the Bosniac Member; or to the Croat Delegates of that body, if the declaration was made by the Croat Member. If the declaration is confirmed by a two-thirds vote of those persons within ten days of the referral, the challenged Presidency Decision shall not take effect.

3. Powers

The Presidency shall have responsibility for:

(*a*) Conducting the foreign policy of Bosnia and Herzegovina.

(*b*) Appointing ambassadors and other international representatives of Bosnia and Herzegovina, no more than two-thirds of whom may be selected from the territory of the Federation.

(*c*) Representing Bosnia and Herzegovina in international and European organizations and institutions and seeking membership in such organizations and institutions of which Bosnia and Herzegovina is not a member.

(*d*) Negotiating, denouncing, and, with the consent of the Parliamentary Assembly, ratifying treaties of Bosnia and Herzegovina.

(*e*) Executing decisions of the Parliamentary Assembly.

(*f*) Proposing, upon the recommendation of the Council of Ministers, an annual budget to the Parliamentary Assembly.

(*g*) Reporting as requested, but not less than annually, to the Parliamentary Assembly on expenditures by the Presidency.

(*h*) Coordinating as necessary with international and nongovernmental organizations in Bosnia and Herzegovina.

(*i*) Performing such other functions as may be necessary to carry out its duties, as may be assigned to it by the Parliamentary Assembly, or as may be agreed by the Entities.

4. Council of Ministers

The Presidency shall nominate the Chair of the Council of Ministers, who shall take office upon the approval of the House of Representatives. The Chair shall nominate a Foreign Minister, a Minister for Foreign Trade, and other Ministers as may be appropriate, who shall take office upon the approval of the House of Representatives.

(*a*) Together the Chair and the Ministers shall constitute the Council of Ministers, with responsibility for carrying out the policies and decisions of Bosnia and Herzegovina in the fields referred to in Article III (1), (4), and (5) and reporting to the Parliamentary Assembly (including, at least annually, on expenditures by Bosnia and Herzegovina).

(*b*) No more than two-thirds of all Ministers may be appointed from the territory of the Federation. The Chair shall also nominate Deputy Ministers (who shall not be of the same constituent people as their Ministers), who shall take office upon the approval of the House of Representatives.

(*c*) The Council of Ministers shall resign if at any time there is a vote of no-confidence by the Parliamentary Assembly.

5. Standing Committee

(*a*) Each member of the Presidency shall, by virtue of the office, have civilian command authority over armed forces. Neither Entity shall threaten or use force against the other Entity, and under no circumstances shall any armed forces of either Entity enter into or stay within the territory of the other Entity without the consent of the government of the latter and of the Presidency of Bosnia and Herzegovina. All armed forces in Bosnia and Herzegovina shall operate consistently with the sovereignty and territorial integrity of Bosnia and Herzegovina.

(*b*) The members of the Presidency shall select a Standing Committee on Military Matters to coordinate the activities of armed forces in Bosnia and Herzegovina. The Members of the Presidency shall be members of the Standing Committee.

Article VI. Constitutional Court

1. Composition

The Constitutional Court of Bosnia and Herzegovina shall have nine members.

(*a*) Four members shall be selected by the House of Representatives of the Federation, and two members by the Assembly of the Republika Srpska. The remaining three members shall be selected by the President of the European Court of Human Rights after consultation with the Presidency.

(*b*) Judges shall be distinguished jurists of high moral standing. Any eligible voter so qualified may serve as a judge of the Constitutional Court. The judges selected by the President of the European Court of Human Rights shall not be citizens of Bosnia and Herzegovina or of any neighboring state.

(*c*) The term of judges initially appointed shall be five years, unless they resign or are removed for cause by consensus of the other judges. Judges initially appointed shall not be eligible for reappointment. Judges subsequently appointed shall serve until age 70, unless they resign or are removed for cause by consensus of the other judges.

(*d*) For appointments made more than five years after the initial appointment of judges, the Parliamentary Assembly may provide by law for a different method of selection of the three judges selected by the President of European Court of Human Rights.

2. Procedures

(*a*) A majority of all members of the Court shall constitute a quorum.

(*b*) The Court shall adopt its own rules of court by a majority of all members. It shall hold public proceedings and shall issue reasons for its decisions, which shall be published.

3. Jurisdiction

The Constitutional Court shall uphold this Constitution.

(*a*) The Constitutional Court shall have exclusive jurisdiction to decide any dispute that arises under this Constitution between the Entities or between Bosnia and Herzegovina and an Entity or Entities, or between institutions of Bosnia and Herzegovina, including but not limited to:

– Whether an Entity's decision to establish a special parallel relationship with a neighboring state is consistent with this Constitution, including provisions concerning the sovereignty and territorial integrity of Bosnia and Herzegovina.

– Whether any provision of an Entity's constitution or law is consistent with this Constitution.

Disputes may be referred only by a member of the Presidency, by the Chair of the Council of Ministers, by the Chair or a Deputy Chair of either chamber of the Parliamentary Assembly, by one-fourth of the members of either chamber of the Parliamentary Assembly, or by one-fourth of either chamber of a legislature of an Entity.

(*b*) The Constitutional Court shall also have appellate jurisdiction over issues under this Constitution arising out of a judgment of any other court in Bosnia and Herzegovina.

(*c*) The Constitutional Court shall have jurisdiction over issues referred by any court in Bosnia and Herzegovina concerning whether a law, on whose validity its decision depends, is compatible with this Constitution, with the European Convention for Human Rights and Fundamental Freedoms and its Protocols, or with the laws of Bosnia and Herzegovina; or concerning the existence of or the scope of a general rule of public international law pertinent to the court's decision.

4. *Decisions.* Decisions of the Constitutional Court shall be final and binding.

Article VII. Central Bank

There shall be a Central Bank of Bosnia and Herzegovina, which shall be the sole authority for issuing currency and for monetary policy throughout Bosnia and Herzegovina.

1. The Central Bank's responsibilities will be determined by the Parliamentary Assembly. For the first six years after the entry into force of this Constitution, however, it may not extend credit by creating money, operating in this respect as a currency board; thereafter, the Parliamentary Assembly may give it that authority.

2. The first Governing Board of the Central Bank shall consist of a Governor appointed by the International Monetary Fund, after consultation with the Presidency, and three members appointed by the Presidency, two from the Federation (one Bosniac, one Croat, who shall share one vote) and one from the Republika Srpska, all of whom shall serve a six-year term. The Governor, who shall not be a citizen of Bosnia and Herzegovina or any neighboring state, may cast tie-breaking votes on the Governing Board.

3. Thereafter, the Governing Board of the Central Bank of Bosnia and Herzegovina shall consist of five persons appointed by the Presidency for a term of six years. The Board shall appoint, from among its members, a Governor for a term of six years.

Article VIII. Finances

1. The Parliamentary Assembly shall each year, on the proposal of the Presidency, adopt a budget covering the expenditures required to carry out the responsibilities of institutions of Bosnia and Herzegovina and the international obligations of Bosnia and Herzegovina.

2. If no such budget is adopted in due time, the budget for the previous year shall be used on a provisional basis.

3. The Federation shall provide two-thirds, and the Republika Srpska one-third, of the revenues required by the budget, except insofar as revenues are raised as specified by the Parliamentary Assembly.

Article IX. General provisions

1. No person who is serving a sentence imposed by the International Tribunal for the Former Yugoslavia, and no person who is under indictment by the Tribunal and who has failed to comply with an order to appear before the Tribunal, may stand as a candidate or hold any appointive, elective, or other public office in the territory of Bosnia and Herzegovina.

2. Compensation for persons holding office in the institutions of Bosnia and Herzegovina may not be diminished during an officeholder's tenure.

3. Officials appointed to positions in the institutions of Bosnia and Herzegovina shall be generally representative of the peoples of Bosnia and Herzegovina.

Article X. Amendment

1. Amendment Procedure. This Constitution may be amended by a decision of the Parliamentary Assembly, including a two-thirds majority of those present and voting in the House of Representatives.

2. Human Rights and Fundamental Freedoms. No amendment to this Constitution may eliminate or diminish any of the rights and freedoms referred to in Article II of this Constitution or alter the present paragraph.

Article XI. Transitional arrangements

Transitional arrangements concerning public offices, law, and other matters are set forth in Annex II to this Constitution.

Article XII. Entry into force

1. This Constitution shall enter into force upon signature of the General Framework Agreement as a constitutional act amending

and superseding the Constitution of the Republic of Bosnia and Herzegovina.

2. Within three months from the entry into force of this Constitution, the Entities shall amend their respective constitutions to ensure their conformity with this Constitution in accordance with Article III (3) (b).

Annex I. Additional Human Rights Agreements to be applied in Bosnia and Herzegovina

1. 1948 Convention on the Prevention and Punishment of the Crime of Genocide

2. 1949 Geneva Conventions I–IV on the Protection of the Victims of War, and the 1977 Geneva Protocols I–II thereto

3. 1951 Convention relating to the Status of Refugees and the 1966 Protocol thereto

4. 1957 Convention on the Nationality of Married Women

5. 1961 Convention on the Reduction of Statelessness

6. 1965 International Convention on the Elimination of All Forms of Racial Discrimination

7. 1966 International Covenant on Civil and Political Rights and the 1966 and 1989 Optional Protocols thereto

8. 1966 Covenant on Economic, Social and Cultural Rights

9. 1979 Convention on the Elimination of All Forms of Discrimination against Women

10. 1984 Convention against Torture and Other Cruel, Inhuman or Degrading Treatment or Punishment

11. 1987 European Convention on the Prevention of Torture and Inhuman or Degrading Treatment or Punishment

12. 1989 Convention on the Rights of the Child

13. 1990 International Convention on the Protection of the Rights of All Migrant Workers and Members of Their Families

14. 1992 European Charter for Regional or Minority Languages

15. 1994 Framework Convention for the Protection of National Minorities

Annex II. Transitional Arrangements

1. Joint Interim Commission

(*a*) The Parties hereby establish a Joint Interim Commission with a mandate to discuss practical questions related to the implementation of the Constitution of Bosnia and Herzegovina and of the General Framework Agreement and its Annexes, and to make recommendations and proposals.

(*b*) The Joint Interim Commission shall be composed of four persons from the Federation, three persons from the Republika Srpska, and one representative of Bosnia and Herzegovina.

(*c*) Meetings of the Commission shall be chaired by the High Representative or his or [her] designee.

2. Continuation of laws

All laws, regulations, and judicial rules of procedure in effect within the territory of Bosnia and Herzegovina when the Constitution enters into force shall remain in effect to the extent not inconsistent with the Constitution, until otherwise determined by a competent governmental body of Bosnia and Herzegovina.

3. Judicial and administrative proceedings

All proceedings in courts or administrative agencies functioning within the territory of Bosnia and Herzegovina when the Constitution enters into force shall continue in or be transferred to other courts or agencies in Bosnia and Herzegovina in accordance with any legislation governing the competence of such courts or agencies.

4. Offices

Until superseded by applicable agreement or law, governmental offices, institutions, and other bodies of Bosnia and Herzegovina will operate in accordance with applicable law.

5. Treaties

Any treaty ratified by the Republic of Bosnia and Herzegovina between January 1, 1992 and the entry into force of this Constitution shall be disclosed to Members of the Presidency within 15 days of their assuming office; any such treaty not disclosed shall be denounced. Within six months after the Parliamentary Assembly is first convened, at the request of any member of the Presidency, the Parliamentary Assembly shall consider whether to denounce any other such treaty.

Source: Text of the Dayton Peace Agreement documents initailed in Dayton, Ohio on Nov. 21, 1995, provided by the Swedish Ministry for Foreign Affairs.

6. Conflicts in and around Russia

VLADIMIR BARANOVSKY

I. Introduction

Russia and most of the post-Soviet states in 1995 were able to avoid major political disturbances in domestic developments, although in a number of cases (such as those of Belarus and some Central Asian and Transcaucasian states) this was mainly achieved by means of consolidating the elements of authoritarianism, undermining the emergence of civil society and the rule of law, and downgrading the principles of human rights and democratic government. The new political élites, all their considerable connections with the *nomenklatura* of Soviet times notwithstanding, seemed increasingly to proceed from the necessity of having their power legitimized by popular vote— even if its fairness has sometimes been seriously questioned by opposition. Most importantly, the parliamentary election in Russia took place in due time, in December 1995, and (contrary to expectations) without any major reports of violations of procedure or falsifications. This election, however, revealed growing public discontent with the government and sharpened the political struggle in the approach to the presidential elections to be held in June 1996.

President Boris Yeltsin's administration continued to proclaim its commitment to the process of reform and indeed promoted the consolidation of the new economic realities—although they increasingly amount to the redistribution of property among and within powerful interest groups and are turning the emerging market economy into a highly centralized, bureaucratized, corrupt and criminalized phenomenon. While claiming certain successes in financial stabilization and a reduction of the extent of industrial decline, the government remained politically vulnerable, seeking to minimize the possibility of social unrest,[1] under pressure from the threat of the restoration of the 'old regime', and increasingly questioned about the genuineness of its overall democratic orientation.[2] Outward assertiveness continued as a compensation

---

[1] According to official statistics, real incomes in Russia fell by 13% in 1995 compared with 1994. An average of 24.7% of the population had incomes below the minimum subsistence level. However, the number of people living below the poverty line decreased steadily from 49.4 million (33%) in Jan. to 28.9 million (20%) in Dec. and the process of income stratification slowed (although the richest 10% of the population had about 27% of the country's total income and the poorest 10% had only 2.5%, with 63% of the population having below-average incomes). Morvant, P., Open Media Research Institute (OMRI), *OMRI Daily Digest*, no. 16, part I (23 Jan. 1996), URL <http://www.omri.cz/Publications/Digests/DigestIndex.html> (hereafter, references to the *OMRI Daily Digest* refer to the Internet edition at this URL address); and *Izvestia*, 23 Jan. 1996.

[2] The president's Human Rights Commission released a report which pointed to 'a visible retreat from democratic achievements' in many areas in 1994–95 and highlighted the increasing militarization of society, the growing tendency to resolve internal conflicts by force and a rise in racial discrimination and intolerance, while the police and 'special services' were winning ever wider and uncontrolled powers.

for domestic failures and as a manifestation of the government's responsiveness to the success of its political opponents.

This chapter addresses the major conflict- and security-related aspects of events in 1995 in and around Russia. Section II focuses on the war in Chechnya, where hostilities and massive violence prevailed over incoherent efforts towards political settlement. Section III presents an overview of the other conflict areas on the territory of the former Soviet Union with special attention to Russia's political and military involvement, and section IV deals with recent security-related developments promoted by Russia in the framework of the CIS.

II. The war in Chechnya

The war in Chechnya which began in late 1994[3] has continued as the most painful development in Russia, accompanied by large-scale violence, claiming many victims, giving rise to a refugee problem, provoking an extremely tense situation in the area of the conflict and affecting the overall political situation in the country.

Hostilities

The poor combat effectiveness of the Russian armed forces was one of the striking revelations of the war in Chechnya. Practically all observers are unanimous that in military terms the operation was extremely badly planned and carried out. Even Defence Minister Pavel Grachev, who in the early stages had presented the forthcoming pacification of Chechnya as a quick and low-cost operation, had to acknowledge the most serious shortcomings in the performance, training, organization and equipment of the troops despatched to the rebellious republic. Merely the fact that reinforcing units sent to Chechnya were made up of elements taken from the whole country and that none of them was fully manned and equipped says much about the state of the Russian armed forces.[4]

The overwhelming preponderance of the Russian armed forces in numbers and in equipment was such that they could not fail steadily to widen their control over the Chechen territory. By mid-1995 the fighters on the side of General Dzhokhar Dudayev, president of the self-proclaimed Chechen Republic, were reported to have been pushed to the mountainous southern part of Chechnya. Their total number, according to some Russian (apparently over-optimistic) estimates, decreased to 1000–1500[5] and these were only able to

Morvant, P., *OMRI Daily Digest*, no. 26, part I (6 Feb. 1996); and American Foreign Policy Council, *Russia Reform Monitor*, no. 100 (AFPC: Washington, DC, 1996).

[3] Baranovsky, V., 'Russia and its neighbourhood: conflict developments and settlement efforts', *SIPRI Yearbook 1995: Armaments, Disarmament and International Security* (Oxford University Press: Oxford, 1995), pp. 240–46.

[4] *Krasnaya Zvezda*, 2 Mar. 1995.

[5] *Krasnaya Zvezda*, 20 June 1995, p. 3.

control 5 per cent of the territory of Chechnya,[6] but their tenacious resistance has turned the conflict into a protracted local war.[7]

Several factors played into the hands of the separatists and undermined the Russian Government's efforts to 'restore constitutional order' in Chechnya.

1. Developments in Chechnya showed once again the inadequacy of regular armed forces in guerrilla warfare.[8] Dudayev's militants, even if defeated in open hostilities, resorted to classic tactics of irregular combat operations, thus denying the Russian units control over the conquered territory and depriving them of targets. Even in Grozny, the capital of Chechnya, the Russian forces long remained vulnerable to attack, despite their strong concentration there.[9]

2. The motivation of the Russian military was poor from the very beginning. The only exception may have been some higher officers expecting quick promotion. According to the General Staff, 557 officers refused to serve in Chechnya. Three deputy defence ministers (generals Gromov, Mironov and Kondratev) criticized the fighting in Chechnya and were removed from their posts.[10] Significant losses, amounting according to official figures to over 2300 killed and about 5500 wounded by the end of the year,[11] did not improve the morale of the troops.

3. The moral mobilization of the Chechens against the Russian invasion, which proved considerable from the very beginning, was significantly reinforced by high civilian casualties; some estimates put them at 36 000 killed and over 100 000 wounded[12]—extremely high figures in proportion to the one million total population of Chechnya. Anti-Russian feelings could only be aggravated by numerous reports of atrocities committed by troops, in particular by the 'special' and Interior Ministry (OMON) forces.[13] However doubtful support for Dudayev may have been, he became a national hero by virtue of Moscow's attempt to resort to force.

---

[6] *Izvestia*, 4 July 1995, p. 1.

[7] Russian Defence Minister Pavel Grachev predicted that hostilities in Chechnya would definitely end by late Apr. 1995. Fuller, L. and Clarke, D., *OMRI Daily Digest*, no. 66, part I (3 Apr. 1995). This turned out to be no more accurate than his earlier prognosis promising to establish control over the whole republic within 72 hours or seize Grozny within 2 hours.

[8] In some senses Russia's experience resembles that of the USA in Viet Nam and the USSR in Afghanistan. Shortcomings in planning, supply and coordination may be only secondary causes of poor military results.

[9] In Sep., the military command assessed the number of Dudayev's combatants in Grozny at 1500; Russian officers recognized that they were only able to control the situation in Grozny in the daytime. *Krasnaya Zvezda*, 23 Sep. 1995, p. 1.

[10] Clarke, D., *OMRI Daily Digest*, no. 71, part I (10 Apr. 1995).

[11] Clarke, D., *OMRI Daily Digest*, no. 240, part I (12 Dec. 1995). According to Gen. Boris Gromov, former Commander of the Soviet 40th Army in Afghanistan, the Russian Army has suffered more serious losses in Chechnya than the Soviet Army did in Afghanistan where in the worst year, 1984, 2227 soldiers were killed. Clarke, D., *OMRI Daily Digest*, no. 34, part I (16 Feb. 1996).

[12] *Izvestia*, 20 June 1995, p. 4. According to the Ministry of the Interior, casualties in the Chechen war amounted to 26 000, approximately half of which were civilians. This official figure is contested: even pro-Moscow Chechen political leader Salambek Khadzhiyev assessed the total number of casualties at 50 000. *Izvestia*, 27 Oct. 1995, p. 5.

[13] The bombing of and assault on the village of Samashki, which was widely reported in the Russian free press as an action amounting to genocide, has become a tragic symbol of the Chechen war.

4. The Russian authorities had to operate under constant pressure of political constraints. Significant opposition to the war on the part of Russian public opinion continued,[14] provoking serious concern among the ruling circles about the forthcoming elections. There was a permanent risk of increasing the discontent of the regional élites in the constituent republics of the Russian Federation, thus undermining its integrity further. The negative international implications for Russia (although less dramatic than might have been expected) also had to be taken into account.[15] All this contributed to disarray within the political leadership in Moscow, preventing the proponents of 'decisive military action' from gaining the upper hand—although the military did often have a free hand when bombing Chechen towns and villages.

Negotiations

Whatever the incentives to seek a political solution, the Russian Government had difficulty in initiating a dialogue with persons whom it had described as bandits and terrorists. Paradoxically, it was one of their most murderous and shocking actions that contributed to opening the way out of the deadlock.

On 14 June, a group of armed Chechen terrorists, headed by a well-known field commander, Shamil Basayev, penetrated the town of Budennovsk in Stavropol *krai* (region), approximately 180 km from Chechnya. Having killed several dozen policemen and civilians, they seized over 1000 hostages, holding them in a local hospital building. The terrorists made the hostages' release conditional on Moscow's agreement to starting negotiations on a political settlement in Chechnya. The scale of the event, as well as unsuccessful attempts by special forces to storm the building, which resulted only in additional casualties[16] and in a dramatic mobilization of the local inhabitants in order to prevent further assaults, led to a serious political crisis affecting Russia's highest echelons of power. In the absence of President Yeltsin (who was attending the meeting of the Group of Seven industrialized countries, G7, in Halifax, Nova Scotia), the decisive move was made by Prime Minister Viktor Chernomyrdin who ordered the establishment of a telephone hot line to the terrorists, publicly accepted their demands for peace talks and provided personal guarantees for their safe return to Chechnya.

This unprecedented and resolute action by the head of government (albeit highly controversial and condemned by his opponents as unacceptable weakness) resulted in a de facto cease-fire in Chechnya and the start of negotiations

---

[14] In reliable polls, 74% of respondents expressed a negative attitude towards attempts to force Chechnya to remain an integral part of Russia. *Segodnya*, 18 July 1995, p. 3.

[15] Among the negative effects of the Chechnya war were the one-year delay in Russia's acceptance as a member of the Council of Europe; the irreparable damage done to the image of 'democratic Russia'; strong reinforcement of perceptions of a continuing Russian policy shift towards 'neo-imperialism'; and the repercussions for the Islamic world's attitude towards Russia. Russia could also be accused of violating the arms control regime: over 1000 tanks and armoured vehicles were used in Chechnya— approximately equal to the total CFE flank quota for the North Caucasus and Leningrad military distrcits (MDs). *Segodnya*, 18 Aug. 1995, p. 3.

[16] The total number of fatalities in Budennovsk was 119. *Izvestia*, 4 July 1995, p. 1.

between representatives of the Russian Government and Dudayev's delegates. Negotiations began several days later in Grozny under the auspices of the mission of the Organization for Security and Co-operation in Europe (OSCE). They brought about an agreement on military questions signed on 30 July.[17]

The main provisions of the agreement included: (*a*) the withdrawal of troops to 2–4 km from the line of contact; (*b*) disarmament of illegal armed formations; (*c*) the withdrawal of Russian troops (conditional on the implementation of the above provisions), with one brigade of the armed forces and one of the interior forces to remain in Chechnya; (*d*) the exchange of prisoners of war; (*e*) the setting up of a supervision commission which would include religious leaders, representatives of local traditional clans (*teips*), international observers and OSCE experts; (*f*) the appointment of a representative of the President of Russia in Chechnya;[18] and (*g*) assistance from the Chechen side in detaining terrorists responsible for the action in Budennovsk. The agreement also envisaged preparations for the forthcoming elections to the presidency of Chechnya and the Russian State Duma, the formation of legitimate institutions and the appointment of representatives of Chechnya in the Russian Parliament. These politically oriented provisions, however, were formulated in rather vague terms.

The practical implementation of the agreement experienced serious difficulties from the very beginning. The issue of prisoners of war became a stumbling-block: the Russian side estimated the number of Russian military detained by the Chechen fighters at about 90, whereas the Chechen side submitted a list of only 5. Russia meanwhile seemed to reject the demands of the Chechen side with respect to some of the militants whom it considered as criminals and responsible for violent actions.[19] Nor was it clear how to disarm the general population, which was in 'illegal' possession of large numbers of weapons and would be reluctant to give them up while the prospects for law and order being re-established in the area were uncertain. As most of these weapons had been acquired at personal expense for the sake of personal security, it was suggested that they be bought up at the current price of approximately $200 per gun. Fifty billion roubles (*c.* $11 million) were allocated for this from the federal budget.[20] Disarmament turned out to be a failure: only a few hundred weapons were turned in during the month of August, and the process later in fact stopped.[21]

Another failed plan concerned a decision to establish 'self-defence forces' in the localities which were to be abandoned by Dudayev's fighters and where the weapons were given up. The aim of this was to quiet the fears of the population in these areas and provide them with security; in fact the scheme in many cases turned into the rearmament of the Chechen irregulars.

[17] *Krasnaya Zvezda,* 5 Aug. 1995, p. 1; and *Segodnya,* 1 Aug. 1995, p. 1.

[18] Oleg Lobov, Secretary of the Security Council of the Russian Federation and close associate of Boris Yeltsin, was nominated.

[19] *Krasnaya Zvezda,* 9 Aug. 1995, p. 1.

[20] Even this would have left at least 10 000 weapons in the hands of the population out of an estimated total of 70 000.

[21] *Izvestia,* 26 Aug. 1995, p. 2; and Parrish, S., *OMRI Daily Digest,* no. 170, part I (31 Aug. 1995).

It seems, however, that the main reasons for the poor start to the peace process were political. The intention to stop hostilities was not accompanied by agreed approaches to the issues which had actually provoked the conflict, the most important of which was Chechnya's status. Putting that question aside at the initial stage of the negotiations was helpful in terms of stopping combat operations, but it left uncertainty about the very core of the conflict. Since this question would have to be addressed in the forthcoming negotiations, both sides were interested in preserving what they had achieved with military means and remained suspicious of each other in tackling practical issues.

The initiation of a peace process also created a legal and political ambiguity. The agreement of 30 July envisaged a settlement on the basis of Russian law which would implicitly mean restoring Chechnya as a constituent part of the Russian Federation. At the same time, the fact that Russia had entered negotiations and concluded an agreement with Dudayev's side implied de facto recognition of what had been proclaimed an illegal regime.[22] Furthermore, this might provide sufficient grounds for questioning the legality of the Russian armed forces' operations in Chechnya. It is significant that the negotiations coincided with the official verdict of the Constitutional Court of the Russian Federation that the president's decree of 9 December 1994 requiring the government to use 'all possible means' to restore law in Chechnya did not represent a violation of the legal norms existing in Russia, as those opposed to the war insisted.[23]

Furthermore, on both sides there were significant forces which were not prepared at any price to endorse a peaceful settlement. In Russia, some influential politicians expressed strong opposition to the search for a compromise in Chechnya.[24] Many of the military considered that the negotiations had been started when the war was practically won and the adversary was close to complete defeat: the separatists, according to this logic, had only used the negotiations as a breathing-space to redeploy and rest their troops. This approach was repeatedly articulated by Defence Minister Grachev, who expressed doubts about the ongoing peace talks.[25] It can also be assumed that the Chechen field commanders were not unanimous about the termination of military activities; moreover, according to Russian estimates, only 30 per cent of the irregulars were effectively controlled by Dudayev's command and the remainder might not abide by the agreement.[26]

There were numerous allegations of hidden resistance to the peace settlement, both at the stage of negotiations and in the process of implementation of the provisions agreed. The main Russian negotiator, Vyacheslav Mikhailov,

---

[22] Significantly, at earlier stages the Russian authorities, even when speculating on possibilities of a peace settlement, had repeatedly rejected the option of direct negotiations with Dudayev, who was officially considered a criminal and ordered to be arrested.

[23] *Segodnya*, 1 Aug. 1995, p. 1.

[24] Petr Shirshov, the Chairman of the Committee on Defence of the Council of Federation, declared that 'peace negotiations in Grozny humiliate the armed forces and the people as a whole'. *Segodnya*, 27 July 1995, p. 2.

[25] Fuller, L., *OMRI Daily Digest*, no. 205, part I (19 Oct. 1995).

[26] *Krasnaya Zvezda*, 5 Aug. 1995, p. 1.

when answering a direct question about the forces in Moscow interested in the continuation of the war, stated bluntly: 'If there were no external factors, we could have agreed long ago'.[27] The agreement was increasingly eroded from September onwards. Incidents continued throughout Chechnya, some days as many as 50 or 60,[28] involving shooting, attacks on the adversary's positions, artillery shelling and numerous casualties daily on both sides. The culmination of this was that the disarmament of the Chechen militants and the withdrawal of Russian troops were suspended indefinitely on 9 October following the attempted assassination of the commander of the Russian forces deployed in Chechnya, Lieutenant-General Anatoliy Romanov, three days earlier.[29] The Russian side started seriously to discuss the possibility of declaring a state of emergency; Dudayev's side threatened to extend the fighting to Russian territory. By the end of 1995 the conflicting parties, without resuming large-scale combat operations, found themselves in a situation of permanent low- and medium-profile military confrontation, with the constant risk of hostilities being significantly broadened.

Prospects for settlement

Paradoxically, the beginning of negotiations in some respects complicated the situation in Chechnya. When accepting Dudayev's side as a partner in negotiations, Moscow in fact relegated to the sidelines its own political allies and clients in the breakaway republic. They felt either betrayed or abandoned, and this immediately resulted in the significant erosion of any support that the efforts of the Russian authorities might have enjoyed in Chechnya. Significantly, even leaders of the institutions which had been set up by Moscow with a clear intention to legitimize the 'restoration of Chechnya' as a constituent part of the Russian Federation started to drift towards a more independent stance. Umar Avturkhanov and Salambek Khadzhiyev, heads of the Moscow-backed Committee for National Accord and Government of National Revival, respectively, which had been set up in 1994, began manoeuvring to be involved in negotiations and at the same time distance themselves from Russia's patronage (presumably not even excluding the option of alliance with Dudayev).[30]

After the beginning of negotiations, Russia tried several times to broaden the political base of its Chechen interlocutors. President Yeltsin even went so far as publicly to accept the possibility of involving the most prominent politician of Chechen origin, Ruslan Khasbulatov, former Speaker of the dissolved Supreme Soviet of the Russian Federation and Yeltsin's main political adversary in the 1993 confrontation in Moscow. However, all these attempts were blocked by the reluctance of Dudayev to share the stakes in his possession with his actual or potential political rivals in Chechnya.

[27] *Argumenty i Fakty*, no. 31 (1995), p. 3.
[28] *Krasnaya Zvezda,* 22 Nov. 1995, p. 1.
[29] Fuller, L., *OMRI Daily Digest*, no. 197, part I (10 Oct. 1995).
[30] *Segodnya*, 12 Aug. 1995, p. 1.

At the end of October, a 'new start' was initiated: Avturkhanov and Khadzhiyev, both of them too closely associated with Russia's intervention, resigned and left the political stage open for Doku Zavgayev, who had been the chairman of the Chechen–Ingush Parliament before Dudayev's time, to become head of government, incarnating a certain legitimacy of the past. It was hoped that he would shift the negotiation process in Chechnya on to an internal political track which would suggest that a political settlement should emerge from talks between the different Chechen factions rather than from negotiations between federal government officials and representatives of Dudayev. Zavgayev manifested an unprecedented readiness to cooperate with the latter, declaring that half of his government were sympathetic to the separatists and expressing willingness to include more of Dudayev's supporters if doing so would promote political stability.[31]

Such statements contradicted Zavgayev's reluctance even to consider the issue of Chechnya's status, which he considered to be unambiguously defined in the Russian Constitution.[32] Moreover, Zavgayev, according to the separatists, lacked the legal or political competence to conclude, on behalf of Chechnya, the agreement on the basic principles of relations with the Russian Federation, which was signed on 8 December.[33] Even more seriously, the prospect of reconciliation was put at risk by the decision to hold the elections in December.

Although none of the parties involved in the conflict denied the need for elections in principle, the key question was whether they could be organized in the presence of the Russian armed forces. At earlier stages, even Russia's authorities and Moscow-backed Chechen politicians had expressed reservations in this respect, conscious that the legitimacy of the result would be doubtful, especially if the elections were boycotted by a significant part of the population of the republic. Thus, in late August 1995 the Russian President's representative in Chechnya, Oleg Lobov, stated that, with the prospects for disarmament and military disengagement of the parties uncertain, it was impossible to set a date for new elections.[34] Even at the end of October, the elections were not expected to be organized in less than six months.[35]

However, while the hopes for a *rapprochement* with Dudayev evaporated, Zavgayev's government, strongly supported by Moscow, opted to hold the elections on 17 December, the day of the parliamentary elections for the whole of the Russian Federation.

The decision to hold 'quick' elections provoked broad opposition. Dudayev's side appealed for a boycott on the grounds that they were designed to legitimize the puppet government and threatened to make it impossible to hold them by resuming large-scale combat operations.[36] In an attempt to wreck

[31] Parrish, S., *OMRI Daily Digest*, no. 218, part I (8 Nov. 1995).
[32] *Obshchaya Gazeta*, 9–15 Nov. 1995, p. 8.
[33] *Krasnaya Zvezda*, 9 Dec. 1995, p. 1.
[34] Parrish, S., *OMRI Daily Digest*, no. 170, part I (31 Aug. 1995).
[35] *Izvestia*, 27 Oct. 1995, p. 5.
[36] *Segodnya*, 29 Nov. 1995, p. 1.

the elections, the Chechen combatants organized a number of battles, including the most serious one of the whole six months of the cease-fire, when they took the town of Gudermes and repulsed an attempt by Russian federal troops to dislodge them.[37] On 9 December Khasbulatov withdrew his candidacy for the presidency, arguing that the vote would give rise to new bloodshed and 'could split Chechnya in two'.[38] A number of Moscow-based human rights groups demanded that the elections be cancelled because they would not be fair, would be held in a 'virtual state of emergency' and would not allow a large proportion of the population, including thousands of refugees, to vote.[39] Several massive protest rallies took place in Grozny.

The elections, held under the heavy protection of the occupation forces providing for security and order (and participating in the vote), brought the expected results. Doku Zavgayev was elected the new head of state, with figures for the turnout varying between 47 and 60 per cent (not verifiable, as no international observers were present: the OSCE mission had left Grozny temporarily for security reasons). However, because the legitimacy of the new leadership was doubtful, the prospects of political stabilization did not improve.

By the end of 1995, events in Chechnya were increasingly developing along the lines of the 'Algerian scenario' or that of Afghanistan at the time of the Soviet intervention, with the government, backed by the Russian armed forces, in control of a considerable part of the territory but unable to suppress numerous groups of combatants operating over the whole of Chechnya. According to Grachev, the Russian armed forces left the mountainous areas of Chechnya and were installed in 17 basing regions over its territory.[40] Yeltsin's statement that 'there are no military means to resolve the conflict in Chechnya' was contradicted by his appeals for 'strikes on Dudayev's strongholds';[41] further significant clashes, such as that provoked in January 1996 by the second hostage-taking by Dudayev's fighters in Kizlyar, Dagestan, may have consolidated the position of the proponents in Moscow of a 'forceful' solution to the Chechen issue and make guerrilla warfare more likely.

On 31 March 1996, after active offensive operations by the Russian troops and in anticipation of the presidential elections, Yeltsin announced a new 'peace plan' for Chechnya envisaging, *inter alia*, the withdrawal of federal armed forces from the territory of the breakaway republic and eventual negotiations, via mediators, with Dudayev's representatives. Offensive operations by Russian troops continued none the less. On 21 April Dzhokhar Dudayev

[37] Fuller, L., *OMRI Daily Digest*, no. 243, part I (15 Dec. 1995).
[38] Fuller, L., *OMRI Daily Digest*, no. 239, part I (11 Dec. 1995).
[39] Belin, L., *OMRI Daily Digest*, no. 240, part I (12 Dec. 1995). By mid-1995 the total number of refugees from Chechnya, according to the UN High Commissioner for Refugees, was 152 000. *Segodnya*, 20 July 1995, p. 2. Significantly, figures provided by the Russian Federal Migration Service were much higher: it estimated that about 610 000 people had abandoned their homes in Chechnya, 487 000 of whom were officially registered with the service during 1995 (200 000 were said to have returned to their homes). Morvant, P., *OMRI Daily Digest*, no. 39, part I (23 Feb. 1996).
[40] *Krasnaya Zvezda*, 17 Nov. 1995, p. 3.
[41] *Segodnya*, 23 Nov. 1995, p. 1; *International Herald Tribune*, 19 Jan. 1996, p. 1; and Russian TV news programme Vremya, 19 Jan. 1996.

was reported killed in a rocket attack. Although his successor Zelimkhan Yandarbiyev is considered to be a firm supporter of independence, the Russian and separatist leaderships met in Moscow on 27 May 1996 and agreed on a complete cease-fire from midnight on 31 May and the release within two weeks of all hostages and other persons forcibly detained. The situation in fact returned to what it had been 10 months earlier, with the issue of Chechnya's future status *vis-à-vis* the Russian Federation still to be settled.

III. Other conflicts in the former Soviet Union

The Trans-Dniester region (Moldova)

The year 1995 started with some positive developments in the settlement of the situation in the Trans-Dniester region.[42] The conflicting parties—Moldova, defending the preservation of its territorial integrity, and the breakaway 'Trans-Dniester Moldovan Republic'—addressed a number of practical issues of mutual interest—finance, communications, the environment and so on. This was stimulated, among other factors, by the economic cooperation agreement between Russia and Moldova elaborated with the participation of representatives of Trans-Dniester.[43] In February, the President of Moldova, Mircea Snegur, and the president of the unrecognized Trans-Dniester Moldovan Republic, Igor Smirnov, signed an agreement to begin restoring the bridges that had been blown up in 1992 and on the gradual removal of customs checkpoints all along the Dniester River.[44] In July the two sides signed three agreements allowing, *inter alia*, limited circulation of the Moldovan currency (the leu) in the Trans-Dniester region.

These achievements, however, were reduced to practically nothing by political developments. In Trans-Dniester the radicals denounced the 'capitulation' to Moldova and pushed the separatist leadership to return to the initial demands for recognition of the breakaway region's sovereignty and independence as a precondition of any further negotiations.[45]

Smirnov, speaking before the Russian State Duma in September 1995, appealed to it either to promote the statehood of the Trans-Dniester region or to make it part of Russia. In response, the State Duma proclaimed the region a part of Russia's sphere of strategic interests and suggested to President Yeltsin that he initiate a trilateral meeting of Russia, Moldova and representatives of the Trans-Dniester region on the issue of recognizing its independence.[46]

---

[42] The Trans-Dniester region saw serious clashes in 1992. The situation had been frozen since then, with the 1994 agreement on the withdrawal of the Russian 14th Army being one of the key elements of stabilization. Amer, R. *et al.*, 'Major armed conflicts', *SIPRI Yearbook 1993: World Armaments and Disarmament* (Oxford University Press: Oxford, 1993), pp. 101–103; Baranovsky, V., 'Conflict developments on the territory of the former Soviet Union', *SIPRI Yearbook 1994* (Oxford University Press: Oxford, 1994), pp. 188–90; and Baranovsky (note 3), pp. 248–49.

[43] *Nezavisimaya Gazeta*, 27 Jan. 1995, p. 2.

[44] *Moscow News*, no. 8 (24 Feb.–2 Mar. 1995), p. 5.

[45] *Jane's Intelligence Review*, vol. 7, no. 11 (Nov. 1995), p. 484.

[46] *Nezavisimaya Gazeta*, 18 Nov. 1995, p. 2.

Although the Russian Foreign Ministry denounced such steps as unfriendly acts towards Moldova and as encouraging the intransigence of the separatists, they certainly contributed to undermining the prospects for a political settlement. The same can be said of the holding of a referendum in the region in December 1995 on a new constitution and on its joining the Commonwealth of Independent States (CIS).[47]

Another complicating factor was the issue of the deployment of Russian troops in the Trans-Dniester region. Although an agreement on their withdrawal had been signed in October 1994, the separatist leadership organized a referendum on the future of the Russian 14th Army; a clear majority of voters requested that it should stay.[48] The separatist leadership also continued to request that the 14th Army's weapons and equipment should remain on its territory,[49] whereas Moldova resolutely insisted on (and Russia had started to prepare for) their withdrawal.[50]

However, the 'strategic arguments' that 'the Russian armed forces have been on the banks of the Dniester region for 200 years and have become an integral element of the military and political balance in this area'[51] seemed to attract increasing sympathy in (if they were not actually initiated by) the authorities in Moscow, who, while not questioning the agreement on withdrawal, appeared to be looking for alternative ways of keeping up the Russian military presence.[52]

President Yeltsin indicated that the question of the time-frame for the Russian units' stay on the territory of Moldova 'could be reconsidered at any moment'.[53] Defence Minister Grachev stated bluntly that he would like 'to keep several mobile units, in high combat readiness, with a total personnel of 3500 in order to preserve peace'.[54] Moldova's acceptance of the establishment of a Russian military base in the Trans-Dniester region following the Russian–Georgian pattern[55] may be a condition of a solution to the conflict.[56]

Abkhazia and South Ossetia (Georgia)

Conflict settlement efforts with respect to Abkhazia and South Ossetia have focused mainly on the issue of the status of these two breakaway regions of Georgia. When addressing the question of the future constitutional order in

---

[47] The new constitution adopted in Dec. 1995 proclaims the Trans-Dniester Moldovan Republic 'a sovereign and independent state', thus rejecting the status of broad autonomy within Moldova. The idea of joining the CIS was supported by 80% of voters in the referendum. *Nezavisimaya Gazeta*, 5 Nov. 1995, p. 3; and *Izvestia*, 26 Dec. 1995, p. 2.

[48] *Izvestia*, 28 Mar. 1995, p. 2 reported a 60% majority in favour of the 14th Army remaining, and *Neue Zürcher Zeitung*, 28 Mar. 1995, a majority of 90%.

[49] *Obshchaya Gazeta*, 16–22 Feb. 1995, p. 1.

[50] *Segodnya*, 6 July 1995, p. 2.

[51] Quoted from an interview with Igor Smirnov, *Segodnya*, 9 Feb. 1995, p. 3.

[52] At the time of writing the agreement on withdrawal had not yet been ratified by the Russian State Duma. *Nezavisimaya Gazeta*, 20 Jan. 1996, p. 3.

[53] *Krasnaya Zvezda*, 29 June 1995, p. 1.

[54] *Segodnya*, 28 June 1995, p. 2.

[55] *Segodnya*, 29 June 1995, p. 1.

[56] *Jane's Intelligence Review*, vol. 7, no. 11 (Nov. 1995), p. 484.

Georgia, its President, Eduard Shevardnadze, has repeatedly insisted on the territorial integrity of the country, at the same time expressing readiness to provide its constituent parts with a considerable degree of autonomy. This would allow Abkhazia to have its own constitution with Abkhaz as an official language (alongside Georgian) and its own state symbols, legislature, executive and judicial systems; South Ossetia would have its own charter.[57] It should be noted, however, that the new constitution approved by the Georgian Parliament on 24 August 1995 does not address the issue of relations with the breakaway regions.[58]

Abkhazia has run itself as a de facto independent state since September 1993 when separatist fighters routed Georgian Government soldiers who had been sent in in 1992 after Abkhazia proclaimed separation from Georgia.[59] Abandoning its earlier demands for total formal independence, Abkhazia is now insisting on a confederative agreement based on recognition of its sovereignty and providing for a loose (in fact, no more than symbolic) union of the two states as equal partners.[60]

Representatives of the Georgian Government and the rebel region held negotiations under the auspices of Russia throughout 1995. The latter, accused of supporting the separatists in the earlier stages of the conflict, had considerably changed its position since establishing closer relations with Shevardnadze, who opted to join the CIS and accepted the deployment of Russian armed forces in Georgia. Georgia, however, required a quid pro quo: it officially stated that it would not ratify the 1994 Treaty on Friendship, Neighbourly Relations and Cooperation with Russia and the attached military-related agreements until its jurisdiction was re-established over the whole of the country.[61] Shevardnadze made it clear that the future of the Russian military bases in Georgia would be called into question unless Russia assisted in restoring the country's unity.[62]

Not surprisingly, Russia focused on developing relations with Georgia as if no Abkhazian pretensions to sovereignty existed. The two sides agreed on re-establishing rail traffic along the Black Sea—that is, through Abkhazia—with Russia taking responsibility for its security, and on the right for Russia to maintain a military base in the Abkhazian town of Gudauta.[63] Strong protests from Abkhazia that it had not been involved or consulted were disregarded.[64] Furthermore, Russian officials have spectacularly alienated themselves from the Abkhazian leadership.[65] The latter was vigorously blamed for intransi-

[57] Bezanis, L., *OMRI Daily Digest*, no. 105, part I (31 May 1995).
[58] Fuller, L., *OMRI Daily Digest*, no. 166, part I (25 Aug. 1995).
[59] Baranovsky 1994 (note 42), pp. 193–95; and Baranovsky (note 3), pp. 251–53.
[60] *Covcas Bulletin*, vol. 5, no. 21 (8 Nov. 1995).
[61] *Krasnaya Zvezda*, 22 Sep. 1995, p. 3. The Georgian Parliament ratified the treaty with Russia on 17 Jan. 1996. Fuller, L., *OMRI Daily Digest*, no. 13, part I (18 Jan. 1996).
[62] Bezanis, L., *OMRI Daily Digest*, no. 214, part I (2 Nov. 1995).
[63] See section IV of this chapter.
[64] *Nezavisimaya Gazeta*, 6 Oct. 1995, p. 3. See also Fuller, L., *OMRI Daily Digest* (note 1), no. 207, part I (24 Oct. 1995); and *OMRI Daily Digest*, no. 65, part I (31 Mar. 1995).
[65] In a public statement on 13 July, the Chairman of the Russian Federation Council, Vladimir Shumeiko, accused the self-proclaimed President of Abkhazia, Vladislav Ardzinba, of genocide and

gence in the negotiations and openly threatened that if they failed Russian military assistance to Georgia would increase; President Yeltsin pledged to take steps to restore Georgian territorial integrity.[66]

Political statements were accompanied by significant practical actions in this direction. A de facto land blockade was established around Abkhazia, from the south and the east by Georgia, and from the north by the Russian Federation.[67] The only remaining outlet to the outside world, the sea route from the capital, Sukhumi, to Turkey used for vital food supplies, was sealed off by Russian warships on 23 October.[68] This blockade was lifted a week later after the Abkhazian delegation refused to continue peace talks, blaming Russia for ceasing to operate as mediator and openly siding with one of the conflicting parties.[69] However, in another effort to tighten the blockade, Russian border guards were instructed to stop allowing the holders of Abkhazian passports to travel to Turkey, the only country that recognized them.[70]

Russia also threatened to withdraw the 3000 peacekeeping troops sent to the Abkhazian–Georgian border in 1994 which were preventing the two sides from resuming hostilities.[71] This threat was echoed by repeated warnings by Georgia that it would not allow an extension of the peacekeepers' mandate[72] and might resort to resolving the problem by military means.[73]

Abkhazia in turn blamed the Russian peacekeepers for employing personnel of the Russian group of forces in the Transcaucasus, allegedly consisting 80 per cent of Georgian nationals; it claimed that agreement had been reached on a Russian–Georgian military operation against Abkhazia[74] and that an invasion was about to start by the end of September.[75] Furthermore, according to unconfirmed reports, Russia transferred to Georgia 12 combat helicopters and spare parts for Su-27 fighters;[76] in January 1996 the security service of Abkhazia released information that the Russian Defence Ministry had agreed to provide Georgia with five large landing ships for carrying out an assault on the Abkhazian part of the Black Sea coast.[77]

compared him to Chechen President Dzhokhar Dudayev. This assessment was endorsed by Russian Foreign Minister Andrey Kozyrev. Fuller, L., *OMRI Daily Digest*, no. 138, part I (18 July 1995).

[66] Parrish, S., *OMRI Daily Digest*, no. 228, part I (22 Nov. 1995); *Segodnya*, 29 Nov. 1995, p. 2; and Rutland, P., *OMRI Daily Digest*, no. 176, part I (11 Sep. 1995).

[67] *Covcas Bulletin*, vol. 5, no. 20 (25 Oct. 1995).

[68] Fuller, L., *OMRI Daily Digest*, no. 207, part I (24 Oct. 1995).

[69] *Nezavisimaya Gazeta*, 5 Nov. 1995, p. 3; and *Covcas Bulletin*, vol. 5, no. 20 (25 Oct. 1995); and vol. 5, no. 21 (8 Nov. 1995). According to later reports, from 30 Oct. 1995 the Abkhazian ships were not allowed to leave from the port of Sukhumi; from 5 Jan. 1996, the port was closed for all foreign ships. *Nezavisimaya Gazeta*, 11 Jan. 1996, p. 3.

[70] Bezanis, L., *OMRI Daily Digest*, no. 222, part I (14 Nov. 1995).

[71] *Krasnaya Zvezda*, 22 June 1995, p. 3.

[72] The Georgian side suspected the commander of the Russian peacekeepers, Gen. Yakushev, of sympathizing with the Abkhazian separatists and supporting them. *Nezavisimaya Gazeta*, 23 May 1995, p. 2. On 26 May the CIS summit meeting in Minsk extended the peacekeeping mandate in Abkhazia until the end of 1995. Mihalka, M., *OMRI Daily Digest*, no. 103, part I (29 May 1995).

[73] *Nezavisimaya Gazeta*, 23 May 1995, p. 2; and *Covcas Bulletin*, vol. 5, no. 20 (25 Oct. 1995).

[74] Fuller, L., *OMRI Daily Digest*, no. 181, part I (18 Sep. 1995).

[75] Interview with Vladislav Ardzinba in *Nezavisimaya Gazeta*, 5 Nov. 1995, p. 3.

[76] *Nezavisimaya Gazeta*, 19 Jan. 1996, p. 3.

[77] *Nezavisimaya Gazeta*, 12 Jan. 1996, p. 3.

The pressure on Abkhazia seemed to have resulted by the end of the year in the prospect of a political settlement. A confidential draft outline of a protocol to end the conflict was made public in November, issuing from negotiations in Moscow between the two parties under Russian mediation. The protocol provided for an Abkhaz Republic with its own constitution, legislature, government, army and budget; a common Georgian–Abkhaz government and legislature, with reserved Abkhaz seats and right of veto; a joint defence policy with coordination of the two armies; and a common currency.[78] This document was rejected by the more uncompromising among the Abkhazian legislators as abandoning the strict confederative pattern.[79]

In Georgia there is also domestic opposition to compromise with Abkhazia.[80] Two questions are the most contentious. The first concerns the Abkhaz army: it is not clear to what extent Georgia would be ready to accept the existence of an autonomous military force with a significant potential for supporting possible future claims for secession. The second is the issue of refugees: Abkhazia refuses to allow the free repatriation of the more than 200 000 Georgians who fled following the fall of Sukhumi in 1993. The UN High Commissioner for Refugees has been able to arrange the return of only about 300 refugees despite two years of work and the expenditure of considerable resources.[81] The problem continues to be one of extreme sensitivity for Georgia, with threats that repatriation could start spontaneously in the absence of a formal agreement[82] and increasing criticism of UN conflict management efforts.[83] Georgia believes that the peacekeeping mission should be broadened and should consist not only in separating the parties but also in promoting the return of the refugees to Abkhazia.[84] At the same time, according to the Abkhazian side, it cannot effectively control the Gala district, which had a predominantly Georgian population before hostilities and where the refugees are in fact returning in great numbers without any official settlement.[85]

In January 1996, at the CIS summit meeting in Moscow, Georgia requested strong collective sanctions, including a de facto economic blockade of Abkhazia.[86] Athough backed by Russia, this request was only partially supported by the CIS heads of states. Five of them[87] were clearly reluctant to

---

[78] Covcas Bulletin, vol. 5, no. 22 (30 Nov. 1995).

[79] Segodnya, 29 Nov. 1995, p. 2.

[80] Nezavisimaya Gazeta, 20 Jan. 1996, p. 3.

[81] Covcas Bulletin, vol. 5, no. 20 (25 Oct. 1995).

[82] Fuller, L., OMRI Daily Digest, no. 138, part I (18 July 1995).

[83] Krasnaya Zvezda, 22 Sep. 1995, p. 3. 'Twelve UN resolutions on the Abkhaz question have remained only on paper', stated Georgian Prime Minister Otar Parsatsia. 'The resolutions have exhausted themselves and can no longer give us anything . . . The cup of patience has long since overflown and it is possible that events may take on an unpredictable direction.' Covcas Bulletin, vol. 5, no. 20 (25 Oct. 1995). In Jan. 1996 the UN Security Council extended the mandate of its 136-man observer mission in Abkhazia until July 1996 and in fact endorsed the approach of Georgia towards conflict management. Nezavisimaya Gazeta, 18 Jan. 1996, p. 3.

[84] Nezavisimaya Gazeta, 11 Jan. 1996, p. 3.

[85] Nezavisimaya Gazeta, 30 Jan. 1996, p. 3.

[86] Nezavisimaya Gazeta, 13 Jan. 1996, p. 1; and 19 Jan. 1996, p. 3.

[87] Belarus, Kyrgyzstan, Tajikistan, Turkmenistan and Uzbekistan—the countries which do not feel directly threatened by separatism.

become excessively involved; the mandate of the peacekeepers was extended till 19 April 1996 but not broadened to include police functions and refugee return enforcement (which might bring about a military confrontation with Abkhazian forces); and economic sanctions can hardly go beyond the existing de facto blockade.[88] Whether increasing political pressure might promote the settlement of this conflict remains to be seen.

In *South Ossetia*, developments during 1995 were much less spectacular, although along similar lines. Moscow's sensitivity about the principle of territorial integrity (reinforced by Chechen separatism in the neighbouring area), together with its strategic objective of consolidating an alliance relationship with Georgia, has left South Ossetians little chance of being reunited with their northern kinsmen living across the mountains in North Ossetia (part of the Russian Federation). Meanwhile, Georgia has pursued a low-key policy, allowing economic imperatives to work and expressing readiness to address in a cooperative way issues such as the return of refugees, the disarmament of illegal units and the resolution of economic problems.[89]

There have been only sporadic violent incidents since 1992, when the Georgian, Ossetian and Russian peacekeepers started to patrol the region. Both Georgia and South Ossetia, pointing to the relative stabilization of the situation, have suggested withdrawing their personnel from the peacekeeping forces and keeping only Russian peacekeepers but in increased numbers.[90]

Negotiations have continued to resolve the status of South Ossetia. While the separatist government publicly still pays lip-service to the objective of independence or union with Russia, privately officials admit that it seems inevitable that South Ossetia will remain part of Georgia, albeit with some degree of sovereignty.[91]

Nagorno-Karabakh (Azerbaijan)

The cease-fire in the area of the conflict has continued since May 1994.[92] The territory of Nagorno-Karabakh and six other administrative districts of Azerbaijan (altogether 20 per cent of its territory) are under the effective control of Karabakh troops.[93] The Lachin land corridor links the breakaway republic and Armenia. The latter denies the presence of its armed forces on the territory of Azerbaijan.[94] Although some sporadic clashes took place in 1995 along the line of contact between Azerbaijani and Armenian troops,[95] the overall military situation can be described as basically frozen.

[88] *Nezavisimaya Gazeta*, 24 Jan. 1996, p. 3.
[89] Fuller, L., *OMRI Daily Digest*, no. 104, part I (30 May 1995).
[90] *Krasnaya Zvezda*, 14 Sep. 1995, p. 1.
[91] *Covcas Bulletin*, vol. 5, no. 20 (25 Oct. 1995).
[92] Baranovsky (note 3), p. 254.
[93] *Krasnaya Zvezda*, 25 May 1995, p. 4.
[94] *Nezavisimaya Gazeta*, 5 Nov. 1995, p. 3.
[95] Bezanis, L., *OMRI Daily Digest*, no. 50, part I (10 Mar. 1995).

After the OSCE decision at its Budapest summit meeting (December 1994) to endorse in principle a peacekeeping operation in Nagorno-Karabakh,[96] the basic problem has been for the parties involved to reach a political decision on the cessation of the conflict. Negotiations continued during 1995 under the auspices of the OSCE Minsk Group,[97] but the expected results were not achieved.[98] The conflicting parties remain far apart on many critical issues, including the problem of refugees, the status of the territory, the return of territories seized, the blockade of Armenia and Nagorno-Karabakh, and security guarantees for the latter.[99]

Nagorno-Karabakh, reluctant to renounce the stakes which effectively guarantee its security, insisted that the existing military and political realities should be taken as the point of departure for a negotiated settlement and would only agree to withdrawal of its troops from the occupied territory in exchange for the definition of its status. The logic of 'status in exchange for territories' was rejected by Azerbaijan.[100] The latter, however, seemed to become more flexible by the end of 1995, when President Geidar Aliev mentioned the possibility of upgrading the status of Karabakh, conditional on the recognition of Azerbaijani sovereignty over the territory. The new constitution of the country gives another former autonomy, Nakhichevan, the status of 'a state within Azerbaijan' and a similar formula might be applied with respect to Karabakh as well.[101]

The broader international context may also have affected developments around the conflict area. The negotiations on the Caspian Sea shelf oil extraction contract and the new pipelines for transferring the oil from Kazakhstan and Azerbaijan to Western Europe have been characterized by dramatic competition between Russian, West European, US, Turkish and Iranian interests, as well as those of the three Transcaucasian states.[102] The discussions on how to ensure stability in Nagorno-Karabakh and who will be the guarantor of the settlement thus touch upon the overall strategic balance in the Transcaucasus.

It should be noted that Azerbaijan, unlike Armenia and Georgia, is very reluctant to provide Russia with military bases on its territory. Azerbaijan also seemed to expect that allowing Russia to circumvent the flank limits embodied in the 1990 Conventional Armed Forces in Europe (CFE) Treaty

---

[96] Baranovsky (note 3), p. 254.

[97] Set up in Mar. 1992 to monitor the situation in Nagorno-Karabakh. The member countries are now (Dec. 1995) Belarus, Finland, France, Germany, Hungary, Italy, Russia, Sweden, Switzerland, Turkey and the USA, plus Armenia and Azerbaijan.

[98] Rutland, P., *OMRI Daily Digest*, no. 176, part I (11 Sep. 1995); Dave, B., *OMRI Daily Digest*, no. 218, part I (8 Nov. 1995); and Bezanis, L., *OMRI Daily Digest*, no. 221, part I (13 Nov. 1995). See also chapter 7, section V of this volume.

[99] *Segodnya*, 20 Sep. 1995, p. 5.

[100] Azerbaijan refused consistently to recognize the independence of Nagorno-Karabakh until the territory which had been seized during earlier fighting was returned. Rutland, P., *OMRI Daily Digest*, no. 172, part I (15 Sep. 1995).

[101] *Nezavisimaya Gazeta*, 5 Dec. 1995, p. 3.

[102] The meeting of US Vice-President Albert Gore and Russian Prime Minister Viktor Chernomyrdin in early Oct. 1995 was reported to have resulted in an agreement on a double pipeline route from Baku—via Armenia and Turkey and via the Russian northern Caucasus. *Krasnaya Zvezda*, 16 Sep. 1995, p. 3; and *Nezavisimaya Gazeta*, 30 Nov. 1995, p. 3; 5 Dec. 1995, p. 3; and 6 Dec. 1995, p. 3.

through temporary force deployment in Armenia and Georgia should be compensated for by the right for it to have more weapons on its own territory.[103]

From this point of view, Russia's sensitivity on the issue of the forthcoming peacekeeping operation in Nagorno-Karabakh is not surprising. The continuing lack of progress in the peace settlement, despite the commitment of the OSCE, and the risk of hostilities resuming may make more convincing the argument in favour of using Russian peacekeepers as the only element that can provide some stability in the region.[104]

Tajikistan

In 1995, the hostilities between government forces and opposition fighters were on a smaller scale than in the previous years.[105] The government claimed that the situation in the country was 'under control and relatively stable'.[106] The opposition Islamic Renaissance Movement of Tajikistan (IRMT) seemed to become more interested in a peaceful settlement—both in the quest for a more respectable international image and because of its failure to unleash broader military action in Tajikistan.[107] The tactic of military pressure against the government was not abandoned, although it mainly took the form of relatively limited but regular clashes in the frontier areas.[108] Within Tajikistan, sporadic terrorist actions took place and a few groups of combatants were reported to be operating. However, the possibility of a military victory for the opposition appeared doubtful.

At the same time the government also faced problems in ensuring effective control over the country. In many areas, especially in the high mountains of Pamir (Gorno-Badakhshan), where the commanders of local self-defence forces represent the only real power, the central government attempted to involve them in the official or semi-official state infrastructure, hoping to make them allies rather than opponents.[109] However, a number of larger-scale armed operations were carried out against the opposition combatants, the most serious incident, involving air bombing, taking place in November in Gorno-Badakhshan.[110]

---

[103] *Nezavisimaya Gazeta*, 5 Dec. 1995, p. 3. Azerbaijan insisted on the military inspection being carried out in Nagorno-Karabakh within the CFE framework.

[104] *Nezavisimaya Gazeta*, 1 Dec. 1995, p. 3.

[105] Baranovsky (note 3), pp. 255–56.

[106] *Krasnaya Zvezda*, 20 July 1995, p. 2.

[107] *Krasnaya Zvezda*, 2 Feb. 1995, p. 3.

[108] The main bases of the Mujahideen are in neighbouring Afghanistan, and it is essential for their activities against the Dushanbe government that they are able to cross the border. The total number of active combatants operating against the border control troops from the territory of Afghanistan was assessed by the Russian side at 1500–2000. *Krasnaya Zvezda*, 2 Feb. 1995, p. 3. During 1994–95, the Russian border control troops registered 799 instances of violation of the Tajik–Afghan frontier, prevented 582 attempts at armed breakthroughs, participated in 260 armed clashes and were under fire *c*. 700 times. *Nezavisimaya Gazeta*, 2 Dec. 1995, p. 3.

[109] *Krasnaya Zvezda*, 8 Sep. 1995, p. 2.

[110] *Nezavisimaya Gazeta*, 1 Dec. 1995, p. 3; and 2 Dec. 1995, p. 3. It should be noted that the government does not have military aircraft. *Nezavisimaya Gazeta*, 23 Nov. 1995, p. 1.

Hostilities hampered the political dialogue between the government and the opposition, which had started in 1994 under strong external pressure. The negotiations did not bring any spectacular results at all in 1995; however, the parties agreed on the continuation of the cease-fire agreement of September 1994, the exchange of prisoners of war and the creation of conditions for the return of refugees.[111] The meeting between the President of Tajikistan, Imamali Rakhmonov, and the IRMT leader, Said Abdullo Nari, which took place in May in Kabul, Afghanistan, may also be included in the positive record of the dialogue.

The list of unfulfilled expectations is much longer—the adoption of a new constitution, the drafting of the law on elections, the organization of free and democratic elections, the involvement of the international institutions during a transitional period and so on. The opposition suggested that 2000 UN peace-keepers be invited, which would not only promote peace but also eliminate suspicions about the imperialist inclinations of Russia.[112]

The government rejected proposals to set up a State Council which would include representatives of the existing authorities and the opposition (40 per cent each) and of national minorities (20 per cent).[113] The idea of establishing security zones which would facilitate the return of refugees was also declined.[114] The opposition, in its turn, considered an offer to accept some ministerial posts, without changing the whole structure of power, as a pure formality.[115] Meanwhile, most of the opposition were prevented from partici-pating in the parliamentary elections held in February 1995, so that the elec-tions failed to provide the regime with democratic credentials.[116]

The Tajik regime remains heavily dependent on Russia. The latter provides 70 per cent of its state budget.[117] The Russian military presence is estimated at 25 000 troops[118] and consists of two elements, border control troops[119] and the 201st Motor Rifle Division officially assigned to the CIS peacekeeping forces which were agreed upon in 1993.[120]

The missions of the two elements from a formal point of view are different. The Russian border control troops—the only effective force capable of protecting the 2000-km long frontiers of Tajikistan, including 1400 km with

[111] *Krasnaya Zvezda*, 20 July 1995, p. 2.

[112] *Nezavisimaya Gazeta*, 24 May 1995, p. 2.

[113] *Nezavisimaya Gazeta*, 20 Apr. 1995, p. 2.

[114] *Nezavisimaya Gazeta*, 23 May 1995, p. 2.

[115] *Nezavisimaya Gazeta*, 23 May 1995 (note 114).

[116] *Segodnya*, 28 Feb. 1995, p. 1; and *Nezavisimaya Gazeta*, 28 Feb. 1995, p. 1; and 2 Mar. 1995, p. 1.

[117] *International Herald Tribune*, 3 Jan. 1995, p. 4.

[118] Lachowski, Z., 'Conventional arms control and security dialogue in Europe', *SIPRI Yearbook 1995* (note 3), p. 781; and chapter 16 in this volume.

[119] The numbers of Russian border control troops in Tajikistan were doubled during 1995, to reach a total of 16 000. *Segodnya*, 28 Dec. 1995, p. 2.

[120] Other elements of the CIS peacekeeping forces include a battalion from Uzbekistan and a company from Kyrgyzstan. The participation of Kazakhstan was suspended by its parliament. *Krasnaya Zvezda*, 23 Sep. 1995, p. 2; and *Nezavisimaya Gazeta*, 23 May 1995, p. 2. The total number of CIS peacekeeping personnel was intended to be 16 000 at the minimum, but the actual number seemed to be significantly below this level. Thus, the 201st Motor Rifle Division (MRD) had less than one-third of its regular staff personnel. *Krasnaya Zvezda*, 23 Sep. 1995, p. 2.

Afghanistan[121]—are to keep fighters, weapons and drugs from entering the country from Afghanistan, thus supporting the Tajik Government. The status of the CIS peacekeeping forces assumes their neutrality; the 1994 cease-fire agreement envisages that 'the CIS collective peacekeeping forces and Russian troops in Tajikistan will fulfil their functions in accordance with the principle of neutrality'.[122] This provision, however, remains a dead letter in the light of their involvement in actions against anti-government combatants. Furthermore, the formal commander of the CIS forces, General Valeriy Patrikeyev, was reported to have been removed because of his 'indecisiveness' in helping the border control troops to defeat 'provocations' by opposition militants along the Tajik–Afghan frontier.[123] Not surprisingly, many of the peacekeeping personnel became victims of terrorist attacks: total casualties in 1995 amounted to several dozen.[124]

This (and other considerations) may be the reason for Russia's increasing pressure on the Tajik Government to be more cooperative in reaching a political settlement with the opposition. This was clearly manifested at the CIS summit meeting in January 1996.[125] The opposition, on its part, increased military pressure against the government and claimed, at the beginning of 1996, to be in control of 70 per cent of Tajik territory.[126]

IV. Developments in the CIS

After four years of existence, the CIS remains as controversial as it has been from the very beginning when it was set up on the ruins of the dissolved Soviet Union. However, in 1995 there have been some new developments affecting the relations between and the policy of the CIS participants in the security field.

Russia's rationales

Russia has manifested a special interest in making the military aspects of relations with the other CIS countries more prominent. This may be attributed to a number of reasons.

First, Russia is concerned with the conflict potential and the risk of armed hostilities within the former USSR. Initiating and promoting security cooperation might be hoped to prevent the conflicts from emerging or to reduce their scope. Second and more importantly, involving the CIS partners in such cooperation would significantly enhance Russia's role within the post-Soviet

---

[121] According to Tajik officials, 90% of the border controllers are citizens of Tajikistan. *Nezavisimaya Gazeta*, 18 Jan. 1996, p. 3.

[122] *Diplomaticheskiy Vestnik*, no. 19–20 (Oct. 1994), p. 37.

[123] *Nezavisimaya Gazeta*, 20 Apr. 1995, p. 2.

[124] *Krasnaya Zvezda*, 23 Sep. 1995, p. 2. Fatal casualties in the 201st MRD numbered 39 in 1993, 35 in 1994 and 23 in 1995. *Krasnaya Zvezda*, 19 Jan. 1996, p. 2.

[125] *Krasnaya Zvezda*, 6 Feb. 1996, p. 1.

[126] Pannier, B., *OMRI Daily Digest*, no. 39, part I (23 Feb. 1996).

space, as it remains militarily by far the most powerful successor state of the former USSR. This, in particular, seems to be considered as an efficient means of preventing the reorientation of the new independent states and neutralizing any tendency to 'geopolitical pluralism' within the post-Soviet space. Third, one of the specific incentives for Russia to become more active in promoting military cooperation and integration within the CIS has been the debates on enlargement of NATO membership. While considering this prospect as a serious challenge to its security, and having failed to convince the Western countries to abandon plans for NATO enlargement eastwards, Russia threatened to respond with a number of countermeasures, including the transformation of the CIS into a military bloc.[127]

The readiness of Russia to create a CIS-based structure similar to the defunct Warsaw Pact was proclaimed by President Yeltsin on 9 September 1995. On 14 September, he signed a decree on 'Russia's strategic course with respect to the CIS member states', stipulating the need 'to move towards forming a collective security system, on the basis of the Tashkent Treaty on Collective Security of 15 May 1992 and bilateral relations between the CIS states, to promote the intention of the member states to unite in a defensive union on the basis of community of interests and military and political goals'. The decree calls for efforts to 'make the CIS countries fulfil their commitment to refrain from participating in alliances and blocs oriented against any other CIS states' and 'gaining their understanding that this region is first of all a zone of the Russian Federation's interests'.[128]

A number of publications authored by high-ranking officers outlined specific components of the proposed CIS military alliance-building.[129] This would include common or joint systems of strategic deployment, communications, intelligence, early warning, air defence, infrastructure, planning, maintenance, command structures and so on. The basic element of collective military security should be provided by regular forces with the capacity for rapid and massive action both in local conflicts and in large-scale warfare. Coalition forces should be created under joint command, with a Joint Chief of Staff under the chairmanship of the head of the General Staff of the Russian Armed Forces. Coalition groups of forces could also be created on a regional basis (the west, the Transcaucasus and Central Asia). Collective forces might be used to prevent military conflicts within member states. The alliance also presumes cooperation in military production, joint measures aimed at conversion, and common use of military research and development (R&D).

Such ambitious plans will undoubtedly face considerable obstacles in terms of practical implementation. Nevertheless, some multilateral and bilateral decisions adopted within the CIS in 1995 may be assessed as contributing to developments along these lines.

---

[127] *Segodnya*, 16 Nov. 1995, p. 2.

[128] *Segodnya*, 22 Sep. 1995, p. 9; and Parrish, S., *OMRI Daily Digest*, no. 181, part I (18 Sep. 1995).

[129] *Nezavisimaya Gazeta*, 26 Feb. 1995, p. 3; *Segodnya*, 20 July 1995, p. 5; *Segodnya*, 30 Sep. 1995, p. 6; and *Krasnaya Zvezda*, 7 Oct. 1995, p. 3.

Promoting military cooperation

At the CIS summit meeting in Almaty, Kazakhstan, in February 1995, the participants adopted a *concept of collective security*. This document, however, is a non-binding memorandum stipulating the intention of the member states to preserve 'peace and stability' within the CIS area.[130]

Much more significant is the agreement, signed at the same summit session, on creating a *joint air defence system* with the aim of restoring control over the airspace of the former USSR.[131] It was also decided to 'study' the possibility of the Baltic states' accession to this agreement.[132] Its implementation will require major efforts to re-create the air defence radar network and, presumably, to preserve the land components of the anti-missile early-warning system.[133] A coordination committee on air defence will be chaired by the Commander-in-Chief of the Russian Air Defence Forces—which, however, does not mean that Russia will be in command of the member states' air defence systems.

At the CIS summit meeting in Minsk, Belarus, in May 1995, the member states signed a treaty on cooperation in *protecting their external borders*.[134] Russia had long advocated this approach, being both reluctant to devote significant resources to manning the intra-CIS frontiers which did not exist in the times of the Soviet Union[135] and concerned by uncontrolled transfers of people, drugs or arms from outside the CIS. At the same time a number of other CIS members, lacking the financial and organizational capacity to arrange efficient border control, are interested in involving Russia.[136] However, since this affects sensitive issues of national sovereignty, it took considerable time and effort to coordinate the approaches of member states.[137] Significantly, the resulting text focuses mainly on 'coordination' of national border control policies, rather than on 'joint protection of the external

---

[130] Baranovsky (note 3), pp. 258–59; and *International Herald Tribune*, 11–12 Feb. 1995, p. 1. For the text, see *Diplomaticheskiy Vestnik*, no. 3 (Mar. 1995), pp. 32–37.

[131] The disintegration of the USSR had dramatic consequences for the country's air defence system, which in fact disappeared after mid-1992. In today's Russia, dense air defence zones are non-existent, with protection provided only to main cities and major military and economic installations. The existing radar location systems do not allow control over low-altitude movements in airspace in virtually any direction; in a southerly direction even middle-altitude control is problematic. *Nezavisimaya Gazeta*, 21 Feb. 1995, p. 2; *Krasnaya Zvezda*, 28 Feb. 1995, p. 2; and *Izvestia*, 10 Mar. 1995, p. 2.

[132] *Diplomaticheskiy Vestnik*, no. 3 (Mar. 1995), p. 31.

[133] Reactivating the temporarily closed radar stations in Belarus and Ukraine will probably be an easy task, whereas in Armenia and Georgia the radar equipment was pillaged and destroyed. *Izvestia*, 10 Mar. 1995, p. 2. The CIS participants agreed that the costs were to be borne by the states where the air defence equipment is located; it is clear, however, that most of them are unable to afford this, and the main costs will be taken over by Russia. In Nov., Russia announced an agreement on assisting Armenia, Georgia, Kazakhstan, Kyrgyzstan, Tajikistan and Uzbekistan to upgrade their air defence systems. Parrish, S., *OMRI Daily Digest*, no. 215, part I (3 Nov. 1995).

[134] For the text, see *Diplomaticheskiy Vestnik*, no. 7 (July 1995), pp. 43–46.

[135] The total length of the 'new frontiers' of Russia is about 14 000 km. *Literaturnaya Gazeta*, 2 Nov. 1994, p. 12.

[136] For example, according to the assessment of the commander of the national border control troops, Valeriy Chkheidze, Georgia will need 10–13 years to organize the protection of its 2000-km land frontiers and 300-km sea frontiers with its own forces, and the costs of establishing one border control post will amount to 1.2 billion roubles (over $250 million). *Krasnaya Zvezda*, 1 Nov. 1995, p. 1.

[137] *Nezavisimaya Gazeta*, 11 Feb. 1995, p. 1.

borders'[138]—although it also entitles the parties to 'take measures for the protection of the frontiers with the help of the necessary contingents from other CIS member states'.[139]

Another dimension of security-related efforts in the CIS framework is *peacekeeping activities*. The CIS decisions in this field only give Russia a multilateral mandate, while the participation of the other member states in peacekeeping efforts within the post-Soviet conflict areas has basically a symbolic character. This pattern has continued through 1995; no significant decisions have been taken apart from prolonging the CIS mandates previously issued for peacekeeping in Abkhazia and Tajikistan. However, a draft concept on prevention and settlement of conflicts on the territory of the CIS states was submitted to the CIS summit meeting in Moscow in January 1996, envisaging, among other steps, joint training of peacekeeping personnel.[140]

Multilateral CIS agreements quite often have a rather general character: their implementation requires concrete actions by the member states on a bilateral basis.[141] Bilateralism has the important advantage that it does not require a search for a multilateral consensus in a situation where all participants have their own agenda and priorities. This fully applies to military cooperation and/or integration: in this field, the most substantial actions are taken bilaterally. Three major developments took place in 1995.

In January, *Russia and Kazakhstan* announced their intention to combine armed forces to create a joint command for planning and training and another joint command for border patrols.[142] This was presented as a dramatic breakthrough in integrating the two states' armed forces within the 'common military and strategic space', a decisive step towards establishing a 'Euro-Asian Union'.[143] 1995 was indicated as the year when practical implementation of the concept of united armed forces would begin.

On 15 September, *Russia and Georgia* signed the treaty on deployment of Russian military bases on Georgian territory as the follow-on to the bilateral 'big' treaty concluded in 1994. Four Russian military bases are entitled to remain on the territory of Georgia for the next 25 years[144] (subject to prolongation for a further five years provided both parties agree). Additional contingents could be deployed in some other areas of Georgia not yet defined.[145] Earlier, Russia and Georgia had also been reported as having agreed on a

[138] This could be compared to the 1993 memorandum signed by Russia and 5 Central Asian states, stipulating that the protection of the frontiers should be assured by joint efforts. *Izvestia*, 13 Jan. 1994, p. 5; and *Nezavisimaya Gazeta*, 15 Jan. 1994, p. 3.

[139] Russian border patrols are deployed in Armenia, Georgia, Kyrgyzstan, Tajikistan and Turkmenistan. Belarus, Kazakhstan, Ukraine and Uzbekistan use their own border guards to protect their frontiers. *Izvestia*, 13 Jan. 1994, p 5.

[140] *Nezavisimaya Gazeta*, 13 Jan. 1996, p. 2.

[141] Thus, as part of the concept of collective CIS border protection, by the end of 1995 the Kazakhstan Air Force received 8 MiG-29s from Russia; more exports of Su-25 close air support planes and Su-27 fighters were expected. Clarke, D., *OMRI Daily Digest*, no. 247, part I (21 Dec. 1995).

[142] *Segodnya*, 21 Jan. 1995, p. 2; and *The Guardian*, 21 Jan. 1995, p. 4. See also chapter 8, section III.

[143] *Krasnaya Zvezda*, 24 Jan. 1995, p. 3.

[144] During negotiations Georgian representatives had requested a 10-year period for maintaining these bases.

[145] *Krasnaya Zvezda*, 19 Sep. 1995, p. 3.

redistribution of the CFE flank quotas, with the Russian side getting the right to 115 tanks, 160 armoured vehicles and 170 artillery systems out of the quotas due to Georgia.[146]

On 9 December, *Russia and Belarus* signed 18 documents significantly upgrading their military cooperation.[147] They focus on joint regional strategic planning by the two ministries of defence, cooperation in military technology, the training of military personnel, joint air patrolling of the borders, joint use of regional groups of forces and the use of the military infrastructure in Belarus by Russia. It was announced that a bilateral treaty on collective security was under preparation, to be signed in the very near future.[148]

Altogether Russia has signed over 200 military-related agreements with the CIS countries; 36 were concluded in 1995.[149]

CIS political patterns

New developments in the military field have in fact followed the emergence of the political composition of the CIS as a framework for the interaction of the successor states of the former USSR. Russia is undoubtedly its centre, economically, politically and militarily; none of the other CIS states can disregard Russia's interests or its ambitions with respect to the post-Soviet space, and all of them seem to put relations with Moscow at the top of their priority lists.

However, the extent and depth of the 'Russian connection' are by no means the same for all the CIS states.

Belarus, under President Alexander Lukashenko and with a predominantly pro-Russian public mood,[150] has manifested its readiness for the closest *rapprochement* with Moscow in all fields—which may eventually result in the reintegration of the two states, with Belarus keeping a symbolic independence, although de facto incorporated into Russia. *Kazakhstan*, on the other hand, aims to consolidate its independence. President Nursultan Nazarbayev's advocacy of a Euro-Asian Union provides a strong incentive to upgrade relations with Russia and at the same time minimize the explosiveness of what might in the long run become the most serious problem for Kazakhstan's statehood, that of the Russian diaspora. Russia and these two countries are emerging as the CIS core area. Significant political preconditions for integration are already satisfied and some practical steps in this direction have already been undertaken.[151]

---

[146] *Georgian Military Chronicle*, Occasional Papers of the Caucasian Institute for Peace, Democracy and Development, vol. 2, no. 1 (Apr. 1995). See also chapter 16, section II in this volume.

[147] *Nezavisimaya Gazeta*, 14 Dec. 1995, p. 3.

[148] *Krasnaya Zvezda*, 10 Dec. 1995, p. 1.

[149] *Krasnaya Zvezda*, 17 Nov. 1995, p. 1.

[150] On 14 May 1995, Belarus held a referendum in which more than 80% of the voters supported the policy of greater integration with Russia. Orttung, R., *OMRI Daily Digest*, no. 193, part I (4 Oct. 1995).

[151] Significantly, Belarus, Kazakhstan and Russia were the first countries to sign, in Jan. 1995, an agreement on forming a customs union. *Izvestia*, 31 Jan. 1995, p. 3. Interestingly, it included a provision that host countries would not make a charge for the stay of another country's armed forces on their territory—which in fact applies only to Russia's armed forces. *Obshchaya Gazeta*, 26 Jan.–1 Feb. 1995, p. 2. On 29 Mar. 1996, Russia, Belarus, Kazakhstan and Kyrgyzstan signed a treaty on further integration

Ukraine's policy, from this perspective, represents an opposite trend. Its lack of enthusiasm for the CIS reflects the character of its relations with Russia.

The overall atmosphere in Russian–Ukrainian relations in 1995 has been basically positive. It was significantly improved by Ukraine's readiness to remove ambiguities concerning its non-nuclear weapon status. On 9 June 1995 President Yeltsin and Ukrainian President Leonid Kuchma signed an agreement on sharing the Black Sea Fleet—the controversial issue which had been on the agenda since 1992.[152] Both sides have been careful to prevent the politically sensitive problem of Crimea from affecting their relations.[153]

However, the long anticipated 'big treaty' between Russia and Ukraine was not signed in 1994 or in 1995. President Kuchma has distanced himself from his predecessor by resolutely abandoning the practice of creating enemy images—but not the goal of consolidating the Ukrainian state and strengthening its position. His policy is far from one of becoming a de facto protectorate of Russia and seems to have provoked bitter disappointment in Moscow. At the same time Kuchma's proclaimed adherence to developing cooperative relations with Russia has made him less vulnerable to domestic criticism, thus reinforcing Ukraine's position in its interaction with Russia. Crises in Ukraine are far from over, but there are significantly fewer of the over-dramatized forecasts of previous years of the disintegration and economic collapse of Ukraine. This could enlarge the field of manoeuvre for Ukraine with respect to Russia.

It is significant that, notwithstanding the proclaimed intention to have a more positive approach towards the CIS, Ukraine has continued its policy of selective participation in the collective agreements elaborated within this structure. It does not sign those documents which are viewed as undermining the role of individual states or promoting supranationalism.[154] Even more importantly, Ukraine's reluctance seems first of all to proceed from the assumption that the CIS is politically dominated by Russia and, for this reason only, cannot be an attractive option. Ukraine refrains from endorsing Russian-led peacekeeping missions in the area of the former Soviet Union.[155] Although

within the CIS; and on 2 Apr. Russia and Belarus signed a treaty on establishing a 'commonwealth', broadly presented as a historic breakthrough in the *rapprochement* of the two Slav states.

[152] According to the agreement, Russia gets 81.7% of the ships and Ukraine 18.3%. *Segodnya*, 10 June 1995, p. 1. There were concerns that implementation of the agreement would face serious difficulties. *Segodnya*, 16 June 1995, p. 9. However, by the end of the year Russia had started to transfer the bases and equipment of the Black Sea Fleet to Ukraine, to keep only Sevastopol as its main basing port and 2 airfields, with personnel to be reduced from 65 000 in 1991 to *c.* 30 000 by the end of 1995 and to 19 000 by the year 2000. *Segodnya*, 2 Dec. 1995, p. 1. It should be noted that Georgia also pretended to be a 'legal heir of the Black Sea Fleet' and requested its part. *Nezavisimaya Gazeta*, 18 Jan. 1996, p. 3.

[153] In Mar. 1995, Ukraine abolished the presidency of Crimea and its constitution. *Nezavisimaya Gazeta*, 21 Mar. 1995, p. 3. This did not provoke any official reaction from Russia because of its engagement in Chechnya. Meanwhile, a new draft of the Ukrainian Constitution gave Crimea the status of autonomous republic, whereas Sevastopol and Kiev received 'special status'.

[154] Thus, Ukraine does not intend to join the CIS customs and payment unions (*Nezavisimaya Gazeta*, 12 Jan. 1996, p. 3), although it seems to be seeking the dismantling of trade barriers.

[155] The Ukrainian Parliament stipulated that Ukraine cannot participate in CIS peacekeeping missions with troops. *Vek*, no. 43 (18–24 Nov. 1994), p. 4.

there had been indications of some readiness to alter its approach,[156] no changes have been registered in this respect in 1995. Meanwhile Ukraine's involvement would be the only way to make the CIS 'collective peacekeeping forces' a genuine multilateral instrument and to relieve Russia of accusations of only using them to interfere in the conflict zones in the former Soviet Union; but, significantly, the possibility of Ukraine's involvement does not seem to excite excessive enthusiasm in Moscow and has been interpreted by some analysts as 'a desire not so much to participate in the preservation of peace . . . as to oppose Russia's expansion in the former Soviet Union'.[157]

Not surprisingly, the prospect of military integration is viewed as especially threatening to Ukraine's independence. President Kuchma has stated bluntly that Ukraine would not enter a CIS military bloc.[158] Ukraine refused to sign the May 1995 treaty on cooperation in protecting the CIS external borders.[159] Its participation in the joint air defence system, apart from being motivated by technical requirements, seems also to proceed from the assumption that ultimate control over the use of air defence means will be held by the member states. By and large, Ukraine appears to have a pragmatic approach towards military cooperation with Russia[160] at the same time as aiming to keep open alternative options.[161]

Exploiting such options seems to be a matter of practical policy in the case of one of three *Transcaucasian states*—Azerbaijan, which has been particularly successful in its policy of gradually reducing its unilateral orientation towards Russia. Most strikingly, this has been achieved by the political manoeuvres of President Aliev, who, when he came to power, was seriously suspected of being strongly supported, if not controlled, by Moscow. However, in 1994–95 Azerbaijan managed to obtain significant guarantees of its independence, first of all by effectively playing the card of the major project for oil extraction from the Caspian Sea shelf. Some Moscow analysts described this dramatically as the beginning of the withdrawal of Russia from the Transcaucasus, calling into question the future of the region as a sphere of

[156] The possibility of Ukraine's participation in peacekeeping in Abkhazia was mentioned by Deputy Defence Minister Ivan Bizhan at the session of the CIS Council of Defence Ministers on 1 Dec. 1994 in Moscow. *Nezavisimaya Gazeta,* 2 Dec. 1994, p. 1. Ukraine's Defence Ministry was reported to have prepared all the documents for sending troops to Nagorno-Karabakh (although this could be arranged within the framework of the OSCE, rather than that of CIS peacekeeping). *Krasnaya Zvezda,* 25 Nov. 1994, p. 11.

[157] *Krasnaya Zvezda,* 25 Nov. 1994, p. 11.

[158] Clarke, D., *OMRI Daily Digest,* no. 203, part I (18 Oct. 1995).

[159] Ukraine refuses to make a distinction between 'external' and 'internal' CIS borders, insisting that state frontiers as such are an essential attribute of independence. *Nezavisimaya Gazeta,* 18 Jan. 1996, p. 3.

[160] The list of questions discussed and agreed upon at the meeting of Russian and Ukrainian defence ministers in Nov. 1995 included: maintenance and financing of parts of the anti-missile early-warning system located in Ukraine; arms purchases from Russia; military cooperation in outer space; transfer of Tu-160 and Tu-95 strategic bombers to Russia; military transit from Russia to Moldova via the territory of Ukraine; and other issues. *Krasnaya Zvezda,* 25 Nov. 1995, p. 1; and 28 Nov. 1995, p. 1.

[161] They are well illustrated by the comments of a high-level Defence Ministry official who was reported to have praised the military programmes of NATO and the USA as being more effective and attractive to Ukraine than those of Russia and the CIS—which might eventually bring about an evolution of the leadership's position on non-affiliation to any bloc. *Krasnaya Zvezda,* 19 Oct. 1994, p. 3.

Russian influence.[162] Russia's decision to close the border with Azerbaijan because of the war in Chechnya (it has been closed since 19 December 1994) was an additional incentive for Baku to consider relations with Iran and Turkey as more promising and stable than those with Russia.[163] Azerbaijan insisted that the planned peacekeeping operation in Nagorno-Karabakh should be multilateral, rather than conducted only by Russia; it also expresses dissatisfaction with the Tashkent Treaty on Collective Security as being only oriented towards defence against external aggression, and demands that it be altered.[164]

It is indicative that Azerbaijan is the only Transcaucasian state which has refused to accept the deployment of Russian armed forces on its territory. Georgia was constrained to do so because alliance with Russia turned out to be the only means to restore its viability. For Armenia it is of the utmost importance because of the geopolitical position of the country and its involvement in the Nagorno-Karabakh conflict. A new political balance and new dividing lines thus seem to be emerging in the Transcaucasus, with a variable geometry pattern of relations between the three states, which are all members of the CIS, and Russia.

Nor in the case of *Moldova* is participation in the CIS equivalent to an alliance-type relationship with Russia. While rejecting any merger with Romania (which was strongly advocated in the initial phase of independence) and developing more balanced, businesslike and flexible relations with Russia, Moldova also seems interested in formulating its own independent foreign policy. It is indicative that, in the debates on how to resist the pressure of Romania, the spectrum of options stretches from joining the CIS security structures to joining NATO.[165] As mentioned above, Moldova continues to insist on the withdrawal of the remaining Russian military personnel from its territory; Russia's suggestion of agreement on establishing a Russian military base was met with a distinct lack of enthusiasm.

The readiness of the *Central Asian states* (other than Kazakhstan) to preserve loyal partnership with Russia does not compensate either for their territorial remoteness or for the relatively limited input they could make in any potential alliance. At the same time most of them may well have reasons not to remain loyal partners of Russia only. In this respect, important efforts are being made to strengthen the links between Central Asian states as distinct from the broader Russia-led pattern and to allow them to operate jointly within the CIS.[166] Information about attempts at consolidation by the Turkic-speaking countries in general in the area of the former Soviet Union and their

[162] *Nezavisimaya Gazeta,* 12 Oct. 1994, p. 3.

[163] According to Azerbaijani officials, restrictions imposed by Russia on the movement of people and goods have resulted, in 1995, in the republic losing some $250 million in trade. Bezanis, L., *OMRI Daily Digest,* no. 38, part I (22 Feb. 1996).

[164] See the interview with the ambassador of Azerbaijan to Russia, Ramiz Rizayev, *Nezavisimaya Gazeta,* 19 Jan. 1996, p. 3.

[165] Both options were mentioned by the Vice-Speaker of the Moldovan Parliament, Nikolae Andronik. *Segodnya,* 1 Dec. 1994, p. 5.

[166] *Nezavisimaya Gazeta,* 19 Jan. 1995, p. 1.

search for independent links with the outside world may be another manifestation of this trend.[167]

By and large, the acceptance of Russia's prominent role in the former Soviet space is proceeding parallel to a cautious but persistent search for alternative options by almost all the actors in the area. There is even less reason to consider the ongoing processes in the post-Soviet space as the benevolent, unqualified subordination of Russia's CIS partners to Russian leadership. Developments within the CIS in 1995 have certainly contributed to increase the role of this post-Soviet institutional framework. It seems premature, however, to regard it as an emerging superstructure encompassing the member states in a new entity which would resemble the dissolved USSR or even re-establish it under the 'USSR minus the Baltics' formula.

Neither are there sufficient grounds to consider the CIS as a multilateral military alliance in the making. The initial reaction of Russia's CIS partners to Moscow-initiated speculations on the subject was rather confused, but even when they support the idea of a military union most of the CIS countries are either unable or unwilling to contribute to it.[168] 'The idea of close cooperation of the CIS states in the military field seems to have no opponents', writes a Russian analyst, 'but its practical implementation is proceeding with great difficulty'.[169]

There is also uncertainty about Russia's interests, goals and resources which might be associated with such plans. For all these reasons, 'the building up of a comprehensive and workable system of CIS collective defence is practically impossible in the foreseeable future. What is possible might be only a simulation of such a building process'.[170] However, in some cases bilateral patterns of military-oriented relationships, if based on the specific pragmatic interests of the parties involved, could indeed develop into fairly advanced forms.

V. Conclusions

In the initial period after the breakup of the USSR, Russia's role in conflict development and conflict management on the territory of the former Soviet Union was often erratic, lacked coordination and produced controversial results. By 1995, it has clearly become less ambivalent and more consolidated and is based on some fundamental parameters of Russian post-Soviet thinking and policy making.

The war in Chechnya reflected both the dramatic failure of Russia in conflict management on its own territory and Moscow's resoluteness in using all

---

[167] On 28 Aug. 1995 the heads of state of the Turkic-language countries of Central Asia and Azerbaijan held their third summit meeting in Bishkek (Kyrgyzstan). *International Observer*, vol. 14, no. 305 (Nov. 1995), p. 423.

[168] Thus, according to Gen. Boris Gromov, former Russian Deputy Defence Minister, Kyrgyzstan would be ready to participate in joint armed forces with only 1 company and Kazakhstan with 2, while Armenia could supply none. *Izvestia*, 10 Dec. 1995, p. 4.

[169] Trenin, D., *Segodnya*, 2 Dec. 1995, p. 6. The article was based on a presentation at the Russian office of the John M. Olin Institute for Strategic Studies.

[170] *Segodnya*, 2 Dec. 1995 (note 169).

means for preserving its perceived interests—a signal which seems to be directed both inward and outward.

In contrast to the recent past, Russia has definitely opted for not under-mining the territorial integrity of its CIS partners and has denied support to separatist forces there, pressuring them to accept autonomous status within arrangements of a federative type. The CIS countries are expected to repay this through loyalty towards Russia—in some cases up to the point of accept-ing its military presence on their territories.

While welcoming the symbolic involvement of the UN and the OSCE in peace settlement efforts, Russia aims to consolidate its own role as the most efficient external pacifier and the major actor in the conflict areas. Operating from the assumption that the post-Soviet space is the area of its vital interests, Russia has actually succeeded in achieving de facto recognition of this by the international community.

In terms of international stability, Russia's increasing role in the post-Soviet space might be rationalized by the possibility that it will marginalize or minimize the scope of conflicts on the territory of the former USSR. Indeed, during 1995 most of them have developed in less dramatic forms than in the recent past. However, according to some assessments, 'it is hardly possible to assume that the peak of armed conflict in the post-Soviet space is already behind us. On the contrary, there are sufficient reasons to expect that develop-ments in 1990–95 were only the prologue to a much higher degree of [aggre-gate] conflict which could involve the whole post-Soviet space or a significant part of it in the medium- and long-term perspective'.[171]

Against this background, reinforcing Russia's positions in some strategic-ally important areas of the 'near abroad' is considered to be of the highest priority. Special emphasis is placed on consolidation within the CIS frame-work, including both political and military components of this process, although the prospects of establishing a CIS-based military alliance remain bleak. It seems to be perceived as an important reserve position in strength-ening opposition to NATO enlargement and in the reconsideration of Russia's former predominantly Western-oriented policy line—which would not necessarily mean re-establishing a confrontational pattern but might allow Russia to take a more independent stance in the international arena, with a more diversified political agenda.

[171] Kosolapov, N., 'Konflikty postsovetskogo prostranstva: politicheskie realii' [Conflicts in the post-Soviet space: political realities], *Mirovaya Ekonomika i mezhdunarodniye otnosheniya*, no. 11 (1995), p. 39.

7. Europe: towards new security arrangements

ADAM DANIEL ROTFELD

I. Introduction

In 1995 the debate and decisions on a new security system in Europe focused on five issues: (*a*) settlement of the conflict in Bosnia and Herzegovina; (*b*) enlargement of NATO and the European Union (EU) to the east; (*c*) the transatlantic partnership, including the US presence in Europe and the European pillar of the Atlantic Alliance; (*d*) the developments in Russia (the war in Chechnya and the difficulties associated with the radical transformation and the domestic reform policy); and (*e*) the discussion initiated by the Organization for Security and Co-operation in Europe (OSCE) on a model for European security for the 21st century. Positions taken on these matters by the USA, individual European states and the EU as a whole revealed both similarities and differences in approaches to and concepts of European security, as well as the practical value of existing structures and the decisions taken within them. While the debate on the future model for security and enlargement of the Western security structures has often been conceptual, the decisions aimed at ending the war in Bosnia and Herzegovina were in a sense a test case of the effectiveness and efficiency of existing structures in the new politico-military situation.[1] In this context, the main focus has been on the problems concerning the changing standing and role of Russia and Germany, shaping new relations between the USA and Europe, transforming the functioning of multilateral security institutions and finding new approaches to the European security system.

European security in the light of the experience in Bosnia and Herzegovina is examined in section II of this chapter. The various standpoints on the eastward enlargement of NATO are presented in section III; and the continued evolution of the EU and the Western European Union (WEU), and the activities of the OSCE in 1995, are assessed in sections IV and V, respectively.

II. European security and the experience of Bosnia

The armed conflict in the former Yugoslavia brought home to the international community the respective strengths and weaknesses of the roles which the main powers, especially the USA, Russia, France, the UK and Germany (the 'Contact Group'), as well as the multilateral security organizations, the United Nations, NATO, the EU, the WEU and the OSCE, can play in European

---

[1] For developments in the former Yugoslavia in 1995 see chapter 5 in this volume.

SIPRI Yearbook 1996: Armaments, Disarmament and International Security

security systems, now and in the future.[2] At an early stage of the conflict, it was thought that the essential role in its solution could be played by the OSCE as the largest, most democratic and, in fact, universal regional security arrangement of all European states and the USA, Canada and the new Central Asian states.[3] The emergency situation mechanisms established by the Berlin CSCE Council of Ministers (19–20 June 1991) were used immediately after the war broke out, but they failed to contain it. As early as the summer of 1991, hopes were pinned mainly on the EU, whose institutions were expected to bring about an end to the armed conflict through joint diplomatic efforts and set in motion peace settlement procedures.[4] All the European security institutions failed, each in its own way, to meet the challenge. In the spring of 1992, after Bosnia and Herzegovina had become engulfed in hostilities as a result of the weakness and inefficacy of the European security institutions, the initiative to seek a settlement to the conflict was taken over by the UN. In 1995 the chief role in restoring peace in the former Yugoslavia was assumed by the USA and NATO.[5]

Efforts to restore peace in 1995 were crowned by the General Framework Agreement for Peace in Bosnia and Herzegovina, initialled in Dayton, Ohio and signed on 14 December in Paris.[6] The Dayton Agreement specifies the roles of NATO, the UN and the OSCE. While the different aspects of restoring peace in Bosnia are clearly intertwined, for practical reasons a division of labour is essential. Thus military matters belong to NATO; political, legal and economic matters fall to the EU; the UN is responsible for the return of refugees and police operations; and humanitarian issues, building democratic institutions, confidence-building measures and regional arms control are supervised by the OSCE. Cooperation among these multilateral security structures is not only desirable, it is also indispensable. Implementing the Agreement will offer important experience in practical collaboration by the great powers and other states within the framework of the existing European regional security structures.

The division of Bosnia and the return of the refugees, as envisaged in the Dayton Agreement, are somewhat contradictory. The re-establishment of a multi-ethnic society and state may not prove compatible with free and demo-

[2] *Lessons of the Western Response to the Crisis in Former Yugoslavia* (Center of International Policy Studies: Rome, May 1995); and Jopp, M., *The Implications of the Yugoslav Crisis for Western Europe's Foreign Relations,* Chaillot Papers, no. 17 (WEU Institute for Security Studies: Paris, Oct. 1994).

[3] As of 31 Dec. 1995 the OSCE (formerly the Conference on Security and Co-operation in Europe, CSCE) comprised 53 states, listed in the Glossary in this volume. Yugoslavia (Serbia and Montenegro) is suspended. '20 Years of the Helsinki Final Act 1976–1995', *OSCE Handbook*, Vienna, 1995, p. 7.

[4] Jacques Delors, former President of the European Commission, while stressing that members of the EC/EU have given 60% of the humanitarian aid and provided 80% of the peacekeeping force to the former Yugoslavia, admitted that it was incapable of stopping the war and had 'failed terribly'. 'Bitter lesson for Europeans', *International Herald Tribune*, 5 Dec. 1995.

[5] 'In the former Yugoslavia, the West European nations have shown that for all their rhetorical commitment to a European foreign policy, they lack the capacity to draft and execute such a policy. They have, unfortunately, demonstrated that they are still satellites of the United States.' Pfaff, W., 'Bosnia pact has not resolved problems in Europe', *International Herald Tribune*, 2 Nov. 1995. See also Woehrel, S. J. and Kim, J., 'Bosnia former Yugoslavia: ongoing conflict and U.S. policy' (Congressional Research Service (CRS), Library of Congress: Washington, DC, 1 Dec. 1995).

[6] See more on the Dayton Agreement in chapter 5 in this volume.

cratic elections under international control. The formalistic treatment of the implementation of the right to self-determination may mean that power is gained by extremists whose activities will thwart the goals laid down in the Agreement.[7] Another problem concerns arms control and disarmament in the former Yugoslavia. In reality, all the parties to the conflict have started to rearm; lifting the arms embargo on Bosnia will do anything but cut back military arsenals.[8] There are many such contradictions. A serious challenge for the international community is the bringing to justice before the International Criminal Tribunal for the Former Yugoslavia of people responsible for war crimes and other violations of international humanitarian law,[9] many of whom still exercise political and military control in various parts of the former Yugoslavia.

Contact Group members have conflicting interests arising from their respective historical, political, cultural and religious ties and affinities with the various ethnic and religious groups of the former Yugoslavia and their desire to neutralize domestic public opinion and reactions to the changing situation in the region. For instance, in Russia the attitude towards the conflict was an important determinant of the positions of the different political groups. Andrey Kozyrev's position on this matter was one of the reasons for sharp criticism of his policy and, eventually, his stepping down as Foreign Minister in January 1996. In turn, President Bill Clinton's commitment to restoring peace in the former Yugoslavia was an instrument for reaffirming US leadership in Europe and the world.

The composition, mandate and work of the Contact Group provided important new experience, for good and for ill, in the search for a body with the character and functions of a kind of European security council. The fact that in spite of, or maybe thanks to, the close historical ties between Russia and Serbia it was possible for NATO and Russia to agree on a common position can hardly be overestimated in contemplating a new system of security in Europe. Despite the different national interests of Russia and its Western partners, consensus and due consideration of the interests of all parties proved possible even in such a delicate matter. It is also telling that Russia's standing has changed, as have the place and role of the Balkans in its policy. It would be anachronistic for Russia to perceive the Balkans as one of its foreign policy priorities. Russia is cautiously acquiring a new understanding of its own

---

[7] This scenario is outlined by Romanenkov, S., 'Ne tshchetny li usiliya mezhdunarodnogo soobschestva?' [Will international efforts not be in vain?], *Segodnya*, 29 Dec. 1995, p. 9.

[8] A conference on disarmament under OSCE auspices began its work in the former Yugoslavia on 5 Jan. 1996, with the intention of achieving an outcome within 6 months.

[9] On 28 Sep. 1992, rapporteurs were given a mandate under the CSCE Moscow Human Dimension Mechanism to Bosnia-Herzegovina and Croatia: 'to investigate reports of atrocities against unarmed civilians in Croatia and Bosnia, and to make recommendations as to the feasibility of attributing responsibility for such acts'. A Tribunal was established on the basis of the Proposal for an International War Crimes Tribunal for the Former Yugoslavia by the Rapporteurs (Corell–Türk–Thune) under the CSCE Moscow Human Dimension Mechanism to Bosnia-Herzegovina and Croatia, 9 Feb. 1992.

capacities appropriate to its real, rather than its historical or imaginary, economic and military potential.[10]

Cooperation in solving the Balkan conflict may change the mutual perceptions of the states participating in the peace process. Russia's consenting to send troop units to act within the general command of NATO under a US general testifies to changes in the policy and psychology of Russia and NATO and may well prove to be an important step in overcoming the negative stereotypes of the period of cold war and confrontation.

The main implication of the Implementation Force (IFOR) operation for NATO is that, for the first time in its history, the Alliance is involved in a military peace enforcement operation. Of wider importance for NATO is the fact that the 16 Allied states were joined by forces from other European states, including Nordic countries, such as Sweden and Finland; Central European states, such as Poland, the Czech Republic and Hungary; and permanently neutral states, Austria and Switzerland.[11] This joint effort is a belated response to one of the most difficult and complex challenges and threats of the post-cold war period. Its successful outcome will be crucial for building a new security structure for Europe.

III. NATO and European security

Since the end of the cold war three main views have been outlined on the future of NATO. First, in various states on both sides of the old East–West divide a belief is voiced that NATO, born of the period of cold war and confrontation, is naturally bound to wither away.[12] The main factor impairing its coherence in the new circumstances is the absence of a clearly defined enemy.[13] At the opposite pole are those who believe that NATO is the key element of the new security structure, with a bright future.[14] The third view is that the future of the Alliance will be determined by how far NATO will manage to acquire not only a declaratory but also a constitutive function in securing peace in the transitional period. As Christoph Bertram observed: 'In times of certainty, institutions mirror the realities of power. In times of

[10] Shmelov, B., 'Chetyre uroka balkanskogo krizisa dlya Rosii' [Four lessons of the Balkan crisis for Russia], *Segodnya*, 29 Dec. 1995, p. 9.

[11] For more on IFOR see chapter 2 in this volume.

[12] This view is officially voiced by Russia and shared by various Western political–scientific circles, and proposals for a new pan-European security structure have emerged. *Die Europäische Sicherheitsgemeinschaft: Das Sicherheitsmodell für das 21. Jahrhundert. Part II: Vom Recht des Stärkeren zur Stärke des Rechts: Plädoyer für eine Europäische Sicherheitsgemeinschaft* [The European security community: Security model for the 21st century. Part II: From the right of the stronger to the strength of law: A plea for a European security community], (Institute for Peace Research and Security Policy, Hamburg University: Hamburg, 1995), pp. 199–358.

[13] As formulated by Carl Schmitt in *Der Begriff des Politischen* [The notion of politics] (Munich–Leipzig, 1932), the essence of politics boils down to the relationship between friend and foe (*Freund Feind Unterstellung*).

[14] This view, as advocated in official NATO documents, has more staunch adherents in Central Europe than in some of the member states. 'The Alliance remains the cornerstone of security and stability in the Euro-Atlantic area', NATO Ministerial Session Communiqué of 29 Nov. 1995, Press Communiqué M-DPC/NPG-2(95)117.

uncertainty, they can shape the realities of power.'[15] In other words, when the rules of the cold war period and bipolar division no longer function, the Alliance's role is to ensure continuity and stability.[16]

In this context, the enlargement and substantial transformation of NATO have been put on the agenda.[17] In 1994–95, NATO decided that it should accept new members for three main reasons. First, collective defence remains essential to European and transatlantic security and is central to US engagement in Europe.[18] Second, the prospect of the new Central and East European (CEE) democracies being admitted to the Alliance provides the nations of Central Europe and the former Soviet republics with additional incentives to strengthen their democratic and legal institutions, ensure civilian control of their armed forces, liberalize their economies and respect human rights, including those of national minorities. As Talbott briefly defined it, 'nations that are encouraged in their aspirations to join NATO are more likely to make a successful transition from their communist past'.[19] Third, the prospect of membership can also foster a greater willingness among these nations to resolve disputes peacefully and contribute to peacekeeping operations. 'Thus the process of expansion can help to promote regional stability and peace.'[20]

In line with decisions adopted at the NATO summit meeting (Brussels, January 1994) and those made by the Allied foreign ministers (Brussels, December 1994), the North Atlantic Council decided 'to initiate the process of examination inside the Alliance to determine how NATO will enlarge, the principles to guide this process and the implications of membership'.[21]

National approaches to this option vary widely: (*a*) for the USA and Western Europe, the main question is how far it fits in with their broader political agenda and, consequently, *how* and *when* to expand and how to deal with the resultant implications;[22] (*b*) for Central Europe NATO enlargement is existential in character and seen as inevitable,[23] while the schedule, criteria, modalities and the composition of the group of potential candidates are still open questions; and (*c*) for Russia, the issue is connected with great-power

[15] Bertram, C., *Europe in the Balance: Securing the Peace Won in the Cold War* (Carnegie Endowment: Washington, DC, Dec. 1995), p. 14.

[16] Compare Kelleher, C. McA., *The Future of European Security: An Interim Assessment* (Brookings Institution: Washington, DC, Dec. 1995), pp. 22–27.

[17] The question is analysed in detail in past *SIPRI Yearbooks*. Compare Rotfeld, A. D., 'Europe: towards a new regional security regime', *SIPRI Yearbook 1994* (Oxford University Press: Oxford, 1994), pp. 205–37; and 'Europe: the multilateral security process', *SIPRI Yearbook 1995: Armaments, Disarmament and International Security* (Oxford University Press: Oxford, 1995), pp. 278–81.

[18] Strobe Talbott stated: 'With the cold war's end, NATO should be open to the new democracies that have regained their independence, that share common values, and that can advance the military and political goals of the Alliance'. Talbott, S., 'Why NATO should grow?', *New York Review of Books*, 10 Aug. 1995, p. 27.

[19] Talbott (note 18), p. 27.

[20] Talbott (note 18), p. 27.

[21] NATO Final Communiqué, Ministerial Meeting of the North Atlantic Council, Brussels, 1 Dec. 1994, Press Communiqué M-NAC-2(94)116. For excerpts see *SIPRI Yearbook 1995* (note 17), p. 306.

[22] Morrison, J. S., *NATO Expansion and Alternative Security Alignments*, McNair Paper 40 (National Defense University: Washington, DC, Apr. 1995), p. 28.

[23] Compare Walesa, L., 'Security Dilemmas of Central Europe', Lecture at SIPRI, Stockholm, 30 Mar. 1995, p. 3. See also interview with Janusz Onyszkiewicz, Deputy to the Polish Sejm (Parliament) and former Defence Minister, in *Rzeczpospolita*, 22 June 1995, p. 24.

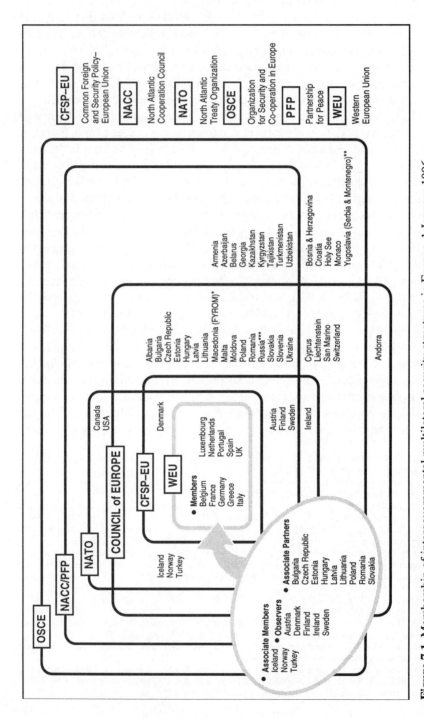

Figure 7.1. Membership of intergovernmental multilateral security structures in Europe, 1 January 1996

* FYROM = Former Yugoslav Republic of Macedonia. ** Suspended since July 1992. *** Russia was admitted to the Council of Europe in February 1996.

status and prestige and is claimed to pose a potential threat to national security; in effect, enlargement of NATO is seen as incompatible with the Russian national *raison d'être*.[24]

The Study on NATO Enlargement

The *Study on NATO Enlargement*,[25] released in September 1995, marked a new stage in the ongoing public debate that has lasted for two years on the desirability and possible consequences of NATO enlargement eastwards. The study represents a political compromise within the Alliance. Its essence, in 82 paragraphs on the purposes and principles of enlargement, consists in the proposition that security is a broad concept embracing political and economic as well as defence components. Security in Europe must be built through a gradual process of integration and cooperation by an interplay of existing multilateral institutions, such as the EU, the WEU and the OSCE, each of which 'would have a role to play in accordance with its respective responsibilities and purposes in implementing this broad security concept'.[26] NATO will remain a purely defensive alliance. The study suggests ways to ensure that enlargement contributes to the stability and security of the entire Euro-Atlantic area without creating a new line of division in Europe; that the North Atlantic Cooperation Council (NACC) and the Partnership for Peace (PFP) contribute concretely to the enlargement process; and that the effectiveness of the Alliance is strengthened through enlargement. It indicates the implications of and necessary preparations for membership and ways in which the enlargement process should proceed. By streamlining NATO decision making it is hoped that the Alliance can accommodate more members without loss of effectiveness. NATO will keep the criteria relevant and avoid undue eastward projection of the burdens of adjustment.

Six key conclusions are defined by the NATO Secretary General:

– NATO enlargement is not aimed against any country or any specific threat . . .
– New members will enjoy all the rights and assume all the obligations of membership under the Washington Treaty—and will need to accept and conform with the principles, policies and procedures adopted by all members of the Alliance at the time that they join;
– As enlargement evolves, the North Atlantic Cooperation Council (NACC) and Partnership for Peace (PfP) will remain vital to building close security cooperation in Europe for both prospective members and those who will not join early or at all;
– The addition of new members to the Alliance will be a parallel process with, and complement, that of the European Union . . .
– Decisions on enlargement will be for NATO itself. Enlargement will be a gradual, deliberate and transparent process, encompassing dialogue with all interested

---

[24] *Russia and NATO*, Report of the Working Group of the Council on Foreign and Defence Policy of the Russian Federation, coordinated by Sergey A. Karaganov, Moscow, published in *Nezavisimaya Gazeta*, special edition, 22 June 1995.
[25] NATO, *Study on NATO Enlargement* (NATO: Brussels, Sep. 1995).
[26] NATO (note 25), para. 1.

partners. There is no fixed or rigid list of criteria. Enlargement will be decided on a case-by-case basis and some nations may attain membership before others. No country outside the Alliance should be given a veto or droit de regard over the process and the eventual decisions taken;

– Allies believe that inviting new members into the Alliance will enhance security for the whole of Europe, including Russia. Thus, they are striving to develop a strong and constructive relationship with Russia, as one cornerstone of a new inclusive and comprehensive security structure in Europe. They seek to develop their relationship with Russia in rough parallel with NATO enlargement.[27]

Western arguments for the enlargement of NATO

The 1995 Report of an Independent Task Force, sponsored by the US Council on Foreign Relations and entitled *Should NATO Expand?*, adopted the following assumption regarding NATO's extension: 'NATO's deepening engagement in the east provides reassurance against unforeseen threats, helps build new militaries that are well integrated into democratic society and capable of operating with NATO forces, and symbolizes the enlargement of the community of established democracies'.[28] The four principal arguments put forward for near-term NATO extension are:

1. For historical, cultural and geopolitical reasons, Western and Central Europe should belong to a security community distinct from that formed by Russia and the other former Soviet republics. Expansion is a historic opportunity to assist the new democracies of Central Europe to consolidate reform and democracy and to avoid the risk of losing the region to internal instability or outside aggression. The ultimate goal should be a stable, cooperative balance between a European and a Euro-Asian security community.

2. Expansion should not alienate Russia and lead to a 'cold peace'. Extending NATO security guarantees to the Central European states would not require forward deployment of troops or fortification of borders. The authors rightly note that: 'if Russian leaders take reform seriously, they will not jeopardize the progress they have made because of NATO expansion'.[29]

3. If NATO does not expand eastwards, it will become irrelevant to Europe's emerging security challenges, lose the support of the citizens of its member states and soon wither away. Expansion would revitalize the Alliance and enhance its relevance to Europe's new strategic landscape.[30]

4. NATO expansion is important to ensure that Germany remains embedded in a cohesive West. The eastward shift of Germany's economic and political

[27] Statement by Secretary General Willy Claes at a press conference at NATO Headquarters, Brussels, 28 Sep. 1995. Reprinted in *NATO Review*, no. 6 (Nov. 1995), p. 10.

[28] *Should NATO Expand?* Report of an Independent Task Force sponsored by the US Council on Foreign Relations (Harold Brown, Chairman; Charles Kupchan, Project Director), (Council on Foreign Relations: New York, 1995), p. 10.

[29] Note 28, p. 11.

[30] 'Only through expansion can NATO complete its transformation from a Cold War military alliance to more of a political forum and integrated military structure for crisis management and joint action in a broader Europe.' Note 28, p. 11.

interests should be accompanied by the eastward expansion of Europe's institutions to ensure that Germany does not become unhinged from them.

The debate focuses on: (*a*) how to enlarge the Alliance without weakening it; (*b*) how to respond positively to the justified expectations and hopes of the new democracies in Central Europe without deepening the sense of threat and isolation in Russia; (*c*) how to include new members without creating new lines of division in Europe; and (*d*) how to involve Russia in the multilateral security process and gain its respect for the standards and norms of democracy, pluralism, political freedoms, human rights, market economy and civilian control of the military.

At the same time proposals are being put forward that the Alliance should protect 'late accessions from vetoes that would make a mockery of NATO's assurances that the door is not closed to any OSCE country'.[31] Last but not least, links with Russia are to be properly taken into account. In a paper published by the Committee on Eastern Europe and Russia in NATO, the necessary transformation of the Alliance is seen to be more easily achieved through a decision on enlargement than by mobilization of public support before such a decision.[32] It suggests that the desired standards and acquiring membership 'may proceed interactively rather than just consecutively'.[33]

It seems that the process of enlarging NATO will result from mutual and two-way adaptation; Russia and other countries would be helped to meet standards, including stabilization of the new democracy, reorientation of the military to a democratic identity and development of market confidence.

Western opponents argue that enlargement should be dependent on the reaction of Russia, and they follow the main Russian reasoning against the inclusion of the CEE states:

1. NATO's eastward enlargement would divide and destabilize Europe. Despite assurances by the Western powers and Central European states, this continues to be Russia's main objection.

2. The decision to enlarge NATO eastwards should be based on Russia's current behaviour, not on assumptions about its past.

3. NATO governments should not promise enlargement unless they are certain of public support. The costs and responsibilities of extending defence guarantees to Central Europe could make it difficult to convince electorates and legislatures in the NATO countries to take an appropriate decision.

4. NATO's formal enlargement in the near future would threaten the political cohesion and military efficacy of the Alliance.[34]

---

[31] Committee on Eastern Europe and Russia in NATO (CEERN), 'Moving forward from NATO's "Study on NATO Enlargement"', Washington, DC, 2 Nov. 1995.

[32] 'In the real world, it is extremely difficult to mobilize the internal political will within NATO to make any major internal transformation of the Alliance.' Note 31, p. 15.

[33] CEERN (note 31), p. 17.

[34] 'NATO requires a consensus to act, and new members with diverse national interests will complicate the task of reaching consensus.' Note 28, p. 14.

The Russian view on NATO enlargement

Russia's negative stance on NATO enlargement has both psychological and politico-military aspects. Psychologically, the majority of the Russian political élite (both the president and the opposition) is not reconciled to the consequences of the breakup of the USSR and the downfall of the totalitarian regimes. There is much evidence that, after a brief period of cooperation with the West, President Boris Yeltsin has increasingly resorted to a traditional anti-Western rhetoric dictated by domestic considerations in which the 'red–brown' opposition determines the agenda. As regards the politico-military aspect, NATO enlargement would mean that Russia would be bordered by Alliance members instead of poorly armed, isolated Central European states susceptible to pressure.

Numerous statements, official documents and expert analyses emphasize that basic Russian national security interests 'call for maintaining friendly if not allied relations' with NATO and the leading Western states.[35] The nearing of NATO to Russia's borders is seen as an attempt to isolate Russia or, worse, as an emerging direct military threat. The issue has in large measure become more part of a domestic game between rival power groups in Russia than an element of a substantial political debate on Russia's future role in the process of shaping the system of international relations. In 1993 Yeltsin stated bluntly: 'We do not see NATO as a bloc opposing us. But it is important to take into account how our public opinion may react to such a step.'[36]

A similar analysis was presented in a study prepared by the Russian Institute of World Economy and International Relations (IMEMO).[37] The authors, like many others, express concern about a reconstruction of the security system in Europe which would lead to NATO's enlargement and also harm the national interests of Russia, but they reject primitive arguments about a threat to Russia posed by 'NATO aggressiveness'. Moreover, they consider the Alliance 'the main factor of stability on the continent'. Statements by Russian politicians, however, were overshadowed by 'countermeasures' taken by Defence Minister Pavel Grachev and the new Foreign Minister, Yevgeniy Primakov.[38] They warned that, in response to NATO expansion, Russia would create a new military bloc, aim its medium-range nuclear missiles at Poland and the Czech

---

[35] President Boris Yeltsin's letter to US President Bill Clinton, 15 Sep. 1993, reprinted in *SIPRI Yearbook 1994* (note 17), pp. 249–50.

[36] Note 35, p. 250.

[37] 'NATO will survive in the foreseeable future, all changes notwithstanding, through internal transformation and adaptation to the changing circumstances. However, the very fact of retaining the immense concentration of the bloc's military potential will not pose a danger to Russia's security, because its main direction is [set] at maintaining stability in Europe and out of its area. Considering that even in the period of confrontation NATO did not have an offensive potential at its disposal, it is all the more characteristic for the present and future conditions.' *Rossiya v sisteme mezhdunarodnikh otnoshenii blizhayshego desatiletiya* [Russia in the system of international relations in the coming decade] (IMEMO: Moscow, 1995), pp. 40–41.

[38] See Grachev's statement of 4 Jan. 1996 in 'Russia links Pact to NATO expansion', *International Herald Tribune*, 5 Jan. 1996, p. 5. In his first public statement as Russia's new Foreign Minister on 12 Jan. 1996, Primakov made clear that he regarded the expansion of the Alliance to include CEE states as a danger. *International Herald Tribune*, 13–14 Jan. 1996, p. 2.

Republic, form a strategic alliance with Iran, and so on. 'In effect, as one expert comments, we are witnessing a clinical [phenomenon of] mass paranoia. . . . Its chief reasons are a prolonged state of indeterminateness, the lack of will in fulfilling promises, and, eventually, a fear and an inadequate assessment of threat resulting in a not always adequate response.'[39]

The debate on NATO enlargement illustrates the dilemma Russia faces: whether to cooperate with the rest of Europe in different fields, including security and arms control, or to return to confrontation and a policy of enmity towards the West. However, Russia's position, like those of the NATO and Central European states, is neither static nor permanent. Views are evolving. At the end of 1995, attention focused not specifically on the issue of enlarging NATO, but on the search for 'special relations' between NATO and Russia.[40] Growing awareness that Russia has no right of veto on enlargement[41] has been accompanied by the conviction that solutions should be sought which would harmonize the security interests of all states concerned. This approach might open prospects of elaborating cooperative instruments which would help alleviate and remove Russia's fears with regard to Alliance enlargement.

Central European arguments

In the period following World War II, the debate on Europe's security focused mainly, if not exclusively, on Western Europe; now, in the post-cold war period, the debate on the future of Europe as a whole focuses on the security of both Russia and Central Europe.

During the cold war, it was widely accepted that overcoming the division of Europe would enable German unification. In fact, events took a different course. Although German unification followed the fall of the Berlin Wall, the division persists between an integrated and secure Europe in the West and a less secure Central Europe still outside the political, economic and military framework unifying Western, Southern and Northern Europe. The 1995 *Poland–NATO* report stated that an effective security system cannot be achieved without the entry of Poland into the EU and NATO. 'Failure in this enterprise will mean the start of a new great European battle for influence in Central Europe.'[42] Similar positions have been taken by Hungary and the

---

[39] Kobrinskaya, I., 'Rasshireniye NATO: kriticheskaya faza vperedi' [NATO enlargement: a critical phase ahead], *Segodnya*, 10 Nov. 1995, p. 9.

[40] From among various options for the settlement of relations between Russia and NATO (a non-aggression pact, a mutual security treaty, agreements on collective security, collective defence or a strategic partnership), some experts favour 'special relations', which would combine mutual security and strategic partnership. Davydov, Y., 'Prorubit li Rossiya okno v NATO?' [Will Russia cut out a window towards NATO?], *Segodnya*, 23 Feb. 1996, p. 7.

[41] Foreign Minister Primakov, during his first visit to a former Eastern bloc country since taking office, admitted in Bratislava, Slovakia, on 29 Feb. 1996 that Russia has 'no veto right' in the matter of NATO expansion, but he stated that it 'would put Russia into a worse geopolitical and military position, not to mention the psychological aspects of the process', *OMRI Daily Digest*, no. 44 (1 Mar. 1996), URL <http://www.omri.cz/Publications/Digests/DigestIndex.html>.

[42] *Report Poland–NATO*, prepared by Poland's 2 former foreign ministers, a former defence minister and his deputy as well as 2 other high-ranking government officials: Andrzej Ananicz, Przemyslaw

Czech Republic. As long as the CEE region is treated as a 'grey zone' or an area of great-power rivalry, stability will not take root in Europe as a whole, and the building of a new European security system will remain a matter of intellectual speculation.[43]

The Central European countries do not perceive a direct concrete threat— there is no such threat from either Russia or other neighbours.[44] Their integration with NATO (and with the EU, the WEU and the Organisation for Economic Co-operation and Development, OECD) would not be seen as a response to direct threats, but rather to the need to reaffirm their place in the cultural, political, military and socio-economic community and civilization of Western states, based on a common system of values. Joining the community is seen not as a temporary, emergency action, but as a historical and strategic goal which will crown the transformation process begun in 1989–90. The CEE states are looking for a security formula to insure against 'finding themselves politically and militarily stranded in the event of a future crisis'.[45] At the same time, understandably, they do not wish to be treated as pawns in the political game, whether as a zone of Russia's actual or potential national security interests or as a function of the West's policy towards Russia.[46]

Central Europe is still not clearly defined. From the historical viewpoint, inclusion in this subregion of peoples and states west of the line that demarcated Eastern from Western Christendom after the Great Schism of 1054 is for the most part not questioned.[47] From the political point of view, these are the four members of the Visegrad Group (Poland, the Czech Republic, Hungary and Slovakia), the three Baltic states (Estonia, Latvia and Lithuania) and Slovenia. In other words, it is not only geography that serves to delimit subregions; often, and perhaps primarily, political considerations are decisive.[48] For this group of states, NATO and the political and military presence of the USA in Europe are of basic importance in shaping a new European security system. As far as the relationship between NATO and the EU is concerned, EU membership would also mean meeting the criteria for admission to NATO

Grudzinski, Andrzej Olechowski, Janusz Onyszkiewicz, Krzysztof Skubiszewski and Henryk Szlajfer, Warsaw, Sep. 1995, p. 33.

[43] See also Towpik, A., 'Nowe warunki bezpieczenstwa europejskiego. NATO z perspektywy Europy Srodkowej' [New premises of European security. NATO from the Central European vantage point], *Rzeczpospolita*, 27 June 1995, p. 27.

[44] It is stated in *Report Poland–NATO* (note 42) that 'Poland is not today in danger.'

[45] Note 42, p. 6.

[46] In Jonathan Dean's view, NATO enlargement would 'frustrate the common Western aim of integrating Russia . . . instead of complementing each other, these two efforts are clashing'. Dean, J. 'Losing Russia or keeping NATO: must we choose?', *Arms Control Today*, vol. 25, no. 5 (June 1995), p. 4.

[47] Mihalka, M., 'Eastern and Central Europe's great divide over membership in NATO', *Transition*, vol. 1, no. 14 (11 Aug. 1995), p. 48.

[48] The example of Poland is very telling in this context: prior to World War II Poland was considered part of Central Europe; after its considerable westward shift under the Potsdam Agreement, it was ascribed to Eastern Europe since, like other Central European countries, it found itself in the Soviet sphere of influence. In the wake of the collapse of the USSR and German unification, Poland's geopolitical location has changed radically, although its borders are unchanged: instead of the 3 former neighbours (the USSR, the GDR and Czechoslovakia) Poland now borders on 7 states: Russia (Kaliningrad area), Lithuania, Belarus, Ukraine, the Czech Republic, Slovakia and Germany. Once again, in accordance with its geography, history and political setting, Poland is part of Central Europe.

rather than vice versa. The main motivation for CEE membership in NATO is to widen the area of stability and security to cover this subregion; Russian opposition is seen by the CEE countries as an attempt to freeze the divisions and petrify the zones of uncertainty and unequal security in Europe.

IV. The EU and the WEU: continued evolution

Enlargement of the European Union

Preparations for the 1996 Intergovernmental Conference (IGC, commonly known as Maastricht II) to be held in Turin were made in 1995. One of the tasks of the IGC is to evaluate the 1992 Maastricht Treaty provisions on a Common Foreign and Security Policy (CFSP). President of the European Commission Jacques Santer wrote in November 1995: 'Today, the Union has a duty to extend that security to the other countries of Eastern Europe. Their integration will be the biggest issue of the next 10 or 20 years because the prospect of a Union of 20 or 25 or even more states turns the entire political, economic and institutional machinery on its head'.[49]

The Copenhagen European Council meeting (21–22 June 1993) defined the criteria to be met by applicant states—stable democratic institutions, adherence to the rule of law, respect for human rights and rights of national minorities, and a sound market economy able to handle intra-Union competition.[50] There was no breakthrough decision on enlargement in 1995, but the ongoing debate has made clear that such a big expansion requires that questions of decision making and power sharing be considered. In short, without the profound institutional changes to be addressed by the IGC in 1996, the Union will be unable to admit new members. Many CEE applicants do not meet the adopted criteria: they would need to adapt their economies and legislations to EU requirements. Although the negotiations are to be conducted individually, at least three categories of candidate state can already be distinguished. According to the criterion of advancement these are: (a) Cyprus and Malta; (b) three of the Visegrad states (the Czech Republic, Hungary and Poland[51]) and Slovenia; and (c) the Baltic states (Estonia, Latvia and Lithuania), Bulgaria, Romania and Slovakia. Unlike in the NATO case, admission will be determined by economic considerations, particularly the costs connected with subsidies or structural funds for the poorest agricultural regions.

[49] Santer, J., 'The European Union's security and defence policy', *NATO Review*, no. 6 (Nov. 1995), p. 4. Such a decision would be a 5th successive stage in enlarging the founding group of 6 states by new members: Denmark, Ireland and the UK (1973), Greece (1981), Spain and Portugal (1986), Austria, Finland and Sweden (1995). The next candidates are Cyprus and Malta; the EU announced that negotiations will begin 6 months after the end of the IGC (probably at the turn of the year 1997/98). Official applications have also been made by Hungary and Poland (1994) and Romania, Slovakia, Latvia and Estonia (1995). At the end of 1995 Bulgaria, the Czech Republic, Lithuania and Slovenia announced their intention to apply for membership.

[50] In the EU enlargement process, the decisions adopted by the Essen Meeting of the European Council, Essen, 9 and 10 Dec. 1994 and the White Book adopted by the European Union (Cannes, June 1995) will also be taken into account.

[51] For many reasons Slovakia, although a member of the Visegrad Group, is increasingly excluded in this context.

The 1995 European Commission document on *The Effects of Enlargement*[52] emphasizes the political implications of admitting new members to the Union. It suggests that enlargement will give new impetus to the European economy and help strengthen security and stability in Europe. The integration process relies today on three pillars: (*a*) the economy; (*b*) foreign and security policy; and (*c*) legal order, justice and internal affairs.

To understand the scale of problems connected with EU expansion eastwards, the considerable gaps in per capita gross domestic product (GDP) should be noted. While average national revenues in the Czech Republic, Hungary, Poland and Slovakia account for one-third of the average for the Union,[53] incomes in some regions of Central Europe are comparable with or even higher than those of Greece and Portugal.

The establishment of the CFSP in the Maastricht Treaty was a genuine conceptual breakthrough.[54] As Jacques Santer observed: 'It committed the WEU defined as the defence component of the European Union to a realignment which will be made even more "complete" by the necessary opening-up to our nearest neighbours'.[55] Such were the assumptions; the relevant treaty provisions remain on paper. In 1995, decisions were taken to review and reexamine them.

The mechanisms for the CFSP decision-making process include the European Council (the heads of state and government), the Council of Foreign Ministers, the European Commission and, in contractual external affairs, the European Parliament.[56] This is a complex process and, more important, many of the Maastricht Treaty contractual provisions 'remain vague and open to interpretation according to the different interests of member-countries'.[57]

Security policies of the West European states are subject to coordination in three frameworks: NATO, the EU and the WEU. This stems from the Maastricht Treaty provisions.[58] In effect, however, the common security of the EU countries (with the exception of Ireland) has so far been based on NATO's potential. Because of the policy of neutrality of three new members in 1995 (Austria, Finland and Sweden), elaboration of a new security arrangement has become a matter of urgency. In practice, this means a rethinking of the mandate and the politico-military role of the WEU.

[52] European Commission, Interim report from the Commission to the European Council on the effects of the policies of the European Union of enlargement to the associated countries of central and eastern Europe, CSE (95)605, Brussels, 6 Dec. 1995. This document was discussed in Madrid by the European Commission in Dec. 1995.

[53] In Romania and Bulgaria the per capita income is only one-fifth of the EU average. See the address by Andrzej Towpik, Under-Secretary of State, Poland's Foreign Ministry, delivered at the joint session of the Foreign Affairs Commission and the Europe Agreement Commission of the Sejm (Parliament), Warsaw, 28 Nov. 1995.

[54] See more on this in Rotfeld in *SIPRI Yearbook 1994* (note 17), pp. 205–37. For the text of Title V of the Maastricht Treaty, the Provisions of a Common Foreign and Security Policy, see the same volume, pp. 251–57.

[55] Santer (note 49).

[56] Jopp, M., *The Strategic Implications of European Integration,* PRIF Reports, no. 35 (Peace Research Institute Frankfurt: Frankfurt, Oct. 1994), p. 11.

[57] Note 56, p. 12.

[58] 'Whereas there is no doubt that WEU has a double function *vis-à-vis* the Union and NATO, the direct relations between the Union and NATO remain largely undefined.' Note 56, p. 13.

A new common security concept for the WEU

On 14 November 1995 the WEU Council of Ministers adopted in Madrid a document identifying the common interests of European countries, the risks and potential threats, as well as 'Europe's new responsibilities in a strategic environment in which Europe's security is not confined to security in Europe and in which Europe has acquired the capability to make its own contribution to the building of a just and peaceful world order'.[59] In May 1994 the WEU Ministers had agreed the criteria for Associate Partnership and in November 1994 the Noordwijk Ministerial Meeting had endorsed conclusions on the formulation of a Common European Defence Policy.[60] In practical terms, this opened the door for participation by CEE states in WEU Council sessions and working groups and also in WEU operations. This can be of practical value in the context of the decisions adopted in Brussels (January 1994),[61] where NATO leaders concluded that the emergence of a European Security and Defence Identity (ESDI) would strengthen the European pillar of the Alliance while reinforcing the transatlantic link. Consequently they authorized the development of 'separable but not separate' capabilities that could be used by NATO or the WEU.

The most interesting part of the WEU document is the section on gaps and deficiencies in European capabilities, identified as (a) crisis management mechanisms, including procedures for force generation and assembly, and command and control procedures; (b) reconnaissance and intelligence; (c) strategic and in-theatre transport capabilities; (d) standardization and interoperability; and (e) the European defence industrial base. The greatest weakness of the WEU is thus operational rather than conceptual. In defining its responses to the gaps and deficiencies the WEU must, in accordance with the Council of Ministers' recommendations, identify and implement policies and new concrete organizational steps to strengthen its politico-military structures; adapt national defence forces while maintaining their effectiveness; reinforce European assets and capabilities; and enhance the European defence industrial base.[62] The document illustrates the wide discrepancy between declared goals and general concepts, on the one hand, and practical operational arrangements, on the other. It is doubtful whether, 'even under the best of circumstances, Europe will in the near future be able to overcome differing foreign policy orientations and national sovereignty concerns to become an international actor in its own right'.[63]

There are both political and economic reasons for this state of affairs. Obviously, with the end of the cold war, the motivation for additional burden-

---

[59] WEU Council of Ministers, *European Security: A Common Concept of the 27 WEU Countries*, Madrid, 14 Nov. 1995, para. 4, p. 1. The document was adopted by all WEU members, associate members, observers and associate partners. Extracts are reprinted in appendix 7A in this volume.

[60] For more details see Rotfeld in *SIPRI Yearbook 1995* (note 17), pp. 271–72.

[61] See the text of the Declaration of the Heads of State and Government Participating in the Meeting of the North Atlantic Council, 11 Jan. 1994, in *SIPRI Yearbook 1994* (note 17), pp. 268–72.

[62] WEU (note 59), paras 181–84.

[63] Sloan, S. R., 'NATO's future: beyond collective defense', *CRS Report for Congress* (Congressional Research Service, Library of Congress: Washington, DC, 15 Sep. 1995), p. 21.

sharing in the military realm is gone. Political changes are easier to make than the financial commitments that the development of independent logistic, intelligence and communications systems, as well as nuclear forces, would necessitate.[64] The revival of the debate on a new role for the WEU in the process of building European security is connected with the evolution of France's position. Its sustained reluctance to commit forces to NATO's integrated command structure notwithstanding, France has signalled some change in its policy by reinvigorating WEU mechanisms in 1995.[65]

Changes in France's position *vis-à-vis* NATO, initiated in 1994, culminated in December 1995 when Foreign Minister Hervé de Charette declared that henceforth France would participate in NATO's military structures.[66] However, France's position generally boils down to the belief that all important decisions should be taken by the North Atlantic Council as authorized by the 1949 North Atlantic Treaty and not by the military structures and mechanisms built up later. An interim attempt at common sense is being made through the Combined Joint Task Forces (CJTF),[67] within which NATO resources and assets can be made available for missions other than collective defence under Article 5 of the North Atlantic Treaty, whether performed under NATO, WEU or other commands.

In the framework of preparations for the 1996 revision of the Maastricht Treaty (at the IGC), on 30 January 1995 the Portuguese President of the WEU Council identified two major issues: 'the common evaluation of European security, including the French proposal for a white paper, and the institutional implications for WEU for a European security and defence identity'.[68] It is not by chance that the EU governments have decided to hold a conference in 1996 to review and revise the treaty provisions on the CFSP. Under Article X of the 1948 Brussels Treaty, member states are entitled to notify the Belgian Government (the depository of the treaty) one year before the expiry of 50 years after signature of their intention to withdraw from the treaty.[69] It would

[64] According to the Royal United Services Institute in London it would require an increase in defence spending from the current European average of 2.5% of GDP by 1.5% (some $107 billion per year into the next century). 'The defence of Europe: it can't be done alone', *The Economist,* 25 Feb. 1995, p. 29.

[65] See Sloan (note 63), pp. 22–24; and Chilton, P., 'Common, collective or combined? Theories of defence integration in the European Union', ed. C. Rhodes and S. Marey, *The State of the European Union (vol. 3): Building a European Polity?* (Lynn Rienner: Boulder, Colo., 1995), pp. 81–109.

[66] Hervé de Charette's speech to the North Atlantic Council, 5 Dec. 1995. He stated that from that time on the French Defence Minister would also 'be able to regularly take part in the work of the Alliance, alongside his colleagues'. See also Grant, R. P., 'France's new relationship with NATO', *Survival*, vol. 38, no. 1 (spring 1996), pp. 58–80.

[67] Report presented to the Political Committee of the North Atlantic Assembly by Jan Petersen (Norway): *Towards a Security Strategy for Europe and NATO*, NAA Political Committee 1995 Reports, Oct. 1995, p. 7.

[68] WEU, The Future of European Security and the Preparation of Maastricht II—Reply to the Fortieth Annual Report of the Council, Report submitted on behalf of the Political Committee by Mrs Aguiar, WEU document 1458, 16 May 1995, p. 6.

[69] The 1948 Brussels Treaty of Collaboration and Collective Self-Defence among Western European States was signed 17 Mar. 1948 and entered into force on 25 Aug. 1948. It was to remain in force for 50 years. In accordance with Art. 10, 'After the expiry of the period of fifty years, each of the High Contracting Parties shall have the right to cease to be a party thereto provided that he shall have previously given one year's notice of denunciation to the Belgian Government'. It should be noted, however, that the WEU was not created by the 1948 Brussels Treaty, but by the Protocols to this Treaty,

be mistaken to consider 1998 a 'deadline', because the 1948 Brussels Treaty (as modified in 1954) would not be terminated automatically after expiry of the 50-year period. A study prepared by the European Strategy Group and the WEU Institute for Security Studies envisages the possible intermeshing of the WEU in the EU by 2005,[70] by which time there might be agreement on the political objectives of building Europe and a solution to the related institutional problems.[71] Institutional links are of special importance in this regard since, in the view of numerous politicians and experts, 'WEU is . . . the only European institution with a contractual link with the Atlantic Alliance from which the whole of the European Union might benefit, the more so, the closer WEU draws to that organization at institutional level'.[72] The crux of the matter is that in the present situation NATO's military structures, in which US forces play the key role, are the only guarantors of European security. US military withdrawal from Europe would make these structures worthless. Thus the political debate in Europe in 1995 centred on whether the IGC will make decisions leading to the WEU becoming the defence pillar of the EU .

The Lisbon Declaration of Ministers of Foreign Affairs and Defence of the WEU confirmed that 'the construction of an integral Europe will remain incomplete as long as it does not include security and defence'.[73] It noted the decision by France, Italy and Spain to organize a land force (EUROFOR) and a maritime force (EUROMARFOR), to be open to other WEU member states. As a follow-up to the decision taken at their previous meeting in Noordwijk,[74] the ministers endorsed a document on a WEU Humanitarian Task Force and tasked the Permanent Council to complete the work on this subject as a matter of priority.[75] The Lisbon meeting defined, for the first time, the common security interests of 27 countries of the European continent.[76]

In sum, meeting the goals and tasks identified in 1995 will be dependent on decisions made by the IGC. They cover essentially two areas: (*a*) adaptation by the transatlantic NATO partners to the European identity emerging under

signed in Paris on 23 Oct. 1954, which came into force on 6 May 1955. The Protocols, negotiated and signed some years before the 1957 Treaty of Rome, were aimed at creating a defensive European alliance including the Federal Republic of Germany.

[70] Stainier, L., 'Common interests, values and criteria for action', ed. L. Martin and J. Roper, *Towards a Common Defence Policy,* Study by the European Strategy Group and the WEU Institute for Security Studies (WEU: Paris, 1995), p. 14.

[71] WEU (note 68), p. 7.

[72] WEU (note 68), p. 15.

[73] Lisbon Declaration of 15 May 1995, reprinted in *Europe/Documents* no. 1933, Atlantic Document, no. 91, 17 May 1995.

[74] WEU Council of Ministers, Noordwijk Declaration, Noordwijk, 14 Nov. 1994. Excerpts of the text are reproduced in *SIPRI Yearbook 1995* (note 17), pp. 302–305

[75] This document, based on the Italian–British proposal on the principles and modalities for establishing a WEU Humanitarian Task Force and on the use of military assets in humanitarian crises, is consistent with para. 3 of the Noordwijk decision. Many other operational aspects were identified in different documents presented to the ministers: WEU's role in evacuation operations, generic planning, intelligence support to the Planning Cell, short-term measures, preliminary conclusions on the formulation of a common European defence policy (approved in the Noordwijk Declaration) (note 74).

[76] 10 WEU members, 3 associate members (NATO states—Iceland, Norway and Turkey), 5 observers (EU states—Austria, Denmark, Finland, Ireland and Sweden), and 9 associate partners (CEE states which have concluded European Agreements with the EU, including the Baltic states).

the security and defence policy within the framework of the WEU;[77] and (b) inclusion of CEE associate partners in the common, comprehensive and cooperative security concept for Europe. For the security of Europe the crucial question is not exactly that of institutional changes within the framework of the security community (NATO, EU/WEU), but one of continued US commitment to the Alliance. Europeans should be prepared for US involvement being weaker than they expect.[78] In other words, three processes will be of significance to European security: (a) enlarging the Alliance to the east; (b) forging a new type of relations between Russia and NATO; and (c) establishing transatlantic cooperation based on shared US–European security interests.

V. The OSCE in 1995: activities and assessment

The first year of the Organization for Security and Co-operation in Europe was 1995. The 1994 decision to make the CSCE a permanent organization[79] was reviewed at the OSCE Ministerial Council Meeting of the foreign ministers in Budapest (7–8 December 1995). In his 1995 Annual Report the OSCE Secretary General stated that the OSCE had strengthened its structures and considerably increased its potential for political consultation and operational conflict management.[80] Among new developments the following were highlighted by the Hungarian Chairman-in-Office (CIO) as being of particular importance: the establishment of a long-term mission in Chechnya and, as part of the OSCE activities in Bosnia and Herzegovina, the appointment of the Ombudsman of the Federation.[81] While neither accomplishment substantially affected the developments in Bosnia or Chechnya, their significance lies in the agreement on a mediation role for the OSCE, especially that by Russia regarding a conflict which was, and still is, considered a domestic matter.[82] The 1994 Budapest Summit Meeting decisions underlined the Organization's role as the primary instrument for early warning, conflict prevention and crisis management.[83] OSCE actions in Chechnya and Bosnia were not only a test of its effectiveness, but also 'broke new ground'[84] for the Organization's activity and brought new experience of consolidated organizational structures.

---

[77] Klaus Kinkel, Minister for Foreign Affairs of Germany, defined this in the following way: 'A key issue on the transatlantic agenda will be the future merging of NATO security and defence structures with those of European integration. NATO must not be weakened, yet Europe must be given a wider scope for action on security matters'. *International Herald Tribune*, 30 Mar. 1995.

[78] Gordon, P. H., 'Recasting the Atlantic Alliance', *Survival*, vol. 38, no. 1 (spring 1996), p. 51.

[79] CSCE, Budapest Document 1994, Budapest Summit Declaration: Towards a Genuine Partnership in a New Era, 6 Dec. 1994, para. 3. The text is reproduced in *SIPRI Yearbook 1995* (note 17), pp. 309–11. For more details see Rotfeld in the same volume, pp. 286–301.

[80] OSCE, *Annual Report 1995 on OSCE Activities submitted by the OSCE Secretary General*, Ref. MC/11/95, Vienna, 30 Nov. 1995.

[81] OSCE, Statement by Hungarian Foreign Minister Laszlo Kovacs, Ref. MC/26/95, Budapest, 7 Dec. 1995.

[82] Russia traditionally interpreted Principle VI of the Helsinki Final Act and Article 2, para. 7, of the UN Charter in a very restrictive way: 'Nothing contained in the present Charter shall authorize the United Nations to intervene in matters which are essentially within the domestic jurisdiction of any state or shall require the Member to submit such matters to settlement under the present Charter'.

[83] Excerpts from the Budapest Decisions can be found in *SIPRI Yearbook 1995* (note 17), p. 310.

[84] OSCE (note 81).

One of the strengthening measures adopted at the Budapest Summit Meeting was the replacement of various OSCE Committees with high-ranking Councils, thereby encouraging states to be represented at a higher political level at OSCE meetings. The first Senior Council Meeting (held in Prague, 30–31 March 1995) reviewed the OSCE role in managing the crisis in Chechnya, preparations for an OSCE multinational peacekeeping force in Nagorno-Karabakh and its role in the former Yugoslavia in support of peace efforts and in preparation for a post-conflict role. OSCE activity and assistance in settling conflicts, reducing tensions in Moldova, Ukraine and Georgia as well as the role played in solving bilateral problems were also reviewed. The OSCE also facilitated the implementation of bilateral agreements such as those between Russia and Latvia on the Skrunda radar station and the Russian military pensioners in Latvia. The Permanent Council in Vienna provided the OSCE with a permanently available political body which strengthened both its consultative and operational functions.

The 20th anniversary of the signing of the 1975 Helsinki Final Act provided a starting-point for a thorough exchange of views, largely future-oriented, on the new role and tasks of the OSCE.[85]

OSCE missions

The first year of the new strengthened OSCE framework saw consultations and negotiations on and the operation of 10 missions[86] and activities of three OSCE representatives: to the Russian–Latvian Joint Commission on Military Pensioners, to the Joint Committee on the Skrunda Radar Station and to the Estonian Government Commission on Military Pensioners.

Preventive diplomacy, conflict prevention and management are seen as the key areas of OSCE activity. New expectations of the OSCE are reflected in the broadened and adjusted mandates of some missions to meet political, military and humanitarian requirements in the field. That all the field missions of the OSCE have involved only 76 authorized seconded personnel[87] shows how much can be achieved with limited human and financial resources. The achievements of some of the missions, particularly those in Estonia, Latvia and Moldova, are beyond question. In other countries, such as Tajikistan and Ukraine, the OSCE presence was but a token of the will to seek peaceful solutions; its task in Bosnia and Herzegovina (Sarajevo) was to support the activity of the ombudsman. Regrettably, the parties engaged in the conflict were not interested in using the potential good offices of the missions.

---

[85] The anniversary was marked on 1 Aug. 1995 in Helsinki at a symposium hosted by the Finnish Government. *OSCE Newsletter* (special issue), vol. 2, no. 8 (Aug. 1995). The Government of the Russian Federation hosted a seminar on a new model of European security (Moscow, 17–18 July 1995). The Swiss Government invited the participants at the original CSCE negotiations to discuss the achievements and perspectives of the OSCE (Geneva, 20 Oct. 1995). Similar seminars and discussions were held in Vienna (June), Hamburg (Sep.), Prague (Oct.) and many other places in Europe.

[86] These 10 missions were in (1) Kosovo, Sandjak and Vojvodina; (2) Skopje; (3) Georgia; (4) Moldova; (5) Tajikistan; (6) Ukraine; (7) Sarajevo; (8) Latvia; (9) Estonia; and (10) Chechnya.

[87] OSCE (note 80), p. 7.

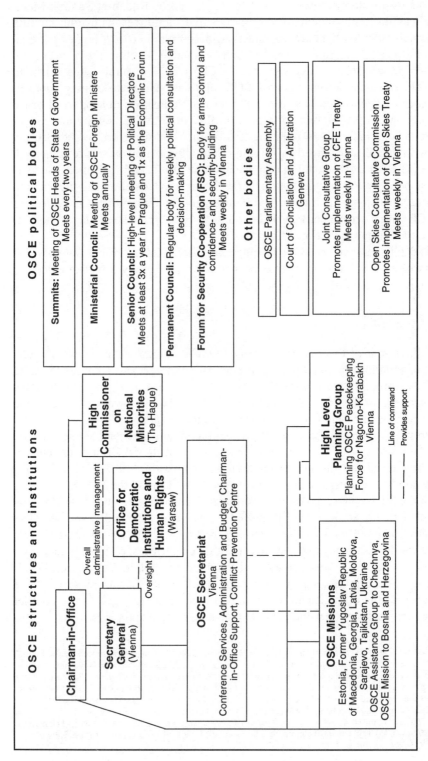

Figure 7.2. The Organization for Security and Co-operation in Europe

The Budapest Summit Meeting decided to deploy a multinational OSCE peacekeeping mission to Nagorno-Karabakh if the parties to the conflict agreed.[88] In July 1995 a High-Level Planning Group (HLPG) for the operation was set up in Vienna (replacing the Initial Operations Planning Group). The HLPG submitted its concept for multinational forces in Nagorno-Karabakh to the Chairman-in-Office. A coordinated effort by the OSCE and the Russian Federation was supplemented by the presence in the area of the personal representative of the CIO with the aim of facilitating a political settlement.[89]

Less known but important examples of the working cooperation between the OSCE and the EU and the WEU in 1995, with UN involvement, were the activities of the Sanctions Coordinator and the Sanctions Assistance Missions (SAMs). More than 200 customs officers and other experts continued their work in seven SAMs located in Albania, Bulgaria, Croatia, Hungary, the former Yugoslav Republic of Macedonia, Romania and Ukraine. Their mandate was to assist and advise the host countries in their implementation of sanctions against the former Yugoslavia (Serbia and Montenegro) in accordance with the relevant UN Security Council solutions.[90]

The High Commissioner on National Minorities

The role of the High Commissioner on National Minorities (HCNM) in OSCE conflict prevention is seldom publicized.[91] In 1995 the HCNM was directly involved in the following countries: Albania—regarding the Greeks in southern Albania; Estonia—primarily regarding the Russian residents; the Former Yugoslav Republic of Macedonia (FYROM)—the Albanian minority; Hungary—the Slovak minority; Kazakhstan and Kyrgyzstan—inter-ethnic relations; Latvia—the Russian population; Moldova—various minority issues; and Ukraine—regarding Crimea.[92] Max van der Stoel assessed his activities in the capacity of High Commissioner as follows: 'The very first lesson I have learned is that it is necessary for the international community to get involved at an early stage, before an emerging conflict has reached dramatic proportions. . . . The second . . . is . . . whether we ought not to pay more attention

[88] OSCE (note 80), p. 14.
[89] On 6 Jan. 1995 the CIO named Jan Eliasson of Sweden and Valentin Lozinsky of Russia as co-chairmen of the Minsk Group (on 21 Apr. 1995 Finland took over the co-chairmanship from Sweden, with Heikki Talvite of Finland as new co-chairman). The personal representative of the CIO on the Nagorno-Karabakh conflict dealt with by the Minsk Conference is Ambassador Stanislaw Przygodzki of Poland (appointed Aug. 1995).
[90] SAM operations were financed by the OSCE, and their Brussels headquarters was financed by the EU. The Sanctions Coordinator's staff undertook in 1995 a series of sanctions-related missions to the Balkan countries and other OSCE states in implementing his mandate to oversee the entire operation and provide basic coordination between all levels and participants in sanctions enforcement. The mandate for SAMS, extended until 30 Dec. 1995, expired because of decisions taken under the Dayton Agreement.
[91] Report prepared by the Office of the OSCE High Commissioner on National Minorities, *The Role of the High Commissioner on National Minorities in OSCE Conflict Prevention* (compiled and edited by Rob Zagman), The Hague, 30 June 1995.
[92] The HCNM has terminated his involvement in Lithuania.

... to the factors that can lead to a conflict'.[93] In this context, he indicated the extremely difficult economic situation of some minorities, which generates the dangers of radicalization and growing extremism. Among factors behind the conflict situations, he also mentioned the lack of government resources to satisfy the cultural and educational needs of minorities.

One example of a conflict-generating situation is the frequent absence of adequate language training facilities.[94] While such issues might appear minor and insignificant, the tensions to which they give rise could be avoided if even very modest means were earmarked for them.[95] The Swedish Government contributed some 5.3 million Swedish crowns for language tuition for the Russian-speaking minority in Latvia in a programme drawn up by the United Nations Development Programme. Finland, Norway and the Netherlands have also promised to contribute to its financing, and discussions are in progress with several other countries for additional support.[96]

The Pact on Stability in Europe

The activity of the HCNM is to some extent still connected with the Pact on Stability in Europe, as adopted in Paris (20 March 1995). In accordance with the Budapest Summit Declaration, the OSCE is the repository of the Pact and is entrusted with monitoring its implementation.[97] The 31st Meeting of the OSCE Permanent Council (March 1995) specified concrete steps with which the Pact should be followed up. The European Union considers the OSCE 'the guardian' of the Pact. The HCNM has been invited to participate in the Central European and Baltic regional round tables.[98] The EU remains financially involved in the follow-up: the PHARE Democracy Programme (initiated as Pologne–Hongrie: action pour la reconversion économique, or Assistance for economic restructuring in the countries of Central and Eastern Europe) as one of the assistance programmes for CEE countries, has been reallocated so as to support implementation of the Pact.

---

[93] M. van der Stoel,, 'Perspectives of the OSCE in tomorrow's Europe', in *From 1975 to 1995 and Beyond: The Achievements of the CSCE—The Perspectives of the OSCE*, Statements of the panellists at the Geneva Seminar on the occasion of the Twentieth Anniversary of the Helsinki Final Act, Geneva, Oct. 1995, pp. 53–54.

[94] Ethnic Russians in the Baltic states, for example, who must pass language tests to become Estonian or Latvian citizens, fail to meet the requirements laid down by the national authorities.

[95] In van der Stoel's view, '[t]he capital needed for conflict prevention would be rather negligible compared with the billions spent for security purposes ... If we would use just 0.01% of the collective defence budgets of all the OSCE states we would already have more than enough to have a very impressive program of conflict prevention'. Note 93, p. 54.

[96] The Russian-speaking minority in Latvia comprises 34% of the population. The aim of the programme is to facilitate the naturalization of this minority in Latvia. Press Release of the Swedish Ministry for Foreign Affairs, 15 Feb. 1996.

[97] Budapest Summit Declaration (note 79). On the origin and analysis of the Pact see Rotfeld in *SIPRI Yearbook 1994* (note 17), pp. 220–22; the text of the French proposal for a Pact on Stability, submitted to the Summit Meeting of the European Council in Copenhagen on 22 June 1993, reprinted in the same volume, pp. 247–49; and Rotfeld in *SIPRI Yearbook 1995* (note 17), pp. 283–85.

[98] See more on this in *SIPRI Yearbook 1995* (note 17), p. 285.

Building democratic institutions

In the search for conflict prevention in Europe minorities and border issues are high on the agenda, however, in the broader sense, long-term security-building on the continent requires the shaping of democratic institutions. The OSCE has been particularly active in this unspectacular and little noticed area.[99] One of the tasks defined by the Budapest Summit Meeting for the Office for Democratic Institutions and Human Rights (ODIHR) was the preparation of a framework for the coordination of election monitoring. After consultations with the Council of Europe, the UN and other relevant international organizations, a framework was presented to the OSCE Permanent Council in May 1995. Its implementation was successfully tested in different parliamentary elections.[100]

Within the OSCE framework a series of international seminars and symposia were held on the rule of law and democratic institutions,[101] on media management,[102] on human dimension implementation[103] and on arms control and security.[104] Other important activities in 1995 were connected with integrating new participating states. The Permanent Council decided to establish an OSCE Liaison Office for Central Asia,[105] and a Voluntary Fund for fostering the integration of recently admitted states was established. In accordance with the Budapest Summit Meeting decision the ODIHIR, the Conflict Prevention Centre (CPC) and the Secretary General organized meetings and seminars in Central Asia, thereby fostering contacts between Central Asian representatives and experts and other OSCE states and international organizations.

A contact point for Roma and Sinti issues within the ODIHR was established with the aim of encouraging development of the organizational

[99] ODIHR activities can be listed as an example. The Office assisted the OSCE mission to Sarajevo; advised the Tajik istan Government with regard to the office of ombudsman; established a network of West and East European ombudsmen; and is preparing a draft manual on national human rights institutions to assist OSCE participating countries in their establishment. Under its auspices, a collection of international documents on 'Human Rights and the Judiciary' (ed. F. Quinn and A. Rzeplinski, ODIHIR: Warsaw, 1995) was published in Russian in 1995, as a reference guide for judges, prosecutors, lawyers, parliamentarians, non-governmental organizations (NGOs) and the media. See also Bloed, A., 'The human dimension of the OSCE: past, present and prospects', *ODIHIR Bulletin*, vol. 3, no. 3 (1995).

[100] During 1995 the following democratic elections to parliaments and local referenda were monitored by observers from OSCE states and NGOs: Kyrgyzstan (5 and 19 Feb.); Estonia (5 Mar.); the local referendum on the inclusion of certain localities in Gagauzia, Republic of Moldova (5 Mar.); local elections in Moldova (16 Apr.); parliamentary elections in Belarus (14 and 18 May); Armenia (5 and 29 July); Latvia (30 Sep. and 1 Oct.); and Croatia (29 Oct.). OSCE (note 80), pp. 18–21.

[101] There were 10 meetings on this subject, the biggest being the Warsaw meeting on Building Blocks for Civil Society: Freedom of Association and NGOs (4–7 Apr. 1995), hosting 286 participants, half of whom represented 123 NGOs.

[102] Seminars were organized in Kishinev, Moldova (11–13 May 1995) and Bishkek, Kyrgyzstan (11–13 Sep. 1995).

[103] The meeting in Warsaw (2–19 Oct. 1995) examined the implementation of the OSCE human dimension commitments and elaborated several recommendations in this regard. See also OSCE, Human Dimension Seminar on the Rule of Law, Selected Materials, ODIHIR, Warsaw, 28 Nov.–1 Dec. 1995.

[104] Seminars were held on Principles Governing Conventional Arms Transfers (Vienna, 20–21 June 1995); on Regional Arms Control in the OSCE (Vienna, 10–12 July 1995); and CSBMs and Arms Control: Application and Compliance (Almaty, Kazakhstan, 16–23 May 1995). The Annual Implementation Assessment Meeting also took place in Vienna, 12–14 Apr. 1995.

[105] OSCE (note 80), para. 6.1.3, p. 24.

capacities of associations of these two ethnic groups and to focus on addressing discrimination and violence against them.

The main new task of the OSCE in 1995 stems from the provisions of the Dayton Agreement: the Organization is to play a key role in post-conflict settlement and in rebuilding the civil society of Bosnia and Herzegovina. The key document in this regard is the decision on OSCE action for peace, democracy and stability in Bosnia and Herzegovina, adopted by the Ministerial Council.[106] The new OSCE mandate comprises three categories: (a) free and fair elections; (b) monitoring human rights; and (c) the negotiating process on arms control, disarmament and confidence- and security-building measures (CSBMs). The OSCE foreign ministers decided that the OSCE 'will supervise the preparation, conduct and monitoring of elections in Bosnia and Herzegovina, certifying when conditions will permit elections to take place'.[107] In accordance with the Dayton Agreement and the relevant Budapest Ministerial Council decisions it should also monitor human rights in Bosnia and appoint an international human rights ombudsman.[108]

The third task for the OSCE, as defined by the Dayton Agreement and Budapest Ministerial Council decisions, is to assist the parties in their negotiations on arms control and CSBMs as well as in the implementation and verification of resulting agreements. The 53 foreign ministers regarded building peace in the former Yugoslavia as a 'historic challenge' presented to the OSCE by the Dayton Agreement[109] or as a 'Herculean task'.[110]

The economic dimension

The economic dimension of the OSCE was the subject of discussion at the Third Meeting of the Economic Forum (Prague, 7–9 June 1995). The Forum considered various aspects of regional cooperation in the fields of trade, investment, infrastructure and their relevance to security.[111] In this context, it is worth taking note of the resolutions on economic affairs, science, technology and environment as adopted by the OSCE Parliamentary Assembly (Ottawa, 8 July 1995).[112]

[106] OSCE, Fifth Meeting of the Ministerial Council, Decisions of the Budapest Ministerial Council Meeting, Decision on OSCE action for peace, democracy and stability in Bosnia and Herzegovina, MC(5).DEC/1, Budapest, 8 Dec. 1995.

[107] OSCE (note 106), Chairman's Summary.

[108] The scope of tasks in this matter is illustrated by the 5-volume Final Report of the Commission of Experts as established pursuant to Security Council Resolution 780(1992) S/194/674, 27 May 1994 and annexes, submitted by the UN Secretary-General to the Security Council, Dec. 1994, vols. II–V, Final Reports and Annexes, New York, 10 Feb. 1995.

[109] OSCE (note 106), Chairman's Summary.

[110] Interview by Ambassador Pekka Ojanen of Finland in the OSCE Review (Published by the Finnish Committee for European Security), vol. 3, no. 4 (1995).

[111] In addition 'The role of tourism in promoting better understanding between different cultures' was discussed in Bucharest (6–8 Nov. 1995). The Bulgarian Government hosted in Sofia an OSCE Seminar on 'The role of trans-European infrastructure for stability and cooperation in the Black Sea region' (15–17 Nov. 1995). OSCE (note 80), p. 24.

[112] The OSCE Parliamentary Assembly (Ottawa, 4–8 July 1995) adopted 3 resolutions corresponding to the 3 baskets of the Helsinki Final Act. The resolution on political affairs and security emphasized the strengthening of the OSCE (exploring the decision-making procedures based on appropriate consensus)

The security model

Work on the security model embraces three spheres: (a) the politico-military field; (b) social, economic and human dimensions; and (c) structural issues, including inter-institutional cooperation (consultation, transparency and the development of the concept of mutually reinforcing institutions),[113] strengthening the OSCE, regional and subregional cooperation[114] and security cooperation beyond the OSCE area.

The effectiveness of existing and new decisions with regard to all the security structures in Europe is assessed through the prism of their commitment to and results in the peaceful settlement of the conflict in Bosnia. OSCE Secretary General Wilhelm Höynck noted:

All our elaborate crisis management manuals, conceived under the conditions of East-West confrontation, are nearly useless. We need new instruments and mechanisms, new approaches to perform this new task well. But we also need a comprehensive and thorough examination of the new challenges and risks. Bosnia and conflicts elsewhere are of immediate concern and call for urgent responses. They do not, however, constitute the essence of the fundamental changes that are occurring; rather they are disturbing and tragic, but an attendant phenomenon. To find comprehensive solutions and not just 'quick fixes', we must look beyond these immediate needs.[115]

Altogether, in the period from the 1994 Budapest Summit Meeting decision to elaborate a Common and Comprehensive Security Model for Europe for the Twenty-First Century (5–6 Dec. 1994) to the end of the Budapest Ministerial Council Meeting (7–8 December 1995), nearly 200 documents and proposals were submitted for formal and informal consideration and negotiation.

The OSCE Ministerial Council in Budapest adopted a decision on a security model for Europe in a document summing up the debate so far and setting the mandate for the near future.[116] It is important to note that the discussion was

and progress being made in the Caucasus and reiterated its concern about the military conflict in the former Yugoslavia. The resolution on democracy, human rights and humanitarian questions stated the need to establish an international criminal law and court covering war crimes. An *Ad Hoc* Committee on a Code of Conduct on Democracy and Human Rights of the Parliamentary Assembly was also established.

[113] The Pact on Stability in Europe, transmitted by the EU to the OSCE for follow-up and implementation in close cooperation with the Council of Europe, may be considered a worthy example of a mutually reinforcing institution.

[114] Alongside the activities of the regional security organizations analysed in this chapter, the Council of Europe (within which the concept of democratic security was elaborated and is now being put into effect) and numerous other subregional structures contribute increasingly to shaping a new security system. These subregional structures are: (a) in Central Europe—the Visegrad Group (the Czech Republic, Hungary, Poland and Slovakia) and the Central European Initiative (10 states); (b) in Northern Europe and the Baltic region—the Nordic Council (5 states), the Baltic Council (3 states), and the Barents Euro-Arctic Council (5 states); (c) in the south—the Black Sea Economic Cooperation (11 states); and (d) on former Soviet territory—the Commonwealth of Independent States (CIS, 12 former Soviet republics) and some other institutions. For details of these institutions see the Glossary in this volume.

[115] Höynck, W., 'What can the OSCE do to manage crises in Europe?', Speech delivered in Pielavesi, 3 Sep. 1995.

[116] OSCE (note 106), Decision on a Common and Comprehensive Security Model for Europe for the Twenty-First Century: a new concept for a new century, MC(5).DEC/2.

not confined to an exchange of views among official state representatives, but that independent experts and researchers were also invited to take part.[117] The ministers discussed and decided on the objectives, guidelines and organization of the future work on a security model. The Ministerial Council resolved to move the work on a security model for Europe into a more operational phase. The aim is to prepare concrete proposals for adoption by the OSCE Lisbon Summit Meeting in late 1996.

The Ministerial Council decided that the security model should proceed in accordance with the following guidelines: to promote strict observance of OSCE principles and commitments; to contribute to the further development of the OSCE and the effective use of its operational capabilities; to promote cooperative approaches to security challenges and risks (including conflict prevention and crisis management); to uphold the comprehensive concept of security and its indivisibility; to develop ways in which complementary and mutually reinforcing organizations work together; to strengthen the relationship between the OSCE and the UN and to contribute to the transparent and democratic evolution of regional and transatlantic organizations.[118]

The debate on expanding NATO and the EU and transforming the WEU is closely related to the work on the security model. While discussions conducted within the OSCE are fairly artificially confined to the OSCE framework, principles and rules, the issue of elaborating a new cooperative security model is at stake. There is a commitment to respect the existing OSCE principles and their new interpretation while agreeing, if necessary, on new principles and norms. The effectiveness of the classic principles which underlay stability in the past must be enhanced to conform with post-cold war conditions. The elimination of the main sources of bloc tensions brings forward the issue of the transparency of any major changes to security organizations. At the operational level, the critical question is how to generate support for peacekeeping, conflict prevention, crisis management and humanitarian relief.

On 1 August 1995 in Helsinki, former German Foreign Minister Hans-Dietrich Genscher argued with the popular view that the Helsinki Final Act fixed the status quo in Europe once and for all. He considered that: 'The CSCE did not stabilize the status quo, but creates a reliable and stable setting in which it could be overcome peacefully, step by step . . . '. He went on to state that in the long run the OSCE will live up to its claims only if it becomes more able to take action and decisions. This entails a number of new initiatives: its decisions should be made binding under international law; its

---

[117] OSCE (note 116); and SIPRI's contribution to the OSCE Seminar on a Common and Comprehensive Security Model for the Twenty-First Century, Vienna, 18–19 Sep. 1995, PC/499/95/Corr. 1, 18 Sep. 1995. SIPRI established an Independent Working Group (IWG) on A Security Model with participation by leading experts, politicians and researchers aimed at producing a report addressing the future security agenda in and for Europe. The first meeting of the IWG was held in Budapest, 2 Dec. 1995.

[118] The Ministerial Council requested the CIO to keep the informal list of risks and challenges to security updated. The 1995 Budapest Meeting recommended a continued wide-ranging discussion on a security model, with broad participation of government officials, non-governmental representatives and academics. Its results should be presented to the 1996 Lisbon Summit Meeting for consideration and assessment. Note 116.

decision-making structure should be improved; and the OSCE presidency's capacity to act should be bolstered. The most heated argument was sparked off by Genscher's idea that 'the OSCE needs a European security council with the same scope as the UN Security Council. Its structure must be such as to make due allowance for the interests of small and medium-sized countries.'[119]

Russian Foreign Minister Andrey Kozyrev presented three steps for moving towards a comprehensive security system:[120]

1. A conceptual stage would be focused on the principles of shaping the model. Among the basic principles, he mentioned *indivisibility of security; comprehensiveness* and a *complex approach* (covering all aspects and spheres: military, political, legal, economic, humanitarian, cultural, ecological and others); *complementarity* of efforts of states and multilateral institutions; and *bridge-building* between different levels and dimensions—bilateral, sub-regional, regional, transregional and global.

2. A second stage, defined as a structural one, might be addressed mainly to the division of labour between different multilateral security structures. Thus Russia abandoned its initial concept of establishing a kind of hierarchy of European organizations.

3. A third stage might establish the basis of comprehensive security as embodied in treaties and international law.

In other words, Genscher and Kozyrev expressed a common desire to adopt a legally binding document, a sort of general treaty for a new security system.

The EU proposals submitted to an OSCE seminar in Vienna on 18–19 September 1995 were an essential contribution to the preparation of a decision on the future system of security.[121] Regarding the definition of challenges to security in the OSCE area the document highlighted the risks, stemming from the domestic situation in states emerging from a totalitarian or one-party system to a democracy, of: fragile political structures; lack of fully pluralist democracy based on free elections; absence of limitations on police or armed forces; ineffective guarantees of human rights and basic freedoms; and incomplete participation of the free media and non-governmental sectors in society. The EU analysis emphasized the inherent difficulties associated with the necessary reform process in the economic field. The absence of adequate infrastructures and communication networks, and the emergence of parallel economies based on speculation, can lead to the spread of organized crime, terrorism and drug trafficking. This, in turn, generates new risks and conflicts in political and security spheres.

---

[119] *OSCE Newsletter*, vol. 2, no. 8 (1995), p. 11.

[120] A. V. Kozyrev's address presented at the Moscow Conference on Twenty Years of the Helsinki Final Act—Towards a new model of European security, 17–18 July 1995. Distributed at the OSCE Seminar on a Common and Comprehensive Security Model for the Twenty-First Century, Vienna, 18–19 Sep. 1995.

[121] EU contribution to the OSCE Seminar on a Common and Comprehensive Security Model for the Twenty-First Century, Vienna, 18–19 Sep. 1995, OSCE ref. PC/477/95, Vienna, 13 Sep. 1995.

It is most likely that a future-oriented cooperative security model will both reassert the commitment to respect OSCE principles and put forward proposals to take account of the new security environment. One positive experience in recent years is the unwritten but widely applied rule of transparency of any major changes introduced by security organizations. A new security system will also generate support for peacekeeping, conflict prevention, crisis management and humanitarian relief in Europe. An increasing role in this new system will be played not only by regional but also subregional security institutions and arrangements.

The concepts and documents discussed within the framework of the work on a security model highlight an important phenomenon: the serious erosion of the state, both as an institution and in its role as the main actor on the international scene. The concomitant weakening and diminished effectiveness of multilateral organizations should be taken into account in the search for new solutions.

VI. Conclusions

Political, diplomatic and material contributions to conflict prevention and crisis management in Europe cannot be confined to one of the functioning structures. None of the European structures or institutions has a monopoly in shaping a comprehensive and common security system for Europe. The main challenge for the existing security arrangements in Europe is how to support the change and assist the CEE states and Russia in their transition to pluralist democracy and market economy while avoiding domestic and international instability.

The debate so far leads to several conclusions.

1. Agreement has emerged as to the goal: such a system would have to ensure security, stability and cooperation among *all* the European, Central Asian and North American states from Vancouver to Vladivostok. Cooperative approaches to security will be developed at the bilateral, subregional and regional levels. What *indivisibility of security* of states means in practice is still an open question. The view that security should now be seen as comprehensive and dynamic in character and embracing both political and military aspects and the economic, ecological and human dimensions is not contested. The integration of the CEE states into Western structures, which is for them a security policy priority and a guarantee of the pursuit of reform, constitutes for NATO and the EU both the challenge of how to reconcile legitimate Russian and CEE security interests and a unique opportunity to influence internal processes in those states by promoting stability in the transitional period.

2. Of equal importance for European security is respect for the 1994 Code of Conduct *between* states and abidance by the adopted principles, norms and

political commitments *within* states.[122] For this reason, there is an urgent need to read anew and redefine some of the fundamental principles governing relations between the states in the region. This applies in particular to the principle of sovereignty in the context of non-intervention and the principle of self-determination in connection with that of the integrity of states.

3. There is a close relationship between domestic and external security. Of vital importance for the new system of security is the practical application of the adopted common system of values: democracy, the rule of law, human rights and fundamental freedoms; market economy; and equal security of participating states. Unfortunately, this catalogue of common values, as laid down in the 1990 Charter of Paris for a New Europe,[123] has not been put into practice and remains mostly a verbal declaration. In other words, an integral part of the comprehensive security system and the main way to prevent conflict should be the shaping of civil societies, democratization of the domestic relations of a state, and respect for adopted principles, rules and norms.

4. In the process of shaping European security, abstract concepts, models and deliberations are far less important than the response to the real needs of preventing conflict and settling crisis. A new system of security will result from evolution and transformation of existing structures rather than an outgrowth of new institutions. Apart from the main organizations (NATO, EU/WEU, OSCE and the Council of Europe), subregional structures such as the Barents Euro-Arctic Council, the Council of Baltic Sea States and the Central European Initiative are bound to play an increasingly substantial role.

5. The adequate readjustment of armed forces to the requirements of the qualitatively new situation and the solution of the difficult problems of conversion, demobilization of troops and civilian control of the military by the democratic institutions of the OSCE states are essential. Arms control and arms reductions in Europe should remain on the list of priorities in shaping a new security system. The new arms control agenda, along with the implementation of the 1990 Treaty on Conventional Armed Forces in Europe and subsequent related agreements, should focus increasingly on the consequences of reductions in armaments, prevention of the development of new arms technologies, arms production and the introduction of an effective regime of arms transfer control, counter-proliferation, and particularly illegal transfers of armaments and arms-manufacturing technology.

The security system will emerge from the collaboration of various structures rather than from just one model. Its architecture will probably resemble concentric circles: for each state the nucleus will be the organization of the defence of its national territory (in some cases based on its own forces; in others, on alliances and agreements); the second circle will be a web of

---

[122] Code of Conduct on Politico-Military Aspects of Security in CSCE, Budapest Document 1994. Budapest Decisions (Chapter VII), Budapest 1994.
[123] The Charter of Paris for a New Europe, Paris, 21 Nov. 1990 is reprinted in Rotfeld, A. D. and Stützle, W. (eds), SIPRI, *Germany and Europe in Transition* (Oxford University Press: Oxford, 1992), pp. 219–26.

bilateral and multilateral security arrangements and agreements (arms control and disarmament); and the third will consist of security organizations and structures whose operation will be ensured by a cooperative and comprehensive security system.

The transition and transformation processes in Europe are unfinished. Russia has definitively lost its position as a superpower but retained its nuclear great power status. As the only unchallenged global superpower the USA is seeking a new role in a volatile security environment. The position of other powers, such as Germany, France and the UK, is about to undergo a dramatic transformation as a result of the common security and foreign policy evolution of the EU. The standing of both the great powers and the military security arrangements in Europe is changing. Plans to enlarge NATO and the EU have prompted more practical thinking in terms of establishing a 'pluralistic security community' (in the sense defined by Karl Deutsch[124]) while avoiding creating new strategic dividing lines or military blocs. NATO, the EU and the OSCE have made progress in redefining and rearranging the security of their own members. The next stage will be implementation of an enlargement strategy with the Central European states accompanied by building a strategic partnership with Russia to engage it in building and integrate it into a European security community. This decision would both revitalize the Atlantic community and offer Russia and its western neighbours a new cooperative security arrangement.

---

[124] Deutsch, K. W., *et al., Political Community and the North Atlantic Area* (Princeton University Press: Princeton, N.J., 1957), p. 5.

Appendix 7A. Documents on European security

EUROPEAN SECURITY: A COMMON
CONCEPT OF THE 27 WEU
COUNTRIES

Madrid, 14 November 1995

Excerpts

INTRODUCTION

1. Over the last decade, many changes have taken place in Europe. A new security architecture is under construction, made possible by the end of the Cold War. In developing the architecture, European States have acknowledged that their security is indivisible, that a comprehensive approach should underlie the concept of security and that co-operative mechanisms should be applied in order to promote security and stability in the whole of the continent. These are being strengthened through international agreements, through declarations aimed at the implementation of the principles, enshrined in the UN Charter, of the sovereign equality and inviolability of internationally recognized borders and through the establishment of international organizations based on common values of democracy, human rights and the rule of law. WEU, EU, NATO, and the OSCE each take these general principles into account when playing their respective roles in the newly emerging security architecture.

2. All European States are committed to the purposes and principles of the United Nations Charter, the OSCE documents and the Stability Pact, and all the States taking part in this common reflection are members of the Council of Europe. No other region of the world has gone so far towards building an international order based on legal instruments.

3. However, with the end of the period of global confrontation embodied in the Cold War, new kinds of security concerns, tension and conflict have emerged, to which Europe and its North American partners must find new answers.

4. WEU countries have decided to examine together the new conditions of their security. The aim of this collective endeavour, itself a contribution to the process of integration—

one of the cornerstones of peace in Europe—is to identify the common interests of Europeans, the risks and potential threats, but also Europe's new responsibilities in a strategic environment in which Europe's security is not confined to security in Europe, and in which Europe has acquired the capability to make its own contribution to the building of a just and peaceful world order.

5. To fulfil that aim, Chapter I analyses the wide range of security challenges that confront Europe. Many of these challenges will be addressed collectively through international cooperation and the process of European integration. As the defence component of the European Union and as a means to strengthen the European pillar of the Atlantic Alliance, WEU is in a position to respond to many of the challenges identified in the politico-military field.

6. Chapter II identifies some of the ways in which WEU countries, in the framework of the emerging European security architecture, can contribute to security and stability in Europe, in neighbouring areas and in the wider world. Special emphasis has been given to the responses WEU can bring to enhancing European capabilities in the field of crisis-prevention and management.

7. Finally, in this exercise for the first time all WEU countries have worked together in such an important matter as their common security. It has proved to be a singular opportunity for a better mutual understanding and provided all participants with the possibility of harmonising their views on WEU's contribution to the emerging security architecture for Europe.

Chapter I

The new European security conditions: challenges and risks

I. THE COMMON SECURITY INTERESTS OF EUROPE

A. The foundations of European Security

8. Europe is witnessing the emergence of a new framework of global security to promote greater stability throughout the continent. Europe and its neighbouring regions have a shared interest in this respect.

9. This new security framework is based on a broad concept of security. The process of European integration has made a major contribution to the security of Europe. This process has created the basis for the development of peaceful relations between European states. A landmark of major importance is the Treaty on European Union. The European Union has become a model of prosperity, stability and peace. It is striving for the economic development and stability of its members and of its partners. As a complement to its economic and commercial weight and commensurate with its wider responsibilities, it is establishing a common foreign and security policy including the eventual framing of a common defence policy, which might, in time, lead to a common defence, compatible with that of the Atlantic Alliance.[1] In this, it will rely in particular on WEU, an integral part of the development of the European Union.

10. The development of an EU Common Foreign and Security Policy, as well as all the earlier, recent and future enlargements of the EU, enhance stability and security on the Continent. The European Agreements, with their clear perspective of membership, mark the need that is felt for developing the involvement of the countries of Central and Eastern Europe in the EU's foreign and security policy. Reinforced political dialogue has been established covering in particular meetings with CFSP bodies from expert to Ministerial level and association with EU joint actions, declarations or démarches.

11. In the Treaty on European Union, WEU, which is an integral part of the development of the European Union, was requested to elaborate and implement decisions and actions of the EU which have defence implications. In June 1992 WEU Ministers agreed that, apart from contributing to the common defence in accordance with Article 5 of the Washington Treaty and Article V of the modified Brussels Treaty respectively, military units made available to WEU could be employed for humanitarian and rescue tasks, peacekeeping tasks and other tasks of combat forces in crisis management. In May 1994 WEU Ministers agreed the arrangements for Associate Partnership, thus involving the countries of Central Europe in WEU's activities. In November that year the Noordwijk Ministerial meeting endorsed preliminary conclusions on the formulation of a Common European Defence Policy.

12. Under their status of association, WEU's Associate Partners can participate in sessions of the WEU Council and working groups and may take part in WEU operations in the framework of the Petersberg Declaration. WEU, as the defence component of the EU and as the means to strengthen the European pillar of the Alliance, is being further developed in full complementarity with the transatlantic nature of the Alliance, and should not duplicate existing structures.

13. NATO continues to play an essential role in reinforcing stability and security in Europe. It has always been a political community of nations committed to promoting shared values and defending common interests. The transatlantic link, embodied by NATO and the substantial North American military presence in Europe, continues to make a crucial contribution to the security of Europe. In November 1991, NATO approved a new strategic concept. This reaffirmed the Alliance's core functions and the importance of the transatlantic link and decided that the creation of a European identity in defence and security issues would underline the preparedness of European nations to take a greater share of responsibility and help to reinforce transatlantic solidarity. At the Brussels summit in January 1994, NATO leaders agreed that the emergence of a European Security and Defence Identity (ESDI) would strengthen the European pillar of the Alliance while reinforcing the transatlantic link. They authorised the further adaptation of the Alliance's political and military structures to reflect its new roles and missions and the development of the emerging ESDI, including the development of separable but not separate capabilities that could be used by NATO or WEU.

14. The democratic revolutions and other historic transformations towards democracy at the end of the 1980's and the early 1990's and the dissolution of the Warsaw Pact brought the Cold War to an end. These developments greatly reduced the risk of massive confrontation and gave a new impetus to the process of European integration. The common historical and cultural heritage of Europe and the new political situation on the continent should be reflected in the new European security framework.

15. The successful transformation of the political, legal and economic systems of the Central and Eastern European countries and

---

[1] As called for in the WEU's Maastricht Declaration.

the process of their integration into European and transatlantic institutions are of fundamental importance for the security and stability of Europe. The enlargement of these institutions should go hand in hand with the strengthening of cooperation with all those European countries that wish it, including Russia and Ukraine.

16. Without prejudice to the efforts and responsibilities of the European Union, WEU and the Atlantic Alliance, the OSCE is performing an important role in promoting stability and cooperation throughout Europe, and with its North American partners, in particular in the field of conflict prevention. The OSCE is currently undertaking a discussion for a common and comprehensive security model for Europe in the 21st century. Bearing in mind the vast array of OSCE activities, the discussion on a Security Model can be expected to reaffirm OSCE's central position in the European security architecture, but without any mandate to control other institutions. The OSCE is, inter alia. an important venue for dialogue with those countries that do not wish or are not likely to become full members of the Western security organizations. The OSCE, as a regional arrangement in the sense of Chapter VIII of the UN Charter, should be further developed into a primary instrument of early warning, conflict prevention and crisis management.

17. The CFE Treaty to which most WEU nations are parties marked a turning point in the arms control and disarmament process in Europe. It remains a cornerstone for European security and stability. The Treaty's full and timely implementation and the preservation of its integrity is of crucial importance.

18. In addition, the agreed confidence and security-building measures enhancing transparency and predictability need to be applied faithfully and, where appropriate, to be developed further.

. . .

D. Responses; enhancing European capabilities

176. In defining its responses to the deficiencies described above, WEU must identify and implement policies and new concrete organizational steps to increase its capability to fulfil the Petersberg tasks and to enhance its contribution to European stability and security.

*Adapt national defence forces while maintaining their effectiveness

177. National defence assets are essential for the security and defence of European countries, underpin collective security and constitute the basis of collective efforts in this field. Nations are undertaking programmes to restructure their armed forces better to meet the new security challenges in crisis prevention and management fields, including peacekeeping. Modernisation of armed forces must include efforts towards greater mobility and interoperability, in order, inter alia, to enable WEU countries to cooperate together in international conflict prevention and management operations.

178. Cooperative efforts including participation in PfP present opportunities of working towards this goal.

179. National defence priorities, at a time when financial resources are necessarily limited, must take account of the obligations entered into vis-a-vis the security organizations (NATO, WEU).

*Strengthen WEU's politico-military structures

180. An important task for WEU in the coming years is to continue to develop its politico-military structures in order to be able to conduct the full range of Petersberg tasks. This includes:

– Developing closer relations with the EU at the political and working levels in respect of actions undertaken at the EU's request in the framework of Article J4 of the Treaty on European Union;

– Improving the close cooperation with NATO;

– Establishing and improving effective liaison and consultation arrangements with other relevant organizations, notably the UN and the OSCE. This will enable the most effective coordination of all the international resources devoted to a particular crisis, including non-military elements. WEU countries could also establish appropriate coordination, when they are involved on a national basis in UN or OSCE peace operations and inform as necessary the WEU Council.

*Reinforce European assets and capabilities

181. In parallel, it is important to examine and reinforce common means for action by developing WEU capabilities that are both effective and credible on a basis of transpar-

ency and complementary with NATO, avoiding unnecessary duplication and capable of undertaking the full range of Petersberg tasks, including the following:

– The implementation of the CJTF concept and the definition of separable but not separate capabilities so as to ensure effective use of CJTF where appropriate by WEU, in that case, under its command;

– Continuing the process of developing national and multinational FAWEUs [Forces Answerable to WEU], developing effective operational links between them and WEU and fully integrating them into WEU planning.

– Examination of the requirements for, and means of generating, strategic lift for the various types of operations envisaged. Thought should be given to the question of military transport aircraft.

– Development of other means for rapid generation of force packages in response to an urgent crisis. The decision on the WEU humanitarian task force will be of use in this area, and provides valuable guidelines for the coordination of military and non-military resources.

– Consideration of how to enhance interoperability between national forces. Given the multinational nature of WEU operations, greater interoperability is an essential objective, and extends to all 27 nations which may potentially take part in operations. There is a need to adopt standard operating procedures compatible with NATO and in accordance with UN principles. The Partnership for Peace programme provides a valuable means of improving interoperability. In this respect greater transparency between PFP and WEU activities would be desirable.

– Consideration of how WEU might benefit more fully from enhanced participation both of Observers and Associate Partners within WEU's activities and Petersberg operations.

– Further development of a WEU exercise and training programme which should be implemented in harmony with that elaborated within NATO. This is essential for interoperability, and to gain practical experience of decision-making procedures at all levels of the organisation.

– The setting up of an Intelligence Section in WEU, which will work on the basis of inputs to be provided by WEU nations, the Satellite Centre, NATO and other relevant sources, and which will be capable of supporting WEU in crisis situations.

– The development of WEU's capacity to use satellite imagery for security purposes by defining the basic conditions for possible WEU participation in a developing multilateral European programme.

– Consideration of the extension of access to a WEU telecommunication system to all WEU nations.

Progress in the above-mentioned areas could be improved by exploring opportunities for burden-sharing and pooling of resources.

182. The various forms of participation in WEU contribute substantially to the ability of WEU to undertake Petersberg tasks. The contribution to these tasks by the Associate Partners should be seen as the manifestation of their intention to contribute to European security and of their aspirations to accede in due course to the modified Brussels Treaty.

183. Restructuring of NATO forces is also being undertaken in the light of the Strategic Concept, with smaller and more mobile forces being an important element. WEU will need to monitor these developments and adapt its planning to cater for the new type of force structures.

* Enhancing the European defence industrial base

184. The demand for defence equipment has changed drastically in the past few years. The defence industrial base in all WEU countries is therefore undergoing major changes. European efforts in the field of crisis prevention and management have to rely on new and different kinds of defence equipment, interoperability being an important feature. The European defence industry is restructuring to adapt to changes in demand. Supplying forces with militarily effective weapons and other equipment requires reliable long-term access to leading edge technology and efficient and responsive suppliers who can respond to common needs. In this respect, the European defence industry should be capable, competitive and commercially sound. WEU countries recognize the need for European armaments cooperation. It was agreed in the WEU Maastricht Declaration to examine further proposals for enhanced cooperation in the field of armaments with the aim of creating a European armaments agency. Such proposals are being examined in the WEAG [Western European Armaments Group] framework.

Source: WEU Council of Ministers, Madrid, 14 Nov. 1995.

MINISTERIAL MEETING OF THE NORTH ATLANTIC COUNCIL HELD AT NATO HEADQUARTERS

Brussels, 5 December 1995

1. Today we are pleased to appoint Mr. Javier Solana as the new Secretary General of the Alliance and Chairman of the North Atlantic Council. We express our deep appreciation for the outstanding contribution and service rendered to our Alliance in this challenging time by Secretary General Willy Claes.

2. We meet as the Alliance is preparing itself for the implementation of the military aspects of the peace agreement for Bosnia-Herzegovina under NATO command and with the participation of other countries. This confirms the key role of the Alliance in ensuring security and stability in Europe, in line with the Alliance's New Strategic Concept. The ongoing transformation and restructuring of our Alliance, which we are determined to carry forward in 1996, has prepared us better to meet this new challenge.

The Alliance's cohesion and solidarity, together with a strong transatlantic link and partnership, are essential to our ability to perform NATO's core functions as well as to undertake an operation of this kind. We reiterate our firm commitment to this partnership, strengthened through a developing European pillar reflecting the emerging European Security and Defence Identity. We welcome the decisions announced by the French Foreign Minister at our meeting expressing France's strong commitment to engage more fully in a changing Alliance and its further transformation, as well as in the development of its European pillar. We also welcome the Transatlantic Initiative of the EU and the US to broaden the foundations of the partnership.

In 1996, the Alliance will continue the steady, measured and transparent progress leading to eventual enlargement.

3. Today, there is genuine hope that a lasting peace can be established in Bosnia-Herzegovina. Decisive action by the Alliance in support of the United Nations in the Former Yugoslavia, together with a determined diplomatic effort, broke the siege of Sarajevo and made a negotiated solution possible. We pay tribute to the men and women involved in Operations SHARP GUARD, DENY FLIGHT and DELIBERATE FORCE. We welcome the agreement initialled in Dayton for peace in Bosnia and Herzegovina. We are looking forward to the conferences in London, Paris and Bonn. We underline the importance of the civil-military interface in the implementation of the peace agreement. Quick and effective implementation of the peace agreement will be crucial for creating the conditions for the restoration of normal life in this war-torn country. We expect the parties to honour their commitments. The basic agreement on Eastern Slavonia and its rapid implementation are vital contributions to stability in the region.

Later today, we will be meeting with our Defence Ministers for a detailed discussion of arrangements for the implementation of the military aspects of a peace plan in Bosnia-Herzegovina and will issue a separate statement.

4. We are pleased that Russia will contribute to the multinational force established to implement the military aspects of the peace agreement for Bosnia-Herzegovina. We attach great importance to this cooperation between NATO and Russia, which will not only help to ensure the successful implementation of the peace settlement but will also assist in building lasting cooperative security structures in Europe. We remain convinced that the construction of such a cooperative European security architecture, with the active participation of Russia, is in the interest of both NATO and Russia, as well as of all other states in the OSCE area. We welcome the agreement in principle reached between Secretary Perry and Minister Grachev on a political consultative mechanism on IFOR operations. We look forward to its being confirmed in a formal agreement between Russia and the Alliance.

We reaffirm our commitment to close, cooperative and far-reaching relations between NATO and Russia, including mutual political consultations and practical security co-operation building on Partnership for Peace and our enhanced dialogue beyond PfP. We have initiated with Russia a dialogue on the future direction our relationship should take. To that end we put forward proposals in September on a political framework document elaborating basic principles for security cooperation as well as for development of permanent mechanisms for consultation. We look forward to a Russian response to our suggestions in carrying forward our fruitful dialogue on these subjects. Relations should be transparent, reflect common objectives, and be rooted in strict compliance with international commitments and obligations.

We are pleased that important consultations have taken place in a 16+1 format. In the course of recent months, we discussed a range of issues related to the situation in the Former Yugoslavia, the proliferation of weapons of mass destruction and the safe and secure dismantlement of nuclear weapons, the CFE Treaty, and the enhancement of our relationship. We are committed to making full use of the potential of existing NATO–Russia agreements and invite Russia to do likewise. In this context, we would especially welcome strengthened and increased Russian participation in NACC and PfP activities.

We affirm our strong support for the ongoing political and economic reforms in Russia. We will improve our information activities in order to promote better understanding of the Alliance, in particular its role in strengthening stability and security in Europe.

5. Democracy, independence, economic development and territorial integrity in all newly independent states are of direct concern to us. They constitute essential factors for stability and security in Europe. We will therefore continue to support actively the endeavours of these states and to develop further our cooperative relationships with them bilaterally as well as through the Alliance's initiatives.

In this context, we reaffirm our support for an independent, democratic and stable Ukraine. We are pleased with the new impetus which was given to NATO–Ukrainian relations during the course of this year. We note with satisfaction Ukraine's active participation in the Partnership for Peace programme and in the North Atlantic Cooperation Council. Reflecting Ukraine's importance and role in European security and stability, we are developing an enhanced relationship in accordance with the objectives agreed during the visit of the Ukrainian Foreign Minister to Brussels in September 1995. We are looking forward to Ukraine's participation in the implementation of an agreed peace plan for Bosnia-Herzegovina, which will contribute significantly to the deepening of our practical cooperation.

6. We intend to continue to develop the North Atlantic Cooperation Council and the Partnership for Peace as permanent features of the evolving European security architecture. They will continue to play an important role in forging strong, lasting links between NATO and all its Partners. By deepening interaction and developing common habits of behaviour, both NACC and the Partnership contribute increasingly to security and stability throughout Europe.

We are pleased that, in less than two years, Partnership for Peace has become firmly established and attracted widespread participation. Building on this momentum, the Alliance should ensure that the Partnership achieves its full potential. With the aim of expanding the scope of the Partnership, we are committed to:

– working with Partners to strengthen the PfP's political-military dimension and current programmes of military cooperation;

– further broadening and deepening the PfP planning and review process;

– providing opportunities for Partners to assume greater responsibilities for shaping their cooperation programmes;

– encouraging greater Partner participation in exercise planning, including the involvement of Partner Liaison Officers from the Partnership Coordination Cell;

– increasing information exchange on bilateral programmes which support PfP.

We welcome steps already taken to develop, broaden and deepen the PfP planning and review process, in particular proposals to individualise and refine the interoperability objectives and opportunities for Partners to bring a greater part of their forces into the planning and review process. We encourage all Partners to take advantage of this process.

We encourage Partners to develop individual, national plans that cover all aspects of Partnership, including civil–military relations, interoperability, defence policy and planning, etc. These plans would serve to give direction to the reform and restructuring of Partner defence establishments so as to make them more compatible with those of NATO. While these would be national plans, we stand ready to provide advice and assistance to our Partners.

To ensure that appropriate resources are available to support the evolution of the Partnership, we have tasked the Council in Permanent Session to provide before our Spring Ministerial a report on the resource and staffing requirements for the Partnership, in the context of the overall report on Alliance budgetary management, structures and procedures which we have already requested.

We are looking forward to tomorrow's meeting with our Partners in the North Atlantic Cooperation Council to discuss the state of our cooperation and to consult on current European security issues. In order to enhance the effectiveness and utility of the NACC, we have instructed the Council in Permanent Session to generate, together with our Partners, a more focused and result-oriented approach to those issues which are central to our cooperation programmes including developing common political objectives where appropriate.

Within the NACC framework, we attach particular importance to programmes designed to give increased emphasis to the development of civil-military relations and the democratic control of armed forces and to the promotion of good neighbourly relations. Building on the dialogue already underway in PfP, we look forward to working with Partners to develop common objectives to assist them in ongoing reform efforts.

We welcome the first steps taken to streamline and harmonise NACC and Partnership structures and procedures, in line with our remit of Noordwijk.

7. We note with satisfaction the progress achieved through NATO's enlargement study, the briefings to our Partners, and Partners' positive responses to our presentations. The study will remain a valuable foundation for the enlargement process.

We have considered the issues raised by Partners which now need to be addressed in greater detail. Accordingly, we have decided that in 1996 the enlargement process will consist of three elements:

– with those Partners who so wish, we would pursue, on an individual basis, intensive bilateral and multilateral consultations, building on the foundation of the enlargement study and the presentations made during the first phase. Any interested Partner would be able to pursue an intensified, individual dialogue with the Alliance.

– through further enhancement of the Partnership for Peace, the Alliance will adopt a programme of practical work that will strengthen ties between the Alliance and all of our Partners. For some Partners these activities will facilitate their ability to assume the responsibilities of membership, while for others they will serve to strengthen their long-term partnership with the Alliance.

– the Alliance will consider what internal adaptations and other measures are necessary to ensure that enlargement preserves the effectiveness of the Alliance. In particular, we must examine the resource and staffing implications of enlargement.

These three elements will constitute the next phase of the enlargement process which

NATO began in January 1994. Intensified dialogue will work in two directions. Interested Partners will learn more about the specific and practical details of Alliance membership; they can review their efforts in terms of the various precepts and principles included in the enlargement study. NATO, in turn, will learn more about what individual Partners could or could not contribute to the Alliance and could begin to identify areas for additional work. Participation in this next phase would not imply that interested Partners would automatically be invited to begin accession talks with NATO.

We have tasked the Council in Permanent Session, with the advice of the NATO Military Authorities, to develop and implement each element of this next phase starting early in 1996, taking into account the conclusions of the study and an assessment of the briefing process. This phase will continue through 1996; we will assess progress at our December 1996 Ministerial and consider the way forward.

8. We affirm the need to continue the efforts initiated by our Heads of State and Government to adapt the political and military structures of the Alliance to take account of the full range of Alliance missions, the admission of new members into the Alliance and the emerging European Security and Defence Identity.

We welcome the progress made, while recognising that much remains to be done to complete this important task. Key to these efforts is the finalisation of the CJTF concept, which is a means to provide separable, but not separate military capabilities that could be employed by NATO or the WEU, including in operations with participating nations outside the Alliance. We are very encouraged by the significant progress that has been made recently within the Alliance and consider that we now have a good basis on which to proceed to final agreement in the near term. We have tasked the Council in Permanent Session to complete, as a matter of urgency, the detailed work necessary to finalise the concept to the full satisfaction of all Allies. We welcome the WEU's continuing readiness to intensify cooperation with NATO on these matters and look forward to further close consultations between the two organisations.

9. We note with satisfaction the increasing ties between NATO and the WEU and are determined to strengthen further our relations and cooperation on the basis of agreed prin-

ciples of complementarity and transparency. We support the improvement of WEU's operational capabilities, which would strengthen the European pillar of our Alliance and enable the European Allies to take greater responsibility for shouldering their share of the common security and defence. We therefore direct the Council in Permanent Session to expedite implementation of the decisions taken in this regard at the Brussels Summit.

We attach importance to the dialogue that has been established between the two organisations, including in Joint Council meetings, on subjects of common concern and are determined to develop them further. In this connection, we have tasked the Council in Permanent Session to identify, in consultation with the WEU, additional areas of our respective activities on which exchanges of information, consultations and cooperation would be of mutual benefit. We also expect a deepening of mutually beneficial NATO–WEU cooperation in the areas of intelligence, strategic mobility and logistics, which would help in developing the WEU's operational capability.

We noted the establishment of EUROFOR and EUROMARFOR by Italy, Portugal, Spain and France and of the Franco-British Euro-Air Group. We welcome the prospect of all of these multinational capabilities becoming available to NATO as well as to the WEU, in keeping with the existing NATO commitments of participating nations, and we look forward to the early definition of the relationship of EUROFOR and EUROMARFOR to NATO. We note Luxembourg's decision to participate in the EUROCORPS and the new operational status, as of 30th November 1995, of the EUROCORPS, which will contribute to the greater operational capability of the European pillar of the Alliance.

We further welcome the 'Common Concept of the 27 WEU Countries on European Security', adopted at the WEU Council in Madrid, which represents an important contribution by the WEU to the process of developing the new European security architecture. We note with particular attention the 'WEU Contribution to the 1996 European Union Inter-Governmental Conference', which is an important contribution for the development of a European Security and Defence Identity and therefore of great relevance to the Alliance. We reiterate our support for the development of this identity, which will strengthen the European pillar of the Alliance and thus the Alliance itself. We expect that further NATO–WEU discussion of these matters will be helpful in attaining this goal.

10. The OSCE has an essential role in European security and in promoting stability on the Continent. We continue to be committed to furthering its comprehensive approach to security and to strengthening its effectiveness, particularly in conflict prevention, management and resolution. From an Alliance perspective, widening the process of democratic development throughout Europe is essential to maintaining security for all of its members. Arms control and confidence-building measures are central elements for further developing cooperative security in Europe, as are the development of norms and standards for democratic control and use of armed forces.

The OSCE will be a valuable partner of the Alliance in the implementation of a peace settlement in Bosnia. We look forward to working together with the OSCE in this endeavour. Its role in the elections process, in monitoring human rights, and in establishing confidence- and security-building measures and arms control in the Former Yugoslavia is central to the peace process. The implementation of the peace settlement will be one promising test ground for cooperation in many areas between our two organisations. We note the proposal to consider the convening of a regional table, in the context of the OSCE 'Pact on Stability'.

We support the continued efforts of the Minsk Group to achieve a political settlement of the conflict in and around Nagorno-Karabakh, which would, along with other conditions, allow the deployment of an OSCE multinational peacekeeping force, as agreed at the Budapest Summit.

We welcome the ongoing efforts of the OSCE assistance group for Chechnya, which is assisting the civilian population, monitoring the human rights situation, and supporting a political settlement of the conflict under OSCE auspices. We urge the parties to pursue meaningful negotiations seeking an end to hostilities and to the continued suffering among the civilian population.

We warmly welcome the recent meeting of the OSCE Chairman-in-Office with the North Atlantic Council and will continue our efforts to improve the pattern of contacts between NATO and the OSCE, including through senior representation at Ministerial meetings and, on a more routine basis, through the International Staff. We will continue to coordinate our contributions to the development of an OSCE Security Model for the 21st Century, which aims at the coherent development of a European security architecture including all participating states.

11. We attach great importance to the full implementation and continued integrity and effectiveness of the CFE Treaty. The Treaty is a cornerstone of European security. The reduction period, completed on 17th November, has resulted in the remarkable, unprecedented destruction of about 50,000 pieces of military equipment in Europe. Transparency and enhanced cooperation between armed forces have been important features of this process, to which NATO has made a major contribution.

However, we note with concern all cases of failure by States Parties to fulfil their Treaty obligations, among them the problem of Russia's flank obligations. We stress that compliance with legally binding obligations is a necessary foundation for good overall relations.

We welcome the 17th November Decision by the Joint Consultative Group, in which the 30 CFE States reconfirm their commitment to the Treaty and agree to find a cooperative solution to the flank problem, which does not diminish the security of any State. In this context, we specially urge all States Parties who have failed to comply with their obligations, to intensify their efforts to reach as quickly as possible such a cooperative solution acceptable to all. These problems should be addressed through an open-minded and constructive dialogue. This will provide a firm basis for the successful outcome of the Review Conference next year and the continued integrity and viability of the Treaty.

12. We reiterate our conviction that security in Europe is greatly affected by security and stability in the Mediterranean. We are satisfied with the talks held this year with a number of Mediterranean non-NATO countries (Egypt, Israel, Mauritania, Morocco and Tunisia) in order to explore the possibilities for a permanent dialogue with countries in the region. In light of the interest shown, we have decided to pursue further the dialogue, with the aim of fostering transparency and achieving a better mutual understanding with the countries to our South, and with a view to contributing to strengthening stability in the Mediterranean region. We welcome the extension of the dialogue to Jordan. Our initiative complements without duplicating other international efforts aimed at fostering stability in this region, in particular the Euro-Mediterranean Conference held in Barcelona in November 1995.

13. The Alliance's continuing success in addressing the political and defence aspects of proliferation, furthered by the work of the Senior Politico-Military Group on Proliferation and Senior Defence Group on Proliferation, demonstrates NATO's resolve to work together on common security concerns and is an important aspect of the Alliance's ongoing adaptation. We welcome and endorse this work as a contribution to enhancing NATO's ability to safeguard the security of its member states in the face of direct risks posed by NBC proliferation. We also welcome the consultations with Cooperation Partners on proliferation issues.

We reiterate our conviction that the indefinite extension of the Treaty on the Non-Proliferation of Nuclear Weapons constitutes a decisive step towards the strengthening of the international non-proliferation regime and of international security. We appeal to all states not yet party to the Treaty to accede to it at the earliest date.

We fully support the ongoing efforts in the Conference on Disarmament towards achievement as the highest priority in 1996 of a global ban on all nuclear testing. We believe that the conclusion of a Comprehensive Test Ban Treaty (CTBT) and a Fissile Material Cut-Off Treaty (FMCT) are important elements in strengthening the international non-proliferation regime, of which the cornerstone is the Nuclear Non-Proliferation Treaty. In this respect, we welcome the decision taken by France, the United Kingdom and United States in favour of a treaty prohibiting all nuclear weapon test explosions and all other nuclear explosions, which will facilitate the adoption of a total and complete test ban.

We welcome the ongoing implementation of the START I Treaty. We note the importance of an early entry into force of the START II Treaty, the Chemical Weapons Convention, and the Open Skies Treaty. We support the ongoing work to strengthen confidence in compliance with the Biological Weapons Convention. We are pleased that the Review Conference of the UN Weaponry Convention in Vienna was able to agree on a new protocol on control of blinding laser weapons, and look forward to it reaching agreement on a substantially strengthened protocol on landmines as the Conference reconvenes in Geneva.

14. International terrorist crimes cannot be justified under any circumstances. They constitute a serious threat to peace, security and stability which can threaten the territorial integrity of states. We reiterate our strong commitment to combat this scourge. We condemn all acts, methods and practices of international terrorism regardless of their origins, causes and purposes.

15. We reaffirm our commitment to the Alliance's common-funded programmes. We consider these programmes vital elements in underpinning our military structures, providing essential operating capability and strengthening Alliance cohesion. We need to ensure that resources are targetted at those programmes which will have the highest priority. We note that work is continuing on the examination of Alliance budgetary management, structures and procedures, and look forward to reports on progress by the time we next meet.

16. The Spring 1996 meeting of the North Atlantic Council in Ministerial Session will be held in Berlin, Germany, on 3rd June.

Source: NATO Final Communiqué, Ministerial Meeting of the North Atlantic Council, Brussels, 5 December 1995, Press Communiqué M-NAC-2 (95)118.

DECISION ON OSCE ACTION FOR PEACE, DEMOCRACY AND STABILITY IN BOSNIA AND HERZEGOVINA

Budapest, 8 December 1995

1. The Ministerial Council welcomes and supports the General Framework Agreement for Peace in Bosnia and Herzegovina initialled on 21 November 1995 and to be signed in Paris on 14 December 1995. In that historic Agreement, the Parties to this tragic conflict call on the OSCE to help ensure that its promise is fulfilled. On behalf of the OSCE, the Council accepts the tasks foreseen in the Agreement and its Annexes.

2. The Parties have requested the OSCE to supervise the preparation and conduct of free and fair elections in Bosnia and Herzegovina. This task is extremely important to ensure a democratic future for that country. The OSCE will also monitor—as requested—the human rights situation in Bosnia and Herzegovina.

3. The Parties have requested the OSCE to help guide the negotiating process to bring about regional stability, to build mechanisms to increase confidence and security, and to establish limitations on the weapons of war. These tasks are essential for a durable peace.

4. The OSCE will be working in concert with a wide range of institutions of the international community. Ministers are fully aware of the considerable demands which will be made upon the international community, including private organizations, in fields such as the needs of the population at the onset of winter, the return of refugees to their country and place of origin, the economic reconstruction and the establishment of a civic society. Participating States will make all efforts to meet these needs to the best of their abilities.

5. The Ministers recognize that the OSCE faces an unprecedented challenge and are aware that it will be judged by its action, not by its words. They are prepared to offer qualified people, the necessary resources, and their constant commitment to meet this challenge. This decision provides a clear mandate for action.

6. To this end, they authorize the Chairman-in-Office, the Secretary General under his direction, and other OSCE bodies and institutions to take all necessary steps to ensure effective and timely implementation of the OSCE's tasks. In this perspective, the Chairman-in-Office will represent the OSCE at the London Conference and other international meetings and conferences connected with the peace settlement. The OSCE will consult and co-operate as appropriate with the United Nations, the Council of Europe and other international organizations active in the field in fulfilling their tasks. In performing these tasks, the Chairman-in-Office will keep the Permanent Council fully informed on a regular basis and will consult with it as appropriate.

7. The Ministerial Council welcomes the opportunity offered by the Paris Conference for reflections on approaches towards ensuring lasting stability and good-neighbourly relations.

8. In anticipation of signature of the Peace Agreement in Paris, the Ministerial Council hereby decides to:

9. Establish a Mission to Bosnia and Herzegovina and pledge that adequate resources and personnel will be provided to carry out its tasks as requested by the Parties to the Agreement. The initial duration of the

Mission will be one year unless the Permanent Council, upon a recommendation of the Chairman-in-Office, decides otherwise;

10. Call for the early appointment of a Head of this Mission by the Chairman-in-Office. Under the authority of the Chairman-in-Office, the Head of Mission will be responsible for implementing the OSCE's tasks in Bosnia and Herzegovina in the fields of elections, human rights monitoring, and facilitating the monitoring of arms control and confidence- and security-building arrangements;

11. Establish, as requested by the Parties in Article II.3 of Annex 3 of the Agreement, the Provisional Electoral Commission, to be chaired by the Head of Mission, in accordance with all the provisions of Article III;

12. Pledge that, in accordance with the Agreement on Civilian Implementation of the Peace Settlement, the OSCE, and in particular the Chairman-in-Office and the Head of Mission, will co-ordinate closely with the High Representative towards the fulfilment of the latter's responsibilities for monitoring implementation of the peace settlement and for co-ordinating the activities of the civilian organizations and agencies in Bosnia and Herzegovina;

13. Authorize the Chairman-in-Office, upon the advice of the Head of Mission and following consultation with the High Representative, and after a substantial discussion, as appropriate, in the Permanent Council, to take the decisions required by Annex 3, Article I.2, regarding conditions for the elections, and Annex 3, Article II.4, regarding the date on which elections can be held;

14. Welcome the initiative of the Government of Sweden to host an informal International Expert Meeting in support of the implementation of Annex 3 on elections;

15. Accept the invitation extended to the OSCE to monitor closely the human rights situation in Bosnia and Herzegovina in accordance with the relevant Annexes of the Agreement;

16. Call for the early appointment of the Human Rights Ombudsman by the Chairman-in-Office;

17. Direct the Mission to co-operate closely with the Office of the Human Rights Ombudsman and the Human Rights Chamber in view of the OSCE's tasks of certifying the conditions for holding elections and providing assistance to the Parties in creating those conditions, and to monitor closely the human rights situation;

18. Agree that the present OSCE Mission in Sarajevo will, upon request, support also the Human Rights Ombudsman. It will be expanded and reorganized into a distinct section of the new Mission;

19. Invite the High Commissioner on National Minorities and the Office for Democratic Institutions and Human Rights to contribute to the implementation of this decision in accordance with their mandates and experience;

20. Welcome the initiative of the Government of Germany to convene, in Bonn, a meeting to initiate the process of confidence- and security-building and arms control anticipated by the Agreement on Regional Stabilization which will be organized under the auspices of the OSCE in accordance with Articles II and IV of Annex 1-B;

21. Welcome the decision of the Chairman-in-Office to designate, at the earliest possible date, after appropriate consultations, including with the most concerned States, (a) Personal Representative(s) to assist the Parties in their respective negotiations under Articles II and IV and in the implementation and verification of resulting agreements, including verification of the holdings declarations called for in Article IV, as soon as the data are submitted;

22. Welcome the commitment of the Parties to the Agreement and the readiness of all other States in the region, to co-operate fully with the OSCE concerning negotiations for a regional arms control agreement, in accordance with the Peace Agreement. The Ministerial Council authorizes the Chairman-in-Office to designate, as anticipated by Article V of the Agreement, as soon as practicable, after appropriate consultations, including with the most concerned States, a Special Representative to help organize and conduct such negotiations under the auspices of the OSCE Forum for Security Co-operation, beginning with agreement on a precise mandate. Parameters to be developed in this mandate will take into account and respect existing arms control rights and obligations including limitations already undertaken on a multilateral basis by certain States in the region; and

23. Offer the full assistance of the OSCE in establishing a Commission for facilitating the resolution of any disputes that might arise in fully implementing the regional arms control agreement of the Parties.

24. The Council takes note of the cost estimate for the operation submitted by the

Secretary General of approximately 245 million Austrian schillings for a twelve-month period. The Council directs the Permanent Council to agree before 15 January 1996 on a budget for the OSCE tasks requested by the Parties in the Peace Agreement to be funded according to established procedures. The Secretary General will assess the acceptability and value of contributions in kind. Before the budget is agreed, the Secretary General is authorized to engage the OSCE on urgent procurement orders and contracts concerning premises for the Mission up to 20% of the above-mentioned cost estimate. The Council determines that the OSCE will seek additional, including non-governmental, sources of funding and directs the establishment of a specific fund to assist in carrying out this decision. The Council welcomes the commitment of the Chairman-in-Office and the Secretary General to ensure that all OSCE action in fulfilment of the tasks in this decision is undertaken as efficiently and expeditiously as possible.

Source: OSCE, Fifth Meeting of the Ministerial Council, Decisions of the Budapest Ministerial Council Meeting, Budapest 1995, CSCE document MC (5).DEC/1, Dec. 1995.

DECISION ON A COMMON AND COMPREHENSIVE SECURITY MODEL FOR EUROPE FOR THE TWENTY-FIRST CENTURY: A NEW CONCEPT FOR A NEW CENTURY

Budapest, 8 December 1995

1. The Ministerial Council notes that, in accordance with the relevant Budapest Summit decision, a broad and comprehensive discussion has been launched on devising a concept of security for the whole OSCE region in the twenty-first century. The Council stresses the importance of the strict observance of all OSCE principles and commitments to ensure security in the century to come. The Council takes note of the progress report presented to it by the Chairman-in-Office and decides to move the work on a security model into a more operational phase, providing opportunities to continue the identification of particular security risks and challenges and examining how the OSCE principles, commitments and mechanisms should be implemented to deal most effectively with the diverse security concerns of participating States. To this end, it endorses follow-up work in preparation for the 1996 Lisbon Summit.

2. A key objective of this discussion is to apply fully the OSCE's unique capabilities and inclusive nature to the development of a common security space based on the OSCE's comprehensive and co-operative concept of security and its indivisibility. Within this space, free of dividing lines, all OSCE participating States and the organizations to which they belong will be able to work together in a constructive, complementary and mutually reinforcing way, building a genuine partnership, in full respect of the free will of their members. While doing so, they will respect the inherent right of each and every participating State to be free to choose or change its security arrangements, including treaties of alliance, as they evolve. Each participating State will respect the rights of all others in this regard. They will not strengthen their security at the expense of the security of other States. Within the OSCE, no State, organization or grouping can have any superior responsibility for maintaining peace and stability in the OSCE region, or regard any part of the OSCE region as its sphere of influence. The basis for our common efforts to design a model is the OSCE principles, including their co-equality, which, together with the high standards represented by our OSCE commitments, remain valid for both inter- and intra-State relationships.

3. The Ministerial Council decides that the work on a model should proceed in accordance with the following guidelines:

– to promote strict observance of OSCE principles and commitments, which is of paramount importance for stability and security in the OSCE region;

– to contribute to the further development of the OSCE and the effective use and strengthening of its operational capabilities;

– to promote co-operative approaches to security challenges and risks, bearing in mind the common commitment of the participating States to promote stability and security, to prevent conflicts, and to manage crises;

– to sustain the OSCE's comprehensive concept of security and its indivisibility in order to promote effective concerted responses to complex security challenges in a spirit of co-operation and solidarity in defence of the OSCE's common values;

– to further develop ways in which complementary and mutually reinforcing org-

EUROPE: NEW SECURITY ARRANGEMENTS 321

anizations work together, including through enhanced dialogue, in the common interests of security and stability in the OSCE area; to develop further the relationship between the OSCE and the United Nations on the basis of the OSCE's position as a regional arrangement under Chapter VIII of the United Nations Charter, and of the relevant provisions of the Budapest Document 1994; and

– to contribute to the transparent and democratic evolution of regional and transatlantic organizations with a view to strengthening confidence, security and stability in the OSCE region.

As work on a concept of security for the twenty-first century proceeds, additional guidelines may be introduced. Such work may benefit from continued contributions by other organizations.

4. In preparation for the Lisbon OSCE Summit, the Ministerial Council entrusts the Chairman-in-Office with the task of intensifying focused discussion on all aspects of a security model, including through a Security Model Committee, under the auspices of the Permanent Council, which can benefit from input from other OSCE fora. The Chairman-in-Office will organize the work, while maintaining its comprehensiveness, in a manner that is consistent with this decision and the attached annex, which is an integral part of the decision. As the work proceeds, specific new measures may be developed for the promotion of all dimensions of security in the OSCE region.

5. With the aim of ensuring a broad, inclusive approach to the work on a security model, the Ministerial Council:

– requests the Chairman-in-Office to keep the issue of 'a common and comprehensive security model for Europe for the twenty-first century' on the agenda of the Senior Council until the 1996 OSCE Lisbon Summit;

– requests the Chairman-in-Office to organize further seminars within the context of the work on a security model, the subjects of which will be agreed upon by the participating States; and

– encourages a wide-ranging discussion on a security model, with broad participation of government officials, non-governmental representatives, and academics.

6. The Council requests the Chairman-in-Office to keep the informal list of risks and challenges to security updated, and to encourage participating States to clarify further their perceptions of specific risks and challenges to their security.

7. Progress achieved and results available at that time will be presented by the Chairman-in-Office to the 1996 Lisbon Summit for consideration and assessment.

———

ANNEX

The Chairman-in-Office will organize the work in the following areas. These areas are indicative only and set no priorities:

– conflict prevention, including early warning and preventive diplomacy
– crisis management and post-conflict rehabilitation
– OSCE peacekeeping
– arms control including confidence-building
– enhanced co-operation in preventing and combating terrorism
– human rights and fundamental freedoms, human contacts, democracy-building
– tolerance-building
– co-operation in preventing and combating aggressive nationalism, racism, chauvinism, xenophobia, anti-semitism and ethnic cleansing
– non-military confidence-building
– co-operation in the fields of migration, refugees and displaced persons
– economic security, including sustainable economic development, well-functioning market economy, and economic co-operation
– co-operation in solving environmental problems and managing disasters
– further development of the concept of complementary and mutually reinforcing institutions, including mechanisms for transparency, consultation and co-operation
– strengthening of the OSCE
– regional co-operation
– co-operation between the OSCE area and the Mediterranean region
– security co-operation beyond the OSCE area
– . . .

Other topics may be agreed upon in the Security Model Committee.

As necessary, the Chairman-in-Office, after appropriate consultations, may set up not more than three informal subsidiary working bodies and, for each working body, appoint a co-ordinator.

———

Source: OSCE, Fifth Meeting of the Ministerial Council, Decisions of the Budapest Ministerial Council Meeting, Budapest 1995, CSCE document MC (5).DEC/2, Dec. 1995.

DECISION ON THE OSCE MINSK PROCESS

Budapest, 8 December 1995

The Ministerial Council

– confirms that the OSCE Minsk Process remains the sole forum for the settlement of the Nagorno-Karabakh conflict;

– commends the determination of the Parties to the conflict to continue to observe the cease-fire established on 12 May 1994;

– urges the Parties to release immediately all POWs and persons detained in connection with the conflict and to provide the ICRC unimpeded access to all places of detention and all detainees;

– supports the efforts of the Co-Chairmen of the Minsk Conference to achieve, in co-ordination with the Chairman-in-Office, a political agreement on the cessation of the armed conflict without any further delay. The implementation of such an agreement will eliminate major consequences of the conflict for all parties and permit the early convening of the Minsk Conference. The signing of the agreement will enable the Permanent Council to take a decision on the establishment of the OSCE peacekeeping operation, based on the valuable recommendations of the High-Level Planning Group, the work of which should continue;

– welcomes the commitments expressed to establish direct contacts, in co-ordination with the Co-Chairmanship, to achieve agreement on the principles governing the resolution of the conflict, and strongly urges that this be done quickly; and

– takes note of the expressed readiness of the Parties to address crucial issues with a view to reaching a compromise as soon as possible.

Source: OSCE, Fifth Meeting of the Ministerial Council, Decisions of the Budapest Ministerial Council Meeting, Budapest 1995, CSCE document MC (5).DEC/3, Dec. 1995.

Part II. Military expenditure, R&D, arms production and trade, 1995

Chapter 8. Military expenditure

Chapter 9. Military research and development

Chapter 10. Arms production

Chapter 11. The trade in major conventional weapons

8. Military expenditure

PAUL GEORGE, BENGT-GÖRAN BERGSTRAND, SUSAN
CLARK and EVAMARIA LOOSE-WEINTRAUB*

I. Introduction

Aggregate world military spending continued to decline over the past year. This is because NATO expenditure, which is the largest component of global military spending, declined by some 5.1 per cent overall in real terms in 1995. However, military spending continues to increase in certain countries and regions, notably in the Middle East and South-East Asia. Malaysia, for example, showed a 6.5 per cent increase in military spending over 1994. Military spending in India and Pakistan, which had been growing quickly in recent years, appears to have stabilized in 1995. Conflict continues to drive military spending in many countries. For example, security expenditure in Algeria has dramatically increased—by 144 per cent ín real terms over 1994—as a result of the Islamic insurgency. Similarly, the civil war in Sri Lanka has resulted in much higher levels of defence expenditure, disappointing the hopes discussed in the *SIPRI Yearbook 1995*.

The lack of reliable information on defence spending for many important countries and regions of the world continues to make it impossible to determine a meaningful figure for total world military spending. China, in particular, presents the analyst with significant problems in determining the accuracy and reliability of its reported data on military spending. Globally, the difficulty of data collection has been compounded by the poor response from many developing countries to SIPRI's requests for military expenditure information in 1995.[1] This is disturbing as the widespread dissemination of military spending information is recognized as one of the major means by which to build confidence between states.

A promising development is that Russia, for the first time, submitted data on its military spending to the UN in 1995 for the years 1992–94. Nevertheless, uncertainty about information on inflation and other economic developments makes it particularly difficult in the case of Russia to assess the country's military spending burden accurately.

---

[1] SIPRI's questionnaires for defence spending information, which are sent to more than 170 countries either through their representatives in Stockholm or directly to the ministries involved, produced only a 12% response. For African countries the response rate was 4%, for Asia 9% and for Central America 6%. Many embassies replied to SIPRI's requests by referring to the relevant defence or finance departments in their respective countries, where invariably follow-up requests failed to generate a reply. Two countries, Cyprus and Peru, explicitly declined to reveal their military spending.

* Section I, the subsection on Russia in section III, section V and section VII were written by P. George, section II by B.-G. Bergstrand, the subsection on Central Asia in section III by S. Clark and sections IV and VI by E. Loose-Weintraub.

SIPRI Yearbook 1996: Armaments, Disarmament and International Security

Section II of this chapter examines developments in NATO, with particular emphasis on the USA. Section III analyses defence budget developments in Russia, including an assessment of the impact of the war in Chechnya on military spending, and provides an overview of developments in the Central Asian republics and a detailed examination of defence expenditure in Kazakhstan. Section IV deals with Australia and New Zealand. In keeping with SIPRI's objective of providing greater coverage of military spending in developing regions, section V examines South Africa and section VI analyses the Central American states.

II. NATO

For nearly a decade, since reaching its highest level in 1987, aggregated NATO military spending has been declining in real terms.[2] The overall spending pattern for 1995, showing a decline in real terms of 5.1 per cent, did not deviate much from the general trend that has marked recent years.

The total NATO spending figure is much influenced by developments in the USA, as US military spending constitutes 58.7 per cent of total NATO spending;[3] in the USA spending fell in 1995 by 6.2 per cent. In the three highest-spending European member states, which together account for another 26.1 per cent of NATO's spending total, military expenditure also fell—in France by 4.4 per cent, in Germany by 0.5 per cent and in the UK by 5.9 per cent.

Similarly, as shown in tables 8A.1 and 8A.2, many other NATO countries such as Italy, the Netherlands, Spain and Canada also show a trend of falling military expenditure. In a few (Denmark, Greece and Norway) spending remains roughly at the same level as in previous years, while only Luxembourg, Portugal and Turkey show a trend of increased military spending, and even in Luxembourg and Turkey spending actually declined in 1995. In Turkey the problem of calculating changes in real terms is further complicated by the difficulty of establishing the rate of inflation.

While overall NATO military spending has decreased, as it has done for nearly a decade, gross domestic product (GDP) has been increasing, so that the military is allocated an ever smaller share of the national income.[4] The share of GDP devoted to military spending may be interpreted as an indicator of how high a priority a country puts on defence and how big an economic burden military spending constitutes. The falling GDP share thus indicates that politically NATO countries currently give much less priority to defence than previously, and that economically the present level of spending is less burdensome.

---

[2] See table 8A.2, appendix 8A.

[3] US military spending as a proportion of total NATO military spending at current prices and current exchange rates. A share calculated in this way gives a fairer result than one based on constant prices.

[4] See table 8A.3, appendix 8A.

Table 8.1. NATO distribution of military expenditure by category, 1986–95

Figures are in US $m. at 1990 prices and exchange rates. Figures in italics are percentage changes from previous year.

		1986	1987	1988	1989	1990	1991	1992	1993	1994	1995
North America											
Canada	Personnel	5 246	5 296	5 280	5 526	5 773	5 144	5 231	4 976	5 238	4 536
	Other oper. exp.	3 426	3 435	3 675	3 461	3 718	3 041	2 966	3 119	2 925	2 838
	Equipment	2 269	2 458	2 338	2 123	1 963	1 885	1 950	2 003	1 773	1 829
	Equip. change		*8.3*	*−4.9*	*−9.2*	*−7.5*	*−4.0*	*3.4*	*2.7*	*−11.5*	*3.2*
USA	Personnel	119 947	118 906	121 771	122 403	112 058	116 206	111 658	104 415	99 075	93 848
	Other oper. exp.	122 627	117 581	115 294	111 829	122 468	75 856	103 418	101 186	76 465	73 602
	Equipment	86 442	87 772	80 317	81 068	75 930	73 435	65 063	59 204	74 179	65 980
	Equip. change		*1.5*	*−8.5*	*0.9*	*−6.3*	*−3.3*	*−11.4*	*−9.0*	*25.3*	*−11.1*
Europe											
Belgium	Personnel	3 050	3 116	3 061	3 175	3 177	3 155	2 455	2 485	2 461	2 487
	Other oper. exp.	1 072	1 018	980	946	924	920	797	732	721	710
	Equipment	643	657	577	468	367	375	308	250	277	232
	Equip. change		*2.2*	*−12.3*	*−18.8*	*−21.7*	*2.3*	*−17.9*	*−18.9*	*10.8*	*−16.3*
Denmark	Personnel	1 414	1 469	1 574	1 584	1 547	1 543	1 502	1 507	1 519	1 533
	Other oper. exp.	668	721	657	612	620	612	577	693	590	591
	Equipment	353	397	391	347	395	426	471	387	411	371
	Equip. change		*12.4*	*−1.5*	*−11.2*	*13.8*	*7.9*	*10.6*	*−17.8*	*6.2*	*−9.8*
Germany	Personnel	19 346	19 960	20 000	20 515	22 049	22 196	22 090	20 183	19 218	19 246
	Other oper. exp.	9 972	10 102	10 262	9 635	8 041	8 980	8 896	8 461	7 460	7 076
	Equipment	8 137	8 155	7 767	7 628	7 491	6 118	5 014	3 772	3 445	3 459
	Equip. change		*0.2*	*−4.8*	*−1.8*	*−1.8*	*−18.3*	*−18.0*	*−24.8*	*−8.6*	*0.4*
Greece	Personnel	2 386	2 379	2 373	2 349	2 476	2 359	2 338	2 311	2 381	2 427
	Other oper. exp.	792	740	656	535	475	498	487	390	454	571
	Equipment	610	663	950	836	827	744	891	918	922	759
	Equip. change		*8.7*	*43.2*	*−12.0*	*−1.2*	*−10.1*	*19.8*	*3.0*	*0.5*	*−17.7*

	1986	1987	1988	1989	1990	1991	1992	1993	1994	1995
Italy										
Personnel	11 648	13 393	13 938	14 266	14 400	15 195	14 653	14 547	14 797	13 876
Other oper. exp.	4 158	4 086	4 630	4 496	4 231	4 077	4 256	4 024	3 835	3 699
Equipment	3 714	4 676	4 943	4 982	4 091	3 864	3 451	3 978	3 496	3 357
Equip. change		25.9	5.7	0.8	-17.9	-5.5	-10.7	15.3	-12.1	-4.0
Luxembourg										
Personnel	60	68	76	72	77	75	84	79	88	86
Other oper. exp.	9	9	17	11	10	10	10	8	12	11
Equipment	2	3	3	4	3	6	5	3	2	5
Equip. change		43.9	-18.1	24.4	-12.4	86.4	-11.1	-44.5	-17.3	97.8
Netherlands										
Personnel	3 827	4 072	4 106	4 101	4 000	3 984	4 125	3 914	3 707	3 679
Other oper. exp.	1 776	1 816	1 520	1 695	1 655	1 653	1 621	1 450	1 329	1 425
Equipment	1 515	1 352	1 542	1 344	1 328	1 126	1 019	923	1 068	948
Equip. change		-10.7	14.1	-12.9	-1.2	-15.3	-9.5	-9.4	15.8	-11.3
Norway										
Personnel	1 475	1 490	1 495	1 435	1 470	1 525	1 563	1 197	1 212	1 178
Other oper. exp.	860	912	899	809	825	734	789	938	965	928
Equipment	653	702	617	836	767	724	871	918	990	854
Equip. change		7.5	-12.2	35.5	-8.2	-5.6	20.2	5.4	7.8	-13.7
Portugal										
Personnel	995	1 027	1 153	1 302	1 371	1 442	1 592	1 523	1 465	1 455
Other oper. exp.	359	322	330	255	246	254	237	277	305	330
Equipment	95	158	183	217	193	164	44	137	78	282
Equip. change		66.6	15.6	18.9	-11.0	-15.3	-73.4	215.8	-43.1	260.6
Spain										
Personnel	..	4 968	5 093	5 540	5 613	5 677	5 639	5 497	5 256	5 345
Other oper. exp.	..	2 159	2 018	2 059	2 082	1 825	1 517	2 047	1 644	1 495
Equipment	2 083	2 469	1 934	1 769	1 150	1 132	884	1 191	969	1 133
Equip. change		18.5	-21.7	-8.5	-35.0	-1.6	-21.9	34.7	-18.7	17.0

Turkey	Personnel	1 509	1 498	1 354	2 027	2 567	2 650	2 799	3 463	3 169	2 295
	Other oper. exp.	1 931	1 653	1 426	1 447	1 515	1 420	1 322	1 252	1 062	896
	Equipment	811	911	856	756	1 063	1 240	1 425	1 455	1 820	2 012
	Equip. change		12.3	-6.1	-11.6	40.5	16.7	14.9	2.1	25.1	10.5
UK	Personnel	16 718	16 599	16 543	16 113	16 149	17 133	16 268	15 796	14 383	13 365
	Other oper. exp.	13 632	13 875	12 072	14 032	14 478	14 175	13 073	8 606	8 685	7 222
	Equipment	10 803	10 513	10 324	8 974	7 120	7 971	6 722	9 441	8 651	9 215
	Equip. change		-2.7	-1.8	-13.1	-20.7	12.0	-15.7	40.4	-8.4	6.5
NATO Europe	Personnel	..	70 040	70 765	72 478	74 896	76 933	75 109	72 503	69 655	66 970
	Other oper. exp.	..	37 414	35 467	36 533	35 102	35 160	33 584	28 877	27 061	24 954
	Equipment	29 419	30 656	30 086	28 162	24 794	23 889	21 105	23 373	22 130	22 626
	Equip. change		4.2	-1.9	-6.4	-12.0	-3.7	-11.7	10.7	-5.3	2.2
NATO total	Personnel	..	194 242	197 817	200 407	192 727	198 283	191 997	181 894	173 968	165 355
	Other oper. exp.	..	158 430	154 436	151 823	161 288	114 057	139 969	133 182	106 451	101 394
	Equipment	118 131	120 886	112 741	111 352	102 688	99 209	88 118	84 581	98 083	90 435
	Equip. change		2.3	-6.7	-1.2	-7.8	-3.4	-11.2	-4.0	16.0	-7.8

Note: France does not return figures giving this breakdown to NATO. NATO data include a fourth category—infrastructure—which is of limited importance for most countries, constituting only a few per cent of their total budget and has been excluded. NATO publishes percentage shares and the totals for the different categories here are calculated using these percentages and total expenditure as shown in table 12A.2. Calculations are based on rounded input data.

Sources: NATO, Financial and Economic Data Relating to NATO Defence, Press release M-DPC-2(94) 125, 14 Dec. 1994; NATO, Financial and Economic Data Relating to NATO Defence, Press release M-DPC-2(95) 115, 29 Nov. 1995; and *NATO Review*, no. 1 (1990), p. 31; no. 1 (1991), p. 33; no. 1 (1992), p. 33; Feb. 1993, p. 33; and Apr. 1994, p. 33.

The present trend of falling military spending in real terms will undoubtedly continue into the next few years, as many NATO countries—not least most of the major spenders mentioned above[5]—have announced plans or indicated that military spending will be cut further. At the end of the 1990s this declining trend may flatten out, leaving military spending stagnant in real terms at the then existing level; but it will continue to decline as a proportion of GDP so long as national incomes continue to grow.

Table 8.1 shows the distribution of military expenditure between different categories—personnel; other operating expenditures; and equipment—for the NATO member countries except France. In general, comparisons between procurement budgets are more difficult than comparisons of military budget totals: definitions differ, countries may not include the same items in their defence budgets, they may classify the different sections of their defence budgets differently and there is no generally agreed borderline between procurement, operations and maintenance (O&M) and research and development (R&D). NATO data, however, are strictly comparable. Of particular interest because of their implications for the defence industry and the arms trade are developments in spending on equipment.

The United States

US defence spending developments in 1995 were mainly influenced by three underlying factors: (a) the more than usually tense budget battle between the President and Congress: the 1996 budget had still not been passed at the time of writing (January 1996); (b) the implementation of the Bottom–Up Review (BUR) and the ongoing debate on new and evolving threat perceptions; and (c) internal management issues like base closures, procurement reform and defence industry problems.

The elections to Congress in November 1994 gave both the House of Representatives and the Senate a Republican majority with the conflicting priorities of a balanced budget, tax reductions and increases in military spending. Defence was not among the top issues during the election, but there was Republican criticism of the Democratic Administration for neglect of the armed forces. In its budget for FY 1996, released in February 1995, the administration requested $258.3 billion in budget authority and $262 billion in outlays.[6] Congress attempted to increase defence spending above the level of the February 1995 budget: on 15 June and on 6 September 1995, the House of Representatives and the Senate passed their respective defence authorization bills, calling for defence spending of $267.3 billion and $264.7 billion, respectively, compared to the administration's proposed authorization of $257.6

---

[5] The exception may here be Germany, where military spending has fallen very rapidly since 1990. This decline may be about to level off.

[6] George, P. et al., 'World military expenditure', SIPRI Yearbook 1995: Armaments, Disarmament and International Security (Oxford University Press: Oxford, 1995), p. 398–99.

billion.[7] One of the most striking differences between the congressional budget proposals and the administration's original budget was that the House and Senate budgets approved expenditure on ballistic missile defences.[8] Politically, the situation is the opposite to what it has been for a long time; Presidents Ronald Reagan and George Bush presented Congress with defence budgets that were then cut by Congress, while President Clinton's defence budgets have been raised by Congress, providing funds that were never requested.[9]

Several of the issues discussed as budget issues relate to a wider security debate. A new, slightly paradoxical, feature in current US budget politics is that many of the congressmen who favour increasing defence spending are also opposed to the USA taking on new international responsibilities, while those who favour cuts in defence spending also advocate greater international commitment. In particular, there has been much opposition to the USA shouldering a bigger peacekeeping burden.[10] At the time of writing it was not certain how much expenditure on peacekeeping Congress would approve. In late November 1995, Clinton offered Congress a compromise, saying that he would approve a higher defence budget that would clear the way for the FY 1996 budget provided that part of the new monies was spent on the Bosnia and other peacekeeping missions instead of new weapon procurement.[11]

On 30 November, President Clinton signed the Defense Appropriations Bill, which provided $243.3 billion for defence appropriations, about $7 billion more than the administration had originally requested.[12] When combined with funding in other defence-related appropriations bills, the resulting expenditure level is roughly consistent with the congressional budget resolutions passed in June.

Within the armed forces, in the aftermath of the BUR, several new studies have been carried out on future force postures, security threats and the costs and affordability of alternatives. In a classified report, the Department of Defense concluded that the BUR was affordable, partly because huge savings would be made on base closures.[13] Even so, suggestions have been put forward that a new comprehensive overview like the BUR must be undertaken

---

[7] Slightly adjusted from the figure that originally appeared in the Feb. 1995 budget. 'More muscular Pentagon bill heads to House floor', *Congressional Quarterly*, 10 June 1995, p. 1659; 'Conflict looms over B-2 and F-22 as bill heads to House floor', *Congressional Quarterly*, 29 July 1995, p. 2292; 'Senate adds billions in weapons to Clinton budget request' and 'Missile provision stalls Senate's final action', *Congressional Quarterly*, 12 Aug. 1995, pp. 2448, 2452; 'Compromise on missile defenses ensures Senate bill's passage', *Congressional Quarterly*, 9 Sep. 1995, p. 2731; 'Analysis: the House and Senate: the sides of the defence spending coin', *Jane's Defence Weekly*, 19 Aug. 1995, p. 15; and 'B-2, subs inhabit legislative limbo', *Defense News*, 11–17 Sep. 1995, p. 4.

[8] See also chapter 9, section III and chapter 14, section VI in this volume.

[9] 'Dead on arrival: Republicans dissect the president's defense budget', *Armed Forces Journal International*, Mar. 1995, p. 10.

[10] 'House votes to sharply rein in US peacekeeping expenses', *Congressional Quarterly*, 18 Feb. 1995, p. 535.

[11] 'Offer to trade defence bill for Bosnia mission', *Financial Times*, 30 Nov. 1995.

[12] Defense Budget Project, *Effect of the FY 1996 Appropriations Act on Major Weapons Programs and Contractors* (Defence Budget Project: Washington, DC, 4 Dec. 1995).

[13] 'Study: budget gap dwarfs all estimates', *Defense News*, 30 Jan.–5 Feb. 1995, p. 12; and 'DoD: Bottom-Up Review is affordable', *Defense News*, 29 May–4 June 1995, p. 1.

soon, perhaps in 1997.[14] Future threats and the need to develop the force posture accordingly have been the subject of some debate, *inter alia* on how questions of technological change should be handled.[15] The need for mobility at all levels, from strategic air transport to the way a group of soldiers operates at the tactical level, seems to be particularly stressed.[16] It is also against this background that the high priority given to the acquisition of new transport aircraft, the C-17,[17] and the V-22 tilt rotor aircraft[18] should be seen. Prepositioning of military equipment is also seen as vital.[19] It is worth noting that some studies point to an increased threat—in spite of present arms control initiatives—from nuclear, biological and chemical weapons, perhaps delivered not only by missiles, bombs or artillery but also by small unmanned aerial vehicles. This may have an impact on future spending priorities.[20]

Other defence spending issues discussed in 1995 which were not directly related to such threat perceptions but were nevertheless important as they would, supposedly, free money and other resources for more urgent tasks were base closures and depot privatization. As force numbers have been cut, the need for an extensive base infrastructure is also declining. In 1991, it was agreed that a non-partisan commission, designed to avoid lobbying and electoral politics, should recommend what bases should be closed, and rounds of base closures were carried out in 1989, 1991 and 1993, many of them of foreign bases. In spite of these closures, the armed forces still had too many bases for the numbers of personnel, and a new review was carried out. A first list of bases to be closed or 'realigned' was presented in late February 1995 and more bases were added later. The closing of some US Air Force bases in California was subject to particular debate and local protest. Nevertheless, in mid-July 1995 President Clinton accepted the recommendations of the commission, calling for the closure of 79 military installations and the realignment of 26 others, which is estimated to save some $19.3 billion over the next 20 years.[21]

It was also proposed that privatization of depots which carry out repair and maintenance, and perhaps also of bases as such, could save money, and in the

---

[14] 'DoD mulls 1997 Bottom-Up Review', *Defense News*, 1117 Sep. 1995, p. 1.

[15] 'Futuristic DoD falters over focus', *Defense News*, 23–29 Jan. 1995, p. 1.

[16] 'Pentagon review reaffirms US mobility stance', *Defense News*, 6–12 Mar. 1995, p. 3; and 'US may send small, mobile units to future war', *Defense News*, 5–11 June 1995, p. 1.

[17] 'C-17 wins praise as commercial option prospects dim', *Defense News*, 10–16 Apr. 1995, p. 34; 'C-17 buy is top question in US military lift strategy', *Defense News*, 3–9 July 1995, p. 9; and 'C-17's performance may spur DoD to buy more aircraft', *Defense News*, 4–10 Sep. 1995, p. 36.

[18] 'US strives to hasten V-22 buys', *Defense News*, 14–20 Aug. 1995, p. 4.

[19] 'US military emphasizes vital role of prepositioned gear', *Defense News*, 10–16 Apr. 1995, p. 22.

[20] 'DoD wargame demonstrates bio warfare's potent threat', *Defense News*, 13–19 Mar. 1995, p. 1; 'US experts: Russian chemical agents are global threat', *Defense News*, 16–22 Oct. 1995, p. 18; and 'US experts fear spread of UAV technology', *Defense News*, 28 Aug.–3 Sep. 1995, p. 12.

[21] 'GOP says proposed cuts fail to pass muster', *Congressional Quarterly*, 4 Mar. 1995, p. 694; 'Pentagon looks for 5th BRAC round', *Jane's Defence Weekly*, 11 Mar. 1995, p. 31; 'Commission expands list of facilities to be cut', *Congressional Quarterly*, 13 May 1995, p. 1339; 'Clinton strains to save jobs at California depot', *Congressional Quarterly*, 8 July 1995, p. 2006; 'Angry Clinton accepts list, seeks to privatize jobs', *Congressional Quarterly*, 15 July 1995, p. 2086; and 'The McClellan factor', *The Economist*, 15 July 1995, p. 39.

coming years privatization may become a more important issue.[22] Another defence economic management question which has been the subject of some debate is the proposal for procurement reform. It has been suggested both that the rules guiding military procurement should be relaxed and that the armed services should give up their right of purchasing weapons themselves to a central Pentagon authority.[23]

III. Russia and Central Asia

Russia[24]

As in previous years, the Russian defence budget allocation for 1995 was subject to considerable lobbying.[25] The government's initial budget plan, submitted to the Duma, the lower house of the Russian Parliament, on 26 October 1994, called for 45.27 trillion roubles (c. $10 billion)[26] in defence spending. During the budget debate in the Duma several amendments were introduced by various political parties arguing for a wide range of increases in the defence budget. After the fourth reading the Duma approved a final figure for defence of 48.6 trillion roubles on 15 March 1995, including a 2 trillion rouble repayment of money owed to the defence industry for weapons manufactured in 1994.[27] Subsequent revisions to the defence budget in August and December 1995 resulted in a total national defence authorization of 59 trillion roubles (c. $13 billion).[28] The breakdown of the defence budget of December 1995 is shown in table 8.2.

As in Soviet times, many additional costs associated with defence appear in other areas of the state budget. The 1995 budget allocates 2.9 trillion roubles ($644 million) for the Border Troops, but this appears under the heading of 'Law Enforcement and State Security'.[29] A number of military-related agencies are now considered to be semi-autonomous and 'civilian' for budgetary purposes. These include the Defence Federal Road-Building Directorate, formerly the Construction Troops, and the Federal Administration of Railway Troops, now attached to the Railways Ministry. These particular kinds of

[22] 'Panel may urge greater emphasis on depot privatization', *Defense News*, 23–29 Jan. 1995, p. 18; 'Officials eye privatizing US military depot operations', *Defense News*, 12–18 June 1995, p. 12; 'DoD wants depot policy to pave way for parterships', *Defense News*, 19–25 June 1995, p. 20; 'DoD looks closer at privatization in effort to cut services' costs', *Defense News*, 25 Sep.–1 Oct. 1995, p. 22; and 'Owens: US military would save by privatizing bases', *Defense News*, 9–15 Oct. 1995, p. 26.

[23] 'DoD panel urges limited oversight of weapon buys' and 'Advantages outweigh risks in DoD procurement reform', *Defense News*, 9–15 Jan. 1995, p. 6, 26; 'GOP takes another swing at procurement overhaul', *Congressional Quarterly*, 7 Oct. 1995, p. 3075; and 'Acquisition reform accord eludes US budget conferees', *Defense News*, 16–22 Oct. 1995, p. 12.

[24] In the analysis and translations from the Russian in this section, the authors are grateful for help provided by Prof. Julian Cooper, Centre for Russian and East European Studies, University of Birmingham.

[25] For a discussion of the Russian defence budget process, see George (note 6), pp. 399–408.

[26] The rate of exchange taken here for the whole of 1995 is 4500 roubles : US$1.

[27] Translation of the defence budget debate provided by the Russian Academy of Sciences, Moscow, 12 May 1995.

[28] *Kommersant-Daily*, 21 Dec. 1995.

[29] *Rossiyskaya Gazeta*, 4 Jan. 1996.

Table 8.2. Russia's defence budget, 1995

Figures are in trillion current roubles. Figures in italics are percentages.

		Percentage of total budget
Operations and maintenance (O&M)	31.880	*53.7*
Procurement	10.275	*17.3*
Research and development (R&D)	4.936	*8.3*
Construction	6.138	*10.4*
Pensions	4.867	*8.2*
Ministry of Defence total	**58.096**	*97.9*
Minatom (nuclear weapons)	1.017	*1.7*
Mobilization	0.250	*0.4*
Other	0.016	*..*
Total defence budget	**59.379**	*100.0*

Note: Budget as approved by President Yeltsin on 27 Dec. 1995.

Source: *Rossiyskaya Gazeta,* 4 Jan. 1996. Analysis provided by Julian Cooper, Centre for Russian and East European Studies, University of Birmingham.

agency have grown appreciably in size as the regular forces and the defence budget have been reduced. There are also substantial non-military allocations to support military R&D. The Russian Space Agency retains much of its traditional military role, but the cost of a contingent of conscripts, drafted in January 1995 to work on the 'civilian' space launch programme, will be paid outside the military budget.[30] It has been suggested that a truer figure for defence expenditure would be around 40 per cent of total expenditure if these and other off-budget items were included.[31]

According to one source, the defence budget was 3.6 per cent of GDP in 1995,[32] which would appear to represent a fall from the level of 1994, estimated by former Prime Minister Yegor Gaidar at 4.3 per cent.[33] In reality it is impossible to tell what the precise figure is because data on inflation, GDP and off-budget items are unavailable or unreliable. A recent study by Gos-komstat, the Russian State Statistics Committee, and the World Bank indicates that the decline in Russian GDP has been less than previously thought and that it is more likely to have fallen by one-third than by a half between 1990 and 1994.[34] Clearly, until such time as Russian statistics can be relied upon all attempts to determine the true level of military expenditure will be problem-atical. According to the budget, the government appears to be aiming to hold defence expenditure at about the same proportion of total government expenditure as last year (around 18–20 per cent), but this is not certain.

[30] Leskov, S., 'Baykonur vne oboronnogo byudzheta nabiraet sobstvennuyu armiyu' [Baykonur outside the defence budget is assembling its own army], *Izvestia,* 28 Dec. 1994, p. 2.

[31] *The Economist,* 23 Sep. 1995, pp. 32, 37.

[32] *Delovoy Mir,* 17 Jan. 1996, p. 3.

[33] 'Gaidar: NATO no threat to Russia', Foreign Broadcast Information Service, in *Daily Report—Central Eurasia (FBIS-SOV),* FBIS-SOV-95-076, 20 Apr. 1995, pp. 18–19.

[34] *The Economist,* 7 Oct. 1995, p. 107.

Russia plans to reduce its armed forces to 1.7 million by the end of 1995, down from 2.3 million at the beginning of 1994.[35] Although the military is committed to a smaller, professional army, this cannot be achieved under present budgetary conditions. Partly in response to budgetary pressures, conscription was extended by six months, to 24 months, on 1 October 1995.

Defence Minister Pavel Grachev has been vociferous in his criticism of the declining defence budget allocation. His displeasure became apparent in October 1995 when he announced that 123 officers, including 23 generals, had been ordered to run for office in December's parliamentary elections to try to gain better representation of the armed forces' interests.[36] Following the 1995 budget allocation, Grachev argued that 83 trillion roubles $18 billion) was the minimum required to maintain morale and combat readiness in an army which was irregularly paid, inadequately housed and short of essential equipment. In the debate over the 1996 defence budget allocation on 25 September 1995, he argued that the needs of the armed forces could not be met in a situation where defence spending has been in dramatic decline since the end of the cold war.[37]

In fact the debate over defence spending is following a familiar pattern, with the Defence Ministry routinely asking for a huge increase in the budget in each funding cycle and the Finance Ministry offering substantially less. An additional problem for the military, however, is that, although the accepted expenditure is far less than the Defence Ministry asks for, even this reduced sum is disbursed erratically, if at all, and carried-over debt simply contributes to shortfalls in defence funding.[38] According to Alexander Piskunov, Deputy Chairman of the Duma Defence Committee, by September 1995 the government debt to the army 'and other fields of defence' was 11.9 trillion roubles ($2.6 billion) or 23.4 per cent of defence spending. The annual budget of food supplies had been used up and the payment of allowances was delayed by more than one month.[39]

The real shortage of funds is having a major impact on force readiness and modernization programmes, as well as retarding the essential military reform process. The Russian Air Force, for example, has seen its capabilities slowly eroded as procurement requirements have been shelved because of budget problems. Spare parts deliveries are reportedly down by some 70 per cent.[40]

The impact of the budget crisis is even more profound at the human level. Military personnel have suffered an enormous decline in their standard of living since the end of the cold war. At the beginning of 1995, up to 130 000 military personnel were said to be without apartments and living in temporary

---

[35] *International Herald Tribune*, 26 Oct. 1994, p. 2. The 1995 budget from its first draft included a target for total manpower of 1 469 000 uniformed servicemen and 600 000 civilians by 1 Jan. 1996. *Nezavisimaya Gazeta*, 3 Nov. 1994, p. 5. The 1996 budget also set a target of 1 469 000 uniformed servicemen by 1 Jan. 1996. *Rossiyskaya Gazeta*, 10 Jan. 1996.

[36] Scott, C., 'Russian army drafted for vote rigging duty', *Sunday Times*, 1 Oct. 1995, p. 18.

[37] 'Grachev urges increased spending by R17–18 trillion', in FBIS-SOV-95-186, 26 Sep. 195, p. 54.

[38] For a description of how defence disbursements are delayed, see George (note 6), pp. 406–07.

[39] 'Duma Defence Committee demands raise in 1996 budget', in FBIS-SOV-95-192, 4 Oct. 1995, p. 29.

[40] 'Cash crunch hits Russian AF', *Forecast International, World Aerospace & Defense Intelligence*, 5 May 1995, pp. 10–11.

accommodation.[41] The military's 1995 budget allocation for food covered only about 25 per cent of its requirements and surplus equipment has been sold off in order to make ends meet. Similarly, emergency rations have been used to feed personnel in several military districts and fleets.[42]

Such funding problems have been standard fare since the collapse of the Soviet Union but they have certainly been compounded during 1995 by the war in Chechnya.

The impact of the war in Chechnya on Russian military spending

The Russian military intervention in the separatist autonomous republic of Chechnya, which began in December 1994, has undoubtedly been a major strain on the defence budget. Exactly how much the operation has cost is, however, a particularly complex issue and involves analysing not only those expenses directly related to military action, such as loss of equipment, additional fuel costs and munitions, but also the cost of reconstructing damaged or destroyed infrastructure and industry. The government has consistently maintained that the expenses of the war will not increase budget outlays but has not provided a definition of how the military operations are financed.[43] The difficulty of assessing the true cost of the campaign is further complicated by the government's efforts to play down the military and financial significance of the conflict. This is probably out of embarrassment at the humiliation the Interior Troops and Russian Army suffered in the first few weeks of the intervention, and also because the extent of the damage to the city of Grozny is evidence that this has been a very costly and badly mismanaged affair.

Even discounting reconstruction costs, the military expenses in Chechnya have clearly been enormous. According to General Vasiliy Vorobev, chief of the Main Administration of Military Budget and Financing of the Defence Ministry, in the first month of the war, from 11 December 1994 until 12 January 1995, expenditure on the operation reportedly amounted to more than 550 billion roubles ($122 million).[44] In February 1995 expenditure on military operations in Chechnya was said to be 12–14 billion roubles daily.[45] According to a source in the Finance Ministry, the military costs of the first 45 days of the war were estimated to have been 800 billion roubles ($177 million), which could mean a total cost for 1995, after inflation, of around 7.5 trillion roubles.[46] In July 1995 the government reported to the Duma that the cost of the war was about 2.5 trillion roubles ($555 million) but this was challenged by Andrey Illarionov, Director of the Institute of Economic Analysis, who put total military spending in Chechnya closer to $6 billion, not

[41] 'General Vorobev on defense budget', in FBIS-SOV-95-001, 3 Jan. 1995, p. 18.

[42] 'Military food, financial shortages detailed', in FBIS-SOV-95-150, 4 Aug. 1995, p. 29.

[43] *Moscow News*, no. 17 (5–11 May 1995), p. 2.

[44] '*Obshchaya Gazeta* on cost of Chechnya war, reconstruction', in FBIS-SOV-95-028-S, 10 Feb. 1995, p. 2.

[45] '*Obshchaya Gazeta* on cost of Chechnya war' (note 44).

[46] 'Internal, external financial cost of Chechnya war weighed', in FBIS-SOV-95-006, 10 Jan. 1995, pp. 19–20.

including assets needed to restore the economy of the republic.[47] In an earlier assessment of the impact of the war, Illarionov argued that defence expenditure jumped to 6.6 per cent of GDP in December 1994 as opposed to 4.1 per cent of GDP for the preceding 11 months.[48]

Given a defence budget of around 60 trillion roubles, the cost of the war would seem manageable if official estimates are to be believed. However, it is far from certain that the government is presenting an accurate picture. Notwithstanding that it is clearly in the military's interest to inflate the seriousness of its financial position, the government's optimistic expenditure figures must be treated circumspectly. It may be concealing the true extent of the economic costs of Chechnya in order to secure continued international financing for its reforms.[49] Official estimates also appear to be based on fragile assumptions that the conflict will soon be over. It is apparent, however, that Moscow faces the prospect of open-ended expenditure in Chechnya for the foreseeable future.

1996 defence budget projections

The disastrous Chechnya operation has exposed the weaknesses in the post-Soviet military reform programme and has led to calls for more defence spending in 1996. The 1996 budget as approved by Yeltsin in December 1995 provides for an increase in defence expenditure in nominal terms to 80 trillion roubles in 1996 (c. $17 billion).[50] This increase is unlikely to keep pace with inflation and it is possible that there will be a reduction in the military budget in real terms. The Defence Ministry had lobbied for an increase to 111 trillion roubles (c. $24.6 billion) for 1996, arguing that the planned budget would keep the armed forces 'on the verge of survival'.[51]

Table 8.3 gives a breakdown of the 1996 approved defence budget. This marks the first occasion since the breakup of the Soviet Union on which the Russian defence budget has been approved in advance of the year to which it applies. The budget does not stipulate any special allocation for the military in connection with Chechnya. It is clear that another acrimonious defence debate is about to begin but it is not evident that the defence budget will necessarily reflect the impact of the Chechnya conflict. Additional expenditures may well be found in other parts of the budget covering internal security matters.

[47] Sigel, T., 'Testing the government's budgetary resolve', *Transition*, vol. 1, no. 21 (17 Nov. 1995), pp. 56–61.

[48] 'Five billion dollars spent on Chechnya', *Baltic Independent*, 5–11 May 1995, p. 6. Part of the increase may have been accounted for by attempts to meet some of the government's payment obligations by the end of the year.

[49] Sutherland, T., 'Chechnya crisis threatens IMF funding', *The Australian*, 18 Jan. 1995, p. 7.

[50] *Rossiyskaya Gazeta*, 10 Jan. 1996 , p. 3.

[51] *Jane's Defence Weekly*, 14 Oct. 1995, p. 11.

Table 8.3. Russia's defence budget, 1996[a]

Figures are in trillion current roubles. Figures in italics are percentages.

		Percentage of total budget
Operations and maintenance (O&M)	41.120	*51.3*
Procurement	13.213[b]	*16.5*
Research and development (R&D)	6.474	*8.1*
Construction	7.637	*9.5*
Pensions	9.899	*12.3*
Defence Ministry total	**78.343**	*97.7*
Minatom (nuclear weapons)	1.512	*1.9*
Mobilization	0.307	*0.4*
Other	0.023	*. .*
Total defence budget	**80.185**	*100.0*

[a] As approved by President Boris Yeltsin, 31 Dec. 1995.

[b] Including 2100 billion roubles to settle debts from 1995.

Sources: *Rossiyskaya Gazeta,* 10 Jan. 1996. Analysis provided by Julian Cooper, Centre for Russian and East European Studies, University of Birmingham.

Central Asia

Since the dissolution of the Soviet Union there have been distinct differences as well as similarities in the ways in which the five Central Asian states[52] have viewed their security concerns and objectives. Kazakhstan has been arguably the strongest proponent of retaining some type of unified force; Uzbekistan was one of the first of the former Soviet republics to establish its own military. While all have recognized the necessity of maintaining a security relationship with Russia in the light of the general appreciation that they cannot effectively ensure their security independently, Turkmenistan has insisted that this relationship develop on a bilateral basis, Uzbekistan's President Islam Karimov pushes for the development of regional security cooperation and would like to see the Commonwealth of Independent States (CIS) focus more on economic issues than on military ones, and the remaining three countries have actively pursued security relations with Russia both bilaterally and through the CIS. Kazakhstan, Kyrgyzstan, Tajikistan and Uzbekistan are all signatories of the May 1992 Tashkent Treaty on Collective Security and have participated in CIS peacekeeping activities; Turkmenistan's President Saparmurad Niyazov has demonstrated a distinct lack of interest in collective CIS security efforts or the joining of any other form of military bloc.

The five states have numerous things in common in security issues, one being that all are focusing on the desirability of creating more mobile forces with modern equipment. They all face problems, either technical or financial,

[52] Kazakhstan, Kyrgyzstan, Tajikistan, Turkmenistan and Uzbekistan.

in maintaining these forces and equipment, but none of them appears to be dedicating significant funds to modernizing or upgrading the combat equipment inherited from the breakup of the Soviet military.

Recent security developments and initiatives in Kazakhstan

In the evolution of Kazakhstan's military force and security posture, several new developments occurred in 1995. Of particular interest to the international community, Kazakhstan officially became a non-nuclear weapon state when the last nuclear devices on its territory were transferred to the Russian Federation in late April 1995.[53] Russia and Kazakhstan are still scheduled to work out compensation arrangements for these withdrawn nuclear missiles. The two countries have, however, already agreed a compensation package for the strategic aviation formerly based in Kazakhstan: Russia began to supply 43 aircraft in November and December 1995, half of which are to be MiG-29s, and another 30 aircraft are to be supplied over the next two years.[54]

Within the Kazakh military, changes in its leadership, force structure and conscription policy all came to the fore in the autumn of 1995. Having been appointed Defence Minister in October 1995, General Alibek Kasymov just one month later announced plans to change Kazakhstan's force structure. He has also suggested that, while security cooperation with Russia will certainly continue, the development of other cooperative relationships—such as with China and the USA—will also be pursued.[55] The air force, air defence and ground forces are to be reorganized, ultimately resulting in a smaller, more mobile and better equipped military. This change should reduce the number of conscripts needed in the future. In November 1995 Kazakhstan extended the period of conscription from 18 to 24 months with effect from the spring 1996 draft; it is expected that the number of conscripts needed annually will be reduced by 25 000–30 000.

The problem of an officer shortage, however, will remain at least for several more years. Between 1992 and 1995, 70 per cent of the officers serving in Kazakhstan left military service. Compounding the difficulties caused by these departures, Kazakhstan, like the other Central Asian states, had a notable lack of ethnic Kazakh officers in the Soviet military: there were only some 2000–3000 Kazakh officers in total. As of 1995, the military is reported to have only two-thirds of the officers it needs, although the Defence Ministry projects that as more native Kazakhs receive officer training this problem will diminish appreciably by 1999. Allowing other nationals to serve as officers in the Kazakh military under contract offers an interim solution.[56]

In terms of security concerns, drug trafficking and drug-related crimes are demanding more and more attention. Where domestic stability and inter-ethnic relations are concerned, demographic changes over the past two years

---

[53] See chapter 14, section IV in this volume.

[54] Reported by Interfax, 8 Nov. 1995, in FBIS-SOV-95-217, p. 61.

[55] Pannier, B., 'Kazakhstan to change military's organization', Open Media Research Institute (hereafter OMRI), *OMRI Daily Digest*, no. 211, part I (30 Oct. 1995).

[56] 'Presidential bulletin', Interfax, 30 Nov. 1995, in FBIS-SOV-95-231, p. 54.

resulting from the exodus of an estimated 900 000 people (over half of whom are Russian) have shifted the ethnic balance so that, whereas before there were almost equal numbers of Kazakhs and Russians, Kazakhs now represent almost half of the population and Russians only about 30 per cent.[57] This change has not reduced tensions between Kazakh officials and Russian Cossack organizations, however.

Interestingly, public opinion polls indicate that most people do not perceive any serious external or internal security threats, whether from China, from NATO or from any member of the CIS. While perceived threats are low, however, the idea of embodying neutrality in Kazakhstan's new constitution did not gain acceptance. The draft published in early July 1995 did include an aspiration 'to a policy of neutrality', but when the final version was approved this clause had been eliminated.[58] Most commentaries pointed out that neutrality simply was not a realistic objective in the light of the country's participation already in the Tashkent Treaty on Collective Security and the various security agreements with Russia, including the stationing of Russian troops on Kazakh soil for at least 20 years.

Bilateral relations with Russia

To one extent or another, all the Central Asian states have reached agreements with Russia on various types of security cooperation arrangements, such as Russian use of military installations in these countries, the ability of Russian military personnel to serve in their armed forces, the supplying of their forces with weapons, equipment and basic living necessities and the training of their officers.

Kazakhstan concluded new or ratified older agreements with Russia in 1995 pertaining to military forces and security in general. In January 1995, the two countries reached agreement on the conditions for Russian citizens to serve under contract in the Kazakh military; in late May, President Nursultan Nazarbayev (in the absence of parliament[59]) ratified it. Most significantly, in February 1995 Kazakhstan and Russia issued a joint declaration on expanding and intensifying their cooperation: clause 10 of this declaration states that 'Kazakhstan and Russia will subsequently proceed from the principle of the use by the armed forces of one party of the facilities and installations located on the territory of the other, considering the parties' endeavour to use their defence potential in the interests of mutual security. To this end, the parties shall as of 1995 embark on the formation of joint armed forces'.[60]

---

[57] These percentages are provided by President Nazarbayev. Kozlov, Yu., 'A new triangle: Russia, Belarus, Kazakhstan emerges', *Nezavisimaya Gazeta*, 15 Nov. 1995, pp. 1, 3, in FBIS-SOV-95-235-S, p. 95.

[58] The draft verion was published in *Kazakhstanskaya Pravda*, 4 July 1995, pp. 1–3, in FBIS-SOV-95-135-S, pp. 76–93. The reference to neutrality was in Article 8.2.

[59] The parliament elected in Mar. 1994 in the first free, multi-party elections in the country was dissolved by the president on 6 Mar. 1995 after the Constitutional Court declared the result of the elections invalid.

[60] Quoted by Neverov, V., 'Draft constitution: without right to error', *Stolichnoe Obozrenie*, 10 Aug. 1995, p. 4, in FBIS-SOV-95-161-S, pp. 59–60.

Table 8.4. Central Asian defence budgets, 1994 and 1995

Country	1994			1995		
	In local currency	In $[a]	As % of total budget	In local currency	In $[a]	As % of total budget
Kazakhstan[b]						
armed forces	7.21 b. tenge	161 m.[c]	8.2	14.4 b. tenge	226 m.	9.6
law enforcement	(6.59) b. tenge	(140 m.)[c]	(7.5)	13.9 b. tenge	218 m.[d]	9.3
Kyrgyzstan	..	..	..	151.1 m. som	13.8 m.[e]	2.5
Tajikistan	34.7 b. roubles	21.0 m.[f]	3.7	..	..	..
Turkmenistan	..	..	..	4.6 b. manats[g]	459.0 m.	7.3
Uzbekistan	990.8 m. sum	39.6 m.[h]	4.7	3.4 b. sum	119.5 m.[i]	5.1

[a] Based on the official exchange rate.

[b] Figures are for the second budget approved, in May 1994, Oct. 1994 and July 1995. For details of what the law enforcement and defence budgets cover, see table 8.5. The 1994 figures for the defence and law enforcement budgets are derived from the IMF Country Report under the heading 'Defense, Public Order and Safety', but the total budget expenditure figure used is the one provided by the Kazakh Government. (The IMF estimates a total expenditure of 119 b. tenge, which would mean that the total spent on defence and law enforcement would be 13.1 per cent of the total budget, rather than 15.7 per cent.)

[c] Exchange rate 44.7 tenge : US$1.

[d] Exchange rate 63.5 tenge : US$1.

[e] Exchange rate 10.96 som : US$1.

[f] Russian roubles. Exchange rate 1650 Russian roubles : US$1.

[g] Exchange rate 10 manats : US$1.

[h] Exchange rate 25 sum : US$1.

[i] Exchange rate 28 sum : US$1.

Sources: 'Edict of the Republic of Kazakhstan . . . 15 March 1995', *Kazakhstanskaya Pravda*, 25 July 1995, pp. 1, 3, in FBIS-SOV-95-152-S, p. 53; 'Appendix to edict of the Republic of Kazakhstan . . . 20 July 1995', *Kazakhstanskaya Pravda*, 25 July 1995, p. 3, in FBIS-SOV-95-152-S, pp. 58–59; Nagimetov, G., 'Our military doctrine ensues from a peace-loving policy', *Novoe Pokolenie*, no. 32 (Sep. 1995), p. 6, in FBIS-SOV-95-181, p. 69; International Monetary Fund, *Republic of Kazakhstan: Background Paper and Statistical Appendix* (IMF: Washington, DC, Jan. 1995), p. 93; 'Republic of Kazakhstan law . . . ', *Kazakhstanskaya Pravda*, 19 Oct. 1994, p. 1, in FBIS-SOV-94-225, p. 62; Dymov, O., 'The army: our pain and our concern', *Kazakhstanskaya Pravda*, 6 Dec. 1994, p. 2, in Joint Publications Research Service, *Central Eurasia: Military Affairs*, JPRS-UMA-94-055, p. 33; Interfax, 9 June 1995, in FBIS-SOV-95-112, p. 79; *Narodnaya Gazeta*, 18 Feb. 1995, p. 1, in FBIS-SOV-95-058-S, p. 56; *Turkmen Press*, 28 Dec. 1994, in FBIS-SOV-95-002, p. 45; Interfax, 23 Sep. 1994, in FBIS-SOV-94-186, p. 63; and information provided to SIPRI by the Foreign Ministry of Uzbekistan.

While both countries continue to maintain their national militaries, this idea of joint command has already been implemented in accordance with another

(July 1995) agreement on establishing joint border forces.[61] Commanded by Kazakh Major General Prohoda, the force also has a coordination council that is led by the heads of Russia's and Kazakhstan's border forces. Currently 15 000 of these joint troops are guarding the Sino-Kazakh border.

Another bilateral accord allows Russia to extend its military communications systems (including fixed-site radio relay and tropospheric and cable communication lines) across Kazakhstan. In return, to the extent possible, Russia will make available to Kazakhstan some of the carrying capacity of its military space communications relay stations.[62]

The final major security initiative between Russia and Kazakhstan pertains to the leasing of Leninsk, the city which supports the Baykonur space launch site. The Baykonur agreement, originally reached in March 1994 and signed by Presidents Yeltsin and Nazarbayev, commits Russia to payment of $115 million annually for a 20-year lease, which can be renewed.[63] Instruments of ratification on the agreement were exchanged in September 1995. By October 1995, the two countries had worked out a draft agreement calling for Leninsk to remain an administrative and territorial entity of Kazakhstan but operating under lease to Russia; as such, it has been designated as the 90th component part of the Russian Federation.[64] The Leninsk lease is also to last 20 years. Russia is to pay for 100 per cent of the city's financing and the terms of the lease apparently stipulate that the money is to be applied to Kazakhstan's repayment of its debt to Russia.

Kazakhstan's defence budget and budget process

Because of frequent changes in Kazakh economic and political life, it is difficult to describe a routine budget process. What it is possible to describe is the procedures called for in the constitution—i.e., how the process should work theoretically[65]—and generally how the process has worked in reality in the past two years.

Each ministry is responsible for preparing a draft budget covering its responsibilities. The Ministry of Finance is to assemble all the components into one budget for submission to Parliament, the Supreme Kenges. The latter consists of two chambers, the Senate and the Mazhilis, and is to discuss the budget and make changes to it in separate sessions, the Mazhilis first, followed by the Senate. Both chambers are allowed to form standing committees which can issue decrees about matters within their jurisdiction; certainly one or more

---

[61] Kazakh Radio First Program, 14.00 h. GMT, 12 July 1995, in FBIS-SOV-95-134, 13 July 1995, p. 74; Verzhbitskaya, N., 'Different states, common border', *Kazakhstanskaya Pravda*, 19 July 1995, p. 1, in FBIS-SOV-95-142, 25 July 1995, p. 71; and Dave, B., 'Russia ready to police Sino-Kazakh border', *OMRI Daily Digest*, no. 201, part I, 16 Oct. 1995.

[62] 'In the corridors of power', *Rossiyskie Vesti*, 27 June 1995, p. 1, in FBIS-SOV-95-124, p. 74.

[63] Agreement between the Russian Federation and the Republic of Kazakhstan on the Basic Principles and Conditions of the Use of the Baykonur Cosmodrome, 28 Mar. 1994; and Contract of Lease of the Baykonur Complex between the Government of the Russian Federation and the Government of the Repubic of Kazakhstan, 10 Dec. 1994.

[64] Leninsk's uncertain status has taken its toll on the population: 50 000 of 100 000 Russian residents there have already reportedly left.

[65] *Kazakhstanskaya Pravda*, 4 July 1995, pp. 1–3, in FBIS-SOV-95-135-S, pp. 76–93.

of these committees would be involved in a review of the budget. During a joint sitting of the Parliament, the two chambers are then to confirm the budget and to make changes to it. It must then be approved by the President.

The primary difficulty in 1994 and 1995 between theory and reality was the absence of a Parliament.[66] For the 1994 state budget, the Cabinet of Ministers, chaired by the Prime Minister, reviewed the assembled draft budget (prepared in segments by the responsible ministries) and decided to submit it to the President for consideration. In late January 1994, in the absence of a legislature, Nazarbayev endorsed it and it was under this budget that the state operated for the first half of 1994. In May, the Cabinet of Ministers, chaired again by the Prime Minister, reviewed the updated budget, which was then submitted to the Senate. In mid-July 1994 the Parliament adopted a budget calling for overall spending to be set at 87.7 billion tenge ($1961 million), while revenues were to amount to 67.5 billion tenge ($1510 million), leaving a deficit equal to 4.6 per cent of estimated GDP.

Within this budget, the Defence Ministry was to receive slightly less than 9 billion tenge ($201 million). The defence budget does not, however, include expenditure on the Ministry of Internal Affairs, the Internal Troops or the Border Forces. On the basis of information contained in the January 1995 report of the International Monetary Fund (IMF) on Kazakhstan,[67] a best estimate of allocations for these latter and other related non-Defence Ministry areas came to about 6.6 billion tenge ($148 million). As table 8.4 illustrates, the defence budget accounted for 8.2 per cent of the total budget of the republic, while law enforcement support came to 7.5 per cent. According to one account, the combined allocations for defence and law enforcement in Kazakhstan in 1992 amounted to only 6.1 per cent of the budget and 11.4 per cent in 1993.[68] So far as they are available, data on the other Central Asian states' defence budgets are also given in the table, although none of the others gives information about similar 'law enforcement' allocations.

Like the Russian Federation and other former Soviet states, Kazakhstan faced tremendous difficulties in trying to implement this budget, above all because of high inflation, lower than projected revenue collection and incremental payments to the various ministries. After the first nine months of the year, numerous reports appeared in the press noting the failure of the budget to meet its objectives. Revenues were only 40 per cent of the level expected. Furthermore, in times of high inflation, when funding is distributed to the ministries in stages rather than in a lump sum as soon as the budget is approved, the purchasing power of what is ultimately received is that much less. For its part, the Defence Ministry was given less than half the planned amount by the Ministry of Finance. After the deduction of some 1.5 billion tenge ($33.5 million) for CIS strategic forces, it was left with an official

[66] The former parliament had dissolved itself in Dec. 1993. New elections in the first free, multi-party elections in the country were held on 7 Mar. 1994. On 1995, see note 59.

[67] International Monetary Fund, *Republic of Kazakhstan: Background Paper and Statistical Appendix* (IMF: Washington, DC, Jan. 1995).

[68] Kasymov, K., 'The government's budget labyrinth', *Ekspress-K*, 11 Aug. 1995, p. 3, in FBIS-SOV-95-160, p. 59.

Table 8.5. Kazakhstan's revised July 1995 budget allocations for defence and law enforcement

Figures are in m. current tenge. Figures in italics are percentages.

Budget item	Amount	Percentage of total budget
General Purpose Forces	13 379.682	*92.6*
Civil Defence Staff and HQ	349.597	*2.4*
Naval forces	344.865	*2.4*
Republic Guard	325.201	*2.3*
Military courts	41.107	*0.3*
Total defence budget	**14 440.452**	*100.0*
Ministry of Internal Affairs	7 648.690	*54.9*
State Committee for Defence of the State Border	2 543.152	*18.2*
Committee for State Security	1 912.374	*13.7*
Internal Troops	1 597.196	*11.5*
Military Border Troops Institute	220.345	*1.6*
State Technical Committee for Information (Protection of Cabinet Ministers)	13.030	*0.1*
Total law enforcement budget	**13 934.787**	*100.0*

Source: Edict of the Republic of Kazakhstan President with the force of law: On the introduction of amendments and additions to edict of the Republic of Kazakhstan President with the force of law no. 2120, dated 15 March 1995, 'On the republic budget for 1995', *Kazakhstanskaya Pravda*, 25 July 1995, pp. 1, 3, in FBIS-SOV-95-152-S, pp. 45–60, 53, 58–59.

budget of 7.2 billion tenge ($161 million) for the year, of which it actually received only 3.5 billion tenge ($78 million).[69] According to the Minister of Finance, only half of the planned overall budget was actually distributed; thus, the Defence Ministry fared as well (or as poorly) as all other ministries.

As stipulated by law, the ministries had prepared their draft 1995 budgets and submitted them to Parliament in December 1994 for debate. As of late February 1995 the Parliament was still considering the proposed budget. On 6 March President Nazarbayev dissolved Parliament and on 15 March 1995 he approved the budget. It specified revenues of 136 billion tenge ($2141 million) and expenditure of 175 billion tenge ($2755 million), of which 18.9 billion ($298 million) was to go to defence and 14.8 billion tenge ($233 million) to law enforcement organs. As with the 1994 budget, this too was revised. According to a presidential edict on 20 July 1995, planned revenue was 111 billion tenge ($1748 million) and expenditure 150 billion ($2362 million), of which defence was allocated 14.4 billion ($226 million) and law enforcement 13.9 billion tenge ($218 million). Table 8.5 provides a further breakdown of these budget items.

---

[69] According to Deputy Defence Minister Major-Gen. A. G. Isengulov, the Defence Ministry actually received only 48% of its allocation in 1994. Dobraya, R., 'Aytkali Isengulov: I agree to declare war on shortcomings in the army', *Kazakhstanskaya Pravda*, 13 May 1995, p. 2, in FBIS-SOV-95-105-S, p. 60.

While the final assessments of the 1995 budget have yet to be made, evidence points to continuing difficulties in meeting expected revenue collection and in the ministries receiving the amount they have been allocated in the official budget. For example, Aytkali Isengulov, adviser to the Defence Minister, noted in September that, for the first six months of 1995, the Ministry had received only 12–15 per cent of the planned budget.[70] Kazakhstan is certainly not alone in experiencing such budgeting problems and some attempt is being made here—as elsewhere in some of the former Soviet states—to retain at the national level only fundamentally national elements of the budget such as defence, while other spending responsibilities are gradually devolved to local administrations.

Observations and conclusions

While the Central Asian states other than Kazakhstan are discussed only briefly here, this overview has sought to impart a sense of the types of challenge facing all these countries. A particular challenge for analysts trying to assess the level of effort being invested in military matters in Central Asia today is the difficulty of obtaining reliable, comprehensive data about defence budgets and actual spending. Much information must be assembled piecemeal, and there are generally no independent (non-governmental) sources of confirmation. In the case of the 1995 Kazakh budget, having 93 per cent of the budget listed as one line-item (for the General Purpose Forces) does not allow an adequate appreciation of how money is specifically to be spent. It is also important not to draw close parallels with defence spending in Western nations, which traditionally have higher manpower costs, for example.

Until these nations discuss such issues more openly, much analysis will have to rely on conjecture.

IV. Oceania

This section focuses on trends and developments in military expenditure in Australia and New Zealand.

Australia

Since World War II Australia has faced the dilemma of how to structure defence policy in the absence of an identifiable threat. Given its size and geography, the distances separating it from major regional military powers and the inhospitable nature of much of its land mass, a sudden major military attack on Australia does not at present seem very probable.

---

[70] Nagimetov, G., 'Our military doctrine ensues from a peace-loving policy', *Novoe Pokolenie*, no. 36 (Sep. 1995), p. 6, in FBIS-SOV-95-181, p. 69.

Table 8.6. Australia's military expenditure allocations, 1991/92–1995/96
Figures are in m. current A$. Figures in italics are percentages.

	1991/92	1992/93	1993/94	1994/95	1995/96[a]
Personnel cost[b]	3 951	4 180	4 696[c]	4 594	3 851
Share of total	*40.2*	*38.2*	*41.7*	*40.8*	*36.1*
O&M[d]	2 974	3 648	3 297	3 335	3 492
Share of total	*30.3*	*33.3*	*29.3*	*29.6*	*32.8*
Procurement[e]	2 223	2 363	2 354	2 388	2 417
Share of total	*22.6*	*21.6*	*20.9*	*21.2*	*22.7*
Construction[f]	443	458	579	640	589
Share of total	*4.5*	*4.2*	*5.1*	*5.7*	*5.5*
R&D[g]	156	224	246	230	226
Share of total	*1.6*	*2.0*	*2.2*	*2.0*	*2.1*
Defence cooperation[h]	75	76	77	78	78
Share of total	*0.8*	*0.7*	*0.7*	*0.7*	*0.7*
Total	**9 822**	**10 949**	**11 249**	**11 265**	**10 653**

[a] Projected amounts.

[b] Includes costs of military pensions, housing assistance, defence force and defence civilian salaries.

[c] From 1993/94 includes payments for accrual-based superannuation of *c.* A$450 million per annum.

[d] Includes administrative costs; production costs; replacement of equipment and stores; repair and overhaul of equipment and stores; rations; fuel; weapons, repair and maintenance of buildings and works and housing for armed forces personnel; and leases and overseas property services.

[e] Includes costs of new major and minor capital equipment.

[f] Includes capital costs for the construction, acquisition and disposal of new buildings, works, property and housing for armed forces personnel.

[g] Consists of the operating costs for the Science and Technology Program of the Department of Defence.

[h] Consists of salaries, allowances, equipment and administration of the Australian Defence Cooperation Projects.

Source: Military expenditure in local currency and current prices for 1991/92–1995/96, received from the Australian Department of Defence (Canberra, Dec. 1995) submitted through the Australian Embassy, Stockholm, Jan. 1996.

Self-reliance was one of the three pillars of overall strategic policy outlined in the 1987 White Paper, *The Defence of Australia,*[71] the remaining two being Australia's alliance with the USA and the commitment to devote a certain level of resources to meet planned objectives. The most recent official document to provide strategic guidance is the *Defence White Paper 1994*, which looks ahead to the year 2000 and beyond.[72] Like its predecessor, it does not identify any specific source of military threat to Australia, but it notes that the

[71] *The Defence of Australia, 1987* (Australian Government Publishing Service: Canberra, Mar. 1987), pp. 1–2.
[72] *Defending Australia: Defence White Paper* 1994 (Australian Government Publishing Service: Canberra, Nov. 1994), p. 158.

end of the cold war has brought about important new uncertainties about the future strategic situation in the region and that it may result in a deteriorating security environment for Australia. The reasoning here is that rapid economic growth will increase the power of the Asian nations while political change is making their policies less predictable. In addition, the strategic role of the USA is changing as it reassesses its global commitments. It is thought that the USA may stage a substantial military withdrawal from the region in the 1990s.

While Australia's treaty relationship with the United States continues to be a key element of its defence policy, the *Defence White Paper 1994* reveals plans to significantly expand regional security partnerships with the countries of the Association of South-East Asian Nations (ASEAN),[73] in particular Indonesia, Malaysia and Singapore. This was demonstrated at the fifth ASEAN summit meeting in Bangkok, on 14–15 December 1995, when Australia announced a security agreement with Indonesia. Under the agreement, the two nations agreed to consult regularly at a ministerial level on matters affecting their common security and to promote beneficial cooperative military activities.[74]

Table 8.6 shows that Australian military expenditure allocations between FYs 1991/92 and 1995/96 increased in nominal terms at the beginning of the 1990s and started to decline in 1995/96. The *Defence White Paper 1994* commits the present government to maintain defence spending at about 2 per cent of GDP. Australia is in the process of preparing for the introduction of a fixed five-year defence budget planning cycle from May 1996 onwards as the basis for 'assured long-term planning', according to Defence Minister Robert Ray.[75] The shift to a clearly defined defence budget cycle is recognized as being particularly important to the capital equipment procurement cycle. Some A$2417 million of new capital equipment programmes have been requested in the 1995/96 defence budget, or about 23 per cent of the total budget of A$10 653 million. While the navy continues to dominate the existing capital equipment acquisition programme with A$890 million (US$662 million) allocated in 1995 for the procurement of ANZAC Class frigates, Collins Class submarines and coastal minehunters, the air force will spend A$390 million (US$290 million) on the upgrading of its 18 P-3C Orion maritime patrol aircraft, updated avionics for its F-111Cs and the Jindalee over-the-horizon radar.[76]

[73] See the Glossary for the membership of ASEAN.

[74] Richardson, M., 'Putting a "building block" of Asian security in place', *International Herald Tribune,* 18 Dec. 1995, pp. 1, 4; 'Australia and Indonesia sign security cooperation accord', *International Herald Tribune,* 19 Dec. 1995, p. 4; Vatikiotis, M. *et al.,* 'Hang on tight', *Far Eastern Economic Review,* 28 Dec. 1995–4 Jan. 1996, p. 16; and McBeth, J. *et al.,* '"Personal pact", Suharto, Keating surprise Asean with security deal', *Far Eastern Economic Review,* 28 Dec. 1995–4 Jan. 1996, pp. 18–21.

[75] la Franchi, P., 'Australia's defence acquisition programme into the 21st century', *Asian Defence Journal,* vol. 25, no. 9 (1 Sep. 1995), pp. 71–77.

[76] Ferguson, G., 'Australian defense spending falls to post-World War II low', *Defense News,* 15–21 May 1995, p. 30.

Table 8.7. New Zealand's military expenditure allocations, 1991/92–1994/95
Figures are in th. current NZ$.

	1991/92	1992/93	1993/94	1994/95
Expenditure				
Operating expenses	862 946	829 566	796 105	788 550
Purchase of fixed assets	147 816	214 505	276 052	270 059
GST on outputs to Crown	186 188	174 784	166 436	160 059
Payment on behalf of the Crown	195 373	–	–	–
Sub-total	*1 392 323*	*1 218 855*	*1 238 593*	*1 218 668*
Receipts				
Sales of fixed assets	50	14 329	10 288	50
Supply of output to other parties	27 585	25 707	11 544	5 730
Receipts on behalf of the Crown	101 357	–	–	–
Sub-total	*128 992*	*40 036*	*21 832*	*5 780*
Total net expenditure	**1 263 331**	**1 178 819**	**1 216 761**	**1 212 888**

Note: GST: government sales tax.
Source: *New Zealand Official Yearbook, 1993* (Statistics New Zealand: Wellington, 1993), p. 58; *1994*, p. 73; and *1995*, p. 106.

Personnel costs take about 36 per cent of the budget. The officer corps is over-large, particularly at major, lieutenant and colonel level, and its cost is excessive.[77] O&M accounts for about 33 per cent of the budget.

New Zealand

New Zealand's defence policy and force structure, like Australia's, are shaped by its remoteness from other powers and it does not perceive direct threats to its security. Because it is a small country with limited fiscal resources, the aim in the present circumstances is to maintain a credible 'minimum' defence force.[78] Military expenditure has been shrinking and its share of GDP has declined from 1.7 per cent in 1992 to 1.4 per cent in 1995.[79] Of the 19994/95 military expenditure budget of *c*. NZ$1.2 billion (US$706 million), NZ$250 million (US$147 million) or 18.8 per cent has been spent on capital acquisition. This will finance part of New Zealand's biggest capital programme—the purchase of two ANZAC Class frigates in a NZ$1.2 billion (US$706 million) contract that will dominate defence budgets until late in the decade. The frigates are two of 10 ordered jointly with Australia.[80]

[77] 'Australia's defence funding fallacies', *Asian Defence Journal,,* vol. 25, no. 5 (May 1995), p. 86.
[78] *The Defence of New Zealand: A Policy Paper* (Government Printing Ltd: Wellington, 1991), pp. 5–8.
[79] *New Zealand Official Yearbook, 1995* (Statistics New Zealand: Wellington, 1995), p. 106.
[80] Mecham, M., 'New Zealand defense geared to "bottom line"', *Aviation Week & Space Technology*, 11 July 1994, pp. 57–58.

V. South Africa

In recognition of its changed political and strategic circumstances, the Government of South Africa has begun a debate on the future of the country's defence policy and requirements. A draft White Paper on national defence was submitted to the parliament in June 1995 and is expected to result in a new defence policy directive in mid-1996. The essence of the emerging policy is that South Africa's military should be inexpensive to maintain in peacetime yet able to build up rapidly in the event of serious hostilities. The military infrastructure is based on a core Professional Force of some 37 000 who can be rapidly reinforced by 275 000 active reserves from the Citizen Force when necessary.

However, South Africa's task of trying to develop a new defence policy that reflects its new security environment is made more complex by the complete political transformation which has resulted from the end of apartheid. South Africa not only faces the difficulty of having to justify continued defence spending in the absence of a visible threat; it also has to temper the economic need to reduce its defence spending with the reality that its new political respectability will ultimately require it to play an expanding role in the broader regional security environment. The essential impact of this situation is that the South African armed forces can expect continued reductions in the resources allocated for defence yet, at the same time, can anticipate being required to prepare for tasks not previously undertaken nor presently defined.

This process is still evolving and it is too early to draw conclusions as to the likely impact that changes in South Africa's strategic outlook might have on defence spending. In the short term, the costs of the post-apartheid integration of various military forces into the new South African National Defence Force (SANDF) represent a substantial strain on the budget. Only the determination of the future role of the South African military in the regional security context will determine precisely what force modernization will be necessary, but there will inevitably be increased pressures on the defence budget as all branches of the armed forces will have to modernize and acquire additional equipment to meet the new commitments that are eventually identified. The exigencies of force integration and modernization therefore have long-term implications for the future direction of South African security policy and will guide military financing decisions into the next century.

South Africa's military expenditure has been declining steadily since 1990, falling steeply by almost 16 per cent in real terms in 1991/92, over 13 per cent in 1992/93 and 5 per cent in 1993/94. As a proportion of GDP it fell from 3.7 per cent to 2.4 per cent over the same period and it will fall further in 1995/96 to about 2.1 per cent of GDP on the basis of current projections.[81] As a percentage of total government expenditure it has been halved since 1989, to about 8 per cent. The levelling off of the reduction in military expenditure

---

[81] Information supplied by the Office of the Secretary of Defence, Pretoria, 6 Dec. 1995.

suggests that the 1995/96 budget allocation of R10 535 billion ($2.9 billion) may represent the bottom of the retrenchment cycle.

Force integration

With the end of apartheid, the process began of consolidating all the armed forces, both 'statutory' and 'non-statutory', that existed before the April 1994 elections into an integrated SANDF.[82] These consisted of the former South African Defence Force (SADF), together with the defence forces of the apartheid-era homelands of Transkei, Bophuthatswana, Venda and Ciskei. The opposition forces consisted primarily of the military wing of the African National Congress Party (ANC), known as Umkhonto we Sizwe, and the Azanian People's Liberation Army (APLA) of the Pan-Africanist Congress (PAC).[83] Total personnel for the integrated SANDF is estimated to have been around 130 000 as of 1 January 1995, representing a 30 per cent increase over pre-integration force levels.

What is interesting about the integration process is that the SANDF is being built up at the same time as plans are being made to down-size it drastically in the near future. Although it is imperative for political reasons to integrate as many of the members of the non-statutory forces who wish to join the SANDF as possible, the reality is that present force levels and commitments cannot be maintained in the face of a declining defence budget. According to Major-General Marius Oelschig, who is in charge of the integration programme, it is expected that the final force structure will require cutbacks of some 30 000 over the next three years.[84] Force levels are expected to stabilize at around 75 000 by the end of the century.[85] Conscription, the traditional method of operating a low-paid force and maintaining the reserves, has been ended and the army will have to find ways to reduce the financial impact of a more expensive professional force by making savings in other areas.

The expansion of the armed forces as a result of integration will also soak up a significant segment of the declining defence allocation. Personnel costs absorb 33 per cent of the total defence budget and salaries are index-linked to inflation. Integration therefore means that non-personnel areas of the defence budget will have to be cut unless additional funds are provided. Nor will down-sizing contribute much in the short term to reducing the pressure on the

---

[82] As agreed upon in the Joint Military Command Council during the pre-election negotiation phase, the terms 'statutory' (constituted under an Act of Parliament) and 'non-statutory' refer to the status of the integrating forces before 27 Apr. 1994. *SANDF Communication Bulletin,* 69/95, 20 July 1995, quoted in Hanson, J. and McNish, S. (eds), *The Republic of South Africa: Prospects and Problems: Proceedings of the Spring Seminar, Toronto, 21 June 1995* (Canadian Institute of Strategic Studies: Toronto, 1995), p. 15.

[83] Members of the Inkatha Freedom Party are not included in the force integration process. O'Brien, K., 'South Africa's new intelligence and security environment', eds J. Cilliers and M. Reichardt, *About Turn: The Transformation of the South African Military and Intelligence* (Institute for Defence Policy: Midrand, 1995).

[84] Oelsschig, M., 'The evolution and management of change in the SANDF', eds Hanson and McNish (note 82), p. 16.

[85] *Jane's Defence Weekly,* vol. 24, no. 9 (2 Sep. 1995), p. 18.

defence budget. Retraining and retrenchment packages will, it is estimated, cost an additional R1.2 billion ($329 million) over the life of the three-year demobilization programme.[86] Savings on personnel costs will not become apparent until FY 1998/99. A 1994 study by the Military Research Group estimated that the total cost of the integration process would be R2036 million and that there is a shortfall of some R954 million in the amount allocated off-budget to cover this.[87]

Force modernization requirements

As the defence budget has declined, there has been a marked decrease in the proportion of resources devoted to procurement funding and a concomitant increase in personnel costs. Procurement fell from about 44 per cent of total military expenditure in 1990 to around 20 per cent in 1995.[88] The government has introduced measures to develop the defence export sector, partly to reduce the unit costs to its own forces of South African-manufactured weapons.[89] However, the prospects for greater South African penetration of the international arms market will be affected by the intense competition among all arms producers to secure new markets since the end of the cold war. Increasing arms sales cannot be relied upon to ease the effects of declining budgets and the army's preference for buying domestic products will probably have to be forsaken in the future.

The capital funding crisis was highlighted in the Defence Ministry's aborted attempt to procure four corvettes for the navy in 1995. The South African Navy (SAN) is the only significant navy south of the Sahara but it lacks true blue-water capability. Apart from South Africa's own requirements to develop its naval potential, it has been proposed that the SAN will serve as the de facto regional navy in the future. To do so, it will need a measure of blue-water capability which requires more and bigger ships. The acquisition of four patrol corvettes is viewed as an essential first step, but plans to put them into service by 1999, at an estimated cost of R1.6 billion ($438 million), were shelved in June 1995 because of budget restraints. This question will be aired again following the conclusion of a defence review in 1996. The navy also needs to prepare to replace older elements of its inventory, such as minesweepers, Daphne submarines and six Minister Class strike craft early in the next century.

Similarly, the South African Air Force (SAAF), although it remains the most effective air force in sub-Saharan Africa, needs to replace its Impala jet

---

[86] *Jane's Defence Weekly* (note 85).

[87] Willett, S. and Batchelor, P., 'The South African defence budget', Military Research Group, Cape Town, Mar. 1994, p. 4.

[88] Information supplied by the Office of the Secretary of Defence, Pretoria, 6 Dec. 1995 in reply to the SIPRI questionnaire.

[89] George, P., 'The impact of South Africa's arms sales policy on regional military expenditure, development and security', Utrikesdepartementet, *Säkerhet och Utveckling i Afrika* [Security and development in Africa], Ds 1996:15 (Utrikesdepartementet: Stockholm, 1996), pp. 237–95 [appendix in English to a report in Swedish].

Table 8.8. South Africa's military expenditure allocations 1990 and 1995
Figures are in m. current Rand.

	1990	Percentage of total	1995	Percentage of total
Personnel cost	3 373	*21.6*	3 613	*34.2*
O&M	3 370	*21.6*	2 299	*21.8*
Procurement	6 917	*44.4*	2 081	*19.7*
Construction	2	*0.1*	64	*0.6*
R&D	1 921	*12.3*	2 478	*23.5*
Total	**15 583**	*100.0*	**10 535**	*100.0*

Source: Office of the Secretary for Defence, Pretoria, South Africa, 6 Dec. 1995 in reply to SIPRI questionnaire.

trainers and the C-160 Transall by 1999, its Mirage F-1AZ and Alouette III helicopters by the year 2000 and the Cheetah fighters by 2010. Its C-130B Hercules should have been replaced before now.[90] The SAAF also needs to acquire combat helicopters and long-range maritime patrol aircraft if it is to be able to monitor South Africa's 2800-km coastline and extensive Exclusive Economic Zone.

The South African Army is the best equipped of all the branches of the armed services, having undergone an extensive modernization programme over the past 15 years.[91] However, funding cuts have not been balanced with a reduction in operational commitments and the army still has as many men performing border protection and internal security tasks as were deployed in Namibia during that conflict.[92] This reflects the serious internal security situation South Africa faces in the post-apartheid era. The South Africa Police Service, despite having grown to 140 000 personnel, is not able to deal with the extent of political and criminal violence the country now faces. As a result, the army is obliged to provide support to the police in areas hit by political unrest. The army has also borne the brunt of costs associated with the integration process.

Because of the nature of its role and the major areas of concern in southern Africa's security environment, the army is most likely to be affected by future demands for South Africa to play a greater role in regional security. The most immediate threat to South Africa stems from the instability that plagues most of southern Africa. Instability is a product of social and economic disparities and leads to internal conflict and the mass migration of people in search of better opportunities. This is not the kind of threat that can be countered by military means. It does, however, increase demands for military and humanitarian aid and the South African military is the only force in the region with

[90] Heitman, H.-R., '$2.9b defence budget marks end to decline', *Jane's Defence Weekly*, 25 Mar. 1995, p. 5.
[91] Heitman, H.-R., Foss, C. F. and Reed, C., 'New army for a new era', *Jane's Defence Weekly*, 29 Apr. 1995, p. 23.
[92] Heitman (note 90).

the logistical skills and professional competence to provide such assistance. These demands are growing in intensity in the region and South Africa is increasingly expected to contribute more to the requirements of peacekeeping and peacemaking in sub-Saharan Africa. Pressures are thus likely to grow on the defence budget.

Defence Minister Joe Modise warned in a speech to the National Assembly on 21 June 1995 that the R10.5 billion defence budget allocation for 1995/96 would not be sufficient to feed and pay South Africa's troops and also buy needed equipment.[93] Any further cuts in the defence budget would make it difficult for South Africa to increase its role in regional security and disaster relief operations.

VI. Central America

This section focuses on security-related issues in Central America—recent developments, the demobilization of the armed forces and the development of defence budgets in El Salvador, Guatemala and Nicaragua. Central America is confronted with the paradox that some countries maintain the most powerful armed forces in its history at a time when their traditional functions, both in politics and in defence, have disappeared.[94]

Of the other countries of the region which are not covered in depth in this section, Belize, Honduras and Panama have not provided military spending data to relevant international organizations or answers to SIPRI's requests for information. Costa Rica abolished its army with the adoption of its new constitution in 1949. It does have paramilitary security forces, but SIPRI has not been able to obtain figures for the budget of these. Panama claims that it has no military expenditure since its army was abolished by a law passed by the National Assembly in August 1994. Mexico is a special case requiring special analysis. The Zapatista rebellion in Chiapas State is no longer threatening the peace of the nation, but much else is. In early 1995 Mexico's smouldering political troubles were exacerbated by a serious crisis of economic confidence, and tension persists after the collapse of the peso, rampant inflation and the effects of structural adjustment on a large part of the population. The security threats to Belize are exclusively external: potential frontier problems exist between Guatemala and Belize, although tensions were little felt during 1995.

Contemporary Central American security issues can be grouped into five broad categories: (a) those which represent a continuation of traditional security concerns dating back to independence and earlier; (b) those that are a direct heritage of the violence of the 1980s; (c) those that reflect continuing issues of civil–military relations; (d) those related to the rise in and increasing globalization of criminal activity; and (e) those involving efforts to develop

---

[93] *Defense News*, 3–9 July 1995, pp. 3, 21.
[94] Rojas, F. (ed.), *Gastos Militar en el América Latina* [Military expenditure in Latin America] (Centro Internacional para el Desarrollo Económico, Facultad Latinoamericana de Ciencias Sociales: Panamá, Aug. 1994), p. 365.

the economy while at the same time defending the environment. Many traditional security concerns have diminished notably in recent years.

In Central America, where political and strategic rivalry between the USA and the former USSR was also a factor, repression escalated and the gravest human rights abuses were committed. In addition, excessive military expenditure prevented the implementation of essential social development programmes. Figures published by SELA (Sistema Ecónomico Latinoamericano, the Latin American Economic System) show that, while development aid has been shrinking in the region, poverty is increasing.[95] In 1992, total development aid to all developing countries amounted to $60 billion, which represented only 0.52 per cent of the developed countries' GDP. Central America received 3.2 per cent of this aid, or $1.9 billion.[96] The conditions attached to the aid have varied from the political and ideological ones typical of the period of the cold war to others based on economic performance.

El Salvador

The signing of the Peace Accord in January 1992 put an end to 12 years of armed conflict, paving the way for faster economic development and improving the economic welfare of the population. The National Reconstruction Plan currently under way will focus on rehabilitating damaged infrastructure and bringing large segments of the population into the economic mainstream.

The Salvadorean Armed Forces have been undergoing a fundamental review and reorganization since the signing of the peace agreement. Manpower has been reduced from 41 700 soldiers in 1985 to 30 500 in 1995.[97] Since the implementation of the peace accords, the armed forces have no political role in the country and have abided by their constitutional mandate to provide for external defence. As of December 1994, the last of the national police administered by the armed forces were supposed to have been demobilized and replaced by the Civil National Police. Instead of the Defence Ministry, the Interior Ministry will deploy the Civil National Police country-wide with a total force of 7000. An élite Anti-Drug Division and an Investigative Division were formed by transferring functions from the Civil National Police, the former taking over the equipment and weapons of the Civil National Police, mainly T-65 rifles. These units have been allocated some $2 million worth of communications equipment, $3 million of computerized systems, as well as 135 vehicles, mainly jeeps and pick-up trucks.[98]

[95] SELA [Sistema Ecónomico Latinoamericano] quoted in *Latin American World Report, Southern Cone Report*, WR-1995-5, 10 Aug. 1995, p. 353.

[96] *Latin American Weekly Report*, WR-95-35, 14 Sep. 1995, p. 415.

[97] International Institute for Strategic Studies, *The Military Balance, 1995–1996* (Oxford University Press: Oxford, 1995), pp. 267, 216.

[98] Montes, J., 'El Salvador: combat arms update', *Jane's Intelligence Review International*, July 1994, pp. 332–35.

Table 8.9. El Salvador's military expenditure allocations, 1990–95
Figures are in m. current colones. Figures in italics are percentages.

	1990	1991	1992	1993	1994	1995
Operating cost[a]	862.5	879.6	917.1	858.4	860.4	860.4
Share of total	*99.2*	*99.0*	*99.0*	*99.2*	*99.3*	*99.3*
Investment cost[b]	9.0	9.0	9.0	8.0	6.0	6.0
Share of total	*1.0*	*1.0*	*1.0*	*0.9*	*0.7*	*0.7*
Total	**871.5**	**888.6**	**926.1**	**866.4**	**866.4**	**866.4**

[a] Includes O&M, personnel (military and civilian) pensions and other social expenditures.
[b] Includes procurement, construction and R&D.
Source: General Humberto Corades Figueroa, Defence Ministry, San Salvador, 6 Nov. 1995.

Total military expenditure for 1994 was 866.4 million colones ($89.4 million) or 9 per cent of central government expenditure (CGE). The data available from the Defence Ministry do not identify whether security and paramilitary expenditures are included in the military budgets.

Following the peace accords and demobilization of the Frente Farabundo Martí para la Liberación Nacional (Farabundo Martí National Liberation Front, FMLN) guerrilla force, El Salvador cut the size of its armed forces substantially but, according to the information available, their funding has remained constant in nominal terms, as shown in table 8.9. It should be emphasized that, in spite of recent efforts at democratization, budget allocations have not been modified accordingly. In the past few years, military spending has been higher than or similar to spending on health and education. For example, in 1993, while defence expenditure accounted for 14.7 per cent of CGE, public health received only 9.5 per cent of the national budget.[99]

Guatemala

Guatemala's endemic guerrilla war differs from similar conflicts in the region in that its character is predominantly ethnic rather than politico-economic. Guerrillas attack military posts and economic targets, the army continues to kill suspected guerrilla supporters and the Civil Patrols, ostensibly volunteer groups of government supporters who patrol rural areas, are responsible for a great many human rights violations. Breakthroughs in the peace process are routinely predicted and just as routinely fall apart.[100] Guatemala's territorial claim to the whole of Belize is another potentially explosive issue, and is further complicated by Mexico's claim to a large portion of the territory in

[99] *Perfil Estadístico Centroamericano FLACSO* [Central American statistical profile], (Facultad Latinoamericana de Ciencias Sociales/Inforpres: Panama, 1993), pp. 1007–1008, 1011.
[100] Millett, R., 'Central America: an overview', *Jane's Intelligence Review Yearbook: The World in Conflict, 1994/95*, pp. 152–57.

Table 8.10. Guatemala's military expenditure allocations, 1990–95
Figures are in m. current quetzals. Figures in italics are percentages.

	1990	1991	1992	1993	1994	1995
Operating cost[a]	372.6	474.9	492.8	561.0	561.1	648.1
Share of total	*90.6*	*90.4*	*92.2*	*93.0*	*93.0*	*89.5*
Investment cost[b]	38.9	50.2	41.7	42.3	42.3	76.3
Share of total	*9.4*	*9.6*	*7.8*	*7.0*	*7.0*	*10.5*
Total	**411.5**	**525.1**	**534.5**	**603.3**	**603.3**	**724.3**

[a] Includes O&M, personnel (military and civilian) pensions and other social expenditures.
[b] Includes procurement, construction and R&D.

Source: Department of Finance of the Army, as reported to the UN, Ministry of National Defence, Guatemala, provided by the Guatemalan Embassy, Stockholm, 10 Dec. 1995.

dispute. Guatemala has not adjusted its claim since the Mexican Government offered in the 1980s to waive its own claims if Guatemala did likewise.

The new President, Alvaro Arzú of the conservative Partido de Avanzada Nacional (National Advance Party, PAN), who took office on 14 January 1996, has promised to curb the power of the military and to increase social spending in the countryside. He may seek to forge alliances with more progressive groups within the military. These groups are believed to favour completion of the peace talks with the Unidad Revolucionaria National Guatemala (United Revolutionary National of Guatemala, URNG) and to want a smaller but more professional army. They are unlikely, however, to tolerate civilian investigation of alleged military involvement in human rights abuses and organized crime, including drug-trafficking, which the URNG, pressure groups and the UN have long sought.

Despite a gradual increase in the strength of the Guatemalan Armed Forces from 31 000 to 44 200,[101] backed by 12 500 paramilitary police and a conscript territorial Defence Force of about 500 000 poorly-armed Indian peasants,[102] Guatemala's insurgency continued throughout the 1990s; it shows little sign of abatement.

Official military expenditure for 1994 was 603.3 million quetzals ($104.9 million). Given inflation of 12 per cent per year, this indicates that reported defence expenditures are projected to decline in real terms. It should be noted that in the latter half of 1994 the government announced across-the-board budget cuts due to fiscal difficulties. The military was slated to lose 20 million quetzals from its budget,[103] although it is unclear whether this cut actually was made or, if it was, from what base it was made, since the 1995 budget

[101] *The Military Balance 1995–1996* (note 97), p. 266.
[102] English, A., 'Guatemala: the unending war', *Jane's Intelligence Review International*, vol. 5 (May 1993), p. 230.
[103] Annual Report on Military Expenditures 1994. Unclassified document submitted to the Committee on Appropriations, House of Representatives by the Department of State in accordance with Section 511 (b) of the Foreign Operations, Export Financing, and Related Programs Appropriations Act, 1993, Washington, DC, Feb. 1995, p. 23.

amounts to 724.3 million quetzals ($127.3 million). In past years the military consistently overspent its allotted budget, receiving funds from other ministries so that its actual share of the budget has usually been higher than initially planned. For example, the defence budget for 1993 reported to the UN was 603.3 million quetzals,[104] while the original Defence Ministry budget for 1993 was 634.2 million quetzals;[105] final reported outlays for 1993 were 692.98 million quetzals.[106]

Nicaragua

In 1990, elections in Nicaragua produced a defeat for the ruling Frente Sandinista para la Liberación Nacional (Sandinista National Liberation Front, FSLN) and made possible a negotiated end to its prolonged civil conflict. The election accelerated the end of external support for internal war, in effect largely removing the nation from the arena of cold war politics. In Nicaragua the basic problem has been the continued control over the military of individuals closely associated with the Sandinistas. Some progress has been made in resolving the situation. In August 1994, the National Assembly approved a new military code which was an important step forward for the democratic process. It provided a framework for institutionalizing civilian control of the armed forces and stipulated among other things that General Humberto Ortega would step down as Commander-in-Chief in February 1995.[107]

Civil–military relations, however, remain one of the main topics of political debate in Nicaragua, contributing to the political divisions which have paralyzed efforts at national reconciliation and economic recovery. From 1990 to 1994, troop numbers were reduced by 81 per cent from nearly 80 000 to 15 200—the fastest demobilization in Latin America.[108] Even so, opponents of the Sandinista People's Army (Ejército Popular Sandinista, EPS) demand that reductions continue to the level of 6000.[109] The government of President Violeta Chamorro has not had the economic or technical basis to meet the costs involved in this for the ex-military—land and housing, technical assistance, financial support and education.

---

[104] See table 8.10.

[105] El Presupuesto Nacional [National budget of Guatemala], received by the Instituto Nacional de Administración Pública, Library and Documentation Centre, Guatemala, Sep. 1995, p. 6.

[106] Annual Report on Military Expenditures 1994 (note 104), p. 7.

[107] Solís, L. and Rojas, F. (eds), De la guerra a la integración: la transición y la seguridad en Centroamérica [From war to integration: the transition and security in Central America] (Fundación Arias para la Paz y el Progreso Humano, Facultad Latinoamericana de Ciencias Sociales: Santiago, Chile, 1995), pp. 165–85.

[108] Castillo, M., 'El profesionalismo militar y la redefinición del papel del Ejército Popular Sandinista' [Military professionalism and the redefinition of the paper for the Sandinista Armed Forces], Paper prepared for the Reúnion del grupo de trabajo de CLASCO fuerzas armadas, sociedad y defensa nacional [Meeting of the CLASCO Working Group on armed forces, society and national defence], Guatemala, Nov. 1994.

[109] Guzmán, L., 'Políticos en uniforme: Un balance de poder del EPS', Problemas de la desmovilización militar en Centroamerica [Problems of military demobilization in Central America], Cuadernos de trabajo, no. 14 (Fundacion Arias para la Paz y el Progreso Humano, Centro para la Paz y la Reconciliacion: San José, July 1993), p. 6.

Table 8.11. Nicaragua's military expenditure allocations, 1992–95
Figures are in US $m. at yearly average exchange rates.[a] Figures in italics are percentages.

	1992	1993	1994	1995
Operating cost[b]	43.4	35.2	33.1	29.4
Share of total	*95.8*	*98.3*	*98.2*	*94.2*
Investment cost[c]	1.9	0.6	0.6	1.8
Share of total	*4..2*	*1.7*	*1.8*	*5.8*
Total	**45.3**	**35.8**	**33.7**	**31.2**
Share of total CGE[d]	*8.7*	*8.6*	*8.1*	*8.0*

[a] As supplied by the Defence Ministry, Managua.
[b] Includes O&M, personnel (military and civilian) pensions and other social expenditures.
[c] Includes procurement, construction and R&D.
[d] Central government expenditure.

Source: UN Definition of Military Budgets, provided by the Nicaraguan Ministry of Defence, through the Nicaraguan Embassy, Stockholm, 6 Dec. 1995.

Nicaragua has reduced military expenditure in conjunction with the downsizing of its army and direct foreign military assistance from the former Soviet Union and Soviet bloc countries has been nearly eliminated. International financial institutions, such as the IMF's Enhanced Structural Adjustment Facility (ESAF), require cuts in overall government spending. It seems, however, that the army's budget has not been reduced in proportion to reductions in troop numbers. This excessive military expenditure increases economic insecurity by creating an opportunity cost in the non-military sector; this then becomes a potential source of internal instability, leading to a vicious circle in which further security expenditure may be required as the government strives desperately to maintain stability.

VII. Conclusions

Although global military spending continued to decline in 1995, heavy reductions in the Western industrialized countries and Russia distorted the overall picture. Many developing countries continue to maintain military expenditure at levels which are out of proportion to their legitimate security requirements. In some cases, internal conflict is driving military expenditure to ever higher levels, thereby limiting the opportunites for governments to address the socioeconomic inequalities which are so often the root cause of violent instability.

Analysis of the impact of these trends on the overall international security environment remains complicated by the absence of reliable information on military expenditure. The lack of meaningful data is a particularly acute problem in determining military expenditure for many African and Latin American countries. Similarly, even where official data are available, their reliability must be seriously questioned in countries such as China and Iran.

Appendix 8A. Tables of military expenditure

PAUL GEORGE, BENGT-GÖRAN BERGSTRAND AND EVAMARIA LOOSE-WEINTRAUB

Sources and methods are explained in appendix 8B. Footnotes appear and conventions used are explained at the end of table 8A.3

Table 8A.1. World military expenditure, in current price figures, 1986–95

Figures are in local currency, current prices.

		1986	1987	1988	1989	1990	1991	1992	1993	1994	1995
NATO[1]											
North America											
Canada	m. C. dollars	10 970	11 715	12 336	12 854	13 473	12 830	13 111	13 293	13 008	12 291
USA	m. dollars	281 105	288 157	293 093	304 085	306 170	280 292	305 141	297 637	288 079	277 834
Europe											
Belgium	m. francs	152 079	155 422	150 647	152 917	155 205	157 919	132 819	129 602	131 955	134 736
Denmark	m. kroner	13 333	14 647	15 620	15 963	16 399	17 091	17 129	17 390	17 293	17 500
France	m. francs	197 080	209 525	215 073	225 331	231 911	240 936	238 874	241 199	246 469	239 600
Germany[2]	m. D. marks	60 130	61 354	61 638	63 178	68 376	65 579	65 536	61 487	58 936	59 925
Greece	m. drachmas	338 465	393 052	471 820	503 032	612 344	693 846	835 458	932 995	1 052 760	1 171 377
Italy	b. lire	19 421	22 872	25 539	27 342	28 007	30 191	30 813	32 364	32 835	32 647
Luxembourg	m. francs	2 390	2 730	3 163	2 995	3 233	3 681	3 963	3 740	4 214	4 164
Netherlands	m. guilders	13 110	13 254	13 300	13 571	13 513	13 548	13 900	13 103	12 990	13 090
Norway	m. kroner	16 033	18 551	18 865	20 248	21 251	21 313	23 638	22 528	23 868	23 787
Portugal	m. escudos	139 972	159 288	194 036	229 344	267 299	305 643	341 904	352 504	360 811	422 586
Spain	m. pesetas	715 306	852 767	835 353	923 375	922 808	947 173	927 852	1 054 902	994 689	1 054 876
Turkey	b. lira	1 868	2 477	3 789	7 158	13 866	23 657	42 320	77 717	156 724	275 273
UK	m. pounds	18 639	19 269	19 290	20 868	22 287	24 380	22 850	22 686	22 250	21 637

		1986	1987	1988	1989	1990	1991	1992	1993	1994	1995
Other Europe											
Albania	m. leks	978	1 011	955	965	990	..	..	3 876	4 515	..
Austria	m. schillings	17 940	16 972	16 597	17 849	17 537	18 208	18 419	19 350	19 744	20 230
Bulgaria	m. leva	[1 203]	[1 396]	1 405	1 682	1 635	3 945	5 762	8 239	12 917	24 000
Croatia³	m. kuna						21.4	190.6	3 043.6	8 120	10 100
Cyprus⁴	m. C. pounds	13.0	15.4	19.1	18.9	22.9	28.6	28.7	116.6	205.0	..
Czech Rep.⁵	m. korunas								│23 777	27 008	27 045
Czechoslovakia⁶	m. korunas	28 300	28 496	29 236	43 784	41 900	43 037	48 503			
Estonia⁷	m. kroons						..	68.0	173.8	326.5	416.7
Finland	m. markkaa	6 100	6 396	7 046	7 411	8 089	9 739	10 206	10 084	9 371	9 018
German DR	m. marks	19 430.1	20 897.4	21 647.0							
Hungary⁸	b. forints	25.8	28.4	38.0	47.7	52.4	54.0	61.2	169.0	79.6	75.4
Ireland	m. Ir. pounds	303.8	292.7	297.4	306.3	359.2	388.0	395.9	404.6	433.0	451.9
Latvia⁹	th. lati								8 512	11 603	14 375
Lithuania¹⁰	m. roubles/m. litai						169.3	2 720.5	│85.9	80.6	136.0
Malta	m. liri	6.5	8.0	7.4	7.4	6.7	7.0	7.8	9.2	10.3	..
Poland	b. 'old' zlotys	381	468	742	2 214	14 945	18 300	26 237	39 803	51 170	58 627
Romania	b. lei	[32.7]	[29.0]	[31.2]	[33.3]	33.8	32.4	158.5	261.6	1 248.3	1 791.3
Slovak Rep.¹¹	m. korunas								8 629	9 614	12 900
Slovenia¹²	m. tolars						4 031	15 437	19 580	24 655	32 420
Sweden	m. kronor	24 552	26 039	28 035	31 037	34 974	35 744	35 302	36 309	37 608	39 908
Switzerland	m. francs	4 776	4 716	4 956	5 431	6 052	6 202	6 249	5 753	5 935	5 938
Yugoslavia¹³	m. new dinars	97	197	568	6 113	5 180	..	..	..	..	..
CIS											
Armenia	m. roubles							250	..	..	..
Azerbaijan¹⁴	m. roubles/m. manats						125.5	6 070.6	56 910	│33 543	..
Belarus¹⁵	m./b. roubles						..	14 967	..	..	│892
Georgia¹⁶	m. roubles/b. coupons						79	3 545	..	..	│38 150
Kazakhstan¹⁷	b. roubles/b. tenge						..	23.7	140.8 │	13.8	28.3
Kyrgyzstan¹⁸	m. roubles/m. som						..	670	..	..	│151

Country	Unit										
Russia[20]	b. roubles	..	..	..	..	..	..	5	58	60	265
Tajikistan	m. roubles	..	..	..	..	..	..	901	7 632	43 004	59 379
Turkmenistan[21]	b. manats	..	..	..	..	..	..	4 750	..	34 700	4.6
Ukraine[22]	b. roubles/ b. karbovanets	..	..	..	..	..	7.0	112.3	547.1	21 597.3	106 200
Uzbekistan[23]	b. roubles/b. sum	..	..	..	..	..	0.2	11.7	207.4	990.8	3 355.4
Middle East											
Bahrain	m. dinars	60.4	60.3	70.4	73.6	81.2	89.2	94.6	94.4	[96.2]	..
Egypt	m. Eg. pounds	3 309	3 364	3 118	3 048	3 504	4 223	4 884	5 413	[5 724]	..
Iran[24]	b. rials	(486)	(473)	(524)	(624)	(727)	(861)	(952)	(1 601)	(2 147)	..
Iraq	m. dinars	..	..	..	..	..	..	..	..	..	..
Israel	m. new shekels	7 523	8 379	9 121	10 566	12 940	[14 778]	18 542	19 164	20 546	25 297
Jordan	m. dinars	249.6	252.8	257.3	251.5	254.7	269.7	272.8	299.6	348.2	..
Kuwait[25]	m. dinars	377	373	476	610	2 585	3 674	1 852	..	..	..
Lebanon	b. Leb. pounds	..	..	..	..	..	..	..	400 742	520 653	539 571
Oman	m. riyals	665.4	583.6	519.0	571.9	656.2	557.4	679.5	650.1	..	..
Saudi Arabia	m. riyals	62 418	60 726	52 150	48 945	50 000	100 000	57 601	61 692	53 549	..
Syria	m. Syr. pounds	14 440	14 327	14 612	16 654	18 429	32 483	33 412	[36 231]	[36 907]	..
UAE	m. dirhams	6 900	5 827	5 827	(5 827)	(5 827)	(5 827)	(5 827)	(5 827)	(5 827)	..
Yemen[26]	m. rials	2 808	3 124	5 533	6 030	10 382	13 227	16 812	..	..	..
South Asia											
Bangladesh	m. taka	7 495	9 080	9 290	10 750	11 450	11 965	13 980	16 095	17 290	..
India	b. rupees	98.2	115.2	129.0	140.4	150.7	160.3	172.5	205.2	231.2	250.1
Nepal	m. rupees	659	739	831	985	1 285	1 577	..	..	..	..
Pakistan	m. rupees	38 471	43 315	46 808	50 261	57 898	67 276	76 554	92 010	97 000	105 737
Sri Lanka	m. rupees	4 704	6 807	5 371	4 574	8 754	11 059	13 590	16 035	(20 018)	32 000
Far East											
Brunei[27]	m. B. dollars	239.9	219.5	358.6	362.8	419.4	..	..	..	..	..
China, P. R.[28]	b. yuan	20.1	21.0	21.8	25.1	29.0	33.0	37.8	42.6	55.1	(63.1)
Indonesia	b. new rupiahs	(1 963)	(1 852)	(1 913)	(2 086)	(2 487)	(2 768)	(3 205)	(3 374)	..	..
Japan	b. yen	3 381	3 563	3 789	4 041	4 301	4 475	4 588	4 627	4 670	4 742

		1986	1987	1988	1989	1990	1991	1992	1993	1994	1995
Korea, North[29]	m. won	3 975	3 971	3 863	4 060	4 314	4 466	4 582	4 692	4 817	..
Korea, South	b. won	4 427.5	4 683.4	5 316.1	6 021.7	6 796.8	8 039.5	8 856.9	9 176.8	10 552.8	11 243.5
Malaysia	m. ringgits	4 075	3 611	2 241	2 761	3 043	4 323	4 500	4 951	5 367	5 980
Mongolia	m. tugriks	790	793	900	850	592	[888]	1 184	2 493	7 214	9 051
Myanmar[30]	m. kyats	1 700	1 355	1 632	3 689	5 160	5 924	8 366	[11 688]	[15 373]	..
Philippines	m. pesos	11 587	12 549	16 788	20 580	23 321	26 010	26 321	28 248	[30 807]	..
Singapore	m. S. dollars	2 564	2 613	2 657	3 080	3 672	4 179	4 252	4 816	4 902	5 395
Taiwan	b. T. dollars	154	149	160	188	211	227	239	254	322	355
Thailand	m. baht	42 147	42 812	44 831	48 846	55 502	64 961	74 625	81 500	88 180	..
Viet Nam	b. dong	..	103	792	2 047	3 319	4 292	[3 730]	3 168	4 730	..
Oceania											
Australia	m. A. dollars	7 280	7 667	7 963	8 538	9 206	9 665	10 385	11 098	11 381	10 959
Fiji	m. F. dollars	16.5	31.3	35.3	43.1	45.2	47.9	45.9	49.4	40.8	..
New Zealand[31]	m. NZ dollars	1 023	1 173	1 336	1 341	1 300	1 210	1 097	1 111	1 021	993
Papua New Guinea	m. kina	36.4	38.5	40.1	45.6	65.6	50.1	56.5	54.4	[56.0]	..
Tonga	th. pa'anga	1 080	1 115	1 138	1 565	1 980	2 269	..	..	..	..
Africa											
Algeria	m. dinars	5 300	5 805	6 084	6 500	[8 470]	10 439	[19 140]	29 810	46 800	154 300
Angola[32]	m./b. kwanzas	32 629	36 585	43 961	58 267	52 391	147 675	484 110	9 707 190	43 521	..
Benin	m. francs	9 100	10 700	11 000	9 100	8 935	[8 018]	[7 100]	[7 610]	..	..
Botswana	m. pulas	65	124	171	207	291	348	..	365	[383]	[423]
Burkina Faso	m. francs	13 658	14 385	15 463	20 173	18 778	..	..	..	17 372	..
Burundi	m. francs	4 780	3 910	..	..	..	..	..	..	..	..
Cameroon	m. francs	50 339	48 165	45 118	48 749	49 674	47 597	49 550	50 811	54 082	..
Cape Verde	m. escudos	357	360	366	..	..	..	215	..	..	..
Central African R.	m. francs	5 892	5 610	..	..	..	..	..	..	..	..
Chad	m. francs	16 850	20 307	..	..	..	..	..	..	..	..
Congo	m. francs	25 625	30 208	..	..	..	..	..	..	..	..
Côte d'Ivoire	m. francs	[36 127]	36 900	38 155	41 368	41 895	40 671	41 503	..	..	..
Djibouti[33]	m. francs	4 632	4 664	4 701	4 705	4 709	4 809	8 000	8 000	..	..

								127	183	. .	. .
Ethiopia	m. birr	969	1 174	1 506	1 769	1 921	1 231	684	681	[747]	. .
Gabon	m. francs	47 100	43 407	. .	. .	. .	. .	. .	. .	. .	. .
Gambia	m. dalasis	. .	. .	. .	. .	20.6	31.0	31.2	24.9	25.5	. .
Ghana	m. cedis	4 605	6 659	4 603	6 106	9 006	15 230	23 242	39 481	. .	. .
Guinea-Bissau	m. pesos	1 251	2 168	. .	8 027	. .	. .	. .	. .	. .	. .
Kenya	m. shillings	2 941	4 111	4 454	4 703	5 648	5 279	5 027	[6 407]	[7 146]	[8 508]
Lesotho	th. maloti	30 539	36 836	38 523	59 321	62 505	62 393	99 243	[103 488]	[92 938]	99 450
Liberia	m. dollars	23.0	25.8	26.5	. .	(56.7)	(20.5)	(21.6)	(35.4)	(41.3)	. .
Libya	m. dinars	819	549	582	. .	. .	. .	. .	. .	. .	. .
Madagascar	m. francs	39.8	39.2	. .	51.3	53.5	55.8	[60.7]	65.6	. .	. .
Malawi	m. kwachas	46.1	47.8	51.7	62.9	66.4	66.5	67.8	69.6	. .	. .
Mali	m. francs	13.0	13.3	14.3	14.7	14.2	[23.5]	16.6	[16.0]	. .	. .
Mauritania	m. ouguiyas	. .	. .	. .	3 230	3 240	3 230	3 430	3 640	3 640	. .
Mauritius	m. rupees	38.7	46.9	62.9	96.1	136.3	164.3	177.9	191.4	. .	. .
Morocco	m. dirhams	6 467	6 687	6 425	7 193	7 873	8 832	10 075	10 093	[10 607]	. .
Mozambique	m. meticais	12 436	41 700	58 200	102 400	136 000	178 000	259 300	416 800	[501 669]	. .
Namibia[35]	m. rand	160.5	190.4	218.7	150.7	123.7	168.7	182.5	180.5	. .	. .
Niger	m. francs	5 000	5 300	5 700	5 749	12 315	. .	. .	. .	. .	. .
Nigeria[36]	m. nairas	(878)	(749)	(1 720)	(2 220)	(2 286)	(2 400)	(3 990)	(4 500)	. .	. .
Rwanda	m. francs	3 050	2 979	2 800	2 809	7 964	13 800	. .	16 582	. .	. .
Senegal	m. francs	28 490	28 784	28 967	30 293	30 685	29 480	. .	. .	. .	. .
Seychelles	m. rupees	60.3	63.4	65.4	73.6	79.2	87.6	105.4	67.1	35.2	55.2
Sierra Leone	m. leones	65	156	293	861	1 876	6 846	13 316	[16 429]	[20 269]	. .
Somalia	m. shillings	2 511	3 000	7 918	4 200	. .	. .	. .	. .	. .	. .
South Africa[37]	m. rand	4 355.7	6 365.7	8 265.1	9 626.2	10 108.4	13 467	12 529	11 538	12 132	11 009
Sudan	m. S. pounds	650	850	. .	. .	. .	. .	. .	. .	. .	. .
Swaziland	m. emalangeni	15.8	16.0	18.7	21.6	34.7	38.7	[43.6]	[54.4]	75.3	. .
Tanzania	m. shillings	4 319	6 090	7 418	8 855	10 823	12 196	. .	. .	. .	. .
Togo	m. francs	9 200	13 047	12 834	13 354	13 817	12 950	11 825	. .	. .	. .
Tunisia	m. dinars	164.2	161.1	199.8	222.2	217.7	224.2	236.7	[251.7]	[272.8]	[289.2]
Uganda	m. shillings	1 836	5 612	14 597	29 760	47 926	60 167	61 711	64 000	. .	. .
Zaire[38]	m./b. zaïres	2 489	7 330	15 010	22 895	. .	. .	33	1 258	. .	. .

		1986	1987	1988	1989	1990	1991	1992	1993	1994	1995
Zambia	m. kwachas	480	637	717	896	2 156	13 785	..	18 798	22 907	..
Zimbabwe	m. Z. dollars	568	652	704	800	950	1 116	1 269	1 437	1 616	1 867
Caribbean											
Bahamas	m. Bah. dollars	10.8	11.7	16.7	18.0	19.0	20.0	..	..	..	..
Barbados	m. Bar. dollars	20.1	21.0	19.1	22.7	27.5	26.2	24.5	26.2	27.0	..
Cuba	m. pesos	1 307	1 300	1 274	1 377	1 380	..	..	..	..	..
Dominican Rep.	m. pesos	201.9	218.9	280.3	332.6	405.8	429.0	798.0	..	..	..
Haiti	m. gourdes	..	..	..	..	..	..	..	..	..	..
Jamaica	m. dollars	123.8	132.1	162.9	206.5	318.2	495.9	643.6	988.7	1 023.2	..
Central America											
Belize	th. B. dollars	..	..	[7 836]	8 711	9 538	9 466	10 584	13 011	[17 240]	..
Costa Rica	b. colones	[1.3]	[1.5]	1.5	1.7	2.0	2.2	3.0	3.9	..	..
El Salvador	m. colones	634.2	686.9	694.9	827.3	871.5	888.6	926.1	866.4	866.4	866.4
Guatemala[39]	m. quetzals	179.5	288.4	317.3	341.2	411.5	525.1	534.5	603.3	603.3	724.3
Honduras	m. lempiras	137.5	141.3	150.0	247.0	276.0	..	..	290.0	..	..
Mexico	m. new pesos	[481.4]	[814.7]	[2 073.6]	[2 643.1]	3 580.6	4 807.6	6 010.8	7 211.4	9 633.5	8 815.9
Nicaragua[40]	m. US dollars	..	..	..	..	177.0	51.1	45.3	35.8	33.7	31.2
Panama[41]	m. balboas	105.0	103.8	102.9	101.9	73.1	78.6	93	..	..	..
South America											
Argentina[42]	australes/pesos	1 669	5 863	27 355	786.4	12 482.6	23 353.7	4 270	4 247	4 712	4 683
Bolivia	m. bolivianos	146.6	173.9	179.5	224.5	356.7	421.9	435.9	482.0	[522.7]	..
Brazil[43]	reais/th. reais	12.0	41.6	428.5	6 786.2	142.2	447.7	4 881.9	..	..	..
Chile[44]	b. pesos	90.0	100.3	126.4	137.5	165.1	203.6	249.4	291.2	334.7	388.1
Colombia	m. pesos	79 058	100 452	155 134	206 518	289 454	344 994	513 961	1 035 025	1 213 554	(1 392 082)
Ecuador	m. sucres	25 598	35 442	61 275	102 000	156 000	[260 000]	[419 825]	..	..	..
Paraguay	m. guaranies	20 097	26 885	32 643	59 654	81 376	141 643	159 110	181 328	201 978	240 000
Peru[45]	b. intis/m.soles	10 720	21 702	90 500	2.0	129.7	478.6	1 001.0	..	..	..
Uruguay	m. new pesos	23	31	58	114	233	363	813	..	..	..
Venezuela	m. bolivares	6 099	9 005	12 934	14 110	24 350	46 896	46 250	..	..	..

Table 8A.2. World military expenditure, in constant price figures, 1986–95

Figures are in US $m., at 1990 prices (CPI-deflated) and exchange rates unless otherwise noted.[46] All notes are at the end of table 8A.3.

	1986	1987	1988	1989	1990	1991	1992	1993	1994	1995
NATO[1]										
North America										
Canada	11 233	11 488	11 631	11 536	11 547	10 413	10 482	10 433	10 191	9 430
USA	335 048	331 215	323 860	320 427	306 170	268 994	284 116	269 111	254 038	238 194
Europe										
Belgium	4 984	5 017	4 806	4 732	4 644	4 579	3 760	3 571	3 551	3 568
Denmark	2 520	2 662	2 714	2 648	2 650	2 697	2 648	2 653	2 587	2 559
France	41 081	42 284	42 243	42 793	42 589	42 875	41 502	41 052	41 260	39 426
Germany[2]	39 889	40 570	40 242	40 146	42 320	39 216	37 697	33 979	31 609	31 448
Greece	3 861	3 856	4 078	3 819	3 863	3 663	3 808	3 716	3 780	3 834
Italy	20 186	22 699	24 113	24 304	23 376	23 706	23 004	23 127	22 556	21 380
Luxembourg	78	89	101	93	97	107	111	102	112	108
Netherlands	7 461	7 598	7 561	7 636	7 421	7 217	7 174	6 590	6 358	6 278
Norway	3 234	3 442	3 279	3 369	3 395	3 293	3 569	3 326	3 473	3 375
Portugal	1 504	1 563	1 738	1 824	1 875	1 925	1 977	1 908	1 861	2 088
Spain	8 827	9 995	9 345	9 668	9 053	8 775	8 113	8 823	7 940	8 037
Turkey	4 532	4 316	3 802	4 398	5 315	5 463	5 747	6 355	6 213	5 336
UK	42 867	42 561	40 646	40 792	39 776	41 087	37 141	36 312	34 742	32 677
NATO Europe	181 025	186 653	184 668	186 223	186 375	184 601	176 253	171 513	166 043	160 114
NATO Total	527 305	529 356	520 159	518 185	504 092	464 008	470 851	451 057	430 271	407 738
Other Europe										
Albania	..			..	66				..	..
Austria[47]	1 726	1 612	1 546	1 622	1 542	1 543	1 507	1 528	1 514	1 516
Bulgaria	(409)	(475)	(472)	(531)	551	306	245	213	223	..
Croatia[3] 1993 prices/exch.r.						[703]	[845]	[851]	[1 096]	[1 312]
Cyprus[4]	33	38	45	43	50	60	56	217	365	..
Czech Rep.[5] 1993 prices/exch.r.								816	842	770

	1986	1987	1988	1989	1990	1991	1992	1993	1994	1995
Czechoslovakia[6]	1 762	1 774	1 816	2 683	2 334	1 520	1 547			
Estonia[7] 1993 prices/exch.r.	..					..	10	13	17	..
Finland	1 975	1 989	2 085	2 058	2 116	2 447	2 499	2 417	2 222	2 113
German DR	..									
Hungary[8]	775	784	907	974	829	637	587	1 323	524	..
Ireland	571	533	530	525	596	623	617	622	650	664
Latvia[9] 1993 prices/exch.r.						1	..	13	13	12
Lithuania[10] 1993 prices/exch.r.						22	3	20	11	13
Malta	22	26	24	24	21	24	24	27	29	
Poland	1 824	1 758	1 776	1 523	1 573	1 090	1 075	1 192	1 150	1 003
Romania[48] 1993 prices/exch.r.	[1 589]	[1 395]	[1 461]	[1 544]	1 507	526	828	385	775	825
Slovak Rep[11] 1993 prices/exch.r.								280	276	338
Slovenia[12] 1993 prices/exch.r.						144	180	173	182	207
Sweden	5 387	5 499	5 572	5 762	5 909	5 540	5 325	5 243	5 295	5 466
Switzerland	7 455	7 255	7 484	7 950	8 407	8 143	7 885	7 023	7 188	7 065
Yugoslavia[13]	4 285	4 351	4 562	3 699	458					
CIS[49]										
Middle East										
Bahrain	162	165	192	215	216	235	250	244	[246]	
Egypt	3 296	2 803	2 208	1 780	1 752	1 764	1 794	1 775	[1 735]	
Iran[24]	(15 556)	(11 776)	(10 131)	(9 865)	(10 673)	(10 793)	(9 498)	(13 175)	(13 439)	
Iraq										
Israel	7 324	6 808	6 374	6 141	6 418	[6 159]	6 903	6 431	6 139	6 762
Jordan	585	593	566	440	384	376	365	383	430	
Kuwait[25] 1989 prices/exch.r.	1 378	1 355	1 704	2 115	8 802	[10 701]	[4 995]			
Lebanon[50]										
Oman	2 213	1 743	1 685	1 572	1 707	1 407	1 658	1 473		
Saudi Arabia	17 077	16 873	14 356	13 336	13 351	25 455	14 676	15 555	15 633	
Syria	3 675	2 283	1 731	1 770	1 642	2 687	2 525	[2 449]	[2 302]	
UAE	2 088	1 662	(1 662)	(1 653)	(1 587)	(1 512)	(1 433)	(1 352)		

South Asia										
Bangladesh	309	342	320	336	331	323	362	416	432	..
India	7 727	8 331	8 530	8 734	8 607	8 038	7 742	8 658	8 853	8 708
Nepal	32	32	33	36	43	46	..	..	..	..
Pakistan	2 376	2 555	2 537	2 525	2 667	2 772	2 881	3 166	2 967	2 858
Sri Lanka	195	263	182	139	219	246	271	287	(330)	432
Far East										
Brunei[27]	140	127	205	204	231	..	..	..	..	..
China, P. R.[28]	6 497	6 243	5 375	5 332	6 069	6 571	6 924	6 668	6 945	(6 121)
Indonesia	(1 443)	(1 246)	(1 190)	(1 220)	(1 350)	(1 373)	(1 477)	(1 425)	..	..
Japan	24 811	26 123	27 572	28 773	29 702	29 916	30 150	30 031	30 115	30 766
Korea, North[29]	..	..	..	..	..	..	..	..	..	..
Korea, South	7 929	8 139	8 624	9 238	9 603	10 393	10 779	10 654	11 531	11 763
Malaysia	1 634	1 445	874	1 048	1 125	1 531	1 522	1 617	1 690	1 794
Mongolia	20	20	23	21	15	[11]	5	3	5	..
Myanmar[30]	580	371	385	685	814	706	818	[867]	[919]	..
Philippines	689	719	884	966	959	901	837	835	[835]	..
Singapore	1 528	1 550	1 553	1 757	2 026	2 230	2 217	2 453	2 423	2 606
Taiwan	6 270	6 045	6 430	7 213	7 782	8 086	8 154	8 394	10 234	10 885
Thailand	1 956	1 939	1 956	2 022	2 169	2 402	2 649	2 794	2 892	..
Viet Nam[51]	..	172	325	482	781	552	[408]	301	402	..
Oceania										
Australia	7 034	6 830	6 611	6 594	6 627	6 742	7 174	7 529	7 579	7 106
Fiji	15	27	27	32	31	30	28	28	23	..
New Zealand[31]	843	835	894	849	776	704	632	632	571	542
Papua New Guinea	47	48	48	52	70	50	54	49	[49]	..
Tonga	1.1	1.1	1.0	1.3	1.5	1.6	..	..	..	..
Africa										
Algeria	859	875	866	847	[945]	926	[1 289]	1 666	2 027	4 962
Angola	..	..	..	..	[1 752]	[2 599]	[2 136]	[2 894]	[1 236]	..
Benin	..	..	..	..	33	[28]	[24]	[25]	..	..

	1986	1987	1988	1989	1990	1991	1992	1993	1994	1995
Botswana	51	90	114	124	156	167	[148]	132	[126]	[126]
Burkina Faso	50	54	56	74	69	..	..	..	50	..
Burundi	37	29	..	..	..	..	..	..	..	..
Cameroon	212	179	178	182	182	172	176	175	173	..
Cape Verde	6.4	6.2	6.1	..	..	..	2.7	..	..	..
Central African R.	19	20	..	..	..	..	..	..	..	..
Chad	64	82	..	..	..	..	..	..	..	..
Congo	99	115	..	..	..	..	..	..	..	..
Côte d'Ivoire	[152]	145	140	151	154	147	145	..	..	..
Djibouti	..	..	..	..	26	22	..	..	..	..
Eritrea[34]	..	..	..	..	..	..	..	..	..	..
Ethiopia	554	689	825	899	928	438	220	212	[221]	..
Gabon	180	167	..	..	..	..	..	..	..	..
Gambia	..	..	..	..	2.6	3.6	3.3	2.5	..	..
Ghana	45	46	24	26	28	40	55	75	..	..
Guinea-Bissau	..	3.8	..	4.9	..	..	..	..	..	..
Kenya	201	260	254	237	246	192	141	[124]	[107]	[129]
Lesotho	19	20	19	26	24	20	28	[26]	[21]	..
Liberia	116	123	116	..	(57)	(10)	(6)	(6)	(4)	..
Libya	..	..	..	..	..	..	..	..	..	..
Madagascar	47	41	..	38	36	34	[33]	32	..	..
Malawi	36	29	24	26	24	22	18	15	..	..
Mali	..	..	53	54	52	[85]	64	[61]	..	..
Mauritania	..	..	..	43	40	38	37	36	34	..
Mauritius	4	4	5	7	9	10	11	10	..	..
Morocco	909	916	859	933	955	992	1 070	1 020	[1 019]	..
Mozambique	..	123	114	143	129	127	127	144	[111]	..
Namibia	102	107	109	65	48	58	54	49	..	..
Niger	16	19	20	21	45	..	..	..	..	..
Nigeria[36]	(304)	(232)	(346)	(297)	(284)	(264)	(304)	(218)	..	..

	[illegible]	[illegible]	[illegible]	[illegible]	[illegible]	140	. .	136	. .	. .
Senegal	99	105	107	112	113	110	. .	. .	. .	. .
Seychelles	12	13	13	14	15	16	19	12	6	10
Sierra Leone	5	5	7	12	12	22	26	[26]	[26]	. .
Somalia	47	44	63	. .	. .	. .	. .	. .	. .	. .
South Africa[37]	2 894	3 641	4 188	4 254	3 908	4 516	3 689	3 098	2 986	2 456
Sudan	789	. .	. .	. .	. .	. .	. .	. .	. .	. .
Swaziland	9	8	9	9	13	14	[14]	[15]	18	. .
Tanzania	57	62	57	54	55	51	. .	. .	. .	. .
Togo	34	48	47	50	51	47	43	. .	. .	. .
Tunisia	249	226	261	269	248	236	235	[241]	[249]	[249]
Uganda	82	83	73	92	112	110	74	72	. .	. .
Zaire[38]	43	68	77	58	. .	. .	. .	. .	. .	. .
Zambia	182	169	122	67	74	247	. .	39	31	. .
Zimbabwe	371	379	381	384	388	370	296	263	242	228
Caribbean										
Bahamas	13	13	18	19	19	19	. .	. .	. .	. .
Barbados	12	12	10	12	14	12	11	11	12	. .
Cuba	. .	. .	. .	. .	. .	. .	. .	. .	. .	. .
Dominican Rep.	92	86	76	62	48	33	58	. .	. .	. .
Haiti	. .	. .	. .	. .	. .	. .	. .	. .	. .	. .
Jamaica	28	28	32	35	44	46	33	42	32	. .
Central America										
Belize	. .	. .	[4]	4	5	4	5	6	[8]	. .
Costa Rica	[28]	[28]	23	23	22	19	21	24	. .	. .
El Salvador	172	150	126	128	109	97	91	72	65	60
Guatemala[39]	78	112	111	107	92	88	81	82	74	82
Honduras	100	100	102	152	138	. .	. .	90	. .	. .
Mexico	[1 287]	[944]	[1 120]	[1 190]	1 273	1 393	1 508	1 665	2 080	1 461
Nicaragua[40]	. .	. .	. .	. .	. .	. .	. .	. .	. .	. .
Panama[41]	107	105	104	103	73	78	77	. .	. .	. .

	1986	1987	1988	1989	1990	1991	1992	1993	1994	1995
South America										
Argentina[42]	2 633	4 146	4 316	3 893	2 560	1 761	2 583	2 323	2 471	2 350
Bolivia	83	86	76	83	112	110	101	103	103	. .
Brazil[43]	1 863	1 961	2 580	2 945	2 031	1 279	1 162	. .	. .	. .
Chile[44]	600	557	610	571	541	547	580	604	620	667
Colombia	404	417	502	531	576	527	618	1 015	961	(908)
Ecuador	178	191	208	197	203	[228]	[238]	. .	. .	. .
Paraguay	43	47	46	67	66	93	90	87	80	. .
Peru[45]	2 157	2 350	1 279	826	691	499	603	. .	. .	. .
Uruguay	200	164	190	207	199	153	204	. .	. .	. .
Venezuela	561	644	716	423	519	745	559	. .	. .	. .

	1986	1987	1988	1989	1990	1991	1992	1993	1994
NATO[1]									
North America									
Canada	2.2	2.1	2.0	2.0	2.0	1.9	1.9	1.9	1.7
USA	6.6	6.3	6.0	5.8	5.5	4.9	5.1	4.7	4.3
Europe									
Belgium	3.0	3.0	2.7	2.5	2.4	2.3	1.9	1.8	1.7
Denmark	2.0	2.1	2.1	2.1	2.1	2.1	2.0	2.0	1.9
France	3.9	3.9	3.8	3.7	3.6	3.6	3.4	3.4	3.3
Germany[2]	3.1	3.1	2.9	2.8	2.8	2.3	2.1	1.9	1.8
Greece	6.1	6.3	6.2	5.7	5.8	5.4	5.6	5.6	5.6
Italy	2.2	2.3	2.3	2.3	2.1	2.1	2.0	2.1	2.0
Luxembourg	1.1	1.2	1.3	1.1	1.1	1.2	1.2	1.1	1.1
Netherlands	3.0	3.0	2.9	2.8	2.6	2.5	2.5	2.3	2.2
Norway	3.1	3.3	3.2	3.3	3.2	3.1	3.4	3.1	3.1
Portugal	3.2	3.1	3.2	3.2	3.1	3.1	3.0	2.9	2.8
Spain	2.2	2.4	2.1	2.0	1.8	1.7	1.6	1.7	1.5
Turkey	4.8	3.3	3.0	3.3	3.5	3.7	3.9	4.0	4.2
UK	4.8	4.6	4.1	4.0	4.0	4.2	3.8	3.6	3.3
Other Europe									
Albania	5.6	5.9	5.6	5.2	5.9	..	..	..	..
Austria	1.3	1.1	1.1	1.1	1.0	0.9	0.9	0.9	0.9
Bulgaria[47]	[3.5]	[3.8]	3.7	4.3	3.6	3.0	3.0	2.9	3.4
Croatia[3]									7.7
Cyprus[4]	0.8	0.9	1.0	0.8	0.9	1.1	1.0	3.6	5.6
Czech Rep.[5]							1	2.7	..
Czechoslovakia[6]	4.1	4.0	4.0	5.8	5.2	4.4			
Estonia[7]						..	0.5	1.3	..
Finland	1.7	1.7	1.6	1.5	1.6	2.0	2.1	2.1	1.8

	1986	1987	1988	1989	1990	1991	1992	1993	1994
German DR	..	..	..	..					
Hungary[8]	2.4	2.3	2.6	2.8	2.5	2.3	2.2	5.1	2.0
Ireland[9]	1.5	1.4	1.3	1.2	1.3	1.4	1.3	1.3	1.2
Latvia[9]								0.6	0.6
Lithuania[10]								0.8	0.5
Malta	1.3	1.5	1.2	1.1	0.9	0.9	0.9	1.0	1.0
Poland	2.9	2.8	2.5	1.9	2.5	2.2	2.3	2.6	2.4
Romania[48]	[3.9]	[3.4]	[3.6]	[4.2]	3.9	1.5	2.6	1.4	1.9
Slovak Rep.[11]								3.1	..
Slovenia[12]						1.1	1.6	1.1	1.1
Sweden	2.6	2.5	2.5	2.5	2.6	2.5	2.4	2.5	2.5
Switzerland	2.0	1.9	1.8	1.9	1.9	1.9	1.8	1.7	1.7
Yugoslavia[13]	4.3	3.9	3.7	2.2	..	..	..		
CIS[49]									
Middle East									
Bahrain	5.0	5.1	5.6	5.5	5.5	6.0	6.2	5.8	[5.3]
Egypt	7.8	6.5	5.1	4.0	3.6	3.8	3.5	3.4	[3.3]
Iran[24]	(3.0)	(2.5)	(2.4)	(2.3)	(2.1)	(1.8)	(1.5)	(1.8)	..
Iraq	..	..	..	..	..	..	..	..	..
Israel	16.9	14.7	13.0	12.3	12.3	[10.9]	11.5	10.4	9.5
Jordan	11.5	11.5	11.4	10.6	9.5	9.4	7.8	7.7	8.2
Kuwait[25]	7.2	6.0	8.2	8.5	48.7	117.4	33.6		
Lebanon[50]	..	..	..	..	..	..	..	..	..
Oman	23.8	19.4	17.7	16.0	16.2	14.2	15.4	12.3	..
Saudi Arabia	23.0	22.0	18.3	15.7	12.8	23.2	12.7	12.7	10.9
Syria	14.4	11.2	7.9	8.0	6.9	10.4	9.0	[9.1]	[8.5]
UAE	8.7	6.7	(6.7)	(5.8)	(4.7)	(4.7)	(4.5)	(4.3)	..
Yemen[26]	7.3	7.2	..	..	..	19.8	18.1	..	..

Bangladesh	1.5	1.6	1.5	1.5	1.5	1.4	1.5	1.6	:
India	3.4	3.6	3.4	3.2	2.9	2.7	2.5	2.7	2.9
Nepal	1.1	1.1	1.0	1.0	1.2	1.2	:	:	:
Pakistan	7.1	6.9	6.5	6.2	6.2	6.0	6.0	6.3	(5.7)
Sri Lanka	2.6	3.5	2.4	1.8	2.7	3.0	3.2	3.2	(3.5)
Far East									
Brunei[27]	4.6	3.7	6.2	6.2	6.4	:	:	:	:
China, P. R.[28]	2.1	1.9	1.5	1.6	1.6	1.6	1.6	1.4	1.3
Indonesia	(1.9)	(1.5)	(1.3)	(1.2)	(1.3)	(1.2)	(1.2)	(1.0)	:
Japan	1.0	1.0	1.0	1.0	1.0	1.0	1.0	1.0	1.0
Korea, North[29]	:	:	:	:	:	:	:	:	:
Korea, South	4.6	4.2	4.0	4.0	3.8	3.7	3.7	3.4	3.5
Malaysia	5.7	4.5	2.5	2.7	2.6	3.3	3.0	3.0	2.9
Mongolia	8.5	8.2	8.7	7.9	5.7	[4.7]	2.5	1.7	:
Myanmar[30]	2.9	2.0	2.1	3.0	3.4	3.2	3.4	[3.4]	[4.2]
Philippines	1.9	1.8	2.1	2.2	2.2	2.1	1.9	1.9	[1.8]
Singapore	6.6	6.1	5.3	5.4	5.5	5.7	5.4	5.4	5.3
Taiwan	5.4	4.6	4.6	4.8	5.0	4.8	4.6	4.4	5.2
Thailand	3.7	3.3	2.9	2.6	2.5	2.6	2.6	2.6	2.4
Viet Nam[51]	:	4.2	6.0	8.4	8.7	6.1	[3.7]	:	:
Oceania									
Australia	2.9	2.7	2.5	2.4	2.4	2.5	2.6	2.7	2.6
Fiji	1.1	2.1	2.2	2.3	2.2	2.2	1.9	1.9	1.6
New Zealand[31]	2.1	2.1	2.1	2.0	1.8	1.7	1.5	1.4	1.2
Papua New Guinea	1.4	1.3	1.3	1.5	2.1	1.4	1.4	1.1	[1.1]
Tonga	1.0	0.9	0.8	1.0	1.1	1.2	:	:	:
Africa									
Algeria	1.8	1.9	1.9	[1.5]	[1.6]	1.3	[2.0]	2.7	3.3
Angola	:	[16.5]	[17.0]	[22.2]	[19.4]	[10.1]	[12.2]	[32.8]	[6.4]
Benin	1.8	2.3	2.3	1.9	1.8	[1.5]	[1.3]	[1.3]	:
Botswana	2.5	3.8	3.7	3.6	4.4	4.7	[4.3]	[4.1]	[3.5]

	1986	1987	1988	1989	1990	1991	1992	1993	1994
Burkina Faso	..	..	..	2.6	2.4	..	..	..	1.2
Burundi	3.4	2.7	..	..	..	..	..	..	..
Cameroon	1.3	1.3	1.2	1.4	1.5	1.5	1.7	1.8	1.3
Cape Verde	2.3	2.0	1.8	..	..	..	0.8	..	..
Central African R.	1.8	1.8	..	..	..	..	..	..	..
Chad	6.0	8.3	..	..	..	..	..	..	..
Congo	4.0	4.4	..	..	..	..	..	..	..
Côte d'Ivoire	[1.1]	1.2	1.2	1.3	1.4	1.4	1.4	..	..
Djibouti	..	..	..	..	6.3	[6.1]	[9.9]	[9.6]	..
Eritrea[34]							(0.4)	(0.5)	[2.6]
Ethiopia	6.5	7.5	9.2	10.2	10.2	6.1	3.0	[2.6]	..
Gabon	3.0	4.2	..	..	..	..	..	..	..
Gambia	..	..	..	..	0.8	1.1	0.7	0.5	..
Ghana	0.9	0.9	0.4	0.4	0.4	0.6	0.8	1.0	..
Guinea-Bissau	2.7	2.3	..	2.2	..	..	..	..	..
Kenya	2.5	3.1	2.9	2.7	2.9	2.4	2.0	[2.0]	[1.7]
Lesotho	5.0	5.1	4.0	4.8	4.0	3.5	4.7	[4.2]	[3.3]
Liberia	2.2	2.3	2.3	..	..	(1.5)	(1.6)	(2.7)	..
Libya	12.7	..	..	..	..	..	..	..	..
Madagascar	1.8	1.4	..	1.3	1.2	1.1	[1.1]	1.0	..
Malawi	2.1	1.8	1.5	1.5	1.3	1.1	1.0	0.8	..
Mali	..	..	..	..	2.1	[3.5]	2.3	[2.1]	..
Mauritania	..	..	..	4.0	3.8	3.5	3.3	3.2	2.9
Mauritius	0.2	0.2	0.2	0.3	0.4	0.4	0.4	0.3	..
Morocco	4.2	4.3	3.5	3.7	3.7	3.7	4.1	3.9	..
Mozambique	10.2	10.6	9.2	10.3	10.1	8.7	8.3	7.6	[3.8]
Namibia	4.8	5.4	4.9	2.9	2.2	2.7	2.5	2.2	[5.8]
Niger	0.8	0.8	0.8	0.8	1.8	..	..	..	..
Nigeria[36]	(1.2)	(0.7)	(1.2)	(1.0)	(0.9)	(0.7)	(0.7)	(0.6)	..
Rwanda	1.8	1.7	1.5	1.5	4.1	6.5	..	7.6	..

Seychelles	4.7	4.5	4.3	4.3	4.0	4.4	4.7	3.2	1.7
Sierra Leone	0.4	0.6	0.7	1.2	1.4	3.0	4.0	[3.8]	[3.9]
Somalia	2.1	1.8	..	..	3.7	—	..	..	..
South Africa[37]	3.0	3.8	4.1	4.0	3.7	4.3	3.7	3.0	2.8
Sudan	2.3	2.0	..	1.0	1.5	..	..	..	..
Swaziland	1.4	1.2	1.1	2.2	2.1	1.7	..	..	..
Tanzania	2.7	2.7	2.2	2.2	2.1	2.8	2.4	..	..
Togo	2.5	3.5	..	..	..	2.0	2.4	[1.7]	..
Tunisia	2.3	2.0	2.3	2.3	2.0	1.9	1.7	1.5	[1.7]
Uganda	2.8	2.5	2.3	2.5	3.0	2.7	1.7	..	..
Zaire[38]	0.5	0.9	0.9	0.7	..	2.7	1.9	..	..
Zambia	3.7	3.2	2.4	1.6	1.9	6.3	..	1.3	..
Zimbabwe	6.8	7.0	6.4	6.1	6.3	5.0	4.4	3.8	3.3
Caribbean									
Bahamas	0.5	0.5	0.6	0.6	0.6	0.7	0.8	..	..
Barbados	0.8	0.7	0.6	0.7	0.8	0.8	0.8	0.8	0.8
Cuba	..	..	1.0	0.8	0.6	0.4	0.7	..	..
Dominican Rep.	1.3	1.1	..	..	..	..	..	..	..
Haiti	..	..	..	..	..	..	..	..	..
Jamaica	0.9	0.8	0.8	0.9	1.0	1.1	0.9	1.0	0.8
Central America									
Belize	..	[0.5]	[1.2]	[1.2]	1.2	1.2	1.1	1.1	[1.6]
Costa Rica	[0.5]	..	0.4	0.4	0.4	0.4	0.3	0.4	..
El Salvador	3.2	3.0	2.5	2.6	2.4	2.1	1.9	1.4	1.2
Guatemala[39]	1.1	1.6	1.5	1.4	1.2	1.2	1.0	0.9	0.8
Honduras	0.9	0.8	0.7	1.0	0.8	0.8	0.6	0.5	..
Mexico	[0.6]	[0.4]	[0.5]	[0.5]	0.5	0.5	0.6	0.6	0.7
Nicaragua[40]	..	..	..	..	..	..	..	..	..
Panama[41]	2.0	1.9	2.2	2.2	1.5	1.5	1.4	1.3	..

	1986	1987	1988	1989	1990	1991	1992	1993	1994
South America									
Argentina[42]	1.7	2.5	2.5	2.4	1.8	1.3	1.9	1.7	1.7
Bolivia	1.6	1.7	1.5	1.5	2.0	1.9	1.8	1.7	1.6
Brazil[43]	0.3	0.4	0.5	0.5	0.4	0.3	0.3	..	..
Chile[44]	2.6	2.2	2.1	1.8	1.8	1.7	1.6	1.6	1.5
Colombia	1.2	1.1	1.3	1.4	1.4	1.3	1.6	2.5	2.2
Ecuador	1.9	2.0	2.0	2.0	1.9	[2.1]	[2.2]	..	..
Paraguay	1.1	1.1	1.0	1.3	1.3	1.7	1.6	1.5	1.5
Peru[45]	3.0	3.0	2.1	1.9	2.0	1.5	1.9	..	..
Uruguay	2.6	1.9	2.1	2.4	2.4	1.8	2.3	..	..
Venezuela	1.2	1.3	1.5	0.9	1.1	1.5	1.1	..	..

1 Official NATO publications provide the data for member countries and reflect NATO's definition of military spending rather than domestic budgetary information.
2 Figures on German military expenditure refer to West Germany up to and including 1990 and to united Germany from 1991.
3 Croatia declared its independence from the former Yugoslavia in June 1991 and was recognized by the European Community in Jan. 1992 and the Unted Nations in May 1992. The constant US dollar figures are calculated using 1993 as the base year.
4 Figures up to and including 1992 may not include full procurement costs. Figures for 1993 are taken from the 1993 submission to the United Nations and for 1994 from the budget approved for the year.
5 The Czech Republic was formed after the breakup of Czechoslovakia on 1 Jan. 1993. The constant US dollar figures are calculated using 1993 as the base year.
6 Czechoslovakia split into the Czech Republic and the Republic of Slovakia on 1 Jan. 1993.
7 Estonia became independent in Sep. 1991. The constant US dollar figures are calculated using 1993 as the base year.
8 The 1993 expenditure increase reflects spare parts and training payments for 28 MiG-29 aircraft from Russia under an agreement which partly settled Russia's $1.76 billion debt to Hungary.
9 Latvia became independent in Sep. 1991. The constant US dollar figures are calculated using 1993 as the base year.
10 Lithuania became independent in Sep. 1991. The constant US dollar figures are calculated using 1993 as the base year. Figures for 1991–92 are in million roubles, for 1993 onwards in million litai. The 1991 figure is taken from Lithuania's Statistics Yearbook 1992 (Methodical Publishing Centre: Vilnius, 1992). It is not clear whether the figure is for the whole year or part of the year.
11 The Slovak Republic was formed after the breakup of Czechoslovakia on 1 Jan. 1993. The constant US dollar figures are calculated using 1993 as the base year.
12 Slovenia declared its independence from the former Yugoslavia in June 1991 and was recognized by the European Community in Jan. 1992 and by the United Nations in May 1992. The constant US dollar figures are calculated using 1993 as the base year.
13 Serbia and Montenegro announced the creation of the Federal Republic of Yugoslavia on 27 Apr. 1992.
14 Figures for 1991–92 are in million roubles. That for 1994 is in million manats and is a budget figure, taken from Finansovye Izvestiya, 28 July–3 Aug. 1994.

15 Figures for 1992–93 are in million roubles, taken from *IMF Economic Review*, no. 11 (1995). That for 1995 is in billion roubles, taken from *Summary of World Broadcasts*, SUW/10368/WA/11, 24 Jan. 1995. All are budget figures. A submission was made by Belarus to the United Nations for 1994 but is stated in a currency which was never official use (vouchers) and has not been used.

16 Figures for 1991–94 are in million roubles. The figure for 1995 is in billion coupons and is a budget figure, taken from *Summary of World Broadcasts*, SU/2202 F/9, 16 Jan. 1995.

17 All figures cover spending for both the armed forces and law enforcement. Figures for 1992–93 are in billion roubles and are taken from *Ländesbericht 1994*. Figures for 1994 onwards are in billion tenge: for source, see table 8.4, chapter 8.

18 Figures for 1991–92 are in million roubles, for 1995 onwards in million som.

19 Figures cover spending both for the armed forces and for law enforcement.

20 Figures for 1992–94 are taken from Russia's submission to the United Nations, Apr. 1995, and include the costs of paramilitary formations. The 1995 figure is the budget figure and does not include expenditure on paramilitary forces. *Rossiyskaya Gazeta*, 4 Jan. 1996.

21 The 1995 figure is in billion manats. Up to and including 1992 the currency was the rouble.

22 Figures for 1991–93 are in billion roubles, for 1994 onwards in billion karbovanets. The 1995 figure is a budget figure, taken from *Golos Ukrainy*, 21 Apr. 1995.

23 Figures for 1991–93 are in billion roubles, for 1994–95 in million sum.

24 Figures from open sources may underestimate Iran's military expenditure. The series should be seen as a trend indicator rather than an expenditure level indicator.

25 Figures include contributions made to the allied forces for the liberation of Kuwait.

26 The People's Democratic Republic of Yemen (South Yemen) and the Yemen Arab Republic (North Yemen) merged in May 1990 to form the Republic of Yemen. Figures from 1984–89 refer to North Yemen and from 1990 to the unified state.

27 Outlays include only allocations made to the Royal Brunei Armed Forces proper.

28 Figures reflect official budget figures only. For a discussion of the debate over the true level of Chinese military expenditure, see Bergstrand, B.-G. *et al.*, 'World military expenditure', *SIPRI Yearbook 1994* (Oxford University Press: Oxford, 1994), pp. 441–48.

29 Figures reflect official figures only and may underestimate North Korea's military expenditure. The lack of reliable economic data makes it difficult to calculate military expenditure in constant US dollars and as a proportion of GDP.

30 Figures reported from open sources may underestimate Myanmar's military expenditure.

31 Figures shown here are based on the *New Zealand Official Yearbook* according to the New Zealand Treasury's outlays, probably on a functional definition of defence. Table 8.7 in chapter 8 is based on the same source but refers to defence expenditure and includes some non-military items.

32 Figures up to and including 1993 are in million kwanzas, and from 1994 in billion kwanzas.

33 Figures for 1992 and 1993 are rounded.

34 Eritrea became independent in 1993.

35 Namibia became independent on 21 Mar. 1990. The Namibian dollar was introduced in Sep. 1993, at par with the South African rand.

36 Official figures are highly unreliable.

37 Figures for 1986–90 are taken from the official budget. For 1991 onwards figures are taken from the returns supplied by the Office of the Secretary for Defence in response to the SIPRI questionnaire and have been revised since publication of the *SIPRI Yearbook 1995*.

38 Because of hyper-inflation in the early 1990s figures are very unreliable. Figures prior to 1991 are in million 'old' zaïres, from 1992 in billion 'new' zaïres.

39 The 1993 figure is that reported to the United Nations. Final reported outlays, however, were 692.98 million quetzals. The 1994 and 1995 figures are budget figures.

40 The lack of reliable economic data for Nicaragua makes it difficult to calculate military expenditure in constant US dollars and as a proportion of GDP. Figures in current prices supplied by Nicaragua to SIPRI were expressed in US dollars.

[41] Panama's Army was abolished by the National Assembly in Aug. 1994. The 1992 figure is taken from *Informe del Contralor General de la República de Panama, 1993* [Annual report of the Comptroller General, 1993], 1 Mar. 1993.

[42] Because of hyper-inflation and currency changes, figures are unreliable. Figures for 1986–88 are in million australes, for 1989–91 in billion australes and for 1992–94 in million pesos.

[43] Because of hyper-inflation and currency changes, figures are unreliable. Figures for 1986–89 are in reais, for 1990–92 in thousand reais.

[44] Figures reported from open sources may underestimate Chile's military expenditure.

[45] Because of hyper-inflation in the late 1980s, figures are unreliable. Figures for 1986–88 are in billion intis, for 1989 onwards in million new soles.

[46] This series is based on the figures provided in the local currency series (table 8A.1), deflated to 1990 price levels and converted into dollars at 1990 period-average exchange rates. Local consumer price indices (CPI) are taken as far as possible from *International Financial Statistics (IFS)* published by the International Monetary Fund. For the most recent years, the CPI is estimated on the basis of the first 3–9 months of the year. Period-average exchange rates are taken as far as possible from *IFS*.

[47] The lack of reliable economic data for Bulgaria makes it difficult to calculate military expenditure in constant US dollars and as a proportion of GDP.

[48] The lack of reliable economic data for Romania makes it difficult to calculate military expenditure in constant US dollars and as a proportion of GDP.

[49] High inflation, volatile exchange rates and the absence of reliable national statistics for all the CIS countries make it difficult to calculate military expenditure in constant US dollars and as a proportion of GDP.

[50] The lack of reliable economic data for Lebanon makes it difficult to calculate military expenditure in constant US dollars and as a proportion of GDP.

[51] Lack of data on inflation makes it impossible to calculate a continuous series in constant 1990 US dollars. Figures up to and including 1989 are calculated using 1989 as the base year, and those for 1990–94 using 1990 as the base year.

[52] The share of gross domestic product (GDP) is calculated in local currency and current prices. GDP data are taken where possible from *IFS* and the UN *National Accounts Statistics: Main Aggregates and Detailed Tables.*

Conventions in tables

. .	Data not available or not applicable	th.	thousand
—	Nil or a negligible figure	m.	million
( )	Uncertain data	b.	billion (thousand million)
[ ]	SIPRI estimate	I	Series break (e.g. for currency changes)

Appendix 8B. Sources and methods

The military expenditure project collects information on and monitors trends in military spending throughout the world. The data provide a solid basis for comparisons and evaluations of military spending and of the economic burden of such expenditure.

Data are presented in three different ways: (*a*) in local currency and current prices, i.e., the basic input data; (*b*) in US dollars and constant prices, to show real changes; and (*c*) as the ratio of military expenditure to gross domestic product (GDP). Tables of military expenditure in current and constant prices, as well as military spending as a share of GDP, are published annually in the *SIPRI Yearbook* where they are presented as a 10-year time-series of military spending for individual countries. For many countries it is not possible to apply an internationally standardized definition of military expenditure. The ambition, therefore, is to provide the best available time-series for each country according to a specific definition for that country.

I. Methods and definitions

The military expenditure database is the basis for the tables published in the *SIPRI Yearbook*.[1] All figures in the *Yearbook* are presented on a calendar-year basis on the assumption that military expenditure occurs evenly throughout the fiscal year. This permits the provision of a uniform picture of trends in military expenditure even though there is no common fiscal year for the budgetary information reported by individual countries. The consumer price index (CPI) is used to deflate current prices into constant values, and period-average market exchange rates are used to convert domestic currencies to US dollars using the base year (currently 1990) exchange rate. The ratio of military expenditure to GDP or gross national product (GNP) is calculated in domestic currency (at current prices).

A basic problem arises from the dearth of disaggregated military spending data for most countries, which makes it difficult to set a common definition of military expenditure for all states throughout the time period covered in the military expenditure series. SIPRI has traditionally used the NATO definition of military expenditure as a broad guideline for all countries. Where possible, the following items are included: all current and capital expenditure on the armed forces and in the running of defence departments and other government agencies engaged in defence projects and space activities; the cost of paramilitary forces, border guards and police when judged to be trained and equipped for military operations; military research and development, testing and evaluation costs; and costs of retirement pensions of service personnel and civilian employees. Items on civilian defence, interest on war debts and veterans' payments are excluded.

The United Nations Unified Reporting System might become a useful source of reliable military expenditure data in the future. However, despite its promise of providing greater disaggregation of data in a uniform fashion, the UN system has thus far proved a disappointment. Few countries report their military spending under the UN

---

[1] *SIPRI Yearbook 1990: World Armaments and Disarmament* (Oxford University Press: Oxford, 1990), appendix 5B, pp. 201–202; *SIPRI Yearbook 1991: World Armaments and Disarmament* (Oxford University Press: Oxford, 1991), appendix 5B, pp. 179–80; and *SIPRI Yearbook 1992: World Armaments and Disarmament* (Oxford University Press: Oxford, 1992), appendix 7B, pp. 269–70.

system and even fewer do so consistently and accurately. Participating states of the Organization for Security and Co-operation in Europe (OSCE) are required to report their military spending along the lines of the UN definition, raising the possibility of far more information on a large number of states becoming available from this source in the future. To date, this resource is restricted for OSCE use only, with free access for representatives of member states. Many governments, however, offer SIPRI the same information in response to individual requests.

II. Sources

The data are collected from national and international publications such as defence budgets, government financial statistics and other economic information and are stored electronically. Supplementary material on military expenditure is collected through systematic scanning and analysis of a wide range of journals, magazines and newspapers. This information is integrated into the database to provide the broadest possible overview of developments in global military expenditure. Where accurate data are not available estimates are made based on economic indicators and trend analysis. SIPRI estimates are presented in square brackets in the military expenditure tables. In some cases data from different sources are contradictory. Where it is not possible for SIPRI to make a definitive judgement on the accuracy of the data these figures are presented in round brackets signifying 'uncertain'. This distinction between SIPRI estimates and uncertain data applies to the military expenditure data only.

For the majority of countries in the SIPRI database, military expenditure estimates are derived primarily from the International Monetary Fund *Government Finance Statistics Yearbook*. Information on the CPI, exchange rates and GDP/GNP are taken from the IMF *International Financial Statistics Yearbook*. Official NATO publications provide the data for member countries and reflect NATO's definition of military spending rather than domestic budgetary information. Data for Central and East European countries are taken primarily from domestic budgets and other official sources provided by their respective embassies in Stockholm or from the ministries of defence in certain countries.

Supplementary information for all countries, particularly for those for which no official information can be found, is sought from a wide variety of sources. In addition to analysing journals, newspapers, defence white papers and standard reference works, the military expenditure project writes to all countries with diplomatic accreditation in Stockholm every year to request current defence budget information. In many cases SIPRI does receive useful material from this effort but, unfortunately, very often information is not forthcoming. Other sources regularly consulted include: the UN publication *National Accounts Statistics: Main Aggregates and Detailed Tables*, *Länderbericht* of the German Statistical Office, *Europa World Yearbook* and Economist Intelligence Unit publications.

9. Military research and development

ERIC ARNETT

I. Introduction

World military research and development (R&D) expenditure in the mid-1990s appears not to exceed $60 billion per year, which represents a reduction of 50–55 per cent in real terms from SIPRI's last estimate.[1] Of the major investors, only India, Japan and South Korea continue to increase their military R&D spending significantly, while the others reduce or hold steady. Spending in the countries of the former Warsaw Treaty Organization (WTO) has decreased dramatically since 1987 and accounts for most of the difference in estimates. Among the major Western countries, France, Italy, Sweden and the USA have all reduced their military R&D expenditure by 25 per cent or more from their cold war peaks of spending.

Despite the often-heard observation that the capacity to innovate and independently produce advanced military technology is proliferating beyond the bounds of control, it remains difficult for any but a few producers to develop military systems embodying advanced technology. Even among the industrialized countries, the imperative for cooperation is growing. Nevertheless, the challenge of coordinating major projects internationally is getting the better of some efforts and fewer products of R&D are entering production. Smaller projects that are more responsive to the participants' national requirements are becoming more popular than grand enterprises.

In particular, major European collaborations have proved to be more complex than expected, and many have failed—as highlighted in the discussion in section III of Spain's initiative to build up its military technology base in 1989–93. Spain has become disenchanted with the model of European defence cooperation that is embodied in multinational consortia in favour of smaller, more practicable bilateral projects that are more responsive to its requirements and capabilities. Sweden, which is also examined in section III, has realized a number of advantages by limiting itself to projects consistent with its novel defence concept and thereby developing sought-after niche technologies. Ironically, Sweden is in a stronger position for cooperation with the NATO states now than is Spain, which took to NATO projects with more gusto in the late 1980s. Both countries remain dependent on the USA for military technology, as do most of the states with which the USA has friendly relations. With its nearest competitor spending less than one-eighth as much on military R&D, the US military technology base continues to maintain and offer important advantages.

[1] Tullberg, R. and Hagmeyer-Gaverus, G., 'World military expenditure', *SIPRI Yearbook 1987: World Armaments and Disarmament* (Oxford University Press: Oxford, 1987), section XII, pp. 153–58.

II. Global trends

SIPRI last reported on world military R&D expenditure in 1987 and on world military R&D as such in 1973.[2] Since then, although the international situation has changed and disarmament progressed, the level of expenditure devoted to military R&D has remained roughly the same or increased as a fraction of military expenditure among most of the states outside the former Soviet bloc. While military R&D remains one of the most active areas of endeavour related to armament, it has also become a more tractable subject for research as more data become available and the role of military R&D in defence planning and international security has come to be understood in a more nuanced way. With this chapter, SIPRI once again presents comprehensive information regarding military R&D on a global scale. This discussion considers only military R&D, not arms production or the arms trade, which are discussed in other chapters of this volume.[3]

Sources of data on military R&D expenditure

In 1996 it is possible to more accurately depict the funds applied globally to military R&D than before (table 9.1 summarizes the 42 countries for which official data were available). This is true as much because the significance of under-reported activity has decreased as because the amount of data regarding reported activity has increased.[4] The government-sponsored military R&D efforts in the states of the former WTO have collapsed, and remaining projects are funded through accounts that are reported to legislative bodies and the United Nations. Of the former WTO states, only Russia remains among the top 20 investors in military R&D.

The reduction of military R&D expenditure in the former WTO states and the measure of additional transparency in the same states increase the confidence in estimates of global investment. Having accounted for the 20 largest investors—with the possible exceptions of Israel[5] and Taiwan—it appears that

---

[2] Forsberg, R., SIPRI, *Resources Devoted to Military Research and Development* (Almqvist & Wiksell: Uppsala, 1972), where there are official data for 22 countries. The *SIPRI Yearbook* reported on military R&D in 1972–74 (only Soviet R&D in 1974) and on military R&D expenditure in 1983–87. The *SIPRI Yearbooks 1994* and *1995* summarized similar data on the major OECD countries in the context of case studies of military R&D in India and China. See Arnett, E., 'Military technology: the case of India', *SIPRI Yearbook 1994* (Oxford University Press: Oxford, 1994), pp. 343–65; and Arnett, E., 'Military technology: the case of China', *SIPRI Yearbook 1995: Armaments, Disarmament and International Security* (Oxford University Press: Oxford, 1995), pp. 359–86.

[3] See chapters 10 and 11 in this volume.

[4] For an overview of sources and methods that is still pertinent, see appendix A of Forsberg (note 2).

[5] David Ivry, the Director-General of the Israeli Defence Ministry, says that the R&D budget is increasing. Fisher, S., 'Interview', *Jane's Defence Weekly*, 31 Jan. 1996, p. 88. The Defence Ministry's figure for R&D in 1994 is $59 million but leaves out special projects. Pedatzur, R., personal communication to E. Sköns, 3 Jan. 1996. One such special project is in the area of missile defence, to which Israel has committed $200 million for 1996–99 in a joint project with the USA, which will spend $300 million. Perry, W. J., 'Address to the Aspin Institute on US national strategy in the Middle East', *Defense Issues*, 6 Feb. 1996.

Table 9.1. Official estimates (1989–95) of government expenditure on military R&D

Figures are in current US$ m. Figure in italics is accurate to one significant digit. Others are accurate to two significant digits.

Country	OECD	UN	Other
USA	39 000 (1995)	..	..
France	4 600 (1993)	4 900 (1994)	..
UK	3 900 (1994)	2 900 (1994)	..
Germany	1 200 (1994)	1 500 (1993)	..
Russia	..	1 200 (1994)	..
China	..	..	*1 000* (1995)
Japan	770 (1994)	1 200 (1994)	..
Italy	520 (1993)	560 (1994)	..
India	..	..	430 (1995/96)
South Korea	..	..	360 (1994)
Sweden	360 (1994)	82 (1994)	..
Spain	270 (1994)	250 (1994)	..
Canada	210 (1992)	87 (1994)	..
Australia	170 (1994)	120 (1990/91)	..
Thailand	..	110 (1991)	..
Switzerland	89 (1991)	..	..
Netherlands	76 (1994)	73 (1994)	..
South Africa	..	..	65 (1994/95)
Brazil	..	48 (1994)	..
Norway	47 (1995)	59 (1993)	..
Poland	..	38 (1994)	..
Ukraine	..	23 (1993)	..
Argentina	..	20 (1994)	..
Finland	19 (1995)	7.7 (1994)	..
Croatia	..	13 (1992)	..
Philippines	..	9.7 (1993)	..
Czech Republic	..	9.7 (1994)	..
Turkey	..	8.6 (1993)	..
Romania	..	6.7 (1992)	..
New Zealand	4.1 (1993)	..	..
Denmark	3.6 (1994)	..	..
Greece	3.0 (1993)	0.29 (1994)	..
Belgium	2.4 (1994)	1.7 (1991)	..
Slovakia	..	1.9 (1994)	..
Portugal	1.8 (1993)	0.45 (1992)	..
Hungary	..	1.6 (1994)	..
Luxembourg	..	1.4 (1994)	..
Malaysia	..	0.52 (1989)	..
Bulgaria	..	0.26 (1994)	..
Belarus	..	0.22 (1994)	..
Namibia	..	0.046 (1992)	..
Peru	..	0.012 (1993)	..

Sources: *OECD Main Science and Technology Indicators,* no. 1 (1994) and no. 2 (1995); United Nations documents A/INF/45/5, 18 Oct. 1990, A/47/303, 30 July 1992; A/47/303/Add. 1, 15 Oct. 1992; A/48/271, 11 Aug. 1993; A/49/190, 29 June 1994; A/49/190/Add. 1, 30 Aug. 1994; A/49/190/Add. 2, 11 Nov. 1994; A/50/277, 20 July 1995; A/50/277/Add. 1, 11 Oct. 1995; and other data provided by national governments.

world military R&D expenditure in the mid-1990s is decreasing, does not exceed $60 billion and is probably closer to $55 billion, of which $39 billion is accounted for by the USA, $50 billion by NATO, and $52 billion by the Organisation for Economic Co-operation and Development (OECD) countries.[6] Despite cuts in R&D spending in China since the death of Mao Zedong and in Russia since the dissolution of the Soviet Union, the same six countries dominate investment in military R&D as in 1987. Japan is approaching their level, and India has announced its intention of doing the same. Since 1987, only India, Japan and South Korea among the top 20 investors have significantly increased their military R&D spending or announced plans to do so.[7]

When SIPRI last reported on military R&D expenditure in 1987, reliable figures were available only from some of the OECD countries and India. Figures furnished by the OECD remain the most useful, since they conform to a common standard: OECD analysts assess which funds are applied to R&D projects of military use regardless of which organ of the government carries out the funded activity. R&D funded by the defence ministry on non-military applications is not counted (e.g., Spanish civilian space research, as discussed below), and R&D funded by other agencies with military applications is counted (e.g., US nuclear weapon research conducted by the Department of Energy). This system provides excellent comparability of data but is not practicable for states that do not have the budget transparency characteristic of the OECD states.

Several states provide figures for military expenditure to the UN, including specific figures for R&D. Despite criticism that the UN form is too cumbersome, it is also insufficient to provide comparable data. Nevertheless, the UN data can be seen as usefully illustrative and are summarized here. However, the figures furnished can diverge quite dramatically from the OECD figures and should be seen as less useful as a basis for comparison.[8] Other national figures are also available directly from the governments concerned, but share with the UN submissions the lack of a common methodology that prevents effective direct comparison. In the case of China, these concerns and questions about appropriate rates of conversion prevent any conclusion being drawn beyond one significant digit.[9]

[6] Compare with the global estimate of $85–100 billion in 1986 according to Acland-Hood, M., 'Military research and development expenditure', SIPRI, *World Armaments and Disarmament: SIPRI Yearbook 1986* (Oxford University Press: Oxford, 1986), pp. 299–307. In real terms, this represents a 50–55% reduction after inflation.

[7] For India's plan, announced in 1995, see the following subsection. For South Korea's plan, adopted in 1992, see Republic of Korea, Ministry of Defense, *Defense White Paper 1992–93* (Korean Institute for Defense Analyses: Seoul, 1992), p. 132 (English translation).

[8] This can usually be ascribed to the peculiarities of the government's organization rather than any attempt to mislead. Sweden's UN figure, for example, corresponds roughly with the budget for the Swedish National Defence Research Establishment (FOA), whereas the OECD figure also includes R&D undertaken by the Defence Matériel Administration, as discussed in section III. Discrepancies for Canada, Finland, Greece and Japan are probably attributable to similar differences in approach. The discrepancy for the UK may stem from the omission of funds for strategic forces from the British return to the UN. UN document A/50/277, 20 July 1995, p. 89.

[9] The estimate of China's expenditure is elaborated in Arnett, 'Military technology: the case of China' (note 2); and Arnett, E., 'Military research and development in southern Asia: limited capabilities despite impressive resources', ed. E. Arnett, SIPRI, *Beyond Threat Perception: Military Technology and*

Military R&D, national goals and research findings

For decades military R&D has been a concern of researchers, who have tried to develop theories of how it might affect security. In general, there is a sense that R&D has a disproportionate significance among military activities. Most fundamentally, the development of new types of weaponry can be a stimulus to additional arms procurement. Some researchers have pushed further, arguing that military R&D is an intrinsically destabilizing force that leads almost inexorably to more military procurement and higher military expenditure.[10] In fact, recent events suggest that states can devote considerable resources to military R&D without motivating the bureaucracy to produce and procure what they invent. This is seen most clearly in cases where states pursue failed R&D initiatives, but R&D without production is becoming an intentional policy in the West.[11] It remains to be seen whether this policy can be sustained, or whether domestic pressure will lead to a reduction in R&D budgets or to an increase in procurement or total military expenditure. Currently, maintaining R&D expenditure appears to act as a constraint on procurement in some cases (as seen most clearly in the case of Germany in table 9.2 and discussed further below), especially if military expenditure is also constrained (see table 9.3).

When military R&D fails to produce outputs of sufficient military value it is more susceptible to broader arguments regarding national goals. These depend strongly on national plans for military and economic development, some of which rely inordinately on the presumed indirect contribution of military R&D to civilian development. Economists have tried to assess the burden placed on the economy by devoting resources—particularly capital and highly skilled labour—to military R&D instead of to other goals, and the magnitude of the social good produced through spin-offs. These questions of opportunity cost are not discussed further here, although they arguably make military R&D more burdensome to the economy than do other types of military expenditure.

These results suggest that it is more fruitful to examine the outputs of military R&D, particularly the potential impact of specific technologies and the ability of states to realize national technology goals. Once the notion of

---

Offensive Capacity in China, India, Pakistan and Iran (Oxford University Press: Oxford, forthcoming). The estimate in table 9.1 that China spends on the order of $1 billion to one significant digit implies that it spends $0.5–1.5 billion.

[10] This was put forward forcefully in Acland-Hood, M., 'Military research and development expenditure', SIPRI, *World Armaments and Disarmament: SIPRI Yearbook 1985* (Oxford University Press: Oxford, 1985), pp. 287: 'large and increasing [R&D] expenditures can be expected to . . . create pressures to increase military expenditure far into the future, independently of the state of political relations then'. Acland-Hood revised this hypothesis in *SIPRI Yearbook 1986* (note 6). Nevertheless, it remains a common argument. See, e.g., Thee, M., 'Science-based military technology as a driving force behind the arms race', eds N. P. Gleditsch and O. Njølstad, *Arms Races: Technological and Political Dynamics* (Sage Publications: London, 1990), p. 118: 'Each new stage in the R&D endeavour becomes a starting-point for a fresh departure to yet another round in the arms spiral'.

[11] See, e.g. , the discussion of 'reconstitution' in Arnett, E. H. and Kokoski, R., 'Military technology and international security: the case of the USA', *SIPRI Yearbook 1993: World Armaments and Disarmament* (Oxford University Press: Oxford, 1993), pp. 307–34; and section III below.

Table 9.2. Trends in expenditure on military R&D as a percentage of expenditure on military equipment in the NATO countries, 1988–95[a]

Country	1988	1989	1990	1991	1992	1993	1994	1995
USA	55.0	53.0	53.0	50.0	57.0	62.0	44.0	50.0
UK	35.0	40.0	51.0	43.0	48.0	34.0	39.0	..
Spain	11.0	24.0	39.0	38.0	42.0	25.0	25.0	..
Germany	18.0	20.0	21.0	23.0	28.0	32.0	32.0	..
Italy	15.0	14.0	10.0	15.0	16.0	12.0	..	..
Canada	9.9	10.0	11.0	10.0	10.0	..	..	..
Netherlands	4.3	5.0	5.6	7.3	7.2	8.0	6.3	..
Norway	8.1	5.6	6.0	5.8	5.2	4.7	4.1	4.7

[a] Includes only those reporting and spending more than $10 m. annually on military R&D.

Sources: OECD Main Science and Technology Indicators, no. 1 (1994); *OECD Main Science and Technology Indicators*, no. 2 (1995); and chapter 8 in this volume.

technological determinism had been disproved,[12] the logical implication that R&D should be steered around potentially destabilizing technologies was taken up.[13] Efforts to evaluate these outputs have become more difficult as the importance of electronics and system upgrades increases and the Revolution in Military Affairs (RMA) threatens to reduce the significance of major systems.[14] Further, in order to judge whether a technology is or might be destabilizing and whether the process of innovation can be steered away from it, it is necessary not only to examine the technology itself, but also the military doctrine into which it is likely to be adopted and the goals of the organizations responsible for R&D and procurement.

Finally, military R&D is not only of interest at the cutting edge of technologies being pursued by the most advanced states. R&D in smaller states can also produce unique, significant innovations, as well as creating new nodes from which technology can be produced and diffused. In short, military R&D has an effect on horizontal as well as vertical proliferation. While sometimes exaggerated, this effect is not insignificant.

[12] Reppy, J., 'Steering military R&D', eds W. A. Smit, J. Grin and L. Voronkov, *Military Technological Innovation and Stability in a Changing World* (Vrije Universiteit Press: Amsterdam, 1992), pp. 85–93; and MacKenzie, D., *Inventing Accuracy: An Historical Sociology of Nuclear Missile Guidance* (MIT Press: Cambridge, Mass., 1990). Technological determinism is the idea that scientists and engineers cannot prevent themselves from inventing undesirable technologies, since there is an imperative that draws them to the most interesting problems, heedless of consequences.
[13] Reppy (note 12).
[14] The RMA, a concept of how information technologies will change military planning and perhaps render major weapon systems obsolete, is summarized in Mazarr, M. J., *The Military Technical Revolution: A Structural Framework* (Center for Strategic and International Studies: Washington, DC, 1993); Odom, W. E., *America's Military Revolution: Strategy and Structure After the Cold War* (American University Press: Lanham, Md., 1993); and Aftergood, S., 'Monitoring military technologies', *Federation of American Scientists Public Interest Report*, Jan./Feb. 1995.

Table 9.3. Trends in expenditure on military R&D as a percentage of total military expenditure in the OECD countries, 1988–95[a]

Country	1988	1989	1990	1991	1992	1993	1994	1995
USA	14.0	13.0	13.0	14.0	13.0	14.0	13.0	14.0
France	11.0	11.0	13.0	12.0	11.0	10.0	..	..
UK	8.8	8.8	9.0	8.2	8.6	8.8	9.7	..
Sweden	7.5	7.3	6.9	8.7	8.0	7.8	6.1	..
Spain	2.3	4.3	5.0	4.9	4.6	3.4	2.9	..
Germany	3.5	3.7	3.8	3.6	3.7	3.6	3.5	..
Australia	3.0	2.9	2.7	2.7	2.6	2.4	2.4	..
Japan	..	1.8	1.9	2.0	2.1	2.3	2.3	..
Italy	3.1	2.8	1.8	2.4	2.4	2.0	..	..
Canada	2.0	1.9	1.8	1.8	1.9		..	..
Norway	1.5	1.4	1.4	1.3	1.2	1.3	1.2	1.2
Switzerland	1.2	1.1	1.1	1.0	..	..	..	..
Netherlands	0.89	0.88	1.0	1.1	1.0	1.1	1.1	..

[a] Includes only those reporting and spending more than $20 m. annually on military R&D.

Sources: OECD Main Science and Technology Indicators, no. 1 (1994); OECD Main Science and Technology Indicators, no. 2 (1995); and chapter 8 in this volume.

India's 1995 'self-reliance plan'

The most striking development in world military R&D in 1995 was India's decision to double the share of its increasing defence budget devoted to military R&D by the year 2000. The Defence R&D Organization's (DRDO) budget was increased to $430 million in 1995 as the government and the parliamentary Defence Committee endorsed a 'self-reliance plan'—known as Plan-2005—meant to reduce the imported content of defence goods to 30 per cent by 2005 by increasing the R&D budget to 10 per cent of the defence budget.[15] If trends continue as expected and the government and legislature are willing to fund this initiative, India will be spending $1 billion annually on military R&D in the next decade (primarily on the programmes shown in table 9.4), not including military nuclear and space activities.

Military R&D was already crowding out a cramped procurement budget before Plan-2005 was announced.[16] Of the DRDO's major projects, none has yet been deployed in any but token numbers. The light combat aircraft (LCA) still requires an engine and an air-to-air missile, on which design work has only just begun.[17] The Agni and Prithvi ballistic missile programmes appar-

---

[15] Lok Sabha Secretariat, Committee on Defence, *Defence Research and Development: Major Projects* (Lok Sabha Secretariat: New Delhi, 1995), p. 6. As shown in table 9.3, only 3 OECD countries spend approximately 10% of their defence budgets on R&D: France, the UK and the USA. The next highest is Sweden at 6.1%.

[16] The tension between R&D and procurement spending in India is examined more closely in Arnett, 'Military technology: the case of India' (note 2).

[17] No design work has yet been done on the missile. Some work has been done on the engine. The LCA is to use an adapted and indigenized US GE F404, much like the Swedish JAS-39 Gripen,

Table 9.4. Major Indian military R&D programmes, 1995

Figures are in 1995 US$ m. The rupee's value against the dollar is volatile.

Project	Past expenditures	1995 budget	Status
Light combat aircraft	700	100	Airframe complete, engine ready 2000? $400 m. required up to 1999
IGMDP[a]	250	100	Prithvi and Trishul accepted by army Akash and Nag in testing
Arjun tank	100	100	9 prototypes delivered to army for trials
Agni ballistic missile	15	..	No additional funding forthcoming $15 m. more required for 5 more tests

[a] IGMDP = Integrated Guided Missile Development Plan, including the Prithvi short-range ballistic missile, the Trishul and Akash air-defence missiles, and the Nag anti-tank missile.

Source: Lok Sabha Secretariat, Committee on Defence, *Defence Research and Development: Major Projects* (Lok Sabha Secretariat: New Delhi, 1995), p. 6.

ently have failed to stir interest in the armed services,[18] while the Arjun tank continues to perform disappointingly in trials.[19] Major projects for nuclear submarines and aircraft-carriers (the latter reportedly allotted $300 million up to 2010) almost certainly will not reach fruition in the foreseeable future.[20]

III. The OECD countries

Among the OECD countries are found most of the world's leading economies and innovative organizations. Of these, the USA is the only country to design and produce a full range of advanced military technologies, albeit with limited dependence on imported components. France, Germany and the UK are able to design and produce complete systems in several important sectors with very little imported content, whereas Italy, Japan, Spain and Sweden are more dependent on co-development, licensed production and imported components despite high levels of innovative capacity. All these countries are seeking greater R&D cooperation, partly to offset costs and partly to ensure access to markets. In Australia, Canada and other states investing less in military R&D, the emphasis is on selection and local adaptation of foreign designs and innovation in limited but important niches.[21]

---

discussed in section III. An entirely new engine would probably cost about $4 billion. Fulghum, D. A., 'LCA's engine designed for extreme conditions', *Aviation Week & Space Technology,* 25 July 1994, p. 45.

[18] Funding for the Agni project was not resumed after the original funds were expended. The air force and army have agreed to accept a total of 100 Prithvi. Lok Sabha (note 15).

[19] The summer 1995 trials were witnessed by members of the Lok Sabha, who reported that problems remained with the propulsion, armament and ergonomics. Lok Sabha (note 15), p. 26.

[20] Bedi, R., 'India will build aircraft carrier for new century', *Jane's Defence Weekly,* 26 Aug. 1995.

[21] According to Richard Brabin-Smith, Australia's Chief Defence Scientist, the Defence Science and Technology Office 'exists primarily to give . . . advice [on foreign procurement]. . . . Everything else is secondary'. Ferguson, G., 'One on one: Richard Brabin-Smith', *Defense News,* 5–11 June 1995.

Table 9.5. Trends in government expenditure on military R&D in OECD countries spending more than $20 m. annually, 1988–95

Figures are in 1990 US$ m.

Country	1988	1989	1990	1991	1992	1993	1994	1995
USA	44 000	43 000	40 000	37 000	37 000	37 000	33 000	33 000
France	4 700	4 800	5 600	5 000	4 700	4 200	..	..
UK	3 600	3 600	3 600	3 400	3 200	3 200	3 400	..
Germany	1 400	1 500	1 600	1 400	1 400	1 200	1 100	..
Japan	..	500	530	580	630	680	680	..
Italy	740	680	420	560	550	470	..	..
Sweden	420	420	410	480	430	410	320	..
Spain	220	420	450	430	370	300	240	..
Canada	230	220	210	190	200	..	..	..
Australia	180	170	160	160	160	150	150	..
Switzerland	89	89	92	85	..	..	..	..
Netherlands	67	67	75	82	73	74	67	..
Norway	50	47	46	42	45	43	41	40

Sources: OECD Main Science and Technology Indicators, no. 1 (1994); and OECD Main Science and Technology Indicators, no. 2 (1995).

The post-cold war trend among the OECD countries is a marked decrease in gross military R&D spending (as shown in table 9.5). Among the most dramatic reductions in the NATO countries, the USA has reduced its spending by 25 per cent since 1988, France by 25 per cent since 1990, and Italy by 36 per cent since 1988. Reductions in Canada, Germany, Norway and the UK have been more modest. The Netherlands and Spain both increased their military R&D expenditure dramatically between 1988 and 1991 (the Netherlands by 22 per cent, Spain by 95 per cent) before returning to approximately the same level in 1994. Among the non-NATO members of the OECD, Sweden has reduced its military R&D spending by 33 per cent since 1991, and Australia and Switzerland have reduced their spending slightly. In contrast to this trend, Japan has increased its military R&D spending by 34 per cent since 1989 with a concomitant increase in the military share of its national R&D effort (see table 9.6), although this remains the lowest among the major states of the OECD.

US presidential candidate Bill Clinton campaigned in 1992 on a promise to reverse the distribution of US Government funding of R&D from 60:40 military-to-civilian to 40:60 while increasing expenditure on military R&D.[22] By the end of 1995, he had made little progress towards keeping either component of that promise; military R&D spending continued its slide to 75 per cent of its 1988 level (most of which reduction came during the Bush Administration) but still consumed 55 per cent of the government's R&D budget (see tables 9.5 and 9.6).

[22] Arnett and Kokoski (note 11). US military R&D expenditure peaked in 1986 at 69.4% of government-funded R&D. *OECD Main Science and Technology Indicators*, no. 1 (1990).

Table 9.6. Trends in government expenditure on military R&D as a percentage of total government expenditure on R&D and total national R&D in OECD countries spending more than $100 m. annually, 1988–95[a]

Country	1988	1989	1990	1991	1992	1993	1994	1995
USA	67.8	65.5	62.6	59.7	58.6	59.0	55.3	54.8
	31.0	28.0	26.0	24.0	24.0	25.0	22.0	..
UK	42.7	43.6	43.7	44.2	40.9	42.5	44.5	..
	19.0	18.0	18.0	18.0	16.0	17.0	..	..
France	37.3	37.0	40.0	36.1	35.7	33.6	..	..
	22.0	21.0	24.0	21.0	19.0	17.0	..	..
Sweden	24.0	24.7	23.6	27.3	24.3	23.5	18.9	..
	..	9.8	..	12.0	..	9.4	..	..
Spain	12.6	19.1	18.4	16.8	14.6	12.5	10.6	..
	7.2	13.0	12.0	10.0	8.4	7.2	6.1	..
Germany	12.4	12.8	13.5	11.0	10.0	8.5	8.4	..
	4.7	4.6	5.0	4.2	4.0	3.5	3.3	..
Australia	11.3	11.2	10.6	9.7	8.9	8.5	7.8	..
	5.0	5.2	4.3	4.5	3.6	..	..	..
Italy	10.4	10.3	6.1	7.9	7.1	6.5	..	..
	6.8	6.0	3.5	4.5	4.3	3.9	..	..
Canada	8.3	7.5	7.1	6.4	6.2	..	..	..
	3.3	3.1	2.8	2.6	2.6	..	..	..
Japan	..	5.1	5.4	5.7	5.9	6.1	6.0	..
	..	0.79	0.79	0.84	0.91	1.0	..	..

[a] First row: Military R&D as a percentage of government R&D expenditure; second row: military R&D as a percentage of national R&D expenditure.

Sources: *OECD Main Science and Technology Indicators,* no. 1 (1994); and *OECD Main Science and Technology Indicators*, no. 2 (1995).

Indeed, the political situation in the USA offers an interesting test of how hard R&D pushes arms procurement. At the end of the cold war the USA terminated and scaled back several large development projects under budget pressure and in the realization that they were not well-suited to post-cold war missions.[23] Despite military lack of interest, Congress has been appropriating money for systems developed by industry in order to demonstrate support both for the military and for the jobs provided by arms production. Most significantly, Congress has pressed the Pentagon to buy V-22 tilt-rotor utility aircraft and more Seawolf submarines and to prepare to buy a national missile defence system,[24] all against military recommendations. It remains to be seen whether this congressional–industrial complex can ultimately overrule the military and force the acquisition of the products of military R&D. In any

[23] In 1997 the Ballistic Missile Defense Organization plans to terminate some of the technology programmes on which it has spent $2–3 billion annually, when others are chosen to proceed into development. Asker, J. R., 'Washington outlook: Kaminski's solution', *Aviation Week & Space Technology*, 12 Feb. 1996, p. 19.

[24] See chapter 14 in this volume.

case, the balance of powers in the USA is unique, and a military decision to scale back production is more likely to be accepted in other political systems.

The US commitment to continuing its dominance in military technology has made it an overwhelmingly popular partner for other OECD states, including those that recently championed European cooperation as a competitive alternative to importing from or co-producing with the USA. (As seen in table 9.1, the USA still accounts for almost 80 per cent of NATO R&D expenditure—increasing its traditional 3:1 lead to 4:1—and 75 per cent of military R&D expenditure in the OECD.) In 1995 the UK chose US Apache attack helicopters over European alternatives, as the Netherlands did in selecting the Apache and the AMRAAM (advanced medium-range air-to-air missile). Denmark, Norway and Sweden also selected the AMRAAM. As discussed below, Spain dropped out of a European frigate programme in favour of an indigenous design that will incorporate US electronics accounting for as much as half of its value. According to Japan's Federation of Economic Organizations, Keidanren, Japan too must co-develop weapons with the USA if it is to retain its current capability.[25]

Nevertheless, German Minister of Defence Volker Rühe reiterated in 1995 that a European goal should be to counter the US 'buy American' policy with an emphasis usually associated with France on buying European.[26] Coordination of European armament development and production was set back in October when the Western European Armaments Group (WEAG) failed to establish a European Armaments Agency as expected.[27] The only silver lining was the creation of a Franco-German armaments agency, which assumed responsibility for the administration of bilateral projects on 1 January 1996. Other European states are said to be welcome to join, but it appears that European cooperation will continue to be expressed most frequently in the form of modest bilateral and trilateral programmes. This has been the case for decades and is explained in somewhat more detail in the context of Spanish R&D below.

Of the OECD countries, France most vividly illustrated the competition between R&D and procurement under a tight budget constraint.[28] Defence Ministry officials said that delays, reductions and cancellations are unavoidable after an 8 per cent decrease in the procurement budget for 1996.[29] France

---

[25] Ebata, K., 'Force cuts are planned as threats are reviewed', *Jane's Defence Weekly*, 3 June 1995, p. 3.

[26] Körner, P., 'German–Swedish defence cooperation', *Military Technology*, Aug. 1995, p. 24.

[27] See also chapter 10, section IV, in this volume.

[28] On West European policies for military R&D and production, see Brzoska, M. and Lock, P. (eds), SIPRI, *Restructuring of Arms Production in Western Europe* (Oxford University Press: Oxford, 1992); and Gummett, P. and Stein, J. A., *European Defence Technology in Transition: Issues for the UK* (Science Policy Support Group: London, 1994).

[29] Sparaco, P., 'French military cuts will force industry changes', *Aviation Week & Space Technology*, 27 Nov. 1995, p. 22; and Sparaco, P., 'Debt-laden France decrees major military cuts', *Aviation Week & Space Technology*, 9 Oct. 1995, p. 30. Thus far the NH-90 and Tiger helicopters, the Trigat anti-tank missile and the future large aircraft transport have been delayed, but no advanced programmes terminated. President Jacques Chirac indicated in 1995 that France will not replace the S3D land-based nuclear missile when it is retired and there is some uncertainty about whether there will be a replacement for the ASMP air-launched missile. See also chapter 10, section IV, in this volume.

has already tried to use European cooperation as a method to broaden the market for its defence goods and thereby increase production and offset reduced domestic procurement, but these programmes have involved compromises on requirements and long lead times.[30] In the end co-development usually leads to co-production, suggesting that it is not likely in itself to affect the ratio of R&D spending to procurement spending or production. This is especially true with the trend in Germany moving strongly towards more R&D relative to production, as suggested by tables 9.2 and 9.3, although Germany is attempting to preserve its production capacity.[31] As a result, France has been left to develop many systems independently, sometimes without even earning revenues through arms sales. The Defence Ministry has launched a strategic review to produce a new five-year plan addressing these problems in the context of the French debt crisis.

The following sections examine two cases in more depth: Spain and Sweden. Together, these states represent the latest—and perhaps the last— major additions to the greater West European military technology base. Spain began cooperating with other European countries more extensively after confirming its entry into NATO in 1986 and has ardently attempted to assimilate itself by pursuing a model of military R&D 'more European than the Europeans'. Sweden, which has long purchased military technology from the NATO countries, has gradually allowed itself to cooperate more directly in R&D projects as its misgivings about the implications for its neutral and nonaligned foreign policy concept fade in the aftermath of the cold war. Perhaps surprisingly, the Swedish approach appears more successful, if expensive. Spain's case suggests the constraints that limit a state's mobility in the hierarchy of military–technology powers, despite remarkable levels of political and economic commitment as well as international cooperation. Sweden's case illustrates the ambitious level of effort necessary for a state simply to develop systems for a neutral and essentially non-offensive military posture and the difficulty faced by small countries in achieving even a limited level of self-reliance.

Spain

Spain is continuing an ambitious post-cold war build-up in its military technology base, but has throttled back its efforts since 1991. As depicted in table 9.5,[32] Spain doubled its expenditure on military R&D in 1989 and has

---

[30] France is still struggling to deploy some of the systems co-developed with Spain beginning in 1986 and discussed below. France stayed out of the Eurofighter consortium because its design (which became the Rafale) lost to the British proposal.

[31] Germany's Economics Minister, Günther Rexrodt, said that the government was only likely to support the ailing military industry through R&D (DM 600 million over the period 1996–99), but not with increased procurement. Matthews, R., 'DASA: applying the corporate medicine', *Jane's Defence Weekly*, 14 Oct. 1995, p. 32.

[32] OECD and Spanish Ministry of Defence estimates of military R&D expenditure diverge, especially after 1993. Ministerio de Defensa, *Memoria de la IV Legislatura, 1990–1993* [Report from the 4th legislature] (Ministerio de Defensa: Madrid, 1993) (in Spanish); and *OECD Main Science and Technology Indicators*, no. 1 (1995), pp. 46, 47, 49. The OECD figures used (table 9.5) do not include defence

sustained a higher level of investment since. Despite a booming economy in the first years of the build-up and cooperation with the most advanced technology powers in NATO, Spain's effort has produced few of the military goods or benefits for the civilian economy that were expected. Spain's emphasis on foreign cooperation led it to invest in systems that do not clearly relate to its own requirements. Spanish defence firms are not necessarily more attractive to foreign partners than they were before, and indigenous programmes have been crowded out. Much of the $2 billion invested since 1989 went to failed projects, so it did not produce any improvement in Spanish security or much employment for production.

The Spanish military technology base was isolated after World War II and remained backward and decentralized. A wave of US imports followed by licensing arrangements after the 1953 bilateral cooperation agreement, the Pact of Madrid, made domestic design of most major systems unnecessary, but exposed Spanish firms to modern technology. In the following decades, Spain's three major producers devoted themselves to four major runs of licensed production: Construcciones Aeronáuticas SA (CASA) to 62 US-designed F-5 fighters, Bazán to 5 US-designed frigates and 8 French-designed submarines (4 of the Daphné Class followed by 4 Agosta Class), and Santa Bárbara to 280 French-designed AMX tanks. Bazán then undertook the construction of an aircraft-carrier and an accompanying battle group. CASA established a strong reputation for its transport aircraft. Domestic and foreign confidence in Spanish engineering increased to such an extent that Spain was readily accepted into technological collaborations after it entered NATO, albeit with some reservations about giving it more than a small role in any given project. Still, there was little domestic investment in military R&D before the initiative of the late 1980s.[33]

As suggested by its timing, Spain's burst of activity in the military R&D field had at least as much to do with domestic politics as with the cold war. With no real feeling of threat from the Soviet bloc, Spain's post-Franco government nevertheless saw the value of engaging the armed forces in outward-looking activities and reducing the officers' interest in internal affairs, especially after the failed coup of 1981. Although the Socialist Workers' Party of Spain (PSOE) was elected in 1982 in part because of anti-NATO feeling, President Felipe González had confirmed the country's entry into NATO and the European Communities (EC) by 1986 because of his party's commitment to cooperative security and a Spanish 'place' in Europe.

Spain's build-up is European in several important senses. First, Spain's choice of projects was heavily influenced by its desire not only to cooperate with European partners but also to develop a security infrastructure—forces and industry—that was appropriate to the new Europe as the PSOE leaders

ministry funds expended on projects judged by OECD analysts to be non-military, particularly space. In 1993, 26.1% of the military R&D budget was devoted to the National Institute for Aerospace Technology (INTA), which is responsible for space projects and various test facilities.

[33] As late as 1981, the Ministry of Defence's R&D budget was only Ptas 0.40 billion, just 1% of its 1989 level. Ministerio de Defensa (note 32), p. 336.

perceived it. This meant striving to invest and innovate at a level comparable to Germany and Italy, if not France. Second, Spain's desire to improve its national science and technology infrastructure was hindered by European Union (EU) regulations limiting subsidization of R&D in all sectors other than the military. If Spain wanted to improve its national technology base, EU rules suggested it must exploit the military R&D loophole.[34]

Further, Spain's ability to invest in military R&D and its outputs was limited by its commitment to achieve economic convergence and thereby economic and monetary union with the rest of Europe. As this entailed shrinking the public sector in ways consonant with the PSOE's Euro-socialist philosophy and the lack of a compelling military threat to Spain's security, defence was an obvious target of opportunity for budget cutters despite accounting only for about 2 per cent of gross domestic product (GDP)—not counting the paramilitary Guardia Civil. Finally, Spain's enthusiastic plunge into cooperative military R&D and subsequent withdrawal into more modest arrangements mirror the aspirations and disappointments of Western Europe as a whole as it sought a more consistent and mutually beneficial approach to military planning.

The Spanish military was given the task of making a full and professional contribution to NATO while the military industry was to redirect its efforts towards achieving self-reliance in military production through cooperation with NATO allies. Then Director General for Armaments and Matériel Juan Fernando Ruíz Montero gave 'strategic independence' as his goal for Spanish military R&D in 1988, defined as 'the greatest possible degree of nationalization . . . without falling for autarkic utopias'. He expected that 90 per cent of Spanish military equipment would be of Spanish design by 2000.[35] European cooperation was intended to promote technology transfers to Spain that would allow indigenous production.

Emphasizing technology transfer and learning from cooperation with other European states, Spain has invested the bulk of its funds since 1989 on major NATO collaborations, particularly the Eurofighter. Early disappointments with these cooperative projects came to a head in 1991 and have since led to more careful tailoring of programmes with partners chosen on the basis of congruent requirements and the technology offered rather than political concerns. Indigenous programmes have continued, albeit with a lower probability of reaching fruition as the domestic procurement budget has been strained. The alternative, design for export, has only been pursued with energy by Bazán, the shipbuilding company.

[34] Reppy, J., personal communication, 9 Feb. 1996. In 1988 the Spanish national R&D effort accounted for only 0.72% of GDP, the lowest in the OECD apart from Greece and Portugal, and about one-third of the EU average (2.0%). *OECD Main Science and Technology Indicators*, no. 2 (1995).

[35] This compares to 35% or 40% in 1988. Cited and translated in Molas Gallart, J., *Military Production and Innovation in Spain* (Harwood Academic Publishers: Chur, Switzerland, 1992), pp. 96, 97. The defence ministry held to this standard in 1990: 'The highest priority goal in the long run is to achieve a higher level of national autonomy . . . the capacity to develop and produce—without anyone's help—new systems and subsystems of great complexity'. Florensa, A. *et al.*, 'Investigación y desarrollo: Salto hacia adelante' [Research and development: a leap forward], *Revista Española de Defensa*, Dec. 1990, p. 11 (in Spanish).

DGAM

Responsibility for Spain's entry into military high technology was delegated to a new organization, the Directorate General for Armaments and Matériel (DGAM). Spanish military planning was reorganized along lines similar to France's after the death of President Francisco Franco in 1975. The Ministry of Defence was created in 1977, with several reorganizations since. As Spain's economy grew faster than that of any other EC state in 1986–90,[36] DGAM rode a wave of prosperity and optimism. As reflected in tables 9.1 and 9.5, Spain's gross expenditure on military R&D during the González build-up ranks it among the highest spenders in Europe and, indeed, the world, with funding surpassing that of India, Italy, South Korea and Sweden in 1990 and twice that of Canada, a country with an economy of roughly the same size. Table 9.6 suggests that the Spanish effort was over-ambitious from the perspective of science and technology policy, bringing Spain to a level of military R&D as a fraction of government-funded and national R&D higher than any non-nuclear country in NATO, in part because of Spain's low rate of spending on other public and private R&D. In fact, the level of military R&D may have made it difficult to afford procurement, as suggested by table 9.2; as the procurement budget declined after 1989, Spain's ratio of military R&D to procurement began to approach that of the UK, a state known for its military technology base's remarkable ability to invent more systems than the industrial base can afford to produce.

In 1986, once Spain had confirmed its position in NATO by a national referendum, DGAM and industry immediately set about joining every possible NATO collaborative R&D effort.[37] From the beginning, the González build-up was seen as a major investment, and one that would involve programmes of international cooperation over and above existing Spanish programmes.[38] Work on projects with limited foreign cooperation remained roughly steady, but NATO cooperation projects were planned to reach over 90 per cent of the military R&D budget. The Spanish philosophy was to 'participate in all those international programmes in which something can be learned'.[39]

By 1989 Spain was participating in 24 cooperative R&D programmes and soon began to realize it might be overextended (see also table 9.7).[40] The 24 programmes were: (*a*) the Eurofighter; (*b*) the future large transport aircraft (FLA); (*c*) the advanced short-range air-to-air missile (ASRAAM); (*d*) the

---

[36] Tsoukalis, L., *The New European Economy* (Oxford University Press: Oxford, 1993), pp. 24–27.

[37] By this time, Spain was already involved in the Eurofighter and NFR-90 programmes.

[38] Spain originally planned for an open-ended crescendo of R&D effort with expenditures reaching Ptas 60 billion in 1992. Fisas Armengol, V., *La Militarització de la Ciència: Els Programmes d'Investigació Militar a Espanya, 1982–1992* [The militarization of science: the programmes of military research for Spain, 1982–1992] (Fundació Jaume Bofill: Barcelona, 1989), p. 83 (in Catalan).

[39] Florensa *et al.* (note 35), p. 8.

[40] Secretary of State for Defence Rafael de la Cruz paraphrased in Gallego, F., 'Spain may cut cooperative R&D', *Jane's Defence Weekly*, 17 June 1989, p. 1222. See also Ministerio de Defensa, *Memoria de la Legislatura, 1986–89* [Report from the legislature] (Ministerio de Defensa: Madrid, 1989), pp. 315–21 (in Spanish); and Fisas (note 38), pp. 122–23.

Table 9.7. Early Spanish collaborative R&D projects (begun by 1989)[a]

Figures are in b. pesetas. Figures in italics are percentages.

Project	Spanish share	Comment
Eurofighter	*13.0*	Production commitment in 1996?
NFR-90	*12.5*	Cancelled 1991, Ptas 1.5 b. spent in 1991
FAMS		NAAWS lost to Aster in 1991, expected outlay: Ptas 23 b.
Aster	*25.0*	Withdrew in favour of NAAWS after spending Ptas 0.4 b.
LAMS	*30.0*	Withdrew in favour of NAAWS 1990
NAAWS	*10.6*	Cancelled 1991, Ptas 0.46 b. spent in 1991
Patiño Class AOR	*50.0*	Commissioned 1995 after Ptas 15 b.
Helios satellite	*7.0*	Helios 1A launched 1995 after Ptas 13 b.
		Spain withdrew from Helios 2 in 1994, but funded Helios 1B in 1996
ASRAAM		Spain withdrew 1989, expected outlay: Ptas 2.6 b.
Trigat	*7.2*	Spain withdrew 1990, expected outlay: Ptas 1.1 b.
APGM-155	*5.0*	Cancelled 1991, Ptas 0.86 b. spent in 1991
A-129 helicopter	*5.0*	Withdrew 1991, Ptas 0.12 b. spent in 1991
MSAM		Cancelled 1991, Ptas 0.086 b. spent in 1991
MSOW	*14.2*	Cancelled 1989
FLA	*10?*	Full-scale development begins in 1996

[a] Expected outlays refer to original project estimates.

NFR = NATO frigate replacement; FAMS = family of anti-air missile systems; LAMS = local area missile system; NAAWS = NATO anti-air warfare system; AOR = auxiliary oil replenishment; ASRAAM = advanced short-range air-to-air missile; APGM = autonomous precision-guided munition; MSAM = medium-range surface-to-air missile; MSOW = modular stand-off weapon; FLA = future large transport aircraft.

Source: Fisas Armengol, V., *La Militarització de la Ciència: Els Programmes d'Investigació Militar a Espanya, 1982–1992* [The militarization of science: the programmes of military research for Spain, 1982–1992] (Fundació Jaume Bofill: Barcelona, 1989), with author's updates.

third-generation anti-tank missile (Trigat); (*e*) the medium-range surface-to-air missile (MSAM); (*f*) the Helios communications and reconnaissance satellite; (*g*) the European data distribution system (EDDS); (*h*) the modular stand-off weapon (MSOW); (*i*) the autonomous precision-guided munition (APGM) for 155-mm artillery; (*j*) the POST-2000 tactical communications system; (*k*) the naval electronic warfare system for helicopters and aircraft (NEWSHA) maritime patrol; (*l*) the Global Positioning System (GPS) for satellite navigation; (*m*) the NATO low-cost ship inertial navigation system (SINS); (*n*) the NATO identification system (NIS); (*o*) the ADA computer language project support environment (APSE); (*p*) the NATO improved Link 11 (NILE) naval communications system; (*q*) the multifunction information distribution system (MIDS); (*r*) the NATO frigate replacement NFR-90; (*s*) the NATO anti-air warfare system (NAAWS); (*t*) the family of anti-air missile systems (FAMS)/local area missile system (LAMS); (*u*) the A-129 Tonal attack helicopter; (*v*) the AOR-90 Patiño Class auxiliary oil replenishment (AOR)/Buque de Aprovisionamiento de Combate (BAC) ship; (w) the aerial command and control system (ACCS) and battlefield information collection and exploitation systems (BICES), command and control (C^2) efforts; and (x) a minehunter.

Tracing the funding and progress of these projects is complicated by erratic official reporting. Although Spain's civilian oversight of the military has made its military technology base one of the most transparent in the world, changing methods of accounting make it impossible to follow any individual project other than the Eurofighter in detail through publicly available reports (see table 9.8).

Spain and Spanish firms soon began dropping out of programmes, losing out to more competitive bids and watching other programmes fall by the way-side. In 1991 alone, DGAM allocated 3 billion pesetas (Ptas), 58 per cent of its non-Eurofighter outlays, to programmes from which it withdrew within the year.[41]

Spain's first foray into NATO cooperation, the eight-nation NFR-90, fore-shadowed much of the NATO experience with cooperative design and production. In 1989 it collapsed into more manageable programmes, like the Trilateral Frigate Cooperation (TFC) programme, which Spain joined with Germany and the Netherlands but left in 1995 in favour of its own F 100 frigate. Even before the NFR-90 project broke up, Spain had joined and pulled out of the German-led Trigat anti-tank missile programme citing budget constraints. In 1989 the ASRAAM and MSOW consortia disintegrated, with Spain opting out of the successor efforts. Spain also picked the wrong partners when selecting team-mates for attack helicopters and SAMs. In 1991 Spain abandoned Italy's project to upgrade its A-129 Mangusta (Mongoose), while NAAWS—the team for which Spain forsook FAMS despite holding a 30 per cent interest in LAMS—lost the competition to Spain's former partners. As a result, Spain is left developing alternative projects indigenously or importing, remaining outside the Eurocopter Consortium.

Spain's first ambivalent experience with NATO cooperation, the NFR-90, may have led to one of its more appropriate new projects: DGAM's largest effort, the F 100 air-defence frigate, which is designed to meet a requirement for four frigates. Spain began detailed design work on the F 100 in January 1996 after withdrawing from the TFC programme in 1995. Spain thus left behind two European partners in favour of the USA, which will provide the Aegis air-defence system for the F 100.[42] In other bilateral efforts, Spain developed the Ptas 9.9 billion Santiago airborne signals intelligence (SIGINT) system with Israel Aircraft Industries,[43] the Patiño Class AOR SNS Mar del

---

[41] These include NFR-90 (Ptas 1.5 billion), APGM-155 (Ptas 858 million), NAAWS (Ptas 465 million), A129 (Ptas 122 million), MSAM (Ptas 86 million.) and Trigat (Ptas 79 million). Luria, R., 'Spanish defense industry faces an uncertain future', *International Defense Review,* Nov. 1992, p. 1103.

[42] Evers, S., and Janssen Lok, J., 'Aegis to equip F 100 frigates', *Jane's Defence Weekly,* 31 Jan. 1996, p. 11.

[43] *Jane's Radar and Electronic Warfare Systems 1994–95* (Jane's Information Group: Coulsdon, Surrey, 1994), pp. 393, 528. Funds for Santiago were included in the 1996 R&D budget request.

Table 9.8. Distribution of Spanish military R&D expenditure, 1987–93

Figures are in m. pesetas. Figures in italics are percentages.

Project	Allocation 1987–89	Share of total	Allocation 1990–93	Share of total
Eurofighter	24.0	*35.2*	98.2	*81.4*
C^2, simulators, arms systems^a	7.6	*11.1*	5.1	*4.2*
Missiles^b	..	..	4.5	*3.7*
Combat vehicles^c	..	..	3.4	*2.8*
Communications and electronic warfare	5.8	*8.5*	2.5	*2.0*
Detection and navigation aids	3.0	*4.4*	2.1	*1.7*
Technology cooperation^d	..	..	1.5	*1.2*
Military computing	..	..	1.0	*0.8*
Munitions and explosives	..	..	0.6	*0.5*
Optronics, infrared, materials	9.6	*14.1*	0.6	*0.5*
Nuclear, chemical and biological defence	..	..	0.1	*0.1*
Total	**68.2**	*100.0*	**120.7**	*100.0*

^{a} Includes anti-tank missile.

^{b} Includes medium-range surface-to-air missiles (MSAM) and family of anti-air missile systems (FAMS).

^{c} Includes F 100 frigates, light attack fighters (EA/A-X) and infantry fighting vehicles (IFVs).

^{d} Includes European Cooperation for the Long-term in Defence (EUCLID).

Sources: Ministerio de Defensa, *Memoria de la IV Legislatura, 1990–93* [Report from the 4th legislature] (Ministerio de Defensa: Madrid, 1993), p. 335 (in Spanish); and Ministerio de Defensa, *Memoria de la Legislatura, 1987–89* [Report from the legislature] (Ministerio de Defensa: Madrid, 1989), p. 337 (in Spanish).

Sur with the Netherlands, and the Austrian–Spanish Cooperative Development (ASCOD) Pizarro infantry fighting vehicle (IFV) with Austria—which features a German MTU engine—all of which will be operational in 1996.[44]

The Eurofighter

Spain's largest R&D programme is its commitment to the four-nation Eurofighter project, which it joined in 1983. Spain retains a 13 per cent holding (compared to 33 per cent each for Germany and the UK and 21 per cent for Italy), reflecting its investment in the $50 billion programme.[45] Typical of the

[44] Prior to the most recent build-up, CASA developed the Airtech CN-235 transport aircraft with Indonesia in 1980–86. The CN-235 was a 50–50 project and is now produced under licence in Turkey. *Jane's All the World's Aircraft 1995–96* (Jane's Information Group: Coulsdon, Surrey, 1994), p. 149.

[45] Lindemann, M., 'Key Eurofighter decision postponed again', *Financial Times*, 22 June 1995. Questions about programme cost arose again in 1995, with the German Federal Audit Office suggesting that life-cycle costs had risen by 50–70%. If true, this would oblige Spain to pay some Ptas 1200 billion (about $10 billion) for its 87 aircraft over the coming years. Shifrin, C. A., 'Eurofighter 2000 testing accelerates', *Aviation Week & Space Technology*, 12 June 1995, p. 79. Spain had already paid Ptas 115 billion (Ptas 66 billion to CASA and Ptas 49 billion to ITP) of the expected Ptas 248 billion for R&D (Ptas 164 billion for development and Ptas 84 billion for definition) in the programme at the end of

PSOE's mixed enthusiasm for European military cooperation is its commitment of Ptas 850 billion to the project (bringing the average life-cycle cost per aircraft to $80 million) in the name of European solidarity combined with the promise to Spanish taxpayers that not one peseta would cross the Pyrenees.

The main Spanish contractor on the Eurofighter is CASA, which has lead design responsibility on the joint structures team as well as the rear fuselage (with Alenia), the right wing (with British Aerospace), and integration and software creation for the communications system.[46] Industria de Turbo Propulsores (ITP), 51 per cent Spanish-owned, is responsible for a few relatively simple parts of the EJ-200 engines. Spain is not committed to the German-selected electronic defence systems, and may develop its own, especially a laser warning receiver, which only Spain and the UK will use on their aircraft. The Spanish firm Indra, through its Eurotronica subsidiary, is an 18 per cent partner in developing the Pirate Infrared Search and Track (IRST) with FIAR and Thorn. In June 1995, Indra joined GEC Marconi and Elettronica in a project to develop the defence aids sub-system (DASS) with a Spanish commitment of 10 per cent, including Ptas 2.4 billion for the first phase of development.[47]

The Eurofighter has been characterized as the embodiment of cold war requirements that are no longer relevant to the needs of the major partners, a criticism that would seem even more germane to Spain. The Eurofighter's main features are its ability to take off from runways that may have been damaged by air or missile attack and to manoeuvre in dogfights with Soviet fighters not far from its own bases. The programme was primarily justified by its ability to defeat the Sukhoi Su-27 and Su-35.[48] Agility, short take-off and landing, and short range do not suit Spain's current military situation any more than they did Spain's cold war role in NATO. Indeed, Spain had little say in developing the requirements for the Eurofighter and almost opted out with France in 1985 when a heavier aircraft with less air-to-ground capability was selected over the French alternative that became the Rafale.[49] In the meantime, CASA's indigenous combat aircraft programmes have stagnated since

1993. Total life-cycle costs to Spain for the programme were projected at an additional Ptas 605 billion in late 1993. Del Vado, S. F., 'El eurocaza del siglo XXI' [The Eurofighter of the 21st century], *Revista Española de Defensa,* Jan. 1994, p. 50 (in Spanish).

[46] Other systems designed in Spain are more prosaic: landing-gear including wheels and brakes, oxygen bottles and equipment, gears, refrigeration, warning lights, valves, pumps, cabin switches and inertial navigation system. Spain's contribution had to be tailored carefully because its partners had doubts about its military industrial capacity and had trouble delegating it its full work share. See, e.g., UK, House of Commons, Defence Committee, *European Fighter Aircraft,* HC Paper 1991/92, no. 299 (Her Majesty's Stationery Office: London, 1992), p. xx.

[47] Florensa, A., 'Fuerza Aérea potenciada' [Air force boosted], *Revista Española de Defensa,* July/Aug. 1995, p. 57 (in Spanish).

[48] Frith, N., 'The European fighter aircraft: potential and prospects', *RUSI Journal,* Apr. 1992. Only China, Russia and Viet Nam operate the Su-27 and only Russia the Su-35. Requirements to operate from poorly prepared runways or under conditions of nuclear attack were relaxed in 1992.

[49] A good brief summary of the requirements process is Elzen, B., Enserink, B. and Smit, W. A., 'Weapon innovation: networks and guiding principles', *Science and Public Policy,* June 1990.

1985, when an indigenous light attack fighter, the EA/A-X, was allowed to languish, only to be revived in 1989 at a very low level of effort.[50]

Independent projects

The crowding-out effect of the Eurofighter on the EA/A-X is suggestive of the mixed result that Spain's build-up has had for its goal of greater indigenous development and production. While technology has been transferred to Spain under the aegis of NATO cooperative programmes, it has been earmarked for use on those projects only and has come at the cost of reduced Spanish control over requirements and facilities. Other projects that were considered a high priority have been given a lower priority or left to others, as in the case of the aircraft-carrier industry.

Perhaps Spain's most impressive feat of indigenous military design and production is the vertical/short take-off and landing (V/STOL) aircraft-carrier *Principe de Asturias,* based on an abandoned US design for a cost-effective sea-control ship and launched in 1989. The *Principe de Asturias* is said to embody 90 per cent Spanish technology (not including aircraft, electronics and weapons), and indeed Spanish shipbuilding remains relatively independent of international cooperation, with only 30 per cent of investment involving foreign firms. Bazán is marketing its experience with aircraft-carriers in hopes of funding independent R&D and has thus far attracted one customer, Thailand. The design of the *Chakri Nareubet* (in honour of the Chakri, Thailand's royal family) was 80 per cent complete in June 1995 and construction 40 per cent complete.[51] It was launched on 20 January 1996, 70 per cent complete, and will carry AV-8S Matador (Killer) V/STOL aircraft when they are retired from Spanish service.[52] The *Chakri Nareubet* will cost $510 million (including electronics and aircraft) and will be delivered in March 1997.[53] Other buyers would have to find their own V/STOL aircraft for a similar ship or accept some technological risk in buying Bazán's first conventional take-off and landing (CTOL) ship, which has been offered to China.[54]

Assessment of the González build-up

The González build-up seems to have shared the fate of European collaboration at large. Spain's period of explosive growth and enthusiasm for European

---

[50] CASA announced in 1995 that the EA/A-X would fly by 2000 and that it was seeking development partners. Spain operates US EF-18 Hornets and French Mirage F-1s, and considered alternatives to Eurofighter, including Russian aircraft and the Gripen, but these were rejected. Garcia in testimony to the Defence Committee of the Congress of Deputies summarized in Del Vado, S. F., 'El EFA continua, asegura Garcia Vargas' [EFA continues, affirms Garcia Vargas], *Revista Española de Defensa,* Dec. 1992, p. 22 (in Spanish).

[51] 'Naval programme: Thailand's offshore patrol helicopter carrier', *Naval Forces,* Apr. 1995, p. 44.

[52] Thailand is expected to pay $90 million for 8 aircraft. Janssen Lok, J., 'Thailand takes East Asia into the carrier age', *Jane's Defence Weekly,* 31 Jan. 1996, p. 23.

[53] Janssen Lok (note 52).

[54] Janssen Lok, J. and Karniol, R., 'Spain offers carrier designs to Chinese', *Jane's Defence Weekly,* 18 Feb. 1995, p. 8. The Spanish offer was of a 22 000-tonne carrier. China may have a requirement for a 44 000-tonne carrier. Arnett, 'Military technology: the case of China' (note 2).

unity and military cooperation coincided with a boom in military science and industry worldwide and optimism about the future of a harmonized European defence production and procurement system. In the rush of the late 1980s, Spanish officials and industrialists feared 'missing the train', a metaphor often used at the time. With the benefit of hindsight, it is not surprising that many projects failed. Unlike the major military technology powers in Europe, Spain was seldom left with a partially developed system to build its own alternative from. In this sense, Spain was not only optimistic, but especially vulnerable. By the early 1990s, it was still struggling to build capacity in new areas while the major European producers were shedding theirs.

For the defence ministry under the González Government the concept of what it meant to be 'European' was problematic. While it might not have been foreseen that Spain's dramatic growth in the 1980s would not be sustained, the major arms producing countries in Europe were not the only model of European defence available. Given Spain's less immediate feeling of threat from the Soviet Union and later Russia and the PSOE's residual anti-militarism, it was predictable that Spain would have a less sustainable commitment to building up the military technology and industrial bases than the others. The defence policy models offered by the other medium powers of NATO and Western Europe instead of the major arms-producing countries might have given Spain a more appropriate and flexible security concept. The Spanish technology base suffered doubly: first, from working as a junior partner on projects unsuited to its unique requirements; and second, from gaining technology only in niches already mastered by others rather than in unique areas where it might become a sought-after partner in later years.

The strategy of redressing weaknesses in the production base was also flawed and in a related way. Not only was Spain attempting to compete in areas where it lacked experience, but the redirection of emphasis left Spanish arms producers with little to make. Even Bazán, which had gone further towards independent modernization than the other major firms and enjoyed a commitment from the government for the largest slice of the procurement pie, was forced to lay off one-fifth of its workforce in 1986–90, almost one-half in 1981–95. With total military sales cut in half, CASA was left to rely on civilian projects and government subsidies while Santa Bárbara, the land-warfare conglomerate that has practically been passed over by the González build-up, has laid off approximately one-half of its workforce and is in danger of bankruptcy.[55]

PSOE's second thoughts

The catastrophic experience of Spain's military technology base in 1991, when so many of the projects in which DGAM had invested came to naught, provoked a dramatic response from the González Administration. In February

[55] Medina, E., 'Chequeo a la industria de defensa' [Check-up on the defence industry], *Revista Española de Defensa*, Jan. 1994, p. 46 (in Spanish). Further cuts will be put off by the 1996 order for 144 Pizarro IFVs.

1992, as the procurement budget dipped to a low of Ptas 86 billion, the new Defence Minister, Julian Garcia Vargas,[56] delivered a five-year procurement plan of unprecedented detail.[57] Budget cuts for 1993, announced in 1992, were so deep that the procurement minister, José Miguel Hernández Vázquez, resigned in protest. Spanish policy for the military industrial base was elucidated in 1993 as encompassing 'total capacity' to maintain systems in operation and to preserve current production capacities with 'sufficient presence' in key niches for Spanish requirements and cooperative projects while supporting economic development.[58] Spain had officially resigned from the pursuit of a massive indigenous military technology and industrial base.

As élite opinion comes to accept that Spain can only prosper in niches and must remain open to cooperation, albeit on safer terms, the emergent debate focuses on the best partners for more modest collaboration. Raúl Herranz, the president of CASA, appears to be strongly committed to CASA as part of a European team of producers competing against their US counterparts.[59] The alternative view, pragmatic in a way almost unimaginable in 1990, is summed up by the observation of Antonio Sanchez Cámara, President of Bazán: 'Can we afford to be dependent on the US for certain key things? My view is, we are anyway, so why bother spending billions. Better concentrate on areas where we have an advantage'.[60]

A new Partido Popular policy for the military technology base?

The new government, led by José María Aznar's Christian Democrat Popular Party (Partido Popular, PP) which was elected in the national elections held on 3 March 1996, is unlikely to dramatically change Spain's military R&D policy. The PP's position on European cooperation is more pragmatic and less ideological than that of the PSOE, so their view of participation in European security arrangements will probably be tempered by a greater willingness to balance European programmes with transatlantic cooperation. The PP's campaign position was that Spain requires 'urgent revitalization of our [its] defence industrial base, now in danger of extinction'; revitalization would come through privatization and international cooperation.[61] This is in part an attempt to position the PP as a better friend to the military than the PSOE, but would not necessarily lead to greater government funding of the military industry. According to the PP's shadow defence minister, Santiago López

[56] As of 3 July 1995, Garcia is on leave from the post. His substitute is Gustavo Suárez Pertierra.

[57] This was part of the Directiva de Defensa Nacional 1/92, which was reaffirmed by a successor plan, Directiva de Defensa Militar 1/95, approved by Suárez 26 Oct. 1995.

[58] Then Secretary of State for Defence Antonio Flos Bassols cited in Medina (note 55), p. 48. Flos also noted the abundance of high-quality *matériel* available second-hand for a good price or gratis through the NATO CFE cascade. Flos resigned in Apr. 1995. His replacement is Juan Ramón Garcia Secades.

[59] Vega Echevarría, J.-J. and Florensa, A., 'Los consorcios europeos son la via del futuro' [European consortia are the way of the future], *Revista Española de Defensa*, May 1994, p. 56.

[60] Janssen Lok and Karniol (note 54), p. 54.

[61] 'Que hacer con la industria militar' [What to do with the military industry], *Revista Española de Defensa*, June 1993, p. 18 (in Spanish).

Table 9.9. Spain and Sweden compared, May 1996

	Spain	Sweden
Governing party	Popular Party	Social Democratic Party
In office since	1996 (coalition)	1994 (coalition)
Joined NATO	1982 (confirmed in 1986)	Not a member
Joined EC/EU	1986	1995
Geographic area (sq. km.)	499 000	411 000
Population, 1993	39 m.	8.8 m.
Gross national product, 1993 (1990 US $m.)	450 000	140 000
Central government expenditure, 1993 (1990 US $m.)	120 000	66 000
Deficit, 1993 (1990 US $m.)	27 000	25 000
Military expenditure, 1993 (1990 US $m.)	5 200	4 700
National R&D expenditure, 1993 (1990 US $m.)	3 900	4 200
Government R&D budget, 1993 (1990 US $m.)	2 200	1 700
Military R&D expenditure, 1993 (1990 US $m.)	300	410
Military industry	Largely government owned	Largely privately owned
Gross domestic product in manufacturing, 1987 (%)	27	24
Manufactures in exports, 1987 (%)	71	84

Sources: CIA, *World Factbook 1994–95* (Brassey's: Washington, DC, 1994); *OECD Main Science and Technology Indicators*, no. 2 (1995); and World Bank, *World Development Report 1989* (Oxford University Press: Oxford, 1989), pp. 169, 195.

Valdivielso, 'From the point of view of equipment, we think that [Spain] is in a worrying situation, but we have to be prudent with additional funding'.[62] Nevertheless, 'boosting research' is among the military items on the PP campaign platform.[63]

Sweden

In contrast to Spain, Sweden has developed an independent defence concept, albeit one that remains dependent on imported technology and remarkable levels of investment in military R&D (see table 9.9).[64] Sweden's expenditure

[62] Tarilonte, E., 'Propuestas del PP en materia de defensa' [Proposals of the PP in the matter of defence], *Revista Española de Defensa*, Mar. 1993, p. 28 (in Spanish).

[63] Tarilonte, E., 'La defensa en los programas electorales' [Defence in the election programmes], *Revista Española de Defensa*, Feb. 1996, p. 25 (in Spanish).

[64] Note that in 1987, when the González build-up began, Spain and Sweden enjoyed roughly comparable levels of industrialization.

on military R&D is much greater than Spain's as a share of government-funded R&D, national R&D and GDP, putting it highest among the non-nuclear weapon states of the OECD in these categories (as seen in table 9.6). Sweden spends almost as much as Italy, a country with five times its GDP, on military R&D, and has long spent at this level.

In recent years Sweden has moved away from a policy of self-reliance in military technology[65] to one of more open and intensive international cooperation as a means to sustain a domestic military industry capable of producing state-of-the-art systems. Much of Sweden's military technology base is still devoted to a project that appears to have value mainly for the symbolic purpose of demonstrating that Sweden can produce combat aircraft with a degree of independence from foreign alliances, the JAS-39 Gripen (Griffin), and the military R&D budget remains high.[66] As a result of the country's economic crisis, all spending is under pressure and Sweden has abandoned some sectors of its military technology and industrial bases. Most significantly, the ability to produce main battle tanks was abandoned in 1991, and the German Leopard was selected as Sweden's new tank in 1995.[67]

One reason Sweden's military R&D effort remains high is the nation's unusual decentralized concept for defending a large territory with a small population (as summarized in table 9.9), which might be characterized as high-technology guerrilla warfare. Air forces are centred on a force of small, maintainable fighter-attack aircraft that can operate from short runways and even rural highways; naval forces comprise corvettes, attack boats and submarines in large numbers without major surface combatants; land forces also operate on the basis of small, mobile units; and all are netted together in a decentralized system of sensors and communications relays that should offer a high level of situation awareness. In a sense, Sweden's armed forces embody not only a non-offensive defence philosophy, but a prescient version of the force envisioned by advocates of the Revolution in Military Affairs.[68]

Given the nature of the RMA, it should not be surprising that Sweden's military posture is technology intensive, requiring a high level of investment in military R&D, while creating relatively few high-profile artefacts. In 1995, three major systems were known to be under development: the Gripen, the SCV 2000 surface combat vessel (ytstridsfartyg) and the Submarine 2000. The remainder of the R&D budget was devoted to missiles, sensors, electronic warfare and low-observability technologies, as summarized in table 9.10.

[65] Sweden previously bought finished systems from the West and produced some systems and components under licence, including the engines for its combat aircraft.

[66] In addition to the funds committed by the Swedish Government, summarized in tables 9.1 and 9.5, Swedish industry contributed more than half as much again through the late 1980s. Hagelin, B., 'Sweden's search for military technology', Brzoska and Lock (note 28), p. 186.

[67] Sweden's Hägglunds still produces armoured, tracked vehicles, one of which, the combat vehicle CV-90, may be adapted as a light tank.

[68] See note 14.

Table 9.10. Major Swedish Government-sponsored military R&D programmes, 1995
Figures are in m. Swedish crowns (SEK).

Project	Status	Comment
JAS-39 Gripen combat aircraft	10 in service	SEK 28 b. through 1994
BAMSE SAM system	Full development in 1998	SEK 2 b. project; SEK 650 m. for 1995–97
Bonus smart artillery shell	Development	SEK 3 b. project with GIAT
StriC C2	In service 1996?	SEK 2 b. contract in 1990
SCV 2000 corvette	Commissioned 1999	SEK 400 m. through 1993; SEK 100 m. in FY 1994/95
S 100B Argus/Erieye AWACS	Delivered 1995	SEK 1 b. contract
Project Viking/Submarine 2000	Concept development	
Torpedo 2000/Type 62	Production in 1997	
Saab Electro-Optical System	Development	

JAS = fighter, attack, surveillance (jakt, attack, spaning); BAMSE SAM = Bofors air-defence missile system surface-to-air missile; StriC = battle management centres (stridslednings-central); SCV = surface combat vessel; AWACS = airborne warning and control system.

Source: Association of Swedish Defence Industries, *The Swedish Defence Industry* (Sveriges Försvarsindustriföreningen: Stockholm, 1994).

Swedish R&D

Military R&D funded by the Swedish Government is spread across several organizations. Basic research is financed by the Swedish National Defence Research Establishment (Försvarets Forskningsanstalt, FOA) and development by the Defence Matériel Administration (Försvarets Materielverk, FMV) and the armed services (see table 9.11). In contrast with Spain, Sweden's military R&D and production are already largely in private hands. The government owns only 25 per cent of Celsius, the public holding company that controls Bofors, Kockums, CelsiusTech and FFV Aerotech. The emphasis has been on the ability of Swedish firms to act as prime contractors integrating projects that include foreign subsystems and components.

Since World War II, the bulk of Sweden's military R&D and the defence effort more generally have focused on defending Sweden's airspace.[69] The Gripen is Sweden's biggest R&D project at present, and indeed ever. Total development costs have amounted to about $2 billion.[70] The Gripen is a smaller and less expensive aircraft than the Eurofighter, with unit costs expected to be in the range of $25–30 million.[71]

[69] This derives in part from Sweden's geography and has only been reinforced by the lessons of the Persian Gulf War. On the importance of air defence, see Hagelin, B. and Wallensteen, P., 'Understanding Swedish military expenditures', *Cooperation and Conflict*, vol. 27 (1992), no. 4, p. 420.
[70] Matthews, R., 'Grip on Gripen changes', *Jane's Defence Weekly*, 10 June 1995, p. 116. Total investment on the programme up to the end of 1995 comes to $4 billion. Hedén, A. and Hansson, H., 'Gripen-projektet: kalla fakta' [The Gripen project: cold facts], *FlygvapenNytt*, no. 2 (1995) (in Swedish).
[71] The average cost rises to $70–80 million each, comparable to the Eurofighter, if all programme costs are included and spread over the fleet.

Table 9.11. FOA R&D costs for 1994/95

Figures are in m. Swedish crowns (SEK).

Project	Allocation
Weapons and protection	132.57
Electronic warfare	103.63
Protection against nuclear, biological and chemical weapons	99.85
Sensors	83.05
Human factors	40.35
Command and control system	37.73
Total	**497.18**

Source: Adapted from FOA, *Årsredovisning 1994/95* [Annual report 1994/95] (FOA: Stockholm, 1995), pp. 16, 20, 24, 28, 32, 38 (in Swedish).

Despite involving almost every Swedish military production firm—including Saab (65 per cent), Volvo Aero (15 per cent), Ericsson (16 per cent) and FFV Aerotech (4 per cent)—the Gripen will have twice as much foreign content (40 per cent) as its predecessor, the AJS-37 Viggen (Thunderbolt). Total programme costs for 1982–2001 were given in January 1995 as 67 billion Swedish crowns (SEK) ($10 billion), including production of the first 140 aircraft in two batches, 11 of which had been delivered by the end of 1995 (1 prototype and 1 production aircraft have crashed). Approximately one-half of production cost outlays go to foreign firms.[72] A third batch of 70–100 aircraft are likely to be bought in the next five-year plan, down from the 160 originally foreseen.

In its air defence role, the Gripen will initially be armed with the US AMRAAM. Sweden is considering participation in two other air-to-air missile programmes. After losing the competition to sell the Gripen to Finland, in part because the USA refused to allow AMRAAM to be included in the package, Sweden cut its order from 500 to 100 missiles. The balance could be made up by a similar missile being discussed by Sweden, France, Germany and the UK, the $1.5 billion future medium-range air-to-air missile (FMRAAM).[73] Similarly, Sweden and the other European nations using the US Sidewinder are discussing the development of a European replacement, known for now as the IRIS-T.[74]

The Gripen is only one component of an elaborate air-defence capability to be coordinated through the new network of StriC battle management centres (stridsledningscentral) being developed by CelsiusTech. When operational, StriC will feed data from a network of airborne and ground-based sensors to Gripen and Viggen fighters and anti-aircraft missile batteries. The airborne sensors have been upgraded with the S 100 Argus AWACS aircraft equipped with the Ericsson FSR 890 Erieye radar, and the ground-based element is due

[72] Of the 44% cited in 1995, 71% is owed in dollars, 14% in pounds, 10% in marks and 5% in francs. 'Swedish defence budget details emerge', *Military Affairs*, 23 Jan. 1995, p. 5.

[73] Gray, B., 'Defence ministry moves on missile for Eurofighter', *Financial Times*, 6 Dec. 1995, p. 8.

[74] Körner (note 26), p. 26.

to be reinforced with SEK 2 billion-worth of SAMs and radars developed under the Bofors air-defence missile system (BAMSE) programme. Bofors is also developing a family of SAMs independently.

After air defence, anti-ship missions have had priority in Swedish planning. A hypothetical invasion force would be engaged from the air in port and at sea and by submarines before coming under fire from coastal defence artillery and attack vessels as it entered Swedish waters. The anti-ship mission has led Sweden to develop advanced anti-ship missiles and an innovative submarine industry that it is reluctant to abandon. Kockums, the Swedish submarine yard, is building three submarines of the new A 19 Gotland Class, ordered in 1990 to begin replacing the 1960s vintage Sjöormen (Seasnake). The first two A 19 submarines were launched in February 1995 and February 1996. A follow-on class, the Submarine 2000 being developed under Project Viking, will represent a further evolution of the Stirling cycle engine technology that permits extended submergences (several weeks at 5 knots) by carrying liquid oxygen. Sweden seeks to maintain its advantages in areas related to operating submarines in shallow and fresh water but is finding it difficult to fund a submarine industry alone. Peter Nordbeck, Commander-in-Chief of the Navy, has stated: 'I can't see how, with my budget, I can maintain a capable submarine fleet if we don't work with partners'. Sweden is competing with an Italo-German consortium for partnership with Denmark and Norway.[75]

As the threat of amphibious invasion has eased, other projects for the anti-ship and port-attack missions have languished or been redirected. While industry has independently funded and promoted a number of smart-weapon projects, the government has shown little interest. Sweden's most advanced air-to-ground weapon is the RBS-15F, the air-launched variant of a coastal defence missile inducted in 1984. Saab has proposed upgrading the RBS-15— as the TSA heavy guided attack weapon (tungt styrt attackvapen) or autonomous stand-off weapon (ASOM)—with terrain-following and target-recognition packages it is developing, but it has not secured government funding.[76] Similarly, Bofors has found it more profitable to cooperate with DASA to develop the Taurus KEPD (kinetic energy penetrator and destroyer) 350, a missile with a Bofors warhead and a German imaging infrared seeker, for the British Royal Air Force's conventional autonomous stand-off munition (CASOM) requirement, one of seven competing projects.[77]

Sweden's other major naval weapon system programme, the SCV 2000 small (400-tonne) stealthy corvette, was envisioned in three variants for air-defence, anti-ship and anti-submarine warfare (ASW). In 1995 the government ordered two SCV 2000s for ASW operations with an option for two

[75] Janssen Lok, J., 'Viking drafted as second Gotland is launched', Jane's Defence Weekly, 21 Feb. 1996, p. 8. Nordbeck added: 'It is for industry to arrange the actual consortium that will do the work'.

[76] This despite the Ministry of Defence finding that the air force's air-to-ground capability was inadequate. Gyldén, N., Sweden's Security Policy: Through the Cold War and Towards the Turn of the Century (Ministry of Defence: Stockholm, 1994), p. 97.

[77] Beal, C., 'DASA/Bofors consortium seeks CASOM success', Jane's International Defence Review, Jan. 1996, pp. 36–37. The KEPD 350 was developed from the DWS submunitions dispenser which entered service with the Swedish Air Force in early 1996, and is not expected to win the competition.

more at a total cost of SEK 1.7 billion for four. The programme absorbed 'just over SEK 100 million' for development in fiscal year (FY) 1994/95, over the total of $60 million spent through 1993. Sweden is also developing Kafus, a fixed underwater reconnaissance system that will replace the current array that seems to have a high false-alarm rate.

Land warfare remains a low priority for Swedish R&D, especially with the decision to buy the Leopard tank instead of a Swedish design. Nevertheless, Swedish firms continue to develop unique weapons in the tradition of the Bofors Bill anti-tank missile, inducted in 1988 and in the midst of evolutionary development. More recently, Bofors and Saab have developed the Strix smart-mortar bomb, and Bofors has entered into an agreement with France's GIAT to develop the Bonus, a smart 155-mm anti-tank submunition similar to the US sense and destroy armour (SADARM).[78] An artillery-spotting radar developed in cooperation with the Norwegian Army was inducted in 1995.

Prospects

Sweden's Social Democratic Government, elected in November 1994 in part to maintain the welfare state, will begin to promulgate a new five-year defence plan in 1996. The Swedish Government is already committed to reducing the defence budget by 5 per cent in 1995–2000. A preliminary report was delivered in June 1995, which will be followed by a second report for the new five-year plan, or 'defence decision', which takes effect on 1 January 1997. The main feature of the plan is a SEK 4 billion (10 per cent) reduction in expenditure, with SEK 2 billion to be cut by 1998, two years early. Some savings may come from the third batch of Gripens.

Even before Swedish entry into the EU in 1995, Swedish defence planning had taken a more European turn,[79] but Sweden will no doubt maintain its current defence concept and its dependence on US technology. The next generation of combat aircraft is likely to be co-developed or imported as Sweden's willingness to be frank about its relationship to the Western arms industry increases.[80]

On 6 December 1995, the Swedish Government presented a bill (1995/96:12) to the parliament restructuring the Swedish military industry. It encouraged Swedish firms to seek foreign cooperation in order to bolster Sweden's ability to produce technologies in four key areas independently: aerospace, submarines, electronic warfare and identification (friend from foe).

---

[78] Bofors is also seeking support to develop a trajectory correctable munition, an artillery round guided from the ground. Hewish, M., 'Smart munitions', *Jane's International Defence Review*, Feb. 1996, pp. 36–37. SADARM is also described in US Congress, Office of Technology Assessment, *New Technology for NATO: Implementing Follow-On Forces Attack* (US Government Printing Office: Washington, DC, 1987).

[79] This was countenanced politically in the 1992 Defence Policy Resolution, which essentially gave the Swedish industry a green light for the endeavours they had been arranging. Gyldén (note 76), p. 102.

[80] At the launch of the Anglo-French company intended to develop the replacement for Eurofighter in Dec. 1995, Gripen was pointedly referred to as another candidate for replacement by the new fighter. De Briganti, G., 'British–French venture boosts future fighter', *Defense News*, 18–24 Dec. 1995, p. 8.

Spain and Sweden: conclusions

Sweden's novel approach to defence planning, while costly, has also made Swedish firms market leaders in niches that make them desirable partners in international collaborations, whereas Spain's efforts to catch up through duplication is less likely to produce unique capabilities for Europe. Ironically, Sweden's independent approach may have led to better prospects for post-cold war cooperation, while Spain's initiative to become 'more European than the Europeans' may leave it better able to develop the next generation of some systems indigenously once the resources devoted to the Eurofighter are released. For both countries, it appears that future cooperation will favour modest projects tailored to their requirements rather than the enormous pan-European undertakings typical of NATO thinking in the 1980s.

IV. Conclusions

It remains difficult for any but a few organizations in a handful of countries to develop advanced systems or enabling technologies, and even those countries that are capable appear less willing to invest what is required. For other states, even the greatest of efforts is likely to be little more than a futile demonstration of their ideological commitment to an unattainable self-sufficiency. Among the countries considered in this chapter, India demonstrates this point vividly. Despite the global trend towards less military R&D as well as lower procurement budgets, 1995 saw the persistence of the view that, in the words of one journalist: 'Technologies of a bewildering variety . . . are suddenly on the loose and the competition to find new ways of putting them to military use is no longer the preserve of the most advanced industrial nations. There is now a free-for-all to acquire weapons which may allow even relatively weak countries the chance to leap-frog their way to battlefield superiority'.[81] Paul Dibb, the Australian hawk, remarked, in the same vein: 'The real danger is . . . the ability of [Asian] states to build the next generation of weapons themselves'.[82] Despite the fact that most countries are beginning to resign themselves to a reduced R&D capability, there remains an erroneous common belief that military R&D will soon release a new wave of weapon proliferation.[83] The discussion in this chapter suggests that such is not the case.

---

[81] Shukman, D., *The Sorcerer's Challenge: Fears and Hopes for the Weapons of the Next Millenium* (Hodder and Stoughton: London, 1995), p. xiii..

[82] Dibb, P., 'The future military capabilities of Asia's great powers', *Jane's Intelligence Review*, vol. 7, no. 5 (May 1995), p. 229.

[83] This divergence of perceptions is noted and tested in Arnett (note 2, China and India) and analysed as a political phenomenon in Arkin, W. M., 'The sky-is-still-falling profession', *Bulletin of the Atomic Scientists*, Mar./Apr. 1994, p. 64; and Spector, L. S., 'Neo-nonproliferation', *Survival*, spring 1995.

10. Arms production

ELISABETH SKÖNS and BATES GILL*

I. Introduction

Restructuring of the arms industry continues worldwide. The developments, forms, progress and obstacles in this process are surveyed in this chapter. The focus is on general trends in production, company strategies and international industrial linkages, while dimensions such as the impact on employment and conversion to civilian production are summarily covered.[1] The transformation of the global arms industry to adjust to a lower level of demand for its products is a vast research field where much work remains to be done.[2]

There is a general downward trend in arms production in most parts of the world—which does not, however, exclude determined efforts to raise the technological level of arms production in many countries, both in the industrialized and in the industrializing worlds. The process of reducing the production capacity for military equipment is reasonably smooth except in China, Russia and Ukraine, which are facing great difficulties in transforming their military industries. In France the tight government–industry relationship has delayed the process of adjustment, but a fundamental change is likely to take place in the near future.

Viewing the global arms industry through the sample of the 'top 100' arms-producing companies in the Organisation for Economic Co-operation and Development (OECD)[3] and developing countries, it seems that the decline in arms sales has decelerated. Their combined arms sales declined by 2 per cent in 1994, as compared with 6 per cent in 1993. Since it is generally agreed that the combined excess capacity in these countries is far from having been eliminated, it can be expected that production and sales will continue to fall during the next few years although possibly at a lower rate. As has been reported in previous editions of the *SIPRI Yearbook*, the companies have by and large

---

[1] For a global survey of trends in conversion during the past decade, see Bonn International Center for Conversion (BICC), *Conversion Survey 1996* (Oxford University Press: Oxford, 1996). Other recent literature on conversion includes Albrecht, U., *Rüstung in der Konversion?* [The conversion of armaments?] (LIT Verlag: Münster and Hamburg, 1994); Bissell, R. E., Report of the Project on Defense Conversion in Developing Countries, Submitted to the IS Institute of Peace, Washington, DC, 1 Aug. 1995; Butterwegge, C. and Grundmann, M. (eds), *Zivilmacht Europa: Friedenspolitik und Rüstungskonversion in Ost und West* [European civil power: peace policy and armaments conversion in East and West] (Bund Verlag: Cologne, 1994); and Gansler, J., *Defense Conversion: Transforming the Arsenal of Democracy* (MIT Press: Cambridge, Mass. and London, 1995).

[2] A survey of research on the military–industrial economy and a list of the most urgent issues to study are provided in Markusen, A. and Weida, W., 'Research, teaching and policy on the military industrial economy', *Peace Economics, Peace Science and Public Policy*, vol. 2, no. 3 (1995), pp. 1–20.

[3] A list of members of the OECD is given in the Glossary.

* Section VI was contributed by Bates Gill.

avoided being adversely affected by the adjustment process, but national costs in the form of structural unemployment are high in many regions.[4]

Restructuring in the USA takes the form primarily of concentration into a few dominant players in each field and is associated with substantial cuts in production capacity. In Western Europe companies continue to focus on costs, fearing competition from the increasingly large US corporations. The concentration process in Europe continues to be slower than in the USA. National markets are smaller and the national restructuring processes have already gone a long way in most European countries. Because there are barriers to mergers into international company structures, military industrial concentration on the European scene tends to take the form of international joint ventures, focused on specific weapon projects or at least categories of weapon. Whether this approach will lead to a significant reduction in the duplication of effort or in weapon costs is as yet not clear.

While concentration, both national and international, facilitates reductions in capacity, it also leads to less competition. This could constitute an additional inducement to growth in the cost of weapon systems. It could also lead to more powerful lobbies for huge military projects.

New military–industrial links are developing in other parts of the world as well, following changes in the international system and in international relations during the 1990s. The break-up of the Soviet Union, the end of the cold war, the peace process in the Middle East, the transformation of South Africa and technological progress and industrial development in East Asia have all had an impact on and are reflected in the global arms industry sector. The former Warsaw Treaty Organization (WTO) member states are gradually reorienting towards NATO-standard equipment and seek to pursue cooperation in this direction. The decline in demand for new Russian equipment is one reason for the increased demand for modernization kits and work for military equipment designed by the former Soviet Union. Israel and South Africa are no longer regarded as politically sensitive cooperation partners and are trying to exploit the emerging niche on the international market of refurbishing military equipment with new electronics, and this will probably result in new military–industrial relations. South Korea has launched an effort to expand its indigenous arms production capability on the basis of its achievements in civilian industry and infrastructure but with less focus on military exports.

China, too, is facing the difficulties of down-sizing as its ambitious effort has begun to show signs of strain. With domestic procurement in considerable decline and few export options, China's military industries must contract, but are ill-prepared to meet commercial challenges. Taking advantage of contraction at the international level, China may be able to use its impressive economic growth to secure access to foreign military technology, especially from Russia and Israel.

---

[4] Global arms industry employment has declined from a peak of 17.5 million in 1987 to 11.1 million in 1995, according to estimates made by BICC. The former cold war adversaries, the NATO and WTO countries, accounted for over 90% of the decline in 1989–95. BICC (note 1), p. 111.

Table 10.1. Regional/national shares of arms sales for the top 100 arms-producing companies in the OECD and the developing countries, 1994 compared to 1993

Figures for arms sales are in US $b. Figures in italics are percentages.

Number of companies, 1994	Region/ country	Share of total arms sales		Arms sales 1994 (US $b.)
		1993	1994	
43	USA	*61.5*	*60.2*	89.3
38	*West European OECD*	*30.9*	*31.5*	46.6
11	France	*12.0*	*11.3*	16.7
11	UK	*9.3*	*10.5*	15.6
8	Germany	*5.3*	*5.0*	7.4
2	Italy	*1.7*	*1.8*	2.7
3	Sweden	*0.9*	*1.2*	1.8
2	Switzerland	*1.0*	*1.0*	1.4
1	Spain	*0.7*	*0.7*	1.0
11	*Other OECD*	*4.9*	*5.5*	8.2
9	Japan	*4.5*	*5.1*	7.5
2	Canada	*0.4*	*0.5*	0.7
8	*Developing countries*[a]	*2.7*	*2.8*	4.1
5	Israel	*1.7*	*1.7*	2.5
2	India	*0.6*	*0.6*	0.9
1	South Africa	*0.4*	*0.4*	0.6
100		***100.0***	***100.0***	**148.1**

Note. Figures may not always add up to totals because of the conventions of rounding.

[a] Four companies in South Korea would be included among the top 100 arms-producing companies in this group if data were available for 1994. See table 10.14.

Source: Appendix 10A.

In the three non-OECD countries on the list, India, Israel and South Africa, arms-producing companies maintained their share in the arms sales of the top 100 companies. This stable share encompassed a relatively large increase in the arms sales of Indian companies (13 per cent), a modest increase for Israeli firms (6 per cent) and a more or less stagnant trend for the South African company.

II. The SIPRI top 100

General trends

The arms sales of the top 100 arms-producing companies in the OECD and the developing countries decreased slightly in 1994. Their combined arms sales amounted to $148 billion in 1994, a decline compared to the previous year of around $3 billion or 2.2 per cent. This represents a deceleration from the previous year, when the arms sales of the top 100 fell by 6 per cent.[5]

---

[5] Because the companies included among the 'top 100' differ from year to year, this figure cannot be directly compared with the figure reported in the *SIPRI Yearbook 1995* for the combined top 100 arms sales in 1993, which was $156 billion. Sköns, E. and Gonchar, Ks., 'Arms production', *SIPRI Yearbook*

In reality, the decline was greater, because for most of the major arms-producing countries an improving exchange rate against the dollar meant that when converted into dollars the decline appeared smaller than it was in their own currencies. This was true for France, Germany, Japan, Switzerland and the UK. The combined arms sales of the companies from these countries therefore declined more in their own currency than as measured in US dollars.

There was a change in the regional shares among the top 100 companies in 1994 (table 10.1). The most notable development is the decline in the US share compared to that of companies in Western Europe.[6] The decline in the arms sales of the leading US companies (by about 4 per cent) reflects the greater intensity of restructuring in the US arms industry, a process which was further accelerated in 1995. The concentration process in the USA is to a great extent driven by down-sizing of production capacity. Most of the US companies listed in table 10.2 are, therefore, in this list because of their sales or acquisitions of arms production units.

In Western Europe, arms sales increased significantly for the leading companies in Italy, Sweden and the UK. In all three countries this was the result of further concentration. The leading companies have acquired other arms-producing companies but without simultaneous rationalization of production. There were also several countries in Western Europe in which the major arms-producing companies experienced significant reductions in arms sales. These include France, Germany and Switzerland. Among the 11 French companies in the list, all but two had declining or stagnant arms sales in 1994, although not as a result of deliberate cuts or divestitures of production units. Among the French companies in table 10.2, none of the instances of reduced arms sales was the result of deliberate policy. The fall in German company arms sales is due to the dramatic decline in domestic orders for military equipment, and is associated with the restructuring of the main German arms-producing company, Daimler Benz Aerospace, DASA.

The increase in the combined share of the nine leading Japanese companies in table 10.1 is illusory, an effect of the appreciation of the yen.[7] However, several individual firms had increased arms sales: the three Japanese companies in table 10.2 with increased arms sales in dollar terms had actual increases as measured in yen of 7–25 per cent. In the three non-OECD countries on the list, arms-producing companies maintained their share in the arms sales of the top 100 companies. This stable share encompassed a relatively large increase in the arms sales of Indian companies (13 per cent), a modest increase for Israeli firms (6 per cent) and a more or less stagnant trend

---

1995: Armaments, Disarmament and International Security (Oxford University Press: Oxford, 1995), p. 455. The average rate of inflation in the OECD countries was 4.1% in 1994.

[6] This is still true, although to a slightly lesser extent, when changes in exchange rates are taken into account: the combined arms sales of the West European companies on the list were constant in dollar terms, while they declined by only 1%, measured in local currency.

[7] While the increase in the combined arms sales of the Japanese firms in the top 100 was over 10% in dollar terms, it was less than 2% measured in yen. Since Japan produces military equipment exclusively for the domestic market, it is the trend in local currency which reflects the actual development of arms-production activities.

Table 10.2. Companies whose arms sales changed the most in 1994 [a]

Figures are in US $m. Figures in italics are percentages.

Company/subsidiary	Country	Sector[b]	Arms sales 1993	Arms sales 1994	Change 1993–94 US $m.	Change 1993–94 %
Companies with decreased arms sales						
Raytheon	USA	El Mi	4 500	3 500	– 1 000	*– 22*
General Motors	USA	Eng El Mi	6 900	5 900	– 1 000	*– 14*
Rockwell International	USA	Ac El Mi	3 350	2 550	– 800	*– 24*
DCN	France	Sh	3 440	2 730	– 710	*– 21*
General Electric	USA	Eng	2 400	1 800	– 600	*– 25*
Carlyle	USA	Ac El Oth	1 200	800	– 400	*– 33*
United Technologies	USA	Ac El Mi	4 200	3 800	– 400	*– 10*
Daimler-Benz	Germany	Ac Eng El MV	3 540	3 200	– 340	*– 10*
Ishikawajima-Harima	Japan	Eng Sh	840	520	– 320	*– 38*
Gencorp	USA	Mi SA/O Oth	850	580	– 270	*– 32*
GIAT Industries	France	A MV SA/O	1 300	1 030	– 270	*– 21*
Dassault Aviation	France	Ac	1 590	1 330	– 260	*– 16*
GTE	USA	El	1 100	850	– 250	*– 23*
Thiokol	USA	Eng SA/O	520	370	– 150	*– 29*
Companies with increased arms sales						
Lockheed Martin[c]	USA	Ac El M	..	14 400	..	..
Loral	USA	El Mi	3 750	5 100	+ 1 350	*+ 36*
Northrop Grumman[d]	USA	Ac El Mi SA/O	4 480	5 600	+ 1 120	*+ 25*
British Aerospace	UK	Ac A El Mi SA/O	5 950	7 030	+ 1 080	*+ 18*
Mitsubishi Heavy Ind.	Japan	Ac MV Mi Sh	2 380	2 730	+ 350	*+ 15*
GKN	UK	Ac MV	200	550	+ 350	*+ 175*
Kawasaki Heavy Ind.	Japan	Ac Eng Mi Sh	1 130	1 450	+ 320	*+ 28*
Westinghouse Electric	USA	El	2 180	2 450	+ 270	*+ 12*
Celsius	Sweden	A El Sh SA/O	930	1 190	+ 260	*+ 28*
Hunting	UK	SA/O	490	670	+ 180	*+ 37*
Bath Iron Works	USA	Sh	600	770	+ 170	*+ 28*
Honeywell	USA	El Mi	300	450	+ 150	*+ 50*
Avondale Industries	USA	Sh	370	510	+ 140	*+ 38*
NEC	Japan	El	390	520	+ 130	*+ 33*
Ericsson	Sweden	El	160	270	+ 110	*+ 69*
Lucas Industries	UK	Ac	390	490	+ 100	*+ 26*
Elbit	Israel	El Oth	230	290	+ 60	*+ 26*

[a] The table includes all parent companies with a change in arms sales of ± $250 million or 25% or more. They are ranked according to their change in arms sales, as calculated in current dollars.

[b] Abbreviations are explained in appendix 10A.

[c] Lockheed and Martin Marietta, which merged into Lockheed Martin, had combined arms sales of $16.6 billion in 1993 ($10.1 billion and $6.5 billion, respectively).

[d] 1993 arms sales are for Northrop, which acquired Grumman in 1993 and subsequently changed its name to Northrop Grumman. Grumman's arms sales were $2700 million in 1993.

Source: Appendix 10A.

Table 10.3. Major international take-overs in the arms industry, 1994–95

Buyer		Company acquired			
Name	Country	Name	Country	Sector	Comments
CAE Inc.	Canada	Trislot System	Belgium	Industrial filters	Price: $7 m.
CAE Inc.	Canada	Ferranti Computer Systems (Aus.)	Australia	Electronics	Renamed CAE Electronics
CAE Inc.	Canada	MRad Pty Ltd	Australia	Flight simulators	Integrated into CAE Electronics (Aus.)
CAE Inc.	Canada	Invertron Simulated Systems	UK	Simulation systems	Price: £6.3m.; from Alvis, UK
Thomson-CSF	France	Indra (24.9% stake)	Spain	Information technology	Price: $25 m.; from Teneo
BGT	Germany	AIC Electronics	USA	Aircraft repair	US FAA approved repair station
Mercedes-Benz	Germany	Up to 15% stake in Oshkosh Truck and take-over of plant	USA	Vehicles	Mercedes-Benz to transfer part of its production of military vehicles to Oshkosh
THC Group	Netherlands	Swan Hunter	UK	Shipbuilding	Price: c. £4.2 m.; from receivers
Rolls Royce	UK	Allison Engine	USA	Aero-engines	Price: $525 m.
Ultra Electronics	UK	Devtek Applied (Devtek)	Canada	Electronics	Price: $16 m.; renamed Hermes Electronics
Allen Bradley (Rockwell)	USA	Allen Bradley Xiamen	China	Military vehicles	Acquired 100% in former joint venture with Xiamen partner
Hughes Electronics	USA	CAE-Link	USA	Simulation	Price: $155 m.; from CAE (Canada)
Lockheed Martin	USA	FMA Fabrica Militar de Aviones	Argentina		25-year management contract
Rockwell International	USA	Part of ASTA (Aero-Space Technologies of Australia)	Australia	Components, Engineering and Defence Division	Price: $29 m.; from Australian Govt.
Sundstrand	USA	Part of Dowty Aerospace (TI Group)	UK	Aero-engines	Price: $8.8 m.; air turbine division
IBM	USA	Part of Tiltan Systems	Israel	Computerized 3-D imaging	51% stake
Hunting Zimbabwe	Zimbabwe	Hunting Aviation	South Africa	Aerospace	

Buyer		Company acquired			
Name	Country	Name	Country	Sector	Comments
Matra Marconi Space (Matra Hachette/GEC)	France/ UK	Part of BAe	UK	Space	Price: £56 m.; space systems div.
Matra Marconi Space (Matra Hachette/GEC)	France/ UK	Part of Ferranti International	UK	Satellite communications	From receivers of Ferranti Int.
Sextant Avionique	France	Mili-Com Electronics	USA	Satellite communications	To be renamed Sextant Electronics
Thomson-CSF	France	Amper Programas	Spain	Communications, avionics	49% stake
Thomson-CSF	France	Defence Group of Thorn EMI	UK	Missiles, optical electronics	Price: $23 m.
Thomson-CSF	France	Redifon	UK	Communications, navigation systems	
Thomson-CSF	France	Rediffusion Simulation (Hughes, USA)	USA	Simulation systems	
Private investors	Domestic and foreign	Government of Brazil	Embraer	Brazil	Foreign investors acquired 33% of the voting stock

Source: SIPRI arms production files.

for the South African company.[8] One Israeli company (Elbit) became a new entrant on the list. Arms sales data for South Korean companies are available for the first time, but only for 1993. In 1993 the combined arms sales of the four companies in South Korea with sales sufficiently high to place them among the top 100 amounted to more than $1725 million, or 1.2 per cent of the 1994 top 100 total (see table 10.14).

International take-overs

As national markets become too small for increasingly expensive design and development of new weapon systems, companies try to extend their activities across borders. These developments are difficult to trace in detail. Looking at the major international take-overs in the arms industry during the past two years, it appears that this is not a dominant feature in the process of consolidation (see table 10.3). One reason for this is the political and legal barriers against international acquisitions. In a survey of the legal restrictions on inter-

[8] These are the trends as measured in local currencies for India and South Africa, while Israeli firms present financial data in US dollars in their company annual reports.

national integration of the arms industry, it was shown that states are using different types of legal instrument to control this process and that these correspond to the national philosophy on the internationalization of arms production. In the UK and the USA such control is exercised through rules on competition, secrecy and acquisitions, in Germany through export control legislation and in France through the government's administrative control over the arms industry.[9]

The main features in the international restructuring of the global arms industry during 1994–95 can be summarized on the basis of table 10.3 as follows:

1. The simulation sector underwent a radical international reorganization.

2. The British arms industry continued to be among the least resistant to foreign take-overs.

3. The acquisition by Rolls Royce (UK) of Allison Engines (USA) represents an unusual acceptance by US authorities of a foreign take-over of a company with leading military technology capabilities.

4. Lockheed Martin's 25-year management and operation contract with Argentina's Fabrica Militar de Aviones (FMA) is a new feature in the internationalization of the global arms industry. It has similarities with a regular take-over but has a more politically acceptable form.[10]

The expected acquisition by Daewoo (South Korea) of Steyr-Daimler-Puch (Austria), which would have represented one of the first major take-overs by a company in an industrializing country of military technology capabilities in an industrialized country, was cancelled.[11]

III. The United States

The restructuring of the US arms industry continued in 1995 and even appeared to accelerate. The process is being driven by the realization in industry and government of the need to cut production capacity. Although the general view is that the process was no more than half completed by the end of 1995,[12] a significant reduction in production capacity has already been achieved. It is characterized by (a) rapid concentration of production capacity into fewer units; (b) a gradual shift of focus from the military aerospace sector to the military electronics sector; (c) high profitability; and (d) a new development of decentralization of production through spin-offs of smaller company

---

[9] Öberg, U., *Nationella säkerhetsintressen, konkurrensrättslig kontroll och försvarsindustriellt samarbete* [National security, merger and anti-trust policy and international cooperation in the defense industry], FOA Report, FOA-R-95-00190-1.3-SE (Swedish National Defence Research Establishment: Stockholm, Nov. 1995), p. 43.

[10] 'Argentine AF facility goes to Lockheed', *Defense News*, 19–25 June 1995; and 'FMA privatization finalized', *World Aerospace & Defense Intelligence*, 30 June 1995, p. 11.

[11] The Daewoo deal was described as agreed during 1995. *Interavia Air Letter*, 23 Oct. 1995, p. 5; *Jane's Defence Weekly*, 4 Nov. 1995, p. 5; and *Defence Industry Digest*, Nov. 1995, p. 15. The only previous examples are a few smaller Israeli take-overs in the USA, but these were related to military–industrial cooperation arrangements.

[12] See, e. g., 'More aerospace mega-mergers on the way', *Interavia Air Letter*, 10 Oct. 1995, p. 6, reporting from a meeting of industry executives and government officials in Oct. 1995.

units. Although it has been a declared policy goal, integration between civil and military production has not advanced very far.[13]

Concentration

Concentration into fewer and larger corporate units is a clear feature. Among the 10 leading US arms-producing companies in 1994, two are the results of 'mega-mergers'—Lockheed Martin and Northrop Grumman. The latter also acquired the remaining half of Vought Aircraft during the year. Loral increased its sales significantly through its acquisition of Federal Systems, a former IBM subsidiary specialized in systems integration.[14]

A multitude of other major acquisitions were agreed in 1995 involving significant transfers of assets, as indicated by the contract values (see table 10.4). The most costly contract was the sale of the defence activities of Westinghouse to Northrop Grumman, primarily in order to fund Westinghouse's recent purchase of a major television network.[15] Another large deal was Raytheon's acquisition of E-Systems, a major contractor in military electronics; this deal was an apparent contradiction to Raytheon's strategy of increasing its commercial activities. The Carlyle Group, which for several years has been buying and selling arms-producing activities with a good profit margin, announced its decision—jointly with Thiokol—to acquire Howmet, a firm which dominates the world market for metal casting for jet aircraft and defence electronics. Hughes Electronics completed its acquisition of CAE-Link, a US subsidiary to a Canadian company specializing in simulation, and also reached an agreement with the Carlyle Group to buy Magnavox, a market leader in military tactical communications, a deal which it was believed would lead to additional concentration in military electronics.[16] Additional mega-mergers are expected during 1996. In late 1995 there were reports of negotiations for a merger between two other leading aerospace companies, Boeing and McDonnell Douglas.[17] At the beginning of 1996 another mega-deal was announced involving Lockheed's acquisition of all the military electronics and systems integration activities of Loral at a price of $9.5 billion.[18]

Changing sectoral focus

During 1993 and 1994 the US consolidation process was most pronounced in the military aerospace sector. In 1995, the focus began to shift to the military electronics sector (see table 10.4), which is likely to become the main sector of acquisition activities in 1996.

[13] Gansler (note 1).

[14] The major mergers and acquisitions in the USA during 1994 are described in Sköns and Gonchar (note 5). Federal Systems has subsequently changed its name to ASIC.

[15] 'Westinghouse sells defence arm for £2.3bn', *The Guardian*, 4 Jan. 1995.

[16] The price of this acquisition was high, corresponding to 97% of the annual revenues of Magnavox.

[17] *Wall Street Journal*, 16 Nov. 1995; and *Washington Post*, 17 Nov. 1995.

[18] 'Lockheed Martin purchases Loral', *World Aerospace & Defense Intelligence*, 12 Jan. 1996, p. 1; and 'Defence integration', *Financial Times*, 9 Jan. 1996.

Table 10.4. Major take-overs in the US arms industry, 1995

Buyer	Seller	Acquired unit	Production of acquired units	
Alliant Tech systems	Hercules	Aerospace business	Aircraft propulsion and munitions	$412 m.
Allied Signal	Northrop Grumman	Precision Products div.	Inertial systems	Undisclosed value (sales $56 m. p. a.)
Boeing	Litton Industries	Precision Gear unit	Helicopter gears and transmissions	Undisclosed value (170 employees)
Carlyle (51%) Thiokol (49%)	Pechiney (France)	Howmet Corp.	Casting for jet aircraft, etc.	$750 m.
General Dynamics	Prudential Insurance	Bath Iron Works	Surface ships	$300 m.
Hughes Electronics	Carlyle	Magnavox Electronic	Military electronics	$370 m.
Litton Industries	Black & Decker	PRC Inc.	Information technology	$425 m.
Litton Industries	Hughes Electronics	Inertial Systems Business of Delco Systems	Maintenance of aircraft avionics, etc.	Letter of intent Sep. 1995
Litton	Imo Industries	Electro-Optical Systems Div.	Electronics	Undisclosed value (sales $110 m. p. a.)
Litton Industries	Teledyne	Electronics Systems div.	Electronics	Undisclosed value; (sales $150 m. p. a.)
Lockheed Martin	General Electric	Part of GE Aircraft Engines	Manufacture of engine controls	MoU Oct. 1995; design units acquired earlier
Loral	Unisys	Defence division	Military electronics systems integration	$862 m.
Northrop Grumman	Westinghouse	Electronic Systems Group	Radar and ASW systems	$3600 m.
Raytheon	E-Systems	E-Systems	Electronics	$2300 m.
Textron		Elco Industries	Fastening products for aerospace and defence	$180 m.
Thiokol	US Govt.	Air Force Plant 78	Motors for ballistic and tactical missiles	Operated by Thiokol for over 30 years
Tracor		GDE Systems	Automatic test systems	Undisclosed value
Tracor	Shareholders	AEL	Military electronics	$116 m.
Triton Services	ITT	Electron Technology Div.	Electron tubes	Undisclosed value

Note. ASW = Anti-submarive warfare.

Source: SIPRI arms production files.

The only major deal in 1995 outside the aerospace and electronics sector was the purchase of one of the largest US Navy shipyards, Bath Iron Works, by General Dynamics, which during the past four years has been one of the major divesting firms, keeping only its tank production (the Abrams) and submarine production (at its Electric Boat yards).[19] The US shipbuilding sector is characterized by hard competition to maintain any activities at a time when orders are contracting sharply. Bath competes with Ingalls shipyard (Litton). Electric Boat, which for decades has been competing with the other main submarine yard, Newport News, was chosen in 1993 as the sole contractor for all future submarine work for the US Navy. In the area of ordnance and ammunition, one sale was stalled in 1995 because of environmental issues—Gencorp's attempt to sell its arms-producing subsidiary Aerojet.[20]

Contraction paralleled by high profits

The contraction of the volume of production in the US military aerospace industry is exceptional. Military aircraft sales declined by 32 per cent in real terms between 1990 and 1995, and missile sales by 54 per cent. In spite of this decline, the US aerospace industry has good profitability. After two years of record profits, net profits after taxes declined in 1995, but were still expected to exceed the profit margins in the US manufacturing industry in general.[21] All major US arms producers reported continued increases in operating profits in their military business.[22] Mergers and acquisitions in the aerospace industry have been followed by large cuts in employment. Employment in the military aircraft, missiles and space sectors has fallen from 627 000 in 1990 to 326 000 in 1995.[23] This is clearly seen at the firm level. Plant closures and reductions in the workforce are common features of consolidation plans. Examples include Lockheed Martin, which will cut employment by 12 000 over five years,[24] Northrop Grumman, which planned to reduce personnel by about 9000 by the end of 1995—a 20 per cent reduction in the combined workforce of the two companies[25]—and Allied Signal's acquisition of Lycoming from Textron in 1994, which will result in the loss of 1200 jobs.[26]

The reduction in military production has not been offset by a corresponding level of investment in civilian production. Most actors involved in restructuring the US arms industry agree that even if market-oriented decisions increase efficiency, the government should play a role to increase civilian production.[27]

---

[19] 'General Dynamic to buy shipyard for $300 million', *Washington Post*, 18 Aug. 1995, p. A1-2. The purchase price for Bath was very low, corresponding to one-third of Bath's annual revenues.

[20] 'Environment woes end Gencorp quest to sell Aerojet unit', *Defense News*, 19–25 June 1995, p. 40.

[21] Aerospace Industries Association (AIA), '1995 year-end review and forecast', Press release, 13 Dec. 1995; and 'US aerospace sales, employment down', *Interavia Air Letter*, 15 Dec. 1995, p. 7.

[22] 'Defence work props up profits for top US firms', *Jane's Defence Weekly*, 4 Nov. 1995, p. 66.

[23] Aerospace Industries Association (note 21), table 9.

[24] 'Defense giants to merge today amid heartache', *Washington Post*, 15 Mar. 1995, pp. C1, C4.

[25] This includes 2400 job losses already decided on due to reduced procurement of the B-2 bomber. 'Northrop Grumman calls layoffs "painful but necessary"', *Defense News*, 26 Sep.–2 Oct. 1994, p. 6.

[26] *Aviation Week & Space Technology*, 9 Oct. 1995, p. 21.

[27] Kapstein, E. B. (ed.), *Downsizing Defense* (Congressional Quarterly: Washington, DC, 1993).

New company strategies

During 1995 a debate started on the costs and benefits from a company per-spective of concentration into large units. The possibility and value of creating broad synergies between different product areas were questioned, an alterna-tive strategy of decentralization towards smaller business units was proposed, and a wave of spin-offs to create more focused units was forecast. According to this view, the extremely large firms that are emerging from the concentra-tion process are unable to respond properly to the market. These therefore have to be split up, possibly after reorganization and contraction.[28]

IV. Western Europe

The adjustment process in Western Europe is characterized by national con-centration and international (European) joint ventures. The reorganization of national arms industries continues, but this process is reaching its limits. In several countries, companies have combined into large units in each sector. In Italy and Sweden, a large segment of arms production has been transferred into one group, Finmeccanica controlling 70 per cent of Italian arms pro-duction and Celsius 50 per cent of Sweden's. National concentration is also strong in the UK, where two major arms-producing companies have exited entirely—Ferranti through bankruptcy, Thorn EMI through divestitures—and Lucas announced in late 1995 that it would try to sell its military operations. In France, national concentration has been slower than in most other European countries because of the special organization of the relations between govern-ment and industry, but this is now changing.

European armaments collaboration

Joint West European armaments projects have a long and uneven history, which has been described in numerous publications.[29] During 1995, the issues of joint procurement and the creation of an open armaments market were dis-cussed in many forums in preparation for the Inter-Governmental Conference (IGC) of the European Union (EU), which in 1996 started to review the Maas-tricht Treaty. Within the Western European Armaments Group (WEAG) of the Western European Union (WEU),[30] studies have been carried out in an ad hoc group, set up in 1993, of the possibility of creating a European Armaments

[28] See, e. g., 'Consolidation trend may give way to focused spin-offs', *Defense News,* 30 Oct.–5 Nov. 1995, p. 24; and '"Mega-merger" strategy rejected by MDC head', *Jane's Defence Weekly,* 4 Nov. 1995, p. 64.

[29] One of the most recent accounts is found in de Vestel, P., Western European Union, Institute for Security Studies, *Defence Markets and Industries in Europe: Time for Decisions?*, Chaillot Paper no. 21 (ISS: Paris, Nov. 1995).

[30] WEAG consists of the 13 former members of the Independent European Programme Group (IEPG), although with different status, depending on their membership in the WEU and the EU. They are the 10 members of the WEU (see the Glossary), Denmark as observer, and Norway and Turkey as associate members.

Agency.[31] Its conclusion was broadly the same as a year before—that 'the conditions for creating an agency that is capable of managing the armaments acquisitions of all WEAG countries have not yet been met. Efforts are focused on the framework and legal structure of the future agency'.[32] At the same meeting it was reported that 'most of the policies had been worked out' for creating an open defence market in Western Europe.[33] There are, however, still major decisions of principle on which consensus is lacking, such as the future relations between the WEU and the EU.

France and Germany decided in December 1995 to create a bilateral armaments agency open for other European countries to join. They have expressed hopes that this agency will develop into a European Armaments Agency, but so far its scope is limited to management of joint armaments projects.[34]

Industrial considerations are becoming increasingly important in government decision making on major arms procurement contracts. One such decision can in some cases determine the future of an entire segment of national industry, because the systems are becoming so large and costly in relation to national markets in Europe. This has an impact on the pace of international collaboration projects, in which work shares and procurement quantities are causing national disputes. Two projects for which this was especially true in 1995 are the Eurofighter-2000 (EF-2000) and the Future Large Aircraft (FLA).[35] Current activities and debates in Europe are focused on five major projects. These are the projects listed in table 10.5.

Decisions to start production of the EF-2000 were expected in 1995 from Italy, Spain and the UK, and in 1996 from Germany. This required agreement between the participating countries on production numbers, work shares, prices and delivery schedules. However, the decision was postponed until 1996 because of political controversies in Germany about the escalating costs of the programme and disagreements over the allocation of production work between the partners. Government audits in both Germany and the UK discovered that the programme had experienced huge cost escalations.[36] The reduction in Germany's requirements (announced in 1992) from 250 to 140 aircraft gave rise to long negotiations for the reapportionment of work shares. The development phase was structured so that national work shares were proportional to the expected number of aircraft to be procured. The issue under dispute was whether this principle should be used for the production phase as

[31] These studies are summarized in Western European Union, Assembly, WEAG: the Course to be Followed, Report submitted on behalf of the Technological and Aerospace Committee by Mrs. Guirado and Lord Dundee, WEU Assembly document no. 1483, 6 Nov. 1995.
[32] Western European Union (note 31).
[33] 'WEAG members discuss reinforcing cooperation among European armaments industries', Atlantic News, 15 Nov. 1995, pp. 3–4.
[34] 'Deutsch-französische Rüstungszusammenarbeit' [Franco-German armaments cooperation], Wehrtechnik, Jan. 1996, pp. 11–13; and 'Germany, France launch joint weapons agency', Jane's Defence Weekly, 17 Jan. 1996, p. 12.
[35] The Horizon anti-air defence frigate has also been delayed by disputes over national work shares. 'France presses Britain, Italy to begin Horizon development', Defense News, 4–10 Dec. 1995.
[36] 'Eurofighter 2000 testing accelerates', Aviation Week & Space Technology, 12 June 1995, p. 78; and 'Eurofighter crash-lands in audit', The Independent, 11 Aug. 1995, p. 2.

Table 10.5. Major European cooperation projects as of 31 December 1995

Project name	Description (first expected delivery)	Countries	Requirement (no.)	Work share (%)	Companies	Status
Eurofighter (EF-2000)[a]	Fighter aircraft (2000/ 2002)	Germany Italy Spain UK	250/140 165/130 100/87 250/250	33/23 21/21 13/14 33/41	DASA Alenia CASA BAe	Awaiting govt. decisions on production
Future Large Aircraft (FLA)	Transport aircraft (2003)	France Germany Italy Spain UK (Belgium) (Portugal) (Turkey)	60 75 44 36 45 ? ? ?	.. 25.95	Aérospatiale DASA Alenia CASA BAe (Shorts) (Sabca/ Sonaca) (OGMA) (TUSAS)	Feasibility study completed 1995; decision 1995 to form Airbus Military Co. (AMC), awaiting govt. approval
(Medium Extended Air Defence Systems) MEADS[b]	Theatre missile defence extended air defence (2005)	France Germany Italy USA	20 20 10 50	20 20 10 50	Aérospatiale Thomson DASA Siemens Alenia Hughes/ Raytheon Lockheed M.	Status of intent Feb. 1995; MoU for project definition due Jan. 1996; industrial teams formed Nov. 1995
Horizon Common New Generation Frigate (CNGF)	Frigate (air defence) (2002)	France Italy UK	4 4 12		DCN (Lorient) Orizzonte (Fincantieri) GEC-Marconi (Yarrow)	MoU for joint devel. July 1994; joint venture Feb. 1995
Trilateral Frigate Cooperation (TFC)[c]	Frigate (air defence) (2001 and 2004)	Germany Nether- lands	3 2	None	Blohm& Voss Royal Schelde	Project definition complete Aug. 1995; contracts expected mid-1996

[a] Requirements and work shares have been revised. Data shown here are those for original plan/assumed number as of end-1995.

[b] For MEADS, data in the column for requirement are instead for programme cost shares.

[c] For TFC there are no work shares, since it is only a loose structure for design collaboration. Spain withdrew from the TFC programme in 1995.

Source: SIPRI arms production files.

well. In early 1996 a preliminary agreement was reached between Germany and the UK to increase German procurement by 40 aircraft to 180, raise its work share to 30 per cent and reduce British procurement by 20 aircraft to

230.[37] However, the approval of the German Parliament, due in 1996, is uncertain.

The FLA project was thrown into disarray in December 1994, when the British Government decided to purchase US C-130J Hercules transport aircraft instead of waiting for the FLA. However, after intensive lobbying from industry, primarily the main participating British company, British Aerospace (BAe), the British Government decided to make this an interim solution and to take part in the FLA project for its long-term requirements, although with a reduced order for FLA aircraft.[38] In October 1995, two of the other collaborators made similar compromises, which are likely to postpone the development of the FLA: Italy decided to buy 19 Hercules aircraft; France decided that it was unable to fund FLA development in the near term and would instead upgrade its Transall transport aircraft.[39] The deep cuts in the French defence budget announced in early 1996 add to the uncertainty about the future of the FLA.

Joint ventures

Development towards large, pan-European arms industry groupings, which has been expected for several years, continues although at a very slow pace. The formation of international joint ventures (see table 10.6) is also a slow process. Several large deals have been under negotiation for two or three years without result. Still, it is clear that this process will continue. In several arms industry sectors all the major European companies are involved in talks on how to combine operations. This is true for the aerospace sector (aircraft, missiles and satellites), for segments of military electronics, and for the ordnance and munitions sector. Less negotiating activity is reported in other sectors, such as military vehicles and shipbuilding. In dual-use sectors, such as aero-engines and components, it is difficult to distinguish defence-related joint ventures from those for civilian production activities.

In military aerospace two broad company agreements were made in 1995, both of which may be expanded to include more partners. Aérospatiale and DASA decided in June to form two joint ventures, to be operational from January 1996—Euromissile Systems (EMSYS) and European Satellite Industries (ESI).[40] The second agreement, although less significant in the short term, could be the first step towards a pan-European cooperation structure for the next generation of fighter aircraft. In December 1995 BAe and Dassault Aviation announced their intention to create a joint venture for research and development (R&D) on technologies for the next-generation fighter aircraft after

[37] 'Bonn behält 30 Prozent an "Eurofighter"-Produktion' [Bonn keeps 30% of Eurofighter production], *Süddeutsche Zeitung*, 20–21 Jan. 1996, p. 1.
[38] The British Government announced in Dec. 1994 that the UK's previous limitation to industrial partnership and government observer status would be upgraded to government participation in 1995. *Jane's All the World's Aircraft, 1995–1996* (Jane's Information Group: Coulsdon, 1995), p. 187.
[39] 'Germans must delay development of FLA', *Defense News*, 23–29 Oct. 1995, p. 6.
[40] 'European companies strengthen ties', *Aviation Week & Space Technology*, 5 June 1995, p. 28.

Table 10.6. International joint ventures in the West European arms industry, 1994–95

Companies	Countries	Joint venture	Purpose
TDA (Thomson/ DASA)	France Germany	RTG-Euromunitions	Joint development of smart munitions
Diehl	Germany		
Thomson-CSF	France Germany	TDA/TDW	Merger of armaments and DASA munitions operations
Thomson-CSF DASA	France Germany	Bayern-Chemie/Protac	Merger of missile propulsion operations
Aérospatiale DASA	France Germany	Euromissile Systems (EMSYS)	Merger of missile operations
Aérospatiale DASA	France Germany	European Satellite Industries (ESI)	Merger of satellite operations, incl. military work
Hispano-Suiza (Snecma) ZF Luftfahrt- technik (ZF)	France Germany	Aerospace Power Transmissions	Project management of transmission for FLA
Messier-Bugatti (Snecma) Dowty (TI Group)	France Germany	Messier-Dowty	Merger of landing gear operations; work for FLA
Thomson-CSF GEC-Marconi	France Germany	Ferranti-Thomson Sonar Systems (FTSS)	GEC-Marconi acquired former Ferranti stake
Redifon (Thomson-CSF) GEC-Marconi	France UK		Cooperation on communication system for the CNGF frigate
DCN Orizzonte GEC-Marconi	France Italy UK	Horizon International Joint Venture Co.	Management of Horizon frigate programme
Thomson-CSF Teneo	France Spain	Indra Sistemas	Indra transformed from Teneo subsidiary to joint venture
Thomson-CSF DASA GEC-Marconi	France Germany UK		Joint development of fire controls for next-generation fighter

Source: SIPRI arms industry files.

the EF-2000 and Rafale around the year 2025 to be able to compete against the large US aerospace corporations.[41]

A deal which was not completed in 1995 was that involving the guided missiles activities of BAe and Matra, but the companies are determined to pur-

---

[41] 'BAe agrees Dassault joint venture', *The Guardian*, 14 Dec. 1995, p. 12; and 'Dassault, BAe in future fighter pact', *Interavia Air Letter*, 15 Dec. 1995, p. 1. The company is to be based in France, led by a British director, initially on a low-level activity of some 25 engineers, but planned to increase successively to 500 employees when all design activities from the parent companies have been transferred.

sue their merger, which would result in the creation of Europe's largest producer of tactical missiles.[42]

Two European teams were formed in November to compete for contracts to develop the NATO Medium Extended Air Defence Systems (MEADS), together with US partner firms, one led by DASA (FRG) and one by Alenia (Italy), both including also Aérospatiale and Thomson (France) and Siemens (FRG). Both teams will also have a US partner company—Lockheed Martin and a Hughes/Raytheon joint venture, respectively.[43] Following the conclusion of the feasibility study for the FLA in 1995, the five participating companies in this project have formally agreed to establish a joint ad hoc subsidiary within Airbus Industrie, to be called Airbus Military Company (AMC).[44]

France

The system of arms production in France in 1995 began a dramatic restructuring process, which is likely to mature for crucial decisions in 1996. This process involves sharp cuts in domestic arms procurement, a new role for the powerful arms procurement agency, and the privatization and mergers of the major arms-producing companies. The new Defence Minister, Charles Millon, decided in June 1995 to form a strategic committee with the task of considering a new military programme plan with particular attention to its implications for the arms industry and with the clear aim of adjusting costs to an affordable level.[45]

Although segments of the industry have undergone the same general developments as those in other West European countries during the 1990s—contraction, diversification, privatization and internationalization—this adjustment process has been inhibited in France by the structure of its system of arms production. The close relationship between the state and the arms industry has resulted in very specific conditions, which have been beneficial to both parties. However, at the same time it has come to impose a considerable burden on French industrial development and innovation.[46] As described in a recent study,[47] it has evolved through the institutionalization of relatively stable balancing of varying interests, covering dimensions such as strategic policy, defence doctrine, and social, industrial and economic considerations.

---

[42] 'UK refuses to aid missile marriage', *The Guardian*, 13 June 1995, p. 12; and 'Slow pace for UK–French joint venture firm', *Jane's Defence Weekly*, 22 July 1995, p. 26.

[43] 'Dasa and Alenia to lead air defence teams', *Jane's Defence Weekly*, 4 Nov. 1995; and 'Ballistic missile defence cooperation in NATO', *Military Technology*, vol. 19, no. 10 (Oct. 1995), pp. 36–39.

[44] 'FLA company announced—just', *Military Technology*, vol. 19, no. 7 (July 1995), p. 68.

[45] The tasks and composition of this committee are described in 'Restructuration, reconversion, recapitalisation' [Restructuring, conversion, recapitalizing], *Tribune Desfossés*, 3 Oct. 1995, pp. 36–37. During Feb. and Mar. 1996, too late for inclusion in this text, several announcements were made which anticipated the conclusions of the review: the merger of the aerospace companies Aérospatiale and Dassault Aviation, and of the missile and electronics producers Matra and Thomson-CSF, and the establishment of a smaller and professional army.

[46] Serfati, C., *Production d'armes: Croissance et innovation* [Arms production: growth and innovation] (Economica: Paris, 1995).

[47] Hébert, J.-P., *Production d'armement: Mutation du système français* [Arms production: changes in the French system] (Documentation française: Paris, 1995).

This has simultaneously satisfied the strategic needs of the state and guaranteed reasonable profit margins to companies. It has also, according to this study, led to a situation of 'contained conversion': the state has striven to delay decisions for as long as possible. Still, there have been de facto cuts in arms industry employment, not through political decisions to reduce the size of the industry,[48] but as a consequence of reduced military output due to insufficient demand and as a result of company decisions to rationalize production.

The challenges to the arms production system are both military and economic. The planned restructuring of the armed forces will lead to radically altered requirements for military equipment. At the same time, the current arms production system is becoming economically unsustainable. This can be observed in the serious losses of several of the main arms-producing companies, leading to dependence on government support, and in the development of unacceptable prices for French weapon systems. The losses accumulated by leading companies are enormous (see appendix 10A). Four of these, all state-controlled, together require government financial support totalling 35 billion francs ($7 billion) during 1996 in order to recover these losses.[49] In a situation when it is a priority for economic policy to reduce the rapidly increasing public debt to fulfil the EU 'convergence' criteria, the state has shown much less willingness than usual to provide unconditional massive financial support.

The restructuring of the system is likely to include a downgrading of the role of the state regulatory authority, la Délégation Générale pour l'Armement (DGA), to the same kind of status as government procurement agencies in other European countries, and as the other side of the coin greater autonomy for the arms-producing companies.

V. Russia[50]

In few other major arms-producing countries has military production dropped as sharply during the 1990s as in the Russian Federation.[51] The decline has been chaotic and to a great extent beyond government control. The goal of the restructuring of the Russian defence complex is a difficult one: 'to achieve a substantial reduction in military production at minimum social cost, and in such a way that an adequate military capability can be maintained, while harnessing, when possible, the military sector's quality resources to the country's

[48] Hébert, J-P. and de Penanros, R., 'French defence industry conversion', *Defence and Peace Economics*, vol. 6 (1995), pp. 212–13.

[49] 'State firms drowning in red ink', *Jane's Defence Weekly*, 21 Oct. 1995, p. 29. This is true for Aérospatiale, Eurocopter, GIAT Industries and SNECMA.

[50] Professor Julian Cooper, Centre for Russian and East European Studies, University of Birmingham, is gratefully acknowledged for his comments on a draft of this section.

[51] The only clear exception is Ukraine, where arms production has dropped to 10% of its 1991 level. Markus, U., 'An ailing military–industrial complex', *Transition*, 23 Feb. 1996, p. 52, citing Radio Rossii, 26 Oct. 1995.

economic revival'.[52] During 1995 the government continued its efforts to come to grips with the situation through a more focused defence industrial policy. Some diversification into civilian production has taken place but the transfer of resources from the military to the civilian sector has been less than expected. This section describes the trends in the output of the Russian arms industry and developments in defence industrial policy during 1995.

Statistics on Russian economic and industrial developments are difficult to interpret and use. In addition to the fact that there are different official series, provided by different public organizations and using different definitions and coverage, there are various other reasons for these weaknesses. One of the more important is the pricing system and the changes in this system, with stepwise liberalization of prices in different segments of the economy. A second reason has to do with the inflationary economy and lack of discipline and clarity in the decision-making and implementation process. The discrepancy between parliamentary allocations and actual disbursements, which is particularly large for the military sector, is a third complicating factor.[53] In addition, production data for Russian enterprises are not a satisfactory indicator of their level of activity because there is still no strong correlation between production and sales: production has been maintained at higher levels than sales through other forms of financing than sales revenues, for example, salary subsidies.[54]

Trends in production

Because the Russian defence complex constituted the core of Russian industry for many years, in fact the most technologically advanced part of it, developments there are intimately linked to the general industrial and economic development of the country. The economic reforms and all the problems inherent in the transition between economic and political systems have seriously impacted on arms production. In addition, military production is directly affected by deep cuts in arms procurement and arms exports.

Military production

According to official Russian statistics, there has been a profound reduction in military production in Russia. By 1995 military production had declined to one-sixth of its level in 1991 (see table 10.7). During 1995 the sharpest reductions in output were in armaments, military communications and radio equipment, and military electronics, while shipbuilding was the only sector with

---

[52] Cooper, J., 'Conversion is dead, long live conversion!', *Journal of Peace Research,* vol. 32, no. 2 (1995), pp. 129–32.
[53] George, P. *et al.*, 'World military expenditure', *SIPRI Yearbook 1995* (note 5), pp. 399–408.
[54] Després, L., 'Financing the conversion of the military–industrial complex in Russia: problems of data', *Communist Economies and Economic Transformation,* vol. 7, no. 3 (Sep. 1995); Shlykov, V., 'Economic readjustment within the Russian defense-industrial complex', *Security Dialogue,* vol. 26, no. 1 (1995), pp. 19–34; and Cooper, J. 'Demilitarizing the Russian defence economy: a commentary', *Security Dialogue,* vol. 26, no. 1 (1995), pp. 35–39.

Table 10.7. Production in the Russian defence complex, rate of change 1991–95
Base: 1991 = 100.

	1991	1992	1993	1994	1995
Military production	100	50	33	20	17
Civilian production	100	100	86	53	40
Total defence complex	100	80	65	39	31
Total industry	100	82	70	56	54

Source: On the defence complex: 'VPK v 1995 godu' [The defence–industrial complex in 1995], *Krasnaya Zvezda,* 17 Feb. 1996 (in Russian), citing data from the State Committee for the Defence Branches of Industry (GKOP), which do not include nuclear weapons and some military-related production of enterprises outside GKOP; on total industry: *Ekonomika i Zhizn*, no. 5 (1995), p. 2; and *Rossiyskaya Gazeta,* 17 Jan. 1996, citing the official Goskomstat data for all industrial production.

rising military production.[55] An increasing number of enterprises are facing serious resource problems: by April 1995, 226 enterprises, research institutes and design bureaux in the defence sector were listed as insolvent.[56]

Although there is no satisfactory measure of the decline in arms procurement,[57] it is clear that it has been dramatic and that it now seems to be decelerating. The drop in expenditure is the result of cuts in the budget adopted by parliament and of the fact that approved allocations are not disbursed in full. During 1995 cuts were smaller than in any year since the 1992 shock: the value of state orders during the first half of the year was only 15 per cent lower than the first half of 1994.[58] The rate of disbursement may not have increased, however: by mid-1995 only 39 per cent of the arms procurement budget for 1995 had been disbursed, while disbursements for the whole of 1994 were about two-thirds of the budget adopted.[59]

The debt accumulated over the years by the armed services because of their inability to pay their suppliers is enormous—18 trillion roubles by the end of 1995, a sum almost twice the nominal arms procurement budget for 1995. The arms industry probably accounts for the greater part of this debt,[60] although

[55] 'Daily: recession deepest in military sectors', *Krasnaya Zvezda,* 12 Aug. 1995, p. 3, in Foreign Broadcast Information Service, *Daily Report—Central Eurasia (FBIS–SOV)* (hereafter FBIS–SOV), FBIS-SOV-95-158, 16 Aug. 1995, p. 39, for mid-1995 results; and 'Defense industry committee optimistic about 1995', *Kommersant Daily,* 26 Dec. 1995, p. 2, in FBIS-SOV-95-248, for full year results.

[56] 'Decline in military production continues', *Krasnaya Zvezda,* 29 Apr. 1995, p. 3. in FBIS-SOV-95-084, 2 May 1995, p. 23.

[57] See also chapter 8, section III in this volume.

[58] Shoumikhin, A., 'View from Russia: the weapon stockpiles', *Comparative Strategy,* vol. 14 (1995), p. 212.

[59] According to Deputy Defence Minister Andrey Kokoshin, of the 10 trillion roubles appropriated in the 1995 national budget for purchases of new hardware, only 39% had reached the Defence Ministry by mid-1995. Interfax, 29 Aug. 1995, 'Commission wants to overhaul defense industry', in FBIS-SOV-95-168, 30 Aug. 1995, p. 31.

[60] The state debt to the defence industry amounted to 9 trillion roubles by Jan. 1996. 'Defense industry owed R9000 bln', *New Europe,* 25 Feb.–2 Mar. 1996, p. 8.

not all of the debt is for military hardware—debts for fuel and municipal services accounted for 2.8 trillion roubles, for instance.[61]

Civilian production

The failure of diversification within the defence complex[62] is seen in the trend in civilian production, which declined by 60 per cent between 1991 and 1995 (see table 10.7). The increase in the civilian share of defence complex production (from 40 per cent in the early 1980s to 70 per cent in 1995) is thus an effect more of falling military production than of conversion or diversification. Output in the defence complex has followed the same general trend as overall industrial production: it has continued to fall but more slowly than in recent years. The rate of decline in overall industrial production stabilized in 1995 at 3 per cent compared to 20 per cent in 1994. The rate of decline in the defence complex fell to roughly 20 per cent in 1995 as compared with 40 per cent in 1994.

Obstacles to civilian diversification include lack of capital investment for alternative production, insufficient demand for civilian products, weak economic signals in favour of diversification and lack of incentives resulting from continued state subsidies to the arms industry. In addition, there are more sophisticated challenges in the long term, if and when the more immediate barriers can be removed. According to one view, one of the more important is the need to change not only the formal institutions and the economic system but also institutionalized practices and routines—to disrupt the 'embedded nature of military technology and production'.[63]

The conversion budget

The Russian defence conversion programme is funded by a combination of federal budget grants, state conversion loans and extra-budgetary sources. It has an even worse record of implementation than the arms procurement budget. The 1995 conversion budget had by November 1995 been funded to only 10–15 per cent.[64] Government assurances in November 1995 that defence enterprises would receive the bulk of the planned amounts for conversion projects by the end of 1995 therefore seemed unrealistic. In addition, a large part, perhaps as much as 80 per cent of the sums disbursed, is devoted not to

---

[61] 'Voennye raskhody pridetsya peresmatrivat' [Military expenditure must be reviewed], *Krasnaya Zvezda*, 17 Jan. 1996, p. 1.

[62] For recent analysis of this failure, see BICC, *Conversion of the Defense Industry in Russia and Eastern Europe*, Report no. 3 (BICC: Bonn, Apr. 1995); and Bernstein, D. (ed.), Center for International Security and Arms Control, Stanford University, *Defense Industry Restructuring in Russia: Case Studies and Analysis* (CISAC: Stanford, Calif., Dec. 1994).

[63] Cronberg, T., *The Entrenchment of Military Technologies: Patriotism, Professional Pride and Everyday Life in Russian Military Conversion*, in BICC (note 62), pp. 65–75.

[64] Interview with Russian Prime Minister Viktor Chernomyrdin, *Rabochaya Tribuna*, 28 Nov. 1995, p. 1, in FBIS-SOV-95-230, 30 Nov. 1995, p. 4.

conversion but to salaries and to the maintenance of social facilities, nursery schools and so on at the enterprises.[65]

Two decisions to speed up the conversion process were taken in late 1995 and early 1996—a government decree to create a state conversion fund and the new federal conversion programme for the period 1995–97 as ratified by government decree.[66] The main task of the new state conversion fund is to promote development and production of civilian products and to ensure uninterrupted funding for conversion projects through the targeted use of federal funds and the attraction of additional extra-budgetary funds. Conversion projects for funding will be selected on a competitive basis and with regard to market considerations.

The conversion programme for 1995–97 sets the target of creating new production capacity for an annual output of civilian goods of 41 trillion roubles, thereby providing 400 000 jobs for employees released from military production and replacing imports of around $1.4 billion.[67] The allocations for the conversion programme amount to the impressive sum of 18.6 trillion roubles, on average 6 trillion roubles per year—almost as much as the entire arms procurement budget. The sources of finance for the programme are the federal budget (7.3 trillion roubles), conversion loans (6.3 trillion roubles) and non-budget sources (5 trillion roubles).[68]

It is, however, unlikely that sufficient investment funding for conversion can be accumulated from the state or from capital generated in industry as a result of domestic arms procurement. This leaves only three sources of funding: profits from civilian production and arms exports, foreign direct investment, and mobilization of Russian money partly deposited in dollars in Russian banks and abroad.[69] The strategy of export-oriented conversion has failed.[70] The ability of Russia to attract foreign direct investment has so far been low.[71] The realistic options therefore appear to be (a) the long-term effects of the transformation of industry into market-driven operation, and (b) attracting investment capital from Russian banks and financial institutions. Both these tracks were pursued during 1995.

---

[65] Private communication with Julian Cooper (note 50); and Renner, M., *Budgeting for Disarmament: The Costs of War and Peace*, World Watch Paper no. 122 (World Watch Institute: Washington, DC, Nov. 1994), p. 40.

[66] 'Russia: defense industry conversion program ratified', *Rossiyskie Vesti*, 24 Jan. 1996, p. 2, in FBIS-SOV-96-017, p. 25.

[67] Decree no. 1239, 16 Dec. 1995. 'Russia: decree on state conversion fund role, leadership', *Rossiyskaya Gazeta*, 18 Jan. 1996, p. 4, in FBIS-SOV-96-014, 22 Jan. 1996, pp. 49–50; see also 'Commission introduces defense conversion program', ITAR-TASS, 19 Sep. 1995, in FBIS-SOV-95-182, 20 Sep. 1995, p. 38.

[68] 'Commission introduces defense conversion program' (note 67).

[69] Després (note 54).

[70] See also chapter 11 in this volume; and Anthony, I. *et al.*, 'The trade in major conventional weapons', *SIPRI Yearbook 1995* (note 5), pp. 491–509.

[71] See, e.g., Sigel, T., 'Bleak prospects for foreign investment', *Transition*, vol. 1, no. 7 (12 May 1995), pp. 52–64.

International cooperation

Attempts are being made to enter international cooperation arrangements, in particular for the purpose of obtaining access to foreign markets, but there are many barriers—competition for previous Soviet armaments markets, differences in certification standards and export control rules, and government protection of Russian military technology.

There are efforts to reconstruct military–technical cooperation within the Commonwealth of Independent States (CIS) group of countries. An important example is the decision in October 1995 to form a new Russian–Ukrainian association, International Aviation Projects, the main industrial partners of which are two aerospace enterprises, Tupolev (Russia) and Antonov (Ukraine). The prospects for restoring cooperation with the Central and East European countries are much more bleak.[72] Most of these countries are oriented towards future membership of NATO and wish to switch to NATO standards and weapon systems.

Cooperation with West European and US companies has had mixed results. Some major cooperation projects in military aerospace and space have continued for several years. Investments in these projects are, however, not expected to have any immediate returns.[73] In 1995 there were reports of an agreement between Yakovlev (Russia) and Lockheed Martin (USA) to cooperate on advanced V/STOL (vertical/short take-off and landing) technology developed by Yakovlev. According to Lockheed, access to Russian technology would result in tremendous cost savings.[74] However, the transfer of technology from Russia to the USA was not approved by the Russian Defence Ministry.[75]

Defence industrial policy

After two failed periods of large-scale conversion of production facilities and labour, new policies are being sought for the restructuring of the Russian arms industry. Two central lines of development are the creation of new forms of industrial structures with the main purpose of integrating production and establishing links between production and sources of investment, and privatization in order to introduce the flexibility required for market-led adjustments. During 1995 these two lines of policy were at the centre of the Russian defence industrial policy debate.

In the course of several reviews during 1995 of progress in restructirong the Russian Defence complex it was concluded that there were serious problems. On the one hand, there were concerns that the national arms production capability would be destroyed. On the other hand there were concerns that 'conver-

---

[72] For a survey of Central and East European arms industries, see a forthcoming SIPRI Research Report by Judit Kiss.

[73] 'Western firms face tough hurdles in CIS', *Aviation Week & Space Technology*, 14 Aug. 1995, pp. 38–39.

[74] 'JAST competitor gets Russian data OK', *Defense News*, 28 Aug.–3 Sep. 1995, p. 10.

[75] 'Defense denies R&D design sale reports to Lockheed', *New Europe*, 15–21 Oct. 1995, p. 13.

sion' or diversification into civilian production was insufficient to replace the loss of technological development and employment in military production.

New industrial structures

The rationale for creating new forms of industrial groups is to replace the industrial structure inherited from the Soviet central planning system. The purpose of these financial–industrial groups (FIGs) is to re-establish links between the various stages in the production process and to combine production with resources for capital investment.[76] Two basic types of FIG are being formed: (a) those which are formed from above by ministerial decision and are usually focused around large industrial enterprises and science and production associations; and (b) those which are created voluntarily and are often centred around banks or other major financial institutions. In addition to the general criticism of the government's failure to address the impact of FIGs on competition, both models have been criticized for shortcomings. FIGs of the first type, lacking significant capital assets, have difficulties in dealing with problems of investment, marketing and technological modernization and therefore easily become an instrument of collective lobbying for state credit. The second type of FIGs, which are often oriented towards short-term speculation in stocks, are in principle unable to manage long-term production programmes effectively.

The MiG-MAPO Group, created by the Mikoyan design bureau (MiG) and the Moscow Aviation Production Organization (MAPO), the main producer of MiG fighter aircraft, has been described as different from both models and therefore more promising. MAPO is consolidating the core of a competitive sector in the Russian economy, which is capable of becoming a centre of growth and modernization for Russian high technology. Since it has broken into the export market it has substantially increased its own investment potential and gained access to the resources of the international capital markets. MAPO's aim is to implement technologically complex and capital-intensive projects for the gradual modification and modernization of its aircraft and for product diversification. This includes in particular creating a new generation of fighters by the end of the century, producing the new MiG-AT trainer, and producing and exporting new models of civil aircraft. These tasks can be carried out only if a large scientific production group with a powerful financial infrastructure is set up.[77]

---

[76] The main pieces of legislation for financial–industrial groups are Presidential Decree no. 2096 'On the formation of financial–industrial groups in the Russian Federation', adopted on 5 Dec. 1993; and the Law on Financial–Industrial Groups, adopted on 30 Nov. 1995. OECD, *The Russian Federation 1995*, OECD Economic Surveys (OECD: Paris, 1995); and *Rossiyskaya Gazeta*, 6 Dec. 1995, p. 3.

[77] 'MiG-MAPO Group seen as new departure', *Krasnaya Zvezda*, 20 May 1995, p. 4, in FBIS-SOV-95-103, 30 May 1995, p. 57.

Privatization

The privatization programme, launched at the end of 1992 and administered by the State Committee for the Management of State Property (GKI, Goskomimushchestvo), classified enterprises by extent of privatization: (*a*) those subject to mandatory privatization; (*b*) those exempted from privatization; and (*c*) those whose privatization is at the discretion of the government or the GKI. In these latter enterprises the government retains a considerable shareholding or keeps a 'golden share' which gives it a veto right over changes in the capital or strategy of the enterprise for a period of two or three years.[78] Of the more than 1800 enterprises supervised by the State Committee for the Defence Branches of Industry (GKOP), 634 were granted free privatization, 430 were exempted from privatization in the period 1993–95, while 677 were to be privatized with a state controlling share and 15 as special projects. For the remaining enterprises in the defence complex, the GKI was still to work out a privatization plan with 'golden shares'.[79]

By mid-1995, wholly stateowned enterprises accounted for only 32 per cent of the volume of production of the defence complex (45 per cent of military production and 25 per cent of civilian output).[80] A plan to accelerate the privatization process in order to increase revenue for the federal budget was rejected in July 1995. Instead, a resolution was passed proposing an extension of the period of assigning 'golden shares' to state enterprises.[81]

Decisions for continued restructuring

In July 1995 there was a long debate in the State Duma, the lower house of the Russian Parliament, 'on the critical situation at military–industrial complex enterprises'.[82] The privatization programme was strongly criticized for not having produced the desired effects on production nor the expected revenues for the state. An analysis by the Duma Committee on Ownership, Privatization and Economic Activity argued that privatization had failed to curb the decline in production, to solve the problem of non-payment or to boost investment activity, while the revenues from it were negligible, and that weak state oversight of the privatization process created additional problems. In several cases,

[78] The programme permits 2 modes of privatization according to the size of the enterprises: large enterprises were to be transformed into joint-stock companies ('corporatization'); small enterprises were to be sold in their entirety; and medium-size enterprises could choose between the 2 modes. Most defence enterprises have been corporatized. The general process of privatization is concisely described in OECD (note 76), pp. 67–81.

[79] Pertsevaya, L., 'Privatization, defense conversion work hand in hand', *Moscow News*, no. 22 (9–15 June 1995); and 'Duma leaders deplore "too-early privatization"', FBIS-SOV-95-141-S, 24 July 1995, pp. 27–29.

[80] 'Duma leaders deplore "too-early privatization"' (note 79). The other 68% were joint-stock companies with and without state participation.

[81] 'Government to pay debts to defense industry', *Segodnya*, 8 July 1995, p. 2, in FBIS-SOV-95-131, 10 July 1995, p. 29; and 'Duma urges assistance for military industries', *Rossiyskaya Gazeta*, 10 Aug. 1995, p. 6, in FBIS-SOV-95-155, 11 Aug. 1995, pp. 26–27.

[82] See note 81.

foreign companies had been able to purchase large stakes, especially in the aviation and electronics sectors.[83]

The resolution passed by the Duma proposed that the government (a) repay the debts to the defence complex for 1994 and the first half of 1995 by 1 August 1995; (b) adopt a monthly schedule of financing arms purchases and R&D work; (c) continue its practice of providing tax relief for defence complex enterprises; (d) elaborate a system for social protection for arms industry workers; (e) accelerate the creation of a state conversion fund; and (f) adopt decisions to ensure that defence complex enterprises' spare capacity is used to produce high-technology civilian products. Last but not least, the Duma expressed the need to give priority to the creation of a legal basis for the activities of defence complex enterprises.[84]

Several of these proposals were adopted towards the end of 1995 and in January 1996, including: (a) a government decree to concentrate major R&D facilities of the arms industry into federal science and technology centres with federal budget support;[85] (b) a law 'On State Defence Orders' regulating the relations between the state (Ministry of Defence) and defence enterprises; and (c) a presidential decree making it possible for defence enterprises to defer payment of tax debts.[86] The law on state defence orders has as its main purpose to provide some government control over arms production and at the same time stabilize economic conditions for arms-producing companies.[87]

These decisions are indicative of the direction of future restructuring of the Russian defence complex under the management of the new Chairman of GKOP from January 1996, Zinoviy Pak. In his first interview in this capacity, he outlined three main goals of Russian defence industrial policy: to define the top priority science and technology areas for the arms industry on the basis of an agreed national armaments development programme; to maintain development programmes for dual-use technologies; and to guarantee continued technological progress in the development of technologies which are critical to national security. He emphasized the importance of forming FIGs in the arms industry and said that he considered foreign investment in the Russian arms industry as one of the most promising means of developing the defence industrial complex, both for its military and for its civilian production.[88]

[83] According to Sergey Burkov, chairman of the committee. 'Government to pay debts to defense industry' (note 81).

[84] 'Government to pay debts to defense industry' (note 81); and 'Duma urges assistance for military industries' (note 81), pp. 26–27.

[85] Adopted 9 Oct. 1995. *Sobranie zakonov Rossiyskoy Federatsii*, no. 42 (1995), pp. 7543–44.

[86] Presidential edict no. 65, 19 Jan. 1996 'On the granting to enterprises and organizations of a deferment of payment of the amounts owed prior to 1 January 1996 in respect of taxes, fines and penalties for violations of tax legislation'; and 'Russia: edict allows deferred payment of back taxes', *Rossiyskaya Gazeta*, 25 Jan. 1996, p. 4, in FBIS-SOV-96-018, 26 Jan. 1996, p. 51.

[87] Adopted by the Duma on 24 Nov. 1995 and signed by the President on 27 Dec. 1995. 'O gosudarstvennom oboronnom zakaze' [The law on state defence], *Krasnaya Zvezda*, 13 Jan. 1996, p. 5; and interview on the significance of the law with Andrey Kokoshin, First Deputy Defence Minister, 'Yeltsin decree boosts defense-related industries', ITAR-TASS, 29 Dec. 1995, in FBIS-SOV-96-001, 2 Jan. 1996, pp. 23–24.

[88] 'Russia defense industry chairman Pak interviewed', *Izvestia*, 9 Feb. 1996, p. 2, in FBIS-SOV-96-030, 13 Feb. 1996, pp. 39–40.

This and the decisions made in December 1994[89] give a somewhat clearer picture of the future development of the Russian arms industry.

VI. China

China's arms industry is facing a critical transition period, characterized by significant down-sizing, commercialization and decentralization of government authority.[90] These changes come in the wake of a major strategic review undertaken in China in the early 1980s which recognized that the long-held Maoist doctrine of 'People's War' was to be replaced by a doctrine enabling the Chinese military to fight 'limited wars under high-tech conditions'.[91]

At the macroeconomic level, while economic reforms of the past 15 years have done much to improve China's overall strength, they have done more to worsen the situation of Chinese defence industries.[92] The sector is in an early stage of contraction, a process that will continue for at least 5–10 years. The Chinese defence industry press and other sources describe difficult times for enterprises in the process of conversion, especially those located in the provincial hinterlands, called the Third Front.[93] These problems include lack of capital and technology, heavy debt, little infrastructural connection to developing markets in the urban and coastal areas, social welfare obligations under the 'work unit' (danwei) system, poor managerial and entrepreneurial skills, and under- and unemployment.[94]

[89] These decisions were to concentrate the arms industry into a smaller number, organized in the form of federal science and technology centres and federally funded enterprises (kazennye), and to release the other enterprises from the defence complex. Sköns and Gonchar (note 5), p. 478.

[90] There are 2 distinct hierarchies of military production in China: (a) ministries, corporations and units under the State Council; and (b) production units operating under the aegis of the People's Liberation Army (PLA). The first might properly be called 'arms industries' and are the focus of this section. The second might be called 'PLA industries'. The military production of the latter tends to be in basic military and medical supplies, not in major conventional weapons.

[91] For more detailed studies of the Chinese defence industry, see Frankenstein, J. and Gill, B., 'Challenges for Chinese defence industries', China Quarterly, no. 143 (June 1996); Frankenstein, J., 'The People's Republic of China: arms production, industrial strategy and problems of history', ed. H. Wulf, SIPRI, Arms Industry Limited (Oxford University Press: Oxford, 1993); and Xie Guang et al. (eds), Dangdai Zhongguo de Guofang Keji Shiye [Modern China's science and technological undertakings of national defence] (Dangdai Zhongguo Chubanshe: Beijing, 1992). On Chinese military technology development, see Arnett, E., 'Military technology: the case of China', SIPRI Yearbook 1995 (note 5), pp. 359–86.

[92] Gill, B., 'The impact of economic reform on Chinese defense industries', eds D. Liu et al., Chinese Military Modernization (Kegan Paul: London, forthcoming 1996); and Shichor, Y., China's Defence Capability: The Impact of Military-to-Civilian Conversion, CAPS Papers no. 8 (Chinese Council of Advanced Policy Studies: Taipei, Apr. 1995).

[93] The Third Front was established in the 1950s and 1960s under Mao Zedong as a strategic manoeuvre to assure continuing defence production in the event of an attack on China's heartland and major cities. Naughton, B., 'The Third Front: defence industrialization in the Chinese interior', China Quarterly, no. 115 (Sep. 1988). For a brief overview of current problems in the Third Front areas, see Gill, B., 'Defensive industry', Far Eastern Economic Review, no. 45 (30 Nov. 1995), p. 62.

[94] Reform of state-owned industries, of which about 30% are defence industries, is expected to cause heavy unemployment. 'Cost of economic reform in China: 18 million jobs', International Herald Tribune, 1–2 July 1995, p. 9.

Arms production and procurement policy

Chinese arms production and procurement policy will probably unfold in two stages over the next 10–15 years. First, and for the near term, China will continue and make minor improvements to its current serial production. In the second stage of this process, looking ahead 7–10 years or more, Chinese defence production and procurement will 'contract the front and give priority to key projects' in order to make the breakthrough towards a more modern military capability. The areas of focus are likely to be more 'high-tech'-oriented and in tune with the current Chinese military doctrine of 'fighting a limited war under modern conditions', including serial production of next-generation fighter and strike aircraft; development of more precise missile strike capabilities, possibly land-attack cruise missiles; production in the area of naval logistics and operations, including possible licensed production of Kilo Class submarines; and production of basic command, control, communications, computer and intelligence (C⁴I) systems, integrating rudimentary satellite and airborne sensors with a limited combined arms operations capability.

In all these areas foreign technology is needed and sought, and has been provided in some cases, particularly from Israel and Russia, to improve the capabilities of these platforms through the integration of more capable subsystems, especially with regard to electronics, guidance, defensive systems, propulsion and weapon systems.

Current trends: contraction, commercialization, decentralization

Contraction

Many of the difficulties faced by the industry derive from its enormous size. Exact assessments of the number and structure of enterprises and numbers of employees involved in defence production are difficult to develop, even for the Chinese authorities. The sector is huge by nearly any measure—in terms of both the number of production units and the number of persons employed. Estimates of the size of the Chinese arms industry range from approximately 1000 production units and 3 million workers to 50 000 production units and 25 million workers.[95] Table 10.8 gives an indication of the size of some units related to defence production.

---

[95] Wei-chin Lee, 'China's defense industry invades the private sector', *SAIS Review*, vol. 15, no. 2 (summer–fall 1995), p. 177. Lee cites *Washington Post*, 17 Mar. 1993, p. A1 for the high estimate. An estimate of 2000 enterprises under the aegis of the State Council is given by Frankenstein and Gill (note 91). An estimate of 5 million arms industry workers is given for 1986 by Huck, B. J., 'Arms industry and conversion in developing countries', ed. Haiyan Qian, *Restructuring the Military Industry: Conversion for the Development of the Civilian Economy* (Publishing House of the Electronic Industry: [Beijing], 1994), p. 86. Basing his figures on Chinese sources, Arnett estimates a defence industry workforce of 3.5 million in the mid-1980s. Arnett, E., 'Military research and development in southern Asia: limited capabilities despite impressive resources', ed. E. Arnett, SIPRI, *Military Technology and Offensive Capacity in Southern Asia* (Oxford University Press: Oxford, forthcoming 1996).

Table 10.8. Major arms-producing enterprises in China, early 1990s

Name	Employees	Defence-related production
Beijing North Vehicle Works	7 000	Heavy military vehicles, howitzers
Chang'an Machinery Plant	12 000	Rifles, heavy machinery, vehicles
Changhe Aircraft Industries Corp.	6 800	Zhi-8 helicopters
Changzhou Lanxiang Machinery Works	5 000	WZ6 turboshaft engines
Chengdu Aircraft Industrial Corp.	20 000	J-7 fighters
Chengdu Engine Co.	20 000	WP6, WP13, WP14 turbojet engines
China Carrier Rocket Institute	27 000	Space launchers
China Jiangnan Space Industries Group	30 000	Satellite and space technologies
China South Aeroengine Co.	20 000	Engines, rocket motors, AAMs
Guangzhou Shipyard	8 000	Luda destroyers, minesweepers
Guiyang Aviation Hydraulic Parts Plant	23 000	Aerospace pumps
Guizhou Aircraft Industrial Corp.	70 000	JJ-7 trainers, AAMs,
Harbin Aircraft Manufacturing Corp.	17 000	SH-6 bombers, Zhi-9A helicopters, Y-12 transport aircraft
Hubei Jiangshan Machinery Plant	7 000	Gearboxes, vehicle parts
Hudong Shipyard	12 000	Jiangwei frigates, fast-attack craft
Inner Mongolia No. 1 Machinery Plant	25 500	Armoured vehicles
Inner Mongolia No. 2 Machinery Plant	23 000	Armoured vehicles
Jiangnan Machinery Plant	11 000	Heavy machinery, vehicles
Jiangnan Shipyard	10 000	Jianghu frigates, Luhu destroyers
Jiangling Machinery Plant	10 000	Vehicle engines, artillery
Jianshe Machine Tools Plant	20 000	Ordnance, rifles
Kunming Ship Equipment Co.	10 000	Naval instruments, electronics
Liaoning Xiangdong Chemical Plant	8 000	Chemicals
Liaoning Qingyang Chemical Corp.	20 000	Chemicals, explosives
Liyang Machinery Corp.	10 000	WP7B turbojet engines
Nanchang Aircraft Manufacturing Co.	20 000	K-8 trainers, Q-5 attack aircraft
Northwest Machinery Plant	13 000	Gas and pressure cylinders
Qing'an Space Equipment Corp.	10 000	Airborne components
Shaanxi Aircraft Co.	10 000	Y-8 transport aircraft
Shandong Machinery Plant	6 000	Weapon testing
Shenyang Aircraft Manufacturing Corp.	30 000	J-8 fighters
Shenyang Liming Engine Corp.	30 000	WP6, WP7 turbojet engines
Wangjiang Machinery Plant	12 000	Mechanical products, gears
Wuchang Shipyard	8 000	Patrol vessels, minesweepers
Xi'an Aircraft Co.	19 730	Y-7 transport aircraft
Xi'an Hui'an Chemical Plant	20 000	Chemicals, solvents, paints
Xi'an Qinchuan Machinery Plant	10 000	Chemicals and ordnance

Note: The table includes those enterprises of 5000 employees or more which are cited in the sources below. Not all workers are directly involved in military production.

Sources: Jin Zhude *et al.* (eds), *Guide to International Corporation* [sic] *and Investment with Enterprises of China's Defense Industry* (China Association for the Peaceful Use of Military Industrial Technology: Beijing, 1993); Tai Ming Cheung, 'Serve the people' and 'Elusive ploughshares', *Far Eastern Economic Review*, 14 Oct. 1993, pp. 64–65, 70; *Jane's All the World's Aircraft, 1995–1996* (Jane's Information Group: Coulsdon, 1995), pp. 48–64, 696–98; and *Jane's Fighting Ships, 1994–1995* (Jane's Information Group: Coulsdon, 1994, pp. 113–40.

Table 10.9. Estimated Chinese production of selected major conventional weapons, 1981–94

Figures for 1981–85 and 1986–90 are five-year averages.

	1981–85	1986–90	1991	1992	1993	1994
Aircraft						
J-7 fighter	48	50	50	50	50	50
J-8 fighter	10	13–16	20–24	20–24	20–24	20–24
H-5 bomber	12–15	0	0	0	0	0
H-6 bomber	5–6	5–6	0	0	0	0
JJ-5 trainer	50	10	0	0	0	0
JJ-6 trainer	50	10	0	0	0	0
JJ-7 trainer	0	0	1	2	2	2
HJ-5 trainer	7	0	0	0	0	0
Q-5 attack	10–12	9–11	8-10	8–10	5	5
Total aircraft	**192–98**	**97–103**	**79–85**	**80–86**	**77–81**	**77–81**
Ships						
Destroyers	<1	<1	1	2	2	1
Frigates	2	2	4	3	2	2
Submarines						
Xia SSBN	0	<1	0	0	0	0
Han attack	<1	<1	0	0	0	0
Ming/Wuhan C patrol	0	<1	1	1	0	1
*Land systems**						
Main battle tanks	490–500	170–210	200	200	150–200	100
Artillery (>100 mm)	200–205	200–250	200–250	200	200	150–200

* Approximately one-half of the land systems shown were exported.

Source: Adapted from Frankenstein, J. and Gill, B., 'Challenges for Chinese defence industries', *China Quarterly,* no. 143 (June 1996).

The contracting trend in Chinese defence production indicated in table 10.9 results from a steep decline in domestic procurement and, to a lesser extent, from a decline in arms exports. The drop in domestic procurement can be traced to two important sources. First, the favourable security situation China has enjoyed since the early 1980s led in large measure to the decision to trim the Chinese armed forces by 25 per cent, which in turn reduced procurement needs. Second, there is evidence that the Chinese armed forces resist procurement of domestically produced systems. The military has begun to demand more sophisticated systems and lobbies hard for the import of foreign weapons and technology (which are often covered by special, 'off-budget' resources). In addition, economic reforms have forced the industries to charge more market-oriented rates and to demand hard currency for those products which incorporate imported sub-systems and technologies, which the services have at times refused to pay for from their own procurement budgets.[96]

[96] For example, the PLA Air Force and naval aviation wing have only a few F-7M fighters because they cannot afford to pay the hard currency demanded by the producers for the Western avionics which

Table 10.10. Volume of Chinese arms exports, 1986–95

SIPRI trend-indicator values[a] expressed in constant 1990 US $m.

1986	1987	1988	1989	1990	1991	1992	1993	1994	1995
1 760	3 214	2 212	1 414	1 222	1 103	1 159	1 284	744	868

[a] See appendix 11C on sources and methods.

Source: SIPRI arms transfer database, 1996.

Table 10.10 shows the decline in the volume of exports for Chinese major conventional weapons—some 60 per cent—since it hit peak levels in 1987. China's past export advantages of low cost and simplicity are being overtaken by the advent of more aggressive and competitive Russian sales which offer good value in comparison to Chinese weapons. Chinese equipment has a poor reputation for quality and sophistication, which places it at a disadvantage as potential clients seek to upgrade their military capabilities, especially in the light of the high-technology warfare exhibited in the 1991 Persian Gulf War.

Commercialization

Now nearly 15 years into the ambitious Chinese defence conversion effort, the programme has a number of success stories, but overall has proved extremely difficult, with most defence enterprises continuing to lose money and facing tough times ahead.[97] Commenting on the looming socio-economic crisis facing the Third Front defence industries in rural Sichuan Province, a Chinese commentator noted that 'most of the factories are on the verge of bankruptcy' and concluded that in their turn to the market 'prospects for success are dubious'.[98] With 55 per cent of China's defence industries in Third Front areas, the conversion effort is both necessary and problematic.[99]

The move into commercial activities diverted resources and expertise from military production. Official statistics show that on average 70 per cent of the outputby value of Chinese defence enterprises under the State Council is for the civilian market. The aim is to raise this figure: some sectors already claim a much higher conversion rate. However, in 1991 *Renmin Ribao* reported that only 40 per cent of the defence industry was engaged in some kind of conversion effort.[100] According to some Western estimates, about 90 per cent of

are in them. Allen, K. W., Krumel, G. and Pollack, J. D., *China's Air Force Enters the 21st Century* (RAND Corporation: Santa Monica, Calif., 1995), p. 224.

[97] The most comprehensive analysis of Chinese defence conversion is provided by Brommelhörster, J. and Frankenstein, J. (eds), *Mixed Motives, Uncertain Outcomes: Defense Industry Conversion in China* (Lynne Reinner: Boulder, Colo., forthcoming 1996). See also Folta, P. H., *From Swords to Plowshares? Defense Industry Reform in the PRC* (Westview Press: Boulder, Colo., 1992).

[98] Pei Jiansheng, 'Market solution eludes remote military–industrial complex', *China Daily Business Weekly*, 6–12 Nov. 1994, p. 7.

[99] This figure was provided in a communication with Jin Zhude, President of the China Association for the Peaceful Use of Military Industrial Technology (CAPUMIT), Nov. 1995.

[100] Foreign Broadcast Information Service, *Daily Report–China (FBIS–CHI)* (hereafter FBIS-CHI), FBIS–CHI, 7 Nov 1991, p. 32, citing *Renmin Ribao*.

Chinese defence production capacity sits idle.[101] Furthermore, it appears that the commercialization effort invests financial and intellectual resources in areas geographically and conceptually outside the traditional centres of arms production with the creation of 'window enterprises' and PLA companies in the prosperous coastal regions of China which are not engaged in military production activities.[102]

On the other hand, the trend towards commercialization may prove advantageous for the industry as a result of 'spin-on' synergies. The Chinese recognize that the future foundation for military technologies will increasingly be commercial technologies. The Vice-Minister of the Commission on Science, Technology, and Industry for National Defence (COSTIND) stated in 1993:

[S]ince national defense high technology itself is frequently a field in which many overlapping technologies are involved, it is becoming increasingly indistinguishable from high technology used in civilian life. The trend toward the interchangeability of military and civilian technology is steadily increasing, and this provides a solid technological basis for the rapid modernization of national defense and for the constant updating of weaponry.[103]

General Liu Huaqing, China's highest-ranking active military officer and Vice-Chairman of the Central Military Commission, said in early 1995 that China 'should pay attention to turning advanced technology for civilian use into technology for military use'.[104] Official Chinese policy appears to view conversion and the commercialization of the industry in an optimistic light, but the problems presented here suggest the difficulties these processes must face.

Decentralization of authority

The trends in China today are towards placing greater decision-making authority in the hands of provincial, municipal and enterprise authorities, to the detriment of authorities in Beijing nominally overseeing the defence enterprises.[105] As the November 1995 White Paper on arms control notes, 'the government departments formerly in charge of military production have already been changed into general corporations [and] will step by step develop into economic entities engaging in research, production, and business'.[106] This

---

[101] 'Making a modern industry', *Jane's Defence Weekly*, 19 Feb. 1994, p. 28.

[102] 'Share-holding system: a new attempt at conversion from military to civilian industry in China', ed. Qian (note 95), p. 96; Tai Ming Cheung, 'Serve the people', *Far Eastern Economic Review*, 14 Oct. 1993, p. 64; and Lu Yishan and Jiu Jichuan, 'Strategic thinking on strengthening international cooperation and promoting conversion from military to civilian industry', ed. Qian (note 95), pp. 236–41.

[103] Xiang Wang, 'Development of modern technology and defense conversion: Interview with Huai Guomo, Vice-Minister of the Commission of Science, Technology and Industry for National Defense', *Conmilit*, no. 196 (May 1993), p. 4.

[104] 'Liu Huaqing urges development of defense technology', translated from *Jiefang Junbao*, 15 Jan. 1995, in FBIS–CHI-95-023, 30 Jan. 1995, p. 30.

[105] This point is based in part on discussions and interviews with Chinese and Western defence and defence industry officials, conducted in China, Nov. 1994, Jan. 1995, Mar. 1995 and Nov. 1995.

[106] People's Republic of China, State Council, *China: Arms Control and Disarmament* (Information Office of the State Council: Beijing, Nov. 1995), pp. 14–15.

gives a freer hand to hundreds of factories, companies and research institutes which are ostensibly subordinate to the ministry-level corporations. The frequency of reorganizations, the trend towards decentralization and the commercialization of defence production enterprises all suggest problems for the near- and medium-term future. Coordinating development and production of defence *matériel* was never easy under the Chinese system,[107] and will only become more difficult under the market conditions currently prevailing in China, which favour the realization of quick profits over long-term planning.

Foreign military technology

Significant near-term improvement in the Chinese defence industrial base will need to rely upon imports of foreign technology and know-how.[108] As China undertakes a much-needed and comprehensive modernization of its armed forces, imports of military technology are particularly needed in the areas of electronics, guidance, defensive systems, propulsion and advanced weapon systems. To date, the principal suppliers of defence-related technology to China have been the Soviet Union/Russia and Israel. In late 1994 and in 1995, new reports surfaced alleging Sino-Israeli cooperation in the development of China's next-generation fighter, rumoured to be based on Lavi technology and dubbed the J-10 in the West.[109] In late 1995 high-ranking Chinese and Russian military officials exchanged a series of visits, and in December the signing of a 'comprehensive agreement on military–technical cooperation' was announced.[110] This agreement probably involves the transfer of a second batch of about 24 Su-27s to China and possibly a technology transfer or licensed production arrangement involving these or other aircraft.[111] Table 10.11 summarizes some of the areas where Russia and China are believed to have defence-related cooperation efforts.

The traditional Chinese practice of reverse engineering or copy production will not apply as easily to newer digital technologies of modern weaponry in which knowledge of the software and how it works becomes far more important than reproduction of the hardware. Yet, given the difficulties which

---

[107] Yan Xuetong, 'China', ed. R. Singh, SIPRI, *Arms Procurement Decision Making* (Oxford University Press: Oxford, forthcoming).

[108] The effect of imports of military technology on the Chinese defence industrial base is discussed in detail in Gill, B. and Kim, T., *China's Arms Acquisitions from Abroad: A Quest for 'Superb and Secret Weapons'*, SIPRI Research Report no. 11 (Oxford University Press: Oxford, 1995).

[109] On the Sino-Israeli development of a new-generation fighter, see Fulghum, D. A., 'New Chinese fighter nears prototyping', *Aviation Week & Space Technology*, 13 Mar. 1995, pp. 26–27; Mann, J., 'Israeli sale of arms technology to China irks US', *International Herald Tribune*, 29 Dec. 1994, p. 1; Barrie, D., 'Chinese tonic', *Flight International*, 9–15 Nov. 1994, p. 16; and 'Israel co-operates with China on secret fighter', *Flight International*, 2–8 Nov. 1994, p. 4.

[110] 'Air force chief ends China visit', ITAR-TASS, 29 Oct. 1995, in FBIS–SOV-95-209, 30 Oct. 1995, p. 18; 'Chinese envoy meets Russian armed forces chiefs', ITAR-TASS World Service, in FBIS–SOV-95-210, 31 Oct. 1995, p. 30; and 'Defence technology agreement signed with China', Interfax, 7 Dec. 1995, in FBIS–SOV-95-236, 8 Dec. 1995, p. 25.

[111] It seems likely that during Boris Yeltsin's planned visit to China in spring 1996 an agreement will be formally concluded, to include the transfer of 24 Su-27s to China and the gradual transfer of technology to allow for the licensed production of Su-27s. 'Russia: Largest aircraft deal to be signed with PRC', *Kommersant Daily*, 7 Feb. 1996, p. 1, in FBIS-SOV-96-028, 9 Feb. 1996, p. 21.

Table 10.11. Defence-related transfers of technology and know-how to China from Russia

Item/technology	Comments
Combat aircraft	Under negotiation for possible co-production of Su-27; training of Chinese Su-27 pilots in Russia
Aircraft engines	Possible technology transfer related to transfer of 100 RD-33 turbofan engines
Submarine and ASW technology	Technology transfer and possible co-production under negotiation as part of Kilo Class submarine deal
Missile technologies	Exchange of experts and scientists to include discussions on guidance systems, testing equipment and cruise missiles

Note. ASW = Anti-submarine warfare.

Sources: Adapted from Gill, B. and Kim, T., *China's Arms Acquisitions from Abroad: A Quest for 'Superb and Secret Weapons'*, SIPRI Research Report no. 11 (Oxford University Press: Oxford, 1995), pp. 65–70, 81–86.

Chinese defence production faces, the acquisition and application of foreign technologies in R&D, production and weapon software and hardware appears to be a promising way forward for the sector. True to its past, however, China is likely to remain cautious to avoid overly-dependent relationships with foreign suppliers, and will continue to seek its long-term goal of an advanced indigenous defence production capability.

VII. Four industrializing countries

Many of the countries outside Europe, North America and the CIS area face the same choice of having to reduce military production in a manner which is acceptable to the economy or trying to export. Restructuring efforts are being made in order to reduce production, but in some cases in order to expand exports or for other reasons, such as inefficiencies in production and military–political goals. Developments there are, however, more difficult to monitor because of the greater secrecy surrounding military production in many of these countries.

Four industrializing countries have companies with annual arms sales high enough to place them among the top 100 arms-producing companies in the world—India, Israel, South Africa and South Korea, countries with great differences in the size and direction of their arms production (table 10.12) and in defence industrial policy. They are also different in terms of openness about their military sector. The governments in India and South Africa are more open about their defence industrial bases. Companies in Israel willingly provide information but not the government. In South Korea, where information on military–industrial activities is a sensitive matter, some new information is becoming available.

Table 10.12. Arms production in four industrializing countries, 1994

Figures are in US $m. Figures in italics are percentages.

	India	Israel[a]	S. Africa	S. Korea
Dominant ownership in arms industry	State	State	State	Private
Arms procurement	2 300[b]	[2 400]	975	5 280[b]
Arms production	1 100	[2 700]	1 065	4 580[b]
Arms production share in GNP	0.4	3.7	0.9	1.4
Arms imports	1 000[c]	>1 400	145	700[b]
Share of procurement from national production				
(a) Locally produced final systems	48	56	..	87
(b) Local content	30	..	60	45–50
Arms exports	41	>1 350	237	27
Share of exports in arms production	3	[>50]	23	0.6[b]
Government military R&D exp.	375	..	65	360
Employment in arms production	185 000	50 000	70 000	60 000
Capacity utilization	68[d]	..	..	60
Population[c] (m.)	898	5	40	44
Area (000 km^2)	3 288	21	1 221	99
GNP[c] (US $m.)	269 500	72 400	118 300	337 800

[a] Data for Israel are estimates in most cases; arms imports from USA only.

[b] 1993 figures.

[c] 1992 figures.

[d] Ordnance Factories only, accounting for roughly half of domestic arms production.

Sources: Data on the military sector: Ministry of Defence, *Annual Report 1994/95* [Government of India: New Delhi, 1995]; Batchelor, P., *The Economics of South Africa's Arms Trade*, Discussion Paper no. 3 (Centre for Conflict Resolution, University of Cape Town: Cape Town, Aug. 1995); Republic of Korea, Ministry of National Defense, *Defense White Paper 1994/95* (Ministry of National Defense: Seoul, 1995); Bonn International Center for Conversion, *Conversions Survey 1996* (Oxford University Press: Oxford, 1996); and the SIPRI arms industry data base. Data on population, area and GNP: *World Development Report 1995*.

India

India's arms industry is basically state-run. It consists mainly of the Ordnance Factories Organization, which includes 39 production entities and 8 'defence public sector undertakings' (DPSUs). The former account for roughly half of India's arms production—military vehicles, artillery, weapon systems, small arms and ammunition—while the latter produce most of the other half—mainly aerospace, electronics equipment and ships. These 47 entities employed about 270 000 people in 1994, of which around 185 000 were in military production.[112] The private sector is small, accounting for no more than 6 or 7 per cent of domestic arms production.[113]

---

[112] These estimates are based on data provided directly by each production unit and with the help of the Ministry of Defence, including separate data for employment in defence production for most units. For the few other units defence employment was estimated on the basis of the defence share in sales.

[113] Roy-Chaudhury, R., 'Defence industries in India', *Asian Strategic Review 1993–94*, p. 268. Private companies are normally small or medium-size companies acting in a sub-contractor role to the

Several public reviews of India's arms industry have come to the conclusion that it is over-dimensioned and inefficient and constitutes a burden on the economy.[114] Capacity utilization in the Ordnance Factories has dropped from 100 to 68 per cent in the six-year period 1988/89–1993/94.[115] The government is trying, although so far with little success, to introduce measures to deal with the problems of excess capacity and inefficiency, including export promotion and diversification into non-military production.

The long-established aim of expanding military exports significantly has not been achieved: military exports were valued at Rs 1250 million in 1993/94, accounting for less than 3 per cent of total arms production.[116] This illustrates the difficulty of entering the international market with low-to-medium military technology.

Diversification into non-military production has been difficult in all seg-ments of the arms industry. The ordnance factories have diversified the least: the share of sales to customers other than the Defence Ministry was 10–20 per cent during the 1990s. Since this 'civilian share' includes sales to paramilitary and police forces, it is not clear if there is any process of civilian diversifica-tion at all.[117] The civilian share is higher for the DPSUs, which were created with a view to closer integration between military and civilian production—up to 88 per cent and increasing for some of them. Shipbuilding companies are trying and have also to some extent been able to diversify into civilian activi-ties, such as maintenance of oil rigs and civilian ship repair.[118] Other com-panies are moving in the opposite direction. For the main electronics enter-prise, Bharat Electronics, military production will become the main business area during the next few years.[119] Private companies, which are often small and integrated as components suppliers to the government arms industry, are finding it difficult to find alternative civilian markets.[120]

Privatization is not a major issue. Hindustan Aeronautics Limited (HAL), the leading aerospace company in India and the largest DPSU, has sought government permission to privatize 20 per cent of the enterprise, but the pur-pose is mainly to raise money for a joint-venture facility with foreign com-

state-owned arms-producing enterprises. They are restricted from final assembly of lethal items, accord-ing to the Industrial Policy Resolution 1956, as amended in 1991. Comment by Singh, A. V., Joint Secretary, Ministry of Defence, Defence Production and Supplies, at a workshop of the SIPRI Project on Arms Procurement Decision Making, New Delhi, 1 July 1995.

[114] See, for example, the annual reports of the Comptroller and Auditor General of India.

[115] As measured in standard man-hours. Capacity utilization in terms of machine-hours dropped from 82% to 74% in the same period. *Report of the Comptroller and Auditor General of India for the year ended 31 March 1994*, no. 8, 1995; and *Union Government, Defence Services (Army and Ordnance Factories)* (New Delhi: Naval Printing Press, 1995), pp. xvii-xviii.

[116] India, Ministry of Defence, *Annual Report 1994/95* [Government of India: New Delhi, 1995], p. 24.

[117] India, Ministry of Defence, *Annual Report 1994/95* (note 116), p. 28.

[118] *Report of the Comptroller and Auditor General* (note 115); and 'India shipmaker wants partners', *Defense News*, 13–19 Feb. 1995, p. 34.

[119] 'Bharat Electronics shows rise in sales', *Defense News*, 24–30 Apr. 1995, p. 25; statement by the chairman of Bharat Electronics, 10 Apr. 1995.

[120] *Report of the Comptroller and Auditor General* (note 115). Exceptions quoted are limited, such as companies like Greaves, which have used their know-how from developing power generator packs for defence systems to supply the civilian market.

panies for helicopter assembly.[121] There is also a government plan to increase private sector involvement in defence projects, but this has not resulted in any significant increase in defence contracts to the private sector.[122]

The local arms industry produces about half of the weapons needed for India's armed forces. India relies to a great extent on foreign technologies, in particular through major programmes of licensed production.[123] The actual rate of self-reliance in defence acquisitions is much lower, officially estimated at 30 per cent.[124] The government target is to increase the local content to 70 per cent of total procurement expenditure by the year 2005, but it is unclear whether there is a realistic strategy to achieve this.[125] The R&D resources required to meet this goal may become an unacceptable burden for the Indian economy, since the priorities in government R&D expenditure already strongly favour defence and space and there is little integration or linkage between military and civilian production.[126]

India has re-established military–industrial cooperation with its traditional partner, the USSR/Russia, in licensed production. HAL has maintained its contacts with suppliers of aerospace parts and components in the former Soviet republics. HAL participates in the joint venture formed with Russian partners in September 1994, Indo-Russian Aviation Ltd, for overhaul, repair, maintenance and updating of aviation equipment of Soviet/Russian origin.[127] HAL is seeking cooperation partners for the Light Combat Aircraft (LCA) project. Several licensed production projects with West European countries are being continued. There is also a new interest in imports from and cooperation with the US arms industry.

Indian enterprises have recently entered several other international cooperation arrangements. Bharat Electronics has started modernizing radar systems with technology transfer from Ericsson (Sweden) and also agreed in 1995 with Thomson-TRT (France) to manufacture Thomson military electronics products.[128] Garden Reach, one of the three shipbuilding DPSUs, has a collaboration agreement with DCN (France).[129]

---

[121] *Defense News*, 13–19 Nov. 1995, p. 50.

[122] 'India's private sector says ministry plan has no teeth', *Defense News*, 21–27 Aug. 1995, p. 25.

[123] These programmes are monitored and reported on in chapter 11 in this volume.

[124] India, Ministry of Defence, *Annual Report 1994/95* (note 116), p. 38.

[125] Arnett, E., 'Military technology: the case of India', *SIPRI Yearbook 1994* (Oxford University Press: Oxford, 1994), pp. 343–65.

[126] Chandrashekar, S., 'Technology priorities for India's development—need for restructuring', *Economic and Political Weekly*, 28 Oct. 1995, pp. 2739–48.

[127] 'India rebuilds aerospace ties with Russia', *Interavia Business & Technology*, Sep. 1994; 'Russia vies to build India's jet trainer', *Defense News*, 14–20 Nov. 1994; and 'About turn for India', *Jane's Defence Weekly*, 17 Dec. 1994.

[128] Memorandum of Understanding signed on 9 Jan. 1995. 'Bharat Electronics Thomson sign pact', *Defense News*, 23–29 Jan. 1995, p. 31.

[129] Agreement signed in June 1994. Garden Reach Shipbuilders and Engineers Ltd, *Annual Report 1994/95*, p. 6; and India, Ministry of Defence, *Annual Report 1994/95* (note 116), p. 34.

Israel

Israel's arms industry is undergoing a rapid reduction. Employment in the state arms production sector has declined from 40 000 in 1991 to 24 000 in 1994 and is planned to be further reduced by mid-1996 to 18 000–19 000, which is considered to be an optimal size.[130] These cuts have created labour unrest and opposition to the contraction of the arms industry.

More than half of arms production in Israel is carried out in three large state-owned companies, Israel Aircraft Industries (IAI), Rafael and TAAS, with combined arms sales of $1900 million in 1994. The next three in size, all private companies, Elbit, El-Op and Koor Industries (through its subsidiary Tadiran), together account for another $700 million in military sales. A third level of producers consists of a number of small, high-technology firms which have entered the arms industry sector comparatively recently.

The state-owned arms industry has incurred heavy losses. The government has therefore imposed stringent recovery programmes with a long-term view to privatization. During the years 1992–94, the combined losses of the three largest state companies amounted to $1600 million.[131] The government has agreed to substantial contributions to the companies' recovery plans, primarily for the retirement of labour. By January 1995 these commitments amounted to $1625 million (for IAI and TAAS) and a further $650 million commitment was planned for Rafael.

The crisis of the Israeli arms industry is an effect more of declining exports than of declining domestic arms procurement. The Israeli arms industry is vulnerable to changes in the international arms market, because the share of exports in military production is high compared to that of most other countries—79 per cent for IAI and 53 per cent for TAAS. Rafael, the national armaments development agency, depends on exports to sell only 28 per cent of its production. In the private sector, the electronics company Elbit exports 82 per cent of its production. While some countries previously did not consider purchasing Israeli military equipment for political reasons, the Middle East peace accord has made the international market accessible for Israeli arms producers.[132] Israeli companies are among the most distinctive suppliers of modernization work for weapon platforms, especially for Russian aircraft and helicopters and for US aircraft, helicopters and tanks. This is an increasing source of income for the Israeli industry. Current Israeli contracts to upgrade Russian-designed MiG fighter aircraft include Cambodia (15 aircraft), the Czech Republic (2) and Romania (100), and there are negotiations for further contracts with the Czech Republic, India and Ukraine.[133]

---

[130] 'Rescuing defense firms costs $2.5b.', *Jerusalem Post,* 14 Jan. 1995, p. 20.

[131] 'Israeli defense industry revamps', *International Defense Review,* no. 6 (1995), p. 81.

[132] The number of countries prepared to buy Israeli military and aerospace equipment has reportedly increased from 70 to 140. 'New horizons for Israel's industry', *Interavia, Business & Technology,* June 1995, pp. 42–50.

[133] 'Israel's special technologies', *Jane's Defence Weekly,* 18 Feb. 1995, p. 33; and 'Israeli aviation firm proposes modernizing MiG-21s', FBIS-SOV-95-135, 14 July 1995, pp. 63–64.

The Israeli arms industry has an exceptional competitive advantage through its strategic relationship with the USA. One of the more technologically sophisticated cooperation projects is the ballistic missile defence programme, focused on the Arrow-2 anti-missile missile, first flight-tested in 1995.[134] The US has funded around three-quarters of the $500 million development costs of this programme, and agreed in 1995 on a new five-year deal with Israel, according to which the USA will provide grants of $40 million per year in addition to the regular military aid package.[135]

South Africa

Although the size of South Africa's arms industry has decreased dramatically during the 1990s,[136] it is still too large for the requirements of South Africa's armed forces. Since coming to power in April 1994 the new government has not given any clear policy guidelines with respect to the future of the domestic arms industry. This policy vacuum has meant that the industry has been reluctant to incur the short-term costs associated with restructuring and reorienting its technological and industrial resources towards the production of civilian goods and services.

The South African arms industry was built up in the context of the UN mandatory arms embargo between 1977 and 1994, and as such occupied a privileged position in terms of access to state resources. The massive investment in domestic arms production capabilities after 1977 created excess production capacity in the early 1980s, and as a result of this South Africa entered the international arms market in 1982. By the end of the 1980s the arms industry was one of the largest and most significant industrial sectors in the national economy and a major exporter of manufactured goods.

As a result of South Africa's improved external security environment, the ending of apartheid and changing government spending priorities, military expenditure, particularly procurement spending, has declined dramatically since 1989, and this has resulted in sharp reductions in the output of the domestic arms industry—by about one-quarter over the past three years. Total employment in the arms industry has declined from 160 000 in 1989 to 70 000 in 1995.[137] Despite the contraction, arms production still accounts for a relatively large part of manufacturing output (around 4 per cent).

Although economic factors were not the primary determinants which led to the establishment of an indigenous arms industry in South Africa, they have

---

[134] 'Arrow test successful', *Jerusalem Post International*, 12 Aug. 1995, p. 24.

[135] 'Israel, US reach new Arrow deal', *Jerusalem Post International*, 13 May 1995, p. 2; and 'US agrees to Arrow fund', *Defense News*, 8–14 May 1995, p. 3.

[136] The background to this decline was described in Ohlson, T., 'South Africa: from apartheid to multi-party democracy', *SIPRI Yearbook 1995* (note 5), pp. 117–45; and Singh, R. P. and Wezeman, P. D., 'South Africa's arms production and exports', *SIPRI Yearbook 1995* (note 5), appendix 14E, pp. 569–82.

[137] Employment in direct arms production was only 48 000 in 1995 according to the South African Defence Industry Association (SADIA). South African Defence Industry Association, Report submitted to the Cameron Commission, 1995, p. 9.

become increasingly important in the domestic debates about the future of this industry, particularly in the context of the government's attempt to reduce the budget deficit while at the same time reallocating spending towards social services.[138]

Arms exports are seen as an important survival strategy for the arms industry. When the UN arms embargo was lifted in May 1994, Armscor, the government arms procurement agency, announced its intention to increase arms exports from about R800 million ($200 million) per year to R1000 million in 1994/95 and further to about R2500 million in the next few years. While this goal has not been achieved (see table 10.13), increased arms exports remain a priority goal and the industry and the Defence Ministry are optimistic about the ability of South Africa to exploit niches in the international arms market.[139]

The government supports the domestic arms industry through its funding of military R&D and provision of international marketing support. Military R&D has in the past accounted for more than 30 per cent of total government R&D expenditure, and, although several major acquisition projects have been cancelled since 1989, it is still taking up a significant share. Almost half of government military R&D funds in 1993 went to private firms through the arms acquisition budget.[140]

The government also supports arms exports through subsidies granted under the General Export Incentive Scheme. Armscor maintains seven overseas offices to provide marketing support, and in fiscal year 1994/95 concluded cooperation agreements with armaments acquisition organizations in three countries—France, Poland and Ukraine—in order to make it possible for South African arms-producing firms to market their products in these countries.[141] Counter-trade is another measure which is used to support the arms industry.[142] A special subsidiary company of Armscor, Macro Countertrade International Ltd, was established in 1993 to facilitate counter-trade agreements with other countries, with a particular focus on the acquisition of

---

[138] The economics of South Africa's arms production have been analysed in several publications by Peter Batchelor, most recently in Batchelor, P., *The Economics of South Africa's Arms Trade*, Discussion Paper no. 3 (Centre for Conflict Resolution, University of Cape Town: Cape Town, Aug. 1995). Much of this section is based on his work.

[139] As illustrated in the interview with South Africa's Defence Minister, Joe Modise, in 'South Africa: National integration, international co-operation and arms sales', *Asian Defence Journal*, no. 4 (1995), pp. 6–8. The implications for regional economic development and security are analysed in George, P., 'The impact of South Africa's arms sales policy on regional military expenditure, development and security', Utrikesdepartementet, *Säkerhet och Utveckling i Afrika* [Security and development in Africa], Ds 1996:15 (Utrikesdepartementet: Stockholm, 1996), pp. 237–95 [appendix in English to a report in Swedish].

[140] 'Survival of the fittest', *Financial Mail*, Oct. 1995, p. 30; and 'Riding the winds of change', *Interavia Business & Technology*, Mar. 1995, p. 22.

[141] Armscor, *Annual Report 1994/95*, p. 22.

[142] According to South Africa's guidelines on counter-trade, all arms import contracts exceeding a value of R5 million must contain an agreement that a sum corresponding to at least 50% of the contract value will be spent in South Africa—as imports from South Africa, as technology transfers to South Africa or as job creation by other means in South Africa. It is also stated in the guidelines that as much as possible of counter-trade exports 'shall be local defence industry products'. Armscor, *Annual Report 1994/95* (note 141), p. 23. Counter-trade is a form of offset in foreign trade.

Table 10.13. South Africa: arms production and arms trade, 1991/92–1994/95

Figures are in m. Rand.

	1991/92	1992/93	1993/94	1994/95
Arms sales by industry	4 826	3 719	4 359	3 773
Arms exports	794	488	886	854
Arms imports	917	697	762	519
Export permits	..	..	559	543
Credits for commercial arms exports	149	205	94	380
Counter-trade	..	..	..	465

Source: South African Defence Industry Association (SADIA), Report submitted to the Cameron Commission, 1995, p. 10; and Armscor, *Annual Report 1994/95*, p. 22.

defence equipment. Joint ventures have also become increasingly important in recent years; in 1995 there were a number of joint ventures between South African firms and overseas firms.[143]

In recent years the arms industry has made a concerted effort to diversify into civilian markets. Denel, the large state-owned group that dominates the domestic arms market, has a stated policy of expanding production for civilian markets. For this purpose, considerable investments are being made in R&D to broaden the company's civilian product range. These diversification efforts have been relatively successful, and Denel has been able to increase the share of its civilian business in turnover from 20 per cent in 1992 to 24 per cent in 1994.[144] Most of the more than 700 private-sector arms-producing companies have also attempted to reduce their dependence upon the domestic defence market. A recent survey of private sector arms-producing companies revealed that for 125 of these firms military sales constitute more than 50 per cent of total output, that for 21 companies this share is over 90 per cent, and that three companies are totally dependent on military sales.[145]

South Korea

South Korea has been producing military equipment since the early 1970s, initially in the form of assembly of foreign systems, but it is above all since the US decision in 1987 to end Foreign Military Sales credits that a determined effort has been made to increase its defence industrial base significantly. This expansion has included most sectors—aerospace, electronics, shipbuilding, vehicles and small arms.

A priority goal is to raise the rate of indigenization. Domestic purchases have gone up to 87 per cent of arms procurement expenditure in 1993, from an

---

[143] See also Singh and Wezeman (note 136).
[144] Denel, *Annual Report 1994/95*, p. 3.
[145] South African Defence Industry Association (note 137).

average of about 60 per cent during the five-year period 1987–91.[146] The ratio of actual local content is, however, significantly lower, since domestic procurement includes a significant share of foreign content in the form of licensed production. If foreign components and raw materials are included, the local content in overall arms procurement is c. 45–50 per cent.[147] This is still a significant rate of self-reliance, even by global comparison. One explanation is that the development of an advanced defence industrial base in South Korea has benefited from the country's rapid economic and industrial development and its strong technological infrastructure. Its shipbuilding industry ranks first in the world in terms of sales, and a new goal is to place its aviation industry among the top 10 in the world.[148] In spite of this, South Korea faces a number of barriers to further indigenization of arms production, primarily structural weaknesses in its national military R&D base and lack of interest on the part of industry in becoming too heavily involved in arms production.[149]

Lack of data has made it impossible to include any South Korean companies in the SIPRI top 100 list. Recently published data for the year 1993, although too late for inclusion in the list for this chapter, show that four companies should be among the top 100.[150] These are Daewoo, Hyundai, Samsung and Korean Air (see table 10.14). The first three are large private corporate conglomerates (chaebols), for which arms sales constitute a small fraction of total turnover, but for some of their subsidiary companies this proportion is much higher. Most of the other 80 companies involved in military production are to varying extents integrated into the production structure of these three conglomerates, primarily as sub-contractors and suppliers of defence-specific components and parts.[151]

Arms production has expanded beyond domestic demand and exports have been falling since the early 1980s. This has resulted in excess capacity and a low rate of capacity utilization. A comparison between the defence and commercial sectors of industry in 1992 showed that the rate of capacity utilization was 60 per cent in defence as against 80 per cent in commercial industry.[152]

---

[146] Amounting to 3680 billion won or $4580 million in 1993. Republic of Korea, Ministry of National Defense, *Defense White Paper 1994/95*, p. 215.

[147] Approximately 2000 billlion won, based on a foreign content of 45% in domestic production. Reed, C., Karniol, R. and Matthews, R., 'South Korean business: diversify for survival', *Jane's Defence Weekly*, 31 July 1993, p. 15.

[148] 'South Korea: aviation industry turnaround now in progress', *International Herald Tribune*, 20 Nov. 1995, p. 15.

[149] Bitzinger, R., 'South Korea's defense industry at the crossroads', *Korean Journal of Defense Analysis*, vol. 7, no. 1 (1995), pp. 233–49.

[150] Charles, F., 'L'industrie de défense de la Corée du Sud' [The defence industry of South Korea], *L'Armement*, no. 14 (Oct./Nov. 1995), pp. 143–52.

[151] 18 prime contractors and 62 sub-contracting firms. *Defense White Paper 1994/95* (note 146). For a comprehensive description of the industrial structure, see Nolan, J. E., *Military Industry in Taiwan and South Korea* (Macmillan: Basingstoke and London, 1986).

[152] Min, S. K., 'Defense Industry of the Republic of Korea: Preparing for the 21st century', paper presented on the 24th Pacific Area Senior Officer Logistics Seminar, Seoul, 17–23 Sep. 1995, p. 25. Brigadier-Gen. Min is Chairman of the Defense Logistics Management Committee, Ministry of National Defense, Republic of Korea.

Table 10.14. Arms sales of the major South Korean arms-producing companies, 1993
Figures are in US $m. Figures in italics are percentages.

Company	Sector	Arms sales est.	Total sales	Arms sales share of total (%)	Profits	No. of employees
Asia Motors	MV	145	1 200	*12*	..	8 276
Daewoo Corp.	A Ac El Mi MV SA/O Sh	[>405]	30 900	*>1.3*	483	77 000
Daewoo Electronics	El	..	..	..	..	..
Daewoo Heavy Ind.	A Ac El[a] Mi MV	165	1 100	*15*	..	8 500
Daewoo Precision Ind.	SA/O	40	200	*21*	..	1 520
Daewoo Shipbuilding and Heavy Machinery	Sh	200	2 200	*9*	..	11 185
Daewoo Telecom	El	..	..	..	..	..
Hanwha	SA/O[b]	185	400	*46*	..	3 500
Hyundai Corp.	MV Sh	[> 300]	36 900	..	11	170 000
Hyundai Heavy Ind.	Sh	..	6 735	..	158	30 725
Hyundai Precision and Ind.	MV	230	1 900	*12*	..	8 340
Kia Machine Tools	SA/O[c]	..	..	..	..	..
Korean Air	Ac	350	3 500	*10*	..	15 400
Lucky-Goldstar Int. Corp.	El Mi Oth	[> 100]	..	..	..	..
Goldstar Electronics	Mi	..	..	..	..	..
Goldstar Precision	El Mi	90	100	*90*	..	1 325
Goldstar Cable	Oth	..	..	..	..	..
Poogsan Metal Corp.	SA/O[d]	185	600	*31*	..	5 455
Samsung Co.	A Ac El Eng Mi MV Sh	670	51 300	*0.9*	520	191 300
Samsung Aerospace (SSA)	Ac El Eng	350	700	*50*	..	4 800
Samsung Electronics (SEC)	El Mi[e]	200	10 200	*2*	..	48 400
Samsung Precisions	Eng	..	..	..	..	..
Samsung Shipbuilding and Heavy Industries (SHI)	A MV Sh	120	400	*30*	..	7 000

[a] Air surveillance radars.
[b] Explosives.
[c] Cannon.
[d] Munitions.
[e] Semi-conductors, communication systems, radars and fire control systems.

Sources: Arms sales: Charles, F., 'L'industrie de défense de la Corée du Sud', *L'Armement*, no. 49 (Oct./Nov. 1995), cited in 'Korea maps its world challenge', *Interavia*, Jan./Feb. 1996, p. 15; industrial codes: Charles, F., 'L'industrie de défense de la Corée du Sud' [The defence industry of South Korea], *L'Armement*, no. 14 (Oct./Nov. 1995), pp. 143–52 (in French); and *Korean Defense Business Directory 1991* (Korea Defense Industry Association: Seoul, 1991); other data: 'The Fortune global 500', *Fortune*, 25 July 1994.

The same study showed that the arms production sector had a higher rate of investment costs to total sales and lower profitability than the commercial sector.[153]

The government has pursued an active policy of promoting its arms industry since its early formation, mainly through tax relief and financial support.[154] More recent measures include increased government expenditure on military R&D, incentives for company-funded military R&D, and efforts to acquire advanced core technology from abroad. Government expenditure on military R&D is planned to increase from 2.9 per cent of the defence budget in 1994 to 5 per cent in 1998.[155] Policies to acquire foreign technology include offset requirements for arms imports and increased international cooperation in military technology. Foreign licensers are required to provide 50 per cent offsets, split between 20 per cent in direct and 30 per cent in indirect offsets.[156]

South Korean arms producers are engaged in many international cooperation projects. The pattern of international cooperation has shifted from strong US dominance in the 1970s and 1980s to greater emphasis on West European countries and some Asian neighbour countries in the 1990s, partly because the latter have offered more favourable terms of cooperation than the USA. Military–industrial cooperation agreements have been established with the governments of France, Germany, Italy, Russia, Spain, Switzerland and the UK in Europe, with Indonesia, Malaysia, the Philippines and Thailand in Asia, and with Canada. Negotiations were under way with the Netherlands in late 1995, and talks were also being pursued with Israel.

Conclusions

The four major industrializing arms-producing countries described in this section have more dissimilarities than similarities.

India's arms industry is inefficient (in terms of productivity) and over-dimensioned (in relation to actual production) with few links to civilian production. It accounts for a small share of gross national product (GNP) but is still absorbing a disproportionate share of national science and high technology resources. There is a significant dependence on foreign technologies through licensed assembly and production.

Israel has a technologically advanced arms industry, which has been built up in close cooperation with the USA. It accounts for a high share of GNP, and currently has great excess capacity, mainly because of the decline in military exports. The size of the arms industry is now being reduced as a matter of

---

[153] Arms production accounted for 10.6% of total industry investment costs, but only 5.5% of total industry sales revenues; and the profit ratio was –4.7% in the arms production sector as against +1.5 per cent in the commercial. There were, however, sector differences: while performance in the land system and shipbuilding sectors was fairly satisfactory, it was poorer in aerospace, arms and ammunition and communications equipment.

[154] The support is regulated mainly in the 1973 Special Law on Defense Industry.

[155] *Defense White Paper 1994/95* (note 146), pp. 112–14.

[156] Reed, Carniol and Matthews (note 147), p. 25. The government is currently reviewing this policy with a view to an upward adjustment of the direct offset ratio. Min (note 152), p. 19.

conscious policy, but there is little interest in diversification and the companies are strongly oriented to increasing their share on the international market. The main policy issue for the government is whether to protect a core of the arms industry to ensure safe national supply of weapon systems or whether to let companies develop even more pronounced export strategies.

The excess capacity of South Africa's arms industry is partly an effect of reduced military budgets but also of its goal of self-sufficiency in armaments during the embargo period. A broad range of armaments are developed and produced, but the level of technology is not as high as that of the Israeli equipment with which many South African companies compete. The choice for South Africa is between on the one hand diversification into civilian products—badly needed after decades of suppression of the material and social needs of the black population—and on the other the hope that export revenues from armaments will benefit the economy at large. If South Africa chooses the latter line, it risks facing the same situation as France and to some extent Israel are now confronting, with dependence on government subsidies, a burden on civilian production, and eventual loss of production and employment.

Like Japan in many ways, South Korea has historically given priority to civilian production and only relatively recently decided to make a serious effort to raise the technological level of its defence industrial base. International cooperation is an important feature in this policy.

Appendix 10A. The 100 largest arms-producing companies, 1994

ELISABETH SKÖNS*

Table 10A contains information on the 100 largest arms-producing companies in the OECD and the developing countries ranked by their arms sales in 1994.[1] Companies with the designation *S* in the column for rank in 1994 are subsidiaries; their arms sales are included in the figure in column 6 for the holding company. Subsidiaries are listed in the position where they would appear if they were independent companies. In order to facilitate comparison with data for the previous year, the rank order and arms sales figures for 1993 are also given. Where new data for 1993 have become available, this information is included in the table; thus the 1993 rank order and the arms sales figures for some companies which appeared in table 13A in the *SIPRI Yearbook 1995* have been revised.

Sources and methods

Sources of data. The data in the table are based on the following sources: company reports, a questionnaire sent to over 400 companies, and corporation news published in the business sections of newspapers and military journals. Company archives, marketing reports, government publication of prime contracts and country surveys were also consulted. In many cases exact figures on arms sales were not available, mainly because companies often do not report their arms sales or lump them together with other activities. Estimates were therefore made.

Definitions. Data on total sales, profits and employment are for the entire company, not for the arms-producing sector alone. Profit data are after taxes in all cases when the company provides such data. Employment data are either a year-end or a yearly average figure as reported by the company. Data are reported on the fiscal year basis reported by the company in its annual report.

Exchange rates. To convert local currency figures into US dollars, the period-average of market exchange rates of the International Monetary Fund, *International Financial Statistics,* was used.

Key to abbreviations in column 5. A = artillery, Ac = aircraft, El = electronics, Eng = engines, Mi = missiles, MV = military vehicles, SA/O = small arms/ordnance, Sh = ships, and Oth = other.

---

[1] For the membership of the Organisation for Economic Co-operation and Development, see the Glossary. For countries in the developing world, see notes to appendix 11A.

* The author gratefully acknowledges the assistance in data collection of Peter Batchelor, Centre for Conflict Resolution (Cape Town), Paul Dunne, Middlesex University (London), Ken Epps (Ontario), Paula Gisower (Buenos Aires), Jean-Paul Hébert, CIRPES (Paris), Peter Hug (Bern), Masako Ikegami (Uppsala), Keidanren (Tokyo), Rudi Leo (Vienna), Rita Manchandi (New Delhi), Arcadi Oliveres, Centre d'Estudis sobre la Pau i el Desarmament (Barcelona), Reuven Pedatzur (Tel Aviv), Giulio Perani (Rome), Gülay Günlük-Senesen (Istanbul), Pierre de Vestel (Brussels) and Werner Voß (Bremen).

Table 10A. The 100 largest arms-producing companies in the OECD and the developing countries, 1994

Figures in columns 6, 7, 8 and 10 are in US $m.

1	2	3	4	5	6	7	8	9	10	11
Rank[a]					Arms sales[b]					
1994	1993	Company[c]	Country	Industry	1994	1993	Total sales 1994	Col. 6 as % of col. 8	Profit 1994	Employment 1994
1	–	Lockheed Martin[d]	USA	Ac El Mi	14 400	0	22 900	63	1 060	170 000
2	2	McDonnell Douglas	USA	Ac El Mi	9 230	9 050	13 176	70	598	65 760
3	5	British Aerospace	UK	Ac A El Mi SA/O	7 030	5 950	10 956	64	214	46 500
4	3	General Motors, GM	USA	Eng El Mi	5 900	6 900	154 950	4	4 900	692 800
5	7	Northrop Grumman[e]	USA	Ac El Mi SA/O	5 600	4 480	6 711	83	35	42 400
S	S	Hughes Electronics (GM)	USA	El Mi	5 590	6 110	14 099	40	925	77 100
6	12	Loral	USA	El Mi	5 100	3 750	5 484	93	288	32 600
7	9	Thomson S.A.	France	El Mi	4 270	4 240	13 400	32	–390	98 700
S	S	Thomson-CSF (Thomson S.A.)	France	El Mi	4 260	4 240	6 554	65	–173	46 825
8	11	Boeing	USA	Ac El Mi	3 800	3 800	21 924	17	856	119 400
9	10	United Technologies	USA	Ac El Mi	3 800	4 200	21 197	18	585	171 500
10	6	Raytheon	USA	El Mi	3 500	4 500	10 013	35	759	60 200
11	13	Daimler-Benz, D-B	FRG	Ac Eng Mv El Mi	3 200	3 540	64 133	5	552	330 550
12	16	GEC	UK	El	3 190	3 210	15 822	20	864	82 250
13	17	Litton Industries	USA	El Sh	3 160	3 170	3 446	92	–152	29 000
S	S	Daimler-Benz Aerospace (D-B)[f]	FRG	Ac Eng El Mi	3 110	3 250	10 719	29	–270	75 580
14	18	General Dynamics	USA	MV Sh	2 860	3 000	3 058	94	321	24 200
15	14	DCN	France	Sh	2 730	3 440	2 788	98	. .	24 900
16	23	Mitsubishi Heavy Industries	Japan	Ac MV Mi Sh	2 730	2 380	28 676	10	784	53 050
17	15	Rockwell International	USA	Ac El Mi	2 550	3 350	11 100	23	634	71 890
18	21	TRW	USA	MV Oth	2 480	2 470	9 087	27	333	64 175
19	20	Aérospatiale Groupe	France	Ac Mi	2 450	2 650	8 747	28	–87	39 555
20	24	Westinghouse Electric	USA	El	2 450	2 180	9 208	27	77	84 400

1	2	3	4	5	6	7	8	9	10	11
Rank[a]					Arms sales[b]		Total sales	Col. 6 as	Profit	Employment
1994	1993	Company[c]	Country	Industry	1994	1993	1994	% of col. 8	1994	1994
21	27	IRI	Italy	Ac Eng El Mi Sh	2 070	1 840	50 275	4	-912	292 700
S	S	Finmeccanica (IRI)	Italy	Ac Eng El Mi	1 860	1 680	7 515	25	1	59 040
22	25	E-Systems	USA	El	1 850	1 870	2 028	91	96	15 760
23	22	General Electric	USA	Eng	1 800	2 400	60 109	3	4 726	221 000
24	26	Tenneco	USA	Sh	1 750	1 860	12 174	14	408	55 000
S	S	Newport News (Tenneco)	USA	Sh	1 750	1 860	1 753	100	200	19 900
25	28	Texas Instruments	USA	El	1 710	1 840	10 315	17	691	56 300
26	29	Textron	USA	Ac Eng MV El Oth	1 600	1 600	9 683	17	433	53 000
S	S	Aérospatiale SNI (Aérospatiale)	France	Ac Mi	1 550	1 640	5 551	28	-1	24 510
27	32	CEA	France	Oth	1 540	1 540	3 275	47	..	17 500
28	38	Kawasaki Heavy Industries	Japan	Ac Eng Mi Sh	1 450	1 130	10 473	14	100	24 266
29	33	Unisys	USA	El	1 400	1 500	7 400	19	101	46 300
S	S	ASIC (Loral)[g]	USA	El Oth	1 400	1 400	1 400	100	58	10 000
30	31	Rolls Royce	UK	Eng	1 360	1 580	4 845	28	124	43 500
31	30	Dassault Aviation	France	Ac	1 330	1 590	1 837	72	47	9 380
32	34	Allied Signal	USA	Ac El Oth	1 300	1 410	12 817	10	759	87 500
33	47	Celsius	Sweden	A El Sh SA/O Oth	1 190	930	1 775	67	99	17 050
34	39	Israel Aircraft Industries	Israel	Ac El Mi	1 150	1 120	1 447	79	-46	13 410
35	46	FMC	USA	A MV Oth	1 100	950	4 051	27	173	21 345
S	S	United Defense (FMC/Harsco)[h]	USA	A MV Oth	1 100	0	1 100	100	100	5 910
36	42	SNECMA Groupe	France	Eng Oth	1 070	1 060	3 408	31	-410	23 720
37	36	GIAT Industries	France	A MV SA/O	1 030	1 300	1 382	75	-526	16 370
38	40	INI [i]	Spain	Ac A MV El Sh	1 020	1 110	20 588	5	-602	130 950
39	44	ITT	USA	El	1 000	970	23 620	4	1 022	110 000
40	–	Lagardère Groupe[j]	France	El Mi Oth	950	970	9 549	10	111	40 300

		Company	Country	Category						
41	51	Mitsubishi Electric	Japan	El Mi	940	820	32 726	3	424	110 575
42	43	Siemens	FRG	El	870	990	52 131	2	1 228	382 000
S	S	Eurocopter Group (Aérospatiale/ DASA, FRG)	France	Ac	860	920	1 657	52	−71	10 025
43	41	GTE	USA	El	850	1 100	19 944	4	2 445	111 200
44	55	Harris	USA	El	840	700	3 336	25	112	28 200
45	37	Carlyle	USA	Ac El Oth	800	1 200	1 263	63	..	..
46	61	Bath Iron Works	USA	Sh	770	600	830	93	48	8 300
47	54	Alliant Tech Systems	USA	SA/O	760	760	789	96	−74	8 200
48	53	Oerlikon-Bührle, O-B	Switzerl.	Ac A El Mi SA/O	750	760	2 785	27	55	17 790
49	48	Bremer Vulkan	FRG	El Sh	740	860	3 708	20	35	25 445
50	52	Diehl	FRG	El Mi SA/O Oth	740	810	1 732	43	..	12 245
S	S	Dornier (Daimler Aerospace)	FRG	Ac El	710	450	1 169	61	..	3 540
S	S	STN Atlas Elektronik (Bremer Vulkan)k	FRG	El	680	780	1 119	61	−16	5 475
S	S	Matra Défense (Lagardère)j	France	Mi Oth	680	..	738	92	..	2 920
S	68	Hunting	UK	SA/O	670	490	1 724	39	22	13 590
52	58	FIAT	Italy	Eng MV	660	660	37 567	2	776	248 180
53	57	Eidgenössische Rüstungs-betriebe	Switzerl.	Ac Eng A SA/O	660	680	721	92	−107	3 635
S	S	Oerlikon-Contraves (O-B)	Switzerl.	A El Mi SA/O	660	670	741	89	38	3 365
54	56	VSEL Consortium	UK	MV Sh	650	690	657	99	100	..
S	S	Vought Aircraft (Northrop)	USA	Ac	650	800	800	81	..	5 200
55	62	Thyssen	FRG	MV Sh	640	590	21 536	3	55	131 865
S	S	Thyssen Industrie (Thyssen)	FRG	MV Sh	640	590	5 001	13	54	42 680
56	59	Denel	S. Africa	Ac A MV El Mi SA/O	600	640	850	71	73	13 800
S	S	SNECMA (SNECMA Groupe)	France	Eng	590	670	1 871	32	−392	12 480
57	49	Gencorp	USA	Ac Eng El Mi SA/O Oth	580	850	1 740	33	−226	12 970
S	S	Aerojet (Gencorp)	USA	-"-	580	850	594	98	25	3 390

1	2	3	4	5	6	7	8	9	10	11
Rank[a]					Arms sales[b]		Total sales	Col. 6 as	Profit	Employment
1994	1993	Company[c]	Country	Industry	1994	1993	1994	% of col. 8 1994	1994	1994
58	60	Hercules	USA	Ac Mi	570	600	2 821	20	274	11 990
59	–	GKN	UK	Ac MV	550	200	4 733	12	141	33 500
60	63	SAGEM Groupe	France	El	540	580	2 466	22	107	14 085
61	66	Ordnance Factories	India	A SA/O Oth	540	510	641	81	..	162 375
62	84	NEC	Japan	El	520	390	36 879	1	346	151 100
63	50	Ishikawajima-Harima	Japan	Eng Sh	520	840	10 011	5	140	27 300
64	87	Avondale Industries	USA	Sh	510	370	510	100	9	6 200
65	83	Lucas Industries	UK	Ac	490	390	3 967	12	–256	45 700
66	67	Dassault Electronique	France	El	490	490	734	67	10	4 075
67	75	Ceridian	USA	El Oth	490	450	916	53	79	7 500
68	64	Rheinmetall	FRG	A MV El SA/O	480	520	1 994	24	..	14 525
69	69	Smiths Industries	UK	El	470	480	1 163	40	122	11 700
70	72	Dyncorp	USA	Ac El	470	470	900	52	..	..
71	86	Racal Electronics	UK	El	450	380	1 437	31	89	11 325
72	–	Honeywell	USA	El Mi	450	300	6 057	7	279	50 800
73	73	Motorola	USA	El	450	470	22 245	2	1 560	132 000
S	S	Bofors (Celsius)	Sweden	A MV SA/O	450	420	491	92	26	4 655
S	S	Agusta Eli (Finmeccanica)	Italy	Ac	450	0	528	85	..	6 445
S	S	CASA (INI)[j]	Spain	Ac	440	440	866	51	25	8 300
74	78	Mitre	USA	El	430	430	..	..	..	..
75	80	Oshkosh Truck	USA	MV	430	420	692	62	13	..
S	S	Agusta (Agusta Eli)	Italy	Ac	420	410	509	83	..	4 580
76	91	Hindustan Aeronautics	India	Ac Mi	410	340	443	93	2.2	35 545
77	77	Teledyne	USA	Eng El Mi	410	440	2 391	17	–8	18 000
78	71	Preussag	FRG	Sh	410	480	14 253	3	151	69 710

		Company	Country							
S	79	HDW (Preussag)	FRG	Sh	410	480	784	52	53	4 070
S	85	CAE!	Canada	El	400	380	810	49	12	:
80	76	TAAS	Israel	A MV SA/O	400	440	460	87	-47	5 000
81	90	Toshiba	Japan	El Mi	400	350	48 228	1	450	190 000
82	82	AT&T	USA	El	400	400	75 094	1	4 710	304 500
S	S	Blohm & Voss (Thyssen Ind.)	FRG	MV Sh	390	320	802	49	-11	4 765
83	88	Esco Electronics	USA	El	390	370	474	82	8	3 700
84	93	Devonport Management	UK	Sh	380	340	418	91	17	5 095
85	65	Thiokol	USA	Eng SA/O	370	520	1 057	35	60	8 000
S	S	SAGEM (SAGEM Groupe)	France	El	360	370	1 183	30	46	5 785
86	81	Rafael	Israel	SA/O OTH	360	420	360	100	-72	4 900
S	S	Hollandse Signaalapparaten (Thomson-CSF, France)	Netherl.	El	360	340	362	99	-49	2 810
87	94	Saab-Scania[m]	Sweden	Ac El Mi Oth	350	320	4 082	9	322	26 650
S	S	Saab Defense (Saab-Scania)	Sweden	Ac Mi Oth	350	0	430	81	:	5 200
S	S	FIAT Aviazione (FIAT)	Italy	Eng	340	260	881	39	:	4 015
88	95	Vosper Thornycroft	UK	Sh	340	320	381	89	38	2 640
89	98	Logicon	USA	Oth	340	320	345	99	20	:
90	89	Koor Industries	Israel	A El	340	350	2 714	13	125	19 555
S	70	Westland (GKN)	UK	Ac	330	480	461	72	29	:
S	S	Sextant Avionique (Thomson-CSF)	France	El	330	340	865	38	:	6 253
91	-	Hitachi Zosen	Japan	Sh	330	:	4 221	8	115	10 500
92	-	Sumitomo Heavy Industries	Japan	A Sh	320	310	4 913	7	-29	:
93	96	Olin	USA	El SA/O Oth	320	320	2 658	12	91	12 800
S	S	GF Oto Melara Breda (Finmeccanica)	Italy	A MV Mi Oth	320	0	:	:	:	:
94	-	Bombardier	Canada	El Mi	310	250	4 352	7	177	37 000
S	S	Tadiran (Koor Industries)	Israel	El	310	300	863	36	39	8 000
S	S	Kockums (Celsius)	Sweden	Sh	300	100	358	84	33	2 635
S	S	CAE-Link (CAE, Canada)[l]	USA	El	300	:	340	88	:	3 100

1	2	3	4	5	6	7	8	9	10	11
Rank[a]					Arms sales[b]		Total sales 1994	Col. 6 as % of col. 8 1994	Profit 1994	Employment 1994
1994	1993	Company[c]	Country	Industry	1994	1993				
S	S	EDS (General Motors)	USA	El	300	300	10 052	3	822	75 400
95	100	SNPE	France	A SA/O	290	310	782	37	26	5 890
96	–	Nissan Motor	Japan	A MV	290	260	58 732	..	–1 672	145 580
97	–	Elbit	Israel	El Oth	290	230	759	38	30	4 635
98	–	Wegmann Group	FRG	MV	280	260	616	45	..	..
S	S	Bazán (INI)[j]	Spain	Eng El Sh	280	330	411	68	–57	7 880
99	97	Sundstrand	USA	Ac Oth	280	320	1 373	20	96	9 200
100	–	Ericsson	Sweden	El	270	160	10 699	3	512	76 145
S	S	Ericsson	Sweden	El	270	160	365	74	..	2 880

[a] Companies with the designation S in the column for rank are subsidiaries. The rank designation in the column for 1993 may not always correspond to that given in table 13A in the *SIPRI Yearbook 1995* because of subsequent revisions. A dash (–) in this column indicates either that the company did not produce arms in 1993, or that it did not exist as it was structured in 1994, in which case there is a zero (0) in column 7, or that it did not rank among the 100 largest companies in the *SIPRI Yearbook 1995*. Other reasons may also apply: see notes below.

[b] A zero (0) in the column for arms sales 1993 indicates that the company did not produce arms in 1993, or that in 1993 the company did not exist as it was structured in 1994. Data for Japan are based on information on military contracts (with the Japan Defense Agency) rather than on sales.

[c] Names in brackets are the names of the parent companies.

[d] Lockheed and Martin Marietta were merged into Lockheed Martin in March 1995. 1994 data are estimated totals for the two companies, since separate data for the two are not available. In 1993, the combined arms sales of the two companies amounted to $16 570 million.

[e] Northrop changed its name to Northrop Grumman in May 1994. Data for 1994 include Grumman and Vought Aircraft since the acquisitions in April and August respectively. Arms sales data for 1993 do not include these.

[f] Formerly DASA. 1993 data are not strictly comparable to data for 1994.

[g] Formerly IBM Federal Systems.

[h] United Defense Limited Partnership was formed in 1994 by the combination of FMC Defense Systems with Harsco's BMY Combat Systems.

[i] The arms-producing subsidiaries of INI were transferred to another state holding company, Teneo, in 1995.

[j] Data for 1993 apply to Matra Hachette, which was then the parent company of Matra Défense.

[k] Data for 1993 apply to the sum of Atlas Elektronik and STN Systemtechnik Nord which were merged into STN Atlas Elektronik from 1 January 1994.

[l] CAE does not include its US subsidiary CAE-Link in its accounts for 1994, because it was sold to Hughes Electronics in 1995. SIPRI has added CAE-Link arms sales and total sales to those of CAE for 1994.

[m] Saab-Scania was separated into two companies in 1995, Saab and Scania.

11. The trade in major conventional weapons

IAN ANTHONY, PIETER D. WEZEMAN and SIEMON T.
WEZEMAN

I. Introduction

The SIPRI global trend-indicator value of international transfers of major conventional weapons in 1995 was $22 797 million in constant (1990) US dollars.[1] The revised estimate for the trend-indicator value for 1994 is $22 842 million—an increase of roughly $1 billion compared with the estimate provided in the *SIPRI Yearbook 1995*. It is usual for the figures for the most recent years to be revised upwards as new and better data become available.[2]

In the period 1991–95 the precipitous decline in the volume of arms transfers recorded for the period 1987–90 appears to have been arrested and there is some evidence of a slight upward trend in deliveries.

Section II surveys the dominant trends in the international arms trade based both on official government data and SIPRI data. In 1995 a third annual report containing returns to the United Nations Register of Conventional Arms was released. The data contained in this report are evaluated in section II.

SIPRI data for deliveries of major conventional weapons have been updated up to and including calendar year 1995. The mid-point in a 10-year time series of SIPRI data coincides with the end of the cold war in 1990. This data set permits a first tentative evaluation of broad patterns in the post-cold war arms trade. Section III examines in greater detail the patterns of arms transfers for selected suppliers and recipients across the 10-year period 1986–95.

II. Developments in 1995

Among suppliers the most notable change in the market share distribution in 1995 was the increase in deliveries by Russia compared with the previous year. According to SIPRI estimates Russia accounted for 17 per cent of all deliveries of major conventional weapons in 1995 compared with only 4 per cent in 1994. Compared with the 43 per cent share recorded for the Soviet Union in 1986 this is still a relatively small share of the global market.

The overall share of the USA in total deliveries recorded for 1995 remained high—43 per cent—but significantly lower than the revised estimate of 56 per

---

[1] The index produced using the SIPRI valuation system enables the aggregation of data on physical arms transfers. The SIPRI system for evaluating the arms trade was designed as a *trend-measuring device*, to permit measurement of changes in the total flow of major weapons and its geographical pattern. A description of the method used in calculating the trend-indicator value is given in appendix 11C.

[2] For this reason it is advisable for readers who require time-series data for periods longer than the 5 years covered in this *Yearbook* to contact SIPRI.

SIPRI Yearbook 1996: Armaments, Disarmament and International Security

cent recorded for 1994. The shares recorded for other leading suppliers—the UK, France and Germany—changed very little compared with 1994.

Six large suppliers—the USA, Russia, FR Germany, the UK, France and China—remain the dominant sources of major conventional weapons. Together they accounted for four-fifths of total deliveries. However, among smaller suppliers the largest increase in recent years was from Canada, accounted for by the delivery of armoured vehicles to Saudi Arabia. Both the Royal Saudi Land Forces (responsible to the Minister of Defence and Aviation, Prince Sultan bin Abdel Aziz Al-Saud) and the Royal Saudi National Guard (responsible to Crown Prince Abdallah bin Abdel Aziz Al-Saud) have been acquiring wheeled armoured personnel carriers in recent years. Each is acquiring a different version of the Swiss MOWAG Piranha.

The Canadian defence industry is largely integrated with that of the USA. In its procurement actions the US Department of Defense treats Canadian contractors in the same manner as US contractors. Moreover, many Canadian companies are subsidiaries of US mother companies. For this reason, a large amount of defence-related exports from Canada are not recorded either in SIPRI data or in published Canadian national statistics.

Saudi Arabian acquisition of armoured vehicles illustrates some of the complexities that can surround international arms transfers. The Royal Saudi Land Forces are acquiring a version of the Piranha under a 1991 contract placed with the Swiss company MOWAG. However, most of the vehicles have been produced in Canada by a subsidiary of the US company General Motors. Special versions of the vehicle (including a version armed with either 81-mm calibre or 120-mm calibre mortar as well as ambulance, recovery vehicle, command post and radar carrying versions) have been produced by a third partner, the British engineering firm GKN.[3]

The versions being acquired by the Saudi National Guard are being sold through the US Foreign Military Sales programme managed by the US Army Tank Automotive Command. However, these vehicles are also being manufactured in Canada (by General Motors, Canada) and in the UK (by GKN).[4] The supply of armoured personnel carriers to Saudi Arabia therefore involves two different customers in the importing government and four different supplier governments. The programme involves three different main contractors (MOWAG, General Motors and GKN) as well as a host of subcontractors.[5]

One new entrant to the group of significant exporting countries in 1995 was Uzbekistan, which transferred 15 large IL-76M Candid transport aircraft to China.

Table 11A.1 in appendix 11A indicates the changing distribution of the arms trade according to different arms importing regions. Among recipients

---

[3] GKN, *Annual Report 1992*, p. 23; and *Jane's Armour and Artillery 1995–96* (Jane's Information Group: Coulsdon, Surrey, 1995), pp. 438–89.

[4] *Jane's Defence Weekly*, 24 Jan. 1996, p. 17.

[5] Major subcontractors include US companies ESC and Delco, and British Aerospace (through its Royal Ordnance subsidiary).

Table 11.1. The 30 leading suppliers of major conventional weapons, 1991–95

The countries are ranked according to 1991–95 aggregate exports. Figures are trend-indicator values expressed in US $m., at constant (1990) prices.

Suppliers	1991	1992	1993	1994	1995	1991–95
1 USA	12 568	13 794	12 802	12 821	9 894	61 879
2 USSR/Russia	4 657	2 841	3 631	962	3 905	15 996
3 Germany, FR	2 520	1 503	1 686	2 483	1 964	10 156
4 UK	1 143	1 099	1 213	1 493	1 663	6 611
5 France	1 071	1 308	1 368	1 021	815	5 582
6 China	1 104	1 158	1 284	744	868	5 158
7 Netherlands	306	316	385	588	448	2 043
8 Italy	346	464	451	338	324	1 923
9 Czechoslovakia[a]	69	213	267	371	326	1 246
10 Israel	172	192	246	231	317	1 159
11 Switzerland	386	330	51	73	132	972
12 Canada	15	131	166	263	301	876
13 Uzbekistan	0	0	0	406	464	870
14 Korea, North	138	86	423	48	48	743
15 Ukraine	16	416	120	107	74	733
16 Sweden	124	123	45	91	221	604
17 Yugoslavia	543	21	0	0	0	564
18 Poland	82	0	1	117	201	402
19 Spain	72	64	53	123	62	374
20 Slovakia	0	0	145	29	178	352
21 Norway	91	0	47	101	35	274
22 Belgium	2	0	0	90	168	260
23 Brazil	43	59	24	61	40	228
24 Korea, South	53	0	48	11	73	184
25 Nicaragua	0	99	53	0	0	152
26 South Africa	35	58	34	0	11	139
27 Austria	20	44	13	23	33	133
28 Pakistan	129	0	0	2	0	130
29 Bulgaria	8	60	21	29	0	118
30 Australia	58	1	10	12	14	96
Others	48	152	157	204	164	725
Total	**25 819**	**24 532**	**24 744**	**22 842**	**22 797**	**120 733**

[a] For the years 1991–92 the data refer to the former Czechoslovakia; for 1993–95 the data refer to the Czech Republic.

Note: The index produced using the SIPRI valuation system is not comparable to official economic statistics, such as gross domestic product, public expenditure or export/import figures. The purpose of the valuation system is to enable the aggregation of data on physical arms transfers. Similar weapon systems require similar values and SIPRI has created an index of trend-indicator values which can be aggregated in a number of different ways. The SIPRI system for evaluating the arms trade was designed as a *trend-measuring device*, to permit the measurement of changes in the total flow of major weapons and its geographical pattern. A description of the method used in calculating the trend-indicator value is given in appendix 11C.

Source: SIPRI arms trade database.

Table 11.2. The 50 leading recipients of major conventional weapons, 1991–95

The countries are ranked according to 1991–95 aggregate imports. Figures are trend-indicator values expressed in US $m., at constant (1990) prices.

	Recipients	1991	1992	1993	1994	1995	1991–95
1	Turkey	954	1 640	2 288	2 089	1 125	8 096
2	Egypt	1 234	1 274	1 191	1 884	1 555	7 138
3	Saudi Arabia	1 208	1 080	2 534	1 309	961	7 092
4	Japan	2 386	1 608	1 260	829	799	6 882
5	Greece	559	2 632	891	1 185	489	5 756
6	India	1 799	1 419	724	445	770	5 158
7	China	188	1 154	1 180	529	1 696	4 747
8	Israel	1 309	1 097	585	976	327	4 293
9	Taiwan	562	503	1 074	1 110	980	4 228
10	Germany, FR	929	1 186	1 136	613	181	4 045
11	Korea, South	604	541	469	485	1 677	3 776
12	Kuwait	597	934	617	98	1 117	3 363
13	Thailand	620	863	162	785	888	3 318
14	Pakistan	603	389	942	888	391	3 212
15	Canada	859	619	326	777	370	2 951
16	Iran	603	283	1 195	522	187	2 790
17	USA	482	517	633	626	508	2 766
18	Indonesia	143	69	370	827	711	2 120
19	Finland	98	698	785	385	243	2 209
20	Spain	126	261	580	863	359	2 189
21	UK	874	1 134	29	24	92	2 151
22	Australia	253	452	750	230	243	1 928
23	Portugal	1 062	3	300	500	5	1 870
24	United Arab Emirates	127	172	465	591	427	1 782
25	France	981	385	137	66	89	1 657
26	Malaysia	58	36	21	359	1 120	1 594
27	Hungary	27	0	1 087	4	144	1 262
28	Afghanistan	1 212	0	0	0	0	1 212
29	Chile	64	247	125	216	386	1 037
30	Netherlands	317	186	126	273	59	961
31	Algeria	561	38	20	175	165	959
32	Myanmar	249	38	358	0	310	956
33	Syria	138	341	188	55	185	908
34	Switzerland	236	286	84	148	138	891
35	Italy	114	79	242	161	254	850
36	Singapore	335	74	116	181	91	797
37	Norway	253	188	144	71	118	775
38	Brazil	157	57	64	247	237	762
39	Bangladesh	154	258	29	92	118	651
40	Bulgaria	411	12	64	1	146	634
41	Argentina	0	15	3	66	515	600
42	Denmark	166	65	42	67	196	535
43	Bahrain	75	64	1	13	353	506
44	Morocco	89	26	147	181	50	493
45	Venezuela	236	68	52	137	0	492
46	Sweden	21	5	36	324	87	473

Recipients	1991	1992	1993	1994	1995	1991–95
47 South Africa	12	400	0	16	39	467
48 Slovakia	0	0	179	36	250	464
49 Belgium	148	93	124	76	24	464
50 Poland	246	49	19	5	143	462
Others	1 381	995	850	1 306	1 483	6 015
Total	**25 819**	**24 532**	**24 744**	**22 842**	**22 797**	**120 733**

a For the years 1991–92 the data refer to the former Czechoslovakia; for 1993–95 the data refer to the Czech Republic.

Note: The index produced using the SIPRI valuation system is not comparable to official economic statistics such as gross domestic product, public expenditure or export/import figures. The purpose of the valuation system is to enable the aggregation of data on physical arms transfers. Similar weapon systems require similar values and SIPRI has created an index of trend-indicator values which can be aggregated in a number of different ways. The SIPRI system for evaluating the arms trade was designed as a *trend-measuring device*, to permit the measurement of changes in the total flow of major weapons and its geographical pattern. A description of the method used in calculating the trend-indicator value is given in appendix 11C.

Source: SIPRI arms trade database.

the most noticeable development in 1995 was the sharp increase in deliveries of major conventional weapons to Asian countries. In 1986 countries in Asia accounted for 26 per cent of deliveries while in 1995 the same countries accounted for 46 per cent of deliveries. In 1986 the Middle East accounted for 31 per cent of total deliveries, which had declined to 23 per cent by 1995, largely as a result of reduced imports by Iraq.

The volume of deliveries of major conventional weapons to countries in South America has increased recently, although this region still accounted for only 5 per cent of total deliveries. Central America, Africa and Oceania continue to show very low levels of demand for major conventional weapons.

Among the countries of Asia, those in the subregion of North-East Asia have recorded some of the sharpest increases in imports in recent years. While the level of imports of major conventional weapons by Japan has fallen consistently during the past five years, deliveries to China and Taiwan have increased sharply. Comparing the volume of deliveries of major conventional weapons in the period 1986–90 with the five years 1991–95, deliveries to China increased ninefold while deliveries to Taiwan almost doubled.[6]

On the Korean Peninsula, South Korea maintained a relatively high volume of imports of major conventional weapons across the period 1986–95. However, the volume of deliveries of major conventional weapons to North Korea

[6] Gill, B. and Kim, T., *China's Arms Acquisitions from Abroad: A Quest for 'Superb and Secret Weapons'*, SIPRI Research Report no. 11 (Oxford University Press: Oxford, 1995).

fell by 98 per cent during this 10-year period. Although North Korea has some defence industrial capacity, it seems unlikely that it could compensate for such a dramatic reduction in imports. Therefore it seems likely that the conventional military capabilities of North Korea have been degraded over the past few years. The impact of the loss of access to traditional sources of arms was compounded for Pyongyang by two decisions taken by Russia in 1995. The first was the decision to replace the bilateral Treaty of Cooperation and Mutual Aid between Russia and North Korea with a new Treaty. Whereas Article 1 of the original Treaty included a commitment that if one party was attacked the other would provide immediate military assistance, the Russian Ministry of Foreign Affairs made it clear that a new Treaty would contain no such commitment.[7] The second was that Moscow and Seoul reached agreement on the rescheduling of Russia's debt to South Korea. According to this agreement part of the debt would be settled by transfers of arms and military equipment. While Russia hoped that this would lead to follow-on sales of military equipment, South Korea appeared to see the agreement as a chance to learn more about the characteristics and capabilities of Soviet-type equipment that forms the core of North Korea's inventory.[8]

Among the countries of the Middle East a noticeable recent trend has been the reduced share of deliveries recorded for the larger countries in the Persian Gulf subregion. In 1986 Iran, Iraq and Saudi Arabia accounted for 57 per cent of deliveries to the overall Middle East region. In 1995 this fell to 22 per cent and Iraq remained subject to a mandatory UN arms embargo. In the mid-1990s some of the smaller Persian Gulf countries are taking delivery of significant quantities of major conventional weapons. Kuwait accounted for only 1 per cent of the overall Middle East market in 1986; by 1995 its estimated share was 10 per cent. The United Arab Emirates accounted for less than 1 per cent of the Middle East market in 1986 and 8 per cent by 1995.[9]

The United States

The United States accounted for 43 per cent of total deliveries in 1995 compared with 56 per cent recorded for 1994. This was a considerable decline in the volume of deliveries of US major conventional weapons. The SIPRI data suggest a reduction of around one-fifth in the volume of US deliveries of major conventional weapons in 1995 compared with 1994.

[7] Kim Kyung-Ho, 'Russia to give no military help to N. K. in war', *Korea Newsreview*, 16 Sep. 1995, p. 10; and Strokan, S., 'Pyongyang build relations anew', *Moscow News*, nos 33–36 (15–21 Sep. 1995), p. 5.

[8] Yurkin, A., 'Russia, South Korea to expand military cooperation', ITAR-TASS in Foreign Broadcast Information Service, *Daily Report–Soviet Union (FBIS-SOV)*, FBIS-SOV-95-188, 28 Sep. 1995, pp. 31–32; and Shim Jae Soon, 'Both sides now: Moscow balances its interests in the two Koreas', *Far Eastern Economic Review*, 30 Nov. 1995. At the end of 1995 it appeared that military technical cooperation between Russia and South Korea was expanding with the decision to establish a full battalion in the South Korean armed forces equipped with the T-80U main battle tank. FBIS-SOV-96-013, 19 Jan. 1996, p. 28.

[9] Because year-by-year trends can be misleading, these shares are calculated using a 3-year moving average.

The five largest recipients of US major conventional weapons in 1995 were Egypt, South Korea, Taiwan, Saudi Arabia and Japan. This was the first time in 10 years that no NATO ally featured among the five largest recipients of US major conventional weapons, probably reflecting two developments: (*a*) the reduced levels of procurement spending by European members of NATO,[10] and (*b*) the process of disposing of second-hand US weapons previously located in Germany, largely completed by the end of 1994.

In spite of these changes it is clear that imports from the United States will remain a central element in the procurement policy of many European countries, including some of the largest. Among the largest arms transfer agreements reached in 1995 were those for the sale of a total of 97 AH-64D Apache attack helicopters to the UK and the Netherlands, 25 C-130J Hercules transport aircraft to the UK and 22 CH-47 Chinook heavy transport helicopters to the UK.

In 1995 the USA agreed to supply 65 BGM-109 Tomahawk Block III cruise missiles to the UK. Originally designed as nuclear weapon delivery systems, these missiles will be supplied in a version designed to carry conventional warheads and will be carried on British-built nuclear-powered submarines. They will be made by the Hughes company. Another US company, Loral, will provide support services that are as important as the missiles themselves. The Block III Tomahawk is guided by a combination of inertial navigation (which incorporates a global positioning system) and a terrain matching system that compares digital maps stored in an onboard computer with images of the surface over which the missile is flying.[11] A European subsidiary of Loral will work closely with British electronics company GEC, which also owns the shipyard where the submarines that will carry Tomahawk are to be built. It is not known how much technology transfer will take place during this process. However, it is likely that the UK will learn a significant amount about how to manage a complex system on the 'electronic battlefield'. The system depends on information gathered from space-based sensors to which the UK does not have independent access and, to this extent, the systems remain dependent on collaboration with the United States for their effective operation.

Russia

According to SIPRI estimates Russia accounted for 17 per cent of total deliveries of major conventional weapons in 1995, a significant increase over the revised estimate of 4 per cent recorded for 1994. Moreover, Russia reached new agreements in 1995 with China, India and South Korea, suggesting that Russia is likely to retain a significant share of the global arms trade in future.

---

[10] The levels of procurement spending by NATO countries are discussed in chapter 8 in this volume. Historically, many European members of NATO have been significant importers of US weapons. This issue is discussed in *The Challenges Facing the European Defence Related Industry: A Contribution for Action at European Level,* Communication from the Commission to the Council, the European Parliament, the Economic and Social Committee and the Committee of the Regions, Brussels, 25 Jan. 1996.

[11] *Defense News*, 23–29 Jan. 1995, p. 38; and *Jane's Defence Weekly*, 11 Nov. 1995, p. 14.

The five most important customers for Russian arms transfers in 1995 were China, Malaysia, India, Viet Nam and Kazakhstan. Of these countries only two—India and Viet Nam—received significant quantities of major conventional weapons from the Soviet Union during the cold war. China (a major recipient of Soviet military assistance until the break in relations in 1960) re-established its military–technical cooperation with the Soviet Union in 1990 and has deepened this cooperation with Russia during the past four years. Malaysia is a new customer for Russia and had no arms transfer relationship with the Soviet Union. Kazakhstan is a newly independent state that was formerly part of the Soviet Union.

Following the dissolution of the USSR, Russia was forced to devise new administrative practices and mechanisms for conducting its arms trade.[12] At the beginning of 1995 four entities were authorized to conduct negotiations with potential foreign customers for Russian arms. These were Rosvooruzhenie (the State Corporation for Trade in Armaments and Military Technical Cooperation); Promexport (the export agency of the State Committee for Defence Industries), Voentech (an agency of the Russian armed forces charged with disposing of surplus equipment) and the fighter aircraft producer MiG-MAPO.[13]

In 1995 there were some further modifications to the administrative arrangements governing arms exports. Under Presidential Decree no. 1008 of 5 October 1995 the State Committee for Military–Technical Policy was charged with supervising the activities of Promexport.[14] The State Committee is under the direct authority of President Boris Yeltsin although First Deputy Prime Minister Oleg Soskovets discharges this authority on his behalf. This decision, together with the dismissal of Victor Glukikh, Chairman of the State Committee for Defence Industries, at the end of 1995, was seen as evidence that more decision-making authority was being centralized under the Presidency.

By the end of 1995, eight enterprises were authorized to negotiate on arms sales and military–technical cooperation with potential foreign customers.[15]

It appears that these decisions were taken as part of an effort to increase the efficiency of Russian arms-export decision making. The changes reflected lessons learned from an evaluation of Russian successes in winning contracts

[12] These changes are described in Anthony, I. *et al.*, 'Arms production and arms trade', *SIPRI Yearbook 1994* (Oxford University Press: Oxford, 1994), p. 462, and Anthony, I., Wezeman, P. D. and Wezeman, S. T., 'The trade in major conventional weapons', *SIPRI Yearbook 1995: Armaments, Disarmament and International Security* (Oxford University Press: Oxford, 1995), pp. 500–509.

[13] MiG-MAPO received its authorization under Decree no. 479 of 6 May 1994: 'On granting enterprises the right to participate in military technical cooperation between Russia and foreign countries'. In addition the joint stock company Aviaexport is authorized to discuss sales of dual-use aircraft with foreign customers. Authorization to conduct export discussions is separate from the case-by-case licensing of arms exports which is also required before a transfer takes place.

[14] The text of Presidential Decree 1008: 'On Russian Federation Military-Technical Cooperation with Foreign Countries' is reprinted in FBIS-SOV-95-201, 18 Oct. 1995, p. 35.

[15] They were: fighter aircraft manufacturer MiG-MAPO; helicopter maker Rosvertol; light arms manufacturer Luzhmash; maker of air defence systems Antei; a hydraulic equipment manufacturer Gydromash; utility vehicle manufacturer Metrovagonmash; component manufacturer Ufa Production Association; and scientific instrument maker Byuro Priborostroyeniya.

in Cyprus, Malaysia and the United Arab Emirates. In each of these cases Russia won contracts in competition with Western suppliers.[16]

Europe

The share of the global supply of major weapons accounted for by members of the European Union (EU) in 1995 remained roughly stable at 25 per cent (compared with 27 per cent in 1994). However, for the first time the data for 1995 include deliveries from the three new members of the EU: Austria, Finland and Sweden.

FR Germany

According to SIPRI estimates FR Germany remained a significant supplier of major conventional weapons in 1995. Its exports of major conventional weapons can be divided into three categories from the perspective of types of transfer: (a) transfers of new major equipment manufactured in Germany; (b) transfers consisting of licences to produce equipment designed in Germany but assembled elsewhere; and (c) transfers of second-hand equipment considered surplus to German requirements. In recent years surplus equipment has accounted for the largest part of German arms exports and this was again the case in 1995. This equipment has originated from the forces of FR Germany and from the inventories of the former German Democratic Republic and has been transferred either free of charge or at low cost to the recipient. A large part of this equipment has been transferred to the NATO Allies—notably Greece and Turkey—as one element of the implementation of the Treaty on Conventional Armed Forces in Europe (CFE). Some equipment has also been transferred to United Nations peacekeeping forces.

The first two categories consist largely of naval equipment and in 1995 there were no commercial agreements for German arms exports outside the naval sector. According to SIPRI estimates for the most recent years, 71 per cent of FR German transfers of major conventional weapons consisted of ships. According to official German data for the same period the figure was between 71 and 82 per cent, depending on the year.

In terms of the distribution of FR German transfers of major conventional weapons, according to SIPRI estimates 71 per cent were transferred to NATO Allies and Organisation for Economic Co-operation and Development (OECD) member states during the period 1991–94.[17] By comparison, according to official German data for the same period, NATO/OECD states accounted for 79 per cent of transfers.

---

[16] *New Times*, July 1995, pp. 48–49; 'Interview with Alexander Kotelkin', *Jane's Defence Weekly*, 23 Sep. 1995, p. 40; and Kotelkin, A., 'Russian aviation export: a breakthrough into the 21st Century', *Military Technology*, Nov. 1995, p. 15. Kotelkin is the General Director of Rosvooruzhenie.

[17] For a list of OECD member states see the Glossary in this volume.

Table 11.3. Exports of weapons by FR Germany, 1991–94
Values are given in b. DM.

	1991	1992	1993	1994
Total exports (commercial and Ministry of Defence)	4.135	2.638	2.577	2.131
Exports to NATO or NATO similar countries	3.242	1.817	2.219	1.814
Exports to other countries	0.893	0.821	0.358	0.317
Percentage of exports of ships	72	82	71	79
FRG total exports	667	676	599	687
Weapons as a percentage of total exports	0.62	0.39	0.43	0.31

Note: 'NATO similar' countries are mostly members of the Organisation for Economic Co-operation and Development (OECD).

Source: Ministry of Economics, Bonn.

Ukraine

Meeting in November 1995 the Ukrainian and Russian ministers of defence agreed, among other things, that 10 Tu-160 Blackjack and 15 Tu-95MS Bear strategic bombers would be sold to Russia by Ukraine. Payment for these aircraft will be in the form of barter. According to Ukrainian Minister of Defence Valeriy Shmarov 'we signed a document according to which experts will estimate the value of the bombers, though payments will be conducted not in cash, but in spare parts which our air force currently needs very much, including engines (which we simply lack), rubber, undercarriages, weapons, launchers and a number of other things which we currently do not produce'.[18]

These aircraft—while theoretically capable of carrying conventional weapons—are not included in the SIPRI aggregate data for major conventional weapons since their primary mission has been the delivery of nuclear weapons.

Official data on the arms trade

While data are available from some governments concerning the value of their arms transfers, using these data for analysis is difficult for reasons discussed below. Since 1992 some governments have been reporting some of their arms imports and exports on a voluntary basis to the United Nations Register of Conventional Arms. These data, though useful, are provided for only a relatively small segment of arms and military equipment—mostly the major weapon platforms—and the United Nations requests that information be provided at a high level of aggregation. Some governments, although by no means all, take advantage of the opportunity to disaggregate the information that they provide to the UN.

[18] FBIS-SOV-95-232, pp. 63–66.

Official data on the value of the arms trade

From table 11.4 it is clear that there are interesting data available from most of the major suppliers about the aggregate value of their arms exports. Using the SIPRI estimates of deliveries of major conventional weapons as a baseline, these countries together probably account for around 87 per cent of total exports. However, the comparability of data from one country to another is very low as each country compiles the data according to a specific national definition of arms transfers. In some cases the data reflect the value of agreements and in other cases the value of equipment delivered. Some of the data are tied to the licensing process and reflect the value of goods for which licences have been issued, even though delivery of the goods or payment may not yet have occurred. Moreover, as some countries (such as France and the USA) require exporters to obtain a licence to negotiate with prospective foreign customers, some licences may never lead to contracts. In some cases the data only include goods which conform to a narrow definition of munitions or weapons of war. In other cases 'dual-use' equipment is also included. Moreover, the comparability of the data across time also cannot be assumed to be perfect. In at least two cases—Sweden and the UK—the range of equipment for which data are recorded changed during this five-year period. This is typical where the process of valuation is associated with the licensing of exports. As the definition of goods to be licensed changes, the data on value go up or down accordingly.

A comprehensive set of official arms transfer statistics disaggregated both by point of origin/destination and by product type would require a harmonization of the basic definitions of what was to be counted and how. This issue is being considered by the World Trade Organization (WTO) as part of a broader set of discussions about how to improve international trade statistics. However, in its 1994 report on military trade, the WTO Task Force on International Trade Statistics underlined five issues that need to be resolved before the main failings of military trade statistics can be remedied:

1. Many governments are generally unwilling to report transactions of military goods. This is primarily for reasons of national security and/or commercial confidentiality, but other reasons include concern about giving advantage to competitors and concerns about the foreign policy implications of activities by domestic anti-arms trade lobbies.

2. There are no internationally agreed definitions for weapon systems; defence-specific military equipment; or non-defence specific military goods and services purchased by the military. The treatment of dual-use capital is unclear, as is the valuation of military aid in kind, barter trade, counter-trade and offsets.

3. Alternative approaches to measurement can be found in official military trade statistics. One is to include all trade undertaken by or on behalf of military establishments; the other is to include only trade in commodities and services with primarily military uses.

Table 11.4. Official data on arms exports, 1990–94

Country	Currency unit	1990	1991	1992	1993	1994
Australia	A$ m.	156.8	168.8			
Canada	C$ m.	158.8	189.2	361.8	335.9	497.4
Czech Republic	US$ m.				167	
FR Germany	DM m.	1 509	4 135	2 638	2 577	2 131
France	FFr b.	35	20.6	20.8	14.5	
Netherlands	HFL m.	531	691	1 007	1 475	1 006
Poland	US$ m.		396.2	67.3		
Russia	US$ b.				1.6	1.71
South Africa	Rand m.	163	752	463	798	854
Sweden[a]	SEK m.	3 327	2 705	2 753	1 216	1 347
Switzerland	SFr m.			258.8	260.3	221
UK[a]	£ m.	1 980	1 862	1 530	1 914	1 798
USA	US$ b.[b]	7.6	8.6	10.3	11	10
	US$ b.[c]	6.2	5.2	2.7	3.4	1.7

[a] Changes in the coverage of data occurred in 1992–93.

[b] Value of security assistance (arms and transfers) by the US Government.

[c] Value of arms and military and certain dual-use equipment to foreign military establishments by US commercial suppliers.

Sources: Answer of Minister of Defence to House of Representatives, Question no. 1004, Canberra, 1991; Annual Reports, Export of Military Goods from Canada 1990, 1991, 1993, 1994, Exports Controls Division, Export and Import Controls Bureau, Department of Foreign Affairs and International Trade, Ottawa; Ministry of Economics, Bonn; Assemblée Nationale, nr 1560, 5 Oct. 1994, Rapport fait au nom de la commision des finances, annex nr 39; Letter from the Minister of Foreign Affairs to the Chairman of the Second Chamber, DAV/PC-N146/95 appendix 2, 18 Aug. 1995, The Hague; Information from the President of the Main Statistics Bureau of Poland; Appendix to the Draft National Policy for the Defence Industry, Defence Industry Working Group, Transnational Executive Council, Sub-council on Defence, Pretoria, 18 Apr. 1994; Regeringens skrivelse 1994/95:183, Redogörelse för den Svenska Krigsmaterielexporten År 1994 [1994 Report on Swedish exports of military equipment], Stockholm; *Österreichische Militärische Zeitschrift,* no. 3 (1995), p. 357; Information from Czech Embassy in Stockholm, 5 July 1994; Moscow ITAR-TASS World Service in Russian 1519 GMT 7 Feb. 1996; *Military Technology,* Oct. 1995, p. 89; Foreign Military Sales, Foreign Military Construction Sales and Military Assistance Facts, as of September 30, 1994, Process Analysis Integration Division Comptroller, DSAA, Washington, DC; *UK Defence Statistics,* 1995 edn, Government Statistical Service, London.

4. Customs declarations are currently inadequate in terms of coverage. Military goods need not pass through customs and, while defence ministries record all imports and have access to domestic defence suppliers for information on exports, they have no obligation to declare this information.

5. Military trade statistics suffer from traditional weaknesses common to other categories of trade statistics. These weaknesses include how to treat a service embodied in a good; how to determine the country of origin/destination where transshipment or intermediate assembly occurs; revisions to

Table 11.5. Government returns to the UN Register for calendar years 1992, 1993 and 1994 as of 1 March 1996

State	Data on imports			Data on exports			Explanation submitted in *note verbale*			Background information		
	1992	1993	1994	1992	1993	1994	1992	1993	1994	1992	1993	1994
Afghanistan	–	–	–	–	–	–	–	yes	–	–	no	–
Albania	nil	–	–	nil	–	–	–	–	–	yes	–	–
Antigua & Barbuda	nil	nil	–	nil	nil	–	–	–	–	no	no	–
Argentina	nil	yes	yes	yes	nil	nil	–	–	–	no	yes	yes
Armenia	–	nil	nil	–	nil	nil	–	–	–	–	no	yes
Australia	yes	yes	yes	nil	nil	nil	–	–	–	yes	yes	yes
Austria	–	nil	yes	yes	nil	nil	–	–	yes	yes	yes	yes
Bahamas	–	–	nil	–	–	nil	–	–	–	–	–	no
Barbados	–	–	nil	–	–	nil	–	–	–	–	–	no
Belarus	nil	nil	–	yes	yes	yes	–	–	–	no	yes	no
Belgium	yes	yes	nil	nil		yes	yes			yes	yes	yes
Belize	–	–	nil	–		nil	–	–	–	–	–	no
Benin	–	–	nil	–	–	nil	–	–	–	–	–	no
Bhutan	nil	nil	nil	nil	nil	nil	–	–	–	no	no	no
Bolivia	yes	–	–	–	–	–	–	–	–	no	–	–
Brazil	yes	yes	yes	yes	nil	nil	–	–	–	yes	yes	yes
Bulgaria	yes	nil	–	yes	yes	yes	–	–	–	yes	yes	yes
Burkina Faso	–	nil	nil	–	nil	nil	–	–	–	–	no	no
Cameroon	–	–	nil	–	–	nil	–	–	–	–	–	no
Canada	yes	yes	yes	yes	yes	yes	–	–	–	yes	yes	yes
Chad	–	–	nil	–	yes	nil	–	–	–	–	no	no
Chile	yes	nil	yes	nil	nil	nil	–	–	–	yes	yes	no
China	yes	nil	yes	yes	yes	yes	–	–	–	no	no	no
Colombia	yes	–	–	nil	–	–	yes	–	–	no	–	–
Comoros	–	nil	–	–	nil	–	–	–	–	–	yes	–
Côte d'Ivoire	–	nil	–	–	nil	–	–	–	–	–	yes	–
Croatia	nil	nil	nil	nil	nil	nil	yes	yes	yes	no	no	no
Cuba	nil	nil	nil	nil	nil	nil	yes	–	–	no	no	no
Cyprus	–	nil	yes	–	nil	nil	–	–	–	–	no	no
Czech Republic	nil	yes	nil	yes	yes	yes	–	–	–	yes	yes	yes
Denmark	yes	nil	yes	nil	yes	nil	–	–	–	yes	yes	yes
Dominica	nil	nil	nil	nil	nil	nil	–	–	–	no	no	no
Dominican Rep.	–	nil	–	–	nil	–	–	–	–	–	no	–
Ecuador	–	–	nil	–	–	nil	–	–	–	–	–	no
Egypt	yes	–	–	yes	–	–	yes	–	–	no	–	–
El Salvador	–	–	–	–	–	–	–	–	–	–	–	yes
Estonia	–	–	yes	–	–	nil	–	–	–	–	–	no
Fiji	nil	nil	nil	nil	nil	nil	yes	–	–	no	no	no
Finland	yes	yes	yes	yes	yes	yes	–	–	–	yes	yes	no
France	nil	nil	yes	yes	yes	yes	–	–	–	yes	yes	yes
Georgia	nil	nil	nil	nil	nil	nil	yes	–	–	no	no	no
Germany	yes	nil	yes	yes	yes	yes	–	–	–	yes	yes	yes
Greece	yes	yes	yes	yes	–	–	yes	–	–	yes	yes	yes
Grenada	nil	nil	nil	bl.	nil	nil	–	–	bl.	no	no	no
Guyana	–	–	nil	–	–	nil	–	–	–	–	–	no
Hungary	nil	yes	yes	nil	nil	–	–	–	–	yes	yes	no
Iceland	nil	nil	nil	nil	nil	nil	yes	–	–	no	no	no
India	yes	nil	yes	yes	yes	nil	–	–	–	no	no	no

Table 11.5 *contd*

State	Data on imports			Data on exports			Explanation submitted in *note verbale*			Background information		
	1992	1993	1994	1992	1993	1994	1992	1993	1994	1992	1993	1994
Indonesia	nil	yes	yes	–	–	–	–	–	–	no	no	no
Iran	yes	yes	yes	nil	nil	nil	–	yes	–	no	no	no
Ireland	nil	nil	yes	nil	nil	nil	–	–	–	no	no	no
Israel	yes	yes	yes	yes	yes	yes	–	–	–	yes	yes	no
Italy	yes	yes	yes	yes	yes	yes	–	–	–	yes	yes	yes
Jamaica	–	–	nil	–	–	nil	yes	yes	yes	no	no	yes
Japan	yes	yes	yes	nil	nil	nil				yes	yes	yes
Jordan	–	nil	–	–	nil	–	–	–	–	–	no	–
Kazakhstan	nil		nil	nil		nil	yes	–	–	no	–	no
Kenya	–	nil	–	–	nil	–	–	–	–	–	no	–
Korea, South	yes	yes	yes	nil	yes	yes	–	–	–	yes	yes	yes
Lebanon	nil	–	–	nil	–	–	yes	–	–	no	–	–
Lesotho	nil	–	–	nil	–	–	yes	–	–	no	–	–
Libya	nil	–	nil	nil	–	nil	yes	–	yes	no	–	no
Liechtenstein	nil	nil	nil	nil	nil	nil	yes			no	no	no
Lithuania	yes	–	–	–	–	–	–	–	–	no	–	–
Luxembourg	nil	nil	–	nil	nil	nil	–	–	–	no	no	no
Madagascar	–	nil	–	–	nil	–	–	–	–	–	no	–
Malawi	–	nil	–	–	nil	–	–	–	–	–	no	–
Malaysia	nil	yes	yes	nil	nil	nil	yes	–	–	no	no	no
Maldives	nil	nil	nil	nil	nil	nil	–	–	–	no	no	no
Malta	yes	nil	nil	nil	nil	nil	–	–	–	no	no	yes
Marshall Islands	–	nil	nil	–	nil	nil	–	–	–	–	no	yes
Mauritania	–	nil	nil	–	nil	nil	–	–	–	no	no	no
Mauritius	–	nil	–	nil	nil	–	yes	–	–	no	no	–
Mexico	–	nil	yes	–	nil	nil	yes	–	–	no	yes	yes
Moldova	–	–	yes	–	–	yes	–	–	–	–	–	no
Mongolia	nil	nil	nil	nil	nil	nil	yes	–	–	no	no	no
Namibia	nil	–	–	nil	–	–	–	–	–	no	–	–
Nepal	yes	nil	nil		nil	nil	–	–	–	no	no	no
Netherlands	yes	yes	yes	yes	yes	yes	yes	yes	–	yes	yes	yes
New Zealand	yes	yes	yes	nil	nil	nil	–	–	–	yes	yes	yes
Nicaragua	–	–	–	–	–	–	yes	–	–	yes	–	–
Niger	n.v.	nil	nil	nil	nil	nil	yes	–	–	no	yes	yes
Nigeria	–	–	–	–	–	–	yes	–	–	no	–	–
Norway	yes	yes	nil	nil	nil	nil	–	–	–	yes	no	no
Oman	–	–	–	–	–	–	yes	–	–	no	–	–
Pakistan	yes	yes	yes	nil	nil	nil	–	–	–	no	no	no
Panama	–	–	nil	–	–	nil	yes	–	–	yes	–	no
Papua New Guinea	nil	–	nil	nil	–	nil	–	–	yes	no	–	no
Paraguay	–	–	–	–	–	–	yes	–	–	no	yes	yes
Peru	yes	yes	yes	bl.	nil	nil	–	–	–	no	no	no
Philippines	yes	yes	yes	nil	–	–	yes	–	–	no	no	no
Poland	yes	nil	nil	yes	yes	yes	–	–	–	yes	yes	yes
Portugal	yes	yes	yes	nil	nil	nil	–	–	–	yes	yes	yes
Qatar	–	–	–	–	–	–	–	–	–	yes	–	–
Romania	yes	nil	yes	yes	yes	yes	–	–	–	no	no	no
Russian Federation	nil	nil	nil	yes	yes	yes	–	–	–	no	no	no
Saint Lucia	nil	nil	nil	nil	nil	nil	–	–	–	–	–	no

State	Data on imports			Data on exports			Explanation submitted in *note verbale*			Background information		
	1992	1993	1994	1992	1993	1994	1992	1993	1994	1992	1993	1994
Saint Vincent & the Grenadines	–	nil	–	–	nil	–	–	–	–	–	no	–
Samoa	–	nil	nil	–	nil	nil	–	–	–	–	no	no
Senegal	nil	–	–	nil	–	–	yes	–	–	no	–	–
Seychelles	nil	–	–	nil	–	–	–	–	–	no	–	–
Sierra Leone	–	–	–	–	–	–	–	–	–	–	yes	–
Singapore	yes	yes	yes	nil	nil	nil	–	–	–	no	no	no
Slovakia	nil	yes	yes	yes	yes	yes	yes	yes	–	no	no	no
Slovenia	nil	nil	nil	nil	nil	nil	yes	–	–	no	no	no
Solomon Islands	nil	–	nil	nil	–	nil	yes	–	–	no	–	no
South Africa	–	–	nil	–	–	yes	yes	–	–	no	–	yes
Spain	yes	yes	yes	nil	nil	nil	–	–	–	yes	yes	yes
Sri Lanka	yes	–	–	–	–	–	yes	–	–	no	–	–
Sweden	yes	yes	yes	yes	yes	nil	–	–	–	yes	yes	yes
Switzerland	nil	nil	nil	nil	yes	nil	–	–	–	yes	yes	yes
Tajikistan	–	–	nil	–	–	nil	–	–	–	–	–	no
Tanzania	nil	nil	nil	nil	nil	nil	–	–	–	no	no	no
Thailand	–	yes	yes	–	–	nil	–	–	–	–	no	no
Trinidad & Tobago	–	nil	–	–	nil	–	–	–	–	–	no	–
Tunisia	–	–	–	–	–	–	yes	–	–	no	–	–
Turkey	yes	yes	yes	nil	nil	nil	–	–	–	yes	no	no
UK	yes	nil	yes	yes	yes	yes	–	–	–	yes	yes	yes
Ukraine	nil	nil	nil	nil	yes	yes	–	–	–	no	no	no
USA	yes	yes	yes	yes	yes	yes	yes	yes	yes	yes	yes	yes
Vanuatu	nil	nil	–	nil	nil	–	yes	–	–	no	no	–
Viet Nam	–	–	nil	–	–	–	–	–	–	–	–	no
Yugoslavia (Serbia & Montenegro)	nil	nil	nil	nil	nil	nil	yes	yes	yes	yes	no	no

Note: n.v. = *note verbale*; bl. = blank.

Source: The composite table of replies of governments to the UN Register, supplied by the United Nations Centre for Disarmament Affairs, 4 Mar. 1996.

published data based on new information or changes in definitions; the time lag in reporting; and the absence of standard quantity units.[19]

Two different approaches to solving some of these problems have been examined. The first relies on reporting by the purchasing agency in the recipient country, supplemented by information from the supplier (either the government or the producer as appropriate). The second approach relies on reporting at the point where the goods cross an international border. The first approach would require a fundamental revision by government purchasing agencies of their attitudes towards public disclosure of defence-related information. In the short term, therefore, the second approach has been adopted by the World Trade Organization. In September 1995, a subcommittee of the

[19] GATT, *Task Force on International Trade Statistics: Military Trade*, Geneva 14–16 Nov. 1994.

World Customs Organization (WCO) discussed possible revisions to the existing Harmonized System of classifying goods proposed by the WTO for application by all WCO members. Modifications could include creating new product identification codes that would allow customs officers to classify military trade into discrete categories and subcategories. The Harmonized System is reviewed every five years and a new schedule came into effect on 1 January 1996. Therefore, if modifications to the Harmonized System were to be accepted, they would not be implemented until after 2000.[20]

The United Nations Register of Conventional Arms

On 13 October the UN Secretary-General presented the third annual report on the United Nations Register of Conventional Arms.[21] By 1 March 1996, 93 governments had submitted data and information on their imports and exports of battle tanks, armoured combat vehicles, large-calibre artillery systems, attack helicopters, combat aircraft, warships and missiles and missile systems—the seven categories of arms defined by UN Resolution 46/36L of 9 December 1991—for calendar year 1994.[22] The status of returns to the UN Register as of 1 March is summarized in table 11.5.

As in earlier years, the UN Register provided official confirmation of some broad trends already visible from non-government data. However, the importance of the UN Register is that this information, because of its official character, can more easily form the basis for bilateral and multilateral discussions between governments. The most important general trends were the large volume of surplus equipment being disposed of by the USA, Germany and, to a lesser extent, the Netherlands. The main recipients of these surplus weapons in 1994 were Greece and Turkey, although another NATO member—Portugal—also received a small quantity of surplus equipment in 1994.

Below this level of general trends it is difficult to establish the flow of weapons because of the lack of consistency in the returns submitted by the member states. This has been a feature of all three of the annual reports on the UN Register.[23]

One form of inconsistency within the Register arises when either the supplier or recipient fails to report. Using the supplier information, for example, it

[20] World Customs Organization, *Observations of the Harmonized System Review Sub-Committee on Proposals by the World Trade Organization Concerning the Possible Incorporation in the HS of Goods for Military Use*, Doc.39.580E, 12 Sep. 1995.

[21] UN, United Nations Register of Conventional Arms: Report of the Secretary General, UN document A/50/547, 13 Oct. 1995.

[22] The background to the establishment of the UN Register and its structure is described in Laurance, E. J., Wezeman, S. T. and Wulf, H., *Arms Watch: SIPRI Report on the First Year of the UN Register of Conventional Arms*, SIPRI Research Report no. 6 (Oxford University Press: Oxford, 1993).

[23] One analysis of the UN Register has suggested that these inconsistencies require 5 remedies: increased participation by governments; a review of the category definitions used in the Register; a consensus on the definition of an arms transfer; greater sharing of national information on arms trade laws and procedures; and the development of a UN consultative mechanism through which governments could address the political and military implications of the data contained in the Register. Laurance, E. J. and Keith, T., *An Evaluation of the Third Year of Reporting to the United Nations Register of Conventional Arms* (Monterey Institute of International Studies, Monterey: Calif., 31 Oct. 1995).

is possible to determine that Egypt received a large quantity of tanks, armoured combat vehicles, large-calibre artillery pieces and combat aircraft in 1994. However, because Egypt did not submit a return for calendar year 1994 it is impossible to confirm this picture of events using official information. Moreover, because the USA provides no supplementary information to elaborate its return to the UN Register it is not possible to determine from the US export return how much if any of this equipment was new and how much was second-hand.

A second form of inconsistency occurs when the recipient and supplier both report but their returns contain different and irreconcilable information. For example, while the United States reported delivering 120 armoured combat vehicles to Greece in 1994, Greece did not report receiving any vehicles.

Nevertheless, as in previous years, the UN Register provided some new information that was not previously known to SIPRI and confirmed some information which was available but either incomplete or insufficiently consistent to include in the annual SIPRI register. The most interesting examples of new information in 1994 were contained in the reports by Bulgaria, Moldova, Poland, Romania, Russia and Slovakia. The information provided by these countries in 1994 was the most valuable element of the UN Register.

Perhaps of most interest were the reports that Poland, Russia and Slovakia exported a significant number of armoured vehicles and artillery to Angola.

III. The pattern of arms transfers after the cold war

Five years after the end of the cold war, how has the international arms trade system changed? This section does not attempt to provide a definitive answer to the question. It sets out first to describe how certain patterns of arms transfer behaviour have changed in the past five years, using the information contained in the SIPRI arms trade database, and, second, to relate these changes to some broad post-cold war developments. The discussion is confined to those issues to which SIPRI data can properly be applied.

The size and shape of the arms trade are determined by deeper events and processes. Measurements and analyses of the arms trade are, according to this perspective, useful empirical tools that can shed some light on the deeper processes themselves.

Three broad categories of development make an impact on the international arms trade: politico-military developments, technology developments and economic developments.[24] All of these developments occur at two levels: the systemic level (meaning both the international system itself and its various

[24] For general discussions of the international arms trade see: Harkavy, R. E., *The Arms Trade and International Systems* (Ballinger: Cambridge, Mass., 1975); Neuman, S. G. and Harkavy, R. E., *Arms Transfers in the Modern World* (Praeger: New York, 1979); Kolodziej, E., *Making and Marketing Arms: The French Experience and its Implications for the International System* (Princeton University Press: Princeton, N.J., 1987); Krause, K., *Arms and the State: Patterns of Military Production and Trade* (Cambridge University Press: Cambridge, 1992); and Laurance, E. J., *The International Arms Trade* (Lexington Books: New York, 1992).

Table 11.6. The leading suppliers and recipients of major conventional weapons
Figures are percentages.

	1986	1987	1988	1989	1990	1991	1992	1993	1994	1995
Suppliers										
6 largest suppliers as % of total deliveries	88	87	86	88	90	89	88	89	85	83
United States	27	28	30	28	34	49	56	52	56	43
USSR/Russia	43	40	38	39	35	18	12	15	4	17
FR Germany	3	2	3	3	5	10	6	7	11	9
United Kingdom	4	5	3	7	5	4	4	5	7	7
China	4	7	6	4	4	4	5	5	3	4
France	9	6	6	7	7	4	5	6	4	4
Recipients										
10 largest recipients as % of total deliveries	64	65	63	63	59	51	58	56	52	52
30 largest recipients as % of total deliveries	86	85	84	86	84	87	93	92	89	86

Source: SIPRI arms trade database.

regional subsystems) and the domestic level in the major supplier and recipient countries which dominate the trade.

Changing patterns in transfers of major conventional weapons

The trade in major conventional weapons has always occurred within a highly concentrated group of states. Table 11.6 indicates the percentage of total deliveries accounted for by the 6 largest suppliers and the 30 largest recipients in the 10-year period 1986–95.

Among suppliers the concentration of deliveries within the six largest suppliers is very high across the period. However, there seems to have been a decrease in the share accounted for by the six largest suppliers in 1994–95. Other suppliers—such as the Netherlands, Canada, Israel, Italy, the Czech Republic and some of the newly independent states on the territory of the former Soviet Union—account for small shares but seem to be increasing their importance as arms suppliers.

The data in the table suggest that while levels of concentration have remained broadly consistent over the 10 years, the distribution of transfers has changed. The most notable feature of the data is the extent to which the share accounted for by the USA increased dramatically after 1989–90 while that accounted for by the USSR and then Russia declined over the same period.

Within the data for the USA there have been very few changes during the period 1986–95. Between 1986 and 1990, 83 per cent of US deliveries of

Table 11.7. The 15 leading recipients of major conventional weapons, 1986–90 and 1991–95

Major recipients 1986–90	Major recipients 1991–95	Countries common to both periods
Afghanistan	Canada	Egypt
Angola	China	India
Czechoslovakia	Egypt	Japan
Egypt	FR Germany	Saudi Arabia
GDR	Greece	Turkey
North Korea	India	
India	Israel	
Iraq	Japan	
Japan	Kuwait	
Poland	Pakistan	
Saudi Arabia	Saudi Arabia	
Soviet Union	South Korea	
Spain	Taiwan	
Syria	Thailand	
Turkey	Turkey	

Source: SIPRI arms trade database.

major conventional weapons were to allies (members of NATO and the Australia, New Zealand and United States Treaty, ANZUS) or close friends (Japan, South Korea, Israel, Egypt and Saudi Arabia). A total of 94 per cent of deliveries were made to the 20 largest recipients of US major conventional weapons. Between 1991 and 1995, 81 per cent of deliveries were made to allies and close friends, while 96 per cent of deliveries were made to the 20 largest recipients.

Between 1986 and 1990, 68 per cent of deliveries from the Soviet Union were made to allies (members of the Warsaw Treaty Organization) or close friends (countries with which the USSR had a Treaty of Friendship). After 1991, 50 per cent of Russian arms deliveries were made to countries which formerly belonged to the group of Soviet allies and friends. This was in spite of the dissolution of the Warsaw Treaty Organization and the decision by Moscow to re-evaluate its relations with important Soviet arms clients in the developing world.

From a recipient perspective, the concentration among the 10 largest recipients appears to have been somewhat reduced over this 10-year period while the level of concentration among the 30 largest recipients has, if anything, increased. There have also been changes in the identity of the largest recipients across the period 1986–95. The 15 recipient countries that received the largest volume of major conventional weapons in this period are listed in table 11.7.

Table 11.8. Diversification of suppliers for selected recipients, 1976–95

	1976–80	1981–85	1986–90	1991–95
Egypt				
Number of suppliers	6	11	9	5
Top supplier (%)	52	67	73	92
Top 3 suppliers (%)	94	87	93	100
Names of top 3 suppliers	USA	USA	USA	USA
	France	China	France	Czech Rep.
	China	France	Italy	Netherlands
India				
Number of suppliers	7	6	9	10
Top supplier (%)	85	76	77	69
Top 3 suppliers (%)	97	99	92	85
Names of top 3 suppliers	USSR	USSR	USSR	Russia
	UK	UK	France	UK
	France	France	UK	Netherlands
Japan				
Number of suppliers	2	3	3	4
Top supplier (%)	99	99	97	97
Top 3 suppliers (%)	100	100	100	100
Names of top 3 suppliers	USA	USA	USA	USA
	FR Germany	FR Germany	Fr Germany	FR Germany
	Switzerland	UK	France	UK
Saudi Arabia				
Number of suppliers	5	8	12	6
Top supplier (%)	72	76	33	73
Top 3 suppliers (%)	98	98	81	94
Names of top 3 suppliers	USA	USA	USA	USA
	France	France	UK	UK
	Italy	Italy	France	Canada
Turkey				
Number of suppliers	6	9	10	8
Top supplier (%)	53	35	46	74
Top 3 suppliers (%)	95	80	82	95
Names of top 3 suppliers	USA	FR Germany	USA	USA
	FR Germany	USA	FR Germany	FR Germany
	Italy	UK	UK	Italy

Source: SIPRI arms trade database.

In the first period, nine of these countries were predominantly or entirely dependent on the Soviet Union and its allies for conventional weapons. In the second period, nine of them were predominantly or entirely dependent on the United States and its allies for conventional weapons. Five countries in the first period and eight countries in the second period are classified as having multiple arms suppliers.[25] On the face of it this would suggest a growing

[25] These classifications are elaborated in Harkavy, R. E., 'The changing international system and the arms trade', eds R. E. Harkavy and S. G. Neuman, *The Arms Trade: Problems and Prospects in the Post-Cold War Period*, Annals of the American Academy of Political and Social Science, vol. 535, special edition, Sep. 1994.

tendency to diversify supply. However, looking at the specific patterns of deliveries to the five countries which appear in both time periods (the right-hand column in table 11.7) raises a question against this finding. An analysis of the specific patterns of the five countries which appeared in the list of major recipients throughout the period 1986–91 is shown from 1976 in table 11.8.

The data suggest that in these five countries the importance of bilateral arms transfers from a single supplier—usually the USA—has increased in the period 1991–95. In Egypt, where there was significant diversification between at least three suppliers prior to 1986, the United States has emerged as the dominant source of supply. In Japan there has been no change in the position of the USA as a virtual monopoly supplier. In Saudi Arabia there is evidence of considerable diversification during the period 1986–90, but there is also evidence that this pattern was reversed during the subsequent five years. In Turkey there is evidence of diversification in the period 1981–90, but again this trend appears to have been reversed. In India there is evidence of the impact of a policy of diversifying suppliers of major conventional weapons.

Observations on the data presented in section III

At the broadest level, the above data tend to reinforce some of the traditional propositions about the trade in major conventional weapons. First, the trade is concentrated among a small number of suppliers and a relatively small number of recipients. The identity of the suppliers conforms closely to the group of major powers as identified by other indicators (such as size of gross domestic product and representation on the UN Security Council). Second, the pattern of arms transfers is heavily dominated by the nature of security arrangements between supplier and recipient. Third, bilateral relationships seem to be durable in the sense that equipment dependencies remain for a considerable period after a change in political alignment.

The data suggest there is much continuity in these very broad patterns of supply, but some elements of discontinuity also appear on closer examination.

The countries previously supplied by the USSR and its allies have found it difficult to find alternative sources of major conventional weapons. By contrast, there is evidence that within the group of states that traditionally relied on the Western Allies for major conventional weapons, the USA has consolidated its dominance at the expense of West European suppliers.

As noted in section II, there is also some support for the suggestion that the importance of motivations other than security assistance is growing. Countries such as Kuwait, Taiwan and the countries of South-East Asia not only face traditional security dilemmas but also have the capacity to pay in hard currency for major systems. This capacity to pay is probably given more weight by suppliers in their decision making compared with such factors as political alignment, access to bases and other facilities considered to have strategic importance and that were weighted more heavily during the cold war.

Appendix 11A. Tables of the volume of the trade in major conventional weapons, 1986–95

IAN ANTHONY, GERD HAGMEYER-GAVERUS, PIETER D. WEZEMAN and SIEMON T. WEZEMAN

Table 11A.1. Volume of imports of major conventional weapons
Figures are SIPRI trend-indicator values, as expressed in US $m., at constant (1990) prices.

	1986	1987	1988	1989	1990	1991	1992	1993	1994	1995
World total	44 854	46 534	39 455	38 284	31 296	25 819	24 532	24 743	22 842	22 797
Developing world	29 583	30 589	22 701	21 759	18 095	13 995	12 072	13 293	13 252	16 073
LDCs	1 731	1 367	2 286	3 496	3 103	1 703	313	414	128	456
Industrialized world	15 271	15 945	16 754	16 525	13 201	11 824	12 460	11 450	9 590	6 724
Africa	3 591	3 218	2 470	2 027	1 708	794	618	313	574	450
Sub-Saharan	2 450	2 599	2 003	575	1 206	144	539	146	203	126
Americas	2 980	3 405	1 819	2 405	1 721	2 321	1 756	1 496	2 301	2 117
North	1 103	1 371	915	781	457	1 347	1 164	1 079	1 512	887
Central	742	327	206	385	443	145	..	3	..	..
South	1 136	1 708	698	1 239	821	829	593	413	789	1 230
Asia	11 702	11 900	11 739	13 914	10 922	9 073	7 074	6 851	6 842	10 140
Europe	11 803	12 626	13 659	13 220	10 212	7 911	9 235	8 433	7 165	4 550
Middle East	14 060	14 831	8 846	5 871	6 354	5 394	5 310	6 853	5 727	5 295
Oceania	718	554	922	847	379	326	539	798	233	245
ASEAN	1 063	1 478	1 371	902	1 231	1 189	1 092	765	2 354	3 379
EU	3 751	3 411	4 781	5 020	3 941	5 429	6 732	4 440	4 617	2 232
NATO	4 722	5 803	6 894	7 467	5 335	7 823	8 989	6 999	7 389	3 993
OECD	7 925	8 473	9 942	10 473	8 460	10 900	12 116	9 973	9 386	5 541
OPEC	10 342	9 990	6 251	6 226	5 803	3 751	2 767	5 317	3 775	3 497
OSCE	12 804	13 832	14 341	13 964	10 625	9 253	10 371	9 213	8 555	5 463

Note: Tables 11A.1 and 11A.2 show the volume of trade for the different regional groupings to which countries are assigned in the SIPRI arms trade database. Since many countries are included in more than one group totals cannot be derived from the tables. The following countries are included in each group:

Developing world: Afghanistan, Algeria, Angola, Argentina, Bahamas, Bahrain, Bangladesh, Barbados, Belize, Benin, Bhutan, Bolivia, Botswana, Brazil, Brunei, Burkina Faso, Burundi, Cameroon, Cape Verde, Central African Republic, Chad, Chile, China, Colombia, Comoros, Congo, Costa Rica, Côte d'Ivoire, Cuba, Cyprus, Djibouti, Dominica, Dominican Republic, Ecuador, Egypt, El Salvador, Equatorial Guinea, Eritrea, Ethiopia, Fiji, Gabon, Gambia, Ghana, Guatemala, Guinea, Guinea-Bissau, Guyana, Haiti, Honduras, India, Indonesia, Iran, Iraq, Israel, Jamaica, Jordan, Kampuchea, Kenya, Kiribati, North Korea, South Korea, Kuwait, Laos, Lebanon, Lesotho, Liberia, Libya, Madagascar, Malawi, Malaysia, Maldives, Mali, Marshall Islands, Mauritania, Mauritius, Mexico, Micronesia, Mongolia, Morocco, Mozambique, Myanmar, Namibia, Nepal, Nicaragua, Niger, Nigeria, Oman, Pakistan, Panama, Papua New Guinea, Paraguay, Peru, Philippines, Qatar, Rwanda, Samoa, Saudi Arabia, Senegal, Seychelles, Sierra Leone, Singapore, Solomon Islands, Somalia, South Africa, Sri Lanka, St Vincent & the Grenadines, Sudan, Surinam, Swaziland, Syria, Tahiti, Taiwan, Tanzania, Thailand, Togo, Tonga, Trinidad & Tobago, Tunisia, Tuvalu, Uganda, United Arab Emirates, Uruguay, Vanuatu, Venezuela, Viet Nam, North Yemen (–1990), South Yemen (–1990), Yemen (1991–), Zaire, Zambia, Zimbabwe.

Least developed countries (LDCs): Afghanistan, Bangladesh, Benin, Bhutan, Botswana, Burkina Faso, Burundi, Cape Verde, Central African Republic, Chad, Comoros, Djibouti, Equatorial Guinea, Eritrea, Ethiopia, Gambia, Guinea, Guinea-Bissau, Haiti, Laos, Lesotho, Liberia, Malawi, Maldives,

Table 11A.2. Volume of exports of major conventional weapons
Figures are SIPRI trend-indicator values, as expressed in US $m., at constant (1990) prices.

	1986	1987	1988	1989	1990	1991	1992	1993	1994	1995
World total	44 854	46 535	39 455	38 284	31 296	25 819	24 533	24 744	22 841	22 797
Developing world	2 775	4 565	3 322	2 056	1 627	1 705	1 725	2 197	1 158	1 410
LDCs	31	91	3	..	..	..	..	..	..	..
Industrialized world	42 079	41 970	36 133	36 228	29 669	24 114	22 808	22 547	21 683	21 387
Africa	85	247	125	..	38	35	88	34	..	11
Sub-Saharan	48	162	63	..	8	35	88	34	..	11
Americas	12 420	13 664	12 047	10 776	10 651	12 632	14 097	13 046	13 146	10 236
North	12 236	13 250	11 747	10 694	10 567	12 582	13 925	12 968	13 084	10 196
Central	..	1	..	1	4	2	99	53	..	..
South	184	413	300	81	79	48	73	24	61	40
Asia	2 013	3 382	2 437	1 564	1 343	1 426	1 262	1 784	1 258	1 561
Europe	29 708	28 702	24 379	25 524	18 994	11 473	8 868	9 555	8 165	10 637
Middle East	604	521	460	410	162	190	216	315	261	337
Oceania	24	18	7	10	108	62	2	10	12	14
ASEAN	14	22	42	8	1	1	4	14	32	28
EU	8 258	7 529	6 772	8 030	6 505	5 622	4 948	5 264	6 290	5 778
NATO	20 132	20 454	17 994	18 359	16 759	18 148	18 704	18 202	19 346	15 726
OECD	20 780	20 932	18 674	19 048	17 477	18 740	19 218	18 354	19 576	16 171
OPEC	98	242	252	26	33	18	..	57	8	25
OSCE	41 945	41 952	36 126	36 218	29 561	24 056	22 793	22 378	21 627	21 180

Mali, Mauritania, Mozambique, Myanmar, Nepal, Niger, Rwanda, Samoa, Sierra Leone, Somalia, Sudan, Tanzania, Togo, Uganda, Vanuatu, Yemen (1991–), North Yemen (–1990), South Yemen (–1990).

Industrialized world: Albania, Armenia (1992–), Australia, Austria, Azerbaijan (1992–), Belarus (1992–), Belgium, Bosnia and Herzegovina (1992–), Bulgaria, Canada, Croatia (1992–), Czechoslovakia (–1992), Czech Republic (1993–), Denmark, Estonia (1991–), Finland, France, Georgia (1992–), FR Germany (–1990), German DR (–1990), Germany (1990–), Greece, Hungary, Iceland, Ireland, Italy, Japan, Kazakhstan (1992–), Kyrgyzstan (1992–), Latvia (1991–), Liechtenstein, Lithuania (1991–), Luxembourg, Macedonia (1992–), Malta, Moldova (1992–), Monaco, Netherlands, New Zealand, Norway, Poland, Portugal, Romania, Russia (1992–), Slovakia (1993–), Slovenia (1992–), Spain, Sweden, Switzerland, Tajikistan (1992–), Turkey, Turkmenistan (1992–), UK, Ukraine (1992–), USA, USSR (–1991), Uzbekistan (1992–), Yugoslavia (–1991), Yugoslavia (Serbia and Montenegro) (1992–).

Africa: Algeria, Angola, Benin, Botswana, Burkina Faso, Burundi, Cameroon, Cape Verde, Central African Republic, Chad, Comoros, Congo, Côte d'Ivoire, Djibouti, Equatorial Guinea, Eritrea, Ethiopia, Gabon, Gambia, Ghana, Guinea, Guinea-Bissau, Kenya, Lesotho, Liberia, Libya, Madagascar, Malawi, Mali, Mauritania, Mauritius, Morocco, Mozambique, Namibia, Niger, Nigeria, Rwanda, Senegal, Seychelles, Sierra Leone, Somalia, South Africa, Sudan, Swaziland, Tanzania, Togo, Tunisia, Uganda, Zaire, Zambia, Zimbabwe.

Sub-Saharan Africa: Angola, Benin, Botswana, Burkina Faso, Burundi, Cameroon, Cape Verde, Central African Republic, Chad, Comoros, Congo, Côte d'Ivoire, Djibouti, Equatorial Guinea, Eritrea, Ethiopia, Gabon, Gambia, Ghana, Guinea, Guinea-Bissau, Kenya, Lesotho, Liberia, Madagascar,

Malawi, Mali, Mauritania, Mauritius, Mozambique, Namibia, Niger, Nigeria, Rwanda, Senegal, Seychelles, Sierra Leone, Somalia, South Africa, Sudan, Swaziland, Tanzania, Togo, Uganda, Zaire, Zambia, Zimbabwe.

Americas: Argentina, Bahamas, Barbados, Belize, Bolivia, Brazil, Canada, Chile, Colombia, Costa Rica, Cuba, Dominica, Dominican Republic, Ecuador, El Salvador, Guatemala, Guyana, Haiti, Honduras, Jamaica, Mexico, Nicaragua, Panama, Paraguay, Peru, St Vincent & the Grenadines, Suriname, Trinidad & Tobago, Uruguay, USA, Venezuela.

North America: Canada, Mexico, USA.

Central America: Barbados, Bahamas, Belize, Costa Rica, Cuba, Dominica, Dominican Republic, Guatemala, Haiti, Honduras, Jamaica, Nicaragua, Panama, El Salvador, St Vincent & the Grenadines, Trinidad & Tobago.

South America: Argentina, Bolivia, Brazil, Chile, Colombia, Ecuador, Guyana, Paraguay, Peru, Suriname, Uruguay, Venezuela.

Asia: Afghanistan, Bangladesh, Bhutan, Brunei, China, India, Indonesia, Japan, Kampuchea, Kazakhstan (1992–), North Korea, South Korea, Kyrgyzstan (1992–), Laos, Malaysia, Maldives, Mongolia, Myanmar, Nepal, Pakistan, Philippines, Singapore, Sri Lanka, Taiwan, Tajikistan (1992–), Thailand, Turkmenistan (1992–), Uzbekistan (1992–), Viet Nam.

Europe: Albania, Armenia (1992–), Austria, Azerbaijan (1992–), Belarus (1992–), Belgium, Bosnia and Herzegovina (1992–), Bulgaria, Croatia (1992–), Cyprus, Czechoslovakia (–1992), Czech Republic (1993–), Denmark, Estonia (1991–), Finland, France, Georgia (1992–), FR Germany (–1990), German DR (–1990), Germany (1990–), Greece, Hungary, Iceland, Ireland, Italy, Latvia (1991–), Liechtenstein, Lithuania (1991–), Luxembourg, Macedonia (1992–), Malta, Moldova (1992–), Monaco, Netherlands, Norway, Poland, Portugal, Romania, Russia (1992–), Slovakia (1993–), Slovenia (1992–), Spain, Sweden, Switzerland, Turkey, UK, Ukraine (1992–), USSR (–1991), Yugoslavia (–1991), Yugoslavia (Serbia and Montenegro) (1992–).

Middle East: Bahrain, Egypt, Iran, Iraq, Israel, Jordan, Kuwait, Lebanon, Oman, Qatar, Saudi Arabia, Syria, United Arab Emirates, North Yemen (–1990), South Yemen (–1990),Yemen (1991–).

Oceania: Australia, Fiji, Kiribati, Marshall Islands, Micronesia, New Zealand, Papua New Guinea, Samoa, Solomon Islands, Tahiti, Tonga, Tuvalu, Vanuatu.

Association of South-East Asian Nations (ASEAN): Brunei, Indonesia, Malaysia, Philippines, Singapore, Thailand, Viet Nam.

European Union (EU): Austria (1995), Belgium, Denmark, Finland (1995), France, FR Germany (–1990), Germany (1990–), Greece, Ireland, Italy, Luxembourg, Netherlands, Portugal, Spain, Sweden (1995), UK.

NATO: Belgium, Canada, Denmark, France, FR Germany (–1990), Germany (1990–), Greece, Iceland, Italy, Luxembourg, Netherlands, Norway, Portugal, Spain, Turkey, UK, USA.

Organisation for Economic Co-operation and Development (OECD): Australia, Austria, Belgium, Canada, Denmark, Finland, France, FR Germany (–1990), Germany (1990–), Greece, Iceland, Ireland, Italy, Japan, Luxembourg, Mexico (1995), Netherlands, New Zealand, Norway, Portugal, Spain, Sweden, Switzerland, Turkey, UK, USA.

Organisation of Petroleum Exporting Countries (OPEC): Algeria, Gabon, Indonesia, Iran, Iraq, Kuwait, Libya, Nigeria, Qatar, Saudi Arabia, United Arab Emirates, Venezuela.

Organization for Security and Co-operation in Europe (OSCE): Albania (1991–), Armenia (1992–), Austria, Azerbaijan (1992–), Belarus (1992–), Belgium, Bosnia and Herzegovina (1992–), Bulgaria, Canada, Croatia (1992–), Cyprus, Czechoslovakia (–1992), Czech Republic (1993–), Denmark, Estonia (1991–), Finland, France, Georgia (1992–), FR Germany (–1990), German DR (–1990), Germany (1990–), Greece, Hungary, Iceland, Ireland, Italy, Kazakhstan (1992–), Kyrgyzstan (1992–), Latvia (1991–), Liechtenstein, Lithuania (1991–), Luxembourg, Macedonia (1995–), Malta, Moldova (1992–), Monaco, Netherlands, Norway, Poland, Portugal, Romania, Russia (1992–), San Marino, Slovakia (1992–), Slovenia (1992–), Spain, Sweden, Switzerland, Tajikistan (1992–), Turkey, Turkmenistan (1992–), UK, Ukraine (1992–), USA, USSR (–1992), Uzbekistan (1992–), Yugoslavia (–1991), Yugoslavia (Serbia and Montenegro) (1992–).

Appendix 11B. Register of the trade in and licensed production of major conventional weapons, 1995

IAN ANTHONY, GERD HAGMEYER-GAVERUS, PIETER D. WEZEMAN and SIEMON T. WEZEMAN

This register lists major weapons on order or under delivery, or for which the licence was bought and production was under way or completed during 1995. 'Year(s) of deliveries' includes aggregates of all deliveries and licensed production since the beginning of the contract. Sources and methods for the data collection, and the conventions, abbreviations and acronyms used, are explained in appendix 11C. Entries are alphabetical, by recipient, supplier and licenser.

Recipient/ supplier (S) or licenser (L)	No. ordered	Weapon designation	Weapon description	Year of order/ of licence	Year(s) of deliveries	No. delivered/ produced	Comments
Algeria							
S: Egypt	(200)	Fahd	APC	1992	1992–95	(200)	For Gendarmerie
France	9	AS-350B Ecureuil	Helicopter	1994	1995	9	For Ministry of Interior security forces
Russia	47	Mi-8T Hip C	Helicopter	1994	1994–95	(47)	
L: UK	3	Kebir Class	Patrol craft	(1990)			
Angola							
S: Poland	52	BMP-2	AIFV	1994	1994–95	(52)	Ex-Polish Army
Spain	2	C-212-300MP Patrullero	Maritime patrol	(1990)			Status uncertain
Switzerland	8	PC-7 Turbo Trainer	Trainer	(1989)	1990	6	Status of last 2 uncertain
Argentina							
S: France	4	AS-550L1 Fennec	Helicopter	1994	1995	(2)	For Navy
	6	MM-38 ShShMS	ShShM system	1979	1985–95	(7)	For 6 Meko 140 Type frigates
	(48)	MM-38 Exocet	ShShM	(1979)	1985–95	(48)	For 6 Meko 140 Type frigates

Recipient/ supplier (S) or licenser (L)	No. ordered	Weapon designation	Weapon description	Year of order/ licence	Year(s) of deliveries	No. delivered/ produced	Comments
Netherlands	6	DA-05	Surveillance radar	(1979)	1985–95	(6)	For 6 Meko 140 Type frigates
	6	WM-28	Fire control radar	(1979)	1985–95	(6)	For 6 Meko 140 Type frigates
USA	40	A-4M Skyhawk II	Fighter/ground attack	1993	1995	(10)	Ex-US Marine Corps; incl 6 TA-4 fighter/trainers; deal worth $125 m incl 8 spare engines, maintenance and support
	(10)	Bell 205/UH-1H	Helicopter	(1993)	1994–95	(10)	Ex-US Army; aid
	3	C-130B Hercules	Transport	1992	1995	3	Ex-US Air Force; aid
	(15)	Super King Air 200/C-12	Transport	(1993)	1995	(1)	Ex-US Air Force and Army
	1	AN/SPS-67	Surveillance radar	1994			On 1 ex-US Navy Newport Class landing ship
	1	Phalanx	CIWS	1994			On 1 ex-US Navy Newport Class landing ship
	1	Newport Class	Landing ship	1994			Ex-US Navy; 2-year lease worth $1.8 m
L: Germany, FR	120	TAM	Main battle tank	1994	1995	120	
	6	Meko 140 Type	Frigate	1980	1985–95	6	Argentine designation Espora Class
	2	TR-1700 Type	Submarine	1977			Original order for 4 cut to 2; Argentine designation Santa Cruz Class
Australia							
S: Canada	3	DHC-8 Dash 8-200	Transport	1994	1995	(3)	Operated by civilian company for Customs; for maritime patrol
	97	LAV-25	AIFV	1992	1994–95	(97)	Deal worth $88 m; incl 33 APCs, 10 ARVs, 9 APC/CPs, 2 ambulances and 10 surveillance versions; Australian designation ASLAV; assembled in Australia
Sweden	8	9LV	Fire control radar	(1991)			For 8 Meko 200ANZ Type (Anzac Class) frigates
	8	Sea Giraffe 150	Surveillance radar	1991			For 8 Meko 200ANZ Type (Anzac Class) frigates
	12	C-130J Hercules II	Transport	1995			Deal worth $670 m
USA	4	P-3B Orion	ASW/maritime patrol	1994	1995	(4)	Ex-US Navy; for training; incl 1 for spares
	8	127mm/54 Mk-42/9	Naval gun	(1989)			For 8 Meko 200ANZ Type (Anzac Class) frigates
	8	AN/SPS-49	Surveillance radar	1993			For 8 Meko 200ANZ Type (Anzac Class) frigates

No.	Weapon designation	Weapon description	Year of order	Year of delivery	No. delivered	Comments
8	Seasparrow VLS	ShAM system	(1991)			For 8 Meko 200ANZ Type (Anzac Class) frigates
..	RIM-7M Seasparrow	ShAM	(1991)			For 8 Meko 200ANZ Type (Anzac Class) frigates
12	RGM-84A Harpoon	ShShM	1995			Deal worth $38 m incl 21 training missiles
L: Germany, FR						
10	Meko 200ANZ Type	Frigate	1989			Incl 2 for New Zealand; option on 2 more for New Zealand; Australian designation Anzac Class
Italy						
6	Gaetta Class	MCM ship	1994			Australian designation Huon Class
Sweden						
6	Type 471	Submarine	1987	1995	1	Deal worth $2.8 b; Australian designation Collins Class
Austria						
S: France						
22	RAC	Surveillance radar	1995	1995		Deal worth $120 m (offsets $340 m)
500	Mistral	Portable SAM	1993	1993–94	(247)	Deal worth $129 m incl launchers (offsets $344 m)
UK						
66	M-109A2 155mm	Self-propelled gun	1994	1994–95	66	Ex-UK Army
USA						
54	M-109A5 155mm	Self-propelled gun	1995	1995		Austrian designation M-109A5Ö; deal worth $48.6 m
..	AIM-9P Sidewinder	Air-to-air missile	(1994)	1995	(144)	For S-35Ö fighters
Bahrain						
S: Netherlands						
25	AIFV/YPR-765	AIFV	(1995)			Ex-Dutch Army
USA						
14	Bell-209/AH-1E	Helicopter	(1993)			Ex-US Army
10	Bell-209/AH-1E	Helicopter	1995			Ex-US Army
6	Bell-209/AH-1E	Helicopter	1995			Ex-US Army; refurbished before delivery
60	M-60A3 Patton II	Main battle tank	(1995)	1995	(60)	Ex-US Army
14	M-60A3 Patton II	Main battle tank	1994	1995	(14)	Ex-US Army
1	AN/SPG-60 STIR	Fire control radar	1995	1995	1	On 1 ex-US Navy FFG-7 Class frigate
1	AN/SPS-49	Surveillance radar	1995	1995	1	On 1 ex-US Navy FFG-7 Class frigate
1	AN/SPS-49	Surveillance radar	1995	1995		On 1 ex-US Navy FFG-7 Class frigate
1	AN/SPS-55	Surveillance radar	1995	1995	1	On 1 ex-US Navy FFG-7 Class frigate
1	I-HAWK SAMS	SAM system	1995	1995		Ex-US Army; aid
1	Phalanx	CIWS	1995	1995	1	On 1 ex-US Navy FFG-7 Class frigate
1	Standard 1 ShAMS	ShAM system	1995	1995	(1)	On 1 ex-US Navy FFG-7 Class frigate
1	WM-28	Fire control radar	1995	1995	1	On 1 ex-US Navy FFG-7 Class frigate
..	MIM-23B HAWK	SAM	1995	1995		Ex-US Army; for 1 I-HAWK SAM system
..	RGM-84A Harpoon	ShShM	1995	1995	(8)	For 1 FFG-7 Class frigate

Recipient/ supplier (S) or licenser (L)	No. ordered	Weapon designation	Weapon description	Year of order/ licence	Year(s) of deliveries	No. delivered/ produced	Comments
	60	RIM-66B Standard 1MR	ShAM	1995	1995	(60)	For 1 FFG-7 Class frigate
	1	FFG-7 Class	Frigate	1995	1995	1	Ex-US Navy
Bangladesh							
S: Czechoslovakia	8	L-39Z Albatros	Jet trainer	(1995)	1995	8	Exchanged for jute
Russia	8	Mi-17 Hip H	Helicopter	(1995)	1995	8	
USA	12	T-37B	Jet trainer	1995	1995	12	Ex-US Air Force; gift
Ukraine	1	An-32 Cline	Transport	(1995)	1995	1	
Belgium							
S: France	714	Mistral	Portable SAM	1988	1991–95	(714)	Deal worth $93 m incl 118 launchers (offsets 75%)
USA	200	AIM-120B AMRAAM	Air-to-air missile	1995	1995		
	545	AIM-9M Sidewinder	Air-to-air missile	1988	1990–95	(545)	Deal worth $49 m
Bolivia							
S: USA	1	C-130B Hercules	Transport	1993	1995	(1)	Ex-US Air Force; deal worth $1 m
Botswana							
S: Netherlands	(50)	Leopard-1V	Main battle tank	1995			Ex-Dutch Army; deal worth $14.3 m incl 279 trucks and 50 recoilless guns
UK	36	Scorpion	Light tank	(1994)	1995	(36)	Incl some ex-Belgian Army Spartan APCs sold to producer and transferred to Botswana
Brazil							
S: France	57	Eryx	Anti-tank missile	1995			
	(100)	Mistral	Portable SAM	1994			
Germany, FR	4	Grajau Class	Patrol craft	1993	1995	4	
Italy	(18)	Model 56 105mm	Towed gun	1995			

No.	Weapon designation	Weapon description	Year of order	Year(s) of deliveries	No. delivered	Comments
6	Albatros Mk-2	ShAM system		1995		For refit of 6 Niteroi Class frigates; deal worth $160 m incl Aspide missiles, 7 RAN-20S and 13 Orion RTN-30X radars
13	Orion RTN-30X	Fire control radar		1995		For refit of 6 Niteroi Class frigates; deal worth $160 m incl 7 RAN-20S radars, 6 Albatros Mk-2 ShAM systems and Aspide missiles
7	RAN-20S	Surveillance radar		1995		For refit of 6 Niteroi Class frigates; deal worth $160 m incl 6 Albatros ShAM system, Aspide missiles and 13 Orion RTN-30X radars
(144)	Aspide	ShAM		1995		For 6 refitted Niteroi Class frigates; deal worth $160 m incl 7 RAN-20S and 13 Orion RTN-30X radars and 6 Albatros Mk-2 ShAM systems
Sweden						
5	Erieye	Airborne radar	1994			Deal worth $125 m; for EMB-120 AEW aircraft
UK						
9	Super Lynx	ASW helicopter	1993			Deal worth $221 m incl refurbishment of 5 Brazilian Lynx to Super Lynx; for Navy
(36)	L-118 105mm	Towed gun	1994	1995	12	Deal worth $60 m incl L-16 81mm mortars
4	MM-38 ShShMS	ShShM system	1994	1995	1	On 4 ex-UK Navy Broadsword Class frigates
8	Seawolf ShAMS	ShAM system	1994	1995	2	On 4 ex-UK Navy Broadsword Class frigates
8	Type 911	Fire control radar	1994	1995	2	On 4 ex-UK Navy Broadsword Class frigates
4	Type 967/968	Surveillance radar	1994	1995	1	On 4 ex-UK Navy Broadsword Class frigates
:	Seawolf	ShAM	1994	1995	(32)	For 4 Broadsword Class frigates
4	Broadsword Class	Frigate	1994	1995	1	Ex-UK Navy; Brazilian designation Greenhalgh Class
USA						
3	River Class	Minesweeper	1994	1995	3	Ex-UK Navy
8	S-61/SH-3D Sea King	Helicopter	1994	1995	6	Ex-US Navy; deal worth $900 000 incl spares and support
14	LVTP-7A1	APC	1995			Deal worth $23 m incl 1 ARV and 1 APC/CP version; for Marines
L: Germany, FR						
3	Type 209/1400	Submarine	1984	1994	1	Brazilian designation Tupi Class
Brunei						
S: Indonesia						
3	CN-235MPA	Maritime patrol	1995			
UK						
3	Yarrow 90m	OPV	1995			Deal worth $948 m

Recipient/ supplier (S) or licenser (L)	No. ordered	Weapon designation	Weapon description	Year of order/ licence	Year(s) of deliveries	No. delivered/ produced	Comments
Bulgaria							
S: Russia	12	Mi-24D Hind D	Combat helicopter	1995	1995	(12)	Ex-Russian Air Force; gift
	100	BMP-1	AIFV	1995	1995	(100)	Ex-Russian Army; gift
	100	T-72	Main battle tank	1995	1995	(100)	Ex-Russian Army; gift
Cambodia							
S: Czechoslovakia	6	L-39Z Albatros	Jet trainer	(1994)	1995	(6)	
Canada							
S: France	28	LG-1 105mm	Towed gun	1994	1995	28	Deal worth $13.2 m
	4 500	Eryx	Anti-tank missile	1992	1993–95	(2 100)	Deal incl 425 launchers (offsets 100%)
Netherlands	24	STIR	Fire control radar	(1985)	1992–95	(20)	For 12 Halifax (City) Class frigates
Sweden	12	Sea Giraffe 150	Surveillance radar	(1985)	1992–95	(10)	For 12 Halifax (City) Class frigates
UK	(152)	MSTAR	Battlefield radar	1994	1995	(152)	For 152 LAV APC/reconnaissance vehicles
USA	12	AN/SPS-49	Surveillance radar	1985	1992–95	(10)	For 12 Halifax (City) Class frigates
	6	Phalanx	CIWS	1990	1994–95	(4)	Deal worth $32 m; for second batch of 6 Halifax (City) Class frigates
	12	RGM-84A ShShMS	ShShM system	1983	1992–95	(10)	For 12 Halifax (City) Class frigates
	12	Seasparrow VLS	ShAM system	1983	1992–95	(10)	Deal worth $75 m incl missiles, for 12 Halifax (City) Class frigates
	..	RGM-84A Harpoon	ShShM	1988	1992–95	(160)	For 12 Halifax (City) Class frigates
	..	RIM-7H Seasparrow	ShAM	1984	1992–95	(271)	Deal worth $75 m incl 12 Seasparrow VLS ShAM systems; for 12 Halifax (City) Class frigates
L: Switzerland	203	LAV-25	AIFV	1993	1994–95	(203)	Deal worth $1.49 b incl option on 411
	240	Piranha 8x8	APC	1995			
USA	100	Bell 412	Helicopter	1992	1994–95	(48)	Deal worth $558 m; Canadian designation CH-146 Griffon

	No.	Weapon designation	Weapon description	Year of order	Year(s) of deliveries	No. delivered	Comments
Chad							
S: Netherlands	2	SA-316B Alouette III	Helicopter	1995	1995	2	Ex-Dutch Army
Chile							
S: Belgium	5	Mirage VBA	Fighter/ground attack	1994	1994	1	Ex-Belgian Air Force; incl 1 Mirage VBP trainer version; deal worth $54 m incl 20 Mirage V MIRSIP fighters
	20	Mirage V MIRSIP	Fighter/ground attack	1994	1994–95	12	Ex-Belgian Air Force Mirage Vs rebuilt to MIRSIP standard; incl 5 trainer version; deal worth $54 m incl 5 Mirage VBA fighters
Canada	1	N M Rogers Class	Ice-breaker	1995	1995	1	Ex-Canadian Coast Guard; Chilean designation Oscar Viel Class
France	..	AM-39 Exocet	Anti-ship missile	1992			For 6 Navy AS-532SC helicopters
	..	Mistral	Portable SAM	(1990)	1991–95	(1 000)	
Israel	1	Phalcon	AEW&C aircraft	(1989)	1995	1	Chilean designation Condor
	4	AMDR	ShAM system	(1989)	1993–95	(2)	For refit of 4 Prat (County) Class destroyers
	(2)	Barak ShAMS	ShAM system	1989	1995	(1)	For refit of 2 Prat (County) Class destroyers
	4	EL/M-2106	Surveillance radar	(1989)	1993–95	(2)	For refit of 2 Prat (County) Class destroyers
	..	Barak	ShAM	1989	1993–95	(64)	For 2 refitted Prat (County) Class destroyers
	..	Python III	Air-to-air missile	(1988)	1992–95	(84)	For modernized Mirage 50 (Pantera) and F-5E (Tigre III) fighters
UK	30	Scorpion	Light tank	1995	1995	15	Ex-UK Army; for Marines
USA	1	AN/SPS-67	Surveillance radar	1995	1995	1	On 1 ex-US Navy Newport Class landing ship
	1	Phalanx	CIWS	1995	1995	1	On 1 ex-US Navy Newport Class landing ship
	1	Newport Class	Landing ship	1995	1995	1	Ex-US Navy; Chilean designation Valdivia Class
L: Spain	29	C-101BB-02 Aviojet	Jet trainer	1984	1986–95	29	Chilean designation T-36/A-36 Halcón; incl some assembled from kits
Switzerland	..	Piranha 8x8D	APC	(1991)	1993–95	52	
UK	..	Rayo	MRL	1995	1995		Status of production uncertain
China							
S: Canada	1	TG-10A Brushfire	Fighter	(1994)			Prior to licensed production

Recipient/ supplier (S) or licenser (L)	No. ordered	Weapon designation	Weapon description	Year of order/ licence	Year(s) of deliveries	No. delivered/ produced	Comments
Russia/USSR	(2)	Ka-27 Helix A	ASW helicopter	(1991)			For Navy
	24	Su-27P Flanker B	Fighter	1995			Incl 2 Su-27UB fighter/trainers
	(200)	T-80U	Main battle tank	1993	1995	(200)	
	..	AA-10a Alamo	Air-to-air missile	1995			For 24 Su-27P fighters
	..	AA-8 Aphid	Air-to-air missile	1995			For 24 Su-27P fighters
	(1 200)	AT-11 Sniper	Anti-tank missile	1993	1995	(1 200)	For 200 T-80U tanks
	2	Kilo Class	Submarine	1994	1995	2	Deal worth $180 m; originally built for Poland and Romania but cancelled; option on more may include licensed production
Uzbekistan	15	Il-76M Candid B	Transport	1993	1994-95	(15)	Ex-Uzbek
L: Canada	..	TG-10B Brushfire	Jet trainer	1994			
France	..	SA-321H Super Frelon	Helicopter	(1981)	1985-95	(11)	Chinese designation Z-8
	(30)	AS-365N Dauphin 2	Helicopter	1988	1992-95	(4)	Chinese designation Z-9A-100 Haitun
Israel	..	Python III	ShAM	(1989)	1990-95	(3 213)	Chinese designation PL-8H
	..	Python III	Air-to-air missile	1990	1990-95	(4 837)	Chinese designation PL-9
Colombia							
S: Brazil	..	EE-11 Urutu	APC	(1994)			
	..	EE-9 Cascavel	Armoured car	(1994)			
Canada	12	Bell 212	Helicopter	(1994)	1994-95	(8)	
Spain	1	Cormoran Class	Fast attack craft	1995	1995	1	Ex-Spanish Navy; refitted before delivery; deal worth $18 m
USA	12	Model 280FX	Helicopter	1994	1995	12	Deal worth $4.1 m
Cyprus							
S: France	50	AMX-30B2	Main battle tank	(1994)	1995		Ex-French Army
Russia	43	BMP-3	AIFV	1995	1995	(20)	Deal worth $68 m
	(344)	AT-10 Bastion	Anti-tank missile	(1995)	1995	(160)	For 43 BMP-3 AIFVs

Recipient / Supplier	No. ordered	Weapon designation	Weapon description	Year of order	Year(s) of deliveries	No. delivered	Comments
Czechoslovakia							
S: Poland	11	W-3 Sokol	Helicopter	1995	1995	11	Exchanged for 10 ex-Czech Air Force MiG-29 fighters
Denmark							
S: France	18	RAC	Surveillance radar	1991	1995	(18)	
	12	TRS-2620 Gerfaut	Surveillance radar	1992	1995	(12)	
Germany, FR	6	TRS-3D	Surveillance radar	1990	1993–95	(5)	For 6 Flyvefisken Class (Stanflex 300 Type) patrol craft/MCM ships
Italy	1	RAT-31SL	Surveillance radar	1995			
Netherlands	14	Leopard 1 ARV	ARV	1993	1993–95	14	Ex-Dutch Army
	8	Leopard 1 BL	Bridge layer	1993	1994–95	8	Ex-Dutch Army
Sweden	(14)	9LV	Fire control radar	(1988)	1989–95	(13)	For 13 Flyvefisken Class (Stanflex 300 Type) patrol craft/MCM ships
Switzerland	10	Eagle	Scout car	1995	1995	10	Option on 17 more
USA	3	F-16A Fighting Falcon	Fighter	1994	1995	3	Ex-US Air Force
	12	MLRS 227mm	MRL	1995			Deal worth $146 m incl 300 rockets, spares and support
	4	Seasparrow VLS	ShAM system	1993			Deal worth $20 m; option on more; for 4 Flyvefisken Class (Stanflex 300 Type) patrol craft/MCM ships
	..	AIM-120A AMRAAM	Air-to-air missile	1994			For F-16 fighters
	840	FIM-92A Stinger	Portable SAM	1991	1994–95	(560)	
	..	RIM-7H Seasparrow	ShAM	(1994)			For 4 Flyvefisken Class (Stanflex 300 Type) patrol craft/MCM ships
Ecuador							
S: Israel	(4)	Kfir C7	Fighter/ground attack	1995			Ex-Israeli Air Force
Egypt							
S: Netherlands	599	AIFV/YPR-765	AIFV	1994	1995	(200)	Ex-Dutch Army; deal worth $135 m incl 12 M-577 APC/CPs and support
	12	M-577A1	APC/command post	1994			Ex-Dutch Army; deal worth $135 m incl 599 AIFV/YPR-765 AIFVs and support

Recipient/ supplier (S) or licenser (L)	No. ordered	Weapon designation	Weapon description	Year of order/ licence	Year(s) of deliveries	No. delivered/ produced	Comments
USA	24	AH-64A Apache	Combat helicopter	1990	1995	(24)	Deal worth $488 m incl 492 AGM-114A missiles; aid
	12	AH-64A Apache	Combat helicopter	1995			Deal worth $518 m incl spares and armament
	(46)	F-16C Fighting Falcon	Fighter	1991	1994–95	(40)	'Peace Vector IV' programme worth $1.6 b incl spare engines and armament; incl 12 F-16D trainer version; from Turkish production line
	2	S-70/UH-60 Blackhawk	Helicopter	1995			Deal worth $42 m incl 2 spare engines, spares and support; for VIP transport
	10	SH-2F Seasprite	ASW helicopter	1994			Ex-US Navy; refurbished to SH-2G before delivery
	76	M-109/SP-122 122mm	Self-propelled gun	1988	1992–95	(76)	Deal worth $96 m
	296	M-113A2	APC	1995	1995	(148)	Ex-US Army; deal worth $36 m
	1	AN/SPG-60 STIR	Fire control radar	1995			On 1 ex-US Navy FFG-7 Class frigate
	2	AN/SPG-60 STIR	Fire control radar	1995			On 2 ex-US Navy FFG-7 Class frigates
	2	AN/SPS-55	Surveillance radar	1995			On 2 ex-US Navy FFG-7 Class frigates
	1	AN/SPS-55	Surveillance radar	1995			On 1 ex-US Navy FFG-7 Class frigate
	1	Phalanx	CIWS	1995			On 1 ex-US Navy FFG-7 Class frigate
	30	Scout	Surveillance radar	1993	1995	(15)	For Coastal Border Surveillance System
	2	Standard 1 ShAMS	ShAM system	1995			On 2 ex-US Navy FFG-7 Class frigates
	1	Standard 1 ShAMS	ShAM system	1995			On 1 ex-US Navy FFG-7 Class frigate
	1	WM-28	Fire control radar	1995			On 1 ex-US Navy FFG-7 Class frigate
	2	WM-28	Fire control radar	1995			On 2 ex-US Navy FFG-7 Class frigates
	7 511	BGM-71D TOW 2	Anti-tank missile	1988	1989–95	(3 500)	
	(36)	RIM-66B Standard 1MR	ShAM	1995			For 1 ex-US Navy FFG-7 Class frigate
	29	UGM-84A SubHarpoon	SuShM	1990	1992–95	(22)	For 4 refitted Romeo Class submarines; deal worth $69 m
	1	FFG-7 Class	Frigate	1995			Ex-US Navy
	3	Swiftships MCM Type	MCM ship	1991	1994–95	(3)	
L: USA	499	M-1A1 Abrams	Main battle tank	1988	1991–95	(404)	Deal worth $2.7 b incl 25 delivered direct
	..	AIM-9P Sidewinder	Air-to-air missile	(1988)	1990–95	(2732)	

Recipient/Supplier (S/L)	No. ordered	Weapon designation	Weapon description	Year of order	Year(s) of deliveries	No. delivered	Comments
Georgia							
S: Finland	8	L-90TP Redigo	Trainer	1992	1994–95	(8)	
Estonia							
S: Finland	1	Silmä Class	OPV	1994	1995	1	Ex-Finnish Frontier Guard; aid
Germany, FR	3	Mi-8T Hip C	Helicopter	(1995)	1995	3	Former GDR equipment; for SAR; aid
	6	Osa I Class	Fast attack craft	(1993)	1995	6	Former GDR equipment; armament removed before delivery; aid
Norway	1	Storm Class	Fast attack craft	1994	1995	1	Ex-Norwegian Navy; armament removed before delivery; gift
Fiji							
S: Australia	3	ASI-315	Patrol craft	1992	1994–95	3	Pacific Forum aid programme
Finland							
S: Italy	1	Bell 412EP/AB-412EP	Helicopter	1995			For Border Guard
Russia	(3)	SA-11 SAMS	SAM system	1995			Deal worth $230 m incl missiles
	(288)	SA-11 Gadfly	SAM	1995			Deal worth $230 m incl 3 SA-11 SAM systems
Sweden	4	Giraffe 100	Surveillance radar	1992	1993–95	(3)	Incl limited assembly in Finland
USA	57	F/A-18C Hornet	Fighter	1992			
	7	F/A-18D Hornet	Fighter/trainer	1992	1995	7	
	(250)	AIM-120A AMRAAM	Air-to-air missile	1992			For 64 F/A-18C/D fighters
	480	AIM-9S Sidewinder	Air-to-air missile	1992			For 64 F/A-18C/D fighters
France							
S: Brazil	80	EMB-312 Tucano	Trainer	1991	1993–95	(36)	Deal worth $170 m
USA	4	E-2C Hawkeye	AEW&C aircraft	1995			For Navy
	5	KC-135A Stratotanker	Tanker/transport	1994			Ex-US Air Force; deal worth $220 m; refurbished to KC-135R before delivery
L: USA	55	MLRS 227mm	MRL	1985	1985–95	55	

Recipient/ supplier (S) or licenser (L)	No. ordered	Weapon designation	Weapon description	Year of order/ licence	Year(s) of deliveries	No. delivered/ produced	Comments
	..	VT-1	SAM	1991	1994–95	633	For Crotale NG SAM and Crotale NG Naval ShAM systems; incl for export
Germany, FR							
S: France	200	Apache/MAW	ASM	1992	1994	(2)	For Tornado IDS fighters; FRG designation MAW
Netherlands	4	LW-08	Surveillance radar	(1989)	1994–95	(2)	For 4 Brandenburg Class (Type 123) frigates
	5	SMART	Surveillance radar	1989	1994–95	(2)	For 4 Brandenburg Class (Type 123) frigates and 1 shore-based training centre
Sweden	8	STIR	Fire control radar	1989	1994–95	(4)	For 4 Brandenburg Class (Type 123) frigates
	(9)	HARD	Surveillance radar	1995			For 3 ASRAD SAM batteries
USA	5	AN/FPS-117	Surveillance radar	1992	1994–95	(5)	Deal worth $94 m incl 2 simulators and spares (offsets 100%); FRG designation RRP-117
	4	Seasparrow VLS	ShAM system	1989	1994–95	(2)	For 4 Brandenburg Class (Type 123) frigates
	96	AIM-120A AMRAAM	Air-to-air missile	1991	1995	48	For modernized F-4F fighters; deal worth $53.6 m; options on 224 more
	96	AIM-120B AMRAAM	Air-to-air missile	1995			
	1 230	BGM-71D TOW 2	Anti-tank missile	1993	1994–95	(1 230)	Deal worth $25 m
	..	RIM-7H Seasparrow	ShAM	1989	1994–95	(32)	For 4 Brandenburg Class (Type 123) frigates
L: Singapore	4	Grajau Class	Patrol craft	1993	1995	(4)	For export to Brazil
USA	4 500	FIM-92A Stinger	Portable SAM	1987	1992–95	(4 500)	
	(1 065)	RIM-116A RAM	ShAM	1985	1989–95	(979)	For Navy
Greece							
S: France	5	TRS-3050 Triton G	Surveillance radar	(1986)	1994–95	(2)	For 5 Jason Class landing ships
	5	TRS-3220 Pollux	Fire control radar	(1986)	1994–95	(2)	For 5 Jason Class landing ships
Germany, FR	(100)	M-113A1	APC	(1995)	1995	100	Ex-FRG Army; aid
	120	ZSU-23-4 Shilka	AAV(G)	1991	1994–95	(120)	Former GDR equipment; part of 'Materialhilfe' programme worth $605 m

Supplier/recipient	No.	Weapon designation	Weapon description	Year of order	Year(s) of deliveries	No. delivered	Comments
	2	Castor 2B	Fire control radar		(1994)	2	On 2 ex-FRG Navy Combattante IIA Type (Tiger Class) fast attack craft
	2	MM-38 ShShMS	ShShM system		(1994)	2	On 2 ex-FRG Navy Combattante IIA Type (Tiger Class) fast attack craft
	2	TRS-3050 Triton	Surveillance radar		(1994)	2	On 2 ex-FRG Navy Combattante IIA Type (Tiger Class) fast attack craft
Netherlands	..	RIM-7M Seasparrow	ShAM	(1988)	1992	(16)	For 4 Meko 200HN Type (Hydra Class) frigates
	2	Combattante IIA Type	Fast attack craft	(1994)	1995	2	Ex-FRG Navy
	177	M-113A1	APC	1991	1994-95	(177)	Ex-Dutch Army
	4	DA-08	Surveillance radar	(1989)	1992	1	For 4 Meko 200HN Type (Hydra Class) frigates
	3	LW-08	Surveillance radar	1992	1993-95	3	On 3 ex-Dutch Navy Kortenaer Class frigates
	3	MW-08	Surveillance radar	1991	1993-95	(3)	For coastal surveillance
	4	MW-08	Surveillance radar	(1989)	1992	1	For 4 Meko 200HN Type (Hydra Class) frigates
	3	RGM-84A ShShMS	ShShM system	1992	1993-95	3	On 3 ex-Dutch Navy Kortenaer Class frigates
	3	Seasparrow ShAMS	ShAM system	1992	1993-95	3	On 3 ex-Dutch Navy Kortenaer Class frigates
	3	STIR	Fire control radar	1992	1993-95	3	On 3 ex-Dutch Navy Kortenaer Class frigates
	8	STIR	Fire control radar	1989	1992	2	For 4 Meko 200HN Type (Hydra Class) frigates
	3	WM-25	Fire control radar	1992	1993-95	3	On 3 ex-Dutch Navy Kortenaer Class frigates
	3	ZW-06	Surveillance radar	1992	1993-95	3	On 3 ex-Dutch Navy Kortenaer Class frigates
	3	Kortenaer Class	Frigate	1992	1993-95	3	Ex-Dutch Navy; deal worth $211 m; Greek designation Elli Class
Norway	..	Penguin Mk-2-7	Anti-ship missile	1993	1994-95	(20)	Deal worth $21 m; for Navy S-70B/SH-60B helicopters; option on more
UK	1	Martello 743-D	Surveillance radar	1995			
USA	12	AH-64A Apache	Combat helicopter	(1991)	1995	6	Deal worth $505 m incl 3 spare engines, support and spares; option on 8 more
	9	Bell 209/AH-1P	Combat helicopter	1994			Ex-US Army; deal worth $2.4 m
	40	F-16C Fighting Falcon	Fighter	1993			'Peace Xenia' programme worth $1.8 b incl 10 spare engines and 40 LANTIRN pods; incl 8 F-16D fighter/trainers
	4	P-3A Orion	ASW/maritime patrol	1994			Ex-US Navy; for training; incl 2 for spares
	4	P-3B Orion	ASW/maritime patrol	1994			Ex-US Navy; lease worth $69 m
	5	S-70/SH-60B Seahawk	ASW helicopter	1991	1994-95	5	Deal worth $161 m; option on 3 more; Greek designation Aegean Hawk

Recipient/ supplier (S) or licenser (L)	No. ordered	Weapon designation	Weapon description	Year of order/ licence	Year(s) of deliveries	No. delivered/ produced	Comments
	4	127mm/54 Mk-42/9	Naval gun	(1988)	1992	1	For 4 Meko 200HN Type (Hydra Class) frigates
	9	MLRS 227mm	MRL	1994			
	6	Phalanx	CIWS	(1993)	1993–95	(6)	For refit of 3 Kortenaer Class frigates
	8	Phalanx	CIWS	1988	1992	2	For 4 Meko 200HN Type (Hydra Class) frigates
	4	RGM-84A ShShMS	ShShM system	1989	1992	1	For 4 Meko 200HN Type (Hydra Class) frigates
	4	Seasparrow VLS	ShAM system	1988	1992	1	For 4 Meko 200HN Type (Hydra Class) frigates
	446	AGM-114A Hellfire	Anti-tank missile	1991	1995	(183)	For 12 AH-64A helicopters
	52	AGM-88B HARM	ARM	1994			Deal worth $27 m incl spares and training equipment; for F-16 fighters
	..	RIM-7H Seasparrow	ShAM	(1992)	1993–95	(72)	For 3 Kortenaer Class frigates
	..	UGM-84A SubHarpoon	SuShM	(1989)	1993–95	(16)	For 8 Type 209 (Glavkos Class) submarines
L: Austria	53	Pandur	APC	1993			Greek designation Leonidas 2; incl c. 90 for export
Germany, FR	267	Steyr 4K-7FA	APC	1987	1990–95	(260)	Deal worth $1.2 b incl 1 delivered direct (offsets $250 m); partly financed by FRG and USA; Greek designation Hydra Class
	3	Meko 200HN Type	Frigate	1988			
Hungary							
S: Germany, FR	20	Mi-24D Hind D	Combat helicopter	1995	1995	20	Former GDR equipment; incl 4 for spares; gift
Russia	97	BTR-80	APC	1995	1995	(97)	
	70	BTR-80	APC	1995	1995	70	For Border Guards
India							
S: France	..	PSM-33	Surveillance radar	1988	1990–95	(6)	
Germany, FR	1	Aditya Class	Support ship	1987			
Italy	(6)	Seaguard TMX	Fire control radar	1993			Option on 1 more
Russia/USSR	8	Bass Tilt	Fire control radar	1983	1989–95	(5)	For 3 Godavari Class (Project 16A Type) frigates
	8	Bass Tilt	Fire control radar	1983	1989–95	(5)	For 8 Khukri Class (Project 25/25A Type) corvettes
	7	Bass Tilt	Fire control radar	(1987)	1991–95	(5)	For 7 Veer/Vibhuti (Tarantul I) Class fast attack craft
	8	Cross Dome	Surveillance radar	(1983)	1989–95	(5)	For 8 Khukri Class (Project 25/25A Type) corvettes

No.	Weapon designation	Weapon description	Year of order	Year(s) of deliveries	No. delivered	Comments
8	Plank Shave	Surveillance radar	(1983)	1989–95	(5)	For 8 Khukri Class (Project 25/25A Type) corvettes
8	SS-N-2 ShShMS	ShShM system	1983	1989–95	(5)	For 8 Khukri Class (Project 25/25A Type) corvettes
7	SS-N-2 ShShMS	ShShM system	1987	1991–95	(5)	For 7 Veer/Vibhuti (Tarantul I) Class fast attack craft
..	SA-N-5 Grail	ShAM	(1983)	1989–95	(200)	For 8 Khukri Class (Project 25/25A Type) corvettes
..	SS-N-2d Styx	ShShM	1983	1989–95	(40)	For 8 Khukri Class (Project 25/25A Type) corvettes
10	MiG-21U Mongol A	Fighter/trainer	1995	1995	10	Ex-Russian Air Force
8	MiG-29SE Fulcrum C	Fighter	1994	1995		
2	MiG-29UB Fulcrum B	Fighter/trainer	1995	1995	2	
12	2S6 Tunguska	AAV(G/M)	1995			
7	Plank Shave	Surveillance radar	(1987)	1991–95	(5)	For 7 Veer/Vibhuti (Tarantul I) Class fast attack craft
3	SS-N-2 ShShMS	ShShM system	1993	1995		For 3 Godavari Class (Project 16A Type) frigates
..	AA-11 Archer	Air-to-air missile	1995	1995	(180)	For 10 MiG-29SE/UB fighters
(192)	SA-19 Grisom	SAM	1995			For 12 2S6 AAV(G/M)s
..	SA-N-5 Grail	ShAM	1987	1991–95	(200)	For 7 Veer/Vibhuti (Tarantul I) Class fast attack craft
..	SS-N-22 Sunburn	ShShM	1992			For 3 Delhi Class (Project 15 Type) destroyers
..	SS-N-2d Styx	ShShM	1987	1991–95	(40)	For 7 Veer/Vibhuti (Tarantul I) Class fast attack craft
..	SS-N-2e Styx	ShShM	1993			For 3 Godavari Class (Project 16A Type) frigates
Slovakia						
35	VT-72B	ARV	1994	1995	35	
UK						
..	Type 968	Surveillance radar	(1994)	1995	1	On 1 ex-UK Navy Leander Class frigate
1	Leander Class	Frigate	1995	1995	1	Ex-UK Navy; armament and most radars removed before delivery
L:						
France						
(15 000)	Milan 2	Anti-tank missile	1992	1993–95	(15 000)	
Germany, FR						
33	Do-228MP	Maritime patrol	1983	1987–95	(31)	For Coast Guard
Korea, South						
8	Sukanya Class	OPV	1987	1990–95	(5)	Incl 4 for Coast Guard
Netherlands						
212	Flycatcher	Fire control radar	(1987)	1988–95	(142)	Indian designation PIW-519
UK						
15	Jaguar International	Fighter/ground attack	1993	1995	(5)	Indian designation Shamsher
2	Magar Class	Landing ship	1985	1994	(1)	
Russia/USSR						
165	MiG-27L Flogger J	Fighter/ground attack	1983	1984–95	(132)	Indian designation Bahadur
..	AT-5a Spandrel	Anti-tank missile	(1988)	1989–95	(5 000)	For BMP-2 AIFVs
7	Tarantul I Class	Fast attack craft	1987	1991–95	(5)	Indian designation Veer or Vibhuti Class

Recipient/ supplier (S) or licenser (L)	No. ordered	Weapon designation	Weapon description	Year of order/ licence	Year(s) of deliveries	No. delivered/ produced	Comments
Indonesia							
S: France	20	LG-1 105mm	Towed gun	1994			Deal worth $17.5 m incl ammunition and support; for Marines
Germany, FR	16	Muff Cob	Fire control radar	1992	1993–95	(12)	Former GDR equipment; on 16 Parchim Class corvettes
	30	Strut Curve	Surveillance radar	1992	1993–95	(26)	Former GDR equipment; on 16 Parchim Class corvettes, 12 Frosch I landing and 2 Frosch II supply ships
	12	Frosch I Class	Landing ship	1992	1993–95	(12)	Part of deal for 39 former GDR ships; refitted before delivery
	2	Frosch II Class	Supply ship	1992	1995	2	Part of deal for 39 former GDR ships; refitted before delivery
	16	Parchim Class	Corvette	1992	1993–95	(12)	Part of deal for 39 former GDR ships; refitted before delivery
Malaysia	20	MD3-160	Trainer	(1994)			In exchange for Malaysian order for CN-235M transports
UK	12	Hawk 100	Jet trainer	1993	1995	(8)	Option on 16 Hawk 100/200 more
	12	Hawk 200	Fighter/ground attack	1993	1995	(8)	Option on 16 Hawk 100/200 more
	..	Scorpion 90	Light tank	1995			Option on more
	(18)	Stormer	APC	1995	1995	(8)	Incl APC/CP and ambulance versions
	(14)	AR-325	Surveillance radar	1989	1991–95	(10)	
L: Germany, FR	4	PB-57 Type	Patrol craft	1993			Indonesian designation Singa Class
Iran							
S: China	(10)	ESR-1	Surveillance radar	1992	1994	5	For 10 Hudong Class fast attack craft
	(10)	Rice Lamp	Fire control radar	1992	1994	5	For 10 Hudong Class fast attack craft
	..	C-802	ShShM	1992	1994	(40)	For 10 Hudong Class fast attack craft
	(10)	C-802 ShShMS	ShShM system	1992	1994	5	For 10 Hudong Class fast attack craft
	(10)	Hudong Class	Fast attack craft	1992	1994	5	For 10 Hudong Class fast attack craft

No.	Weapon designation	Weapon description	Year of order	Year(s) of deliveries	No. delivered	Comments
..	[...]	Mobile SSM system				
(100)	T-72M1	Main battle tank	(1991)	1993–95	(10)	
1	Kilo Class	Submarine	(1993)	1994–95	(100)	Status uncertain; Iranian designation Tareq Class
(16)	SS-N-22 Sunburn	ShShM	1993	1995	(12)	For use in existing coast defence system
Israel						
S: France						
4	AS-565SA Panther	ASW helicopter	1994			Deal worth $48 m; sold through USA; partly financed by USA; for Navy
Germany, FR						
2	Dolphin Class	Submarine	1991			Deal worth $570 m; financed by FRG
Russia						
45	BRDM-2	Scout car	1994	1995	15	Ex-Russian army; for PLO police in Gaza; gift
USA						
14	Bell-209/AH-1E	Helicopter	(1995)	1995	(4)	Ex-US Army
21	F-15I Strike Eagle	Fighter/bomber	1994	1995	(2)	Deal worth $1.76 b (offsets $1 b); financed by USA
4	F-15I Strike Eagle	Fighter/bomber	1995			
6	S-65A/CH-53D Stallion	Helicopter	1992	1994–95	(6)	Ex-US Air Force; deal worth $13.2 m
..	TA-4J Skyhawk	Fighter/trainer	(1992)	1994–95	(10)	Ex-US Navy
42	MLRS 227mm	MRL	1995			Deal worth $108 m incl 1500 rockets
6	M-577A2	APC/command post	1993	1995	(6)	Ex-US Army
28	M-577A2	APC/command post	1995	1995	(28)	Ex-US Army
3	AN/SPS-55	Surveillance radar	1989	1994–95	3	On 3 Saar 5 Type (Eilat Class) corvettes
3	Phalanx	CIWS	(1989)	1994–95	3	On 3 Saar 5 Type (Eilat Class) corvettes
3	RGM-84A ShShMS	ShShM system	(1989)	1994–95	3	On 3 Saar 5 Type (Eilat Class) corvettes
300	AIM-9S Sidewinder	Air-to-air missile	1990	1993–95	(300)	Deal worth $32 m incl support
..	FIM-92A Stinger	Portable SAM	(1993)	1993–95	(300)	
..	RGM-84A Harpoon	ShShM	(1989)	1994–95	(48)	For 3 Saar 5 Type (Eilat Class) corvettes
3	Saar 5 Class	Corvette	1989	1994–95	3	Built to Israeli design; some weapon systems fitted in Israel; Israeli designation Eilat Class
Italy						
S: Germany, FR						
8	Do-228-200	Transport	1990	1992–95	(8)	For Army
UK						
24	Tornado ADV F Mk-3	Fighter	1994	1995	12	Ex-UK Air Force; 10-year lease worth $360 m incl $200 m for logistical support
USA						
..	Sky Flash	Air-to-air missile	1994	1995	(48)	For 24 Tornado ADV fighters
13	AV-8B Harrier II Plus	Fighter/ground attack	1990			Deal worth $522 m; assembled in Italy; for Navy
42	AGM-65G Maverick	ASM	1994			Deal worth $25 m; for Navy AV-8B fighters

Recipient/ supplier (S) or licenser (L)	No. ordered	Weapon designation	Weapon description	Year of order/ licence	Year(s) of deliveries	No. delivered/ produced	Comments
	33	AIM-120A AMRAAM	Air-to-air missile	1994			Deal worth $23 m; for Navy AV-8B fighters
	..	BGM-71D TOW 2	Anti-tank missile	1987	1990–95	(1 320)	For Army A-129 helicopters
L: France	23 000	Milan 2	Anti-tank missile	1984	1985–95	(17 433)	Incl 18 for Army, 32 for Police, 25 for Coast Guard;
USA	..	Bell 412/AB-412	Helicopter	1980	1982–95	(97)	incl production for export
Japan							
S: Italy	4	127mm/54	Naval gun	(1988)	1993–95	2	For 4 Kongo Class destroyers
UK	6	BAe-125-800	Transport	1992	1995	3	For SAR; Japanese designation U-125A
USA	2	Boeing 767 AWACS	AEW&C aircraft	1993			Deal worth $840 m
	2	Boeing 767 AWACS	AEW&C aircraft	1994			Deal worth $773 m
	1	BAe-125/RH-800	Transport	1995			For SAR; Japanese designation U-125A; option on 20 more
	1	C-130H Hercules	Transport	1995			Deal worth $43 m
	..	S-76C	Helicopter	1993	1994	1	For Maritime Safety Agency; for SAR
	36	MLRS 227mm	MRL	1993	1994–95	(18)	Deal worth $362 m
	12	AN/SPG-62	Fire control radar	(1988)	1993–95	(6)	For 4 Kongo Class destroyers
	2	AN/SPY-1D	Surveillance radar	1992	1995	(1)	Part of Aegis air defence system for 2 Kongo Class destroyers
	1	AN/SPY-1D	Surveillance radar	(1993)			Part of Aegis air defence system for fourth Kongo Class destroyer
	1	Patriot SAMS	SAM system	(1994)	1995	1	
	6	Phalanx	CIWS	1988	1993–95	(4)	Deal worth $66 m; for 3 Kongo Class destroyers
	2	Phalanx	CIWS	1993			Deal worth $7.7 m; for 1 Kongo Class destroyer
	3	RGM-84A ShShMS	ShShM system	1994	1995	(1)	For 3 Kongo Class destroyers
	3	Standard VLS	ShAM system	1990	1995	(1)	Part of Aegis air defence system for 3 Kongo Class destroyers
	75	AGM-84A Harpoon	Anti-ship missile	1990	1991–95	(75)	Deal worth $125 m
	16	AGM-84A Harpoon	Anti-ship missile	1994	1995	(6)	

Country/Supplier	No. ordered	Weapon designation	Weapon description	Year of order	Year(s) of deliveries	No. delivered	Comments
	56	RIM-66M Standard 2	ShAM	1994	1995	(19)	For Kongo Class destroyers
	:	RIM-7H Seasparrow	ShAM	1993		(56)	For Kongo Class destroyers
L: France	:	MO-120-RT-61 120mm	Mortar	1992	1993–95	160	Deal worth $13.4 m
Germany, FR	:	FH-70 155mm	Towed gun	(1982)	1984–95	417	
Italy	3	Sparviero Class	Fast attack craft	1990	1993–95	3	Deal worth $170 m; option on 3 more; Japanese designation PG-01 Class
USA	52	Bell 205 Kai/UH-1J	Helicopter	1991	1992–95	52	For Army
	83	Bell-209/AH-1S	Combat helicopter	1982	1984–95	77	For Army
	58	CH-47D Chinook	Helicopter	(1984)	1986–95	52	Incl for Army
	3	EP-3C Orion	ELINT aircraft	1992	1993–95	3	For Navy
	37	F-15J Eagle	Fighter	1987	1992–95	37	Incl F-15DJ fighter/trainers
	..	Hughes-500/OH-6D	Helicopter	1977	1978–95	206	For Army and Navy
	66	P-3C Orion	ASW/maritime patrol	1985	1987–94	57	For Navy
	52	S-70/SH-60J Seahawk	ASW helicopter	1988	1991–95	37	For Navy; incl 21 for SAR
	64	S-70/UH-60J Blackhawk	Helicopter	1988	1991–95	19	Incl 18 for Navy
	2	UP-3D Orion	EW aircraft	1994	1995	1	For Navy
	1 330	AIM-7M Sparrow	Air-to-air missile	1990	1990–95	986	Deal worth $477 m
	..	BGM-71C I-TOW	Anti-tank missile	(1983)	1985–95	7 604	
Jordan							
S: USA	12	F-16A Fighting Falcon	Fighter	(1995)			Ex-US Air Force
	..	F-16B Fighting Falcon	Fighter/trainer	(1995)			Ex-US Air Force
	4	S-70/UH-60L Blackhawk	Helicopter	1995			Deal worth $67 m incl 2 spare engines, spares and support
	(50)	M-60A3 Patton II	Main battle tank	(1995)	(1995)		Ex-US Army
Kazakhstan							
S: Russia	8	MiG-29 Fulcrum C	Fighter	(1995)	1995	8	Aid
Korea, North							
S: Kazakhstan	24	KS-19 100mm	Anti-aircraft gun	1995	1995	24	Ex-Kazakh Army

Recipient/ supplier (S) or licenser (L)	No. ordered	Weapon designation	Weapon description	Year of order/ licence	Year(s) of deliveries	No. delivered/ produced	Comments
Russia/USSR	4	Fire Can	Fire control radar	1995	1995	4	Ex-Kazakh Army
	..	Drum Tilt	Fire control radar	(1979)	1981–94	(15)	For Soju Class fast attack craft
	..	Drum Tilt	Fire control radar	(1987)	1990–95	(5)	For Taechong II (Mayang) Class patrol craft
	..	Square Tie	Surveillance radar	(1979)	1981–94	(15)	For Soju Class fast attack craft
	..	SS-N-2 ShShMS	ShShM system	(1979)	1981–94	(15)	For Soju Class fast attack craft
L: China	..	Romeo Class	Submarine	1973	1975–92	(15)	
Russia/USSR	..	SA-16	Portable SAM	(1989)	1992–95	(80)	
Korea, South							
S: France	984	Mistral	Portable SAM	1992	1993–95	(600)	Deal worth $180 m incl 130 launchers (offsets 25%)
Italy	3	127mm/54	Naval gun	(1993)			For 3 KDX-2000 Type frigates
Netherlands	2	Goalkeeper	CIWS	(1991)			For 1 KDX-2000 Type frigate
	4	Goalkeeper	CIWS	1995			For 2 KDX-2000 Type frigates
	1	MW-08	Surveillance radar	1994			For 1 KDX-2000 Type frigate; option on more
	2	STIR	Fire control radar	(1992)			For 1 KDX-2000 Type frigate; option on more
Russia	..	BMP-3	AIFV	1995			Payment for Russian debt to South Korea; for technical evaluation
	..	T-80U	Main battle tank	1995			Payment for Russian debt to South Korea; for technical evaluation
	..	AT-7 Saxhorn	Anti-tank missile	1995			Payment for Russian debt to South Korea; for technical evaluation
	..	SA-18	Portable SAM	1995			Payment for Russian debt to South Korea; for technical evaluation
UK	(16)	ST-1802	Fire control radar	(1987)	1989–95	16	For second batch of 16 Po Hang Class corvettes
USA	48	F-16C Fighting Falcon	Fighter	1991	1994–95	(17)	Incl 36 assembled from kits; deal worth $2.52 b incl 72 licensed production, 12 spare engines and 20 LANTIRN pods
	8	P-3C Orion Update 3	ASW/maritime patrol	1990	1995	(8)	Deal worth $840 m incl spare engines, training and spares

No.	Weapon designation	Weapon description	Year of order	Year of delivery	No. delivered	Comments
..	… 200mm	Self-propelled gun	1995	1995	13	Ex-US Army
275	M-48A5 Patton	Main battle tank	1995	1995	275	Ex-US Army
3	AN/SPS-55	Surveillance radar	1994			For 3 KDX-2000 Type frigates
9	AN/TPQ-36	Tracking radar	1992			Deal worth $14 m
6	AN/TPQ-37	Tracking radar	1994	1995	6	Deal worth $106 m incl field radios
1	RGM-84A ShShMS	ShShM system	(1992)			For 3 KDX-2000 Type frigates
2	Seasparrow VLS	ShAM system	(1994)			Deal worth $57 m; for 2 KDX-2000 Type frigates
28	AGM-84A Harpoon	Anti-ship missile	1992	1995	(28)	Deal worth $58 m incl support; for P-3C ASW aircraft
130	AGM-88A HARM	Anti-radar missile	1992			For F-16 fighters
190	AIM-120A AMRAAM	Air-to-air missile	1993			For F-16 fighters
300	AIM-9S Sidewinder	Air-to-air missile	1994	1994–95	(200)	Deal worth $34 m incl spares and support
(72)	RGM-84A Harpoon	ShShM	(1992)			For 3 KDX-2000 Type frigates
..	RIM-7H Seasparrow	ShAM	1992			For KDX-2000 Type frigates; deal worth $12.7 m
L: Germany, FR						
2	Type 209/1200	Submarine	1987	1994–95	2	In addition to 1 delivered direct; Korean designation Chang Bogo Class
3	Type 209/1200	Submarine	1989	1995	1	Korean designation Chang Bogo Class
3	Type 209/1200	Submarine	1994			Deal worth $510 m; Korean designation Chang Bogo Class
USA						
72	F-16C Fighting Falcon	Fighter	1991			Deal worth $2.52 b incl 48 delivered direct, 12 spare engines and 20 LANTIRN pods
242	M-109A2 155mm	Self-propelled gun	1989	1991–95	242	Deal worth $260 m
(234)	M-109A2 155mm	Self-propelled gun	1995			Deal worth $50 m
(833)	K-1 ROKIT	Main battle tank	1981	1984–95	775	Developed for Korean production
Kuwait						
S: Egypt						
2	AN/TPS-63	Surveillance radar	(1993)	1994	1	For 8 P-37BRL Type fast attack craft
France						
8	MRR-3D	Surveillance radar	1995			Deal worth $54 m
1	TRS-22XX	Surveillance radar	1995			
8	P-37BRL Type	Fast attack craft	1995			Deal worth $475 m incl $10 m for training
Italy						
11	Skyguard SAMS	SAM system	(1988)	1989–91	(6)	Kuwaiti designation Amoun
Russia						
(27)	BM-23 300mm Smerch	MRL	1994	1995	6	

Recipient/ supplier (S) or licenser (L)	No. ordered	Weapon designation	Weapon description	Year of order/ licence	Year(s) of deliveries	No. delivered/ produced	Comments
	(20)	BMP-2	AIFV	1994	1994–95	(20)	For BMP-3 AIFVs
	..	BMP-3	AIFV	1994	1995	(60)	For 20 BMP-2 AIFVs
	(480)	AT-10 Bastion	Anti-tank missile	(1994)	1995	(480)	
	(80)	AT-4 Spigot	Anti-tank missile	1994	1994–95	(80)	
UK	16	EMB-312 Tucano	Trainer	1989	1995	(16)	
	254	MCV-80 Desert Warrior	AIFV	1993	1995	(21)	Deal worth $740 m (offsets 30%); incl APC/CP, repair and ARV versions
USA	(250)	Starburst	Portable SAM	1994	1995	(250)	Deal worth $80 m incl 50 launchers
	16	M-113A3	APC	1992	1994–95	(16)	Deal worth $32 m incl 30 M-577A3 APC/CPs; part of deal worth $4 b; option on 109 more
	218	M-1A2 Abrams	Main battle tank	1992	1994–95	(114)	Deal worth $4 b incl 46 M-88A1 ARVs, 16 M-113A3 APCs, 30 M-577A3 APC/CPs and spares
	30	M-577A3	APC/command post	1992	1994–95	(30)	Deal worth $32 m incl 16 M-113A3 APCs; part of deal worth $4 b; option on 22 more
	46	M-88A1	ARV	1992	1995	(23)	Deal worth $4 b incl 218 M-1A2 tanks, 16 M-113A3 APCs, 30 M-577A3 APC/CPs and spares
	6	I-HAWK SAMS	SAM system	1992			Part of deal worth $2.2 b
	5	Patriot SAMS	SAM system	(1993)	1995	(2)	Deal worth $327 m incl 210 missiles (offsets 30%)
	40	AGM-84A Harpoon	Anti-ship missile	1988	1995		For F/A-18C/D fighters
	..	BGM-71C I-TOW	Anti-tank missile	1993	1995	(20)	For MCV-80 AIFVs
	210	MIM-104 PAC-2	SAM	(1993)	1995	(105)	Deal worth $327 m incl 5 Patriot SAM systems (offsets 30%)
	342	MIM-23B HAWK	SAM	1992			Part of deal worth $2.2 b
Latvia							
S: Czechoslovakia	20	D-30 122mm	Towed gun	(1994)	1995	20	Ex-Czech Army; aid
	25	M-53 100mm	Towed gun	1994	1995	25	Ex-Czech Army; aid
Norway	1	Storm Class	Fast attack craft	1994	1995	1	Ex-Norwegian Navy; armament removed before transfer; gift

Lebanon

No.	Weapon designation	Weapon description	Year of order	Year of delivery	No. delivered	Comments
S: USA						
225	M-113A2	APC	1995	1995	225	Ex-US Army; deal worth $37 m
118	M-113A2	APC	1994	1994	(92)	Ex-US Army; aid
Lithuania						
S: Germany, FR						
3	Osa I Class	Fast attack craft	1993	1995	3	Former GDR equipment; armament removed before delivery; aid
Norway						
1	Storm Class	Fast attack craft	1994	1995	1	Ex-Norwegian Navy; armament removed before delivery; gift
Malaysia						
S: France						
2	MM-40 ShShMS	ShShM system	1993			For 2 Lekiu Class frigates
16	MM-40 Exocet	ShShM	1993			For 2 Lekiu Class frigates
Indonesia						
(6)	CN-235	Transport	1995	1995	(3)	In exchange for Indonesian order for 20 MD3-160 trainers and Proton cars; deal worth $102 m; option on 14 more
Italy						
2	Albatros Mk-2	ShAM system	1995	1995		On 2 Assad Class corvettes
2	Otomat/Teseo ShShMS	ShShM system	1995	1995		On 2 Assad Class corvettes
2	RAN-12L/X	Surveillance radar	1995	1995		On 2 Assad Class corvettes
4	RTN-10X	Fire control radar	1995	1995		On 2 Assad Class corvettes
(12)	Aspide	ShAM	1995	1995		For 2 Assad Class corvettes
(24)	Otomat Mk-2	ShShM	1995	1995		For 2 Assad Class corvettes
	Assad Class	Corvette	1995	1995		Originally built for Iraq but embargoed
Korea, South						
47	KIFV	APC	1995	1995	47	Deal worth $29.3 m; incl APC/CP version
Netherlands						
2	DA-08	Surveillance radar	1992			For 2 Lekiu Class frigates
Russia						
18	MiG-29S Fulcrum C	Fighter	1994	1995	18	Deal worth $600 m (offsets $220 m incl $150 barter trade); incl 2 MiG-29UB fighter/trainers
. .	AA-10a Alamo	Air-to-air missile	1994	1995	(105)	For 18 MiG-29S fighters
. .	AA-11 Archer	Air-to-air missile	1994	1995	(216)	For 18 MiG-29S fighters
Sweden						
2	Sea Giraffe 150	Surveillance radar	1992	1992		For 2 Lekiu Class frigates
UK						
18	Hawk 200	Fighter/ground attack	1990	1994–95	(18)	Deal worth $740 m incl 10 Hawk 100 jet trainers, armament, training and support
2	Martello 743-D	Surveillance radar	1990	1992–95	(2)	Deal worth $190 m

Recipient/ supplier (S) or licenser (L)	No. ordered	Weapon designation	Weapon description	Year of order/ licence	Year(s) of deliveries	No. delivered/ produced	Comments
	2	Seawolf VLS	ShAM system	1992			On 2 Lekiu Class frigates
	4	ST-1802SW	Fire control radar	1993			On 2 Lekiu Class frigates
	32	Seawolf VL	ShAM	1993			For 2 Lekiu Class frigates
	504	Starburst	Portable SAM	1993	1995	(125)	
	2	Lekiu Class	Frigate	1992			Deal worth $600 m incl spares, training and support
USA	5	C-130H-30 Hercules	Transport	1995	1995	5	
	8	F/A-18D Hornet	Fighter/trainer	1993			Option on 10 more (offsets $250 m)
	30	AGM-65D Maverick	ASM	1993			For F/A-18D fighters
	25	AGM-84A Harpoon	Anti-ship missile	1993			For F/A-18D fighters
	20	AIM-7M Sparrow	Air-to-air missile	1993			For F/A-18D fighters
	40	AIM-9S Sidewinder	Air-to-air missile	1993			For F/A-18D fighters
L: Switzerland	20	MD3-160	Trainer	1993	1995	12	More built for export and civilian customers
Mauritius							
S: Chile	1	Guardian Class	OPV	1994			Canadian design produced in Chile; deal worth $14.6 m
Mexico							
S: Belgium	(95)	Timoney Mk-5	APC	(1994)	1994–95	(95)	Ex-Belgian Air Force and Gendarmerie
S: Sweden	..	RBS-70 Mk-2	Portable SAM	(1993)	1994–95	(20)	For Air Force
Moldova							
S: Romania	..	TAB-77	APC	(1993)	1994	30	Ex-Romanian Army
Morocco							
S: Denmark	2	Osprey 55 Type	OPV	1990			Moroccan designation El Hahiq Class
S: France	2	OPV-64	OPV	1993	1995	1	Moroccan designation Rais Bargacia Class

Moroccan designation Rais Bargacia Class

No. ordered	Weapon designation	Weapon description	Year of order	Year(s) of deliveries	No. delivered	Comments
Myanmar						
S: China						
24	A-5M Fantan	Fighter/ground attack	(1992)	1995	(12)	
10	F-7M Airguard	Fighter	(1993)	1995	(10)	
2	FT-7	Fighter/trainer	(1993)	1995	(2)	
(50)	Type 69-II	Main battle tank	1993	1995	(50)	
6	Hainan Class	Patrol craft	1994			
Namibia						
S: India						
2	SA-315B Lama	Helicopter	1994	1995	(2)	Deal worth $5.5 m incl 2 SA-316B helicopters
2	SA-316B Alouette III	Helicopter	1994	1995	(2)	Deal worth $5.5 m incl 2 SA-315B helicopters
USA						
1	Learjet 31A	Transport	(1995)	1995	1	For VIP transport
Netherlands						
S: Canada						
7	CH-47C Chinook	Helicopter	(1993)	1995	2	Deal worth $16 m; ex-Canadian Air Force; refurbished to CH-47D in USA before delivery
France						
17	AS-532U2 Cougar	Helicopter	1993			Deal worth $242 m (offsets 120%)
Germany, FR						
15	FH-70 155mm	Towed gun	1995	1995	15	Ex-FRG Army
USA						
12	AH-64A Apache	Combat helicopter	1995			On loan until arrival of AH-64D; deal worth symbolic $12
30	AH-64D Longbow	Combat helicopter	1995			Deal worth $686 m (offsets $873 m)
6	CH-47D Chinook	Helicopter	1993			
8	RGM-84A ShShMS	ShShM system	1990	1991–95	(8)	Deal worth $25 m; for 8 Karel Doorman (M) Class frigates
8	Seasparrow VLS	ShAM system	1985	1991–95	(8)	For 8 Karel Doorman (M) Class frigates
..	AGM-114A Hellfire	Anti-tank missile	1995			For AH-64D/A; deal worth $127 m
200	AIM-120A AMRAAM	Air-to-air missile	1995			
..	RGM-84A Harpoon	ShShM	1988	1991–95	(128)	For 8 Karel Doorman (M) Class frigates
..	RIM-7H Seasparrow	ShAM	1985	1991–95	(128)	For 8 Karel Doorman (M) Class frigates
UAE						
6	L-118 105mm	Towed gun	(1995)	1995	6	Ex-UAE Army; for Marines

Recipient/ supplier (S) or licenser (L)	No. ordered	Weapon designation	Weapon description	Year of order/ licence	Year(s) of deliveries	No. delivered/ produced	Comments
New Zealand							
S: Australia	2	Meko 200ANZ Type	Frigate	1989			Deal worth $554.7 m; option on 2 more
Sweden	2	9LV	Fire control radar	1991			For 2 Meko 200ANZ Type frigates
	2	Sea Giraffe 150	Surveillance radar	1991			For 2 Meko 200ANZ Type frigates
USA	2	127mm/54 Mk-42/9	Naval gun	(1989)			For 2 Meko 200ANZ Type frigates
	2	AN/SPS-49	Surveillance radar	(1993)			For 2 Meko 200ANZ Type frigates
	2	Phalanx	CIWS	1994			Deal worth $17.6 m; for refit of 2 Leander Class frigates
	2	Seasparrow VLS	ShAM system	1992			For 2 Meko 200ANZ Type frigates
	..	RIM-7M Seasparrow	ShAM	(1991)			For 2 Meko 200ANZ Type frigates
Nigeria							
S: France	72	VBL	Scout car	(1992)	1993–95	(72)	
Switzerland	7	PC-7 Turbo Trainer	Trainer	(1993)			
UK	..	MBT Mk-3	Main battle tank	1990	1992–95	(80)	Deal worth $282 m; order may be for up to 150
L: USA	60	Air Beetle T-18	Trainer	1992	1993–95	(36)	Developed for Nigerian production from RV-6A home-built
Norway							
S: Finland	22	XA-185	APC	1994	1995	(22)	For Norwegian UN forces; option on more
France	7 200	Eryx	Anti-tank missile	1993	1995	(200)	Deal worth $115 m incl 424 launchers; option on more (offsets incl production of components)
	400	Mistral	Portable SAM	1990	1992–95	(400)	Deal worth $60 m (offsets 75%); for refit of Hauk Class fast attack craft
Italy	3	RAT-31S	Surveillance radar	1994			
Netherlands	16	M-577A1	APC/command post	1994	1995	16	Ex-Dutch Army; deal worth $659 000
Sweden	104	CV-9030	AIFV	1994	1995	2	Deal worth $241 m (offsets $184 m); option on more
UK	2	S-61/Sea King HAR-3	Helicopter	1993	1995	(1)	Deal worth $22.2 m

Supplier	No.	Weapon designation	Weapon description	Year of order	Year of deliveries	No. delivered	Comments
USA	4	AWS-9	Surveillance radar	1994	1994–95	(4)	Deal worth $29 m; for refit of 4 Oslo Class frigates
	12	MLRS 227mm	MRL	1995	1995		Deal worth $199 m incl rockets, practice rockets, spares and support
	24	AN/TPQ-36A	Fire contol radar	1994	1995	(2)	For Norwegian Advanced Surface-to-Air Missile System
	148	AIM-120A AMRAAM	SAM	1994	1995	(30)	Deal worth $106 m; for Norwegian Advanced Surface-to-Air Missile System
	7 612	BGM-71D TOW 2	Anti-tank missile	1985	1987–95	(7 612)	Deal worth $126 m incl 300 launchers and spares
Oman							
S: France	2	Crotale NG Naval	ShAM system	1992			For 2 Qahir Class (Muheet Type) corvettes
	2	DRBV-SIC	Fire control radar	(1992)			For 2 Qahir Class (Muheet Type) corvettes
	2	MM-40 ShShMS	ShShM system	1992			For 2 Qahir Class (Muheet Type) corvettes
	..	MM-40 Exocet	ShShM	1992			For 2 Qahir Class (Muheet Type) corvettes
	..	VT-1	SAM	1992			For Crotale NG ShAM system for 2 Qahir Class (Muheet Type) corvettes
	3	Vigilante 400 Type	Patrol craft	1993	1995	2	Omani designation Al Bushra Class; option on 5 more
Netherlands	2	MW-08	Surveillance radar	1992			For 2 Qahir Class (Muheet Type) corvettes
	2	STING	Fire control radar	(1992)			For 2 Qahir Class (Muheet Type) corvettes
South Africa	24	G-6 Rhino 155mm	Self-propelled gun	1994	1995	(12)	Deal worth $120 m
Switzerland	5	Skyguard	Fire control radar	1995			For use with 10 GDF-005 AA guns
UK	12	Hawk 200	Fighter/ground attack	1990	1994–95	(12)	Deal worth $225 m incl 4 Hawk 100 jet trainers
	4	Challenger ARV	ARV	1993	1995	(2)	Deal worth $225 m incl 18 Challenger 2 tanks, 2 training tanks and 4 Stormer APC/CPs
	18	Challenger 2	Main battle tank	1993	1995	(6)	Deal worth $225 m incl 4 ARVs, 2 training version and 4 Stormer APC/CPs; option on 18 more
	80	Piranha 8x8	APC	1994	1995	(20)	Deal worth $138 m; incl ARV, APC/CP, 81mm mortar carrier and other versions; option on 46 more
	..	Rapier Mk-2	SAM	1992			Deal worth $71 m incl modernization of Rapier SAM systems
	..	Starstreak	SAM	1993			

Recipient/ supplier (S) or licenser (L)	No. ordered	Weapon designation	Weapon description	Year of order/ licence	Year(s) of deliveries	No. delivered/ produced	Comments
USA	2	Qahir Class	Corvette	1992			Deal worth $265 m; 'Muheet Project'
	(96)	AIM-9L Sidewinder	Air-to-air missile	1990	1993–95	(96)	For 16 Hawk 100/200 jet trainers/fighters
Pakistan							
S: China	25	K-8 Karakorum 8	Jet trainer	1987	1994–95	(12)	Incl assembly; some components produced in Pakistan; option on more, incl licensed production
France	..	T-85-IIAP	Main battle tank	1990	1992–95	(282)	For Army and Navy
	..	Mistral	Portable SAM	(1991)	1994	(50)	Deal worth $100 m; for 3 Agosta 90B Type submarines
	..	SM-39 Exocet	SuShM	1994			
	2	Agosta 90B Type	Submarine	1994			Incl 1 assembled in Pakistan; deal worth $750 m incl 1 licensed production
	1	Eridan Class	MCM ship	1992	1995	1	In addition to 1 ex-French Navy and 1 licensed production
Lebanon	10	Mirage IIIE	Fighter	1994			Ex-Lebanese Air Force
Netherlands	6	DA-08	Surveillance radar	1994			For refit of 6 Amazon Class (Type 21) frigates
Sweden	6	9LV	Fire control radar	1994			For refit of 6 Amazon Class (Type 21) frigates
UK	3	Lynx HAS-3	ASW helicopter	1994	1994–95	3	Ex-UK Navy; option on 3 more
USA	10	Bell-209/AH-1S	Combat helicopter	1990			Deal worth $89 m incl spare engines and support; embargoed 1992–95
	3	P-3C Orion Update 2	ASW/maritime patrol	(1990)			Deal worth $240 m incl spares and support; embargoed 1992–95
	24	M-198 155mm	Towed gun	1988			Embargoed 1992–95
	..	AN/TPQ-36	Tracking radar	(1990)			Deal worth $65 m; embargoed 1992–95
	4	AN/TPQ-37	Tracking radar	(1985)	1987–89	(3)	
	28	AGM-84A Harpoon	Anti-ship missile	1990			For P-3C ASW/maritime patrol aircraft; embargoed 1992–95
	360	AIM-9L Sidewinder	Air-to-air missile	1988			For F-16 fighters; embargoed 1992–95
L: China	(450)	T-69-II	Main battle tank	(1990)	1991–95	330	Deal worth $1.2 b

	No.	Weapon designation	Weapon description	Order date	Delivery date	No.	Comments
France	..	Anza 2	SAM	(1988)	1989–95	650	Deal worth $750 m incl 2 delivered direct
	1	Agosta 90B Type	Submarine	1994			In addition to 1 ex-French Navy and 1 delivered direct
	1	Eridan Class	MCM ship	1992			
Italy	..	Skyguard	Fire control radar	(1988)	1989–95	94	For use with GDF-002 35mm AA guns
USA	755	M-113A2	APC	1989	1991–95	755	
Peru							
S: Ukraine	3	An-32 Cline	Transport	1994			Option on 3 more
Philippines							
S: Korea, South	3	F-5A Freedom Fighter	Fighter/ground attack	(1995)	1995	3	Ex-South Korean Air Force; aid
	5	Sea Dolphin Class	Patrol craft	1995	1995	5	Ex-South Korean Navy; aid
Russia	20	Yak-18T	Lightplane	(1993)	1994–95	(10)	
USA	5	MD-530MG Defender	Helicopter	1993	1994–95	(5)	
	12	Commando V-300	APC	1993	1995	(12)	Deal worth $18.2 m incl 12 Commando V-300 FSV AIFVs
	12	Commando V-300 FSV	AIFV	1993	1995	(12)	Deal worth $18.2 m incl 12 Commando V-300 APCs
L: UK	142	FS-100 Simba	APC	1992	1994–95	(61)	Deal worth $46 m incl 8 delivered direct
Poland							
S: Czechoslovakia	10	MiG-29 Fulcrum	Fighter	1995	1995	10	Ex-Czech Air Force; exchanged for 11 W-3 Sokol helicopters; incl 1 MiG-29UB fighter/trainer
Germany, FR	18	Mi-24D Hind D	Combat helicopter	1995			Former GDR equipment; gift
L: USA	(2)	PA-34-200T Seneca III	Transport	(1994)	1995	1	For VIP transport
Russia/USSR	..	An-28	Transport	(1992)	1993–95	4	Incl maritime patrol version
Portugal							
S: UK	1	Watchman	Surveillance radar	1993	1995	(1)	NATO aid

Recipient/ supplier (S) or licenser (L)	No. ordered	Weapon designation	Weapon description	Year of order/ licence	Year(s) of deliveries	No. delivered/ produced	Comments
Qatar							
S: France	12	Mirage 2000-5	Fighter	1994			
	..	VBL	Scout car	(1992)	1993-95	(16)	
	4	Crotale NG Naval	ShAM system	1992			For 4 Vita Class fast attack craft
	4	MM-40 ShShMS	ShShM system	1992			For 4 Vita Class fast attack craft
	4	TRS-3051 Triton	Surveillance radar	(1992)			For 4 Vita Class fast attack craft
	..	MICA EM	Air-to-air missile	1994			Deal worth $280 m incl R-550 missiles; for 12 Mirage 2000-5 fighters
	500	Mistral	Portable SAM	1990	1992-95	(400)	
	..	MM-40 Exocet	ShShM	1992			For 4 Vita Class fast attack craft
	..	R-550 Magic 2	Air-to-air missile	1994			Deal worth $280 m incl MICA EM missiles; for 12 Mirage 2000-5 fighters
Netherlands	4	Goalkeeper	CIWS	1992			For 4 Vita Class fast attack craft
	4	STING	Fire control radar	(1992)			For 4 Vita Class fast attack craft
UK	4	Vita Class	Fast attack craft	1992			Deal worth $200 m
Romania							
S: USA	4	C-130B Hercules	Transport	1995			Ex-US Air Force
	5	AN/FPS-117	Surveillance radar	1995			Deal worth $82 m
L: France	..	SA-330 Puma	Helicopter	1977	1978-94	(190)	Incl production for export
USA	96	Bell-209/AH-1F	Helicopter	1995			
Russia/USSR	..	SA-7 Grail	Portable SAM	(1978)	1978-95	(450)	
Saudi Arabia							
S: Canada	1 117	LAV-25	AIFV	1990	1992-95	(1 030)	Deal worth $700 m; incl 111 LAV-TOW tank destroyers, 130 LAV-90mm armoured cars, 73 LAV-120mm mortar carriers and 449 in other versions; for National Guard

	No. ordered	Weapon designation	Weapon description	(1990)	1995	No. delivered	Comments
France	..	Piranha 8x8	APC	1994	1995	(20)	Incl several versions
	2	Castor 2J	Fire control radar	1994			On 2 Improved La Fayette Class (F-3000S Type) frigates
	2	Crotale Naval ShAMS	ShAM system	1994			On 2 Improved La Fayette Class (F-3000S Type) frigates
	2	DRBV-26C	Surveillance radar	1994			On 2 Improved La Fayette Class (F-3000S Type) frigates
	2	MM-40 ShShMS	ShShM system	1994			On 2 Improved La Fayette Class (F-3000S Type) frigates
	2	Sea Tiger Mk-2	Surveillance radar	1994			On 2 Improved La Fayette Class (F-3000S Type) frigates
	..	MM-40 Exocet	ShShM	1994			For 2 Improved La Fayette Class (F-3000S Type) frigates
	..	VT-1	Ship-to-air missile	1990			For 2 Improved La Fayette Class (F-3000S Type) frigates
	2	La Fayette Class	Frigate	1994			Part of deal worth $3.42 b incl other weapons, construction of a naval base, training and support (offsets 35%)
Switzerland	(20)	PC-9	Trainer	1994	1995	2	Sold through UK as part of 'Al Yamamah II' deal
UK	20	Hawk 100	Jet trainer	1993			Part of 'Al Yamamah II' deal
	(60)	Hawk 200	Fighter/ground attack	1993			Part of 'Al Yamamah II' deal
	48	Tornado IDS	Fighter/bomber	1993			Part of 'Al Yamamah II' deal
USA	..	Piranha 8x8	APC	1990	1992–93	94	Incl several versions
	8	C-130H Hercules	Transport	1990	1992	(1)	Deal worth $320 m incl 2 C-130H-30 version
	72	F-15S Strike Eagle	Fighter/bomber	1992	1995	(4)	Deal worth $9 b incl 24 spare engines, 48 LANTIRN pods and armament
	8	S-70/UH-60 Blackhawk	Helicopter	1992			Deal worth $225 m; for MedEvac use
	150	M-60A3 Patton II	Main battle tank	1990	1994–95	150	Ex-US Army; deal worth $206 m
	2	AN/TPS-70	Surveillance radar	1993	1994–95	(2)	'Peace Pulse' programme worth $18 m
	13	Patriot SAMS	SAM system	1992	1995	(4)	Deal worth $1.03 b incl 1 SAM system for training and 761 MIM-104 PAC-2 missiles
	900	AGM-65D Maverick	ASM	1992	1995	(50)	Deal worth $9 b incl 72 F-15S fighters, 24 spare engines and 48 LANTIRN pods; incl AGM-65G version

Recipient/ supplier (S) or licenser (L)	No. ordered	Weapon designation	Weapon description	Year of order/ licence	Year(s) of deliveries	No. delivered/ produced	Comments
	300	AIM-7M Sparrow	Air-to-air missile	1992	1995	(20)	Deal worth $9 b incl 72 F-15S fighters, 24 spare engines and 48 LANTIRN pods
	300	AIM-9S Sidewinder	Air-to-air missile	1992	1995	(20)	Deal worth $9 b incl 72 F-15S fighters, 24 spare engines and 48 LANTIRN pods
	761	MIM-104 PAC-2	SAM	1992	1995	(250)	Deal worth $1.03 b incl 13 operational and 1 training Patriot SAM systems
Sierra Leone							
S: Belarus	(2)	Mi-24D Hind D	Combat helicopter	1994	1995	(2)	Ex-Belarussian Air Force
Singapore							
S: France	150	Mistral	Portable SAM	1992	1994–95	(150)	Deal incl also 30 launchers; incl for Navy
Israel	6	Barak ShAMS	ShAM system	(1992)			For 6 Victory Class corvettes; status uncertain
	..	Barak	ShAM	(1992)			For 6 Victory Class corvettes; status uncertain
Jordan	7	F-5E Tiger II	Fighter	1994			Ex-Jordanian Air Force; deal worth $21 m
Netherlands	5	Fokker 50 Enforcer 2	ASW/maritime patrol	1991	1994–95	5	
Sweden	4	Landsort Class	MCM ship	1991	1994–95	2	Incl assembly of 3 in Singapore
	1	Sjöormen Class	Submarine	1995			Ex-Swedish Navy; refitted before delivery; for training
UK	(18)	FV-180 CET	AEV	1993	1994–95	(18)	
	18	FV-180 CET	AEV	1995			
USA	6	CH-47D Chinook	Helicopter	1994			Incl for SAR
	8	F-16C Fighting Falcon	Fighter	1994			Deal worth $890 m incl 10 F-16D fighter/trainers; 'Peace Carven II' programme
	10	F-16D Fighting Falcon	Fighter/trainer	1994			Deal worth $890 m incl 8 F-16C fighters; 'Peace Carven II' programme
	50	AIM-7M Sparrow	Air-to-air missile	1993			For F-16C/D fighters
	30	AIM-9S Sidewinder	Air-to-air missile	1994			For F-16C/D fighters

	No.	Weapon designation	Weapon description	Year of order	Year of delivery	No. delivered	Comments
Slovakia							
S: Russia	7	MiG-29S Fulcrum C	Fighter	1995	1995	7	Payment for Russian debts to Slovakia
	1	MiG-29UB Fulcrum B	Fighter/trainer	1995	1995	1	Payment for Russian debts to Slovakia
Slovenia							
S: Canada	5	Bell 412	Helicopter	1994	1994–95	(5)	Part of deal worth $30 m incl 2 Bell 206B helicopters (offsets 100%)
South Africa							
S: Switzerland	60	PC-7 Turbo Trainer	Trainer	1993	1994–95	(42)	Deal worth $130 m (offsets 55%); assembled in South Africa
USA	1	C-130B Hercules	Transport	1995			Ex-US Air Force; gift; option on 3 more
Spain							
S: France	840	Mistral	Portable SAM	1991	1992–95	(600)	Deal worth $154 m incl 200 launchers (offsets 50%)
Germany, FR	108	Leopard 2	Main battle tank	1995	1995	54	Ex-FRG Army
	..	Leopard 2 KWS	Main battle tank	1995	1995		
Italy	1	RAN-30X	Surveillance radar	(1991)	1995	(1)	For Meroka CIWS on 1 Patino Class support ship
	1	RAN-30X	Surveillance radar	(1993)			For Meroka CIWS on 1 LPD Type AALS
	2	RAT-31S	Surveillance radar	1992			Deal worth $23.4 m (offsets 150%); option on 2 more
	2	Mirage F-1B	Fighter/trainer	1994			Ex-Qatari Air Force; deal worth $132 m incl 11 Mirage F-1C fighters and spares
Qatar	11	Mirage F-1C	Fighter	1994			Ex-Qatari Air Force; deal worth $132 m incl 2 Mirage F-1B fighter/trainers and spares
UK	56	L-118 105mm	Towed gun	1995			Deal worth $63 m incl ammunition
USA	8	AV-8B Harrier II Plus	Fighter/ground attack	1992	1995		Deal worth $257 m; for Navy; assembled in Spain
	24	F/A-18A Hornet	Fighter	1995	1995	6	Ex-US Navy; option on 6 more; deal worth $288 m; refurbished before delivery
	6	RF-4C Phantom II	Reconnaissance plane	1995	1995	3	Ex-US Air Force
	6	S-70B/SH-60B Seahawk	ASW helicopter	1991	1992	2	Deal worth $251 m, for FFG-7 (Santa Maria) Class frigates

Recipient/ supplier (S) or licenser (L)	No. ordered	Weapon designation	Weapon description	Year of order/ licence	Year(s) of deliveries	No. delivered/ produced	Comments
	1	TAV-8B Harrier II	Fighter/trainer	1992			Deal worth $25 m; for Navy
	83	M-110A2 203mm	Self-propelled gun	1991	1993-95	(48)	CFE cascade; ex-US Army
	(31)	M-577A2	APC/command post	1993	1995	(15)	Ex-US Army
	2	AN/SPS-10	Surveillance radar	1994	1994-95	2	On 2 ex-US Navy Newport Class landing ships
	2	AN/VPS-2 Modified	Fire control radar	(1991)	1995	(2)	For 2 Meroka CIWS on 1 Patino Class support ship
	2	AN/VPS-2 Modified	Fire control radar	(1993)			For 2 Meroka CIWS on 1 LPD Type AALS
	2	Phalanx	CIWS	1994	1994-95	2	On 2 ex-US Navy Newport Class landing ships
	2	Newport Class	Landing ship	1994	1994-95	2	Ex-US Navy; lease worth $4.6 m incl spares and training
L: UK	4	Sandown/CME Type	MCM ship	1993			Deal worth $381 m
USA	(2 000)	BGM-71F TOW-2	Anti-tank missile	1987	1995	100	Deal incl also 200 launchers
Sri Lanka							
S: China	3	Haizhui Class	Patrol craft	1994			
Israel	3	Kfir C7	Fighter/ground attack	(1995)	1995	3	Ex-Israeli Air Force
Ukraine	3	An-32 Cline	Transport	(1995)			
	3	Mi-17 Hip H	Helicopter	(1995)			
Sudan							
S: Kyrgyzstan	1	Mi-24D Hind D	Combat helicopter	(1995)	1995	1	Ex-Kyrgyz Air Force
Sweden							
S: France	2	AS-332B Super Puma	Helicopter	1993	1994-95	2	Swedish designation Hkp-10; for SAR
	..	TRS-2620 Gerfaut	Surveillance radar	1993	1993-95	(40)	Deal worth $17.7 m; for CV-90 AAV(G)s
Germany, FR	350	BMP-1	AIFV	1994	1995	2	Former GDR equipment; Swedish designation Pbv-501

	No.	Weapon designation	Weapon description	Year of order	Year of delivery	No. delivered	Comments
	120	Leopard 2 KWS	Main battle tank	1994			Deal worth $770 m incl 160 ex-FRG Army Leopard 2 tanks (offsets 100%, incl assembly of 91); option on 90; Swedish designation Strv-122
	(800)	MT-LB	APC	1993	1993–95	(346)	Former GDR equipment; deal worth $10.3 m incl 228 2S1 SP gun chassis for spares; incl 200 for spares; Swedish designation Pbv-401
USA	2	Gulfstream IV	Transport	1992	1995	2	Modified for ELINT use in Sweden; Swedish designation Tp-102
	100	AIM-120A AMRAAM	Air-to-air missile	1994			Deal worth $190 m (offsets 100%); for JAS-39 fighters
Switzerland							
S: USA	34	F/A-18C/D Hornet	Fighter	1993			Deal worth $2.3 b; incl 8 F/A-18D trainer version
	150	AIM-120A AMRAAM	Air-to-air missile	1988			For 34 F/A-18C/D fighters
	..	AIM-9L Sidewinder	Air-to-air missile	(1988)			For 34 F/A-18C/D fighters
	12 000	BGM-71D TOW 2	Anti-tank missile	(1985)	1988–95	(7 275)	Deal worth $209 m incl 400 launchers and night vision sights; assembled in Switzerland
	3 500	FIM-92A Stinger	Portable SAM	1988	1993–95	(2 250)	Deal worth $315 m (offsets 70% incl production of components)
Syria							
S: Korea, North	(150)	SS-1 Scud C	SSM	1989	1991–95	(140)	Part of deal worth $1.6 b; status uncertain
Russia	54	MiG-29S Fulcrum C	Fighter	1994			Part of deal worth $1.6 b; status uncertain
	350	T-72M	Main battle tank	1994			Part of deal worth $1.6 b; status uncertain
	..	SA-16 Gimlet	Portable SAM	1994			Part of deal worth $1.6 b; status uncertain
Slovakia	171	T-72M	Main battle tank	1992	1993–95	(115)	Part of deal for 252 T-72 tanks, of which 81 delivered from Czechoslovakia before break-up
Taiwan							
S: France	60	Mirage 2000-5	Fighter	1992			Deal worth $2.6 b (offsets 10%); option on 40 more
	6	DRBV-26C	Surveillance radar	1995			For 6 La Fayette (Kang Ting) Class frigates
	6	TRS-3051 Triton	Surveillance radar	1995			For 6 La Fayette (Kang Ting) Class frigates

Recipient/ supplier (S) or licenser (L)	No. ordered	Weapon designation	Weapon description	Year of order/ licence	Year(s) of deliveries	No. delivered/ produced	Comments
	(1 500)	MICA	Air-to-air missile	(1992)			Deal worth $1.2 b incl R-550 missiles; for 60 Mirage 2000-5 fighters
	(500)	R-550 Magic 2	Air-to-air missile	1992			Deal worth $1.2 b incl MICA missiles; for 60 Mirage 2000-5 fighters
	6	La Fayette Class	Frigate	1991			Deal worth $4.7 b, Taiwanese designation Kang Ting Class
Italy USA	1	Te Kuan Class	Survey ship	1993	1995	1	
	26	Bell-206/OH-58D Kiowa	Combat helicopter	1992	1993-95	(26)	Deal worth $367 m
	18	Bell-209/AH-1W	Combat helicopter	1992	1993-95	(18)	Option on more
	12	C-130H Hercules	Transport	1993	1993-94	(8)	Deal worth $620 m incl spares and support
	4	E-2C Hawkeye	AEW&C aircraft	1993	1994-95	(4)	Deal worth $700 m (offsets 10%)
	150	F-16A Fighting Falcon	Fighter	1992			Deal worth $5.8 b incl spare engines, AIM-7M and AIM-9S missiles; incl 30 F-16B fighter/trainers
	60	T-38 Talon	Jet trainer	1993	1994-95	(22)	Ex-US Air Force; lease
	160	M-60A3 Patton II	Main battle tank	1991	1995	(60)	Ex-US Army; deal worth $91 m
	4	M-88A1	ARV	1990	1995	(4)	
	:	AN/FPS-117	Surveillance radar	1992			
	7	AN/SPG-60 STIR	Fire control radar	(1989)	1993-95	(3)	For 7 FFG-7 (Cheng Kung) Class frigates
	2	AN/SPS-10	Surveillance radar	1994			On 2 ex-US Navy Newport Class landing ships
	7	AN/SPS-49	Surveillance radar	(1989)	1993-95	(3)	For 7 FFG-7 (Cheng Kung) Class frigates
	(3)	Patriot MADS	SAM system	1994			Deal worth $1.3 b incl missiles
	7	Phalanx	CIWS	1991	1993-95	(3)	For 6 FFG-7 (Cheng Kung) Class frigates
	2	Phalanx	CIWS	1994			On 2 ex-US Navy Newport Class landing ships
	6	Phalanx	CIWS	1995			Deal worth $75m incl 6 Mk 75 76mm guns, spares and ammunition; for 6 La Fayette (Kang Ting) Class frigates
	1	Standard VLS	ShAM system	1993			Deal worth $103 m incl spares and support; for PFG-2 (Tien Tan) Class frigate
	7	Standard 1 ShAMS	ShAM system	1989	1993-95	(3)	For 7 FFG-7 (Cheng Kung) Class frigates
	7	WM-28	Fire control radar	(1989)	1993-95	(3)	For 7 FFG-7 (Cheng Kung) Class frigates

No.	Weapon designation	Weapon description	Year of order	Year(s) of deliveries	No. delivered	Comments
664	AUW-114A Hellfire	Anti-tank missile	(1991)	1993–95	(684)	For Bell 206/OH-58D and Bell 209/AH-1W helicopters
600	AIM-7M Sparrow	Air-to-air missile	1992			For 150 F-16A/B fighters
900	AIM-9S Sidewinder	Air-to-air missile	1992			For 150 F-16A/B fighters
200	MIM-104 PAC-2	SAM	1994			For 3 Patriot MADS SAM systems
..	RIM-116A RAM	ShAM	1993			For PFG-2 (Tien Tan) Class frigates
97	RIM-66B Standard 1MR	ShAM	1991	1993–95	(97)	Deal worth $55 m incl spares and support; for FFG-7 (Cheng Kung) Class frigates
..	RIM-66B Standard 1MR	ShAM	(1995)	1995	(23)	For FFG-7 (Cheng Kung) Class frigates
4	Aggressive Class	Minesweeper	1994	1995		Ex-US Navy; deal worth $2.5 m
2	Newport Class	Landing ship	1994			Ex-US Navy; lease
L: USA 7	FFG-7 Class	Frigate	1989	1993–95	3	Taiwanese designation Cheng Kung Class

Thailand

Supplier	No.	Weapon designation	Weapon description	Year of order	Year(s) of deliveries	No. delivered	Comments
S: Austria	18	GHN-45 155mm	Towed gun	1995	1995	18	Deal worth $130 m
Canada	20	Bell 212	Helicopter	1993			Shelter-based version
	(4)	ADATS SAMS	SAM system	1993	1994–95	(4)	For 4 ADATS SAM systems
	..	ADATS	SAM	1993	1994–95	(32)	Most weapons and electronics fitted in Thailand
China	2	Naresuan Class	Frigate	1989	1994–95	2	For VIP transport
France	3	AS-332B Super Puma	Helicopter	1995	1995		Deal worth $136 m; option on 4–6 more
Germany, FR	3	Do-228-200MP	Maritime patrol	1995	1995		For 2 Naresuan Class frigates
Italy	6	G-222	Transport	1994	1994–95	(6)	For 2 Naresuan Class frigates
Netherlands	2	LW-08	Surveillance radar	1995	1995	(2)	
	4	STIR	Fire control radar	1992	1994–95	(4)	
Spain	2	C-212-200 Aviocar	Transport	1995	1995	(2)	
	9	Harrier Mk-50/AV-8S	Fighter/ground attack	1995			Incl 2 Harrier Mk-54/TAV-8S fighter/trainers; deal worth $90 m; for Navy
UK	1	Chakri Naruebet Class	Aircraft carrier	1992			Deal worth $228 m without armament and radars
	2	Jetstream 41	Transport	1995	1995	1	For Army
USA	17	A-7E Corsair II	Fighter/ground attack	1994	1995	(8)	Ex-US Navy; incl 3 for spares; deal worth $81.6 m incl 4 TA-7C trainer version; for Navy
	3	E-2C Hawkeye	AEW&C aircraft	1991			Deal worth $382 m incl support

Recipient/ supplier (S) or licenser (L)	No. ordered	Weapon designation	Weapon description	Year of order/ licence	Year(s) of deliveries	No. delivered/ produced	Comments
	12	F-16A Fighting Falcon	Fighter	1991	1995	(6)	Deal worth $547 m incl 6 F-16B fighter/trainers, spares and support
	6	F-16B Fighting Falcon	Fighter/trainer	1991	1995	6	Deal worth $547 m incl 12 F-16A fighters, spares and support
	6	S-70B/SH-60B Seahawk	ASW helicopter	1993	1995	(1)	Deal worth $186 m incl spare engines, support and spares; for Navy
	6	S-76/H-76 Eagle	Helicopter	1995			
	4	TA-7C Corsair II	Fighter/trainer	1994	1995	4	Ex-US Navy; deal worth $81.6 m incl 17 A-7E fighters; for Navy
	2	127mm/54 Mk-42/9	Naval gun	1992	1994	1	On 2 ex-US Navy Knox Class frigates
	2	127mm/54 Mk-45	Naval gun	(1990)	1994–95	(2)	For 2 Naresuan Class frigates
	52	M-113A3	APC	1995			Deal worth $85 m incl 12 M-577A3 APC/CPs, 18 M-901A3 tank destroyers; incl 9 ambulance, 12 M-1063 mortar carriers, 10 ARV versions and 21 M-125A3 mortar carriers
	12	M-577A3	APC/command post	1995			Deal worth $85 m incl 52 M-113A3A3 APCs and 18 M-901A3 tank destroyers
	101	M-60A3 Patton II	Main battle tank	1995			Ex-US Army; deal worth $127 m
	18	M-901 ITV	Tank destroyer	1995			Deal worth $85 m incl 12 M-577A3 APC/CPs and 52 M-113A3A3 APCs
	2	AN/SPG-53	Fire control radar	1992	1994	1	On 2 ex-US Navy Knox Class frigates
	2	AN/SPS-10	Surveillance radar	1992	1994	1	On 2 ex-US Navy Knox Class frigates
	2	AN/SPS-40B	Surveillance radar	1992	1994	1	On 2 ex-US Navy Knox Class frigates
	1	AN/SPS-52C	Surveillance radar	1994			For 1 Chakri Naruebet Class aircraft carrier
	2	LAADS	Surveillance radar	1993	1995	(1)	Deal worth $11.8 m
	1	Phalanx	CIWS	1994			For 1 Chakri Nareubet Class aircraft carrier
	2	Phalanx	CIWS	1992	1994	1	On 2 ex-US Navy Knox Class frigates
	2	RGM-84A ShShMS	ShShM system	(1991)	1994–95	(2)	For 2 Naresuan Class frigates
	2	RGM-84A ShShMS	ShShM system	1992	1994	1	On 2 ex-US Navy Knox Class frigates
	2	Seasparrow VLS	ShAM system	(1991)	1994–95	(2)	For 2 Naresuan Class frigates

No.	Weapon designation	Weapon description	Year of order	Year of delivery	No. delivered	Comments
3	W-2100	Surveillance radar	1995			Deal worth $180 m incl communication network, training and support
..	RGM-84A Harpoon	ShShM	(1991)	1994–95	(32)	For 2 Naresuan Class frigates
(48)	RIM-7H Seasparrow	ShAM	(1991)	1994–95	(48)	For 2 Naresuan Class frigates
2	Knox Class	Frigate	1992	1994	1	Ex-US Navy; 5-year lease worth $4.3 m; Thai designation Phutthayotfa Chulalok Class

Tunisia

	No.	Weapon designation	Weapon description	Year of order	Year of delivery	No. delivered	Comments
S: Czechoslovakia	(12)	L-59 Albatros	Jet trainer	1994	1995	(12)	

Turkey

	No.	Weapon designation	Weapon description	Year of order	Year of delivery	No. delivered	Comments
S: Canada	10	Bell 206L LongRanger	Helicopter	1993	1995	(10)	Deal worth $25 m incl licensed production of 14
France	20	AS-532U2 Cougar	Helicopter	1993	1995	(10)	Deal worth $253 m (offsets $162 m)
	14	TRS-22XX	Surveillance radar	(1989)	1993–95	(8)	Deal worth $150 m (offsets $63 m); incl 10 assembled in Turkey
Germany, FR	2	100mm Modèle 1953	Naval gun	1995	1995	2	On 1 ex-FRG Navy Rhein Class depot ship
	70	M-48 AVLB	Bridge layer	1995	1995	70	Ex-FRG Army; part of 'Materialhilfe 3' aid programme
	39	M-88A1	ARV	1995	1995	39	Ex-FRG Army; part of 'Materialhilfe 3' aid programme
	1	DA-02	Surveillance radar	1995	1995	1	On 1 ex-FRG Navy Rhein Class depot ship
	2	M-45	Fire control radar	1995	1995	2	On 1 ex-FRG Navy Rhein Class depot ship
	197	RATAC-S	Battlefield radar	1992	1995	(30)	Incl assembly in Turkey
	1	FPB-57	Fast attack craft	1993			Turkish designation Yildiz Class
	1	Meko 200 Type	Frigate	1990	1995	1	Deal worth $465 m incl licensed production of 1; Turkish designation Barbaros Class
	1	Meko 200 Type	Frigate	1994			Deal worth $525 m incl licensed production of 1; Turkish designation Barbaros Class
	1	Rhein Class	Depot ship	1995	1995	1	Ex-FRG Navy; part of 'Materielhilfe 3' aid programme
Italy	20	AB-206B	Helicopter	1994	1995	(10)	Deal worth $18.7 m; for training
	100	M-113A1	APC	(1991)	1994–95	(100)	CFE cascade; ex-Italian Army
	3	RAT-31SL	Surveillance radar	1995			

Recipient/ supplier (S) or licenser (L)	No. ordered	Weapon designation	Weapon description	Year of order/ licence	Year(s) of deliveries	No. delivered/ produced	Comments
	4	Seaguard	Fire control radar	1990	1995	2	For 2 Meko 200 Type (Barbaros Class) frigates
	4	Seaguard	Fire control radar	(1994)			For 2 Meko 200 Type (Barbaros Class) frigates
	2	Seaguard TMX	Fire control radar	1991	1994–95	(2)	For 5 FPB-57 Type (Yildiz Class) fast attack craft
	2	Seaguard TMX	Fire control radar	(1990)	1995	1	For 2 Meko 200 Type (Barbaros Class) frigates
	(48)	Aspide	ShAM	(1990)	1995	(24)	For 2 Meko 200 Type (Barbaros Class) frigates
Netherlands	3	MW-08	Surveillance radar	1995			For 3 FPB-57 Type (Yildiz Class) fast attack craft
	3	STING	Fire control radar	1995			For 3 FPB-57 Type (Yildiz Class) fast attack craft
	4	STIR	Fire control radar	(1994)			For 2 Meko 200 Type (Barbaros Class) frigates
Russia	19	Mi-17 Hip H	Helicopter	(1994)	1995	(5)	Deal worth $65 m; for Gendarmerie
UK	2	AWS-6	Surveillance radar	(1991)	1994–95	(2)	For 2 FPB-57 Type (Yildiz Class) fast attack craft
	2	AWS-6	Surveillance radar	(1990)	1995	1	For 2 Meko 200 Type (Barbaros Class) frigates
	2	AWS-6	Surveillance radar	(1992)			For 2 Meko 200 Type (Barbaros Class) frigates
	2	AWS-9	Surveillance radar	(1990)	1995	1	For 2 Meko 200 Type (Barbaros Class) frigates
	2	AWS-9	Surveillance radar	(1994)			For 2 Meko 200 Type (Barbaros Class) frigates
USA	2	KC-135A Stratotanker	Tanker/transport	1995	1995	2	Ex-US Air Force; lease until delivery of KC-135R tanker/transports in 1997
	7	KC-135A Stratotanker	Tanker/transport	1994			Ex-US Air Force; refurbished to KC-135R before delivery
	10	P-3A Orion	ASW/maritime patrol	1991			Ex-US Navy; status uncertain
	12	SH-2F Seasprite	ASW helicopter	1994			Ex-US Navy; deal worth $115 m incl support and 2 for spares; refurbished before delivery; for Navy
	2	SH-2F Seasprite	ASW helicopter	1994			Ex-US Navy; for spares; deal worth $115 m incl 12 refurbished SH-2F helicopters
	2	127mm/54 Mk-45	Naval gun	(1990)	1995	1	For 2 Meko 200 Type (Barbaros Class) frigates
	2	127mm/54 Mk-45	Naval gun	(1992)			For 2 Meko 200 Type (Barbaros Class) frigates
	24	MLRS 227mm	MRL	1993			Deal worth $289 m incl 1772 rocket pods, spares and support
	(250)	M-113A2	APC	(1991)	1994–95	(250)	CFE cascade; ex-US Army
	2	AN/SPS-49	Surveillance radar	1995			On 2 ex-US Navy FFG-7 Class frigates
	5	AN/TPQ-36	Tracking radar	1992	1995	(2)	Deal worth $28 m

Supplier	No. ordered	Weapon designation	Weapon description	Year of order	Year(s) of deliveries	No. delivered	Comments
	2	Phalanx	CIWS	1995			On 2 ex-US Navy FFG-7 Class frigates
	2	RGM-84A ShShMS	ShShM system	(1991)	1994–95	(2)	For 2 FPB-57 Type (Yildiz Class) fast attack craft
	2	RGM-84A ShShMS	ShShM system	1990	1995	1	For 2 Meko 200 Type (Barbaros Class) frigates
	2	RGM-84A ShShMS	ShShM system	(1994)			For 2 Meko 200 Type (Barbaros Class) frigates
	2	Seasparrow ShAMS	ShAM system	1990	1995	1	For 2 Meko 200 Type (Barbaros Class) frigates
	2	Seasparrow VLS	ShAM system	1994			For 2 Meko 200 Type (Barbaros Class) frigates
	(274)	AGM-65G Maverick	ASM	1991	1993–95	(274)	
	100	AGM-88A HARM	Anti-radar missile	1993	1994–95	(100)	For F-16 fighters
	80	AIM-120A AMRAAM	Air-to-air missile	1993			Deal worth $52 m; for F-16 fighters
	200	AIM-9M Sidewinder	Air-to-air missile	(1992)	1993–95	(310)	Deal worth $23 m
	310	AIM-9S Sidewinder	Air-to-air missile	1990			Deal worth $30 m incl training missiles
	500	AIM-9S Sidewinder	Air-to-air missile	1994			Deal worth $55 m incl 30 training missiles
	:	RGM-84A Harpoon	ShShM	(1991)	1994–95	(32)	For 2 FPB-57 Type (Yildiz Class) fast attack craft
	40	RGM-84A Harpoon	ShShM	1990	1995	(20)	Deal worth $62 m
	16	RGM-84A Harpoon	ShShM	1994			
	16	RGM-84A Harpoon	ShShM	1995			Deal worth $15.3 m
	(72)	RIM-66B Standard 1MR	ShAM	1995			For 2 ex-US Navy FFG-7 Class frigates
	:	RIM-7H Seasparrow	ShAM	(1994)			For 2 Meko 200 Type (Barbaros Class) frigates
	:	UGM-84A SubHarpoon	SuShM	(1993)	1994–95	(12)	For 4 Type 209/1400 (Preveze Class) submarines
	2	FFG-7 Class	Frigate	1995			Ex-US Navy; deal worth $7 m; Turkish designation Gaziantep Class
L: Canada	14	Bell 206L LongRanger	Helicopter	1993	1994–95		Deal worth $25 m incl 10 delivered direct
Germany, FR	2	FPB-57 Type	Fast attack craft	1991	1994–95	2	Deal worth $143 m; Turkish designation Yildiz Class
	2	FPB-57 Type	Fast attack craft	1993			Deal worth $250 m incl 1 delivered direct; Turkish designation Yildiz Class
	1	Meko 200 Type	Frigate	1990			Deal worth $465 m incl 1 delivered direct; Turkish designation Barbaros Class
	1	Meko 200 Type	Frigate	1994			Deal worth $525 m incl 1 delivered direct; Turkish designation Barbaros Class
Spain	4	Type 209/1400	Submarine	1987		2	Turkish designation Preveze Class
UK	50	CN-235M	Transport	1991	1992–95	19	Deal worth $550 m incl 2 delivered direct
	:	Shorland S-55	APC	(1990)			Incl for Gendarmerie; also produced for export
USA	40	F-16C Fighting Falcon	Fighter	1992	1994–95	(20)	Deal worth $2.8 b incl 12 spare engines

Recipient/ supplier (S) or licenser (L)	No. ordered	Weapon designation	Weapon description	Year of order/ licence	Year(s) of deliveries	No. delivered/ produced	Comments
	40	F-16C Fighting Falcon	Fighter	1994			Deal worth $1.8 b
	650	AIFV	AIFV	1988	1990–95	275	Deal worth $1.08 b incl 830 APC, 48 tank destroyer and 170 APC/mortar carrier version (offsets $705 m)
	170	AIFV-AMV	APC/mortar carrier	1988	1993–95	130	Deal worth $1.08 b incl 650 AIFV, 830 APC and 48 tank destroyer version (offsets $705 m)
	830	AIFV-APC	APC	1988	1991–95	680	Deal worth $1.08 b incl 650 AIFV, 48 tank destroyer and 170 APC/mortar carrier version (offsets $705 m)
UK							
S: USA	25	C-130J Hercules II	Transport	1994			Deal worth $1.56 b (offsets 100%)
	3	CH-47D Chinook	Helicopter	1993	1995	(1)	UK designation Chinook HC Mk-2
	14	CH-47D Chinook	Helicopter	1995			Deal worth $365 m incl 8 MH-47E helicopters; UK designation Chinook HC Mk-2
	8	MH-47E Chinook	Helicopter	1995			Deal worth $365 m incl 14 CH-47D helicopters; UK designation Chinook HC Mk-3
	2	Phalanx	CIWS	1994			Deal worth $25 m incl spares and support; for support ships
	3	Phalanx	CIWS	(1993)			For 1 Ocean Class AALS
	210	AIM-120A AMRAAM	Air-to-air missile	1992	1995	(70)	Deal worth $228 m incl support; for Navy Sea Harrier FRS-2 fighters
	65	BGM-109 Tomahawk	SLCM	(1995)			Deal worth $142 m
L: USA	67	AH-64D Longbow	Attack helicopter	1995			Deal worth $3.95 b (offsets 100%)
	..	AGM-114A	Anti-tank missile	1995			UK designation Brimstone; for AH-64D helicopters
	..	BGM-71A TOW	Anti-tank missile	1980	1982–95	33699	

	No. ordered	Weapon designation	Weapon description	Year of order	Year(s) of deliveries	No. delivered	Comments
S: Australia	7	CH-47C Chinook	Helicopter	1991	1994–95	(7)	Ex-Australian Air Force; for Army
Canada	102	Bell 206B JetRanger 3	Helicopter	1993	1993–95	(102)	For Army; for training; US designation TH-67A Creek; option on 20 more
Israel	12	Piranha 8x8	APC	1994	1995	12	For National Guard
	1 725	K-6 120mm	Mortar	1990	1991–95	(1 615)	US designation M-120 or M-121
UK	113	Firefly 160	Trainer	1992	1993–95	113	Deal worth $54.8 m; US designation T-3A Firefly; incl assembly in USA
	20	Shorts 330UTT	Transport	1993	1995	(10)	Ex-civilian; deal worth $100 m; refurbished to C-23B+ Sherpa before delivery
L: Italy	12	Lerici Class	MCM ship	1986	1993–95	(4)	US designation Osprey Class
Japan	(180)	Beechjet 400T	Transport	1990	1991–95	(130)	Deal worth $628 m; for training; US designation T-1A Jayhawk
Netherlands	..	WM-28	Fire control radar	(1973)	1977–95	(112)	For several US Navy ships; incl 31 for export; US designation Mk-92
Switzerland	(711)	PC-9	Trainer	1995	1995		Incl 339 for Navy
UK	199	Hawk	Jet trainer	1986	1988–95	(58)	For Navy; US designation T-45A Goshawk
	436	L-119 105mm	Towed gun	1987	1991–95	(220)	US designation M-119
	13	Ramadan Class	Patrol craft	1990	1992–95	(13)	US designation Cyclone Class
United Arab Emirates							
S: France	7	AS-565SA Panther	ASW helicopter	1995			For Abu Dhabi; deal worth $235 m
	390	Leclerc	Main battle tank	1993	1994–95	(55)	Deal worth $4.6 b incl 46 ARV version (offsets 60%)
	46	Leclerc ARV	ARV	1993	1995	(2)	
	..	AM-39 Exocet	Anti-ship missile	1995	1995	(10)	Deal worth $60 m incl modification of UAE AS-332 helicopters to ASW/anti-ship version
	..	AS-15TT	Anti-ship missile	1995			For 7 AS-565SA helicopters
Germany, FR	12	G-115T	Trainer	1995			Deal worth $5.5 m; option on 12 more
Indonesia	7	CN-235	Transport	1992	1993–95	(7)	Deal worth $108 m
Italy	(6)	Bell 412SP/AB-412SP	Helicopter	1991	1992–95	(6)	Deal worth $30 m incl spares and support; for Dubai
Netherlands	87	M-109A3 155mm	Self-propelled gun	1995			Ex-Dutch Army; refurbished before delivery for $33 m; incl 2 training version; for Abu Dhabi

Recipient/ supplier (S) or licenser (L)	No. ordered	Weapon designation	Weapon description	Year of order/ licence	Year(s) of deliveries	No. delivered/ produced	Comments
Romania	10	SA-330 Puma	Helicopter	1994			Deal worth $37 m; for Abu Dhabi
Russia	(150)	BMP-3	AIFV	(1994)	1994–95	(150)	For Dubai
	(1 200)	AT-10 Bastion	Anti-tank missile	(1994)	1994–95	(1 200)	For 150 BMP-3 AIFVs
UK	4	Hawk	Jet trainer	(1994)	1995	4	For Mirage 2000 fighters
	..	Al Hakim	ASM	1985	1994	328	Deal worth $150 m; for Abu Dhabi
USA	10	AH-64A Apache	Combat helicopter	1994			Deal worth $54.9 m
	2	C-130H-30 Hercules	Transport	1991			Part of deal worth $300 m
	1	AN/TPS-70	Surveillance radar	1993	1995	(1)	
	(1)	LASS	Surveillance radar	1993	1995	(1)	
	360	AGM-114A Hellfire	Anti-tank missile	1994			For 10 AH-64A helicopters
Viet Nam							
S: Russia	6	Su-27P Flanker B	Fighter	(1994)	1995	6	Deal worth $200 m
	2	Bass Tilt	Fire control radar	1995			For 2 Tarantul I Class fast attack craft
	2	Plank Shave	Surveillance radar	1995			On 2 Tarantul I Class fast attack craft
	2	SS-N-2 ShShMS	ShShM system	1995			On 2 Tarantul I Class fast attack craft
	(108)	AA-10a Alamo	Air-to-air missile	(1994)	1995	(108)	For 6 Su-27P fighters; may incl other AA-10 versions
	(72)	AA-11 Archer	Air-to-air missile	(1994)	1995	(72)	For 6 Su-27P fighters
	(80)	SA-N-5 Grail	ShAM	1995			For 2 Tarantul I Class fast attack craft
	(16)	SS-N-2d Styx	ShShM	1995			For 2 Tarantul I Class fast attack craft
	2	Tarantul I Class	Fast attack craft	1994			For 2 Tarantul I Class fast attack craft
Yugoslavia							
S: Kazakhstan	226	SA-16 Gimlet	Portable SAM	1995	1995	226	Incl also 57 launchers; illegal delivery
Zimbabwe							
S: France	..	AS-332L Super Puma	Helicopter	(1994)	1995	1	For VIP transport

Abbreviations and acronyms

AA	Anti-aircraft
AALS	Amphibious assault landing ship
AAV(G)	Anti-aircraft vehicle (gun-armed)
AAV(M)	Anti-aircraft vehicle (missile-armed)
AAV(G/M)	Anti-aircraft vehicle (gun- and missile-armed)
AEV	Armoured engineer vehicle
AEW	Airborne early-warning
AEW&C	Airborne early-warning and control
AIFV	Armoured infantry fighting vehicle
APC	Armoured personnel carrier
APC/CP	Armoured personnel carrier/command post
ARM	Anti-radar missile
ARV	Armoured recovery vehicle
ASM	Air-to-surface missile
ASW	Anti-submarine warfare
CDS	Coast defence system
CIWS	Close-in weapon system
ELINT	Electronic intelligence
EW	Electronic warfare
incl	Including/includes
MCM	Mine countermeasures (ship)

MRL	Multiple rocket launcher
OPV	Offshore patrol vessel
SAM	Surface-to-air missile
SAR	Search and rescue
ShAM	Ship-to-air missile
ShShM	Ship-to-ship missile
SuShM	Submarine-to-ship missile
VIP	Very important person
VLS	Vertical launch system

Conventions:

. .	Data not available or not applicable
–	Negligible figure (< 0.5) or none
( )	Uncertain data or SIPRI estimate
m	million (10^6)
b	billion (10^9)

Appendix 11C. Sources and methods

I. The SIPRI sources

The sources of the data presented in the arms trade registers are of five general types: newspapers; periodicals and journals; books, monographs and annual reference works; official national documents; and documents issued by international and inter-governmental organizations. The registers are largely compiled from information contained in around 200 publications searched regularly.

Published information cannot provide a comprehensive picture because the arms trade is not fully reported in the open literature. Published reports provide partial information, and substantial disagreement among reports is common. Therefore, the exercise of judgement and the making of estimates are important elements in compiling the SIPRI arms trade data base. Order dates and the delivery dates for arms transactions are continuously revised in the light of new information, but where they are not disclosed the dates are estimated. Exact numbers of weapons ordered and delivered may not always be known and are sometimes estimated—particularly with respect to missiles. It is common for reports of arms deals involving large platforms—ships, aircraft and armoured vehicles—to ignore missile armaments classified as major weapons by SIPRI. Unless there is explicit evidence that platforms were disarmed or altered before delivery, it is assumed that a weapons fit specified in one of the major reference works such as the *Jane's* or *Interavia* series is carried.

II. Selection criteria

SIPRI arms trade data cover five categories of major weapons or systems: aircraft, armour and artillery, guidance and radar systems, missiles, and warships. Statistics presented refer to the value of the trade in these five categories only. The registers and statistics do not include trade in small arms, artillery under 100-mm calibre, ammunition, support items, services and components or component technology, except for specific items. Publicly available information is inadequate to track these items satisfactorily.

There are two criteria for the selection of major weapon transfers for the registers. The first is that of military application. The aircraft category excludes aerobatic aeroplanes and gliders. Transport aircraft and VIP transports are included only if they bear military insignia or are otherwise confirmed as military registered. Micro-light aircraft, remotely piloted vehicles and drones are not included although these systems are increasingly finding military applications.

The armour and artillery category includes all types of tanks, tank destroyers, armoured cars, armoured personnel carriers, armoured support vehicles, infantry combat vehicles as well as multiple rocket launchers, self-propelled and towed guns and howitzers with a calibre equal to or above 100 mm. Military lorries, jeeps and other unarmoured support vehicles are not included.

The category of guidance and radar systems is a residual category for electronic-tracking, target-acquisition, fire-control, launch and guidance systems that are either (*a*) deployed independently of a weapon system listed under another weapon category (e.g., certain ground-based SAM launch systems) or (*b*) shipborne missile-launch or point-defence (CIWS) systems. The values of acquisition, fire-control, launch and guidance systems on aircraft and armoured vehicles are included in the value of the respective aircraft or armoured vehicle. The reason for treating shipborne systems separately is that a given type of ship is often equipped with numerous combinations of different surveillance, acquisition, launch and guidance systems.

The missile category includes only guided missiles. Unguided artillery rockets, man-portable anti-armour rockets and free-fall aerial munitions (e.g., 'iron bombs') are excluded. In the naval sphere, anti-submarine rockets and torpedoes are excluded.

The ship category excludes small patrol craft (with a displacement of less than 100 t), unless they carry cannon with a calibre equal to or above 100 mm; missiles or torpedoes; research vessels; tugs and ice-breakers. Combat support vessels such as fleet replenishment ships are included.

The second criterion for selection of items is the identity of the buyer. Items must be destined for the armed forces, paramilitary forces, intelligence agencies or police of another country. Arms supplied to guerrilla forces pose a problem. For example, if weapons are delivered to the Contra rebels they are listed as imports to Nicaragua with a comment in the arms trade register indicating the local recipient. The entry of any arms transfer is made corresponding to the five weapon categories listed above. This means that missiles and their guidance/launch vehicles are often entered separately under their respective category in the arms trade register.

III. The value of the arms trade

The SIPRI system for arms trade evaluation is designed as a *trend-measuring device*, to permit measurement of changes in the total flow of major weapons and its geographic pattern.[1] Expressing the evaluation in monetary terms reflects both the quantity and quality of the weapons transferred. Aggregate values and shares are based only on *actual deliveries* during the year/years covered in the relevant tables and figures.

The SIPRI valuation system is not comparable to official economic statistics such as gross domestic product, public expenditure and export/import figures. The monetary values chosen do not correspond to the actual prices paid, which vary considerably depending on different pricing methods, the length of production runs and the terms involved in individual transactions. For instance, a deal may or may not cover spare parts, training, support equipment, compensation, offset arrangements for the local industries in the buying country, and so on. Furthermore, to use only actual sales prices—even assuming that the information were available for all deals, which it is not—military aid and grants would be excluded, and the total flow of arms would therefore not be measured.

Production under licence is included in the arms trade statistics in such a way as to reflect the import share embodied in the weapon. In reality, this share is normally high in the beginning, gradually decreasing over time. However, as SIPRI makes a single estimate of the import share for each weapon produced under licence, the value of arms produced under licence agreements may be slightly overstated.

---

[1] Additional information is contained in Brzoska, M., 'The SIPRI price system', *SIPRI Yearbook 1987: World Armaments and Disarmament* (Oxford University Press: Oxford 1987), appendix 7D; Sköns, E., 'Sources and methods', *SIPRI Yearbook 1992: World Armaments and Disarmament* (Oxford University Press: Oxford, 1992), appendix 8D; and SIPRI, *Sources and Methods for SIPRI Research on Military Expenditure, Arms Transfers and Arms Production*, SIPRI Fact Sheet, Stockholm, Jan. 1995.

Part III. Non-proliferation, arms control and disarmament, 1995

12. Multilateral military-related export control measures

IAN ANTHONY and THOMAS STOCK

I. Introduction

In 1995 changes occurred in the membership of multilateral military-related export control regimes: the Australia Group, the Missile Technology Control Regime (MTCR) and the Nuclear Suppliers Group (NSG).[1] Romania became the 29th member of the Australia Group, while Brazil, Russia and South Africa became members of the MTCR, bringing its membership to 28 states. New Zealand and South Africa became members of the NSG, increasing its membership to 31 states. In the European Union (EU), the regulation developed to address exports of dual-use technologies entered into force on 1 July 1995. In addition, one new regime—the Wassenaar Arrangement on Export Controls for Conventional Arms and Dual-Use Goods and Technologies—was established, subject to approval of the member governments, on 18 December 1995 at a meeting of high-level officials of the 28 founding member states in The Hague. This new regime is expected to be established formally in 1996.

With the implementation of the EU Regulation and the creation of the Wassenaar Arrangement, the emphasis of multilateral export regulation has been expanded to include new categories of goods and technologies. Section II discusses the regimes for controls on conventional weapon and dual-use technology transfers, including the framework and terms of reference of the new Wassenaar Arrangement. Section III describes developments in 1995 in the two nuclear regimes, section IV the regime to regulate chemical and biological exports, and section V the MTCR. Appendix 12A discusses the possible impact of multilateral export controls on transfers of one specific dual-use technology—digital telecommunications.

The process of harmonizing membership across the multilateral regimes continued in 1995. In the area of transfers of nuclear materials and technology, during the cold war period the Soviet Union and other members of the Warsaw Treaty Organization (WTO) were involved in development of the Nuclear Suppliers Group. The other regimes, however, were founded around a core

---

[1] For background information about the structure and terms of reference of 6 multilateral regimes and for developments up to the end of 1994, see Anthony, I. *et al.*, 'Multilateral weapon-related export control measures', *SIPRI Yearbook 1995: Armaments, Disarmament and International Security* (Oxford University Press: Oxford, 1995), pp. 597–633.

Table 12.1. Membership of multilateral weapon-related export control regimes, as of 1 January 1996

State	Zangger Committee 1974	NSG[a] 1978	Australia Group[b] 1985	MTCR[c] 1987	EU dual-use regulation 1994	Wassenaar Arrangement[d] 1995
Argentina		x	x	x		
Australia	x	x	x	x		x
Austria	x	x	x	x	x	x
Belgium	x	x	x	x	x	x
Brazil	x			x		
Bulgaria	x	x				
Canada	x	x	x	x		x
Czech Republic	x	x	x			x
Denmark	x	x	x	x	x	x
Finland	x	x	x	x	x	x
France	x	x	x	x	x	x
Germany	x	x	x	x	x	x
Greece	x	x	x	x	x	x
Hungary	x	x	x	x		x
Iceland			x	x		
Ireland	x	x	x	x	x	x
Italy	x	x	x	x	x	x
Japan	x	x	x	x		x
Luxembourg	x	x	x	x	x	x
Netherlands	x	x	x	x	x	x
New Zealand		x	x	x		x
Norway	x	x	x	x		x
Poland	x	x	x			x
Portugal	x	x	x	x	x	x
Romania	x	x	x			
Russia	x	x		x		x
Slovakia	x	x	x			x
South Africa	x	x		x		
Spain	x	x	x	x	x	x
Sweden	x	x	x	x	x	x
Switzerland	x	x	x	x		x
Turkey						x
UK	x	x	x	x	x	x
USA	x	x	x	x		x

Note: The years in the column headings indicate when the regime was created.

[a] The Nuclear Suppliers Group.

[b] The European Commission is represented in the Australia Group as an observer.

[c] The Missile Technology Control Regime.

[d] The Wassenaar Arrangement is the only regime listed in this table which has not yet entered into force.

group of states which were associated with the system of alliances and security arrangements led by the United States. Since the end of the cold war, the membership of regimes has gradually been harmonized until, by the end of 1995, most of the former members of the WTO and the European states that were neutral or non-aligned during the cold war had become members of one or more of the multilateral regimes.

At the end of 1995 membership of the regimes had expanded to include Argentina and South Africa—neither traditionally associated with the core group of states engaged in multilateral export regulation. Nevertheless, membership was still confined to a group of 34 countries. Moreover, in recent years members of the regimes have increasingly emphasized those activities that set the terms and conditions on which technology transfer can occur rather than the denial aspects of export controls.

There is no formal link between the NSG and the 1968 Non-Proliferation Treaty (NPT) or between the Australia Group and either the 1972 Biological Weapons Convention (BWC) or the 1993 Chemical Weapons Convention (CWC). International responsibility to prevent proliferation is greatest in the case of chemical and biological weapons because of the universal prohibition of the use, development, production and transfer of these weapons through the BWC and CWC.[2] The particular status given to nuclear weapon states in the NPT—which has no equivalent in either the CWC or BWC—has made it more difficult to secure comprehensive membership of the NPT.[3] There is no multilateral convention or treaty that addresses the issue of ballistic missile possession or use.

As a result of changes in technology and markets, the regulation of international technology transfer is increasingly seen by governments as a collaborative exercise. Regimes provide them with a forum for discussion, exchange of information, lobbying and bargaining in support of national policy objectives. However, even if governments can build a consensus on the conditions for technology transfer, collaboration between government and industry and within companies is necessary to implement these policies.

Approaches to export control

Government objectives can be of a political nature (the US preference), they can be economic, or they can be narrowly focused on non-proliferation concerns.

There is no consensus within any of the regimes that they should attempt to coerce states whose *political* behaviour is considered unacceptable by regime members. However, the USA does use its export regulations in this way and is a central actor in each of the multilateral regimes. In 1995 the USA continued to employ coercive trade and investment policies as an element in its bilateral relations with Iran. On 15 March 1995 President Bill Clinton expanded US

---

[2] See chapter 15 in this volume for a discussion of chemical and biological weapon and arms control issues.

[3] See chapters 13 and 14 in this volume for a discussion of nuclear weapon and arms control issues.

sanctions against Iran to include a ban on all trade and investment, including the purchase of Iranian oil by US companies.[4] The action was explained by Secretary of State Warren Christopher as part of a wider policy 'to use our diplomatic and economic measures and our military deterrent to contain Iran and to pressure it to cease its unacceptable actions'. These 'unacceptable actions' included proliferation concerns but also included actions not related to proliferation; specifically, the charges are that Iran is 'the foremost sponsor of international terrorism' and that it 'seeks to undermine the Middle East peace process'.[5]

From public statements by US officials it is not fully clear whether the removal of the current Iranian Government is considered to be necessary to achieve this change in behaviour. In testimony before the House of Representatives International Relations Committee, Under Secretary of State Peter Tarnoff and Representative Lee Hamilton had the following exchange:

Rep. Hamilton: Secretary Christopher said that we must isolate Iraq and Iran until there is a change in their government, a change in their leadership—that's a direct quote. Does that mean that our policy is to overthrow the government of Iraq? Of Iran?

Mr Tarnoff: . . . with respect to the government of Iran, we are not seeking to overthrow that government.[6]

While other governments object to aspects of Iran's behaviour—particularly its opposition to the Middle East peace process—there is a dispute about how to attempt to change it. Some members of the multilateral regimes favour a policy of 'critical dialogue' with Iran.[7]

The focus of the regimes on dual-use technologies associated with weapon production as well as on weapons themselves has led to suspicions that the regimes are a form of *economic* warfare.[8] In 1995, for example, some governments continued to argue that the activities of the Australia Group are not consistent with Article XI of the Chemical Weapons Convention, which relates to economic and technological development. Under Article XI, parties pledge to facilitate the fullest possible exchange of chemical materials and related information for purposes not prohibited by the convention. Several governments argue that, since export controls are a barrier to trade, they cannot be consistent with this commitment.[9] However, this argument assumes that the alternative to multilateral regimes is free trade. Since export controls are

---

[4] These sanctions became effective on 7 May 1995. *Letter from the President to the Speaker of the House of Representatives and the President of the Senate, 6 May 1995* (White House, Office of the Press Secretary: Washington, DC, 8 May 1995).

[5] Secretary of State Warren Christopher, State Department Press Briefing, 1 May 1995, reproduced in *US Department of State Dispatch*, vol. 6, no. 9 (8 May 1995).

[6] 'House hears Tarnoff, Reidel testimony on US policy on Iran', *Wireless File (Europe)* (United States Information Agency: Washington, DC, 13 Nov. 1995). URL <gopher://pubgopher.srce.hr:70/00/usis/casopisi/wf/european%20WF%2013.11.95>.

[7] 'House hears Tarnoff, Reidel testimony on US policy on Iran' (note 6).

[8] Anthony *et al.*, *SIPRI Yearbook 1995* (note 1).

[9] 'Statement by the representative of Nigeria on behalf of the African Group presented at the opening of the tenth session of the Preparatory Commission for the OPCW on 3 April 1995', PrepCom document PC-X/14, 3 Apr. 1995.

given expression through national legislation (whose legitimacy is not questioned), the abolition of the regimes could make trade regulation less rather than more efficient, with even greater barriers to technology transfer.[10] Moreover, if there were no regulations that sought to prevent unwanted forms of proliferation, some states—notably the USA—might argue for other measures (perhaps including the use of force) to prevent the spread of nuclear, chemical and biological weapons.

The debate on CWC Article XI reflects the misunderstanding or, alternatively, the lack of trust between 'North' and 'South'. The main question to be resolved is whether current export licensing measures reflect a general way of thinking among the developed countries or whether they are the result of the former weapon procurement programmes of a few countries, most notably Iraq.

It is also argued that extending controls on technology transfer to include dual-use technologies conflicts with obligations accepted in trade-related international negotiations by the governments of countries which are major sources of technology. Negotiations on technology transfer have taken place since the early 1970s, first within the United Nations Conference on Trade and Development (UNCTAD), then within the framework of the General Agreement on Tariffs and Trade (GATT) and most recently within the World Trade Organization. Throughout these discussions it was clear that, while access to technology could be regulated to a greater or lesser degree, neither technology suppliers nor recipients would waive the right to take actions seen as necessary for their national security.[11]

Consequently, even close allies have not entirely deregulated transfers of dual-use items and technologies. For example, under the simplified licensing procedures announced by President Clinton in October 1995, exports of specified computers to Australia, Canada, Japan, Mexico, New Zealand and Western Europe still required general licences. Licensing requirements were also simplified for exports to South America, South Korea, the Association of South-East Asian Nations (ASEAN), the Czech Republic, Hungary, Poland, Slovakia, Slovenia and South Africa, but more elaborate licensing procedures were required for transfers to other countries.[12]

---

[10] This argument is made in, e.g., Bertsch, G. K., Cupitt, R. T. and Elliot Gower, S. (eds), *International Cooperation on Nonproliferation Export Controls: Prospects for the 1990s and Beyond* (University of Michigan Press: Ann Arbor, Mich., 1994).

[11] This requirement was explicit in the draft UN Code of Conduct and was also written into the text of the Final Act and Agreement Establishing the World Trade Organization, General Agreement on Tariffs and Trade, Uruguay Round (including GATT 1994), Marrakesh, 15 Apr. 1994. URL <http://ananse.irv.vit.no/trade_law/gatt/nav/toc.html>. In Article XXI of the GATT 1994 agreement there is a specific security exception which states that 'Nothing in this Agreement shall be construed . . . to prevent any Member from taking any action which it considers necessary for the protection of its essential security interests . . . relating to traffic in arms, ammunition and implements of war and to such traffic in other goods and materials as is carried on directly or indirectly for the purpose of supplying a military establishment . . . '. See also *Draft International Code of Conduct on the Transfer of Technology: Report and Notes by Experts on the Outstanding Issues*, United Nations Conference on Trade and Development (UNCTAD) document TD/CODE TOT/52, 5 Aug. 1988.

[12] *Export Controls on Computers*, White House Fact Sheet, 6 Oct. 1995. For the members of ASEAN, see the glossary at the front of this volume.

The third rationale for the regimes is that they contribute to *non-proliferation* objectives, preventing proliferation that could have a negative impact on regime member states. In the past, regimes have targeted technologies that are related to the development or production of weapons of mass destruction. However, in the control list associated with the 1994 EU dual-use regulation, one section is reserved for digital telecommunications equipment—a technology which is neither inherently military in character nor directly associated with a weapon system but which could have military applications.[13] Secure and effective communications are recognized to be an important factor in successful military operations. For this reason digital communications systems dedicated to military application usually require export licences. It is often said that there has been a convergence between military and civil telecommunications technology or that civilian technology is superior to (rather than just different from) military technology in this area. Therefore, the question arises whether a country that would be denied a licence for a military communications system can achieve the same capabilities by purchasing unlicensed civilian technologies.

II. Conventional weapon and dual-use technology export controls

The Wassenaar Arrangement

After over two years of discussions, the representatives of 28 states established the Wassenaar Arrangement on Export Controls for Conventional Arms and Dual-use Goods and Technologies at a meeting of high-level officials in the Netherlands on 18 December 1995. It was agreed that the work of the Arrangement would involve both plenary meetings and supporting activities and that a secretariat would be based in Vienna, Austria.[14]

Following the decision of November 1993 to lift the embargo implemented through the Coordinating Committee on Multilateral Export Controls (COCOM), a group of 23 states entered into discussion of a follow-on regime.[15] The original intention was to have the regime in place in March 1994, when the lifting of the COCOM embargo was implemented. However, the process of defining a new regime was delayed by unresolved questions about its membership, scope and terms of reference.

The central membership issue was whether or not to invite Russia to participate in the new regime.[16] The United States opposed the membership of Russia in the Wassenaar Arrangement until the Russian Government under-

---

[13] See also appendix 12A in this volume.

[14] The Wassenaar Arrangement on Export Controls for Conventional Arms and Dual-Use Goods and Technologies, Final Declaration by 28 states, signed at Wassenaar, the Netherlands, 19 Dec. 1995.

[15] The 5 countries which subsequently joined the discussions were the Czech Republic, Hungary, Poland, Russia and Slovakia. For the membership of COCOM as of Mar. 1994, see Anthony *et al.*, *SIPRI Yearbook 1995* (note 1), p. 598.

[16] For a discussion of the lifting of the COCOM embargo and the issue of Russian membership of the new forum to replace it, see Anthony *et al.*, *SIPRI Yearbook 1995* (note 1).

took not to conclude new arms transfer agreements with Iran and to clarify the scope and content of arms transfers to be made in the framework of a 1989 agreement between the Soviet Union and Iran.[17] Under this agreement it is believed that deliveries of equipment to Iran would continue until 1999.[18]

These issues were discussed by Presidents Clinton and Yeltsin on four occasions: in April 1993, January 1994, September 1994 and May 1995, by which time a general agreement had been reached. Under this agreement President Yeltsin agreed to supplement his pledge not to permit new agreements between Russia and Iran by clarifying the extent of previous and pending arms transfers to Iran. The detailed aspects of this issue were to be discussed in the US–Russian Joint Commission on Economic and Technological Cooperation (known as the Gore–Chernomyrdin Commission). On 1 July 1995 the Commission concluded its fifth meeting in Moscow under the joint chairmanship of Russian Prime Minister Viktor Chernomyrdin and US Vice-President Al Gore.[19] At this meeting the USA received the clarification that it had sought, and it was confirmed that Russia would be invited as a founding member of the Arrangement.[20]

Other countries that are believed to be considering membership of the Wassenaar Arrangement include Argentina, Bulgaria, Romania, South Africa, South Korea and Ukraine. Some of these countries are expected to join soon after it becomes operational. The issue of Chinese membership has been raised periodically, although there has been no formal indication from China about its interest or willingness to join the Arrangement.[21]

As a principle, membership of the Arrangement is not closed but is conditionally open. Any state which meets the conditions of membership is free to apply. In so far as they are known, the conditions for membership are similar to those for other regimes. The state must have national legal and administrative mechanisms that allow it to implement decisions arrived at by the group; it must comply with international non-proliferation treaties and agreements; and, since the Arrangement works by consensus, it must be accepted by the existing members.

At a September 1995 meeting of the 28 states (including Russia) held to discuss the establishment of the regime, they agreed that the Wassenaar

---

[17] Goldman, S., Katzman, K. and Davis, Z. S., *Russian Nuclear Reactor and Conventional Arms Transfers to Iran*, Congressional Research Service Report 95-641F (Library of Congress, CRS: Washington, DC, 23 May 1995).

[18] *Balkan News and East European Report*, 14–20 May 1995, p. 39.

[19] The Commission was established at the summit meeting of Presidents Clinton and Yeltsin in Vancouver in Apr. 1993. It is oriented towards discussions of cooperation in the fields of energy, space, science and technology and is intended to ensure that bilateral relations between Russia and the USA continue to be addressed at the highest levels. See also chapter 14 in this volume.

[20] 'Chernomyrdin–Gore Commission outcome assessed', *Izvestia*, 4 July 1995, p. i (in Russian), in Foreign Broadcast Information Service, *Daily Report–Central Eurasiya* (hereafter FBIS-SOV), FBIS-SOV-95-128, 5 July 1995, pp. 4–6; Pushkov, A., 'Success in space, problems on earth', *Moscow News*, 7–13 July 1995, p. 1; and 'Complete understanding with US on arms to Iran', Interfax, 22 July 1995, in FBIS-SOV-95-141, 24 July 1995, p. 5.

[21] *Arms and Technology Transfers: Security and Economic Considerations Among Importing and Exporting States* (UNIDIR: Geneva, 1995), p. 102.

Arrangement had five main objectives. The arrangement should enable the participants to:

a) promote greater transparency and responsibility with regard to transfers of armaments and sensitive dual-use goods and technologies;

b) prevent the acquisition of armaments and sensitive dual-use items for military end uses, if the behaviour of a state is, or becomes, a cause for serious concern of the participants;

c) focus on the threats to international peace and security which may arise from transfers of armaments and sensitive dual-use goods and technologies in cases where the risks are judged greatest. However, the new arrangement would:
• not be directed against any state or group of states;
• not impede bona fide civil transactions;
• not interfere with the rights of states to acquire legitimate means with which to defend themselves;

d) provide for an appropriate exchange of information, on a voluntary basis, and assess the scope for co-ordinating national control policies, in order to ensure that trade in arms and dual-use goods and technologies is carried out responsibly;

e) welcome, on a global and non-discriminatory basis, prospective adherents complying with agreed criteria.[22]

The undertakings in the Arrangement are to be implemented through national export controls, and it was stressed that the decision to transfer or to deny any item remains the sole responsibility of each government.

The founding member states also discussed whether or not the Arrangement should be directed at a specific group of countries whose behaviour was considered to be of concern. The preference of the United States was to specify target countries. According to Assistant Secretary of State Thomas McNamara, the Arrangement has two major goals: (a) to prevent destabilizing build-ups of weapons in regions of tension such as South Asia and the Middle East 'by establishing a formal process of transparency, consultation, and, where appropriate, adopting common policies of restraint'; and (b) to '[d]eal firmly with states whose behaviour is today a cause of concern, such as Iraq, Iran, North Korea, and Libya'.[23]

In the end, the founding members of the Wassenaar Arrangement did not agree on a list of target countries—which could then have been modified only by consensus of the group. Rather than leave the decision about when a specified target country was no longer a cause for concern to a group decision, states preferred to retain the flexibility to modify national export policies and regulations without the need for external consent.

To achieve these goals the regime partners would share intelligence on global trends and threats to peace and stability, consult closely about the dangers they see arising, provide information about trade in arms and sensitive dual-use goods and technologies to countries in regions of conflict, and define

[22] 'New multilateral export control arrangement', Press Statement from the High Level Meeting of representatives of 28 states, Wassenaar, the Netherlands, 11–12 Sep. 1995.

[23] '"New Forum" will guard against destabilizing arms buildup', Wireless File (United States Information Service, US Embassy: Stockholm, 21 Sep. 1995, p. 16.

common approaches to these countries.[24] Information that may be shared will include notification of applications to export controlled goods that have been denied. At the time of writing, final agreement on the lists of controlled items had not been reached. At least at the first stage of its development, the Arrangement does not appear to include prior notification of forthcoming contracts for controlled goods. However, the current terms of reference of the Arrangement are seen as the first step in a process whose outcome is not yet determined.

The European Union Regulation

On 19 December 1994 an EU Regulation on the Control of Exports of Dual-Use Goods was accepted by the EU Council of Ministers. The regulation had been developed by the European Community (EC) Commission in consultation with the competent authorities in the member states as part of the effort to complete the internal market in the framework of the 1986 Single European Act.[25]

The main arguments for the EU Regulation were practical. With a single, EU-wide regulation, exporting companies would not need to monitor and adapt to a large number of different national practices. In the framework of the Single Market it was hoped that licences could be eliminated for transfers of non-military goods between member states. Moreover, decisions about where to produce goods for export outside the perimeter of the EU could be taken more on the basis of efficiency and cost if potential distortions arising from different export licensing procedures for non-military goods were eliminated.

In practice, both establishing and implementing the EU Regulation proved to be difficult. Negotiations lasted from early 1991 until December 1994, when the Regulation and a joint-action decision taken in the context of Article J.3 of the 1992 Maastricht Treaty were agreed.[26]

Modifications to the list of destinations and commodities subject to the EU Regulation can only be made by the member states and not by the European Commission, which has an executive role, In addition, there is not total uniformity among the member states about licensing practices and procedures. Some states retain some specific national licensing requirements where certain goods are concerned. The European Commission is tasked with monitoring the impact of implementing the regulation and decision and will report on this to the member states.

[24] '"New Forum" will guard against destabilizing arms buildup' (note 23).
[25] For a more detailed discussion of the EU Regulation, see Anthony *et al.*, *SIPRI Yearbook 1995* (note 1), pp. 616–19.
[26] European Union Council Regulation no. 2281/94 and Council Decision 94/9842/CFSP, both of 14 Dec. 1994.

III. Nuclear export controls: the Zangger Committee and Nuclear Suppliers Group

The Zangger Committee and the Nuclear Suppliers Group were established in 1974 and 1978, respectively. The Zangger Committee agreed a list of items which would, if exported to a non-nuclear weapon state that was not a party to the NPT, trigger the application of International Atomic Energy Agency (IAEA) safeguards. The NSG is a forum for discussing and coordinating export control policies with the objective of averting the acquisition of nuclear weapons by non-nuclear weapon states.[27]

In 1995 modifications were made to the trigger list by the members of the Zangger Committee.[28] Two countries joined the NSG during the year—New Zealand and South Africa—bringing its membership to 31 states. Moreover, the members of the NSG made it clear that South Korea was expected to join once the necessary national legal and administrative arrangements were complete. South Korea currently adheres to the NSG guidelines on a voluntary basis.[29] Representatives of Ukraine and the EU attended the 1995 NSG plenary meeting as observers. The NSG members also revised the annexes to the Guidelines for Transfers of Nuclear-related Dual-use Equipment, Material and Related Technology.[30]

After the end of the COCOM embargo in March 1994, the COCOM members agreed to implement the COCOM lists of controlled items (including the International Atomic Energy List) on a global basis, pending the establishment of the new Wassenaar Arrangement. When the Wassenaar Arrangement is formally established, the former members of COCOM will no longer be obliged to implement these lists through national regulations.

IV. Chemical and biological export controls: the Australia Group

The Australia Group was established in 1985 with 15 members, with the goal of preventing or at least hinderfing further proliferation of chemical weapons (CW), following evidence that Iraq was developing CW capabilities based on trade with international suppliers.[31] The Group developed lists of chemicals known to be key precursors or precursors for the production of chemical warfare agents. After making certain amendments and changes, in 1992 the Aus-

---

[27] For a more detailed discussion of the Zangger Committee and the NSG, see Anthony et al., SIPRI Yearbook 1995 (note 1), pp. 601–607; and chapter 13 in this volume.

[28] The modifications were published as IAEA document INFCIRC/209/Rev.1/Mod.3, Oct. 1995.

[29] Nuclear Suppliers Group Plenary Meeting, 5–7 Apr. 1995, Finnish Ministry of Foreign Affairs, Press statement.

[30] The revised guidelines were published as IAEA document INFCIRC/254/Rev.2/Part 2, Oct. 1995.

[31] For a more detailed discussion of the Australia Group, see Anthony et al., SIPRI Yearbook 1995 (note 1), pp. 611–12.

tralia Group arrived at a list consisting of 54 chemicals.[32] In 1988 the Group realized that in addition to control of precursor chemicals there was a need to develop a warning list of potential equipment for CW agent production, which was adopted in 1989 and has been further amended since then.

Growing concern about BW proliferation resulted in lists of biological agents, animal pathogens and plant pathogens subject to export control (since 1992) and dual-use biological equipment.[33]

At the autumn 1994 meeting of the Australia Group, the members decided to reduce the number of their plenary meetings from two to one each year. Romania participated in the October 1995 meeting in Paris for the first time, increasing the membership to 29 states. At their 1995 meeting, the members also agreed several amendments to the list of biological weapon-relevant materials and equipment.[34] The members expressed 'a strong belief that full adherence to the Chemical Weapons Convention (CWC) and the Biological and Toxin Weapons Convention (BTWC) will be the only way to bring about a permanent global ban on CBW'.[35] Although by the end of 1995 only 19 of the 29 members had ratified the CWC, the members stated that they all plan to be among the first 65 states to ratify it.[36]

In taking the necessary legislative steps to ratify the CWC, the members pledged that they would take steps to ensure that 'all relevant national regulations promote the object and purpose of the CWC and will be fully consistent with it upon its entry into force'.[37] This statement reflected the ongoing debate about the role of the Australia Group after the entry into force of the CWC.

The Australia Group stresses the importance of Article I of the CWC, which requires that no party should ever 'assist, encourage or induce, in any way, anyone to engage in any activitity prohibited to a State Party under this Convention'.[38] The meeting concluded that 'national export licensing policies in the chemical sphere therefore fulfil the obligations established under Article I of the CWC.'[39]

With respect to Article XI of the CWC (Economic and Technological Development), the Group stated at the 1995 meeting that measures such as national export licensing are 'consistent with the undertaking in Article XI of the CWC to facilitate the fullest possible exchange of chemical materials and

---

[32] For more information, see Mathews, R. J., 'A comparison of the Australia Group list of chemical weapon precursors and the CWC scheduled chemicals', *Chemical Weapons Convention Bulletin*, no. 21 (Sep. 1993), pp. 1–3.

[33] For details, see Anthony *et al., SIPRI Yearbook 1995* (note 1), pp. 614–15.

[34] These amendments were made taking into account recent developments, especially the discoveries about the Iraqi BW programme made in 1995.

[35] 'Press Release: Australia Group Meeting, October 1995', Australia Group Document AG/Oct95/Press/Chair/16.

[36] For the full list of states which have signed or ratified the CWC as of 1 Jan. 1996, see annexe A in this volume.

[37] 'Press Release . . .' (note 35).

[38] For the text of the Chemical Weapons Convention, see *SIPRI Yearbook 1993: World Armaments and Disarmament* (Oxford University Press: Oxford, 1993), appendix 14A, pp. 735–56.

[39] 'Press Release . . .' (note 35).

related information for purposes not prohibited by the Convention, as they are focused solely on preventing assistance to activities banned under the CWC'.[40]

Romania, which ratified the CWC in February 1995, had expressed a desire to join the Australia Group for several years. In 1992 it presented Government Decision No. 594, a new export control regime for the non-proliferation of nuclear, chemical and biological weapons and of missiles carrying such weapons.[41] This decision introduced a licensing requirement, end-use controls and lists of items subject to export control, among them technologies and items related to chemical and biological weapons. Government Decision No. 434 of 1993 established a National Agency for Export Control, renamed the National Agency for Control of Strategic Exports and of the Prohibition of Chemical Weapons in May 1994 after the National Authority for implementing the CWC was created.[42] Finally, on 29 July 1994, Government Ordinance no. 31 adjusted the structure and responsibilities of the new organization, and when this Ordinance came into force in November 1994 Romania completed its preparations for membership of the Australia Group.

The continuing debate on Article XI of the CWC and the future of the Australia Group is mainly focused on two positions. The first is that Article XI has to ensure the 'free and unhampered transfer of chemicals' and the second is that every state party to the CWC has the right to take national measures (including export controls) in accordance with the obligation under Article I not to assist anyone 'to engage in any activity prohibited to a State Party'. During 1995 this debate continued in the Preparatory Commission (PrepCom) of the Organisation for the Prohibition of Chemical Weapons (OPCW)[43] as well as in other forums. In general, countries from the South see the Australia Group (and other regimes such as the MTCR) as an effort to deny technology. They feel that the measures applied 'have discriminatory implications well beyond the military realm'.[44] At the April 1995 PrepCom Plenary Meeting, the African Group stated:

in the area of development of economic and technological cooperation the Commission has made no significant break-through. The African Group reaffirms its commitment to the implementation of Article XI of the Convention, particularly on the issues relating to the removal of all measures at regional levels and all other arrangements that restrict or impede trade, development and exchange of information,

---

[40] 'Press Release . . .' (note 35).

[41] Conference on Disarmament document CD/1178, 15 Jan. 1993.

[42] 'Romania: an up-date', *Proceedings: Regional Seminar on National Implementation of the Chemical Weapons Convention*, Brno, Czech Republic, 1–2 June 1994, Occasional Paper no. 5, Provisional Technical Secretariat for the Organisation for the Prohibition of Chemical Weapons, pp. 49–52.

[43] For information on 1994, see Stock, T., Geissler, E. and Trevan, T., 'Chemical and biological arms control', *SIPRI Yearbook 1995* (note 1), p. 734; and chapter 15 in this volume.

[44] Moodie, M., 'Beyond proliferation: the challenge of technology diffusion', *Washington Quarterly*, vol. 18, no. 2 (1995), pp. 183–202.

research and transfer of technology for purposes not prohibited under the Convention.[45]

Western Europe and Other Countries (the WEOG countries), a group defined under the future Executive Council of the CWC, responded by stating: 'The WEOG countries are committed to full and timely implementation of all aspects of the CWC, including Article XI, and to this end, will ensure that their relevant national regulations are consistent with the object and purpose of the CWC at the time of its entry into force for each of them'. In particular, they reiterated 'their support for free and responsible trade and believe that the use of export licensing will be a critical element in ensuring that the essential goal of the Convention—stemming the proliferation of chemical weapons—will be carried out fully and effectively'.[46]

An important, positive aspect of Article XI is that it facilitates the exchange of information on issues concerning the chemical industry, technology, chemistry, trade and technology transfer. In 1994 it became clear to many states that, if chemical trade among the parties to the CWC is to be facilitated, the implementation of Article XI should be seen from a more practical standpoint:[47] actual trade barriers between North and South must be identified, and it must be considered whether the existence of export control regimes is really the most significant impediment to trade and technology transfer.

One way to overcome some specific impediments to trade would be for states to inform each other about regulations, investment guidelines, environmental regulations and health guidelines in a timely and efficient manner. With this in mind, it was suggested during PrepCom deliberations that a library or database be established to help 'promote economic and technological development in the field of chemistry'.[48] Such a library might include the following subjects: producers and suppliers of chemicals and chemical technology, dangerous properties of chemicals and the handling of chemicals, commercial and technical use of chemicals, sources of standards, and national and international regulations on trade in chemicals and chemical technologies, including transport regulations, customs duties and taxes.

V. The Missile Technology Control Regime

In 1995 three countries joined the MTCR—Brazil, Russia and South Africa—bringing its membership to 28 states.

---

[45] 'Statement by the representative of Nigeria on behalf of the African Group presented at the opening of the tenth session of the Preparatory Commission for the OPCW on 3 April 1995', PrepCom document PC-X/14, 3 Apr. 1995.

[46] 'Statement by the WEOG at the tenth plenary session of the Preparatory Commission for the Organisation for the Prohibition of Chemical Weapons', PrepCom document PC-X/24, 25 Apr. 1995.

[47] This was based on the PrepCom's request for a Permanent Technical Secretariat (PTS) study on that issue (see Note by the Executive Secretary, 'Request for data on types of information to be contained in a possible database to be established under Article XI', PC-IX/B/1, 13 Oct. 1994) and a paper submitted by Australia (see 'Non-paper: Information for Article XI Database', 6 Nov. 1994).

[48] 'Expert Group on Technical Cooperation and Assistance: Seventh Report', PrepCom document PC-X/B/WP.13, 16 Mar. 1995.

In 1995 the Brazilian Government was in the process of introducing national legislation to enforce controls on exports of missile and related dual-use technologies.[49] The President of Brazil, Fernando Henrique Cardoso, discussed Brazilian membership of MTCR in a meeting with President Clinton in April 1995. At the Bonn plenary meeting of MTCR partners held on 10–12 October 1995, they agreed to admit Brazil. The Equipment and Technology Annex to the MTCR Guidelines was also amended at this plenary meeting.[50]

The issue of missile transfers has been a significant sub-component of the US–Soviet/Russian bilateral dialogue about strategic weapons.[51] Russian exports of surface-to-surface ballistic missiles were discussed in the Gore–Chernomyrdin Commission. In addition to cooperation in space exploration, environmental monitoring from space and development of new scientific and technical knowledge about future aircraft that could fly close to the limit of or outside the earth's atmosphere, the commercial exploitation of space is also considered by the Commission. The former ballistic missile production industry in Russia will serve the satellite launch market (in which Russia could be among the market leaders). However, US assistance in this transformation has been conditional on Russian policy towards ballistic missile transfers.

In September 1993 Russia and the USA signed a Memorandum of Understanding which committed Russia to apply the MTCR Guidelines on the sale of missiles and related high-technology goods and services. However, it was not until the July 1995 meeting of the Gore–Chernomyrdin Commission that agreement was reached that Russia would participate in all aspects of the MTCR.[52]

In 1993 South Africa modified its national export regulations in the Non-proliferation of Weapons of Mass Destruction Act (Act no. 87) to include missiles and related dual-use technologies. On 13 May 1994, in Government Notice no. R888 issued by the Department of Defence, the South African Government introduced a licensing requirement for all items which fall within the limitations of the MTCR.[53] With these steps the South African Government acquired the legal authority and administrative capacity to implement its MTCR obligations. On 3 October 1994 South Africa and the USA signed a bilateral missile-related import–export agreement which restated South Africa's intention to abide by the MTCR Guidelines and included provisions by which South Africa could import space launch vehicles (SLVs) to put satellites into orbit. The two countries issued a joint statement describing mea-

[49] *Defense News*, 24–30 Apr. 1995, p. 6.

[50] 'Missile Technology Control Regime holds plenary meeting in Bonn', Press Statement by Ministry of Foreign Affairs, FR Germany, 12 Oct. 1995. These amendments were subsequently introduced into the list of items controlled under the EU dual-use regulation.

[51] The US–Soviet dialogue on ballistic missile exports dates back to at least 1990. Shuey, R., *Missile Proliferation: A Discussion of US Objectives and Policy Options*, Congressional Research Service Report 90-120F (Library of Congress, CRS: Washington, DC, 21 Feb. 1990). See also chapter 14 in this volume.

[52] 'Talks to focus on missile technology', *Segodnya*, 27 June 1995, p. 2 (in Russian), in FBIS-SOV-95-123, 27 June 1995, pp. 3–4; 'Moscow to join export, missile technology bodies', Interfax, 30 June 1995, in FBIS-SOV-95-127, 3 July 1995, p. 24.

[53] Reproduced in [South African] *Government Gazette* (Pretoria), vol. 347, no. 15720 (13 May 1994).

sures that South Africa would take to terminate its own research programme to develop a space launch vehicle.[54]

In 1995 MTCR members implemented a 'no undercut' policy that had been agreed at the plenary meeting in Stockholm in October 1994. According to this policy the MTCR partners will inform one another of cases where a licence for an item contained on the MTCR Equipment and Technology Annexe has been denied. Other partners agree not to approve new licences for the same item to the same country. This measure should reduce the possibility that MTCR members can gain competitive advantages over each other in the commercial area by adopting different interpretations of the regime guidelines.

[54] *US Department of State Dispatch*, vol. 5, no. 42 (17 Oct. 1994), p. 694.

Appendix 12A. Transfers of digital communications system technology

IAN ANTHONY

I. Introduction

Any armed forces which acquire an effective and secure communications system will have enhanced their military capabilities very significantly. The USA and its allies are currently investing large sums of money in developing new and more effective communications systems. However, it is unlikely that any monopoly over such systems could be defended indefinitely.[1] The number of countries which are interested to acquire such systems is growing. According to the Ministry of Post and Telecommunications in China, engineers are constructing a 'rapid combat system' based primarily on 'satellite communications, and secondarily on mobile land receiving stations, digital microwave and remote-controlled switching systems and other such emergency components. This network will include 200 000 kilometers of high-grade fiber-optic cable, 50 000 kilometers of microwave transmission cable and 156 land-based receiving stations.'[2] Communications systems specially designed or adapted for military use are subject to export controls in most if not all countries where they are produced. However, to extend export controls over civilian products with potential military applications, three conditions have to be met.

1. There has to be a problem of national security that is sufficiently important to justify action.
2. The security benefits derived from controls must outweigh the economic and political costs involved in introducing them.
3. There must be a characteristic of the market or product which makes controls feasible.

II. An overview of the market for military and civilian telecommunications

One trend within both civilian and military market sectors is the move from analogue systems to digital systems. Both systems transmit information via waves. However,

---

[1] In this context a secure system means communication with minimal risk of either a technical breakdown in the system or the interception and reading of traffic. For a survey of recent investments in digital communications by the armed forces in North America and Western Europe, see 'The digital battlefield', Supplement to *Defense News*, Sep. 1995.

[2] Cited in 'Modern weapons enter production: PLA better equipped', *Inside China Mainland*, Jan. 1996, pp. 37–38. In 1995 the United States Defense Science Board concluded that future adversaries of the USA are unlikely to attempt to acquire major combat systems 'because they can't compete with us on tactical aircraft or stealthy submarines or stealthy aircraft. What do they buy? They buy information for information warfare, weapons of mass destruction and the capability to hide much of what they have'. White, J., 'The compelling case for modernization', *Defense Issues*, vol. 10, no. 89 (18 Sep. 1995). URL <http://www.dtic.dla.mil:80/defenselink/pubs/di95/di1089.html>.

digital systems construct waves by converting information into binary language, the language of computers. Analogue systems, on the other hand, use vibration to modulate sound waves. The message is carried by reinterpreting the precise modulation of the wave. Although both digital and analogue systems can transmit not just sound but also pictures and text, digital systems are generally acknowledged to offer higher quality and greater reliability in transmission. Moreover, digital signals make it easier to exchange information between machines that in the past were separate—telephones, televisions and monitors, telefaxes and computers. This appendix is concerned only with digital systems.

Conventional cables or optical fibres carry the bulk of data and voice traffic in a national telephone system. Data and voice traffic can also be carried via satellites in microwave transmissions.[3]

In the future, land-mobile systems are expected to carry a higher percentage of the traffic. While digital land-mobile radio systems are generally contained among a specific group of users, digital mobile telephone systems have mostly been developed in collaboration with national telecommunications companies and depend on national telephone networks to carry a major part of the traffic. The emergence of satellite-borne cellular networks (such as the Iridium system based on 66 low-earth orbit satellites and other similar planned systems) may at some later date allow a global telecommunications system to compete with national networks.

Telecommunications systems that have characteristics normally associated with military applications can have civilian applications. For example, civilian police forces, trucking companies and taxi firms may use communications systems that have some features in common with military land-mobile radios. In the reverse case, it would be necessary to license telecommunications equipment and technologies that were developed entirely with civilian use in mind if such equipment could meet military needs or were sold to a military user.

The market for civilian telecommunications can be divided into two sectors: equipment suppliers and equipment operators. In the past, operators have mostly been state-owned monopolies. However, the structure of this market is beginning to change and is expected to change further. Equipment operators (i.e., providers of network services) need not own physical assets (such as cables, optical fibres or switches) but may be private companies that manage networks on behalf of the customer, which may still be a state-owned utility. Managing and operating equipment is a much larger economic activity than equipment supply, accounting for perhaps 90 per cent of total telecommunications sales. Most recent developments in digital telecommunications have been market driven and the market for civilian equipment is much larger than that for military equipment. Moreover, while the global military market is not growing, many observers anticipate significant future growth in the civilian market.

The fact that this civilian market is still very dynamic has meant that the outcome of discussions currently under way about technical standards for civilian digital telecommunications is having an impact on military systems. Martin Libicki has observed that in the absence of agreed technical standards an integrated system is

---

[3] Satellites can offer a supplement to terrestrial civilian telephone networks but they are not an alternative. For example, using satellites would not be practical in heavily populated, built-up areas. Digital telecommunications satellites and the technologies central to their development are of great interest to military users. These satellites are also subject to export controls in many of the countries which produce them, although new producers—e.g., Brazil, Israel and South Africa—are emerging.

reduced to a series of 'islands of connectivity' that raise costs and reduce flexibility and ease of use.[4] It is therefore likely that national and international standards will be developed (either by administrative decision or by decisions in the marketplace). Agreement on regulations affecting trade in the telecommunications sector is an important objective of the World Trade Organization (WTO) in 1996.[5]

Some of the most important customers for military equipment—notably the USA—have conceded the need for civilian markets to drive technology development in the future. Emmett Paige, Assistant Secretary for Defense for Command, Control, Communications and Intelligence, has observed that in building its future global command and control system the USA will reject proprietary systems even if they seem cost effective at the time of initial purchase. According to Paige, 'we have learned our lesson—standardize the interfaces, using commercial standards whenever possible . . . so the component software (and hardware) systems can rapidly evolve and be integrated into a stable matrix of interoperable systems'.[6]

Whereas governments are likely to play an important role in negotiating and delivering major items of military equipment, the international trade in civilian technologies with potential military applications is more likely to be conducted by industry. From a supplier perspective, the market for telecommunications is dominated by a small number of companies in North America and Western Europe. For major systems the most important companies are Alcatel-Alsthom (France), Ericsson (Sweden), GEC-Plessey (UK), Motorola (USA), Northern Telecom (Canada) and Siemens (Germany). Other companies have a powerful position in specific subsystems. For example, Nokia (Finland) provides handsets for mobile digital systems. At first sight, a market that is dominated on the supply side by a small number of companies located in industrialized countries should not create major difficulties to export control. However, significant barriers do exist.

Factors complicating export control

It would be of concern to industry if governments established regulations restricting international trade in telecommunications products and services on national security grounds.

Apart from the fact that the market is very large, telecommunications are recognized to be an important element in other economic activities. If export controls prevented the development of telecommunications infrastructure, networks and services for civilian purposes, they would significantly reduce the efficiency of economic activity in general.[7] In addition, telecommunications companies tend to make a high investment in research and development (R&D) and can legitimately claim to be

[4] Libicki, M., 'Standards: the rough road to the common byte'. URL <http://www.ndu.edu:80/ndu/inss/actpubs/act001/ai.html>.

[5] 'Brittan sees bright future for US–EU partnership', *Wireless File* (United States Information Service, US Embassy: Stockholm, 2 Nov. 1995), p. 6.

[6] Paige, E., 'Retaining the edge on current and future battlefields', *Defense Issues*, vol. 10 no. 85 (22 Aug. 1995). URL <http///www.dtic.dla.mil:80/defenselink/pubs/di95/di1085.html>. The UK has taken a similar decision. Miller, D., 'Rationalizing telecommunications: the British DFTS', *Jane's International Defense Review*, Jan. 1996, p. 35. For a discussion of national regulations in the USA, see Crandall, R. W., 'Waves of the future', *Brookings Review*, winter 1996, pp. 26–29.

[7] UNCTAD Ad Hoc Working Group on Trade Efficiency, Draft Guidelines on Key Sectors for Trade Efficiency: Telecommunications, UNCTAD document TD/B/WG.2/11/Add.5 (Geneva, 2 May 1994). Apart from the reduction in economic activity, the market for civil telecommunications is regarded as a key growth area both by equipment manufacturers and by systems operators.

among the 'technology drivers' within their national economies. Therefore, the issue of whether the costs of export controls outweigh the benefits is a very significant one for both suppliers and recipients. The political costs of technology denial are also likely to be high because a country that cannot acquire an efficient telecommunications system is likely to be disadvantaged in many ways.

The structure and certain aspects of the telecommunications market also raise questions about the feasibility of designing controls that can be effective without being a major barrier to legitimate civilian trade.

Companies that supply integrated systems tend to have a high dependence on materials and technologies that they buy from other countries and also a high dependence on sales outside the country in which they are incorporated. They also tend to be highly international in their organization with many subsidiary companies in other countries responsible for production, marketing and distribution of products.

By definition, telecommunications puts a high premium on systems. Telecommunications equipment suppliers not only provide larger customers with many individual items of equipment but also integrate that equipment into a system. The capacity for systems integration is regarded as an important product. It is likely that the supplying company and the recipient (probably a state-owned operator) will have to cooperate at many levels and for some time during and after installation.[8] Moreover, to ensure that the equipment works properly and that a buyer is trained to use it effectively some human exchanges and training will be required. It is very unlikely that an operator can use equipment effectively if only written documentation is transferred.[9] Moreover, as noted above, providing network services is also becoming a major business activity. As one observer has noted, 'if networks become "non-excludable" international public goods, then it is likely that the backward linkage into digital telecommunications technologies will also become more difficult to regulate'.[10]

In some of the largest potential new markets for digital communications—notably in Central and Eastern Europe and in parts of Asia—market access is likely to be conditional on at least a degree of transfer of technology and know-how. This may include not only technology related to equipment manufacturing but also systems integration skills.

As a result, export controls can only be effective if the telecommunications industry cooperates in implementation. No single country or group of companies has yet established an unassailable position either as a source of universally accepted technological standards or in market share. In this environment the competition between countries and companies is fierce and the incentives to open new markets are great. Nevertheless, the companies which dominate the market for digital telecommunications all adopt policies of full cooperation in export control. Although the fastest growing markets for advanced telecommunications products and services are outside North America and Western Europe, these are still by far the largest and most impor-

---

[8] As noted above, the market for operating telecommunications systems is also beginning to change. In future it is likely that private companies will have a larger role in managing and operating civilian telecommunications networks.

[9] The same arguments apply in market sectors such as computer hardware and software. Harvey, J. *et al.*, *A Common-Sense Approach to High Technology Export Control* (Center for International Security and Arms Control, Stanford University: Stanford, Calif., Mar. 1995); and Goodman, S., Wolcott, P. and Burkhart, G., *Building on the Basics: An Examination of High-performance Computing Export Control Policy in the 1990s* (Center for International Security and Arms Control, Stanford University: Stanford, Calif., Nov. 1995).

[10] David Mussington, RAND Corporation, personal communication with the author, 26 Jan. 1996.

tant markets. While acts of illegality by individual employees are always possible, evading laws and regulations in force in Canada, the USA or the EU would not be a worthwhile general policy for any large company. As the Swedish company Ericsson has noted, 'such activities could result in export sanctions, including fines and denial of export privileges, against the employer involved, their company and possibly the Ericsson Group as a whole. Such sanctions could seriously affect not only the company's or operating unit's ability to obtain foreign-controlled technology, and to pursue export opportunities, but could also have far-reaching negative effects on the entire Ericsson Group'.[11]

After assessing these factors, the European Union has decided to implement licensing procedures for telecommunications equipment. Category 5, 'telecommunications and information security', of the EU Regulation, which entered into force on 1 July 1995, lists those items that require an export licence before leaving the territory of the European Union. The category includes communications systems that employ digital technology and includes both mobile and fixed systems. While the category includes both digital radios and telephones, in the framework of the EU Regulation land-mobile radios are subject to stricter controls than telephones. Under the regulation 'portable (personal) radiotelephones for civil use, e.g. for use with commercial civil cellular radio-communications systems, containing encryption, when accompanying their users' are explicitly exempted from control.[12] For company licensing practices, this makes it necessary to determine whether or not a customer is a civilian end-user.

III. Similarities and differences in civilian and military telecommunications technology

Military command and control has traditionally been divided into strategic, tactical and unit levels. Strategic command systems usually involve communication between fixed sites or bases. This communication between bases can be (and in many countries is) an integrated part of the national telephone network, although there are usually special arrangements (such as the installation of redundant lines) to adapt the civilian system for military use. Tactical and unit-level military communications are more likely to be based on mobile systems.

The military applications of mobile, portable radios have long been acknowledged. However, the coordination of battlefield initiatives and the transmission of a stream of data about enemy activities have become progressively more important. Historically, most advanced industrial countries have pursued dedicated military R&D programmes to provide increasingly sophisticated communications systems to their armed forces.

Technology development is permitting the command and control hierarchy to be reorganized. The US, Canadian and many European armed forces are investing in new digital communications systems organized as networks within which information processed at higher levels of command can be passed directly to field commanders

---

[11] 'Ericsson internal export control procedures', Unpublished manuscript, Ericsson, Stockholm, 6 Nov. 1995. For similar points of view from other suppliers, see Ebata, K., 'Report on Japanese dual-use export controls: background, policy and prospects', Unpublished manuscript, Oct. 1995, pp. 22–24; and *The Export Control Manager* (Department of Trade and Industry: London, 1995).

[12] 'Council Decision of 19 December on the joint action adopted by the Council on the basis of Article J.3 of the Treaty on European Union concerning the control of exports of dual-use goods', *Official Journal of the European Communities*, vol. 37 (31 Dec. 1994).

and vice versa. As these systems are introduced, military communications systems should reflect what is considered to be optimal from a command perspective rather than what is technically possible.

To operate on the battlefield, communications systems must have certain characteristics not previously expected in civilian systems. The system must have a minimal failure rate and be easy to repair, maintain and support. The system must be 'user friendly' in its operation so that all members of a unit and not just specialists can quickly learn how to operate it. A military communications system must continue to function when one or more of its parts are disabled or malfunctioning and it must be able to withstand efforts to jam or disrupt signals. The messages transmitted must be secure—through encryption or frequency hopping—in ways that make it difficult or impossible for an enemy to read them.[13] Military systems tend to require a very high level of physical durability or 'ruggedness'.[14]

Differences between military and civilian user requirements are becoming progressively fewer. Business users increasingly require enhanced security and there is growing interest in providing telecommunications services to civilian users in remote locations—where the costs of laying a terrestrial network of cables or optical fibres would be great. In these cases the requirements for a rugged civilian digital communications system could be as demanding as those in the military area.

Military users have become interested in taking advantage of commercial technologies and networks in cases where this could save them the cost and necessity of building parallel systems. In October 1995, US Admiral William Owens observed that by the year 2000 in the civilian area 'the data rate of communications [will go] up not by 10 per cent or by 20 per cent but by 20,000 times. Ten thousand times more data will be able to be exchanged. It is possible for the military to take good advantage of that, plug into that fiber optic network'.[15]

In addressing some manufacturing problems the civilian sector has also found solutions which appear to be superior to those adopted in specialist military programmes. For example, factory tests by Motorola in the USA suggest that the failure rate of micro-electronic components produced in the civilian facilities operated by the company are many times lower than in dedicated military production facilities.[16]

The convergence has not all occurred because of changes in civilian demand. The nature of military demand has also changed. Traditionally military establishments have stockpiled components to reduce their vulnerability to cut-offs in supply. Military establishments have also insisted on a high degree of independent capacity to repair and maintain the systems they operate. Under budget pressures both practices are being re-examined and closer collaboration with manufacturers and private service providers is a likely future trend.

---

[13] Harbor, B., *Technological Divergence in the Development of Military and Civil Communications Systems: The Case of Ptarmigan and System X* (Centre for Information and Communication Technologies, University of Sussex: Falmer, July 1989).

[14] According to its military specification, a US military radio must survive being dropped onto a concrete floor from a height of 1 metre and a 'splash test' using a water jet with a pressure of 2 kg per square centimetre.

[15] 'Czech PFP exercise provides U.S. with good lessons', *Wireless File (Europe)* (United States Information Agency: Washington, DC, 12 Oct. 1995). URL <gopher://pubgopher.srce.hr:70/00/usis/casopisi/wf/European%20WF%20.12.10.95>.

[16] This is attributed to the different regulatory environment for civilian and military production. In particular, it is suggested that technical specifications which must be followed if goods are to be sold to the military cannot keep pace with the rate of improvement being introduced in civilian products under pressure of market competition. Gansler, J., 'Transforming the US defence industrial base', *Survival*, vol. 35, no. 4 (winter 1993/94), pp. 135–36.

The escalating costs of R&D are also likely to make it more difficult for producer countries to support parallel military and civilian digital telecommunications programmes insulated from one another. In particular in areas such as switching systems and network development there are likely to be pressures for sharing R&D costs and perhaps also the costs of maintaining and operating telecommunications networks.

Civilian telephone networks require fully automatic and very powerful switching systems to handle the high and increasing volume of traffic. While peacetime traffic within a military network is much lower than in a civilian counterpart, the escalating need for rapid exchanges of large amounts of information during high intensity military operations also requires a high capacity for switching and traffic management.[17] However, the specific nature of the demand is different. Civilian traffic consists of very large numbers of people sending messages through the system at random and the switching systems are designed to cope with this pattern of use. Military communications may require that a single message be transmitted to many recipients simultaneously or in a very short period of time. If the information cannot be transmitted rapidly then it may be of little or no use to the recipient. In this respect military communications are more similar to information broadcasting than civilian telephone communication.

IV. Summary and implications

This discussion suggests that, under economic and technological cross-pressures, some of the boundaries dividing military and civilian research, development, production and deployment in the area of digital telecommunications are becoming increasingly difficult to draw. It also suggests that this is most true at the level of components and certain individual manufactured goods. At the level of integrated systems, there are some more important differences between specific military and civilian requirements. However, military and civilian users share a growing need for skills that allow them to construct and manage complex telecommunications networks.

Close cooperation between buyer and seller is a normal practice in the area of civilian telecommunications. Therefore, it would be difficult for a recipient to conceal military applications. However, it is possible that skills learned from constructing and managing civil networks could be applied in the military sphere. For smaller items— such as handsets—which can be sold to operators, retail outlets or to other agents, it is technically much more difficult to monitor and control their transfer or use. However, because they are only a small part of a system, they cannot provide any useful capability to the recipient on their own.

It is also true that a purely civilian digital communications system could be of some military value. Against an advanced adversary this value would not be very high because key elements of even mobile networks—such as cellular base stations—are fixed and their location is known. Therefore they would be vulnerable to destruction or jamming. A civilian system could give greater military capabilities where a potential adversary did not have the capability to disrupt or destroy the system. Because of the limited range over which civilian cellular networks operate, such a communications system would mostly be of value to forces operating on their own national territory.

---

[17] For example, the transfer of digital maps and digital images to forward units requires a very high capacity.

The use of civilian mobile telecommunications by the military in these circumstances would be a lesser concern than their use by terrorists or non-state military forces. However, this would be a different kind of problem from those considered in this chapter.

Although it is not likely that a company could unknowingly provide a major communications system to an unauthorized user, there could nevertheless be cases where the need for licensing creates problems for a company. Such cases occur, for example, where the military owns or operates civil communications networks or companies in the buyer country. In some countries the military is also tasked with assisting in economic and technological development. Licensing problems can then arise where a ministry of defence or the armed forces own and operate manufacturing facilities that make products for both military and civilian markets. This is the case in, for example, China and some Latin American countries.

In these cases, sales could be to a military end-user even if the products are intended for civilian end-use and, without assurances and information from the buyer, it could be difficult for a supplier to receive authority to export. In cases involving transfers of production technology, the regulation of retransfers—the sale to third parties of products produced under a license agreement—will also become an important issue.

To operate successfully it is in the interest of telecommunications companies to comply with all the laws and regulations in all the countries where they operate. Therefore, because of their international structure, most major telecommunications companies have to invest a significant amount in developing and implementing export control compliance procedures. While a general framework for control procedures can be developed for the whole company, it is necessary for each subsidiary to tailor its procedures to the national regulations in force in the country where it is operating. Virtually all the major telecommunications companies either operate in the USA or import some parts, software or technical data of US origin.

These items may have to be licensed under US export law after they are incorporated into other products. Therefore, more than one set of export control procedures will often apply to certain advanced telecommunications equipment. The EU Regulation on export of dual-use goods has not removed the need to monitor national export regulations even in the European context as individual member states are still free to exert additional national controls if they choose.[18]

---

[18] 'Ericsson internal export control procedures' (note 11).

13. The nuclear non-proliferation regime after the NPT Review and Extension Conference

JOHN SIMPSON

I. Introduction

In 1995 two seemingly contradictory events occurred: on the one hand, the 1968 Non-Proliferation Treaty (NPT)[1] was made permanent and a universal nuclear non-proliferation regime based on it appeared to be attainable; on the other, the tensions within the regime over the handling of non-compliance questions, and between treaty parties over progress towards nuclear disarmament, became more visible. The legal foundations of the regime were made secure by the decision on the NPT, yet its objectives and the steps that could and should be taken to reinforce it are likely to cause sustained debate and diplomatic friction in the future. The core of such debate will be whether the main task of the treaty regime is to prevent nuclear proliferation by the non-nuclear weapon states within it or whether it is to facilitate both the disarmament of the five declared nuclear weapon states (China, France, Russia, the United Kingdom and the United States) and the removal of the ambiguity that surrounds the nuclear weapon status of three states (India, Israel and Pakistan) which are parties neither to the NPT nor to a regional nuclear non-proliferation treaty.[2]

This is not a new debate: it has existed since the mid-1960s, when the NPT was being negotiated. However, it is now acquiring enhanced international prominence, in part because of the consistent increase in the number of parties to the treaty—from the first NPT Review Conference in 1975 until the opening of the 1995 NPT Review and Extension Conference on 17 April and indeed until the end of the year.[3] In addition, Brazil, a non-NPT party, has accepted equivalent commitments to NPT membership by bringing the regional 1967 Treaty of Tlatelolco fully into force in its territories (see section III).

---

[1] The text of the NPT is reproduced in Kokoski, R., SIPRI, *Technology and the Proliferation of Nuclear Weapons* (Oxford University Press: Oxford, 1995), pp. 255–58.

[2] The NPT defines a nuclear weapon state as 'one which has manufactured and exploded a nuclear weapon or other nuclear explosive device prior to 1 January 1967' (Article IX.3). By implication, all other states are non-nuclear weapon states. South Africa provides a precedent for a state which has manufactured nuclear devices and entered the NPT as a non-nuclear weapon state once it has dismantled its weapons and manufacturing capability.

[3] By the end of the year there were 183 NPT ratifications; see annexe A in this volume. The 9 UN member states which were not parties to the NPT as of 1 Jan. 1996 were Andorra, Angola, Brazil, Cuba, Djibouti, India, Israel, Oman and Pakistan.

Near universality of NPT membership has placed the three non-NPT states with unsafeguarded nuclear facilities—India, Israel and Pakistan—in a more politically visible position than before, enhancing pressure on them to move away from their ambiguous nuclear stance as Argentina, Brazil and South Africa have done. It has also increased the salience of universality as a goal for the NPT and for the non-proliferation regime. As NPT universality nears demands for the 'nuclear weapon five' to engage in a clearly defined, and some would argue time-bound, programme of disarmament are being strengthened, while pressure is increasing on the 'ambiguous three' to act to clarify their status and to accede to the NPT as non-nuclear weapon states.

These strengthened demands have occurred in the context of a change in the nature of multilateral nuclear disarmament negotiations. They are no longer exercises in political rhetoric aimed at influencing the leaderships of non-aligned states and publics in nuclear weapon states and their allies. Rather, there now exists a serious search for disarmament agreements that will reinforce and extend the existing non-proliferation regime by constraining nuclear weapon potentials and inventories. As a consequence, measures which can both contribute to the disarmament of the existing nuclear weapon states and place constraints on those states which remain outside the NPT, such as a comprehensive test ban treaty (CTBT) and a fissile material production cut-off,[4] have acquired near-universal support and thus become attainable political goals.

These radical changes in the nuclear non-proliferation context all contributed to shaping the outcome of the 1995 NPT Review and Extension Conference. At the same time, the activities of at least three non-nuclear weapon parties to the treaty—the Democratic People's Republic of Korea (North Korea), Iran and Iraq—were the subject of close scrutiny and accusations of non-compliance, highlighting the issues of how the rules of the non-proliferation regime should be specified and enforced, the basis for imposing restrictions on exports to NPT parties, and the desirability of changing the conceptual basis and the detailed application of the system of safeguards administered by the International Atomic Energy Agency (IAEA). In the light of these developments, this chapter offers an analysis of how the indefinite extension of the NPT was achieved; its implications for the future of the treaty and its nuclear non-proliferation regime; regional proliferation and non-proliferation developments, including the creation of additional nuclear weapon-free zones (NWFZs); and developments in demand- and supply-side elements of the regime, including security assurances and IAEA safeguards.

[4] See chapter 14 in this volume.

II. The 1995 NPT Review and Extension Conference

The outcome of the conference

On 11 May 1995, the NPT Review and Extension Conference decided without a vote to recognize that a majority of the parties favoured the treaty having an indefinite duration.[5] This decision was not taken by consensus, nor by a unanimous vote of the parties: rather, the minority recognized its inability to prevail on this issue. Moreover, this was one of three decisions taken simultaneously. The other two decisions involved amendments to the process for reviewing the implementation of the treaty[6] and a set of detailed 'yardsticks' for evaluating that implementation.[7] While the three decision documents had no legal relationship to each other, politically the future of the treaty will almost certainly be dependent on the effective execution of the two collateral decisions.[8] In addition, the conference subsequently passed a resolution calling for the creation of a zone free of nuclear weapons and other weapons of mass destruction in the Middle East,[9] which some Arab states linked politically to the decision on the duration of the NPT. Having made the duration decision, the conference proved unable to agree on the text of a final declaration. This was mainly because of disagreement over whether Article VI of the NPT, the nuclear disarmament article, had been complied with by the nuclear weapon states.[10]

Events prior to the conference

The NPT was signed in 1968 and entered into force in 1970. It forms the foundation of the nuclear non-proliferation regime, as it is the only global legal instrument through which a state can commit itself to non-nuclear weapon status. Article VIII.3 of the NPT mandated that five years after its entry into force a conference of the parties should be held to review its implementation and that at intervals of five years thereafter conferences could be convened if a majority of the parties submitted a proposal to this effect to the

[5] *Extension of the Treaty on the Non-Proliferation of Nuclear Weapons*, Presented to the conference as NPT/CONF.1995/L.6, proposed by the President, reported in the Final Document of the Conference as NPT/CONF.1995/32/DEC.3, 11 May 1995. The text is reproduced in appendix 13A in this volume.

[6] *Strengthening the Review Process for the Treaty*, Presented to the conference as NPT/CONF.1995/L.4, proposed by the President, reported in the Final Document of the Conference as NPT/CONF.1995/32/DEC.1, 11 May 1995. The text is reproduced in appendix 13A in this volume.

[7] *Principles and Objectives for Nuclear Non-Proliferation and Disarmament*, Presented to the conference as NPT/CONF.1995/L.5, proposed by the President and reported in the Final Document of the Conference as NPT/CONF.1995/32/DEC.2, 11 May 1995. The text is reproduced in appendix 13A in this volume.

[8] Dhanapala, J., 'The outcome of the 1995 Nuclear Non-Proliferation Treaty (NPT) Review and Extension Conference', *Disarmament in the Last Half Century and its Future Prospects*, Disarmament: Topical Papers 21 (United Nations: New York, 1965), p. 56.

[9] *Resolution on the Middle East*, Presented to the conference as NPT/CONF.1995/L.8 (as amended), and sponsored by the Russian Federation, the UK and the USA. Reported in the Final Document of the Conference as NPT/CONF.1995/32/RES.1, 11 May 1995.

[10] Article VI obliges the parties to 'pursue negotiations in good faith on effective measures relating to cessation of the nuclear arms race at an early date and to nuclear disarmament, and on a treaty on general and complete disarmament under strict and effective international control'.

depositary governments. Such conferences have been held every five years since 1975.

The 1975 conference established three important precedents for future gatherings: that conferences would be preceded by a series of meetings of a Preparatory Committee (PrepCom); that the detailed work on the review would be undertaken by dividing the text of the NPT and of its preamble between two (later three) Main Committees; and that the objective of the conferences should be to agree a final consensus declaration on the results of the review. The review conferences were able to agree such a final declaration only in 1975 and 1985; in 1980 and 1990 this proved impossible, mainly owing to disagreement over the implementation of Article VI, and more particularly the lack of progress towards a CTBT.

The NPT contains a clause, in Article X.2, which had the effect of postponing any decision on the duration of the treaty for 25 years after its entry into force. A majority of its parties could then choose between three alternative options: making the treaty permanent, terminating it after a further fixed period or extending it for a series of fixed periods. This led to the 1995 NPT conference consisting of the process for taking that decision, superimposed on a quinquennial review of the implementation of the treaty.

Four one-week meetings of its PrepCom, spread over 23 months, preceded the 1995 conference, and an additional intersessional meeting convened in the days immediately before it opened. The main tasks of these preparatory meetings were to agree on the agenda, rules of procedure and conference officers. Decisions on these issues were seen to enhance or reduce the ability of caucus groups to exercise pressure and influence over substantive matters, and the debates at the first three PrepCom meetings were far from harmonious.[11] The fourth PrepCom meeting, in January 1995, was more productive and agreed the officers for the conference, its agenda and the rules of procedure, with two exceptions. The first exception was the modalities of taking a vote on the duration decision, should this prove necessary. The second exception was whether that decision should be reported in the final declaration from the conference or in a separate document. The intersessional meeting on 14–15 April failed to find an acceptable formula for voting on the duration options, but it confined the area of disagreement to whether the vote should be by public or secret ballot.[12]

Inherent in the PrepCom debates were different perceptions of the role and focus of the conference. Some parties regarded the decision on the duration of the treaty as the priority issue and saw the review of its implementation as secondary. Other parties wanted to use the conference process to pressure the nuclear weapon states into nuclear disarmament and regarded a nonpermanent treaty as offering more frequent and effective opportunities for

[11] For details of events at these meetings see Goodby, J. E. Kile, S. and Müller, H., 'Nuclear arms control', *SIPRI Yearbook 1995: Armaments, Disarmament and International Security* (Oxford University Press: Oxford, 1995), section IV, pp. 668–70.

[12] This disagreement centred on Article 28(3) of the Conference's Rules of Procedure. See *Draft Rules of Procedure*, NPT/CONF.1995/PCIII/CRP.2, 20 Sep. 1994 and *Rules of Procedure*, NPT/CONF. 1995/28, 9 May 1995.

political leverage. As a consequence, many parties perceived the conference primarily as a review conference, with the duration decision to be addressed at the end of the review process and heavily dependent on its results.

These differing views on the nature of the conference were reflected in the way parties approached it. Many states in the Western and Eastern caucus groups, which were strongly committed to the treaty having an indefinite duration, had a clear objective to achieve and mounted a bilateral lobbying campaign in its favour in the capitals of states parties which had not made such a commitment. Although the states in the Non-Aligned Movement (NAM) caucus group[13] were opposed to an indefinite duration for the treaty, they failed to agree on an alternative duration option at their meetings prior to the conference and thus had no positive objective to campaign for in the weeks before the conference. One consequence was that, at least in respect of the duration decision, the outcome of the 1995 NPT Review and Extension Conference was conditioned by many activities outside the conference, whereas the outcome of previous review conferences had been determined largely within them.

When the conference began the result of a vote by the parties on the duration of the treaty remained problematic.[14] Many parties preferred a decision taken by consensus to one reached by voting, as the former would highlight the underlying support for the regime, while the latter would emphasize the disagreements between its parties. The heart of the differences over the duration decision apparently was not the inherent desirability of an indefinite extension but the political leverage some states believed could be obtained over the nuclear weapon powers by an alternative decision. This led to considerable analysis in both governmental and non-governmental circles on strategies for bridging these differences, and two ideas emerged as possible solutions. The first was to amend the review process to offer greater opportunity for applying leverage to the nuclear weapon states over disarmament.[15] The second was to devise a set of short-term disarmament and non-proliferation goals or yardsticks to evaluate the implementation of the NPT.[16]

[13] The states of the NAM are listed in the glossary at the front of this volume.

[14] It is unclear how many of the parties to the treaty were committed to permanence when the conference opened. A US non-governmental organization estimated this number as 84; 90 states comprised a majority of the parties. Campaign for the NPT Press Advisory, 20 Apr. 1995.

[15] This idea was first proposed in non-governmental circles and discussed at a Programme for Promoting Nuclear Non-Proliferation (PPNN) conference for delegates to the First Committee of the UN General Assembly in Oct. 1994. See Dunn, L. A., 'High noon for the NPT', *Arms Control Today*, July/Aug. 1995, p. 3; and *Strengthening the Review Process for the Treaty* (note 6), p. 9. It was also discussed at a meeting of the Group of Seven (G7) leading industrialized nations in early 1995 at the initiative of Canada, but received a lukewarm reception from the nuclear weapon states present.

[16] Although the idea of reformulating Article VI in a form which would identify realistic steps that the nuclear weapon states might take had been discussed in non-governmental circles as early as the summer of 1993, the development of the 'yardsticks' emerged from events in Southern Africa in the month immediately before the NPT conference started. These compelled the South African Government to clarify its position on the desirable duration of the treaty. In the belief that non-proliferation, like human rights, was an international norm that was absolute and could not be time-limited, a principled decision was taken to support the permanence of the NPT. However, there was no desire to see the removal of pressure on the nuclear weapon states, and the idea of performance 'yardsticks' in the disarmament and other areas was therefore developed and promoted in association with changes to the review process to substitute for any political leverage that a non-permanent treaty would have generated.

Events during the conference[17]

When the conference opened on 17 April 1995, 175 of the NPT parties were present. Initial plenary statements were made by individual states and by the European Union (EU), and a small working group was convened to recommend a method for voting on the extension options. On the second day of the conference the Foreign Minister of South Africa, a member of the NAM, made a statement committing South Africa to a permanent NPT but proposing changes to the review process and the creation of yardsticks for assessing progress in implementing the treaty.[18] The three Main Committees tasked with reviewing specific elements of the treaty initiated their work at the end of the first week, while Canada started gathering co-sponsors for a 'bare' resolution proposing that the NPT should be made permanent. Its aim was to attract more than 90 co-sponsors and thus demonstrate conclusively that a majority of the parties were in favour of a permanent treaty. Mexico also circulated a draft resolution which left blank the period of extension but contained commitments to a time-bound framework for disarmament and other measures, thus linking them legally to any duration decision.

By the end of the second week Conference President Ambassador Jayantha Dhanapala of Sri Lanka initiated informal consultations on ways around the apparent impasse between the proponents and opponents of indefinite extension and asked the South African delegation to produce draft documents elucidating their proposals for amending the review process and creating yardsticks to evaluate the implementation of the NPT. The president created a private Presidential Consultation forum of approximately 20 delegation leaders and their advisers to negotiate 'a declaration of principles on nuclear non-proliferation and nuclear disarmament, a strengthening of the review process of the treaty and an agreement on the universality of the treaty especially in the Middle East'.[19]

These ideas formed the core of the South African Foreign Minister's plenary speech in the opening week of the conference.

[17] Many articles have been written describing and analysing events at the conference and their implications. See in particular '1995 Review and Extension Conference', *Strategic Digest (India)*, vol. 25, no. 7 (1995), pp. 901–54; Andemicael, B., Opelz, M. and Priest, J., 'Measure for measure: the NPT and the road ahead', *IAEA Bulletin 37*, no. 3 (1995), pp. 30–38; Delpech, T., 'Non-prolifération nucléaire: Les enjeux après la prorogation du TNP' [Nuclear non-proliferation: the stakes after the extension of the NPT], *Les Études du CERI*, no 11 (Jan. 1996); Dhanapala (note 8); Dunn (note 15); Fischer, D., 'The peaceful use of nuclear energy and non-proliferation after the 1995 NPT Review and Extension Conference', *Disarmament in the Last Half Century and its Future Prospects* (note 8), pp. 169–74; Johnson, R., 'Indefinite extension of the Non-Proliferation Treaty: risks and reckonings', *ACRONYM Report*, no. 7, 1995; Kelle, A., 'The nuclear non-proliferation regime after the NPT Extension Conference: the tasks ahead', *International Spectator*, vol. 30, no. 4 (Oct./Dec. 1995), pp. 148–55; Rauf, T. and Johnson, R., 'After the NPT's indefinite extension: the future of the global non-proliferation regime', *Nonproliferation Review*, vol. 3, no. 1 (fall 1995), pp. 28–42; Sanders, B., 'The 1995 NPT Review and Extension Conference: an overview', *Contemporary Security Policy*, vol. 16, no. 3 (Dec. 1995), pp. 421–28; and Shaker, M., 'The outcome of the 1995 NPT Review and Extension Conference' (note 8), pp. 57–64.

[18] Statement by the Foreign Minister of the Republic of South Africa, Mr Alfred Nzo, to the 1995 Review and Extension Conference of the Parties to the Treaty on the Non-Proliferation of Nuclear Weapons (NPT), 19 Apr. 1995, p. 3.

[19] Dhanapala (note 8), p. 54.

At the end of the third week, three duration resolutions were formally submitted to the conference. The first resolution was organized by Canada and co-sponsored by a majority of the parties; it was a 'bare' resolution for the indefinite extension of the treaty.[20] The second resolution, sponsored only by Mexico (not a member of the NAM), linked in a single legal document an indefinite duration for the treaty with disarmament and other commitments by the nuclear weapon states.[21] The third resolution was co-sponsored by Indonesia, the Chairman of the NAM and 10 other 'like-minded states'; in a single legal document it tied the extension of the NPT for 25-year periods to disarmament and other commitments similar to those envisaged by Mexico.[22] This situation gave the president and all parties conclusive proof that there was a majority in favour of a permanent treaty. It also removed pressure to agree a definitive procedure for voting,[23] although continuing lack of agreement on this issue deterred the majority from pushing for an immediate vote on indefinite extension of the NPT, rather than continuing to negotiate on a 'package deal' which could produce an unopposed duration decision.

The president's consultations on the package deal centred on the two documents the South African delegation had been asked to prepare: *Strengthening the Review Process of the Treaty* and *Principles and Objectives for Nuclear Non-Proliferation and Disarmament*. After the submission of the three formal duration proposals, the president's consultative group incorporated some of the ideas in the Mexican and the NAM 'like-minded state' proposals into the two South African documents. By 10 May a package existed which was intended to produce an unopposed decision to make the NPT permanent; it consisted of the political commitments contained in the *Strengthening the Review Process* and *Principles and Objectives* draft decision documents and a legal decision document making the NPT permanent on the basis of recognition that a majority of the parties favoured this.

Throughout the conference, the United States engaged in extensive private consultations on the position taken by Egypt and some other Arab states that they would not 'renew' the treaty unless a commitment was obtained from Israel to accede to it. No such commitment was forthcoming, and as a consequence a resolution was tabled by 14 Arab states on 9 May 1995 calling on Israel to accede to the NPT 'without delay'.[24] It was implied that the 14 Arab states might withhold their support from a package deal on the duration of the NPT if the resolution was not linked to that package. This situation was

---

[20] NPT/CONF.1995/L.2., 5 May 1995, had 104 co-sponsors. Towards the end of the second week of the conference, this initiative was in danger of becoming becalmed well short of 90 co-signatories, and some thought was given to abandoning it. It was then carried beyond the 90 figure by NAM states freed from their reluctance to commit themselves to a permanent treaty in advance of their Bandung meeting, held on 25–27 Apr., and by the inability of that meeting to agree a common position on duration.

[21] NPT/CONF.1995/L.1/Rev.1, 5 May 1995.

[22] NPT CONF.1995/L.3, 5 May 1995, co-sponsored by Indonesia, Iran, Jordan, Korea (North), Malaysia, Mali, Myanmar, Nigeria, Papua New Guinea, Thailand and Zimbabwe.

[23] During the final week the issue of the procedures for voting was 'resolved' by agreeing a document which specified in detail how voting would take place in both a secret and open mode, but left it to the Conference to decide which method to use if the decision was to be taken by a vote. NPT/CONF. 1995/28.

[24] NPT/CONF.1995/L.7, 9 May 1995.

resolved when the three depositary states co-sponsored a new draft resolution on the Middle East on 11 May, which did not name Israel but which called for the universality of the NPT and the implementation of comprehensive IAEA safeguards by all states in the region.[25] After minor amendments were made to this draft resolution, it proved acceptable to all treaty parties. The way was then open for the NPT to be made permanent. The president presented the three draft decision documents to the conference, and all were accepted without a vote. The resolution on the Middle East was then presented by the depositaries and again accepted without a vote.[26] One aspect of these decisions was that North Korea had withdrawn from participation in decision making at the conference on 9 May 1995.

Approximately 36 hours remained for the conference to agree the final declaration. The three Main Committees had spent the two middle weeks of the conference drafting detailed documents and had handed their reports to the Drafting Committee for integration into a single draft declaration. Main Committees II and III had nearly reached agreement on their texts, but Main Committee I (dealing with the commitments of the nuclear weapon states) was far from producing a consensus document. By 11 May the Drafting Committee had made further advances towards producing a text from the material supplied by Main Committees II and III, but serious differences remained on those elements of the draft final declaration which dealt with the nuclear weapon states' compliance with the NPT, and, in particular, the description and evaluation of their nuclear disarmament record. Despite the intervention of the president and the heads of delegation who had previously engaged in consultations with him, agreement was not reached on the wording of key aspects of these matters. As a consequence the conference terminated without agreement on a final declaration.[27] While the conference succeeded in making the treaty permanent, it failed to make formal comment on key NPT compliance issues, such as the activities of Iraq and North Korea.

[25] NPT/CONF.1995/L.8 (as amended).

[26] Considerable misunderstanding, disagreement and uncertainty exist over the nature of these decisions. No one doubts that they were taken without a vote. However, since the operative clause of the duration decision was that the conference 'decides that, as a majority exists among states party to the Treaty for its indefinite extension, in accordance with article X, para. 2, the Treaty shall continue in force indefinitely', it merely recognized a legal fact, and thus cannot be read as implying that all the parties were in favour of this option or necessarily acquiesced to it once it existed. Hence it was not a positive consensus decision, but a negative one of deciding without a vote. On that basis several parties felt free to voice their disagreement with the decision in their remarks after it had been taken. The 2 collateral decision documents and the Middle East resolution, however, do appear to be consensus documents as they contain expressions of view from which no party dissented. However, in its statement after the decisions had been taken, China did indicate that it had not changed its position on comprehensive IAEA safeguards as a condition for trading with non-parties, and thus appeared to dissent from para. 12 of the *Principles and Objectives* decision document.

[27] The 1995 NPT conference did produce a final document, NPT/CONF.1995/32, comprising 3 elements: Organisation and Work of the Conference; Documents Issued at the Conference; and Summary Records and Verbatim Records. This contains the reports from all the Main Committees that the Drafting Committee was working on. In addition, the IAEA circulated INFCIRC/174 (IAEA: Vienna, 12 June 1995) at the request of Australia. This contained the first part of the Final Document and the texts of the review of the treaty undertaken by Main Committees II and III.

The future of the NPT conference process

While the 1995 NPT conference created a permanent NPT, it also mandated significant changes in the way NPT issues will be handled in the future. In addition, the failure to agree a final declaration (as was also the case for the 1980 and 1990 review conferences) reinforced the view that different methods of reporting on its implementation were needed. Debate over how non-proliferation issues should be handled in the context of the NPT review system thus seems inevitable. At the centre of such a debate will be the documents on *Strengthening the Review Process* and on *Principles and Objectives*. They were negotiated for a dual purpose: to provide an alternative means of generating political leverage over the nuclear weapon states, and to offer a more focused method of addressing non-proliferation and disarmament issues at NPT review conferences. The implementation of the new arrangements involves significant political decisions. Failure to take these decisions will be seen as reneging on the political bargain built into the 1995 duration package. Indeed, it can be argued that the legal decision does not guarantee the permanency of the treaty, and thus of its linked regime. That will depend on how the collateral political commitments are implemented, and some observers have suggested that non-compliance in this area could be a basis for withdrawal from the NPT.

The strengthened NPT review process comprises several distinct elements. First, a review conference every five years is now mandatory.[28] Second, in each of the three years preceding all future review conferences, the PrepCom will meet for 10 working days to 'consider principles, objectives and ways to promote the full implementation of the treaty, including its universality, and to make recommendations thereon to the Review Conference'.[29] It will also consider whether the goals contained in the second collateral document have been attained.[30] As NPT PrepCom meetings have traditionally dealt almost exclusively with procedural questions, these constitute major changes in the review process. Perhaps more significantly, a conference to discuss substantive disarmament and non-proliferation issues will now convene in four years out of every five, rather than once every five years, thus offering a forum for more timely consideration of emerging treaty non-compliance questions.

Two other significant decisions were taken concerning future review conferences. First, although they will continue to operate with three Main Committees, 'subsidiary bodies could be established . . . for specific issues relevant to the Treaty, so as to provide for a focused consideration of such issues'. One of the tasks of NPT PrepCom meetings will be to create such 'bodies'.[31] Second,

---

[28] *Strengthening the Review Process for the Treaty* (note 6), para. 2.

[29] *Strengthening the Review Process for the Treaty* (note 6), para. 2. The decision to hold a mandatory review conference every five years is argued by some to have significant legal implications, as de facto it amends Article VIII.3 of the NPT ('At intervals of five years thereafter, a majority of the Parties to the Treaty may obtain, by submitting a proposal to this effect to the Depositary Governments, the convening of further conferences with the same objective of reviewing the operation of the Treaty.'). See Shaker (note 17), p. 64.

[30] *Strengthening the Review Process for the Treaty* (note 6), para. 4.

[31] *Strengthening the Review Process for the Treaty* (note 6), para. 6.

the 1995 conference prescribed that 'Review Conferences should look forward as well as back . . . and identify the areas in which, and the means through which, further progress should be sought in future [and] address specifically what might be done to strengthen the implementation of the Treaty and achieve its universality'.[32] This frees them from the constraint, inherent in their previous remit, of focusing exclusively on reviewing the implementation of the treaty in the previous five years.

The first of the annual NPT PrepCom meetings with a redefined remit will be held in 1997, but it is already clear that the collateral decision documents have left unresolved many relevant and significant issues. Among the practical matters are whether more permanent and strengthened secretariat arrangements will be needed to support these new procedures; where the PrepCom meetings will be held and who will convene them; their detailed scheduling, given the congested timetable of arms limitation and disarmament meetings; and how continuity of national personnel and policy will be sustained over the new four-year review process.

The most significant of the substantive questions is probably whether the PrepCom meetings will be 'mini-review conferences', with all relevant NPT issues on the agenda and a remit to monitor and recommend action on events relevant to the operation of the NPT and the regime. One alternative is for them to focus sequentially in 1997, 1998 and 1999 on the work allocated to each of the three Main Committees. Another issue is whether the PrepCom meetings should produce a report on their work, either to give direction to their annual meetings or as a vehicle for making recommendations to the quinquennial NPT review conferences or directly to bodies such as the IAEA, the Disarmament Commission (DC) or the United Nations Security Council.

The decisions taken in New York in May 1995 create a potent new instrument for unconstrained examination of non-proliferation and disarmament issues at future NPT review conferences, and to an extent yet to be determined at annual NPT PrepCom meetings. How it will be used may depend on actions taken before and at the 1997 PrepCom meeting. The decisions have also created a potential new disarmament agenda-setting forum operating alongside those already being serviced by the United Nations, but how it will relate to these other forums remains unclear. Of particular relevance in this context will be whether a UN Special Session on Disarmament (UNSSOD IV) will be convened in 1997, and what impact its activities will have on the strengthened NPT review process and vice versa.

The decision document on *Principles and Objectives for Nuclear Non-Proliferation and Disarmament* offers a set of criteria against which progress in relevant areas can be measured. It can also be viewed as a contemporary interpretation of the short- and medium-term objectives that parties should pursue in order to implement their commitments under the NPT. The criteria are grouped under seven headings: Universality; Non-Proliferation; Nuclear Disarmament; Nuclear-Weapon-Free Zones; Security Assurances; Safeguards;

---

[32] *Strengthening the Review Process for the Treaty* (note 6), para. 7.

and Peaceful Uses. The two most significant of these criteria are those under Universality, which was placed at the beginning of the document to signal the importance of this issue in the non-proliferation regime, and those under Disarmament, which include the time-bound target of completion of a CTBT in 1996. The document is viewed by some of those who drafted it as a dynamic text, capable of being updated by successive review conferences, thus enabling the NPT to adapt to changing circumstances without the need for amendment. The incremental and cooperative approach which underpins it is seen as seeking to change the nature of the nuclear disarmament and non-proliferation debate in the diplomatic community from rhetorical sloganeering and conflict on long-term objectives to hard-headed bargaining and cooperation on shorter-term but more attainable ones.

The existence of the *Principles and Objectives* document raises several practical questions for the NPT review process. The first is how the updating of this document is to be undertaken—through the normal committee procedures or via presidential consultations similar to those in 1995 that created it. The second is whether its existence will lead to a radical change in the nature of the review process, with review conferences no longer seeking to produce a final declaration reporting on the past implementation of the NPT article by article, but instead using different methods of conducting their business, such as evaluating the degree to which the criteria in the *Principles and Objectives* document have been met, and making proposals for amendment to this document in the light of changing circumstances.[33] Parties may be more prepared to consider such changes as a consequence of the failure of the 1995 conference to agree a final declaration.

For many parties, the 'success' of the 1995 NPT conference can only be evaluated in 1997–2000, when the new structures within which debates determining the treaty's political future will take place are brought into operation. The issues likely to determine the outcome of such an evaluation will be whether negotiation on a CTBT has been completed by the end of 1996; whether the new arrangements for the review process are implemented in an atmosphere of cooperation rather than conflict from 1997 onwards; and what effect UNSSOD IV would have on the situation. One irony is that the evolution of the first and last of these issues seems likely to be conditioned by the actions of states which are non-parties to the NPT, particularly India.

The success of the revised NPT review arrangements may also be heavily dependent on whether they enable parties to respond rapidly and coherently to alleged acts of treaty non-compliance. This issue was raised at the 1995 conference by the Sri Lankan delegation, who argued for the creation of a perma-

---

[33] The less than satisfactory nature of the existing structure of NPT review conferences was already under discussion before the 1995 conference. For arguments related to this and some ideas on alternative ways of conducting these conferences, see Sanders, B., *NPT Review Conferences and the Role of Consensus*, Issue Review no. 4 (Mountbatten Centre for International Studies for the Programme for Promoting Nuclear Non-Proliferation: Southampton, UK, Apr. 1995).

nent NPT executive committee on compliance.[34] In parallel, one US non-governmental organization (NGO) issued a report advocating the creation of a UN proliferation rapporteur, supported by a small staff and reporting directly to the Security Council.[35] No action was taken on either suggestion at the conference, perhaps in part because it may have been feared that such innovations would be used to raise allegations of non-compliance by the nuclear weapon states with Article VI of the NPT. However, the decision document on *Strengthening the Review Process* did confer on NPT review conferences, and possibly their PrepComs, the power to create 'subsidiary bodies'. Such bodies might include executive committees. Thus while no overt action was taken in 1995 to create more permanent institutions to support the NPT, the revised NPT review process may offer a favourable context for such a development.

The consequences of the conference for nuclear non-proliferation

While the issues of nuclear disarmament and Israeli nuclear capabilities may have been central to the discussions on the duration of the NPT, such issues often appear somewhat divorced from the implementation of export control guidelines, bilateral diplomatic pressures on other potential proliferators, measures needed to strengthen the IAEA safeguards system and safeguards compliance questions that are the main agenda items for many national officials and intelligence organizations tasked with preventing nuclear proliferation. Given that context, three conclusions can be drawn about the consequences of the 1995 NPT conference for the nuclear non-proliferation regime as a whole.

First, making the NPT permanent avoided the potentially damaging consequences inherent in other outcomes. Although this extension decision was seen by many parties as sustaining an undesirable status quo, it did give confidence that nuclear non-proliferation would remain an international norm indefinitely, that IAEA safeguards would continue to be operative and that nuclear disarmament could proceed on a stable basis. Any other outcome, whether an extension for a fixed period or periods, or a stalemate from which no duration decision emerged, would have put in doubt the commitment of the parties to the permanence of that status quo and the maintenance of the activities associated with it. In short, this outcome consolidated the basis for most of the activities currently subsumed under the nuclear non-proliferation regime.

A second seemingly contradictory conclusion is that an important new trend is reflected by the emphasis in both the review debates and the *Principles and Objectives* decision document on universality, nuclear disarmament and the promotion of measures which have both nuclear disarmament and non-proliferation functions, such as a CTBT. Nuclear disarmament and non-

---

[34] Statement by Ambassador H. L. De Silva, Permanent Representative of Sri Lanka to the United Nations at the 1995 Review and Extension Conference of the Parties to the Treaty on the Non-Proliferation of Nuclear Weapons, New York, 19 Apr. 1995.

[35] See *Confronting the Proliferation Danger: The Role of the U.N. Security Council*, A Report of the UNA–USA Project on the Security Council and Nonproliferation (United Nations Association of the United States of America: New York, 1995).

proliferation activities are starting to converge as the possibilities of creating a universal and dynamic non-proliferation regime and a continuing process of nuclear disarmament appear to be increasing, even if these activities remain highly problematic. Without the guarantees provided by the non-proliferation regime nuclear weapon states are unlikely to give up their nuclear weapons. Without a process of nuclear disarmament, particularly one involving China, it is unlikely that India will contemplate acceding to the NPT, and thus Pakistan also. In addition, it now seems prudent to evaluate new disarmament and non-proliferation arrangements in the light of a potential 'nuclear-disarmed' world. Also, several of the industrialized allies of the USA and the former USSR, which until 1991 actively supported non-proliferation but not nuclear disarmament, now regard nuclear disarmament as an equally important policy objective to nuclear non-proliferation and are taking initiatives to pursue it. The creation of the Canberra Commission by the Australian Government is a case in point.[36]

The third conclusion is that if the purposes of NPT review conferences include providing guidance and generating new initiatives to enable the nuclear non-proliferation regime to adapt to changed circumstances, past conference structures and processes have not been conducive to achieving these objectives. The amended review process may have the potential to overcome some of these deficiencies. However, it is at an early stage of development, and much effort will be needed in 1997–2000 to implement the changes necessary to enable the treaty and its linked regime to meet future non-proliferation challenges.

III. Regional proliferation developments and initiatives

Since 1990 regional proliferation concerns have centred largely on the few parties to the NPT that have been alleged to be seeking nuclear weapons in breach of their legal commitments; on nuclear smuggling from the former USSR and other developments related to its breakup; and on those states which are not NPT parties but which have unsafeguarded nuclear facilities. Regional non-proliferation initiatives have taken several forms, most notably the negotiation and implementation of regional NWFZ agreements. Following the end of the East–West confrontation, all nuclear weapon states perceive such regional initiatives as developments to be encouraged, and as a consequence much greater scope now appears to exist for introducing and reinforcing them.

Africa

The main development in Africa in 1995 was agreement on the creation of a NWFZ covering the continent. The African Nuclear-Weapon-Free Zone Treaty, known as the Treaty of Pelindaba, was finalized at a joint meeting of

---

[36] The Canberra Commission is described in the glossary at the front of this volume.

the Organization of African Unity (OAU)–UN Group of Experts and an Inter-governmental Group of Experts, held in South Africa on 29 May–2 June 1995. Minor amendments were subsequently made to the treaty at a session of the OAU's Council of Ministers on 21–23 June, and the amended text was forwarded to the UN General Assembly in September 1995.[37] A signing cere-mony was held in Cairo on 11 April 1996.

The treaty differs from its other regional predecessors in several significant respects. The area of application is 'the territory of the continent of Africa, island states members of OAU and all islands considered by the Organisation of African Unity in its resolutions to be part of Africa' (Article 1.(a)).[38] It thus excludes any large sea areas, although 'territorial seas and archipelagic waters' are included. All the territory of the state of Egypt is within the NWFZ, including Sinai. Each party to the treaty undertakes not to conduct any actions related to the acquisition of nuclear explosive devices and to prohibit the stationing and testing of such devices on its territory (Articles 3–5). It also undertakes to declare, and either destroy or convert to civil uses, any capacity for the manufacture of such devices; to dismantle any devices that have been produced prior to the entry into force of the NPT; and to allow the IAEA and an African Commission on Nuclear Energy to verify that these undertakings have been implemented (Article 6). Finally, each party agrees to prohibit the dumping of radioactive waste within the zone (Article 7).

Although attempts were made to place limitations on enrichment of uran-ium, separation of plutonium and possession of such materials, this did not survive into the final treaty text. However, the final text does make clear that parties to the treaty are only to supply nuclear materials in future to states that accept comprehensive IAEA safeguards, thus prohibiting new transfers to India, Israel and Pakistan (Article 9.(c)). It also contains undertakings to apply physical protection measures to nuclear installations within the zone (Article 10), and on non-participation in attacks on them (Article 11). An African Commission on Nuclear Energy, which will meet annually, is to be created to enforce compliance with the treaty, and conferences of the parties will be held every two years (Articles 12 and 14). Withdrawal from the treaty can only occur after 12 months' notice (Article 20).

Details of a complaints procedure and mechanisms for the settlement of dis-putes are contained in Annex IV of the treaty. These provide for a detailed challenge inspection procedure, concluding with the conduct of on-site inspec-tions by the IAEA. Three protocols are attached to the treaty for signature by extra-zonal states. Protocol I contains an unconditional negative security assurance for all states in the NWFZ from each of the five nuclear weapon states; Protocol II is a commitment by those same states not to participate in any testing of nuclear weapons in the zone. Protocol III, which is open for sig-nature by France and Spain only, binds those states to apply the provisions of the treaty to territories for which they are internationally responsible.

---

[37] United Nations document A/50/426, 13 Sep. 1995. The text is reproduced in appendix 13A in this volume.
[38] Text from United Nations document A/50/426 (note 37).

A key feature of the treaty is that it leaves ambiguous the status of the Chagos Archipelago, which is part of the British Indian Ocean Territories but over which Mauritius claims sovereignty. One of its islands, Diego Garcia, houses a US military base. Although Article 1 and Annex I appear to indicate that the archipelago falls within the zone, Protocol III is not open for signature by the UK, and thus the implication is that the archipelago falls outside the zone.

South-East Asia

Although a South-East Asian NWFZ had been discussed for many years, the speed with which it was finally agreed surprised most observers. One permissive factor was that after the NPT conference the United States apparently indicated to Indonesia that it would not oppose such a development.[39] Following the 29th meeting of the standing committee of the foreign ministers of the Association of South-East Asian Nations (ASEAN), the Treaty on the South-East Asia Nuclear Weapon-Free Zone was signed in Bangkok on 15 December 1995 by the leaders of the seven members of ASEAN—Brunei Darussalam, Indonesia, Malaysia, the Philippines, Singapore, Thailand and Viet Nam—at their fifth summit meeting. It was also signed by Cambodia, Laos and Myanmar (formerly Burma).[40]

There is considerable similarity between the Bangkok and Pelindaba treaties, except that the former has no provision for dismantling existing nuclear weapons or devices, and it is mandatory for all parties to accede to the 1986 Convention on Early Notification of a Nuclear Accident. Also, its only protocol is one through which the nuclear weapon states can provide negative security assurances to the parties. However, its geographic coverage includes the exclusive economic zones (EEZs) of the state parties, while the article covering foreign ships and aircraft is not preceded by the disclaimer in the Pelindaba treaty that it is 'without prejudice to the purposes and objectives of the treaty'.[41] China has reportedly objected to the EEZ provisions, as it claims areas of the South China Sea regarded by ASEAN states as within their EEZ, and thus within the zone, while both China and the United States reportedly regard its provisions covering foreign ships and aircraft as potentially restricting their freedom to move nuclear-powered vessels or nuclear-armed ships or aircraft through the area.[42] Unless the treaty is amended, such objections may affect their willingness to sign the protocol.

---

[39] *International Herald Tribune*, 18 Sep. 1995.

[40] The text of the treaty was contained in a press release issued by the ASEAN summit meeting in Bangkok and is also reproduced in appendix 13A in this volume.

[41] See note 40.

[42] *Disarmament Diplomacy*, no. 1 (Jan. 1996), pp. 35–36.

The South Pacific

The main development in the South Pacific in 1995 was the recommencement of nuclear testing by France at Mururoa Atoll on 5 September, and the protests in the area following the announcement of this decision by French President Jacques Chirac on 13 June.[43] Included in this decision was a commitment to dismantle and decommission the site once the testing series was completed. This appears to have opened the door to the announcement by France, the UK and the USA on 20 October that they would join China and the Russian Federation in signing the protocols to the 1985 South Pacific Nuclear Free Zone (Rarotonga) Treaty in the first half of 1996. (All three nations did so on 25 March 1996.[44])

Latin America

Following amendment of the 1967 Treaty for the Prohibition of Nuclear Weapons in Latin America and the Caribbean (Treaty of Tlatelolco) in August 1992, Argentina, Brazil and Chile waived the entry into force provision in 1994, allowing the treaty to enter into force for them.[45] Between January and March 1995 three additional states—Guyana, Saint Kitts (Christopher) and Nevis, and Saint Lucia—ratified the treaty, and Cuba signed it (and ratified it in February 1996). Cuba's ratification meant that all states in the zone were now parties to the treaty, and, as all other conditions had been fulfilled, the treaty came fully into force at that point.[46] In addition, Argentina acceded to the NPT in February 1995 and Chile in May 1995, leaving Brazil and Cuba as the only parties to the Treaty of Tlatelolco which were not parties to the NPT.[47]

North-East Asia

The nuclear status of North Korea has been a source of proliferation concern to many governments since the early 1980s[48] and continued to be so in 1995. In October 1994, North Korea and the USA signed an Agreed Framework, by which North Korea would close its existing indigenously constructed nuclear facilities, remain a party to the NPT and eventually allow the IAEA to apply full Agency safeguards procedures to its facilities. In return, North Korea was

[43] See also chapter 14 and appendix 14A in this volume.

[44] *International Herald Tribune*, 20, 21 and 22 Oct. 1995 and 26 Mar. 1996.

[45] Müller, H., 'The nuclear non-proliferation regime beyond the Persian Gulf War and the dissolution of the Soviet Union', *SIPRI Yearbook 1992: World Armaments and Disarmament* (Oxford University Press: Oxford, 1992), pp. 100–101; and Lockwood, D., 'Nuclear arms control', *SIPRI Yearbook 1993: World Armaments and Disarmament* (Oxford University Press: Oxford, 1993), pp. 571–72. For parties to the Treaty of Tlatelolco as of 1 Jan. 1996, see annexe A in this volume.

[46] *PPNN Newsbrief*, no. 32 (4th quarter 1995), p. 2.

[47] *PPNN Newsbrief*, no. 29 (1st quarter 1995), p. 2; and *PPNN Newsbrief*, no. 30 (2nd quarter 1995), p. 5.

[48] For the background to the situation in North Korea, see *SIPRI Yearbook 1995* (note 11), pp. 653–56. See also chapter 3 in this volume.

to be provided with the finance to import two light-water reactors (LWRs) over a 10-year period and with heavy fuel oil to substitute for the nuclear power its planned indigenous reactors would have generated. While this arrangement appeared to condone non-implementation of the full NPT/IAEA safeguards system for a period of years, it also had the effect of going beyond the constraints of that system in denying to North Korea materials and facilities with which it might make nuclear weapons. However, the uncertainty over whether North Korea already possesses sufficient plutonium to make a weapon will remain until the end of the decade, if not beyond, while the arrangement appeared to reward North Korea for non-compliance with its IAEA and NPT commitments.

During 1995 the process of implementing the Agreed Framework started. Difficulties were rapidly encountered over how the origin of the reactor was to be characterized in contract documents. Since much of the finance, the design and the components would come from South Korea, it wished the reactor to be described as a South Korean-supplied reactor. North Korea was adamant that it should be described as a US-supplied reactor. A further area of disagreement was that North Korea insisted that IAEA safeguarding activities in the country were being conducted under the terms of the Framework Agreement and their purpose was solely to verify the freeze on its indigenous programme. However, the IAEA insisted the safeguarding activities were being conducted under the terms of its NPT INFCIRC/153 Model Safeguards Agreement[49] and thus covered all materials and related facilities in North Korea.

The disagreement over how to characterize the reactor led North Korea to threaten to withdraw from its commitments under the Agreed Framework in early March and to restart its frozen indigenous programme. In parallel, Japan, South Korea and the USA established the Korean Peninsula Energy Development Organization (KEDO) to raise the finance for the reactors and to organize their construction. Several rounds of North Korean–US bilateral discussions in April and May 1995 failed to resolve the issue of whether South Korea or the USA would be named as the supplier of the reactors. In June, however, after three weeks of negotiations in Malaysia, agreement was reached on this issue—that the reactors would not be specified explicitly as being of South Korean design.

While this issue was being resolved, work progressed on creating KEDO, and in August 1995 it held its first general meeting. In addition, supplies of fuel oil to North Korea commenced in 1995. By 15 December KEDO was able to sign a contract with North Korea to supply two 1000-Megawatt-electric (MWe) reactors at a cost of $4.5 billion, with completion expected in 2003. The (South) Korean Electrical Power Corporation was to be the prime contractor. The contract apparently specifies that the freeze on the North Korean indigenous programme will continue. The IAEA will be permitted to

---

[49] The Structure and Content of Agreements Between the Agency and States Required in Connection with the Treaty on the Non-Proliferation of Nuclear Weapons, IAEA document INFCIRC/153 (corrected), (IAEA: Vienna, 1983), is reprinted in Howlett, D. and Simpson, J. (eds), *Nuclear Non-Proliferation: A Reference Handbook* (Longman: Harlow, 1992), pp. 175–92.

resume full safeguards inspections, including special inspections, in late 1998 or early 1999, when a significant proportion of the project is completed. The spent fuel from the 5-MWe research reactor will be transferred out of the country when key nuclear components are delivered for the reactors. Finally, when the first LWR is completed, North Korea will start to dismantle its indigenous graphite-moderated reactors, with this process being completed by the time the second LWR is finished.[50] These arrangements appear to be a practical way of resolving the area of most acute proliferation concern on the Korean peninsula, but a full evaluation of their effectiveness may not be possible for several years.

Although North and South Korea signed an agreement in December 1991 to set up a nuclear weapon-free Korean peninsula and create a Joint Nuclear Control Committee (JNCC) to supervise it, agreement on how to achieve these objectives has remained elusive. The two sides agreed to hold a summit meeting in July 1994, but the death of North Korean President Kim Il Sung led to the talks being postponed. Direct contacts had not resumed at the end of 1995. Thus a regional approach to the proliferation problems on the Korean peninsula appears to have been rejected by North Korea in favour of bilateral North Korean–US negotiations.

South Asia

The nuclear proliferation threat in South Asia arises from the ambiguity surrounding the nuclear programmes of India and Pakistan. India exploded a nuclear device in 1974 and has unsafeguarded fissile material production facilities capable of having produced sufficient fissile materials for tens of weapons. However, most analysts believe it has no stockpile of assembled weapons. Pakistan has a centrifuge enrichment plant, which has provided it with sufficient highly enriched uranium (HEU) for a small number of weapons, and it has admitted to having components which, if put together, would constitute a nuclear device. US sources indicate that Pakistan ceased production of this material in the early 1990s under heavy pressure from the USA. It is also building a natural uranium, heavy water reactor at Khushab of 40-MWe capacity which will not automatically be subject to IAEA safeguards and which could produce significant quantities of plutonium once it becomes operational after 1996.

Attempts to prevent these two regional rivals openly declaring their nuclear weapon status have been hampered by the structural characteristics of their nuclear relationship, with the Pakistan capability being perceived as stimulated by the conventional military threat from India, while India's capability appears to have been conditioned by China's actions. This asymmetry has meant that Pakistan has sought a regional solution for the problem, while India has insisted on a global one. As a consequence of this disagreement over the

---

[50] Material for this section is drawn from *PPNN Newsbrief*, no. 29 (1st quarter 1995), pp. 6–8; *PPNN Newsbrief*, no. 30 (2nd quarter 1995), pp. 12–14; *PPNN Newsbrief*, no. 31 (3rd quarter 1995), pp. 16–18; and *PPNN Newsbrief*, no. 32 (4th quarter 1995), pp. 11–12.

context in which the situation should be addressed, recent non-proliferation efforts have consisted mainly of bilateral initiatives by the USA towards the two countries on both an official and an NGO basis. These initiatives have sought to remove friction in US bilateral relations with both states, in order to facilitate more productive exchanges over proliferation matters.

The main initiatives towards Pakistan have been directed at ameliorating the operation of the Pressler Amendment, contained in subsection 620E(e) of the US International Security and Development Cooperation Act of 1985.[51] This mandated that no military or economic assistance was to be provided to Pakistan unless the US president had certified on an annual basis that Pakistan did not possess a nuclear explosive device and that the provision of such aid would significantly reduce the likelihood of it doing so. In October 1990 President George Bush decided he could not sign the annual certification, and consequently the export of some 28 F-16 fighter aircraft and other military material, which had already been paid for by Pakistan, was suspended. In 1995 several attempts were made to develop ways of reimbursing these payments, while the US–Pakistan Defense Consultative Group met for the first time since 1990.[52] In September, the US Senate voted in favour of a one-time waiver of the amendment to allow Pakistan to receive the proceeds of the sale of the F-16s and for the other military material to be transferred to it.[53]

In the case of India, US Secretary of Defense William Perry signed a military cooperation agreement during a visit in January 1995, and in September the two states conducted bilateral security talks in Washington. However, attempts to improve relations were complicated by India's opposition to any waiver of the application of the Pressler Amendment to Pakistan. It is also reported that the USA sought to persuade both India and Pakistan to agree on unilateral declarations that they would not build miniaturized nuclear warheads and deploy them on missiles.[54]

These US initiatives appear to have been stimulated by a fear that time may be running out on efforts to prevent overt nuclear proliferation in South Asia. Although both India and Pakistan are assumed to have a capability for aircraft delivery of nuclear devices, India is moving towards deploying its indigenously designed and produced Prithvi missile, while Pakistan is reported to have Chinese-supplied M-11 missiles in storage and ready to be deployed in response.[55] Such a missile arms race may generate pressures for warheads with a wide radius of destruction, including nuclear warheads.

Global developments have also had a significant impact on the regional situation. Negotiation of a fissile-material production cut-off agreement in the CD in Geneva did not start in 1995 because of disagreement over the mandate,[56] specifically over whether stockpiles should be covered by the agreement. Pak-

---

[51] See *SIPRI Yearbook 1995* (note 11), p. 658.
[52] *Defence News*, 29 May–4 June 1995; and *Defence News,* 5–11 June 1995.
[53] *Washington Post*, 22 Sep. 1995.
[54] *Washington Post*, 27 July 1995.
[55] International Institute for Strategic Studies, *The Military Balance 1995–1996* (Oxford University Press: Oxford, 1995), p. 152.
[56] See chapter 14 in this volume.

istan has been particularly concerned about this proposal, as any agreement stopping future fissile material production would leave it with lower stocks of unsafeguarded nuclear materials than India, and thus in a position of disadvantage in potential future weapon numbers. For its part, India appears to have been discomforted by the outcome of the 1995 NPT conference which emphasized the increasing political and economic costs generated by India's ambiguous nuclear stance. These include a ban on all nuclear-related imports which will continue until, and unless, India accepts a comprehensive IAEA safeguards agreement.[57]

In December 1995, US surveillance satellites were reported to have detected unusual activities at Pokaran, the site of India's 1974 nuclear test in the Rajasthan desert, while India also appeared to be attempting to have a ban on all nuclear weapon development activities and a time-bound framework for disarmament incorporated into the text of the CTBT—thus changing it from a treaty simply banning nuclear test explosions and making it unacceptable in its new form to the USA and some other nuclear weapon states.[58] Whether these actions should be interpreted as preparing the ground for an Indian nuclear testing programme to be initiated before a CTBT is agreed or as an attempt to prevent the only time-bound disarmament objective in the NPT *Principles and Objectives* being achieved, and thus to make a harmonious implementation of the new NPT review process more difficult, or both, may become clearer in 1996. Any nuclear test explosion in South Asia would place great strain on US non-proliferation policies for it would bring into operation the Glen Amendment of 1977 to the Foreign Assistance Act of 1961, which bars aid to any non-nuclear weapon state which explodes a nuclear device.[59] Draconian sanctions would automatically apply to trade and economic assistance to the state involved, but they could also have similar consequences for US bilateral non-proliferation policies to those generated by the Pressler Amendment in relation to Pakistan, in that they would forbid the use of conventional military transfers or other forms of assistance as tools to persuade it not to conduct another explosion.

The Middle East

Three issues form the focus for nuclear proliferation and non-proliferation concerns in the Middle East: Israel and a Middle East NWFZ, Iraq and Iran.

The starting-point for discussions on a Middle East NWFZ was an Israeli desire to engage the Arab states in direct discussion on this issue, with the

[57] This condition, on 'new supply arrangements' was contained in para. 12 of the *Principles and Objectives* decision document. The ban was reinforced on a regional level by Article 9 (c) of the Pelindaba treaty. Only China, in its statement after the duration decision indicating how it proposed to apply IAEA safeguards, signalled that it might not impose the ban.

[58] *PPNN Newsbrief*, no. 32 (4th quarter 1995), pp. 5–6.

[59] This amendment, Section 670, was contained in the International Security and Development Cooperation Act of 1977. Subsection (b) bars aid to any country which transfers a nuclear explosive device or receives or detonates a nuclear explosive device. The president may provide aid if he certifies that termination would hinder non-proliferation objectives or otherwise jeopardize the common defence and security.

Arab states responding by arguing for Israeli accession to the NPT. Part of the Middle East peace process which started in Madrid in October 1991 involved the creation of an Arms Control and Regional Security (ACRS) Working Group, although it proved unable to make any significant progress in addressing nuclear issues as Israel was not prepared to accept constraints on its nuclear capabilities until the peace process had been completed.[60] For some Arab states, however, such constraints were an essential part of that process. In December 1995, indications emerged from Egyptian–Israeli discussions that Prime Minister Shimon Peres and President Hosni Mubarak had reached an understanding under which Egypt would cease its pressure for immediate denuclearization in return for a commitment that Israel would sign a treaty creating a NWFZ in the region one year after peace had been established with Lebanon and Syria. At the same time, Peres came close to openly admitting that Israel had nuclear weapons by reportedly saying that 'after peace arrives, we'll be in a Middle East free of nuclear weapons'.[61]

The issue of whether Iraq had provided the United Nations Special Commission on Iraq (UNSCOM) and the IAEA with full information on its programmes to produce weapons of mass destruction continued to concern the UN Security Council.[62] In April 1995, the IAEA issued a report indicating that information was still sparse on Iraq's gas centrifuge enrichment activities and on its weaponization efforts in the second half of 1990.[63] On 8 August, two of Saddam Hussein's sons-in-law, one of whom had been in charge of Iraq's nuclear weapon programme, defected to Jordan. Soon after this event, Iraq provided UNSCOM with thousands of additional documents on its programmes to produce weapons of mass destruction, including some which detailed two previously unknown aspects of the nuclear programme. One of these was a crash programme, started in the summer of 1990, to produce a nuclear explosive device by April 1991 from safeguarded enriched uranium already in the country. A second was an unsuccessful effort to develop radiological weapons using cobalt-60 and caesium. When the IAEA submitted its semi-annual report to the UN Security Council in October, it again emphasized that there was no certainty that all the relevant documents had been revealed, while the Chairman of UNSCOM indicated that some of its assessments of the Iraqi programme would need to be reconsidered in the light of the new documentation. Reports also circulated that since 1991 Iraq had continued to acquire technology relevant to the production of ballistic missiles, including some which had originated from dismantled nuclear delivery systems, and that it had imported centrifuge equipment from a European manufacturer.[64]

[60] See Kemp, G. and Pressman, J., 'The Middle East: continuation of the peace process', *SIPRI Year-book 1995* (note 11), pp. 191–92; and chapter 4 in this volume.

[61] *PPNN Newsbrief*, no. 32 (4th quarter 1995), p. 2.

[62] See also chapter 15 in this volume.

[63] United Nations Security Council document S/1995/287, 11 Apr. 1995.

[64] *PPNN Newsbrief*, no. 31 (3rd quarter 1995), pp. 17–18; and *PPNN Newsbrief*, no. 32 (4th quarter 1995), p. 13.

US policy makers, in common with some policy makers in Israel, remain convinced that their intelligence sources indicate that Iran is actively pursuing a policy to acquire nuclear weapons, even though the IAEA can find no evidence to demonstrate that Iran is not complying with its commitments under the NPT and its IAEA safeguards agreement.[65] The consequences of this for non-proliferation policies were found in disagreements between the United States on the one hand, and the Russian Federation and China on the other, over the plans by the latter two states to provide Iran with nuclear technologies that it could legitimately receive under the NPT.

In the case of the Russian Federation, the issue centred on a contract, signed in January 1995, under which it would complete two German-designed power reactors at Bushehr, and negotiations that were believed to be taking place for two further reactors and gas centrifuge equipment. The USA applied pressure on Russia to cancel the deal, and the issue was raised at the Clinton–Yeltsin summit meeting in early May. This resulted in Russian officials offering assurances that the gas centrifuge deal would not go ahead, while the reactor sale was remitted to the US–Russian Joint Commission on Economic and Technological Cooperation (known as the Gore–Chernomyrdin Commission) for further consideration.[66] The latter did not cause the deal to be abandoned, and by the end of 1995 attention focused on the issue of how used fuel from the reactors was to be disposed of, with one authoritative Russian source indicating that Iran would either store the fuel or send it to Russia to be reprocessed, with Iran taking back the high-level waste and the recovered fissile materials, rather than the plutonium in the fuel remaining in Russia as had been previously believed.[67]

The differences between China and the USA centred on China's negotiations to sell two 300-MWe power reactors and associated fuel production facilities to Iran. This issue was raised at the foreign minister level just before the NPT conference in April 1995. Although China publicly rejected the US pressure, problems appear to have arisen subsequently over the supply of the reactors, with the Chinese Foreign Minister stating that the deal was 'suspended for the time being'.[68]

In both the Russian and Chinese cases many commentators pointed out that there was an inconsistency between the US opposition to the transfer of LWRs to Iran and its position on the transfer of such reactors to North Korea, which was the central element in the North Korean–US Framework Agreement. For their part US officials noted that the North Korean reactor deal was an incentive to bring North Korea into compliance with the NPT, whereas the USA believes that Iran is violating the NPT and therefore not entitled to receive the benefits promised therein.

[65] *New York Times*, 10 Jan. 1995. See also chapters 12 and 14 in this volume.
[66] *PPNN Newsbrief*, no. 30 (2nd quarter 1995), pp. 14–15; see also chapters 12 and 14 in this volume.
[67] *Nucleonics Week*, 9 Nov. 1995.
[68] *PPNN Newsbrief*, no. 30 (2nd quarter 1995), p. 15; and *PPNN Newsbrief*, no. 31 (4th quarter 1995), p. 7.

IV. Demand- and supply-side initiatives

One way of viewing the nuclear non-proliferation regime is to regard it as a multifaceted mechanism for reducing the demand for nuclear weapon possession and for making it more difficult to acquire such weapons: both a demand- and supply-side regime. On the demand side, three areas of activity have been particularly significant: reductions in the perception that nuclear weapons have great utility in national defence policies, enhanced security assurances and strengthened IAEA safeguards, including those on fissile materials in military stockpiles. On the supply side, activity has focused mainly on strengthening national export control systems and their international guidelines, particularly those of the Nuclear Suppliers Group (NSG), and the creation of a new system of controls to replace the Coordinating Committee on Multilateral Export Controls (COCOM).[69]

Reducing the salience of nuclear weapons

The main source of perceptions on the utility of nuclear weapons is the activities of the nuclear weapon states. If they are prepared to forgo nuclear weapons, this is a key indicator that such weapons lack security and political value. Thus their actions and commitments in this area have considerable long-term non-proliferation significance. All the nuclear weapon states except China have engaged in well-publicized nuclear weapon reductions, both by cutting back on stockpile numbers and by removing from their stockpiles categories of weapons committed to specific roles. As a consequence, most 'war-fighting' weapons have now been retired, and at least one nuclear weapon state, the United Kingdom, is committed to having only a single strategic system with limited numbers of warheads by the end of the decade.[70] In addition, the *Principles and Objectives* document that came out of the NPT conference contained a programme of action which included: 'The determined pursuit by the nuclear-weapon States of systematic and progressive efforts to reduce nuclear weapons globally, with the ultimate goal of eliminating those weapons'.[71] This followed a joint statement by France, Russia, the UK and the USA in which they 'solemnly reaffirmed their commitment, as stated in Article VI, to pursue negotiations in good faith on effective measures relating to nuclear disarmament, which remains our ultimate goal'.[72]

This is not to argue, of course, that the elimination of nuclear weapons is imminent. On the contrary, at the end of 1995 several indicators suggested

[69] See also chapter 12 in this volume.

[70] Letter dated 21 April 1995 from the Head of the Delegation of the United Kingdom of Great Britain and Northern Ireland addressed to the Secretary-General of the 1995 Review and Extension Conference of the Parties to the Treaty on the Non-Proliferation of Nuclear Weapons, NPT/CONF.1995/24, 21 Apr. 1995, para. 40 (c)–(e).

[71] *Principles and Objectives for Nuclear Non-Proliferation and Disarmament* (note 7), para. 4.(c).

[72] Declaration dated 6 April 1995, annexed to letter dated 17 April 1995 from the Representatives of France, the Russian Federation, the United Kingdom of Great Britain and Northern Ireland and the United States of America addressed to the Secretary-General of the 1995 Review and Extension Conference of the Parties to the Treaty on the Non-Proliferation of Nuclear Weapons, NPT/CONF.1995/20.

that the movement towards nuclear disarmament was weakening. Concerns over biological and chemical weapon proliferation led to assertions in the USA that nuclear weapons had a continuing role to play in deterring the threat from use of these weapons, even if deployed by NPT parties which had been furnished with negative security assurances. Russia had not ratified the 1993 START II Treaty, and the USA had refused to move forward with 'START III'.[73] US security partners supported the continued reliance on nuclear deterrence of non-nuclear threats through NATO and bilateral alliances. Russia's doctrine has been similar to that of NATO since the renunciation of no-first-use in 1993, while China is also alleged to be considering revisions to its nuclear doctrine.[74]

Security assurances

Multilateral security assurances can be regarded as a necessary collateral measure to convince non-nuclear weapon states that not possessing nuclear weapons does not detract from their security. They may also be perceived as a 'halfway house' towards the delegitimization of such weapons and nuclear disarmament. They have in the past been provided by existing nuclear weapon states in two forms: negative assurances that nuclear threats would not be mounted and implemented against non-nuclear weapon states; and positive assurances of assistance in the event of such threats and their implementation. The negative assurances were given through a series of unilateral declarations and through protocols to NWFZ treaties; the positive ones through UN Security Council Resolution 255.[75] These assurances were regarded by many non-nuclear weapon states as inadequate in two respects: the unilateral negative ones had weak legal status, as they were not contained in an international agreement or treaty, while only the three NPT depositary states had offered positive ones, which were in themselves not regarded as going beyond commitments already contained in the UN Charter.

In the run-up to the 1995 NPT conference, the five nuclear weapon states met frequently in Geneva to try to reach agreement on a new security assurance document. However, this proved difficult to produce, and what eventually emerged was UN Security Council Resolution 984.[76] Among other things, it noted a series of unilateral statements on security assurances made by representatives of the five nuclear weapon states to the CD in Geneva, in which China offered a much less restricted set of assurances than the other four states.[77] Resolution 984 also explicitly covered both positive and negative

[73] See the discussion in chapter 14.

[74] Johnston, A. I., 'China's new "old thinking": the concept of limited deterrence', *International Security*, vol. 20, no. 3 (winter 1995/96).

[75] United Nations document S/RES/255, 19 June 1968.

[76] United Nations Security Council document S/RES/984, 11 Apr. 1995. The text is reproduced in appendix 13A in this volume.

[77] These statements were annexed to letters sent to the Secretary-General of the United Nations by the Permanent Representatives of China (A/50/155-S/1995/265), France (A/50/154-S/1995/264), Russia (A/50/151-S/1995/261), the UK (A/50/152-S/1995/262) and the USA (A/50/153-S/1995/263) in New York on 5–6 Apr. 1995.

security assurances, specifying measures to be taken in the areas of settlement of disputes, humanitarian assistance and compensation for victims. This initiative was regarded as unsatisfactory by many NPT parties, however, with the result that the *Principles and Objectives* document stated that 'further steps should be considered to assure non-nuclear weapon States party to the Treaty against the use or threat of use of nuclear weapons. These steps could take the form of internationally legally binding instrument'.[78]

IAEA safeguards

IAEA safeguards serve to provide assurances that other states are not pursuing nuclear weapon programmes and seeking to 'break out' of the NPT to nuclear weapon status, thus generating a proliferation chain reaction.[79] However, until 1991 the comprehensive safeguards applied to NPT non-nuclear weapon state parties, known as INFCIRC/153 safeguards, were oriented mainly towards detecting diversion of declared nuclear materials from their specified uses through material accountancy techniques. Following the revelations of Iraq's clandestine nuclear weapon development programme, the IAEA sought to strengthen its safeguards regime to provide enhanced confidence in its assurances of non-diversion of declared nuclear materials and to be in a position to detect undeclared materials and related clandestine nuclear weapon activities. Several measures to achieve this objective were implemented by the IAEA Board of Governors over the next two years, including confirming the right of the Agency to use special inspections; demanding that parties provide design information on facilities under construction or undergoing modification at the earliest possible moment; and initiating a system of reporting to the Agency the imports and exports of specified equipment and nuclear and non-nuclear materials.[80]

In the summer of 1993, the IAEA embarked on a major initiative, known as 'Programme 93 + 2', intended to lead to a strengthened and more cost-effective safeguarding system.[81] The intention was to retain material accountancy as the cornerstone of the system but to implement arrangements for much improved transparency over all aspects of national nuclear activities, through innovations such as enhanced inspection and data-collection arrangements. This would give the Agency an augmented basis for comparing information derived from material accountancy activities and from other sources, rather than having to rely on the former source alone. The IAEA Board of Governors endorsed the general direction of the programme in March 1995, and in June the Board was presented with a two-part document detailing

---

[78] *Principles and Objectives for Nuclear Non-Proliferation and Disarmament* (note 7), para. 8.

[79] See Dunn, L. A. and Overholt, W. H., 'The next phase in nuclear proliferation research', *Orbis*, vol. 20, no. 2 (summer 1976), especially pp. 509–16.

[80] Fischer, D., Sanders, B., Scheinman, L. and Bunn, G., *A New Nuclear Triad: The Non-Proliferation of Nuclear Weapons, International Verification and the International Atomic Energy Agency*, PPNN Study Three (Mountbatten Centre for International Studies for Programme for Promoting Nuclear Non-Proliferation: Southampton, UK), 1992.

[81] See *SIPRI Yearbook 1995* (note 11), p. 667; and the glossary at the front of this volume.

specific proposals to achieve its aims. Part I consisted of those measures which it was agreed could be implemented through the Agency's existing legal authority under INFCIRC/153 or the IAEA Statutes; Part II comprised those measures which some states believed could only be implemented if additional legal powers were given to the Agency. The Board approved the implementation of the Part I measures at its June 1995 meeting and began discussing Part II measures at its December meeting. The main difficulty with these additional proposals appears to be whether the IAEA should negotiate their implementation on a state-by-state basis, thus allowing it to activate them immediately in those states which believe that Part II measures are covered by existing legal authority, or whether it should first negotiate generic amendments or additional protocols to the existing standard safeguards agreement, INFCIRC/153, and then ask all parties to ratify them.

The practical consequence of these decisions is that in early 1996 the Agency will start implementing several modifications to the existing safeguards system. These include collecting environmental samples at declared facilities where the IAEA has an established right of access; acquiring information not previously requested but covered by existing legal instruments, such as data on uranium mining, processing and conversion plants; and seeking details of past nuclear activities. The innovations still under discussion are the right of access to sites which do not contain nuclear material but where activities have been declared to exist that are 'functionally' related to fuel-cycle operations (e.g., heavy-water plants); the right of access to all parts of a site declared to contain nuclear materials, in order that environmental sample collection can be undertaken; and a requirement for an expanded declaration by each state giving a complete description of its nuclear fuel cycle, not just a statement of the nuclear materials within its jurisdiction and their location.[82]

The end of the cold war and the collapse of the USSR led to large numbers of nuclear weapons being retired and dismantled, and thus to increases in the stockpiles of HEU and plutonium not covered by the IAEA or the European Atomic Energy Community (Euratom) safeguards systems. The NPT permits non-nuclear weapon states to stockpile these materials so long as they are covered by safeguards. Both of these situations are regarded by some observers as constituting significant proliferation risks. This has led to calls for greater transparency as regards both civil and military fissile material stockpiles and to attempts to introduce a new framework for their management. In January 1995, Belgium, France, Germany, Japan, Switzerland, the UK and the USA agreed in principle to publish annual statements of their inventories of civil-use plutonium, as part of a move towards greater transparency. In addition, these states plus China and Russia initiated discussions outside the IAEA context on a new framework agreement for the international management of plutonium.[83] The first results of this initiative came in September 1995, when

[82] See *PPNN Newsbrief*, no. 31 (3rd quarter 1995), pp. 11–12; and *Strengthening the Effectiveness and Improving the Efficiency of the Safeguards System*, Report of the Director General [of the IAEA] to the General Conference, GC(39)/17, 22 Aug. 1995.

[83] *Nucleonics Week*, 26 Jan. 1995.

all nine states were reported to have reached agreement on a format they would use for releasing information on their national stockpiles of plutonium and other nuclear materials.[84]

The Nuclear Suppliers Group[85]

The 1995 annual plenary meeting of the Nuclear Suppliers Group (NSG) was held in Helsinki on 5–7 April, with Finland in the chair. The 31 NSG members at this meeting included the new entrants New Zealand and South Africa.

The 1995 plenary meeting reviewed the Guidelines for Transfers of Nuclear-related Dual-use Equipment, Material and Related Technology and revised the annexes.[86] It agreed that in future the guidelines would not only list the nuclear equipment and materials which would only be exported to a state if it accepted comprehensive IAEA safeguards, but also technologies associated with these items.[87]

The meeting also considered extending membership to Belarus, Brazil, Kazakhstan, Ukraine (present as an observer) and Mexico and expressed the expectation that South Korea would join.[88] One basic requirement for NSG membership is the existence of an effective national export control system. South Korea submitted its application for membership on 4 October, was accepted at a meeting of NSG officials in Vienna on 13 October, and will thus attend the next annual meeting as the 32nd NSG member.[89]

V. Conclusions

An observer who suggested in 1990 that, by the end of 1995, 183 states would be parties to the NPT and that the treaty would be made permanent without formal opposition would have been accused of gross over-optimism. Yet that situation now exists. Moreover, NPT parties were prepared, following the Iraq experience, to widen the role that they wished the IAEA safeguards system to perform and to accept significantly enhanced monitoring of their nuclear activities. In addition, two new NWFZ treaties were in existence in Africa and South East Asia, while the 1967 Treaty of Tlatelolco was about to come fully into force. Using these criteria, the nuclear non-proliferation regime can be argued to have been immeasurably strengthened in the five years since 1990.

[84] *Atoms in Japan*, vol. 39, no. 10 (Oct. 1995), pp. 17–18. This states that information is to be released on the amount of material in each nuclear facility, the amount to be recovered from dismantled weapons and how much of this is to be used commercially, the amount of plutonium in used fuel sent overseas for reprocessing and received from overseas clients for this purpose, and the amount in spent fuel.

[85] See also chapter 12, section III, in this volume. For the list of NSG members and observers in 1995, see table 12.1 in chapter 12.

[86] The revised guidelines were published as IAEA document INFCIRC/254/Rev.2/Part 2, Oct. 1995.

[87] *PPNN Newsbrief*, no. 30 (2nd quarter 1995), p. 5.

[88] Nuclear Suppliers Group Plenary Meeting, 5–7 Apr. 1995, Finnish Ministry of Foreign Affairs, Press statement.

[89] *Korea Newsreview*, vol. 24, no. 42 (21 Oct. 1995), p. 4.

Yet this judgement may run the risk of being regarded as superficial by the end of the century if some current trends continue. The near-universalization of the NPT has had the effect of isolating politically the three states with unsafeguarded nuclear facilities that remain outside it—India, Israel and Pakistan. India displays symptoms which could be interpreted as a willingness to undermine the NPT-based non-proliferation regime by its principled rejection of the treaty and its insistence that its path to global disarmament is the only correct one. At the same time, it is clear that difficult choices lie ahead for nuclear non-proliferation policies, particularly those of the United States. Strategies for dealing with NPT non-compliance and restraining the nuclear proliferation activities of states outside the treaty may lead to judgements that 'carrots' are necessary to influence the behaviour of such states, even though their provision may run counter to global norms and consensual rules and appear to reward regime renegades. Comparison of US policies towards Iran and North Korea, and the international dissonance that has accompanied them, illustrate the problems and consequences of the discrimination that can arise from this source. Yet such contradictions appear almost inevitable if effective policies are to be designed to handle the future nuclear situations in South Asia and the Middle East.

The end of the East–West conflict has separated the interests of the nuclear weapon states in continuing to possess nuclear weapons from those of many of their past allies and has served to create the potential for a significant nuclear weapon state/non-nuclear weapon state split within the nuclear non-proliferation regime over progress towards nuclear disarmament. The politics of both nuclear non-proliferation and nuclear disarmament are thus changing slowly but inexorably, in line with the weakening of the political structures imposed by the bipolar ideological divide of the years after 1945. The core of the diplomatic disputes over the NPT, the demand that the division between nuclear and non-nuclear weapon states be eliminated, is slowly starting to move from the realm of political rhetoric to that of reality. This suggests that one issue for the changed review process created at the 1995 NPT conference may be how to manage the slow transition from a nuclear-armed to a nuclear-disarmed world in a manner which provides assurances of security for both the states currently within the NPT and the small minority that now remain outside it. In doing so, confidence will need to be enhanced that the non-proliferation regime is able to handle effectively future non-compliance situations of the type that have arisen within it in the past five years and to provide assurances that no advantages will accrue to renegades breaking out from either the non-proliferation or the disarmament elements of an increasingly integrated global nuclear weapon management regime.

Analysts of the contemporary scene may therefore have to look to the future to understand the present. One version of this future is a reversion to the past: renewed hostility between a greater Russia on the one hand and China, Europe and the USA on the other. Yet that scenario ignores the forces of intra-state disorder and decentralization of authority that appear likely to dominate the future as well as the cross-cutting integrating force of economic globalism.

Under this latter scenario, the existence of nuclear weapons and stockpiles of fissionable material in unstable countries may themselves represent a major global threat if they cease to be subject to secure control. At the same time, the utility of such weapons in roles other than deterring their use against the national territories of the nuclear weapon states by other such states is increasingly coming into question. The former, more pessimistic, perspective on the future might thus see 1995 as the high point of global efforts to prevent nuclear weapon proliferation and to move towards global disarmament. The latter, more optimistic, perspective suggests that the 1995 NPT conference may mark the start of the final stage in making the existing NPT-based nuclear non-proliferation regime universal, as well as the end of the first stage in the construction of a regime to facilitate a non-nuclear weapon world.

Appendix 13A. Documents on nuclear arms control and non-proliferation

EXTENSION OF THE TREATY ON THE NON-PROLIFERATION OF NUCLEAR WEAPONS

New York, 11 May 1995

The Conference of the States Party to the Treaty on the Non-Proliferation of Nuclear Weapons (hereinafter referred to as 'the Treaty') convened in New York from 17 April to 12 May 1995, in accordance with articles VIII,3 and X,2 of the Treaty,

Having reviewed the operation of the Treaty and affirming that there is a need for full compliance with the Treaty, its extension and its universal adherence, which are essential to international peace and security and the attainment of the ultimate goals of the complete elimination of nuclear weapons and a treaty on general and complete disarmament under strict and effective international control,

Having reaffirmed article VIII,3 of the Treaty and the need for its continued implementation in a strengthened manner and, to this end, emphasizing the Decision on Strengthening the Review Process for the Treaty and the Decision on Principles and Objectives for Nuclear Non-Proliferation and Disarmament also adopted by the Conference,

Having established that the Conference is quorate in accordance with article X,2 of the Treaty,

Decides that, as a majority exists among States party to the Treaty for its indefinite extension, in accordance with its article X,2, the Treaty shall continue in force indefinitely.

Source: Text reproduced from NPT/CONF. 1995/32/DEC.3. Presented to the Conference as NPT/CONF.1995/L.6, proposed by the President.

STRENGTHENING THE REVIEW PROCESS FOR THE TREATY

New York, 11 May 1995

1. The Conference examined the implementation of article VIII,3, of the Treaty and agreed to strengthen the review process for the operation of the Treaty with a view to assuring that the purposes of the Preamble and the provisions of the Treaty are being realized.

2. The States party to the Treaty participating in the Conference decided, in accordance with article VIII,3, of the Treaty, that Review Conferences should continue to be held every five years and that, accordingly, the next Review Conference should be held in the year 2000.

3. The Conference decided that, beginning in 1997, the Preparatory Committee should hold, normally for a duration of 10 working days, a meeting in each of the three years prior to the Review Conference. If necessary, a fourth preparatory meeting may be held in the year of the Conference.

4. The purpose of the Preparatory Committee meetings would be to consider principles, objectives and ways in order to promote the full implementation of the Treaty, as well as its universality, and to make recommendations thereon to the Review Conference. These include those identified in the Decision on Principles and Objectives for Nuclear Non-Proliferation and Disarmament adopted on 11 May 1995. These meetings should also make the procedural preparations for the next Review Conference.

5. The Conference also concluded that the present structure of three Main Committees should continue and the question of an overlap of issues being discussed in more than one Committee should be resolved in the General Committee, which would coordinate the work of the Committees so that the substantive responsibility for the preparation of the report with respect to each specific issue is undertaken in only one Committee.

6. It was also agreed that subsidiary bodies could be established within the respective Main Committees for specific issues relevant to the Treaty, so as to provide for a focused consideration of such issues. The establishment of such subsidiary bodies would be recommended by the Preparatory Committee for each Review Conference in relation to the specific objectives of the Review Conference.

7. The Conference agreed further that Review Conferences should look forward as well as back. They should evaluate the results of the period they are reviewing, including

the implementation of undertakings of the States parties under the Treaty, and identify the areas in which, and the means through which, further progress should be sought in the future. Review Conferences should also address specifically what might be done to strengthen the implementation of the Treaty and to achieve its universality.

Source: Text reproduced from NPT/CONF. 1995/32/DEC.1 as published in NPT/CONF. 1995/32 (Part I). Presented to the Conference as NPT/CONF.1995/L.4, proposed by the President.

PRINCIPLES AND OBJECTIVES FOR NUCLEAR NON-PROLIFERATION AND DISARMAMENT

New York, 11 May 1995

Reaffirming the preamble and articles of the Treaty on the Non-Proliferation of Nuclear Weapons,

Welcoming the end of the cold war, the ensuing easing of international tension and the strengthening of the trust between States,

Desiring a set of principles and objectives in accordance with which nuclear non-proliferation, nuclear disarmament and international cooperation in the peaceful uses of nuclear energy should be vigorously pursued and progress, achievements and shortcomings evaluated periodically within the review process provided for in article VIII (3) of the Treaty, the enhancement and strengthening of which is welcomed,

Reiterating the ultimate goals of the complete elimination of nuclear weapons and a treaty on general and complete disarmament under strict and effective international control,

The Conference affirms the need to continue to move with determination towards the full realisation and effective implementation of the provisions of the Treaty, and accordingly adopts the following principles and objectives:

Universality

1. Universal adherence to the Treaty on the Non-Proliferation of Nuclear Weapons is an urgent priority. All States not yet party to the Treaty are called upon to accede to the Treaty at the earliest date, particularly those States that operate unsafeguarded nuclear facilities. Every effort should be made by all States parties to achieve this objective.

Non-proliferation

2. The proliferation of nuclear weapons would seriously increase the danger of nuclear war. The Treaty on the Non-Proliferation of Nuclear Weapons has a vital role to play in preventing the proliferation of nuclear weapons. Every effort should be made to implement the Treaty in all its aspects to prevent the proliferation of nuclear weapons and other nuclear explosive devices, without hampering the peaceful uses of nuclear energy by States parties to the Treaty.

Nuclear disarmament

3. Nuclear disarmament is substantially facilitated by the easing of international tension and the strengthening of trust between States which have prevailed following the end of the cold war. The undertakings with regard to nuclear disarmament as set out in the Treaty on Non-Proliferation of Nuclear Weapons should thus be fulfilled with determination. In this regard, the nuclear-weapon States reaffirm their commitment, as stated in article VI, to pursue in good faith negotiations on effective measures relating to nuclear disarmament.

4. The achievement of the following measures is important in the full realization and effective implementation of article VI, including the programme of action as reflected below:

(*a*) The completion by the Conference on Disarmament of the negotiations on a universal and internationally and effectively verifiable Comprehensive Nuclear-Test-Ban Treaty no later than 1996. Pending the entry into force of a Comprehensive Test-Ban Treaty, the nuclear-weapon States should exercise utmost restraint;

(*b*) The immediate commencement and early conclusion of negotiations on a non-discriminatory and universally applicable convention banning the production of fissile material for nuclear weapons or other nuclear explosive devices, in accordance with the statement of the Special Coordinator of the Conference on Disarmament and the mandate contained therein;

(*c*) The determined pursuit by the nuclear-weapon States of systematic and progressive efforts to reduce nuclear weapons globally, with the ultimate goal of eliminating those weapons, and by all States of general and complete disarmament under strict and effective international control.

Nuclear-weapon-free zones

5. The conviction that the establishment of internationally recognized nuclear-weapon-free zones, on the basis of arrangements freely arrived at among the States of the region concerned, enhances global and regional peace and security is reaffirmed.

6. The development of nuclear-weapon-free zones, especially in regions of tension, such as in the Middle East, as well as the establishment of zones free of all weapons of mass destruction should be encouraged as a matter of priority, taking into account the specific characteristics of each region. The establishment of additional nuclear-weapon-free zones by the time of the Review Conference in the year 2000 would be welcome.

7. The cooperation of all the nuclear-weapon States and their respect and support for the relevant protocols is necessary for the maximum effectiveness of such nuclear-weapon-free zones and the relevant protocols.

Security assurances

8. Noting United Nations Security Council resolution 984 (1995), which was adopted unanimously on 11 April 1995, as well as the declarations by the nuclear-weapon States concerning both negative and positive security assurances, further steps should be considered to assure non-nuclear-weapon States party to the Treaty against the use or threat of use of nuclear weapons. These steps could take the form of an internationally legally binding instrument.

Safeguards

9. The International Atomic Energy Agency (IAEA) is the competent authority responsible to verify and assure, in accordance with the statute of the IAEA and the Agency's safeguards system, compliance with its safeguards agreements with States parties undertaken in fulfilment of their obligations under article III(1) of the Treaty, with a view to preventing diversion of nuclear energy from peaceful uses to nuclear weapons or other nuclear explosive devices. Nothing should be done to undermine the authority of the IAEA in this regard. States parties that have concerns regarding non-compliance with the safeguards agreements of the Treaty by the States parties should direct such concerns, along with supporting evidence and information, to the IAEA to consider, investigate, draw conclusions and decide on necessary actions in accordance with its mandate.

10. All States parties required by article III of the Treaty to sign and bring into force comprehensive safeguards agreements and which have not yet done so should do so without delay.

11. IAEA safeguards should be regularly assessed and evaluated. Decisions adopted by its Board of Governors aimed at further strengthening the effectiveness of IAEA safeguards should be supported and implemented and the IAEA's capability to detect undeclared nuclear activities should be increased. Also States not party to the Treaty on the Non-Proliferation of Nuclear Weapons should be urged to enter into comprehensive safeguards agreements with the IAEA.

12. New supply arrangements for the transfer of source or special fissionable material or equipment or material especially designed or prepared for the processing, use or production of special fissionable material to non-nuclear-weapon States should require, as a necessary precondition, acceptance of IAEA full-scope safeguards and internationally legally binding commitments not to acquire nuclear weapons or other nuclear explosive devices.

13. Nuclear fissile material transferred from military use to peaceful nuclear activities should, as soon as practicable, be placed under IAEA safeguards in the framework of the voluntary safeguards agreements in place with the nuclear-weapon States. Safeguards should be universally applied once the complete elimination of nuclear weapons has been achieved.

Peaceful uses of nuclear energy

14. Particular importance should be attached to ensuring the exercise of the inalienable right of all the parties to the Treaty to develop research, production and use of nuclear energy for peaceful purposes without discrimination and in conformity with articles I, II and as well as III of the Treaty.

15. Undertakings to facilitate participation in the fullest possible exchange of equipment, materials and scientific and technological information for the peaceful uses of nuclear energy should be fully implemented.

16. In all activities designed to promote the peaceful uses of nuclear energy, preferential treatment should be given to the non-nuclear-weapon States party to the Treaty, taking the needs of developing countries particularly into account.

17. Transparency in nuclear-related export controls should be promoted within the

framework of dialogue and cooperation among all interested States party to the Treaty.

18. All States should, through rigorous national measures and international cooperation, maintain the highest practicable levels of nuclear safety, including in waste management, and observe standards and guidelines in nuclear materials accounting, physical protection and transport of nuclear materials.

19. Every effort should be made to ensure that the IAEA has the financial and human resources necessary in order to meet effectively its responsibilities in the areas of technical cooperation, safeguards and nuclear safety. The IAEA should also be encouraged to intensify its efforts aimed at finding ways and means for funding technical assistance through predictable and assured resources.

20. Attacks or threats of attack on nuclear facilities devoted to peaceful purposes jeopardize nuclear safety and raise serious concerns regarding the application of international law on the use of force in such cases, which could warrant appropriate action in accordance with the provisions of the Charter of the United Nations.

The Conference requests that the President of the Conference bring this decision, the Decision on Strengthening the Review Process of the Treaty and the Decision on the Extension of the Treaty to the attention of the heads of State or Government of all States and seek their full cooperation on these documents and in the furtherance of the goals of the Treaty.

Source: Text reproduced from NPT/CONF. 1995/32/DEC.2. Presented to the Conference as NPT/CONF.1995/L.5, proposed by the President.

AFRICAN NUCLEAR-WEAPON-FREE ZONE TREATY

Text forwarded to the UN Secretary-General by the Chairman of the Group of Experts, 2 August 1995

PELINDABA TEXT OF THE AFRICAN NUCLEAR-WEAPON-FREE ZONE TREATY
(as amended by the OAU Council of Ministers, 23 June 1995)

The Parties to this Treaty,

Guided by the Declaration on the Denuclearization of Africa, adopted by the Assembly of Heads of State and Government of the Organization of African Unity (hereinafter referred to as OAU) at its first ordinary session, held at Cairo from 17 to 21 July 1964 (AHG/Res.11(1)), in which they solemnly declared their readiness to undertake, through an international agreement to be concluded under United Nations auspices, not to manufacture or acquire control of nuclear weapons,

Guided also, by the resolutions of the fifty-fourth and fifty-sixth ordinary sessions of the Council of Ministers of OAU, held at Abuja from 27 May to 1 June 1991 and at Dakar from 22 to 28 June 1992 respectively, (CM/Res.1342 (LIV) and CM/Res.1395 (LVI)), which affirmed that the evolution of the international situation was conducive to the implementation of the Cairo Declaration, as well as the relevant provisions of the 1986 OAU Declaration on Security, Disarmament and Development,

Recalling United Nations General Assembly resolution 3472 B (XXX) of 11 December 1975, in which it considered nuclear-weapon-free zones one of the most effective means for preventing the proliferation, both horizontal and vertical, of nuclear weapons,

Convinced of the need to take all steps in achieving the ultimate goal of a world entirely free of nuclear weapons, as well as of the obligations of all States to contribute to this end,

Convinced also that the African nuclear-weapon-free zone will constitute an important step towards strengthening the non-proliferation regime, promoting cooperation in the peaceful uses of nuclear energy, promoting general and complete disarmament and enhancing regional and international peace and security.

Aware that regional disarmament measures contribute to global disarmament efforts,

Believing that the African nuclear-weapon-free zone will protect African States against possible nuclear attacks on their territories,

Noting with satisfaction existing NWFZs and recognising that the establishment of other NWFZs, especially in the Middle East, would enhance the security of States Parties to the African NWFZ,

Reaffirming the importance of the Treaty on the Non-Proliferation of Nuclear Weapons (hereinafter referred to as the NPT) and the need for the implementation of all its provisions,

Desirous of taking advantage of article IV of the NPT, which recognizes the inalienable right of all States Parties to develop research on, production and use of nuclear energy for peaceful purposes without discrimination and to facilitate the fullest possible exchange of equipment, materials and scientific and technological information for such purposes,

Determined to promote regional cooperation for the development and practical application of nuclear energy for peaceful purposes in the interest of sustainable social and economic development of the Africa continent,

Determined to keep Africa free of environmental pollution by radioactive wastes and other radioactive matter,

Welcoming the cooperation of all States and governmental and non-governmental organizations for the attainment of these objectives,

Have decided by this treaty to establish the African NWFZ and hereby agree as follows:

Article 1. Definition/Usage of terms

For the purpose of this Treaty and its Protocols:

(*a*) 'African nuclear-weapon-free zone' means the territory of the continent of Africa, islands States members of OAU and all islands considered by the Organization of African Unity in its resolutions to be part of Africa;

(*b*) 'Territory' means the land territory, internal waters, territorial seas and archipelagic waters and the airspace above them as well as the sea bed and subsoil beneath;

(*c*) 'Nuclear explosive device' means any nuclear weapon or other explosive device capable of releasing nuclear energy, irrespective of the purpose for which it could be used. The term includes such a weapon or device in unassembled and partly assembled forms, but does not include the means of transport or delivery of such a weapon or device if separable from and not an indivisible part of it;

(*d*) 'Stationing' means implantation, emplacement, transport on land or inland waters, stockpiling, storage, installation and deployment;

(*e*) 'Nuclear installation' means a nuclear-power reactor, a nuclear research reactor, a critical facility, a conversion plant, a fabrication plant, a reprocessing plant, an isotope separation plant, a separate storage installation and any other installation or location in or at which fresh or irradiated nuclear material or significant quantities of radioactive materials are present.

(*f*) 'Nuclear material' means any source material or special fissionable material as defined in Article XX of the Statute of the International Atomic Energy Agency (IAEA) and as amended from time to time by the IAEA.

Article 2. Application of the Treaty

1. Except where otherwise specified, this Treaty and its Protocols shall apply to the territory within the African nuclear-weapon-free zone, as illustrated in the map in annex I.

2. Nothing in this Treaty shall prejudice or in any way affect the rights, or the exercise of the rights, of any state under international law with regards to freedom of the seas.

Article 3. Renunciation of nuclear explosive devices

Each Party undertakes:

(*a*) Not to conduct research on, develop, manufacture, stockpile or otherwise acquire, possess or have control over any nuclear explosive device by any means anywhere;

(*b*) Not to seek or receive any assistance in the research on, development, manufacture, stockpiling or acquisition, or possession of any nuclear explosive device;

(*c*) Not to take any action to assist or encourage the research on, development, manufacture, stockpiling or acquisition, or possession of any nuclear explosive device.

Article 4. Prevention of stationing of nuclear explosive devices

1. Each Party undertakes to prohibit, in its territory, the stationing of any nuclear explosive device.

2. Without prejudice to the purposes and objectives of the treaty, each party in the exercise of its sovereign rights remains free to decide for itself whether to allow visits by foreign ships and aircraft to its ports and airfields, transit of its airspace by foreign aircraft, and navigation by foreign ships in its territorial sea or archipelagic waters in a manner not covered by the rights of innocent passage, archipelagic sea lane passage or transit passage of straits.

Article 5. Prohibition of testing of nuclear explosive devices

Each Party undertakes:

(*a*) Not to test any nuclear explosive device;

(*b*) To prohibit in its territory the testing of any nuclear explosive device;

(*c*) Not to assist or encourage the testing of any nuclear explosive device by any State anywhere.

Article 6. Declaration, dismantling, destruction or conversion of nuclear explosive devices and the facilities for their manufacture

Each Party undertakes:

(a) To declare any capability for the manufacture of nuclear explosive devices;

(b) To dismantle and destroy any nuclear explosive device that it has manufactured prior to the coming into force of this Treaty;

(c) To destroy facilities for the manufacture of nuclear explosive devices or, where possible, to convert them to peaceful uses;

(d) To permit the International Atomic Energy Agency (hereinafter referred to as IAEA) and the Commission established in article 12 to verify the processes of dismantling and destruction of the nuclear explosive devices, as well as the destruction or conversion of the facilities for their production.

Article 7. Prohibition of dumping of radioactive wastes

Each Party undertakes:

(a) To effectively implement or to use as guidelines the measures contained in the Bamako Convention on the Ban of the Import into Africa and Control of Transboundary Movement and Management of Hazardous Wastes within Africa in so far as it is relevant to radioactive waste;

(b) Not to take any action to assist or encourage the dumping of radioactive wastes and other radioactive matter anywhere within the African nuclear-weapon-free zone.

Article 8. Peaceful nuclear activities

1. Nothing in this Treaty shall be interpreted as to prevent the use of nuclear science and technology for peaceful purposes.

2. As part of their efforts to strengthen their security, stability and development, the Parties undertake to promote individually and collectively the use of nuclear science and technology for economic and social development. To this end they undertake to establish and strengthen mechanisms for cooperation at the bilateral, subregional and regional levels.

3. Parties are encouraged to make use of the programme of assistance available in IAEA and, in this connection, to strengthen cooperation under the African Regional Cooperation Agreement for Research, Training and Development Related to Nuclear Science and Technology (hereinafter referred to as AFRA).

Article 9. Verification of peaceful uses

Each Party undertakes:

(a) To conduct all activities for the peaceful use of nuclear energy under strict non-proliferation measures to provide assurance of exclusively peaceful uses;

(b) To conclude a comprehensive safeguards agreement with IAEA for the purpose of verifying compliance with the undertakings in subparagraph (a) of this article;

(c) Not to provide source or special fissionable material, or equipment or material especially designed or prepared for the processing, use or production of special fissionable material for peaceful purposes to any non-nuclear-weapon State unless subject to a comprehensive safeguards agreement concluded with IAEA.

Article 10. Physical protection of nuclear materials and facilities

Each Party undertakes to maintain the highest standards of security and effective physical protection of nuclear materials, facilities and equipment to prevent theft or unauthorized use and handling. To that end each Party, *inter alia*, undertakes to apply measures of physical protection equivalent to those provided for in the Convention on Physical Protection of Nuclear Material and in recommendations and guidelines developed by IAEA for that purpose.

Article 11. Prohibition of armed attack on nuclear installations

Each Party undertakes not to take, or assist, or encourage any action aimed at an armed attack by conventional or other means against nuclear installations in the African nuclear-weapon-free zone.

Article 12. Mechanism for compliance

1. For the purpose of ensuring compliance with their undertakings under this Treaty, the Parties agree to establish the African Commission on Nuclear Energy (hereafter referred to as the Commission) as set out in annex III.

2. The Commission shall be responsible *inter alia* for:

(a) Collating the reports and the exchange of information as provided for in article 13;

(b) Arranging consultations as provided for in annex IV, as well as convening conferences of Parties on the concurrence of simple majority of State Parties on any matter arising from the implementation of the Treaty;

(c) Reviewing the application to peaceful nuclear activities of safeguards by IAEA as elaborated in annex II;

(d) Bringing into effect the complaints procedure elaborated in annex IV;

(e) Encouraging regional and sub-regional programmes for cooperation in the peaceful uses of nuclear science and technology;

(f) Promoting international cooperation with extra-zonal States for the peaceful uses of nuclear science and technology.

3. The Commission shall meet in ordinary session once a year, and may meet in extra-ordinary session as may be required by the complaints and settlement of disputes procedure in annex IV.

Article 13. Report and exchanges of information

1. Each Party shall submit an annual report to the Commission on its nuclear activities as well as other matters relating to the Treaty, in accordance with the format for reporting to be developed by the Commission.

2. Each Party shall promptly report to the Commission any significant event affecting the implementation of the Treaty.

3. The Commission shall request the IAEA to provide it with an annual report on the activities of AFRA.

Article 14. Conference of Parties

1. A Conference of all Parties to the Treaty shall be convened by the Depositary as soon as possible after the entry into force of the Treaty to, *inter alia*, elect members of the Commission and determine its headquarters. Further conferences of State Parties shall be held as necessary and at least every two years, and convened in accordance with paragraph 2 (b) of article 12.

2. The Conference of all Parties to the Treaty shall adopt the Commission's budget and a scale of assessment to be paid by the State Parties.

Article 15. Interpretation of the Treaty

Any dispute arising out of the interpretation of the Treaty shall be settled by negotiation, by recourse to the Commission or another procedure agreed to by the Parties, which may include recourse to an arbitral panel or to the International Court of Justice.

Article 16. Reservations

This Treaty shall not be subject to reservations.

Article 17. Duration

This Treaty shall be of unlimited duration and shall remain in force indefinitely.

Article 18. Signature, ratification and entry into force.

1. This Treaty shall be open for signature by any state in the African nuclear-weapon-free zone. It shall be subject to ratification.

2. It shall enter into force on the date of deposit of the twenty-eighth instrument of ratification.

3. For a signatory that ratifies this Treaty after the date of the deposit of the twenty-eighth instrument of ratification, it shall enter into force for that signatory on the date of deposit of its instrument of ratification.

Article 19. Amendments

1. Any amendments to the Treaty proposed by a Party shall be submitted to the Commission, which shall circulate it to all Parties.

2. Decision on the adoption of such an amendment shall be taken by a two-thirds majority of the Parties either through written communication to the Commission or through a conference of Parties convened upon the concurrence of a simple majority.

3. An amendment so adopted shall enter into force for all parties after receipt by the Depositary of the instrument of ratification by the majority of Parties.

Article 20. Withdrawal

1. Each Party shall, in exercising its national sovereignty, have the right to withdraw from this Treaty if it decides that extraordinary events, related to the subject-matter of this Treaty, have jeopardized its supreme interests.

2. Withdrawal shall be effected by a Party giving notice, which includes a statement of the extraordinary events it regards as having jeopardized its supreme interest, twelve months in advance to the Depositary. The Depositary shall circulate such notice to all other parties.

Article 21. Depositary functions

1. This Treaty, of which the Arabic, English, French and Portuguese texts are equally authentic, shall be deposited with the Secretary-General of OAU, who is hereby designated as Depositary of the Treaty.

2. The Depositary shall:

(a) Receive instruments of ratification;

(b) Register this Treaty and its Protocols

pursuant to article 102 of the Charter of the United Nations;

(c) Transmit certified copies of the Treaty and its Protocols to all States in the African nuclear-weapon-free zone and to all States eligible to become party to the Protocols to the Treaty, and shall notify them of signatures and ratification of the Treaty and its Protocols.

Article 22. Status of the annexes

The annexes form an integral part of this Treaty. Any reference to this Treaty includes the annexes.

ANNEX I. [see map overleaf]

ANNEX II. SAFEGUARDS OF THE INTERNATIONAL ATOMIC ENERGY AGENCY

1. The safeguards referred to in subparagraph (b) of the article 9 shall in respect of each Party be applied by the International Atomic Energy Agency as set forth in an agreement negotiated and concluded with the Agency on all source or special fissionable material in all nuclear activities within the territory of the Party, under its jurisdiction or carried out under its control anywhere.

2. The Agreement referred to in paragraph 1 above shall be, or shall be equivalent in its scope and effect to, the agreement required in connection with the Treaty on the Non-Proliferation of Nuclear Weapons (INFCIRC/153 corrected). A party that has already entered into a safeguards agreement with the IAEA is deemed to have already complied with the requirement. Each Party shall take all appropriate steps to ensure that the Agreement referred to in paragraph 1 is in force for it not later than eighteen months after the date of entry into force for that Party of this Treaty.

3. For the purpose of this Treaty, the safeguards referred to in paragraph 1 above shall have as their purpose the verification of the non-diversion of nuclear material from peaceful nuclear activities to nuclear explosive devices or for purposes unknown.

4. Each Party shall include in its annual report to the Commission, in conformity with art. 13, for its information and review, a copy of the overall conclusions of the most recent report by the International Atomic Energy Agency on its inspection activities in the territory of the Party concerned, and advise the Commission promptly of any change in those conclusions. The information furnished by a Party shall not be, totally or partially, dis-closed or transmitted to third parties, by the addressees of the reports, except when that Party gives its express consent.

ANNEX III. AFRICAN COMMISSION ON NUCLEAR ENERGY

1. The Commission established in article 12 shall be composed of twelve Members elected by Parties to the Treaty for a three-year period, bearing in mind the need for equitable geographical distribution as well as to include Members with advanced nuclear programmes. Each Member shall have one representative nominated with particular regard for his/her expertise in the subject of the Treaty.

2. The Commission shall have a Bureau consisting of the Chairman, the Vice-Chairman and the Executive Secretary. It shall elect its Chairman and Vice-Chairman. The Secretary-General of the Organization of African Unity, at the request of Parties to the Treaty and in consultation with the Chairman, shall designate the Executive Secretary of the Commission. For the first meeting a quorum shall be constituted by representatives of two-thirds of the Members of the Commission. For that meeting decisions of the Commission shall be taken as far as possible by consensus or otherwise by a two-thirds majority of the Members of the Commission. The Commission shall adopt its rules of procedure at that meeting.

3. The Commission shall develop a format for reporting by States as required under articles 12 and 13.

4. (a) The budget of the Commission, including the costs of inspections pursuant to annex IV to this Treaty, shall be borne by the Parties to the Treaty in accordance with a scale of assessment to be determined by the Parties;

(b) The Commission may also accept additional funds from other sources provided such donations are consistent with the purposes and objectives of the Treaty;

ANNEX IV. COMPLAINTS PROCEDURE AND SETTLEMENT OF DISPUTES

1. A Party which considers that there are grounds for a complaint that another Party or a Party to Protocol III is in breach of its obligations under this Treaty shall bring the subject-matter of the complaint to the attention of the Party complained of and shall allow the latter thirty days to provide it with an explanation and to resolve the matter. This

Annex I. Map of an African Nuclear-Weapon-Free Zone

Appears without prejudice to the question of sovereignty

Prince Edward and Marion Is.

may include technical visits agreed upon between the Parties.

2. If the matter is not so resolved, the complainant Party may bring this complaint to the Commission.

3. The Commission, taking account of efforts made under paragraph 1 above, shall afford the Party complained of forty-five days to provide it with an explanation of the matter.

4. If, after considering any explanation given to it by the representatives of the Party complained of, the Commission considers that there is sufficient substance in the com-

plaint to warrant an inspection in the territory of that Party or territory of a party to Protocol III, the Commission may request the International Atomic Energy Agency to conduct such inspection as soon as possible. The Commission may also designate its representatives to accompany the Agency's inspection team.

(a) The request shall indicate the tasks and objectives of such inspection, as well as any confidentiality requirements;

(b) If the Party complained of so requests, the inspection team shall be accompanied by representatives of that Party provided that the inspectors shall not be thereby delayed or otherwise impeded in the exercise of their functions;

(c) Each Party shall give the inspection team full and free access to all information and places within each territory that may be deemed relevant by the inspectors to the implementation of the inspection;

(d) The Party complained of shall take all appropriate steps to facilitate the work of the inspection team, and shall accord them the same privileges and immunities as those set forth in the relevant provisions of the Agreement on the Privileges and Immunities of the International Atomic Energy Agency;

(e) The International Atomic Energy Agency shall report its findings in writing as quickly as possible to the Commission, outlining its activities, setting out relevant facts and information as ascertained by it, with supporting evidence and documentation as appropriate, and stating its conclusions. The Commission shall report fully to all States Parties to the Treaty giving its decision as to whether the Party complained of is in breach of its obligations under this Treaty;

(f) If the Commission considers that the Party complained of is in breach of its obligations under this Treaty, or that the above provisions have not been complied with, States Parties to the Treaty shall meet in extraordinary session to discuss the matter;

(g) The States Parties convened in extraordinary session may as necessary, make recommendations to the Party held to be in breach of its obligations and to the Organization of African Unity. The Organization of African Unity may, if necessary, refer the matter to the United Nations Security Council;

(h) The costs involved in the procedure outlined above shall be borne by the Commission. In the case of abuse, the Commission shall decide whether the requesting State Party should bear any of the financial implications.

5. The Commission may also establish its own inspection mechanisms.

PROTOCOL I

The Parties to this Protocol,

Convinced of the need to take all steps in achieving the ultimate goal of a world entirely free of nuclear weapons as well as the obligations of all States to contribute to this end,

Convinced also that the African Nuclear-Weapon-Free Zone Treaty, negotiated and signed in accordance with the Declaration on the Denuclearization of Africa (AHG/Res.11(1)) of 1964, resolutions CM/Res.1342 (LIV) of 1991 and CM/Res.1395(LVI) Rev.1 of 1992 of the Council of Ministers of the Organization of African Unity and United Nations General Assembly Resolution 48/86 of 16 December 1993, constitutes an important measure towards ensuring the non-proliferation of nuclear weapons, promoting cooperation in the peaceful uses of nuclear energy, promoting general and complete disarmament, and enhancing regional and international peace and security,

Desirous of contributing in all appropriate manners to the effectiveness of the Treaty,

Have agreed as follows:

Article 1

Each Protocol Party undertakes not to use or threaten to use a nuclear explosive device against:

(a) Any Party to the Treaty; or

(b) Any territory within the African nuclear-weapon-free zone for which a State that has become a Party to Protocol III is internationally responsible as defined in annex I.

Article 2

Each Protocol Party undertakes not to contribute to any act that constitutes a violation of the Treaty or of this Protocol.

Article 3

Each Protocol Party undertakes, by written notification to the Depositary, to indicate its acceptance or otherwise of any alteration to its obligation under this Protocol that may be brought about by the entry into force of an amendment to the Treaty pursuant to article 20 of the Treaty.

Article 4

This Protocol shall be open for signature by China, France, the Russian Federation, the United Kingdom of Great Britain and Northern Ireland and the United States of America.

Article 5

This Protocol shall be subject to ratification.

Article 6

This Protocol is of a permanent nature and shall remain in force indefinitely, provided that each party shall, in exercising its national sovereignty, have the right to withdraw from this Protocol if it decides that extraordinary events, related to the subject-matter of this Protocol, have jeopardized its supreme interests. It shall give notice of such withdrawal to the Depositary twelve months in advance. Such notice shall include a statement of the extraordinary events it regards as having jeopardized its supreme interests.

Article 7

This Protocol shall enter into force for each State on the date of its deposit with the Depositary of its instrument of ratification or the date of entry into force of the Treaty, whichever is later.

In witness whereof the undersigned, being duly authorized by their Governments, have signed this Protocol.

PROTOCOL II

The Parties to this Protocol,

Convinced of the need to take all steps in achieving the ultimate goal of a world entirely free of nuclear weapons as well as the obligations of all States to contribute to this end,

Convinced also that the African Nuclear-Weapon-Free Zone Treaty, negotiated and signed in accordance with the Declaration on the Denuclearization of Africa (AHG/Res.11(1)) of 1964, resolutions CM/Res.1342 (LIV) of 1991 and CM/Res.1395(LVI)/Rev.1 of 1992 of the Council of Ministers of the Organization of African Unity and United Nations General Assembly resolution 48/86 of 16 December 1993, constitutes an important measure towards ensuring the non-proliferation of nuclear weapons, promoting cooperation in the peaceful uses of nuclear energy, promoting general and complete disarmament, and enhancing regional and international peace and security,

Desirous of contributing in all appropriate manners to the effectiveness of the Treaty,

Bearing in mind the objective of concluding a treaty banning all nuclear tests,

Have agreed as follows:

Article 1

Each Protocol Party undertakes not to test or assist or encourage the testing of any nuclear explosive device anywhere within the African nuclear-weapon-free zone.

Article 2

Each Protocol Party undertakes not to con-tribute to any act that constitutes a violation of the Treaty or of this Protocol.

Article 3

Each Protocol Party undertakes, by written notification to the Depositary, to indicate its acceptance or otherwise of any alteration to its obligation under this Protocol that may be brought about by the entry into force of an amendment to the Treaty pursuant to article 20 of the Treaty.

Article 4

This Protocol shall be open for signature by China, France, the Russian Federation, the United Kingdom of Great Britain and Northern Ireland and the United States of America.

Article 5

This Protocol shall be subject to ratification.

Article 6

This Protocol is of a permanent nature and shall remain in force indefinitely, provided that each Party shall, in exercising its national sovereignty, have the right to withdraw from this Protocol if it decides that extraordinary events, related to the subject-matter of this Protocol, have jeopardized its supreme interests. It shall give notice of such withdrawal to the Depositary twelve months in advance. Such notice shall include a statement of the extraordinary events it regards as having jeopardized its supreme interests.

Article 7

This Protocol shall enter into force for each State on the date of its deposit with the Depositary of its instrument of ratification or the date of entry into force of the Treaty, whichever is later.

In witness whereof the undersigned, being duly authorized by their Governments, have signed this Protocol.

PROTOCOL III

The Parties to this Protocol,

Convinced of the need to take all steps in achieving the ultimate goal of a world entirely free of nuclear weapons as well as the obligations of all States to contribute to this end,

Convinced also that the African Nuclear-Weapon-Free Zone Treaty, negotiated and signed in accordance with the Declaration on the Denuclearization of Africa (AHG/Res.11(1)) of 1964, resolutions CM/Res.1342 (LIV) of 1991 and CM/Res.1395(LVI)/Rev.1 of 1992 of the Council of Ministers of the Organization of African Unity and United Nations General Assembly resolution 48/86 of 16 December 1993, constitutes an important measure towards ensuring the non-proliferation of nuclear weapons, promoting cooperation in the peaceful uses of nuclear energy, promoting general and complete disarmament, and enhancing regional and international peace and security,

Desirous of contributing in all appropriate manners to the effectiveness of the Treaty,

Have agreed as follows:

Article 1

Each Protocol Party undertakes to apply, in respect of the territories for which it is de jure or de facto internationally responsible situated within the African nuclear-weapon-free zone, the provisions contained in articles 3, 4, 5, 6, 7, 8, 9 and 10 of the Treaty and to ensure the application of safeguards specified in annex II of the Treaty.

Article 2

Each Protocol Party undertakes not to contribute to any act that constitutes a violation of the Treaty or of this Protocol.

Article 3

Each Protocol Party undertakes, by written notification to the Depositary, to indicate its acceptance or otherwise of any alterations to its obligation under this Protocol that may be brought about by the entry into force of an amendment to the Treaty pursuant to article 20 of the Treaty.

Article 4

This Protocol shall be open for signature by France and Spain.

Article 5

This Protocol shall be subject to ratification.

Article 6

This Protocol is of a permanent nature and shall remain in force indefinitely provided that each Party shall, in exercising its national sovereignty have the right to withdraw from this Protocol if it decides that extraordinary events, related to the subject-matter of this Protocol, have jeopardized its supreme interests. It shall give notice of such withdrawal to the Depositary twelve months in advance.

Such notice shall include a statement of the extraordinary events it regards as having jeopardized its supreme interests.

Article 7

This Protocol shall enter into force for each State on the date of its deposit with the Depositary of its instrument of ratification or the date of entry into force of the Treaty, whichever is later.

In witness whereof the undersigned, being duly authorized by their Governments have signed this Protocol.

Source: Text reproduced from United Nations General Assembly document A/50/426, 13 Sep. 1995.

TREATY ON THE SOUTHEAST ASIA NUCLEAR WEAPON-FREE ZONE

Bangkok, 15 December 1995

The States Parties to this Treaty:

Desiring to contribute to the realization of the purposes and principles of the Charter of the United Nations;

Determined to take concrete action which will contribute to the progress towards general and complete disarmament of nuclear weapons, and to the promotion of international peace and security;

Reaffirming the desire of the Southeast Asian States to maintain peace and stability in the region in the spirit of peaceful coexistence and mutual understanding and cooperation as enunciated in various communiques, declarations and other legal instruments;

Recalling the Declaration on the Zone of Peace, Freedom and Neutrality (ZOPFAN) signed in Kuala Lumpur on 27 November 1971 and the Programme of Action on ZOPFAN adopted at the 26th ASEAN Ministerial Meeting in Singapore in July 1993;

Convinced that the establishment of a Southeast Asia Nuclear Weapon-Free Zone, as an essential component of the ZOPFAN, will contribute towards strengthening the security of States within the Zone and towards enhancing international peace and security as a whole;

Reaffirming the importance of the Treaty on the Non-Proliferation of Nuclear Weapons (NPT) in preventing the proliferation of nuclear weapons and in contributing towards international peace and security;

Recalling Article VII of the NPT which

recognizes the right of any group of States to conclude regional treaties in order to assure the total absence of nuclear weapons in their respective territories;

Recalling the Final Document of the Tenth Special Session of the United Nations General Assembly which encourages the establishment of nuclear weapon-free zones;

Recalling the Principles and Objectives for Nuclear Non-Proliferation and Disarmament, adopted at the 1995 Review and Extension Conference of the Parties to the NPT, that the cooperation of all the nuclear-weapon States and their respect and support for the relevant protocols is important for the maximum effectiveness of this nuclear weapon-free zone treaty and its relevant protocol;

Determined to protect the region from environmental pollution and the hazards posed by radioactive wastes and other radioactive material;

Have agreed as follows:

Article 1. Use of Terms

For the purposes of this Treaty and its Protocol:

(*a*) 'Southeast Asia Nuclear Weapon-Free Zone', hereinafter referred to as the 'Zone', means the area comprising the territories of all States in Southeast Asia, namely, Brunei Darussalam, Cambodia, Indonesia, Laos, Malaysia, Myanmar, Philippines, Singapore, Thailand and Vietnam, and their respective continental shelves and Exclusive Economic Zones (EEZ);

(*b*) 'territory' means the land territory, internal waters, territorial sea, archipelagic waters, the seabed and the sub-soil thereof and the airspace above them;

(*c*) 'nuclear weapon' means any explosive device capable of releasing nuclear energy in an uncontrolled manner but does not include the means, transport or delivery of such device if separable from and not an indivisible part thereof;

(*d*) 'station' means to deploy, emplace, emplant, install, stockpile or store;

(*e*) 'radioactive material' means material that contains radionuclides above clearance or exemption levels recommended by the International Atomic Energy Agency (IAEA)'

(*f*) 'radioactive wastes' means material that contains or is contaminated with radionuclides at concentrations or activities greater than clearance levels recommended by the IAEA and for which no use is foreseen; and

(*g*) 'dumping' means

(*i*) any deliberate disposal at sea, including seabed, and subsoil insertion of radioactive wastes or other matter from vessels, aircraft, platforms or other man-made structures at sea, and

(*ii*) any deliberate disposal at sea, including seabed and subsoil insertion, of vessels, aircraft, platforms or other man-made structures at sea containing radioactive material,

but does not include the disposal of wastes or other matter incidental to, or derived from the normal operations of vessels, aircraft, platforms or other man-made structures at sea and their equipment, other than wastes or other matter transported by or to vessels, aircraft, platforms or other man-made structures at sea, operating for the purpose, of disposal of such matter or derived from the treatment of such wastes or other matter on such vessels, aircraft, platforms or structures.

Article 2. Application of the Treaty

1. This Treaty and its Protocol shall apply to the territories, continental shelves and EEZ of the States Parties within the Zone in which the Treaty is in force.

2. Nothing in this Treaty shall prejudice the rights or the exercise of these rights by any State under the provisions of the United Nations Convention on the Law of the Sea of 1982, in particular with regard to freedom of the high seas, rights of innocent passage, archipelagic sea lanes passage or transit passage of ships and aircraft, and consistent with the Charter of the United Nations.

Article 3. Basic Undertakings

1. Each State Party undertakes not to, anywhere inside or outside the Zone:

(*a*) develop, manufacture or otherwise acquire, possess or have control over nuclear weapons;

(*b*) station or transport nuclear weapons by any means; or

(*c*) test or use nuclear weapons.

2. Each State Party also undertakes not to allow, in its territory, any other State to:

(*a*) develop, manufacture or otherwise acquire, possess or have control over nuclear weapons;

(*b*) station nuclear weapons; or

(*c*) test or use nuclear weapons.

3. Each State Party also undertakes not to:

(*a*) dump at sea or discharge into the atmosphere anywhere within the Zone any radioactive material or wastes;

(*b*) dispose radioactive material or wastes on land in the territory of or under the jurisdiction of other States except as stipulated in Paragraph 2(e) of Article 4; or

(c) allow, within in territory, any other State to dump at sea or discharge into the atmosphere any radioactive material or wastes.

4. Each State Party undertakes not to:

(a) seek or receive any assistance in the commission of any act in violation of the provisions of Paragraphs 1, 2 and 3 of this Article; or

(b) take any action to assist or encourage the commission of any act in violation of the provisions of Paragraphs 1, 2 and 3 of this Article.

Article 4. Use of Nuclear Energy for Peaceful Purposes

1. Nothing in this Treaty shall prejudice the right of the States Parties to use nuclear energy, in particular for their economic development and social progress.

2. Each State Party therefore undertakes:

(a) to use exclusively for peaceful purposes nuclear material and facilities which are within its territory and areas under its jurisdiction and control;

(b) prior to embarking on its peaceful nuclear energy programme, to subject its programme to rigorous nuclear safety assessment conforming to guidelines and standards recommended by the IAEA for the protection of health and minimization of danger to life and property in accordance with Paragraph 6 of Article III of the Statute of the IAEA;

(c) upon request, to make available to another State Party the assessment except information relating to personal data, information protected by intellectual property rights or by industrial or commercial confidentiality, and information relating to national security;

(d) to support the continued effectiveness of the international non-proliferation system based on the Treaty on Non-Proliferation of Nuclear Weapons (NPT) and the IAEA safeguards system; and

(e) to dispose radioactive wastes and other radioactive material in accordance with IAEA standards and procedures on land within its territory or on land within the territory of another State which has consented to such disposal.

3. Each State Party further undertakes not to provide source or special fissionable material, or equipment or material especially designed or prepared for the processing, use or production of special fissionable material

to:

(a) any non-nuclear-weapon State except under conditions subject to the safeguards required by Paragraph 1 of Article III of the NPT; or

(b) any nuclear-weapon State except in conformity with applicable safeguards agreements with the IAEA.

Article 5. IAEA Safeguards

Each State Party which has not done so shall conclude an agreement with the IAEA for the application of full scope safeguards to its peaceful nuclear activities not later than eighteen months after the entry into force for that State Party of this Treaty.

Article 6. Early Notification of a Nuclear Accident

Each State Party which has not acceded to the Convention on Early Notification of a Nuclear Accident shall endeavour to do so.

Article 7. Foreign Ships and Aircraft

Each State Party, on being notified, may decide for itself whether to allow visits by foreign ships and aircraft to its ports and airfields, transit of its airspace by foreign aircraft, and navigation by foreign ships through its territorial sea or archipelagic waters and overflight of foreign aircraft above those waters in a manner not governed by the rights of innocent passage, archipelagic sea lanes passage or transit passage.

Article 8. Establishment of the Commission for the Southeast Asia Nuclear Weapon-Free Zone

1. There is hereby established a Commission for the Southeast Asia Nuclear Weapon-Free Zone, hereinafter referred to as the 'Commission'.

2. All States Parties are *ipso facto* members of the Commission. Each State Party shall be represented by its Foreign Minister or his representative accompanied by alternates and advisers.

3. The function of the Commission shall be to oversee the implementation of this Treaty and ensure compliance with its provisions.

4. The Commission shall meet as and when necessary in accordance with the provisions of this Treaty including upon the request of any State Party. As far as possible, the Commission shall meet in conjunction with the ASEAN Ministerial Meeting.

5. At the beginning of each meeting, the Commission shall elect its Chairman and such other officers as may be required. They shall hold office until a new Chairman and other officers are elected at the next meeting.

6. Unless otherwise provided for in this Treaty, two-thirds of the members of the Commission shall be present to constitute a quorum.

7. Each member of the Commission shall have one vote.

8. Except as provided for in this Treaty, decisions of the Commission shall be taken by consensus or, failing consensus, by a two-thirds majority of the members present and voting.

9. The Commission shall, by consensus, agree upon and adopt rules of procedure for itself as well as financial rules governing its funding and that of its subsidiary organs.

Article 9. The Executive Committee

1. There is hereby established, as a subsidiary organ of the Commission, the Executive Committee.

2. The Executive Committee shall be composed of all States Parties to this Treaty. Each State Party shall be represented by one senior official as its representative, who may be accompanied by alternates and advisers.

3. The functions of the Executive Committee shall be to:

(a) ensure the proper operation of verification measures in accordance with the provisions on the Control System as stipulated in Article 10;

(b) consider and decide on requests for clarification and for a fact-finding mission;

(c) set up a fact-finding mission in accordance with the Annex of this Treaty;

(d) consider and decide on the findings of a fact-finding mission and report to the Commission;

(e) request the Commission to convene a meeting when appropriate and necessary;

(f) conclude such agreements with the IAEA or other international organizations as referred to in Article 18 on behalf of the Commission after being duly authorized to do so by the Commission; and

(g) carry out such other tasks as may, from time to time, be assigned by the Commission.

4. The Executive Committee shall meet as and when necessary for the efficient exercise of its functions. As far as possible, the Executive Committee shall meet in conjunction with the ASEAN Senior Officials Meeting.

5. The Chairman of the Executive Committee shall be the representative Chairman of the Commission. Any submission or communication made by a State Party to the Chairman of the Executive Committee shall be disseminated to the other members of the Executive Committee.

6. Two-thirds of the members of the Executive Committee shall be present to constitute a quorum.

7. Each member of the Executive Committee shall have one vote.

8. Decisions of the Executive Committee shall be taken by consensus or, failing consensus, by two-thirds of the members present and voting.

Article 10. Control System

1. There is hereby established a control system for the purpose of verifying compliance with the obligations of the States Parties under this Treaty.

2. The Control System shall comprise:

(a) the IAEA safeguards system as provided for in Article 5;

(b) report and exchange of information as provided for in Article 11;

(c) request for clarification as provided for in Article 12; and

(d) request and procedures for a fact-finding mission as provided for in Article 13.

Article 11. Report and Exchange of Information

1. Each State Party shall submit reports to the Executive Committee on any significant event within its territory and areas under its jurisdiction and control affecting the implementation of this Treaty.

2. The States Parties may exchange information on matters arising under or in relation to this Treaty.

Article 12. Request for Clarification

1. Each State Party shall have the right to request another State Party for clarification concerning any situation which may be considered ambiguous or which may give rise to doubts about the compliance of that State Party with this Treaty. It shall inform the Executive Committee of such a request. The requested State Party shall duly respond by providing without delay the necessary information and inform the Executive Committee of its reply to the requesting State Party.

2. Each State Party shall have the right to request the Executive Committee to seek

clarification from another State Party concerning any situation which may be considered ambiguous or which may give rise to doubts about compliance of that State Party with this Treaty. Upon receipt of such a request, the Executive Committee shall consult the State Party from which clarification is sought for the purpose of obtaining the clarification requested.

Article 13. Request for a Fact-Finding Mission

A State Party shall have the right to request the Executive Committee to send a fact-finding mission to another State Party in order to clarify and resolve a situation which may be considered ambiguous or which may give rise to doubts about compliance with the provisions of this Treaty, in accordance with the procedure contained in the Annex to this Treaty.

Article 14. Remedial Measures

1. In case the Executive Committee decides in accordance with the Annex that there is a breach of this Treaty by a State Party, that State Party shall, within a reasonable time, take all steps necessary to bring itself in full compliance with this Treaty and shall promptly inform the Executive Committee of the action taken or proposed to be taken by it.

2. Where a State Party fails or refuses to comply with the provisions of Paragraph 1 of this Article, the Executive Committee shall request the Commission to convene a meeting in accordance with the provisions of Paragraph 3(e) of Article 9.

3. At the meeting convened pursuant to Paragraph 2 of this Article, the Commission shall consider the emergent situation and shall decide on any measure it deems appropriate to cope with the situation, including the submission of the matter to the IAEA and, where the situation might endanger international peace and security, the Security Council and the General Assembly of the United Nations.

4. In the event of breach of the Protocol attached to this Treaty by a State Party to the Protocol, the Executive Committee shall convene a special meeting of the Commission to decide on appropriate measures to be taken.

Article 15. Signature, Ratification, Accession, Deposit and Registration

1. This Treaty shall be open for signature by all States in Southeast Asia, namely, Brunei Darussalam, Cambodia, Indonesia, Laos, Malaysia, Myanmar, Philippines, Singapore, Thailand and Vietnam.

2. This Treaty shall be subject to ratification in accordance with the constitutional procedure of the signatory States. The instruments of ratification shall be deposited with the Government of the Kingdom of Thailand which is hereby designated as the Depositary State.

3. This Treaty shall be open for accession. The instruments of accession shall be deposited with the Depositary State.

4. The Depositary State shall inform the other States Parties to this Treaty on the deposit of instruments of ratification or accession.

5. The Depositary State shall register this Treaty and its Protocol pursuant to Article 102 of the Charter of the United Nations.

Article 16. Entry Into Force

1. This Treaty shall enter into force on the date of the deposit of the seventh instrument of ratification and/or accession.

2. For States which ratify or accede to this Treaty after the date of this seventh instrument of ratification or accession, the Treaty shall enter into force on the date of deposit of its instrument of ratification or accession.

Article 17. Reservations

This Treaty shall not be subject to reservations.

Article 18. Relations with Other International Organizations

The Commission may conclude such agreements with the IAEA or other international organizations as it considers likely to facilitate the efficient operation of the Control System established by this Treaty.

Article 19. Amendments

1. Any State Party may propose amendments to this Treaty and its Protocol and shall submit its proposals to the Executive Committee, which shall transmit them to all the other States Parties. The Executive Committee shall immediately request the Commission to convene a meeting to examine the proposed amendments. The quorum required for such a meeting shall be all the members of the Commission. Any amendment shall be adopted by a consensus decision of the Commission.

2. Amendments adopted shall enter into force 30 days after the receipt by the Deposit State of the seventh instrument of acceptance from the States Parties.

Article 20. Review

Ten years after this Treaty enters into force, a meeting of the Commission shall be convened for the purpose of reviewing the operation of this Treaty. A meeting of the Commission for the same purpose may also be convened at anytime thereafter if there is consensus among all its members.

Article 21. Settlement of Disputes

Any dispute arising from the interpretation of the provisions of this Treaty shall be settled by peaceful means as may be agreed upon by the States Parties to the dispute. If within one month, the parties to the dispute are unable to achieve a peaceful settlement of the dispute by negotiation, mediation, enquiry or conciliation, any of the parties concerned shall, with the prior consent of the other parties concerned, refer the dispute to arbitration or to the International Court of Justice.

Article 22. Duration and Withdrawal

1. This Treaty shall remain in force indefinitely.

2. In the event of a breach by any State Party of this Treaty essential to the achievement of the objectives of this Treaty, every other State Party shall have the right to withdraw from this Treaty.

3. Withdrawal under Paragraph 2 of Article 22, shall be effected by giving notice twelve months in advance to the members of the Commission.

In witness whereof, the undersigned have signed this Treaty.

Done at Bangkok, this fifteenth day of December, one thousand nine hundred and ninety-five, in one original in the English language.

ANNEX. PROCEDURE FOR A FACT-FINDING MISSION

1. The State Party requesting a fact-finding mission as provided in Article 13, hereinafter referred to as the 'requesting State', shall submit the request to the Executive Committee specifying the following:

(*a*) the doubts or concerns and the reasons for such doubts or concerns;

(*b*) the location in which the situation which gives rise to doubts has allegedly occurred;

(*c*) the relevant provisions of the Treaty about which doubts of compliance have arisen; and

(*d*) any other relevant information.

2. Upon receipt of a request for a fact-finding mission, the Executive Committee shall:

(*a*) immediately inform the State Party to which the fact-finding mission is requested to be sent, hereinafter referred to as the 'receiving State', about the receipt of the request; and

(*b*) not later than 3 weeks after receiving the request, decide if the request complies with the provisions of Paragraph 1 and whether or not it is frivolous, abusive or clearly beyond the scope of this Treaty. Neither the requesting nor receiving State Party shall participate in such decisions.

3. In case the Executive Committee decides that the request does not comply with the provisions of Paragraph 1, or that it is frivolous, abusive or clearly beyond the scope of this Treaty, it shall take no further action on the request and inform the requesting State and the receiving State accordingly.

4. In the event that the Executive Committee decides that the request complies with the provisions of Paragraph 1, and that it is not frivolous, abusive or clearly beyond the scope of this Treaty, it shall immediately forward the request for a fact-finding mission to the receiving State, indicating, *inter alia*, the proposed date for sending the mission. The proposed date shall not be later than 3 weeks from the time the receiving State receives the request for a fact-finding mission. The Executive Committee shall also immediately set up a fact-finding mission consisting of 3 inspectors from the IAEA who are neither nationals of the requesting nor receiving State.

5. The receiving State shall comply with the request for a fact-finding mission referred to in Paragraph 4. It shall cooperate with the Executive Committee in order to facilitate the effective functioning of the fact-finding mission, *inter alia*, by promptly providing unimpeded access of the fact-finding mission to the location in question. The receiving State shall accord to the members of the fact-finding mission such privileges and immunities as are necessary for them to exercise their functions effectively, including inviolability of all papers and documents and immunity from arrest, detention and legal

process for acts done and words spoken for the purpose of the mission.

6. The receiving State shall have the right to take measures to protect sensitive installations and to prevent disclosures of confidential information and data not related to this Treaty.

7. The fact-finding mission, in the discharge of its functions, shall:

(*a*) respect the laws and regulations of the receiving State;

(*b*) refrain from activities inconsistent with the objectives and purposes of this Treaty;

(*c*) submit preliminary or interim reports to the Executive Committee; and

(*d*) complete its task without undue delay and shall submit its final report to the Executive Committee within a reasonable time upon completion of its work.

8. The Executive Committee shall:

(*a*) consider the reports submitted by the fact-finding mission and reach a decision on whether or not there is a breach of this Treaty;

(*b*) immediately communicate its decision to the requesting State and the receiving State; and

(*c*) present a full report on its decision to the Commission.

9. In the event that the receiving State refuses to comply with the request for a fact-finding mission in accordance with Paragraph 4, the requesting State through the Executive Committee shall have the right to request for a meeting of the Commission. The Executive Committee shall immediately request the Commission to convene a meeting in accordance with Paragraph 3(e) of Article 9.

PROTOCOL TO THE TREATY ON THE SOUTHEAST ASIA NUCLEAR WEAPON-FREE ZONE

The States Parties to this Protocol,

Desiring to contribute to efforts towards achieving general and complete disarmament of nuclear weapons, and thereby ensuring international peace and security, including in Southeast Asia;

Noting the Treaty on the Southeast Asia Nuclear Weapon-Free Zone, signed at Bangkok, on the fifteenth day of December, one thousand nine hundred and ninety-five;

Have agreed as follows:

Article 1

Each State Party undertakes to respect the Treaty on the Southeast Asia Nuclear Weapon-Free Zone, hereinafter referred to as the 'Treaty', and not to contribute to any act which constitutes a violation of the Treaty or its Protocol by States Parties to them.

Article 2

Each State Party undertakes not to use or threaten to use nuclear weapons against any State Party to the Treaty. It further undertakes not to use or threaten to use nuclear weapons within the Southeast Asia Nuclear Weapon-Free Zone.

Article 3

This Protocol shall be open for signature by the People's Republic of China, the French Republic, the Russian Federation, the United Kingdom of Great Britain and Northern Ireland and the United States of America.

Article 4

Each State Party undertakes, by written notification to the Depositary State, to indicate its acceptance or otherwise of any alteration to its obligations under this Protocol that may be brought about by the entry into force of an amendment to the Treaty pursuant to Article 19 thereof.

Article 5

This Protocol is of a permanent nature and shall remain in force indefinitely, provided that each State Party shall, in exercising its national sovereignty, have the right to withdraw from this Protocol if it decides that extraordinary events, related to the subject-matter of this Protocol, have jeopardized its supreme national interests. It shall give notice of such withdrawal to the Depositary State twelve months in advance. Such notice shall include a statement of the extraordinary events its regards as having jeopardized its supreme national interests.

Article 6

This Protocol shall be subject to ratification.

Article 7

This Protocol shall enter into force for each State Party on the date of its deposit of its instrument of ratification with the Depositary State. The Depositary State shall inform the other States Parties to the Treaty and to this Protocol on the deposit of instruments of ratification.

In witness whereof the undersigned, being duly authorised by their Governments, have signed this Protocol.

Source: Text reproduced from ASEAN Summit *Press Release*, 15 Dec. 1995.

UNITED NATIONS SECURITY COUNCIL RESOLUTION 984 ON SECURITY ASSURANCES

Adopted in New York, 11 April 1995

The Security Council,

Convinced that every effort must be made to avoid and avert the danger of nuclear war, to prevent the spread of nuclear weapons, to facilitate international cooperation in the peaceful uses of nuclear energy with particular emphasis on the needs of developing countries, and reaffirming the crucial importance of the Treaty on the Non-Proliferation of Nuclear Weapons to these efforts,

Recognizing the legitimate interest of non-nuclear-weapon States Parties to the Treaty on the Non-Proliferation of Nuclear Weapons to receive security assurances,

Welcoming the fact that more than 170 States have become Parties to the Treaty on the Non-Proliferation of Nuclear Weapons and stressing the desirability of universal adherence to it,

Reaffirming the need for all States Parties to the Treaty on the Non-Proliferation of Nuclear Weapons to comply fully with all their obligations,

Taking into consideration the legitimate concern of non-nuclear-weapon States that, in conjunction with their adherence to the Treaty on the Non-Proliferation of Nuclear Weapons, further appropriate measures be undertaken to safeguard their security,

Considering that the present resolution constitutes a step in this direction,

Considering further that, in accordance with the relevant provisions of the Charter of the United Nations, any aggression with the use of nuclear weapons would endanger international peace and security,

1. *Takes note* with appreciation of the statements made by each of the nuclear-weapon States (S/1995/261, S/1995/262, S/1995/263, S/1995/264, S/1995/265), in which they give security assurances against the use of nuclear weapons to non-nuclear-weapon States that are Parties to the Treaty on the Non-Proliferation of Nuclear Weapons;

2. *Recognizes* the legitimate interest of non-nuclear-weapon States Parties to the Treaty on the Non-Proliferation of Nuclear Weapons to receive assurances that the Security Council, and above all its nuclear-weapon State permanent members, will act immediately in accordance with the relevant provisions of the Charter of the United Nations, in the event that such States are the victim of an act of, or object of a threat of, aggression in which nuclear weapons are used;

3. *Recognizes further* that, in case of aggression with nuclear weapons or the threat of such aggression against a non-nuclear-weapon State Party to the Treaty on the Non-Proliferation of Nuclear Weapons, any State may bring the matter immediately to the attention of the Security Council to enable the Council to take urgent action to provide assistance, in accordance with the Charter, to the State victim of an act of, or object of a threat of, such aggression; and *recognizes also* that the nuclear-weapon State permanent members of the Security Council will bring the matter immediately to the attention of the Council and seek Council action to provide, in accordance with the Charter, the necessary assistance to the State victim;

4. *Notes* the means available to it for assisting such a non-nuclear-weapon State Party to the Treaty on the Non-Proliferation of Nuclear Weapons, including an investigation into the situation and appropriate measures to settle the dispute and restore international peace and security;

5. *Invites* Member States, individually or collectively, if any non-nuclear-weapon State Party to the Treaty on the Non-Proliferation of Nuclear Weapons is a victim of an act of aggression with nuclear weapons, to take appropriate measures in response to a request from the victim for technical, medical, scientific or humanitarian assistance, and affirms its readiness to consider what measures are needed in this regard in the event of such an act of aggression;

6. *Expresses* its intention to recommend appropriate procedures, in response to any request from a non-nuclear-weapon State Party to the Treaty on the Non-Proliferation of Nuclear Weapons that is the victim of such an act of aggression, regarding compensation under international law from the aggressor for loss, damage or injury sustained as a result of the aggression;

7. *Welcomes* the intention expressed by certain States that they will provide or support immediate assistance, in accordance with the Charter, to any non-nuclear-weapon State Party to the Treaty on the Non-Proliferation of Nuclear Weapons that is a victim of an act of, or an object of a threat of, aggression in which nuclear weapons are used;

8. *Urges* all States, provided for in Article VI of the Treaty on the Non-Proliferation of Nuclear Weapons, to pursue negotiations in good faith on effective measures relating to nuclear disarmament and on a treaty on general and complete disarmament under strict and effective international control which remains a universal goal,

9. *Reaffirms* the inherent right, recognized under Article 51 of the Charter, of individual and collective self-defence if an armed attack occurs against a member of the United Nations, until the Security Council has taken measures necessary to maintain international peace and security;

10. *Underlines* that the issues raised in this resolution remain of continuing concern to the Council.

Source: Text reproduced from United Nations Security Council Resolution 984, 11 Apr. 1995. Sponsored by China, France, the Russian Federation, the United Kingdom of Great Britain and Northern Ireland, and the United States of America.

14. Nuclear arms control

SHANNON KILE and ERIC ARNETT

I. Introduction

The year 1995 was one of progress in nuclear arms control, although there were indications that the political momentum towards further arms reductions and technological limitations was waning. In the light of the 'unfinished business' remaining on the arms control agenda, 1996 will be a watershed year in which the five declared nuclear weapon states, which still possess over 20 000 nuclear weapons, move either decisively to advance that agenda or noticeably away from it.

In 1995 the Conference on Disarmament (CD) made considerable progress towards concluding negotiations on a comprehensive test ban treaty (CTBT) and achieved a mandate to negotiate a treaty banning the production of fissile material for nuclear explosives. The implementation of the reductions in strategic nuclear delivery vehicles mandated by the 1991 Treaty on the Reduction and Limitation of Strategic Offensive Arms (START I Treaty) proceeded ahead of schedule in the five states parties. Bilateral cooperation between the USA and Belarus, Kazakhstan, Russia and Ukraine also intensified over the course of the year, with the US-funded Cooperative Threat Reduction programme delivering large-scale assistance to the former Soviet republics to facilitate their nuclear disarmament and demilitarization activities.

Despite consensus at the CD, the Non-Proliferation Treaty (NPT) Review and Extension Conference, and the UN General Assembly that the CTBT should be completed in 1996, there were also signs in 1995 that it might not be. China's positions in particular will have to be adjusted if this deadline is to be met, but several other issues remain to be resolved. Furthermore, despite its mandate, the CD did not begin to negotiate the fissile material convention. The US–Russian relationship was fraught with difficulties, with the prospects for Russian ratification of the 1993 Treaty on Further Reduction and Limitation of Strategic Offensive Arms (START II Treaty) looking increasingly gloomy and several cooperative denuclearization projects becoming the subjects of controversy. Negotiations between Russia and the USA to clarify the 1972 Anti-Ballistic Missile (ABM) Treaty also remained in an impasse; the USA proceeded with the testing of a new advanced-capability theatre missile defence (TMD) interceptor despite the lack of agreement with Russia over the permissibility of such tests under the terms of the ABM Treaty. China, France

* Sections IV, V and VI were written by S. Kile and sections II, III and VII by E. Arnett. Data for the nuclear forces tables and for figure 14.1 were provided by Robert S. Norris, of the Natural Resources Defense Council (NRDC), and William M. Arkin.

SIPRI Yearbook 1996: Armaments, Disarmament and International Security

and the UK also indicated that deployment of new missile defence systems could have repercussions for their nuclear force planning.

This chapter reviews the principal nuclear arms control and non-proliferation developments in 1995. Section II presents data on the nuclear weapon inventories. Section III describes the progress of negotiations at the CD on a comprehensive nuclear test ban treaty and on a fissile material production cut-off agreement. Section IV examines the changes under way in the strategic nuclear forces of the START I parties as they implement the reductions mandated by the treaty; it also looks at the travails of the follow-on START II Treaty and assesses the prospects for its ratification. Section V reviews the status of Cooperative Threat Reduction programme assistance in the former Soviet republics. Section VI describes the continuing deadlock between Russia and the USA over the scope of the ABM Treaty and the moves in the US Congress to commit the USA to develop and deploy a national missile defence system.

II. Tables of nuclear forces

At the beginning of 1996, there were well over 20 000 nuclear weapons in the operational inventories of the NPT nuclear weapon states:[1] 7947 strategic and 1150 tactical warheads for the USA; 7235 strategic and over 4000 tactical warheads for Russia;[2] 300 warheads for the UK; just over 500 warheads for France; and approximately 300 strategic and perhaps 150 tactical warheads for China.[3] There were fewer than 100 warheads in Israel.[4] The strategic nuclear force deployments are summarized for the NPT nuclear weapon states in tables 14.1–14.5. The tables include only the strategic nuclear weapons of the USA, Russia and China, not their tactical nuclear weapons. The figures in the tables are best estimates based on public information but contain some uncertainties, as reflected in the notes. Figures for China are especially uncertain.

[1] NPT Article IX.3 defines a nuclear weapon state as 'one which has manufactured and exploded a nuclear weapon or other nuclear explosive device prior to 1 January, 1967', hereafter in this chapter called an 'NPT nuclear weapon state'.

[2] If bomber aircraft in Ukraine are not counted since they are not fully operational and their nuclear weapons have been returned to Russia, the CIS total for strategic nuclear weapons falls to 6875. According to a recent report, only 1 of the Russian Typhoon Class submarines is operational; if the missiles from the others are not counted, the CIS total falls to 6329. Handler, J., 'Russia ready for START III', *Bulletin of the Atomic Scientists*, Jan./Feb. 1996, p. 11.

[3] Israel, which is also known to have nuclear weapons, is not an NPT state party and may have conducted a nuclear test in 1979. Miller, M. M., 'Israel', ed. E. Arnett, SIPRI, *Nuclear Weapons after the Comprehensive Test Ban: Implications for Modernization and Proliferation* (Oxford University Press: Oxford, 1996).

[4] Israel has enough plutonium for 55–95 weapons, according to figures in table 14.7, section III. They are thought to be deployed on gravity bombs and Jericho 1, Jericho 2 and perhaps Lance missiles. Arnett, E., 'Implications of the comprehensive test ban for nuclear weapon programmes and decision making', Arnett (note 3).

Table 14.1. US strategic nuclear forces, January 1996

Type	Designation	No. deployed	Year first deployed	Range (km)[a]	Warheads x yield	Warheads in stockpile
Bombers						
B-52H[b]	Stratofortress	76	1961	16 000	ALCM 5–150 kt	1 000
					ACM 5–150 kt	400
B-1B[c]	Lancer	82	1986	19 000 }	Bombs, various	1 400
B-2[d]	Spirit	8	1994	11 000 }		
Total		**166**				**2 800**
ICBMs						
LGM-30G[e]	Minuteman III	525		13 000		1 575
	Mk 12	..	1970		3 x 170 kt	*600[h]*
	Mk 12A	..	1979		3 x 335 kt	*975[h]*
LGM-118A	MX/Peacekeeper	50	1986	11 000	10 x 300 kt	500
Total		**575**				**2 075**
SLBMs						
UGM-96A[f]	Trident I C-4	192	1979	7 400	8 x 100 kt	1 536
UGM-133A[g]	Trident II D-5	192		7 400		1 536
	Mk-4	..	1992		8 x 100 kt	*1 152[h]*
	Mk-5	..	1990		8 x 475 kt	*384[h]*
Total		**384**				**3 072**

[a] Range for aircraft indicates combat radius, without in-flight refuelling.

[b] B-52Hs can carry up to 20 air-launched cruise missiles (ALCMs)/advanced cruise missiles (ACMs) each, but only about 1000 ALCMs and 400 ACMs are available for deployment. The Nuclear Posture Review (NPR) released on 22 Sep. 1994 recommended retaining 66 aircraft. Currently, the B-52Hs are consolidated at 2 bases, with the 2nd Bomb Wing at Barksdale Air Force Base (AFB), Louisiana, and the 5th Bomb Wing at Minot AFB, North Dakota. In 1995, 18 B-52s were retired; another 10 will be retired in 1996. By the end of 1996 there will be 2 wings of 28 aircraft each, plus 10 for spares and training.

[c] The B-1B can carry up to 24 B61 and/or B83 nuclear gravity bombs. Four have crashed and 1 is used as a ground trainer at Ellsworth AFB, South Dakota, and is not considered operational. The USA has begun to 'reorient' all its B-1Bs to exclusively conventional (i.e., non-nuclear) missions. This transition is already occurring (and is reflected in the table), although the START II Treaty has not entered into force. By the end of 1997 the B-1 will be out of the SIOP (Single Integrated Operational Plan [for strategic nuclear weapons]) altogether. Currently, 11 B-1Bs serve with the Air National Guard at McConnell AFB, Kansas; 45 are at Dyess AFB, Texas, 37 at Ellsworth AFB, and 2 test planes are at Edwards AFB, California. The aircraft will count towards START I Treaty limits but not towards START II Treaty limits.

[d] The first B-2 bomber was delivered to the 509th Bomb Wing at Whiteman AFB, Missouri, on 17 Dec. 1993. Four more were delivered in 1994 and 3 in 1995—on 16 Feb., 26 June and 14 Nov. Five are scheduled for delivery in 1996, 1 in 1997, and the 20th and last B-2 is scheduled for delivery on 31 Jan. 1998. Five of the 6 aircraft now in the test programme will be modified to achieve operational capability. Initially, the first 16 B-2s will be capable of carrying only the B83 nuclear gravity bomb. Eventually, all 20 operational B-2s will be capable of carrying the B61 and B83 bombs. The 509th Bomb Wing will have 2 squadrons, the 393rd and the 715th, each with 8 planes.

Table 14.1 *Notes, contd*

e The 500 Minuteman III intercontinental ballistic missiles (ICBMs) are being consolidated. On 4 Oct. 1995 the first of 150 Minuteman IIIs at Grand Forks AFB, North Dakota, began to be shifted to Malmstrom AFB, Montana. The transfer will proceed at the rate of about 1 missile per week over a 3-year period. When completed, there will be 200 Minuteman IIIs at Malmstrom AFB and 150 each at Minot AFB, North Dakota, and Warren AFB, Wyoming. According to the NPR, the plan is to remove the 3 warheads on the Minuteman III missile and replace them with a single W87 warhead taken from the 50 MX missiles that will be retired.

By the end of 1995 all 450 Minuteman IIs had been removed from their silos. On 18 May 1995 the last Minuteman II was removed from its silo at Whiteman AFB, Missouri. On 10 Aug. 1995 the last Minuteman II was removed from its silo at Malmstrom AFB. The last Minuteman II at Ellsworth AFB, South Dakota, had been removed in Apr. 1994. Work continued in blowing up silos in accordance with the START I Treaty. By the end of 1995, over 100 silos had been blown up at Ellsworth and some 25 at Whiteman. Silo destruction will eventually take place at Grand Forks with the elimination of the 150 silos that once housed Minuteman IIIs, after transfer of the missiles to Malmstrom. When the START II Treaty is implemented, the 50 former MX silos at Warren will also have to be destroyed. A $4.5 billion programme is under way to improve the capability of the Minuteman III missile and to extend its operational life to the year 2020. There are 3 major parts to the programme: updating consoles at launch control centres; improving guidance systems; and 'repouring' new solid propellant in 2 of the missile's 3 stages.

f The W76 warheads from the Trident I missiles are being fitted on Trident II submarines home-ported at King's Bay, Georgia, and are supplemented by 400 W88 warheads, the number of warheads built before production was halted.

g One new Ohio Class Trident submarine, the *USS Maine* (SSBN-741), the 16th of the class, joined the fleet in a commissioning ceremony on 29 July 1995. The last 2 Trident submarines (*USS Wyoming* and *USS Louisiana*) will be delivered in 1996 and 1997, respectively. Two major decisions in the NPR are to reduce the number of nuclear-powered, ballistic-missile submarines (SSBNs) to 14 (all Ohio Class) by retiring 4 SSBNs based in Bangor, Washington, and to purchase additional Trident II D-5 submarine-launched ballistic missiles (SLBMs) for 4 submarines that currently carry the Trident I SLBM. When START II is implemented the number of warheads per missile is planned to be reduced to 5.

h The total for these figures appears above them; they should not be added in the totals below for ICBMs and SLBMs.

Sources: William J. Perry, Secretary of Defense, *Annual Report to the President and the Congress,* Mar. 1996, pp. 213–18; William J. Perry, Secretary of Defense, *Annual Report to the President and the Congress,* Feb. 1995, pp. 163–66; START I Treaty Memorandum of Understanding, Sep. 1990; START I Treaty Memorandum of Understanding, 5 Dec. 1994; START I Treaty Memorandum of Understanding, 1 July 1995; Senate Committee on Foreign Relations, START II Treaty, Executive Report 104-10, 15 Dec. 1995; US Air Force Public Affairs, personal communications; *Bulletin of the Atomic Scientists*; and Natural Resources Defense Council (NRDC).

Table 14.2. Russian strategic nuclear forces, January 1996

Type	NATO designation	No. deployed	Year first deployed	Range (km)[a]	Warheads x yield	Warheads in stockpile
Bombers						
Tu-95M[b]	Bear-H6	31	1984	12 800	6 x AS-15A ALCMs, bombs	186
Tu-95M[b]	Bear-H16	57	1984	12 800	16 x AS-15A ALCMs, bombs	912
Tu-160[c]	Blackjack	25	1987	11 000	12 x AS-15B ALCMs or AS-16 SRAMs, bombs	300
Total		**113**				**1 398**
ICBMs[d]						
SS-18[e]	Satan	186	1979	11 000	10 x 550–750 kt	1 860
SS-19[f]	Stiletto	150	1980	10 000	6 x 550 kt	900
SS-24 M1/M2[g]	Scalpel	36/10	1987	10 000	10 x 550 kt	460
SS-25[h]	Sickle	345	1985	10 500	1 x 550 kt	345
Total		**727**				**3 565**
SLBMs[i]						
SS-N-18 M1	Stingray	208	1978	6 500	3 x 500 kt	624
SS-N-20[j]	Sturgeon	120	1983	8 300	10 x 200 kt	1 200
SS-N-23	Skiff	112	1986	9 000	4 x 100 kt	448
Total		**440**				**2 272**

[a] Range for aircraft indicates combat radius, without in-flight refuelling.

[b] According to the 1 July 1995 START I MOU, the Bear bombers are deployed as follows: Bear-H16s—19 at Mozdok (Russia), 17 at Ukrainka (Russia), and 21 at Uzin (Ukraine); and Bear-H6s—2 at Mozdok, 25 at Ukrainka and 4 at Uzin (Ukraine). The 40 Bear-H bombers (27 Bear-H6s and 13 Bear-H16s) that were based in Kazakhstan were withdrawn to Russia, including some 370 AS-15 ALCM warheads. The 25 Bear bombers in Ukraine are poorly maintained and not fully operational.

[c] Nineteen Blackjacks are based in Ukraine at Priluki. The remaining 6 are in Russia—1 at the Zhukovsky Flight Research Centre just south of Moscow and 5 at Engels AFB near Saratov. The Blackjacks at Priluki are poorly maintained and not fully operational. An agreement announced on 24 Nov. 1995 calls for Ukraine to eventually return the 19 Blackjacks, 25 Bears and more than 300 cruise missiles to Russia. The precise timing of the transfer and the amount of money to be paid were not made public. It is likely that most of the aircraft will be used for spare parts to support the bombers in Russia, with only a very few, if any at all, returning to service.

[d] Deactivation and retirement of ICBMs and their launchers proceed through at least 4 stages. In stage 1, an ICBM is removed from alert status by electrical and mechanical procedures. Next, warheads are removed from the missile. In stage 3 the missile is withdrawn from the silo. Finally, to comply with START I elimination provisions, the silo is blown up and eventually filled in with concrete. The number of missiles and warheads will vary depending on which stage the analyst chooses to feature.

[e] In the Sep. 1990 START I MOU, the USSR declared 104 SS-18s in Kazakhstan (at Derzhavinsk and Zhangiz-Tobe) and 204 in Russia (30 at Aleysk, 64 at Dombarovski, 46 at Kartaly and 64 at Uzhur). By the end of 1995 all SS-18s in Kazakhstan and 18 in Russia are considered to be non-operational, leaving 186 in Russia. On 25 Apr. 1995 the Russian Strategic Missile Forces Chief-of-Staff, Col.-Gen. Viktor Yesin, stated that all the SS-18 warheads that were formerly in Kazakhstan had been transferred to Russia. In Apr. the first SS-18 silos

Table 14.2 *Notes, contd*

in Kazakhstan were blown up. Under the START I Treaty, Russia is permitted to retain 154 SS-18s. If the START II Treaty is fully implemented, all SS-18 missiles will be destroyed, but Russia may convert up to 90 SS-18 silos for deployment of single-warhead ICBMs.

f In the original START I Treaty MOU, the USSR declared 130 SS-19s in Ukraine and 170 in Russia. The Nov. 1995 agreement (see note *c*) also included the sale of 32 SS-19s, once deployed in Ukraine, to Russia. Some SS-19s in Russia are being withdrawn from service.

g Of the original 56 silo-based SS-24 M2s, 46 were in Ukraine at Pervomaysk and 10 in Russia at Tatishchevo. By the end of 1995 only the 10 in Russia were considered operational. All 36 rail-based SS-24 M1s are in Russia—12 each at Bershet, Kostroma and Krasnoyarsk.

h SS-25s are deployed in both Russia and Belarus. SS-25 deployment in Belarus peaked in Dec. 1991 at 81 missiles at Lida and Mozyr. By the end of 1995 the number had decreased to 18, with 9 at each base. It is doubtful, but still unclear, whether any SS-25 warheads remain in Belarus. The SS-25, which is assembled at Votkinsk in Russia, is the only Russian strategic weapon system still under production. On 20 Dec. 1994 Russia flight-tested a variant of the SS-25. Several flight-tests were conducted during 1995. This silo-based variant, all parts of which are produced in Russia, is planned to supplement the mobile force.

i Approximately one-half of the SSBN fleet has been withdrawn from operational service. It is assumed here that all the Yankee Is, Delta Is and Delta IIs and 1 Delta III have been withdrawn from operational service, leaving 26 SSBNs of 3 classes (13 Delta IIIs, 7 Delta IVs and 6 Typhoons). All these SSBNs are based on the Kola Peninsula (at Nerpichya, Olenya and Yagelnaya) except for 9 Delta IIIs which are based at Rybachi (15 km south-west of Petropavlovsk) on the Kamchatka Peninsula. No additional SSBN production is expected before the year 2000.

j A follow-on to the SS-N-20, called the SS-N-26, is in development and is expected to be flight-tested soon and deployed during this decade. A second SLBM, for a new class of SSBN that might replace the Typhoon and Delta IV, is also under development.

Sources: START I Treaty Memorandum of Understanding, 1 Sep. 1990; START I Treaty Memorandum of Understanding, 5 Dec. 1994; START I Treaty Memorandum of Understanding, 1 July 1995; 'Nuclear notebook', *Bulletin of the Atomic Scientists*, Mar./Apr. 1996, pp.62–63; International Institute of Strategic Studies (IISS), *The Military Balance 1995–1996* (Oxford University Press: Oxford, 1995), pp. 289–92; and Natural Resources Defense Council (NRDC).

Table 14.3. British nuclear forces, January 1996[a]

Type	Designation	No. deployed	Date deployed	Range (km)[b]	Warheads x yield	Warheads in stockpile
Aircraft[c]						
GR.1	Tornado[d]	96	1982	1 300	1–2 x 200–400 kt bombs	100[e]
SLBMs						
A3-TK	Polaris	48	1982[f]	4 700	2 x 40 kt	70[g]
D-5	Trident II	16	1994[h]	7 400	4–6 x 100 kt	128

a The US nuclear weapons for certified British systems have been removed from Europe and returned to the USA, specifically for the 11 Nimrod anti-submarine warfare (ASW) aircraft based at RAF St Magwan, Cornwall, UK, the 1 Army regiment with 12 Lance launchers and the 4 Army artillery regiments with 120 M109 howitzers in Germany. Squadron No. 42, the Nimrod maritime patrol squadron, disbanded in Oct. 1992, but St Magwan will remain a forward base for Nimrods and will have other roles. The 50 Missile Regiment (Lance) and the 56 Special Weapons Battery Royal Artillery were disbanded in 1993.

b Range for aircraft indicates combat radius, without in-flight refuelling.

c The Royal Air Force will operate 8 squadrons of dual-capable Tornado GR.1/1A aircraft. These include: 4 squadrons at RAF Bruggen, Germany (Nos 9, 14, 17 and 31); 2 squadrons previously based at Marham which were redeployed to RAF Lossiemouth, Scotland, in 1994 (they replaced the Buccaneer S2B in the maritime strike role and were redesignated Nos 12 and 617); and 2 reconnaissance squadrons at RAF Marham (Nos 2 and 13). Each squadron has 12 aircraft.

d The US Defense Intelligence Agency (DIA) has confirmed that the RAF Tornados 'use two types of nuclear weapons, however exact types are unknown'. The DIA further concludes that each RAF Tornado is capable of carrying 2 nuclear bombs, 1 on each of the 2 outboard fuselage stations.

e The total stockpile of WE-177 tactical nuclear gravity bombs was estimated to have been about 200, of which 175 were versions A and B. The C version of the WE-177 was assigned to selected Royal Navy Sea Harrier FRS.1 aircraft and ASW helicopters. The WE-177C existed in both a gravity-bomb and a depth-bomb modification. There were an estimated 25 WE-177Cs, each with a yield of approximately 10 kt. Following the Bush–Gorbachev initiatives of 27 Sep. and 5 Oct. 1991, British Secretary of State for Defence Tom King said: 'we will no longer routinely carry nuclear weapons on our ships'. On 15 June 1992 the Defence Minister announced that all naval tactical nuclear weapons had been removed from surface ships and aircraft, that the nuclear mission would be eliminated and that the 'weapons previously earmarked for this role will be destroyed'. The 1992 White Paper stated: 'As part of the cut in NATO's stockpile we will also reduce the number of British free-fall [gravity] nuclear bombs by more than half'. A number of British nuclear bombs were returned to the UK from bases in Germany. On 4 Apr. 1995 the government announced that the remaining WE-177s would be withdrawn by the end of 1998.

f The 2-warhead Polaris A3-TK (Chevaline) SLBM was first deployed in 1982 and has now completely replaced the original 3-warhead Polaris A-3T SLBM, first deployed in 1968. *HMS Revenge* was retired in 1992. *HMS Renown* returned to service in late 1993 after a long refit. *HMS Resolution* was retired during 1995. *HMS Repulse* will be retired in 1997, followed by *Renown* in 1998. Chevaline warheads are being dismantled.

g It is now thought that the UK produced only enough warheads for 3 full boatloads of missiles, or 48 missiles, with a total of 96 warheads. In Mar. 1987 French President Mitterrand stated that Britain had '90 to 100 [strategic] warheads'.

h *HMS Vanguard* went on its first patrol in Dec. 1994. The first test-firing of a Trident II SLBM from *HMS Victorious*, the second submarine of the class, took place on 24 July 1995 at the Eastern Test Range off the coast of Florida. A second firing took place in Aug. The first patrol is scheduled for early 1996. The Ministry of Defence announced that 'each [Trident] submarine will deploy with no more than 96 warheads, and may carry significantly fewer'; the table assumes 4 warheads per missile.

Sources: Norris, R. S., Burrows, A. S. and Fieldhouse, R. W., *Nuclear Weapons Databook Vol. V: British, French and Chinese Nuclear Weapons* (Westview: Boulder, Colo., 1994), p. 9; and Secretary of State for Defence, *Statement on the Defence Estimates 1995*, Cmnd 2800 (Her Majesty's Stationery Office: London, May 1995).

Table 14.4. French nuclear forces, January 1996

Type	No. deployed	Year first deployed	Range (km)[a]	Warheads x yield	Warheads in stockpile
Land-based aircraft					
Mirage IVP[b]	18	1986	1 570	1 x 300 kt ASMP	15
Mirage 2000N/ASMP	45[c]	1988	2 750	1 x 300 kt ASMP	45
Carrier-based aircraft					
Super Étendard	24	1978	650	1 x 300 kt ASMP	20[d]
Land-based missiles					
S3D[e]	18	1980	3 500	1 x 1 Mt	18
Hadès[f]	[30]	[1992]	480	1 x up to 80 kt	30
SLBMs[g]					
M-4A/B	64	1985	6 000	6 x 150 kt	384

[a] Range for aircraft assumes combat mission, without in-flight refuelling, and does not include the 90- to 350-km range of the Air-Sol Moyenne Portée (ASMP) air-to-surface missile. President Chirac announced on 23 Feb. 1996 that he had decided to modernize the ASMP. The French company Aérospatiale will build the ASMP Plus. It will have a range of 500 km, enter service in 2007 and be deployed with Mirage 2000N and Rafale aircraft.

[b] The ageing Mirage IVP fleet is scheduled to be retired in 1996 and 1997. The Air Force plans to purchase 235 Rafale aircraft, with a first wing of 20 operational by mid-2002. A portion of them are to be certified nuclear-capable and carry the ASMP in about 2005. A severe French budget crisis may alter these plans.

[c] Only 45 (3 squadrons—EC 1/4 and EC 2/4 at Luxeuil and EC 3/4 at Istres) of the 75 Mirage 2000N aircraft have nuclear missions.

[d] The Super Étendard achieved a nuclear capability in 1981 with the AN 52 bomb, and eventually all 3 squadrons were capable of carrying this gravity bomb. From Apr. 1989, the Super Étendard began receiving the ASMP missile, and by mid-1990 24 aircraft (2 squadrons) were capable of carrying the ASMP. The third squadron relinquished its AN 52s (and thus its nuclear role) in July 1991. Plans call for the Rafale M to replace the Super Étendard in the nuclear role, beginning in about 2005. The Navy plans to purchase a total of 86 aircraft, of which the first 16 will perform an air-to-air interceptor role.

[e] President Chirac announced on 23 Feb. 1996 that the S3D will be retired over the next 2 years, cancelling earlier plans to retain them until 2010.

[f] Although the first regiment was activated at Suippes in eastern France on 1 Sep. 1991, the plan to deploy Hadès was shelved soon thereafter and the missiles and warheads were placed in storage. The programme had an original goal of 60 launchers and 120 missiles and was eventually cut to 15 launchers and 30 missiles. The Pluton short-range ballistic missile has been retired. Chirac announced on 23 Feb. 1996 that the Hadès weapon system would be dismantled.

[g] On returning from its 58th and final operational patrol on 5 Feb. 1991, SSBN *Le Redoutable* was retired along with the last MSBS (Mer-Sol Balistique Stratégique) M20 missiles. The remaining 5 submarines (*Le Terrible, Le Foudroyant, L'Indomptable, Le Tonnant* and *L'Inflexible*) are capable of carrying the MSBS M-4A/B missile. Although there are 80 launch tubes on the 5 SSBNs, only 4 sets of missiles were bought, and the number of TN 70/71 warheads in the stockpile is thus calculated to be 384, probably with a small number of spares. *Le Triomphant* was launched on 13 July 1993 and will enter service, with the M45 SLBM, in 1996, followed by *Le Téméraire* in 2000 and *Le Vigilant* in 2002 or 2003. President Chirac announced on 23 Feb. 1996 that the 4th submarine would be built. He also stated that a new SLBM, known as the M51, will replace the M45 and be ready for service in

the period 2010–15. On 15 Feb. 1995 an M45 was successfully test-fired from *Le Triomphant* for the first time. The M45 will carry the TN 75 nuclear warhead, which was tested in 1995.

Sources: Norris, R. S., Burrows, A. S. and Fieldhouse, R. W., *Nuclear Weapons Databook Vol. V: British, French and Chinese Nuclear Weapons* (Westview: Boulder, Colo., 1994), p. 10; *Air Actualités: Le Magazine de l'Armée de l'Air*; and Address by M. Jacques Chirac, President of the Republic, at the École Militaire, Paris, 23 Feb. 1996.

Table 14.5. Chinese nuclear forces, January 1996

Type	NATO designation	No. deployed	Year first deployed	Range (km)	Warheads x yield	Warheads in stockpile
Aircraft[a]						
H-5	B-5	30	1968	1 200	1 x bomb	
H-6	B-6	120	1965	3 100	1 x bomb	150
Q-5	A-5	30	1970	400	1 x bomb	
Land-based missiles[b]						
DF-3A	CSS-2	50	1971	2 800	1 x 1–3 Mt	50
DF-4	CSS-3	20	1980	4 750	1 x 1–3 Mt	20
DF-5A	CSS-4	7	1981	>13 000	1 x 3–5 Mt	7
DF-21	CSS-6	36	1985–86	1 800	1 x 200–300 kt	36
SLBMs[c]						
JL-1	CSS-N-3	12	1986	1 700	1 x 200–300 kt	12

[a] All figures for bomber aircraft are for nuclear-configured versions only. Hundreds of aircraft are also deployed in non-nuclear versions. Aircraft range is equivalent to combat radius. The force is assumed to have 150 nuclear gravity bombs, with estimated yields of between 10 kt and 3 Mt. The new H-7 aircraft (NATO designation B-7) was scheduled for deployment in 1995 but may not have entered production and may or may not be nuclear-capable. The H-5 and Q-5 may no longer be in service as nuclear-capable.

[b] China defines missile ranges as follows: short-range, < 1000 km; medium-range, 1000–3000 km; long-range, 3000–8000 km; and intercontinental-range, > 8000 km. The nuclear capability of the medium-range M-9 missile is unconfirmed, so it is not included. China is also developing 2 other ICBMs. The DF-31, with a range of 8000 km and carrying one 200- to 300-kt warhead, is scheduled for deployment in the late 1990s; the 12 000-km range DF-41 is scheduled for deployment around 2010 and may be MIRVed if China develops that capability.

[c] Two JL-1 SLBMs are presumed to be available for rapid deployment on a single Golf Class test ballistic-missile submarine (SSB). The 8000-km range JL-2 (NATO designation CSS-N-4), to carry one 200- to 300-kt warhead, will be available in the late 1990s. It is to be carried by the 09-4 SSBN, which may not be available until after the turn of the century.

Sources: Norris, R. S., Burrows, A. S. and Fieldhouse, R. W., *Nuclear Weapons Databook Vol. V: British, French and Chinese Nuclear Weapons* (Westview: Boulder, Colo., 1994), p. 11; Lewis, J. W. and Hua, D., 'China's ballistic missile programs: technologies, strategies, goals', *International Security*, vol. 17, no. 2 (fall 1992), pp. 5–40; International Institute of Strategic Studies (IISS), *The Military Balance 1995–1996* (Oxford University Press: Oxford, 1995), p. 176; and Arnett, E., 'Military technology: the case of China', *SIPRI Yearbook 1995: Armaments, Disarmament and International Security* (Oxford University Press: Oxford, 1995), pp. 380–83.

III. Arms control at the Conference on Disarmament

The Geneva-based Conference on Disarmament, the UN arms control negotiating forum, was the scene of the only nuclear arms control negotiations in
1995. Despite a full agenda of proposed negotiations, the CD had only two
formal mandates in 1995: for a comprehensive test ban treaty and a treaty
banning fissile material production. There was significant progress in the
CTBT negotiations in 1995, with near-consensus on the crucial issue of the
treaty's scope. Negotiations were not held on a fissile material production cut-
off treaty, and most observers are pessimistic about progress in the near term.

The comprehensive nuclear test ban

Despite the express wishes of Russia and the Group of 21 (G-21) formerly
non-aligned states,[5] a CTBT was not agreed in 1995. Nevertheless, substantial
progress was made, particularly on the issue of scope, and most observers
expect the treaty to be opened for signature in 1996. Indeed, at the NPT
Review and Extension Conference in May 1995, all but three members of the
CD committed themselves to complete the CTBT by the end of 1996. (Brazil,
India and Pakistan are not NPT parties and did not participate in the conference, but all three are members of the G-21.)

As the CTBT negotiations entered their second year at the CD, progress
slowed for several reasons despite the completion of a working draft, or
'rolling text', in 1994.[6] First, many participants anticipated or were involved
in preparations for the 1995 NPT Review and Extension Conference. While
some issues were resolved—in part to create a favourable atmosphere for the
conference (for example, France and the UK dropped their insistence on permitting tests in 'exceptional circumstances', and the USA withdrew its provision for an 'easy exit' after 10 years)—most were left to wait until the broader
question of the international non-proliferation regime was resolved.[7] Similarly, French arms control policy remained paralyzed by a divided government
until Jacques Chirac was elected president on 10 May 1995. Chirac's election,
followed in the same month by the adjournment of the NPT Conference and a
Chinese nuclear test, left the CD awaiting the outcome of his government's
review of French testing policy. For these reasons, serious negotiations did not
begin until the third round, which convened on 31 July 1995.

---

[5] For the members of the G-21 (now 19 states), see the glossary at the front of this volume.

[6] For a summary of progress in 1994 and more detail on the main issues, see Arnett, E., 'The compre-
hensive nuclear test ban', *SIPRI Yearbook 1995: Armaments, Disarmament and International Security*
(Oxford University Press: Oxford, 1995), pp. 697–718. See also the reports from R. Johnson in *Nuclear
Proliferation News* (London).

[7] See chapter 13 in this volume for a discussion of the NPT Review and Extension Conference.

Chinese and French nuclear tests[8]

It was known that China expected to test at least once or twice in 1995.[9] In late 1994 reports began to emerge that China planned to conduct as many as five more tests. In early 1995 China refined its public position on entry into force, suggesting that it might continue testing after signing the CTBT and would stop testing only when the treaty had entered into force. (All the nuclear weapon states but China have signed the 1969 Vienna Convention on the Law of Treaties, which obliges them not to 'defeat the object and purpose' of a treaty once they have signed it.) After the second and last Chinese test of the year, on 17 August, the Japanese Government was reportedly informed that China would test only twice more before the CTBT enters into force.[10]

France was much less ambiguous. President Chirac commissioned a review of French testing policy soon after he assumed office. Since few official responsibilities were changed by the election (the government was already run by Chirac's Conservative Party under the government of President François Mitterrand), the review quickly came to a conclusion. Chirac announced on 13 June that, as expected, France would conduct a single campaign of nuclear tests before signing the CTBT. He emphasized that the tests would be conducted between September 1995 and May 1996, that they would not be used to develop new types of nuclear weapon, and that France would then sign the treaty and never test again. Chirac speculated further that France might abandon its force of land-based missiles.[11] In July he was more specific about the purposes of the tests: 'It is a question of testing our new nuclear warhead [the TN 75 for the M45 submarine-launched ballistic missile (SLBM)], then of testing, with two tests, the security, safety and reliability of our primaries and their capacity for ageing. Finally, that leaves four tests. In total, seven or eight tests, according to the circumstances, which will permit us to acquire the technology of simulation'.[12]

Despite the widespread expectation that France would resume testing after the May 1995 election and Chirac's effort to put the decision in a positive light,[13] the international response to the decision was even more negative than expected. The CD negotiations reached an impasse for the remainder of the

[8] For data on nuclear tests, see appendix 14A.

[9] For a summary of forecasts, see Arnett, *SIPRI Yearbook 1995* (note 6), p. 710.

[10] *Tokyo Shimbun*, 25 Aug. 1995, in Foreign Broadcast Information Service, *Daily Report–Technology Arms Control (FBIS-TAC)*, FBIS-TAC-95-005, 13 Oct. 1995.

[11] Lewis, J. A. C., 'France lifts ban on nuclear tests', *Jane's Defence Weekly*, 24 June 1995.

[12] 'M. Chirac explique les raisons techniques des essais nucléaires français' [Mr Chirac explains the technical reasons for French nuclear tests], *Le Monde*, 14 July 1995, p. 3. The article contains an explanation that the test of the TN 75 will qualify or certify its performance characteristics, and the 2 reliability tests will verify the yield of warheads that might be contaminated by the decay of materials or otherwise degraded by age. These purposes of the tests were confirmed by the Foreign Ministry in Ministère des Affaires Étrangères, 'Political–military aspects', *About the Final Series of French Nuclear Tests*, 1995. Version current on 20 Dec. 1995, URL <http://www.france.diplomatie.fr/frmonde/essa1.gb.html>. See also James, B., 'Q&A: questioning Paris's rationale for nuclear testing', *International Herald Tribune*, 17 July 1995, p. 2. A primary is the fission trigger for a thermonuclear bomb.

[13] In addition to the assurances Chirac gave when announcing the tests, France had reiterated in May that it understood that the NPT was intended to lead to the abolition of nuclear weapons. See also chapter 13 in this volume.

second round of the 1995 session, but the later progress was ascribed by many to the more constructive role France had taken.[14] Poland's Ambassador, Ludwik Dembinski, chairman of the CD Ad Hoc Committee on a Nuclear Test Ban, went so far at the end of the 1995 session as to give France most of the credit for the year's advances: 'What really has affected negotiations here was the declaration of France that they are willing to conclude the treaty in 1996. . . . This was much more important from the point of view of the conference than the series of nuclear tests announced at the same time'.[15]

Scope

While differences remain on the scope of the CTBT, most of these are in areas where the ultimate conclusion is not difficult to predict. More importantly, the other Permanent Five (P5) members of the UN Security Council accepted the position of China and the G-21 that the treaty should not permit hydronuclear experiments—explosions that trigger a nuclear chain reaction and release a very small amount of nuclear energy. While the P5 did not accept the language proposed by the G-21, which would ban any explosion that 'releases nuclear energy', the negotiating record is likely now to reflect the fact that the ambiguous language in the treaty, first proposed by Australia in its 1994 draft treaty, is meant implicitly to ban hydronuclear experiments.[16] France was the first to announce its position (9 August), but was quickly followed by the USA (11 August) and the UK (14 September). Russia's position remained unclear as of early 1996.

China continued to insist that peaceful nuclear explosions (PNEs) should be permitted under the CTB, despite indications in 1994 that it would bow in the face of the proposal's lack of support.[17] In 1995 China not only maintained its position on PNEs but also mustered a range of arguments which suggested that it was committed to this position. According to Chinese officials, the

[14] This had been expected after a pre-election report highlighted the linkage between the tests and France's willingness to accept a more restrictive scope. Garwin, R., Kidder, R. and Paine, C., *A Report on Discussions Regarding the Need for Nuclear Test Explosions to Maintain French Nuclear Weapons under a Comprehensive Test Ban* (Federation of American Scientists and Natural Resources Defense Council: Washington, DC, 1995). Robert Bell of the US National Security Council publicly confirmed that France's positive role in the CTB negotiations could be credited not only to the tests, but also to the USA sharing computer simulation codes. *National Public Radio Morning Edition*, 13 Oct. 1995. A US Defense Department official explained in Nov. that cooperation with France would include information regarding safety and reliability, an exchange in which France would also be providing the USA with useful information. Arnett, E., 'US planning nuclear cooperation after the CTB', *Bulletin of the Atomic Scientists*, May/June 1996.

[15] Higgins, A. G., 'Nuclear ban', Associated Press, 21 Sep. 1995. See also Butler, D., 'Physicists warm to French nuclear tests', *Nature*, vol. 377 (21 Sep. 1995); Arnett, E., 'Nuclear testing: what's at stake?', *Life and Peace Review* (Uppsala), vol. 9, no. 3 (1995); and 'WPQ: French nuclear tests', *Arms Control and Disarmament Quarterly Review*, no. 38 (July 1995), p. 38.

[16] Conference on Disarmament document CD/NTB/WP.222, 8 Mar. 1995 reflects the Australian position (which differs only slightly from the draft tabled by Australia in 1994, CD/NTB/WP.49) and CD/NTB/WP.244, 27 June 1995, the G-21 position (the latter was tabled by India). CD/NTB/WP.49 is reproduced in Arnett, E. (ed.), *Implementing the Comprehensive Test Ban: New Aspects of Definition, Organization and Verification*, SIPRI Research Report no. 8 (Oxford University Press: Oxford, 1994).

[17] Chinese officials had indicated informally that China would accept a CTBT that banned PNEs and did not ban the first use of nuclear weapons. Arnett, *SIPRI Yearbook 1995* (note 6).

potential contribution of PNEs to economic development is guaranteed by Article V of the NPT and was demonstrated by the Soviet and US programmes, which, they claimed, were only abandoned for political reasons.[18] China would permit PNEs only after they were approved by the CTBT's decision-making body and would allow inspections to demonstrate that the PNE device was not a nuclear weapon. Some Chinese officials would be willing to accept a 'temporary ban' on PNEs that would be reconsidered if the economic potential of the technology were realized.[19]

Verification

In addition to the progress on the scope of the CTBT, the CD made considerable progress on verification in 1995, agreeing that the treaty's internationally operated monitoring network would comprise 50 alpha (primary) seismic stations[20] in continuous contact with the treaty's International Data Centre (IDC), 100–150 beta (secondary) stations and 11 hydroacoustic arrays. There would also be 20–100 atmospheric monitoring stations, perhaps supplemented by aircraft, and 12–70 infrasound stations. These are judged to be adequate to detect any test as small as 1 kiloton. Distinguishing small tests from earthquakes or non-nuclear explosions and detecting tests below 1 kt would also be possible under some circumstances but not always reliably. Ambiguities that could not be cleared up by consultation and clarification could lead to inspections. There remain disagreements regarding both whether information from sources other than the IDC, for example, from governments, may be presented during the consultation (with China, Iran and Pakistan opposing any use of outside information) and how many states must approve an inspection to prevent it from being blocked. Without information from outside sources, it would appear to be practically impossible to detect hydronuclear experiments or other low-yield tests, much less make the case for an inspection.

Prospects

In early 1995, Russia and the G-21 states called for the CTBT to be completed by the end of the year. In May the states parties to the NPT affirmed that the CTBT should be completed by the end of 1996, echoing the official positions of China and the USA. On 1 July US Secretary of Defense William Perry gave the most specific time-frame yet articulated by an official: 'We expect to sign this treaty in the beginning of next year, in order [for it] to enter into force in the fall of 1996, provided that France and China have conducted their tests

[18] Chinese officials say that they became aware of the potential of PNEs from participants in the Soviet programmes. Personal communication. See also Arnett (note 14); and Findlay, T., *Nuclear Dynamite: The Peaceful Nuclear Explosions Fiasco* (Brassey's Australia: Rushcutters Bay, NSW, 1990).

[19] Unnamed official paraphrased in Wu Yun, *China's Policy Towards Arms Control and Disarmament: From Passive Responding to Active Leading* (China Institute of Contemporary International Relations: Beijing, 1995), p. 8.

[20] In Aug. 1995, only 27 of these stations were participating in verification experiments being run by the Group of Scientific Experts. Conference on Disarmament document CD/1341, 22 Aug. 1995.

before that period'.[21] Despite these optimistic assessments, the chairman of the negotiations said in July 1995 that finishing the treaty in 1996 was 'possible, but it will be very difficult'.[22]

By the end of 1995 the outlook for a swift conclusion was good, if not excellent. The consensus that the treaty should ban all tests, even hydronuclear experiments, makes it much simpler to develop verification provisions. (Permitting hydronuclear experiments under the treaty might require special measures to distinguish them from low-yield tests. Although detecting hydronuclear experiments will be a verification challenge, it is similar to that posed by tests below 1 kiloton and therefore poses no distinct new problem.) It remains to be seen how quickly negotiators will play their remaining bargaining-chips in other areas, but most of them are of rapidly diminishing value for anything but obstruction now that the most important outlines of the treaty have been firmly drawn. In addition, several states have attempted to link the CTBT to other disarmament measures. India in particular demanded late in the year that the CTBT contain a commitment to complete nuclear disarmament in a specified period (10 years), independent of the NPT.

If some observers and participants became more pessimistic about the prospects for concluding the CTBT and others began to question its relevance after the NPT Review and Extension Conference and the resumption of French testing, in 1995 there was also a renewed appreciation of the CTBT's contribution as 'a valuable barrier and hedge against any *new* qualitative arms race', in the words of John Holum, director of the US Arms Control and Disarmament Agency (ACDA).[23] Indeed, if successfully concluded, the CTBT will prevent the nuclear weapon states from developing, weaponizing and certifying the technologies underlying very-low-yield nuclear weapons (so-called mini-nukes and micro-nukes) and third-generation weapons, despite growing interest in these technologies in some quarters, particularly in the USA. These constraints on modernization complement the widely appreciated effects on the acquisition of nuclear weapons by new countries. The possibility that more conservative governments will be brought in by elections in 1996 in India, Israel, Russia and the USA makes swift progress at the beginning of the year important.

[21] 'US leaves France isolated on nuclear testing', Agence France Presse (AFP), 1 July 1995. US Ambassador John Holum was more specific: 'President Clinton is committed to concluding the complete text of the agreement by April—the end of the first part of the 1996 CD session', which adjourns on 29 Mar. 'US presses for comprehensive nuclear test ban treaty', Wireless File (United States Information Service, US Embassy: Stockholm, 18 Oct. 1995). A more likely time-frame is that laid out by Australian Ambassador Richard Starr: 'In practice the treaty needs to be available for signature by autumn of 1996, that is at the commencement of UNGA 51. . . . The Conference [on Disarmament] will have to sign off by the end of June 1996 on a completed text . . . so that preparations for signature . . . in September can commence'. 'Statement by H. E. Mr Richard Starr, UNGA 50, First Committee' (Australian Mission to the United Nations: New York, 1995), p. 2. The CD adjourns for the year on 13 Sep. 1996.

[22] Hanley, C. J., 'Nuclear countdown', Associated Press, 17 July 1995.

[23] Holum, J., Remarks to the National Security Forum, Chicago, Illinois, 7 June 1995 (ACDA: Washington, DC, 1995), p. 2 (emphasis in original). The effects of the CTB on nuclear weapon programmes and decision making are examined in Arnett (note 3).

Table 14.6. Estimated inventories of weapon-grade plutonium and uranium in the NPT nuclear weapon states, 31 December 1993

Figures are central estimates, in tonnes.

State or region	Plutonium	% in weapons	Highly enriched uranium (weapon-grade equivalent)	% in weapons
Commonwealth of Independent States	131 ± 20%	30	1 025 ± 30%	20
USA	85 ± 3%	40	640 ± 10%	30
France	4.8 ± 30%	40	25 ± 20%	40
China	3.5 ± 50%	30	20 ± 25%	40
UK	2.4 ± 20%	40	10 ± 25%	60

Source: Adapted from Albright, D. *et al., SIPRI Yearbook 1995: Armaments, Disarmament and International Security* (Oxford University Press: Oxford, 1995), table 9.2, p. 320.

The ban on production of fissile material for nuclear explosives

The CD achieved a mandate for a fissile material production cut-off in 1995, but only by avoiding specific language on the purpose and extent of the treaty.[24] The mandate reads:

1. The Conference on Disarmament decide to establish an Ad Hoc Committee on a 'Ban on the production of fissile material for nuclear weapons or other nuclear explosive devices'.
2. The Conference directs the Ad Hoc Committee to negotiate a non-discriminatory, multilateral and internationally and effectively verifiable treaty banning the production of fissile material for nuclear weapons or other nuclear explosive devices.
3. The Ad Hoc Committee will report to the Conference on the progress of its work before the conclusion of the 1995 session.[25]

Although the committee was formed, it never met and therefore had no progress to report at the end of the year.

Supporters of the ban in the P5 states see it as a way of codifying their de facto cut-off of production of highly enriched uranium (HEU) and plutonium in special military facilities. This not only locks in their production freeze at a time when all of them have huge surpluses but would for the first time also limit the military nuclear facilities in the threshold states—the non-NPT states with military nuclear programmes: India, Israel and Pakistan—and perhaps ultimately open them to international inspection.

India and Pakistan did not block the cut-off mandate, but both strongly suggested that, for the negotiations to succeed, they must address the problem

---

[24] The primary considerations to be borne in mind while negotiating the treaty are summarized in Berkhout, F. *et al.*, 'A cutoff in the production of fissile material', *International Security*, vol. 19, no. 3 (winter 1994/95), pp. 167–202. See also Simpson, J., 'Nuclear arms control and an extended non-proliferation regime', *SIPRI Yearbook 1994* (Oxford University Press: Oxford, 1994), pp. 605–29; and Lockwood, D., 'Nuclear arms control', *SIPRI Yearbook 1994*, section VI, pp. 659–64.
[25] Conference on Disarmament document CD/1299, 24 Mar. 1995.

Table 14.7. Estimated inventories of weapon-grade plutonium and uranium in the non-NPT states, 31 December 1993 and 1994

Figures are central estimates, in tonnes.

State or region	Plutonium 31 Dec. 1993	Highly enriched uranium (weapon-grade equivalent) 31 Dec. 1994
Israel	$0.44 \pm 25\%$	–
India	$0.35 \pm 30\%$	–
Pakistan	–	$0.21 \pm 30\%$

Source: Albright, D. *et al., SIPRI Yearbook 1995: Armaments, Disarmament and International Security* (Oxford University Press: Oxford, 1995), table 9.2, p. 320.

of fissile material more comprehensively. (Israel, which is an observer and not a member of the CD, has not made a formal statement on the cut-off.) Proposals include declaring and reducing existing stocks, regulating production of fissile materials in non-military plants,[26] and halting the production of tritium in addition to HEU and plutonium.

IV. The START treaties

The 1991 START I and 1993 START II treaties form the twin pillars of an arms control treaty regime which is gradually shaping a more stable and transparent strategic environment of shrinking nuclear arsenals.[27] In 1995 the treaties continued to occupy a crucial position on the international arms control agenda, although their prominence was overshadowed to some extent by other nuclear weapon issues, such as France's resumption of nuclear testing.[28]

At the beginning of 1995, the uncertainty surrounding the START regime had considerably diminished. The entry into force of the START I Treaty in December 1994, one of the key items of unfinished business left over from the cold war, had settled the fate of the Soviet strategic nuclear weapons based outside Russia and paved the way for the deeper reductions in the Russian and US nuclear arsenals mandated by the START II Treaty. However, the year ended with the prospects for implementing these deeper cuts cast increasingly into doubt, as neither the US nor the Russian legislature had ratified the treaty. In a reversal of the nuclear arms control situation prevailing throughout most

[26] Roughly 150 000 kg of plutonium had been separated by the end of 1993 by Belgium, France, Germany, India, Japan, Russia, the USA and the UK. Albright, D., Berkhout, F. and Walker, W., SIPRI, *Plutonium and Highly Enriched Uranium 1996: World Inventories, Capabilities and Policies* (Oxford University Press: Oxford, forthcoming 1996).

[27] For a description of the provisions of the START I Treaty, see Cowen Karp, R., 'The START Treaty and nuclear arms control', *SIPRI Yearbook 1992: World Armaments and Disarmament* (Oxford University Press: Oxford, 1992), pp. 13–26. For a description of the provisions of the START II Treaty, see Lockwood, D., 'Nuclear arms control', *SIPRI Yearbook 1993: World Armaments and Disarmament* (Oxford University Press: Oxford, 1993), pp. 554–59.

[28] Lewis, F., 'Nuclear protesters should start worrying about START II', *International Herald Tribune*, 16–17 Sep. 1995, p. 6.

of the cold war, START II faced little organized opposition in the US Senate, while its approval by the Russian Duma was in doubt. As 1995 ended, the possibility loomed that the treaty would not be ratified and that the START regime, which encompasses the only international legally binding agreements shaping the post-cold war US–Russian strategic nuclear balance, would not be fully implemented.

Implementation of the START I Treaty

The START I Treaty was signed by US President George Bush and Soviet President Mikhail Gorbachev in Moscow on 31 July 1991, following nearly a decade of negotiations.[29] The treaty entered into force on 5 December 1994, when the leaders of the five Lisbon Protocol signatory states exchanged the instruments of ratification at a summit meeting of the Conference on Security and Co-operation in Europe (CSCE) held in Budapest, Hungary.[30]

The START I Treaty requires Russia and the USA to make phased reductions in their strategic nuclear forces over a seven-year implementation period to no more than 1600 strategic nuclear delivery vehicles (SNDVs) and 6000 treaty-accountable nuclear warheads; it also sets out interim reduction deadlines. The treaty obligates Belarus, Kazakhstan and Ukraine to eliminate entirely all the former Soviet strategic nuclear forces based on their territories. In anticipation of the treaty's entry into force, Russia and the USA made considerable progress in 1994 in implementing START-mandated force reductions. The process of deactivating and eliminating strategic nuclear weapon systems was also well under way in Belarus, Kazakhstan and Ukraine in accordance with their denuclearization commitments.

According to a senior US Defense Department official, by the spring of 1995 the United States had deactivated (by removing the warheads from the launch vehicles) all the land- and sea-based missile systems scheduled to be eliminated under START I.[31] These included 450 warheads from Minuteman II intercontinental ballistic missiles (ICBMs) and 3456 warheads from Poseidon (C-3) and Trident I (C-4) SLBMs. In addition, all the B-52 heavy bombers scheduled for dismantlement had been retired to an elimination facility at Davis-Monthan Air Force Base (AFB), Arizona.[32] By mid-1995 the USA had, in accordance with START elimination rules, destroyed 290 missile

---

[29] For more detail on the developments clearing the way for the START I Treaty's entry into force, see Goodby, J., Kile, S. and Müller, H., 'Nuclear arms control', *SIPRI Yearbook 1995* (note 6), pp. 636–39.

[30] At a 23 May 1992 meeting of foreign ministers in Lisbon, Portugal, the three non-Russian former Soviet republics with strategic nuclear weapons based on their territories—Belarus, Kazakhstan and Ukraine—signed a protocol with Russia and the USA making them signatories to START I. Excerpts from the text of the Lisbon Protocol are reproduced in *SIPRI Yearbook 1993* (note 27), appendix 11A, pp. 574–75.

[31] Walter B. Slocombe, Under-secretary of Defense for Policy, Prepared remarks before the Senate Armed Services Committee, 17 May 1995. The deactivated weapon systems remain START-accountable, however, until they have been rendered permanently inoperative in accordance with the procedures specified in the START Treaty's Conversion or Elimination Protocol. Cowen Karp (note 27).

[32] Lockwood, D., 'START I enters into force, clears way for START II approval', *Arms Control Today*, vol. 25, no. 1 (Jan./Feb. 1995), p. 26.

launch vehicles out of a total of 684–834 launchers to be eliminated or converted (depending on force planning decisions); it had also eliminated 230 B-52 heavy bombers out of a planned total of 386. These reductions put the USA below the first START I intermediate ceiling on launchers (2100) that comes into effect in December 1997.[33]

Russia also proceeded with the elimination or conversion of its strategic nuclear forces. US officials had previously expressed concern over what they perceived to be the slow pace of Russia's implementation of its START I-mandated force reductions.[34] However, according to data contained in the Memorandum of Understanding (MOU) exchanged by the signatory states as part of the START I Treaty's entry into force,[35] Russia was in some respects ahead of the USA in implementing these reductions; as of December 1994 Russia had removed from START accountability 378 ICBM silos (primarily for obsolescent SS-11 and SS-13 missiles) while the USA had eliminated 41.[36] By mid-1995, Russia had destroyed 630 missile launchers and heavy bombers.[37] Together with the reductions made in Belarus, Kazakhstan and Ukraine, these cuts put Russia and the other three former Soviet republics close to meeting the second intermediate ceiling (1900) on launchers that does not take effect until December 1999.[38]

On 24 November Russia announced that it planned to purchase 32 six-warhead SS-19 ICBMs from Ukraine. According to the Commander-in-Chief of the Strategic Rocket Forces, Colonel-General Igor Sergeyev, the acquisition of the additional missiles would 'allow Russia's nuclear potential to be maintained at the necessary level until 2009'.[39] They will be used as spares and for parts to support the deployed SS-19 force. Some Defence Ministry officials have proposed that Russia be allowed to deploy more than the 105 SS-19

---

[33] Prepared Statement of Secretary of Defense William J. Perry to the Senate Foreign Relations Committee, 1 Mar. 1995, *Defense Issues*, vol. 10, no. 25 (1995); and Lockwood, D., 'US–Russian strategic weapons dismantlements', *Arms Control Today*, vol. 25, no. 4 (May 1995), p. 32.

[34] Remarks prepared for delivery by Secretary of Defense William J. Perry to the Henry L. Stimson Center, 20 Sep. 1994, Office of Assistant Secretary of Defense for Public Affairs, News release, no. 535-94, 20 Sep. 1994, p. 4; and Starr, B., 'Perry wants speedier Russian disarmament', *Jane's Defence Weekly*, vol. 22, no. 13 (1 Oct. 1994), p. 6.

[35] The parties are required to update every 6 months the MOU data on the number, type and location of the strategic nuclear weapons on their territories. In accordance with a treaty protocol on inspection and monitoring activities, baseline inspections to verify the MOU data began 45 days after the treaty entered into force and were completed 120 days thereafter.

[36] Lockwood, D., 'New data on the strategic arsenal of the former Soviet Union', *Jane's Intelligence Review*, vol. 7, no. 6 (June 1995), p. 247. The USA has made less progress in eliminating ICBMs from START accountability since it—in contrast to the Russian practice—has chosen to first deactivate all the missiles slated for elimination before beginning the destruction of the silo complexes. By the end of 1995, the USA had eliminated 125 Minuteman II silos.

[37] Carnegie Endowment for International Peace and the Monterey Institute of International Studies, *The Nuclear Successor States of the Soviet Union: Nuclear Weapons and Sensitive Exports Status Report*, no. 3 (July 1995), pp. 7–9.

[38] Perry (note 33).

[39] Quoted in Clarke, D., 'Russia to buy Ukrainian missiles, bombers', Open Media Research Institute (OMRI), *OMRI Daily Digest*, vol. 1, no. 229 (27 Nov. 1995). URL <http://www.omri.cz/Publications/Digests/DigestIndex.html> (hereafter, references to *OMRI Daily Digest* refer to the Internet edition at this URL address); and 'Russia to buy nuclear missiles and bombers from Ukraine', *Nuclear Proliferation News*, no. 37 (15 Dec. 1995), p. 24.

ICBMs 'downloaded' to a single warhead each that are permitted under the terms of the START II Treaty.[40]

By the end of 1995 Ukraine had made some progress in fulfilling its pledge to eliminate all the former Soviet strategic nuclear weapons based on its territory.[41] It continued to deactivate the 176 ICBMs that the Soviet Union had declared as deployed there in the 1990 START I MOU by removing nuclear warheads from the launch vehicles. By the end of October, 80 of the 130 SS-19 ICBMs in Ukraine had been deactivated.[42] The 46 SS-24 missiles based in silos at Pervomaysk had already been deactivated by the previous November in accordance with the schedule set out in the 14 January 1994 Trilateral Statement signed by the presidents of Russia, Ukraine and the USA.[43] Over 75 per cent of the 1734 former Soviet nuclear warheads based in Ukraine had been transferred to Russia by the end of 1995; the approximately 450 remaining warheads are scheduled to be transferred to Russia for dismantlement by mid-1996.[44]

The fate of the 44 former Soviet heavy bombers (19 Tu-160 'Blackjack' and 25 Tu-95 'Bear' aircraft) based at two airfields in Ukraine was resolved after protracted bargaining between Kiev and Moscow. In the spring of 1995, Ukrainian and Russian negotiators reached an agreement under which the bombers, along with their approximately 300 air-launched cruise missiles (ALCMs), would be returned to Russia in exchange for a $190 million reduction in Ukraine's debt to Russia.[45] Russian officials subsequently indicated that they were not interested in the return of the aircraft, most of which had seriously deteriorated in storage and were no longer in condition to fly.[46] Nevertheless, on 24 November the Commander-in-Chief of the Russian Air Force, Colonel-General Petr Deineken, announced that Russia would purchase the aircraft and their cruise missiles as part of a broader military cooperation deal with Ukraine.[47]

---

[40] For a discussion of Russian defence planners' concerns about a strategic 'window of vulnerability' developing vis-à-vis the USA in the first decade of the next century, see Bluth, C., 'The Russian view of its strategic nuclear arsenal', Jane's Intelligence Review, vol. 6, no. 6 (June 1994), pp. 266–67.

[41] The transfer to Russia of the former Soviet tactical nuclear weapons stockpiled on Ukrainian territory was completed in May 1992.

[42] Markus, U., 'Ukrainian disarmament update', OMRI Daily Digest, vol. 1, no. 212 (31 Oct. 1995).

[43] For a description of the Trilateral Statement, see Lockwood, D., 'Nuclear arms control', SIPRI Yearbook 1994 (note 24), pp. 641–43, and for the text of the Statement see appendix 16A, pp. 677–78.

[44] Clarke, D., 'Missile chief updates weapons in near abroad', OMRI Daily Digest, vol. 1, no. 103 (29 May 1995); and Norris, R. and Arkin, W., 'Russian (CIS) strategic nuclear forces, end of 1995', Bulletin of the Atomic Scientists, vol. 52, no. 2 (Mar./Apr. 1996), pp. 62–63.

[45] 'Russia set to buy back ex-Soviet bombers', Jane's Defence Weekly, vol. 23, no. 11 (18 Mar. 1995), p. 23; and Clarke, D., 'Fleet impasse holds up bomber deal', OMRI Daily Digest, vol. 1, no. 111 (8 June 1995). Russian personnel are reported to have removed the guidance system software from the cruise missiles stored in Ukraine. See, e.g., Lockwood, D., 'Nuclear weapon development', SIPRI Yearbook 1994 (note 24), p. 296.

[46] Norris, S. and Arkin, W., 'Estimated Russian (CIS) stockpile, September 1995', Bulletin of the Atomic Scientists, vol. 51, no. 5 (Sep./Oct. 1995), p. 61.

[47] Clarke (note 39); and Ukraininform, 28 Nov. 1995, in Foreign Broadcast Information Service (FBIS), Daily Report–Central Eurasia, FBIS-SOV-95-228, 28 Nov. 1995, pp. 54–55. The aircraft are not expected to return to service and are likely to be used to provide spare parts for other Russian Air Force bombers.

On 24 April 1995 Kazakhstan became the first of the former Soviet republics to fulfil its pledge to become a non-nuclear weapon state when it transferred to Russia the last of 898 nuclear warheads removed from the 104 SS-18s ICBMs based at Derzhavinsk and Zhangiz-Tobe. (The 40 Bear-H strategic bombers and their associated AS-15 ALCMs inherited by Kazakhstan from the former Soviet Union had been flown back to Russia in early 1994.)[48] The destruction of the SS-18 launch silos has been considerably slowed by a series of disputes between Moscow and Almaty. After protracted negotiations over cost-sharing arrangements, on 12 April Russian Strategic Rocket Forces personnel began readying the silo complexes for destruction in accordance with START elimination rules; the process is expected to be completed by the end of 1996.[49]

The withdrawal from Belarus to Russia of the last of the 81 SS-25 ICBMs based at Mozyr and Lida proceeded less smoothly. In early July 1995 Belarussian President Alexander Lukashenko announced that he had suspended 'indefinitely' the withdrawal of the 18 SS-25 missiles scheduled to be transferred to Russia at the end of the month.[50] The move, which reportedly was connected with the government's efforts to reduce its debt to Russia, threw into doubt Belarus' commitments under the NPT and START I to remove all nuclear weapons from its territory.[51] However, on 5 August 1995 the Belarussian Foreign Ministry issued a clarification that the withdrawal of the weapons had not been halted but merely slowed owing to Russia's reluctance to take financial responsibility for the ecological damage left behind after the missiles' withdrawal.[52]

The START II Treaty

The START II Treaty was signed by US President George Bush and Russian President Boris Yeltsin on 3 January 1993. The treaty bans all land-based strategic ballistic missiles with multiple independently targetable re-entry vehicles (MIRVs) and commits both parties to make phased reductions in their strategic nuclear forces to no more than 3500 deployed warheads by the year 2003.[53] This ceiling represents approximately one-third the size of the US and Soviet strategic nuclear arsenals before the signing of START I in July 1991.

---

[48] 'US congratulates Kazakhstan for removal of nuclear weapons', *Wireless File* (United States Information Service, US Embassy: Stockholm, 26 May 1995), p. 5; Clarke, D., 'Kazakhstan free of nuclear weapons', *OMRI Daily Digest*, vol. 1, no. 82 (26 Apr. 1995); and Lockwood (note 36), p. 248.

[49] 'Kazakhstan begins eliminating ICBM silos', ITAR-TASS, 24 Apr. 1995, in FBIS-SOV-95-078, 24 Apr. 1995, p. 73.

[50] 'Belarus suspends START I withdrawals', *Nuclear Proliferation News*, no. 30 (7 Aug. 1995), p. 6; and 'Lukashenko on suspending withdrawal of nuclear weapons', Minsk Interfax-West, 24 July 1995, in FBIS-SOV-95-142, 25 July 1995, p. 64.

[51] The fate of the nuclear warheads is unclear. However, US officials suggested that their transfer to Russia may have been completed. Enginsoy, U., 'Belarus hold Russian nukes', *Defense News*, vol. 10, no. 33 (21–27 Aug. 1995), pp. 1, 28.

[52] Markus, U., 'Belarusan disarmament update', *OMRI Daily Digest*, vol. 1, no. 152 (7 Aug. 1995).

[53] START II does not limit the number of nuclear warheads held in inactive stockpiles. The US Department of Defense reportedly plans to maintain an additional 2500 nuclear warheads as a hedge

US ratification

In the United States, President Bush submitted the START II Treaty to the Senate for its advice and consent on 15 January 1993. The Senate moved promptly to consider ratification of the treaty, with the Foreign Relations Committee initiating hearings in May 1993, involving President Bill Clinton and former Bush Administration officials. However, the hearings there and in the Armed Services and Intelligence committees were suspended in August 1993 because of the diplomatic impasse over the future nuclear weapon status of Ukraine that was blocking entry into force of the START I Treaty.[54]

With the accession of Ukraine to the NPT as a non-nuclear weapon state and the subsequent entry into force of the START I Treaty in December 1994, the US Senate again took up its consideration of START II ratification. The Foreign Relations Committee completed its hearings in March 1995, followed by the Armed Services Committee in May. Little opposition to the treaty was voiced in the hearings, and the testimony given by most government officials and independent experts strongly endorsed its ratification.[55]

Senate action on the treaty was stymied, however, by the legislative logjam created at the end of April by the chairman of the Foreign Relations Committee, Senator Jesse Helms. Asserting his chairmanship prerogatives, Helms halted all action in the committee in order to compel the Clinton Administration to accept passage of legislation to reorganize parts of the US foreign affairs bureaucracy.[56] On 5 September 1995 the Senate adopted with strong bipartisan support a non-binding 'sense of the Senate' resolution expressing its view that it should 'promptly consider giving its advice and consent to ratification of the START II Treaty and the Chemical Weapons Convention'.[57] This view was immediately echoed by President Clinton, who urged the Senate to complete its deliberations as soon as possible.[58] After intensive bargaining, Helms announced in December that he would accept a compromise reorganization plan.[59]

The agreement between Helms and senior Democrats in the Senate ended the impasse that had halted action in the Foreign Relations Committee and

against potential nuclear threats. Hitchens, T., 'Study: US underestimates nuclear arsenal numbers, cost', *Defense News*, vol. 10, no. 29 (17–23 July 1995), p. 14.

[54] The entry into force of the START I Treaty was a precondition for the START II Treaty to be able to come into force, since all the START I provisions—including the verification regime—apply to START II (except for specific modifications, such as for the bomber counting rules). Lockwood (note 27), pp. 556–59.

[55] Lockwood, D., 'DOD officials endorse START II during final Senate hearing', *Arms Control Today*, vol. 25, no. 5 (June 1995), pp. 27–29.

[56] The impasse in the Senate also blocked final hearings on the ratification of the Chemical Weapons Convention. Keeny, S., 'Holding US security hostage', *Arms Control Today*, vol. 25, no. 8 (Oct. 1995), p. 2; and Lippman, T., 'Head-on collision on weapons pact', *International Herald Tribune*, 14 Nov. 1995, p. 2.

[57] *Congressional Record*, 5 Sep. 1995, p. S12619.

[58] 'President urges Senate to ratify START II, CWC treaties', *Wireless File* (United States Information Service, US Embassy: Stockholm, 6 Sep. 1995), p. 11.

[59] Doherty, C., 'Helms in deal to end freeze on arms pact, nominees', *Congressional Quarterly*, vol. 53, no. 48 (9 Dec. 1995), p. 3753; and 'Helms gives ground', *International Herald Tribune*, 18 Dec. 1995, p. 8.

paved the way for a vote on START II ratification. As expected, the treaty won the overwhelming endorsement of the Senate. On 26 January 1996, it was approved by a vote of 87 to 4.[60]

Russian ratification proceedings

In Russia, President Yeltsin submitted the START II Treaty to the Supreme Soviet for ratification on 9 February 1993. Before it was able to take action on the treaty, however, the Soviet-era legislature was dissolved in the constitutional crisis in the autumn of 1993. Yeltsin did not promptly re-submit the treaty to the new parliament elected in December 1993 because of Ukraine's dilatory behaviour in honouring its denuclearization pledges; its submission was further delayed by the pressing economic and political problems that were occupying the Duma, including the crisis in Chechnya. Against the background of a growing nationalist backlash against the treaty among parliamentary deputies, Yeltsin submitted START II to the Duma on 20 June 1995. He also designated Defence Minister Pavel Grachev and then Foreign Minister Andrey Kozyrev as his official representatives in the parliamentary debates on ratification.[61]

Under the provisions of the Russian Constitution approved in December 1993, treaty ratification requires a simple majority vote in both the lower (Duma) and upper (Federation Council) houses of parliament; some observers believe that the Federation Council is likely to defer to the deliberations of the Duma with regard to START II ratification.[62] Within the Duma, the International Affairs Committee, assisted by the Defence Committee, are the principal parliamentary bodies responsible for considering START II ratification. The Duma has appointed Vladimir Lukin, chairman of the International Affairs Committee, to oversee the ratification proceedings.[63]

Hearings in the Duma began on 11 July 1995, when the two committees convened a joint closed-door session to receive testimony from government officials, military officers and defence industry representatives. The confidential testimony is reported to have generally favoured ratification of the treaty, albeit with a number of important conditions.[64] The committees held an open

---

[60] 'US Senate ratifies START II as Congress loiters on ABM brink', *Disarmament Diplomacy*, no. 2 (Feb. 1996); and 'Clinton, Christopher welcome "historic" Senate START II vote', *European Wireless File* (United States Information Agency: Washington, DC, 30 Jan. 1996). Version current on 2 Feb. 1996, URL <gopher://pubgopher.srce.hr:70//11/usis/casopisi/wf>.

[61] 'START II representatives named', Moscow Interfax (in Russian), 27 June 1995, in FBIS-SOV-95-124, 28 June 1995, p. 10.

[62] Lepingwell, J., 'START II and the politics of arms control in Russia', *International Security*, vol. 20, no. 2 (fall 1995), p. 78.

[63] Nazarkin, Y. and Jones, R., 'Moscow's START II ratification: problems and prospects', *Arms Control Today*, vol. 25, no. 7 (Sep. 1995), pp. 8–9.

[64] Zhuravlev, P., 'START II Treaty submitted for ratification', *Segodnya*, 13 July 1995, p. 2, in FBIS-SOV-95-134, 13 July 1995, pp. 34–35; and 'Duma begins hearings on START II Treaty', *OMRI Daily Digest*, vol. 1, no. 136 (14 July 1995).

hearing on 18 July in which government officials also supported treaty ratification.[65]

On 17 October the committees convened a closed-door hearing to examine the financial and economic implications of START II ratification. The hearing reportedly revealed intensified opposition to several key treaty provisions and underscored the extent to which ratification had become linked to broader Russian security policy concerns.[66] It also highlighted a growing complaint among deputies that the Yeltsin Government was seeking to push START II through the legislature without first preparing a document similar to the USA's 1994 Nuclear Posture Review, explaining the impact of the treaty on Russia's strategic nuclear deterrence capabilities.[67]

No further legislative action on the treaty was taken before the parliamentary elections held in December, in which former communist and anti-Western nationalist factions made significant gains in the Duma. In the wake of the elections, even proponents of START II considered the prospects for its ratification to have diminished.[68] However, it continued to be backed by the senior military leadership and key political figures, albeit with some reservations,[69] and its fate in the Duma was by no means sealed as 1996 began.

START II and Russian security concerns

The START II Treaty has been a source of controversy among Russian parliamentarians, independent experts and newspaper editorial writers since it was signed in 1993 and has to some extent become a hostage to the vicissitudes of post-Soviet domestic politics. The ratification proceedings have served to crystallize opposition to the general direction of Russian foreign policy under President Yeltsin and former Foreign Minister Kozyrev.[70]

In addition, broader Russian security policy concerns not directly connected with the merits of the treaty itself have increasingly entered into the START II debate. Mounting tensions in Russia's relations with the United States have diminished the prospects for ratification by creating an atmosphere of suspicion and mistrust.[71] In this regard, the treaty's greatest vulnerability in the Duma derives from Russian concerns about the scale and pace of current US ballistic missile defence (BMD) programmes, which are perceived as under-

[65] 'Foreign Ministry, military favor START II ratification', Moscow Interfax, 18 July 1995, in FBIS-SOV-95-138, 18 July 1995, p. 6.

[66] Spector, L., 'START II ratification in Russia', Nuclear Non-proliferation Network Bulletin Board (CompuServe), 23 Oct. 1995, message no. 1334.

[67] Konovalov, A., Korshunov, S. and Oznobishchev, S., 'Twilight of arms control', Nezavisimaya Gazeta, 26 Oct. 1995, pp. 1, 5, in FBIS-SOV-95-212, 2 Nov. 1995, p. 40.

[68] Associated Press, 'Russians question nuclear treaty', International Herald Tribune, 30 Jan. 1996, p. 7.

[69] Hitchens, T. and Zhigulsky, A., 'Russia may fail to ratify START II by April deadline', Defense News, vol. 11, no. 5 (5–11 Feb. 1996), p. 16.

[70] Sorokin, K., 'Russia after the crisis: the nuclear strategy debate', Orbis, vol. 38, no. 1 (winter 1994), pp. 19–40; see also Arbatov, A. (ed.), Implications of the START II Treaty for US–Russian Relations, Report no. 9 (Henry L. Stimson Center: Washington, DC, 1993).

[71] Golts, A., 'Crisis of confidence threatens START II', Krasnaya Zvezda, 20 July 1995, p. 3, in FBIS-SOV-95-140, 21 July 1995, pp. 5–6.

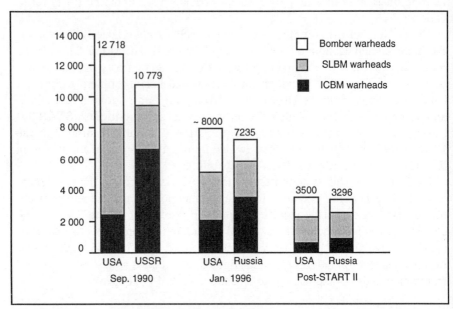

Figure 14.1. US and Soviet/Russian strategic nuclear forces: 1990, 1996 and after implementation of the START II Treaty

Note: ICBM and SLBM warhead attributions are based on the START I Treaty Memorandum of Understanding. Bomber loadings are based on the START II Treaty Memorandum of Understanding. Figures for Jan. 1996 do not include strategic nuclear delivery systems which have been deactivated or retired although they remain treaty-accountable according to the START counting rules.

Strategic nuclear forces September 1990

US delivery vehicles

ICBMs: 450 Minuteman IIs; 500 Minuteman IIIs; 50 Peacekeepers (MX).
SLBMs: 192 Poseidon (C-3); 384 Trident Is (C-4); 96 Trident IIs (D-5).
Bombers: 66 B-52Gs; 95 B-52Hs; 97 B-1Bs.

Russian delivery vehicles

ICBMs: 326 SS-11s; 40 SS-13s; 188 SS-17s; 308 SS-18s; 300 SS-19s; 56 SS-24s (silo-based); 33 SS-24s (rail-mobile); 288 SS-25s (road-mobile).
SLBMs: 192 SS-N-6; 280 SS-N-8; 12 SS-N-17; 224 SS-N-18s; 120 SS-N-20s; 112 SS-N-23s.
Bombers: 17 Tu-95 Bear A/B; 46 Tu-95 Bear G; 57 Tu-95 Bear-Hs (equipped to carry 16 nuclear cruise missiles each); 27 Tu-95 Bear-Hs (equipped to carry six nuclear cruise missiles each); 15 Tu-160 Blackjacks.

Current strategic nuclear forces, January 1996

US delivery vehicles

ICBMs: 525 Minuteman IIIs; 50 Peacekeepers (MX).
SLBMs: 192 Trident Is (C-4); 192 Trident IIs (D-5).
Bombers: 76 B-52Hs; 82 B-1Bs; 8 B-2s.

Russian delivery vehicles

ICBMs: 186 SS-18s; 150 SS-19s; 10 SS-24s (silo-based); 36 SS-24s (rail-mobile); 345 SS-25s (road-mobile).

SLBMs: 208 SS-N-18s; 120 SS-N-20s; 112 SS-N-23s.

Bombers: 57 Tu-95 Bear-HS (equipped to carry 16 nuclear cruise missiles each); 31 Tu-95 Bear-Hs (equipped to carry 6 nuclear cruise missiles each); 25 Tu-160 Blackjacks.

Post-START II strategic nuclear forces, projected*

US delivery vehicles

ICBMs: 450/500 Minuteman IIIs downloaded to 1 warhead each.

SLBMs: 336 Trident IIs (D-5) downloaded to 5 warheads each.

Bombers: 32 B-52Hs (equipped to carry 20 ALCMs/ACMs each); 30 B-52Hs (equipped to carry 12 ALCMs/ACMs each); 20 B-2s.

Russian delivery vehicles

ICBMs: 605 SS-25s (road-mobile); 90 SS-25s based in converted SS-18 silos); 105 SS-19s downloaded to 1 warhead each.

SLBMs: 176 SS-N-18s; 120 SS-N-20s downloaded to 6 warheads each; 112 SS-N-23s.

Bombers: 35 Tu-95 Bear-Hs (equipped to carry 16 nuclear cruise missiles each); 20 Tu-95 Bear-Hs (equipped to carry 6 nuclear cruise missiles each); 10 Tu-160 Blackjacks.

* Assumptions for Russian strategic forces under START I and START II:

ICBMs: It is assumed that Russia will give its Strategic Rocket Forces enough priority to find sufficient economic resources eventually to build and deploy 700 SS-25s (road-mobile and silo-based) and/or a road-mobile follow-on. If fewer ICBMs are deployed more SSBNs could be retained for the force still to reach 3500 warheads, if that figure remains a goal. If more ICBMs are deployed fewer SSBNs could be retained.

SLBMs: Admiral Felix Gromov, Commander-in-Chief of the Russian Navy, indicated in 1993 that Russia plans to retain 176 SS-N-18 SLBMs on 11 Delta III submarines. The US Director of Naval Intelligence stated that the future SSBN force will consist of 24 submarines.

Bombers: An agreement announced at the end of Nov. calls for Ukraine to eventually return the 19 Blackjack bombers, 25 Bear bombers and more than 300 cruise missiles to Russia. The precise timing of the transfer was not made public. It is assumed that not all the bombers will return to service.

Sources: *For US forces*: START I Treaty Memorandum of Understanding, Sep. 1990; START I Treaty Memorandum of Understanding, 5 Dec. 1994; START I Treaty Memorandum of Understanding, 1 July 1995; Senate Committee on Foreign Relations, START II Treaty, Executive Report 104–10, 15 Dec. 1995; William J. Perry, Secretary of Defense, *Annual Report to the President and the Congress*, Mar. 1996, pp. 213–18; William J. Perry, Secretary of Defense, *Annual Report to the President and the Congress*, Feb. 1995, pp. 87–88; US Air Force Public Affairs, personal communications; *Bulletin of the Atomic Scientists*; Natural Resources Defense Council (NRDC); and authors' estimates.

For Russian forces: Arbatov, A. (ed.), *Implications of the START II Treaty for US–Russian Relations* (Henry L. Stimson Center: Washington, DC, 1993), p. 6; Sorokin, K. E., 'The Nuclear Strategy Debate', *Orbis* , vol. 38, no. 1 (winter 1994), pp. 19–40; Statement of Ted Warner, Senior Defense Analyst, RAND Corporation, before the Senate Foreign Relations Committee, 3 Mar, 1992, as cited in *The START Treaty*, Senate Hearing 102–607, Part 1 (US Government Printing Office: Washington, DC, 1992), pp. 228–29; START I Treaty Memorandum of Understanding, Sep. 1990; Gromov, F., 'Reforming the Russian Navy', *Naval Forces,* vol. 14, no. 4 (1993), p. 10; Office of Naval Intelligence, Director of Naval Intelligence Posture Statement (June 1994), p. 13; and authors' estimates.

mining the ABM Treaty as a cornerstone of strategic stability.[72] Parliamentarians and defence officials have unambiguously linked the outcome of the START II debate with continued US adherence to the provisions of the ABM Treaty.[73] Russian critics of the Clinton Administration's proposals to clarify the scope of the ABM Treaty to permit the development of a new generation of advanced-capability theatre missile defence systems argue that the acceptance of these proposals will create a loophole in the treaty that will effectively render it a dead letter. In his 20 June letter transmitting the START II Treaty to the Duma, President Yeltsin emphasized that the treaty 'can be fulfilled only provided the United States preserves and strictly complies with the bilateral ABM Treaty'.[74]

The US Senate's approval in September 1995 of an amendment to the 1996 defence authorization bill requiring the United States to 'develop for deployment' by the year 2003 a multi-site nationwide missile defence system raised particular concern in Moscow; such a system is seen as being gravely destabilizing for the US–Russian strategic balance in a post-START world of reduced nuclear arsenals.[75] As one Russian analyst has pointed out, military planners in Russia interpreted the Senate's 'develop for deployment' formula essentially to mean 'develop and deploy'.[76] One obvious option for countering an anticipated US deployment of a nationwide missile defence system would be for Russia to halt its nuclear arms reductions mandated by the START I Treaty and to retain the MIRVed land-based ICBMs, especially the 'heavy' SS-18 missiles, scheduled for elimination under the terms of START II.

In the course of the Duma ratification debate, the START II Treaty also became entangled with another highly contentious security policy issue—that of NATO enlargement.[77] Western proposals to extend NATO membership to the former Warsaw Pact member states of Central and Eastern Europe have aroused opposition across the political spectrum in Moscow. Within the Duma, the issue of NATO enlargement contributed to the unleashing of a nationalist backlash that has considerably undermined support for START II ratification. Assessing the prospects for securing the Duma's approval of the treaty, Lukin warned that 'it would be harder to get approval of the deal at a

[72] See section V below. For further discussion, see Arbatov, A., 'The ABM Treaty and theatre missile defence', *SIPRI Yearbook 1995* (note 6), pp. 681–717.

[73] In conjunction with the ratification hearings, Russia's Deputy Foreign Minister Georgiy Mamedov told the Duma on 18 July that 'if the US does not strictly adhere to the ABM Treaty . . . there can be no question of ratification'. Quoted in 'Duma wary of START II as Congress nears ABM crossroads and US and Russian negotiators struggle on', *Nuclear Proliferation News*, no. 30 (7 Aug. 1995), pp. 5–6.

[74] Quoted in Nazarkin and Jones (note 63), p. 11.

[75] Keeny, S., 'Compromise meriting a veto', *Arms Control Today*, vol. 25, no. 7 (Sep. 1995), p. 2; and Nadein, V., 'US Senate deals blow to missile equilibrium', *Izvestia*, 5 Aug. 1995, p. 3, in FBIS-SOV-95-152, 8 Aug. 1995, pp. 6–7.

[76] Nazarkin, Y., 'START II hangs in the balance', *Defense News*, vol. 10, no. 44 (6–12 Nov. 1995), p. 19.

[77] Reuter, 'Russia links pacts to NATO expansion', *International Herald Tribune*, 5 Jan. 1996, p. 5. According to one Russian observer, some parliamentary deputies envision a deal 'swapping ratification of the START II Treaty for a promise concerning the nonenlargement of NATO'. Fedorov, Y., 'What is behind the bargaining over START II?', *Moskovskie Novosti*, no. 42 (25 June–2 July 1995), p. 14, in FBIS-SOV-95-145-S, 28 July 1995, pp. 1–2. See also chapter 7 in this volume.

time when our former allies are being unilaterally turned into NATO members despite our warnings that this is unacceptable to Russia'.[78]

Criticism of START II in Russia

Critics of the START II Treaty in Russia have raised a number of technical and budgetary concerns about the treaty's provisions, arguing that they are inequitable for Russia and disproportionately benefit the USA. While a final decision is likely to be made on the basis of prevailing political sentiments, these concerns do carry significant weight in the START II ratification debate and have led to calls from some parliamentarians and defence experts to incorporate modifications into the treaty as binding ratification conditions.

One of the principal complaints is that START II requires Russia to eliminate the most powerful and important component of its strategic nuclear forces—multiple-warhead land-based ballistic missiles—while allowing the United States to retain the most formidable component of its 'triad' of strategic forces—the Trident SLBM. Although some critics acknowledge that the elimination of MIRVed ICBMs can promote a more stable strategic nuclear balance, they complain that doing so requires Russia to undertake a costly, long-term restructuring of the composition of its strategic forces that it can scarcely afford.[79] In contrast, the USA can preserve most of its present forces, including the air- and sea-based weapons in which it enjoys a comparative technological advantage.[80]

A related argument of START II critics is that Russia bears a disproportionate cost burden in implementing the treaty—one that is prohibitive in the light of the poor state of the Russian economy. They argue that, even with financial assistance to expedite the disarmament process, Russia must still spend substantial sums of money to safely dismantle the large numbers of land- and sea-based ballistic missile systems scheduled for elimination under the treaty. In addition, Russia will have to invest scarce budgetary resources to develop and procure hundreds of new single-warhead ICBMs if it intends to maintain a rough numerical parity with the USA's strategic forces.[81]

Proponents of ratification point out, however, that Russia in any case cannot afford to maintain many of the ballistic missiles scheduled for elimination

---

[78] Quoted in Zhigulsky, A., 'START 2 opposition mounts', *Defense News*, vol. 10, no. 20 (22–28 May 1995), p. 18.

[79] Based on START I force loading attributions, in Dec. 1994 approximately 65% of Russia's deliverable strategic nuclear warheads were deployed on ICBMs. Russia's post-START II force plans call for more than half of its deliverable warheads to be deployed on submarine-launched ballistic missiles. However, according to a senior Russian Navy officer, recent funding shortfalls threaten to drastically reduce the Navy's strategic nuclear submarine fleet. Gavrilenko, A., '"Typhoon" almost lost from sight behind barrage of decisions', *Krasnaya Zvezda*, 26 July 1995, p. 1, in FBIS-SOV-95-145, 28 July 1995, pp. 31–33.

[80] A confidential report circulating in the Duma reportedly recommends that START II be ratified only if amended to permit Russia to retain some land-based MIRVed ICBMs. Parrish, S., 'Duma report recommends START II revisions', *OMRI Daily Digest*, vol. 1, no. 209 (26 Oct. 1995).

[81] Russia has halted production of heavy bombers and is not expected to produce new ballistic missile-launching submarines this decade. A follow-on ICBM to the single-warhead SS-25, the Topol M (RS-12M), is expected to form the backbone of the Strategic Rocket Forces by the year 2005. 'Russia tests home-grown version of SS-25 ICBM', *Arms Control Today*, vol. 25, no. 1 (Jan./Feb. 1995), p. 27.

under START II, despite the high priority given to the strategic forces in the defence budget.[82] Duma Speaker Gennadiy Seleznev predicted in early January 1996 that many of his fellow communist deputies would reluctantly support the treaty because Russia 'simply [does] not have the economic means' to maintain current strategic nuclear force levels.[83] Proponents also point out that Russia's strategic nuclear arsenal is set to decline regardless of the outcome of the START II debate, since the country will not be able to afford to keep force levels at even the reduced START I ceilings.[84] In this regard, they claim, START II ratification actually works to Russia's advantage, since it mandates equally deep cuts in the US strategic nuclear forces.[85]

While conceding that START II will impose significant cuts in US forces, a number of Russian critics argue that the key problem lies in the fact that the treaty, at least in its present form, leaves open a worrying possibility of US circumvention.[86] They complain that START II requires Russia to dismantle all its MIRVed ICBMs—in particular, its 10-warhead SS-18 missiles—while allowing the USA to 'download' and retain all its Minuteman III ICBMs and highly accurate, long-range Trident II SLBMs. Since the treaty's downloading provisions do not require the destruction of the missile 'bus', or platform, upon which nuclear warheads are loaded on a ballistic missile, START II thereby places the USA in a better position than Russia to stage a rapid 'break-out' from the treaty regime and achieve a strategically significant advantage in the number of deployed warheads.[87] In a similar vein, critics of the treaty charge that the US Air Force could easily 'switch labels' on its modern B-1B bombers and restore them to their original strategic nuclear mission.[88]

[82] Koretskiy, A., 'START II hearings: cuts are in order because there are no maintenance funds', *Kommersant Daily*, 20 July 1995, p. 4, in FBIS-SOV-95-139, pp. 4–5. Both the SS-18 and SS-24 ICBMs were manufactured at Dnepropetrovsk in Ukraine; the cost of building a new factory complex in Russia to recondition existing missiles or to manufacture new ones is deemed to be prohibitively high.

[83] 'Seleznev endorses START II Treaty', *OMRI Daily Digest,* vol. 1, no. 32 (14 Feb. 1996). Seleznev added, however, that an enlargement of NATO or a US withdrawal from the ABM Treaty would kill any chance of ratification by the Duma.

[84] Senior Russian military officials have repeatedly warned that the lack of financing will adversely affect the readiness levels and service lives of the strategic forces. See, e.g., the interview with Col.-Gen. Viktor Yesin, Chief of Staff of the Strategic Rocket Forces, in Dolinin, A., 'Nuclear missile parity is an outmoded concept', *Krasnaya Zvezda*, 2 Sep. 1995, p. 4, in FBIS-SOV-95-172, 6 Sep. 1995, pp. 33–34. One US analyst has projected that current trends in defence spending mean that in the next decade the Russian strategic forces are likely to deploy fewer strategic nuclear warheads—possibly as few as 1300—than permitted under the START II limits. Handler, J., 'The future of the Russian strategic forces', *Jane's Intelligence Review*, vol. 7, no. 4 (Apr. 1995), pp. 162–65.

[85] Golts, A., 'Why Russia has let its nuclear arsenal go for soap and sausage', *Komsomolskaya Pravda,* 5 Sep. 1995, p. 7, in FBIS-SOV-95-175, 11 Sep. 1995, pp. 38–39.

[86] See, e.g., Obolensky, G., 'START II: who will have to reduce the missiles?', *Krasnaya Zvezda*, 25 July 1995, p. 3, in FBIS-SOV-95-145, 28 July 1995, pp. 1–2.

[87] In announcing the results of the Pentagon's Nuclear Posture Review in Sep. 1994 (see below), the US Secretary of Defense stressed that the USA intended to retain the flexibility to reconstitute its strategic nuclear forces by rapidly 'uploading' warheads on land- and sea-based ballistic missiles. Transcript of press conference remarks by Secretary of Defense William J. Perry, Office of Assistant Secretary of Defense for Public Affairs, News release no. 546-94, 22 Sep. 1994.

[88] Nazarkin and Jones (note 63), pp. 11–12; and Bluth (note 40).

Support for START II in Russia

While senior military officials and members of the Yeltsin Government have acknowledged shortcomings in the START II Treaty, they have not set out to comprehensively overhaul—and thereby possibly derail—the accord, which they see as on balance enhancing Russia's security interests. They contend that many of the treaty's problems can be remedied through adjustments in implementation after its entry into force. For example, the deadline for the completion of the treaty's final reductions could be extended beyond the year 2003 to ease the financial burden on Russia.[89]

Russian proponents of ratification point out that START II promises to create a more transparent and stable strategic environment that leaves Russia with a still highly robust nuclear deterrent to potential aggression. Moreover, it offers long-term defence budget savings, consistent with Russia's strategic force planning goals and the potential of Russia's military industries. It also reduces by 50 per cent the number of SLBM warheads the USA planned to deploy under START I and contains new bomber counting rules that will sharply reduce the USA's advantage in the number of deployed strategic nuclear warheads permitted by the treaty. However, against the background of increasingly assertive nationalist sentiment in the parliament and the general souring of US–Russian relations, particularly over the issue of ballistic missile defences and NATO enlargement, even supporters of START II concede that they face an uphill struggle in the ratification proceedings.

Beyond START II?

Despite the START II Treaty's uncertain prospects in the Duma, senior Russian Government officials have given serious consideration to a follow-on treaty that would further reduce nuclear arsenals. In a 26 September 1994 speech delivered before the UN General Assembly, President Yeltsin broached the idea of taking further steps to limit strategic nuclear weapons, proposing a 'treaty on nuclear security and strategic stability' among the nuclear weapon states aimed at reducing the number of warheads and delivery vehicles in their arsenals.[90] The idea of making deeper cuts, beyond those mandated by START II, has been an appealing one in Moscow because it goes some way towards solving Russian force structure problems arising from the severe constraints on defence resources—in particular, the costly challenge of modernizing its strategic forces in order to maintain numerical parity with those of the USA.[91] However, in the light of the perceived threat posed to the

---

[89] The START II Treaty provides for interim reductions to be accomplished 7 years after the entry into force of START I. This means that these interim reductions must be made by 5 Dec. 2001, leaving only 1 year to complete all remaining START II reductions before the 1 Jan. 2003 deadline.

[90] UN General Assembly document A/48/PV.5, 26 Sep. 1994.

[91] Nazarkin and Jones (note 63), p. 14. The deputy chief of the Naval Operations Directorate, Rear Admiral Aleksey Ovcharenko, proposed that Russia and the USA agree to cut their respective strategic forces to half the START II levels, arguing that doing so 'would make it possible to abandon the development of a number of expensive strike systems and to work for the long-term future'. Gavrilenko (note 79), p. 32.

integrity of the ABM Treaty by US theatre missile defence programmes, Russian officials have adopted an increasingly negative attitude to making deeper nuclear arms reductions.

Proposals for further cuts in strategic nuclear forces have received only a tepid welcome from Clinton Administration officials. This reticence reflects in part the Administration's preoccupation with securing the ratification of START II rather than with moving beyond the treaty. It also reflects the conservative 'lead but hedge' force planning guidelines contained in the Pentagon's September 1994 Nuclear Posture Review (NPR), a comprehensive review which established strategic and tactical nuclear force levels to the year 2003. While setting out modest cuts in US warhead requirements, the NPR slowed the political momentum towards further arms reductions and preserved the option of undertaking a future build-up 'in the event of a reversal of reform in Russia'.[92]

Despite the souring of US–Russian relations, the Clinton Administration has not ruled out a START III Treaty. At their May 1995 summit meeting in Moscow Presidents Yeltsin and Clinton reaffirmed their desire to 'begin discussions' on nuclear arms reductions beyond those mandated by START II.[93] Senior Pentagon officials have emphasized, however, that any discussions of further reductions are predicated upon the assumption that START I and START II will be fully implemented.[94]

V. Cooperative threat reduction

The Nunn–Lugar programme

Alarmed by the spectre of 'loose nukes' finding their way out of the disintegrating USSR and into the hands of rogue states or terrorist organizations, in November 1991 Congress approved the Soviet Nuclear Threat Reduction Act.[95] Known as the 'Nunn–Lugar programme' after its sponsors, Senators Richard Lugar and Sam Nunn, this legislation provided for the transfer of up to $400 million from the fiscal year (FY) 1992 Defense Department budget to facilitate the 'transportation, storage, safeguarding, and destruction of nuclear and other weapons in the Soviet Union . . . and to assist in the prevention of weapons proliferation'.[96] In October 1992 Congress approved the transfer of an additional $400 million under the Former Soviet Union Demilitarization Act. Together, these initiatives established a cooperative arms control forum, known as the Safe and Secure Dismantlement (SSD) Talks, to facilitate bilat-

---

[92] Perry (note 87).

[93] Slocombe (note 31).

[94] Perry (note 34).

[95] For a highly influential report examining the nuclear weapon-related dangers attending the breakup of the Soviet Union, see Campbell, K. *et al.* (eds), *Soviet Nuclear Fission*, CSIA Studies in International Security no. 1 (Center for Science and International Affairs, John F. Kennedy School of Government, Harvard University: Cambridge, Mass., 1991).

[96] *Congressional Record*, 27 Nov. 1991, S18798, cited in Lockwood (note 24), pp. 665–66.

eral US assistance to Belarus, Russia, Kazakhstan and Ukraine for their denu-clearization activities.[97]

In 1993 Congress approved the Cooperative Threat Reduction Act, which expanded the objectives of the Nunn–Lugar programme beyond consolidating the former Soviet nuclear weapon arsenal in Russia and ensuring its custodial safety. The Cooperative Threat Reduction (CTR) programme encompasses a wider range of non-proliferation and demilitarization activities, which are focused primarily on dismantling strategic weapons and associated infra-structure; they are also broadly aimed at stabilizing the former Soviet Union's nuclear weapon design and manufacturing complex and converting it, where feasible, to non-military pursuits.

The CTR programme has come under fire from critics in the former Soviet republics as early and sometimes exaggerated expectations about its results have been disappointed. One of the principal complaints is about the slow progress made in implementing many CTR projects. In addition, political sup-port for the programme has dwindled in the former Soviet republics as the economic and social problems arising from the demilitarization of their nascent market economies continue to mount.[98]

In the USA, the political mood in the Republican-controlled US Congress turned increasingly against the Nunn–Lugar programme in 1995. Critics complained about the executive branch's slow pace in obligating and dis-bursing the money appropriated for projects. Some Republican lawmakers in the House also voiced concern that the scope of the programme had become too wide, with Pentagon money being spent on 'non-defence' projects, such as housing for demobilized Strategic Rocket Forces troops and the conversion of military industries, that are not directly related to weapon dismantlement and destruction activities.[99] As a sign of its waning support for the programme, Congress voted to provide only $300 million in Nunn–Lugar funding for FY 1996 compared with the Clinton Administration's $371 million request.[100]

In response to these criticisms, supporters of the Nunn–Lugar programme argue that its technological and financial assistance has been instrumental in helping Russia and the other former Soviet republics to overcome obstacles to meeting their disarmament obligations. They also point out that many of the delays occurred in the initial definition and negotiation phase of a complex programme; the programme is now shifting to an implementation phase, and the pace of its provision of assistance is accelerating.[101]

[97] Goodby, Kile and Müller (note 29), pp. 645–47.
[98] Shields, J., 'Conference findings on the Nunn–Lugar Cooperative Threat Reduction program: donor and recipient country perspectives', *Nonproliferation Review*, vol. 3, no. 1 (autumn 1995), pp. 66–75.
[99] Erlich, J., 'Nunn–Lugar may survive scrutiny from GOP', *Defense News*, vol. 10, no. 1 (9–15 Jan. 1995), p. 6; and Hiat, F., 'Progress slight in program to destroy Soviet nuclear arms', *International Herald Tribune*, 13 Feb. 1995, p. 5. Support for the Nunn–Lugar programme has also been eroded by the tendency of many legislators to consider it a form of foreign aid, which is generally unpopular in Congress.
[100] Towell, P., 'Bill with troops' pay raise clears; veto likely over missile policy', *Congressional Quarterly*, vol. 53, no. 50 (23 Dec. 1995), p. 3900.
[101] See, e.g., Lockwood, D., 'The Nunn–Lugar program: no time to pull the plug', *Arms Control Today*, vol. 25, no. 5 (June 1995), pp. 9–10; and Goodby, Kile and Müller (note 29), pp. 646–47.

Table 14.8. US Cooperative Threat Reduction programme: summary of assistance as of 31 December 1995

Figures are in US $m.

Programme area name	Notified	Obligated
Chain of custody	357.1	272.7
Demilitarization	226.7	225.1
Destruction and dismantlement	567.0	382.0
Other programme support[a]	85.4	59.6
Total	**1 236.2**	**939.4**

[a] Includes funds obligated for non-agreement assistance, e.g., Defense and Military Contacts, Defense Enterprise Fund, Arctic Nuclear Waste and Other Assessments/Administration Costs.

Source: US Department of Defense.

A June 1995 report issued by the US General Accounting Office (GAO) supported this latter claim, stating that the Pentagon has made considerable progress in obligating and disbursing CTR funds, as well as in enhancing CTR programme planning, since the last review in June 1994. The GAO report noted that the amount of obligated funds had more than doubled between June 1994 and May 1995 and that disbursements had more than tripled over the same period. The GAO report also noted that the Pentagon had made progress in conducting audits to ensure that CTR aid was being used for the purposes intended. In addition, the CTR programme had been streamlined by the transfer of nine projects from the Department of Defense to the Departments of State, Energy and Commerce, beginning in FY 1996.[102]

Implementation of CTR programmes

As shown in table 14.8, Cooperative Threat Reduction programme assistance falls into three general categories of activity: chain of custody; weapon destruction and dismantlement; and demilitarization. By the end of the year the USA had committed nearly $1.25 billion to the support of CTR programmes in Belarus, Kazakhstan, Russia and Ukraine. Table 14.9 summarizes the status of the programme assistance.

Dismantlement and destruction

In FY 1995 the largest share of CTR programme assistance was earmarked for the dismantlement and destruction of strategic nuclear delivery vehicles and their associated launchers.[103] Nunn–Lugar money has supported the procure-

[102] General Accounting Office, *Weapons of Mass Destruction: Reducing the Threat from the Former Soviet Union—an Update* (GAO/NSIAD-95-165), 9 June 1995, pp. 10–12.

[103] Cooperative Threat Reduction Program: Summary of Obligations and Disbursements by Country/Project, Assistant to the Secretary of Defense, Office of Cooperative Threat Reduction, 6 Nov. 1995.

ment of US-made equipment, such as mobile cranes, excavators, plasma cutters and shears, for use in the dismantlement and elimination of ICBM silos, SLBM tubes and heavy bombers. It also has been obligated to assist Russia in developing suitable technologies for chemical weapon dismantlement as well as to establish a government-to-government communications link to report progress in implementing the START I Treaty.[104]

Over the course of 1995 the Pentagon increased Nunn–Lugar funding for projects to facilitate the dismantlement and destruction of strategic nuclear weapons. On 1 April 1995 the USA and Ukraine amended a 1993 agreement to provide up to an additional $20 million in US assistance for the elimination of SS-19 and SS-24 ICBMs and their silos located in Ukraine. This amendment increased to $205 million the agreed CTR programme assistance to Ukraine for eliminating ICBMs and silos and disposing of highly toxic liquid rocket propellant.[105] Earlier programme assistance facilitated the removal of warheads from missiles and their return to Russia. On 3 April 1995 the USA and Russia signed an amendment adding up to $20 million to the previously agreed $130 million in CTR assistance to expedite the dismantlement of land- and sea-based ballistic missiles and their launchers.[106] According to Russian officials, the transport and disposition of liquid rocket fuel was one of the worst bottlenecks in the dismantlement process.[107] On 28 June 1995 the USA and Russia signed an agreement earmarking an additional $12 million for dismantlement and destruction projects.[108]

Chain of custody

By the end of 1995, $357 million had been included in agreements for fissile material physical control and accounting (MPC&A), export controls, weapon transport and storage security, and nuclear reactor safety. On 3 April 1995 Russian Defence Minister Grachev and US Secretary of Defense Perry signed an agreement providing $17 million for diagnostic railcars to assess conditions of railway tracks and reduce the probability of accidents involving trains transporting nuclear weapons.[109] They also signed an agreement for $3 million in Nunn–Lugar assistance to improve the security of facilities storing nuclear weapons, including enhanced weapon inventory management and tracking systems.[110]

One of the Nunn–Lugar programme's highest priorities is to create an effective MPC&A regime to account for, protect and control fissile material

---

[104] Goodby, Kile and Müller (note 29), pp. 647–48.

[105] 'US assists Ukraine with nuclear weapons dismantlement', Office of Assistant Secretary of Defense for Public Affairs, News release no. 164-95, 1 Apr. 1995.

[106] 'US assists Russia with weapons dismantlement and weapons security', Office of Assistant Secretary of Defense for Public Affairs, News release no. 163-95, 3 Apr. 1995.

[107] General Accounting Office (note 102), p. 13; and Ptichkin, S., 'Asymmetrical poison', *Rossiyskaya Gazeta*, 20 July 1995, p. 3, in FBIS-SOV-95-141, 24 July 1995, pp. 6–7.

[108] 'Gore and Chernomyrdin announce expansion of Nunn–Lugar cooperation', Fact Sheet, Office of the Vice President, 30 June 1995.

[109] The transport of nuclear warheads is considered to be one of the most vulnerable points along the warhead chain of custody.

[110] 'US assists Russia with weapons dismantlement and weapons security' (note 106).

Table 14.9. US Cooperative Threat Reduction programme assistance to Belarus, Kazakhstan, Russia and Ukraine, notified and obligated, as of 31 December 1995

Figures are in US $m.

Agreement	Notified	Obligated
Belarus		
Government to Government Communications Link	2.3	1.0
Defense Enterprise Fund	5.0	5.0
Defense and Military Contacts	7.5	0.5
Emergency Response Training/Equipment	5.0	5.0
Environmental Restoration (Project Peace)	25.0	16.9
Export Control Assistance	16.3	9.6
Industrial Partnerships	20.0	19.6
Material Control and Accountability	3.0	2.6
Strategic Offensive Arms Elimination	16.0	0.1
Science and Technology Centre	5.0	4.9
Total	**105.1**	**65.2**
Kazakhstan		
Government to Government Communications Link	2.3	0.8
Defense Enterprise Fund	7.0	7.0
Defense and Military Contacts	0.9	0.2
Emergency Response Training/Equipment	5.0	2.5
Export Control Assistance	7.3	3.1
Industrial Partnerships	15.0	14.9
Material Control and Accountability	8.0	7.6
Strategic Offensive Arms Elimination	70.0	33.6
Nuclear Infrastructure Elimination	7.0	1.5
Science and Technology Centre	9.0	8.9
Total	**131.5**	**80.1**
Russia		
Defense Enterprise Fund	10.0	10.0
Defense and Military Contacts	11.6	7.2
Emergency Response Training/Equipment	15.0	14.2
Export Control Assistance	2.3	0.6
Industrial Partnerships	38.0	37.3
Material Control and Accountability	45.0	42.6
Strategic Offensive Arms Elimination	162.0	126.6
Science and Technology Centre	35.0	34.9
Security Enhancements for Russian Railcars	21.5	21.5
Fissile Material Containers	50.0	47.8
Fissile Material Storage Facility Design	15.0	15.0
Fissile Material Storage Facility Equipment	75.0	30.6
Weapons Security Storage	5.0	0.6
Weapons Security Transportation	27.0	23.8
Armoured Blankets	5.0	3.2
Chemical Weapons Destruction Assistance	55.0	37.6
Arctic Nuclear Waste	30.0	28.9
Research and Development Foundation	10.0	10.0
Total	**612.4**	**492.4**

Agreement	Notified	Obligated
Ukraine		
Defense and Military Contacts	5.0	1.5
Emergency Response Training/Equipment	5.0	3.1
Export Control Assistance	13.3	6.6
Government to Government Communications Link	2.4	0.7
Industrial Partnerships	50.0	49.8
Material Control and Accountability	22.5	21.6
Multilateral Nuclear Safety Initiative	11.0	11.0
Science and Technology Centre	15.0	14.9
Strategic Nuclear Arms Elimination	215.0	163.1
Nuclear Infrastructure Elimination	10.0	0.0
Total	**349.2**	**272.3**

Source: US Department of Defense.

stockpiles in the former Soviet Union, primarily in Russia. While there have been no verified reports of the theft or diversion of significant amounts of weapon-grade fissile materials, the serious security shortcomings that have been identified at many Russian nuclear facilities have heightened anxiety about nuclear smuggling and led to calls for urgent action.[111] However, as FY 1995 drew to a close, only a small fraction of the money obligated for improving MPC&A had actually been spent and little of the contracted equipment had been delivered.[112]

Cooperative efforts to improve MPC&A in Russia have been hampered by bureaucratic delays in Washington, particularly in connection with spending Defense Department money, and by suspicion and hesitation within Russia's powerful Ministry of Atomic Energy (Minatom) about involving the USA so intimately in the activities of its once highly secret nuclear installations. However, the urgency of concerns about the security of Russian nuclear facilities has prompted moves to expedite the implementation of cooperative MPC&A projects.[113] In late August, a working group set up under the auspices of the Gore–Chernomyrdin Commission (see below) selected five laboratories and research institutes in Russia as priority sites for upgrading the security of the weapon-usable fissile material stored there.[114] The assistance to be provided

[111] Testimony of David Osias, National Intelligence Officer for Strategic Programs, Central Intelligence Agency, before the Subcommittee on Europe, Senate Foreign Relations Committee, 22 Aug. 1995. Russian Interior Minister Viktor Yerin reported in Feb. 1995 that 80% of the nuclear facilities in Russia lacked the basic equipment needed to detect the theft of fissile material. 'New Russian measures to secure fissile material', *Arms Control Today*, vol. 25, no. 2 (Mar. 1995), p. 31.

[112] Lockwood (note 101), p. 11.

[113] Beginning in FY 1996, CTR programmes in this area will be transferred to the Department of Energy (DOE), which has greater flexibility than the DOD in implementing agreements with local contractors.

[114] 'US–Russia experts plan intensification of nuclear safety and security cooperation', *Nuclear Nonproliferation News*, no. 34 (12 Oct. 1995), p. 14.

includes portal monitoring sensors, non-destructive assay equipment, nuclear material detectors and physical protection equipment.[115]

In addition, a number of programmes operating outside the auspices of the Nunn–Lugar programme have intensified efforts to improve fissile material control and accounting procedures.[116] Under the Department of Energy's 'lab-to-lab programme', US and Russian national laboratories have established cooperative links aimed at implementing an effective MPC&A regime.[117] This 'bottom–up' strategy has been fruitful in combating the nuclear leakage problem, not least because Department of Energy rules allow US funds to be spent on Russian goods and services in developing a locally designed and produced MPC&A system. It has been cited as a cost-effective and generally successful threat reduction approach that might be applied on a larger scale to other, less technical areas.[118]

Demilitarization

Nunn–Lugar demilitarization efforts include projects to convert defence industries (primarily plants producing items related to weapons of mass destruction) to non-military production, provide housing for demobilized Strategic Rocket Forces personnel and establish centres for scientific cooperation. At the end of 1995, $216 million had been obligated for demilitarization activities.

The International Science and Technology Centre (ISTC), which opened in Moscow in March 1994, became the subject of controversy in Washington in 1995. Funded by Nunn–Lugar money and other foreign contributions, the ISTC has provided non-military employment for some 8000 engineers and scientists in the former Soviet Union who previously worked on nuclear and chemical weapons and missile delivery system technology.[119] In its report on CTR activities, the GAO noted that scientists receiving Centre funds may also continue to be employed by institutes engaged in weapons work. This led to charges on Capitol Hill that the CTR programme subsidizes Russia's development of new weapons of mass destruction.[120]

A senior Pentagon official acknowledged that some recipients of ISTC grants may indeed temporarily continue to do weapon-related work while they are making the transition to civilian pursuits; however, the crucial point is that

---

[115] 'US assists Russia with nuclear materials security', Office of the Assistant Secretary of Defense for Public Affairs, News release no. 032–95, 24 Jan. 1995.

[116] 'US–Russia experts plan intensification of nuclear safety and security cooperation' (note 114), p. 14.

[117] Lockwood (note 101), p. 12.

[118] Johnson, K., *US–FSU Nuclear Threat Reduction Programs: Effectiveness of Current Efforts and Prospects for Future Cooperation*, Center for International Security Affairs, Los Alamos National Laboratory, Aug. 1995, pp. 20–29.

[119] A second centre was established in Kiev in July 1994, with two others in the planning stages for Belarus and Kazakhstan. For a description of the role of these centres in efforts to stem the 'brain drain' of weapon experts from the former Soviet Union, see De Andreis, M. and Calogero, F., *The Soviet Nuclear Weapon Legacy*, SIPRI Research Report no. 10 (Oxford University Press: Oxford, 1995), pp. 47–51.

[120] Gertz, B., 'Russia uses Pentagon fund in constructing new nukes', *Washington Times*, 23 May 1995, p. A12.

they continue to do this work in Russia and not in an aspiring nuclear weapon state, which is the principal aim of the programme.[121] Earlier in the year the Pentagon had announced that it would increase its contribution to the ISTC in Moscow by $10 million, bringing the total US contribution to $35 million.[122]

The US–Russian HEU Agreement

In 1995 major progress was made in resolving a dispute that was threatening to unravel the 1993 US–Russian agreement which provides for conversion of the highly enriched uranium (HEU) recovered from scrapped former Soviet nuclear warheads into fuel for civilian nuclear power plants.[123] A protocol to the agreement was signed on 30 June 1995 in Moscow during talks between US Vice-President Al Gore and Russian Prime Minister Viktor Chernomyrdin that addressed shortcomings in the original deal that had led to Russian threats to pull out of it.[124]

The HEU Agreement was initially hailed as a significant step in reducing the risk of diversion or theft of the weapon-usable fissile material recovered from dismantled warheads. It would also provide a steady flow of hard currency into the Russian Treasury, part of which must be used for 'the conversion of defence enterprises, enhancing the safety of nuclear power plants, environmental clean-up of polluted areas and operation of facilities' for converting HEU into low-enriched uranium (LEU).

Under the terms of the agreement, the United States Enrichment Corporation (USEC), a quasi-governmental agency, would purchase from Russia over 20 years up to 500 tonnes of HEU extracted from nuclear warheads for use as civilian reactor fuel.[125] The agreement specified that Russia would blend down the ex-warhead material to 4.4 per cent LEU; not less than 10 t of HEU per year would be purchased in the first five years, and not less than 30 t per year thereafter. The total deal is valued at nearly $12 billion, although prices are negotiated each year to reflect international market conditions.[126]

The implementation of the HEU Agreement was quickly stymied by a dispute between Russia and the USA over the price of the blended LEU to be delivered to US fuel fabricators. A more serious complication arose because the agreement did not provide for Russia to be promptly paid for the natural uranium it used to dilute the weapon-grade HEU. It specified that Russia

---

[121] Press conference remarks of Ashton Carter, Assistant Secretary of Defense for International Security Policy, Department of Defense news briefing, 23 May 1995.

[122] 'US assists Russia with weapons dismantlement and weapons security' (note 106).

[123] For the text of the HEU Agreement, see *SIPRI Yearbook 1994* (note 24), appendix 16A, pp. 673–75.

[124] Medeiros, E., 'Gore–Chernomyrdin talks resolve several outstanding issues', *Arms Control Today*, vol. 25, no. 9 (Sep. 1995), pp. 26, 32.

[125] The USA stipulated that Russia first had to work out revenue sharing arrangements with Belarus, Kazakhstan and Ukraine for the value of the fissile material extracted from the former Soviet nuclear warheads withdrawn from their territories.

[126] Bukharin, O., 'Weapons to fuel', *Science & Global Security*, vol. 4, no. 2 (1994), pp. 189–212. The first shipment of Russian LEU under the agreement arrived in Ohio in late June 1995. Lippman, T., 'First shipment of uranium arrives from Russia', *Washington Post*, 25 June 1995, p. A6.

would be paid upon delivery of the diluted uranium for the work done in blending it down, worth about $8 billion; Russia would be paid for the uranium itself—worth approximately $4 billion—only when the material was sold on the US commercial market. However, an agreement suspending US Commerce Department 'anti-dumping' regulations prevented the sale of Russian-origin uranium on the US market until after the suspension agreement expired in 2003, meaning that the remaining payment to Russia would be delayed for years.[127]

With the head of Minatom, Viktor Mikhailov, threatening to find other buyers for the HEU, the dispute was discussed during the 29–30 June 1995 meeting of the US–Russian Joint Commission on Economic and Technological Cooperation (the Gore–Chernomyrdin Commission). While the protocol signed at the meeting did not resolve all the disputes surrounding the agreement, such as the issue of price, it did provide for measures to ensure simultaneous payment to Russia for both the blending work and the uranium itself. The USEC agreed to pay for the full value of Russian uranium upon delivery, pending congressional authorization for the president to waive anti-dumping restrictions. The USEC also agreed to advance $100 million to Minatom as a 'good faith gesture' so that it could continue its uranium blending work.[128]

The two sides also agreed at the June meeting of the Gore–Chernomyrdin Commission to work out measures to allow sampling of the HEU being blended down at the Tomsk and Sverdlovsk facilities to verify that it had in fact been extracted from newly dismantled Russian nuclear warheads rather than from stockpiles of HEU not previously used in weapons or from other sources; in return Russia would be allowed to inspect USEC facilities to verify that the blended LEU was used for civilian purposes.[129] Bilateral talks to implement the monitoring procedures made little progress, however, as the Russian Government was unwilling to allow the high degree of intrusion at its blending facilities needed to verify that no cheating was occurring. At the end of the year criticism mounted in the USA about the Clinton Administration's inability to verify that the diluted HEU purchased from Russia had indeed been extracted from dismantled nuclear weapons.[130]

Fissile material stockpile agreements

In 1995 the USA and Russia continued negotiations begun the previous year on comprehensive confidence-building measures to increase the transparency of their fissile material stockpiles. These efforts were given high-level impetus

[127] Mathews, J., 'National security blunder', *Washington Post*, 5 May 1995, p. 6; and Broad, W., 'US deal with Russia to salvage uranium is fast unravelling', *International Herald Tribune*, 13 June 1995, pp. 1, 6.

[128] 'US and Russia find tentative way ahead on uranium sale', *Nuclear Proliferation News*, no. 30 (7 Aug. 1995), p. 7; and Lippman, T., 'US vows faster payment to Russia on uranium deal', *Washington Post*, 6 July 1995, p. A17.

[129] Medeiros, E., 'Gore–Chernomyrdin talks resolve several outstanding issues', *Arms Control Today*, vol. 25, no. 7 (Sep. 1995), pp. 26, 32.

[130] Broad, W., 'Clinton scrambling to show A-arms pacts are verified', *International Herald Tribune*, 30 Jan. 1996, p. 5.

at the summit meeting between Presidents Clinton and Yeltsin held in Moscow on 9–10 May. The two leaders signed a Joint Statement on the Transparency and Irreversibility of the Process of Reducing Nuclear Weapons in which they called for the conclusion of agreements for a regular exchange of detailed information on aggregate stockpiles of nuclear weapons and fissile materials, for reciprocal monitoring at storage facilities of fissile material removed from nuclear warheads and declared to be 'excess to national security requirements', and for other measures 'as necessary' to enhance confidence in reciprocal declarations on fissile material stockpiles. The two presidents also pledged that their respective countries would not manufacture nuclear weapons from newly produced fissile material or from the excess fissile material removed from weapons.[131]

Russian–US talks continued throughout the year in the Joint Working Group on Safeguards, Transparency and Irreversibility (ST&I), a forum created under the auspices of the Gore–Chernomyrdin Commission for negotiations to establish a new arms control regime covering the large US and Russian holdings of fissile material. The measures proposed by Washington are based on a comprehensive notion of transparency, in which the bilateral exchange of classified data on aggregate warhead and fissile material stockpiles would be linked with ambitious reciprocal monitoring and inspection arrangements. These arrangements would permit each country to inspect, with few exceptions, every facility in the other's nuclear weapon production complex. They would also permit the inspection of all components removed from dismantled warheads.

Despite the push given to the ST&I talks by the Clinton–Yeltsin Joint Statement, they subsequently made little headway. The key stumbling-block has been the inability of the two sides to reach a data-exchange cooperation agreement, which is the necessary legal precursor to the broader transparency measures being negotiated. A planned November meeting of negotiators in Moscow was cancelled at the last minute by Russian officials, who cited a new inter-agency policy review involving the Atomic Energy, Defence and Foreign Ministries.[132] US negotiators expressed concern that the agreement had become an increasing political liability in the run-up to the presidential elections in Russia, with officials there unwilling to share sensitive nuclear weapon information for fear of being accused by hard-line nationalists of betraying state secrets.[133]

---

[131] 'Joint Statement on the Transparency and Irreversibility of the Process of Reducing Nuclear Weapons, 10 May 1995', *Wireless File* (United States Information Service: US Embassy, Stockholm, 10 May 1995), pp. 16–17.

[132] Hitchens, T., 'US fears Russia vote may stymie nuke talks', *Defense News*, vol. 11, no. 8 (26 Feb.–3 Mar. 1996), p. 4.

[133] Hitchens (note 132); and Parrish, S., 'Russia blocks progress on nuclear agreements', *OMRI Daily Digest*, vol. 2, no. 15 (22 Jan. 1996).

The reactor shut-down agreement

At their May 1995 summit meeting in Moscow, Clinton and Yeltsin also urged progress in implementing the plutonium reactor shut-down agreement signed at the 23 June 1994 meeting of the Gore–Chernomyrdin Commission. This agreement obligates Russia and the USA to end the production of plutonium for military purposes no later than the year 2000; a side agreement prohibits the restarting of reactors already closed.[134]

Despite the agreement, Minatom refused to accelerate the shut-down of its three remaining dual-purpose reactors in the Siberian cities of Seversk (in a complex formerly known Tomsk-7) and Zheleznogorsk (in a complex formerly known as Krasnoyarsk-26) since these facilities also generate heat and electricity for the surrounding communities; it also refused to allow US inspectors to verify that the plutonium produced there was no longer being used to manufacture nuclear weapons. Minatom officials insisted that the USA pay or at least help secure financing for building replacement reactors. The US Government refused to underwrite the cost of constructing new power plants and rejected Minatom's proposal to jointly develop a new advanced reactor programme. In an effort to resolve the impasse, the two presidents called for greater bilateral cooperation in identifying and financing alternative energy sources.[135] On 5 December a Minatom spokesman announced that the three reactors would be shut down by 2000; they are to be replaced by smaller reactors not capable of producing weapon-grade plutonium.[136]

VI. The ABM Treaty and ballistic missile defence

The debate over ballistic missile defences and the future of the 1972 ABM Treaty intensified during 1995.[137] The stalled negotiations in the Standing Consultative Committee (SCC) between the United States and Russia over a US proposal to clarify the scope of the ABM Treaty remained a potent source of acrimony in US–Russian relations.[138] In Washington, the Republican-dominated Congress approved a defence authorization bill that would commit the USA to developing and deploying a multi-site nationwide ballistic missile defence system—a specific contravention of the 1974 Protocol to the ABM

[134] 'Fact Sheet: Gore–Chernomyrdin Commission', US Department of State, Bureau of Public Affairs, 21 Sep. 1994. The USA halted its production of plutonium in 1988; Russia declared that it had halted the production of plutonium for military purposes on 1 Oct. 1994. The reactor shut-down agreement reinforces US and Russian support for a multilateral convention banning the production of fissile material for military purposes.

[135] Medeiros (note 129), p. 32.

[136] Agence France Presse International News (in English), 5 Dec. 1995, in FBIS-SOV-95-234, 6 Dec. 1995, p. 27.

[137] The ABM Treaty was signed by the United States and the Soviet Union on 26 May 1972 and entered into force in October of that year. Amended in a Protocol in 1974, it is now in force for the USA and Russia as the legal successor to the USSR. For the text of the ABM Treaty; the Agreed Statements, Common Understandings and Unilateral Statements; and the 1974 Protocol, see Stützle, W., Jasani, B. and Cowen, R., SIPRI, *The ABM Treaty: To Defend or Not to Defend?* (Oxford University Press: Oxford, 1987), appendix, pp. 207–13.

[138] The SCC is the body established in the ABM Treaty to address questions about its implementation.

Treaty, which limits the parties to no more than one site each.[139] The year drew to a close amid a growing chorus of warnings from arms control advocates that an evisceration or outright abandonment of the ABM Treaty would spell the end of the remarkable post-cold war achievements in reducing US and Russian strategic nuclear arsenals.

The demarcation debate

The issue of ballistic missile defence reappeared on the arms control agenda in 1993, when the USA initiated discussions with Russia in the SCC to clarify the ABM Treaty to permit the testing and deployment of a new family of US advanced-capability theatre ballistic missile defence systems.[140] The Clinton Administration has argued that the new TMD systems are needed to protect US troops and allies in future conflicts from adversaries who might be armed with long-range ballistic missiles.[141] Russia has strenuously opposed US efforts to exclude advanced-capability TMD systems from the constraints of the ABM Treaty. It argues this would open the door to the deployment of US missile defence systems with considerable 'inherent capabilities' against Russian strategic nuclear forces and thereby undermine the stabilizing logic of mutual assured destruction codified in the treaty. Russian officials have also been anxious to halt or severely curtail planned US TMD programmes in order to forestall an expensive new qualitative arms race that Russia would scarcely be able to afford.[142]

The SCC proposal put forward by the USA in November 1993 sought to define missile defence systems according to their 'demonstrated capabilities' against ballistic targets. Specifically, a missile defence interceptor would be regarded as strategic only if it had been tested against a target with a maximum speed exceeding 5 km/second.[143] An interceptor system not tested against targets exceeding this speed would fall outside the constraints of the ABM Treaty.

Russia rejected the US demarcation proposal as being too permissive and countered with a proposal in January 1994 that missile defence systems tested against targets moving faster than 5 km/second or that had interceptor speeds

[139] The ABM Treaty obligates both countries not to undertake to build a nationwide defence system against strategic ballistic missile attack and limits the development and deployment of missile defences. Among other provisions, it prohibits the 2 parties from giving air defence missiles, radars or launchers the technical capability to counter strategic ballistic missiles or from testing them in a strategic ABM mode. Arbatov (note 72), p. 681.

[140] TMD systems occupy a 'grey zone' and are not formally subject to the restrictions imposed by the ABM Treaty, which limits only strategic ABM systems. However, the demarcation between strategic and theatre ballistic missiles is not clearly defined and the technical characteristics of defences against them overlap considerably.

[141] For a description of the 'core' US TMD programmes, see Arbatov (note 72), pp. 682–86.

[142] Feodosyev, V., 'What will US Senate decision lead to?', *Krasnaya Zvezda*, 8 Sep. 1995, p. 3, in FBIS-SOV-95-175, 11 Sep. 1995, pp. 23–24; Felgengauer, P., 'Agreement reached on "defining" the concept of tactical ABM', *Segodnya*, 11 May 1995, p. 1, in FBIS-SOV-95-091, 11 May 1995, pp. 2–3; and Crossette, B., 'Russian minister opposing US missile plan', *New York Times*, 25 Apr. 1995, p. 4.

[143] This corresponds to a missile with a range of approximately 3000 km. The re-entry speed of ICBM warheads is approximately 6–7 km/second. Arbatov (note 72), p. 690.

exceeding 3 km/second would fall under the provisions of the ABM Treaty. In March 1994 this approach was rejected by the USA as being too restrictive, since the proposed limits on interceptor speeds would preclude the development of its 'upper tier' TMD programmes. Negotiations followed in the SCC in which a series of new interceptor-velocity and target-velocity parameters were proposed; however, little headway was made on reaching a compromise agreement, and the demarcation talks were stalled by the autumn of 1994.

The Clinton–Yeltsin joint statement on TMD

Amid signs of a hardening of positions, US and Russian officials met in London in April 1995 to prepare a draft statement on ballistic missile defences for the following month's summit meeting between Presidents Clinton and Yeltsin. In an effort to move the demarcation issue forward, the two sides reportedly agreed to defer discussion of specific technical parameters and instead to work out a statement of general principles that would serve as guidelines for later talks on which TMD systems would be permitted under the ABM Treaty.[144]

At their May summit meeting in Moscow, Clinton and Yeltsin issued a joint statement setting out 'basic principles to serve as a basis for further discussions' on the issue of TMD system demarcation. While reaffirming the ABM Treaty as 'a cornerstone of strategic stability', they agreed that Russia and the USA 'have the option to establish and deploy effective theatre missile defence systems' as long as doing so does not 'lead to violation or circumvention of the ABM Treaty'. The TMD systems to be deployed must not 'pose a realistic threat to the strategic nuclear forces of the other side' and must not 'be tested to give such systems that capability'. In addition, Clinton and Yeltsin agreed that the scale of future TMD system deployments—'in number and geographic scope'—by either side must be 'consistent with theater ballistic missile programs confronting that side'.[145]

US officials described the joint statement as offering a more flexible 'force-on-force' criterion by which theatre systems could be distinguished from strategic BMD systems by examining the overall impact of one side's TMD on the other side's overall strategic forces.[146] According to US SCC Commissioner Stanley Riveles, the principles set out in the statement make clear that the ABM Treaty does not apply to TMD systems 'that may simply have a theoretical capability against some strategic missiles but which would not be militarily significant in the context of operational considerations such as numbers and locations of deployments, system characteristics and realistic

[144] Pfeiffer, T. and Lockwood, D., 'Clinton to seek TMD understanding with Yeltsin at Moscow summit', *Arms Control Today*, vol. 25, no. 4 (May 1995), pp. 22, 30.
[145] 'Text of Clinton–Yeltsin joint statement on theatre missile defence systems', 10 May 1995, *Wireless File* (note 131), p. 14.
[146] Gertz, B., 'Nuclear talks strategy pondered', *Washington Times*, 22 May 1995, p. A6.

engagements scenarios'.[147] This view was immediately challenged by arms control advocates, who pointed out that the ABM Treaty expressly prohibits parties from giving individual non-ABM systems or their components an inherent ABM capability.[148]

The joint statement failed to break the impasse in the TMD demarcation talks between Washington and Moscow. On 22 June the USA reportedly put forward a proposal for a cooperative arrangement under which each side would determine independently whether ABM interceptors with speeds beyond 3 km/second are ABM Treaty-compliant.[149] This proposal was rejected in a diplomatic note from Moscow as not being 'in accord with the demarcation principles agreed upon' in the joint statement and as possibly leading 'to irreconcilable differences concerning compliance with the ABM Treaty as a result of possible differing interpretations'.[150] The note suggested instead a return to discussion of Russia's earlier demarcation proposal based on limiting the maximum speed of missile interceptors.

The Clinton Administration showed little interest in continuing formal discussions in the SCC, preferring to take up the demarcation issue at the political level. A meeting in November between US Under-secretary of State Lynn Davis and Russian Deputy Foreign Minister Georgiy Mamedov reportedly made progress in breaking the impasse, with the two sides reaching an 'agreed framework' for resolving the TMD demarcation issue. According to this framework, tests of missile defence systems against ballistic missile targets with a maximum flight speed of 5 km/second will be permitted. Missile defence systems that have a 'demonstrated' interceptor speed of 3 km/second or less and have been tested against permitted target missiles will also be considered ABM Treaty-compliant.[151] This clarification of the treaty would allow for the development and deployment of 'core' US TMD systems, including the Army's Theater High Altitude Area Defense (THAAD) missile. The agreed framework did not address the status of higher-speed TMD systems (that is, those with interceptor speeds exceeding 3 km/second), such as the US Navy's Upper-Tier system currently under development. The USA has already declared that this system will be treaty-compliant. However, at a press conference held in Moscow on 8 December, a Russian Foreign Ministry spokesman denied that the framework agreement reached by Russia and the USA would

---

[147] Remarks delivered by Stanley Riveles, US Commissioner, Standing Consultative Committee, to the Eighth Multinational Conference on Theater Missile Defense, London, United Kingdom, US Arms Control and Disarmament Agency, Office of Public Affairs, 6 June 1995, p. 4.

[148] See, e.g., Medeiros, E., 'US, Russia set new "principles" to address ABM–TMD dispute', *Arms Control Today*, vol. 25, no. 5 (June 1995), pp. 21, 23. These prohibitions were intended to prevent the deployment of highly capable TMD systems which could form the basis for a rapid break-out from the treaty regime.

[149] Gertz, B., 'Moscow balks at ABM proposal', *Washington Times*, 19 July 1995, p. A5.

[150] Cited in Gertz (note 146). See also Mendelsohn, J., 'ABM Treaty remains threatened by continuing US push for TMD', *Arms Control Today*, vol. 25, no. 7 (Sep. 1995), pp. 28, 33.

[151] 'Breakthrough reported in US–Russia ABM talks', *Nuclear Proliferation News*, no. 37 (15 Dec. 1995), pp. 24–25; and Cerniello, C., 'US, Russia agree on framework for ABM–TMD "demarcation" talks', *Arms Control Today*, vol. 25, no. 10 (Dec. 1995–Jan. 1996), p. 21.

permit the development and deployment of advanced-capability US TMD systems.[152]

Congress and missile defence

The efforts of the Clinton Administration to reach an agreement with Russia on the testing and deployment of TMD systems within the framework of the ABM Treaty came under increasing fire throughout 1995 from the new Republican-controlled Congress. House and Senate Republicans complained that the demarcation negotiations in effect allowed Russia to constrain the ability of the USA to defend its allies and troops in the field.[153] In the run-up to the Moscow summit meeting between Clinton and Yeltsin, 50 Republican senators sent a letter to the White House on 1 May expressing their opposition to any deal with Russia that would limit US TMD programmes.[154]

The mounting criticism from Congress prompted the Clinton Administration to proceed with development of core US TMD programmes, despite the absence of any agreement with Russia on their compliance with the ABM Treaty. On 21 April the US Army and the Ballistic Missile Defense Organization (BMDO) conducted the first flight test of the THAAD missile.[155] The Clinton Administration had originally prohibited THAAD flight testing until ABM Treaty compliance issues were resolved but reversed itself in early 1995 by unilaterally declaring the tests to be treaty-compliant.[156]

In addition, the Administration's pledge to preserve the integrity of the ABM Treaty collided with moves in Congress to require the Pentagon to build a nationwide BMD system to protect the population of the USA. On 6 September 1995 the US Senate approved an amendment to the 1996 defence authorization bill, the Missile Defense Act of 1995, instructing the Defense Department to 'develop an affordable and operationally effective' nationwide ballistic missile defence system 'capable of attaining initial operational capability by the year 2003', at which time Congress would vote on its deployment. The wording of the amendment represented a compromise with the language contained in a 3 August version of the Senate bill requiring the Pentagon to deploy within seven years a multi-site, nationwide BMD system.

In December a new dispute arose between congressional Republicans and the Clinton Administration over national missile defence (NMD). The Republican-drafted wording of the House–Senate conference committee report for the 1996 defence authorization bill required the Pentagon to deploy

---

[152] Parrish, S., 'Foreign Ministry denies ABM deal with US', *OMRI Daily Digest*, vol. 1, no. 239 (11 Dec. 1995).

[153] Gildes, K., 'Lawmakers continue to seek abolishment of ABM Treaty', *Defense Daily*, 18 May 1995, p. 250; and Gertz, B., 'Clinton, Yeltsin agree on missiles', *Washington Times*, 11 May 1995, p. A4.

[154] Associated Press, 'Proposed treaty limits wouldn't stop efforts to guard troops from missiles', *Washington Times*, 5 May 1995, p. A6.

[155] Fulghum, D., 'THAAD successful in first, but simple, test flight', *Aviation Week & Space Technology*, 1 May 1995, pp. 25–26.

[156] Lovece, J., 'Pentagon expected to call THAAD flight tests treaty-compliant', *Defense Week*, 3 Jan. 1995, p. 3; and Pfeiffer and Lockwood (note 144), p. 22.

by 2003 an NMD system capable of protecting all the 50 states. In the message to Congress accompanying his 28 December veto of the authorization bill, President Clinton argued that this provision would set the USA on a 'collision course with the ABM Treaty' and jeopardize continued Russian implementation of the START I Treaty as well as Russian ratification of START II.[157] A leading Senate Democrat characterized the bill's missile defence language as an 'anticipatory breach' of the ABM Treaty.[158] To ensure enactment into law of the stalled 1996 defence budget, congressional leaders subsequently agreed to delete the missile defence provision from the authorization bill, although they left a $740 million increase in the national missile defence account.[159]

VII. Conclusions: a watershed in 1996

Russia and the USA were noticeably approaching a watershed in their nuclear arms control relations at the end of 1995. While both proceeded ahead of schedule in eliminating the nuclear weapons slated for dismantlement under the START I Treaty, by December it was not clear that START II would be ratified by Russia or that further reductions were possible. After the June 1996 Russian presidential elections, there are likely to be clearer indications as to whether Russia is prepared to continue along the road of arms control. If not, reductions will nonetheless have been greater than many had anticipated a few years before.

At the end of 1995 US–Russian negotiations to clarify the ABM Treaty remained deadlocked. An evisceration or abandonment of the ABM Treaty would have spillover effects not only for START II but also for nuclear force planning in China, France and the UK, all of which have suggested that deployment of new missile defences would require them to take compensatory measures, which in turn might require nuclear testing.[160]

Events in 1996 will demonstrate how far behind the nuclear weapon states are willing to leave the cold war, or indeed whether they will leave it behind at all. There is good reason to believe that the CTB treaty will be opened for signature in 1996 and that Russia and the USA will find a *modus vivendi* for the ABM Treaty, START II and further arms reductions. Nevertheless, despite a renewed push by the non-nuclear weapon states in 1995 for the global elimination of nuclear weapons in the near term,[161] it appears that the process of reducing them to zero, if it continues, will do so only gradually, taking decades rather than years.

---

[157] Quoted in Erlich, J. and Finnegan, P., 'Compromise on missile shield eases budget snag', *Defense News*, vol. 11, no. 3 (23–28 Jan. 1996), p. 4.

[158] Towell, P., 'ABM language disputed', *Congressional Quarterly,* vol. 53, no. 50 (23 Dec. 1995), p. 3898.

[159] Erlich and Finnegan (note 157).

[160] Arnett, E., 'Implications of the comprehensive test ban for nuclear weapon programmes and decision making', Arnett (note 3).

[161] See chapter 13 in this volume.

Appendix 14A. Nuclear explosions, 1945–95

RAGNHILD FERM

I. Introduction

In 1995 significantly more nuclear tests[1] were conducted than in the past two years. China carried out two tests and France five during the year. All the tests in 1993 (one) and 1994 (two) were conducted by China. France had not tested since 1991.

The last Soviet test was carried out on 24 October 1990, the last US test on 23 September 1992 and the last British test on 26 November 1991.

II. The United States and the United Kingdom

On 30 January 1995 President Bill Clinton announced that the US test moratorium—in effect since October 1992—will be extended until a comprehensive test ban treaty (CTBT) has entered into force. According to a 1995 Department of Energy (DOE) press release the USA is, however, planning a series of six 'subcritical high-explosive experiments with nuclear material' to test the reliability of US nuclear warheads as well as to maintain the capabilities of the test site and support nuclear test readiness. These experiments will also help maintain the skills of the experts at the test site, should full-scale US nuclear testing ever resume.[2] They will be carried out underground at the Nevada Test Site and are designed not to reach nuclear criticality, that is, there will not be a nuclear explosion. Six subcritical tests are planned: two for 1996 and four for 1997.

The United Kingdom has not been able to continue its testing programme during the US test moratorium since it has since 1962 conducted its tests in cooperation with the USA at the US test site in Nevada.

III. Russia

Since the break-up of the Soviet Union, Russia has not conducted any nuclear tests.

From time to time Russian authorities provide new information about the former Soviet testing programme; in 1995 a Russian tabulation of all Soviet tests was compiled from official records.[3] The revised total for Soviet explosions is the same—715 explosions, including 124 peaceful nuclear explosions (PNEs)—but the new information clarified when the tests took place and the distribution between atmospheric and underground explosions. In the revised data for the USSR, there were 12 more atmospheric tests conducted before 1963 and 12 fewer underground explosions after 1963; 456 tests were conducted at the Semipalatinsk test site in

---

[1] The term nuclear 'test' denotes explosions conducted in nuclear weapon test programmes. The tables in this appendix list all nuclear explosions, including so-called peaceful nuclear explosions (PNEs) and the atomic bombs dropped on Hiroshima and Nagasaki in 1945.

[2] 'New contractor announced for Nevada Test Site: secretary outlines plans for site', *DOE News*, US Department of Energy press release, 27 Oct. 1995.

[3] *USSR Nuclear Tests, August 1949 through October 1990* (All-Russian Scientific Research Institute of Experimental Physics [VNIIEF] Sarov: Moscow, 1995).

Kazakhstan (116 in the atmosphere and 340 underground) and 130 at the Novaya Zemlya test site (88 in the atmosphere, 39 underground and 3 under water). The remaining 129 tests, many of which were PNEs, were conducted in various places in the Soviet Union.[4]

Although the Semipalatinsk test site was closed by the Kazakh authorities in 1991, Russia has not yet formally terminated its activities on Novaya Zemlya. The site on the southern island has not been used since 1975, but one or two tests per year were conducted at the northern site in 1976–90.

IV. France

On 13 June 1995, newly elected President Jacques Chirac announced that a new series of eight French nuclear tests would take place.[5] He stated that France was obliged to complete this series of tests to ensure the safety, security and reliability of the French deterrence forces and to develop its simulation programme. In spite of worldwide protests, France resumed its nuclear testing on 5 September with the explosion of a device of less than 10 kilotons at its test site on Mururoa in the Tuamouto archipelago in eastern French Polynesia. The next French test was conducted at the nearby atoll Fangataufa and was announced by French authorities to be of the order of 100 kt. Estimates of the three remaining tests during the year were in the range of 20–80, 5–20 and 10–40 kt, respectively.[6] After the sixth test, conducted on Mururoa on 27 January 1996, France announced the 'definitive end' of its test programme.[7]

In August 1995 the French Government for the first time published a complete list of all its nuclear tests since 1960.[8] It was admitted that in three cases (twice in 1966 and once in 1973) the tests had caused contamination.

On 20 October 1995 France, together with the USA and the UK, announced that it would sign the Protocols to the 1985 South Pacific Nuclear Free Zone Treaty (Treaty of Rarotonga), which it did on 25 March 1996. Under Protocol 3 of the treaty, the declared nuclear weapon states undertake not to test any nuclear explosive device anywhere within the zone.

V. China

Unlike the other declared nuclear weapon states, China has never had a test moratorium. It claims that it needs to finalize its nucler programme and stresses that it has conducted only a few tests altogether (43), compared with, for example, the USA, which has carried out over 1000 tests. It has pledged to stop testing completely when a CTBT has entered into force. The yields of the two tests in 1995 carried out at the Chinese test site north-west of Lake Lop Nor in the Xinjiang Province were in the range of 50–200 kt.

---

[4] 'Known nuclear tests worldwide, 1945–1995', *Bulletin of the Atomic Scientists*, vol. 52, no. 3 (May/June 1996), pp. 61–63, based on information from *USSR Nuclear Tests . . .* (note 3).

[5] *Le Monde*, 15 June 1995.

[6] These yields (except for that of the second test) are estimated by the Australian Seismological Centre, which states that empirical equations have been used. However, there is no single agreed formula for the determination of yields.

[7] *Le Monde*, 31 Jan. 1996

[8] *Le Monde*, 2 Aug. 1995.

Table 14A.1. Registered nuclear explosions in 1995

Date	Origin time (GMT)	Latitude (deg)		Longitude (deg)		Region	Body wave magnitude[a]
China							
15 May	04.06	41.	N	89.	E	Lop Nor	6.5
17 Aug.	01.00	41.	N	89.	E	Lop Nor	6.4
France							
5 Sep.	21.30	21.	S	139.	W	Mururoa	4.8
1 Oct.	23.30	22.	S	138.	W	Fangataufa	5.5
27 Oct.	22.00	21.	S	139.	W	Mururoa	5.5
21 Nov.	21.30	21.	S	139.	W	Mururoa	5.0
27 Dec.	21.30	21.	S	139.	W	Mururoa	5.2

[a] Body wave magnitude (m_b) indicates the size of the event. In order to be able to give a reasonably correct estimate of the yield it is necessary to have detailed information, for example, on the geological conditions of the area where the test is conducted. Giving the m_b figure is therefore an unambiguous way of listing the size of an explosion. m_b data for the Chinese tests were provided by the Swedish National Defence Research Establishment (FOA) and data for the French tests by the Australian Seismological Centre, Australian Geological Survey Organisation, Canberra.

Table 14A.2. Estimated number of nuclear explosions, 16 July 1945–31 December 1995

a = atmospheric; u = underground

Year	USA[a]		USSR/Russia		UK[a]		France		China		India		Total
	a	u	a	u	a	u	a	u	a	u	a	u	
1945	3	–	–	–	–	–	–	–	–	–	–	–	3
1946	2[b]	–	–	–	–	–	–	–	–	–	–	–	2
1947	–	–	–	–	–	–	–	–	–	–	–	–	–
1948	3	–	–	–	–	–	–	–	–	–	–	–	3
1949	–	–	1	–	–	–	–	–	–	–	–	–	1
1950	–	–	–	–	–	–	–	–	–	–	–	–	–
1951	15	1	2	–	–	–	–	–	–	–	–	–	18
1952	10	–	–	–	1	–	–	–	–	–	–	–	11
1953	11	–	5	–	2	–	–	–	–	–	–	–	18
1954	6	–	10	–	–	–	–	–	–	–	–	–	16
1955	17[b]	1	6[b]	–	–	–	–	–	–	–	–	–	24
1956	18	–	9	–	6	–	–	–	–	–	–	–	33
1957	27	5	16[b]	–	7	–	–	–	–	–	–	–	55
1958	62[c]	15	34	–	5	–	–	–	–	–	–	–	116
1959	–	–	–	–	–	–	–	–	–	–	–	–	–[d]
1960	–	–	–	–	–	–	3	–	–	–	–	–	3[d]
1961	–	10	58[b]	1	–	–	1	1	–	–	–	–	71[d]
1962	39[b]	57	78	1	–	2	–	1	–	–	–	–	178
1963[e]	4	43	–	–	–	–	–	3	–	–	–	–	50
1964	–	45	–	9	–	2	–	3	1	–	–	–	60
1965	–	38	–	14	–	1	–	4	1	–	–	–	58

Year	USA[a] a	USA[a] u	USSR/Russia a	USSR/Russia u	UK[a] a	UK[a] u	France a	France u	China a	China u	India a	India u	Total
1966	–	48	–	18	–	–	6	1	3	–	–	–	76
1967	–	42	–	17	–	–	3	–	2	–	–	–	64
1968	–	56[f]	–	17	–	–	5	–	1	–	–	–	79
1969	–	46	–	19	–	–	–	–	1	1	–	–	67
1970	–	39	–	16	–	–	8	–	1	–	–	–	64
1971	–	24	–	23	–	–	5	–	1	–	–	–	53
1972	–	27	–	24	–	–	4	–	2	–	–	–	57
1973	–	24[g]	–	17	–	–	6	–	1	–	–	–	48
1974	–	22	–	21	–	1	9	–	1	–	–	1	55
1975	–	22	–	19	–	–	–	2	–	1	–	–	44
1976	–	20	–	21	–	1	–	5	3	1	–	–	51
1977	–	20	–	24	–	–	–	9	1	–	–	–	54
1978	–	19	–	31	–	2	–	11	2	1	–	–	66
1979	–	15	–	31	–	1	–	10	1	–	–	–	58
1980	–	14	–	24	–	3	–	12	1	–	–	–	54
1981	–	16	–	21	–	1	–	12	–	–	–	–	50
1982	–	18	–	19	–	1	–	10	–	1	–	–	49
1983	–	18	–	25	–	1	–	9	–	2	–	–	55
1984	–	18	–	27	–	2	–	8	–	2	–	–	57
1985	–	17	–	10	–	1	–	8	–	–	–	–	36[h]
1986	–	14	–	–	–	1	–	8	–	–	–	–	23[h]
1987	–	14	–	23	–	1	–	8	–	1	–	–	47[h]
1988	–	15	–	16	–	–	–	8	–	1	–	–	40
1989	–	11	–	7	–	1	–	9	–	–	–	–	28
1990	–	8	–	1	–	1	–	6	–	2	–	–	18
1991	–	7	–	–	–	1	–	6	–	–	–	–	14
1992	–	6	–	–	–	–	–	–	–	2	–	–	8[i]
1993	–	–	–	–	–	–	–	–	–	1	–	–	1[i]
1994	–	–	–	–	–	–	–	–	–	2	–	–	2[i]
1995	–	–	–	–	–	–	–	5	–	2	–	–	7[i]
Total	**217**	**815**	**219**	**496**	**21**	**24**	**50**	**159**	**23**	**20**	**–**	**1**	**2 045**

[a] All British tests from 1962 have been conducted jointly with the USA at the Nevada Test Site, so the number of US tests is actually higher than indicated here. The British Labour Government observed a unilateral moratorium on testing in 1965–74.

[b] One of these tests was carried out under water.

[c] Two of these tests were carried out under water.

[d] The UK, the USA and the USSR observed a moratorium on testing in the period Nov. 1958–Sep. 1961.

[e] On 5 Aug. 1963 the USA, the USSR and the UK signed the Partial Test Ban Treaty (PTBT), prohibiting nuclear explosions in the atmosphere, in outer space and under water.

[f] Five devices used simultaneously in the same explosion (a peaceful nuclear explosion, PNE, to develop peaceful uses for atomic energy) are counted here as one explosion.

[g] Three devices used simultaneously in the same explosion (a peaceful nuclear explosion, PNE, to develop peaceful uses for atomic energy) are counted here as one explosion.

[h] The USSR observed a unilateral moratorium on testing in the period Aug. 1985–Feb. 1987.

Table 14A.2 *Notes contd*

i The USSR has observed a moratorium on testing from Oct. 1991 and the USA since Oct. 1992; France observed a moratorium from Apr. 1992 until the president announced in June 1995 that a new series of tests would be started.

Table 14A.3. Estimated number of nuclear explosions, 16 July 1945–31 December 1995

USA^{a,b}	USSR/Russia	UK^a	France^b	China	India	**Total**
1 032	715	45	209	43	1	**2 045**

a All British tests from 1962 have been conducted jointly with the USA at the Nevada Test Site, so the number of US tests is actually higher than indicated here.

b This total includes tests for safety purposes, irrespective of the yields and irrespective of whether they have caused a nuclear explosion or not.

Sources for tables 14A.1–14A.3

Swedish National Defence Research Establishment (FOA), various estimates; Reports from the Australian Seismological Centre, Bureau of Mineral Resources, Geology and Geophysics, Canberra; *Krasnaya Zvezda*, 13 Sep. 1990; *Pravda*, 24 Oct. 1990; US Department of Energy (DOE), *Summary List of Previously Unannounced Tests* (DOE: Washington, DC, 1993); US Department of Energy (DOE), *Nuclear Detonations Redefined as Nuclear Tests* (DOE: Washington, DC, 1994); Norris, R. S., Burrows, A. S. and Fieldhouse, R. W., 'British, French and Chinese nuclear weapons', *Nuclear Weapons Databook*, Vol. V (Natural Resources Defense Council (NRDC): Washington, DC, 1994); 'Assessment of French nuclear testing' (Direction des centres d'experimentations nucleaires [DIRCEN] and Commissariat à l'Energie Atomique [CEA]); 'Known nuclear tests worldwide, 1945–1995', *Bulletin of the Atomic Scientists*, vol. 52, no. 3 (May/June 1996), pp. 61–63; and *USSR Nuclear Tests, August 1949 through October 1990* (All-Russian Scientific Research Institute of Experimental Physics [VNIIEF] Sarov: Moscow, 1995).

15. Chemical and biological weapon developments and arms control

THOMAS STOCK, MARIA HAUG and PATRICIA RADLER

I. Introduction

In 1995, the 80th anniversary of the first use of chemical weapons (CW) in modern history, a number of events occurred that were related to chemical and biological warfare (CBW) and disarmament.[1] Efforts continued to obtain the 65 ratifications needed to bring the Chemical Weapons Convention (CWC) into force. In March 1995 an incident in the Tokyo underground system involving the nerve agent sarin illustrated how vulnerable societies are to terrorism and particularly to chemical agent attacks.

New information about the advanced state of the Iraqi biological weapon (BW) programme demonstrated that it was possible for a country to develop a sophisticated offensive BW programme and to keep its nature and extent secret for several years. Data on the Iraqi CW and missile programmes proved the suspicion that Iraq had not fully disclosed its past activities to be well founded. Owing to these events, to increasing concern about proliferation and to evaluation of the 1991 Persian Gulf War, CBW defence is receiving increased attention from policy makers and defence establishments.

The destruction of chemical weapons continued to be a major problem, particularly in Russia. Foreign support for the Russian CW destruction programme increased, although doubts remain as to Russia's ability to destroy its stockpile within the timeframes envisaged under the CWC. Both Russia and the USA must consider public opinion and environmental concerns when destroying chemical weapons. In both Russia and the USA the estimated cost of CW destruction continued to increase. At the end of 1995 neither Russia nor the USA, the two major possessors of chemical weapons, had ratified the CWC.

The number of CWC ratifications in 1995 was twice that in 1994, but an additional 18 ratifications are needed in order for the convention to enter into force. The setting up of the international machinery for the future Organisation for the Prohibition of Chemical Weapons (OPCW) in The Hague progressed, but various issues that require political compromise or technical solution remain to be resolved.

The Fourth Review Conference of the 1972 Biological Weapons Convention (BWC) will be held in late 1996, and efforts intensified to prepare for the addition of a verification protocol to the BWC. An Ad Hoc Group was estab-

---

[1] On 22 Apr. 1915 German troops used chemical agents (chlorine) as a method of warfare at the Battle of Ypres. This event is recognized as the first use of chemical weapons in modern warfare.

lished as proposed at the 1994 Special Conference to suggest appropriate measures to strengthen the BWC; it held three meetings in 1995.

II. Chemical weapon developments in 1995

Allegations of CW use

In 1995 there were allegations of CW use in armed conflicts in Chechnya, Mexico, Myanmar (formerly Burma), Sri Lanka, the former Yugoslavia and on the border between Ecuador and Peru. However, most of these cases were either unsubstantiated or disproved. Apart from the 1980–88 Iraq–Iran War, most recent allegations of CW use have occurred in remote regions of internal conflict that are difficult for unbiased experts to reach or investigate. In many cases local populations that claim to be victims of CW use do not possess the education or training to identify chemical weapons. Use of tear gas is often mistaken for CW use, as are a variety of illnesses, unusual odours or fumes. Allegations of CW use can also be used to gain international support or to create sympathy.

In the *former Yugoslavia,* Bosnian Serbs, Bosnian Government forces and Croatian regular army troops were all accused of using CW in over a dozen incidents in 1995.[2] None of these accusations was confirmed by independent experts, and there were no reports of deaths having resulted from the alleged attacks. The agents said to have been used ranged from ambiguous 'poison gas' to CS, phosgene, nerve gas and BZ.[3] Only one incident was reported in detail in the Western press: it was claimed that Bosnian Serbs had used an incapacitating gas in the attack on Zepa in July.[4] Serb forces reportedly wore protective masks in several gas attacks during the siege of Zepa, and Bosnian gas victims needed several days to recover from the effects of the gas.[5] Western experts speculated that the gas that may have been used was BZ, which was supported by statements made by specialists from the former Yugoslav Army's CW programme who claimed that the Serbs had 'inherited the capacity to produce BZ'.[6] Earlier, in July 1995, a Russian press report accused Bosnian Government troops of using poison gas near Sarajevo, quoting the chairman of the military for the Serb-held region of Sarajevo, Nedelko Prstoyevich, as saying: 'this criminal act gives Serbs the right to retaliate in kind'.[7] This statement typifies those which followed the charges and countercharges of CW use in the war in the former Yugoslavia.

---

[2] '24 May', '3 June', '4 June', '29 June', '10 July', '19 July', '24 July', '26 July', '28 July', '13 August', *Chemical Weapons Convention Bulletin,* no. 29 (Sep. 1995), pp. 18, 19, 24, 26, 28, 29, 32; and Institute for Defense and Disarmament Studies, *Arms Control Reporter* (IDDS: Brookline, Mass.), sheet 704.E-2.131, Oct. 1995.

[3] '24 May', '24 July', *Chemical Weapons Convention Bulletin,* no. 29 (Sep. 1995), pp. 18, 29; and *Arms Control Reporter* (note 2).

[4] Hedges, C., 'Bosnia troops cite gassings at Zepa', *New York Times,* 27 July 1995.

[5] Hedges (note 4).

[6] Hedges (note 4).

[7] ['Use of chemical weapons in Sarajevo'], *Krasnaya Zvezda,* 4 July 1995, p. 3 (in Russian).

In the *Russian Federation* it was reported that chemical weapons had been used by Russian troops in Chechnya in December 1994 and January 1995, claims denied by the Russian Government.[8] On the other hand, in January 1995 a Russian military subcommittee claimed to have verified that Chechen rebels had used a chlorine-type gas and hydrogen cyanide in attacks on Russian troops.[9] In August 1995 reports of Russian use of chemical weapons that caused damage to the skin of people living in Avtury, Chechnya,[10] proved to be scabies and other illnesses related to poor sanitation.[11]

In *Myanmar* in February 1995 Karen ethnic minority forces claimed that government troops had used chemical weapons in an assault on their camp.[12] Thai military authorities investigating the claim found no evidence of CW use.[13] In April there were unsubstantiated reports that refugees fleeing from Myanmar to Thailand became ill as a result of a CW attack by the Army of Myanmar.[14]

In late November 1995 the *Sri Lankan* Army reported that it had been attacked by Tamil Tigers using an unidentified gas.[15] In February 1995 *Ecuador* accused *Peru* of aerial spraying of CW during their continuing border conflict, charges denied by Peru.[16] In March 1995 in *Mexico* the National Commission for Democracy in Mexico claimed that the Mexican Army was considering the use of chemical weapons against Zapatista rebels.[17]

CW production, possession and procurement

As of 1995 only Russia and the USA had publicly admitted that they possess a CW arsenal. However, intelligence agencies allege that a number of other states have offensive CW programmes. It is difficult to verify these allegations, but reports may indicate CW proliferation. The countries discussed below are among those alleged in 1995 to possess chemical weapons.

Iran has allegedly produced mustard, chlorine, phosgene and hydrogen cyanide and is said to have the capacity to produce nerve agents, such as sarin,

---

[8] 'Chechen vice president: Russians using chemical weapons', in Foreign Broadcast Information Service, *Daily Report–Central Eurasia (FBIS-SOV)*, FBIS-SOV-94-246, 22 Dec. 1994, p. 25; 'Further report', in Joint Publication Research Studies, *Arms Control and Proliferation Issues* (JPRS-TAC) JPRS-TAC-95-003-L, 17 Jan. 1995, p. 19; and 'Use of chemical weapons in Chechnya denied', in FBIS-SOV-94-241, 15 Dec. 1994, p. 40.

[9] 'Duma leader on chemical weapons use, aid', in FBIS-SOV-95-003, 5 Jan. 1995, p. 25.

[10] 'Chechens show symptoms of chemical poisoning', in FBIS-SOV-95-156, 14 Aug. 1995, pp. 12–13; and 'Allegations of chemical weapons use investigated', in FBIS-SOV-95-164, 24 Aug. 1995, pp. 4–6.

[11] 'Experts say no chemical weapons used in Avtury', in FBIS-SOV-95-165, 25 Aug. 1995, p. 6.

[12] Richardson, M., 'Burma's drive on rebels angers neighbors', *International Herald Tribune*, 22 Feb. 1995, p. 4.

[13] 'No evidence of chemical weapon use by Burma', in Foreign Broadcast Information Service, *Daily Report–East Asia (FBIS-EAS)*, FBIS-EAS-95-079, 25 Apr. 1995, p. 68.

[14] '1,200 flee to Thailand to escape fighting', *New York Times*, 28 Apr. 1995, p. A3.

[15] 'Gas mot lankesisk militär' [Gas against Lankan military], *Svenska Dagbladet*, 26 Nov. 1995, p. 8 (in Swedish).

[16] *Arms Control Reporter*, sheet 704.E-2.127, Oct. 1995.

[17] Lopez, A. B., 'Genocido quimico en Chiapas' [Chemical genocide in Chiapas], *El Financiero*, 6 Mar. 1995, p. 42 (in Spanish).

and possibly V agents.[18] In 1995 it was reported that the Iranian CW stockpile consisted of between several hundred and 2000 tonnes (t) of various CW agents.[19] In January and February 1995 both the German and the US governments issued separate intelligence reports stating that Iran was building CW production facilities utilizing material supplied by German and Indian companies.[20] India denied the allegations.[21] One of the CW facilities allegedly being built is located in Bandar Abbas.[22] Iran is also alleged to possess CW production facilities that have been operating for some years located in Qazun, A Razi, Bashwir and Damghan.[23] In March 1995 US Secretary of Defense William Perry claimed that Iran was deploying CW on a number of islands in the Straits of Hormuz, including the island of Abu Musa.[24] An Iranian foreign ministry spokesman denied these allegations.[25]

The *former Yugoslav Army* reportedly had a CW production facility at Potoci near Mostar, Bosnia.[26] This facility was alleged to be capable of producing sarin, mustard and other agents and was reportedly dismantled in 1992 and moved to Lucani in southern Serbia.[27] In November 1995 British experts claimed that Serbia possessed the capability to produce sarin but that sarin had not been transferred to the Bosnian Serbs.[28]

European and US intelligence reports claimed that a plant with 13 automated production lines, which *Libya* opened in September 1995 near Rabta, is a CW production facility capable of producing mustard.[29] Libya denied the allegations, stating that the $20 million plant is for the production of pharmaceuticals.[30] The plant is near the site of an alleged unfinished CW production facility that was mysteriously destroyed by fire in 1990.[31] Libya claims that the initial plant was sabotaged by German, Israeli and US intelligence services.[32] It has also been reported that Libya is building a CW production facility near Tarhunah, south-east of Tripoli.[33]

---

[18] 'Iran's weapons of mass destruction', *Jane's Intelligence Review*, Special Report no. 6, 1995, pp. 16–17; and Adams, J., 'Iran making chemical arsenal', *Sunday Times*, 5 Feb. 1995, p. 15.

[19] 'Iran's weapons of mass destruction' (note 18), p. 17.

[20] Adams (note 18); and Dettmer, J., 'Tehran building deadly gas plant', *Washington Times*, 30 Jan. 1995, p. A1.

[21] 'India denies role in toxic gas', *Washington Times*, 2 Feb. 1995, p. A17.

[22] Adams (note 18).

[23] Dettmer (note 20).

[24] 'US warns of Iran buildup in Gulf', *International Herald Tribune*, 23 Mar. 1995, p. 7.

[25] 'Allegations "lack military sense"', in Foreign Broadcast Information Service, *Daily Report–Near East and South Asia* (FSBIS-NES), FBIS-NES-95-058, 27 Mar. 1995, p. 70.

[26] Stock, T., 'Chemical weapons', *SIPRI Yearbook 1994* (Oxford University Press: Oxford, 1994), p. 327.

[27] Bartholomew, R., 'The Balkans and chemical warfare: a possibility?', *ASA Newsletter*, 11 Oct. 1995, pp. 1, 7.

[28] Bellamy, C., 'Fears over Serbia's poison gas factories', *The Independent*, 27 Nov. 1995, p. 10.

[29] 'Libya opens Rabta chemical plant', *Jane's Intelligence Review Pointer*, vol. 2, no. 11 (Nov. 1995), p. 3.

[30] 'Libya opens Rabta chemical plant' (note 29).

[31] Walker, C., 'West's doubts linger as Libya opens chemical plant', *The Times*, 22 Sep. 1995; and Lundin, J., 'Chemical and biological warfare', *SIPRI Yearbook 1991: World Armaments and Disarmament* (Oxford University Press: Oxford, 1991), p. 92.

[32] Walker (note 31).

[33] 'Libya opens Rabta chemical plant' (note 29).

Reports in the spring of 1995 claimed that US intelligence sources believe that *North Korea* possesses approximately 1000 t of chemical weapons, including blister, nerve, blood and tearing agents and that it has an annual production capacity of 4500 t of CW agents.[34] Chemical weapons are reportedly produced at a factory in Kanggye; precursors are produced in a chemical plant in Hyesan; and the main CW storage facilities are located at the Maram Materials Company and the Chihari Chemical Company.[35]

In October 1995 the Federal Security Service of *the Russian Federation* accused former Chairman of the Committee on Convention Problems of Chemical and Biological Weapons Anatoly Kuntsevich of involvement in the smuggling of 800 kg of toxic agents to Syria.[36] Kuntsevich, then a candidate for the state Duma, denied the allegations and stated that the charges might have been politically motivated since, at the time they were made, the US Senate was discussing ratification of the CWC and Russian President Boris Yeltsin was in the USA.[37]

Old and abandoned chemical weapons and CW munitions dumped at sea

The most important developments in 1995 with respect to abandoned chemical weapons were the Japanese fact-finding missions in China. According to China, Japan abandoned over 2 million CW munitions and over 100 t of toxic agents in China during World War II.[38] On 26 February–13 March 1995 a Japanese team visited China and sealed and removed three containers of mustard and lewisite found near Chuzhou and three containers of diphenylchloroarsine found in Nanjing.[39] This was the first time that Japan officially admitted that it had abandoned chemical weapons in China. In June a Japanese team removed 366 rusted, but identifiably Japanese, chemical weapons from two sites in Jilin Province, China.[40] Although most of the negotiations between China and Japan on abandoned chemical weapons remain secret, it is clear that such fact-finding and recovery missions will continue in the future. Official Chinese newspapers estimate the cost for recovery and destruction of abandoned CW in China at over $1 billion.[41]

---

[34] 'Military estimates DPRK chemical arms stocks', in FBIS-EAS-95-073, 17 Apr. 1995, p. 52; and 'N. Korea: chemical weapons', *Yonha* (telex), 21 Mar. 1995.

[35] 'DPRK chemical weapons can reportedly kill 40 million people', in Foreign Broadcast Information Service, *Daily Report–Arms Control and Proliferation Issues* (FBIS-TAC), FBIS-TAC-95-003, 29 June 1995, p. 8.

[36] 'Daily comments on Kuntsevich smuggling charges', in FBIS-SOV-95-207, 26 Oct. 1995, p. 33; 'Senior official accused of smuggling chemical weapons', Open Media Research Institute, *OMRI Daily Digest*, 23 Oct. 1995; and Mirzayanov, V., 'Dismantling the Soviet/Russian chemical weapons complex: an insider's view', *Chemical Weapons Disarmament in Russia: Problems and Prospects*, report no. 17 (Henry L. Stimson Center: Washington, DC, Oct. 1995), p. 32.

[37] 'Daily comments on Kuntsevich smuggling charges' (note 36); and 'Kuntsevich calls smuggling charges "absurd"', in FBIS-SOV-95-205, 24 Oct. 1995, p. 25.

[38] 'Some information on discovered chemical weapons abandoned in China by a foreign state', Conference on Disarmament document CD/1127, CD/CW/WP.384, 18 Feb. 1992.

[39] 'Japan disposes of CW left behind', *Jane's Defence Weekly*, vol. 23, no. 131 (Apr. 1995), p. 19.

[40] Reuter, 'Japan, China to discuss WW2 chemical arms disposal', 7 June 1995.

[41] United Press International, Beal, T., 'China wants disposal of Japanese bombs', 17 Aug. 1995, via Nexis.

In January 1995 a representative of the Polish armed forces stated that Poland would have to destroy a stockpile of adamsite from World War II at an estimated cost of $2.8 million.[42]

A NATO-sponsored workshop was held in Kaliningrad, Russia, in January 1995 on the problems associated with sea-dumped chemical weapons, particularly those dumped in the Baltic and North seas.[43] Sea-dumped chemical munitions were much discussed in the UK in 1995, especially after British Gas encountered sea-dumped conventional munitions when it began laying an underwater pipeline linking Scotland and Northern Ireland.[44] Responding to a parliamentary inquiry, British Ministry of Defence (MOD) representatives stated that approximately 120 000 t of British chemical weapons were dumped off the coast of Britain in 1945–49 and an additional 25 000 t of chemical weapons (including about 17 000 t of captured German tabun-filled bombs) were dumped between 1955 and 1957.[45] There were no British CW sea-dumping operations after 1957.[46] The CW dump sites are located 80–160 km west of the Hebrides, 130 km north-west of Northern Ireland, 400 km south-west of Land's End and in Beaufort's Dyke in the Irish Sea.[47] The chemical weapons at Beaufort's Dyke comprise approximately 14 000 t of phosgene artillery rockets in crates.[48] A total of 24 ships containing chemical weapons were scuttled at other sites at depths of 500–4200 m.[49] There are no detailed records of these various CW sea-dumping operations or of British CW sea dumping in international waters far from the UK.[50]

CW destruction

Although the 1990 Russian–US Bilateral Destruction Agreement[51] has yet to be ratified by Russia and the USA, both countries continued to proceed with their CW destruction programmes.

---

[42] 'Poland to destroy chemical weapons within ten years', *PAP* [Polish News Agency] *News Wire*, 9 Jan. 1995.

[43] James, B., 'Deep-sixed chemical weapons', *International Herald Tribune*, 5 Jan. 1995, p. 8.

[44] Edwards, R., 'Danger from the deep', *New Scientist,* vol. 148, no. 2004 (18 Nov. 1995), pp. 16–17.

[45] *Hansard* (Commons), 'Chemical weapons', vol. 254, no. 39 (27 Jan. 1995), col. 448; and *Hansard* (Commons), 'Hazardous waste (dumping at sea)', vol. 264, no. 146 (20 Oct. 1995), col. 387.

[46] *Hansard* (Commons), 'Sea dumping (munitions)', vol. 257, no. 83 (31 Mar. 1995), col. 875.

[47] *Hansard* (note 45).

[48] *Hansard* (Commons), 'Chemical weapons', vol. 254, no. 49 (9 Feb. 1995), col. 412.

[49] Hencke, D., 'Records lost of chemicals and arms dumped at sea', *The Guardian*, 28 Apr. 1995, p. 9.

[50] Hencke (note 49).

[51] The Agreement between the United States of America and the Union of Soviet Socialist Republics on Destruction and Non-Production of Chemical Weapons and on Measures to Facilitate the Multilateral Convention on Banning Chemical Weapons, commonly called the Bilateral Destruction Agreement or BDA, was signed on 1 June 1990. The text of the agreement is reproduced in *SIPRI Yearbook 1991* (note 31), pp. 536–39. The Russian Federation took over all Soviet international obligations and treaties and is the sole inheritor of Soviet obligations under this agreement. It is the only state of the former Soviet Union to possess CW stockpiles.

CW destruction in the Russian Federation

Russia did not begin destruction of its chemical weapon stockpile of 40 000 t in 1995, but progress was made in various political and other aspects of the CW destruction programme. On 25 March 1995 President Yeltsin signed a decree on CW destruction in Russia, stating that the weapons would be destroyed at facilities collocated with the current storage sites at Pochep (Bryansk oblast), Maradikovsky (Kirov oblast), Leonidovka (Penza oblast), Shuchye (Kurgan oblast), Gorny (Saratov oblast) and Kizner and Kambarka (Republic of Udmurtia).[52] On 6 July the Russian Government approved a draft law for the destruction of CW which was submitted to the Duma on 16 September 1995,[53] and in December 1995 the Chemical Weapons Destruction Act was introduced in the Duma.[54]

A plan for CW destruction in Russia (which did not require ratification by the Duma) was adopted by the government on 26 October 1995.[55] It called for beginning destruction with the bulk lewisite stored at Kambarka and the bulk mustard and lewisite stored at Gorny. When the two destruction facilities are operational they are projected to have a combined annual destruction capacity of 1850 t of agent.[56] There are 7500 t of bulk blister agents to be destroyed at the two sites.[57] Once destruction at Kambarka and Gorny has begun the plan calls for the destruction of the approximately 32 500 t of CW in munitions that are stored at the remaining five sites.[58] All Russian chemical weapons are to be destroyed and the destruction facilities decommissioned by 2009.[59]

In October 1995 the planned cost of the destruction programme was estimated at 16.6 trillion roubles (then equivalent to approximately $3.5 billion).[60] Earlier, in July, the government had announced that the total cost of CW destruction in Russia would be $6 billion, of which $500 million would be dedicated to verification costs.[61] The July figure is apparently more realistic. In August 1995 the chief of staff of the Russian armed forces requested

---

[52] 'Yeltsin signs decree on chemical weapons destruction', *OMRI Daily Digest*, 27 Mar. 1995.

[53] 'Government approves plan for destruction of chemical weapons', *OMRI Daily Digest*, 7 July 1995; and 'Yeltsin submits chemical weapons destruction bill to Duma', *OMRI Daily Digest*, 18 Sep. 1995.

[54] *Moscow News*, no. 49 (15–21 Dec. 1995), p. 2; and 'Statement by the head of the delegation of the Russian Federation at the twelfth session of the Preparatory Commission for the OPCW on 13 December 1995', PrepCom document PC-XII/18, 13 Dec. 1995, p. 1. In Mar. 1996 the Decree of the Government of the Russian Federation, no. 305, 21 Mar. 1996, was adopted. It contains the federal programme Destruction of Chemical Weapons Stockpiles in the Russian Federation.

[55] 'Russian government endorses chemical weapons destruction program', *OMRI Daily Digest*, 27 Oct. 1995.

[56] 'Government adopts program for CW elimination', in FBIS-SOV-95-208, 27 Oct. 1995, p. 43.

[57] 'Government adopts program for CW elimination' (note 56).

[58] 'Government adopts program for CW elimination' (note 56).

[59] According to decree no. 305 (note 54). 'Russian government endorses chemical weapons destruction program' (note 55); and *Moscow News* (note 54).

[60] 'Russian government endorses chemical weapons destruction program' (note 55); and *Moscow News* (note 54).

[61] ['It has to be done, but the funding to carry it out is lacking'], *Kommersant Daily*, 8 July 1995 (in Russian).

510 billion roubles (approximately $110 million) from the government for CW destruction for budget year 1996.[62]

Several countries are assisting Russia with its CW demilitarization. According to US sources, Russian officials have estimated that 35–50 per cent of the total Russian CW destruction costs will have to come from international assistance.[63] In 1995 the *Netherlands* joined those countries offering assistance by pledging technical assistance to the future destruction facility in Kambarka.[64] The *Swedish* National Defence Research Establishment (FOA) has allocated approximately $500 000 to various projects at the Kambarka facility, including a risk assessment.[65] *Germany* has allocated approximately $4.5 million to the destruction facility in Gorny for fiscal year (FY) 1995. By the end of FY 1995 Germany had provided approximately $11 million in financial assistance.[66]

The *USA* remains the largest donor of CW destruction assistance to Russia. It has allocated $55 million to CW destruction in Russia, and as of May 1995, $22.5 million had been specified for various projects and $7.3 million had been disbursed. US assistance is directed primarily at the destruction of nerve agents, which constitute approximately 80 per cent of the Russian stockpile, and it covers three projects: (*a*) preparation of a comprehensive implementation plan for Russian CW destruction, (*b*) establishment of an analytical CW destruction laboratory, and (*c*) conducting of a joint Russian–US evaluation of Russian CW destruction technology. Relatively little of the $55 million had been disbursed by the end of 1995 owing to delays in the selection of a site for the analytical destruction laboratory, for which $30 million is allocated. The US Department of Defense (DOD) will submit an additional request for $234 million for Russian CW destruction assistance for FY 1996 and 1997. These funds will be for the construction of a CW destruction facility with an annual destruction capacity of 500 t. The construction cost of the facility is estimated at more than $500 million and will require funding through 2001.[67]

Chemical weapon destruction in Russia continues to be of concern to those living near destruction sites. In October 1995 the Green Cross organized the first public hearing on CW destruction in Saratov, Russia.[68] Russian Government and military representatives, national experts, researchers, environmentalists and representatives of the citizens of Gorny attended the hearing, as did

[62] 'Chief of staff on chemical weapons destruction', *OMRI Daily Digest*, 2 Aug. 1995.
[63] US General Accounting Office (GAO), *Weapons of Mass Destruction: Reducing the Threat from the Former Soviet Union*, appendix II, *Destruction and Dismantlement Projects*, GAO/NSIAD-95-165, CTR: an update, 9 June 1995.
[64] The monetary value of the assistance has not yet been agreed. 'Russian-Dutch MoU', *Jane's Defence Weekly*, vol. 24, no. 22 (2 Dec. 1995), p. 8.
[65] 'Svensk stöd för förstöring av kemiska vapen i Ryssland' [Swedish support for destruction of chemical weapons in Russia], Regeringsbeslut 8 [Governmental decision 8], Ministry for Foreign Affairs, 19 Jan. 1995, H90, (in Swedish).
[66] GAO (note 63).
[67] GAO (note 63).
[68] Timashova, N., ['We will destroy chemical weapons even if it means ecological damage'], *Izvestia*, 17 Oct. 1995, p. 2 (in Russian).

grass-roots environmental activists from US CW destruction sites.[69] Despite public outreach efforts numerous citizen groups in both Russia and the USA continue to express dissatisfaction with the current CW destruction plans in both countries.

CW destruction in the United States

As in previous years, the US chemical weapon destruction programme experienced delays and cost increases in 1995. In July the US General Accounting Office (GAO) reported that the estimated total cost of the US CW destruction programme had risen to $11.9 billion.[70] Initial cost estimates had been underestimated owing largely to two factors; *(a)* costs were based on 24-hour-per-day destruction operations, which are not yet feasible, and *(b)* there were initially insufficient operational testing data from the prototype destruction facility, Johnston Atoll Chemical Agent Disposal System (JACADS), which is located on Johnston Atoll in the Pacific Ocean, south-west of Hawaii.[71] As of July 1995 approximately $2 billion had been spent on the US CW destruction programme, but only two of the nine planned destruction facilities had been built and approximately 2 per cent of the stockpile destroyed.[72]

Delays in the US CW destruction programme in 1995 resulted mainly from the failure to issue certain state permits. The destruction facility in Tooele, Utah, completed trial burns at one of its two liquid incinerators in August 1995, and destruction operations were scheduled to begin in September.[73] However, a state permit to begin operation had still not been issued to the facility at the end of 1995 and would not be issued until a pre-operational survey had been completed.[74] Construction of the destruction facility at Anniston, Alabama, was scheduled to begin in August 1995, but a state building permit had not yet been issued by December 1995.

Despite delays the destruction programme made some progress in 1995. In July JACADS successfully completed destruction of its entire stockpile of more than 72 000 M-55 nerve agent rockets,[75] and in November 1995 JACADS completed destruction of its MC1 sarin-filled 750-lb (340 kg) bombs.[76] In addition, JACADS has destroyed over 45 000 CW projectiles and 134 tonne containers since operations began in 1990.[77]

---

[69] Green Cross, 'Final statement', First Public Hearing on the Problem of the Destruction of Chemical Weapons in the Saratov Region, Saratov, 17–19 Oct. 1995.

[70] This is a large increase over the initial 1985 total cost estimate of approximately $1.7 billion and almost double the 1991 cost estimate of $6.5 billion. GAO, *Chemical Weapons Disposal: Issues Related to DOD's Management*, GAO/T-NSIAD-95-185, 13 July 1995.

[71] GAO, *Chemical Stockpile Disposal Program Review*, GAO/NSIAD-95-66R, 12 Jan. 1995.

[72] GAO (note 70).

[73] 'Trial burns begin at the Tooele chemical agent disposal facility', *Chemical Demilitarization Update*, vol. 3, no. 5 (Sep. 1995), p. 5.

[74] 'Preoperational survey of TOCDF', *Chemical Demilitarization Update*, vol. 3, no. 6 (Nov. 1995), p. 6.

[75] 'JACADS destroys its M-55 rocket stockpile', *Chemical Demilitarization Update*, vol. 3, no. 5 (Sep. 1995), p. 1.

[76] Program Manager for Chemical Demilitarization, Public Affairs Office, US Army, 'Army destroys all MC-1 bombs at Johnston Atoll', *Press Release*, no. 95-16 (15 Dec. 1995).

[77] 'JACADS destroys its M-55 rocket stockpile' (note 75).

In December 1994 the US Army released a report evaluating the storage life of M-55 rockets, of which there are approximately 478 000 in the US CW stockpile.[78] The report found that there is a less than one in one million chance that a non-leaking rocket would auto-ignite before 2013.[79] For leaking munitions the chances may be greater since rockets exposed to chemical agents may have a shorter 'shelf-life'. In March 1995 low levels of sarin were detected leaking from gaskets on the doors of a filter unit at JACADS.[80] The gaskets were replaced and monitoring procedures enhanced following the leak. In August, 35 M-55 sarin-filled rockets were discovered to be leaking or in danger of leaking at the Anniston depot, and they were sealed in leak-proof containers.[81] Since 1982, at the Anniston depot alone, 373 rockets and 92 other CW have had to be repackaged and sealed to contain leaks.[82]

A total of $575.5 million was appropriated for US CW destruction in FY 1995.[83] The budget estimate for CW destruction for FY 1996 was initially $746.7 million, but this figure was reduced by the Senate Committee on Appropriations to $631.7 million in July 1995.[84] The Committee modified its prohibition on federal funds being spent on feasibility studies for the transport of CW, and the 1996 budget allows for such studies. However, at the same time the Senate Committee stated that it 'is convinced that armed convoys of lethal chemical weapons moving through hundreds of miles of populated cities and counties is unacceptable'.[85] The Committee reiterated that no additional CW would ever be moved to Johnston Atoll. The final appropriation for FY 1996 was $672.3 million.[86]

Alternative CW destruction technologies

While the USA is still officially planning to use incineration as a method of destruction at all of its planned destruction facilities, the US Army is conducting intensive studies of alternative technologies for agents that are stored in bulk. There are only two sites in the USA where alternative destruction technologies are being considered: Aberdeen Proving Ground, Maryland, and Newport Chemical Activity, Indiana (both are bulk-agent-only sites). US testing of two alternative destruction technologies—neutralization, and neu-

---

[78] US Army Chemical Stockpile Disposal Program, 'Army releases report on M55 rocket storage life evaluation', *Press Release*, 23 Jan. 1995.

[79] US Army Chemical Stockpile Disposal Program (note 78).

[80] 'Likely source of low-level agent release at Johnston Island identified', *Chemical Demilitarization Update*, vol. 3, no. 4 (May 1995), p. 5.

[81] '35 leaking rockets containerized at Anniston', *Chemical Demilitarization Update*, vol. 3, no. 6 (Nov. 1995), p. 5.

[82] '35 leaking rockets containerized at Anniston' (note 81).

[83] *Department of Defense Appropriation Bill, 1996, Report* (US Government Printing Office: Washington, DC, 1995), p. 199.

[84] *Department of Defense Appropriation Bill* (note 83).

[85] *Department of Defense Appropriation Bill* (note 83), p. 200.

[86] *Congressional Record*, 22 Jan. 1996, p. H358. Congressional Record Online via GPO Access, Version current on 30 Jan. 1996, URL <wais.access.gpo.gov>.

tralization followed by biodegradation—began in July 1995.[87] Gas-phase chemical reduction is also being studied by the US Army.[88]

The UK announced in March 1995 that it would build a pilot plant for the destruction of old CW munitions by the use of an electrochemical oxidative process (the Silver II process).[89] The plant will be located at Porton Down.

In 1995 alternative demilitarization technologies were discussed at several conferences.[90]

III. Implementation of the CWC

Since the CWC was opened for signing in January 1993, the number of states which have signed it has reached 160,[91] and 47 states have submitted their instruments of ratification to the Secretary-General of the United Nations.[92] The CWC will enter into force 180 days after a total of 65 states have deposited their ratifications. In 1993 it was hoped that only 18 months would be needed for this process, but this proved unrealistic and the convention did not to enter into force at the earliest possible date, January 1995.

There are several reasons for the slower than anticipated ratification process, including: *(a)* the unrealistic estimates of the time needed for individual states to prepare for national implementation; *(b)* the complexity of implementation of the CWC, which involves many administrative, legal and technical problems; *(c)* the time-consuming drafting of implementing legislation and establishing of implementing agencies; and *(d)* the complexity of preparing indus-

---

[87] 'Alternative technologies update: Army prepares for bench-scale testing', *Chemical Demilitarization Update*, vol. 3, no. 5 (Sep. 1995), p. 3.

[88] 'Eli Eco says US Army to review chemical disposal technology', *Dow Jones News*, 14 Nov. 1995.

[89] '23 March', *Chemical Weapons Convention Bulletin*, no. 28 (June 1995), p. 23.

[90] 'Army holds workshop on advances in alternative demilitarization technologies', *Chemical Demilitarization Update*, vol. 3, no. 6 (Nov. 1995), p. 1. See also NATO, 'NATO workshop on nuclear and chemical contamination in the countries of the former Soviet Union: cleanup. management and prevention', *Press Release*, no. 95(11), 9 Feb. 1995; NATO, 'NACC seminar on demilitarization and disarmament in transition: socio-economic consequences to be held in Minsk, Republic of Belarus, 22–24 March 1995', *Press Release*, no. 95(22), 15 Mar. 1995; NATO, 'NATO advanced research workshop on scientific advances in alternative demilitarization technologies 24–25 April in Warsaw', *Press Release*, no. 95(30), 19 Apr. 1995; NATO, 'Meeting of NATO committees on the challenge of modern society (CCMS) with cooperation partners', *Press Release*, no. 95(32), 26 Apr. 1995; NATO, 'NACC workshop on "Polish experiences in defence conversion" Warsaw/Lowicz, Poland, 21–24 May 1995', *Press Release*, no. 95(38), 8 May. 1995; and NATO, 'NATO/CCMS meeting on protection of civil populations from toxic material spills during movement of military goods, October 17–19, 1995', *Press Release*, no. 95(96), 10 Oct. 1995. Version current on 24 Jan. 1996, URL <http://www.nato.int/docu/home.htm>.

[91] Uzbekistan signed the CWC on 24 Nov. 1995, bringing the total number of signatory states to 160. PrepCom document PC/CWC-S.R./12, 8 Jan. 1996.

[92] During 1995 the following states deposited their instruments of ratification: Tajikistan, 11 Jan. 1995; Mongolia, 17 Jan. 1995; Armenia, 27 Jan. 1995; Finland, 7 Feb. 1995; Oman, 8 Feb. 1995; Romania, 15 Feb. 1995; France, 2 Mar. 1995; Switzerland, 10 Mar. 1995; Croatia, 23 May 1995; Monaco, 1 June 1995; the Netherlands, 30 June 1995; Denmark, 13 July 1995; Peru, 20 July 1995; Algeria, 14 Aug. 1995; Austria, 17 Aug. 1995; Poland, 23 Aug. 1995; Ecuador, 6 Sep. 1995; South Africa, 13 Sep. 1995; Japan, 15 Sep. 1995; Canada, 26 Sep. 1995; Argentina, 2 Oct. 1995; Slovak Republic, 27 Oct. 1995; El Salvador, 30 Oct. 1995; Georgia, 27 Nov. 1995; Namibia, 27 Nov. 1995; Italy, 6 Dec. 1995; Côte d'Ivoire; 12 Dec. 1995; and Morocco, 28 Dec. 1995; PrepCom document PC/CWC-S.R./12, 8 Jan. 1996; and PrepCom, Media and Public Affairs Branch, 'Morocco ratifies the Chemical Weapons Convention', *Press Release*, no. 83 (4 Jan. 1996).

try to submit declarations. Delays in ratification may also be attributed to the fact that some states are waiting for Russia and the USA to ratify the CWC. The convention would lose much of its authority and credibility were it to enter into force without these two states.

Given the current pace of ratifications and information provided by signatory states on their progress towards ratification, the Provisional Technical Secretariat (PTS) estimates that the CWC may enter into force by late 1996 or early 1997.[93]

At the 1993 signing ceremony the Paris Resolution was adopted to establish the Preparatory Commission for the OPCW (PrepCom).[94] The Paris resolution aimed to take all necessary measures to ensure the rapid and effective establishment of the future OPCW, to develop detailed procedures and to set up the necessary infrastructure for the OPCW.

The PrepCom is composed of all signatory states, and its work is conducted in plenary sessions, working groups and expert groups. Working Group A deals primarily with organizational issues (e.g., rules of procedure, staff and finance matters, preparation of the budget and programme of work), while Working Group B details procedures for verification, technical cooperation and assistance.[95] The expert groups prepare recommendations on specific issues which are subject to the approval of the working groups and the plenary sessions. All PrepCom decisions are taken by consensus. The PTS assists the PrepCom and is charged with building up the future OPCW and its Technical Secretariat (TS) as well as facilitating the dissemination of information to signatory states on all aspects of the implementation of the convention.[96]

The Preparatory Commission for the OPCW

Three plenary sessions were held in 1995 (3–7 April, 24–27 July and 11–14 December). As in the past it was difficult to obtain the participation of the required 50 per cent of all signatory states in these sessions (see table 15.1). It is the goal of the PrepCom that both the USA and Russia will be among the original ratifiers of the convention. The PTS assumes that the 1990 Russian–US Bilateral Destruction Agreement will have entered into force at the time of entry into force of the CWC.[97]

In March 1995 the PTS formally requested that the World Customs Organisation (WCO) introduce sub-headings for chemical substances into its harmonized commodity description and coding system (HS) to facilitate tracking

---

[93] 'Report of the Executive Secretary, part 1: retrospective on 1995', PrepCom document PC-XII/11, 7 Dec. 1995, p. 1.

[94] Resolution establishing the Preparatory Commission for the Organisation for the Prohibition of Chemical Weapons (i.e., the Paris Resolution), paras 10–15.

[95] Provisional Technical Secretariat of the Preparatory Commission for the Organisation for the Prohibition of Chemical Weapons, Information Series 2 (revision 3) Jan. 1995, p. 1.

[96] Information Series 2 (note 95), p. 2.

[97] 'Budget and programme of work 1995', vol. 1, PrepCom document PC-VIII/A/WP.1(1), 15 July 1994, p. 34.

Table 15.1. Attendance at 1995 plenary sessions of the Preparatory Commission

Plenary session	Date	Number of signatory states in attendance	Number of signatory states	Rate of attendance	Number of ratifications
10	3–7 Apr. 1995	88	159	55.3	27
11	24–27 July 1995	93	159	58.5	32
12	11–14 Dec. 1995	87	160	54.4	45

Sources: 'Report of the Commission', PrepCom document PC-X/23, 7 Apr. 1995; 'Report of the Commission', PrepCom document PC-XI/17, 27 July 1995; and 'Report of the Commission', PrepCom document PC-XII/17, 14 Dec. 1995.

the import and export of scheduled chemicals through existing national customs controls.[98] Collaboration with the WCO Secretariat and participation in a November 1995 HS Committee meeting will enable finalization of the chemical nomenclature before the next HS committee meeting in April 1996.[99]

At the April 1995 10th plenary session of the PrepCom many states expressed concern about the use of sarin by terrorists in Japan. The Chairman of the PrepCom and a number of states stressed the importance of bringing the CWC into force soon in order to rapidly secure its benefits.[100]

At the 11th plenary session in July 1995 the proposed Programme of Work and Budget for 1996 was approved. The budget is in two parts. Part I ($15.5 million) was decreased from the 1995 budget ($17 million) because several one-time expenditures have now been made.[101] The funds for Part II of the budget, which will become available on deposit of the 65th ratification of the CWC, were increased to $18.2 million to allow for expansion to the full strength of 369 staff members, including the first group of 140 inspectors.[102] Of the total contributions from signatory states assessed for Part I of the budget in 1995, 94.1 per cent were received in the first 10 months of the year. This collection rate considerably exceeds the average United Nations collection rate of approximately 65–70 per cent.[103]

The OPCW Confidentiality Policy was adopted in 1995,[104] but it must be formally approved at the first conference of states parties. It outlines the responsibilities of the OPCW, the Director-General, the Technical Secretariat, the inspection team, the future states parties and the observers as regards the

[98] 'Report by the Executive Secretary, the intersessional period 3 Dec. 1994–31 Mar. 1995', PrepCom document PC-X/10, 31 Mar. 1995, p. 5–6.
[99] 'Report of the Executive Secretary, part 1: retrospective on 1995' (note 93), pp. 13–14.
[100] 'Report by the Chairman of the Commission', PrepCom document, PC-X/11, 30 Mar. 1995, pp. 1–2.
[101] Such as procurement of computers. 'Report of the Commission', PrepCom document PC-XI/17, 27 July 1995, p. 3.
[102] 'Report of the Commission' (note 101).
[103] 'Report of the Executive Secretary, part 1: retrospective on 1995' (note 93), p. 7.
[104] 'Report of the Commission' (note 101), p. 5.

handling and protection of confidential information.[105] It also establishes a Confidentiality Commission to deal with alleged breaches of confidentiality.

The 10th plenary session reorganized the work of the PrepCom to: *(a)* streamline the substantive work of the expert groups, *(b)* make best use of experts from the signatory states present at The Hague, and *(c)* encourage the participation of all delegates.[106] Eleven 'clusters' were set up, each of which corresponds to one or more experts groups. The chairman of Working Group A or B will coordinate work between plenary sessions, convene meetings with an expert group when appreciable progress has been made and consult with delegations.[107]

In September and October 1995 the current and former chairmen of the PrepCom and the Executive Secretary attempted to speed up the ratification process in Russia and the USA by visits to both countries. Discussions were held with senior administration officials and with senior representatives of the legislatures of both countries.[108] By the end of 1995 neither state had ratified the CWC.

In 1995 progress was made in establishing the General Training Scheme for future inspectors and in approving technical specifications for many items of inspection equipment. However, there are several issues, some of more than two years duration, which show no sign of early resolution. Much remains to be done to finalize the Inspection Manual, to reach agreement on the technical aspects of declaration requirements and to find solutions to disputes—including those related to challenge inspections,[109] the ultimate scope of the OPCW Analytical Database, old and abandoned chemical weapons, and chemical weapon production facilities.[110]

Working Group A

In Working Group A, the Expert Group on Data Systems considered issues related to the Information Management System (IMS), security, national offers and the Information Systems Branch budget for 1995.[111] In November 1995 the OPCW IMS Security Study, a study to define adequate security measures for sensitive information obtained from declarations and inspections,

[105] 'Expert Group on Confidentiality', PrepCom document PC-XI/B/WP.8, 23 June 1995, and its annex.

[106] 'Report of the Executive Secretary, part 2: the intersessional period 22 July–7 Dec. 1995', PrepCom document PC-XII/11, 7 Dec. 1995, p. 8; and 'Note of the Executive Secretary, work of the commission during the intersessional period between its eleventh and twelfth session', PrepCom document PC-XI/9, 21 July 1995, pp. 1–2.

[107] Dunworth, T., 'Progress in The Hague: building the Organisation for the Prohibition of Chemical Weapons, quarterly review no. 11', *Chemical Weapons Convention Bulletin*, no. 29 (Sep. 1995), p. 6.

[108] 'Report of the Executive Secretary, part 1: retrospective on 1995' (note 93), p. 2.

[109] With respect to challenge inspection many delegations, however, argue that the 'solution to disputes related to challenge inspections' is already adequately taken care of in the CWC text under Article IX, paras 22 and 23.

[110] 'Report of the Executive Secretary, part 1: retrospective on 1995' (note 93), p. 3.

[111] 'Expert Group on Data Systems: tenth report', PrepCom document PC-X/A/WP.1, 9 Feb. 1995, p. 1.

was submitted to the task forces and the Expert Group on Data Systems.[112] The IMS will have two components (critical and non-critical) to provide appropriate, secure and cost-effective protection for data.[113] An internal evaluation concluded that funding for the IMS in the 1996 budget is insufficient,[114] and the Executive Secretary has begun to act to address this problem.[115]

The Draft Media and Public Affairs Policy was provisionally approved by the PrepCom.[116] It establishes rules for contacts with news media by OPCW personnel and incorporates the recommendations of the Expert Group on Confidentiality.[117] It states that the OPCW should 'promote the image of the OPCW as an accessible international organisation which provides balanced, timely and objective information'. Information 'specifically related to a State Party' may be released 'only at the request of or with the express consent of the State Party to which this information refers'. The inspected state must ensure that the news media do not interfere with the work of the inspection team.[118]

The Finance Group discussed the OPCW Financial Regulations and OPCW Financial Rules[119] and decided to include regulations on procurement, on reimbursable expenses with regard to inspection of facilities and on the establishment of a Special Fund for Challenge Inspections. The group worked on the first OPCW budget (i.e., for the first year after entry into force of the CWC).[120]

Working Group B

At the end of 1994 a number of issues for which Working Group B is responsible remained unsettled.[121] In 1995, political differences between delegations prevented substantive progress, and important issues continued to be unre-

[112] 'Note by the Executive Secretary: security study on the Information Management System of the OPCW', PrepCom document PC-XII/A/3, 8 Nov. 1995.

[113] 'Expert Group on Data Systems: tenth report' (note 111).

[114] 'Note by the Executive Secretary, Programme of work and budget: 1995 and 1996', PrepCom document PC-XII/A/4, 10 Nov. 1995; and 'Report of the Executive Secretary, part 1: retrospective on 1995' (note 93), p. 6.

[115] 'Expert Group on Data Systems: thirteenth report', PrepCom document PC-XII/A/WP.3, 17 Nov. 1995, p. 1–2; and 'Report of the Executive Secretary, part 1: retrospective on 1995' (note 93), p. 6.

[116] 'Report of the Commission', PrepCom document PC-X/23, 7 Apr. 1995, p. 4.

[117] 'Final report on the formal consultations on OPCW media and public affairs policy', PrepCom document PC-X/A/WP.5, 8 Mar. 1995, attachment, p. 5.

[118] 'Final report on the formal consultations on OPCW media and public affairs policy' (note 117).

[119] 'Finance Group: report of the eighth meeting', PrepCom document PC-XII/A/WP.2, 3 Nov. 1995, p. 1.

[120] The first year's budget will be divided into two parts, one on verification costs and one on administrative and other costs. 'Finance Group: report of the eighth meeting' (note 119), pp. 8–11; and 'Note by the Executive Secretary: methodology and assumptions for the OPCW budget', PrepCom document PC-XII/A/1, 16 Oct. 1995.

[121] The topics selected for Working Group B on the basis of the Paris Resolution, the CWC, the reports of the Expert Groups and consultations with delegations are: old and abandoned CW, CW, CWPFs, inspection procedures, challenge inspections, health and safety, sampling and analytical procedures, training, chemical industry issues, assistance and protection issues, economic and technological development, confidentiality, approved equipment, model facility agreements and other agreements. 'Report of the Chairman of the Commission and the Executive Secretary on improved methods of work of the Commission', PrepCom document PC-IX/8, 2 Dec. 1994, appendix, pp. 7–14.

solved, although some of the Working Group B expert groups reached agreement on certain technical aspects of implementation of the CWC.

In the first half of 1995 the Expert Group on Safety Procedures worked on the draft OPCW Health and Safety Regulations which address health and safety in the workplace, in the OPCW Laboratory and during inspections,[122] but 1995 ended without final agreement on the draft.[123] A Task Force on Medical Treatment developed procedures for treatment of persons exposed to chemical agents.[124]

The Expert Group on Chemical Industry Issues worked on a model facility agreement for Schedule 2 facilities, but agreement was not reached.[125] Issues related to the information required in a declaration (e.g., whether 'production by synthesis' includes biochemical and biologically mediated processes,[126] the method of reporting aggregate national data for Schedule 2 and 3 chemicals and the declaration of castor bean processing plants) remained unsettled.[127] In addition, the final provisions regarding scheduled chemicals in low concentrations (including mixtures) could not be agreed.[128]

The interpretation of Article XI (Economic and Technical Development) remained controversial.[129] The Expert Group on Technical Co-operation and

[122] 'Expert Group on Safety Procedures: fourth report', PrepCom document PC-X/B/WP.8, 16 Feb. 1995, pp. 1–2.

[123] 'Expert Group on Safety Procedures: sixth report', PrepCom document PC-XI/B/WP.7, 23 June 1995; and 'Expert Group on Safety Procedures: seventh report', PrepCom document PC-XII/B/WP.5, 1 Nov. 1995. However, the group approved two documents: 'Principles of the medical treatment of chemical poisoning' and 'Medical fitness standards for employees of the OPCW'.

[124] 'Expert Group on Safety Procedures: fourth report' (note 122), p. 2. Two documents were approved on the assessment of the effectiveness of antidotes and the cost-effective selection of medications: 'Format for the presentation of material concerning the treatment of chemical casualties' and 'Operational requirements and technical specifications relating to medications and equipment to be used in the chemical casualty treatment kit'.

[125] The group received advice on the legal status of model facility agreements and existing facility agreements. 'Note by the Executive Secretary: legal opinion on the respective legal status of model agreements and of facility agreements', PrepCom document PC-XI/B/4, 15 May 1995; and 'Expert Group on Chemical Industry Issues: ninth report', PrepCom document PC-XI/B/WP.1, 27 Apr. 1995, pp. 1–2.

[126] The CWC defines production generally as 'its formation through chemical reaction', and Part IX of the Verification Annex discusses production of discrete organic chemicals 'by synthesis'. In contrast, the initial definition of toxic chemicals in Article II of the CWC states 'regardless of whether they are produced in facilities, in munitions or elsewhere'. The question whether facilities producing DOCs by biosynthesis should be excluded by limited interpretation of 'production by synthesis' is still unresolved.

[127] There is debate on what CWC negotiators meant by 'aggregate national data'. Sutherland, R. G. et al., 'Declaration thresholds and aggregate national data', SIPRI–Saskatchewan–Frankfurt Group, eds T. Kurzidem et al., Effective Implementation of the Chemical Weapons Convention: Proceedings of a Conference held at Bad Homburg, Germany, 8–10 Sep. 1995 (SIPRI–Saskatchewan–Frankfurt Group: Frankfurt am Main, Dec. 1995), pp. 176–177; and 'Expert Group on Chemical Industry Issues: ninth report' (note 125), pp. 1–2. Ricin, which is listed on Schedule 1 of the CWC, is extracted from castor beans.

[128] Sutherland et al. (note 127), pp. 178–179; and 'Expert Group on Chemical Industry Issues: ninth report' (note 125), p. 1–2.

[129] The article states that the parties shall 'undertake to facilitate . . . in the fullest exchange of chemicals, equipment and scientific and technical information'. Controversy on this issue is related to the position of some states that Article XI should ensure the 'free unhampered transfer of chemicals' for peaceful purposes and to the position that future States Parties are bound under Article I not to 'assist . . . anyone to engage in any activity prohibited' under the CWC. Stock, T., Geissler, E. and Trevan, T., 'Chemical and biological arms control', SIPRI Yearbook 1995: Armaments, Disarmament and International Security (Oxford University Press: Oxford, 1995), p. 734; and chapter 12 in this volume, which includes a discussion of Article XI and the Australia Group.

Assistance reviewed a study by the PTS on the use of databases to facilitate the exchange of information relating to economic and technological developments in chemistry.[130] Signatory states are encouraged to submit documentation to the data bank,[131] but the major source of data will be commercial databases. An experimental Internet site was established by the PTS to assist National Authorities by providing information on the work of the PrepCom, the CWC and its implementation.[132]

The Expert Group on Inspection Procedures approved documents specifying the general requirements and technical specifications for health and safety equipment, and for a set of sample collection kits for munitions.[133] Agreement was reached on rules for 'sanitizing' information unrelated to an inspection from data collected by inspectors,[134] and on technical items to be used as inspection equipment.[135] Reports by Specialist Task Forces on analytical issues were approved.[136] An inspected state will receive a copy of all inspection data, and if the inspected state 'has reasons to believe' that information not related to the purposes of the inspection has been recorded, the information will be removed by the inspection team in the presence of a representative of the inspected state.[137]

The Expert Group on Confidentiality set up general principles for handling and protecting confidential information related to inspections;[138] these are included in the Draft OPCW Policy on Confidentiality which was approved at the 11th plenary meeting.[139] Information obtained in an on-site inspection will be classified according to the wishes of the inspected state.[140] The problem of liability for damage caused by a breach of confidentiality by the Technical

---

[130] 'Report of the Executive Secretary, the intersessional period 3 Dec. 1994–31 Mar. 1995' (note 98), pp. 17–18.

[131] 'Note from the Executive Secretary', PrepCom document PC-VI/B/3, 28 Jan. 1994, and 'Report of the Executive Secretary, the intersessional period 3 Dec. 1994–31 Mar. 1995' (note 98), p. 18.

[132] 'Note by the Executive Secretary, The establishment of a temporary Secretariat Internet site', PrepCom document PC-XI/B/7, 30 June 1995. URL <http://www.opcw.nl/>.

[133] 'Expert Group on Inspection Procedures: seventh report', PrepCom document PC-X/B/WP.9, 2 Feb. 1995, p. 2, and its annexes 2 and 3.

[134] 'Expert Group on Inspection Procedures: seventh report' (note 133), pp. 2–3, and its annex 1, 'Measures in relation to approved equipment following inspection activities'. An additional two documents were approved which concern inspection procedures and equipment, 'Expert Group on Inspection Procedures: tenth report', PrepCom document PC-XII/B/WP.6, 2 Nov. 1995, concerning GC/MS sample preparation kit and sampling and analysis during investigation of alleged use.

[135] For technical specifications for boots and a flammability/explosive/air quality monitor, see 'Expert Group on Inspection Procedures: ninth report', PrepCom document PC-XI/B/WP.6, 21 June 1995, p. 2; and on sample transport kits for small and large samples, 'Report of the Executive Secretary, part 2: the intersessional period 22 July–7 Dec. 1995' (note 106), p. 22.

[136] 'Expert Group on Inspection Procedures: eighth report', PrepCom document PC-XI/B/WP.5, 19 June 1995, p. 2, 'Criteria for acceptable performance of laboratories in proficiency testing'; and 'Expert Group on Inspection Procedures: ninth report' (note 135), pp. 1–2, 'Standard operating procedure for preparation of test samples for OPCW/PTS proficiency tests'; additionally, the group approved the results of the evaluation of the IR spectra and the architecture of the OPCW Analytical Database System.

[137] 'Expert Group on Inspection Procedures: seventh report' (note 133), annex 1, p. 12.

[138] 'Expert Group on Confidentiality: sixth report', PrepCom document PC-X/B/WP.2, 15 Dec. 1994, p. 2, and its annex.

[139] 'Report of the Commission', PrepCom document PC-XI/17, 27 July 1995, pp. 5–6; and OPCW Policy on Confidentiality as annexed to PrepCom document PC-XI/B/WP.8, 23 June 1995.

[140] 'Expert Group on Confidentiality: sixth report' (note 138), annex, p. 12.

Secretariat should be addressed 'as it arises, by applying existing principles of public international law and private international law and by using the dispute resolution mechanisms in the CWC'.[141] There is still no agreement on: (a) the possible exercise of national jurisdiction where immunity is waived by the Director-General or in cases of serious breach of confidentiality by a staff member of the TS; (b) the application of national jurisdiction to natural or legal persons who have breached confidentiality; (c) the compensation for loss caused by a breach of confidentiality; and (d) the operating procedures for the Confidentiality Commission.[142]

Assistance from signatory states enabled the Expert Group on Training to near completion of the General Training Scheme for inspectors.[143] On the recommendation of the expert group, the PTS hosted three workshops to discuss and harmonize the offers for Module 1 training courses.[144] Five states offered M1 Basic courses[145] (all were certified except the Russian course). Nine states made 11 offers for M2 Specialist Application courses, and 6 were certified. In addition, nine states offered to provide access to facilities for M3 on-site inspection training.[146]

The Expert Group on Challenge Inspection made little progress in 1995; agreement was reached only on illustrative examples of information to be included in 'all appropriate information on the basis of which the concern (of possible non-compliance) has arisen' and on the format for an inspection mandate for conducting a challenge inspection.[147] No progress was made on establishing objective criteria to evaluate whether a request for a challenge inspection has been abused and for compensation in the event of abuse.[148]

Definition of 'usability' of old chemical weapons is an important question which has been discussed for three years by the Expert Group on Old and

---

[141] 'Expert Group on Confidentiality: seventh report', PrepCom document PC-X/B/WP.7, 8 Feb. 1995, p. 3.

[142] 'Expert Group on Confidentiality: eighth report', PrepCom document PC-XI/B/WP.8, 23 June 1995, p. 4.

[143] 'Report of the Executive Secretary, part 1: retrospective on 1995' (note 93), p. 3.

[144] 'Expert Group on Training: seventh report', PrepCom document PC-X/B/WP.12, 1 Mar. 1995, pp. 5–6. The first workshop, 16–17 May, was on Basic Course training. 'Report of the Executive Secretary, the intersessional period 1 Apr.–21 July 1995', PrepCom document PC-XI/8, 21 July 1995, p. 19. The second workshop was held on 18–19 Sep. 1995, 'Expert Group on Training, ninth report', PrepCom document PC-XII/B/WP.7, 1 Dec. 1995, p. 2; and the third workshop, 20–22 Sep. 1995, was on Trainee Evaluation, 'Expert Group on Training, ninth report', PrepCom document PC-XII/B/WP.7, 1 Dec. 1995, p. 3.

[145] France, India, the Netherlands, Russia and the USA. 'Report of the Executive Secretary, part 1: retrospective on 1995' (note 93), pp. 12–13.

[146] 'Expert Group on Training: ninth report' (note 144); 'Report of the Executive Secretary, part 2: the intersessional period 22 July–7 Dec. 1995' (note 106), p. 2; and 'Report of the Executive Secretary, part 1: retrospective on 1995' (note 93), pp. 12–13.

[147] 'Report of the Executive Secretary, the intersessional period 3 Dec. 1994–31 Mar. 1995' (note 98), p. 17; 'Expert Group on Challenge Inspections: fourth report', PrepCom document PC-XI/B/WP.9, 11 July 1995; and 'Expert Group on Challenge Inspection: fifth report', PrepCom document PC-XII/B/WP.3, 17 Oct. 1995, p. 1.

[148] 'Report of the Executive Secretary, part 2: the intersessional period 22 July–7 Dec. 1995' (note 106), p. 21.

Abandoned Chemical Weapons.[149] No agreement was reached owing to the differing political views of the delegations.

The Expert Group on Chemical Weapons Issues also could not reach agreement.[150] Major differences remained on the content of declarations and verification requirements in relation to former CW production facilities, a draft model facility agreement for them, their conversion for purposes not prohibited by the CWC[151] and the cost of verification.[152] The secretariat presented a first draft of a format for the inspection report for a CW storage facility.[153]

A Russian paper on the definition of a CW production facility caused controversy at the 10th plenary session.[154] Russia suggested that it might interpret the CWC as excluding from inspection, destruction, or conversion requirements most or all of the facilities at which it formerly produced chemical weapons. The paper was not supported by any other state. The USA and other countries stated that the Russian position was unacceptable, that it violated the integrity of the CWC and constituted a principal obstacle to progress in the preparation for entry into force.[155] Discussion on this topic continued in the expert group, but no progress was made. In December 1995, the Russian delegation indicated that it was willing to reconsider the definition of CW production facilities.[156]

Working Group B made progress in 1995, although its achievements on important verification issues were limited.[157] Final agreement was not reached on: CW production facilities, old and abandoned CW, the declaration handbook, challenge inspections, the inspection manual, low concentrations of chemicals under Schedules 2 and 3, and discrete organic chemicals.[158]

[149] 'Expert Group on Old and Abandoned Chemical Weapons: sixth report', PrepCom document PC-XI/B/WP.11, 13 July 1995, pp. 1–2.

[150] 'Report of the Executive Secretary, the intersessional period 3 Dec. 1994–31 Mar. 1995' (note 98), p. 18; and 'Report of the Executive Secretary, part 2: the intersessional period 22 July–7 Dec. 1995' (note 106), p. 23.

[151] 'Expert Group on Chemical Weapons Issues: fourth report', PrepCom document PC-X/B/WP.15, 23 Mar. 1995, p. 2.

[152] 'Report of the Executive Secretary, part 2: the intersessional period 22 July–7 Dec. 1995' (note 106), p. 23.

[153] 'Expert Group on Chemical Weapons Issues: fourth report', PrepCom document PC-X/B/WP.15, 23 Mar. 1995, p. 3.

[154] 'Russian Federation, the issue of declaration of chemical weapons production facilities', PrepCom document PC-X/B/WP.14, 23 Mar. 1995.

[155] 'Report of the Commission', PrepCom document PC-XI/17, 27 July 1995, p. 2; and Dunworth (note 107), p. 6.

[156] 'Statement by the head of the delegation of the Russian Federation at the twelfth session of Preparatory Commission for the OPCW on 13 December 1995', PrepCom document PC-XII/18, 13 Dec. 1995, pp. 1–3.

[157] 'Report of the Executive Secretary, part 1: retrospective on 1995' (note 93), p. 3.

[158] DOCs are defined as all compounds of carbon except for its oxides, sulfides and metal carbonates, identifiable by chemical name, by structural formats, if known, and by Chemical Abstracts Service registry number if assigned.

The Provisional Technical Secretariat

In early 1995 the Provisional Technical Secretariat presented a paper prioritizing the tasks of Working Group B and the PrepCom.[159] At the end of 1995 much of the necessary inspection and laboratory equipment had been procured by the PTS.[160]

The PTS interviewed 341 candidates for the job of inspector by the end of 1995. Of these, 251 were found suitable or borderline candidates, but only 94 (38 per cent) of those are citizens of states which have ratified the CWC. There is a sufficient number of well-qualified candidates to allow selection among suitable or borderline candidates and to ensure geographical diversity for the following positions: CW munitions specialists, analytical chemists, medical specialists and technicians. The outlook is more pessimistic for industry inspectors. More than one-third of the candidates for these positions stated during interviews that they might be unavailable should the secretariat call them for training.[161]

The PTS released a Model Act to Implement the CWC,[162] which is designed to assist signatory states which possess no chemical weapons and which have little or no chemical industry. It covers both approval and implementation of the CWC,[163] but has been criticized by states and non-governmental organizations (NGOs) as too general, especially as regards its provisions on National Authorities. It also does not address the General Purpose Criterion,[164] which ensures that potential new chemicals that are not covered by the schedules will fall under the scope of the CWC. In addition, the Model Act suggests that signatory states adopt a provision so that in a conflict between the convention and national law the CWC would prevail. The suggested provision reiterates the principle that no state can claim that its laws justify non-compliance with

---

[159] These included: (a) arrangements for inspector recruitment and training; (b) the question how and when facilities that produce low concentrations of Schedule 2 and 3 chemicals in process or waste streams must be declared, a question that must be answered in order to permit the Declaration Handbook to be finalized; (c) the coverage of production by synthesis of DOC; (d) questions related to the development of the Inspection Manual; (e) criteria for the evaluation of the risk of particular facilities to the object and purpose of the Convention and formats for the inspection mandate and inspection reports; (f) model agreements for both CW-related and industry facilities; (g) the definition of CW production facilities; (h) old and abandoned CW issues; (i) the OPCW's Information Management System; and (j) the OPCW's staff rules and regulations. 'Background discussion paper prepared by the Secretariat, the current status of the Commission's activities and priority tasks for Working Group B for the remainder of the current and the next intersessional period', PrepCom document PC-X/B/WP.10, 22 Feb. 1995.

[160] 'Report of the Executive Secretary, part 1: retrospective on 1995' (note 93), p. 3; and 'Report of the Executive Secretary, the intersessional period 3 Dec. 1994–31 Mar. 1995' (note 98), p. 3.

[161] 'Report of the Executive Secretary, part 2: the intersessional period 22 July–7 Dec. 1995' (note 106), p. 15.

[162] 'Note by the Executive Secretary, model national implementing legislation', PrepCom document PC-XI/7, 18 July 1995.

[163] 'Report of the Executive Secretary, the intersessional period 1 Apr.–21 July 1995' (note 144), p. 3.

[164] However, the General Purpose Criterion is not mentioned in the CWC. The alternative would be to include the definition of chemical weapons.

an international treaty.[165] However, the status of international treaties is normally determined by the constitution of a country. The suggested provision could thus easily conflict with existing constitutional regulations.

In September 1995 a Basic Course for Personnel of National Authorities was held in The Netherlands. It was designed for the personnel of National Authorities of signatory states which possess no chemical weapons and which will thus need to make only limited declarations.[166] A workshop on communication was held in May 1995,[167] and a trial exercise involving sending and receiving 'mock declarations' followed by a workshop to discuss the exercise was held in October and November 1995.[168]

In cooperation with Belarus, Cameroon, Côte d'Ivoire, Cuba, Ethiopia and South Korea regional seminars on national implementation were organized in Minsk, Yaoundé, Yamoussoukro, Havana, Addis Ababa and Seoul, respectively.

One-third of the signatory states have embassies or missions in Brussels, and many states, mostly developing countries, are unable to attend all of the PrepCom meetings, including plenary meetings. Owing to this and in an attempt to enhance the universality of the CWC, various outreach strategies have been proved by the PTS and the NGOs to enable these countries to attend PrepCom meetings and to be informed of the developments in the PrepCom.[169] To this end, a workshop on national implementation legislation organized by the PTS, the Harvard Sussex Program on CBW Armament and Arms Limitation, and the SIPRI–Saskatchewan–Frankfurt Group was held on 25 October 1995, in Brussels, for representatives of African, Caribbean and Pacific countries.[170]

---

[165] See Article 27 of the Vienna Convention on the Law of Treaties 1969. Elias, T. O., *The Modern Law of Treaties* (Oceana: Dobbs Ferry, N.Y., 1974), p. 236.

[166] 'Note by the Executive Secretary, invitation to propose candidates for a basic course for personnel of National Authorities', PrepCom PC-XI/B/2, 12 Apr. 1995. The course took place on 11–29 Sep. 1995; 49 persons from 38 member states participated. Teachers were provided from the Netherlands, Switzerland, the UK and SIPRI. 'Report of the Executive Secretary, part 2: the intersessional period 22 July–7 Dec. 1995' (note 106), p. 9.

[167] The workshop on communication was held on 17–19 May 1995. 'Report of the Executive Secretary: the intersessional period 1 Apr.–21 July 1995' (note 144), p. 6; Report of the Executive Secretary, part 2: The intersessional period 22 July–7 Dec. 1995' (note 106), pp. 9–10; and 'Note by the Executive Secretary, Communications workshops', PrepCom document PC-XI/B/5, 2 June 1995.

[168] The trial declaration exercise was conducted on 12–18 Oct. 1995 and the workshop on 6–8 Nov. 1995. 'Report of the Executive Secretary, part 2: the intersessional period 22 July–7 Dec. 1995' (note 106), pp. 9–10; and 'Note by the Executive Secretary, trial declaration exercise on communication and second communications workshop', PrepCom document PC-XII/B/1, 27 Aug. 1995.

[169] Note by the Executive Secretary, 'The Brussels Project', PrepCom document PC-XII/4, 2 Nov. 1995.

[170] Preparatory Commission for the Organisation for the Prohibition of Chemical Weapons, Provisional Technical Secretariat, External Relations Division, Media & Public Affairs Branch, 'Workshop on national implementation and legislation of the Chemical Weapons Convention', *Press Release*, no. 74 (26 Oct. 1995).

National implementation

Several states which have ratified the CWC in 1995 made public their national implementation legislation.[171] The organizational set-up of the National Authority must be addressed in national legislation. Other obligations may also be fulfilled, such as: (*a*) ascertaining that the domestic legislation of a state ensures the discharge of its responsibilities under the CWC, (*b*) satisfying declaration obligations under Articles III and VI, (*c*) being prepared to receive inspections, (*d*) meeting its obligations under Articles X and XI, (*e*) ensuring that requirements are observed regarding confidential information received by a state, and (*f*) making certain that National Authority personnel are knowledgeable as regards their rights and obligations.[172]

In 1995, among others, Canada, Japan and the Netherlands enacted implementing legislation.[173] The Canadian legislation passed both houses of parliament and royal assent was granted. Italy's draft ratification law was approved by its parliament on 8 November 1995,[174] but an ordinance providing detailed provisions on declaration and verification is needed. The UK allocated time on its parliamentary calendar to consider the draft CWC bill.[175] All three readings of the draft bill have taken place, and it is expected that ratification

---

[171] *Finland*, 'Regeringens proposition till Riksdagen om godkännande av vissa bestämmelser i konventionen om förbud mot utveckling, produktion, innehav, och användning av kemiska vapen samt om deras förstöring' [Government proposal to Parliament on approval of certain provisions in the CWC]; *Romania*, 'Decision on some measures for implementing the International Convention on the Prohibition of the Development, Production, Stockpiling and the Use of Chemical Weapons and on their Destruction', no. 211, 18 May 1994; *Switzerland*, 'Botschaft betreffend das Übereinkommen über der Entwicklung, Herstellung, Lagerung und des Einsatzes chemischer Waffen und über die Vernichtung solcher Waffen (Chemiewaffenübereinkommen, CWÜ)' [Message concerning the agreement about the development, production, stockpiling and use of chemical weapons and about the destruction of such weapons (CWC)], 20 Apr. 1994 (draft), and 'Ausführungsverordnung zum Chemiewaffenübereinkommen (CWÜVO)' [Ordinance to the CWC]; *the Netherlands*, 'Goedkeuring van het 31 januari 1993 te Parijs tot stand gekomen Verdrag tot verbod van de ontwikkeling, de produktie, de aanleg van voorraden en het gebruik van chemische wapens en inzake de vernietiging van deze wapens, met bijlagen, 23 910 (R 1515)', Vergaderjaar 1994–1995, Tweede Kamer der Staten-General [Ratification of the CWC by the Dutch Parliament]; Regels betreffende de uitvoering van het Verdrag tot verbod van de ontwikkeling, de produktie, de aanleg van voorraden en het gebruik van chemische wapens en inzake de vernietiging van deze wapens (Uitvoeringswet verdrag chemische wapens) 23 911' [National implementation law for the CWC] Vergadejaar 1994–1995, Tweede Kamer der Staten-Generaal; *Denmark*, Lovforslag no. L231, Folketinget 1994–95, Forslag til Lov om inspektioner, erklærings-afgivelse og kontrol i medfør af De Forenede Nationers konvention om forbud mod kemiske våpen' [Proposal for regulations on inspections, declarations and verification], 19 Apr. 1995; *South Africa*; 'Act no. 87 of 1993: Non-Proliferation of Weapons of Mass Destruction Act, 1993', *Government Gazette*, vol. 337, no. 14919 (2 July 1993); *Japan*, 'Law no. 65, Law on Prohibition of Chemical Weapons and Regulations etc., of Special Chemicals'; *Canada*, 'Bill C-87, An Act to implement the Convention on the Prohibition of the Development, Production, Stockpiling and Use of Chemical Weapons and on their Destruction', 1st reading, May 1, 1995, 1st session, 35th Parliament, 42–43–44 Elizabeth II, 1994–95; and *Italy*, Legge, 18 Nov. 1995, no 496. 'Ratifica ed esecuzione della Convenzione sulla proibizione dello sviluppo, produzione, immagazzinaggio ed uso di armi chimiche e sulla loro distribuzione, con annessi, fatta a Parigi il 13 Gennaio 1993' [Ratification and implementation of the CWC]; *Gazzetta Ufficiale*, serie generale 376 (25 Nov. 1995).

[172] Stock, Geissler and Trevan (note 129), p. 740.

[173] Note 171.

[174] Note 171

[175] There is a draft act: 'Chemical Weapons Convention, Consultation Paper on a Bill to implement the Chemical Weapons Convention in the UK', 7 July 1995; and Chemical Weapons Bill, House of Commons 1995/96 [Bill 2] (Her Majesty's Stationery Office: London, 16 Nov. 1995).

will take place in early 1996. The British draft bill explicitly mentions the General Purpose Criterion, which requires transparency mechanisms to ensure compliance with the CWC. The British National Authority will be required to publish an annual report on its activities, and an Advisory Board will be established to which the National Authority will report twice annually.[176]

In India implementation legislation is pending before parliament and will likely be considered before the end of the winter session.[177] Belarus,[178] Brazil, Cameroon, China, Costa Rica, the Czech Republic, Ethiopia, Latvia, Pakistan, Papua New Guinea and Ukraine[179] are also close to completing their national implementation procedures and may be able to deposit their instruments of ratification in early 1996. In New Zealand the Chemical Weapons (Prohibition) Bill was introduced into parliament and referred to the Foreign Affairs and Defence Select Committee for public submissions and comment.

The European Council reiterated the admonition of the European Union (EU) that its members ratify the CWC at the earliest opportunity so that it can enter into force.[180] It is the expressed wish of the EU that its members should be among the original 65 ratifiers.

In the USA Senator Jesse Helms, Chairman of the Senate Foreign Relations Committee, blocked early ratification of the CWC[181] by refusing to schedule debate on the convention in the Senate Foreign Relations Committee. However, in late 1995 a compromise was reached, and the CWC is to be placed on the Senate calendar by 30 April 1996.[182]

In Russia the draft act for the destruction of CW was introduced in the Duma in December 1995,[183] thus removing one major obstacle to ratification. The President's Committee on CBW Convention Problems has the primary responsibility for implementation of the CWC.

[176] Robinson, J. P., 'The chemical weapons bill: what more is needed?', Paper presented at the Chemical Weapons Bill: Background Briefing, Royal Society of Chemistry, London, 20 Nov. 1995, p. 15.

[177] Dunworth, T., 'Progress in The Hague: building the Organisation for the Prohibition of Chemical Weapons, quarterly review no. 12', Chemical Weapons Convention Bulletin, no. 30 (Dec. 1995), p. 4.

[178] 'Republic of Belarus, ratification and implementation of the Convention', PrepCom document PC-X/B/WP.16, 3 Apr. 1995.

[179] 'Report of the Commission', PrepCom document PC-XI/17, 27 July 1995, p. 2; and 'Statement by the Head of the Delegation of Pakistan at the Eleventh Session of the Preparatory Commission for OPCW on 25 July 1995', PrepCom document PC-XI/15.

[180] Conclusions of the European Council, Madrid, 15–16 Dec. 1995. Version current on 21 Dec. 1995, URL <http://www.cec.lu/record/madr-c3.html>.

[181] Helms refused to debate the CWC in the Senate Foreign Relations Committee in an attempt to pressure President Clinton to dismantle at least two of the following agencies: the US Information Agency, the Arms Control and Disarmament Agency and the Agency for International Development. Defence News, vol. 10, no. 38 (25 Sep.–1 Oct. 1995), p. 2; and International Herald Tribune, 14 Nov. 1995, p. 2.

[182] Oja, I., 'Strid om vapenavtal' [Battle over weapon agreement], Dagens Nyheter, 10 Dec. 1995, p. A9 (in Swedish); and Wireless File (United States Information Service: US Embassy, Stockholm, 15 Dec. 1995), pp. 3–4.

[183] Note 54.

Industry concerns

Chemical industry representatives met in The Hague with the PrepCom Expert Group on Chemical Industry Issues, in their third combined meeting, on 26–27 June 1995.[184] Industry was briefed on the status of preparations for entry into force of the CWC. The meeting addressed declaration requirements for the chemical industry, the Declaration Handbook, the use of databases to meet Article XI requirements and model agreements for industry facility agreements.[185] Industry representatives stressed that the pace of the ratification process should accelerate in order to achieve entry into force as soon as possible.[186]

The chemical industry noted that chemical manufacturers need: *(a)* to better identify and quantify the volume of international trade potentially affected by the CWC; and *(b)* to have the remaining areas where there is uncertainty resolved quickly. It is the view of the chemical industry that the PrepCom must take decisions on these topics as soon as possible.[187]

The Committee on Relations with the Host Country

The headquarters agreement is a controversial issue, and discussion between the PrepCom and the Netherlands continued in 1995. The 1994 headquarters agreement and the Paris Resolution both state that the Netherlands will contribute to the cost of the building.[188]

In 1995 the design of the building was refined, but progress was slow on obtaining the necessary legal documents.[189] Problems arose about the method of calculating increases in rent, about guarantees to be given by the Netherlands to cover potential problems arising from possible late entry into force of the CWC and about the legal immunity of both the PrepCom and the OPCW.[190] Additionally, if the bilateral agreement between Russia and the

---

[184] Delegations from 34 states parties, industry representatives from 21 states parties and industry manufacturers associations took part. 'Report of the Executive Secretary, the intersessional period 1 April–21 July 1995' (note 144).

[185] 'Expert Group on Chemical Industry Issues: chairman's summary of the combined meeting with chemical industry', PrepCom document PC-XI/B/WP.10, 27 June 1995, pp. 2–4.

[186] 'Report of the Executive Secretary, the intersessional period 1 April–21 July 1995' (note 144) p. 6.

[187] Walls, M. P., 'The role of declaration in implementation of the CWC: The view of U.S. industry', SIPRI–Saskatchewan–Frankfurt Group (note 127), p. 76.

[188] Stock, Geissler and Trevan (note 129), p. 736; and 'Agreement between the Preparatory Commission for the Organisation for the Prohibition of Chemical Weapons and the Kingdom of the Netherlands concerning Headquarters of the Commission', PrepCom document PC-VI/6, 23 Feb. 1994; and the Paris Resolution (note 94), annex 3, paras 5–9.

[189] 'Report of the Executive Secretary, part 1: retrospective on 1995' (note 93), p. 4.

[190] Section 5-6 of the Paris Resolution states that The Hague and the Netherlands will pay for rent of office space for a limited time. The question of immunity is linked to the problem of whether the PrepCom or the OPCW will have legal responsibility if the entry into force of the CWC is delayed or does not occur.

USA is not in force when the CWC enters into force, the OPCW building will be inadequate since additional inspectors will be required.[191]

The role of non-governmental organizations

Non-governmental organizations are not allowed to take part in the negotiations of the PrepCom. However, NGOs are encouraged to take part in various activities for dissemination of information and to continue to play an important role in the implementation of the CWC. Certain NGOs possess expertise on various CW issues, the history of the negotiations, verification and implementation aspects, legal issues, and the like.[192] There are areas, particularly on the national level, where these NGOs can support implementation of the CWC.[193] These areas include: support,[194] mediation,[195] transmission,[196] and warning or guidance.[197]

In September 1995 the SIPRI–Saskatchewan–Frankfurt Group organized a conference on the Effective Implementation of the CWC. For the first time representatives from various National Authorities, the chemical industry, the PTS and NGOs were brought together to share information and to suggest solutions to problems related to implementation of the CWC.[198] The Pugwash Study Group on the Implementation of the Chemical and Biological Weapons Conventions organized a workshop in the spring of 1995 on the CWC schedules and its General Purpose Criterion.[199] The American Bar Association organized a programme in February 1995 on Implementing the CWC that brought together experts from the US executive branch, academia and industry.[200] These activities and the active participation of some NGOs in regional semi-

[191] In the Soviet–US Bilateral Destruction Agreement (note 51), tha appointment of an additional 120 inspectors is discussed. However, in the absence of the agreement, the actual number of extra inspectors depends on the level of verification of Russian and US CW deemed necessary by the states parties.

[192] Such as the SIPRI–Saskatchewan–Frankfurt Group, the Harvard–Sussex Programme, the Henry L. Stimson Center, the Pugwash Conferences on Science and World Affairs and the Kellman/Tanzman Group.

[193] Stock, T., Kurzidem, T., Radler, P. and Sutherland, R., 'CWC implementation: targeting the important groups and the role of NGOs—an overview', Occasional Paper no. 10, Paper prepared for the Regional Seminar on National Implementation of the Chemical Weapons Convention, Yaoundé, Cameroon, 13–15 Feb. 1995.

[194] Dissemination of information, support of the training of national inspectors and legal support in the process of drafting the necessary national legislation.

[195] There could be a need to mediate between: (a) the National Authority and the facility operator, (b) the facility operator and chemical manufacturers associations, and (c) the chemical industry, especially the CMA, and the future National Authority.

[196] Informing about the ongoing international implementation process and making available the experience of other states parties with implementation.

[197] Informing the concerned public if delays in implementation should occur because of unexpected administrative difficulties or inaction on the part of legislative bodies.

[198] There were approximately 80 participants from 21 nations. 'List of participants', SIPRI–Saskatchewan–Frankfurt Group (note 127), pp. 267–71. Additionally, the SIPRI–Saskatchewan–Frankfurt Group published 12 papers on various topics related to the CWC; some are reproduced in SIPRI–Saskatchewan–Frankfurt Group (note 127), pp. 144–207.

[199] 3rd Workshop of Pugwash Study Group on the Implementation of the Chemical and Biological Weapons Convention, Noordwijk, the Netherlands, 19–21 May 1995.

[200] Sonreel Seminar Series, 'Implementing the Chemical Weapons Convention: the nuts and bolts of compliance', Washington, DC, 7 Feb. 1995, sponsored by the American Bar Association, Section of Natural Resources, Energy, and Environmental Law.

nars have demonstrated the useful contributions that NGOs can make to national implementation.

IV. Biological weapons and arms control

The Fourth Review Conference of the Biological Weapons Convention will be held on 25 November–13 December 1996. In 1995 efforts focused on working out measures for a future verification regime for the BWC. Many states parties feel that the BWC needs to be strengthened by the addition of an intrusive verification regime. There were few allegations of the possession or use of biological weapons in 1995. Approximately 10–12 countries are alleged to possess offensive BW programmes.[201]

Allegations of BW use and possession

Allegations that the Government of Myanmar was using biological weapons on the Thai–Myanmar border against the Karen ethnic minority continued in 1995,[202] but these allegations could not be confirmed.[203] The initial allegation occurred in August 1993, and the disease described was similar to cholera or shigella.[204] The symptoms that had been present in those affected in 1993 reappeared in 1994 in people living in another area, 100 km south of Bilin.[205]

In July 1995 in his annual Report to Congress on Adherence to and Compliance with Arms Control Agreements President Clinton expressed doubt about the compliance with the BWC of eight countries: China, Egypt, Iran, Iraq, Libya, Russia, Syria and Taiwan.[206] The report claimed that Russia had deactivated some research and production facilities but that others may still be able to produce BW agents. The report also stated that Egypt had developed BW agents in 1972 and that there is no evidence that it has abandoned these efforts. It also claimed that Iran has produced BW agents and apparently weaponized a small quantity of them.

In May 1995 a report by the Director of the US Defense Intelligence Agency (DIA) stated that Russia denied 'weaponization' and stockpiling of biological warfare agents and claimed that Russia had 'misrepresented the

---

[201] Latter, R., 'The proliferation of nuclear, biological and chemical weapons', *Jane's Intelligence Review Yearbook 1994/95*, pp. 16–19.

[202] 'Burma and biological weapons', *Jane's Intelligence Review*, vol. 7, no. 11 (Nov. 1995), p. 518.

[203] '10 July', *Chemical Weapons Convention Bulletin*, no. 29 (Sep. 1995), p. 26.

[204] 'Burma and Biologicals: BW?', *ASA Newsletter*, no. 47 (1 Apr. 1995), 95-2, p. 12.

[205] 'Myanmar', *Asian Recorder*, vol. 40, no. 50 (10–16 Dec. 1994), p. 24439; 'Rebels claim Myanmar using possible biological warfare agents', *ASA Newsletter*, no. 45 (21 Dec. 1994), 94-6, p. 16.

[206] *Arms Control Reporter*, sheets 701.B.142–43, Aug. 1995; Gertz, B., 'China has biological arsenal, Congress told', *Washington Times*, 15 July 1995, p. A2; Smith, J., 'U.S. accuses China of germ weapons work', *Washington Post*, 15 July 1995, p. A18; and 'Arms control compliance report cites concerns about Russia, China', *Chemical & Engineering News*, vol. 73, no. 31 (31 July 1995), p. 17. An earlier report from the Arms Control and Disarmament Agency (ACDA) was submitted to Congress in response to the congressional requirement in Section 51 of the Arms Control and Disarmament Act. ACDA, *Adherence to and Compliance with Arms Control Agreements* (ACDA: Washington, DC, 30 May 1995); and ACDA, *Threat Control through Arms Control: Report to Congress, 1994* (ACDA: Washington, DC, 13 July 1995).

size, scope and maturity of the former Soviet programme and the current programme'.[207]

In August 1995 there were allegations that Iran was attempting to develop biological weapons with the aid of Russian scientists.[208] Clinton's report to Congress stated that Syria and Libya were both developing an offensive BW capability and that there was insufficient evidence to determine whether or not Taiwan was engaged in prohibited activities.[209] In addition, the report claimed that China likely maintains an offensive BW programme. China categorically denied these allegations as 'groundless and utterly irresponsible'.[210]

In February 1995 a report by unidentified US intelligence sources alleged that information and material from the former South African BW programme may have proliferated to Libya, which is alleged to have a BW programme.[211] The former South African regime conducted a secret CW and BW programme in the mid-1980s, and it is alleged that the weapons developed in that programme were to be used to assassinate anti-apartheid leaders at home and abroad. The programme was terminated in 1993 by then President F. W. de Klerk.[212] The current President of South Africa, Nelson Mandela, has stated that the country no longer has such a programme and has 'no connection with any country, including Libya, in regard to chemical and biological weapons programmes'.[213]

Japan

In 1995, the 50th anniversary of the end of World War II, significant amounts of information became available about the Japanese biological weapon programme in the 1930s and 1940s.[214] Already in November 1994 it was confirmed that the Japanese Imperial Army operated at least four BW units in China in World War II.[215] Top-secret experiments using BW killed at least 3000 people from China, Korea, Mongolia and Russia. However, the exact

[207] 'Russia denies biological weapon stockpiling', *Jane's Defence Weekly*, vol. 23, no. 19 (13 May 1995), p. 5.

[208] Adams, J., 'Russia helps Iran to build bio-weapons', *Sunday Times*, 27 Aug. 1995, p. 14.

[209] '13 July', *Chemical Weapons Convention Bulletin*, no. 29 (Sep. 1995), pp. 26–27; *Threat Control through Arms Control* (note 206); and 'ACDA annual report is informative, clear-headed effort', *Congressional Record*, 14 July, pp. S10076–77, from *Congressional Record Online* via GPO Access. Version current on 30 Jan. 1996, URL <wais.access.gpo.gov>.

[210] New China News Agency, Beijing, 'US accusation on biological weapons "groundless and utterly irresponsible"', 18 July 1995, in *BBC* [British Broadcasting Corporation] *Summary of World Broadcasts* (BBC-SWB), 19 July 1995.

[211] Adams, J., 'Gadaffi lures South Africa's top germ warfare scientists', *Sunday Times*, 26 Feb. 1995.

[212] Taylor, P., 'Toxic S. African arms raise concern', *Washington Post*, 28 Feb. 1995, p. A14.

[213] Reuters World Service, Boyle, B., 'S. African arms scientists may be in Libya-Mandela', 2 Mar. 1995, via Nexis.

[214] Hadfield, P., 'Wartime skeletons return to haunt Japan', *New Scientist*, vol. 145, no. 1966 (25 Feb. 1995), pp. 12–13; and Harris, S. H., *Factories of Death: Japanese Biological Warfare 1932–45 and the American Cover Up* (Routledge: London, 1994).

[215] 'Confirmed: germ warfare unit operated in China', in JPRS-TAC-95-003-L, 17 Jan. 1995, pp. 5–6.

number of deaths may have been 10 times greater.[216] In February 1995 former members of Unit 731, the main biological warfare unit in the Japanese Imperial Army, provided information about the activities of the unit.[217] In April 1995 the Japanese Government was petitioned by a group of 41 Chinese citizens seeking compensation as victims of Japanese aggression during World War II. Several of them claimed to have been victims of BW experiments.[218] In the summer of 1995 a symposium on the activities of Unit 731 was held in Harbin, China.[219]

Status of the BWC

Participation in the BWC and confidence-building measures under the BWC

In 1995 no additional states acceded to the BWC. As of 31 December 1995, 133 states were states parties to the BWC.[220]

The ninth round of information exchange on the BWC confidence-building measures (CBMs) in 1995 elicited more responses than in previous years. As of 15 April 1995, only 31 states had submitted declarations,[221] but by September 1995 a total of 51 states had done so.[222] The number of states which have participated in the information exchange at least once is now 71, 6 more than in 1994. The six states were: Bhutan, Côte d'Ivoire, Laos, Papua New Guinea, Saint Lucia and San Marino.

The Ad Hoc Group in Geneva

The Special Conference held in Geneva in September 1994 decided to establish an Ad Hoc Group, 'to consider appropriate measures, including possible verification measures, and draft proposals to strengthen the Convention, to be included, as appropriate, in a legally binding instrument'.[223] It was decided that

---

[216] 'Berichte über Menschenversuche der Japaner in China' [Reports on experiments on humans in China by the Japanese], *Frankfurter Allgemeine Zeitung*, 24 Nov. 1994, p. 8; and 'China finds another germ lab used by Japan in war killings', *International Herald Tribune*, 24 Nov. 1994, p. 6.

[217] '7 February', *Chemical Weapons Convention Bulletin*, no. 27 (Mar. 1995), p 30; and 'Atrocities', *Press Democrat*, 11 Feb. 1995.

[218] Kyodo News Service, Tokyo, 'First group of Chinese war victims to lodge compensation claim with government', 26 Apr. 1995, in *BBC-SWB*, 27 Apr. 1995; and Kyodo News Service, Tokyo, 'China backs move to compensate some war victims', 4 May 1995, in *BBC-SWB*, 5 May 1995.

[219] It was organized by the Chinese Institute of the Academy of Social Sciences and a Japanese international symposium committee and included experts from both countries, as well as some victims of the BW experiments. Xinhua News Agency, Beijing, 'Japan war anniversary: research published on Japanese bacteriological warfare', 11 Aug. 1995, in *BBC-SWB*, 14 Aug. 1995; and United Press International, Tharp, D., [Untitled report], 8 Aug. 1995, via Nexis.

[220] See annexe A in this volume; and 'List of States Parties to the Convention on the Prohibition of the Development, Production and Stockpiling of Bacteriological (Biological) and Toxin Weapons and on their Destruction', BWC/AD HOC GROUP/INF.3, 6 July 1995.

[221] UN Centre for Disarmament Affairs document CDA/14-95/BW-III, 10 May 1995.

[222] UN Centre for Disarmament Affairs document CDA/14-95/BW-III/Add.1 and Add.2, 12 Sep. 1995.

[223] Special Conference of the States Parties to the Convention on the Prohibition of the Development, Production and Stockpiling of Bacteriological (Biological) and Toxin Weapons and on Their Destruction, 'Final report', Geneva, 19–30 Sep. 1994, BWC/SPCONF/1, pp. 10–11.

measures considered by the Ad Hoc Group 'should be formulated and implemented in a manner designed to protect sensitive commercial proprietary information and legitimate national security needs' and should 'avoid any negative impact on scientific research, international cooperation and industrial development'.[224]

The first session of the Ad Hoc Group was held on 4–6 January 1995 in Geneva and attended by representatives from 49 states parties.[225] A system was set up to address the four main provisions of the mandate: *(a)* definitions of terms and objective criteria, *(b)* CBMs and transparency measures, *(c)* measures to promote compliance, and *(d)* measures related to Article X.[226]

The second meeting of the Ad Hoc Group was held on 10–21 July 1995[227] with representatives from 52 states parties. Four Friends of the Chair[228] presented papers on the four main provisions.[229] Various proposals were made at the meeting, including a suggestion to strengthen 'measures to promote compliance' by establishing criteria for the submission of declarations, for future on-site inspection measures and for other measures based on surveillance activities. It was also proposed that declarations to strengthen compliance with the BWC be submitted if any one or any combination of the following were present: military biological defence programmes or facilities, high-containment facilities, work with listed pathogens and toxins, aerobiology or aerosol dissemination, production microbiology, genetic manipulation and equipment as well as other criteria such as transfer data and vectors. Several delegations expressed the view that 'triggers' for declarations and their content must be differentiated so that the activities, facilities and events of greatest relevance to the BWC are declared.

The on-site measures discussed were: validation and information visits, routine visits and inspections, and short-notice visits and challenge inspections. The feasibility of visits and inspections to demonstrate compliance and to protect against the loss of commercial proprietary information, especially in the pharmaceutical industry and vaccine production facilities, was demonstrated by a series of British trial inspections[230] and by Canada and the Netherlands in

---

[224] 'Final report' (note 223), p. 10.

[225] The chairman was Ambassador Tibor Tóth (Hungary). Ad Hoc Group of the States Parties to the Convention on the Prohibition of the Development, Production and Stockpiling of Bacteriological (Biological) and Toxin Weapons and their Destruction, 'Procedural report', BWC/AD HOC Group/3, 6 Jan. 1995. The Vice-Chairmen Ambassador Richard Starr (Australia) and Ambassador Jorge Berguno (Chile).

[226] 'Procedural report' (note 225).

[227] United Nations Office at Geneva, 'Negotiations on strengthening prohibition on biological weapons to be held in Geneva, 10 to 21 July', *Press Release*, no. DC/95/32 (3 July 1995), pp. 1–2.

[228] Dr Ali Mohammadi (Iran), Ambassador Tibor Tóth (Hungary), Stephen Pattison (UK) and Ambassador Jorge Berguno (Chile).

[229] Pearson, G. S., 'On course for strengthening the BTWC', *ASA Newsletter*, no. 50 (11 Oct. 1995), 95-5, pp. 1, 10–11; and *Arms Control Reporter*, sheet 701.B.141–2, Aug. 1995.

[230] 'United Kingdom BTWC practice compliance inspection (PCI) programme: summary report', BWC/SPCONF/WP.2, 20 Sep. 1994; and 'UK practice inspection: pharmaceutical pilot plant', BWC/CONF.III/VEREX/WP.147, 24 May 1994.

a joint trial inspection.[231] Investigation of alleged use[232] was considered key to any system of measures to strengthen the BWC and would focus on initiation, implementation, judgement and unusual outbreaks of disease. Voluntary multilateral information sharing and various off-site surveillance measures were considered as possible CBMs.[233]

A framework for future discussion of 'confidence building and transparency measures' emhasizing scope, specific measures and legal issues was outlined, and the role of existing or enhanced CBMs in such a system was discussed.

The discussion of 'definitions of terms and objective criteria' focused on developing a list of human pathogens and toxins, and the following papers were presented: *(a)* a list of human, animal and plant pathogens and toxins, which might be developed for specific measures to strengthen the BWC; *(b)* a set of criteria, proposed to be used in combination for the development of a list of human pathogens and toxins; and *(c)* a note recording the views on definition of terms and objective criteria.[234]

Twelve general elements for the 'implementation of Article X' were outlined based on national papers and discussions. They included the scope and content of scientific and technical exchange, institutional arrangements and ways to enhance cooperation.[235]

The mandate of the Ad Hoc Group and discussion at the 1995 meeting[236] suggest the following measures: *(a)* declarations and notifications, *(b)* on-site visits and inspections, *(c)* investigation of alleged use, and *(d)* multilateral information sharing.[237] In addition, most participants held the view that definitions and lists for particular measures may be prepared if the scope of the prohibition under Article I of the BWC is not undermined or redefined. A legally binding protocol to strengthen the BWC may be feasible, but the text of the BWC would remain unchanged. The regime envisaged would contain a component to deter violators, and Article X measures would have to be developed on a multilateral basis.

At least two additional sessions of the Ad Hoc Group will be held prior to the Fourth Review Conference of the BWC. It is doubtful that the Ad Hoc Group will have completed its work or that a verification protocol will be ready by the Fourth Review Conference.

---

[231] The Netherlands and Canada, 'Bilateral trial inspection in a large vaccine production: a contribution to the evaluation of potential verification measures', BWC/CONF.III/VEREX/WP.112, May 1993.

[232] Working Paper submitted by South Africa, 'Investigating alleged use of biological weapons', Ad Hoc Group of the States Parties to the Convention on the Prohibition of the Development, Production and Stockpiling of Bacteriological (Biological) and Toxin Weapons and on their Destruction, BWC/AD HOC GROUP/11, 10 July 1995.

[233] 'Procedural Report of the Ad Hoc Group of the States Parties to the Convention on the Prohibition of the Development, Production and Stockpiling of Bacteriological (Biological) and Toxin Weapons and on their Destruction', BWC/AD HOC GROUP/28, 24 July 1995.

[234] Pearson (note 229).

[235] *Arms Control Reporter*, sheet 701.B.141–2, Aug. 1995.

[236] The third meeting took place on 27 Nov.–8 Dec. 1995 in Geneva. Ad Hoc Group of the States Parties to the Convention on the Prohibition of the Development, Production and Stockpiling of Bacteriological (Biological) and Toxin Weapons and on their Destruction, 'Procedural report', BWC/AD HOC GROUP/29, 12 Dec. 1995.

[237] Pearson (note 229).

British–Russian–US meetings

The British–Russian–US 1992 Joint Statement on Biological Weapons initiated a trilateral process to address concerns about Russian compliance with the BWC.[238] The three nations agreed to permit inspections and visits to both non-military and military BW facilities.[239] US concerns about Russian compliance, which continued to be expressed even after the initial visits, were discussed at an April 1995 meeting between the Russian Defence Minister and the US Secretary of Defense.[240] It was agreed that working groups would be formed and that the exchange of information on problems connected with biological weapons would be expanded.[241] However, in July 1995 the Director of the US Arms Control and Disarmament Agency stated that the USA is still "'not satisfied" about Russian activities at plants where legitimate biological activities are "co-located" with former biological weapons (BW) efforts'.[242]

V. UNSCOM activities

In 1995 the United Nations Special Commission on Iraq (UNSCOM)[243] continued its verification and monitoring activities. At the end of 1994 Iraq had been hopeful that the sanctions imposed on it under UN Security Council Resolution 661 would be lifted,[244] and in early 1995 some Security Council members[245] favoured doing so. This did not occur owing in large part to the discovery in 1995 of new information about the Iraqi BW programme.

New data were provided by Iraq about its chemical and nuclear weapon programmes and about its missile capability.[246] In 1995 Iraq also acknowledged the existence of a radiological weapon programme.[247] In 1987 that programme had conducted research and development (R&D) work to explore the use of radiological weapons as a means of territory denial. In addition, in 1995 Iraq admitted that is had produced major subsystems of Scud-type engines and had conducted a covert programme to develop and produce a surface-to-surface

[238] Geissler, E., 'Biological weapon and arms control developments', *SIPRI Yearbook 1994* (note 26), p. 718; and Stock, Geissler and Trevan, *SIPRI Yearbook 1995* (note 129), p. 742.
[239] Stock, Geissler and Trevan, *SIPRI Yearbook 1995* (note 129), p. 742.
[240] *Arms Control Reporter*, sheet 701.B.137–8, Aug. 1995.
[241] 'More on Perry, Grachev talks', in FBIS-SOV-95-064, 4 Apr. 1995, pp. 5–6.
[242] Porth, J. S., 'Arms problems with Russia underline need for binding accords', *Wireless File* (United States Information Service, US Embassy: Stockholm, 19 July 1995), pp. 14–15.
[243] Ekéus, R., 'The United Nations Special Commission on Iraq', *SIPRI Yearbook 1992: World Armaments and Disarmament* (Oxford University Press: Oxford, 1992), pp. 509–30; Ekéus, R., 'The United Nations Special Commission on Iraq: activities in 1992', *SIPRI Yearbook 1993: World Armaments and Disarmament* (Oxford University Press: Oxford, 1993), pp. 691–703; Trevan, T., 'UNSCOM: activities in 1993', *SIPRI Yearbook 1994* (note 26), pp. 739–58; and Stock, Geissler and Trevan, *SIPRI Yearbook 1995* (note 129), pp. 725–60.
[244] United Nations Security Council document S/RES/661 (1990), 6 Aug. 1990.
[245] These were France, Russia and China.
[246] For detailed information see United Nations Security Council documents S/1995/284, 10 Apr. 1995; S/1995/494, 20 June 1995; S/1995/864, 11 Oct. 1995; and S/1995/1038, 17 Dec. 1995.
[247] United Nations Security Council document S/1995/1038 (note 246).

missile subsequent to the adoption of UN Security Council Resolution 687, the so-called cease-fire resolution.[248]

UNSCOM found that almost every time Iraq submitted a Full, Final and Complete Declaration (FFCD), there were so many subsequent changes and adjustments that, in time, the initial declaration was no longer valid.

The 7 August 1995 defection to Jordan of General Hussein Kamel Hassan, who had been in charge of the Iraqi weapon acquisition programme, led to a significant change in Iraqi willingness to cooperate with UNSCOM. However, the new Iraqi openness was insufficient grounds for lifting the sanctions.

The Baghdad Monitoring and Verification Centre

The Baghdad Monitoring and Verification Centre (BMVC)[249] was established in August 1994. By October 1994 it was operating in a 'test mode' and focusing on its future tasks under the UNSCOM mandate: continuous monitoring and verification of Iraqi compliance, and control of imports and exports. The BMVC monitors activities related to missiles, chemical and biological weapons and coordinates monitoring of nuclear weapon activities with the International Atomic Energy Agency (IAEA).[250]

The 'baseline missile inspection process' was completed in August 1994.[251] Thereafter UNSCOM performed numerous inspections (see table 15.2) at a variety of missile facilities, and by October 1995, 40 video cameras had been installed at 16 facilities.[252] Iraq is required to present 10 per cent of its missiles for verification three times per year.

The BMVC chemical monitoring team completed its baseline inspections of 62 chemical sites and 18 universities, colleges and research institutes by October 1995; over 200 monitoring inspections have taken place. Additional information from Iraq in August 1995 will lead to inspections at newly identified sites.

BW monitoring began on 4 April 1995. Owing to the dual-use nature of biotechnology and the ease with which civilian facilities can be converted for BW purposes, there is a need for broad monitoring. By October 1995 at least 79 sites throughout Iraq had been included in the BW monitoring and verification regime. Following the interim monitoring period (October 1994–March 1995),

[248] United Nations Security Council document S/1995/1038 (note 246).

[249] United Nations Security Council documents S/1994/489, 22 Apr. 1994; S/1994/750, 24 June 1994; and S/1994/1422, 15 Dec. 1994.

[250] Experts working at the BMVC are responsible for export and import controls, biological and chemical laboratories, aerial inspections, a photographic laboratory, an imagery library and communication with New York and Vienna. They control and maintain all remote-controlled sensors installed by the inspection teams at different sites in Iraq. In addition, logistical support staff, such as helicopter and ground transportation, and translation/interpretation services are part of the centre. A total of 80 personal will be employed at the BMVC. The aim is to rotate staff at the centre every 3–6 months. The first monitoring group (missiles) began work at the BMVC on 17 Aug. 1994. United Nations Security Council document S/1994/1138, 7 Oct. 1994.

[251] Baseline inspections are conducted at sites that will be subject to future monitoring and verification to prepare monitoring and verification protocols for the sites.

[252] United Nations Security Council document S/1995/864 (note 246).

the monitoring group conducted over 150 inspections (April–October 1995), including 20 inspections of the facility at Al Hakam.[253]

Plans for future monitoring and verification

On 2 October 1991 the UN Secretary-General submitted a report to the Security Council on UNSCOM's plan for ongoing monitoring and verification of Iraq's compliance with the relevant parts of section C of Security Council Resolution 687.[254] The plan contained annexes with lists of items relevant to the implementation of monitoring and verification in Iraq. Under the plan an import and export monitoring system will come into effect once the sanctions on Iraq have been lifted. Both Iraq and the supplier states will be required to notify UNSCOM of all exports of listed equipment and materials. If an item is found in Iraq, the import of which was not notified, then the assumption would be that it was procured for prohibited purposes.

The past three years have made it clear that the annexes from the 1991 draft plan should be revised to include a precise listing of items to be notified under the import and export control mechanism. In March 1995 revised annexes and lists for future monitoring and verification of Iraq's compliance with the relevant parts of section C of Security Council Resolution 687 were presented to the Security Council.[255] In July 1995 the Sanctions Committee approved an UNSCOM–IAEA joint proposal for the import and export control mechanism,[256] and that mechanism now awaits approval by the Security Council.[257]

The past Iraqi BW programme

In February 1995 the Executive Chairman of UNSCOM, Rolf Ekéus, noted that UNSCOM still lacked baseline data on the past Iraqi BW programme.[258] Of particular concern was the discovery that Iraq had imported 20–30 t of growth media in 1988–89. Iraq claimed that the material had been used for medical diagnostic purposes, but such uses require only small amounts. The type of growth media that had been imported is suitable for the production of

---

[253] New information about Iraq's BW programme has shown that Al Hakam was the main facility for this programme.

[254] United Nations Security Council document S/22871/Rev.1, 2 Oct. 1991.

[255] United Nations Security Council document S/1995/208, 17 Mar. 1995, lists items related to CW, BW and missile activities such as chemicals, equipment, biological equipment, micro-organisms, bacteria, mycoplasma, rickettsia, viruses, human and animal pathogens, other organisms and toxins, bio-hazard containment and decontamination items, fermentation equipment, equipment for biological processing, detection equipment, equipment capable of being used in the development, production, construction, modification or acquisition of missile systems, propellants, chemicals for propellants, flight control and detection equipment, etc. United Nations Security Council document S/1995/215, 23 Mar. 1995, lists items related to nuclear activities.

[256] United Nations Security Council document S/1995/864 (note 246).

[257] United Nations Security Council document S/1995/1038 (note 246).

[258] Noch Unklarheiten über Iraks B-Waffen' [Still uncertainties about Iraq's BW], *Süddeutsche Zeitung*, 24 Feb. 1995, p. 7; and Reuter, 'UN Inspectors seek more Iraqi arms data', *International Herald Tribune*, 20 Feb. 1995.

Table15.2. UNSCOM inspections in 1995 (in-country dates)

Type of inspection/date	Team
Chemical	
2 Oct. 1994–14 Jan. 1995	CG 1
11–21 Jan. 1995	CW23/UNSCOM108
16–22 Jan. 1995	CW22/UNSCOM107
14 Jan.–15 Apr. 1995	CG 2
16 Apr.–26 Sep. 1995	CG 3
16–20 Sep. 1995	CW25/UNSCOM124
9–15 Dec. 1995	CW26A/UNSCOM129A
Biological	
28 Dec. 1994–31 Jan. 1995	IBG 1
10–22 Jan. 1995	BW18/UNSCOM109
20 Jan.–6 Feb. 1995	BW19/UNSCOM110
23 Jan.–3 Feb. 1995	BW22/UNSCOM113
3–17 Feb. 1995	BW20/UNSCOM111
3–17 Feb. 1995	BW21/UNSCOM112
12–18 Mar. 1995	BW23/UNSCOM115
24 Mar.–6 Apr. 1995	BW24/UNSCOM116
1 Feb.–3 Apr. 1995	IBG 2
4 Apr.–7 Aug. 1995	BG 1
27 Apr.–16 May 1995	BW25/UNSCOM 118
15–26 July	BW26/UNSCOM 121
19 Aug.–3 Sep. 1995	BW27/UNSCOM125
27 Sep.–11 Oct. 1995	BW28/UNSCOM126
8 Aug. –9 Nov. 1995	BG2
7–15 Dec. 1995	BW29/UNSCOM 127
Ballistic missile	
27–31 Jan. 1995	MG 2C
22 Feb.–30 May1995	MG 3
6–14 Mar. 1995	BM31/UNSCOM103
25 May–1 June 1995	BM32/UNSCOM100
30 May–27 Aug. 1995	MG 4
25–30 July 1995	BM33/UNSCOM122
20–24 Aug. 1995	MG 4A
27 Aug.–12 Nov. 1995	MG 5
27 Sep.–1 Oct. 1995	BM34/UNSCOM123
9–15 Dec. 1995	BM35/UNSCOM130
Nuclear	
16 Dec. 1994–13 Jan. 1995	NMG 94-06
12 Jan.–2 Feb. 1995	NMG 95-01
2–28 Feb. 1995	NMG 95-02
28 Feb.–16 Mar. 1995	NMG 95-03
16 Mar.–6 Apr. 1995	NMG 95-04
6–26 Apr. 1995	NMG 95-05
27 Apr.–10 May 1995	NMG 95-06
11–30 May 1995	NMG 95-07
31 May–20 June 1995	NMG 95-08
21 June–9 July 1995	NMG 95-09
10–30 July 1995	NMG 95-10

Type of inspection/date	Team
31 July–10 Aug. 1995	NMG 95-11
11–29 Aug. 1995	NMG 95-12
30 Aug.–11 Sep. 1995	NMG 95-13
9–19 Sep. 1995	IAEA 28/UNSCOM 131
12 Sep.–3 Oct. 1995	NMG 95-14
4–22 Oct. 1995	NMG 95-15
17–25 Oct. 1995	IAEA 29/UNSCOM 132
22 Oct.–9 Nov. 1995	NMG 95-16
9–20 Nov. 1995	NMG 95-17
20 Nov.–12 Dec. 1995	NMG 95-18
Export/import mission	
22 Apr.–6 May 1995	UNSCOM 119
Special missions	
7–31 Jan. 1995	
7–21 Jan. 1995	
13–26 Jan. 1995	
13–16 Mar. 1995	
12–28 Jan. 1995	
23 Jan.–14 Feb. 1995	
25 Jan.–4 Feb. 1995	
19–23 Feb. 1995	
22–28 Feb. 1995	
28 Feb.–18 Mar. 1995	
16–29 Mar 1995	
24–27 Mar. 1995	
4–23 May 1995	
14–17 May 1995	
29 May–1 June 1995	
19–22 June 1995	
22 June–2 July 1995	
30 June–2 July 1995	
2–10 July 1995	
4–6 Aug. 1995	
7–12 Aug. 1995	
17–20 Aug. 1995	
24 Aug.–2 Sep. 1995	
24 Aug.–18 Sep. 1995	
5–14 Sep. 1995	
17–20 Sep. 1995	
29 Sep.–1 Oct. 1995	
19–25 Oct. 1995	
24–26 Nov. 1995	
27–29 Nov. 1995	
29 Nov.–3 Dec. 1995	

a CW = chemical weapons, MG = Missile Monitoring Group, BM = ballistic missiles, IBG = Interim Monitoring Group, NMG = Nuclear Monitoring Group, BW = biological weapons, CG = Chemical Monitoring Group, and BG = Biological Monitoring Group.

Source: Information from UNSCOM spokesman, 18 Dec. 1995.

anthrax and botulinum toxin.[259] On investigation, UNSCOM was only able to account for 22 t of the 39 t of complex growth media that had been imported in 1988 by the Iraqi Technical and Scientific Materials Import Division.[260]

Technical talks in Baghdad in March 1995 were unable to resolve remaining questions. Iraq continued to claim that there had been only a basic military biological research programme at Salman Pak which had begun work in 1986 and ceased in 1990. The programme allegedly employed only 10 persons.[261] An April report by UNSCOM to the Security Council stated that despite a new declaration from Iraq in March 1995 it was still not possible to 'account definitively for all the materials and items which may have been used' in the biological warfare programme 'and are known to have been acquired by Iraq'.[262] The report stated that the design features of the facility at Al Hakam, which Iraq claimed was a single-cell protein plant for the production of animal feed, were more consistent with the requirements of a BW agent facility.

In June 1995 Iraq acknowledged for the first time that it had an offensive biological weapon programme which included the production of BW agents. Iraq continued to deny that there had been 'weaponization' of agents.[263] On 4 August 1995 Iraq presented another FFCD on its BW programme to UNSCOM; it also denied that there had been weaponization of BW agents. Six days after the defection of General Hussein Kamel Hassan to Jordan, on 13 August, Ekéus received a letter inviting him to Baghdad. On 17 August 1995 Iraq informed UNSCOM during a meeting in Baghdad that it would cooperate and that there would now be full transparency. Iraq claimed that General Hussein Kamel had concealed information about the prohibited programmes. Iraq then disclosed an extensive BW programme and admitted to weaponization activities.[264] Ekéus later stated at a press conference that while significant new data had been provided, documentation to verify the new information was lacking. Before leaving Baghdad the UNSCOM team was given documentation about Iraqi nuclear, biological, chemical (NBC) and missile activities. Ekéus visited Jordan where he spoke with General Hussein Kamel, who supplied additional information.[265]

In November 1995 Iraq submitted a new FFCD on biological weapons, its third for the year. The disclosures made by Iraq since August 1995 were included, but major deficiencies remained. UNSCOM has evidence that the Iraqi BW programme was more extensive than has been admitted, and Iraq continues to fail to provide precise figures about the amounts of BW agents and munitions which were produced, weaponized and destroyed.[266]

[259] United Nations Security Council document S/1995/284 (note 246).
[260] Iraq's hospital consumption in 1987–94 was 200 kg of growth media per annum. It is normally packed in 0.1 to 1-kg packages. The media imported by Iraq in 1988 were packaged in 25–100 kg drums. In addition, the manufacturers' guarantee for this growth media is 4 to 5 years.
[261] United Nations Security Council document S/1995/284 (note 246).
[262] United Nations Security Council document S/1995/284 (note 246).
[263] United Nations Security Council document S/1995/864 (note 246).
[264] United Nations Security Council document S/1995/864 (note 246).
[265] 'Ekéus on defector information, biological weapons', in FBIS-NES-95-170, 1 Sep. 1995, pp. 24–29.
[266] United Nations Security Council document S/1995/1038 (note 246).

UNSCOM obtained additional information in September 1995 about several new designs for long-range missile systems (up to 3000 km), which Iraq was in the process of developing.[267] Such missiles would have been capable of reaching other regions, including parts of Europe, and if supplied with BW warheads would have presented a major threat not only to the Middle East, but to other regions as well. Table15.3 presents a chronology of the Iraqi BW programme as of the autumn of 1995.[268]

The past Iraqi CW programme

UNSCOM oversaw the destruction of both bulk and weaponized CW agents in the following quantities: 30 t of tabun, 70 t of sarin and 600 t of mustard.[269] A total of 480 000 l of CW agents, more than 28 000 chemical weapon munitions and nearly 1 800 000 kg and 648 barrels of 45 different precursor chemicals were destroyed.[270] The destruction of Iraq's CW weaponry, including precursor chemicals and other militarily relevant chemicals, was successfully completed in April 1994.[271]

On the basis of Iraqi data and the FFCD of March 1995, the Iraqi CW programme consisted of the following:[272] mustard gas production that started in 1981 with a total output 2850 t,[273] and nerve agent production that began in 1984 with a total output of 210 t of tabun[274] and 790 t of sarin and GF (cyclosarin).[275] An R&D programme for VX was carried out in 1987–88, and 260 kg of VX[276] were produced.[277]

In October 1995 Iraq declared that its March 1995 FFCD was inadequate.[278] It is now clear that the VX programme began in 1985 and ran until December 1990. More important, VX was produced on an industrial scale, and in a November 1995 FFCD Iraq admitted to the production of 1.8 t of VX in 1988 and an additional 1.5 t in 1990.[279] There is now evidence that in early 1989 Iraq possessed the necessary quantities of precursors for large-scale production of VX.[280]

---

[267] United Nations Security Council document S/1995/864 (note 246).

[268] The following data on the Iraqi BW programme are based on United Nations Security Council document S/1995/864 (note 246); and United Nations Security Council document S/1995/1038 (note 246). See also Starr, B., 'Iraq reveals a startling range of toxic agents', *Jane's Defence Weekly*, vol. 24, no. 19 (11 Nov. 1995), p. 4.

[269] United Nations Security Council document S/1995/284 (note 246).

[270] United Nations Security Council document S/1995/494 (note 246).

[271] A full report of this is contained in United Nations Security Council document S/1994/750, 24 June 1994.

[272] United Nations Security Council document S/1995/284 (note 246).

[273] The agent purity was at least 80%, and it was stable in storage. Iraq earlier declared 3080 t.

[274] Iraq had previously declared 250 t. The tabun had a maximum purity of 60%.

[275] Iraq had previously declared 812 t. Sarin was also of maximum purity of 60%.

[276] Iraq had previously declared 160 kg.

[277] United Nations Security Council document S/1995/284 (note 246).

[278] United Nations Security Council document S/1995/864 (note 246).

[279] United Nations Security Council document S/1995/1038 (note 246).

[280] In Sep. 1995 Iraq admitted having acquired sufficient precursors for the production of several hundred tonnes of VX. United Nations Security Council document S/1995/864 (note 246).

Table 15.3. The Iraqi biological weapon programme as of autumn 1995

Year	Activity
1974	Iraq adopts a policy to acquire biological weapons.
1975–78	R&D activities conducted at Al Salman; work ends in 1978.
1985	Work resumes on the BW programme at Muthanna State Establishment; research on anthrax and botulinum toxin; no agent production occurs.
1987	BW programme is transferred back to Al Salman; new equipment is acquired and research shifts to application of agents as BW; effects on larger animals studied, including field trials and work in inhalation chamber; start of full-scale production phase for a BW programme.
1988	Initial weapon field trials start; botulinum toxin production in one 450-litre (l) fermenter; in Mar. first field trials conducted at Muthanna range with anthrax simulants and botulinum toxin. Decision taken to build a new site for BW production at Al Hakam; two 1850-l and seven 1480-l fermenters from the Veterinary Research Laboratories are transferred to the site with the 450-l fermenter line from Taji (for botulinum toxin production); production of aflatoxin starts in May at Al Salman; production later moves to Fudaliyah; a total of 1850 l are produced; advanced research for the BW programme is conducted on: *(a) Clostridium perringens* (since Apr.), *(b)* trichothecene mycotoxins (since May), *(c)* ricin, *(d)* wheat cover smut (1987–88), and *(e)* several viruses (e.g., haemorrhagic conjunctivitis virus, rotavirus, camel pox virus).
1989	Production of approximately 1500 l of anthrax at Al Salman (concentrated to 150 l). At Al Hakam production of botulinum toxin for weapon purposes starts in Apr. and of anthrax in May; in Nov. 122-mm rocket weaponization trials are held.
1990	First live firings take place in May; in Aug. trials with R400 aerial bombs are conducted; in Aug., after the invasion of Kuwait, a 'crash' programme on BW is launched and the imperatives of production and weaponization take over; by Dec. 100 R400 bombs are filled with botulinum toxin, 50 with anthrax and 16 with aflatoxin; in addition, 13 Al Hussein warheads are filled with botulinum toxin, 10 with anthrax and 2 with aflatoxin.
1991	In Jan. field trials are conducted with spray tanks based on a modified aircraft drop tank;[a] all weapons are deployed in early Jan. at four locations, where they remain throughout the Persian Gulf War.
1995	Iraq has declared the production of at least: *(a)* 19 000 l of concentrated botulinum toxin (nearly 10 000 l were filled into munitions); *(b)* 8500 l of concentrated anthrax (nearly 6500 l were filled into munitions); and *(c)* 2200 l of concentrated aflatoxin (nearly 1580 l were filled into munitions).

[a] The plan was to mount the tanks on either a piloted fighter aircraft or a remotely piloted aircraft and to spray a maximum of 2000 l of anthrax.

Source: United Nations Security Council document S/1995/864, 11 Oct. 1995.

After Iraq's declaration of its BW programme and weaponization, the material balance for declared munitions, especially CW munitions, was no longer valid. New information was obtained about Iraqi efforts in the CW weaponization programme.[281] By the end of 1995 UNSCOM was unable to rule out the existence in Iraq of stocks of VX, its direct precursors[282] and undeclared munitions.[283]

Evaluation of findings

In its October report to the Security Council UNSCOM stated that Iraqi 'biological and chemical weapons have been subject to conflicting presentations by Iraqi authorities . . . On the one side, it was explained that the biological and chemical weapons were seen by Iraq as a useful means to counter a numerically superior force; on the other, they were presented as a means of last resort for retaliation in the case of a nuclear attack on Baghdad'.[284]

Following its November 1995 review of Iraqi compliance, the Security Council chose not to lift the sanctions imposed on Iraq.[285] Iraq has yet to meet the requirement of submitting a final FFCD, especially as regards its biological, chemical and missile programmes. In the absence of these data, the future monitoring and verification regime cannot provide complete assurance that Iraq has not retained some parts of its former weapon programmes.

VI. Chemical and biological defence

Recent years have seen consolidation of the lessons learned in the Persian Gulf War,[286] and there is now increased emphasis on CBW defence.[287] Effective protective and detection measures, together with intrusive arms control treaties such as the CWC and BWC, should constitute an effective web of deterrence.[288]

According to a US DOD study the detection, identification and characterization of BW agents is the main deficiency in the capability of the US military

---

[281] Among others, in Apr. 1990 Iraq conducted long-range missile flight tests with chemical warheads. It has admitted to the development of binary sarin-filled artillery shells, 122-mm rockets and aerial bombs.

[282] There was still uncertainty about what had been done with more than 200 t of phosphorus pentasulfide and diisopropylamine (from the VX programme).

[283] United Nations Security Council document S/1995/864 (note 246).

[284] United Nations Security Council document S/1995/864 (note 246).

[285] 'UNO-Sanktionen gegen Irak erneut verlängert' [UN sanctions against Iraq again prolonged], *Süddeutsche Zeitung*, 10 Nov. 1995, p. 7.

[286] Pearson, G. S., 'Chemical and biological defence: an essential security requirement', *Proceedings of the Fifth International Symposium on Protection Against Chemical and Biological Warfare Agents, Stockholm, Sweden, June 11–16, 1995*, FOA-R-95-00122-4.9-SE (National Defence Research Establishment: Umeå, Sweden, June 1995), pp. 11–23.

[287] Porteus, H., 'Grappling with the BW genie', *International Defense Review*, vol. 28, no. 3 (1995), pp. 32–34; and Tyson, P., 'Protection to the force', *Defense News Marketing Supplement*, vol. 10, no. 40 (1995), pp. 16, 18 and 20.

[288] Pearson, G. S., 'Chemical and biological defence: an essential national security requirement', *RUSI Journal*, vol. 140, no. 4 (Aug. 1995), pp. 20–27.

to counter weapons of mass destruction.[289] The USA is deficient in the following areas: detection, characterization and defeat of underground weapons of mass destruction facilities, vaccines against BW and biological and chemical agent defeat. A war-game in July 1995, simulating the widespread use of chemical and biological weapons including a domestic terrorist attack with BW, raised many questions about the adequacy of US policy, military doctrine and operational planning to counter weapons of mass destruction.[290] In the autumn of 1995 the US Deputy Secretary of Defense approved the formation of a Counter-Proliferation Council in the DOD. Its main purpose is to coordinate policy on combating NBC weapons. For FY 1996 the DOD plans to spend approximately $3.8 billion on technology procurement associated with countering weapons of mass destruction.[291] The US Marine Corps is considering forming a special unit capable of responding to future CW or BW terrorist attacks.[292] These new efforts to improve the US capability to counter weapons of mass destruction are part of the overall Counterproliferation Support Programme (CSP) for which $108 million was requested in the FY 1996 budget, in addition to $3.8 billion for the planned CSP programmes.[293]

Prior to the Persian Gulf War BW defence was given a low priority by the US armed services. In 1993 the Joint Program Office (JPO) for Biological Defense was established.[294] It is tasked with bringing order to the BW detection arena[295] and solving problems associated with the lack of a vaccine production capability. Its most important task is to develop and field a BW detector and to create standardized tests and evaluation regimes for BW defence components. The Light Detection and Ranging sensor that detects clouds carrying BW agents is among the new systems being considered for BW detection.[296] Efforts are also under way to meet the threat posed by CBW production facilities.[297]

Increasing concern about the possibility of biological warfare led Australia to establish a modest biological defence and disarmament programme in

[289] Starr, B., 'CW detection is top of US shortfall list', *Jane's Defence Weekly*, vol. 23, no. 23 (10 June 1995), p. 26.

[290] Hitchens, T., 'Wargame finds U.S. falls short in biowar', *Defense News*, vol. 10, no. 34 (28 Aug.–3 Sep. 1995), pp. 1, 18.

[291] Starr, B., 'DoD sets up council to focus anti-NBC policy', *Jane's Defence Weekly*, vol. 24, no. 19 (1 Nov. 1995), p. 6.

[292] Hitchens, T. and Holzer, R., 'Marines chief plans bio-chem unit', *Defense News*, vol. 10, no. 23 (21–27 Aug. 1995), pp. 3, 29; and 'USMC Commandant unveils new unit plan', *Jane's Defence Weekly*, vol. 24, no. 8 (26 Aug. 1995), p. 5.

[293] Erlich, J. and Hitchens, T., 'Counterproliferation efforts await requirement review', *Defense News*, vol. 10, no. 44 (6–12 Nov. 1995), p. 20.

[294] 'Preparing for the worst', *Jane's Defence Weekly*, vol. 23, no. 22 (3 June 1995), p. 24.

[295] Contracts have been awarded to US companies by the US Army Chemical and Biological Defense Command at Aberdeen Proving Ground. 'Firms research into biological detection', *Jane's Defence Contracts*, Aug. 1995, p. 5.

[296] Cooper, P., 'Lab seek biological early warning', *Defense News*, vol. 10, no. 31 (7–13 Aug. 1995), p. 10.

[297] Hitchens, T. and Oliveri, F., 'USAF considers ways to smother chemical weapons', *Defense News*, vol. 10, no. 38 (25 Sep.–1 Oct. 1995), p. 4.

1995.[298] In the UK the first NBC defence regiment was formed in 1995.[299] The regiment, which is specially trained in detection and reconnaissance measures related to CBW, will support existing NBC defence units at all levels, respond to possible terrorist acts, and deal with chemical leaks and disasters.

In June 1995 the Fifth International Symposium on Protection Against Chemical and Biological Warfare Agents was held in Stockholm.[300] The scope of the symposium was expanded to include protection against biological warfare—reflecting the recognized need for a 'two-track' defence against the entire spectrum of CW and BW agents and for improved arms control measures.[301]

VII. Other CBW-related developments

The Tokyo nerve gas attack and CBW terrorism

The single CW incident that received the greatest press coverage in 1995 was the sarin attack on the Tokyo underground on 20 March, which resulted in 12 deaths and over 5500 injuries. Relatively few people died because of the quick reaction of the Tokyo emergency services, the rapid identification of the poison as nerve gas and the corresponding medical response of hospitals. These factors, added to the fact that the sarin was not in its purest form at the time of dispersal, may have saved hundreds of lives.

Tokyo police sources stated that they found five separate packages containing a total of 11 plastic pouches on trains on the Marunouchi, Chiyoda and Hibiya underground lines. The pouches were punctured with umbrellas with sharpened tips, releasing gas. Later investigations revealed that the packages contained sarin and acetonitrile. The trains of the three lines were scheduled to arrive at the Kasumigaseki station in the heart of the federal government district between 8:09 and 8:13 a.m. Two of the five packages released gas at the station while the other three were discovered either before or after the trains stopped at the Kasumigaseki station.[302]

On 16 May 1995, the leader of the Aum Shinrikyo (Supreme Truth) religious cult, Shoko Asahara, was arrested with a number of his followers.[303] Asahara and six other cult leaders were formally indicted on 6 June for murder

[298] 'Australia studies biological defense', *International Defense Review*, vol. 28, no. 6 (June 1995), p. 10.

[299] 'UK forms first NBC regiment', *Strategic Digest*, vol. 25, no. 4 (Apr. 1995), p. 515.

[300] *Proceedings* (note 286). The symposium was attended by more than 700 experts from 34 countries.

[301] Pearson, G. S., 'Fifth International Symposium on Protection Against Chemical and Biological Warfare Agents: an overview', *ASA Newsletter*, no. 49 (10 Aug. 1995), 95-4, pp. 1, 10–11.

[302] Purver, R., 'Chemical and biological terrorism: the threat according to the open literature', Canadian Security Intelligence Service, unclassified document, June 1995, p. 153; Kristof, N. D., 'Japanese indict leader of cult in gas murders', *New York Times*, 7 June 1995; Croddy, E., 'Urban terrorism: chemical warfare in Japan', *Jane's Intelligence Review*, vol. 7, no. 11 (Nov. 1995), p. 521; and Strasser, S. *et al.*, 'Nerve gas terror', *Newsweek*, vol. 125, no. 14 (3 Apr. 1995), p. 11.

[303] Two weeks before the attack Aum Shinrikyo had published a book detailing the characteristics of sarin and two other nerve agents and had stated that nerve gas was 'the new weapon of Armageddon'. Purver (note 302), p. 160.

702 NON-PROLIFERATION, ARMS CONTROL, DISARMAMENT, 1995

in connection with the 20 March attack.[304] Asahara maintained his innocence until October 1995, when he confessed to masterminding the attack.[305]

A few days after the 20 March attack Japanese police searched cult facilities near Kamikuishiki, a village at the foot of Mount Fuji. Ostensibly, police were looking for a missing notary public, but the search resulted in the discovery of approximately 2 t of chemicals, sophisticated laboratory equipment, CW protective equipment and sarin degradation products.[306] There were 500 drums of several chemicals, including phosphorus trichloride, hexane, isopropyl alcohol and sodium fluoride.[307] Almost a year earlier, in July 1994, residents of the village had reported eye irritation and nausea from fumes coming from the compound and had filed a complaint. During a search, police found sarin residue near the cult compound but made no further investigation as there had been no injuries. The cult then made a countercharge against the villagers for defamation, and Asahara claimed that the government was trying to poison cult members.[308]

As more information on the activities of the cult surfaced, a connection was made with an incident which occurred on 27 June 1994 in a residential section of the town of Matsumoto, where 7 people died and over 200 were injured.[309] It was believed that a release of sarin was to blame, but the case had remained unsolved. Asahara admitted to Aum Shinrikyo involvement in the Matsumoto incident when he confessed in October to ordering the Tokyo underground attack.[310] It was later discovered that the attack had been aimed specifically against a judge involved in a lawsuit against Aum Shinrikyo.[311]

Other Aum Shinrikyo CBW activities became known in 1995. For example, in 1993–94 a company owned by the cult held a station property in Western Australia.[312] Cult members imported various chemicals and obtained others through legitimate sources in Australia for use at the property. Following the March 1995 attack in Tokyo, Australian Federal Police investigated activities at the property. Dead sheep were found and samples were analysed for traces of chemicals; evidence was found suggesting that nerve agents may have been used on the sheep.[313] There was no evidence that cult members had produced nerve agents from the chemicals obtained in Australia.

In July Aum Shinrikyo members confessed to spreading anthrax virus in the streets of Tokyo in 1993.[314] The attack had gone unnoticed as there had been

[304] Kristof (note 302).

[305] Nakamoto, M., 'Asahara "admits poison gas role"', *Financial Times*, 5 Oct. 1995, p. 4.

[306] Kristof, N. D., 'Japanese police find chemicals and gas masks at site of a cult', *New York Times*, 23 Mar. 1995, p. 1; and 'Nerve-gas residue found at Japan cult site', *Boston Globe*, 8 Apr. 1995, p. 4.

[307] Croddy (note 302).

[308] Purver (note 302), p. 160.

[309] 'Discovering a Japanese cult's deadly designs for doomsday', *Jane's Defence Weekly*, vol. 24, no. 20 (18 Nov. 1995), p. 25.

[310] Nakamoto (note 305).

[311] Croddy (note 302), p. 523.

[312] Director, Chemical Weapons Office, *Annual Report of the Director of Safeguards 1994–95* (Department of Foreign Affairs and Trade: Canberra, 1995), p. 19.

[313] Kristof, N. D., 'Police say cult tested gas in Australia', *International Herald Tribune*, 12 May 1995, p. 4.

[314] 'Cult members tell of virus spray', *International Herald Tribune*, 27 July 1995, p. 4.

no casualties. Searches of the cult's compound in Kamikuishiki turned up 160 barrels of growth medium and botulism-producing bacteria, indicating that the cult was also involved in BW activities.[315] Aum Shinrikyo activities were also investigated in Russia, where the cult claimed to have over 30 000 members.[316] Japanese press reports alluded to Russian complicity in the attacks, which was quickly denied by Russian authorities.[317] Following the Tokyo attack it was revealed that a Russian woman associated with the cult had been a victim of nerve agent poisoning.[318] Russian authorities closed down the cult's operations in Russia on 29 March 1995.[319]

Aum Shinrikyo's 'chemical team leader', Masami Tsuchiya, later confessed that the cult had produced approximately 30 kg of sarin in its compound near Mount Fuji over a period of two years.[320] It was discovered that Aum Shinrikyo had, at least experimentally, produced sarin, tabun, soman, phosgene and VX and worked with biological agents such as botulinum toxin and anthrax.[321] The cult allegedly murdered two former cult members by VX injection in late 1994.[322]

Various terrorist CW attacks and threats of attack occurred in Japan after the Tokyo underground attack. On 19 April 1995, in Yokohama, 571 people were treated after 'noxious' gas was released from three locations near the main train station. Police initially reported the gas to be phosgene,[323] but a former criminal gang member, Koji Hara, later admitted to and was arrested for the attack, claiming he had used tear gas.[324] On 21 April, 29 people were hospitalized after being overcome by fumes in a Yokohama department store, and on 25 April, 4 people were hospitalized after a liquid was released outside a restaurant in the town of Maebashi.[325] None of the injuries sustained in these attacks was serious. A potentially more dangerous attack occurred on 5 May 1995 when two bags were found set ablaze in the men's lavatory at the Shinjuku underground station in Tokyo.[326] One bag contained two litres (l) of powdered sodium cyanide and the other held 1.5 l of sulphuric acid, which when combined would have produced hydrogen cyanide gas. Underground guards extinguished the fire and rapidly evacuated the area, and there were no casualties. On 4 July a cleaning woman found the same combination of chemicals

[315] Pollack, A., 'Japanese police say they found germ-war material at cult site', *New York Times*, 29 Mar. 1995, p. 10.

[316] Stanley, A., 'Russians close branch of Japanese cult linked to nerve gas', *New York Times* (international edn), 30 Mar. 1995, p. A8.

[317] 'FSK official on "Russian connection" with sect', in FBIS-SOV-95-064, 4 Apr. 1995, p. 15.

[318] Croddy (note 302).

[319] Stanley (note 316).

[320] Croddy (note 302), p. 521.

[321] 'Discovering a Japanese cult's deadly designs for doomsday' (note 309).

[322] Croddy (note 302), p. 523.

[323] Kristof, N. D., '24 Japanese afflicted by fumes', *International Herald Tribune*, 12 Apr. 1995, p. 5.

[324] 'Ex-gang member admits Yokohama gas attacks', *International Herald Tribune*, 7 July 1995, p. 4.

[325] Purver (note 302), p. 181.

[326] Purver (note 302), p. 181.

together with a timer device at the Kayabacho underground station in Tokyo.[327] Police disarmed the device and there were no injuries.

In response to the CW attacks the Japanese Government passed laws against the manufacture, import or possession of nerve gas.[328] The attacks were also a primary factor in accelerating Japan's ratification of the CWC, which occurred on 15 September 1995.

The Tokyo attack appeared to have initiated several other CW terrorist threats around the world. An anonymous letter and video tape threatened an attack in April 1995 at Disneyland in California.[329] In June right-wing groups in Chile threatened to release sarin in the Santiago underground system unless former head of the secret police General Manuel Contreras was released from prison.[330] German authorities announced in July that right-wing neo-nazi groups in Germany were experimenting with toxic chemicals.[331] In February 1995, prior to the Tokyo attack, a US federal court found two members of a radical anti-tax group, the Patriots Council, guilty of possessing ricin in violation of the Biological Weapons Anti-Terrorism Act of 1989. One of the accused had planted castor beans on his property and extracted 0.7 grams of ricin from the beans he harvested.[332] In all the above-mentioned cases no attack was carried out.

The Tokyo incident provoked a worldwide re-examination of preparedness for CBW attacks by terrorist groups against civilian populations. Security was heightened in undergrounds in London, Moscow, New York and San Francisco, among other locations.[333] A statement by US Senator Sam Nunn reflects the increased seriousness with which CBW terrorism in now regarded: 'the scenario of a terrorist group either obtaining or manufacturing and using a weapon of mass destruction is no longer the stuff of science fiction or adventure movies. It is a reality which has already come to pass, and one which, if we do not take appropriate measures, will increasingly threaten us in the future'.[334]

Gulf War Syndrome

Despite numerous studies in recent years there is still no adequate explanation for the cause of Gulf War Syndrome—a variety of ailments afflicting veterans

---

[327] 'Another cyanide bomb is diffused in Tokyo subway', *International Herald Tribune*, 5 July 1995, p. 1.

[328] Guest, R., 'Japan moves to ban sarin after attack', *Electronic Telegraph*, 19 Apr. 1995. URL <http://www.telegraph.co.uk/et/access>.

[329] Lippman, T. W., 'Troops were sent to Disneyland after threat of a gas attack', *International Herald Tribune*, 24 Apr. 1995, p. 4.

[330] 'Chile sarin threat', *Jane's Defence Weekly*, vol. 23, no. 24 (17 June 1995), p. 12.

[331] 'Gefährliche Giftmischer' [Dangerous poison mixers], *Der Spiegel*, vol. 49, no. 27 (1995), p. 16 (in German).

[332] de Fiebre, C., '2 convicted of possessing deadly poison', *Star Tribune*, 1 Mar. 1995, p. 1B.

[333] Lii, J. H., 'In subways elsewhere, a heightened state of alert', *New York Times*, 21 Mar. 1995, p. A6.

[334] Nunn, S., 'Opening statement to the US Senate Permanent Subcommittee on Investigations, Hearing on Global Proliferation of Weapons of Mass Destruction', 31 Oct. 1995.

of the 1991 Persian Gulf War.[335] However, two separate studies concluded that the syndrome could be caused by a combination of pyridostigmine bromide (an anti-nerve agent, pre-treatment drug), DEET (an insect repellent applied to the skin) and permethrin (an insecticide applied to clothing and blankets).[336] A study carried out by researchers at Duke University in North Carolina on chickens and a second carried out by the US DOD on rats found that combining these chemicals causes nerve damage, which may account for some of the undiagnosed illnesses known as Gulf War Syndrome. The majority of cases of Gulf War Syndrome have occurred in the US military (approximately 2000), and approximately 500 cases have been reported in Great Britain, 40–50 cases in Canada, approximately 10 cases in the Czech Republic and a small number of cases in Norway.[337] However, there are, for example, no reported cases of the syndrome in the Egyptian, French, Moroccan, Saudi Arabian or Syrian militaries or among the Kuwaiti or Saudi civilian populations.[338] A number of the members of these groups (e.g., the French forces) did not receive the anti-nerve agent, pre-treatment drug pyridostigmine bromide or other CBW preventive shots.[339]

Another possible cause of some of the illnesses was discovered by researchers at Robert Wood Johnson Medical Center in New Jersey who found that 40 of 43 veterans complaining of Gulf War Syndrome had chronic inflammation of the upper airways, restricting the rate of air flow to the lungs, possibly because of exposure to smoke and effluents from burning Kuwaiti oil wells.[340] Some Gulf War veteran and activist groups claim that the illnesses may be linked to vaccines meant to counter the effects of biological weapons, namely anthrax.[341] Others maintain that the illnesses result from the alleged use of chemical or biological weapons by Iraq in the Persian Gulf War, although a study by the Institute of Medicine of the US National Academy of Sciences concluded in June 1995 that the illnesses 'are not the result of chemical, biological, or toxin warfare, or accidental exposures to stored weapons or material'.[342] Regardless of this finding, approximately 2000 veterans are suing several multinational corporations for $1 billion for allegedly selling chemicals to Iraq, which allowed it to build up a CBW capability.[343]

[335] Brown, D. 'Gulf War Syndrome study pinpoints no single cause', *Washington Post*, 14 Dec. 1994, p. A2.

[336] Kleiner, K., 'Did toxic mix cause Gulf sickness?', *New Scientist*, vol. 1461, no. 1974 (22 Apr. 1995), p. 5.

[337] Department of the Army, Walter Reed Army Medical Center, *International Coalition: Reports of Symptoms*, memorandum (Department of the Army: Washington, DC, 18 Jan.1994). Version current on 7 Dec. 1995, URL <http://www.ides.com/Gulf_War/international/internat.html>; and House of Commons Defence Committee, *Gulf War Syndrome, Eleventh Report*, House of Commons, 1994/95 no. 197 (Her Majesty's Stationery Office: London, 25 Oct. 1995), p. xviii.

[338] Department of the Army (note 337).

[339] House of Commons Defence Committee (note 337).

[340] 'Airway blockage may explain Gulf War Syndrome symptoms', *Chemical and Engineering News*, vol. 73, no. 23 (5 June 1995), p. 29.

[341] Evans, M., 'Gulf troops say effects of drugs were kept secret', *The Times,* 2 Feb. 1995, p. 2.

[342] 'No chemical weapons used in Gulf, panel says', *Washington Times*, 1 June 1995, p. A6.

[343] 'No chemical weapons used in Gulf, panel says' (note 342).

The DOD has appropriated up to $500 000 annually to the National Academy of Sciences to review studies related to illnesses among Gulf War veterans, and the first such report was issued in January 1995.[344] In February the US Department of Veterans Affairs published its final regulation on monthly compensation payments to Gulf War veterans with undiagnosed illnesses.[345] In March 1995 President Clinton formed a Presidential Advisory Committee on Gulf War veteran illnesses. In October the US House of Representatives legislated an extension to the end of 1998 of guaranteed medical treatment for veterans suffering from Gulf War Syndrome.[346]

The British Government agreed in July 1995 to conduct more research on Gulf War Syndrome, but it has been criticized by Gulf War veteran groups for responding unsatisfactorily to illness claims.[347] In October 1995 the Defence Committee of the House of Commons published its 11th report, a detailed account of claims, research and symptoms associated with Gulf War Syndrome.

VIII. Conclusions

With 28 new ratifications of the CWC in 1995 progress was made towards implementation of the convention. However, 18 ratifications are still needed to achieve the 65 necessary for entry into force. The earliest realistic estimate for entry into force of the CWC is the end of 1996 or early 1997. The apparent reasons for the delay are related to the fact that substantial time and effort are required to set up the legal and organizational framework for ratification and implementation.

It is highly desirable that the major possessors of CW stockpiles, Russia and the USA, are among the first 65 ratifiers. If not, the future OPCW and Technical Secretariat will need to be rethought, since current planning for verification activities under the CWC assumes that the 1990 Russian–US Bilateral Destruction Agreement will be in force.

The work of the PrepCom progressed in 1995, but there is still not final agreement on a number of issues, including those related to declaration and verification. Some issues may be solved when 65 ratifications have been deposited and it becomes clear which states will comprise the first conference of states parties. Political debate continues on the interpretation of Article XI. There is a clear indication that some of the thinking from the CWC negotiations in Geneva has been transferred to The Hague, especially to the expert groups. However, these groups are only part of that implementation structure. The preparations for national implementation undertaken by many states show strong commitment to the CWC.

[344] Department of Veterans Affairs, Office of Public Affairs, News Service, *VA Fact Sheet* (Department of Veteran Affairs: Washington, DC, June 1995). Version current on 26 Jan. 1996, URL <http://www.gulfwar.org/vafacts1.html>.
[345] 'VA Fact Sheet' (note 344).
[346] 'Medical treatment for Gulf War vets is extended by House', *Congressional Quarterly*, vol. 53, no. 41 (21 Oct. 1995), p. 3213.
[347] Norton-Taylor, R., 'Gulf illness study cleared', *The Guardian*, 28 July 1995, p. 4.

What is most needed is the political will to solve the major remaining problems. There is still reason to believe that the CWC can be implemented in an effective and efficient manner.

In 1995 UNSCOM continued its activities in Iraq to fulfil its mandated obligations. The disclosure of the past Iraqi BW programme was of major significance. In addition, the completeness and accuracy of the information supplied by Iraq about its CW, missile and nuclear programmes were questioned. Iraq not only produced large amounts of botulinum toxin, anthrax and aflatoxin but also had weaponized these agents and may have been prepared to use them as a last resort. New information on the Iraqi CW programme proved that VX had been produced and that Iraq possessed the necessary quantities of precursors for large-scale production of VX. Questions must be asked about how Iraq managed to keep its BW programme and the magnitude of its other weapons of mass destruction programmes secret and how information on these programmes remained so well hidden despite four years of UNSCOM inspections. It is clear that a full, final and complete declaration of Iraq's NBC and missile programmes has not yet been made. Unless this occurs, it is unlikely that the sanctions on Iraq will be lifted in the near future.

In 1995 UNSCOM activities concentrated on the installation of a permanent monitoring system to verify Iraqi compliance with the requirements outlined in the cease-fire resolution. The BMVC is now fully functional and carried out several on-site inspections in 1995. Under the plan for future monitoring and verification of Iraqi compliance with the cease-fire resolution, a detailed import and export control system has been approved. It will enter into force following the lifting of sanctions.

Issues related to strengthening the BWC received greater attention in 1995 than in the past. The newly established Ad Hoc Group of Experts held three meetings in 1995 and considered various measures to strengthen the BWC. In particular, it addressed definitions of terms, lists of bacteriological (biological) agents and toxins, the incorporation of CBMs into a legally binding regime and a system of measures to promote compliance with the BWC. Despite progress in the development of provisions to strengthen the BWC, it is doubtful that a verification protocol will be ready for the Fourth Review Conference of the BWC in late 1996. There was slightly greater participation in the ninth round of the information exchange.

Analysis of the lessons from the Persian Gulf War and increasing concern about terrorist use of CW or BW made it apparent that, in addition to the need for effective CW and BW arms control measures, more effective protection and detection measures are needed. The incidents involving sarin in the Tokyo underground system in March 1995 turned terrorist scenarios involving CW into reality and raised the question of how to prevent such incidents in the future. It is impossible to construct a totally secure control system, but the entry into force of the CWC, strengthening of the BWC and effective national legislation will make it more difficult for terrorists to manufacture, procure or use CW or BW in the future.

There is still no clear explanation of Gulf War Syndrome, but studies in 1995 indicated that it is unlikely that it was caused by Iraqi use of CW or BW.

Allegations of chemical and biological weapon use in 1995 were confined to disproved or unsubstantiated incidents in areas that were difficult for experts to reach. This pattern is consistent with allegations from previous years.

The destruction of chemical weapons in both Russia and the USA remains a matter of concern. The overall cost of destruction in the USA has grown to $11.9 billion; for Russia the cost is estimated at approximately $6 billion. The US JACADS facility continues to operate, and in 1995 it successfully destroyed all the M55 nerve-agent rockets stored at the facility. At the Tooele and Anniston facilities destruction programmes were delayed owing to lack of state and local permits. Russia is in the process of enacting a chemical weapon destruction law, but the Russian CW destruction programme faces major financial problems even though Germany, the Netherlands, Sweden and the USA continue to donate funds and expertise to it.

The problem of old chemical munitions dumped at sea continued to receive attention, especially in Europe, where concerns were expressed about the environmental impact of these weapons. In 1995 Japan officially admitted that it had abandoned CW in China in World War II.

A number of events related to chemical and biological weapons and related disarmament measures achieved prominence in 1995. Perhaps the most dramatic of these was the terrorist use of chemical weapons in Japan. The world must now contend not only with states, but also with individuals who are willing to acquire and use these weapons of mass destruction. The manner in which CBW disarmament and prohibition regimes address these threats in the future will have significant impact on whether or not the world will one day be rid of chemical and biological weapons.

16. Conventional arms control and security cooperation in Europe

ZDZISLAW LACHOWSKI

I. Introduction

Since the end of the cold war the Organization for Security and Co-operation in Europe (OSCE) participating states have been confronted with vexing questions concerning the new scope, tasks, role and place of conventional arms control in the European security setting. The post-cold war period changed the premises of arms control. Preventive diplomacy, crisis management and other forms of peace missions and arrangements seemed effectively to replace the traditional arms control approaches in the new, cooperative environment. The first half of the 1990s was primarily the era of arms control implementation, and only the most necessary changes were made to accommodate the existing agreements to the new circumstances.

In 1995 the need for arms control and security cooperation was emphasized regionally with the evident peacekeeping failure and the US-led enforced peace arrangements in Bosnia and Herzegovina and, Europe-wide, with the completion of the final reduction phase of the 1990 Treaty on Conventional Armed Forces in Europe (the CFE Treaty)[1] and of the reductions agreed under the 1992 Concluding Act of the Negotiation on Personnel Strength of Conventional Armed Forces in Europe (the CFE-1A Agreement).[2] The longstanding issue of the flank zone was the main concern in treaty implementation endeavours during the year; however, more importantly, there were attendant disquieting attempts at renegotiation of the treaty. The Forum for Security Co-operation (FSC) focused increasingly on arms control implementation and a future arms control framework, and the OSCE was entrusted with a more active arms control mission in Bosnia and Herzegovina at the end of the year. Despite expectations that the Open Skies Treaty would enter into force in 1995, the ratification process was held up by the failure of Russia, Belarus and Ukraine to ratify the treaty.[3]

---

[1] The CFE Treaty and Protocols are reprinted in Koulik, S. and Kokoski, R., SIPRI, *Conventional Arms Control: Perspectives on Verification* (Oxford University Press: Oxford, 1994), pp. 211–76.

[2] The text of the CFE-1A Agreement is reprinted in *SIPRI Yearbook 1993: World Armaments and Disarmament* (Oxford University Press: Oxford, 1993), pp. 683–89.

[3] By the end of 1995, 22 states had ratified the Open Skies Treaty. For the treaty to enter into force, the deposit of 20 instruments of ratification is required, including those of the depositaries (Canada and Hungary) and of states parties whose individual allocation of passive quotas is 8 or more. For information and data on the Open Skies Treaty, see 'Summaries and status of other multilateral agreements' in annexe A of this volume. For the text of the treaty see *SIPRI Yearbook 1993* (note 2), appendix 12C, pp. 653–71.

This chapter covers the major issues relating to European arms control and security cooperation in the OSCE area in 1995. Appendix 16A reviews the implementation of confidence- and security-building measures (CSBMs), as agreed in the Vienna Document 1994,[4] and appendix 16B surveys foreign military presence in the OSCE area.

II. The CFE Treaty: the end of the reduction period

The CFE Treaty set equal ceilings within its Atlantic-to-the-Urals (ATTU) application zone on the treaty-limited equipment (TLE) of the groups of states parties, originally the NATO and the former Warsaw Treaty Organization (WTO) states (now 30 states parties), essential for launching surprise attack and initiating large-scale offensive operations. The reduction of excess TLE was to be completed in three one-year phases by 16 November 1995. The first phase was successfully completed in November 1993, with roughly one-third of the states' liabilities reduced. More than 70 per cent of the reduction liabilities were cut back by the end of 1994.

The major questions on the agenda of or related to CFE Treaty implementation in 1995 discussed here are: *(a)* the reduction process; *(b)* verification of the third phase of the TLE reduction period; *(c)* the flank issue; *(d)* the linkage between the CFE Treaty and NATO enlargement; *(e)* the future of the CFE Treaty; and *(f)* CFE-related arms transfers.

Reduction of TLE holdings

To comply with the CFE Treaty ceilings excess TLE items were to be destroyed or disabled in other ways provided for in the Protocol on Reductions. Each state party was to have eliminated its reduction liability in each of the five categories of conventional armaments and equipment limited by the CFE Treaty by the end of the third reduction phase.[5]

At the end of 1994, Russian TLE had been reduced by about 38 200 items (including some 2000 holdings declared to be beyond the Urals). However, the rate of reductions and destruction was uneven. By the end of March 1995, NATO Allies had destroyed more than 90 per cent of their military liabilities and planned to finalize their reduction process by 16 November. On 23 May 1995 Germany, with the biggest CFE reduction obligations after Russia, had completed scrapping its heavy weapon systems or converting them to non-military purposes. Since mid-1992, 16 private firms at 16 sites in Germany had destroyed about 8600 of some 11 000 TLE items, a large proportion of which were from the former East German *Nationale Volksarmee* arsenal. Part of the reduction commitment was met by the sale or transfer of weapons (c. 500 tanks, 1400 armoured combat vehicles (ACVs) and 400 artillery systems) to allied partners. The cost of reduction was estimated at more than

---

[4] The Vienna Document 1994 is reprinted in *SIPRI Yearbook 1995: Armaments, Disarmament and International Security* (Oxford University Press: Oxford, 1995), pp. 779–820.
[5] The CFE Treaty (note 1), Article VIII, para. 4(C).

DM100 million ($72.3 million), excluding the cost of disposition of the ammunition.[6]

The group of non-NATO states parties as a whole, however, lagged considerably behind at that time, and had only destroyed or disabled about 70 per cent of the total.[7] While several Central European states were reducing their liabilities according to schedule, the situation in Belarus, Ukraine, Russia and the Caucasian republics prompted NATO concern about non-compliance. In the middle of the year it was reported that some Central and East European signatories, faced with the huge costs of destroying their holdings, were trying to dispose of TLE surpluses by intensifying equipment exports.[8] Germany was also selling or giving away old East German military equipment stocks in large quantities around the world.

The high cost of destruction continued to be a problem, frequently raised by some former WTO states. Belarus was a borderline case, having stopped its reduction process on 23 February 1995, citing economic crisis and strategic concerns (the latter concern, possible NATO enlargement, was soon dropped, however). This attempt at blackmail elicited sharp reactions from NATO states, which in early March presented a joint *démarche* to the Minsk authorities against the unilateral breach of the treaty.[9] In mid-April, Belorussian Defence Minister Anatol Kastenko said that Belarus would like to sell some tanks instead of dismantling them, estimating the cost of destroying one tank at 1.5 million roubles (*c.* $1350).[10] During an August 1995 visit to Minsk, German Foreign Minister Klaus Kinkel urged his hosts to abide by their CFE Treaty obligations. However, Belarus continued to insist on receiving $12–15 million in aid from the West, which Western experts found excessive.[11] Kinkel promised that the European Union and Germany would cover part of the destruction costs if there were 'positive signals' from Minsk regarding reductions.[12] Belorussian officials complained in particular that 25 per cent of the national budget is being spent on the cleanup after the 1986 Chernobyl disaster. In September, the Belorussian authorities sent first signals of their intention to resume arms destruction, having received special equipment and

[6] 'Waffen systeme vorzeitig zerstört' [Weapon systems destroyed before schedule], *Frankfurter Allgemeine Zeitung*, 24 May 1995.

[7] *International Herald Tribune*, 8–9 Apr. 1995.

[8] 'C. European nations sell arms to comply with CFE', *Defense News*, 19–25 June 1995, p. 44.

[9] 'NATO warnt Weißrußland vor Bruch des KSE-Vertrags' [NATO warns Belarus against breach of the CFE Treaty], *Frankfurter Allgemeine Zeitung*, 9 Mar. 1995.

[10] Institute for Defense and Disarmament Studies, *Arms Control Reporter* (IDDS: Brookline, Mass.), sheet 407.B.517, 1995. According to the Belorussian Foreign Ministry, it received from the OSCE the right to export 298 decommissioned T-80 tanks. 'Minsk cuts costs to fulfil nuclear commitments', *Foreign Broadcast Information Service, Daily Report Central Asia (FBIS-SOV)*, FBIS-SOV-95-156, 14 Aug. 1995, p. 71.

[11] Belarus was accused by US experts of seeking ways to profit by using more expensive means of destruction. *Defense News*, 14–20 Aug. 1995, p. 4. Poland offered to destroy part of the Russian and Belorussian TLE, but no contract was agreed. *Warsaw Voice*, 24 Sep. 1995, p. 7.

[12] *Frankfurter Allgemeine Zeitung*, 22 Aug. 1995. According to President Lukashenko, in the wake of his decision to suspend the destruction of armaments, Germany and the USA allegedly pledged $230 million [*sic*] to the reduction programme. He expressed his hope that the first $100 million 'pledged by the West' would arrive soon. 'Lukashenko on resumption of weapons destruction', Moscow INTERFAX in English, FBIS-SOV-95-195, 10 Oct. 1995, p. 80.

Table 16.1. Russia's reductions outside the CFE Treaty application area and the Black Sea Fleet reductions, 31 December 1995

Area	Tanks		ACVs		Artillery		Total red.	%
	Liab.	Red.	Liab.	Red.	Liab.	Red.		
From beyond the Urals	6 000	1 264	1 500	685	7 000	3 453	5 402	37.3
Black Sea Fleet naval infantry/coastal defence	602	375	1 725	1 059	1 080	862	2 296	67.4

Sources: Estimates based on Moscow Interfax in English, 1 Jan. 1996, in FBIS-SOV-96-001, 2 Jan. 1996, pp. 10–11; and Selected data on the implementation of the CFE Treaty obligations, Permanent Mission of the Slovak Republic to the OSCE, 19 Dec. 1995.

materials from abroad for this purpose. These signals were soon followed by President Alexander Lukashenko's declaration to this effect.[13] In mid-October, the main Borisov repair works resumed the scrapping of tanks and ACVs. However, the chance of Belarus meeting the 16 November 1995 deadline was gone.[14]

On 12 September Belarus, Kazakhstan, Russia and Ukraine announced that they would be unable to meet their CFE obligations, for technological and political reasons.[15] Control over naval infantry and coastal defence holdings, under their joint command as part of the Black Sea Fleet, presented the main obstacle to implementation by Russia and Ukraine. Under the 14 June 1991 pledge they must jointly reduce 602 tanks, 1725 ACVs and 1080 artillery systems,stationed within the ATTU zone.[16] At the end of 1995, two-thirds of the Baltic Sea Fleet liabilities had been scrapped. In October, Ukrainian officials claimed that they could not meet the goal until the division of the Black Sea Fleet with Russia was settled.[17] In early November, the Ukrainian Foreign

[13] 'General Portnov confirms arms destruction to resume', Minsk Radio Minsk Network in Belorussian, 20 Sep. 1995, FBIS-SOV-95-182, 20 Sep. 1995, p. 73. 'Lukashenka: Destruction of conventional arms resumed', Moscow Interfax in English, 28 Sep. 1995, FBIS-SOV-95-189, 28 Sep. 1995, p. 63. In Oct. Belarus announced that it earmarked nearly 5 billion Belorussian roubles (*c.* $450 000) for the resumption of the reduction. 'Prime Minister estimates cost of arms destruction', Minsk BELAPAN in English, 12 Oct. 1995, FBIS-SOV-95-197, 12 Oct. 1995, p. 63.

[14] Belorussian Deputy Foreign Minister Andrei Sannikov announced that the Joint Consultative Group had agreed to extend the time frame of treaty implementation by Belarus until 26 Apr. 1996. *Krasnaya Zvezda*, 28 Nov. 1995, FBIS-SOV-95-229, 29 Nov. 1995, p. 51.

[15] OMRI (Open Media Research Institute), *OMRI Daily Digest*, no. 178 (13 Sep. 1995), URL <http://www.omri.cz/Publications/Digests/DigestIndex.html> (hereafter, references to the *OMRI Daily Digest* refer to the Internet edition at this URL address). In Kazakhstan, this concerned part of the equipment transferred by the USSR beyond the Urals in 1990 and 1991, and which it pledged to destroy under the politically binding statement of 14 June 1991. In Sep. 1993, the Kazakh, Russian and Uzbek defence ministers agreed on the quotas of weapons each state should eliminate. Lachowski, Z., 'Conventional arms control and security co-operation in Europe', *SIPRI Yearbook 1994* (Oxford University Press: Oxford, 1994), p. 569.

[16] Statement by the Government of the USSR, 14 June 1991, reprinted in *Arms Control Reporter*, sheets 407.D.80–82, 1991.

[17] 'Ukraine, Belarus unable to meet CFE deadline', Kiev INTELNEWS in English, FBIS-SOV-95-201, 18 Oct. 1995, p. 51. At the end of Nov. 1995, the defence ministers of Russia and Ukraine reportedly signed an agreement, in a series of other military accords, concerning the disputed flank limitation issue. *OMRI Daily Digest*, no. 229 (27 Nov. 1995).

Ministry stated that its conventional weapon reductions were completed on 31 October, excluding the equipment attached to the Black Sea Fleet.[18]

Head of the Main Armoured Troops Department of the Russian Defence Ministry Colonel-General Alexander Galkin stated on 3 November that of the equipment moved east of the Urals (6331 tanks and 1988 ACVs) only 1518 tanks and 983 ACVs had been destroyed.[19] Deputy Chief of the General Staff Dmitriy Kharchenko later said that Russia would be unable to meet the 31 December deadline for their destruction, as only about one-quarter of the tanks, half of the ACVs and half of the artillery systems had been destroyed (see table 16.1), and about 100 billion roubles ($20 million) were needed to complete the task of scrapping the other roughly 9000 holdings. Russia proposed that the December deadline be extended until the end of 1998.[20]

The civil war and the military presence in Chechnya, the creation of an army in the northern Caucasus and uncertainty about the reduction of TLE beyond the Urals (the Russian military claims that much of it is too rusty or obsolete to merit the cost of deliberate destruction[21]), as well as the Black Sea Fleet dispute, cast doubt on Russia's meeting its CFE reduction obligations. On 15 November, Defence Minister Pavel Grachev told a news conference that Russia was not prepared to meet the CFE Treaty deadline, for 'financial and other reasons',[22] but on 20 November Kharchenko announced that Russia had fulfilled its treaty obligations by destroying 3520 tanks, 6004 ACVs, 1096 artillery pieces, 1021 combat aircraft and 99 attack helicopters.[23] None the less, the naval and coastal defence as well as the east-of-the Urals holdings remained Russia's liability. Another problem which must be addressed is that of the Russian holdings in Armenia, Georgia and Moldova.[24]

[18] *Segodnya*, 3 Nov. 1995, p. 8.

[19] *OMRI Daily Digest,* no. 216 (6 Nov. 1995). These figures include the holdings agreed under the two, political and legal, 14 June 1991 pledges. Compare tables 20.4 and 20.5 in Lachowski, Z., 'Conventional arms control and security dialogue in Europe', *SIPRI Yearbook 1995* (note 4), pp. 768–69.

[20] 'Russia unable to scrap arms in Central Asia by deadline', Moscow Interfax in English, 21 Nov. 1995, FBIS-SOV-95-224, 21 Nov. 1995, p. 27; and 'Gen. Kharchenko on failure to scrap military hardware', FBIS-SOV-96-001, 2 Jan. 1996, pp. 10–11. The east-of-the-Urals equipment was deployed to Russian Asia, Kazakhstan, Turkmenistan and Uzbekistan.

[21] The West suggested a simplified form of destruction by filling a tank with concrete. Russia refused to apply such a method because of the unprofitable nature of the operation (the material cannot be recycled). 'Russia unable to scrap arms in Central Asia by deadline' (note 20).

[22] 'Moscow calls for amendment to treaty', Moscow Interfax in English, 16 Nov. 1995, FBIS-SOV-95-222, 17 Nov. 1995, p. 17; and *OMRI Daily Digest,* no. 224 (16 Nov. 1995).

[23] 'Official claims Russia complied with CFE obligations', Moscow Interfax in English, 16 Nov. 1995, FBIS-SOV-95-222, 17 Nov. 1995, p. 17. Different figures were supplied by the Russian Defence Ministry press centre: 3188 tanks, 5419 ACVs, 660 artillery pieces, 1029 aircraft and 99 combat helicopters; however, they were said not to include the coastal defence and naval infantry. 'CFE treaty obligations said fulfilled', Moscow ITAR-TASS in English, 20 Nov. 1995, FBIS-SOV-95-224, 21 Nov. 1995, p. 16. The same figures were reported to the Conflict Prevention Centre (CPC) in Vienna.

[24] In autumn 1995 Armenia notified the CFE Joint Consultative Group that Russia is temporarily stationing 40 tanks, 55 ACVs and 81 artillery pieces on the former's territory. *Nezavisimaya Gazeta*, 5 Dec. 1995, p. 3. The question of the temporary stationing of equipment has been raised by Azerbaijan in the JCG in connection with the flank issue. A Georgian source estimates that Russia has roughly 300 tanks, 750 ACVs and 300 heavy artillery pieces deployed in Georgia and Armenia. 'The current condition of the Group of Russian Troops in Transcaucasia (GRTT)', *Georgian Military Chronicle* (Occasional Papers of the Caucasian Institute for Peace, Democracy and Development), vol. 2, no. 2 (Apr. 1995). According to the Georgian–Russian agreement, Russia could temporarily maintain 115 tanks, 160 ACVs and 170 artillery pieces. The agreement has not yet been ratified. *Krasnaya Zvezda*,

Armenia and Azerbaijan were also among the countries that failed to comply with the treaty because of inadequate resources or facilities. Poland, with one of the biggest reduction obligations, completed the destruction and disposal of its liabilities in mid-September,[25] and the Czech Republic, Hungary, Romania and Slovakia had also destroyed or converted their excess TLE by the end of October.

At the end of 1995, according to CPC estimates, 49 696 heavy weapons were verified scrapped or converted to non-military use since November 1992. NATO had cut nearly 16 500 items and the former WTO states had reduced over 33 200 items (including Russia's 10 400—see tables 16.3 and 16.4).

Verification

The CFE Treaty inspection and verification regimes require unprecedented openness at military installations throughout the area of application. Along with the reductions, this has made the treaty a cornerstone of European security and stability. Under the provisions of the treaty, the states parties continued to inspect declared sites and objects of verification (OOVs). The passive declared-site inspection quotas were equal to 10 per cent of a state's notified OOVs during the reduction period. Declared information and the findings of inspection teams were reported to the Joint Consultative Group (JCG), the principal CFE Treaty verification and compliance mechanism, composed of representatives from all 30 states parties. Over 2100 intrusive on-site inspections have been carried out at military installations since the signing of the treaty (see table 16.2) to confirm the equipment reductions, and valuable experience was gained during the three-year period. The inspection process provided cooperative experience and established confidence among states parties. No major breaches were reported. Given the many participants and numerous complex procedures involved, the verification part of the CFE regime is clearly a success.[26]

In 1995, NATO sponsored two meetings on verification issues. On 9 and 10 March, at the Alliance headquarters in Brussels, a second workshop on the NATO verification database (VERITY) in support of the CFE Treaty (the first was in February 1994) hosted representatives from the foreign ministries and national verification organizations of 13 North Atlantic Cooperation Council (NACC) partners (Kazakhstan did not participate). Partner countries now access VERITY directly to report on inspections conducted and retrieve

---

24 Nov. 1995, p. 3, FBIS-SOV-95-227, 27 Nov. 1995, p. 69. The Russian troops in Moldova reportedly have 120 tanks, 130 ACVs and 129 artillery pieces. Griboncea, M., 'Rejecting a new role for the former 14th Russian army', *Transition*, 22 Mar. 1996, p. 40.

[25] Poles even claimed that, unlike in other countries, their arms destruction turned out to be profitable. 'CFE treaty fulfilled. "Irreversible" disarmament concluded', *Warsaw Voice*, 24 Sep. 1995, p. 7.

[26] Govan, G. G., 'An in-depth look at on-site inspections', *Arms Control Today*, vol. 25, no. 7 (Sep. 1995), p.18. In Dec. 1995, Turkey was denied the right previously granted by Armenia to conduct an aerial inspection of Russian units in that country, with no explanation for the change of position. *OMRI Daily Digest*, no. 240 (12 Dec. 1995).

Table 16.2. Inspections hosted and conducted by states parties during the baseline validation period and the reduction period, 1993–95

State	Inspections Hosted	% of total	Con-ducted	% of total	State	Inspections Hosted	% of total	Con-ducted	% of total
Armenia	13	0.59	3	0.14	Moldova	5	0.23	0	0.00
Azerbaijan		0.00		0.00	Netherlands	31	1.42	78	3.69
Belarus	82	3.75	5	0.24	Norway	4	0.18	28	1.32
Belgium	23	1.05	57	2.69	Poland	94	4.30	81	3.83
Bulgaria	169	7.73	60	2.84	Portugal	4	0.18	10	0.47
Canada	2	0.09	65	3.07	Romania	168	7.69	72	3.40
Czech Rep.	250	11.44	96	1.47	Russia	349	15.97	346	16.35
Denmark	9	0.41	31	59	Slovakia	84	3.84	28	1.32
France	65	2.97	142	6.71	Spain	39	1.78	74	3.50
Georgia		0.00		0.00	Turkey	68	3.11	59	2.79
Germany	196	8.97	262	12.38	UK	61	2.79	189	8.93
Greece	21	0.96	6	0.28	Ukraine	274	12.54	46	2.17
Hungary	83	3.80	64	3.02	USA	55	2.52	246	11.63
Italy	34	1.56	60	2.84					
Luxembourg	2	0.09	8	0.38	**Total**	**2 185**	**100.00**	**2116**	**100.00**

Source: Selected data on the implementation of the CFE Treaty obligations, Permanent Mission of the Slovak Republic to the OSCE, 19 Dec. 1995.

official CFE information. At the workshop, the participants acquainted themselves with the system and exchanged views and verification experience.[27]

On 11–13 October, at NATO headquarters, the Alliance's Verification Coordinating Committee (VCC) organized its fifth seminar with the 14 NACC partners on cooperation in the verification and implementation of conventional arms control agreements, including the CFE Treaty and the Vienna Document 1994. As at the previous seminars, discussion focused on four areas of special relevance to the treaty: joint inspections of declared sites; joint inspections of main battle tanks, ACVs, combat aircraft and attack helicopter reductions; joint training courses; and sharing of information stored in VERITY.[28]

Nearly 700 inspections have been conducted since January 1993 by Allied teams to check figures provided by the signatory states, and another 950 inspections to monitor the destruction of surplus TLE in the ATTU area. Non-NATO states participated in 250 NATO-conducted inspections, and Allied states took part in 20 inspections carried out by Central and East European states. According to NATO sources, VERITY is intensively used: it contains reports from about 1700 inspections and, by October 1995, 126 experts from 26 countries had accessed the database 9600 times.[29] In January 1995, the

[27] NATO VERITY workshop with Cooperation Partners, *NATO Press Release*, vol. 95, no. 21 (8 Mar. 1995).
[28] NATO Seminar with Cooperation Partners on implementation of conventional arms control agreements, *NATO Press Release*, vol. 95, no. 94 (9 Oct. 1995).
[29] *Atlantic News*, no. 2760 (25 Oct. 1995), pp. 3–4.

Table 16.3. CFE reductions and holdings, 1 January 1996

State[a]	Tanks				ACVs				Artillery				Aircraft				Helicopters			
	Ceil.	Liab.	Red.	Hold.	Ceil.	Liab.	Red.	Hold.	Ceil.	Liab.	Red.	Hold.	Ceil.	Liab.	Red.	Hold.	Ceil.	Liab.	Red.	Hold.
Armenia	220	0	0	102	220	159	18	285	285	0	0	225	100	0	0	6	50	0	0	7
Azerbaijan[b]	220	216	0	275	220	727	0	810	285	103	0	336	100	0	0	49	50	0	0	15
Belarus[b]	1 800	1 873	1 381	2 183	2 600	1 435	1 118	2 839	1 615	0	3	1 533	294	130	84	338	80	0	0	79
Belgium	334	28	28	334	1 099	284	284	704	320	58	58	316	232	0	0	169	46	0	0	46
Bulgaria	1 475	794	794	1 475	2 000	332	332	1 985	1 750	404	410	1 750	235	100	100	235	67	0	0	44
Canada	77	0	0	0	277	0	0	0	38	0	0	6	90	0	0	0	0	0	0	0
Czech Rep.	957	1 123	1 123	953	953	1 217	1 217	1 363	767	1 409	1 409	767	230	51	57	187	50	0	0	36
Denmark	353	146	146	343	316	0	0	303	553	0	0	552	106	0	1	75	12	0	0	12
France	1 306	39	39	1 289	3 820	570	570	3 556	1 292	149	149	1 251	800	0	0	667	396	66	66	317
Georgia	220	0	0	–	220	0	0	–	285	0	0	–	100	0	0	–	50	0	0	–
Germany	4 166	2 566	2 566	3 034	3 446	4 257	4 257	2 622	2 705	1 623	1 623	2 056	900	140	140	578	306	0	0	224
Greece	1 735	1 013	1 099	1 735	2 534	447	447	2 324	1 878	505	517	1 878	650	0	14	489	30	0	0	6
Hungary	835	510	510	835	1 700	65	212	1 540	840	207	207	840	180	0	28	144	108	0	0	59
Italy	1 348	300	324	1 164	3 339	537	537	2 993	1 955	205	205	1 939	650	0	0	522	139	56	57	138
Moldova	210	0	0	0	210	0	0	209	250	0	0	155	50	0	0	27	50	0	0	0
Netherlands	743	0	0	734	1 080	261	261	1 012	607	59	59	580	230	0	0	182	50	22	91	0
Norway	170	127	127	170	225	57	57	203	527	17	17	246	100	0	0	75	0	0	0	0
Poland	1 730	1 120	1 130	1 721	2 150	301	935	1 455	1 610	741	770	1 581	460	61	121	400	130	0	0	92
Portugal	300	0	0	186	430	0	0	367	450	0	0	320	160	0	0	105	26	0	0	0
Romania	1 375	1 591	1 591	1 375	2 100	973	973	2 073	1 475	2 423	2 423	1 471	430	78	78	373	120	0	0	16
Russia[c]	6 400	3 187	3 188	5 608	11 480	5 419	5 419	10 140	6 415	658	660	6 298	3 416	1 004	1 029	2 989	890	99	99	829
Slovakia	478	578	578	478	683	443	443	683	383	679	679	383	115	30	30	114	25	0	0	19
Spain	794	371	481	630	1 588	0	0	1 199	1 310	87	88	1 210	310	0	0	188	90	0	0	28
Turkey	2 795	1 060	1 060	2 608	3 120	0	5	2 450	3 523	122	122	3 103	750	0	115	383	103	0	0	20
UK	1 015	183	183	662	3 176	30	30	2 574	636	0	0	536	900	0	0	640	371	5	5	342
Ukraine[c]	4 080	1 974	1 974	4 039	5 050	1 545	1 551	4 896	4 040	0	0	3 727	1 090	550	550	1 008	330	0	0	270
USA	4 006	192	639	1 213	5 372	0	0	2 181	2 492	0	5	831	784	0	0	222	431	0	0	164
Ex-WTO	20 000	12 966	12 269	19 044	30 000	12 613	12 218	28 278	20 000	6 624	6 561	19 066	6 800	2 004	2 077	5 870	2 000	99	99	1 466
NATO	19 142	6 025	6 692	14 102	29 822	5 996	6 448	22 488	18 286	2 825	2 843	14 824	6 662	140	270	4 295	2 000	149	219	1 297
Total	39 142	18 991	18 961	33 146	59 822	18 609	18 666	50 766	38 286	9 449	9 404	33 890	13 462	2 144	2 347	10 165	4 000	248	318	2 763

[a] Iceland, Kazakhstan and Luxembourg have no weapon limits in the application zone. [b] Reduction continues. [c] TLE belonging to the Black Sea Fleet not included.

Source: Selected data on the implementation of the CFE Treaty obligations. Permanent Mission of the Slovak Republic to the OSCE, 19 Dec. 1995.

Table 16.4. Total TLE liabilities and reductions, 1 January 1996

State[a]	Total liability	% of total	Actual reduction	State[a]	Total liability	% of total	Actual reduction
Armenia	159	0.32	18	Netherlands	342	0.69	411
Azerbaijan[b]	1 046	2.12	0	Norway	201	0.41	201
Belarus[b]	3 438	6.95	2586	Poland	2 223	4.50	2 956
Belgium	370	0.75	370	Portugal	0	0.00	0
Bulgaria	1 630	3.30	1636	Romania	5 065	10.24	5065
Canada	0	0.00	0	Russia[c]	10 364	20.96	10 395
Czech Rep.	3 800	7.69	3 806	Slovakia	1 730	3.50	1 730
Denmark	146	0.30	147	Spain	458	0.93	569
France	824	1.67	824	Turkey	1 182	2.39	1 302
Georgia	0	0.00	0	UK	218	0.44	218
Germany	8 586	17.37	8 586	Ukraine[c]	4 069	8.23	4 075
Greece	1 518	3.07	2 077	USA	192	0.39	644
Hungary	782	1.58	957	**Ex-WTO**	**34 306**	**69.39**	**33 224**
Italy	1 098	2.22	1 123	**NATO**	**15 135**	**30.61**	**16 427**
Moldova	0	0.00	0	**Total**	**49 441**	**100.00**	**49 696**

[a] Iceland, Kazakhstan and Luxembourg have no weapon limits in the application zone.

[b] Reduction continues.

[c] TLE belonging to the Black Sea Fleet not included.

Source: Selected data on the implementation of the CFE Treaty obligations, Permanent Mission of the Slovak Republic to the OSCE, 19 Dec. 1995.

Forum for Security Co-operation agreed to the VCC request for an end-user station on the OSCE communication network to register CSBM and CFE notifications.[30]

The participants also discussed the challenges facing CFE states parties in the next phase. The end of the reduction period marked the start of the 120-day residual level or 'second baseline' validation period, when the parties will verify the TLE holdings in units remaining from the completion of the three-year reduction period. The follow-on residual period, commencing in mid-March 1996, will usher in frequent on-site inspections of these units to monitor annual data exchanges by all states parties. Over a period of 120 days more than 400 inspections are planned, including some 70 in Russia. Implementation issues will be on the agenda of the May 1996 Review Conference, and the CFE verification regime will continue for the duration of the treaty.

The VCC seminar was the last gathering of all the interested parties before entry into force of the CFE Treaty. Participants agreed to organize other seminars and workshops for the verification teams and a workshop on how NACC countries can contribute to VERITY.

[30] OSCE Forum for Security Cooperation, *Journal* (Vienna), no. 97 (18 Jan. 1995).

The flank issue

The flank question remained the main bone of contention, notably between Russia and most of the other parties.[31] At least since the outbreak of the war in Chechnya, if not earlier, it was clear to other CFE states parties that Russia was unlikely to abide by the flank provisions in Article V of the treaty. Indeed, the increase of Russian heavy weapons and troops in the Caucasus region suggested that Moscow's approach to this issue was military rather than political. The Atlantic Alliance and other states repeatedly urged Russia to comply with the treaty, advising the use of all available alternatives and loopholes: negotiations with other flank zone countries to secure a portion of their entitlements; reassignment of armoured infantry fighting vehicles (AIFVs) to interior security forces in the zone (Article XII); temporary deployments (Article V, 1c); agreements with other flank states on changes in maximum holdings (Article VII, 3), (see table 16.5); deferral of reducing TLE assigned to naval infantry and coastal defence units pending a settlement on the ownership of the Black Sea Fleet; and calling for revisions at the May 1996 Review Conference. The piecemeal composition of TLE that would result, however, would continue to constrain Russia's freedom to use forces in the area considerably and, as was rightly observed, Russian reluctance to make use of these loopholes stemmed not so much from domestic security concerns as from a strategic desire to radically restructure its (southern) flank force.[32] It remained to be seen how the signatories would resolve what was a deliberate policy of *faits accomplis* in violation of Article V of the treaty.

The Russian demands have become even more insistent since the start of the conflict in Chechnya, which led Russia to argue that it could implement the treaty 'only in a stable setting'.[33] In April, both Defence Minister Grachev and Foreign Ministry spokesman Grigoriy Karasin reaffirmed that Russia could not comply with all the limitations on its flanks. On 18 April, a US State Department spokesman again urged against unilateral steps which would avoid meeting CFE Treaty limits.[34] On 26 April, the Commander-in-Chief of the Russian Ground Forces, Colonel-General Vladimir Semyonov, announced that Russia was to create a new army in the northern Caucasus by 1 June. The 58th Army was to be based on an army corps stationed in Vladikavkaz, North

[31] In autumn 1993, Russia and Ukraine formally opened discussions on the flank zone. Because of flank limitations, Russia was allowed to deploy only 18% of its TLE (including that in storage) in the Leningrad and North Caucasus Military Districts (MDs), together covering more than half of its European territory; Ukraine could have only 17% of its tanks, 7% of its ACVs and 25% of its artillery units deployed on one-quarter of its territory (the former Odessa MD). The deployment asymmetry is also illustrated by the fact that Russia could have 6 times more tanks and 15 times more ACVs in the tiny Kaliningrad region than in the whole flank zone. Regarding the flank issue in 1993 and 1994, see Lachowski (note 15), pp. 571–74, and Lachowski (note 19), pp. 769–73. See also Falkenrath, R. A., 'The CFE flank dispute: Waiting in the wings', *International Security*, vol. 19, no. 4 (spring 1995), p. 118–44.

[32] Audritsch, M. R., 'Russia's equipment holdings on the flanks', *Jane's Intelligence Review*, vol. 7, no. 12 (Dec. 1995), p. 547.

[33] 'Grachev: Russia has insufficient weapons on southern flank', Moscow Interfax in English, 16 Apr. 1995, FBIS-SOV-95-073, 17 Apr. 1995, p. 29.

[34] *Wireless File* (United States Information Service, US Embassy: Stockholm, 18 Apr. 1995).

Ossetia, with some 2500 tanks. While admitting that the new army would 'not go well with the CFE Treaty', Semyonov stated that Russia's interests should prevail over the terms of the treaty.[35] The unilateral Russian decision came as a surprise to other CFE states parties, which protested immediately. Western governments said they would review their positions, and Germany even threatened to reconsider the aid package to Russia. NATO indicated once more that the treaty provisions offer some flexibility on force deployment in the flanks, but there was no desire to let this become a major issue. Western diplomats and experts believed that, as the new 58th Army was to be created from forces already in the area, a 'constructive' approach should prevail vis-à-vis Russian policy in the region, where a threat of a prolonged guerrilla war existed.[36]

The Russian–US summit meeting on 9–10 May in Moscow brought about a first significant change in the US position.[37] US President Bill Clinton admitted that 'some modifications are in order', and declared US willingness both to seek ways to preserve the integrity of the treaty and compliance with it and to 'respond to Russia's legitimate security interests'. No details were agreed upon, and the USA urged that Russia and Ukraine should seek adjustments 'within the parameters of the Treaty'.[38] German Foreign Minister Kinkel concurred, expressing an understanding for Russia's security interests and advising it to 'find a way' of complying with the CFE Treaty.[39]

The possibility of Russia changing the flank provisions led to increased anxiety among the NATO states directly concerned, and a sharp reaction from Turkey which threatened retaliatory steps.[40] It was also pointed out that failure by Russia to abide by the terms of the CFE Treaty could also jeopardize billions of dollars in the US Nunn–Lugar aid programme which is contingent on the US President certifying that Russia complies with all arms control obligations. The NATO ministerial session communiqué of 30 May reaf-

[35] 'Semjonow: Interessen Rußlands wichtiger als KSE-Vertrag' [Semyonov: Russia's interests more important than the CFE Treaty], Frankfurter Allgemeine Zeitung, 27 Apr. 1995; and Atlantic News, no. 2713 (28 Apr. 1995).
[36] Wireless File, 27 Apr. 1995; and The Independent, 27 Apr. 1995, p. 13.
[37] A change in the US position was earlier signalled by Arms Control and Disarmament Agency (ACDA) Director John Holum on 8 May 1995. OMRI Daily Digest, no. 90 (10 May 1995).
[38] The US position on treaty 'modification' is outlined in Sullivan, A. (USIA White House Correspondent), 'Joint Press conference in Moscow. Clinton cites progress on security issues at Moscow summit', Wireless File, 11 May 1995.
[39] Atlantic News, no. 2719 (25 May 1995); and 'Ruehe, Kinkel say CFE treaty "must be preserved"', Hamburg DPA in German, 23 May 1995, Foreign Broadcast Information Service Report, Arms Control and Proliferation Issues (FBIS-TAC), FBIS-TAC-95-003, 29 June 1995, p. 117.
[40] 'Turkey threatens buildup if Russia defies CFE limits', Defense News, 22–28 May 1995, p. 16. In estimating the military balance in northern Europe, a Norwegian report concluded that 'there continues to exist considerable offensive military capabilities on the Russian side', but '[i]t is difficult to see that Russia at the present time will be capable of launching a more comprehensive attack in the North' and that 'there no longer exists a current threat of invasion against South Norway from the sea, or through Southern Sweden. Norwegian Atlantic Committee, The Military Balance in Northern Europe 1994–1995, Oslo 1995, pp. 26–27. During the year, however, while pointing to 'new challenges coming from the north-western territory of Russia, and namely—military and civilian nuclear activity in the Kola Peninsula', Norway decided to resign from its self-imposed constraints on military activities near the Russian borders and conduct exercises together with its NATO allies. Felgengauer, P., 'Norvegia opasa-yetsia ugrozy z severo-vostoka' [Norway afraid of threat from north-east], Segodnya, 6 Dec. 1995, p. 2.

Table 16.5. Potential Russian holdings in the flank zones with the maximum use of available alternatives as permitted under the CFE Treaty

	Tanks	ACVs	Artillery
Russian flank entitlements	700	580	1 280
Internal security (art XII.1)	0	600	0
Temporary deployment (art V.1)	153	241	140
Subtotal (exclusive Russian control)	**853**	**1421**	**1420**
Temporary deployment to other flank areas (art V.1)	306	482	280
Other state-permitted flank increases over inventory, as of Jan. 94 (art VII.3)	480	246	416
Subtotal (dependent on other states cooperating)	**786**	**728**	**696**
Total	**1 639**	**2 149**	**2 116**

Source: Audritsch, M. R., 'Russia's equipment holdings on the flanks', *Jane's Intelligence Review*, vol. 7, no. 12 (Dec. 1995), p. 549.

firmed that the integrity of the treaty should be preserved and that full implementation by November 1995 would provide 'the essential basis for a constructive and comprehensive review process at the CFE Review Conference in 1996, as foreseen in the treaty, in the spirit of cooperative security'.[41]

In the course of summer 1995 Russia continued to make proposals and to take further steps with regard to the Caucasus. In July, the Russian delegation to the JCG suggested that a zone be declared exempt from CFE Treaty obligations (an 'exclusive zone' like that in south-western Turkey). Alongside this, the policy of *fait accompli* continued, with President Boris Yeltsin signing a decree on 4 July permitting the permanent deployment of Russian military units in Chechnya. According to Grachev a motorized rifle division with 'several auxiliary units' as well as 'sub-units of interior troops' would be permanently stationed in the republic.[42]

On 19 July, Russia came up with new demands to be allowed to deploy some 1250 tanks, 3900 ACVs and 1400 artillery units in excess of the flank limits, including 360 tanks, 1690 ACVs and 400 artillery pieces above the allowed limits in the southern flank (see table 16.6).[43] Another complication for the Joint Consultative Group (JCG) was the Russian weapons deployed in Armenia, Georgia and Ukraine; Armenia had already agreed to surrender part of its TLE quota to Russia and Georgia had initialled a similar agreement.[44]

On 22 September in the JCG, on behalf of NATO, the Turkish representative presented proposals to address Russian and Ukrainian concerns regarding flank limits, particularly in the North Caucasus. By that time, according to US

[41] *Atlantic News*, no. 2721 (1 June 1995), Annex.

[42] ITAR-TASS reported that a combined army group built around the 58th Army was at that time temporarily stationed in Chechnya, including the 106th Combined Marine Regiment and the 16th Guard Independent Motorized Brigade. *OMRI Daily Digest*, no. 129 (5 July 1995).

[43] 'Cold war monster won't lie down', *Financial Times*, 18 Aug. 1995.

[44] For Russia's estimated holdings in Armenia and Georgia, see note 24.

Table 16.6. Russian proposals with regard to the flank zone, 1994–95

	Tanks	ACVs	Artillery
Autumn 1994 proposals			
Flank zone total	1 100[a]	3 000	2 100
North Caucasus MD	600	2 200	1 000
Summer 1995 proposals			
Flank zone total	1 950	4 500	2 700
North Caucasus MD	1 060	2 270	1 680
Russian presence (Sep. 1995 US estimates)			
Flank zone total	3 000	5 500	3 000
North Caucasus MD	1 700	3 600	1 500
Flank zone entitlements	700	580	1 280

[a] Russian General Staff Chief Mikhail Kolesnikov proposed raising the number of tanks to 1500.

Sources: *Atlantic News*, no. 2660 (7 Oct. 1994), p. 2; *Financial Times*, 18 Aug. 1995, p. 3; and *Atlantic News*, no. 2751 (22 Sep. 1995), p. 2.

Defense Department estimates, Russia had increased its troops in that region to some 1700 tanks, 3600 ACVs and 1500 artillery pieces. Altogether in the flank area it had approximately 3000 tanks, 5500 ACVs and 3000 artillery systems.[45] NATO's proposals included:

1. Removing from the flank zone the Volgograd and Astrakhan *oblasts* in the North Caucasus Military District (MD): the Pskov, Novgorod and Vologda *oblasts* from the Leningrad MD; and the Odessa *oblast* from the Odessa MD;

2. To allay concerns of other states parties with regard to redrawing the map, Russia and Ukraine should agree to the following measures:

(*a*) verification: additional inspections in the flank and former flank *oblasts* beyond those they are required to host under the CFE Protocol on Inspections;

(*b*) information: (i) supplementary information on the status and disposition of forces in the flank and former flank areas; (ii) transfer of TLE between the two parts of the Russian flank zone should be particularly subject to notification; and (iii) Russia and Ukraine should provide treaty-required data on forces in this area, including internal security forces, every six months instead of once a year;

(*c*) constraints: the states should agree to exercise restraint with regard to equipment deployments, to ensure that this map realignment does not result in destabilizing force concentrations.

It was also suggested at the JCG that the 30 CFE states parties undertake commitments to preserve the integrity of the treaty and resolve outstanding implementation issues in a cooperative way; pledge full compliance by the November deadline and reconfirm their commitment to comply fully with all

[45] *OMRI Daily Digest*, no. 182 (20 Sep. 1995).

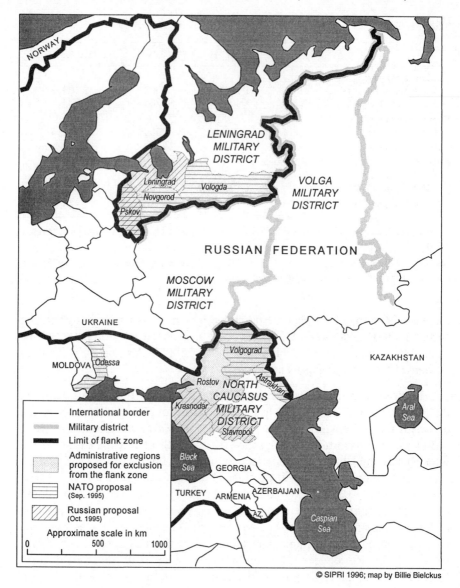

© SIPRI 1996; map by Billie Bielckus

Figure 16.1. Changes proposed for the CFE Treaty flank zone map realignment

its provisions; and agree not to station conventional armed forces on the territory of another state party beyond levels agreed with that state (and only in accordance with Article V).

Moreover, Russia and Ukraine were to reaffirm their commitment to implement the legally binding pledge of 14 June 1991 on naval infantry and coastal defence holdings; and Russia was to confirm its political commitment regarding the equipment moved beyond the Urals. Russia would also withdraw as quickly and transparently as possible substantial amounts of excess equipment from the current flank zone. Agreement on the gerrymandering and other measures would be negotiated within the JCG which would conclude with an extraordinary conference, if possible before 17 November 1995, and submitted to the Review Conference in 1996.[46]

Consequently, at the end of September Norway announced its willingness to accept some revision concerning the military districts of Russia's northern flank in return for a greater number of inspections and more transparency.[47]

The NATO proposal, while meeting most of Russia's demands for more tanks and artillery, would require the destruction or removal of additional ACVs.[48] Russia considered that the NATO offer took 'insufficient' account of its security needs and interests: for example, the proposal to exclude the Novgorod and Vologda regions from the flank zone was considered 'somewhat belated' and disadvantageous (while also seen as 'a step in the right direction') by Russia which 'does not have any arms subject to limitation in these oblasts'.[49] During his visit in late October to the USA, President Yeltsin presented a counter-proposal concerning the exclusion of the Leningrad, Pskov and Volgograd *oblasts* and of the Stavropol and Krasnodar *krays* with the Republic of Adygea.[50] A week later, on 28 October, Grachev announced that he and US Defense Secretary William Perry had reached a compromise on the flank, somewhat different from the earlier NATO proposals: the Krasnodar and Stavropol *krays*, as demanded by Russia, and the Rostov-on-the Don and Volgograd *oblasts*, as reportedly agreed additionally by the USA, would be excluded from the southern part of the flank zone and included in the CFE Extended (Rear) Zone,[51] and Russia agreed that the Leningrad *oblast* would remain in the northern flank.[52] The Perry–Grachev compromise was reported to have led to differences between the USA and its NATO allies and partners. Turkey rejected it immediately, and the Baltic states, Finland and Norway also issued reservations. Including Rostov in the list of southern *oblasts* for the rear

---

[46] *Atlantic News*, no. 2752 (27 Sep. 1995), pp. 1–2.

[47] *Arms Control Reporter*, sheet 407.B.522, 1995.

[48] 'The CFE treaty: can it survive?', *IISS Strategic Comments*, no. 8 (12 Oct. 1995).

[49] Reportedly, such a proposal was included in Yeltsin's message to President Clinton and British Prime Minister John Major in Dec. 1994. Since then (i.e., after the outbreak of the war in Chechnya) it was said to have become outdated. See interview with Deputy Chief of the General Staff Dmitriy Kharchenko for *Krasnaya Zvezda*, 18 Nov. 1995, pp. 1, 2. *Segodnya*, 28 Sep. 1995, p. 1 reported the Russian insistence on 'excluding from the treaty's applicability a separate part of territory'.

[50] Kharchenko interview (note 49).

[51] Russia's Extended and Expanded Central Zones include the Moscow MD, the Volga MD and the Kaliningrad Region. According to the Russian Defence Ministry Russia could station up to 4275 tanks, 9945 ACVs and 3825 artillery pieces there. 'Ministry source on alterations needed to CFE Treaty.', Moscow Interfax in English, 11 Nov. 1995, FBIS-SOV-95-218, 13 Nov. 1995, p. 18.

[52] In this context, Grachev went on to state that Russia would retain a 'margin of manoeuvre' to deploy troops and heavy weapons in its northern flank, thanks to its exclave in Kaliningrad. *Atlantic News*, no. 2762 (1 Nov. 1995), p. 3. See also 'Bestimmungen des KSE-Vertrages sollen geändert werden [CFE Treaty provisions should be changed], *Frankfurter Allgemeine Zeitung*, 30 Oct. 1995. US Defense Secretary William Perry claimed that the compromise consisted in Russia restraining itself from increasing the numbers of its troops and equipment in its north-western territory. *Segodnya*, 31 Oct. 1995; and 'Perry sees no significant Russian threat to Baltics', *Baltic Independent*, 24–30 Nov. 1995, p. 1. On the other hand, a diplomatic source in Vienna claimed that actually the Russian Leningrad *oblast* concession was false since Russia had not intended to deploy more troops there. 'Moscow seen excluding southern regions from CFE', AFP in English, 31 Oct. 1995, FBIS-SOV-95-211, 1 Nov. 1995, p. 14.

zone was especially likely to be fiercely opposed by Turkey, worried by the prospect of increased Russian military and political influence in the northern Caucasus.[53]

In the meantime, General Semyonov announced that the actual amount of armaments in the northern part of the flank (the Leningrad MD) met the CFE Treaty requirements, while those for the southern flank had not been met.[54]

On 17 November, the JCG agreed the basic elements of an approach towards a solution of the flank question,[55] including map realignment, but several important details remained. Three groups of issues were outstanding:

1. *Geographical issues*. There was no agreement between Russia and the USA or within NATO (mainly because of Turkey's opposition[56]), let alone consensus of all 30 parties, as to which *oblasts* should be 'redrawn' (i.e., not included in the flank zone).

2. *'Benchmarks'*. A timetable for reductions would be needed to get Russia in compliance with the limits for the redefined flank zone.

3. *Transparency and constraints*. Increased verification and notification would be required as well as specific constraints applying to the redrawn *oblasts*.[57]

In a joint statement the 30 CFE states parties pledged to seek solutions to these issues. It was also agreed that additional inspections of the new regions should be negotiated. Any revisions were to be signed and formally adopted at the May 1996 Review Conference.[58] The JCG decision to continue to discuss the flank issue taking into account Russia's position was greeted with satisfaction by the latter.[59]

NATO's ministerial meeting of 5 December 1995 noted 'with concern', among other things, Russia's failure to meet the flank obligations, and welcomed the agreement by all 30 parties to find a cooperative solution to the problem, 'which will not diminish the security of any state'.[60] The USA urged

---

[53] 'Arms treaty hits obstacles', *The Guardian*, 3 Nov. 1995.

[54] 'Semyonov: Russia will fulfil CFE Treaty by 16 Nov', Moscow Interfax in English, 3 Nov. 1995, FBIS-SOV-95-214, 6 Nov. 1995, p. 22.

[55] 'CFE Consultative Group revises approach to flank force problem', Unofficial transcript: 11/17 State Dept. CFE Briefing, *Wireless File*, 17 Nov. 1995, pp. 16–22.

[56] On 20 Nov. Turkey once again urged Russia to comply with all aspects of the CFE Treaty. *OMRI Daily Digest*, no. 227 (21 Nov. 1995). Both the USA and Russia tried to persuade Turkey to change its position. It was later reported that Turkey might be willing to accept an unspecified modification in the Treaty as long as it met its security needs. *OMRI Daily Digest*, no. 231 (29 Nov. 1995).

[57] Note 55.

[58] *Arms Control Reporter*, sheet 407.B.527, 1996. The compromise reached at the CFE First Review Conference in Vienna in May 1996 excluded the following areas from the flank zone: the Pskov, Volgograd and Astrakhan oblasts; parts of the Rostov oblast and the Krasnodar kray; and the Odessa oblast (Ukraine).

[59] *Segodnya*, 24 Nov. 1995, p. 1. Foreign Ministry spokesman G. Krasin stated, 'for the first time, the RF's partners officially admitted that the problem of flank limits, as raised by Russia and Ukraine, should be solved in the light of political reality in Europe, as changed after the signing of the treaty'. Ukraine took a less definitive position: Defence Minister Valeriy Shmarov said Ukraine would abide by the flanks limits if the Russian and Ukrainian proposals were denied; but if Russia's proposed changes were accepted, Ukraine would want similar ones. *Arms Control Reporter*, sheet 407.B530, 1996.

[60] Final Communiqué of the Ministerial Meeting of NATO. Eurosec text: Final Communiqué 12/5, Brussels, 5 Dec. 1995.

its NATO allies quickly to resolve the dispute with Russia on flank limitations in the CFE Treaty.[61]

In its more than two-year history, the flank issue has fallen victim to legal rigour and political inflexibility. Owing to Western intransigence, Russia's demands were too long dismissed at the JCG or referred to the 1996 Review Conference; at the same the military build-up in the Caucasus region was either neglected or deplored. It was only in the last months before the CFE reduction deadline that the NATO states decided to look for face-saving solutions to remedy the situation. Since the map is not an integral part of the treaty, it is argued that its redrawing would not require a new ratification process. Russian non-compliance with Article V was considered a 'technical' failure and that could be papered over. However, the changes require full agreement by all 30 states parties and at least some of them may deem it necessary to review them in accordance with their national legislatures.

The handling of the CFE issue by Russian diplomats, particularly the flank problem, has met with repeated domestic criticism. The main attacks have come from the Defence Ministry, focusing on the military–strategic aspects. A political assessment of the failures of the Russian foreign service pointed to: (a) poor preparation of the negotiating process within the JCG, as illustrated by the case of the 58th Army; (b) engagement in a 'numbers' debate and a concomitant inability effectively to link the issue of the flank parameters with the new processes in Europe; (c) absence of effective attempts to resolve the flank issue with the other former Soviet republics concerned; (d) insufficient preparation of Russian arguments for a review of the flank limits in the wake of the autumn 1995 NATO proposals; and (e) lack of proper diplomatic work with the Central Asian states on the equipment transferred beyond the Urals in 1990–91, leaving Russia entirely responsible for its destruction.[62]

The CFE Treaty and NATO enlargement

The issue of NATO expanding to the east was the main issue in the European security policy debate in 1995. The CFE Treaty also became an element of the enlargement dialogue between Russia and NATO, if somewhat indirectly. The issue had two general aspects, political and military.

By alluding to or threatening the possibility of pulling out of the CFE Treaty if NATO expanded eastwards, Russia created a linkage between the two issues. The Alliance has chosen to stick to full treaty implementation and thus proved unable or unwilling to establish a stronger link between these two questions and use the treaty as a lever in its policy *vis-à-vis* Russia, mainly from fear of undermining the treaty and of adversely affecting the reform

[61] US Secretary of State Warren Christopher told the NATO foreign ministers that the working group meeting in Vienna should intensify its work and that 'policy-making officials, with decision-making authority' from national capitals should join it no later than mid-Feb. *OMRI Daily Digest,* no. 236 (6 Dec. 1995), p. 1.

[62] Konovalov, A., Korshunov, S. and Oznobischchev, S., 'Twilight of arms control. What the new Russian foreign ministry leadership should do', *Nezavisimaya Gazeta,* 26 Oct. 1995, pp. 1, 5, FBIS-SOV-95-212, 2 Nov. 1995, pp. 38–39.

process in Russia. Some Western experts have made some suggestions as to how to reconcile NATO expansion with amendments to the CFE Treaty.[63] Signals from Moscow in this context were mixed, especially in the first part of the year, reflecting infighting among various actors at all levels of the government and a measure of uncertainty on how to respond to the 'threat'. In general, however, Russia, while in a weaker position with regard to the CFE Treaty, did not hesitate to use it as an instrument of policy in response to the challenge of NATO expansion to the east.

The Russian Foreign Ministry persisted for the most part in cooperative efforts to seek compromise solutions.[64] In early 1995 there were signs that a compromise on the two issues was being considered in the Russian Foreign Ministry. In the spring, Russian officials were reported to have hinted at some moves the West could make to soften the blow of NATO admitting former Central European satellites of the Soviet Union. These included a promise that new members of the Alliance would not host foreign troops or nuclear weapons; clearer Western recognition of Russian special interests in the former Soviet Union; and a revision of the terms of the CFE Treaty.[65]

This line of policy stood in sharp contrast to the positions of the Russian Defence Ministry and General Staff. At the end of March Chief of the General Staff Mikhail Kolesnikov sharply criticized the idea of enlargement, saying that it would render the CFE Treaty void.[66] In his talks with US Defense Secretary William Perry on 3 April in Moscow, Defence Minister Grachev warned that the treaty might be suspended, and threatened that 'countermeasures could be taken' (such as the creation of new formations, redeployment of armed forces and closer security ties among CIS states) if NATO expanded eastwards too quickly. Thus it was indicated that the CFE Treaty could become the hostage of Russia's discontent with NATO.[67] Familiar allegations of the ill-will on the part of the West, which 'instinctively senses the possibility of further increasing the imbalance of forces on the continent in

---

[63] See, e.g., Sharp, J. M. O., 'Task for NATO I: move east and revise the CFE', *The World Today*, Apr. 1995, pp. 67–70. A summer 1995 report by the Bertelsmann Stiftung proposed the inclusion of the Alliance's new Central and East European (CEE) members within its own collective ceiling, while the contingents allocated by the treaty for these states could be redistributed among Russia and the other Soviet republics. Moreover, NATO could agree on additional ceilings for forces stationed in the CEE states, in order to ensure that the Alliance did not concentrate substantial forces along the borders with Russia. Bertelsmann Stiftung, Interim Report of a Working Group on 'CFSP and the future of the European Union', prepared in collaboration with the Research Group on European Affairs (University of Munich) and the Planning Staff of the European Commission (DG1A), July 1995, p. 18.

[64] 'Karasin favors new treaty', Moscow ITAR-TASS in English, 13 Apr. 1995, FBIS-TAC-95-003, 29 June 1995, p. 54. A high-ranking Foreign Ministry official told the Interfax Agency in spring 1995 that 'Russia can hardly be expected to withdraw from the CFE Treaty. . . . Taken as whole, the Treaty meets Russian interests because it imposes similar restrictions on NATO. If Russian withdraws from the Treaty, the alliance will face no restrictions, either, and this is not in Russia's interests.' 'What Russian Defence Minister Pavel Grachev said on the issue in question must be regarded as the expression of his ministry's rather than the government's views', summed up Interfax. 'Foreign Ministry critical of Clinton CFE stance', Interfax in English, FBIS-TAC-95-003, 29 June 1995, p. 58.

[65] *Financial Times*, 22 Mar. 1995.

[66] *Financial Times*, 18–19 Mar. 1995.

[67] *The Independent*, 4 Apr. 1995.

its favour', have also reappeared.[68] These and other warnings and threats were becoming increasingly prevalent over Russian diplomacy's more sophisticated persuasion and search for politically constructive solutions.[69]

The highly charged atmosphere in Russia's domestic affairs in the face of the coming elections and NATO's expected decision on criteria for admitting new members put increasing pressure on Russian diplomats to change course and take a tougher stance.[70] In autumn 1995, as the CFE Treaty deadline approached, NATO and Russian diplomatic activities increased and the tone of their statements sharpened. Russian Foreign Ministry officials variously denied any links between NATO enlargement schemes and CFE Treaty amendments.[71] Although both the West and Russia firmly denied any linkage or bargaining between the Alliance's planned enlargement and conventional arms treaty revisions, such speculations persisted, especially after NATO's new CFE proposals were announced.[72]

Veiled Russian threats met with Western criticism. In October, US Arms Control Association representatives took up the issue of linkage and the risk of Russia withdrawing from the treaty. They noted that the fate of the Nunn–Lugar legislation is at stake and that the CFE Treaty and CFE-1A Agreement also put constraints on German force levels, a factor that should be carefully weighed by Russia.[73]

There are also major military–strategic implications at stake. Bloc-based numerical ceilings corresponding to the political division were logical, convenient and workable in the cold war period but have become obsolete and constraining. In the emerging multipolar environment it is extremely difficult, if at all possible, for CFE negotiators to find an equally clear and satisfactory system of quantitative limits. Accommodation of NATO newcomers (possibly the Czech Republic, Hungary, Poland and Slovakia) in the CFE Central Zone would have to affect Germany (also in this zone) painfully if the treaty's 'groups of states' balance were to be retained; virtually no equipment could be based in Germany, which appears unrealistic.

Russia has complained that the ratio of its conventional forces *vis-à-vis* NATO's would worsen in the event of NATO enlargement (to *c.* 7:10). Moreover, the collapse of the USSR and the formation of new post-Soviet states

---

[68] See, e.g., Melnikov, I., 'Driving Russia into a corner: Operation of CFE Treaty', *Moskovskaya Pravda*, 12 July 1995, FBIS-SOV-95-135, 14 July 1995, pp. 11–13; and Golts, A., 'NATO expansion: time out or a slow run up? "Research" by the atlanticists fails to answer that question', *Krasnaya Zvezda*, 11 Oct. 1995, p. 3, FBIS-SOV-95-197, 12 Oct. 1995, p. 26.

[69] See e.g., Kharchenko, D., 'We cannot allow others to solve their security problems at Russia's expense', *Krasnaya Zvezda*, 12 July 1995, p. 3.

[70] Compare 'Karasin favors new treaty' (note 64). Among significant Russian political parties, only Yegor Gaidar's Russia's Democratic Choice claimed to have no objections to NATO enlargement, provided the flank issue is settled. 'Gaydar sees "no threat" to interests', Moscow ITAR-TASS in English, 21 Sep. 1995, FBIS-SOV-95-184, 22 Sep. 1995, p. 18.

[71] 'Kozyrev against "deals" for expansion', Moscow ITAR-TASS in English, 21 Sep 1995, FBIS-SOV-95-184, 22 Sep. 1995, p. 17; and *OMRI Daily Digest,* no. 191 (2 Oct. 1995).

[72] Compare 'L'OTAN est prête à faire des concessions *vis-à-vis* de Moscou pour s'élargir vers l'Est' [NATO is ready to make concessions *vis-à-vis* Moscow to expand eastwards], *Le Monde*, 22 Sep. 1995; and Sychev A., 'Russia allowed to transfer tanks to Caucasus, but only as compensation for NATO's eastward expansion', *Izvestia*, 20 Sep. 1995, pp. 1, 2.

[73] *Wireless File*, 24 Oct. 1995, pp. 19, 22–23.

weakened Russia's control of the armed forces of its neighbours. However, Western experts believe that Russia's claims and pursuit of CFE Treaty renegotiation stem less from the fear of being at a military disadvantage than from its renewed interest in modernizing its strategic forces.[74] All this notwithstanding, at the end of 1995, NATO did not seem to be giving much concern to the implications of NATO enlargement for the CFE Treaty regime.[75]

On 15 November, Pavel Grachev asserted that Moscow's willingness to 'compromise' on CFE issues would be contingent on NATO not expanding, saying that if NATO did expand, 'we will no doubt form some defensive, military and political, alliance of our own'.[76] A few days later, a senior Russian Foreign Ministry official made the most direct linkage between the CFE and NATO enlargement issues, stating that the treaty would be rendered obsolete if the Alliance expanded eastwards, as such a move would endanger Russia's interests and force it to withdraw. However, he went to say that the treaty could be saved if it was amended to reflect national, rather than cold-war bloc forces. This would mean expanding the CFE regime to include the 53 OSCE states (a 'CFE-2' treaty).[77]

By the end of the year Russia had managed to avoid the creation of a NATO–CFE linkage and had succeeded in allaying what it saw as adverse tendencies on both fronts where it was clearly at a disadvantage. The question of NATO enlargement was postponed for an unspecified time, and NATO had agreed to amendments to the CFE flank provisions. Furthermore, Russia continued to blackmail the West with the threat of pulling out of the conventional arms control regime in the event of enlargement.[78]

The CFE-2 concept

With the CFE Treaty reduction process drawing to a close and the Review Conference scheduled for May 1996, the attempt to look beyond the treaty in

[74] *Defense News,* 11–17 Dec. 1995, pp. 1, 42.

[75] In NATO, *Study on NATO Enlargement* (NATO: Brussels, Sep. 1995), it is stated that that '. . . possible implications of NATO's enlargement for the CFE can only be assessed when the actual enlargement is taking place. Since there is no decision as yet on the timing and the scope of NATO's enlargement, it would be premature to draw any conclusions at this stage' (para. 21).

[76] *Segodnya,* 16 Nov. 1995, p. 2. Concepts of a Russian-led military and political alliance have appeared time and again, but Defence Ministry sources reportedly view such a response to NATO expansion as rather 'premature'. Unconfirmed official reports from the end of Oct. claimed that to meet a perceived threat of NATO enlargement Russia would deploy tactical nuclear weapons in western Russia, Belarus, Kaliningrad and on Russian Baltic Fleet warships. Such a doctrine would also require amending the flank provisions of the CFE Treaty. Lyasko, A., 'Although the doctrine is new, it resembles the old one', *Komsomol'skaya Pravda,* 29 Sep. 1995, p. 2. See also Korotchenko, I. and Karpov, M., 'Russian nuclear missiles will be retargeted at Czech Republic and Poland. Such a proposal is being prepared by RF Armed Forces General Staff in the event of NATO's real expansion toward east', *Nezavisimaya Gazeta,* 7 Oct. 1995, FBIS-SOV-95-195, 10 Oct. 1995, pp. 34–35.

[77] 'Foreign Ministry: Why Russia may back out of CFE Treaty', Moscow Interfax in English, 20 Nov. 1995, FBIS-SOV-95-224, 21 Nov. 1995, p. 15.

[78] One analyst points out a smarter approach that Russia could adopt—settling the flank issue as quickly as possible in order to be in a good position to argue that the limits imposed by the CFE Treaty on Russia and the other parties are fundamental to European security, thus confounding those who support NATO expansion. Mendelsohn, J., 'The view from Moscow', *Arms Control Today,* vol. 25, no. 10 (Dec. 1995/Jan. 1996), p. 2.

its bloc-related shape is under way. For some time Russia's protests about discrimination have been accompanied by proposals to adapt the agreement to the new realities. The prospect of NATO expanding to the east led to some suggestions, but they have not yet taken the shape of formal proposals. Russia has tried to promote renegotiation of the treaty as part of a new comprehensive security model for Europe and the Russian delegation submitted a paper to the OSCE Senior Council meeting in Prague in April 1995.[79] The main premises of the proposed CFE-2 treaty are as follows:

1. It will provide for further cuts, 15–20 per cent below present CFE levels.

2. The bloc limits should be replaced by national levels and quotas which should not exceed, and might possibly be lower than, the preceding quantitative ceilings. This should also apply to the inspection and verification regimes.

3. The intention of East European states to join NATO provides a basis for the revision of the CFE Treaty and the negotiation of a new one.

4. In line with harmonization efforts in the field of OSCE arms control, the CFE-2 agreement should include all OSCE states and zone limits should be dropped or replaced by subregional limits based on a quite different approach.

5. Since it would embrace all OSCE states, the new treaty should most appropriately be negotiated within the OSCE, which would give it real security functions and make it the basis of a security structure for Europe.[80]

This issue has since been raised by Russia in bilateral and multilateral (OSCE) talks with other CFE states parties and was in particular discussed during President Yeltsin's visit to the USA, at the US–Russian summit meeting in Hyde Park in October.[81] At the JCG, while carefully avoiding any reference to NATO enlargement, the Russian delegation later proposed the introduction of a 'sufficiency rule' for alliances at reduced arms levels and the elaboration of a mechanism for 'applying the Treaty in extraordinary circumstances'.

East European CFE-related arms transfers

Reports of the 'cascading' of excess weapons among the former WTO states appeared in late spring 1995. After the visit of Russian Prime Minister Viktor Chernomyrdin to Sofia in May, and that of former commander of the WTO armed forces Marshal Viktor Kulikov, now a military adviser to the Russian Defence Minister, to Bulgaria in June, the latter announced that it would receive $500 million worth of 1970s-vintage military equipment from Russia. The package would include 100 T-72 tanks, 100 BMP-1P AIFVs and 12

---

[79] *Financial Times*, 4 Apr. 1995.

[80] 'Moscow and Kiev do not have to violate the treaty on conventional forces in Europe. The empire's successors can redistribute the USSR's quota', *Segodnya*, 5 May, p. 3, FBIS-TAC-95-003, 29 June 1995, p. 57.

[81] 'Karasin: Russia favors modernizing CFE Treaty', Moscow Interfax in English, 31 Oct. 1995, in FBIS-SOV-95-211, 1 Nov. 1995, p. 14.

Mi-24 attack helicopters.[82] Later, Russia was reported to have offered Bulgaria 360 T-72 tanks and 12 MiG-29 jet fighters (worth $500 million) in return for Bulgarian bonds exchangeable for property.[83] The move could be seen as an apparent effort to stave off Bulgaria's desire to join NATO and to countervail NATO's cascade transfers. There were also reports of Hungary receiving 97 Russian ACVs and other equipment in debt repayment.[84]

III. Implementation of the CFE-1A Agreement

The 1992 CFE-1A Agreement sets ceilings on various categories of the land-based conventional armed forces of the 30 states parties in the ATTU zone. It is politically binding and not subject to ratification by parliaments. The national personnel limits as laid down in CFE-1A came into force in parallel with the CFE Treaty limits on armaments.

A number of changes were made or initiated in 1995 aiming at reductions in manpower, the creation of professional armies and adaptation to the new tasks and challenges facing armed forces in Europe. In CEE countries, conscription was retained because of financial difficulties and high unemployment. On 15 March 1995, Germany, while keeping conscription, announced a massive restructuring plan. Of its 734 military installations 19 were to be closed and a further 28 reduced in size as the armed forces were cut by 32 000 servicemen to 338 000.[85] Army divisions were to be reduced to 7 (from 12 in 1991), combat brigades to 22. The length of military service was to be cut from 15 to 10 months. The biggest troop reductions were to be in the land forces (24 400), with smaller cuts in air and naval forces (5800 and 1800, respectively). A 53 600-strong crisis response force, while fully integrated into the national military structures, was to be trained for crisis contingencies, conflict prevention and civilian evacuations.

In March 1995, Belgium released its last conscripts and turned to a professional army, envisaging an armed force of 40 000 men by 1997/98.[86] In addition the Netherlands announced in January 1996 that as from Sep. 1996 its armed forces will become professional.[87] The Czech and Hungarian armies also plan further personnel cuts and reduction of their conscription periods.[88]

In February 1996, President Jacques Chirac presented sweeping defence changes planned by France including creation of an all-volunteer army, cut by more than 100 000.[89]

---

[82] *OMRI Daily Digest*, no. 112 (9 June 1995) and no. 128 (3 July 1995); and *Jane's Defence Weekly*, 15 July 1995, p. 12.

[83] *OMRI Daily Digest*, no. 138 (18 July 1995).

[84] *OMRI Daily Digest*, no. 148 (1 Aug. 1995).

[85] *Frankfurter Allgemeine Zeitung*, 15 Mar. 1995; and *Defense News*, 20–26 Mar. 1995, p. 6, and 29 May–4 June 1995, p. 10.

[86] 'Belgien: Das Ende der allgemeinen Wehrpflicht–Neuorganisation der Streitkräfte' [Belgium: the end of general compulsory military service—reorganization of the military forces], *Österreichische Militärische Zeitschrift*, no. 3 (1995), p. 346.

[87] *Neue Zürcher Zeitung*, 31 Jan. 1996.

[88] *Jane's Intelligence Review*, Jan. 1996, pp. 6–7; and *The Guardian*, 2 Mar. 1996.

[89] *Le Monde*, 24 Feb. 1996.

Table 16.7. CFE-1A Agreement ceilings and manpower holdings, 1 January 1996

State[a]	Ceilings	Holdings 1 Jan. 1996	State	Ceilings	Holdings 1 Jan. 1996
Armenia	60 000	60 000	Moldova	20 000	11 119
Azerbaijan	70 000	68 548	Netherlands	80 000	44 638
Belarus	100 000	85 190	Norway	32 000	22 605
Belgium	70 000	46 341	Poland	234 000	233 870
Bulgaria	104 000	99 778	Portugal	75 000	43 982
Canada	10 660	681	Romania	230 000	198 135
Czech Rep.	93 333	62 769	Russia[c]	1 450 000	818 474
Denmark	39 000	29 266	Slovakia	46 667	45 832
France	325 000	310 185	Spain	300 000	172 869
Georgia[b]	40 000		Turkey	530 000	527 670
Germany	345 000	293 266	UK	260 000	229 326
Greece	158 621	158 621	Ukraine	450 000	400 686
Hungary	100 000	66 051	USA	250 000	107 166
Italy	315 000	277 823			
Luxembourg	900	730			
			Total former WTO	**2 998 000**	**2 150 452**
			Total NATO	**2 791 181**	**2 265 792**
			Total	**5 789 181**	**4 416 244**

[a] Iceland and Kazakhstan have no military manpower in the zone of application.

[b] Georgia did not declare its manpower holdings.

[c] In the ATTU zone only.

Source: Selected data on the implementation of the CFE Treaty obligations, Permanent Mission of the Slovak Republic to the OSCE, 19 Dec. 1995.

The Russian armed forces continued to be plagued by a variety of troubles: budgetary squeeze; contempt for institutions; absence of motivation to serve in the ranks; bullying; bribery and cheating; food shortages; weapon trading; and concomitant draft evasion. In the autumn the Russian Federation Council extended the service of current conscripts from 18 to 24 months. Military manpower was reported to be at 63 per cent of the approved level.[90] Facing continued extensive draft dodging, Grachev announced in November that the Russian Army will be at least 100 000 men below the authorized strength of 1.7 million—on 1 January 1996 it would consist of between 1.55 and 1.6 million servicemen.[91] The troubles notwithstanding, the Defence Minister indicated at the same time the desirability of changing the criterion of the

---

[90] *International Herald Tribune*, 17 Oct. 1995. A report by the Bundestag's Defence Committee, as revealed by the daily *Süddeutsche Zeitung* of 27–28 Jan. 1996, found the Russian forces to be in 'deep crisis': 51 of the 81 divisions are not operational; half of the 28 brigades are not battle-ready; only the airborne units and the two divisions earmarked for international peacekeeping missions are combat-ready. The air force and the navy are equally troubled by a lack of equipment, fuels and maintenance. In contrast, nuclear weapons are sufficiently secured and under the control of the command structures.

[91] 'Grachev: army to be under 100 000 men under strengthM, Moscow ITAR-TASS in English, 10 Nov. 1995, FBIS-SOV-95-218, 13 Nov. 1995, p. 32. For financial reasons the Russian Defence Minister ruled out professional armed forces.

national armed force's strength, based on the density of troops per kilometre 'of the front' or of the border.[92]

Ukraine announced early in 1995 that it would be compelled to reduce its armed forces by a further 60–65 000 because of financial troubles. The Ukrainian Government reaffirmed in early 1996 that it intends to cut its armed forces from 470 000 to 350 000 by the end of 1996.[93]

IV. The Forum for Security Co-operation

The Forum concentrated increasingly on arms control issues in 1995, in line with Decision V of the 1994 Budapest Document.[94]

In January 1995, on Swedish initiative, the Special Committee of the FSC decided to be referred to simply as the Forum for Security Co-operation (with which it was synonymous). Other changes were introduced to enhance its effectiveness, such as extending the rotating chairmanship of the FSC to one month, broadening the tasks of the chairman, and so on, to ensure better continuity. The Forum also conducted work on CSBM implementation.[95]

The expansion of FSC tasks decided upon in Budapest had led to some controversy over the priorities of its work or even the validity of the 1992 Helsinki Programme of Immediate Action.[96] There was also disagreement as to whether the two working groups, established in early November 1994, should be revived or whether a new work structure would be more desirable. In early 1995 various delegations submitted their views on the further work, including the Polish proposal for a European agency on arms control/ verification and the Dutch proposal to discuss implementation issues in a standing working group. The controversy was resolved in early April with the calling into being of two new subsidiary working groups:

1. Group A was to focus on continuing in accordance with the FSC mandate in the 1992 Helsinki Document; developing new approaches to items in the mandate, taking account of the specific characteristics of the armed forces of individual states; monitoring and discussing implementation measures, decisions and commitments adopted by the Forum; preparing the Annual Implementation Assessment Meeting; and

2. Group B was to address future challenges and risks to military security and, in particular, to develop a framework for building, maintaining and improving stability and security both in the OSCE region as a whole and on a

---

[92] 'Grachev speaks on debate over size of Russian army', Moscow Mayak Radio Network, 9 Oct. 1995, FBIS-SOV-95-195, 10 Oct. 1995, p. 47. While illustrating this demand with other countries' ratio of manpower per km of borders, he failed, however, to note that those states do not possess border troops of the type Russia has. *OMRI Daily Digest*, no. 195 (6 Oct. 1995).

[93] *Nezavisimaya Gazeta*, 29 Feb. 1996, p. 7.

[94] This section is based on the reports on FSC activities in 'OSZE-Tätigkeitsbericht' [OSCE activity report], *Österreichische Militärische Zeitschrift*, nos 2–6 (1995), and on FSC documentation.

[95] For CSBM implementation in 1995 see appendix 16A in this volume.

[96] 'OSZE-Tätigkeitsbericht' [OSCE activity report], *Österreichische Militärische Zeitschrift*, no. 2 (1995), p. 204.

regional level; within this framework, Group B was to determine an agenda for establishing new measures of arms control.[97]

FSC seminars on conventional arms transfers and regional arms control

Within Group A, the FSC decided to hold two seminars in Vienna, one on principles governing conventional arms transfers and another on regional arms control in the OSCE area.

The first seminar took place on 20–21 June 1995. It addressed: national export legislation; control lists; licences; enforcement practices and procedures; and possibilities for better international cooperation in preventing undesirable or unauthorized transfers, particularly of light weapons and small arms. A questionnaire on national policies and procedures for the export of conventional arms and related technology was sent to the participating states before the seminar. A number of recommendations were made for each topic, such as publishing guidelines on arms transfers as a common standard in all participating states; developing consistent control lists for conventional arms and related technology to avoid duplication of efforts internationally; providing national control lists and forms of licences for circulation through the CPC; specifying the minimum information for licence applications; establishing national contact points and compiling and disseminating a list of contact points through the CPC; and a number of measures on enforcement. The latter included effective sanctions against illegal arms exports; establishing specialized agencies to prosecute those guilty of violations; establishing a central office to collect information from the monitoring, licensing and prosecution areas; regulating international cooperation in preventing and combating violations through enforcement; and guidelines for international cooperation in combating illegal arms exports, including the establishment of 'contact points' to facilitate cooperation between monitoring and investigatory bodies across national boundaries. Some of them later found their way to the FSC decision on a seminar follow-up (distribution of the questionnaire by the CPC to the states; national publication of guidelines; provision of national control lists; a list of contact points). In the light of the seminar's outcome, Group A was entrusted with continuing the analysis of how to improve transparency and cooperation in arms transfers.[98]

The other seminar, held at US initiative from 10 to 12 July, sought to stimulate discussion on regional arms control, laid down in both the Helsinki Document (1992) and Budapest (1994) Decisions but not yet sufficiently addressed in the framework of the Forum. Various concepts and ideas were presented: elaboration of a catalogue of possible regional measures (Poland, UK); laying down principles for regional tables (Austria); and regional verification (UK). Sweden suggested that 'regional security cooperation' should be pursued rather than 'regional arms control', which was seen as shift-

---

[97] FSC, *Journal*, no. 109 (5 Apr. 1995), Annex.
[98] FSC, *Journal*, nos 118 (28 June 1995) and 121 (19 July 1995), Annex 1.

ing the focus from effect to process. Basic principles for regional measures were identified: complementarity of regional and OSCE-wide measures; harmonization of regional measures and existing commitments; flexibility of measures to fit specific regional needs; linkage of measures with broader OSCE conflict prevention/crisis management endeavours; open-ended participation for all states wishing to take part in regional talks; political will to enter regional talks by the parties concerned.[99] In light of the experience in the former Yugoslavia and other conflict-ridden places (such as the Baltic states, the Caucasus and Central Asia), the role of regional tables as well as of conflict-preventing and post-conflict settlement measures was stressed. As a result of the seminar the FSC instructed Group A to adjust its agenda in order to give priority to the development of regional measures. Consequently, Group A started to devote its attention at least twice monthly to the development of regional measures.[100]

Harmonization

In Group A the question of harmonization of arms control obligations continued to be stalled. Russia stuck to its concept of creating a single pan-European arms control regime, soon starkly confronted with its own unilateral action (forming the 58th Army in the Caucasus) calling its compliance with the CFE Treaty into question. Western delegations were prepared to continue talks only on information exchange and verification provided the relevant provisions of the Vienna Document 1994 would be simultaneously supplemented. Austria indicated its interest in the integral implementation of the CFE Treaty and demanded agreement on identifying harmonization goals prior to further negotiation.[101] Once a month, the group discussed implementation, as some delegations put increasing emphasis on the group dealing solely with this issue.[102]

Framework for arms control

In Group B, the USA sought to clarify the meaning of the term 'framework for arms control', as formulated in the Budapest Decisions. This approach was criticized by other delegations as potentially sacrificing the pan-European arms control regime at the cost of regional measures. Eventually it was agreed that a first exchange of views on the specific military challenges for security should be held in order to consider future arms control negotiations.

On 24 July NATO submitted a working paper on arms control under the lengthy and rather vague title 'Contribution to the further reflection of the Forum for Security Cooperation on the development of a framework for arms control'. While stressing the purpose of building and enhancing the security

---

[99] FSC seminar on regional arms control in the OSCE area, Chairman's Summary, FSC document FSC/185/95, 18 July 1995.

[100] FSC document FSC.DEC/16, 4 Oct. 1995.

[101] 'OSZE-Tätigkeitsbericht' [OSCE activity report], *Österreichische Militärische Zeitschrift*, no. 4 (1995), p. 449.

[102] *Arms Control Reporter*, sheet 402.B.335, 1995.

partnership among OSCE states, the need to address specific security problems as part of an overall OSCE structure, creating a web of interlocking and mutually reinforcing security agreements and providing structural coherence to the interrelationship between existing and future arrangements, it proposed negotiation of both OSCE-wide arms control measures and regional approaches based on the principles of sufficiency, transparency (through information exchange), verification and the acceptance of limits on forces. It is proposed that such measures 'be negotiated separately, but would be integral to the framework concept and annexed to it in the same way as existing agreements'. The methods proposed for building, maintaining and improving stability and security in the OSCE area were:

1. Evaluate the effectiveness of past and current OSCE arms control and confidence- and security-building efforts, enhance existing and develop new measures/agreements to address both new and continuing security challenges;

2. Develop more effective implementation assessment methods;

3. Move discussion of regional security issues in the FSC to a more practical and concrete phase in order to define specific challenges to regional stability;

4. Develop measures on a regional or OSCE-wide basis to enhance transparency and confidence regarding military forces and activities of OSCE states;

5. Seek commitments by partners to regional or other agreements not binding on all other OSCE states to provide information on the implementation of these agreements to all the participating states of the OSCE, as agreed by the signatories of such agreements.[103]

V. Regional CSBMs and arms control

The OSCE is to pursue regional stability and arms control under the General Framework Agreement for Peace in Bosnia and Herzegovina, the Dayton Agreement, and broker, implement and monitor two sets of negotiations, on CSBMs and arms control.

Confidence- and security-building measures

As parties to the Annex 1B Agreement on Regional Stabilization of the Dayton Agreement,[104] the Republic of Bosnia and Herzegovina, Croatia, the Federal Republic of Yugoslavia (Serbia and Montenegro), the Federation of Bosnia and Herzegovina and the Republika Srpska agreed to devise a regional structure for stability, to include CSBMs based on the Vienna Document 1994 of the Negotiations on Confidence- and Security-Building Measures as well as regional CSBMs and measures for subregional arms control. To be negotiated within 45 days of the entry into force of the Annex (14 December 1995 when the Agreement was signed), the measures would initially cover: (a) restric-

---

[103] FSC document FSC/192/95, 24 July 1995.

[104] General Framework Agreement for Peace in Bosnia and Herzegovina, Dayton, Ohio, 14 Dec. 1995, Annex 1B, Regional Stabilization. Reprinted in appendix 5A in this volume.

tions on military deployments and exercises in certain geographical areas; (b) restraints on the reintroduction of foreign forces; (c) restrictions on locations of heavy weapons; (d) troop and heavy weapon withdrawals; (e) disbandment of special operations and armed civilian groups; (f) notification of planned military activities including international military assistance and training programmes; (g) identification and monitoring of weapon production capabilities; (h) immediate data exchange on holdings in the five weapon categories covered by the CFE Treaty;[105] and (i) immediate establishment of military liaison missions between the heads of the armed forces of the Federation of Bosnia and Herzegovina and the Republika Srpska.

The parties also agreed not to import any arms for 90 days after the Annex entered into force nor to import heavy weapons[106] or heavy weapon ammunition, mines, military aircraft or helicopters for 180 days or until an agreement on armament levels takes effect.

On 26 January 1996 the CSBM Agreement was reached between the Bosnian Government, the Bosnian-Croat Federation and the Bosnian Serbs.[107] The Agreement is largely based on the 1994 Vienna CSBM Document but includes additional restrictions and restraining measures on military movements, deployments and exercises, not previously addressed by the OSCE. It provides for exchange of military information and data relating to major weapon and equipment systems; notification of changes in command structures or equipment holdings; risk-reduction mechanisms and cooperation; and notification and observation of and constraints on certain military activities. Military activities will be subject to notification if they include 1500 troops, 25 tanks, 40 ACVs, 40 artillery pieces, 3 combat aircraft or 5 combat helicopters; and if they involve flights by 60 or more sorties of combat aircraft and/or combat helicopters. During 1996 and 1997 the parties may only conduct one military manoeuvre involving more than 4000 troops, 80 tanks, 100 ACVs, 100 artillery pieces, 15 combat aircraft or 20 combat helicopters. Thereafter the parties will be subject to similar constraints with specified parameters. There are also strict territorial limits. No party shall conduct or participate in the notifiable exercises within 10 km of international borders; either side of the Inter-Entity Boundary Line between the Federation and the Republika Srpska; the city limits of Gorazde, Brcko and the Posavina Corridor; or the territory transferred from one entity to another. The other measures embrace withdrawal of forces and heavy weapons to cantonments/barracks or other designated areas; restrictions on locations of heavy weapons; notification of disbandment of special operations and armed civilian groups; identification and monitoring of weapons; military contacts and cooperation; verification and inspection regime; and communications. The parties are also committed to

---

[105] Artillery pieces are defined as those of 75-mm calibre and above (the CFE Treaty set the threshold at 100-mm calibre for heavy artillery).

[106] Heavy weapons refer to all tanks and ACVs, all artillery of 75-mm calibre and above, all mortars of 81-mm and above and all anti-aircraft weapons of 20-mm and above.

[107] For the text, see Agreement on Confidence- and Security-Building Measures in Bosnia and Herzegovina. Version current on 5 Mar. 1996, URL ‹http://www.fsk.ethz.ch/osze/docs/bosag.html›.

contribute to the prevention of the proliferation of weapons of mass destruction.[108]

Subregional arms control

OSCE negotiations to reach agreement on levels of armaments and establish voluntary limits on military manpower of the three Bosnian parties and the Federal Republic of Yugoslavia (Serbia and Montenegro) and Croatia were to commence within 30 days of the entry into force of the Annex, based on the following criteria: population size, current military holdings, defence needs and relative force levels in the region. Also by mid-January 1996, the parties were to report their inventories of heavy weapons in accordance with the format laid down in the Vienna Document 1992 and taking account of the special considerations of the region. The agreement is to establish numerical limits on CFE-type equipment holdings.[109] If agreement is not reached within 180 days of the Annex taking effect (i.e., by 6 June 1996), then limits based on the approximate 5:2:2 ratio of the parties shall apply (which would mean NATO sending in weapons to redress the current military imbalance). The determined holdings of Yugoslavia will provide the baseline, and the limits will be 75 per cent of the baseline for Yugoslavia; 30 per cent for Croatia; and 30 per cent for Bosnia and Herzegovina (allocated on the basis of a 2:1 ratio between the Federation of Bosnia and Herzegovina and the Republika Srpska).

In the first months of 1996, the arms control negotiations have encountered a number of obstacles (chiefly delays in provision of data on weapon holdings and questions of enforcement). The US drive to rearm the Federation's troops (the 'equip and train' programme) met with opposition from the European allies, afraid of impairing the chances for genuine reconciliation, undermining the Vienna talks and precipitating a regional arms race rather than building a regional military balance. Observers have envisaged that the talks would pick up momentum in the last weeks prior to the June deadline.[110]

The OSCE assists the parties in their negotiations on CSBMs and armaments and manpower agreements as well as in their implementation and verification (including verification of declared holdings). In line with the relevant provisions of the Dayton Agreement the OSCE Ministerial Council meeting in early December 1995 authorized the Chairman-in-Office to designate a Special Representative to help organize and conduct regional arms control negotiation under the auspices of the FSC.[111] The precise mandate for

---

[108] Ambassador Istvan Gyarmati of Hungary chaired the CSBM negotiation. Reviewing the Agreement, two BASIC analysts draw attention to two potential loopholes (absence of a provision preventing introduction of fresh foreign forces; and lack of restrictions on international training programmes, mentioned in the Dayton Agreement) and the somewhat idealistic tone of some of the provisions (military contacts and cooperation between the former warring sides). Kokkinides, T. and Plesch, D., 'Confidence-building and arms control in Bosnia', *BASIC Reports* (British American Security Information Council), no. 50, 21 Feb. 1996, pp. 4–5.

[109] See note 102.

[110] Note 108, pp. 5–6.

[111] OSCE, Fifth Meeting of the Ministerial Council, Decisions of the Budapest Ministerial Council Meeting, Decision on OSCE action for peace, democracy and stability in Bosnia and Herzegovina,

the Representative is to take account of and respect 'existing arms control rights and obligations including limitations already undertaken on a multi-lateral basis by certain states in the region.'[112] The OSCE also promised to help establish a Commission to facilitate the resolution of any disputes that might arise in implementing the regional arms control agreement.

VI. Conclusions

With the end of the cold war and the conclusion of landmark agreements on arms control, disarmament and CSBMs, the belief prevailed that other cooperative security instruments and mechanisms, such as peacekeeping, preventive diplomacy and crisis management, would take over the major role in ensuring stability and security. Arms control took second place in the public eye. However, the failure to contain the spread of conflicts has shown that implementation and further development of agreements on arms control, disarmament and confidence-building, while they are neither the sole nor the primary condition for the enhancement of political and military security, as was often the case in the cold war period, are essential. In the run-up to the end of the century, arms control will have to find a strong conceptual and practical footing as part of the ongoing process of fundamental transformation of security relations.

In the mid-1990s, conventional arms control issues embrace: (*a*) the pursuit of full implementation of existing agreements and arrangements; (*b*) further development of these agreements to adapt them to the post-cold war situation and create a 'web of interlocking and mutually reinforcing' security accords; and (*c*) new negotiations and approaches effectively to address military challenges and risks not addressed by the 'grand' treaties and other arrangements of the first half of the decade.

In 1995 nearly 50 000 heavy weapons were cut back by 30 states parties to the CFE Treaty. Along with massive Russian troop withdrawals from Central Europe and the Baltic states in 1994, this established an unprecedented core of military stability and predictability in Europe. These and other arms control and related accomplishments have proved the continuing willingness of OSCE states to pursue and abide by the principles of cooperative security. Against the generally positive background, adverse developments and a certain military assertiveness persist in Russia. The CFE flank dispute flared up in 1995, with repeated threats by the Russian military to withdraw from the treaty. The belated NATO response resulted in a makeshift redrawing of the map, but this did not seem to satisfy Russia. While talks continue on the flank issue, Russia proposes sweeping changes aiming at de facto renegotiation of the treaty,

---

MC(5).DEC/1, Budapest, 8 Dec. 1995. The text is reproduced in appendix 7A in this volume. The talks are chaired by Ambassador Vigleik Eide of Norway.

[112] In this context, Bulgaria, Greece and Romania made a reservation to the effect that the negotiation should not affect the limitation under CFE and CFE-1A accords. *Interpretative statement under para. 79 (Chapter 6) of the Final Recommendations of the Helsinki Consultations*, MC(5). DEC/1, 8 Dec. 1995. Annex 2.

presenting the JCG and the May 1996 Review Conference with a difficult task. NATO insists on full implementation of the treaty, but its eastward enlargement will call for a thorough reassessment and a new approach to the conventional arms balance on the European continent.

The existing procedures and mechanisms are not adequate to the new requirements and environment, and the 'old thinking' still prevails among arms control experts and decision makers. On the other hand, there is still no clear-cut concept of how to apply arms control to subregional and internal conflicts. The conceptual failure stems partly from the lack of determined political leadership and mission and partly from the fear of undermining and dismantling the existing European arms control and security foundations. The international community, therefore, continues to stick to its slightly modified instruments while facing the new types of crisis and conflict and the concomitant urgent need to address them with new tools.

Classical arms control, with its emphasis on calculating balances, is neither helpful nor sensible in the face of the qualitatively different challenges and threats posed by the new security environment. Future limitations and reductions are more likely to result from a political exercise than from 'bean counting'. With the collapse of the bloc division, the trends and changes, mostly driven by budgetary squeezes, which are taking place in armed forces (high technological inputs and operational developments; rapid reaction, mobile and professional forces *versus* the old-type armies) will make numerical balances increasingly unattainable and outdated. Moreover, subregional stability and arms control arrangements will make this even more complex and difficult. Thus, cooperative, stability-enhancing measures, including coercive ones like those in Bosnia and Herzegovina, are gaining in prominence.

Facing the failure to stave off and resolve the conflicts raging in eastern and south-eastern Europe, and unable to apply the traditional arms control instruments, the OSCE states have decided to give priority to developing a new framework for arms control which assumes forging a common understanding of the current and likely future military security challenges, devising measures and approaches appropriate to specific problems arising from regional tensions and instabilities while ensuring complementarity between regional and OSCE-wide approaches. Intensive efforts to elaborate a compromise OSCE text in this regard have unfortunately been thwarted by Russia, evidently seeking to avoid having its room for manoeuvre constrained with regard to the CFE Treaty and the arms control agenda, and the Budapest Ministerial Council (7–8 December 1995) was unable to agree on the arms control framework. On the other hand, the negotiations on regional arms control and CSBMs in and around the former Yugoslavia, if accompanied by strong political will and concerted efforts, stand a chance to help enhance mutual confidence, reduce the risk of conflict and inject stability into this conflict-ridden area.

Appendix 16A. The Vienna CSBMs in 1995

ZDZISLAW LACHOWSKI

I. Introduction

Organization for Security and Co-operation in Europe (OSCE) participants paid greater attention to confidence- and security-building measures (CSBMs) in 1995 and addressed a wider range of arms control issues. In addition to the provisions of the Vienna Document 1994 of the Negotiations on Confidence- and Security-Building Measures they were bound by the mandate of the December 1994 CSCE/OSCE Review Conference and Summit Meeting in Budapest to strengthen the implementation of CSBMs, with special emphasis on regional stability and complementarity between regional and OSCE-wide approaches. At the Annual Implementation Assessment Meeting (AIAM) and the OSCE Forum for Security Co-operation (FSC) discussions were marked by a more active assessment of the application and applicability of CSBMs and a search for possible future measures. The General Framework Agreement for Peace in Bosnia and Herzegovina (the Dayton Agreement) envisaged the negotiation of a regional structure for stability, including confidence- and security-building measures based on the Vienna Document 1994 and to be supplemented by regional CSBMs and measures for subregional arms control.[1]

II. Implementation

The Annual Implementation Assessment Meeting

At the Annual Implementation Assessment Meeting, held 13–15 March 1995 in the framework of the FSC, concern was expressed about Russian military activities in Chechnya in the light of its Vienna Document obligations. The Russian delegation considered CSBM provisions on notification and the invitation of observers to be inapplicable during the domestic crisis and argued that transparency about the conflict was ensured by the mass media coverage; that the aim of military action in Chechnya was to defend Russia's territorial integrity and it did not endanger the security of any state; and that the allegedly stabilizing situation in Chechnya made it possible to provide military information.

These arguments were questioned and rejected on all counts by other OSCE delegations. They stressed the applicability of CSBMs in 'all-weather' conditions, including internal crisis situations, and considered mass media coverage to be no substitute for Vienna Document notification. The claim that no security threat exists was considered counter to the principle of indivisibility of security in the OSCE area. Nevertheless the discussion at the AIAM was reported to have been 'constructive and cooperative'.[2]

It was proposed that a special body be established in the FSC to deal with day-to-day implementation, and that the AIAM continue to deal with general problems and

---

[1] For more details see section VI in chapter 16 in this volume.
[2] 'OSZE Tätigkeitsbericht' [OSCE Activity Report], *Österreichische Militärische Zeitschrift*, no. 3 (1995), p. 342.

Table 16A.1. Information exchanged pursuant to Vienna Documents 1992 and 1994

Figures show the percentage of the total number of participating states that submitted information, 1992–95.

	Military forces	Defence planning/ military budgets	Annual calendars and constraining provisions
1992	79	46	58
1993	68	43	66
1994	75	48	70
1995	83	57	58

Source: Sweden's Informal Working Paper, OSCE FSC Document 431/95, Vienna, 12 Mar. 1995; information provided to SIPRI by the Conflict Prevention Centre.

long-term planning. In this context, the Polish proposal for a European verification agency reappeared. It was agreed that the Conflict Prevention Centre (CPC) would examine these suggestions to enable the FSC to start up the planned implementation working group.

With regard to the follow-up to the AIAM, a number of proposals and suggestions were made, ranging from improvements to the Vienna Document 1994 to a conceptual debate on possible future measures (new techniques and measures, e.g., differentiated regional regimes; ways of adapting the OSCE-wide regime to meet regional needs; the role of the AIAM in embracing non-CSBM issues; widening the time-frame of the AIAM, etc.). As a result a number of amendments clarifying or streamlining the Vienna Document 1994 were adopted by the FSC and annexed to the document (concerning invitations to observe certain notifiable military activities and replies thereto and defence planning information exchange).

The dilemma of better implementation and further development of CSBMs, often raised at previous AIAMs, remains. The 1996 AIAM will be held 4–6 March 1996.

The implementation record

Overall, Vienna Document implementation was found to have been better than in preceding years. Some 'new' participants failed to contribute to the annual information exchange in 1995 (the five Central Asian republics—Kazakhstan, Kyrgyzstan, Tajikistan, Turkmenistan and Uzbekistan). A total of 45 participating states supplied information on military forces in the course of the year. However, the provision of defence planning information, introduced by the Vienna Document 1994, was much less successful—more than half the states had failed to send it in or had provided incomplete documentation by the time of the AIAM (although 31 states had supplied this information by December 1995). During the year, 35 states announced plans to deploy major weapons and equipment systems, and 29 of them used the automated data exchange. Twelve participating states have submitted additional CSBM information (white papers, etc.).

Military activities

Supplementing the Vienna Document 1994 with the new parameters concerning military activities has had no immediate impact on the number of military exercises

Table 16A.2. CBM/CSBM notification and observation thresholds, 1975–94

Document	Notification	Observation
Helsinki Final Act 1975	25 000 troops (voluntary, 21 days in advance; area: European states, USSR and Turkey—250-km strip east of the western borders)	No parameters, voluntary, on a bilateral basis
Stockholm Document 1986	13 000 troops or 300 battle tanks, or 3 000 troops amphibious landing (obligatory, 42 days in advance; area: from the Atlantic 'to the Urals'). Air force included in notification if at least 200 sorties by aircraft, excluding helicopters, are flown	17 000 troops or 5 000 troops in amphibious landing parachute drop or parachute drop
Vienna Document 1990	Ditto	Ditto
Vienna Document 1992	9 000 troops or 250 battle tanks, or 3 000 in amphibious landing or parachute drop (obligatory, 42 days in advance; area: Europe plus new Central Asian republics). Air force included in notification if at least 200 sorties by aircraft, excluding helicopters, are flown	13 000 troops or 300 tanks; 3 500 airborne landing or parachute drop
Vienna Document 1994	9 000 troops or 250 battle tanks, 500 ACVs, or 250 self-propelled and towed artillery pieces, mortars and multiple-rocket launchers (100-mm calibre and above); 3 000 in amphibious landing, heliborne landing or parachute drop (obligatory, 42 days in advance; area: Europe plus the Central Asian republics). Air force included in notification if at least 200 sorties by aircraft, excluding helicopters, are flown	13 000 troops or 300 tanks or 500 ACVs or 250 artillery pieces, mortars and multiple rocket launchers (100-mm and above); 3 500 in airborne landing, heliborne landing or parachute drop

subject to notification. During the first half of the 1990s it was clear that the tendency to conduct several major manoeuvres each year continued. Of the planned notifiable activities in 1995,[3] only five exercises were carried out: two Strong Resolve 95 manoeuvres (field training exercise (FTX) and amphibious landing); the command post exercise (CPX) Baptise Pegasus 95; the Adventure Exchange 95 (not reported by SIPRI in 1995); and the CPX/FTX Cold Grouse 95. Three notified activities were cancelled: the FTX FMOE 95 in Sweden (cancelled in January 1995); the Mistral 95 in the western Mediterranean Sea; and FTX Dynamic Mix 95 in the Central/Eastern Mediterranean Sea. Observers were invited to three exercises, two of which had been carried out under the Bulgarian–Greek Athens Document of 1993 (which sets lower thresholds than those of the Vienna Document).

SIPRI has been informed of four manoeuvres (three by NATO and one by Finland) subject to notification planned for 1996. As a novelty, the CPC has also been informed of the deployment of the British contingent in the NATO Peace Implementation Force (IFOR) totalling 13 568 troops.

Constraining provisions concerning military activities exceeding the thresholds of 40 000 troops or 900 battle tanks or the frequency of major manoeuvres, introduced under the Vienna Document 1992, have never been used.

---

[3] Lachowski, Z., 'The Vienna confidence- and security-building measures', *SIPRI Yearbook 1995: Armaments, Disarmament and International Security* (Oxford University Press: Oxford, 1995), appendix 20A, table 20A.

Table 16A.3. Calendar of planned notifiable military activities in 1996, exchanged by 15 Nov. 1995

States/Location	Dates/Start window	Type/Name of activity	Area	Level of command	No. of troops	Type of forces or equipment	No. and type of divisions	Comments
1. Finnish forces in Finland	16–23 Apr.	Kymi 96	Kouvola-Lappeenranta-Kotka-Hamina	Eastern cmd	12 816	Land forces and air support	3 jaeger brigs	..
2. Denmark, France, Greece, Italy, Netherlands, Portugal, Spain, Turkey, UK, USA	22 Sep.–10 Oct.	CPX Dynamic Mix 96	To be determined	CINC-SOUTH	3 000	Amphibious landing	..	Assault, anti-air warfare, strike warfare
3. Belgium, Canada, Denmark, France, Italy, Netherlands, Spain, Turkey, UK, USA in Italy	30 Sep.–10 Oct.	FTX/STX Dynamic Mix 96	Sea, Cap Teulada Range, Pian di Spille Range	Div. level, CINC-SOUTH	9 600 troops (excl. naval forces)	Naval/amphibious forces	..	..
4. Belgium, Denmark, Germany, France, Italy, Netherlands, Norway, UK, USA in Germany	15 Oct.–15 Nov.	CPX/CAX Atlantic Resolve	Grafenwoehr and Kaiserslauten areas	Army group NATO AFCENT—HQ; MNJTF—the deploying organization	15 000 300 Belgian; 400 French; 1 200 German 300 Italy; 300 Dutch; 300 Norwegian; 225 British; 11 975 US	Land, air, naval and a marine corps	2 mech. divs, 2 arm. divs	Joint multinational event to train corps-size HQ commanders and staff in a spectrum of politico-military activities from OOTW through mid-intensity exercises: two politico-military exercises, a staff planning exercise, a deployment exercise, a non-combatant evacuation order exercise and a multi-spectrum conflict.
Begium, France, Germany, Luxembourg, Spain[a]	17 Nov.–2 Dec. 1995	CPX Baptise Pegasus 95	Area delimited by Charleroi, Namur, Luxembourg, Dijon, Troyes	Army corps; Eurocorps HQ	9 000	Land forces	4 divs and corps troops	Cmd posts (corps, div, brig, and bttln) deployed in the field

[a] Corrected and supplemented information on the 1995 exercise.
Note: AFCENT = Allied Forces Central Europe; arm = armoured; brig = brigade; CAX = computer assisted exercise; CINCSOUTH = Commander-in-Chief Allied Forces Southern Europe; cmd = command; CPX = command post exercise; div = division; FTX = field training exercise; mech = mechanized; MNJTF = Multinational Joint Task Force; OOTW = operations other than war; STX = staff training exercise (?).

By 20 December 1995, 63 evaluation visits had been paid (some of them were hosted voluntarily by states), including 47 to formations/units of ground forces and 16 to those of air forces. SIPRI was also informed of 16 inspections conducted during the year. According to the (incomplete) information obtained by SIPRI, both forms of verification functioned well, without major discrepancies or obstacles. The three air base visits in 1995 brought the total of this type of military visit since 1991 to 26. Of a total of 45 participating states with air forces, nine have not yet hosted an air base visit; they all are supposed to extend invitations by January 1997.

III. Conclusions

In 1995 some headway was made at both interstate and intra-state levels. The record of implementation of the Vienna Document has improved with more states providing more complete information as envisaged under its terms. The annual assessment surveyed implementation and made successive proposals and suggestions to streamine it. More important, however, was the more active addressing of regional, subregional and sub-state confidence and security building. The Chechen crisis put CSBM implementation to a severe test and made the participants address the issues of their 'fair-weather' *versus* 'bad-weather' character and intra-state applicability more vigorously. The Dayton accords and the OSCE involvement in the peace process in Bosnia will both certainly prompt some further effort in the FSC towards developing and integrating OSCE-wide and regional CSBMs and other stabilizing arrangements.

Appendix 16B. Foreign military presence in the OSCE area

ZDZISLAW LACHOWSKI

I. Introduction

In the wake of the big Russian troop withdrawals in the first half of the 1990s the focus of foreign military presence in the area of the Organization for Security and Co-operation in Europe (OSCE) has shifted from the centre of the Eurasian continent to its peripheries. The character and tasks of foreign troops have also been modified.[1] Peacekeeping and peace-enforcing forces are deployed along the south-eastern and eastern rims of the OSCE area, from Bosnia to Central Asia. Their roles differ, however: while in the former Yugoslavia they constitute a cooperative security effort, in the Commonwealth of Independent States (CIS) area their 'collective' security goals are ambivalent, with the neighbouring big power being the chief 'peacekeeper'. Aside from the declared tasks of protecting the southern borders of Russia and the CIS, they seem to be preparing the ground to strengthen the predominant military presence and political influence. In 1995 Russia made a series of moves to further uphold its military influence in the former Soviet republics. US and other Allied military presence in Western Europe and Germany in particular, which was warranted by the bloc confrontation in the past, is steadily declining. This appendix reviews foreign troop deployments and withdrawals in Europe and post-Soviet Central Asia in 1995.

II. The area of the former Soviet Union

In the course of 1995 Russia tried to strengthen ties with its CIS partners by making efforts to breathe some life into the idea of CIS collective security.[2] For different reasons the most ardent advocates of collective security efforts at present are Belarus, Kazakhstan and Kyrgyzstan, which, together with Russia, constitute the core of the Commonwealth.[3] The agreement of the 10 February summit meeting in Almaty was of little consequence, approving only continued peacekeeping operations in Tajikistan and guidelines for a joint air defence system.[4] However, Colonel-General V. Semyonov, Commander-in-Chief of the Russian Ground Forces, soon questioned whether a joint CIS air defence system could be set up quickly when the elements of the old system in the Caucasus were 'in shambles' and Azerbaijan, Moldova and

---

[1] The Turkish occupation of part of Cyprus, not discussed in this section, is an exception.

[2] See also section IV of chapter 6 in this volume.

[3] On 29 Mar. 1996, the presidents of these 4 countries signed a series of agreements 'with an aim to further integrate these states'. OMRI (Open Media Research Institute), *OMRI Daily Digest*, no. 65 (1 Apr. 1996), URL <http://www.omri.cz/Publications/Digests/DigestIndex.html>. (hereafter, references to the *OMRI Daily Digest* refer to the Internet edition at this URL address). On 2 Apr. 1996 a union was formed by Russia and Belarus.

[4] This followed the Russian–Kazakh agreement of late Jan. 1995 to merge some army units and tighten military cooperation. 'Former Soviet states adopt joint air-defense plan', *Defense News*, 20–26 Feb. 1995, p. 4.

Turkmenistan had failed to sign the agreement.[5] Owing to the evident reluctance and misgivings of Russia's partners, successive CIS ministerial meetings during the year barely managed to agree on any substantive defence matters beyond extending the CIS mandate in Tajikistan.[6]

On 18 April Russian Foreign Minister Andrey Kozyrev suggested that Russia reserve a special right to intervene militarily to protect its compatriots in the 'near abroad',[7] and later he called for Russian military bases across CIS territory to tighten military cooperation and deter external threats.[8]

On 14 September President Boris Yeltsin signed a decree outlining Russian strategy towards the CIS which, among other things, called for the formation of a military alliance in order to create an effective collective defence system. However, the idea met with lukewarm reactions from most other CIS leaders.[9]

In the meantime Russian military personnel located in other CIS countries continued servicing and preparing former Soviet military equipment and installations for redeployment to Russia, 'peacekeeping', serving as military advisers and specialists for the individual national armed forces and ensuring border security in cooperation with national units.[10]

The Baltic states after Russian withdrawal

After the completion of Russian troop withdrawals from the Baltic states in 1994, a number of problems remained. The issue of military transit between Russia and Lithuania, which caused much political controversy in 1994, was settled in January 1995 by extending military transit regulations, established in the 18 November 1993 agreement for Russian troops pulling out of Germany, until the end of the year. Both sides made concessions. Lithuania gave up its demand that all countries abide by its regulations on dangerous and military cargoes, and Russia stopped insisting on a special treaty on military transit.[11] Nevertheless, Lithuania complained about numerous violations of its airspace by Russian aircraft.[12]

---

[5] 'Gen. Semenov: CIS army will be "eventually" set up', Moscow Interfax in English, 23 Feb. 1995, in *Foreign Broadcast Information Service, Daily Report Central Asia (FBIS-SOV)*, FBIS-SOV-95-037, 24 Feb. 1995, p. 2. It was estimated that building the system would take at least 5 years. In May, Col-Gen. Viktor Prudnikov, chief of Russia's air defence troops and chairman of the CIS air defence coordinating committee, asserted that such a system might be constructed by the end of 1996. *OMRI Daily Digest*, no. 91 (11 May 1995). In Mar. Russian–Georgian talks started on developing Georgia's air defence system.

[6] In general, CIS efforts so far look better on paper than in reality, being declaratory rather than substantive in character. It was reported in early Oct. that the foreign ministers of the 12 CIS countries had agreed on 'an entire packet of documents' on the formation of a 'CIS collective security system', but no details were revealed. *OMRI Daily Digest*, no. 193 (4 Oct. 1995). In Nov. Grachev announced an agreement on helping Armenia, Georgia, Kazakhstan, Kyrgyzstan, Tajikistan and Uzbekistan upgrade their air defence systems. *OMRI Daily Digest*, no. 215 (2 Nov. 1995).

[7] Kozyrev cited the emigration of 240 000 Russians from other CIS countries as evidence of the abuse of their rights outside Russia. *OMRI Daily Digest*, no. 77 (19 Apr. 1995).

[8] *Financial Times*, 7 July 1995.

[9] The Belorussian President supported the idea. Compare 'Only Lukashenko prepared to form bloc', *Izvestia*, 16 Sep. 1995, p. 3. Later, in Oct., Georgian Defence Minister Vardiko Nadibaidze declared that a CIS military bloc is 'inevitable'. *OMRI Daily Digest*, no. 203 (18 Oct. 1995).

[10] Woff, R. A., *The Armed Forces of the Soviet Union: Evolution: Structure and Personalities* (Carmichael and Sweet: Portsmouth, UK, 1995), pp. A1–8.

[11] In parallel, an agreement granting Lithuania the status of 'most-favoured nation' was reached. *Baltic Independent*, 27 Jan.–2 Feb. 1995, p. 1.

[12] *Baltic Independent*, 14–20 Apr. 1995, p. 5 and 3–9 Nov. 1995, p. 5.

The problem of some 2000 retired Russian servicemen who stayed in Latvia illegally after the Russian military withdrawal remained unsettled. By 1 March less than half of them had registered for temporary residence permits, due at the end of April. Both sides assumed a compromise position. Russia asked to extend their stay until the end of 1995 so that their resettlement in Russia could be arranged.[13]

In July and early October, the Russian Duma ratified the July 1994 treaties with Estonia on social guarantees for retired Russian servicemen and the withdrawal of Russian troops from Estonia, respectively.[14] However, Estonia postponed ratification of the treaties with Russia on the grounds that it was unclear which Estonian laws would have to be changed by the ratification.[15] The Estonian Parliament ratified the two agreements on 20 December, adding four explanatory declarations to that on troop withdrawal. The agreement on retired servicemen was also complemented with a declaration that it only applied to military personnel in Estonia who had received pensions from Russian sources before it was signed.[16]

In accordance with the 30 July 1994 agreement, Russia completed the dismantlement of two nuclear reactors at Paldiski and handed over the former Soviet submarine training base at Paldiski to Estonia on 26 September 1995.[17]

The only remaining Russian military installation is the Skrunda radar station in Latvia, which is to cease its work by the end of August 1998 and to be dismantled by February 2000. With OSCE assistance, the implementation of the Skrunda radar agreement between Latvia and Russia has been facilitated.

Damage to the environment in the three Baltic states and the costly clean-up of waste at former Soviet military sites are problems yet to be solved.

Russian military presence in the Transcaucasus

Russian military involvement in handling political and military instability in the Transcaucasus was further intensified in 1995.[18] About 25 000 Russian troops were stationed in the region at the end of 1994—the Group of Russian Forces in the Transcaucasus (GRFT). However, the war in Chechnya and possible redeployments may have changed Russian manpower strengths in the Transcaucasus during 1995. In the spring, Russia was reported to have as many as 312 tanks, 749 ACVs and 312 heavy artillery pieces in Georgia and Armenia.[19] One concern for Russia in consolidating its position in the region is that the entire post-Soviet air defence system in the region is in disarray, begging for reconstruction. In October, Russian–Georgian and Russian–Armenian tactical air combat joint training exercises were held.

On 20–22 March, Russian Defence Minister Pavel Grachev held talks in Tbilisi, *Georgia* on a broad spectrum of bilateral military and technical cooperation issues including the status and number of Russian bases and the creation of a Transcaucasus

[13] *Baltic Independent*, 17–23 Mar. 1995, p. 5.
[14] *Baltic Independent*, 13–19 Oct. 1995, p. 3.
[15] The ratification ran up against the opposition of the Estonian Parliament which demanded that ratification should not take place before a new border treaty has been concluded with Russia. *Baltic Independent*, 24–30 Nov. 1995, p. 2 and 8–14 Dec. 1995, p. 2.
[16] *OMRI Daily Digest*, no. 248 (22 Dec. 1995).
[17] *Baltic Independent*, 29 Sep.–5 Oct. 1995, p. 2.
[18] See also chapter 6 in this volume.
[19] 'The current condition of the Group of Russian Troops in Transcaucasia (GRTT)', *Georgian Military Chronicle* (Occasional Papers of the Caucasian Institute for Peace, Democracy and Development), vol. 2, no. 2 (Apr. 1995).

air defence system. An agreement was initialled to define the future status of Russian troops which had remained deployed since 1991 with no formal status.[20] It was agreed that a fourth base, the Abkhazian Bombora military airfield near Gudauta, would be made available to Russia. In early 1995, it was reported that 226 T-72 tanks and 221 artillery systems and other weapons were stationed in the Akhalkalaki and Batumi bases.[21] The talks on the air-defence system led to the opening on 1 June of two Soviet-era radar stations and a command post controlling airspace around Tbilisi. Reaching agreement on Russian help in 'restoring Georgia's territorial integrity' in the Georgian–Abkhazian dispute (in early 1995 Russia was reported to have started handing over military equipment to the Georgian armed forces while pressing Abkhazia to come to terms with Georgia[22]), Prime Minister Viktor Chernomyrdin and Georgian President Eduard Shevardnadze paved the way to signing a series of agreements on military cooperation on 15 September. These included the long-anticipated agreement allowing Russia formally to lease the four military bases in this republic for 25 years with an option on a further 5-year period.[23] According to the agreement, there should be no more than 25 000 Russian servicemen in Georgia.[24] On 17 January 1996, the Georgian Parliament ratified the 3 February 1994 Treaty on Friendship and Cooperation with Russia.

The Russian–Georgian agreements in 1995 were accompanied by a number of similar agreements with *Armenia*, concluded by Presidents Boris Yeltsin and Levon Ter-Petrosyan in Moscow on 16 March. An agreement was signed on the deployment of a motor-rifle division at a Russian military base in the north-western town of Gyumri and a Russian command group in Erevan. In total, 82 tanks, 193 ACVs and 100 heavy artillery pieces of the Russian forces are said to be stationed in the republic. A joint air defence post is also planned to reinforce the Russian base.[25] On 23 March, a joint Armenian–Russian military exercise took place in Armavir under Russian command. In November Armenia ratified the agreement on the establishment of a single CIS air defence system.[26]

Azerbaijan continued to reject Russian offers of closer military cooperation. In October in Baku, a Russian delegation discussed military cooperation, including renewed Russian use of the over-the-horizon radar station at Gebele and the creation of a unified air defence system.[27] In November, the Russian Government was reported to have offered to support Azerbaijan's efforts in the OSCE Minsk Group to regain Nagorno-Karabakh if Baku granted Russia military basing rights. Azerbaijani Parliament Speaker Rasul Gulev stated in another context that Moscow seeks to regain control of a major Soviet-era early-warning radar complex in Azerbaijan as part of a trade-off involving the terms of the Nagorno-Karabakh settlement.

[20] In 1994 Russia and Georgia signed a protocol of intent for Russia to keep 3 bases in Georgia: the Vaziani airfield, *c.* 30 km south of Tbilisi, linking the Russian Group of Forces in the Transcaucasus with Russia; Akhalkalaki (147th Motor Rifle Division); and Batumi (145th Motor Rifle Division).

[21] Note 18.

[22] E.g., in Sep. Russian Deputy Foreign Minister Boris Pastukhov threatened to withdraw the 3000 Russian peacekeepers who have policed the Abkhazian–Georgian border since Oct. 1993. *OMRI Daily Digest*, no. 176 (11 Sep. 1995).

[23] Kakheli, I., 'Military bases in a country of "active neutrality"', *Obshchaya Gazeta*, 2–8 Nov. 1995, p. 4; and *OMRI Daily Digest*, nos 176 (11 Sep. 1995) and 181 (18 Sep. 1995).

[24] 'The Russian Federation's Defence Ministry's military bases in Georgia', *Georgian Military Chronicle* (Occasional Papers of the Caucasian Institute for Peace, Democracy and Development), vol. 2, no. 6 (Oct. 1995).

[25] Moscow Interfax in English, 16 Mar. 1995, FBIS-SOV-95-052, 17 Mar. 1995, pp. 5–6.

[26] FBIS-SOV-95-224, 21 Nov. 1995, p. 53.

[27] *OMRI Daily Digest*, no. 196 (9 Oct. 1995).

Russian military presence in Ukraine, Belarus and Moldova

Ukraine continued its careful quest for greater politico-military freedom *vis-à-vis* Russia. Some 12 000 Russian servicemen still serve in the Black Sea Fleet. Despite some progress on the fate of the Fleet, as announced time and again during the year, the issue was not resolved. About 1500 Russian personnel service the 43rd Strategic Rocket Army nuclear facilities in Vinnitsa. In August, Ukraine announced a change in the proportion of ethnic Ukrainians in its armed forces, from 45 to 59 per cent.

Belarus took further steps to tighten its political, economic and military ties with Russia in 1995. The agreements of 21 February established even closer military cooperation, and included the location of two early-warning systems on Belorussian territory under Russian jurisdiction.[28] The main role of the 25–30 000 Russian troops in Belarus is to guard and maintain the remnants of the former Soviet arsenal and the long-range aviation assets in Baranovichi. Belorussian–Russian agreements said that withdrawal of the Russian nuclear regiments should be complete by late 1995. Seven out of nine regiments of the strategic rocket forces (with 81 mobile SS-25 Topol missiles) had been returned to Russia by early 1995, but President Alexander Lukashenko unexpectedly ordered a halt to the pull-out of the last two regiments (with 18 SS-25s) in July, claiming it was 'a gross political error' in the light of the coming unification with Russia. Like the February decision to halt reductions under the Treaty on Conventional Armed Forces in Europe (CFE) this was prompted by economic considerations.[29] In August Lukashenko urged Russia to 'make better use' of its defence cooperation with Belarus.[30] In December Belarus signed an agreement with Russia to conclude the missile withdrawal by September 1996. Withdrawal of equipment and troops will take several more months.[31]

Disagreement continued as to whether the Russian troops in Trans-Dniester should be withdrawn as a result of of a political solution, as demanded by Russia, or *alongside* a political settlement, as called for by *Moldova*. The former 14th Army, renamed the Operational Task Force, and elements of the 27th (Peacekeeping) Motor-Rifle Division constitute the core of the Russian military presence in Moldova. Pulling out the 5000-strong Russian contingent from the self-proclaimed Transdniester republic is very problematic.[32] Russia cites the still volatile situation in the area and the possibility of renewed armed conflict, as well as the logistics of transporting huge amounts of ammunition through Ukraine and the costs involved. Disposal of munitions is also controversial, destruction methods meeting local opposition on environmental grounds; it was repeatedly stopped and started during the year.[33] All

---

[28] *OMRI Daily Digest*, no. 38 (22 Feb. 1995).

[29] *Izvestia*, 6 July 1995, pp. 1–2. Later, a Belorussian official claimed that the hold-up was caused by Belorussian concern about the ecological mess they left behind. 'Official on withdrawal Russian strategic units', Moscow Interfax in English, 10 July 1995, FBIS-SOV-95-132, 11 July 1995, p. 56. Belarus also demanded cancellation of $400 m. debts for Russian natural gas. *Defence News*, 21–27 Aug. 1995, pp. 1, 28.

[30] *OMRI Daily Digest*, No. 167 (28 Aug. 1995).

[31] Moscow Interfax in English, 9 Dec. 1995, FBIS-SOV-95-237, 11 Dec. 1995, p. 68. All this may be called into question by the formation of a union by Russia and Belarus.

[32] According to Moldovan estimates, the former 14th Army included 4 infantry brigades, an artillery regiment, a tank battalion, an anti-aircraft brigade, a reconnaissance battalion, a communication battalion, Dniester and Delta battalions and a border guard regiment, equipped with 16 T-64 tanks, 18 122-mm howitzers, 50 120-mm mortars and over 5000 guns. 'Composition of Dniester's illegal armed formations detailed', INFOTAG in English, 7 Apr. 1995, FBIS-SOV-95-069, 11 Apr. 1995, p. 63.

[33] The total ammunition stored in the Trans-Dniester area amounts to 410 000 t, of which 50 000 t cannot be removed for technical reasons and have to be destroyed on the spot.

this was compounded until recently by the fact that the army was composed predominantly of local inhabitants.[34] The Russian Duma, dominated by nationalists and conservatists, strongly opposes military withdrawal from Moldova, issuing bills to this effect and refusing to ratify the 21 October 1994 agreement.[35] Implementation of the agreement on a three-year withdrawal started in early 1995;[36] but it was a slow process because of resistance from the Trans-Dniester authorities and Lieutenant-General Alexander Lebed, seeking excuses to delay and obstruct the pull-out. Grachev's visit to Moldova on 26–27 June produced a new agreement on the withdrawal, complementing that of October 1994 and providing for three stages: two for the withdrawal of equipment and munitions and a third for that of army personnel. At the same time, Moldova rejected Russia's request to deploy 3500 soldiers to help keep the peace in Trans-Dniestria.[37] In the autumn Russia seemed to be seeking to maintain its military presence there. In autumn and winter, in the tripartite joint commission monitoring Trans-Dniestria, Russia again proposed that its troops be given the status of peacekeepers.[38] In November, Russia and Ukraine signed a protocol on the transit through Ukraine of Russian troops from Trans-Dniestria.[39]

Central Asia

National armed forces in the five former Soviet republics in Central Asia are characterized by the lack of an indigenous officer corps: some 90 per cent of the officers are Slavs, mostly Russian. Russian troops are welcomed by the host states and play a stabilizing role in Central Asia, both internally and externally. They are chiefly presented as a defence against external threats (including Islamic fundamentalism), but protection of autocratic ruling élites dependent on Russia and the maintenance of domestic stability seem to be most critical. Central Asia's strategic dependence on Russia is twofold, based on: (a) a collective security arrangement under the aegis of the CIS and led by Russia, with Kazakhstan as its leading advocate (as part of a 'Euro-Asian Union'), followed by Kyrgyzstan, Tajikistan and Uzbekistan; and (b) bilateral agreements with Russia, as in the case of Turkmenistan.[40] During the year Russia signed additional military agreements with its Central Asian partners, strengthening its role in the region.

Russia's dilemma with regard to *Tajikistan* is whether to try for a more representative government, which implies a risk of undermining its loyal Tajik allies, or press on with a military solution. The 25 000-strong CIS Collective Peacekeeping Force in

---

[34] 'Russian army withdrawal unrealistic, Lebed says', *Balkan News*, 29 Jan.–4 Feb. 1995. In the 26 Mar. 1995 referendum in the Trans-Dniester area, 93% of those voting were in favour of the continued presence of the former 14th Army. *Neue Zürcher Zeitung*, 28 Mar. 1993, p. 3. In Nov. 1995, Grachev announced that all the conscripts from the Dniester area had been dismissed and replaced by Russian conscripts, making the former 14th Army 'fully Russian'. *OMRI Daily Digest*, no. 221 (13 Nov. 1995).

[35] *OMRI Daily Digest*, nos 83 (27 Apr. 1995) and 122 (23 June 1995).

[36] *Izvestia*, 4 Feb. 1995, p. 1. Two engineering brigades were planned to be withdrawn in 1995.

[37] *OMRI Daily Digest*, nos 123 (26 June 1995) and 124 (27 June 1995).

[38] FBIS-SOV-95-228, 28 Nov. 1995, p. 25; FBIS-SOV-95-238, 12 Dec. 1995, p. 23; and FBIS-SOV-95-250, 29 Dec 1995, p. 39–40.

[39] *OMRI Daily Digest*, no. 229 (27 Nov. 1995).

[40] For figures on the Russian military presence in Central Asia in 1994 see Lachowski, Z., 'Conventional arms control and security dialogue in Europe', *SIPRI Yearbook 1995: Armaments, Disarmament and International Security* (Oxford University Press: Oxford, 1995), p. 781. For a fuller analysis see Menon, R., 'In the shadow of the Bear: Security in post-Soviet Central Asia', *International Security*, vol. 20, no. 1 (summer 1995), pp. 149–81.

Tajikistan, with the largest Russian force deployed outside Russia's borders, consists mainly of Russian personnel (24 000, including 16 000 on the borders). It comprises the 201st Motor Rifle Division and the Tajik Operation Group of the Russian border troops. This presence puts a heavy financial burden on Russia (c. 80 per cent of the cost of 'peacekeeping'). During the year Russia took a number of steps to help Tajikistan strengthen its army, which could be seen as seeking to decrease the role of Russian troops in fighting opposition forces.[41] In March a 1500-man joint Russian–Tajik–Uzbek 'peacekeeping' exercise was held in Tajikistan (the third since 1991) to give 'a display of force for those who may cherish plans to destabilize the situation in the region'.[42]

The Russian military in *Kazakhstan* are mainly military advisers, staff officers, commanders, technical specialists and scientists at the Baikonur space station. After initial quarrels and disputes over a range of issues inherited from Soviet times, a series of military and related agreements in 1994–95 provided a basis for closer cooperation between the states. Eight military cooperation agreements, signed on 20 January 1995, included arrangements to merge their forces and create joint commands for planning and training and one to police the Chinese border. All were ratified by July. In August agreement was reached on outstanding issues regarding Baikonur, the Leninsk complex and related security matters.[43] It was announced in October that the 1000-km Sino-Kazakh border is patrolled by about 15 000 Russian and Kazakh soldiers.[44] In January 1996, 16 additional agreements were signed with Russia, providing for further military assistance, training of Kazakh forces, joint air defence operations and equipment.[45]

III. Foreign military presence in Western Europe

The numbers of foreign troops in Western Europe, particularly in Germany, have diminished steadily since the end of the cold war. The end of the bloc confrontation, German unification, the CFE Treaty, the collapse of the Warsaw Treaty Organization (WTO), the breakup of the USSR and Soviet/Russian troop withdrawals from Central Europe in 1994 all contributed to reorganization and reductions in foreign military presence. In Germany, the total number of foreign troops has fallen from 400 000 to c. 165 000 since 1989.

US presence

At the beginning of 1995 there were about 150 000 US troops in Western Europe, including some 100 000 in Germany, 14 000 in the UK and 12 000 in Italy. Some 17 000 were distributed among the small contingents in other Allied European states and the US 6th Fleet in the Mediterranean.[46] In June, US Under-Secretary of Defense Joseph Nye confirmed that Europe remains the forward-based platform for

---

[41] FBIS-SOV-95-070, 12 Apr. 1995, p. 80; and *OMRI Daily Digest*, no. 146 (28 July 1995).

[42] *OMRI Daily Digest*, no. 64 (30 Mar. 1995); and FBIS-SOV-95-062, 31 Mar. 1995, p. 72.

[43] Wolff, R., 'Kazakh-Russian relations: an update', *Jane's Intelligence Review*, vol. 7, no. 12 (Dec. 1995), p. 567. However, disagreements have been reported to persist over the lease of the Baikonur cosmodrome and a number of other military sites in Kazakhstan to the Russian Defence Ministry. *OMRI Daily Digest*, no. 57 (20 Mar. 1996).

[44] *OMRI Daily Digest*, no. 201 (16 Oct. 1995); and FBIS-SOV-95-199, 16 Oct. 1995, p. 81.

[45] *OMRI Daily Digest*, no. 20 (27 Jan. 1996).

[46] 'Zum Stande der NATO-Streitkräfte in Europa-Mitte' [On the situation of the NATO armed forces in Central Europe], *Österreichische Militärische Zeitschrift*, no. 5 (1995), p. 563.

Table 16B. Allied forces stationed in Germany

State/Type of forces		No. of troops		
		1989	31 Dec. 1994	31 Dec. 1996
Belgium		27 300	11 800	2 150
France		44 000	22 000	22 000
UK	British Army of the Rhine	58 000		26 250
	Royal Air Force Germany	12 000		6 250
	Total	**70 000**	**35 000**	**32 500**
Canada		7 900	100	100
The Netherlands	Land	6 000		
	Air force	2 000		
	Total	8 000	5 700	2 500
USA	US Army Europe	204 400	75 000	61 000
	UA Air Force Europe	41 400	16 000	15 400
	Total	**245 800**	**91 000**	**76 500**
Total		**403 000**	**165 600**	**135 750**

Source: Based on *Allierte Truppen und multinationale Streitkräftestrukturen in Deutschland* [Allied troops and the multinational armed force structures in Germany], Presse- und Informationsamt der Bundesregierung. Referat Außen- und Sicherheitspoliti, Bonn, Jan. 1995, p. 22.

coordination of US troops throughout the world.[47] The long-standing issue of 'burden-sharing' led the US House of Representatives to vote in mid-1995 for reducing the number of US troops in Europe to as few as 25 000 unless the European Allies pay a bigger share of the costs. The Clinton Administration criticized the idea of a cut-back as threatening to 'compromise the President's ability to protect US interests not only in Europe but throughout the world'.[48]

Germany

The status of foreign troops changed after unification. Since 18 March 1993, a new agreement regulates the stationing of allied forces on German territory, which replaced the former 12 agreements and administrative regulations.

At the end of 1994, the US Army had only 345 installations in 47 garrisons, to be reduced to 249 installations in 39 bases by the end of 1996. Britain said that its armed forces at 28 sites in Germany would be reduced to about 32 500 in 1995. French forces in Germany have been halved to 22 000 at 18 sites since mid-1990. Belgium and the Netherlands, while carrying out drastic reductions in their respective armies, are to cut their forces in Germany to rather symbolic strengths of about 2000 and 2500 troops, respectively, by the end of 1997. Canada withdrew its last troops in 1993, retaining about 100 men at the NATO headquarters and in the airborne warning and control system (AWACS) unit.[49]

---

[47] *Frankfurter Allgemeine Zeitung*, 9 June 1995.

[48] 'US threatens Europe troop cuts', *International Herald Tribune*, 16 June 1995.

[49] *Allierte Truppen und multinationale Streitkräftestrukturen in Deutschland* [Allied forces and multinational armed force structures in Germany], Presse- und Informationsamt der Bundesregierung. Referat Außen- und Sicherheitspolitik, Bonn, Jan. 1995, pp. 6–10, 11–13. Compare note 45, pp. 563–66.

17. Land-mines and blinding laser weapons: the Inhumane Weapons Convention Review Conference

JOZEF GOLDBLAT

I. Introduction

A Review Conference of the Convention on Prohibitions or Restrictions on the Use of Certain Conventional Weapons Which May Be Deemed to Be Excessively Injurious or to Have Indiscriminate Effects (CCW Convention),[1] often referred to as the 'Inhumane Weapons' Convention, was held in Vienna on 25 September–13 October 1995, with two additional sessions in 1996. The CCW Convention was opened for signature in 1981 and entered into force in 1983. It is an 'umbrella treaty' to which specific agreements can be added as protocols. Protocol I prohibits the use of any weapon whose primary effect is to injure by fragments which cannot be detected in the body by the use of X-rays. Protocol II restricts the use of mines, booby-traps and other devices, and aims to prevent or reduce civilian casualties caused by these devices during and after hostilities. Protocol III restricts the use of incendiary devices.[2]

The CCW Convention has attracted relatively few adherents; by 31 December 1995, 57 states had ratified it.[3] Paradoxically, a number of African and Asian states (e.g., Afghanistan, Angola, Cambodia, Mozambique and Somalia) that have suffered greatly from the effects of inhumane conventional weapons, mainly land-mines, are not yet parties to the Convention. Some of these states participated as observers at the Review Conference together with other non-parties. Representatives of nearly 70 non-governmental organizations (NGOs), including the Vietnam Veterans of America Foundation, Human Rights Watch, Physicians for Human Rights and the International Campaign to Ban Landmines, followed the proceedings. The International Committee of the Red Cross (ICRC) submitted reports and working papers to the Review Conference proposing changes to the wording of the CCW Convention and organized symposia and working groups prior to the Review Conference. In addition, the NGOs and the ICRC launched international media campaigns to ban anti-personnel mines. The campaign employs advertisements that are designed to mobilize public opinion and to stigmatize the production, stockpiling, transfer and use of anti-personnel mines.

---

[1] The text of the CCW Convention and Protocols I–III is reproduced in Goldblat, J., SIPRI, *Agreements for Arms Control: A Critical Survey* (Taylor & Francis: London, 1982), pp. 296–302.

[2] For an assessment of the convention and of the preparatory work for its revision, see Goldblat, J., 'Inhumane conventional weapons: efforts to strengthen the constraints', *SIPRI Yearbook 1995: Armaments, Disarmament and International Security* (Oxford University Press: Oxford, 1995), pp. 825–35.

[3] For the parties to the CCW Convention and Protocols I–III, see annexe A in this volume.

SIPRI Yearbook 1996: Armaments, Disarmament and International Security

The main tasks of the Review Conference were: (*a*) to strengthen the provisions of Protocol II on the use of land-mines, booby-traps and other devices; and (*b*) to consider the proposal for an additional protocol to restrict the use of certain laser weapons.[4] Only the second task was completed, and an additional protocol was adopted.[5] The Review Conference decided to continue its work on 15–19 January and on 22 April–3 May 1996 in Geneva. The session held in January 1996 resolved certain problems of a technical nature, but many other problems remained to be solved.

II. Land-mines

On 19 January 1996, the President of the Review Conference submitted a report which included a draft revision of Protocol II.[6] The draft incorporated the views of the delegations with the intent of providing a basis for negotiation at the concluding session of the Review Conference, held on 22 April–3 May 1996.

Anti-personnel land-mines

The focus of the discussion was on the detectability of anti-personnel land-mines and the methods for their self-destruction and self-deactivation.

In the President's draft, an 'anti-personnel mine' is defined as a mine that is 'primarily' designed to be exploded by the presence, proximity or contact of a person and one which will incapacitate, injure or kill one or more persons.[7] The humanitarian impact of anti-personnel land-mines on civilians is far in excess of their military utility. The Secretary-General of the United Nations has characterized them as 'weapons of mass destruction' that are 'both perverse and insidious'.[8]

All types of mine fall under at least one of four categories: blast, fragmentation, directional or bounding mines. Blast mines are the most common. They rely on the energy released by an explosive charge to harm the target, but the explosive effect is usually enhanced by fragmentation caused by the blast. In fragmentation mines the blast serves mainly to shatter the mine and to hurl its fragments over as wide an area as possible. Directional mines rely chiefly on fragmentation and utilize the harmful effects of preformed metal fragments of

---

[4] The term 'laser' stands for light amplification by stimulated emission of radiation. Lasers have various civilian and military applications. The CCW Convention Review Conference dealt with military lasers for anti-personnel use.

[5] The text of the protocol is reproduced as appendix 17A in this volume.

[6] CCW Review Conference document CCW/CONF.I/WP.4*/Rev.1, 19 Jan. 1996. The definitions in this section are based on 'Article 2 definitions' of the President's draft of Protocol II.

[7] The ICRC objects to the use of the word 'primarily'. It argues that if a munition is designed so that it can be used both as an anti-personnel mine and for some other purpose it should be considered an anti-personnel mine; otherwise it may escape the restrictions to be introduced by the amended protocol. This applies, for example, to anti-tank mines that are designed to have anti-personnel characteristics. Statement issued by the ICRC, Geneva, Jan. 1996.

[8] Boutros Boutros-Ghali, 'Statement to the International Meeting on Mine Clearance', Geneva, 6 July 1995; see United Nations document SG/SM/5679, 7 July 1995.

selected size and shape which travel at high velocity in a predetermined arc. In bounding mines a small explosive charge is detonated and propels the mine upwards, scattering fragments—which may be preformed—over a far wider area than would be possible with a surface or buried mine of similar size. All such mines can be activated by pressure, trip wire, electronic or remote control, or by a combination of these methods.[9]

Mines kill or inflict wounds that usually result in surgical amputation, and survivors require extended hospital care. The amputees need physical therapy and prosthetic devices to lead a normal life, and some are so disfigured that they need psychological counselling to cope with the trauma. At least 250 000 people have been disabled by land-mines, and the number is increasing.[10]

Most of the anti-personnel land-mines currently in use are easy to manufacture and expensive to remove.[11] They are deemed to have a defensive role when used as a barrier to protect national borders or vital military or economic installations, or as an impediment to the deployment of enemy troops in locations advantageous to an attacker. They are also used on a much larger scale, however, by both regular and irregular forces as offensive weapons to desolate entire regions, disrupt agriculture and damage the economic infrastructure. According to the text of Protocol II now in force, parties to an armed conflict must keep records on minefields, but this is rarely done.

The controversy over the detectability of mines

In the President's draft the use of anti-personnel mines which are not detectable is to be prohibited. Agreement was not reached to prohibit the use of the so-called 'anti-handling device' which is part of, linked to, attached to or placed under the mine, and which causes the mine to explode when an attempt is made to tamper with it.[12] Agreement could also not be reached on whether or not mines that are designed to be exploded by the presence, proximity or contact of a tank or other vehicle should be covered by the requirement of detectability.[13]

It has been proposed that anti-personnel mines incorporate in their construction a material or device that enables detection of the mine by commonly available technical mine detection equipment and provides a response signal equivalent to the signal produced by eight grams or more of iron in a single

---

[9] ICRC, *Symposium on Anti-Personnel Mines*, Report, Montreux, 21–23 Apr. 1993.

[10] Roberts, S. and Williams, J., *The Enduring Legacy of Landmines* (Vietnam Veterans of America Foundation: Washington, DC, 1995).

[11] Parlow A., 'Toward a global ban on landmines', *International Review of the Red Cross*, July/Aug. 1995. See also the section on 'mine clearance' in this chapter.

[12] Issues related to the use of anti-handling devices are summarized in an informal background paper submitted by the delegation from the Netherlands. See CCW Review Conference document CCW/CONF.I/CRP.5, 18 Jan. 1996.

[13] Such mines are larger than anti-personnel mines and, unless altered, require heavy pressure (generally more than 100 kg) to set them off.

coherent mass.[14] This obligation would apply only to anti-personnel mines produced after the adoption of the amended Protocol II. Anti-personnel mines produced before its adoption might have attached to them, prior to their emplacement (and in a manner 'not easily removable'), a material or device making them detectable instead of having such a material or device incorporated in their construction. The latter obligation, although relatively easy to fulfil since the parties would not have to provide information about mines in their stockpiles or those newly produced, would not need to be complied with immediately. At the time of its notification of consent to be bound by the amended protocol, each party would be free to declare that it would defer compliance for a period of up to eight years from the entry into force of Protocol II—the period presumably needed for acquisition of the capability to introduce the necessary changes to mines.[15] Assuming that it would take some three years for the amended protocol to enter into force (as was the case with the CCW Convention itself), the situation could remain unchanged for over a decade.

Although allowing a long transition period, during which the parties would be invited to minimize only 'to the extent feasible' the use of non-detectable anti-personnel mines, is not compatible with humanitarian objectives, most delegations to the Review Conference expressed a desire for a 'grace period'. Russia wanted a period longer than eight years. The representative of China stressed the military utility of mines and recognized no need for their detection, especially if the mines were equipped with self-destruct and self-deactivating mechanisms (see below).[16] It is, however, widely recognized that the greatest measure of safety is provided by finding a mine and physically rendering it harmless.

The controversy over self-destruction and self-deactivation of mines

The presence of metal in a mine does not guarantee that the mine will be detected and can be safely removed. This is especially true for mines laid in soil rich in iron or on former battlegrounds that contain large numbers of metal fragments, including spent cartridges. In order to deal with this and other uncertainties, the President's draft proposes that remotely delivered anti-personnel mines—those delivered by artillery, missile, rocket, mortar or similar means, or dropped from an aircraft—should be designed and constructed so that no more than 5 (or 10) per cent of the activated mines would fail to self-destruct within 30 days after emplacement. (Mines delivered from a

[14] Low metallic content contributes greatly to the difficulties in mine detection in Bosnia and Herzegovina, where some 2 million land-mines are reported to have been laid. See USIS Geneva *Daily Bulletin*, 26 Jan. 1996.

[15] The US Delegation to the Review Conference demonstrated how a piece of metal can be fixed onto a mine to make it detectable. The ease with which this can be done renders the need for deferral questionable.

[16] The Deputy Director of the Disarmament Division of the Chinese Foreign Ministry said that 'if mines are used properly and responsibly, they are a very effective means of self-defence'. Quoted in the newsletter of the International Campaign to Ban Landmines, *CCW News* (Geneva), 19 Jan. 1996.

land-based system from less than 500 metres are not considered to be 'remotely delivered', provided they are used in accordance with the relevant articles of Protocol II.) In order to function automatically the self-destruct mechanism must be incorporated in the mine or externally attached to it. Each mine would be required to be equipped with a backup self-deactivation feature designed and constructed so that, together with the self-destruct mechanism, no more than 1 of 1000 activated mines would function as mines 120 days after emplacement. 'Self-deactivation' means automatically rendering a mine inoperable by means of the irreversible exhaustion of a component, such as a battery, that is essential to the operation of the mine.

It is not clear how the envisaged failure rate of the above mechanisms could be ensured and kept within permissible limits. Their reliability is particularly important in the case of mines which are remotely delivered in large quantities and which cannot be accurately mapped. Anti-personnel mines which have not been remotely delivered, such as those emplaced by hand, would have to meet the requirements for self-destruction and self-deactivation only if used outside marked areas monitored by military personnel and protected by fencing or other means to ensure the exclusion of civilians. However, in conditions of military action a party to an armed conflict exposed to a direct enemy attack might be relieved from the obligation not to lay mines unequipped with self-destruct and self-deactivation mechanisms outside marked and fenced areas. Such an 'escape clause' would considerably weaken the constraints and could even nullify them.

According to the President's draft, if a party cannot comply immediately with the requirements for the self-destruction and self-deactivation of mines, it might declare at the time of its notification of consent to be bound by the amended Protocol II that it would defer compliance for a period of up to eight years with respect to mines produced prior to the entry into force of the amended protocol. During the period of deferral the parties would undertake to minimize 'to the extent feasible' the use of anti-personnel mines that are not equipped with both self-destruct and self-deactivation mechanisms. With respect to remotely delivered anti-personnel mines, the parties would have to comply with either the requirement for self-destruction or the requirement for self-deactivation; with respect to other anti-personnel mines, they would have to comply with at least the requirement for self-deactivation. Owing to these reservations, mines that did not meet the required specifications could continue to be in use for a long period. In the absence of international controls it would not be possible to ascertain reliably if a mine had been produced before or after entry into force of Protocol II, or if it was actually designed and produced according to the proper specifications.

The deferral period of 8 years was suggested by the President; other proposals ranged from 3 to 17 years. Bulgaria proposed that the length of the transition period might be related to an international exchange or provision of relevant technology and suggested that an appropriate formulation to that effect be incorporated in Protocol II.

The use of remotely delivered mines other than anti-personnel mines (e.g., anti-tank mines) would be prohibited unless they are self-deactivating and/or equipped with an effective mechanism for self-destruction or self-neutralization so that they would cease to function as mines as soon as they no longer served the military purpose for which they were intended. A 'self-neutralizing' mechanism is an automatically functioning mechanism which renders a munition inoperable. Here, too, the parties might defer compliance—for the same period as that envisaged for other mines—with the relevant provision of the amended protocol as regards mines produced prior to its adoption. During the period of deferred compliance, anti-tank mines and anti-vehicle mines would be allowed to be used only if they were delivered in a controlled manner, similar to delivery from a vehicle, and if their position were recorded in accordance with the Technical Annex to Protocol II.

Assessment of the main controversies

From the humanitarian standpoint restrictions on the use of mines by changes in their construction are insufficient; the parameters of the proposed modifications are not even verifiable. Only absolute assurance that a previously mined area is free of activated mines would make that area safe and usable. However, obtaining such assurance is impossible; failures of self-destruct and self-deactivating mechanisms are inevitable. If Protocol II were adopted as proposed in the President's draft, this could be seen as legitimizing the use of mines that are technically more sophisticated than those currently in use.

The suggested provision for transition periods for the implementation of the new obligations could further weaken the effects of the provisions of Protocol II. It would allow the parties to continue their current practices for many years. Since some 2–5 million mines are believed to be newly emplaced every year, while only 100 000 mines are removed annually, the humanitarian crisis caused by land-mines scattered in more than 60 countries (mostly in the developing world) would become even more acute.[17]

Other controversies over mines[18]

Mine clearance

According to the President's draft, after the cessation of hostilities each party would be responsible for clearing the minefields under its control. If a party no longer exercises control over areas in which mines have been laid, it should provide to the responsible party the assistance needed to remove them.

---

[17] These figures were given in the text distributed to participants at the CCW Review Conference by the UN Department of Humanitarian Affairs, Geneva, 1996.

[18] These issues were discussed mainly at the Sep.–Oct. 1995 session of the Review Conference but were hardly addressed at the Jan. 1996 session.

Indeed, a legally binding undertaking by all parties to cooperate in clearing areas where there are mines would be necessary.[19] Experts estimate that removing the existing 110 million active mines would take more than 1000 years under current conditions if no new mines were laid. (On average, one mine-clearer is killed and two others are injured for every 5000 mines removed.[20]) Parties could reach agreement among themselves as well as with international organizations on the provision of technical and material assistance to mine-clearance activities. The UN Voluntary Trust Fund, established by the UN Secretary-General in 1994, should have at its disposal sufficient resources to meet requests for such assistance. However, the International Meeting on Mine Clearance in July 1995 raised less than one-third of the UN's goal of $75 million for the fund.

Transfer

In the past 25 years more than 255 million land-mines have been produced, including approximately 190 million anti-personnel mines. In the 1990s the global production of mines averaged close to 5 million per year. Approximately 100 companies in at least 55 nations have produced more than 360 different types of anti-personnel mine. Thirty-six nations are known to have exported land-mines, and almost all of the land-mines laid in the most affected countries come from foreign sources. Their prices vary. For example, the Chinese Type 72 anti-personnel mine is widely available for $3 but is sometimes sold for as little as $1. Many other conventional mines sell for less than $10 but some improved types can cost hundreds of dollars.[21]

According to the President's draft, mines whose use is to be prohibited would also be prohibited from being transferred to any recipient, while for mines whose use is to be restricted the parties would be required to exercise 'restraint' in their transfer. In particular, anti-personnel mines would not be permitted to be transferred to states not bound by Protocol II unless the recipient applied the protocol, took steps to adhere to it in accordance with the article requiring detectability and so notified the Depositary of the Convention. No mines would be transferred to any recipient other than a state or its agent or agencies.

The provisions of the President's draft would not significantly reduce the availability of anti-personnel land-mines if technically less developed countries were supplied with 'safer' models. They could lead to the resumption of exports by states that have proclaimed moratoria on transfer.[22] (As of March 1996 over 30 countries had declared moratoria, most of which are either

---

[19] Mine clearance is distinct from mine breaching. The former aims to rid an entire area of mines as effectively as possible, while the latter aims to clear a path for troops or vehicles through a minefield.

[20] Information provided by the ICRC.

[21] Goose, S., *Antipersonnel Landmine Producers and Exporters* (Human Rights Watch Arms Project: New York, Sep. 1995).

[22] The 1995 UN General Assembly urged states that have not yet done so to declare moratoria on the export of anti-personnel land-mines. See UN document A/RES/50/70, 12 Dec. 1995.

limited in time or qualified.[23]) In the longer run, only an internationally binding prohibition on all transfer of anti-personnel mines can be durable.

Consultation and compliance

The President's draft proposes that the parties pledge to consult and cooperate with each other on all issues related to the functioning of Protocol II. To this end conferences would be held on an annual basis in addition to periodic review conferences of the CCW Convention.

The provisions of the 1949 Geneva Conventions[24] on the protection of victims of war relating to measures for the suppression of breaches would apply to Protocol II. Each party would have to take appropriate measures to prevent and suppress any breaches, and an act committed 'wilfully or wantonly' and causing death or serious injury to the civilian population would be treated as a grave breach. However, no international mechanism is envisaged to determine whether the provisions of Protocol II have been violated and, if so, by whom. China, India and Pakistan, for example, are opposed to the establishment of such a mechanism. Lack of procedures to verify compliance with the assumed obligations could reduce the effectiveness of the adopted rules.

Scope of application

The applicability of the revised Protocol II to non-international armed conflicts remains to be formally agreed. The matter is important because most armed conflicts in recent years have been intra-state,[25] and it is in such conflicts that most mines are laid. According to existing humanitarian law non-international armed conflicts are those which occur between the armed forces of a state and dissident armed forces or other organized armed groups which, under responsible command, 'exercise such control over a part of the state's territory as to enable them to carry out sustained and concerted operations'.[26] This definition, formulated many years ago, appears too narrow in the light of recent conflicts, in particular those in Somalia and the former Yugoslavia.

Summary

The most effective way to deal with the danger posed by anti-personnel land-mines is to prohibit—not restrict or regulate—their production, stockpiling, transfer and use, and to establish international control over compliance with

[23] Certain countries renounced the use and/or further production of anti-personnel land-mines. See ICRC information sheet EAA/6, Dec. 1995; *CCW News*, 15 Jan. 1996; and *New York Times*, 17 Mar. 1996.
[24] Schindler, D. and Toman, J., *The Laws of Armed Conflicts* (Martinus Nijhoffs: Dordrecht, the Netherlands, 1988), pp. 367–594.
[25] See also chapter 1 in this volume.
[26] The 1977 Protocol Additional to the Geneva Conventions of 12 Aug. 1949, and Relating to the Protection of Victims of Non-International Armed Conflicts (Protocol II), Article 1, reproduced in ICRC, *Protocols Additional to the Geneva Conventions of 12 August 1949* (ICRC: Geneva, 1977), pp. 90–101.

the prohibition. A complete ban would be more easily verifiable than partial solutions.

The suggested changes in the construction of mines could create a new, lucrative division of the arms industry and increase the trade in arms, but they would not address the central issue of the use of these inhumane weapons. Many governments are unable or unwilling to make anti-personnel mines detectable, self-destructing and self-deactivating; this may be because of the costs involved, which may be prohibitive, or for security reasons. Those governments which are prepared to do so may be tempted in time of armed conflict to use the new types of mine in greater numbers than the old ones to compensate for a possible loss of effectiveness caused by facilitated clearing, self-destruction and self-deactivation.

It is unlikely that the radical measures suggested above will be agreed at the current CCW Convention Review Conference. Amendments to the protocols of the convention must be adopted, as was the convention itself, by consensus. However, consensus among the parties on the prohibition of all anti-personnel land-mines appears unattainable. If a total ban were to be negotiated, a special diplomatic conference would need to be convened, independent from the CCW Convention Review Conference and open to all states—both parties and non-parties to the current convention. Its participants could then draft and possibly adopt by a majority decision, rather than by consensus, a comprehensive treaty, separate from the CCW Convention. The initiative to convene such a conference might be taken by a group of states which have stated that they favour the elimination of anti-personnel land-mines.[27]

III. Blinding laser weapons

Main provisions of Protocol IV

On 13 October 1995, the Review Conference of the CCW Convention decided to annex a Protocol on Blinding Laser Weapons to the CCW Convention as Protocol IV.[28] The protocol prohibits the use of laser weapons that are specifically designed to cause permanent blindness to unenhanced vision (i.e., to the naked eye or to the eye with corrective eyesight devices such as prescription glasses or contact lenses).

The term 'weapons specifically designed' means those weapons having as their sole combat function, or as one of their combat functions, to cause permanent blindness (Article 1). 'Permanent blindness' is defined as irreversible loss of vision that cannot be corrected and which is seriously disabling with no prospect of recovery (Article 4). 'Serious disability' is described as visual acuity of less than '20/200 Snellen' measured using both eyes (Article 4). This

---

[27] This group includes Austria, Belgium, Canada, Colombia, Denmark, Estonia, Mexico, the Netherlands, New Zealand, Norway, the Philippines, Slovenia, South Africa, Sweden and Switzerland. Among US politicians and high-ranking military officers there is also growing support for the outlawing of anti-personnel mines. See *International Herald Tribune,* 18 Mar. 1996.

[28] CCW Convention Review Conference document CCW/CONF.I/7, 12 Oct. 1995. The text of Protocol IV is reproduced as appendix 17A in this volume.

means that a disabled person cannot see at 20 feet (approximately 6 m) what a person with normal vision can see at 200 feet (approximately 60 m).[29] This language was introduced into the text of Protocol IV on the insistence of the US Delegation. It would seem redundant unless the intent were to legitimize the production of lasers which cause damage to eyesight below a specified (although uncontrollable) threshold, but this does not appear to be the case.[30] The United Kingdom stated that it did not possess and 'currently' had no plans to develop or procure any laser weapon designed to blind enemy troops permanently or 'to disrupt' their eyesight temporarily.[31]

Protocol IV forbids the transfer of blinding laser weapons to any recipient. Blinding as an incidental or collateral effect of military use of other laser systems, including lasers used against optical equipment, is exempt from the prohibition.

Assessment of Protocol IV

Although the military utility of blinding laser weapons is limited, the adoption of Protocol IV of the CCW Convention was an important achievement. Blinding is a particularly abhorrent way of wounding the enemy and is more debilitating than most battlefield injuries because sight provides 80–90 per cent of a person's sensory stimulation.[32] Protection against the threat of blinding laser weapons is virtually impossible.[33] Blinding cannot be considered a military necessity and belongs to that category of generally condemned methods of warfare which cause superfluous injury or unnecessary suffering and which must be expressly prohibited by international law.

For the first time since the 1868 Declaration of St Petersburg[34] (which prohibited the employment of projectiles of a given weight that are explosive or charged with 'fulminating' or inflammable substances) a new weapon, developed and reportedly also tested,[35] has been prohibited before being used on the

---

[29] As regards the term 'permanent', some experts argue that it is impossible to design a laser that can blind only temporarily. Lasers that might only dazzle at the far range of their beam could blind at closer distance. See ICRC, *Blinding Weapons: Reports of the Meetings of Experts Convened by the International Committee of the Red Cross on Battlefield Laser Weapons, 1989–1991* (ICRC: Geneva, 1993), p. 339. In a number of countries 'blindness' is defined as a visual acuity corresponding to less than 10% of normal vision, but this definition is applied only for rehabilitation purposes. (Oral communication from the World Health Organization.)

[30] Reportedly, there is little support among senior US military officers for the military utility of blinding. See Graham, B., 'Pentagon, in a shift, outlaws lasers used to blind enemy', *International Herald Tribune*, 21 Sep. 1995.

[31] House of Commons, *Official Report* (Her Majesty's Stationery Office: London, 19 Jan. 1995).

[32] See *Blinding Weapons* (note 29), p. 336.

[33] Existing protective goggles shield only against laser beams of known wavelengths. Full protection would require goggles which block out all wavelengths and thereby deprive the protected person of the ability to see. See *Human Rights Watch Arms Project*, vol. 7, no. 1 (Sep. 1995); and ICRC paper DDM/JUR.PH. LDB, 16 Nov. 1994.

[34] See Goldblat (note 1), pp. 120–21.

[35] According to press reports, the China North Industries Corporation exhibited a weapon described as a 'laser interference device' at arms exhibitions in Manila and Abu Dhabi, and advertised one of its major applications as injuring eyesight. See *International Defense Review*, vol. 28 (May 1995); *Jane's Pointer*, vol. 2, no. 6 (June 1995); and *Military Technology*, vol. 19, issue 5 (May 1995). The USA field-tested prototypes of various laser-weapon systems. In Aug. 1995 the US Army signed a contract for the

battlefield. It is also the first time that both the use and the transfer of a specific weapon has been banned by the international humanitarian law of armed conflict.

Protocol IV does, however, have several weaknesses. The production of blinding laser weapons has not been outlawed, and the blinding of persons using optical devices has not been banned. Such devices, including binoculars, magnify the intensity of the laser beam and increase the potential for blindness. For example, a member of a tank crew who was looking through a periscope could be permanently blinded by an anti-*matériel* laser that has been designed mainly to destroy or damage optical devices.

The parties are required to take all feasible precautions—which should include training of the military and other 'practical measures'—to avoid causing blindness with laser systems other than those specifically designed to inflict damage to vision. However, the term 'feasible' can lend itself to different interpretations. The relevant paragraph of Protocol IV might better have unequivocally established the rule that blinding as a method of warfare is prohibited. Such wording would have banned all practices that are intended or which can be expected to cause blindness. An exception for laser systems for targeting and range-finding purposes could be justified if blindness caused by them was not intentional. Laser systems aimed at destroying optical equipment can hardly be considered legitimate, because they are expected to destroy human eyesight in most cases, unless and until effective means are universally used as standard equipment to prevent such injuries.[36]

Differentiation between intentional and accidental blinding with laser weapons may be difficult, but this should not be impossible if a consistent pattern of violations were discerned. In the event of suspicion, an international enquiry including a fact-finding mission could be conducted. Unfortunately, Protocol IV provides no verification measures.

Protocol IV applies only to international armed conflicts. The proposal for extending its scope to cover non-international armed conflicts received general support but was not included in the final draft.[37]

Protocol IV will enter into force in accordance with Article 5 of the Convention six months after the date on which 20 states have notified their consent to be bound by it. For states which notify their consent to be bound by Protocol IV after that date, the protocol will enter into force six months after the

production of its most advanced portable laser-weapon system, the so-called Laser Countermeasure System, which subsequently was cancelled. See Graham, B., 'Army laser weapon becomes first casualty of new policy', *Washington Post*, 13 Oct. 1995. Other nations alleged to have laser-weapon programmes include France, Germany, Israel, Russia and the UK. See Human Rights Watch, *US Blinding Laser Weapons* (Human Rights Watch: New York, 21 May 1995).

[36] By using indirect viewing mechanisms, the operators of electro-optical devices could protect themselves from the blinding effects of anti-*matériel* lasers, but such mechanisms are not widely available. The user of a laser against optical equipment must therefore assume that he may blind personnel operating such equipment.

[37] According to an informal understanding reached in Vienna, the wording of any future agreement extending the scope of the laser protocol to non-international armed conflicts would be the same as that to be adopted for the land-mines protocol. This understanding was reaffirmed by 135 states in a resolution passed at the International Conference of the Red Cross and the Red Crescent, held in Dec. 1995 in Geneva.

date of notification. Several delegations to the Review Conference suggested that the six-month requirement be dropped so that Protocol IV might enter into force without delay, but such a change would require an amendment to the CCW Convention. On 12 December 1995, the UN General Assembly commended Protocol IV to all states, with a view to achieving the widest possible adherence to this instrument 'at an early date'.[38]

---

[38] UN document A/RES/50/74, 10 Jan. 1996.

Appendix 17A. Protocol IV to the Inhumane Weapons Convention

ADDITIONAL PROTOCOL TO THE CONVENTION ON PROHIBITIONS OR RESTRICTIONS ON THE USE OF CERTAIN CONVENTIONAL WEAPONS WHICH MAY BE DEEMED TO BE EXCESSIVELY INJURIOUS OR TO HAVE INDISCRIMINATE EFFECTS

Adopted in Vienna, 12 October 1995

ARTICLE 1. ADDITIONAL PROTOCOL

The following protocol shall be annexed to the Convention on Prohibitions or Restrictions on the Use of Certain Conventional Weapons Which May Be Deemed to Be Excessively Injurious or to Have Indiscriminate Effects ('the Convention') as Protocol IV:

Protocol on Blinding Laser Weapons (Protocol IV)

Article 1

It is prohibited to employ laser weapons specifically designed, as their sole combat function or as one of their combat functions, to cause permanent blindness to unenhanced vision, that is to the naked eye or to the eye with corrective eyesight devices. The High Contracting Parties shall not transfer such weapons to any State or non-State entity.

Article 2

In the employment of laser systems, the High Contracting Parties shall take all feasible precautions to avoid the incidence of permanent blindness to unenhanced vision. Such precautions shall include training of their armed forces and other practical measures.

Article 3

Blinding as an incidental or collateral effect of the legitimate military employment of laser systems, including laser systems used against optical equipment, is not covered by the prohibition of this Protocol.

Article 4

For the purpose of this Protocol 'permanent blindness' means irreversible and uncorrectable loss of vision which is seriously disabling with no prospect of recovery. Serious disability is equivalent to visual acuity of less than 20/200 Snellen measured using both eyes.

ARTICLE 2. ENTRY INTO FORCE

This Protocol shall enter into force as provided in paragraphs 3 and 4 of Article 5 of the Convention.

Source: CCW document CCW/CONF.I/7, 12 Oct. 1995.

Annexes

Annexe A. Arms control and disarmament agreements

Annexe B. Chronology 1995

Annexe A. Arms control and disarmament agreements

RAGNHILD FERM

I. Summaries and status of the major multilateral arms control agreements, as of 1 January 1996

Notes

1. The agreements are listed below in the order of the date on which they were signed or adopted; the date on which they entered into force is also given.

2. The Russian Federation, constituted in 1991 as an independent sovereign state, has confirmed the continuity of international obligations assumed by the Soviet Union. The other former Soviet republics which were constituted in 1991 as independent sovereign states have subsequently signed, ratifed, acceded or succeeded to agreements in order to become signatories/parties.

3. The Federal Republic of Germany and the German Democratic Republic merged into one state in 1990. All agreements to which the Federal Republic of Germany (West Germany) was a party are in force for the united Germany.

4. The Yemen Arab Republic and the People's Democratic Republic of Yemen merged into one state in 1990. According to a statement by the united Yemen state, all agreements which either state has entered into are in force for Yemen.

5. Czechoslovakia split into two states, the Czech Republic and Slovakia, in 1993. Both states have succeeded to all agreements to which Czechoslovakia was a party.

6. The Federal Republic of Yugoslavia split into several separate states in 1991–92. The international legal status of what remains of the former Yugoslavia—Yugoslavia (Serbia and Montenegro)—is ambiguous, but since it considers that it is the same entity the name 'Yugoslavia' remains in these lists. (The former Yugoslav republics of Bosnia and Herzegovina, Croatia, Macedonia and Slovenia have succeeded, as independent states, to several agreements.)

7. Taiwan, while not recognized as a sovereign state by some nations, is listed as a party to those agreements which it has signed and ratified.

8. Unless otherwise stated, the treaties in this annexe are open to all states for signature, ratification, accession or succession.

9. For a few major treaties, the substantive parts of the most important reservations and/or declarations are given in footnotes below the list of parties. For fuller declarations and/or reservations, see *SIPRI Yearbook 1995*, annexe A.

10. A complete list of UN member states and year of membership appears in the glossary at the front of this volume. Not all the parties listed in this annexe are UN member states.

Protocol for the prohibition of the use in war of asphyxiating, poisonous or other gases, and of bacteriological methods of warfare (Geneva Protocol)

Signed at Geneva on 17 June 1925; entered into force on 8 February 1928.

The protocol declares that the parties agree to be bound by the prohibition, which should be universally accepted as part of international law.

Parties (132): Afghanistan, Albania, Algeria, Angola,[1] Antigua and Barbuda, Argentina, Australia, Austria, Bahrain,[1] Bangladesh,[1] Barbados, Belarus, Belgium,[1] Benin, Bhutan, Bolivia, Brazil, Bulgaria, Burkina Faso, Cambodia, Cameroon, Canada,[1] Cape Verde, Central African Republic, Chile, China,[1] Côte d'Ivoire, Cuba, Cyprus, Czech Republic, Denmark, Dominican Republic, Ecuador, Egypt, Equatorial Guinea, Estonia, Ethiopia, Fiji,[1] Finland, France,[1] Gambia, Germany, Ghana, Greece, Grenada, Guatemala, Guinea-Bissau, Holy See, Hungary, Iceland, India, Indonesia, Iran, Iraq,[1] Ireland, Israel,[2] Italy, Jamaica, Japan, Jordan,[3] Kenya, Korea (North),[1] Korea (South),[1] Kuwait,[1] Laos, Latvia, Lebanon, Lesotho, Liberia, Libya,[1] Liechtenstein, Lithuania, Luxembourg, Madagascar, Malawi, Malaysia, Maldives, Malta, Mauritius, Mexico, Monaco, Mongolia, Morocco, Nepal, Netherlands,[4] New Zealand, Nicaragua, Niger, Nigeria,[1] Norway, Pakistan, Panama, Papua New Guinea,[1] Paraguay, Peru, Philippines, Poland, Portugal,[1] Qatar, Romania, Russia,[4] Rwanda, Saint Kitts (Christopher) and Nevis, Saint Lucia, Saudi Arabia, Senegal, Sierra Leone, Slovakia, Solomon Islands, South Africa,[1] Spain, Sri Lanka, Sudan, Swaziland, Sweden, Switzerland, Syria, Tanzania, Thailand, Togo, Tonga, Trinidad and Tobago, Tunisia, Turkey, Uganda, UK, Uruguay, USA,[4] Venezuela, Viet Nam,[1] Yemen, Yugoslavia

[1] The protocol is binding on this state only as regards states which have signed and ratified or acceded to it. The protocol will cease to be binding on this state in regard to any enemy state whose armed forces or whose allies fail to respect the prohibitions laid down in it.

[2] The protocol is binding on Israel only as regards states which have signed and ratified or acceded to it. The protocol shall cease to be binding on Israel as regards any enemy state whose armed forces, or the armed forces of whose allies, or the regular or irregular forces, or groups or individuals operating from its territory, fail to respect the prohibitions which are the object of the protocol.

[3] Jordan undertakes to respect the obligations contained in the protocol with regard to states which have undertaken similar commitments. It is not bound by the protocol as regards states whose armed forces, regular or irregular, do not respect the provisions of the protocol.

[4] The protocol shall cease to be binding on this state with respect to use in war of asphyxiating, poisonous or other gases, and of all analogous liquids, materials or devices, in regard to any enemy state if such state or any of its allies fail to respect the prohibitions laid down in the protocol.

Signed but not ratified: El Salvador

Treaty for collaboration in economic social and cultural matters and for collective self-defence (Brussels Treaty)

Signed at Brussels on 17 March 1948; entered into force on 25 August 1948.

The treaty provides for close cooperation of the parties in the military, economic and political fields.

Original parties (5): Belgium, France, Luxembourg, Netherlands, UK

Accessions (2): Germany, Italy

See also the Protocols of 1954.

Convention on the prevention and punishment of the crime of genocide (Genocide Convention)

Adopted at Paris by the UN General Assembly on 9 December 1948; entered into force on 12 January 1951.

Under the convention any commission of acts intended to destroy, in whole or in part, a national, ethnic, racial or religious group as such is declared to be a crime punishable under international law.

Parties (121): Afghanistan, Albania,* Algeria,* Antigua and Barbuda, Argentina,* Armenia, Australia, Austria, Bahamas, Bahrain,* Barbados, Belarus,* Belgium, Bosnia and Herzegovina, Brazil, Bulgaria,* Burkina Faso, Cambodia, Canada, Chile, China,* Colombia, Costa Rica, Côte d'Ivoire, Croatia, Cuba, Cyprus, Czech Republic, Denmark, Ecuador, Egypt, El Salvador, Estonia, Ethiopia, Fiji, Finland,* France, Gabon, Gambia, Georgia, Germany, Ghana, Greece, Guatemala, Haiti, Honduras, Hungary,* Iceland, India,* Iran, Iraq, Ireland, Israel, Italy, Jamaica, Jordan, Korea (North), Korea (South), Kuwait, Laos, Latvia, Lebanon, Lesotho, Liberia, Libya, Liechtenstein, Luxembourg, Macedonia (Former Yugoslav Republic of), Malaysia,* Maldives, Mali, Mexico, Moldova, Monaco, Mongolia,* Morocco,* Mozambique, Myanmar (Burma), Namibia,* Nepal, Netherlands, New Zealand, Nicaragua, Norway, Pakistan, Panama, Papua New Guinea, Peru, Philippines,* Poland,* Romania,* Russia,* Rwanda,* Saint Vincent and the Grenadines, Saudi Arabia, Senegal, Seychelles, Singapore,* Slovakia, Slovenia, Spain,* Sri Lanka, Sweden, Syria, Taiwan, Tanzania, Togo, Tonga, Tunisia, Turkey, Uganda, UK, Ukraine,* Uruguay, USA,* Venezuela,* Viet Nam,* Yemen,* Yugoslavia, Zaire, Zimbabwe

*With reservation and/or declaration upon ratificaton, accession or succession.

Signed but not ratified: Bolivia, Dominican Republic, Paraguay

Geneva Convention (IV) relative to the protection of civilian persons in time of war

Signed at Geneva on 12 August 1949; entered into force on 21 October 1950.

The convention establishes rules for the protection of civilians in areas covered by war and on occupied territories.

Parties (186): Afghanistan, Albania,* Algeria, Andorra, Angola,* Antigua and Barbuda, Argentina, Armenia, Australia,* Austria, Azerbaijan, Bahamas, Bahrain, Bangladesh, Barbados,* Belarus,* Belgium, Belize, Benin, Bhutan, Bolivia, Bosnia and Herzegovina, Botswana, Brazil, Brunei, Bulgaria,* Burkina Faso, Burundi, Cambodia, Cameroon, Canada, Cape Verde, Central African Republic, Chad, Chile, China,* Colombia, Comoros, Congo, Costa Rica, Côte d'Ivoire, Croatia, Cuba, Cyprus, Czech Republic,* Denmark, Djibouti, Dominica, Dominican Republic, Ecuador, Egypt, El Salvador, Equatorial Guinea, Estonia, Ethiopia, Fiji, Finland, France, Gabon, Gambia, Georgia, Germany,* Ghana, Greece, Grenada, Guatemala, Guinea, Guinea-Bissau,* Guyana, Haiti, Holy See, Honduras, Hungary,* Iceland, India, Indonesia, Iran,*Iraq, Ireland, Israel,* Italy, Jamaica, Japan, Jordan, Kazakhstan, Kenya, Kiribati, Korea (North),* Korea (South),* Kuwait,* Kyrgyzstan, Laos, Latvia, Lebanon, Lesotho, Liberia, Libya, Liechtenstein, Luxembourg, Macedonia (Former Yugoslav Republic of), Madagascar, Malawi, Malaysia, Maldives, Mali, Malta, Mauritania, Mauritius, Mexico, Micronesia,[1] Moldova, Monaco, Mongolia, Morocco, Mozambique, Myanmar (Burma), Namibia, Nepal, Netherlands, New Zealand, Nicaragua, Niger, Nigeria, Norway, Oman, Pakistan,* Panama, Papua New Guinea, Paraguay, Peru, Philippines, Poland,* Portugal,* Qatar, Romania,* Russia,* Rwanda, Saint Kitts (Christopher) and Nevis, Saint Lucia, Saint Vincent and the Grenadines, Samoa (Western), San Marino, Sao Tome and Principe, Saudi Arabia, Senegal,

Seychelles, Sierra Leone, Singapore,* Slovakia,* Slovenia, Solomon Islands, Somalia, South Africa, Spain, Sri Lanka, Sudan, Suriname,* Swaziland, Sweden, Switzerland, Syria, Tajikistan, Tanzania, Thailand, Togo, Tonga, Trinidad and Tobago, Tunisia, Turkey, Turkmenistan, Tuvalu, Uganda, UK, Ukraine,* United Arab Emirates, Uruguay,* USA,* Uzbekistan, Vanuatu, Venezuela, Viet Nam,* Yemen,* Yugoslavia,* Zaire, Zambia, Zimbabwe

* With reservation and/or declaration upon ratification, accession or succession.

[1] According to the provisions of Article 153, the convention shall come into force six months after the deposit of the instrument of ratification. This state ratified the convention in the second half of 1995 and the convention entered into force for that state in 1996.

Protocols to the 1948 Brussels Treaty (Paris Agreements on the Western European Union)

Signed at Paris on 23 October 1954; entered into force on 6 May 1955.

The protocols modify the 1948 Brussels Treaty, allowing the Federal Republic of Germany and Italy to become parties in return for controls over German armaments and force levels (annulled, except for weapons of mass destruction, in 1984). The Protocols to the Brussels Treaty are regarded as having created the Western European Union (WEU). (Portugal and Spain became members of the WEU in 1988 and Greece in 1994.)

Antarctic Treaty

Signed at Washington, DC, on 1 December 1959; entered into force on 23 June 1961.

Declares the Antarctic an area to be used exclusively for peaceful purposes. Prohibits any measure of a military nature in the Antarctic, such as the establishment of military bases and fortifications, and the carrying out of military manoeuvres or the testing of any type of weapon. The treaty bans any nuclear explosion as well as the disposal of radioactive waste material in Antarctica, subject to possible future international agreements on these subjects.

In accordance with Article IX, consultative meetings are convened at regular intervals to exchange information and hold consultations on matters pertaining to Antarctica, as well as to recommend to the governments measures in furtherance of the principles and objectives of the treaty.

The treaty is subject to ratification by the signatories and is open for accession by UN members or by other states invited to accede with the consent of all the contracting parties whose representatives are entitled to participate in the consultative meeting provided for in Article IX.

Parties (42): Argentina,[†] Australia,[†] Austria, Belgium,[†] Brazil,[†] Bulgaria, Canada, Chile,[†] China,[†] Colombia, Cuba, Czech Republic, Denmark, Ecuador,[†] Finland,[†] France,[†] Germany,[†] Greece, Guatemala, Hungary, India,[†] Italy,[†] Japan,[†] Korea (North), Korea (South),[†] Netherlands,[†] New Zealand,[†] Norway,[†] Papua New Guinea, Peru,[†] Poland,[†] Romania,* Russia,[†] Slovakia, South Africa,[†] Spain,[†] Sweden,[†] Switzerland, UK,[†] Ukraine, Uruguay,*[†] USA[†]

Note: Turkey acceded on 24 January 1996.

* With reservation and/or declaration upon ratification, accession or succession.

[†] Party entitled to participate in the consultative meetings.

The Protocol on Environmental Protection to the Antarctic Treaty (Madrid Protocol) was signed in 1991. Not in force as of 1 April 1996.

Treaty banning nuclear weapon tests in the atmosphere, in outer space and under water (Partial Test Ban Treaty, PTBT)

Signed at Moscow on 5 August 1963; entered into force on 10 October 1963.

Prohibits the carrying out of any nuclear weapon test explosion or any other nuclear explosion: (*a*) in the atmosphere, beyond its limits, including outer space, or under water, including territorial waters or high seas; and (*b*) in any other environment if such explosion causes radioactive debris to be present outside the territorial limits of the state under whose jurisdiction or control the explosion is conducted.

Parties (124): Afghanistan, Antigua and Barbuda, Argentina, Armenia, Australia, Austria, Bahamas, Bangladesh, Belarus, Belgium, Benin, Bhutan, Bolivia, Botswana, Brazil, Bulgaria, Canada, Cape Verde, Central African Republic, Chad, Chile, Colombia, Costa Rica, Côte d'Ivoire, Croatia, Cyprus, Czech Republic, Denmark, Dominican Republic, Ecuador, Egypt, El Salvador, Equatorial Guinea, Fiji, Finland, Gabon, Gambia, Germany, Ghana, Greece, Guatemala, Guinea-Bissau, Honduras, Hungary, Iceland, India, Indonesia, Iran, Iraq, Ireland, Israel, Italy, Jamaica, Japan, Jordan, Kenya, Korea (South), Kuwait, Laos, Lebanon, Liberia, Libya, Luxembourg, Madagascar, Malawi, Malaysia, Malta, Mauritania, Mauritius, Mexico, Mongolia, Morocco, Myanmar (Burma), Nepal, Netherlands, New Zealand, Nicaragua, Niger, Nigeria, Norway, Pakistan, Panama, Papua New Guinea, Peru, Philippines, Poland, Romania, Russia, Rwanda, Samoa (Western), San Marino, Senegal, Seychelles, Sierra Leone, Singapore, Slovakia, Slovenia, South Africa, Spain, Sri Lanka, Sudan, Suriname, Swaziland, Sweden, Switzerland, Syria, Taiwan, Tanzania, Thailand, Togo, Tonga, Trinidad and Tobago, Tunisia, Turkey, Uganda, UK, Ukraine, Uruguay, USA, Venezuela, Yemen, Yugoslavia, Zaire, Zambia

Signed but not ratified: Algeria, Burkina Faso, Burundi, Cameroon, Ethiopia, Haiti, Mali, Paraguay, Portugal, Somalia

Treaty on principles governing the activities of states in the exploration and use of outer space, including the moon and other celestial bodies (Outer Space Treaty)

Signed at London, Moscow and Washington, DC, on 27 January 1967; entered into force on 10 October 1967.

Prohibits the placing into orbit around the earth of any objects carrying nuclear weapons or any other kinds of weapons of mass destruction, the installation of such weapons on celestial bodies, or the stationing of them in outer space in any other manner. The establishment of military bases, installations and fortifications, the testing of any type of weapons and the conduct of military manoeuvres on celestial bodies are also forbidden.

Parties (94): Afghanistan, Algeria, Antigua and Barbuda, Argentina, Australia, Austria, Bahamas, Bangladesh, Barbados, Belarus, Belgium, Benin, Brazil,* Bulgaria, Burkina Faso, Canada, Chile, China, Cuba, Cyprus, Czech Republic, Denmark, Dominican Republic, Ecuador, Egypt, El Salvador, Equatorial Guinea, Fiji, Finland, France, Germany, Greece, Guinea-Bissau, Hungary, Iceland, India, Iraq, Ireland, Israel, Italy, Jamaica, Japan, Kenya, Korea (South), Kuwait, Laos, Lebanon, Libya, Madagascar,* Mali, Mauritius, Mexico, Mongolia, Morocco, Myanmar (Burma), Nepal, Netherlands, New Zealand, Niger, Nigeria, Norway, Pakistan, Papua New Guinea, Peru, Poland, Romania, Russia, San Marino, Saudi Arabia, Seychelles, Sierra Leone, Singapore, Slovakia, South Africa, Spain, Sri Lanka, Sweden, Switzerland, Syria, Taiwan, Thailand, Togo, Tonga, Tunisia, Turkey, Uganda, UK, Ukraine, Uruguay, USA, Venezuela, Viet Nam, Yemen, Zambia

* With reservation and/or declaration upon ratification, accession or succession.

Signed but not ratified: Bolivia, Botswana, Burundi, Cameroon, Central African Republic, Colombia, Ethiopia, Gambia, Ghana, Guyana, Haiti, Holy See, Honduras, Indonesia, Iran, Jordan, Lesotho, Luxembourg, Malaysia, Nicaragua, Panama, Philippines, Rwanda, Somalia, Trinidad and Tobago, Yugoslavia, Zaire

Treaty for the prohibition of nuclear weapons in Latin America and the Caribbean (Treaty of Tlatelolco)

Signed at Mexico, Distrito Federal, on 14 February 1967; entered into force on 22 April 1968. The treaty was modified and amended in 1990, 1991 and 1992.

Prohibits the testing, use, manufacture, production or acquisition by any means, as well as the receipt, storage, installation, deployment and any form of possession of any nuclear weapons by Latin American countries.

The parties should conclude agreements with the IAEA for the application of safeguards to their nuclear activities.

Under *Additional Protocol I* the extra-continental or continental states which, *de jure* or *de facto*, are internationally responsible for territories lying within the limits of the geographical zone established by the treaty (France, the Netherlands, the UK and the USA) undertake to apply the statute of military denuclearization, as defined in the treaty, to such territories.

Under *Additional Protocol II* the nuclear weapon states—China, France, Russia (at the time of signing, the USSR), the UK and the USA—undertake to respect the statute of military denuclearization of Latin America, as defined and delimited in the treaty, and not to contribute to acts involving a violation of the treaty, nor to use or threaten to use nuclear weapons against the parties to the treaty.

The treaty is open for signature by all the Latin American republics, all other sovereign states situated in their entirety south of latitude 35⁰ north in the western hemisphere, and (except for a political entity the territory of which is the subject of an international dispute) all such states which become sovereign, when they have been admitted by the OPANAL General Conference. Additional Protocol I is open to France, the Netherlands, the UK and the USA; and Additional Protocol II to China, France, Russia (at the time of signing the USSR), the UK and the USA.

Parties to the original treaty (30) (Not all the parties have signed and ratified the amendments): Antigua and Barbuda,[1] Argentina, Bahamas,[1] Barbados,[1] Belize,[1] Bolivia,[1] Brazil,[1,2] Chile,[1†] Colombia,[1†] Costa Rica,[1†] Dominica, Dominican Republic,[1†] Ecuador,[1†] El Salvador,[1†] Grenada,[1] Guatemala,[1†] Haiti,[1] Honduras,[1†] Jamaica,[1†] Mexico,[1†] Nicaragua,[1,2†] Panama,[1†] Paraguay,[1†] Peru,[1†] Saint Lucia, Saint Vincent and the Grenadines, Suriname,[1†] Trinidad and Tobago,[1†] Uruguay,[†] Venezuela[1†]

Parties to Additional Protocol I: France,[4] Netherlands,[†] UK,[5] USA[6†]

Parties to Additional Protocol II: China,[7] France,[8] Russia,[9] UK,[5] USA[10]

† Parties with safeguards agreements in force with the International Atomic Energy Agency (IAEA).

Ratified but not in force as of 1 January 1996: Guyana, Saint Kitts (Christopher) and Nevis

Signed but not ratified: Cuba

[1] The treaty is in force for this country in accordance with Article 28 (Article 29 of the amended Treaty), which waived the requirements for the entry into force of the treaty, specified in that article.

[2] Brazil stated that, according to its interpretation, the treaty gives the signatories the right to carry out, by their own means or in association with third parties, nuclear explosions for peaceful purposes, including explosions which involve devices similar to those used in nuclear weapons.

[3] Nicaragua stated that it reserved the right to use nuclear energy for peaceful purposes such as the removal of earth for the construction of canals, irrigation works, power plants, and so on, as well as to allow the transit of atomic material through its territory.

[4] France declared that Protocol I shall not apply to transit across French territories situated within the zone of the treaty, and destined for other French territories. The protocol shall not limit the participation of the populations of the French territories in the activities mentioned in Article 1 of the treaty, and in efforts connected with the national defence of France. France does not consider the zone described in the treaty as established in accordance with international law; it cannot, therefore, agree that the treaty should apply to that zone.

[5] When signing and ratifiying Protocols I and II, the UK made the following declarations of understanding: The treaty does not permit the parties to carry out nuclear explosions for peaceful purposes unless and until advances in technology have made possible the development of devices for such explosions which are not capable of being used for weapon purposes. The signing and ratification by the UK could not be regarded as affecting in any way the legal status of any territory for the international relations of which the UK is responsible, lying within the limits of the geographical zone established by the treaty. Should any party to the treaty carry out any act of aggression with the support of a nuclear weapon state, the UK would be free to reconsider the extent to which it could be regarded as bound by the provisions of Protocol II.

[6] The USA ratified Protocol I with the following understandings: The provisions of the treaty do not affect the exclusive power and legal competence under international law of a state adhering to this Protocol to grant or deny transit and transport privileges to its own or any other vessels or aircraft irrespective of cargo or armaments; the provisions do not affect rights under international law of a state adhering to this protocol regarding the exercise of the freedom of the seas, or regarding passage through or over waters subject to the sovereignty of a state. The declarations attached by the USA to its ratification of Protocol II apply also to Protocol I.

[7] China declared that it will never send its means of transportation and delivery carrying nuclear weapons to cross the territory, territorial sea or airspace of Latin American countries.

[8] France stated that it interprets the undertaking contained in Article 3 of Protocol II to mean that it presents no obstacle to the full exercise of the right of self-defence enshrined in Article 51 of the UN Charter; it takes note of the interpretation by the Preparatory Commission for the Denuclearization of Latin America according to which the treaty does not apply to transit, the granting or denying of which lies within the exclusive competence of each state party in accordance with international law. In 1974, France made a supplementary statement to the effect that it was prepared to consider its obligations under Protocol II as applying not only to the signatories of the treaty, but also to the territories for which the statute of denuclearization was in force in conformity with Protocol I.

[9] The USSR signed and ratified Protocol II with the following statement:
The USSR proceeds from the assumption that the effect of Article 1 of the treaty extends to any nuclear explosive device and that, accordingly, the carrying out by any party of nuclear explosions for peaceful purposes would be a violation of its obligations under Article 1 and would be incompatible with its non-nuclear weapon status. For states parties to the treaty, a solution to the problem of peaceful nuclear explosions can be found in accordance with the provisions of Article V of the NPT and within the framework of the international procedures of the IAEA. The USSR declares that authorizing the transit of nuclear weapons in any form would be contrary to the objectives of the treaty.

Any actions undertaken by a state or states parties to the treaty which are not compatible with their non-nuclear weapon status, and also the commission by one or more states parties to the treaty of an act of aggression with the support of a state which is in possession of nuclear weapons or together with such a state, will be regarded by the USSR as incompatible with the obligations of those countries under the treaty. In such cases the USSR reserves the right to reconsider its obligations under Protocol II. It further reserves the right to reconsider its attitude to this protocol in the event of any actions on the part of other states possessing nuclear weapons which are incompatible with their obligations under the said protocol.

[10] The USA signed and ratified Protocol II with the following declarations and understandings: Each of the parties retains exclusive power and legal competence, to grant or deny non-parties transit and transport privileges. As regards the undertaking not to use or threaten to use nuclear weapons against the parties, the USA would consider that an armed attack by a party, in which it was assisted by a nuclear weapon state, would be incompatible with the treaty. Article 18, para. 4 permits, and US adherence to Protocol II will not prevent, collaboration by the USA with the parties to the treaty for the purpose of carrying out explosions of nuclear devices for peaceful purposes in a manner consistent with a policy of not contributing to the proliferation of nuclear weapon capabilities.

Treaty on the non-proliferation of nuclear weapons (NPT)

Signed at London, Moscow and Washington, DC, on 1 July 1968; entered into force on 5 March 1970.

Prohibits the transfer by nuclear weapon states, to any recipient whatsoever, of nuclear weapons or other nuclear explosive devices or of control over them, as well as the assistance, encouragement or inducement of any non-nuclear weapon state to manufacture or otherwise acquire such weapons or devices. Prohibits the receipt by non-nuclear weapon states from any transferor whatsoever, as well as the manufacture or other acquisition by those states, of nuclear weapons or other nuclear explosive devices.

Non-nuclear weapon states undertake to conclude safeguard agreements with the International Atomic Energy Agency (IAEA) with a view to preventing diversion of nuclear energy from peaceful uses to nuclear weapons or other nuclear explosive devices.

The parties undertake to facilitate the exchange of equipment, materials and scientific and technological information for the peaceful uses of nuclear energy and to ensure that potential benefits from peaceful applications of nuclear explosions will be made available to non-nuclear weapon parties to the treaty. They also undertake to pursue negotiations in good faith on effective measures relating to cessation of the nuclear arms race at an early date and to nuclear disarmament, and on a treaty on general and complete disarmament.

In 1995, 25 years after the entry into force of the treaty, in accordance with Article X, a conference was convened to decide whether the treaty would continue in force indefinitely or would be extended for an additional fixed period or periods. It was decided that the treaty should remain in force indefinitely.

Parties (183): Afghanistan,[†] Albania, Algeria, Antigua and Barbuda, Argentina, Armenia,[†] Australia,[†] Austria,[†] Azerbaijan, Bahamas, Bahrain, Bangladesh,[†] Barbados, Belarus,[†] Belgium,[†] Belize, Benin, Bhutan,[†] Bolivia,[†] Bosnia and Herzegovina, Botswana, Brunei,[†] Bulgaria,[†] Burkina Faso, Burundi, Cambodia, Cameroon, Canada,[†] Cape Verde, Central African Republic, Chad, Chile, China,[1] Colombia, Comoros, Congo, Costa Rica,[†] Côte d'Ivoire,[†] Croatia,[†] Cyprus,[†] Czech Republic,[†] Denmark,[†] Dominica, Dominican Republic,[†] Ecuador,[†] Egypt,[†2] El Salvador,[†] Equatorial Guinea, Eritrea, Estonia, Ethiopia,[†] Fiji,[†] Finland,[†] France,[†3] Gabon, Gambia,[†] Georgia, Germany,[†] Ghana,[†] Greece,[†] Grenada, Guatemala,[†] Guinea, Guinea-Bissau, Guyana, Haiti, Holy See,[†] Honduras,[†] Hungary,[†] Iceland,[†] Indonesia,[†] Iran,[†] Iraq,[†] Ireland,[†] Italy,[†] Jamaica,[†] Japan,[†] Jordan,[†] Kazakhstan,[†] Kenya, Kiribati,[†] Korea (North),[†] Korea (South),[†] Kuwait, Kyrgyzstan, Laos, Latvia,[†] Lebanon,[†] Lesotho,[†] Liberia, Libya,[†] Liechtenstein,[†4] Lithuania,[†] Luxembourg,[†] Macedonia (Former Yugoslav Republic of), Madagascar,[†] Malawi,[†] Malaysia,[†] Maldives,[†] Mali, Malta,[†] Marshall Islands, Mauritania, Mauritius,[†] Mexico,[†5] Micronesia, Moldova, Monaco, Mongolia,[†] Morocco,[†] Mozambique, Myanmar (Burma),[†] Namibia, Nauru,[†] Nepal,[†] Netherlands,[†] New Zealand,[†] Nicaragua,[†] Niger, Nigeria,[†] Norway,[†] Palau, Panama, Papua New Guinea,[†] Paraguay,[†] Peru,[†] Philippines,[†] Poland,[†] Portugal,[†] Qatar, Romania,[†] Russia,[†] Rwanda, Saint Kitts (Christopher) and Nevis, Saint Lucia,[†] Saint Vincent and the Grenadines,[†] Samoa (Western),[†] San Marino, Sao Tome and Principe, Saudi Arabia, Senegal,[†] Seychelles, Sierra Leone, Singapore,[†] Slovakia,[†] Slovenia, Solomon Islands,[†] Somalia, South Africa,[†] Spain,[†] Sri Lanka,[†] Sudan,[†] Suriname,[†] Swaziland,[†] Sweden,[†] Switzerland,[†4] Syria,[†] Taiwan, Tajikistan, Tanzania, Thailand,[†] Togo, Tonga,[†] Trinidad and Tobago,[†] Tunisia,[†] Turkey,[†] Turkmenistan, Tuvalu,[†] Uganda, UK,[†] Ukraine,[†] United Arab Emirates, Uruguay,[†] USA,[†] Uzbekistan, Vanuatu, Venezuela,[†] Viet Nam,[†] Yemen, Yugoslavia,[†] Zaire,[†] Zambia,[†] Zimbabwe[†]

† Safeguards agreements in force with the International Atomic Energy Agency (IAEA), as required by the treaty, or concluded by a nuclear weapon state on a voluntary basis. For Russia (at the time of signing the USSR), the UK, Ukraine and the USA, the IAEA safeguards provide only for non-military nuclear installations.

[1] China stated that the nuclear weapon states should undertake: (a) not to be the first to use nuclear weapons at any time and under any circumstances; (b) not to use or threaten to use nuclear weapons against non-nuclear weapon countries or nuclear-free zones; and (c) to support the establishment of nuclear weapon-free zones, respect the status of such zones and assume corresponding obligations. All states that have nuclear weapons deployed outside of their boundaries should withdraw all those weapons back to their own territories.

[2] Egypt called upon nuclear weapon states to promote research and development of peaceful applications of nuclear explosions in order to overcome all the difficulties at present involved therein.

[3] An agreement between France, the European Atomic Energy Community (Euratom) and the IAEA for the application of safeguards in France had entered into force in 1981. The agreement covers nuclear material and facilities notified to the IAEA by France.

[4] Liechtenstein and Switzerland define the term 'source or special fissionable material' in Article III of the treaty as being in accordance with Article XX of the IAEA Statute, and a modification of this interpretation requires their formal consent; they will accept only such interpretations and definitions of the terms 'equipment or material especially designed or prepared for the processing, use or production of special fissionable material', as mentioned in Article III of the treaty, that they will expressly approve.

[5] On signing the treaty, Mexico stated, inter alia, that none of the provisions of the treaty shall be interpreted as affecting in any way whatsoever the rights and obligations of Mexico as a state party to the treaty of Tlatelolco. It is the understanding of Mexico that 'at the present time' any nuclear explosive device is capable of being used as a nuclear weapon and that there is no indication that 'in the near future' it will be possible to manufacture nuclear explosive devices that are not potentially nuclear weapons. However, if technological advances modify this situation, it will be necessary to amend the relevant provisions of the treaty in accordance with the procedure established therein.

Treaty on the prohibition of the emplacement of nuclear weapons and other weapons of mass destruction on the seabed and the ocean floor and in the subsoil thereof (Seabed Treaty)

Signed at London, Moscow and Washington, DC, on 11 February 1971; entered into force on 18 May 1972.

Prohibits emplanting or emplacing on the seabed and the ocean floor and in the subsoil thereof beyond the outer limit of a 12-mile seabed zone any nuclear weapons or any other types of weapons of mass destruction as well as structures, launching installations or any other facilities specifically designed for storing, testing or using such weapons.

Parties (92): Afghanistan, Algeria, Antigua and Barbuda, Argentina,[1] Australia, Austria, Bahamas, Belarus, Belgium, Benin, Botswana, Brazil,[2] Bulgaria, Canada,[3] Cape Verde, Central African Republic, China,[4] Congo, Côte d'Ivoire, Croatia, Cuba, Cyprus, Czech Republic, Denmark, Dominican Republic, Equatorial Guinea, Ethiopia, Finland, Germany, Ghana, Greece, Guinea-Bissau, Hungary, Iceland, India,[5] Iran, Iraq, Ireland, Italy,[6] Jamaica, Japan, Jordan, Korea (South), Laos, Latvia, Lesotho, Libya, Liechtenstein, Luxembourg, Malaysia, Malta, Mauritius, Mexico,[7] Mongolia, Morocco, Nepal, Netherlands, New Zealand, Nicaragua, Niger, Norway, Panama, Philippines, Poland, Portugal, Qatar, Romania, Russia, Rwanda, Sao Tome and Principe, Saudi Arabia, Seychelles, Singapore, Slovakia, Slovenia, Solomon Islands, South Africa, Spain, Swaziland, Sweden, Switzerland, Taiwan, Togo, Tunisia, Turkey, UK, Ukraine, USA, Viet Nam,[8] Yemen, Yugoslavia,[9] Zambia

Signed but not ratified: Bolivia, Burundi, Cambodia, Cameroon, Colombia, Costa Rica, Gambia, Guatemala, Guinea, Honduras, Lebanon, Liberia, Madagascar, Mali, Myanmar (Burma), Paraguay, Senegal, Sierra Leone, Sudan, Tanzania, Uruguay

[1] Argentina stated that it interprets the references to the freedom of the high seas as in no way implying a pronouncement of judgement on the different positions relating to questions connected with international maritime law. It understands that the reference to the rights of exploration and exploitation by
coastal states over their continental shelves was included solely because those could be the rights most
frequently affected by verification procedures. Argentina precludes any possibility of strengthening,
through this treaty, certain positions concerning continental shelves to the detriment of others based on
different criteria.

[2] Brazil stated that nothing in the treaty shall be interpreted as prejudicing in any way the sovereign
rights of Brazil in the area of the sea, the seabed and the subsoil thereof adjacent to its coasts. It is the
understanding of Brazil that the word 'observation', as it appears in para. 1 of Article III of the treaty,
refers only to observation that is incidental to the normal course of navigation in accordance with international law.

[3] Canada declared that Article I, para. 1, cannot be interpreted as indicating that any state has a right to
implant or emplace any weapons not prohibited under Article I, para. 1, on the seabed and ocean floor,
and in the subsoil thereof, beyond the limits of national jurisdiction, or as constituting any limitation on
the principle that this area of the seabed and ocean floor and the subsoil thereof shall be reserved for
exclusively peaceful purposes. Articles I, II and III cannot be interpreted as indicating that any state but
the coastal state has any right to implant or emplace any weapon not prohibited under Article I, para. 1
on the continental shelf, or the subsoil thereof, appertaining to that coastal state, beyond the outer limit of
the seabed zone referred to in Article I and defined in Article II. Article III cannot be interpreted as indicating any restrictions or limitation upon the rights of the coastal state, consistent with its exclusive
sovereign rights with respect to the continental shelf, to verify, inspect or effect the removal of any
weapon, structure, installation, facility or device implanted or emplaced on the continental shelf, or the
subsoil thereof, appertaining to that coastal state, beyond the outer limit of the seabed zone referred to in
Article I and defined in Article II.

[4] China reaffirmed that nothing in this treaty shall be interpreted as prejudicing in any way the
sovereign rights and the other rights of the People's Republic of China over its territorial sea, as well as
the sea area, the seabed and subsoil thereof adjacent to its territorial sea.

[5] The accession by India is based on its position that it has full and exclusive rights over the continental shelf adjoining its territory and beyond its territorial waters and the subsoil thereof. There cannot,
therefore, be any restriction on, or limitation of, the sovereign right of India as a coastal state to verify,
inspect, remove or destroy any weapon, device, structure, installation or facility, which might be
implanted or emplaced on or beneath its continental shelf by any other country, or to take such other
steps as may be considered necessary to safeguard its security.

[6] Italy stated, *inter alia*, that in the case of agreements on further measures in the field of disarmament
to prevent an arms race on the seabed and ocean floor and in their subsoil, the question of the delimitation of the area within which these measures would find application shall have to be examined and
solved in each instance in accordance with the nature of the measures to be adopted.

[7] Mexico declared the treaty cannot be interpreted to mean that a state has the right to emplace
weapons of mass destruction, or arms or military equipment of any type, on the continental shelf of
Mexico. It reserves the right to verify, inspect, remove or destroy any weapon, structure, installation,
device or equipment placed on its continental shelf, including nuclear weapons or other weapons of mass
destruction.

[8] Viet Nam stated that no provision of the treaty should be interpreted in a way that would contradict
the rights of the coastal states with regard to their continental shelf, including the right to take measures
to ensure their security.

[9] In 1974, the Ambassador of Yugoslavia transmitted to the US Secretary of State a note stating that in
the view of the Yugoslav Government, Article III, para. 1, of the treaty should be interpreted in such a
way that a state exercising its right under this article shall be obliged to notify in advance the coastal
state, in so far as its observations are to be carried out 'within the stretch of the sea extending above the
continental shelf of the said state'.

Convention on the prohibition of the development, production and stockpiling of bacteriological (biological) and toxin weapons and on their destruction (BW Convention)

Signed at London, Moscow and Washington, DC, on 10 April 1972; entered into force on 26 March 1975.

Prohibits the development, production, stockpiling or acquisition by other means or
retention of microbial or other biological agents, or toxins whatever their origin or

method of production, of types and in quantities that have no justification of prophylactic, protective or other peaceful purposes, as well as weapons, equipment or means of delivery designed to use such agents or toxins for hostile purposes or in armed conflict. The destruction of the agents, toxins, weapons, equipment and means of delivery in the possession of the parties, or their diversion to peaceful purposes, should be effected not later than nine months after the entry into force of the convention.

Parties (133): Afghanistan, Albania, Argentina, Armenia, Australia, Austria, Bahamas, Bahrain, Bangladesh, Barbados, Belarus, Belgium, Belize, Benin, Bhutan, Bolivia, Bosnia and Herzegovina, Botswana, Brazil, Brunei, Bulgaria, Burkina Faso, Cambodia, Canada, Cape Verde, Chile, China, Colombia, Congo, Costa Rica, Croatia, Cuba, Cyprus, Czech Republic, Denmark, Dominican Republic, Ecuador, El Salvador, Equatorial Guinea, Estonia, Ethiopia, Fiji, Finland, France, Germany,* Ghana, Greece, Grenada, Guatemala, Guinea-Bissau, Honduras, Hungary, Iceland, India,* Indonesia, Iran, Iraq, Ireland,* Italy, Jamaica, Japan, Jordan, Kenya, Korea (North), Korea (South), Kuwait, Laos, Lebanon, Lesotho, Libya, Liechtenstein, Luxembourg, Malaysia, Maldives, Malta, Mauritius, Mexico,* Mongolia, Netherlands, New Zealand, Nicaragua, Niger, Nigeria, Norway, Oman, Pakistan, Panama, Papua New Guinea, Paraguay, Peru, Philippines, Poland, Portugal, Qatar, Romania, Russia, Rwanda, Saint Kitts (Christopher) and Nevis, Saint Lucia, San Marino, Sao Tome and Principe, Saudi Arabia, Senegal, Seychelles, Sierra Leone, Singapore, Slovakia, Slovenia, Solomon Islands, South Africa, Spain, Sri Lanka, Suriname, Swaziland, Sweden, Switzerland,* Taiwan, Thailand, Togo, Tonga, Tunisia, Turkey, Uganda, UK, Ukraine, Uruguay, USA, Venezuela, Viet Nam, Yemen, Yugoslavia, Zaire, Zimbabwe

* With reservation and/or declaration upon ratification, accession or succession.

Signed but not ratified: Burundi, Central African Republic, Côte d'Ivoire, Egypt, Gabon, Gambia, Guyana, Haiti, Liberia, Madagascar, Malawi, Mali, Morocco, Myanmar (Burma), Nepal, Somalia, Syria, Tanzania, United Arab Emirates

Convention on the prohibition of military or any other hostile use of environmental modification techniques (Enmod Convention)

Signed at Geneva on 18 May 1977; entered into force on 5 October 1978.

Prohibits military or any other hostile use of environmental modification techniques having widespread, long-lasting or severe effects as the means of destruction, damage or injury to states party to the convention. The term 'environmental modification techniques' refers to any technique for changing—through the deliberate manipulation of natural processes—the dynamics, composition or structure of the Earth, including its biota, lithosphere, hydrosphere and atmosphere, or of outer space. The understandings reached during the negotiations, but not written into the convention, define the terms 'widespread', 'long-lasting' and 'severe'.

Parties (63): Afghanistan, Algeria, Antigua and Barbuda, Argentina, Australia, Austria, Bangladesh, Belarus, Belgium, Benin, Brazil, Bulgaria, Canada, Cape Verde, Chile, Cuba, Cyprus, Czech Republic, Denmark, Dominica, Egypt, Finland, Germany, Ghana, Greece, Guatemala, Hungary, India, Ireland, Italy, Japan, Korea (North), Korea (South),* Kuwait, Laos, Malawi, Mauritius, Mongolia, Netherlands,* New Zealand, Niger, Norway, Pakistan, Papua New Guinea, Poland, Romania, Russia, Saint Lucia, Sao Tome and Principe, Slovakia, Solomon Islands, Spain, Sri Lanka, Sweden, Switzerland, Tunisia, UK, Ukraine, Uruguay, USA, Uzbekistan, Viet Nam, Yemen

* With reservation and/or declaration upon ratification, accession or succession.

Signed but not ratified: Bolivia, Ethiopia, Holy See, Iceland, Iran, Iraq, Lebanon, Liberia, Luxembourg, Morocco, Nicaragua, Portugal, Sierra Leone, Syria, Turkey, Uganda, Zaire

Protocol (I) additional to the 1949 Geneva Conventions, and relating to the protection of victims of international armed conflict

Signed at Bern on 12 December 1977; entered into force on 7 December 1978.

The protocol confirms that the right of the parties to an international armed conflict to choose methods or means of warfare is not unlimited and that it is prohibited to use weapons or means of warfare which cause superfluous injury or unnecessary suffering.

Parties (143): Albania, Algeria,* Angola,* Antigua and Barbuda, Argentina,* Armenia, Australia,* Austria,* Bahamas, Bahrain, Bangladesh, Barbados, Belarus, Belgium,* Belize, Benin, Bolivia, Bosnia and Herzegovina, Botswana, Brazil, Brunei, Bulgaria, Burkina Faso, Burundi, Cameroon, Canada,* Cape Verde, Central African Republic, Chile, China,* Colombia, Comoros, Congo, Costa Rica, Côte d'Ivoire, Croatia, Cuba, Cyprus, Czech Republic, Denmark,* Djibouti, Dominican Republic, Ecuador, Egypt,* El Salvador, Equatorial Guinea, Estonia, Ethiopia, Finland,* Gabon, Gambia, Georgia, Germany,* Ghana, Greece, Guatemala, Guinea, Guinea-Bissau, Guyana, Holy See,* Honduras, Hungary, Iceland,* Italy,* Jamaica, Jordan, Kazakhstan, Korea (North), Korea (South),* Kuwait, Kyrgyzstan, Laos, Latvia, Lesotho, Liberia, Libya, Liechtenstein,* Luxembourg, Macedonia (Former Yugoslav Republic of), Madagascar, Malawi, Maldives, Mali, Malta,* Mauritania, Mauritius, Mexico, Micronesia,[1] Moldova, Mongolia,[1] Mozambique, Namibia, Netherlands,* New Zealand,* Niger, Nigeria, Norway, Oman,* Panama,[1] Paraguay, Peru, Poland, Portugal, Qatar,* Romania, Russia,* Rwanda, Saint Kitts (Christopher) and Nevis, Saint Lucia, Saint Vincent and the Grenadines, Samoa (Western), San Marino, Saudi Arabia,* Senegal, Seychelles, Sierra Leone, Slovakia, Slovenia, Solomon Islands, South Africa,[1] Spain,* Suriname, Swaziland,[1] Sweden,* Switzerland,* Syria,* Tajikistan, Tanzania, Togo, Tunisia, Turkmenistan, Uganda, Ukraine, United Arab Emirates,* Uruguay, Uzbekistan, Vanuatu, Viet Nam, Yemen, Yugoslavia,* Zaire, Zambia, Zimbabwe

* With reservation and/or declaration upon ratification, accession or succession.

[1] In accordance with the provisions of Article 95.2, the protocol enters into force for a party six months after the deposit of its instrument of ratification or accession. This state ratified or acceded to the protocol in the second half of 1995 and the protocol entered into force for that state in 1996.

Convention on the physical protection of nuclear material

Signed at Vienna and New York on 3 March 1980; entered into force on 8 February 1987.

The convention obliges the parties to protect nuclear material for peaceful purposes during transport across their territory or on ships or aircraft under their jurisdiction.

Parties (53): Antigua and Barbuda, Argentina,* Armenia, Australia, Austria, Belarus, Belgium,[†] Brazil, Bulgaria, Canada, Chile, China,* Croatia, Czech Republic, Denmark,[†] Estonia, Euratom,*[†] Finland, France,*[†] Germany,[†] Greece,[†] Guatemala, Hungary, Indonesia,* Ireland,[†] Italy,*[†] Japan, Korea (South),* Liechtenstein, Lithuania, Luxembourg,[†] Mexico, Mongolia,* Netherlands,*[†] Norway, Paraguay, Peru,* Philippines, Poland,* Portugal, Romania, Russia,* Slovakia, Slovenia, Spain,*[†] Sweden, Switzerland, Tunisia, Turkey,* UK,[†] Ukraine, USA, Yugoslavia

* With reservation and/or declaration upon ratification, accession or succession.

† Belgium, Denmark, France, Germany, Greece, Ireland, Italy, Luxembourg, Netherlands, Spain and the UK signed as Euratom member states.

Signed but not ratified: Dominican Republic, Ecuador, Haiti, Israel, Morocco, Niger, Panama, South Africa

Convention on prohibitions or restrictions on the use of certain conventional weapons which may be deemed to be excessively injurious or to have indiscriminate effects (CCW Convention, or 'Inhumane Weapons' Convention)

Signed at New York on 10 April 1981; entered into force on 2 December 1983.

The convention is an 'umbrella treaty', under which specific agreements can be concluded in the form of protocols.

Protocol I prohibits the use of weapons intended to injure by fragments which are not detectable in the human body by X-rays.

Protocol II prohibits or restricts the use of mines, booby-traps and similar devices.

Protocol III restricts the use of incendiary weapons.

Protocol IV, adopted in Vienna on 12 October 1995 and on 12 December 1995 commended by the UN General Assembly to all states to adhere to it, prohibits the use of laser weapons specifically designed to cause permanent blindness to unenhanced vision. Not in force as of 1 April 1996.

Parties (57): Argentina,[1] Australia, Austria, Belarus, Belgium, Benin,[1] Bosnia and Herzegovina, Brazil, Bulgaria, Canada, China, Croatia, Cuba, Cyprus,[2] Czech Republic, Denmark, Ecuador, Finland, France,[3] Germany, Greece, Guatemala, Hungary, India, Ireland, Israel, Italy, Japan, Jordan,[1] Laos, Latvia, Liechtenstein, Malta, Mexico, Mongolia, Netherlands,* New Zealand, Niger, Norway, Pakistan, Poland, Romania,[1] Russia, Slovakia, Slovenia, South Africa,[1] Spain, Sweden, Switzerland, Togo,[1] Tunisia, Uganda,[1] UK, Ukraine, Uruguay, USA, Yugoslavia

[1] In accordance with Article 5.2, the convention enters into force for a state six months after the deposit of the instrument of ratification or accession. This state deposited its instruments of ratification or accession in the second half of 1995 and the convention entered into force for this state in 1996.

Signed but not ratified: Afghanistan, Egypt, Iceland, Luxembourg, Morocco, Nicaragua, Nigeria, Philippines, Portugal, Sierra Leone, Sudan, Turkey, Viet Nam

[1] The accession of Benin refers only to Protocols I and III of the convention.

[2] Cyprus declared that the provisions of Article 7, para. 3b, and Article 8 of Protocol II of the convention will be interpreted in such a way that neither the status of peacekeeping forces or missions of the UN in Cyprus will be affected nor will additional rights be, *ipso jure*, granted to them.

[3] France ratified only Protocols I and II. It made this reservation: Not being bound by the 1977 Additional Protocol I to the Geneva Conventions of 1949, France considers that para. 4 of the preamble to the convention on prohibitions or restrictions on the use of certain conventional weapons, which reproduces the provisions of Article 35, para. 3, of Additional Protocol I, applies only to states parties to that protocol. France will apply the provisions of the convention and its three protocols to all the armed conflicts referred to in Articles 2 and 3 common to the Geneva Conventions of 1949.

South Pacific nuclear free zone treaty (Treaty of Rarotonga)

Signed at Rarotonga, Cook Islands, on 6 August 1985; entered into force on 11 December 1986.

Prohibits the manufacture or acquisition by other means of any nuclear explosive device, as well as possession or control over such device by the parties anywhere inside or outside the zone area described in an annex. The parties also undertake not to supply nuclear material or equipment, unless subject to IAEA safeguards, and to prevent in their territories the stationing as well as the testing of any nuclear explosive device. Each party remains free to allow visits, as well as transit, by foreign ships and aircraft.

The Treaty of Rarotonga is open for signature by members of the South Pacific Forum. Protocol 1 is open to France, the UK and the USA; Protocol 2 to China, France, Russia, the UK and the USA; and Protocol 3 to China, France, Russia, the UK and the USA.

Under *Protocol 1*, France, the UK and the USA would undertake to apply the treaty prohibitions relating to the manufacture, stationing and testing of nuclear explosive devices in the territories situated within the zone, for which they are internationally responsible.

Under *Protocol 2*, China, France, Russia (at the time of signing, the USSR), the UK and the USA would undertake not to use or threaten to use a nuclear explosive device against the parties to the treaty or against any territory within the zone for which a party to Protocol 1 is internationally responsible.

Under *Protocol 3*, China, France, the UK, the USA and Russia (at the time of signing, the USSR) would undertake not to test any nuclear explosive device anywhere within the zone.

Parties (11): Australia, Cook Islands, Fiji, Kiribati, Nauru, New Zealand, Niue, Papua New Guinea, Samoa (Western), Solomon Islands, Tuvalu

Signed but not ratified: Vanuatu

Parties to Protocol 1: 0
Parties to Protocol 2: China, Russia
Parties to Protocol 3: China, Russia

Note: On 25 March 1996, France, the UK and the USA signed the three protocols to the Rarotonga Treaty. Not in force as of 1 April 1996.

Treaty on conventional armed forces in Europe (CFE Treaty)

Signed at Vienna on 19 November 1990; entered into force on 9 November 1992.

The treaty sets ceilings on five categories of military equipment (battle tanks, armoured combat vehicles, artillery pieces, combat aircraft and attack helicopters) in an area stretching from the Atlantic Ocean to the Ural Mountains (the Atlantic-to-the-Urals, ATTU, zone).

The treaty was negotiated and signed by the member states of the Warsaw Treaty Organization (WTO) and NATO within the framework of the CSCE (from 1 January 1995 the OSCE).

The **Tashkent Document**, signed by former Soviet republics with territories within the ATTU zone (except the Baltic states) at Tashkent on 15 May 1992, includes the Agreement on the Principles and Procedures for Implementing the CFE Treaty (**Tashkent Agreement**), establishing maximum levels for holdings of armaments and equipment for implementation of the treaty and a number of certain types of helicopters not subject to CFE Treaty limits. The Document also includes a Declaration by which the states recognize how to implement the CFE Treaty after the breakup of the USSR.

All the CFE Treaty parties signed, at Oslo, on 5 June 1992, the Final Document of the Extraordinary Conference of the States Parties to the CFE Treaty (**Oslo Document**), introducing modifications, necessary because of the emergence of new states as a consequence of the breakup of the USSR.

Parties (30): Armenia, Azerbaijan, Belarus, Belgium, Bulgaria, Canada, Czech Republic, Denmark, France, Georgia, Germany, Greece, Hungary, Iceland, Italy, Kazakhstan, Luxembourg, Moldova, Netherlands, Norway, Poland, Portugal, Romania, Russia, Slovakia, Spain, Turkey, UK, Ukraine, USA

The concluding act of the negotiation on personnel strength of conventional armed forces in Europe (CFE-1A Agreement)

Signed by the parties to the CFE Treaty at Helsinki on 10 July 1992; entered into force simultaneously with the CFE Treaty.

The agreement limits the personnel of the conventional land-based armed forces within the ATTU zone.

Vienna Documents 1990, 1992 and 1994 on Confidence- and Security-Building Measures

The Vienna Documents were adopted by all the CSCE states. The Vienna Document 1994 was adopted at Vienna on 28 November 1994.

The **Vienna Document 1990** on Confidence- and Security-Building Measures (CSBMs) repeats many of the provisions in the 1986 Stockholm Document on CSBMs and Disarmament in Europe and expands several others. It establishes a communications network and a risk reduction mechanism. The **Vienna Document 1992** on CSBMs builds on the Vienna Document 1990 and supplements its provisions with new mechanisms and constraining provisions. **The Vienna Document 1994** on CSBMs amends and expands the previous Vienna Documents.

The Vienna Documents were signed by all members of the Conference on Security and Co-operation in Europe (from 1 January 1995 the OSCE).

Treaty on open skies

Signed at Helsinki on 24 March 1992; not in force as of 1 April 1996.

The treaty obliges the parties to submit their territories to short-notice unarmed surveillance flights. The area of application stretches from Vancouver, Canada, eastwards to Vladivostok, Russia.

The Open Skies Treaty was negotiated between the member states of the Warsaw Treaty Organization (WTO) and NATO. It is also open for signature by the former Soviet republics. For six months after entry into force of the treaty, any other OSCE member state may apply for accession. The treaty will enter into force when 20 states have ratified it, including all parties with more than eight 'passive quotas' (Belarus, Canada, France, Germany, Italy, Russia, Turkey, Ukraine, UK, USA).

22 ratifications deposited: Belgium, Bulgaria, Canada, Czech Republic, Denmark, France, Germany, Greece, Hungary, Iceland, Italy, Luxembourg, Netherlands, Norway, Poland, Portugal, Romania, Slovakia, Spain, Turkey, UK, USA

Signed but not ratified: Belarus, Georgia, Kyrgyzstan, Russia, Ukraine

Convention on the prohibition of the development, production, stockpiling and use of chemical weapons and on their destruction (Chemical Weapons Convention, CWC)

Opened for signature at Paris on 13 January 1993; not in force as of 1 April 1996.

The Convention prohibits not only the use of chemical weapons (prohibited by the 1925 Geneva Protocol) but also the development, production, acquisition, transfer and stockpiling of chemical weapons. Each party undertakes to destroy its chemical weapons and production facilities. The convention will enter into force 180 days after the deposit of the 65th instrument of ratification.

47 ratifications deposited: Albania, Algeria, Argentina, Armenia, Australia, Austria, Bulgaria, Canada, Cook Islands, Côte d'Ivoire, Croatia, Denmark, Ecuador, El Salvador, Fiji, Finland, France, Georgia, Germany, Greece, Italy, Japan, Lesotho, Maldives, Mauritius, Mexico, Monaco, Mongolia, Morocco, Namibia, Netherlands, Norway, Oman, Paraguay, Peru, Poland, Romania, Seychelles, Slovakia, South Africa, Spain, Sri Lanka, Sweden, Switzerland, Tajikistan, Turkmenistan, Uruguay

Note: Brazil, the Czech Republic and Papua New Guinea had ratified the convention as of 1 April 1996.

Signed but not ratified: Afghanistan, Azerbaijan, Bahamas, Bahrain, Bangladesh, Belarus, Belgium, Benin, Bolivia, Brunei, Burkina Faso, Burundi, Cambodia, Cameroon, Cape Verde, Central African Republic, Chad, Chile, China, Colombia, Comoros, Congo, Costa Rica, Cuba, Cyprus, Djibouti, Dominica, Dominican Republic, Equatorial Guinea, Estonia, Ethiopia, Gabon, Gambia, Ghana, Guatemala, Guinea, Guinea Bissau, Guyana, Haiti, Holy See, Honduras, Hungary, Iceland, India, Indonesia, Iran, Ireland, Israel, Kazakhstan, Kenya, Korea (South), Kuwait, Kyrgyzstan, Laos, Latvia, Liberia, Liechtenstein, Lithuania, Luxembourg, Madagascar, Malawi, Malaysia, Mali, Malta, Marshall Islands, Mauritania, Micronesia, Moldova, Myanmar (Burma), Nauru, Nepal, New Zealand, Nicaragua, Niger, Nigeria, Pakistan, Panama, Philippines, Portugal, Qatar, Russia, Rwanda, Saint Kitts (Christopher) and Nevis, Saint Lucia, Saint Vincent and the Grenadines, Samoa (Western), San Marino, Saudi Arabia, Senegal, Sierra Leone, Singapore, Slovenia, Swaziland, Tanzania, Thailand, Togo, Tunisia, Turkey, Uganda, UK, Ukraine, United Arab Emirates, USA, Uzbekistan, Venezuela, Viet Nam, Yemen, Zaire, Zambia, Zimbabwe

II. Summaries and status of the major US–Soviet/Russian agreements, as of 1 January 1996

Treaty on the limitation of anti-ballistic missile systems (ABM Treaty)

Signed by the USA and the USSR at Moscow on 26 May 1972; entered into force on 3 October 1972.

The treaty obligates the parties not to undertake to build a nation-wide defence system against strategic ballistic missile attack and limits the development and deployment of permitted missile defences.

A protocol to the ABM Treaty, introducing further numerical restrictions on permitted ballistic missile defences, was signed in 1974.

Treaty on the limitation of underground nuclear weapon tests (Threshold Test Ban Treaty, TTBT)

Signed by the USA and the USSR at Moscow on 3 July 1974; entered into force on 11 December 1990.

The parties undertake not to carry out any individual underground nuclear weapon test having a yield exceeding 150 kilotons.

Treaty on underground nuclear explosions for peaceful purposes (Peaceful Nuclear Explosions Treaty, PNET)

Signed by the USA and the USSR at Moscow and Washington, DC, on 28 May 1976; entered into force on 11 December 1990.

The parties undertake not to carry out any underground nuclear explosion for peaceful purposes having a yield exceeding 150 kilotons or any group explosion having an aggregate yield exceeding 150 kilotons.

Treaty on the elimination of intermediate-range and shorter-range missiles (INF Treaty)

Signed by the USA and the USSR at Washington, DC, on 8 December 1987; entered into force on 1 June 1988.

The treaty obliges the parties to destroy all land-based missiles with a range of 500–5500 km (intermediate-range, 1000–5500 km; and shorter-range, 500–1000 km) and their launchers by 1 June 1991. The INF Treaty was implemented before this date.

Treaty on the reduction and limitation of strategic offensive arms (START I Treaty)

Signed by the USA and the USSR at Moscow on 31 July 1991; entered into force on 5 December 1994.

The treaty requires the USA and Russia to make phased reductions in their offensive strategic nuclear forces over a seven-year period. It sets numerical limits on deployed strategic nuclear delivery vehicles (SNDVs)—ICBMs, SLBMs and heavy bombers—

and the nuclear warheads they carry. In the May 1992 Protocol to Facilitate the Implementation of the START Treaty (**Lisbon Protocol**), Belarus, Kazakhstan and Ukraine also assumed the obligations of the former USSR under the treaty. They pledged to eliminate all the former Soviet strategic weapons on their territories within the seven-year reduction period and to join the NPT as non-nuclear weapon states in the shortest possible time.

Treaty on further reduction and limitation of strategic offensive arms (START II Treaty)

Signed by the USA and Russia at Moscow on 3 January 1993; not in force as of 1 April 1996.

The treaty requires the USA and Russia to eliminate their MIRVed ICBMs and sharply reduce the number of their deployed strategic nuclear warheads to no more than 3000–3500 each (of which no more than 1750 may be deployed on SLBMs) by 1 January 2003 or no later than 31 December 2000 if the USA and Russia reach a formal agreement committing the USA to help finance the elimination of strategic nuclear weapons in Russia.

Annexe B. Chronology 1995

RAGNHILD FERM

For the convenience of the reader, key words are indicated in the right-hand column, opposite each entry. They refer to the subject-areas covered in the entry. Definitions of the acronyms can be found on page xvi.

3 Jan.	The UN Secretary-General issues a supplement to the 1992 *Agenda for Peace.*	UN
20 Jan.	Kazakh President Nazarbayev and Russian President Yeltsin sign an agreement, in Moscow, to establish joint armed forces, with a joint command for military planning and training and for patrols along their borders with China. They also pledge to cooperate closely on security and foreign matters.	Russia/ Kazakhstan
24 Jan.	Ukraine's Ministry of Defence issues a statement that Ukraine has fulfilled all the conditions stipulated in the START I Treaty (Lisbon Protocol) with regard to transferring ICBMs out of Ukraine.	START; Ukraine
30 Jan.	US President Clinton announces that the USA will extend its moratorium on nuclear testing (in effect since Oct. 1992) until the entry into force of a CTBT. In addition, the USA drops its earlier proposal for a clause allowing the parties to withdraw from a CTBT after 10 years.	USA; CTBT
8 Feb.	The UN Security Council authorizes the establishment of UN Angola Verification Mission (UNAVEM) III to help in the implementation of the 20 Nov. 1994 Lusaka Protocol between the warring parties in Angola.	UN; Angola
8 Feb.	China gives assurances that it will not use or threaten to use nuclear weapons against Kazakhstan.	China/ Kazakhstan; Security guarantees
10 Feb.	At the CIS summit meeting in Almaty, an agreement is signed on creation of a joint air defence system with the aim of restoring control over the airspace of the former USSR.	CIS
22 Feb.	British Prime Minister Major and Irish Prime Minister Bruton present, in Belfast, a Joint Framework Document for All-party Constitutional Talks on a Durable Settlement for Northern Ireland.	Northern Ireland; UK; Ireland
20–21 Mar.	At a meeting held in Paris, the Pact on Stability in Europe (a 1993 French proposal) is adopted by over 50 states. The instruments and procedures are handed over to the OSCE.	Europe; OSCE

23 Mar.	The Conference on Disarmament (CD) decides to establish an Ad Hoc Committee on a Ban on the Production of Fissile Material for Nuclear Weapons or Other Nuclear Explosive Devices. The CD directs the Ad Hoc Committee to negotiate a 'non-discriminatory, multilateral, and internationally and effectively verifiable treaty'.	CD; Fissile material
31 Mar.	The UN Mission in Haiti (UNMIH) takes over responsibility for Haiti from the US-led Multinational Force (MNF).	UN; Haiti
31 Mar.	The failed UN Operation in Somalia (UNOSOM) is terminated. The withdrawal is assisted by a seven-nation operation ('United Shield').	UN; Somalia
6 Apr.	At the CD the five declared nuclear weapon states each pledges that it will not use nuclear weapons against non-nuclear states parties to the NPT and will come to the assistance of a non-nuclear weapon state attacked with, or threatened by the use of, nuclear weapons.	CD; NPT; Security guarantees
11 Apr.	The UN Security Council unanimously adopts Resolution 984, taking note of the security assurances given by the nuclear weapon states not to use nuclear weapons against non-nuclear weapon states parties to the NPT. The Council recognizes the legitimate interest of non-nuclear weapon states parties to the NPT to receive assurances that the Security Council, and above all its nuclear weapon state permanent members, will act immediately in accordance with the UN Charter in the event that such states are the victim of an act of, or the object of a threat of, aggression in which nuclear weapons are used.	UN; NPT; Security guarantees
17 Apr.– *12 May*	The NPT Review and Extension Conference is held in New York. As the delegates agree that a majority of the parties endorse an indefinite extension of the NPT, there is no formal vote. A Declaration of Principles and Objectives for Nuclear Proliferation and Disarmament as well as a decision on strengthening the review process are also adopted.	NPT
18 Apr.	At the NPT Review and Extension Conference, the British Foreign Secretary announces that the UK has ceased the production of fissile material for explosive purposes.	UK; Fissile material
24 Apr.	The Foreign Ministry of Kazakhstan announces that all nuclear warheads that Kazakhstan inherited from the former Soviet Union are transferred to Russia, in accordance with its pledge to become a non-nuclear weapon state.	Kazakhstan/ Russia; START
1 May	The Croatian Army launches a major offensive against UNPA (UN Protected Area) Sector West in Western Slavonia and regains control.	Former Yugoslavia

9–10 May	Russian President Yeltsin and US President Clinton, meeting in Moscow, issue a joint statement setting out the basic principles for the development and deployment of theatre missile defence systems under the 1972 ABM Treaty. The two presidents also sign a Declaration on the Transparency and Irreversibility of the Process of Reducing Nuclear Weapons, urging cooperative efforts to safeguard fissile material stockpiles from their countries' nuclear weapon complexes. The declaration calls for the rapid negotiation of agreements to exchange, on a regular basis, detailed information on aggregate stockpiles of nuclear warheads and fissile materials.	Russia/USA; ABM; Fissile material
15 May	At a WEU Council meeting, held in Lisbon, 27 states (the fully fledged members, the Observers, the Associate Members and the Associate Partners) approve a document which defines their common interests and the risks facing European security. Before the opening of the meeting France and Spain sign documents on the constitution of two joint forces, the rapid operational Euroforce (EUROFOR) and the European maritime force (EUROMARFOR).	WEU
29 May– 2 June	An OAU–UN Group of Experts, meeting in Pelindaba, South Africa, reaches agreement on the draft text of a treaty establishing an African Nuclear-Weapon-Free Zone.	NWFZ; Africa; OAU
31 May	At the NACC meeting in Noordwijk, the Netherlands, Russia approves the PFP Individual Partnership Programme (IPP) document and the Document on a Broader, More Intense Dialogue.	NACC; Russia; PFP
13 June	French President Chirac announces that France will end its moratorium on nuclear testing and will carry out eight underground explosions in French Polynesia between Sep. 1995 and May 1996, halt all tests by May 1996 and sign a CTBT.	France; CTBT
13 June	The USA and North Korea sign, in Kuala Lumpur, an agreement concerning the implementation of their nuclear agreement signed in Oct. 1994.	USA/North Korea
23 June	The Heads of State of the OAU, meeting in Addis Ababa, adopt the amended text of the Treaty on an African Nuclear-Weapon-Free Zone (the Treaty of Pelindaba) (see *29 May–2 June*). The treaty is forwarded to the UN Secretary-General on 2 Aug.	NWFZ; Africa; OAU
11 July	The Bosnian enclave Srebrenica, a declared safe area, falls to the Bosnian Serb Army. UN peacekeepers are forced to withdraw. Zepa falls on 25 July.	Bosnia/Bosnian Serbs
30 July	A peace agreement on Chechnya, negotiated under the auspices of the OSCE, is signed in Grozny by the Russian and Chechen sides. (On 31 July the Russian Constitutional Court declares that the invasion of Chechnya was legal.)	Chechnya/ Russia

4 Aug.	The Croatian Army launches a major offensive against the Krajina Serbs, shelling Knin and launching air raids. By 9 Aug. it is in full control of UNPA Sector North and South.	Croatia/Krajina
7–11 Aug.	Israeli Foreign Minister Peres and Chairman of the PLO Arafat, meeting in Taba, Egypt, reach agreement concerning further Palestinian territory and authority and Israel's military redeployment from the West Bank.	Israel/Palestine
10 Aug.	In a statement to the CD, France says that France will support a CTBT, prohibiting any nuclear weapon test or any other nuclear explosion.	France; CTBT
11 Aug.	US President Clinton announces that the USA now supports a CTBT, prohibiting any nuclear weapon test or any other nuclear explosion.	USA; CTBT
17 Aug.	At an UNSCOM meeting in Baghdad, Iraq discloses for the first time that it has a full-scale programme for the development of biological weapons (after two of Iraqi President Saddam Hussein's sons-in-law had defected to Jordan, on 8 Aug.).	Iraq; UNSCOM; BW
30 Aug.	NATO launches air strikes against Bosnian Serb military targets in Bosnia, retaliating for Bosnian Serb attacks on Sarajevo. The UN Rapid Reaction Force backs the NATO attack.	NATO/Bosnian Serbs
31 Aug.	At the annual conference of French ambassadors, held in Paris, French President Chirac announces that France will, 'when the time comes', take an initiative with its main partners concerning the 'Europeanization' of its nuclear deterrent force.	Nuclear weapons; France/Europe
8 Sep.	The foreign ministers of Bosnia, Croatia and Yugoslavia (Serbia and Montenegro), meeting in Geneva with representatives of the Contact Group (France, Germany, Russia, the UK and the USA), sign an agreement covering the basic principles of a peace accord (Principles for a Comprehensive Peace Settlement in Bosnia-Herzegovina), including the continued existence of Bosnia within its present international borders.	Former Yugoslavia
13 Sep.	The foreign ministers of Greece and the Former Yugoslav Republic of Macedonia (FYROM) sign, at UN Headquarters in New York, an Interim Accord establishing a new relationship between the two countries.	Greece/ Macedonia
14 Sep.	Russian President Yeltsin signs a decree outlining Russian policy towards the countries of the CIS. The decree calls for close economic ties and urges a move towards forming a common security system on the basis of the 1992 Tashkent Treaty on Collective Security.	Russia/CIS

21 Sep.	The CD adopts a proposal to admit 23 new states to the CD, with the date of their full admission to be decided by the CD 'at the earliest possible date'.	CD
22 Sep.	At the CFE Joint Consultative Group (JGC) meeting, held in Vienna, NATO proposes making certain flank zone *oblasti* (administrative regions) in Russia and Ukraine part of the rear zone in which more treaty-limited equipment (TLE) may be deployed. In return, Russia and Ukraine would agree to more verification, information and constraining measures in the original flank zone.	CFE; NATO; Russia
22 Sep.	The IAEA General Conference adopts Resolution GC(39)/46 requesting the Director General to continue to develop the measures proposed under 'Programme 93 + 2' in order to bring about a more effective and efficient system covering all nuclear material in all peaceful nuclear activities within the territory of a state which has concluded a comprehensive safeguards agreement.	IAEA
25 Sep.– 13 Oct.	A Review Conference of the 1981 Convention on Prohibitions or Restrictions on the Use of Certain Conventional Weapons Which May Be Deemed to be Excessively Injurious or to Have Indiscriminate Effects (the Certain Conventional Weapons, CCW, Convention) is held in Vienna. The parties agree to a new Protocol IV, restricting the use of blinding laser weapons, but fail to reach consensus on revisions to the existing protocol on land-mines (Protocol I).	CCW
26 Sep.	NATO presents to Russia a draft proposal for a political framework for NATO–Russian relations, beyond the PFP.	NATO/Russia
26 Sep.	The foreign ministers of Bosnia and Herzegovina, Croatia and Yugoslavia (Serbia and Montenegro), meeting at the US Mission to the UN, announce that they have reached agreement on Further Agreed Basic Principles.	Former Yugoslavia
28 Sep.	Israeli Prime Minister Rabin and PLO Chairman Arafat, meeting in Washington, sign, in the presence of US President Clinton, the King of Jordan and Egyptian President Mubarak, an agreement on extended PLO government on the West Bank.	Israel/ PLO
28 Sep.	NATO presents a study to the NACC and PFP states on a possible enlargement of NATO membership, the *Study on NATO Enlargement,* explaining the goals and principles of enlargement and the conditions that candidate countries must fulfil.	NATO; NACC; PFP
5 Oct.	US President Clinton announces a 60-day cease-fire in Bosnia and Herzegovina to allow for peace talks. (The cease-fire becomes effective on 12 Oct.)	Bosnia; USA

20 Oct.	France, the UK and the USA jointly announce their intention to sign, in the first half of 1996, the Protocols to the 1985 South Pacific Nuclear Free Zone Treaty (Treaty of Rarotonga).	NWFZ; USA, UK; France
23 Oct.	Russian President Yeltsin and US President Clinton, meeting north of New York, at Hyde Park, agree that Russian troops will participate in supervising the peace in Bosnia and Herzegovina.	Russia/USA; Bosnia
24 Oct.	The largest gathering of the world's leaders in history, on the occasion of the 50th Anniversary of the UN, adopts at UN headquarters in New York a Declaration urging the redirection of the UN to greater service to humankind.	UN
30 Oct.	French President Chirac and British Prime Minister Major, meeting in London, issue a declaration on a common nuclear doctrine. They state that the aim is to mutually strengthen deterrence while retaining the independence of the nuclear forces of the two states.	UK/France; Nuclear weapons
1 Nov.	Peace talks between Bosnia, Serbia and Croatia, with the USA and the EU as moderators, open in Dayton, Ohio, USA.	Former Yugoslavia
4 Nov.	Israeli Prime Minister Yitzhak Rabin is assassinated in Tel Aviv by an Israeli religious nationalist.	Israel
9 Nov.	The governments of the member states of the OAS, meeting in Santiago, agree to recommend the application of several confidence-building measures in Latin America.	OAS; CSBM
12 Nov.	Croatia and Serbia sign an agreement providing for the reintegration of Eastern Slavonia into Croatia (the Basic Agreement on the Region of Eastern Slavonia, Baranja and Western Sirmium).	Croatia/Serbia
14 Nov.	The WEU Council of Ministers, meeting in Madrid, adopts a Document on European Security, identifying Europe's new responsibilities in a strategic environment in which Europe's security is not confined to security in Europe.	WEU
16 Nov.	China issues through its official press agency a policy document on arms control, expressing its opposition to the US proposal to deploy ballistic missile defence systems in Asia to protect Japan and US military forces.	China; BMD
17 Nov.	The final reduction phase of the CFE Treaty ends. Some states parties have failed to comply. All parties pledge to seek solutions to the flank issue (see *22 Sep.*), including new definitions of the flank regions, a new timetable, and more transparency and constraints.	CFE

21 Nov.	The General Framework Agreement for Peace in Bosnia and Herzegovina (the Dayton Agreement), is initialled by Serb President Milosevic, Croatian President Tudjman and Bosnian President Izetbegovic in Dayton, Ohio, USA. The agreement includes a new constitution for Bosnia and Herzegovina. An Implementation Force (IFOR), predominantly consisting of NATO forces, to stay in the area for one year, is established.	Former Yugoslavia
22 Nov.	The UN Security Council unanimously adopts Resolution 1021 on conditional suspension of general sanctions against Yugoslavia (Serbia and Montenegro). (Russia abstains from voting.)	UN; Former Yugoslavia
26 Nov.	Australia announces the establishment of the Canberra Commission on the Elimination of Nuclear Weapons. The Commission will report to the 51st session of the UN General Assembly and to the CD.	Canberra Commission
28 Nov.	The Russian and NATO defence ministers, meeting in Brussels, agree to establish a joint consultative committee to allow Russian forces to operate in Bosnia and Herzegovina under US as opposed to NATO command, in IFOR.	Russia/NATO; Bosnia
30 Nov.	At a ceremony in Laon, France, the Eurocorps (made up of the forces of Belgium, France, Germany, Luxembourg and Spain) is declared operational.	Eurocorps
3 Dec.	At a meeting in Madrid between the USA and the EU, US President Clinton, Spanish Prime Minister González and the President of the European Commission sign The New Transatlantic Action Plan, including measures for transatlantic cooperation to respond to global challenges and efforts to promote peace and stability, democracy and development throughout the world and a joint EU–US Action Plan.	USA/EU
5 Dec.	The French Foreign Minister announces in Brussels that France will return to its seat in the NATO Military Committee. (France left NATO's military bodies and its integrated military structure in 1966.)	NATO/ France
7–8 Dec.	The OSCE Ministerial Council, meeting in Budapest, adopts a document on OSCE action for peace, democracy and stability in Bosnia and Herzegovina.	OSCE; Bosnia
8–9 Dec.	A Peace Implementation Conference for Bosnia and Herzegovina is held in London to plan the post-war reconstruction of Bosnia.	Bosnia
9 Dec.	The Russian and Belarussian defence ministers sign, in Minsk, documents significantly upgrading military cooperation between the two states.	Russia/Belarus

12 Dec.	The UN General Assembly adopts resolutions on arms control and disarmament, calling for *inter alia* an early conclusion of a CTBT and a halt to all testing, transparency in armaments, a moratorium on export of anti-personnel land-mines, and nuclear weapon-free zones in South Asia and Africa.	UN
14 Dec.	The General Framework Agreement for Peace in Bosnia and Herzegovina is signed in Paris by Serb President Milosevic, Croatian President Tudjman and Bosnian President Izetbegovic.	Bosnia
14–15 Dec.	At the summit meeting of the Association of South-East Asian Nations (ASEAN), held in Bangkok, the Treaty on the Southeast Asia Nuclear Weapon-Free Zone is signed by the ASEAN member states and Burma, Cambodia and Laos.	ASEAN; NWFZ
16 Dec.	North Korea and the Korean Peninsula Energy Development Organization (KEDO, a US-led international consortium financed mainly by South Korea and Japan) sign, in New York, an agreement implementing the North Korean–US Agreed Framework signed on 21 Oct. 1994. Under the agreement KEDO will provide North Korea with two light-water reactors to replace its existing graphite-based models.	North Korea/KEDO
18 Dec.	At a meeting of high-level officials in Wassenaar, the Netherlands, the Wassenaar Arrangement on Export Controls for Conventional Arms and Dual-use Goods and Technologies is provisionally set up, to be formally established in 1996.	Export control
20 Dec.	The UN Protection Force (UNPROFOR) in the former Yugoslavia is formally replaced by IFOR (Implementation Force), under the command of NATO.	UN; NATO; Former Yugoslavia

About the contributors

Dr Ramses Amer (Sweden) is a Research Associate at the Department of Peace and Conflict Research, Uppsala University. His recent publications include *The United Nations and Foreign Military Interventions: A Comparative Study of the Application of the Charter*, 2nd edn (1994) and *Peace-keeping in a Peace Process: The Case of Cambodia*, Report no. 40 (1995). He has contributed articles to international journals and has written reports on issues of Asian security.

Dr Ian Anthony (United Kingdom) is Leader of the SIPRI Arms Transfers Project. He is editor of the SIPRI volumes *Arms Export Regulations* (1991) and *The Future of Defence Industries in Central and Eastern Europe* (1994), and author of *The Naval Arms Trade* (SIPRI, 1990) and *The Arms Trade and Medium Powers: Case Studies of India and Pakistan 1947–90* (1991). He has written or co-authored chapters for the *SIPRI Yearbook* since 1988.

Dr Eric Arnett (United States), an engineer, is Leader of the SIPRI Military Technology and International Security Project. In 1988–92 he was Senior Programme Associate in the Program on Science and International Security and Director of the Project on Advanced Weaponry in the Developing World at the American Association for the Advancement of Science. He is the editor of the SIPRI volumes *Implementing the Comprehensive Test Ban: New Aspects of Definition, Organization and Verification*, SIPRI Research Report no. 8 (1994), *Nuclear Weapons After the Comprehensive Test Ban: Implications for Modernization and Proliferation* (1996) and *Military Capacity and the Risk of War: China, India, Pakistan and Iran* (forthcoming, 1996). His research is supported by the W. Alton Jones and John D. and Catherine T. MacArthur Foundations.

Dr Vladimir Baranovsky (Russia) is Leader of the SIPRI Project on Russia's Security Agenda. He holds the position of Senior Researcher at the Institute of World Economy and International Relations in Moscow where he was Head of the International Security Section (1986–88) and Head of the European Studies Department (1988–92). He is the author of *Politicheskaya integratsiya v Zapadnoy Evrope* [Political integration in Western Europe] (1983), *Evropeyskoye soobshchestvo v mezhdunarodnykh otnosheniyakh* [The European Community in the international relations system] (1986) and *Zapadnaya Evropa: voenno-politicheskaya integratsiya* [Western Europe: military and political integration] (1988), and co-editor of *Zapadnoevropeyskaya integratsiya: politicheskie aspekty* [West European integration: political aspects] (1985); *Strany Yuzhnoy Evropy v sovremennom mire* [The countries of Southern Europe in the modern world] (1990); *1992: noviye khorizonty Zapadnoy Evropy* [1992: new horizons of Western Europe] (1993) (all in Russian); and *In from the Cold: Germany, Russia and the Future of Europe* (1992). He has contributed to a number of books and journals and to the *SIPRI Yearbook* since 1993.

Bengt-Göran Bergstrand (Sweden) was in 1994–96 a Researcher on the SIPRI Military Expenditure Project, while on leave as Senior Researcher from the Swedish National Defence Research Establishment (FOA). He has contributed to the *SIPRI Yearbook* since 1994.

Anthony Borden (United States) is a graduate of Yale University. An editor and journalist, he is one of the founding directors of the London-based Institute for War and Peace Reporting, in London, and editor of its journal *War Report*. He has contributed chapters to Marc S. Miller (ed.), *The State of the Peoples: A Global Human Rights Report on Societies in Danger* (1993) and *The Common Interest* (1987).

Richard Caplan (United States) is a Research Fellow at the Institute for War and Peace Reporting, London, and a MacArthur Junior Research Fellow at the Department of War Studies, King's College, London. His writings on the former Yugoslavia include *Post-Mortem on UNPROFOR* (1996) and chapters in *With No Peace to Keep: United Nations Peacekeeping and the War in the Former Yugoslavia* (1995) and *A Global Agenda: Issues Before the United Nations* (1994). He is the co-editor (with John Feffer) of *Europe's New Nationalism: States and Minorities in Conflict* (1996).

Susan Clark (United States) is a member of the Research Staff at the Institute for Defense Analyses, USA. Her work focuses primarily on the foreign and security policies of the former Soviet states. She was a contributor to and editor of *Soviet Military Power in a Changing World* (1991) and *Gorbachev's Agenda: Changes in Soviet Domestic and Foreign Policy* (1989), and co-author of *The USSR and the Western Alliance* (1990). She is a contributor to M. Mandelbaum (ed.), *Central Asia and the World* (1994) and L. Aron and K. Jensen (eds), *The Emergence of Russian Foreign Policy* (1994). Her articles have also appeared in *Jane's Intelligence Review* and *ORBIS*.

Margareta Eliasson (Sweden) is a Desk Officer for West Africa at the Swedish International Development Agency (SIDA). She was previously Project Coordinator for Africa Groups of Sweden.

Ragnhild Ferm (Sweden) is Leader of the SIPRI Arms Control and Disarmament Documentary Survey Project. She has published chapters on nuclear explosions, the comprehensive test ban and arms control agreements, and the annual chronologies of arms control and political events in the *SIPRI Yearbook* since 1982. She is the author of brochures and leaflets on SIPRI research topics in Swedish.

Dr Trevor Findlay (Australia) is Leader of the SIPRI Peacekeeping and Regional Security Project. He is a former Australian diplomat, specializing in arms control, and was Senior Research Fellow at and Acting Head of the Peace Research Centre, Australian National University, Canberra. He is founding editor of the quarterly journal *Pacific Research*. He is author of *Nuclear Dynamite: The Peaceful Nuclear Explosions Fiasco* (1990), *Peace Through Chemistry: The New Chemical Weapons Convention* (1993) and the SIPRI Research Reports *Cambodia: The Legacy and Lessons of UNTAC* (1995) and *Challenges for the New Peacekeepers* (1996).

Mary Jane Fox (USA) is a Ph.D. candidate at the Department of Peace and Conflict Research at Uppsala University. She holds a dual BA (Honours) in Political Science and Religion from Rutgers University.

Paul George (Canada) is Leader of the SIPRI Military Expenditure Project. He was previously an international security consultant in Ottawa, Canada, working on projects with a number of agencies and institutes. He has served as Visiting Professor and Chair of Military and Strategic Studies at Acadia University in Nova Scotia and as a Lecturer in Political Geography and International Relations at Carleton University in Ottawa. His recent publications include research reports on good governance, democratic development, military expenditure and regional security issues for the Canadian International Development Agency and a chapter in *Säkerhet och Utveckling i Afrika* [Security and Development in Africa] (1996), published by the Swedish Ministry for Foreign Affairs.

Dr Bates Gill (United States) is Leader of the Project on Security and Arms Control in East Asia at SIPRI. Formerly, he was Fei Yiming Professor of Comparative Politics at the Johns Hopkins University Center for Chinese and American Studies in Nanjing, China. He is the author of *The Challenge of Chinese Arms Proliferation: US Policy for the 1990s*, Strategic Studies Monograph Series (1993), co-author (with Taeho Kim) of *China's Arms Acquisitions from Abroad: A Quest for 'Superb and Secret Weapons'*, SIPRI Research Report no. 11 (1995) and co-author (with Richard Bitzinger) of *Gearing Up for High-Tech Warfare?: Chinese and Taiwanese Defense Modernization and the Implications for Confrontation Across the Taiwan Strait, 1995–2005* (1996).

Jozef Goldblat (Sweden) is Senior Lecturer at the Graduate Insitute of International Studies in Geneva, Consultant to the UN Institute for Disarmament Research (UNIDIR) and Vice-President of the Geneva International Peace Research Institute (GIPRI). He has written reports, articles and books on truce supervision, the arms race and disarmament problems. From 1969 to 1989 he directed the Programme of Arms Control and Disarmament Studies at SIPRI. He is the author of *Arms Control: A Guide to Negotiation and Agreements* (1994) and *The Nuclear Non-Proliferation Regime: Assessment and Prospects* (forthcoming, 1996).

Gerd Hagmeyer-Gaverus (Germany) is Researcher on the SIPRI Arms Transfers Project. He was formerly a Researcher at the Centre for Social Science Research at the Free University of Berlin, where he co-authored several research reports. He has contributed to chapters on military expenditure and arms trade in the *SIPRI Yearbook* since 1985.

Olga Hardardóttir (Iceland) is a Research Assistant on the SIPRI Peacekeeping and Regional Security Project. She was previously employed at SIPRI as a librarian.

Maria Haug (United States) was in 1995 a Research Assistant on the SIPRI Chemical and Biological Warfare Project. She was a Research Assistant at the Center for Nonproliferation Studies at the Monterey Institute of International Relations in 1993–95. In 1994 she worked as an intern and consultant to the Provisional Technical Secretariat of the Preparatory Commission of the Organisation for the Prohibition of Chemical Weapons (OPCW) in The Hague.

Ann-Sofi Jakobsson (Sweden) is a Ph.D. student at the Department of Peace and Conflict Research, Uppsala University. She is a contributor to the *SIPRI Yearbook 1995*.

Dr Peter Jones (Canada) is Leader of SIPRI's Middle East Security and Arms Control Project. Prior to joining SIPRI in October 1995, he worked for the Canadian

Department of Foreign Affairs and International Trade for seven years, focusing on security and arms control issues. He is the author of *International Peacekeeping: An Annotated Bibliography* and several articles on maritime security, peacekeeping, verification and Open Skies.

Jaana Karhilo (Finland) was a Research Assistant on the SIPRI Peacekeeping and Regional Security Project (1994–96). She previously did research on the CSCE and contributed a chapter to *Science and Research in the Service of Peace* (1992). She is co-editor of *Perspectives on Security* (1993) and contributed to the *SIPRI Yearbook 1995*.

Shannon Kile (United States) is a Research Assistant on the SIPRI Project on Russia's Security Agenda. He contributed to the *SIPRI Yearbook* in 1993 and 1995, and is the author of a chapter in the SIPRI Research Report *The Future of the Defence Industries in Central and Eastern Europe* (1994).

Dr Zdzislaw Lachowski (Poland) is Researcher on the SIPRI Project on Building a Cooperative Security System in and for Europe. He was previously Researcher at the Polish Institute of International Affairs, where he examined problems of European security and the CSCE process in particular and issues concerning West European political integration. He has published extensively on these subjects. He is co-editor of *Wizje Europy* [Visions of Europe] (1989, in Polish), and has contributed to the *SIPRI Yearbook* since 1992.

Evamaria Loose-Weintraub (Germany) is a Research Assistant on the SIPRI Military Expenditure Project. She was previously Research Assistant on the SIPRI Arms Trade Project. She is co-author of a chapter in the SIPRI volume *Arms Export Regulations* (1991) and the SIPRI Research Report *The Future of the Defence Industries in Central and Eastern Europe* (1994), and contributed to the *SIPRI Yearbook* in 1984–88 and 1992–94. Her current research fields are military expenditure in the Central and East European countries and South American military expenditure and economic development.

Dr Kjell-Åke Nordquist (Sweden) is Assistant Professor at the Department of Peace and Conflict Research, Uppsala University. He is co-author (with Christer Ahlström) of *Casualties of Conflict* (1991), prepared for the Red Cross/Red Crescent Movement's World Campaign for the Protection of Victims of War, and author of *Peace After War: On Conditions for Durable Inter-State Boundary Agreements* (1992). He is presently working on internal autonomy as conflict resolution in armed conflicts and has co-authored chapters on major armed conflicts in the *SIPRI Yearbook* since 1990.

Thomas Ohlson (Sweden) is a political scientist and economist, working with the Department of Peace and Conflict Research, Uppsala University. In 1982–87 he was Leader of the SIPRI Arms Trade Project, and in 1987–90 a Researcher at the Centre for African Studies in Maputo, Mozambique. He edited *Arms Production in the Third World* (1986) and *Arms Transfer Limitations and Third World Security* (1987), and is the co-author of *Arms Transfers to the Third World, 1971–85* (1987), all SIPRI volumes. He co-authored chapters in the *SIPRI Yearbook* in 1982–87 and 1995. His recent publications include *The New is Not Yet Born: Conflict and Conflict Resolution in Southern Africa* (1994), *The South African Tripod* (1994) and several articles on Southern Africa.

Patricia Radler (Sweden) was in 1994–96 a Research Assistant on the SIPRI Chemical and Biological Warfare Project. Her work centred on national implementation of the Chemical Weapons Convention. She is co-editor of *Effective Implementation of the Chemical Weapons Convention*, Proceedings of a Conference held at Bad Homburg, Germany, 8–10 September 1995.

Dr Adam Daniel Rotfeld (Poland) is Director of SIPRI and Leader of the SIPRI Project on Building a Cooperative Security System in and for Europe. He was head of the European Security Department in the Polish Institute of International Affairs, Warsaw in 1978–89. He was a member of the Polish Delegation to the Conference on Security and Co-operation in Europe (CSCE) and Personal Representative of the CSCE Chairman-in-Office to examine the settlement of the conflict in the Trans-Dniester region (1992–93). He is the author or editor of over 20 books and more than 200 articles on the legal and political aspects of relations between Germany and the Central and East European states after World War II (recognition of borders, the Munich Agreement and the right of self-determination), human rights, CSBMs, European security and the CSCE process. He is co-editor of the SIPRI volume *Germany and Europe in Transition* (1991) and *Europejski System bezpieczenstwa* in statu nascendi [European security system in statu nascendi] (1990, in Polish). He has written chapters for the *SIPRI Yearbook* since 1991.

Anna Schnell (Sweden) holds a Masters degree in Business Administration and Political Economy. She presently works at Save the Children (Swedish chapter), International Department, in Stockholm. She previously worked at UNICEF, Middle East and Northern Africa Section, in New York.

John Simpson (United Kingdom) is Professor of International Relations and Director of the Mountbatten Centre for International Studies, University of Southampton, and Programme Director of the Programme for Promoting Nuclear Non-Proliferation (PPPN). He is a member of the UN Secretary-General's Advisory Board for Disarmament Matters and co-editor (with Darryl Howlett) of *The Future of the Non-Proliferation Treaty* (1995).

Elisabeth Sköns (Sweden) is Leader of the SIPRI Arms Production Project. She has contributed to most editions of the *SIPRI Yearbook* since 1983. Her most recent publications include chapters on the internationalization of the arms industry in the SIPRI volume *Arms Industry Limited* (1993) and in the *Annals of the American Academy of Political and Social Science* (1994); *Weapon Supplies to Trouble Spots*, a background report for the UNDP *Human Development Report 1994* (1994); and a chapter on Sweden's defence industrial policy in *The Arms Production Dilemma* (1994).

Margareta Sollenberg (Sweden) is a Research Assistant with the Armed Conflicts Data Project at the Department of Peace and Conflict Research, Uppsala University. She is editor of *States in Armed Conflict 1994* (1995) and contributed to the *SIPRI Yearbook 1995*.

Dr Thomas Stock (Germany) is Leader of the SIPRI Chemical and Biological Warfare Project and Series Editor of the SIPRI Chemical & Biological Warfare Studies. He is an analytical chemist, with research experience in analytical chemistry and chemical toxicology. He is co-author of chapters in the SIPRI volumes *Non-Production by Industry of Chemical-Warfare Agents: Technical Verification under a Chemical Weapons Convention* (1988), *Verification of Conventional Arms Control in Europe: Technological Constraints and Opportunities* (1990) and *Control of Dual-Threat Agents: The Vaccines for Peace Programme* (1994). He is co-editor of *National Implementation of the Future Chemical Weapons Convention* (1990), *Verification after the Cold War: Broadening the Process* (1994) and *The Challenge of Old Chemical Munitions and Toxic Armament Wastes* (forthcoming, 1996). He has contributed to the *SIPRI Yearbook* since 1991 and has written extensively on the verification and national implementation of chemical disarmament accords and on old and abandoned chemical weapons.

Professor Peter Wallensteen (Sweden) has held the Dag Hammarskjöld Chair in Peace and Conflict Research since 1985 and is Head of the Department of Peace and Conflict Research, Uppsala University. He has recently published studies of the operation and reforms of the UN Security Council and is author of *From War to Peace: On Conflict Resolution in the Global System* (1994). He has co-authored chapters in the *SIPRI Yearbook* since 1988.

Pieter D. Wezeman (Netherlands) is a Research Assistant on the SIPRI Arms Transfers Project. He is a contributor to the *SIPRI Yearbook 1995*.

Siemon T. Wezeman (Netherlands) is a Research Assistant on the SIPRI Arms Transfers Project. He is the co-author (with Edward J. Laurance and Herbert Wulf) of *Arms Watch: SIPRI Report on the First year of the UN Register of Conventional Arms*, SIPRI Research Report no. 6 (1993), (with Bates Gill and J. N. Mak) of *ASEAN Arms Acquisitions: Developing Transparency.* (1995) and (with John Sislin) of *1994 Arms Transfers: A Register of Deliveries From Public Sources*, a SIPRI/MIIS (Monterey Institute of International Relations) study (1995). He has also been a contributor to the *SIPRI Yearbook* since 1993.

Carl Johan Åsberg (Sweden) is a PhD student at the Department of Peace and Conflict Research, Uppsala University. He is co-author of *States in Armed Conflict 1993* (1994).

SIPRI Yearbook 1996: Armaments, Disarmament and International Security

Oxford University Press, Oxford, 1996, 830 pp.
(Stockholm International Peace Research Institute)
ISBN 0-19-829202-3

ABSTRACTS

ROTFELD, A. D., 'Introduction: towards a pluralistic security system', in *SIPRI Yearbook 1996*, pp. 1–12.

The end of the cold war started a process of fundamental change of the international system. Numerous major accomplishments in the areas of arms control, armament reduction and disarmament indicate that these issues have not lost their importance, although they are often overshadowed by new risks and threats. New threats which undermine world security are 'ripening' on the peripheries of great-power global politics. One of the main new risks is the domestic weakness of many states whose governments are losing control of internal developments. As a result, some states are sliding into anarchy and ungovernability. There is still a chance that the security dilemma of global powers—national interests vs. shared values—may be superseded by the concept of a pluralist security community as defined 40 years ago by Karl Deutsch.

SOLLENBERG, M. and WALLENSTEEN, P., 'Major armed conflicts', in *SIPRI Yearbook 1996*, pp. 15–30.

In 1995, 30 major armed conflicts were waged in 25 locations around the world, compared with 32 major conflicts and 28 conflict locations in 1994 (revised data for 1994). As in 1994, all the major armed conflicts in 1995 were internal, or intrastate, rather than between states. However, foreign forces were involved in some of the conflicts. Only one conflict—that in Bosnia and Herzegovina—was ended during the year through a comprehensive peace treaty which included military and civilian provisions, as well as ways of addressing the incompatibilities behind the conflict.

FINDLAY, T., 'Armed conflict prevention, management and resolution', in *SIPRI Yearbook 1996*, pp. 31–74.

The General Framework Agreement on Bosnia and Herzegovina and a separate agreement on Croatia constituted the most spectacular peacemaking achievement of the year. Largely favourable developments also continued in the Middle East peace process and Haiti. Peace accords were struck in Angola and Liberia, although implementation remained unsteady. Chechnya, Sri Lanka and Sudan faced renewed conflict despite peace efforts. UN peacekeeping contracted significantly, but reform efforts continued. Conflict prevention was given new emphasis and regional organizations moved to enhance their capabilities for conflict prevention, management and resolution. Peace enforcement was used to great effect in Bosnia but at the cost of marginalizing the UN. The USA, Russia and the conflicting parties themselves often played key roles in particular peace processes.

KARHILO, J., 'Redesigning Nordic military contributions to multilateral peace operations', in *SIPRI Yearbook 1996*, pp. 101–16.

In the 1990s the Nordic countries of Denmark, Finland, Norway and Sweden have re-evaluated the policy and structure of their military contributions to UN peacekeeping operations in keeping with national and cooperative security considerations. The UN stand-by force system, maintained since the 1960s in all four countries, has been replaced in Denmark by an International Brigade for NATO and UN tasks, retained in Norway alongside a new NATO rapid reaction commitment and was under review in Finland and Sweden in 1995. Despite the current organizational differences, the Nordic countries uphold a tradition of extensive institutional and operational cooperation in peacekeeping.

FINDLAY, T., 'Reform of the United Nations', in *SIPRI Yearbook 1996*, pp. 117–32.

In its 50th anniversary year the UN underwent intense scrutiny as to its past performance, current state and future prospects. Overshadowing everything, however, was its dire financial situation caused by non-payment of assessed contributions by many members, especially the USA. As in the immediately preceding years, reform proposals proliferated during the year, most notably those relating to the Security Council, rationalization and better integration of the sprawling UN system and democratization, but no fundamental ones were implemented. At the end of 1995, however, the UN faced the frightening prospect that without a long-term solution to its near insolvency, its staff numbers would be slashed, its mandate severely crimped and its very future called into question.

GILL, B., 'The divided nations of China and Korea: discord and dialogue', in *SIPRI Yearbook 1996*, pp. 133–59.

Military tensions dominate relations between the two Koreas and between mainland China and Taiwan. However, in recent years, significant developments in other spheres—economic, political and humanitarian—offer promise that these disputes can be resolved peacefully. For mainland China and Taiwan, a groundwork for resolution of basic non-political issues was established, while economic and person-to-person linkages deepen year-by-year. The two Koreas have held prime ministerial-level discussions while slowly expanding trade relations; the activities of the Korean Peninsula Energy Development Organization (KEDO) offer other opportunities for dialogue. Economic relations hold the greatest promise as a foundation upon which to slowly construct peaceful settlements.

JONES, P., 'The Middle East peace process', in *SIPRI Yearbook 1996*, pp. 161–89.

Progress was achieved on the Israeli–Palestinian track with the signature of the Interim Agreement, while the Palestinian Authority and the Israeli Government intensified the fight against terror. The murder of Prime Minister Yitzhak Rabin, however, demonstrated that terrorism remains a threat in the region. The Israeli–Syrian talks were stalled for much of the year, before reviving after Rabin's assassination. Much remains to be done, and Israeli and US elections scheduled for 1996 are looming. The Israeli–Jordanian Peace Treaty was implemented smoothly in 1995. The multilateral track of the peace process made progress in 1995 but is limited by the need for further bilateral achievements, particularly between Israel and Syria.

BORDEN, A. and CAPLAN, R., 'The former Yugoslavia: the war and the peace process', in *SIPRI Yearbook 1996*, pp. 203–31.

The Croatian Government launched two military offensives on Serb-held enclaves in Croatia which radically altered circumstances there and in Bosnia and Herzegovina. Coinciding with a shift in US policy and unexpected military reverses for the Bosnia Serbs, this contributed to the achievement of a cease-fire in Bosnia and the Dayton Agreement. Both in the military arrangements and in its constitutional provisions, however, the Agreement entrenches the ethnic divisions which gave rise to the conflict in the first place. In the Former Yugoslav Republic of Macedonia, despite a breakthrough in relations with Greece and the presence of UNPREDEP, political stability remained fragile and relations between the Slavs and ethnic Albanians remain tense.

BARANOVSKY, V., 'Conflicts in and around Russia', in *SIPRI Yearbook 1996*, pp. 251–78.

During 1995, Russia and most of the other post-Soviet states were able to avoid major domestic political disturbances. With the exception of the dramatic conflicts in Chechnya and (to a lesser extent) in Tajikistan, the conflicts on the territory of the former USSR are less severe. The large-scale hostilities in Chechnya continued in the face of incoherent efforts to achieve a political settlement. Within the CIS, Russia has strengthened and consolidated its position, pursuing a less erratic and more pragmatic policy involving a renunciation of any moves to undermine the territorial integrity of CIS partners, the denial of support to separatist forces and pressure on these forces to accept autonomous status within federative-type arrangements.

ROTFELD, A. D., 'Europe: towards new security arrangements', in *SIPRI Yearbook 1996*, pp. 279–308.

While the debate on a future security model has often been conceptual, the decisions aimed at ending the war in Bosnia and Herzegovina were in a sense a test case of effectiveness and efficiency of the existing structures in the new politico-military situation. The debate and decisions on a new security system in Europe were focused in 1995 on extending the Western security structures (NATO and EU/WEU) to the east; the transatlantic partnership, including the US presence in Europe; and the internal developments in Russia. The discussion initiated by the OSCE on a security model highlights the serious erosion of the state, both as an institution and in its role as the main actor on the international scene. There is a search for solutions which would both revitalize the Atlantic community and offer an enlargement strategy towards the Central European states, accompanied by building a cooperative security arrangement with Russia and its Western neighbours.

GEORGE, P., BERGSTRAND, B.-G., CLARK, S. and LOOSE-WEINTRAUB, E., 'Military expenditure', in *SIPRI Yearbook 1996*, pp. 325–58.

Despite a continuing decline in aggregate world military spending most reductions have occurred in the major spending states of the past, the Western democracies and the former Soviet Union. Persistently high—and growing—levels of military spending in many countries make much of the world an increasingly unstable and dangerous place. Upward pressures on military budgets are evident throughout East Asia, Southeast Asia and South America and spending levels remain unjustifiably high in many African countries. There is no room for complacency if wasteful and dangerous levels of military spending are to be brought under control.

ARNETT, E., 'Military research and development', in *SIPRI Yearbook 1996*, pp. 381–409.

World military R&D expenditure in the mid-1990s probably does not exceed $60 b., a real reduction of more than 50 per cent from 1987. Spending in the countries of the former Warsaw Treaty Organization accounts for most of the difference. France, Italy and the USA have also reduced their spending by 25 per cent or more from their cold-war peaks. The USA continues to spend more than eight times as much as its nearest competitor. Of the major investors, only India, Japan and South Korea continue to increase their spending significantly. The challenge of coordinating major projects internationally is getting the better of some efforts, particularly in Europe.

SKÖNS, E. and GILL, B., 'Arms production', in *SIPRI Yearbook 1996*, pp. 411–55.

Contraction and consolidation of the arms industry continue worldwide. The process of capacity reduction is fairly smooth except in Russia and China, which are facing great difficulties in transforming their military industries, and to some extent France. The drop in arms production, although decelerating, will continue, since excess capacity is far from eliminated. This decline is associated with structural unemployment but profitability remains high. The fall in Russian military production is dramatic—to one-sixth of the 1991 level—and civilian diversification limited. China's ambitious conversion effort shows signs of strain due to its commercial inexperience, but it will take several years before a full picture develops.

ANTHONY, I. and STOCK, T., 'Multilateral military-related export control measures', in *SIPRI Yearbook 1996*, pp. 537–51.

In 1995 the membership of the Nuclear Suppliers Group (NSG), the Australia Group and the Missile Technology Control Regime (MTCR) continued to expand. Modifications were made to the Zangger Committee trigger list and to the lists of equipment and technology subject to control in the NSG, Australia Group and MTCR. In December 1995, subject to the approval of the 28 participating member governments, a new multilateral regime was established to address the issue of export controls on conventional arms and dual-use goods and technologies. This new regime, known as the Wassenaar Arrangement, had been under discussion for more than two years. The Wassenaar Arrangement will provide a forum in which governments can, without commitment, exchange information and views about export controls and possible security threats that might arise from transfers of arms or dual-use equipment.

ANTHONY, I., WEZEMAN, P. D. and WEZEMAN, S. T., 'The trade in major conventional weapons', in *SIPRI Yearbook 1996*, pp. 463–83.

According to SIPRI estimates the global trend-indicator value of foreign deliveries of major conventional weapons in 1995 was $22 797 billion in constant (1990) US dollars. This represents a slight increase over the revised estimate for 1994, suggesting that the fall in the volume of deliveries of major conventional weapons recorded since the end of the cold war has come to an end. Among suppliers, the most notable change was the relatively high share of deliveries by Russia in comparison with 1994. Russia accounted for 17 per cent of total deliveries in 1995 compared with 4 per cent in 1994. The USA remained the largest supplier in 1995, accounting for 43 per cent of deliveries. Among recipients the most noticeable trend has been the growing share of total deliveries accounted for by countries in North-East Asia. Deliveries to China and Taiwan have increased sharply in recent years.

SIMPSON, J., 'The nuclear non-proliferation regime after the NPT Review and Extension Conference', in *SIPRI Yearbook 1996*, pp. 561–89.

In 1995 the Treaty on the Non-Proliferation of Nuclear Weapons (NPT) was made permanent at the Review and Extension Conference, and proposals were agreed to change its review mechanism. When implemented from 1997 onwards, more focused meetings of its 182 parties will occur on a near-annual basis. The Conference underlined the increasing political salience of the nuclear-weapon ambiguity surrounding India, Israel and Pakistan as the NPT approaches universality, and how the nuclear non-proliferation regime and the nuclear disarmament process are starting to merge. Regional developments have included agreement on nuclear weapon-free zone treaties covering Africa and South-East Asia.

KILE, S. and ARNETT, E., 'Nuclear arms control', in *SIPRI Yearbook 1996*, pp. 611–55.

The CD made progress on the CTB in 1995 and achieved a mandate for a convention banning the production of fissile material for military purposes. Although implementation of START I proceeded ahead of schedule, START II remained unratified and US–Russian discussions to clarify the application of the ABM Treaty to tactical missile defences remained deadlocked. The US-funded programme of cooperation to facilitate denuclearization and demilitarization intensified and became embroiled in domestic controversies in Russia and the USA. The year 1996 is likely to be a watershed, in which nuclear arms control either grinds to a halt or is reinvigorated.

FERM, R., 'Nuclear explosions, 1945–95', in *SIPRI Yearbook 1996*, pp. 656–60.

In 1995 the USA, Russia and the UK continued to abide by their unilateral moratoria on nuclear weapon tests. In spite of worldwide protests France resumed its nuclear testing, and between September and December conducted five tests. After an additional test in January 1996 France declared the 'definitive end' of its test programme. China carried out two nuclear explosions and stated that it needs to continue testing until a CTBT has entered into force. New information on Soviet nuclear tests is now available. These data indicate that there were 12 more atmospheric tests conducted (before 1963) and 12 fewer underground (after 1963) compared to the 1995 Yearbook tables on nuclear explosions.

STOCK, T., HAUG, M. and RADLER, P., 'Chemical and biological weapon developments and arms control', in *SIPRI Yearbook 1996*, pp. 661–708.

In 1995 a terrorist nerve gas attack in Tokyo focused attention on chemical weapons (CW). Allegations of the possession or use of CW were consistent with those in previous years. Several possible causes of the Gulf War Syndrome were identified. The cost of destroying CW continued to increase, and remains a major problem, particularly for Russia. The UN Special Commission on Iraq (UNSCOM) discovered that Iraq had a more advanced biological weapon (BW) programme than it had declared, including weaponized BW agents. The number of ratifications of the CWC increased to 47, with 18 more ratifications needed for it to enter into force. The work of the Preparatory Commission progressed, but issues related to verification and declaration were not finalized. The Ad Hoc Group of Experts was established in Geneva to consider various measures to strengthen the BWC.

LACHOWSKI, Z., 'Conventional arms control and security cooperation in Europe', in *SIPRI Yearbook 1996*, pp. 709–39.

Arms control must find a strong conceptual and practical footing as part of the ongoing fundamental transformation of security relations. In 1995 nearly 50 000 heavy weapons were cut back by 30 states parties to the CFE Treaty. This reduction, together with Russian troop withdrawals from Central Europe and the Baltic states in 1994, have created an unprecedented core of military stability and predictability in Europe. The CFE flank dispute flared up with threats by the Russian military to withdraw from the Treaty. NATO insists on full CFE implementation, but its eastward enlargement requires a new approach to the conventional arms balance. The problem of how arms control can be applied to subregional and internal conflicts, challenges and threats remains. The OSCE has decided to give priority to developing a new framework for arms control, but the Budapest Ministerial Council of December 1995 was unable to agree on it. The negotiations on regional arms control and CSBMs in the former Yugoslavia may contribute to enhancing mutual confidence, reducing the risk of conflict and injecting stability into this conflict-ridden area.

GOLDBLAT, J., 'Land-mines and blinding laser weapons: the Inhumane Weapons Convention Review Conference', in *SIPRI Yearbook 1996*, pp. 753–64.

Efforts to strengthen the Inhumane Weapons Convention yielded the first positive result in October 1995, with the adoption of Protocol IV, which prohibits or restricts the use of laser weapons specifically designed to cause permanent blindness to unenhanced vision. Protocol IV has not established a rule unequivocally outlawing all practices intended or expected to cause blindness. No progress was made in 1995 with regard to the prohibition and restriction on the use of anti-personnel land-mines. The necessity to render such mines detectable, self-destructing and self-deactivating is widely recognized, but controversy could not be resolved over the reliability of the modifications which are to be made in their construction and over the length of the transition period needed to make the modifications. The only effective way to deal with the danger inhumane weapons pose is to prohibit them. A special diplomatic conference would need to be convened to negotiate such a ban.

Errata

SIPRI Yearbook 1995: Armaments, Disarmament and International Security

Page 60, line 10 from the bottom should read:	'into peacekeeping.[120] By the end of the year significant progress had been made in'.
Page 63, the last line, last paragraph of the sub-section on 'UNMOT (Tajikistan)' should read:	'maintain close contacts with the CIS force and CSCE Mission in Tajikistan.[138]'.
Page 69, second full paragraph, the first line should read:	'In July the General Assembly's Advisory Committee on Administrative and'.
Page 611, the end of line 1 should read:	'Transfers of Schedule 3'.
Page 722, table 18A.1, the second entry under China in the column for Latitude, should read:	'41. N'.
Page 769, line 12 of the text should read:	'Altogether roughly 38 200 (including naval, coastal and beyond-the-Urals holdings) TLE items'.
Page 871, in the summary of the START II Treaty, line 3 should read:	'which no more than 1750 may be deployed on SLBMs) by 1 January 2003 or no'.
Page 877, in the entry for '21 July', line 4 should read:	'observers (UNOMIG) in the area is increased to monitor'.

Errors which appeared in the index are not listed separately.

INDEX

Ferranti 422
FFV Aerotech 405, 406
FIAR 399
FIAT 459
FIAT Aviazione 461
Fiji 362, 367, 373
Finland:
  IFOR and 111
  military expenditure 360, 366, 371
  NATO and 110, 111
  peacekeeping 101, 108–12
  rapid reaction force 108, 110–11
  Russia and 116
  UN and 108–109, 110
  USSR and 108
Finmeccanica 422, 458
fissile material:
  management of 586–87
  production ban 2, 10, 562, 579–80, 611, 625–26
FLA (future large transport aircraft) 395, 423, 424, 425
Flash, Operation 207
FMC 458
FMRAAM missile 406
Framework Agreement see Dayton Agreement
France:
  Africa and 65
  arms exports 464
  arms industry 414, 418, 422, 423, 427–28
  Burundi and 38
  Comoros and 71
  Germany, co-production with 391
  military expenditure 326, 359, 365, 371
  military expenditure on research and development 9, 381, 388, 389, 391–92
  NATO and 294
  nuclear disarmament 583
  nuclear forces 618
  nuclear tests 1–2, 42, 576, 620, 621–22, 657, 658, 659, 660, 789, 790
  Rapid Reaction Force (with UK) 63, 216
  WEU and 294
Franco, President Francisco 395
Freitas do Amaral, Diogo 131
Friends of IGADD 73
FUERZAS UNIDAS–PKO '95 69

Gabon 363, 368, 374
Gaidar, Yegor 334
Galbraith, Peter 207
Galkin, Colonel-General Alexander 713
Gambia 363, 368, 374
Garcia Vargas, Julian 402
GATT Agreement 126, 541

Gaza 161, 162, 163, 166, 167, 169–74, 187
  see also Interim Agreement on the West Bank and the Gaza Strip
GEC 457, 469
GEC Marconi 399
Gencorp 459
General Dynamics 421, 457
General Electric 458
General Framework Agreement see Dayton Agreement
General Motors 457, 464
Geneva Convention (IV) 771–72
Geneva Conventions (1977) 780
Geneva Protocol (1925) 77
genocide 131
Genocide Convention (1948) 771
Genscher, Hans-Dietrich 304–305
Georgia:
  Abkhazia 2, 18, 68, 73, 261–65, 272, 748
  CIS and 262, 264–65, 272
  military expenditure 360
  North Ossetia 265
  OSCE and 297
  Russia and 18, 71, 262, 263, 272–73, 276, 747–48
  South Ossetia 71, 261, 262, 265
German Democratic Republic:
  military equipment given away 711
  military expenditure 360, 366, 372
Germany, Federal Republic of:
  arms exports 464, 471
  arms industry 418, 423–25
  chemical weapons 704
  France, co-production with 391
  military expenditure 326, 327, 359, 365, 371
  military expenditure on research and development 385, 388, 389, 392
  NATO and 286–87
  Russia and 668
  USA and 752
GF Oto Melara Breda 461
Ghana:
  military expenditure 363, 368, 374
  peacekeeping 65
Gharekhan, Chinmaya 41
GIAT 408, 458
GKN 460, 464
Gligorov, President Kiro 225, 226
Glukikh, Victor 470
Golan Heights 175, 176, 177, 178, 179
Goldstone, Richard 42, 43
González, President Felipe 393, 400–1
Gorazde 63, 215, 218, 220, 227
Gorbachev, President Mikhail 627
Gore, Al 206, 543, 550, 645, 647, 648, 649
Gore–Chernomyrdin Commission 543, 550, 582, 645, 647, 648, 649, 650

chemical weapon attack in 661, 673,
701–704, 708
co-production 391
Korea and 139, 140, 141
Middle East and 186, 187
military expenditure 361, 367, 373
military expenditure on research and
development 9, 381, 384, 388, 389
peacekeeping 60
Jericho 162 *see also* Interim Agreement on
the West Bank and the Gaza Strip
Jerusalem 162, 163, 165, 167, 169, 172, 173
Jiang Zemin 148–49, 151, 153, 155
Joint Commission on Economic and
Technological Cooperation *see* Gore–
Chernomyrdin Commission
Johnston Atoll 669, 670
Jordan:
  Hassan defects to 692, 696
  Israel, peace treaty with 161
  military expenditure 361, 366, 372
  USA and 181
Jovanovic, Vladislav 208
Judaea and Samaria 164, 169
judicial system, international 42

Kabul 37, 38, 268
Kama, Laïty 43
Karadzic, Radovan 210, 211, 212, 215, 218,
219, 221, 223, 224, 227
Karasin, Grigoriy 718
Karimov, President Islam 338
Kastenko, Anatol 711
Kasymov, General Alibek 339
Kawasaki 458
Kazakhstan:
  armed forces and 339–40
  arms imports 470
  denuclearization 10, 339
  military expenditure 341, 342–45, 360
  nuclear tests 657
  nuclear weapons 1, 339, 627, 628, 629–30,
  644, 788
  oil 266
  peacekeeping 338
  Russia and 272, 273, 338, 340, 342, 750,
  751, 752
  START and 788
Kenya 43, 74, 363, 368, 374
Khadzhiyev, Salambek 257, 258
Kharchenko, Dmitriy 713
Khasbulatov, Ruslan 257, 259
Kim Il Sung 136, 142, 156, 578
Kim Jong Il 156
Kim Young Sam 136
Kinkel, Klaus 711, 719
Kinzer, Major General Joseph 50
Kittani, Ismail 53

Kizlyar 259
Kockums 405, 407, 461
Kolesnikov, Mikhail 726
Koo Chen-fu 145, 147
Koo-Wang talks 145, 147, 152, 158
Koor Industries 461
Korean Air 452
Korean Armistice Agreement (1953) 134,
154
Korea, North:
  Agreed Framework (1994), with USA
  136–38, 154, 582, 789, 794
  arms imports 467–68
  chemical weapons 665
  flooding 141, 143–44
  IAEA and 577–78
  infiltrators killed 153
  Japan and 139, 140, 141
  military expenditure 362, 367, 373
  NPT and 136
  nuclear activities 562, 568, 576–78
  nuclear reactors 136, 137, 138, 577
  nuclear weapons and 154
  oil for 138
  plutonium 577
  Russia and 468
  UN and 143
  USA and 70, 136, 137, 153–54, 157,
  576–77, 588
Korea, South:
  arms exports 452, 453
  arms imports 467
  arms industry 444, 445, 451–54, 455
  arms production 412
  cooperation agreements 454
  elections 156
  KOTRA 141
  military expenditure 361, 367, 373
  military expenditure on research and
  development 9, 381, 384
  peacekeeping and 60
  political scandal 156
  public opinion on North 143
  unification and 138, 157
  US troops in 154
Korean Peninsula:
  Agreed Framework (1994) 136–38, 154,
  582, 789, 794
  Basic Agreement 134, 136
  Denuclearization Declaration 134–35, 578
  dialogue in 133, 134–44
  DMZ 134, 135
  economic relations 138–41
  humanitarian ties 141–44, 158
  investments 139–40, 141
  JNCC 578
  joint communiqué (1972) 134
  KEDO 136–38, 577, 794

Middle East:
Arms Control and Regional Security
(ACRS) Working Group 182–85, 188
CBMs 184
conflict in 19, 20, 24–25
Environment Working Group 186, 188
EU and 186
Japan and 186, 187
maritime agreements 184
military expenditure 9, 325, 361, 366, 372
nuclear weapon-free zone 563, 580–81
peace process 2, 19–20, 161–89:
documents on 190–202
Final Status Talks 163, 166, 169, 171,
173, 187, 189
Interim Agreement on the West Bank
and Gaza Strip 161, 169–74, 191–202
Madrid Conference 189
multilateral track 181–88
opposition to 163, 164–65, 189
progress 8
Taba Joint Statement 168–69, 190
territorial questions 166
Refugee Working Group 187, 188
Regional Communications Network 183
Regional Development Bank 185–86
Regional Economic Development
Working Group (REDWG) 185–86, 188
Regional Security Centre 184
Russia and 184
USA and 70, 177, 178, 179
Water Resources Working Group 187, 188
water rights 168, 172, 176
MiG–MAPO Group 434, 470
Mikhailov, Viktor 648
Mikhailov, Vyacheslav 256–57
military exercises 741–43
military expenditure:
data on 325
SIPRI sources and methods 379–80
tables on 359–76
taxes on 129–30
trends 325–58
world 325
world decline 9
military expenditure on research and
development:
data sources 382–84
national goals 385
procurement and 385
reductions in 9, 381, 384
technology and 385, 386
trends 382–88, 558
world 381, 382–88
military technology, cooperation and 381
Millon, Charles 427
Milosevic, President Slobodan 209, 210, 212,
216, 221, 223, 227, 230

mines 753, 754–61
MINUGUA (UN Mission for the
Verification of Human Rights and of
Compliance with the Commitments of the
Comprehensive Agreement on Human
Rights in Guatemala) 39, 40, 80
MINURSO (UN Mission for the Referendum
in Western Sahara) 47, 78
MINUSAL (UN Mission in El Salvador) 45,
80
Mischief Reef 71
Mitchell, Senator George 70
Mitre 460
Mitsubishi 457, 459
Mitterrand, President François 621
Mladic, General Ratko 212, 217, 218, 221,
223
Modise, Joe 353
Moi, President Daniel Arap 73
Moldova:
conflict in 260–61
military expenditure 361
OSCE and 297, 299
peacekeeping and 60
Russia and 71, 260, 261, 276, 749–50
MOMEP (Military Observer Mission
Ecuador/Peru) 70
Mongolia 362, 367, 373
Morocco 363, 368, 374
Mostar 213
Motorola 460, 557
MOWAG 464
Mozambique:
military expenditure 363, 368, 374
peace operations in 3
UN and 44, 59
MTCR (Missile Technology Control
Regime) 537, 549–51:
membership 538
Mubarak, Hosni 65, 184, 581
multilateralism 5
Mururoa Atoll 576, 657
mustard gas 664, 665
Myanmar:
biological weapon allegations 686
chemical weapon allegations 662, 663
conflict in 20, 27, 72
military expenditure 362, 367, 373

NACC (North Atlantic Cooperation Council)
67, 105, 285
Nagorno-Karabakh 2, 18, 19, 26, 67, 265–67,
297, 299, 748
Nakhichevan 266
Namibia 363, 368, 374
Nari, Said Abdullo 268

Sergeyev, Colonel-General Igor 628
Sextant Avionique 461
Seychelles 363, 369, 375
Shevardnadze, President Eduard 262, 748
Shmarov, Valeriy 472
Siemens 427, 459
Sierra Leone:
    conflict in 17, 21, 29, 40–41, 74
    military expenditure 363, 369, 375
    UN and 41
Singapore 362, 367, 373
SIPRI–Saskatchewan–Frankfurt Group 681,
    685
Sirmium 209
Slavonia see Eastern Slavonia, Western
    Slavonia
Slovakia 360, 366, 372, 479
Slovenia:
    arms embargo 61
    military expenditure 360, 366, 372
Smirnov, Igor 260
Smith, Lieutenant-General Rupert 214, 215
Smiths Industries 460
SNECMA Groupe 458, 459
Snegur, President Mircea 260
SNPE 462
Soko, Smiljko 205
Somalia:
    conflict in 21, 29, 33, 74
    military expenditure 363, 369, 375
    UN and 38, 41, 61
soman 703
Song Young-dae 142
Soskovets, Oleg 470
South Africa:
    ANC 350
    apartheid 349
    arms embargo 450
    arms exports 351, 450
    arms industry 413, 444, 445, 449–51
    arms production 412
    force integration 350–51
    force modernization 351–53
    joint ventures 451
    military expenditure 349–53, 363, 369,
      375, 449
    military expenditure on research and
      development 450
    MTCR and 550–51
    NPT and 566, 567
    nuclear weapons 562
    peacekeeping and 60, 65, 66
South America:
    conflict in 19, 20, 21, 30
    military expenditure 364, 370, 376
South Asia:
    military expenditure 361, 367, 373
    nuclear programmes 578–80

South China Sea 71, 575
South Ossetia see under Georgia
South-East Asia:
    conflicts in 19
    military expenditure 325
    see also following entry
Southeast Asia Nuclear Weapon-Free Zone,
    Treaty on (1995) 575, 601–609, 794
Southern African Development Community
    (SADC) 66
Spain:
    arms industry 393–403, 423
    Canada and 42
    co-production 391, 392, 393, 394,
      395–400, 401
    DGAM 395–98
    European frigate programme 391
    military build-up 393–94, 400–401
    military expenditure 326, 328, 359, 365,
      371
    military expenditure on research and
      development 384, 388, 389, 392–403
    military technology 381
    NATO and 393, 394, 395, 396, 397
    PP (Partido Popular, Christian Democrat
      Popular Party) 402, 403
    PSOE (Socialist Workers' Party of Spain)
      393, 394, 399, 401, 402
    threat assessment 401
Spratley Islands 71
Srebrenica 44, 45, 63, 212, 215, 217–19,
    220, 223, 227, 789
Sri Lanka:
    chemical weapon allegations 662, 663
    conflict in 18, 20, 27, 31, 70
    military expenditure 325, 361, 367, 373
    NPT and 566, 571–72
SSD (Safe and Secure Dismantlement Talks)
    640
ST&I (Safeguards, Transparency and
    Irreversibility) talks 649
START I (1991) 1, 611, 626, 627–30, 631,
    634–35, 654, 785–86
START II (1993) 1, 584, 611, 626, 630–39,
    654, 655, 786
START III 584, 639–40
state:
    erosion of 306
    peoples and 121
    sovereignty of 5
STN Atlas Elektronik 459
Stockholm Document (1986) 742
Stoel, Max van der 299
Storm, Operation 208
Strasser, Captain Valentine 40
Submarine 2000 404, 407